Handbook of Sensory Physiology

Volume VIII

Perception

By

S.M.Anstis J.Atkinson C.Blakemore O.Braddick T.Brandt
F.W.Campbell S.Coren J.Dichgans P.C.Dodwell P.D.Eimas J.M.Foley
R.Fox L.Ganz M.Garrett E.J.Gibson J.S.Girgus M.M.Haith
Y.Hatwell E.R.Hilgard D.Ingle G.Johansson B.Julesz M.Konishi J.R.Lackner
E.Levinson A.M.Liberman L.Maffei T.Oyama A.Pantle
E.Pöppel R.Sekuler C.F.Stromeyer M.Studdert-Kennedy H.-L.Teuber R.K.Yin

Edited by

Richard Held Herschel W. Leibowitz
Hans-Lukas Teuber

With 254 Figures and 7 Anaglyphs

Springer-Verlag Berlin Heidelberg NewYork 1978

Richard Held

Massachusetts Institute of Technology Dept. of Psychology, E10–139,
Cambridge, MA 02139 (USA)

Herschel Leibowitz

Psychology Department, Pennsylvania State University
417 Moore Building, University Park, PA 16802 (USA)

Hans-Lukas Teuber

Massachusetts Institute of Technology

ISBN 3-540-08300-6 Springer-Verlag Berlin · Heidelberg · New York
ISBN 0-387-08300-6 Springer-Verlag New York · Heidelberg · Berlin

Library of Congress Cataloging in Publication Data. Main entry under title: Perception. (Handbook of sensory physiology; v. 8) Bibliography: p. Includes index. 1. Senses and sensation. 2. Perception-Physiological aspects. 3. Visual perception. I. Anstis, S.M. II. Held, Richard. III. Leibowitz, Herschel W. IV. Teuber, Hans Lukas. V. Series. [DNLM: 1. Perception. WL700 H236 v. 8] QP351.H34 vol. 8 [QP441] 591.1′82′08s [152.1] 78-9830

Printed in Germany

Typesetting, printing and binding: Universitätsdruckerei H. Stürtz AG, Würzburg

2122/3120-543210

Hans-Lukas Teuber

1916–1977

Hans-Lukas Teuber, Professor and Head of the Department of Psychology at the Massachusetts Institute of Technology, lost his life on January 4, 1977 while swimming off Virgin Gorda in the British Virgin Islands. Professor Teuber had won world-wide recognition as a leader in psychology and in the neurosciences. His pioneering research into the behavioral after-effects of brain injury, begun during the final years of World War II in collaboration with Professor Morris Bender, led to his recognition as an authority on the relationship between brain and behavior. His work, which encompassed both basic and clinical investigations, provided a foundation for contemporary neuropsychology and its integration with related disciplines.

He was born in Berlin on August 7th, 1916, was graduated from the College Français and attended the University of Basel. In 1941, embarking from Switzerland on a perilous journey, he emigrated to the United States. He received his Ph.D. in experimental psychology from Harvard University in 1947 and joined the faculty of the New York University College of Medicine that year. It was there that he guided his small psychological laboratory into comprehensive research efforts on the psychological effects of brain injury on human behavior.

In 1961, Teuber moved to M.I.T., where he had been made Head of the Psychology Section and where he re-established his laboratory. Three years later, he became Head of what in a very short time was to be known as a unique and distinguished *brain sciences* department at that institution, created by him to reflect his conception of what such a department should be—a center where endeavors as diverse as neuroanatomy, experimental psychology, and psycholinguistics could flourish and yet form a genuine and quite interdisciplinary whole. His more than 200 papers and monographs reflect not only this broad interdisciplinary approach to the fundamental questions in his chosen field but also his remarkable ability to integrate basic and clinical research.

He enjoyed an unusually close relationship with both the North American and European psychological and neuroscience communities. Returning to post-war Europe for the first time in 1957 to attend the International Psychological Congress in Brussels, he found himself embarked on a trip which was to solidify his ties with his European colleagues. Throughout the subsequent twenty years, he traveled with increasing frequency to Europe to promote the interchange of scientific information and personnel, to lecture, and to serve on numerous committees and study groups. He was a member of the organizing committee for the *Handbook of Sensory Physiology,* published by Springer Verlag, and edited the volume on Perception in this series. The only extended period away from his home institution was in 1971–72 when Oxford University bestowed upon him the honor of Eastman Professor.

A much abbreviated list of recognitions by his colleagues includes election to the U.S. National Academy of Sciences, the French Psychological Society, the U.S. Society of Experimental Psychologists, recipient of the Lashley Award for Research in Neurobiology from the American Philosophical Society, and the Kenneth Craik Award in experimental psychology from Cambridge University. In the spring of 1975, he was awarded two honorary doctorates: one from the Medical Faculty of the Université Claude Bernard of Lyon, France, and the other, a month later, from the Psychological Faculty of the University of Geneva, Switzerland. He had just received the prestigious James R. Killian, Jr. Faculty Achievement Award from the Massachusetts Institute of Technology and was preparing the Killian Lectures in connection with that honor at the time of his death. A memorial service was held on January 19, 1977, the last of the two dates set aside for the planned Killian Lectures.

Teuber's career was firmly rooted in both the European and North American psychological communities: His father, a student of Karl Stumpf, founded the primate research station on Tenerife, one of the Canary Islands, where Professor Wolfgang Köhler carried out his famous studies during World War I. Teuber particularly cherished his personal and professional friendship with Köhler, one of the founders of the Psychologische Forschung, the antecedent of Psychological Research. Luke, as Teuber was known to his many friends, was always a congenial and enthusiastic host and succeeded in making both his New York University and Massachusetts Institute of Technology departments, as well as his home, a "natural" stopping-off place for traveling scientists, both foreign and domestic, interested in experimental psychology, neurophysiology, perception, brain injury, and language. A dedicated and skillful teacher, he took a warm personal interest in students and colleagues, an unusually large percentage of whom occupy prominent positions throughout the world, not only in psychology but in related disciplines. A gifted linguist, he could read fluently in Latin, Ancient Greek, English, French and German, and was well known for his comprehensive and inspiring lectures in the latter three languages. He never hesitated to give freely of his time when requested, either for institutions or individuals, and served as an advisor on a broad spectrum of consulting committees throughout the world, including National Aeronautics and Space Administration the National Institutes of Health, the International Brain Research Organization, and editorial boards of various journals.

He is survived by his wife, Marianne, who shared his professional work to a remarkable extent, and by two sons, Andreas and Christopher.

Herschel Leibowitz Richard Held

Preface

This volume was designed to focus on the problems of perception and originally was to have been solely edited by Professor Hans-Lukas Teuber who was a member of the editorial board which initiated production of the Handbook. Accordingly, he issued invitations to a number of researchers in perception asking them to contribute chapters written in a style described in his words:

> *"...we hope that no author will feel constrained to undertake a major search of the literature; he could write, instead, on an area in which he has been quite active himself, and where most of the issues are immediately obvious to him. In this way, the writing of the chapter should be enjoyable rather than a chore; it should result in a personal account of the state of a given area rather than in an encyclopedic treatise... the field deserves this sort of summary review, particularly if it is pointed toward the future and speeds the convergence of developments in sensory physiology and psychological studies of perception."*

With the growing burden of national and international commitments including departmental headship, Professor Teuber felt that it would be wise to share the editorial responsibilities for this volume and accordingly, asked Professors Richard Held and Herschel Leibowitz to co-edit the volume with him in the same spirit as outlined in his invitation to authors. They agreed to help in this task. Following Professor Teuber's tragic death in January 1977, Professors Held and Leibowitz have completed his work and guided the volume to the final publication stage.

Professor Teuber had originally planned to prepare a chapter on Perceptual Effects of Cerebral Lesions for this volume which would provide an overview of the field and indicate directions for future research. Teuber viewed his work on the behavioral aftereffects of brain injury providing a special perspective on the normal function of the brain in perception as well as other capacities. It was this perspective that made his accounts of pathology of such interest and value to scientist and clinician alike. It led him to leave no stone unturned in his search for understanding of normal function in the disciplines of which he was intellectual master—ranging through the brain sciences as well as those of behavior. It enriched his contributions to a degree rarely attained in the science. Those familiar with his unique style, his breadth of knowledge, and his unparalleled ability to summarize, synthesize, and inspire, will appreciate that his chapter would have been a most welcome contribution to the literature. When his premature death eliminated this possibility, the editors proposed to publish (in lieu of a formally prepared chapter) Professor Teuber's last major address, "The Brain and Human Behaviour", presented as an invited paper to the International Congress of Psychology in Paris in the summer of 1976. Permission to reproduce this chapter was kindly given by Professor Paul Fraisse, President of the International Congress, and is gratefully acknowledged. Although this treatment goes beyond the topic of perception, the chapter reflects his ability to integrate major developments coming from a wide variety of disciplines and suggests promising bases for future research.

R. Held H. Leibowitz

Introduction

Why should a Handbook of Sensory Physiology include a volume devoted to the topic of perception? In one traditional approach, the senses have been regarded as the mind's windows on the world meaning that they are the source of perceptions of that world. In another tradition, perceptual processes are regarded as having their own rules independent of the senses. But in this view, processes in the central nervous system are regarded as correlated with perception. From both points of view, perception is indissolubly bound up with sensory and neuronal processes. The real problem consists in delineating the relationship. To what extent does sensory stimulation and its sequelae constrain perception and to what extent is perception a process with laws intrinsic to it and constrained only by the dynamics of the central nervous system?

New progress in our understanding of central processing in sensory systems has provided exciting leads in the search for the central correlates of perception. For example, the discovery of single neurons in the visual cortex selectively sensitive to oriented edges was, perhaps prematurely, enthusiastically greeted by investigators of vision as the potential neural substrate for form perception. The revelation of the tuning of these cells for orientation soon found its parallel in perceptual experiments demonstrating such tuning by means of psychophysical methods. Many more examples could be cited. They have made the last decade or two a creative period for advancement in the field—for progress related both in fact and in theory to advances in knowledge of the physiology and anatomy of the nervous system.

A volume of this sort is, by its nature, selective. The interests and scope of its editors and the type of approach to the subject matter have delimited the contributions in the volume. We can make no claim to inclusiveness and we recognize that some important areas may have been omitted. We have attempted, first of all, to cover areas of perception to which neuronal mechanisms can be plausibly related. Other areas are covered which are important but whose underlying neuronal substrates cannot yet be profitably related to the nervous system.

The earliest chapters are devoted to feature filters and channels. These entities, closely related in principle to the single units of neurophysiology, represent at this time an attempt to define an alphabet for perception. If the elements can be defined, then perhaps we can understand percepts as concatenations of these elements. So runs the logic behind regarding them as the most basic subject matter of the volume. Two chapters under the topic of depth and distance next raise some issues concerning the metrical aspects of perception, about the spatial framework within which are organized the subjects which have names and can be recognized and discriminated.

Comparison of perceptual capacities across species can, in principle, explain the relevance to perception of differing neuronal structures as well as providing a useful perspective on man, the species of principal concern to us. Developmental studies can similarly cast light on the relation of neural structure and function and their perceptual correlates as both change over time. Deprivation experiments have, in recent years, aroused the hope that a direct correlation of function with neuronal mechanisms might be achieved. For example, if the class of all cortical neurons sensitive to vertical and near-vertical edges is eliminated in an animal by a deprivation procedure, then failure by that altered brain in discriminating vertical lines might be expected. The classic issue of the role of experience in the development of perceptual capacity has been approached in part by the technique of deprivation.

Under Complex Aspects of Perception we have included chapters on the perception of pattern, of illusions, of the classic aftereffects, and of the recognition of faces, that most complex of meaningful patterns. All of the former deal with spatially distributed stimuli, the temporal dimension being of secondary, if any relevance. Of temporal patterns important to perception, none is more so than the human artifact of speech to which two chapters are devoted. Turning to the combination of spatial and temporal dimensions, we have four chapters devoted to aspects of vision which involve both dimensions. Two chapters are devoted to aspects of perception related to spatial and postural stability, involving the relevant sensory systems. The final chapter (by the late Hans-Lukas Teuber) deals primarily with perceptual and behavioral effects of cerebral lesions and the reasons for including this chapter in its present form are discussed in the Preface.

Contents

List of Contributors

ANSTIS, S.M., Dept. of Psychology, York University, 4700 Keele St, Downsview, Ont. M3J 1P3, Canada

ATKINSON, J., Psychological Laboratory, Downing Street, Cambridge CB2 3EB, Great Britain

BLAKEMORE, C., Physiological Laboratory, Downing Street, Cambridge CB2 3EG, Great Britain

BRADDICK, O., Psychological Laboratory, Downing Street, Cambridge CB2 3EB, Great Britain

BRANDT, T., Neurologische Klinik mit klinischer Neurophysiologie, Krupp Krankenanstalten, Wittekindstraße 30, D-4300 Essen, FRG

CAMPBELL, F.W., Psychological Laboratory, Downing Street, Cambridge CB2 3EG, Great Britain

COREN, S., Department of Psychology, University of British Columbia, Vancouver V6T IW5, Canada

DICHGANS, J., Neurologische Klinik der Universität Tübingen, Liebermeisterstr. 18–20, D-7400 Tübingen, FRG

DODWELL, P.C., Department of Psychology, Queen's University, Kingston, Ont., Canada

EIMAS, P.D., Walter S. Hunter Laboratory of Psychology, Brown University, Providence, RI 02912, USA

FOLEY, J.M., Department of Psychology, University of California, Santa Barbara, CA 93106, USA

FOX, R., Psychology Department, Vanderbilt University, Nashville, TN 37240, USA

GANZ, L., Department of Psychology, Stanford University, Stanford, CA 94305, USA

GARRETT, M., Psychology Department, Massachusetts Institute of Technology, Cambridge, MA 02139, USA

GIBSON, E.J., Psychology Department, Cornell University, Ithaca, NY 14850, USA

GIRGUS, J.S., Department of Psychology, Princeton University, Princeton, New Jersey, 08540, USA

HAITH, M.M., Department of Psychology, University of Denver, Denver, CO 80210, USA

HATWELL, Y., UER de Psychologie et Sciences de l'Education, Université des Sciences Sociales, Boite Postale 47/X, F-38040 Grenoble, France

HILGARD, E.R., Department of Psychology, Stanford University, Stanford, CA 94305, USA

INGLE, D., Psychology Department, Brandeis University, Waltham, MA, USA

JOHANSSON, G., Psykologiska Institutionen, Uppsala Universitet, Box 227, S-75101 Uppsala, Sweden

JULESZ, B., Bell Laboratories, Sensory and Perceptual Processes Department, Murray Hill, NJ 07974, USA

KONISHI, M., California Institute of Technology, Division of Biology 216–76, Pasadena, CA 91125, USA

LACKNER, J.R., Psychology Department, Brandeis University, Waltham, MA, USA

LEVINSON, E., Cresap Neuroscience Laboratory, Washington University, St. Louis, MO, 63130, USA

LIBERMAN, A.M., Haskins Laboratories, New Haven, CT 06511, USA

MAFFEI, L., Laboratorio di Neurofisiologia del CNR, Via S. Zeno, 51, 56100 Pisa, Italy

OYAMA, T., Department of Psychology, Chiba University, Yayoi-cho, Chiba-shi, 280, Japan

PANTLE, A., Psychology Department, Miami University, Oxford, OH 45056, USA

PÖPPEL, E., Institut für Medizinische Psychologie, Ludwig-Maximilians-Universität, Schillerstraße 42, D-8000 München 2, FRG

SEKULER, R., Cresap Neuroscience Laboratory, Northwestern University, 2021 Sheridan Road, Evanston, IL 60201, USA

STROMEYER, C.F., Division of Applied Sciences, Harvard University, 29 Oxford Street, Cambridge, MA 02138, USA

STUDDERT-KENNEDY, M., Haskins Laboratories, New Haven, CT 06511, USA

TEUBER, H.-L., Massachusetts Institute of Technology, Department of Psychology E10–014, Cambridge, MA 02139, USA

YIN, R.K., The Rand Corporation, 2100 M Street, N.W., Washington, DC 20037, USA

I. Basic Features

A. Feature Filters and Channels

Chapter 1

Channels in Vision: Basic Aspects

O. BRADDICK, F.W. CAMPBELL, J. ATKINSON, Cambridge (GB)

With 16 Figures

Contents

A. Receptive Fields and Channels

KENNETH J.W. CRAIK (1914–1945), while discussing how the human visual system recognized objects, wrote:

> Now in mathematics it is legitimate to seek transformations through which certain quantities (such as the physical laws of nature and the velocity of light in relativity theory) remain invariant. In fact, the action of various physical devices which "recognize" or respond identically to certain simple objects can be treated in terms of such transformations. Thus the essential part of physical "recognizing" instruments is usually a filter—whether it be a mechanical sieve, an optical filter,

> or a tuned electrical circuit—which "passes" only quantities of the kind it is required to identify and rejects all others. Mathematically, the situation here is that, in a perfect filter, the transformation leaves the desired quantity unaltered, but reduces all others to zero.

So, CRAIK saw clearly that to separate anything from a population of similar or different things one needs a filter. To separate say, eggs into small and large we need only one sieve; but to separate them into small, medium, and large we require two filters, that is, a low-pass plus a high-pass filter. These can be physically separate, as in the case of the egg filters, or combined into one as in the case of many electronic filters or all mechanical resonators, like a tuning fork.

A fundamental insight of sensory physiology is that there are many parallel pathways within a sensory system, each specialized to carry information about a different type of stimulus element. In the visual system, the most obvious way in which this is true is that within the retina, optic nerve, and visual cortex, information from different parts of the visual field is carried by separate neural elements. This is apparent from the anatomy and gross physiology. Thus, when it became possible to record the activity of single neurons in the visual pathway, an immediate question was: where does light have to appear in the field of view, in order to activate a given neuron? The answer to this question was conveniently expressed in terms of the neuron's *receptive field* (HARTLINE, 1938). It was soon apparent that a cell not only had a receptive field within which it responded to light, but that sub-areas could be mapped according to the nature of the response to a small flash. In certain areas the response was excitatory, while in others it was inhibitory. So besides being specialized to deal with a particular area of the visual field, a neuron responded optimally to a particular distribution of light within that area.

In the retinal ganglion cells (KUFFLER, 1953) and certain cortical cells (HUBEL and WIESEL, 1962) of the cat the response to a pattern of light appeared to be well predicted by considering the summation of the effects of the pattern on the excitatory and inhibitory zones as mapped out with small flashed spots of light. Thus for these cells, the receptive field concept provided a clear and adequate way to describe a neuron's spatial properties. Figure 1 shows such a map. However, in many other cases, such as the frog's ganglion cells (BARLOW, 1953; MATURANA et al., 1960) and the "complex" cortical cells of cat (HUBEL and WIESEL, 1962), a neuron can have a marked selectivity for certain spatial patterns of light, but one which is impossible to predict from any attempt to define excitatory and inhibitory zones of the receptive field. The spatial properties of such neurons have sometimes been summed up by the description of a *trigger feature*—the pattern of light (e.g., a dark convex moving edge in the case of certain frog ganglion cells) which optimally activates the cell. This is not to say that such neurons do not have receptive fields. They do, since they respond to stimulation only in a certain region of the visual field; but no receptive field map can show their pattern-responsive properties.

The receptive field description is also incomplete when we consider responsiveness to properties of the stimulus other than its spatial distribution. Visual

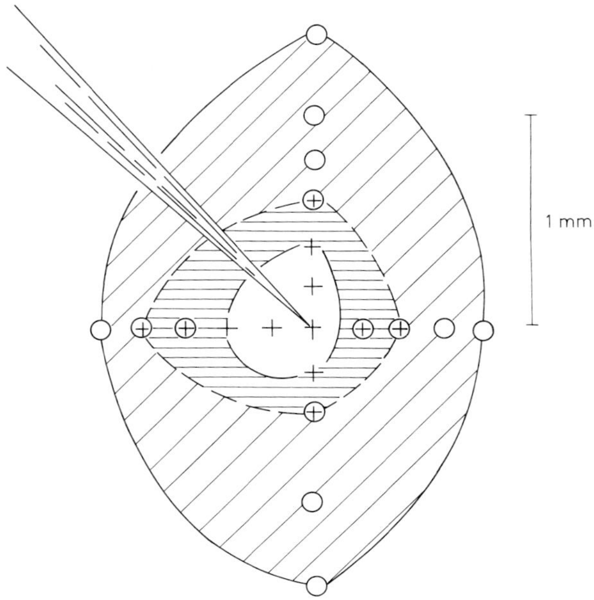

Fig. 1. Example of receptive field of ganglion cell in cat retina. In the three concentric zones, flashed spot elicits "on," "on-off," and "off" responses respectively. (From KUFFLER, 1953)

neurons may be specific to color, or to direction of stimulus motion. Again, these could be expressed as trigger features of the stimulus.

Another way to describe cell properties is to use the receptive field concept, but to extend it to dimensions of the stimulus other than the two dimensions of the visual field. Figure 2, for instance, shows the responsiveness of a cortical neuron as a function of the stimulus orientation. Such an "orientation field" may be plotted whether or not the spatial receptive field has an oriented shape. That is, it can describe a complex cell as well as a simple cell. Figure 3 is another example, showing responsiveness of a monkey lateral geniculate cell to wavelength. It extends the analogy to spatial receptive fields, in that both excitatory and inhibitory zones of the wavelength dimension are represented.

This description is probably best where a neuron's specificity is for a certain range of a continuous variable in the stimulus, such as position, orientation, or wavelength. Where the specificity is more complex or discrete, simple definition of a trigger feature is easier. In the case of continuous variables, we can regard the dimension as being divided into separate smaller ranges for neural analysis. Plotting the various receptive fields together on the dimension of analysis will show how this division of labor occurs. An independent structural element of the system, dealing with its particular subrange of the stimulus dimension, we shall call a *channel*. This rather noncommittal term is appropriate where psychophysical experiments demonstrate the existence of separate processing of different subranges, but cannot tell us exactly what the separate structures are. Sometimes, "channel" is used to mean a population of neural units, which

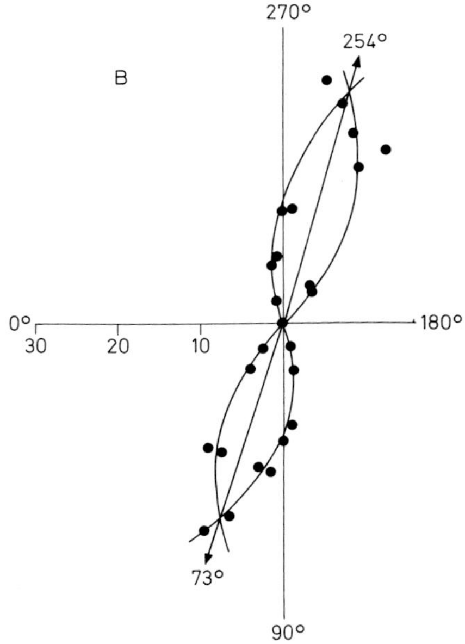

Fig. 2. "Receptive field" in the domain of orientation measured in visual cortical neuron in cat. Radial distance of each point is proportional to impulse rate elicited by drifting grating of that orientation. (From CAMPBELL et al., 1968)

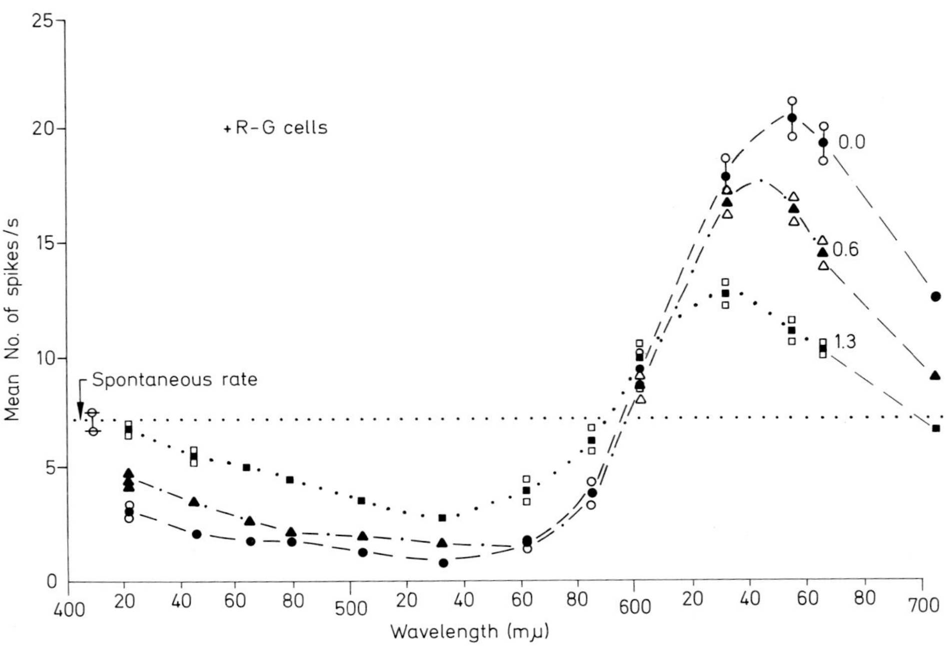

Fig. 3. "Receptive field" in the domain of wavelength: mean result (at three luminance levels) for geniculate cells of similar type in monkey. Dotted line indicates resting discharge rate of cells; thus when a colored flash gives lower impulse rate, existence of inhibition at that wavelength is indicated. (From DEVALOIS et al., 1966)

share some dimensional specificities although they may differ in others, e.g. receptive field position. This issue, and the fundamentals of the channel concept generally, are lucidly discussed in some detail by GRAHAM (in press).

We shall consider here the visual analysis of two important stimulus dimensions; the orientation of contours, and the size (spatial frequency) of visual objects. Among the other dimensions that have been studied along the same lines are motion and stereoscopic disparity. Most of the principles of the analysis of processing channels were in fact first introduced in the study of color. YOUNG (1802) enunciated the idea that different structures in the visual system responded to different ranges of wavelength, and the work of STILES (1959) is an unequalled example of the use of selective adaptation to determine psychophysically the properties of individual channels.

B. Psychophysical Techniques of Channel Analysis

While physiological techniques can examine the response of a particular element of the visual system, in a psychophysical experiment we are necessarily dealing with the response of the system as a whole. Indirect arguments are therefore necessary to derive the properties of channels from psychophysical results. These usually take the following general form: stimuli A and B interact in their psychophysical effects; for instance stimulus A makes stimulus B less detectable. Stimuli A and C do not interact in this way. Therefore some structure exists common to the visual processing of both A and B, where their effects interact. C, however, is not processed in the same way by this structure. Thus, the structure deals only with a subset of stimuli. If that subset is a portion of the range of some stimulus dimension—e.g., if A and B are lines of similar orientation, while C is separated in orientation from A and B—then the structure is a selective channel in the sense outlined above.

In the widely used method of *selective adaptation,* the interaction is the reduction in sensitivity to one stimulus that follows prolonged exposure to another. This reduction in sensitivity is found to be greatest for stimuli close to the adapting stimulus along some stimulus dimension, while it is small or absent for stimuli which are sufficiently different. An example is the orientation-specific adaptation first reported by GILINSKY (1968). The inference in this case is that if the orientations of two stimuli are sufficiently different, they are transmitted by separate orientation-specific channels. These channels may be adapted by stimulation, independently of one another.

Masking also involves one stimulus selectively reducing the detectability of another. In this case, however, the two stimuli are presented simultaneously rather than successively. CAMPBELL and KULIKOWSKI (1966) used this method to investigate orientation selective channels: again the argument is that, if one grating affects the detection of another of nearby orientation, they must be interacting within a channel. *Summation of subthreshold stimuli* may also be used as the interaction defining a channel. Two stimuli [e.g. gratings of different spatial frequency (SACHS et al., 1971; GRAHAM and NACHMIAS, 1971)] are presented simultaneously and superimposed, each at such a low contrast level that it would not be detected if presented alone. If the two stimuli are processed by a common channel, with detection depending on the output of that channel, then in combination they may exceed the detection threshold. If, however, they are processed by different channels, in which detection occurs independently, there will be no such summation, and the only increase in detectability should be due to the "probability summation" when either of two independent low-probability events can lead to detection.

Quantitative data about channel characteristics can be derived from threshold summation data with relatively few and straightforward assumptions. This can be done less readily with selective adaptation or masking, since the details of the processes underlying these phenomena are unknown or controversial. However, the summation method is experimentally more laborious than adaptation or masking, and these latter methods have provided a good deal of our qualitative and rough quantitative picture of channel properties.

The specificity and limitations of any single method must be realized. First, each method depends on a specific interaction. The processes involved in different interactions must be different at least in part, and may even involve different structures in the visual system. The channel specificity revealed by a single method is in fact the range of a particular interaction, and other interactions may show a different range. Such differences in results would not invalidate any particular method. However, similarities in the range of different interactions along the same stimulus dimensions would certainly enhance the power and generality of the channel idea.

Secondly, as well as depending on a specific interaction, each method determines that interaction for a particular psychophysical function. In the methods outlined above that function has been the detection of contrast. However, other functions may be used. Notably, interactions may affect judgments of the value of a stimulus on the dimension for which the channels are selective. For instance, adaptation to a particular spatial frequency affects the apparent spatial frequency of subsequently viewed gratings (BLAKEMORE and SUTTON, 1969). This phenomenon implies that the activity of frequency-selective channels is actually involved in the perception of spatial frequency. The observations on contrast threshold could only show that selective channels existed and were involved in the detection of contrast.

C. The Use of Spatially Periodic Stimuli

Most of the experimental work to be described uses stimuli which are one-dimensionally periodic luminance distributions (gratings). The luminance profile is very frequently sinusoidal, and the major experimental variables are the spatial frequency and contrast (amplitude/mean luminance) of the sinusoid.

The idea of using visual stimuli based on the Fourier series is by no means new, for Ernst Mach in 1866 designed a mechanical device for adding together the harmonics (in variable phase and amplitude) to produce gratings of any waveform (see RATLIFF, 1965, pages 291 and 292). Mach wrote:

> On the occasion of these experiments I tired of painting sectors and devised a simple device by means of which one can at least represent a very great number of different light curves. This is based on the Fourier series.

However, there is no record of Mach having ever used his Fourier synthesizer.

Fourier analysis allows the description of any waveform as a sum of sinusoidal components. Thus, if a system is linear, and its transmission of a sine-wave input of different frequencies is known, its transmission of any other input can be predicted as the sum of the transmitted sine-wave components. In the psychophysical context, "transmission" means the contribution to the perceived image of a component in the visual input, most easily assessed by determining the contrast sensitivity (1/contrast threshold) of an observer to that component.[1]

The determination of contrast sensitivity to sinusoidal gratings over the spatial frequency range ("modulation transfer function" or MTF) is valuable for two reasons. First, as compared with acuity as a measure of the spatial performance of the visual system, it yields much more information: it tells us how the system behaves over the whole range from very coarse to very fine spatial variations, and not just how it behaves at its upper limit. Secondly, if the visual system can be treated as linear, it can provide a quite general description of performance: the detectability of any pattern could be predicted from a knowledge of the sensitivity to its Fourier components.

Following SCHADE's (1956) determination of the spatial MTF for vision, CAMPBELL and ROBSON (1968) tested whether it could predict the detectability of complex gratings. They found that it could; a complex grating (e.g., of square-wave profile) became detectable when its contrast was such that one of its sinusoidal components would be detectable if present alone. This suggested that, at threshold at least, linear analysis was applicable to the visual system.

Data of this type can be approached in terms of two alternative models of the visual system; single-channel and multi-channel. The single-channel model regards the system as a spatial filter, whose characteristics are defined by the modulation transfer function. The output of this system is the filtered version of the input spatial wave form, and detectability depends on a threshold criterion, e.g. of peak-to-trough amplitude, being applied to this waveform. The multi-channel model supposes that each narrow band of spatial frequencies is dealt with by an independent channel. The modulation transfer function is then the envelope of the sensitivities of these separate channels. Detection occurs indepen-

[1] The work of GEORGESON and SULLIVAN (1975) shows that, for suprathreshold gratings, the apparent contrast of high and low spatial frequencies is not attenuated as the threshold MTF would predict. The implication is that the threshold MTF reflects the transmission characteristics of the peripheral visual system, but that this is corrected for in the signals that mediate perceived contrast. GEORGESON and SULLIVAN point out that a multichannel system (see below) would be well suited to perform this correction.

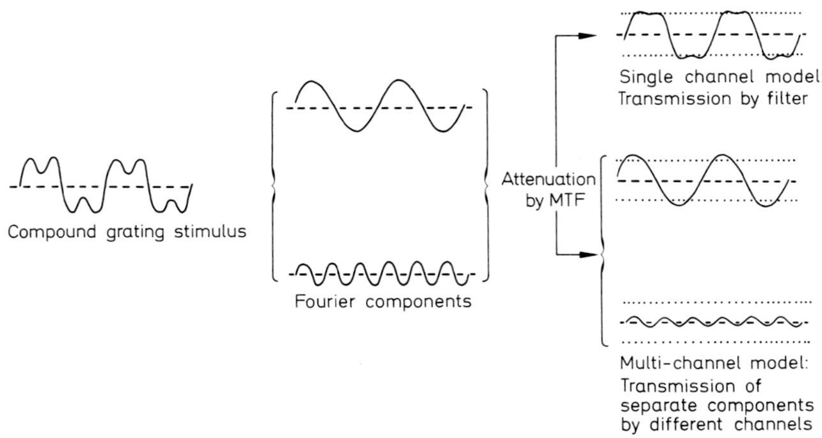

Fig. 4. Transmission of compound grating stimulus, according to single- and multi-channel models. In multi-channel model *(below on right)* two frequency components of grating are transmitted by separate channels, the signal in each channel being attenuated to a different degree because MTF has different values at the two spatial frequencies. In diagram amplitude of signal in channel signaling fundamental spatial frequency exceeds threshold (dotted lines) but that in channel signaling higher harmonic does not. Detection will therefore occur, due only to fundamental-frequency channel. In single-channel model *(above on right)* the two components are attenuated by different amounts according to MTF, just as in multi-channel model. However, they are not transmitted separately in visual system. The signal transmitted in single channel is sum of these two attenuated components. In diagram, this combined signal exceeds threshold and detection will occur

dently in any channel when the signal in that frequency band, attenuated according to the sensitivity of that channel, reaches a threshold criterion. The models are illustrated diagrammatically in Figure 4.

The multi-channel model implies that the visual system performs an approximate Fourier analysis of the input stimulus, with separate channels signaling the various Fourier components. The distinction between this idea, and the use of Fourier analysis as a mathematical tool, must be understood. To describe patterns in Fourier terms, and to specify visual performance by the MTF, does not involve the assumption that the visual system processes spatial frequencies independently, only that it can be treated as approximately linear.

For both single- and multi-channel models, threshold for a high-frequency square-wave or sawtooth grating should be that of the fundamental component. This is what CAMPBELL and ROBSON found. However, other features of their data are not consistent with the single-channel model. The inconsistencies appear in cases where two or more components of a complex wave form would be expected to contribute markedly to the output modulation. The sensitivity is less in these cases than the single-channel model predicts. This is an example of the study of channels by subthreshold summation; the effects of modulation in different frequency bands did not summate as the single-channel model required and the conclusion drawn was that the different frequency components were transmitted by different channels. CAMPBELL and ROBSON also showed that a sine- and a square-wave grating became distinguishable at the contrast where the third harmonic component would be detectable on its own. This result is very naturally predicted from the multi-channel model; the two gratings are distinguished by the presence of activity in the third harmonic channel. The single-channel model cannot tackle the problem without ad hoc assumptions.

This theoretical and experimental approach naturally leads to the properties of the channels being specified in the domain of spatial frequency; they can be described as spatial filters which are tuned to transmit a certain frequency band. However, it should be remembered that a description in the Fourier domain always has an equivalent in spatial terms, and vice versa.

As an example, let us take a plausible model for the receptive field sensitivity profile of a retinal ganglion cell; that it consists of a Gaussian distribution of excitatory sensitivity, and a broader concentric Gaussian distribution of inhibitory sensitivity (ENROTH-CUGELL and ROBSON, 1966). Thus, the overall sensitivity profile is the difference of two Gaussians differing in standard deviation. It is qualitatively apparent that a cell with such a receptive field will show little response to gratings whose period is much narrower than the excitatory region, and also little response to gratings of such low frequency that both excitatory and inhibitory regions fall well within a single half-period. There will be some intermediate frequency, with a half-period comparable to the width of the excitatory zone, which yields a strong response. Thus, such a cell has the properties of a crudely tuned spatial frequency channel. This can be determined more exactly by taking the Fourier transform of the sensitivity profile. The Fourier transform of a Gaussian is itself a Gaussian whose S.D. is inversely related to that of the original (a narrow spatial range implies a broad spatial frequency band and vice versa). Thus, if the inhibitory radius is taken to be n times the excitatory, the spatial frequency (f) sensitivity is of the form $[K_1 e^{-f^2} - K_2 e^{-(nf)^2}]$. Figure 5 shows an example of Gaussian excitatory and inhibitory sensitivity profiles, and a resulting contrast sensitivity function. Functions developed from this have been fitted to psychophysical channel data (SACHS et al., 1971; BLAKEMORE and CAMPBELL, 1969). (This is not to imply the frequency channels are believed to be ganglion cells.)

Similarly, given a hypothetical or empirical frequency sensitivity function, a line-spread function can be derived from it giving the spatial profile of a receptive field which would have that frequency response. Strictly, then, representations of channel properties in the spatial domain and the Fourier domain are equivalent and the choice between them is a matter of taste. This statement must be qualified in three ways.

First, the Fourier representation is often mathematically more convenient. To predict the response of a channel to a given stimulus object, one simply multiplies the frequency spectrum of the object by the transfer function. In the spatial domain, the more complicated operation of convoluting the object profile with the line-spread function is necessary.

Secondly and more importantly, the discussion of Fourier representations here has been incomplete in that it has not touched on phase information. The frequency spectrum of an object does not contain all the information necessary to reconstruct the spatial pattern of the original object, because the

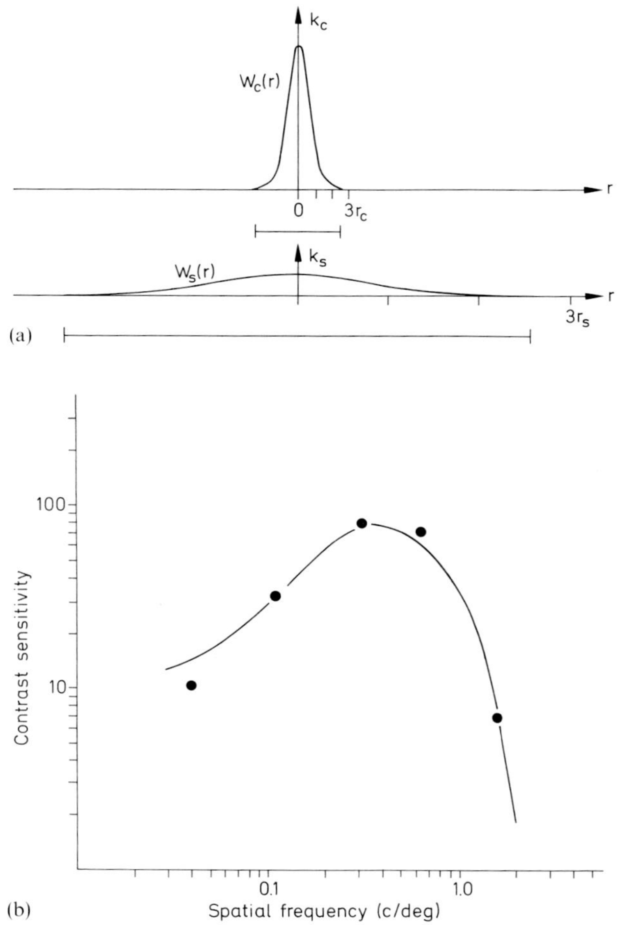

Fig. 5. (a) Hypothetical Gaussian spatial sensitivity profiles, for excitatory *c* and inhibitory *s* processes of retinal ganglion cell. Overall sensitivity profile would be difference of these two functions. (b) Contrast sensitivity function derived from this sensitivity profile. In this example two parameters have been adjusted to fit experimental physiological data from a particular ganglion cell (solid circles). They are (a) ratio of radii of inhibitory and excitatory profiles, which in this case was taken as 5.5, and (b) ratio of total areas under the two profiles, which in this case was 0.90. Latter figure, implying that total excitatory and inhibitory sensitivities of cell are almost balanced, varies little from cell to cell. (From ENROTH-CUGELL and ROBSON, 1966)

frequency components will produce quite different results if added together in different phase relationships. Similarly the frequency response of a channel does not *uniquely* specify a receptive field. A complete Fourier representation does contain all the information (as real and imaginary parts, sine and cosine terms, or amplitude and phase functions, according to convention). Such a representation of channel properties would be difficult to derive experimentally, and usually only the amplitude of the response to different frequencies is given.

It is possible that the neglect of phase information is not just a shortcoming of method, but may reflect an actual property of the channels. That is, a channel might respond similarly to a component of a given spatial frequency, irrespective of its phase. Such a property could not be specified by a spatial receptive field profile. It would indicate a striking nonlinearity (since the effects of waves 180° out-of-phase could not sum to zero) and thus linear analysis would be strictly inapplicable to such as system. Nonetheless, such a channel would very naturally be described as a "spatial frequency detector" and would defy simple description in the spatial domain. Neural units with this property have been described in cat retina (the Y-cells of ENROTH-CUGELL and ROBSON, 1966 — see Section F) and it is implied by HUBEL and WIESEL's (1962) definition of a complex cortical cell.

Conversely, there may be cases (see Section G) where the relative phase of frequency components in the object is critical for the response of a channel. In such cases a description of the spatial frequency response would not adequately characterize the channel, and a description in the spatial domain might be more appropriate.

Thirdly, the most illuminating way to describe channels depends on our theory of their functional role. To speak of a "bar detector" with a particular spatial profile implies that it is used for seeing bars. If we believe that, by virtue of its frequency selectivity, it is involved in a visual Fourier analysis of many complex scenes, the term "spatial frequency channel", and a specification in the frequency domain, may be more appropriate. This view would be supported by the finding of DE VALOIS et al. (1977) that cortical cells show a greater selectivity to grating frequency than to bar width.

D. Spatial Frequency Selectivity

I. Adaptation and Masking Experiments

The model of multiple independent channels, each responsible for the detection of contrast over a limited band of spatial frequencies, has been supported by adaptation experiments. PANTLE and SEKULER (1968) showed that exposure to a square-wave grating of high contrast affected the subsequent detection of gratings of nearby spatial frequencies. The detailed interpretation of this experiment is complicated by the presence of higher harmonics in a square-wave, but BLAKEMORE and CAMPBELL (1969) found a similarly frequency-specific elevation of the contrast threshold for a sinusoidal grating, following 60 s exposure to a high-contrast sinusoid (Fig. 6).

The degree of specificity is conventionally expressed as the width at half-height of the function expressing the adaptation effect against spatial frequency. Thus, the exact value of bandwidth depends on the scale of measurement used for

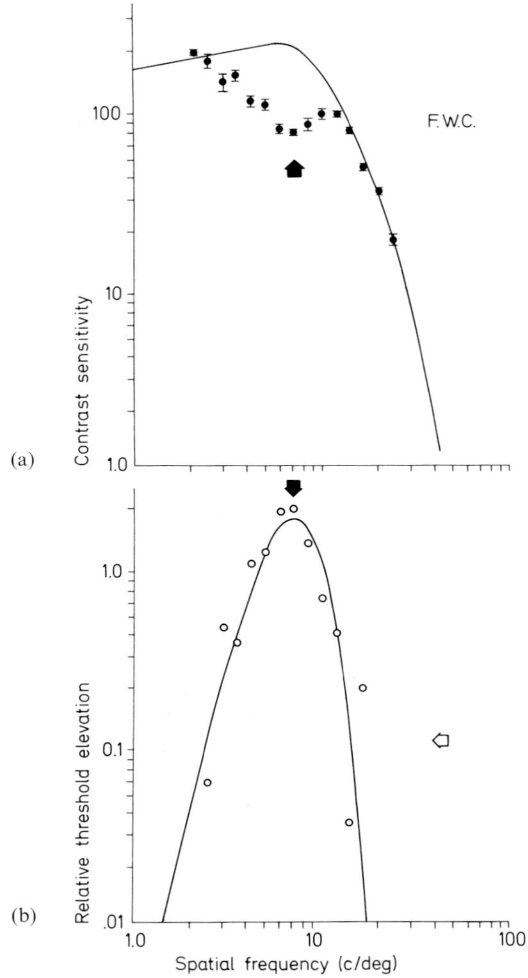

Fig. 6. (a) Solid line is contrast sensitivity function in absence of adaptation, and data points are contrast sensitivities following adaptation to grating of 7.1 c/°. (b) Relative threshold elevation due to adaptation, expressed as sensitivity ratio minus one. In each plot, adapting frequency is indicated by solid arrow. (From BLAKEMORE and CAMPBELL, 1969)

the adaptation effect. Using BLAKEMORE and CAMPBELL's measure of "relative threshold elevation" the width at half-height is about 1.2 octaves of spatial frequency (i.e. 0.6 octaves either side of the adaptation frequency). Using a different measure (the equivalent contrast transform; see section E) and a slightly different adaptation experiment, BLAKEMORE et al. (1973) found a full width at half-height of 0.75 octaves. By any measure, at about $1^1/_2$ octaves on either side of the adaptation frequency no threshold elevation is detectable. If it is assumed that each spatial frequency is detected by the channel whose sensitivity peaks at that frequency, then the function shows the extent to which channels are adapted at different distances (on the frequency axis) from the adapting frequency, and hence the width of the frequency band capable of adapting a single channel. BLAKEMORE and CAMPBELL showed that a similar function could be obtained for any adapting frequency in the range 3–20 c/deg, and concluded that there was a large number of these relatively narrow-band channels, with their frequencies for peak sensitivity closely spaced throughout this range.

These after-effects were not simply retinal after-images, since they occurred when the subject scanned his eyes across several grating cycles during the adaptation phase (and JONES and TULUNAY-KEESEY, 1975, have shown similar adaptation with phase-reversing gratings stabilized in their retinal position). The adaptation of retinal ganglion cells with center-surround receptive field organization might show spatial frequency bandpass characteristics. However, the fact that the adaptation transfers to some extent between the eyes, and that the effect is specific to gratings close in orientation to the adapting grating, implies that the channels are cortically located. Further evidence that the channels are not retinal ganglion cells comes from GRAHAM'S (1972) study of the effects of luminance. At low luminance levels the low-frequency drop in the psychophysical contrast sensitivity function becomes flatter, which is consistent with the behavior of ganglion-cell responses (ENROTH-CUGELL and ROBSON, 1966). However, GRAHAM found that the individual channels revealed by grating adaptation did not change their bandwidth, only their overall sensitivity. The implication is that the spatial properties of individual channels are determined not by the relationships within ganglion-cell receptive fields, but by combining the outputs of a number of ganglion cells with a certain spatial relationship. Direct neurophysiological evidence from cats, and from evoked potential measurement in humans, for cortical spatial frequency channels is discussed in the chapter by MAFFEI.

A variant on the technique of adaptation and subsequent test, which yields similar results, is to present superimposed masking and test stimuli simultaneously. These experiments have used one-dimensional visual noise, filtered to a limited frequency band, as a masking stimulus. CARTER and HENNING (1971) showed that narrow-band noise had a more severe masking effect on a grating containing 160 cycles than on a single cycle and suggested that this was because the single cycle contains a broad range of frequency components, which can be detected by channels that are not influenced by the narrow-band noise. Using broad-band noise, they estimated that the bandwidth of the noise that was effective in masking the grating was 1–2 octaves. STROMEYER and JULESZ (1972) measured the masking effects of noise bands whose high- and low-frequency cut-offs varied relative to the test grating spatial frequency. Their results agreed well with BLAKEMORE and CAMPBELL'S: when the test frequency fell about 0.6 octave outside the noise band, the relative threshold elevation was reduced by one-half, while if the noise band was kept centered on the test frequency and increased in width, the maximum masking was obtained with a 2-octave noise bandwidth and noise outside that band was apparently ineffective in masking.

II. Subthreshold Summation

Experiments on subthreshold summation, like those on adaptation and masking, show that only nearby spatial frequencies interact. GRAHAM and NACHMIAS (1971) measured the contrast thresholds for various combinations of a sinusoidal grating and its third harmonic. They found that these compound gratings were detected at the level where one or other component reached its threshold contrast. The thresholds were the same whether the two components were in peaks-add or peaks-subtract phase, even though the peak-to-trough amplitude of the wave form passed by a single-channel filter would be very different in these two cases. They concluded that contrast at the two frequencies was being detected by independent channels whose bandwidths were sufficiently narrow that they were unaffected by the other frequency, $1^1/_2$ octaves away.

SACHS et al. (1971) pursued this line of experimentation further. They studied compound gratings whose frequencies were as close as 4:5 in ratio. The analysis was complex, because facilitation due to signals summating in the same channel had to be distinguished from probability summation. They concluded that the frequencies of two components could be very close and yet detection could be independent: their estimates of the sensitivity of the channel centered on 14 c/deg show a bandwidth at half-height of about 0.4 octaves.

How can this figure be reconciled with the considerably greater bandwidths obtained from adaptation studies? GRAHAM in press and STROMEYER and KLEIN (1975) have presented an argument that the bandwidth estimated from subthreshold summation is an underestimate. The argument rests on the plausible supposition that grating contrast at a given frequency is not detected by a unitary detector looking at a wide spatial extent, but by a population of probabilistically independent, spatially local, detector channels. The detection rate found for a spatially extended grating stimulus will then depend on probability summation of detections by these independent local channels. Now these channels will not be equally stimulated. This can be seen by considering a compound grating with two components close in spatial frequency; spatial "beats" will appear with some regions showing high contrast and others low. Taking this into account, it turns out that the detection probability by a set of channels with a given frequency response is less than would be expected if all spatial locations contributed equally to detection. A wider spatial frequency bandwidth is therefore required to predict a given detection rate for a compound grating, than was supposed from the calculations of SACHS et al.

On the other hand, the simple interpretation of the adaptation experiments can also be questioned. To take the bandwidth of the adaptation effect as the bandwidth of channel sensitivity requires the assumption that adaptation is an after-effect of prolonged excitation of the channel. DEALY and TOLHURST (1974), however, have pointed out that adaptation may be an after-effect not of a channel's excitation, but of its inhibition.

They examined the effect of adapting gratings of various contrasts on a test grating of a different frequency. Now the channel detecting the test frequency is presumably narrower than the whole MTF, so that the threshold for this channel at the adapting frequency must be higher than the threshold for the system as a whole at that frequency. Nevertheless, a measurable reduction in sensitivity to the test frequency is produced by adapting gratings of any contrast above threshold, so adaptation of a channel appears to be possible without that channel having been stimulated in the adapting phase.

The result, then, suggests that a wider range of frequencies can adapt a channel than can stimulate it for detection. If the adaptation is an after-effect of inhibition, this implies that a channel has a broad inhibitory bandwidth centered on the same frequency as its narrow excitatory bandwidth. That is, "receptive fields" in the spatial frequency domain show a lateral inhibition phenomenon similar to that known in the spatial domain. This principle may be very widely pervasive in the neural processing of stimulus dimensions.

These arguments, then, by suggesting that the summation experiments yield an underestimate and the adaptation experiments an overestimate of a channel's excitatory sensitivity, may make these data quantitatively consistent. The masking experiments, on this view, would be manifesting the simultaneous effects of inhibition and therefore would be expected to agree, as they do, with the adaptation experiments.

III. Spatial Extent and the Lowest Adaptable Channel

The argument above raised the question of the spatial extent of individual independent channels. A narrow frequency bandwidth implies broad spatial extent, and vice versa. In fact the channels must be local to particular regions of the visual field, because the adaptation effects are coarsely localized. The picture which emerges is neither one of spatial point-by-point analysis of visual information, nor of very narrow-band spatial frequency analysis of the whole visual field, but an intermediate one in which information about each local area of the visual field is carried by a set of moderately narrow-band frequency channels.

The finite spatial extent of channels relates to the question of the "lowest adaptable channel." Blakemore and Campbell (1969) found that adaptation to frequencies below 3 c/° produced threshold elevation peaking at 3 c/°, suggesting that this frequency was the lowest at which a selective channel could be found. Tolhurst (1973), however, showed that this was a function of screen size, and with a larger screen demonstrated a "lowest adaptable channel" at 1.5 c/°. Presumably a certain spatial extent of grating is necessary to stimulate a channel effectively. Tolhurst's work showed that the finding of a lowest adaptable channel was nonetheless significant, since it was a specific feature of the detection of stationary gratings; with moving gratings adaptation specific to much lower frequencies was possible with the same screen size. This is one of the lines of evidence for distinct populations of detectors, one restricted to relatively high spatial frequencies that is responsive to static stimuli, and one responsive to temporal change over the lower part of the spatial frequency range (see Section F).

IV. Interaction Between Channels

Although the definition of channels involves their mutual independence in some respect, the channels so defined may and do show interactions when tested in other ways. We have already suggested that a wider range of frequencies may inhibit a channel than excite it, a phenomenon which could be due to inter-channel inhibition. Other evidence for such an effect comes from adaptation to compound waveforms. TOLHURST (1972a) found that adaptation to a high-contrast square-wave grating, while it produced some threshold elevation at the third harmonic frequency, did not produce as much as the third harmonic sinusoidal component when the latter was present alone. He suggested that the adapting effect of the third harmonic was reduced by inter-channel inhibition from the fundamental frequency.

Inhibition between frequency-selective channels may also be the explanation of the "monocular rivalry" effect described by ATKINSON and CAMPBELL (1974): two spatial frequency components of a compound grating appeared to fluctuate in their relative visibility, as if the channels responsible for the detection of the two were mutually competing. This interaction, however, depended on the phase relation between the two components (see Section H.II.).

HENNING et al. (1975) report a rather different sort of interaction between frequency components widely separated in spatial frequency. They used a stimulus in which the contrast of a "carrier" grating was modulated at a low spatial frequency. This has a frequency spectrum of three components: the central "carrier" frequency and two symmetrically placed sidebands. The modulation frequency is much lower than these and is not present in the spectrum (Fig. 7). Despite this, the compound stimulus had a large masking effect on a grating at the modulation frequency, and vice versa. None of the individual components showed this effect. This may imply that a channel responds not only to a particular frequency band, but also to the corresponding spatial periodicity in components well outside that band. It must imply some extension of the idea of independent linear spatial frequency channels.

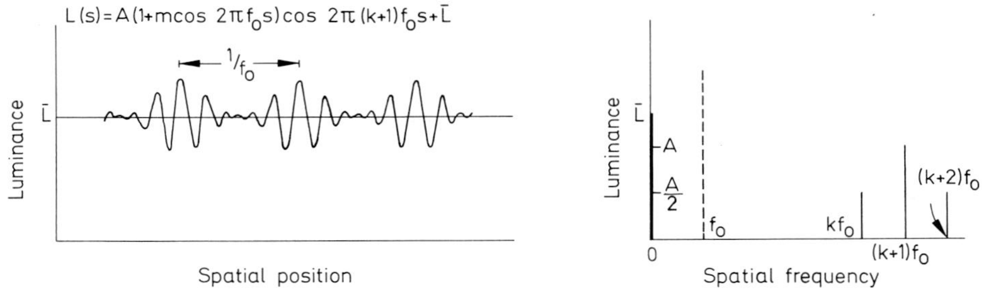

Fig. 7. Luminance profile (left) and spatial frequency spectrum (right) of contrast modulated grating. No spectral component is present at modulation frequency f_0. (From HENNING et al., 1975)

V. Spatial Frequency Channels and Size Perception

The experiments reviewed demonstrated the existence of spatial frequency channels involved in the detection of contrast. If there are distinct channels responding to different spatial frequencies, it becomes very plausible to suppose that the distribution of activity among these channels is the means by which the spatial frequency content of an image is coded in the visual system. No experiment on contrast threshold can prove this, however. To show that the channels serve in the perception of spatial frequency, frequency or size judgment and not just detection must be studied. BLAKEMORE and SUTTON (1969) and BLAKEMORE et al. (1970) have shown that exposure to a high-contrast grating produces a change in the perceived spatial frequency of gratings viewed afterward: gratings of a somewhat lower spatial frequency than the adapting pattern are matched to lower than their true frequency, and those of somewhat higher spatial frequency to higher than their true frequency.

This effect can readily be understood in terms of tuned spatial frequency channels. The estimated bandwidth of these channels implies that a grating excites a range of channels, with maximum excitation of the channel tuned to the stimulus frequency. The perceived spatial frequency will depend on this pattern of activity; a simple assumption is that the frequency perceived is that to which the most active channel is tuned. Now prolonged exposure to a grating depresses the excitability of channels tuned around the grating frequency. A test grating of a slightly different frequency will then produce a reduced effect in these channels. This adaptation will be much less in the channels on the "far side" (in the frequency domain) of the test frequency. The peak in the distribution of activity will thus be shifted to channels tuned to frequencies further away from the adapting frequency (Fig. 8) producing the observed change in perception. There will be no perceived frequency shift at the adapting frequency itself, since the effect there is a symmetrical depression of the pattern of activity. The shift will also be small at frequencies far from the adapting frequency, where there is little adaptation of the channels. Thus the effect, as observed, will reach a maximum for frequencies slightly off the adapting frequency (Fig. 9).

The idea that the same depression of sensitivity is responsible for the threshold elevation and perceived frequency shift effects is supported by their qualitative similarities, and quantitatively by the experiment of BLAKEMORE and NACHMIAS (1971). They examined the reduction of both effects when the adapting and test gratings differed in orientation. They could compare the magnitude of threshold elevation with that of frequency shift by means of the "equivalent contrast transform": that is, the adapting contrast in the same orientation as the test which gave the same sized effect as the full-contrast adaptation at an orientation different from the test. In these terms the sensitivities of the two adaptation effects to variations in adapting orientation were quantitatively the same.

A different type of evidence for the involvement of tuned channels in size perception comes from BAGRASH et al. (1974). THOMAS and his co-workers

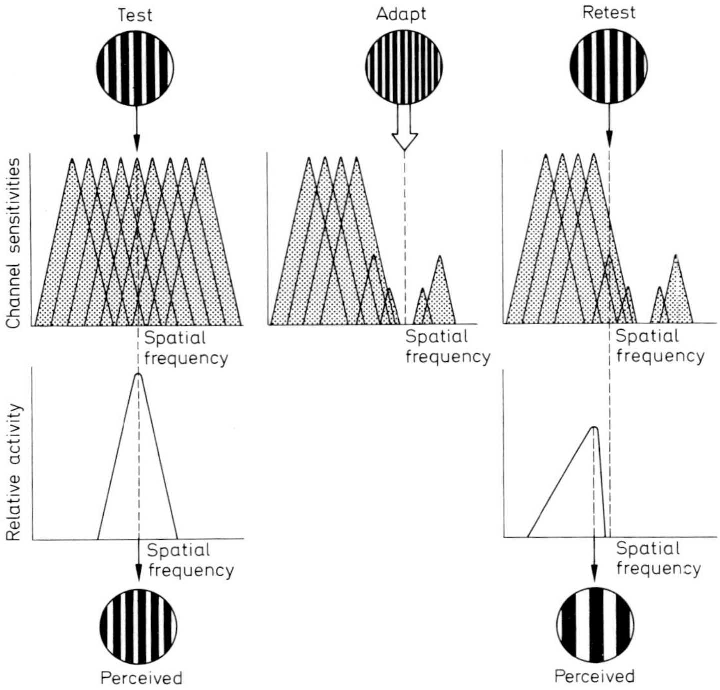

Fig. 8. Model for shift in perceived spatial frequency following adaptation. *Left:* sensitivity profiles of set of spatial frequency channels before adaptation, and distribution of activity in them resulting from presentation of test grating. *Center:* sensitivity profiles of same channels following prolonged exposure to adapting grating. Greatest depression of sensitivity is for channel tuned to adapting frequency. *Right:* distribution of activity in adapted channels, when test stimulus is presented following adaptation. Peak of distribution, which corresponds to spatial frequency perceived, is shifted to channel tuned to lower frequency. (Diagram is illustrative rather than quantitatively accurate: symmetrical sensitivity profiles of equal height are not realistic, and degree of adaptation is exaggerated)

(THOMAS et al., 1968; THOMAS, 1970; BAGRASH, 1973) have shown that size-selective mechanisms must be postulated to account for the *detection* of different sized patches. BAGRASH et al. (1974) looked at both detection and size estimation in a single experiment. Their stimuli consisted of a patch and a surrounding annulus which varied in relative brightness. When the annulus is relatively dim, it tends to inhibit detection, i.e. detection is by a mechanism tuned to the size of the central patch, and the reported size of the detected patch corresponds to the central patch. When the annulus is brighter, it summates with the patch for detection, i.e. detection is by a mechanism tuned to the size of the patch plus annulus (or larger), and in these conditions the reported size is larger. Thus, the size of the patch seen corresponded to the mechanism hypothesized to be responsible for its detection. Hopefully, further studies may indicate whether these mechanisms are to be identified with those studied by the grating experiments.

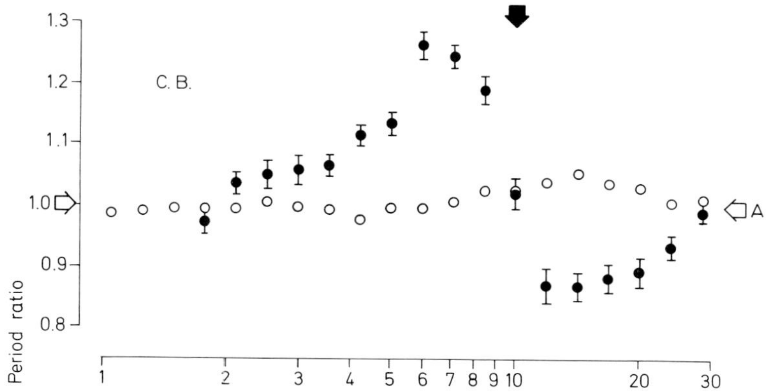

Fig. 9. Perceived spatial frequency shift. Subject was required to match apparent spatial frequency of test grating with that of adjustable grating in unadapted region of visual field. Ordinate is ratio of periods of test and matching gratings, and abcissa is spatial frequency of test grating. Before adaptation *(open circles)* no systematic error in matching is found. After adaptation to grating of 10 c/° *(solid arrow)* matching frequency is shifted away from adapting frequency on either side *(filled circles)*. Greatest shift is at frequencies slightly above and below adapting frequency. (From BLAKEMORE et al., 1970)

E. Orientational Selectivity

I. Masking, Adaptation, and Summation

The interactions between gratings described in the last section occur only if the gratings are similar in orientation. In fact, the orientation specificity of masking and adaptation effects was investigated before their spatial-frequency specificity. CAMPBELL and KULIKOWSKI (1966) showed that simultaneous masking between gratings was a function of their relative orientation, and GILINSKY (1968) showed that preadaptation to a high-contrast grating increased the exposure duration necessary to detect a test grating of the same orientation. These results pointed to the existence in the human visual system of orientation-sensitive neurons like those discovered by HUBEL and WIESEL (1962, 1968) in the striate cortex of cat and monkey.

Quantitatively, CAMPBELL and KULIKOWSKI expressed their results in terms of the minimum contrast for masking gratings of various orientations necessary to produce threshold elevation for a superimposed vertical test grating (of the same spatial frequency). They found that this contrast measure fell to half for gratings oriented ±12° away from the test. When the test grating was at 45°, the orientation selectivity was not as sharp (about ±15°). This coarser tuning at oblique orientations is consistent with a wide variety of evidence that visual performance is generally poorer with oblique than with vertical or horizontal stimuli.

Blakemore and Nachmias (1971) examined the effect of variously oriented high-contrast adapting gratings on the sensitivity to a vertical test grating. The adapting and test gratings were successive. Using their "equivalent contrast transform", the half-height point is the orientation which produces the same adaptation as a vertical adapting grating of half the contrast. In Blakemore and Nachmias' experiment, this occurred with gratings $\pm 7°$ from the vertical. Movshon and Blakemore (1973) found similar figures ($6^1/_2°$ and $8^1/_2°$ for two subjects) and showed that the orientation tuning, when measured in terms of equivalent adapting contrasts, did not vary with spatial frequency. These values are rather smaller than Campbell and Kulikowski's, and the reasons for this discrepancy have not been resolved; the measures used would be expected to be closely related. Differences between subjects, between stimulus conditions, between simultaneous and successive effects, and in treatment of data may be responsible. In any case, all the data suggest that the tuning of orientation channels in man is finer than that in cat, where the analysis of the impulse rate of cortical units shows half-widths mostly in the range $\pm 10°$ to $\pm 30°$ (Campbell et al., 1968).

The method of subthreshold summation has also been applied to the question of orientation tuning, by Kulikowski et al. (1973). As in the case of spatial frequency, it appears to imply much finer tuning than that found in adaptation experiments. Kulikowski et al. inferred that channel sensitivity fell to half at $\pm 3°$ from the peak. The same arguments may apply to orientation as to spatial frequency tuning: on the one hand, adaptation and masking may depend on inhibitory mechanisms which act over a broader bandwidth than the excitation of a single channel; on the other hand, an interpretation of summation data that does not include probability summation between independent areas of the pattern is likely to overestimate the sharpness of the excitatory tuning of channels.

Orientation, then, seems to share the importance of spatial frequency as a dimension of visual analysis. Each of the channels which transmit visual spatial information filters quite a narrow band of these dimensions jointly. The rough Fourier analysis performed by the visual system is two dimensional, as suggested by Kabrisky (1967) and Pollen et al. (1971) (although their proposals for its cortical embodiment are unlikely to be correct). Each channel responds to a limited area of the two-dimensional Fourier domain, corresponding to a spectral component of a certain orientation and frequency.

II. Inhibitory Effects Between Orientations

Lateral inhibition in the spatial domain is a well-established fact. It has been widely suggested that there might be an analogous interaction between detectors responding to adjacent parts of the orientation dimension. We have already discussed the equivalent suggestion for spatial frequency, and the possibility that such inter-channel inhibition might be responsible for selective adaptation effects.

Perhaps the most direct psychophysical demonstration of such inhibition is the phenomenon of "monocular rivalry" (CAMPBELL et al., 1973). If two superimposed sinusoidal gratings are observed, they alternate in perceptual dominance, in the way that would be expected if there was mutual inhibition between the channels detecting them. This alternation only occurs if the angle between the gratings is greater than about 15° (suggesting that nonoverlapping populations of orientation channels must be activated for the effect to occur), and occurs most vigorously when the angle is about 45° or greater. The latter figure is much greater than the range of inhibitory interaction usually postulated (e.g., to explain orientation contrast effects), and must lead to doubt as to whether the same kind of inhibition can explain all the phenomena.

Simultaneous contrast of orientations has been known for a long time under the guise of various illusion figures (e.g., those named for Zöllner and Hering). These effects could be readily explained if inhibition due to one line or grating shifted the distribution of activity in orientation channels that determined the perceived orientation of a second line or grating, and recent measurements of orientation contrast effects have been interpreted in this way (WALLACE, 1969; BLAKEMORE et al., 1970). To generate a significant shift, the inhibition must decrease quite sharply with orientation difference.

In the analogous phenomenon of the simultaneous spatial frequency shift (spatial frequency contrast), KLEIN et al. (1974) have shown that a surrounding annulus of grating can induce the effect without affecting the threshold for the grating in the center, and argue from this that spatial frequency contrast and threshold elevation depend on mechanisms at different levels of visual processing. However TOLHURST and THOMPSON (1975), in the case of orientation contrast, showed that the difference is due to the fact that threshold is determined by the center of the test patch, which is far enough from the annulus to be unaffected. Apparent orientation of a suprathreshold grating is determined by the patch as a whole, and is contributed to heavily by the region close to the inducing annulus. Thus, the two effects can both be ascribed to the same orientation channels, and, they argue, to inhibitory interactions between them. Apart from its specific argument, this study illustrates the importance of considering how a population of units contribute jointly to perception.

A variety of other effects invite the hypothesis of inter-channel inhibition. ANDREWS (1965) was one of the first to propose it; he found great variance in the perceived orientation of briefly exposed short lines and suggested that the accuracy of perception in longer exposures was due to a sharpening of response specificity by slow-acting inhibition. ATKINSON (1972) has found that differently oriented after-images show mutual inhibition of visibility.

III. The Tilt After-Effect

We have described simultaneous and successive orientation-specific effects on threshold, and simultaneous effects on perceived orientation; the successive effect on perceived orientation completes the picture. This tilt after-effect has been extensively studied since it was first reported by VERNON (1934) and GIBSON and RADNER (1937).

Work on the tilt after-effect is marked by striking disagreements on essentials: the effect occurs only close to the vertical and horizontal axes (GIBSON and RADNER, 1937; CAMPBELL and MAFFEI, 1971) or it is found for 45° lines also (KÖHLER and WALLACH, 1944; LENNIE, 1972): an "indirect effect" on orientations 90° away from the adapting orientation is found (GIBSON and RADNER, 1937; MORANT and HARRIS, 1965; CAMPBELL and MAFFEI, 1971) or is not found (KOHLER and WALLACH, 1944; PRENTICE and BEARDSLEE, 1950; LENNIE, 1972); with grating stimuli, the effect is spatial frequency specific (WARE and MITCHELL, 1974) or it is not (CAMPBELL and MAFFEI, 1971; PARKER, 1972).

There have been two classes of theoretical approach to the tilt after-effect. One is that it is due to the adaptation of basic neural mechanisms of contour detection—in modern terms, adaptation-induced shifts in the pattern of activity in orientation channels. The other is that it is due to a more global revision of the subjective horizontal-vertical frame of reference. Each of the points of disagreement above is relevant to this theoretical division, and the persistence of the disagreements makes it likely that phenomena of both types occur, singly or mixed together, depending on the exact experimental procedures. So, while the tilt after-effect must surely yield information about orientation channels, that information is difficult to disentangle until we can confidently isolate these two effects that apparently contribute to it.

The degree of interocular transfer of the tilt after-effect and of threshold elevation has been compared in attempts to determine whether they have a common origin. CAMPBELL and MAFFEI (1971) found 100% transfer of the tilt after-effect but their conclusion that this (and the lack of spatial frequency specificity that they found) implied a different mechanism from threshold elevation (which shows incomplete transfer) has been challenged by COLTHEART (1974). In fact, the degree of transfer found depends on the dominance of adapted and tested eyes (WARE and MITCHELL, 1974). Therefore, in the absence of systematic tests of the transfer of both effects, in the same subjects and *in both directions between dominant and nondominant eyes,* no comparisons can be made of the two effects.

F. Temporal Properties of Channels

Temporal modulation of a grating (whether by drifting at constant velocity, or by contrast reversal of a stationary grating) alters an observer's contrast sensitivity (ROBSON, 1966; VAN NES et al., 1967). The difference in sensitivity between a static and a modulated grating is not the same throughout the spatial frequency range. At low spatial frequencies sensitivity is much higher when there is temporal modulation at a moderate frequency, while at high spatial frequencies the sensitivity is the same, or lower, for the modulated than for the static grating.

On the multi-channel model, this spatio-temporal interaction could arise in two ways. The spatial properties of individual channels could be a function of temporal modulation, e.g. excitatory and inhibitory processes could have different time constants. Alternatively, a distinct population of channels might be activated by temporally modulated stimuli. These channels would be more sensitive to low spatial frequencies than the channels revealed by experiments with static stimuli.

Psychophysical evidence favors the second alternative. One line of evidence that two distinct mechanisms are involved is that two distinct thresholds can be observed as the contrast of a temporally modulated grating is raised (VAN NES et al., 1967). When the stimulus is first distinguishable from a constant uniform field, temporal change is visible but the spatial structure is very indistinct. The spatial pattern becomes visible at a higher contrast. KEESEY (1972), using a stabilized retinal image of a flickering line, showed that these two thresholds varied independently with temporal frequency, and proposed that a distinct mechanism was responsible for each. This argument has been pursued by KULIKOWSKI and TOLHURST (1973). They showed that the thresholds behaved differently with spatial frequency also. At low spatial frequencies (below about 3–4 c/°) the threshold for detecting flicker is much lower than that for spatial pattern; the familiar low-frequency cut is sharp for the latter but shallow and at lower frequencies for the former. At high spatial frequencies the detection threshold and the pattern threshold coincide, and the stimulus is not seen to flicker at threshold. KULIKOWSKI and TOLHURST conclude that there are two sets of channels. One, whose activity leads to the perception of temporal modulation, requires temporal transients but is sensitive only to low or medium spatial frequencies. The other, responsible for pattern vision, responds well to low temporal frequencies but not to high, and to high spatial frequencies but not to low (Fig. 10).

TOLHURST (1973) used an adaptation technique to examine the separate properties of these two types of channel. Adaptation to stationary gratings did not yield selective threshold elevation to low spatial frequencies (see Section D.III.). If the adaptation and test gratings were moving, however, threshold elevation peaking at the adapting spatial frequency could be demonstrated down to the lowest spatial frequency used (0.66 c/°). In another experiment the test grating moved, while the adapting stimulus was stationary. The threshold elevation in this case was much less than that for a moving adapting grating. Thus, the channels responding to temporally modulated and to static gratings could be adapted independently, and the movement-sensitive channels were again shown to be the more sensitive to low spatial frequencies. As in the experiments described earlier, only when threshold was presumed to be determined by the movement-sensitive channels, was the temporal modulation visible at threshold.

A possible objection to this account, in terms of channels with distinct temporal properties, is that the small eye movements occurring during fixation

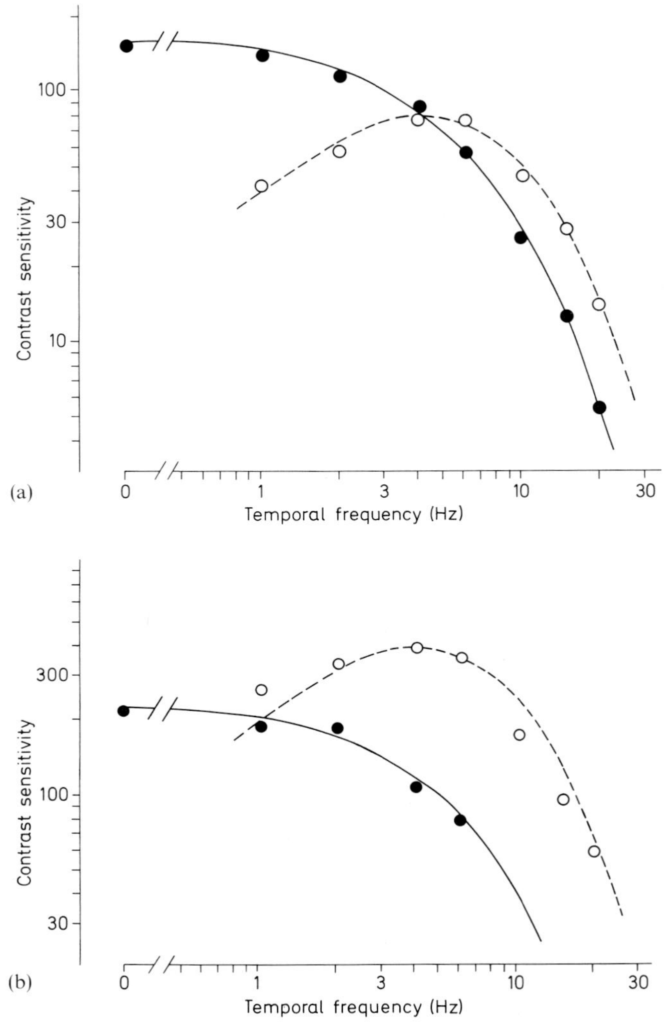

Fig. 10. (a) Contrast sensitivities for temporally modulated grating of high spatial frequency (12 c/°). Continuous line and solid circles indicate sensitivity for perception of spatial pattern, while broken line and open circles indicate sensitivity for detecting flicker. Modulation was sinusoidal contrast reversal of stationary grating. (b) As (a), but with grating of spatial frequency 0.8 c/°. Note change of vertical scale. Pattern and flicker thresholds are presumed to reflect activity of different mechanisms. (From KULIKOWSKI and TOLHURST, 1973)

may produce effective temporal transients at high spatial frequencies but not at low. This cannot explain, however, why distinct pattern and flicker thresholds should be observed, especially in KEESEY's experiment where image stabilization abolished temporal transients due to eye movements.

The two types of channel implied by these psychophysical experiments correlate well with the distinction between two classes of retinal ganglion cell in the cat, called X- and Y-cells by ENROTH-CUGELL and ROBSON (1966) and sustained and transient cells by CLELAND et al. (1971). The X- or sustained cells show linear spatial summation, small receptive fields (and hence a good response to high spatial frequencies but a poor response to low), and a sustained temporal response. The Y- or transient cells are spatially nonlinear and respond to lower spatial frequencies than X-cells in the corresponding retinal region. Their rapid transient temporal response means that they respond poorly to low temporal frequencies and well to high. The sustained/transient distinction exists among neurons in the lateral geniculate nucleus also (CLELAND et al., 1971), with each class receiving its input from the corresponding class of retinal ganglion cell. The two systems may well continue separately into the striate cortex (STONE and HOFFMAN, 1971; MAFFEI and FIORENTINI, 1973), which is consistent with the idea that their activity could yield distinct sensations, of spatial pattern and flicker (or movement) respectively.

G. Other Spatial Specificities

There is a recent body of evidence that the relatively narrow-band spatial-frequency channels discussed in Section D are not the only system involved in the detection of spatial contrast. TOLHURST (1972b) used an adaptation stimulus with the luminance profile shown in Figure 11. Such a stimulus appears to have a boundary between two areas of uniform brightness (the Craik-Cornsweet illusion) (O'BRIEN, 1958). Adaptation to this pattern, with fixation scanning over the area of the spatial transient to produce uniform light adaptation, elevated contrast threshold for a similar pattern of the same polarity but not to the same extent for a pattern of the reverse polarity. Both these patterns have the same spatial frequency content, so the channel that is adapted must be sensitive not only to the frequencies present but also to their phase relation.

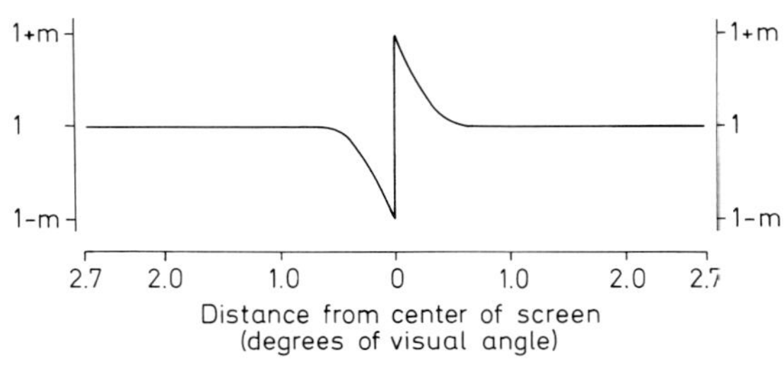

Fig. 11. Luminance profile of stimulus used by TOLHURST to adapt possible edge-detectors. It appears as an edge between two uniform areas, the brighter being on right in this case. The absence of real luminance difference between the two sides avoids possibility of differential light adaptation of the two parts of the retina. m is contrast of pattern. (From TOLHURST, 1972b)

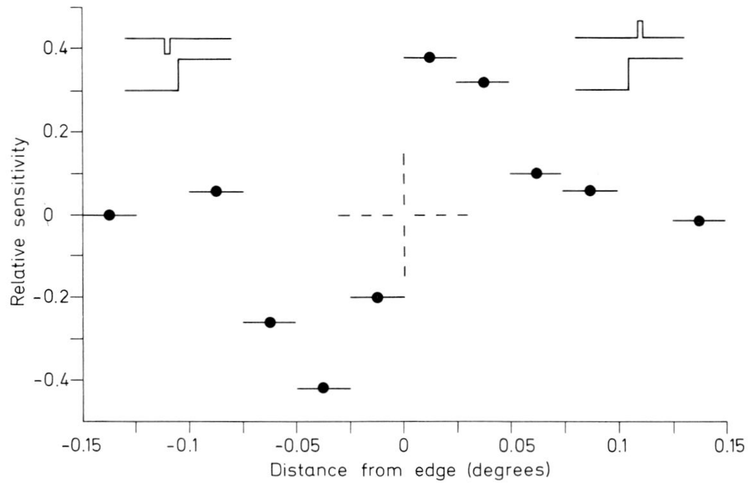

Fig. 12. Sensitivity profile of channel detecting an edge, obtained from subthreshold summation of edge with bright and dark lines in various positions. Each point was derived as follows: contrast of line was set to some subthreshold value, and threshold contrast for added edge determined. This was repeated for other values of line contrast, and slope of function relating threshold edge contrast to line contrast taken as measure of relative sensitivity of edge detector to line stimulus at that point. Bar through each point represents line width. (From SHAPLEY and TOLHURST, 1973)

This selectivity could be embodied in a spatial sensitivity profile which has odd symmetry, like the stimulus profile. Such channels can be called edge-detectors, and have their counterparts in cortical receptive fields described by HUBEL and WIESEL (1962, 1968) in cat and monkey.

The detection of edges has been explored in more detail by SHAPLEY and TOLHURST (1973) and KULIKOWSKI and KING-SMITH (1973), both using the method of subthreshold summation. They mapped the spatial sensitivity profile of the channel detecting an edge by testing the degree of summation with a subthreshold line at varying distance from the edge. SHAPLEY and TOLHURST's results are shown in Figure 12. The profile is very localized, points of peak positive and negative sensitivity being separated by about 0.1 deg. The spatial frequency response of the detector (as derived from the spatial profile and also tested experimentally by summation with subthreshold gratings) is broad and insensitive compared to the spatial frequency channels, so it presumably plays little part in detecting sinusoidal gratings. SHAPLEY and TOLHURST present evidence that it is the critical channel for the detection of Craik-Cornsweet edges, low-frequency square-wave gratings, and narrow ramps.

KULIKOWSKI and KING-SMITH (1973) also investigated the detection of a single fine line by the same methods. The detector responsible was found to have a fairly broad frequency sensitivity function, corresponding to a spatial sensitivity profile with a central excitatory peak about 0.1° wide and flanking inhibitory tails. This is probably too broadly tuned in the frequency domain to be a spatial frequency channel, though the "grating detector" bandwidth which the authors compare it with is likely to be artefactually narrow, for reasons discussed in Section D. Besides frequency channels and edge-detectors, then, there may be line- or bar-detectors.

This evidence for a variety of detectors, however, is not conclusive. The studies mentioned above assumed a fixed threshold for each detector. GRAHAM (1975) shows that if probability summation is allowed for, then the data could be explained by a number of relatively narrow-band spatial frequency channels, each contributing probabilistically to the detection of the target. Adaptation experiments, while less susceptible to quantitative analysis, may therefore provide the firmer line of evidence.

TOLHURST (1972b) and SHAPLEY and TOLHURST (1973) raise the interesting possibility that there is a specific perceptual appearance associated with the activity of each type of detector. A fuller development of this idea must come to grips with the problem of how the detectors interact above threshold. It promises the possibility of using recognition, rather than detection, experiments to determine the nature of the mechanism responding to a particular stimulus.

H. The Integration of Information Across Channels

I. Pattern Recognition in the Frequency Domain

The idea that the visual system filters information through an array of selective channels has proved to be a powerful one in the understanding of psychophysical and physiological phenomena. However, in real life vision is used to direct complex behavior which must draw together information from the whole spectrum of channels. Although the essence of a channel is its independence of others, the information it yields is unlikely to be useful in isolation.

This is not to say that, following the visual system's rough Fourier analysis, there must be any "resynthesis", in the sense of an inverse operation restoring a representation in the space domain. The visual system does not exist to recreate the retinal image; it exists to derive from the image the information we need. If the information is transformed into the frequency domain, then useful relationships must be extracted from it in that form. Discovering and understanding these relationships is the challenge facing us.

A simple first suggestion was made by BLAKEMORE and CAMPBELL (1969). The problem of pattern recognition is the problem of how invariances are detected, one of which (an atypically simple one to specify) is size invariance. Now when a visual object is scaled in size, the spatial frequencies of all its spectral components are altered by the scaling factor, and the ratios between them are unchanged. If, therefore, the system was organized so that frequency *ratios* could be readily extracted, size invariance in recognition could be readily achieved. The fact that channel bandwidth appears to be roughly constant in terms of octaves, rather than absolute increments of frequency or period, suggests that the presence of activity at two points of the array "*n* channels apart" might represent a fixed frequency ratio.

The need to manipulate optical information arises for engineers and optical physicists, as well as for human beings and cats. The blossoming technologies of the digital computer and the laser have made it convenient, as well as theoretically attractive, for many of these manipulations to be performed in the Fourier domain, for example the selection of particular spatial frequency components for removal or enhancement (ANDREWS, 1972). Work in this field can provide provocative ideas about the image processing that goes on in human perception.

KABRISKY, GINSBURG, and their co-workers have explored the consequences of filtering out the higher spatial frequency components of the visual input. The resulting low-pass filtered image, for example, has lost much of the detailed variation between different exemplars of the same alphabetic character, thus easing the long-standing problem of character recognition (KABRISKY, 1970; GINSBURG, 1971; CARL and HALL, 1972). It also emphasises many of the classic "Gestalt" organizational properties of patterns, including many of the well-known geometrical illusion figures (GINSBURG, 1971a; GINSBURG et al., 1972). It is plausible that these phenomena depend on the processing of a low-pass filtered section of the frequency spectrum. This raises an interesting problem, for the high spatial frequencies rejected by such a filter are not, of course invisible to the subject when the illusion or Gestalt phenomena appear. Attention must be distributed in a variable way among the channels dealing with different parts of the frequency spectrum. For certain perceptual judgments, information from the low frequency channels is used; for others, information from the high frequency channels (GINSBURG, 1971b, p. 66). A simulation of the type of information which could be extracted, as attention is shifted between different bands of frequency, is shown in Figure 13. The global forms present in the image are transmitted most prominently in the low frequency band, but for information about details such as the number, the high spatial frequencies must be examined.

GINSBURG (1973) suggests that in the reversing triangles figure (Fig. 14), the perceived fluctuations in the dominant direction of the triangles are due to fluctuating dominance of the channels transmitting different regions of the two-dimensional Fourier spectrum—in this case, regions distinguished by orientation rather than spatial frequency. The fact that in this figure, the whole group of triangles change their dominant orientation in unison, certainly strongly suggests that the fluctuation is occurring in a system where a spatially extended area is handled in a unitary way. This is the case, of course, in a Fourier representation. The fluctuation seems likely to be closely akin to the "monocular rivalry" phenomenon discussed earlier, and in fact ATKINSON et al. (1973) found that the two phenomena varied with pattern size in a similar way.

The interplay of parallel processing in different spatial-frequency channels can also be observed in stereoscopic vision. JULESZ (1971), by selective filtering and masking, has shown that stereoscopic disparities can be detected if either high or low frequency bands are presented to both eyes, but not if different, nonoverlapping frequency bands are presented to the two eyes. It has been a puzzle in the past how the same stereoscopic display could simultaneously

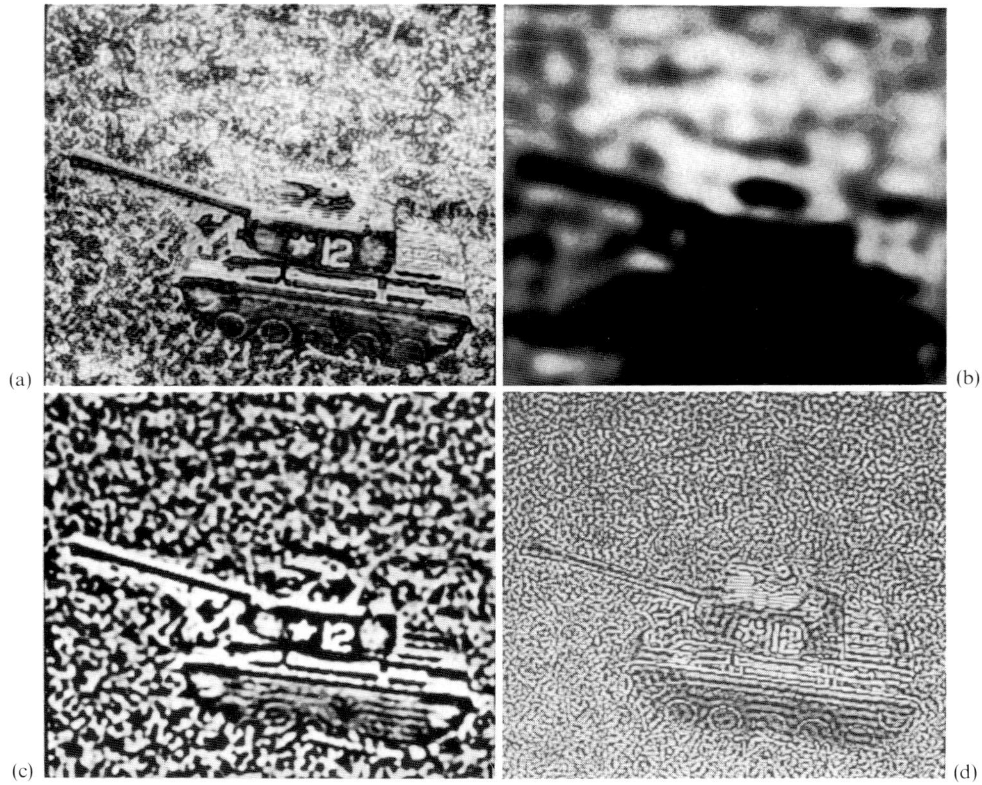

Fig. 13. (a) Original photographic image. (b) Same image filtered to pass low spatial frequencies only. (c) As (b), but with only medium spatial frequencies passed. (d) As (b), but with only high spatial frequencies passed. (Courtesy of H.C. ANDREWS)

yield stereoscopic depth and double vision or rivalry, for instance in pairs of patterns that are similar in overall arrangement but different in detail (KAUFMAN, 1964). Now we can suggest that the stereoscopic disparity is being detected in the low-frequency band, while the mismatch leading to rivalry is simultaneously detected by the high-frequency channels (BRADDICK, 1968; JULESZ, 1971).

It was pointed out in Section D that it is most unlikely that any unitary spatial frequency channel looks at the whole visual field. Rather, the frequency analysis is local. Indeed, if pattern recognition in the Fourier domain is to apply to objects or characters, rather than to whole scenes, such spatially restricted analysis is what is required. This raises the intriguing question: if an object is recognized by its local spectrum, over what area is that spectrum computed by the system, and is that area fixed or is it determined by visual information present in the pattern?

The latter suggestion is consistent with what may be called the "Abraham Lincoln phenomenon" from its demonstration by HARMON (1971). A coarsely

Fig. 14. "Reversing triangles" figure. At any instant the triangles appear to point in a particular direction. This perceived direction fluctuates, and when it does so all tringles appear to change together

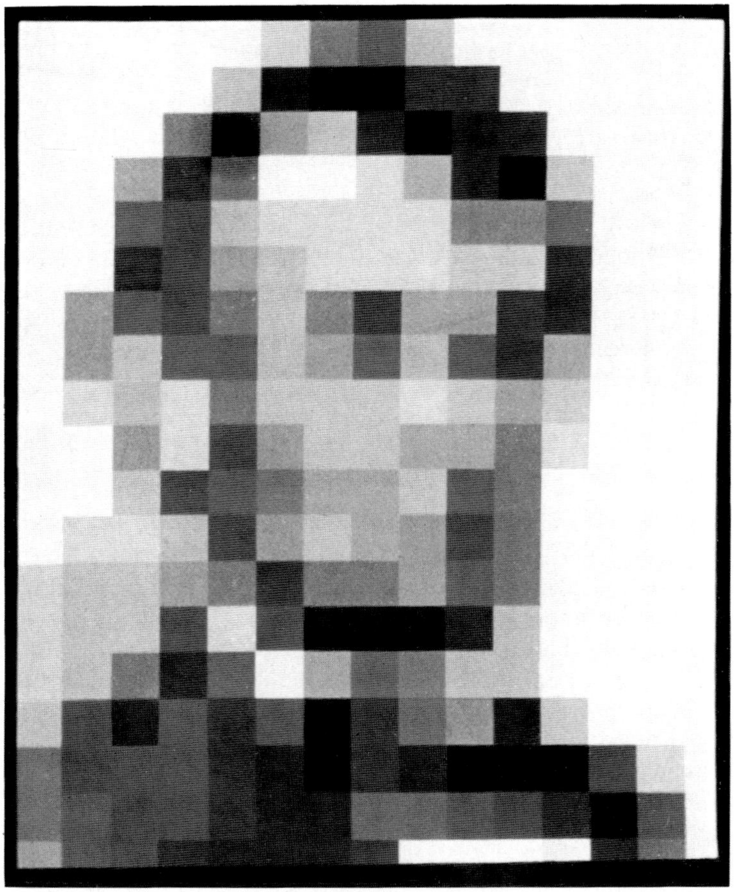

Fig. 15. Coarsely sampled and quantized picture. If high spatial frequencies introduced by quantization are removed (e.g. by viewing from distance or by screwing up your eyes), picture may be easily recognized. These operations do not, of course, restore high frequencies lost in sampling process, indicating that it is not loss of these frequencies that is responsible for difficulty of recognition. (Courtesy of LEON D. HARMON, Bell Laboratories)

quantized picture (Fig. 15) is very difficult to recognize. The damaging effect of quantization is not due to removal of high spatial frequencies in the original, since easy recognition can be restored if the quantized picture is blurred. It must therefore be the "irrelevant" high spatial frequencies which are introduced by the block quantization that affect recognition. These are removed again by the blurring.

A hypothesis for the effect of the high-frequency quantization noise is that it divides the picture into blocks which are analyzed separately, and that low frequencies which cross many blocks (and which carry the face information) are not analyzed. However, these low frequencies may readily be analyzed in the absence of the quantization noise. A variety of other displays may be devised in which high spatial frequencies apparently mask much lower frequencies in similar fashion.

This type of explanation is challenged by HARMON and JULESZ'S (1973) experiments on the effect. They found that filtering out all but the very high frequency part of the quantization noise left a picture which, while criss-crossed by fine lines, was quite recognizable; while filtering out this very-high-frequency portion, but leaving the two octaves of noise above the band carrying picture information, gave an effect very similar to the unfiltered quantized picture. They concluded that recognition was damaged by masking from an adjacent frequency band, as in the masking of a grating by noise within the "critical band" demonstrated by STROMEYER and JULESZ (1972). Two octaves is a very wide band, however; from the grating experiments relatively little effect would be expected from the upper part of this band. To make a strong case that critical-band masking explains the effect, one would like to see recognition abolished by noise that was restricted to the band *immediately* above the picture frequencies.

II. Information About Phase

The frequency power spectrum of a pattern has lost a great deal of the information present in the pattern, namely the relative phase of the frequency components. This is information to which we are certainly visually sensitive. To take an extreme case, broad-band noise has the same (flat) power spectrum as a single point, but they certainly look very different. A model of the visual system as a spectral analyzer must incorporate this sensitivity.

TOLHURST'S (1972b) adaptation experiment with Craik-Cornsweet edges, discussed in Section G, is a demonstration that phase sensitivity is a property of some individual channels as well as of the visual system as whole. STROMEYER et al. (1973) have a somewhat similar demonstration; they exposed their subjects to alternating complex gratings that differed only in the relative phase of their components, and in color; e.g. a green right-facing sawtooth wave alternated with a red left-facing sawtooth. They found an after-effect of perceived color contingent on the phase relations in the (achromatic) test stimulus. An interesting point was that they only found this phase specificity if the frequency ratio

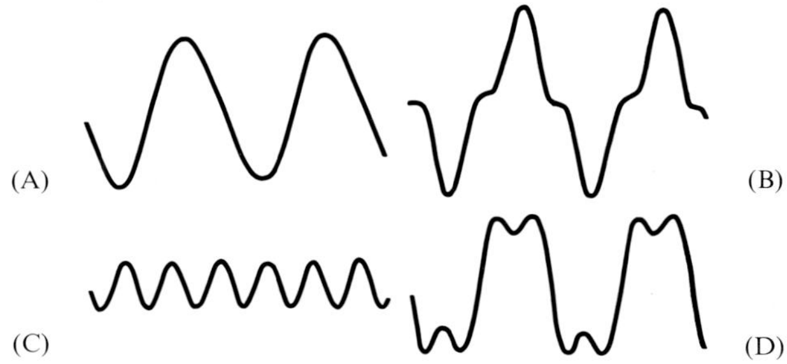

Fig. 16. (A) Sine-wave of frequency *f*. (B) Sine-wave of frequency *3f*. (C) Profile of compound grating obtained by adding A and B in "peaks-add" phase. (D) Profile of compound grating obtained by adding A and B in "peaks-subtract" phase

of the components was 1:3 or less, implying that the phase-sensitive mechanism was only available for relatively close frequencies.

Another phase-sensitive effect is the monocular rivalry of two grating components of different frequency (ATKINSON and CAMPBELL, 1974). A compound grating of component frequencies *f* and *3f*, in which the components are in peaks-add or peaks-subtract phase (see Fig. 16), is perceptually stable. For intermediate phase relationships, however, vigorous perceptual fluctuations are observed. In part, these fluctuations consist of the disappearance and reappearance of one or other component. There are also fluctuations, however, in which both components are visible but in which the appearance of the compound oscillates between resembling a compound of peaks-subtract (or "square-wave-like") phase and one of peaks-add (or "triangle-wave-like") phase (FURCHNER and GINSBURG, 1976). FURCHNER and GINSBURG also found that the proportion of the time that one of these resemblances dominated could be influenced by preadaptation to a peaks-add or peaks-subtract compound. This experiment suggests that, rather than a mechanism transmitting information about the entire range of phase, there exist specific mechanisms responding to these particular phase relationships. The proposed "edge" and "bar" detectors discussed in Section G might be such mechanisms.

Although we are certainly sensitive to phase, NACHMIAS and WEBER (1975) have shown that phase relations in a compound grating cannot be detected at the contrast threshold for that grating; there is a definite interval of contrast in which both components are visible, but their phase relation cannot be perceived. This may represent the interval between the threshold of narrow-band mechanisms capable of detecting each component separately, and broader-band phase-sensitive mechanisms that are less sensitive. MERCHANT (1965) has suggested that this interval may be much more marked in peripheral than in foveal vision. ATKINSON, CAMPBELL and FRANCIS (1976) find that, for spatial frequencies above about 8 c/deg, dots or bars in a linear array clearly appear as discrete, but it is not possible to perceive how many are present, even within the normal limit of accurate numerosity judgements. Is it possible that at high frequencies narrow-band mechanism can tell us that spatial contrast is present, but there are no broad-band mechanisms to pin it down in phase or position? These stimulus situations—very low contrast, peripheral vision, or high spatial frequency—may illustrate what vision is like when frequency but not phase information is available.

The problem of phase information promises to be a center of research activity in spatial vision. It appears at the moment that its solution will be found, not in the integration of information from narrow-band spatial frequency channels, but in the integration of information from these with information from broad-band mechanisms tuned to particular significant phase relationships.

This section, and this chapter, can only sketch the beginnings of an approach to the awesome problems of how we unify the information impinging on our retinae, to give us the visual world in which we live and act. We can end as we began with a quotation from Kenneth CRAIK:

> All this may sound very confused, but there does seem to be a problem how the parts of a spatial pattern become, in human perception, interrelated and unified in a way in which external isolated points in space do not seem to be, and to a greater extent even than sequences of events in time are in the outer world.

This problem is still present whether we are unifying points in space, or points in Fourier transform space.

References

Andrews, D.P.: Perception of contours in the central fovea. Nature (Lond.) **205**, 1218–1220 (1965).

Andrews, H.C.: Digital computers and image processing. Endeavour **31**, 88–94 (1972).

Atkinson, J.: Visibility of an afterimage in the presence of a second afterimage. Percept. Psychophys. **12**, 257–262 (1972).

Atkinson, J., Campbell, F.W.: The effect of phase on the perception of compound gratings. Vision Res. **14**, 159–162 (1974).

Atkinson, J., Campbell, F.W., Fiorentini, A., Maffei, L.: The dependence of monocular rivalry on spatial frequency. Perception **2**, 127–133 (1973).

Atkinson, J., Campbell, F.W., Francis, M.R.: The magic number 4 ± 0: A new look at visual numerosity judgements. Perception. **5**, 327–334 (1976)

Bagrash, F.M.: Size-selective adaptation: psychophysical evidence for size-tuning and the effects of stimulus contour and adapting flux. Vision Res. **13**, 575–599 (1973).

Bagrash, F.M., Thomas, J.P., Shimamura, K.K.: Size-tuned mechanisms: correlation of data on detection and apparent size. Vision Res. **14**, 937–942 (1974).

Barlow, H.B.: Summation and inhibition in the frog's retina. J. Physiol. (Lond.) **119**, 69–88 (1953).

Blakemore, C., Campbell, F.W.: On the existence of neurons in the human visual system selectively sensitive to the orientation and size of retinal images. J. Physiol. (Lond.) **203**, 237–260 (1969).

Blakemore, C.B., Carpenter, R.H.S., Georgeson, M.A.: Lateral inhibition between orientation detectors in the human visual system. Nature (Lond.) **228**, 37–39 (1970).

Blakemore, C.B., Muncey, J.P.J., Ridley, R.M.: Stimulus specificity in the human visual system. Vision Res. **13**, 1915–1933 (1973).

Blakemore, C.B., Nachmias, J.: The orientational specificity of two visual after-effects. J. Physiol. (Lond.) **213**, 157–174 (1971).

Blakemore, C.B., Nachmias, J., Sutton, P.: The perceived spatial frequency shift: Evidence for frequency selective neurons in the human brain. J. Physiol. (Lond.) **210**, 727–750 (1970).

Blakemore, C.B., Sutton, P.: Size adaptation: a new aftereffect. Science **166**, 245–247 (1969).

Braddick, O.J.: Binocular fusion and perceptual analysis. Ph.D. dissertation, University of Cambridge (1968).

Campbell, F.W., Cleland, B.G., Cooper, G.F., Enroth-Cugell, C.: The angular selectivity of visual cortical cells to moving gratings. J. Physiol. (Lond.) **198**, 237–250 (1968).

Campbell, F.W., Gilinsky, A.S., Howell, E.R., Riggs, L.A., Atkinson, J.: The dependence of monocular rivalry on orientation. Perception **2**, 123–125 (1973).

Campbell, F.W., Kulikowski, J.J.: Orientation selectivity of the human visual system. J. Physiol. (Lond.) **187**, 437–445 (1966).

Campbell, F.W., Maffei, L.: The tilt aftereffect: a fresh look. Vision Res. **11**, 833–840 (1971).

Campbell, F.W., Robson, J.G.: Application of Fourier analysis to the visibility of gratings. J. Physiol. (Lond.) **197**, 551–566 (1968).

Carl, J.W., Hall, C.F.: The application of filtered transforms to the general classification problem. IEE Trans. Comput. **C-21**, 785–790 (1972).

Carter, B.E., Henning, G.B.: The detection of gratings in narrow-band visual noise. J. Physiol. (Lond.) **219**, 355–365 (1971).

Cleland, B.G., Dubin, M.W., Levick, W.R.: Sustained and transient neurones in the cat's retina and lateral geniculate nucleus. J. Physiol. (Lond.) **217**, 473–496 (1971).

Coltheart, M.: Review of "Annual Review of Psychology". Quart. J. exp. Psychol. **26**, 661–662 (1974).

• Craik, K.J.W.: The nature of psychology. Sherwood, S.L. (ed.). Cambridge: Cambridge University Press 1966.

Dealy, R.S., Tolhurst, D.J.: Is spatial adaptation an aftereffect of prolonged inhibition? J. Physiol. (Lond.) **241**, 261–270 (1974).

DeValois, R.L., Abramov, I., Jacobs, G.H.: Analysis of response patterns of LGN cells. J. opt. Soc. Amer. **56**, 966–977 (1966).

De Valois, R.L., Albrecht, D.G., Thorelli, L.: Bar or gratings? Vision: 1977 Dedicatory Symposium at Univ. Houston Coll. Optom. (1977).

Enroth-Cugell, C., Robson, J.G.: The contrast sensitivity of retinal ganglion cells of the cat. J. Physiol. (Lond.) **187**, 517–552 (1966).

Furchner, C., Ginsburg, A.P.: Phase effects in pattern rivalry and classification. Paper read at Ass. Res. Vis. Opthal., Sarasota (1976).

• Georgeson, M.A., Sullivan, G.D.: Contrast constancy: deblurring in human vision by spatial frequency channels. J. Physiol. (Lond.) **252**, 627–656 (1975).

Gibson, J.J., Radner, M.: Adaptation, after-effect, and contrast in the perception of tilted lines. I. Quantitative Studies. J. exp. Psychol. **20**, 453–467 (1937).

Gilinsky, A.S.: Orientation-specific effects of patterns of adapting light on visual acuity. J. opt. Soc. Amer. **58**, 13–18 (1968).

Ginsburg, A.P.: Psychological correlates of a model of the human visual system. Proc. 1971 Nat. Aerospace Electronics Conference (NAECON), pp. 283–290. Dayton, Ohio: IEEE Trans. on Aerospace and Electronic Systems (1971 a).

Ginsburg, A.P.: Psychological correlates of a model of the human visual system. MS dissertation GE/EE/715-2. Wright-Patterson AFB, Ohio: Air Force Institute of Technology (1971 b).

Ginsburg, A.P.: Perceptual correlates of a two-dimensional spatial frequency model of the human visual system (abstract). J. opt. Soc. Amer. **64**, 257 (1974).

Ginsburg, A.P., Carl, J.W., Kabrisky, M., Hall, C.F., and Gill, R.A.: Psychological aspects of a model for the classification of visual images. In Rose, J. (ed.) Advances in Cybernetics and Systems, **3**, 1289–1306, Gordon and Breach, London (1976).

Graham, N.: Spatial frequency channels in the human visual system: Effects of luminance and pattern drift rate. Vision Res. **12**, 53–68 (1972).

Graham, N.: Spatial frequency channels in human vision: detecting edges without edge detectors. In: Visual coding and adaptability. Harris, C.S. (ed.). Hillsdale, N.J.: Lawrence Erlbaum Assocs. (in press).

Graham, N., Nachmias, J.: Detection of grating patterns containing two spatial frequencies: A comparison of single channel and multichannel models. Vision Res. **11**, 251–259 (1971).

Harmon, L.D.: Some aspects of recognition of human faces. In: Pattern recognition in biological and technical systems. Grüsser, O.J. (ed.). Berlin-Heidelberg-New York: Springer 1971.

Harmon, L.D., Julesz, B.: Masking in visual recognition: effects of two dimensional filtered noise. Science **180**, 1194–1197 (1973).

Hartline, H.K.: The response of single optic nerve fibres of the vertebrate eye to illumination of the retina. Amer. J. Physiol. **121**, 400–415 (1938).

Henning, G.B., Hertz, B.G., Broadbent, D.E.: Some experiments bearing on the hypothesis that the visual system analyses spatial patterns in independent bands of spatial frequency. Vision Res. **15**, 887–898 (1975).

Hubel, D.H., Wiesel, T.N.: Receptive fields, binocular interaction and functional architecture in the cat's visual cortex. J. Physiol. (Lond.) **160**, 106–154 (1962).

Hubel, D.H., Wiesel, T.N.: Receptive fields and functional architecture of monkey striate cortex. J. Physiol. (Lond.) **195**, 215–243 (1968).

Jones, R.M., Tulunay-Keesey, U.: Local retinal adaptation and spatial frequency channels. Vision Res. **15**, 1239–1244 (1975).

Julesz, B.: Foundations of Cyclopean perception. Chicago: Univ. of Chicago Press 1971.

Kabrisky, M.: A proposed model for visual information processing in the human brain. In: Models for the perception of speech and visual form. Wathen-Dunn, W. (ed.). Cambridge, Mass.: MIT Press 1967.

Kabrisky, M., Tallman, O., Day, C.M., Radoy, C.M.: A theory of pattern perception based on human physiology. Ergonomics **13**, 129–142 (1970).

Kaufman, L.: On the nature of binocular disparity. Amer. J. Psychol. **78**, 1–20 (1964).

Keesey, U.T.: Flicker and pattern detection: a comparison of thresholds. J. opt. Soc. Amer. **62**, 446–448 (1972).

Klein, S., Stromeyer, C.F., Ganz, L.: The simultaneous spatial-frequency shift: a dissociation between the detection and perception of gratings. Vision Res. **14**, 1421–1432 (1974).

Köhler, W., Wallach, H.: Figural after-effects: an investigation of visual processes. Proc. Amer. phil. Soc. **88**, 269–357 (1944).

Kuffler, S.W.: Discharge pattern and functional organisation of mammalian retina. J. Neurophysiol. **16**, 37–68 (1953).

Kulikowski, J.J., Abadi, R., King-Smith, P.E.: Orientational selectivity of grating and line detectors in human vision. Vision Res. **13**, 1479–1486 (1973).

Kulikowski, J.J., King-Smith, P.E.: Spatial arrangement of line, edge, and grating detectors revealed by sub-threshold summation. Vision Res. **13**, 1455–1478 (1973).

Kulikowski, J.J., Tolhurst, D.J.: Psychophysical evidence for sustained and transient detectors in human vision. J. Physiol. (Lond.) **232**, 149–162 (1973).

Lennie, P.: Mechanisms underlying the perception of orientation. Ph.D. dissertation, University of Cambridge, 1972.

Maffei, L., Fiorentini, A.: The visual cortex as a spatial frequency analyser. Vision Res. **13**, 1255–1267 (1973).

Maturana, H.R., Lettvin, J.Y., McCulloch, W.S., Pitts, W.H.: Anatomy and physiology of vision in the frog. J. gen. Physiol. **43**, 129–172 (second suppl.) (1960).

Merchant, J.: Sampling theory for the human visual sense. J. opt. Soc. Amer. **55**, 1291–1295 (1965).

Morant, R.B., Harris, J.R.: Two different after-effects of exposure to visual tilts. Amer. J. Psychol. **78**, 218–226 (1965).

Movshon, J.A., Blakemore, C.B.: Orientational specificity and spatial selectivity in human vision. Perception **2**, 53–60 (1973).

Nachmias, J., Weber, A.: Discrimination of simple and complex gratings. Vision Res. **15**, 217–224 (1975).

Nes, F.L. van, Koenderick, J.J., Nas, H., Bouman, M.A.: Spatiotemporal modulation transfer function in the human eye. J. opt. Soc. Amer. **57**, 1082–1088 (1967).

O'Brien, V.: Contour perception, illusion, and reality. J. opt. Soc. Amer. **48**, 112–119 (1958).

Pantle, A., Sekuler, R.: Size detecting mechanisms in human vision. Science **162**, 1146–1148 (1968).

Parker, D.M.: Contrast and size variables and the tilt after-effect. Quart. J. exp. Psychol. **24**, 1–7 (1972).

Pollen, D.A., Lee, J.R., Taylor, J.H.: How does the striate cortex begin the reconstruction of the visual world? Science **173**, 74–77 (1971).

Prentice, W.C.H., Beardslee, D.C.: Visual "normalization" near the vertical and horizontal. J. exp. Psychol. **40**, 355–364 (1950).

Ratliff, F.: Mach bands: Quantitative studies on neural networks in the retina. San Francisco: Holden-Day 1965.
Robson, J.G.: Spatial and temporal contrast sensitivity functions of the human eye. J. opt. Soc. Amer. **56**, 1141 (1966).
Sachs, M., Nachmias, J., Robson, J.G.: Spatial frequency channels in human vision. J. opt. Soc. Amer. **61**, 1176–1186 (1971).
Schade, O.H.: Optical and photoelectric analog of the eye. J. opt. Soc. Amer. **46**, 721–739 (1956).
Shapley, R.M., Tolhurst, D.J.: Edge detectors in human vision. J. Physiol. (Lond.) **229**, 165–183 (1959).
Stiles, W.S.: Color vision: the approach through increment-threshould sensitivity. Proc. nat. Acad. Sci. (Wash.) **45**, 100–113 (1959).
Stone, J., Hoffman, K.P.: Conduction velocity of afferents to cat visual cortex: a correlation with cortical receptive field properties. Brain Res. **32**, 460–466 (1971).
Stromeyer, C.F., Julesz, B.: Spatial-frequency masking in vision: Critical bands and spread of masking. J. opt. Soc. Amer. **62**, 1221–1232 (1972).
Stromeyer, C.F., Klein, S.: Evidence against narrow-band spatial frequency channels in vision: the detectability of frequency modulated gratings. Vision Res. **15**, 899–910 (1975).
Stromeyer, C.F., Lange, A.F., Ganz, L.: Spatial frequency phase effects in human vision. Vision Res. **13**, 2345–2360 (1973).
Thomas, J.P.: Model of the function of receptive fields in human vision. Psychol. Rev. **77**, 121–134 (1970).
Thomas, J.P., Rourke, D.L., Wilder, D.G.: Inhibitory effect of less intense stimuli upon the increment threshold for a narrow test line. Vision Res. **8**, 537–542 (1968).
Tolhurst, D.J.: Adaptation to square wave gratings: Inhibition between spatial frequency channels in human visual system. J. Physiol. (Lond.) **226**, 231–248 (1972a).
Tolhurst, D.J.: On the possible existence of edge-detector neurones in the human visual system. Vision Res. **12**, 797–804 (1972b).
Tolhurst, D.J.: Separate channels for the analysis of the shape and the movement of a moving visual stimulus. J. Physiol. (Lond.) **231**, 385–402 (1973).
Tolhurst, D.J., Thomson, P.G.: Orientation illusions and after-effects: inhibition between channels. Vision Res. **15**, 967–972 (1975).
Vernon, M.D.: The perception of inclined lines. Brit. J. Psychol. **25**, 186–196 (1934).
Wallace, G.K.: The critical distance of interaction in the Zöllner illusion. Percept. Psychophys. **5**, 261–264 (1969).
Ware, C., Mitchell, D.E.: The spatial selectivity of the tilt aftereffect. Vision Res. **14**, 735–737 (1974).
Young, T.: On the theory of light and colours. Phil. Trans. **92**, 12–48 (1802).

Chapter 2

Spatial Frequency Channels: Neural Mechanisms

L. MAFFEI, Pisa, Italy

With 19 Figures

Contents

When one is concerned with the investigation of spatial frequency channels in the visual system, one often has to face the use of periodical visual stimuli which are generated on television displays by means of the sophisticated techniques of modern electronics. However, many physiologists and psychologists have criticized periodical stimuli as being visually unnatural and maintain that our visual world is composed of more complicated stimuli such as bars and edges at various orientations. Admittedly, the experimental visual world utilized by visual scientists is very limited and most of the time it is seemingly irrelevant and uninteresting to the subjects of the experiment. Without a doubt, the familiarity of objects and the emotions evoked in recognizing them are essential factors underlying pattern perception. Numerous experiments, both old and new, indicate that the capabilities of our visual systems are molded, at least in part, by our previous experience of the external world.

Despite these criticisms, spatial periodic stimuli, or gratings with a rectangular or sinusoidal luminance profile, have proved to be very convenient for psycho-

Fig. 1. The Parthenon

physical and neurophysiologic experiments on vision. Figure 1 is a reproduction from some work by Ictinus and Callicrates who might be referred to, in modern terms, as two Ph.D. students of Phidias, a professor of that time. The work was published long ago in the Acropolis of Athens with the title *Parthenon* and I think it quite sufficiently shows that periodical stimuli are not just diabolical inventions of modern electronics and can be quite pleasant and natural to look at.

Indeed, sinusoidal gratings are the simplest unidimensional light distribution and any light distribution in the retinal image can be expressed as the sum of its sinusoidal components, according to the Fourier theory. Thus, one can study how the visual system detects simple gratings of various spatial frequencies with the hope of understanding how it would behave for more complex waveforms.

The use of gratings as visual stimuli at the neuronal level has been prompted mainly by two factors. First, the attempt to find a possible neural substrate for the hypothesis postulated by CAMPBELL and ROBSON (1968) that information concerning the retinal image is transmitted to higher centers through separate spatial frequency channels. Second, the utility in providing a quantitative analysis of how the neurons of the various stages of the visual pathway respond to the size of the visual stimulus. For a long time attention has been concentrated on how the neurons analyze the orientation parameters of visual stimuli at the cortical level.

Neglecting color, the variables encountered in sine-wave gratings are spatial frequency, contrast, average luminance, position in the visual field (or in the receptive field when dealing with single cell), and orientation.

In the following, I have tried to select and review a series of experiments from psychophysical, electrophysiologic, and behavioral studies which seem to me to combine, giving an overall insight into how spatial information is analyzed in the visual system.

The first part of this chapter describes the neural processing of the parameters of a sinusoidal grating, such as spatial frequency, contrast, and spatial phase; the second part will deal with neural correlates of several phenomena of adaptation to gratings.

A. Analysis of Spatial Frequency

The spatial frequency of a grating is defined as the number of bars per degree of visual angle. In the chapter by F.W. CAMPBELL et al., the human contrast sensitivity as a function of spatial frequency has already been extensively discussed. Here we shall concentrate on how the single neurons of the various stations of the visual pathway, retina, lateral geniculate body, superior colliculus, and striate cortex, respond to gratings of various spatial frequency. The results are qualitatively similar for the monkey (CAMPBELL et al., 1969b; Schiller et al., 1976) and for the cat (ENROTH-CUGELL and ROBSON, 1966; CAMPBELL et al., 1969a; MAFFEI and FIORENTINI, 1973) although the data for the cat are more complete and systematic. These data show how the parameter spatial frequency is progressively analyzed at the various stations of the visual pathway. From the retina to the cortex there is a progressive tuning of the single neurons to a given spatial frequency (Fig. 3).

I. Retinal ganglion and Lateral Geniculate Nucleus (LGN) Cells

The pioneering work at the retinal level was done by ENROTH-CUGELL and ROBSON in 1966. They showed that cat retinal ganglion cells respond to a grating drifting over the receptive field by a modulation of their frequency of discharge. Figure 2 shows that the retinal ganglion cell discharge is modulated in synchrony with the passage of the bars of the grating across the cell receptive field. They described two classes of retinal ganglion cells, one (X cells) in which the spatial integration that occurs over the receptive field is, at a first approximation, linear and one (Y cells) in which spatial integration is clearly nonlinear.

If one analyzes the peak-to-peak amplitude of discharge modulation as a function of the spatial frequency of the stimulus, one obtains curves which

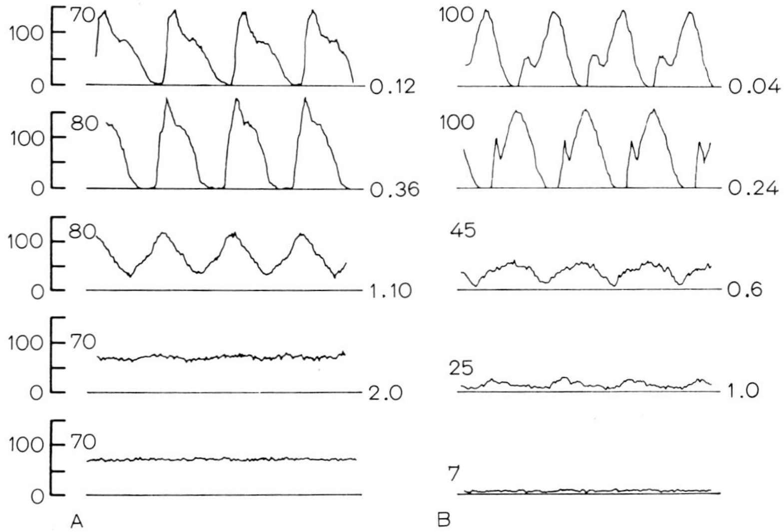

Fig. 2A and B. Responses from (A) on-center and (B) off-center Y-cell to sinusoidal grating pattern of different spatial frequencies but same contrast (0.4) drifting across their receptive fields. Spatial frequency (c/°) is shown at right of each zero line. Lowest records in (A) and (B) show responses to uniformly illuminated field. Mean pulse density of discharge (pulses/s) is given to left of each trace. (From ENROTH-CUGELL and ROBSON, J. Physiol. **187**, 1966)

vary for different cells and are related to the size of the receptive field of them, in such a way that the smaller the receptive fields, the higher the spatial frequency at which the cell responds with the maximum modulation of its discharge. The response curves of five retinal ganglion cells are reported in Figure 3A. All five ganglion cells have their receptive field within the area centralis, the area of greatest acuity in the cat. It is immediately apparent that even if the cells are in the same part of the retina and are therefore signaling information about the same objects in the outside visual world, the optimum spatial frequency of the different cells may occur anywhere in a frequency range of a factor of 10 or more. A difference has been observed between X and Y cells (ENROTH-CUGELL and ROBSON, 1966; CLELAND et al., 1971): the cells with higher cut-off frequency and more pronounced low frequency attenuation are of type X.

Lateral geniculate cells have a qualitatively similar behavior to that of ganglion cells (Fig. 3B) although, interestingly different quantitatively. As for the retina, the range of spatial frequencies to which cells are sensitive varies for different cells. However, in comparison with the retinal cells, the LGN neurons, and especially those of type X, show a decisively more pronounced, low frequency attenuation. For a long time much speculation has occurred (see BRINDLEY, 1970) as to what role the lateral geniculate body could play in the analysis of visual spatial information. It now seems that this station could be given a role in the progressive tuning of visual neurons to spatial frequency.

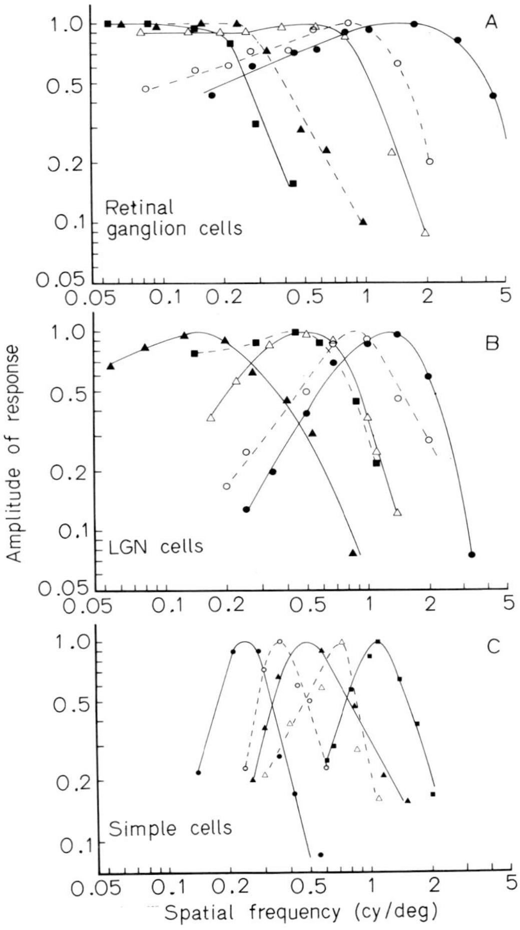

Fig. 3A–C. Responses of retinal ganglion cells (A) lateral geniculate cells (B) and simple cells of striate cortex (C) to a sinusoidal grating, as function of spatial frequency. Ordinates represent amplitude of averaged responses to passage of single period of grating over cell receptive field. Maximal amplitude of response of each cell has been taken as one. All 15 cells are recorded in correspondence of area centralis. Average luminance of grating 2 cd/m^2, contrast 20%. (A) *Filled squares*: off-center cell type *Y*, diameter of receptive field center 2°. *Filled triangles*: on-center cell, type *X*, diameter of receptive field center 1°. *Open triangles*: on-center cell type *Y*, diameter of receptive field center 1°. *Open circles*: on-center cell type *X*, diameter for receptive field center 0.5°. *Filled circles*: on-center cell, type *X*, diameter of receptive field center 0.5°. (B) *Filled triangles*: off-center cell, type *Y*, dia. of receptive field center 0.5°. *Filled squares*: on-center cell, type *Y*, dia. of receptive field center 1–2°. *Open triangles*: on center cell type *X*, dia. of receptive field center 1°. *Open circles*: on-center cell, type *X*, dia. of receptive field center 0.3°. *Filled circles*: on-center cell, type *X*, dia. of receptive field center 0.3°. (C) *Filled circles*: unit with on-center region of 1–2° width, flanked by two off regions. *Open circles*: unit with receptive field of same type as previous one, but with very weak off-flanks. On-center region of 1° width. *Filled triangles*: unit with bipartite receptive field consisting of on-region of 1.3° flanked by one off region of 0.7° width. *Open triangles*: unit with bipartite receptive field of total width 0.9°. *Filled squares*: unit with bipartite receptive field of total width 0.6°. In (A) and (B) velocity of grating was 4 grating periods/s. In (C) velocity of grating was constant and of order of 2°/s. Control experiments showed that peak and shape of simple cell spatial frequency tuning curves are rather insensitive to variations of velocity of grating (redrawn from Vision Res. **13**, 1973)

II. Simple and Complex Cortical Cells

The response of cortical neurons to gratings of various spatial frequencies has been investigated by Campbell et al. (1969a), Maffei and Fiorentini (1973), and Ikeda and Wright (1974). Simple and complex cells differ in their receptive size and their functional organization when mapped with spots or bars of light, and similarly, they differ in their response to sinusoidal gratings. Ikeda and Wright (1974, 1975), find that there is some overlapping in the spatial properties of these two classes of cells. Maffei and Fiorentini (1973, and unpublished results) find that the two classes of cells have different response properties. The criteria that Maffei and Fiorentini followed for classifying simple and complex cells are similar to those followed by Hubel and Wiesel (1962) and by Pettigrew et al. (1968). More specifically: *Simple cells*—small receptive fields, little or no spontaneous discharge, preference for moving stimuli of low speed (1–5°/s). For a large percentage of cells of this class it was possible to map the receptive field in regions of on- or off-type response. *Complex* cells—comparatively large receptive field, spontaneous discharge in the absence of stimulus, preference for moving stimuli of relatively high speed (5–15°/s). More than 50 per cent of these cells give on-off responses to a light spot flashed at any position within their receptive field.

The simple cells respond to a moving grating by a modulation of their discharge frequency, similarly to what occurs for retinal and LGN cells. The response curves for five simple cells are presented in Figure 3C. As for retinal and LGN neurons, the various simple neurons are sensitive to different spatial frequency ranges. The frequency at which the response is maximum for the 48 cells investigated varied between 0.2 and 3 c/°. Most important, however, is the fact that the range of frequency at which most of the simple cells are sensitive is very narrow: each cell is tuned to a well-defined spatial frequency and is practically insensitive to a stimulus frequency twice or half the peak response frequency. The selectivity of most simple cells for spatial frequency is comparable to the selectivity of simple cells for orientation.

These narrow tuning curves for spatial frequency of simple cells could be the neural substrate for the spatial frequency channels that have been postulated on the basis of psychophysical experiments (Campbell and Robson, 1968; Blakemore and Campbell, 1969; Blakemore et al., 1970; Sachs et al., 1971; Maffei and Fiorentini, 1972).

The complex cells respond to a moving sinusoidal grating by an overall increase of their average discharge. In contrast with simple cells, however, for most complex cells there is no modulation of the discharge frequency synchronous with the passage of a single bar of the grating across its receptive fields, except when the grating period is greater than the width of the receptive field. For this reason, the responses of complex cells to moving gratings were evaluated by measuring the average discharge as a function of the spatial frequency. The results for five complex cells are reported in Figure 4. Ikeda and Wright (1975) recently reported data showing that both simple and complex cells can be subdivided into transient and sustained. The sustained cells, both simple and complex, would have narrow spatial frequency channels, whereas

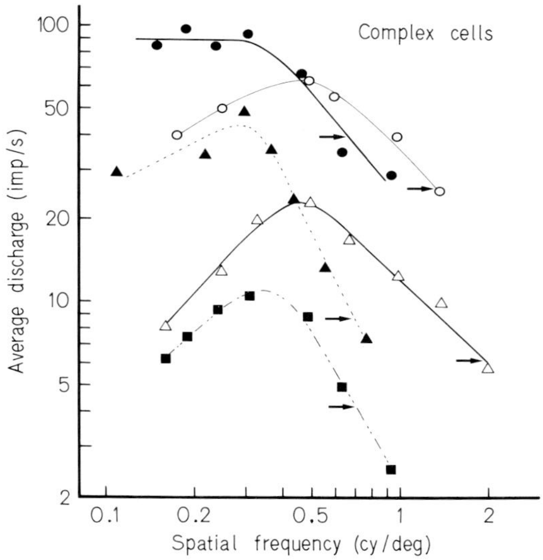

Fig. 4. Response of complex cells of striate cortex to a sinusoidal grating, as function of spatial frequency. Ordinates represent average discharge of cell evaluated over 1-min period while grating was moving at constant velocity over cell receptive field. Velocity was such to maximize cell discharge and was of order of several °/s. Other experimental conditions as for Fig. 1. Width of receptive field: 6° (*filled circles*), 5° (*open circles*), 3° (*filled triangles*), 1–5° (*open triangles*), 3° (*filled squares*). Arrows indicate average discharge of cell in absence of stimulus. (From MAFFEI and FIORENTINI Vision Res. **13**, 1973)

the channels of transient cells would be flat at low spatial frequencies. These authors claim that the distinction between narrow and broad spatial frequency channels should be referred to sustained and transient cortical cells rather than to simple and complex.

MAFFEI and FIORENTINI (unpublished observations) do not find simple cells with no low frequency attenuation. Furthermore they stress that, in the context of the analysis of spatial frequencies, the simple and complex cells cannot be considered a single family. As mentioned above, the complex cells do not respond to a drifting grating with a modulation of their rate of discharge as simple cells do. A direct comparison between the spatial frequency channels of simple and complex cells, therefore, is meaningless since they are obtained by analyzing different variables.

In Figure 3 I have stressed the elaboration of spatial information from the retina, geniculate, and up to the simple cells of cortex since, at these three successive stages of the visual pathway, the response to a drifting grating has similar effects on the cell discharge. Therefore, the spatial frequency channels at these stages can be obtained by analyzing the same parameter of the cell discharge.

The bandwidth of the spatial frequency tuning curves of cortical cells and in particular of simple cells are largely independent of the temporal frequency or velocity of the stimulus (BISTI, MAFFEI, PIRCHIO and ROMANIN-JACUR, in

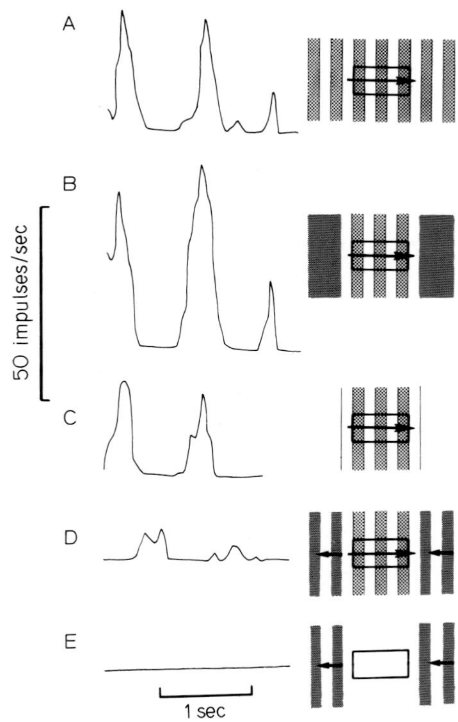

Fig. 5. Average responses of a simple cell to a grating of practically unlimited extent (top control trace) drifting over the receptive field, or to a grating limited by two masks at various distances from the receptive field center, as illustrated in the right part of the figure. The bottom trace was obtained by stimulating with the drifting grating two regions on either side of the receptive field, while a 2° strip through the receptive field was unformly illuminated. Velocity of the grating: 2°/s. Spatial frequency: 0.7 c/°. (From MAFFEI and FIORENTINI, Vision Res. **16**, 1976)

preparation) and of the average luminance (BISTI, CLEMENT, MAFFEI and MECACCI, 1977).

The selectivity for spatial frequency reflects the properties of the cell receptive field in that receptive field size and preferred spatial frequency are correlated (MAFFEI and FIORENTINI, 1977).

Moreover a large percentage of these cells (especially simple) show an optimal response when the area of the stimulus grating exceeds the extent of the cell receptive field and covers adjacent parts of the visual field. These adjacent parts are unresponsive *per se* in the sense that when stimulated in isolation they do not elicit any response from the cell. The optimal extent of the stimulus corresponds to 4–5 cycles of the grating of the preferred spatial frequency. An example is reported in Figure 5. The top trace represents the response to an optimal grating (0.7 c/°) of practically unlimited extent. The second trace from top is the response to the same grating when the grating is limited by two masks so that only a strip of the same width as the receptive field remains exposed. The amplitude of the response is dramatically reduced. By progressively displacing the masks from the edges of the receptive field the response of the cell increases. This property seems to indicate that this class of cells acts as periodicity detectors.

1. Visual Acuity of Simple and Complex Cells of the Cat

Visual acuity in man can be determined by measuring the smallest angle of resolution subtended by the distance between two spots or lines, or by the spacing of a periodic bar pattern. The limit of resolution of a cortical neuron can be tested in a similar way, assuming that a cell is able to resolve the bars of a grating when it gives separate responses to the single bars. Using this method, it was found that the simple cells resolve grating up to 5–6 c/°, while complex cells have their maximum resolution around 1 c/°. Behavioral experiments have shown that the visual acuity of the cat is around 5.5–6 c/° (SMITH, 1936; BISTI and MAFFEI, 1974; for other references, see BERKLEY, 1976).

2. Comments

The experiments were done under the same conditions at the various levels of the visual pathway to make possible a comparison of the processing of spatial information by neurons in the retina, LGN, and visual striate cortex.

The progressive narrowing of the response curves from the retina to the LGN and to the simple cortical cells (Fig. 3A, B, C) suggests that these are three successive stages in the elaboration process of spatial information. At the three stations the tuning to spatial frequencies is more pronounced in the cells of type X. There is some evidence that most of the simple cells receive an X input (STONE and HOFFMANN, 1971).

Since the pioneer work by HUBEL and WIESEL (1962), the property of cortical cells which has been emphasized, even overemphasized, is their selectivity to the orientation of the stimulus. It now emerges quite clearly that most of the cortical cells of the cortex are also extremely specific for spatial frequencies to an extent which is comparable to, or greater than, their selectivity to orientation.

III. Superior Colliculus Cells

As for the response to drifting gratings, the cells of the superior colliculus of the cat can be subdivided into two classes. About 50% of them are completely insensitive to drifting sinusoidal gratings of moderate contrast, while the other 50% of the cells, however, are sensitive and show response curves which are very similar to those of the complex cells of the cortex (Fig. 6). After chronic ablation of visual areas 17, 18, 19, and Clare-Bishop, the number of collicular cells sensitive to drifting gratings is greatly reduced and the response curves become somewhat broader and more similar to those observed for retinal ganglion cells (BISTI and SIRETEANU, 1976).

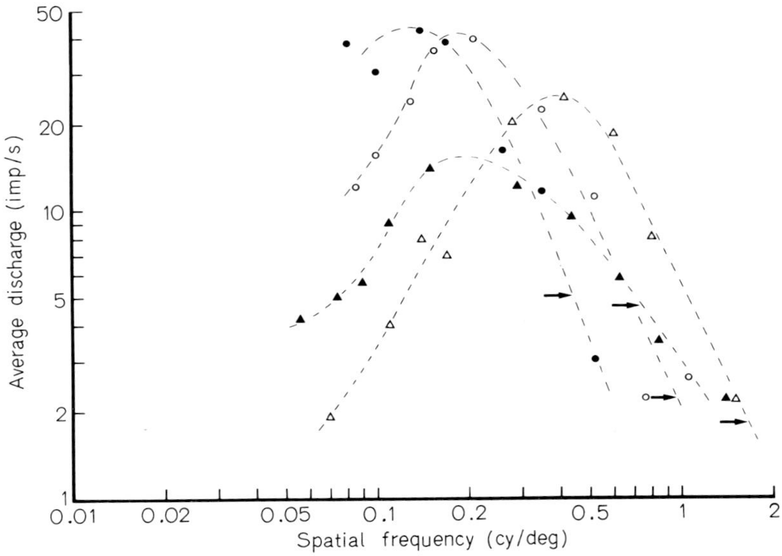

Fig. 6. Response of collicular cells to a sinusoidal grating as function of spatial frequency. Ordinates represent average discharge of cell evaluated over 1 min period while grating was moving at constant velocity over cell receptive field. Velocity such to maximize cell discharge. Other experimental conditions as for Figs. 3 and 4. Open and filled circles are nondirectional units. Open and filled triangles are directional units. Arrows indicate average discharge of each cell in absence of stimulus. (From BISTI and SIRETEANU, Vision Res. **16**, 1976)

The similarity of responses between collicular and complex cells is not surprising since it had been demonstrated (PALMER and ROSENQUIST, 1974) that the cortical afferents to the superior colliculus originate from the complex cells of layer 5 of the cortex.

B. Analysis of Spatial Phase

In a preceding chapter the psychophysical experiments concerning the analysis of spatial phase have been extensively discussed. Here we will limit ourselves to the analysis of this parameter at the neuronal level. The relative position of the stimulus with respect to a reference point of the receptive field is defined as *spatial phase*.

It has recently been suggested by POLLEN et al. (1971) and POLLEN and TAYLOR (1973) that the phase of the stimulus is coded by a cortical cell in terms of the delay of its response. Indeed these authors found that for complex cells the responses to a bright spot flashed at different positions on the receptive field have delays that differ by a few milliseconds. This hypothesis cannot

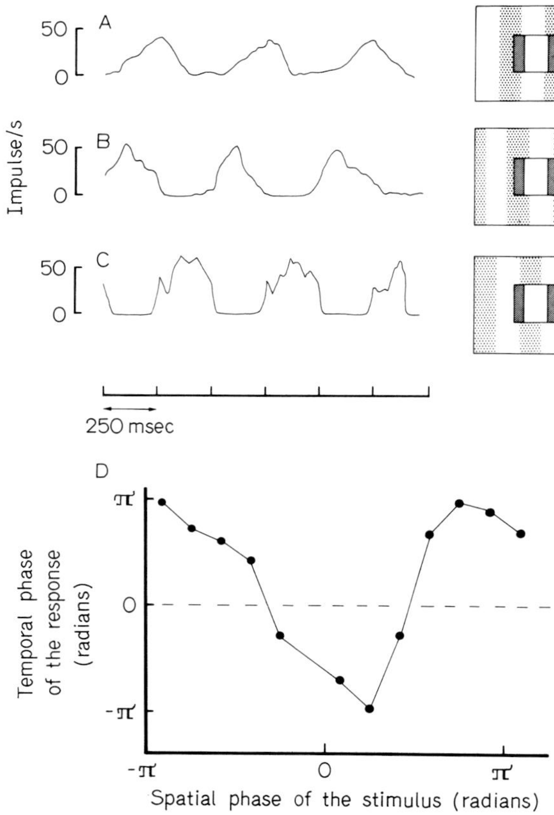

Fig. 7A–D. Variation of responses of a simple cortical cell to an alternating grating as function of position of stimulus over cell receptive field. (A), (B), and (C) represent averaged responses to a sinewave grating of 0.28 c/° alternating in phase at rate of 2 Hz and set at three different positions with respect to cell receptive field, as indicated on left. Times at which phase of stimulus grating was reversed are indicated on time scale. (D) Time of occurrence of peak in response plotted as function of stimulus position (spatial phase). Time of occurrence of peak is expressed in terms of fraction of stimulus period (500 ms), put equal to 2π (temporal phase). Receptive field consisted of on-region (*white*) and two flanking off-regions (*black*). (From Maffei and Fiorentini, Vision Res. **13**, 1973)

apply to the case when the stimulus is a grating because the various parts of the receptive field are stimulated simultaneously.

Maffei and Fiorentini (1973) looked for an alternative mechanism for the transmission of phase information.

The stimulus was a stationary grating, the contrast of which was alternated in time at a rate of 2–4 Hz. In this way the brighter regions of the grating replaced the darker regions and vice versa, 2–4 times in a second, while the average luminance remained constant. Responses were obtained for several spatial phases, i.e., several positions of the stimulus with respect to the cell's receptive field.

For any given phase of the stimulus, the record consisted of a series of periodic responses with the same temporal period as the stimulus (Fig. 7). It is apparent from the records that the time of occurrence of the peaks varies with the spatial phase of the stimulus. If the time to the peak is measured from each record and plotted against the spatial phase, the graph of Figure 7 is obtained. The ordinate (temporal phase) is the time of occurrence of the peak expressed as a fraction of the stimulus period. The temporal phase of the response varies rather regularly with its spatial phase.

On the basis of these results, the hypothesis has been formulated that the spatial phase of the stimulus is coded in terms of the temporal phase of the response. The phase of the response to a periodic stimulus is a different parameter from the delay of the response to a flash. The phase shifts in the responses probably result from the interplay of various contributions of the excitatory and inhibitory regions of the simple cell receptive field, as was shown to occur in retinal ganglion cells (MAFFEI and CERVETTO, 1968).

A similar experiment was performed on complex cells. About 50% of these cells, however, do not even respond to stationary alternating gratings. In those complex cells which respond to this stimulus, the temporal phase of the response was found to be independent of the spatial phase of the stimulus.

C. Analysis of Contrast in Retinal, Geniculate, and Cortical Cells

For a sine-wave grating of constant average luminance, this quantity is proportional to the amplitude of its luminance profile. The contrast of the grating is defined as:

$$C = \frac{L_{max} - L_{min}}{L_{max} + L_{min}}$$

where L_{max} and L_{min} are the maximum and minimum luminances of the bars, respectively.

A few years ago, CAMPBELL and MAFFEI (1970) investigated human visual-evoked potentials in response to sinusoidal gratings, the phase of which was alternated in time. They found that for each spatial frequency the amplitude of the evoked potential was linearly related to the logarithm of the contrast of the grating (Fig. 8). Moreover, they found that extrapolation of the regression line between evoked potential amplitude and logarithm of contrast to zero amplitude predicts the psychophysical contrast threshold (Fig. 8).

Subsequently FIORENTINI and MAFFEI (1973), by a method of binocular matching, demonstrated that the contrast perceived by a human subject (subjec-

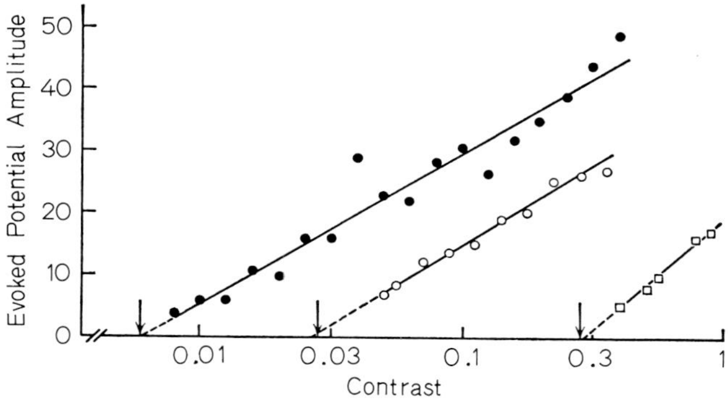

Fig. 8. Human; evoked potentials. Three sets of results were obtained at spatial frequencies of 3.5, 9, and 18 c/° from left to right. Arrows indicate psychophysical threshold obtained at each frequency. Evoked potential amplitude is measured in relative units. (From CAMPBELL and MAFFEI, J. Physiol. **207**, 1970)

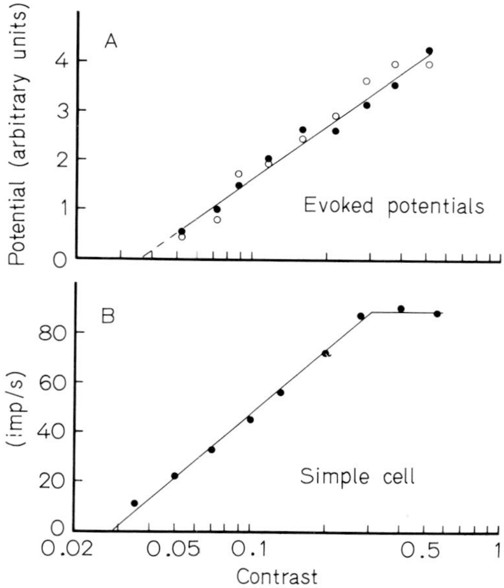

Fig. 9. (A) Amplitude of visual-evoked potentials recorded from cat in response to an alternating grating of 1.3 c/°. (From CAMPBELL et al., J. Physiol. **229**; 1973.) (B) Amplitude of response of simple cell of striate cortex of cat to grating of 0.45 c/° moving across cell receptive field. (MAFFEI and FIORENTINI, Vision Res. **13**, 1973)

tive contrast) is linearly related to the log contrast of the grating at any given spatial frequency over a range from threshold to more than 1 log unit above threshold. Still more recently CAMPBELL et al. (1973), used in the cat the same technique of the evoked potentials as for the human subjects and found again a linear relationship between the amplitude of evoked potentials and the logarithm of contrast (Fig. 9A). Since the relation held for the experimental animal, it has become possible to ask the question of how and in which class of cells in the visual pathway, contrast is elaborated. A linear relation between the amplitude of the cell response and the logarithm of stimulus contrast was found to hold for one class of cells in the visual cortex, i.e., the so-called simple cells (Fig. 9B). Neither retinal nor geniculate units showed such relation. For the complex cells of the striate cortex, the relation was found to be linear only in a small proportion of the units investigated. The conclusion was proposed that the logarithmic relation observed in the evoked potentials of the cat and man, as well as at a perceptual level, could probably be due to the outcome of an elaboration carried out also at simple cell level.

Comments

Many lines of experimental evidence suggest that in the cat the class of simple cells of the cortex has the properties required for an analysis of spatial frequency: the various cells are tuned to different spatial frequencies. In addition they can encode the amplitude of the sinusoidal components (contrast of the image) and their spatial phase, in terms of two different parameters of their responses. These characteristics of the simple cells may recall qualitatively the

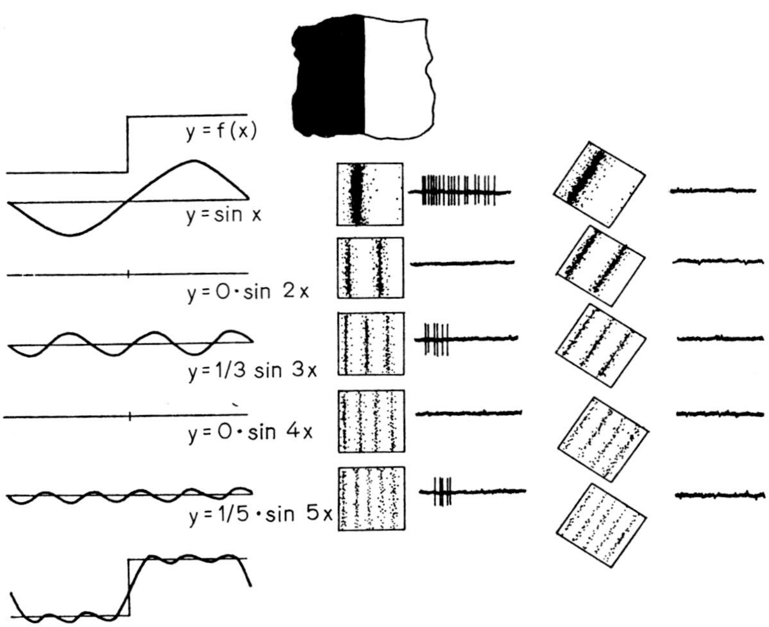

Fig. 10. Scheme illustrating expansion of a gradient of illumination into Fourier series by visual cortical receptive fields. (From GLEZER et al., Vision Res. **13**, 1973)

behavior of Fourier analyzers, although simple cells also exhibit nonlinear properties, for example in the processing of contrast.

The suggestion that the visual system could work like a Fourier analyzer is also suggested by recent findings by GLEZER et al. (1973), POLLEN and RONNER (1975), and GLEZER et al. (1976) who found in the visual area 18 of the cat that some complex cells respond better to gratings than to any other visual stimulus. Moreover, these cells are sensitive to the number of cycles of the gratings. They have also found that in some orientational columns the different cells are sensitive to a different number of cycles of the grating. They formulate the hypothesis that these groups of cells, taken together, could transmit a matrix of information concerning the harmonics of a complex image of a given orientation. The model is illustrated in Figure 10 in which GLEZER et al. (1973) report the expansion of a step function into Fourier series. Shown on the right are receptive field sets within two columns of different orientation and the corresponding responses to the step stimulus. The receptive fields oriented parallel to the edge would give responses with amplitudes proportional to the expansion coefficients. Columns where receptive field are not parallel to the edge do not respond to it. The model is certainly of some interest in my opinion, however, the experimental evidence supporting it is still rather weak.

D. Architectural Organization of Spatial Frequency Detectors in the Visual Cortex: Spatial Frequency Rows

HUBEL and WIESEL (1962, 1965, 1968) have shown that areas 17 and 18 have a highly ordered spatial organization with respect to the cell preferred orientation. When the microelectrode penetration is perpendicular to the surface of the cortex, the preferred stimulus orientation of cells remains approximately the same from surface to white matter. The slab of the cortex within which the cells have the same preferred orientation has been called "orientation column." HUBEL and WIESEL have recently investigated also the spatial organization of the visual cortex with respect to the cell preferred orientation in tangential penetrations (HUBEL and WIESEL, 1974). They have shown that in the monkey, for tracks of the electrode of the order of 1 mm or more the orientation changes orderly from one cell to the next, reaching a total rotation of 180° in less than 1 mm.

MAFFEI and FIORENTINI (1977) have examined the distribution of cortical cells in the cat with respect to the preferred spatial frequency of the stimulus both in perpendicular and in tangential penetrations. The findings are suggestive of a quite precise organization of area 17 with respect to this parameter. The architecture of cortical cells according to the preferred spatial frequency of the stimulus seems to be somewhat complementary to that for orientation in that when one parameter is constant the other usually varies and viceversa. More

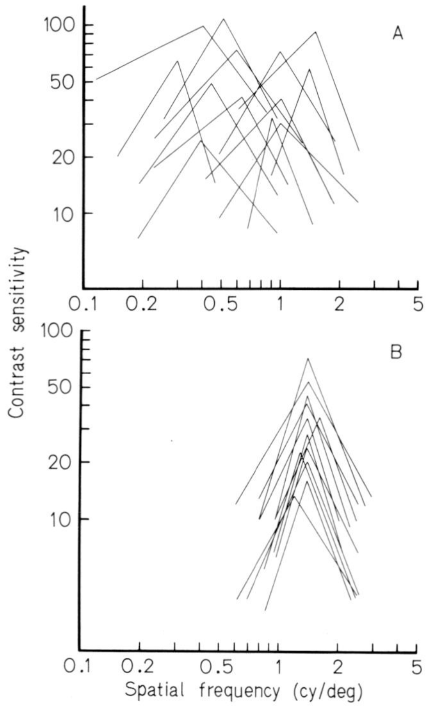

Fig. 11. (A) Contrast sensitivity curves of 13 neurons recorded in a penetration perpendicular to the cortical surface in area 17. All the cells had approximately the same preferred stimulus orientation (vertical). The ordinates represent the reciprocal of contrast threshold (contrast in percent). (B) Contrast sensitivity curves of 12 neurons recorded in a tangential penetration perpendicular to the medial plane in area 17 (layer IV). All the neurons were classified as simple. (From MAFFEI and FIORENTINI, Vision Res. **17**, 1977)

explicitely, in penetrations perpendicular to the surface of the cortex (columns), the cells maintain approximately the same preferred orientation but show a large spectrum of preferred spatial frequencies. In penetrations parallel to the surface of the cortex, on the contrary, the preferred orientation usually changes orderly from cell to cell, but the preferred spatial frequency remains practically invariant.

Examples of the contrast sensitivity curves for cells recorded in an orientation column and in a tangential penetration are reported in Figure 11 (A and B, respectively). Other examples of how the orientation and preferred spatial frequency vary in tangential penetrations are reported in Figure 12.

The architectural organization in terms of spatial frequency of cortical cells corresponds, at a first approximation, to their receptive field size. Indeed, MAFFEI and FIORENTINI (1977) have shown that when a large number of cells are considered, a correlation between the preferred spatial frequency of the stimulus and the size of the receptive field becomes apparent.

A sketch of a two-dimensional architectural organization of the striate cortex is reported in Figure 13, where cells located in the same column have the same

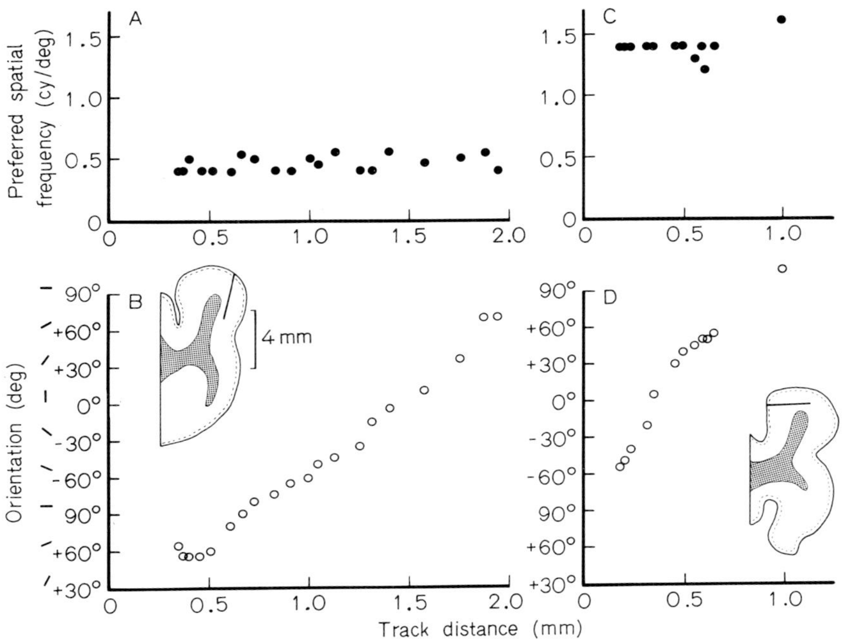

Fig. 12A–D. Preferred spatial frequency and orientation of cells recorded in tangential penetrations, as functions of microelectrode track distance. (A) and (B) Penetration in the coronal plane very close to the medial surface (see inset). (C) and (D) Penetration perpendicular to the medial plane (see inset). In (A) and (B) 15 cells were classified as simple and 5 were unclassified. In (C) and (D) all the cells were classified as simple. (From MAFFEI and FIORENTINI, Vision Res., **17**, 1977)

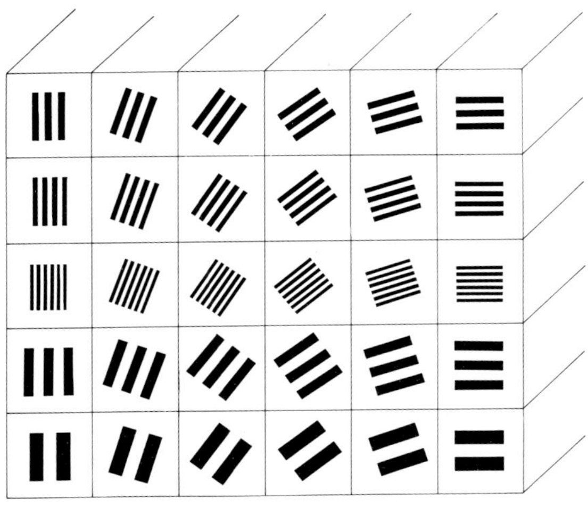

Fig. 13. Sketch of a coronal section of the cat striate cortex describing the possible arrangement of receptive fields according to their preferred spatial frequency and orientation. The gratings in each row have the same period and those in each column have the same orientation

preferred orientation but a variety of preferred spatial frequencies (and of receptive field sizes), while cells in the same layer or sublayer have different preferred orientations, but virtually the same preferred spatial frequency.

The architectural arrangement of cells in a two-dimensional array according to these two stimulus parameters, i.e., orientation and spatial frequency, recalls the columns and rows of a matrix, where column stands for orientation and row stands for spatial frequency. The position of each neuron in the array is specified by two indices, j and k, expressing two functional properties of the neuron: j is the column index (orientation) and k is the row index (spatial frequency):

$$\begin{matrix} a_{1,1} & a_{2,1} & \cdots & \cdots & a_{n,1} \\ a_{1,2} & a_{2,2} & \cdots & \cdots & \cdots \\ \cdots & \cdots & \cdots & a_{j,k} & \cdots \\ a_{1,n} & \cdots & \cdots & \cdots & \cdots \end{matrix}$$

One could speculate that this matrix transforms the two-dimensional light distribution of the stimulus in a neural image encoded in terms of orientation and spatial frequency. If we consider the matrix corresponding to a hypercolumn (where the preferred cell orientation covers a range of 180° and all the cells look at the same area of the visual field) then the simultaneous activation of a number of elements of this matrix would be the neural correlate of a visual object contained in that area.

E. Neural Adaptation to Gratings

BLAKEMORE and CAMPBELL (1969) showed that prolonged observation of a high contrast grating greatly reduces the visibility of a low contrast grating of the same spatial frequency. One can experience this effect by inspecting the upper left grating in Figure 14 for about 1 min. After this adaptation period the central grating can hardly be detected. This phenomenon is highly selective for orientation and spatial frequency: the visibility of a grating of low contrast is not affected by adaptation to grating of different orientation and spatial frequency. Using this technique, BLAKEMORE and CAMPBELL (1969) were able to define the widths of the spatial frequency channels. For the neurophysiologist the next logical question was: Does the phenomenon of perceptual adaptation have a neural correlate in a given class of cells? And if so, is it possible to use the technique of adaptation at the neuronal level for a description of the spatial frequency channels? In other words, is it possible to repeat the experiment of BLAKEMORE and CAMPBELL in a single neuron? The experiment supplies a

Fig. 14. Perceptual adaptation to gratings. Grating at upper left and central grating have same spatial frequency, but latter has lower contrast. If one looks at upper left grating for about 1 min with gaze moving around small circle and then looks at low-contrast grating, latter grating seems invisible for few seconds. Looking at horizontal grating or at vertical grating of different spatial frequency, it has no effect on visibility of central grating. (Modified from BLAKEMORE and CAMPBELL, J. Physiol. **203**, 1969)

positive answer and indicates again that the simple cells of the cortex are the neural substrate for the spatial frequency channels. The evidence for this conclusion was offered by experiments performed by MAFFEI et al. (1973). A grating of low contrast (three times the threshold) was drifted over the receptive field of single visual units and the average rate of discharge recorded for 1 min,

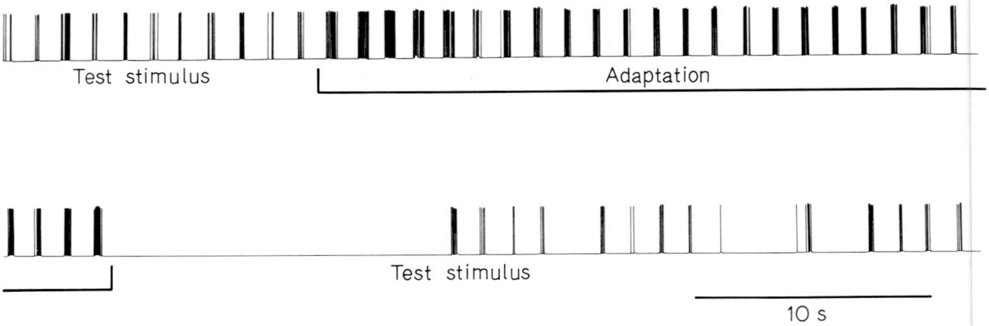

Fig. 15. Adaptation of a simple cell to a grating. Spike activity of simple cell of striate cortex was recorded on penwriter. Stimulus was a grating oriented at preferred orientation of cell and drifting in its preferred direction. Average luminance of grating was kept constant at 2 cd/m^2. Clusters of spikes in record are responses of cell to single period of grating. In first and last parts of record (test stimulus), contrast was 6%, three times threshold. During 1 min period of adaptation, contrast was raised to about 55%. After adaptation period, cell did not respond at all to test stimulus for 14 s and slowly recovered in another 15 s. (From MAFFEI et al., Science **182**, 1973)

then the contrast was set at the highest available value and the cell was exposed to this stimulus (adapting stimulus) for 1 min, after which the contrast was lowered again to its initial value and the response to the test stimulus was recorded for at least another minute. Retinal ganglion and geniculate cells did not show any phenomenon of adaptation, whereas the simple cells of the striate cortex showed this phenomenon without exception. Figure 15 illustrates the adaptation of a simple cell. The top record shows the response to a drifting grating of a relatively low contrast (the test stimulus) and then the response to the adapting grating of high contrast. The bottom record shows the end of the adaptation period and the subsequent slow recovery of the response to the test grating. In this case, the response to the test stimulus returned to its initial value in about 30 s. For all simple cells examined, the recovery time after 1 min of adaptation varied from 20–25 s to 2 min. As for the complex cells, they fell into two classes: most of them did not show any appreciable adaptation effect, of those that did, however, the effect was rather short, of at most 10–15 s.

These results suggest that perceptual adaptation to gratings is the outcome of neural phenomena of adaptation such as the one observed in the single cells of the cat striate cortex. As mentioned for perceptual adaptation in man, the simple cell adaptation is also selective for orientation and spatial frequency: there is no adaptation when the orientation or the spatial frequency of the adapting (high contrast) or the test grating falls outside the orientation or spatial frequency channel of the cell. The adaptation effect of a simple cell of the cortex as a function of the spatial frequency of the test grating, is illustrated in Figure 16. The open circle curve is reported for comparison, and like Figure 3, describes the channel as a function of the spatial frequency of a drifting grating of moderate contrast (10%). It can be noted that the widths

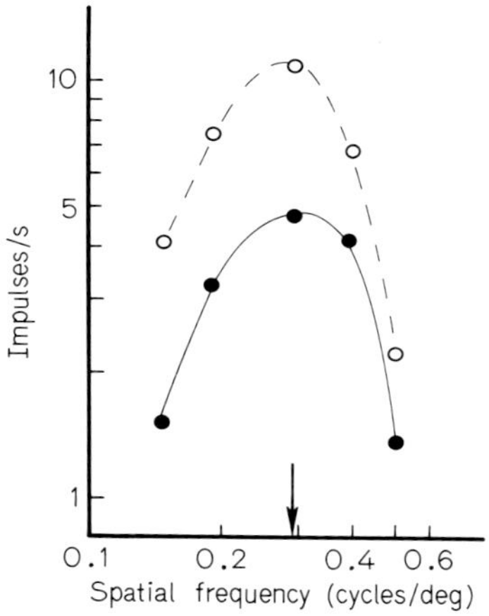

Fig. 16. Spatial frequency selectivity of a simple cell adaptation to a high contrast grating. Open circles illustrate spatial frequency channel of a simple cell obtained by measuring average discharge in response to drifting grating of various spatial frequencies at moderate contrast. Filled circles indicate average discharge of same cell in response to a drifting grating of moderate contrast (0.05) at spatial frequencies reported in abscissae following exposure for 1 min to a high contrast drifting grating of fixed spatial frequency (0.29 c/°). Frequency of adapting grating is indicated by arrow

of the channels are approximately the same when determined directly as a response to drifting grating or with the adaptation technique.

The phenomenon of the adaptation of the simple cells should not be mistaken for the well-known phenomenon of light and dark adaptation. The test and adapting grating have the same average luminance and differ only in contrast. Moreover, several control experiments demonstrate that the effect is not due to nonspecific fatigue of the cell under the high contrast stimulation. In this context a surprising finding is that the cells adapt even when the receptive field, as defined by a flashing luminous bar, is to a large extent, or even completely, masked so that the cell response to the adapting grating is abolished or reduced to a discharge rate lower than the test response (Fig. 17). This experiment, discussed in detail elsewhere (MAFFEI and FIORENTINI, 1974), implies that the cell response to gratings is influenced by many inputs to the cell and that some of them form a fringe around its receptive field enlarging the visual space participating in the analysis of the grating stimulus.

The results of the adaptation of simple cell to grating are also relevant to the problem of hierarchical organization of cortical cells. HUBEL and WIESEL in 1962 proposed a model of neural anatomical connections in which the receptive field of complex cells is built from the projection of simple cells. This model implies that the input to complex cells is neural information already elaborated by simple cells. The fact that complex cells either do not adapt or, if they do adapt, recover faster than simple cells, is not easy to reconcile with the HUBEL and WIESEL hypothesis. Also other features of complex cell responses shed some doubt on the HUBEL and WIESEL model. In the previous

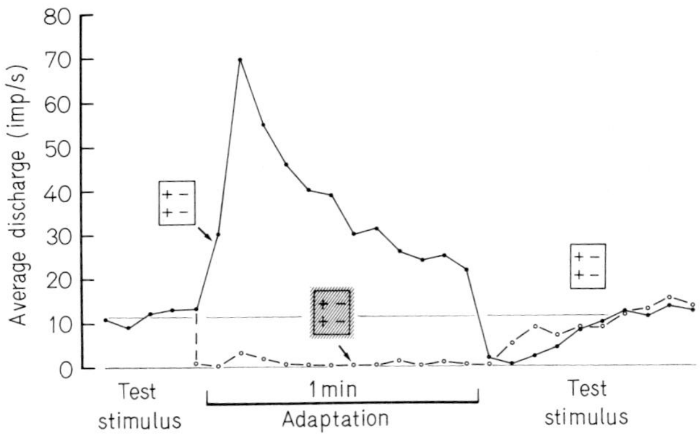

Fig. 17. Tracings are continuous records of discharge rate of cell averaged for 55 s intervals before, during, and after adaptation. Continuous tracing illustrates experiment similar to that reported in Fig. 15. In test stimulus conditions, grating of low contrast (0.04) was drifting over cell receptive field. In adaptation stimulus condition, grating of same spatial frequency but of high contrast replaced test stimulus. Dotted tracing illustrates results of experiment when receptive field, as determined by flashing luminous bar, is completely masked during adaptation

section on "Analysis of Spatial Frequency," it was pointed out that responses of the complex cells to gratings are rather different from those of simple cells. Their activity is not correlated with the single bars of the gratings and the ranges of spatial frequency sensitivity of the complex cells are more uniform than for simple cells.

It appears likely that the complex cells work in parallel, rather than in series, with simple cells in the processing of visual information. It might be supposed that the X-chain is devoted to the analysis of spatial information, while the Y-pathway is involved in other visual functions, for instance, movement perception.

F. Long-term Adaptation to Spatial Frequency in Kittens

Another series of experiments in kittens show how strong and how selective the phenomenon of adaptation to gratings can be for spatial frequency. The experiment is, in its philosophy and procedure, closely related to those of HIRSCH and SPINELLI (1970) and BLAKEMORE and COOPER (1970). They demonstrated that if a kitten is brought up in a visual environment containing only bars of a given orientation, the visual cortex of the kitten develops only neurons subserving that orientation. The new experiment takes into account that cortical visual neurons, besides being very selective for the orientation of the visual stimulus, are very specific for spatial frequency. In this experiment, a grating

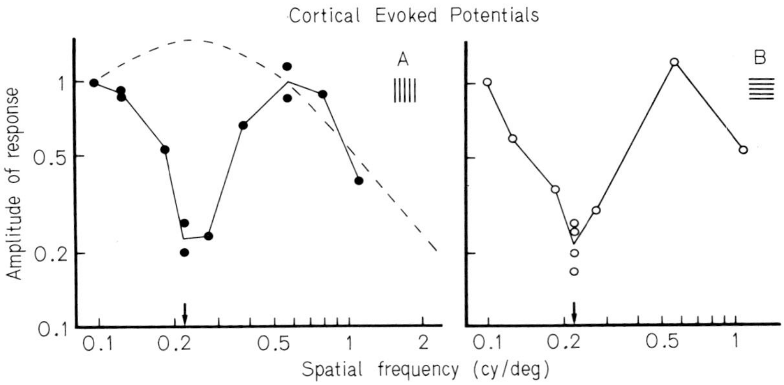

Fig. 18 A and B. Amplitude of cortical-evoked potentials as function of spatial frequency of stimulus grating for kitten exposed to grating of 0.22 c/°. (A) Points represent amplitude of evoked potentials (in arbitrary units) in response to vertical grating having contrast of 20% and alternating in phase at 8 Hz. For spatial frequency of pre-exposure (indicated by arrow in figure) and for two other spatial frequencies on either side of it, recordings were repeated twice at different times. Dashed line was obtained by fitting results from similar experiment performed under same experimental conditions in control kitten 3 months old. This kitten was reared in normal visual environment. (B) Amplitude of evoked potentials from same kitten as in (A) (exposed to 0.22 c/° grating) in response to horizontal grating. Other experimental conditions as in (A). (From MAFFEI and FIORENTINI, Science **186**, 1974)

of a given spatial frequency is offered to the kitten as its only visual experience. The spatial frequencies used for the kittens' exposure were those corresponding to the peak of the contrast sensitivity curve of the cat. Cortical and geniculate neural responses to a grating of the same spatial frequency as that to which the animals were exposed are reduced as compared with the responses to other frequencies. This reduction of cortical and geniculate responses was independent of the orientation of the grating.

In Figure 18 the amplitude of evoked potentials in response to alternating sinusoidal gratings of moderate contrast is reported as a function of the frequency of the stimulus. The spatial frequency at which the kitten was pre-exposed for 2–4 h per day between the third week and third month of age was 0.22 c/° and is indicated in the figure by the arrow. It is clear that the amplitude of the evoked potentials is much smaller for the frequencies around 0.22 c/° than for lower or higher frequencies. This dip in the curve is even more evident when compared with the analogous curve obtained for the same value of contrast in a control kitten (Fig. 14, *dashed curve*). This curve peaks just around 0.2 c/°.

The results of Figure 18 A are relative to a vertical grating, that is a grating parallel to the grating of exposure. In the same kitten, a similar dip in the spatial frequency curve was obtained for the evoked potentials in response to a horizontal grating (Fig. 18 B) and for oblique gratings.

The result of the experiment indicates that the effect of grating exposure is spatial frequency selective but not orientation selective. This observation suggests that the neurons of the lateral geniculate body, or of the retina, the responses of which are not sensitive to stimulus orientation, could be first

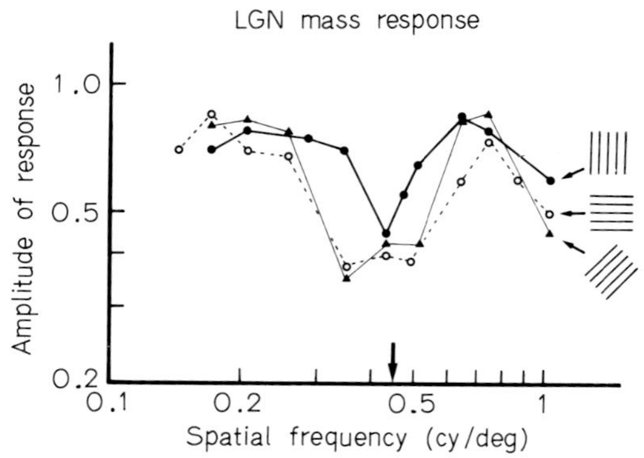

Fig. 19. Amplitude of mass response of lateral geniculate body *(LGN)* recorded from optic radiations in response to alternating gratings of various orientations (vertical, horizontal, and 45° from vertical) and spatial frequencies. Recordings were performed on kitten pre-exposed to grating of 0.45 c/°, as indicated by thick arrow in figure. Contrast of stimulus grating was 30% and its frequency of alternation 8 Hz. (From MAFFEI and FIORENTINI, Science **186**, 1974)

affected by the exposure to gratings. Mass activity recorded from the optic radiations (Fig. 19) and from the optic tract in response to sinusoidal gratings alternated in phase show that an effect similar to that observed for cortical evoked potentials is present at geniculate body level (Fig. 19) while absent in the optic tract. Figure 19 reports the amplitudes of evoked potentials recorded from the optic radiation as a function of spatial frequency and for various orientations of the grating. In this case the frequency of the grating at which the kitten had been exposed was 0.45 c/°. All three curves for the vertical, horizontal and oblique grating show a dip in the region of this frequency. A reduction in sensitivity for the spatial frequency of exposure was also found at the single unit level, both in some geniculate cells and in some complex neurons of the striate cortex.

Subsequently on the same kittens on which electrophysiologic experiments were performed the contrast sensitivity was measured using behavioral techniques.

The behavioral findings (FIORENTINI and MAFFEI, 1978, in press) are in agreement with the electrophysiologic results. Indeed they show that the psychophysical contrast sensitivity is decreased at the spatial frequency of exposure and that this fact holds for horizontal as well as for vertical test gratings.

Qualitatively speaking the long-term adaptation to gratings in kittens gives results similar to those observed in man or in adult cats for short-term adaptation. There are two main differences: a) in kittens the neural modifications brought about by the exposure are probably permanent (MAFFEI and FIORENTINI, 1974); b) the modification of neural responses seems to occur primarily at geniculate level.

The results of experiments on kittens on adaptation to gratings seem to be, in contradiction with the concept, generally accepted, according to which exposure to a given pattern during the critical period increases the sensitivity of the visual system for that pattern. The results reported show an instance in which this sensitivity is decreased.

G. Feature, Frequency Detectors or Both?

The electrophysiologic results we have reviewed suggest the conclusion that the visual system possesses all the necessary hardware for a spatial frequency analysis of visual information. Supporting this conclusion is the existence of neurons that are sensitive to amplitude, phase, and spatial frequency of the various harmonics and which show the phenomenon of adaptation to gratings in a way that seems directly correlated with the psychophysics. If the hypothesis that cortical cells are spatial frequency detectors is correct, feature detectors would be synthesized somewhere, somehow by an organized convergence of frequency detectors. Evidence along this line has recently been given by psychophysic experiments (MAFFEI AND FIORENTINI, 1972). Two sinusoidal gratings, the first and the third harmonic of a square-wave, were presented separately to the two eyes of a human subject. What the subject perceives is a compound pattern resulting from the neural superposition of the two gratings. The pattern perceived is a square-wave very similar to the pattern seen monoptically when the two gratings are physically superimposed. From these experiments it was concluded that the information about the amplitude and phase of two sinusoidal stimuli presented separately to the two eyes can be synthesized by the visual system. The hypothesis that cortical cells act as frequency detectors, of course, does not exclude the possibility that frequency detectors could coexist in harmony with certain families of specialized feature detectors. It is reasonable for the nervous system to develop a specialized hardware for features which are particularly relevant to the animal's life. Evidence in favor of this hypothesis seems to be suggested by recent psychophysic experiments (TOLHURST, 1972; SHAPLEY and TOLHURST, 1973; and KULIKOWSKI and KING-SMITH, 1973).

The mere existence of spatial frequency channels could not mean that the visual system actually functions according to a Fourier scheme of analysis and synthesis. One could maintain that cortical cells selective for spatial frequencies could be included in the class of feature detectors as such, like the orientation and edge detectors described by HUBEL and WIESEL. They could have the task of analyzing discontinuities in light intensity and the relative limits of it, i.e. the columns and the arch between them, the branches of a tree, and so on. In this case the periodicity of the pattern would not be a necessary factor. We could call them *spacing detectors*. More likely, they could function as *texture detectors*. In other words, they could be the feature detectors for striped patterns such as the texture of surface made of a relatively high number of cycles of the same pattern. In this context it is relevant to mention experiments now in progress in this laboratory. They clearly indicate that the responsiveness of a class of cortical cells increases with the area of the grating and hence, the actual number of bars present in the gratings when the spatial frequency is held constant. This means that for these cortical cells, the receptive field is much larger than that determined with the classical method of moving—that of flashing a luminous bar. The classical concept of a receptive field is no longer adequate when considering these detectors. The receptive field is a description of the input properties of a visual neuron and it can be related to the overall output of the visual system in very particular cases. If one wants to correlate neural activity with the actual perception of complex visual stimuli, the consideration of cortical cell activity in isolation from millions of their neural neighbors seems to me rather naive. Probably the complicated cross-talk of a given set of cells is, on purely theoretical grounds, if anything, a less misleading hypothesis.

One can certainly find a way of including cortical cells selective for spatial frequencies in the class of feature detectors, either as spacing or texture detectors. However, common sense suggests that an animal can not have as many feature detectors as all the different features existing in the external world. In my opinion, it is more parsimonious to think that cortical visual cells show a set of common properties adequate for the detection of the various features. Since most visual patterns, in our visual experience, can be shown mathematically to be composed of a series of spatial frequencies, the hypothesis that at least a class of cortical cells function as spatial frequency detectors seems to be, at the present time, more economical than to suppose an infinity of detectors for the infinite number of visual patterns. It is only a working hypothesis, but I think it is worth experimental effort to prove or to disprove it. This procedure in which one tries to verify or to disprove a hypothesis is an old but valid scientific method, advocated by, among others, Galileo Galilei, a famous citizen of Pisa.

References

Berkley, M.A.: Cat visual psychophysics: neural correlate and comparison with man. Progr. Psychobiol. physiol. Psychol. **6**, 63–119 (1976).

Bisti, S., Maffei, L.: Behavioural contrast sensitivity of the cat in various visual meridians. J. Physiol. (Lond.) **241**, 201–210 (1974).

Bisti, S., Sireteanu, R.C.: Sensitivity to spatial frequency and contrast of visual cells in the cat superior colliculus. Vision Res. **16**, 247–251 (1976).

Bisti, S., Clement, R., Maffei, L., Mecacci, L.: Spatial frequency and orientation tuning curves of visual neurones in the cat: effects of mean luminance. Exp. Brain Res. **27**, 335–345 (1977).

Blakemore, C., Campbell, F.W.: On the existence in the human visual system of neurones selectively sensitive to the orientation and size of retinal images. J. Physiol. (Lond.) **203**, 237–260 (1969).

Blakemore, C., Cooper, G.F.: Development of the brain depends on the visual environment. Nature (Lond.) **228**, 477–478 (1970).

Blakemore, C., Nachmias, J., Sutton, P.: The perceived spatial frequency shift: evidence for frequency selective neurones in the human brain. J. Physiol. (Lond.) **203**, 237–260 (1970).

Brindley, G.S.: Physiology of the Retina and Visual Pathway. 2nd Ed. London: E. Arnold, 1970.

Campbell, F.W., Cooper, G.F., Enroth-Cugell, Christina: The spatial selectivity of the visual cells of the cat. J. Physiol. (Lond.) **203**, 223–235 (1969a).

Campbell, F.W., Cooper, G.F., Robson, J.G., Sachs, M.B.: The spatial selectivity of visual cells of the cat and the squirrel monkey. J. Physiol. (Lond.) **204**, 120–121 (1969b).

Campbell, F.W., Maffei, L.: Electrophysiological evidence for the existence of orientation and size detectors in the human visual system. J. Physiol. (Lond.) **207**, 635–652 (1970).

Campbell, F.W., Maffei, L., Piccolino, M.: The contrast sensitivity of the cat. J. Physiol. (Lond.) **229**, 719–731 (1973).

Campbell, F.W., Robson, J.G.: Application of Fourier analysis to the visibility of gratings. J. Physiol. (Lond.) **197**, 551–566 (1968).

Cleland, B.G., Dubin, M.W., Levick, W.R.: Sustained and transient neurones in the cat's retina and lateral geniculate nucleus. J. Physiol. (Lond.) **217**, 423–496 (1971).

Enroth-Cugell, C., Robson, J.G.: The contrast sensitivity of retinal ganglion cells of the cat. J. Physiol. (Lond.) **187**, 517–552 (1966).

Fiorentini, A., Maffei, L.: Contrast perception and electrophysiological correlates. J. Physiol. (Lond.) **231**, 61–69 (1973).

Fiorentini, A., Maffei, L.: Selective impairment of contrast sensitivity in kittens exposed to periodic gratings. J. Physiol. (Lond.) 1978 (in press)

Glezer, V.D., Dudkin, K.N., Tsherbach, T.A. Gauselman, V.E.: Studies on spatial frequency filters in the visual cortex. Their characteristics and structural organization, in Information Processing in the Visual System, Proc. of the IV Symposium on Sensory System Physiology, V.D. Glezer ed., pp. 51–58 (Leningrad, 1976).

Glezer, V.D., Ivanoff, V.A., Tscherbach, T.W.: Investigation of complex and hypercomplex receptive fields of visual cortex of the cat as spatial frequency filters. Vision Res. **13**, 1875–1904 (1973).

Hirsch, H.V.B., Spinelli, D.N.: Visual experience modifies distribution of horizontally and vertically oriented receptive fields in cats. Science **168**, 869–871 (1970).

Hubel, D.H., Wiesel, T.N.: Receptive fields, binocular interaction and functional architecture in the cat's visual cortex. J. Physiol. (Lond.) **160**, 106–154 (1962).

Hubel, D.H., Wiesel, T.N.: Receptive fields and functional architecture in two non-striate visual areas (18 and 19) of the cat. *J. Neurophysiol.* **28**, 229–289 (1965).

Hubel, D.H., Wiesel, T.N.: Receptive fields and functional architecture of monkey striate cortex. J. Physiol. (Lond.) **195**, 215–243 (1968).

Hubel, D.H., Wiesel, T.N.: Sequence regularity and geometry of orientation columns in the monkey cortex. J. comp. Neurol. **158**, 267–294 (1974).

Ikeda, H., Wright, M.J.: Evidence for "sustained" and "transient" neurones in the cat's visual cortex. Vision Res. **14**, 133–136 (1974).

Ikeda, H., Wright, M.J.: Spatial and temporal properties of "sustained" and "transient" neurones in area 17 of the cat's visual cortex. Exp. Brain Res. **22**, 362–382 (1975).

Maffei, L., Cervetto, L.: Dynamic interactions in retinal receptive fields. Vision Res. **8**, 1299–1303 (1968).

Maffei, L., Fiorentini, A.: Processes of synthesis in visual perception. Nature (Lond.) **240**, 479–481 (1972).

Maffei, L., Fiorentini, A.: The visual cortex as a spatial frequency analyser. Vision Res. **13**, 1255–1267 (1973).

Maffei, L., Fiorentini, A., Bisti, S.: Neural correlate of perceptual adaptation to gratings. Science **182**, 1036–1038 (1973).

Maffei, L., Fiorentini, A.: Geniculate neural plasticity in kittens after exposure to periodic gratings. Science **186**, 447–449 (1974).

Maffei, L., Fiorentini, A.: The unresponsive regions of visual cortical receptive fields. Vision Res. **16**, 1131–1139 (1976).

Maffei, L., Fiorentini, A.: Spatial frequency rows in the striate visual cortex. Vision Res. **17**, 257–264 (1977).

Kulikowski, J.J., King-Smith, P.E.: Spatial arrangement of line, edge and grating detectors revealed by subthreshold summation. Vision Res. **13**, 1455–1478 (1973).

Palmer, L.A., Rosenquist, A.C.: Visual receptive fields of single striate cortical units projecting to the superior colliculus in the cat. Brain Res. **67**, 27–42 (1974).

Pettigrew, J.D., Nikara, T., Bishop, P.O.: Responses to moving slits by single units in cat striate cortex. Exp. Brain Res. **6**, 373–390 (1968).

Pollen, D.A., Lee, J.R., Taylor, J.H.: How does the striate cortex begin the reconstruction of the visual world. Science **173**, 74–77 (1971).

Pollen, D.A., Ronner, S.F.: Periodic excitability changes across the receptive fields of complex cells in the striate and parastriate cortex of the cat. J. Physiol. (Lond.) **245**, 667–697 (1975).

Pollen, D.A., Taylor, J.H.: The striate cortex and the spatial analysis of visual space, in The Neurosciences: Third Study Program. Worden, F., and Schmitt, F.O., eds., (Cambridge: M.I.T. Press, 1973).

Sachs, M.B., Nachmias, J., Robson, J.G.: Spatial frequency channels in human vision. J. opt. Soc. Amer. **61**, 1176–1186 (1971).

Shapley, R.M., Tolhurst, D.J.: Edge detectors in human vision. J. Physiol. (Lond.) **229**, 165–183 (1973).

Schiller, P.H., Finlay, B.L., Volman, S.F.: Quantitative studies of single-cell properties in monkey striate cortex. III Spatial Frequency. J. Neurophysiol. **39**, 1334–1351 (1976).

Smith, K.U.: Visual discrimination in the cat. IV. The visual acuity of the cat in relation to stimulus distance. J. gen. Physiol. **49**, 297–313 (1936).

Stone, J., Hoffmann, K.P.: Conduction velocity of afferents to cat visual cortex: a correlation with cortical receptive field properties. Brain Res. **32**, 460–466 (1971).

Tolhurst, D.J.: On the possible existence of edge detector neurons in the human visual system. Vision Res. **12**, 797–804 (1972).

Chapter 3

Physiological Basis of Motion Perception

ROBERT SEKULER, ALLAN PANTLE, and EUGENE LEVINSON,
Evanston, Illinois, and Oxford, Ohio (USA)

With 11 Figures

Contents

A. Introduction

The perception of visual motion has fascinated psychophysicists for well over a century. During that time there has been a steady accumulation of information about motion without much accompanying theoretical structure. One recent development in visual physiology has begun to provide the basis for such a structure: the discovery in the mammalian visual system of *directionally selective* neurons, single cells that respond differentially to targets moving in different directions through the cells' receptive fields. The likelihood that similar direction-selective cells play a role in the motion perception of humans (GRÜSSER and GRÜSSER-CORNEHLS, 1973) has heightened the psychophysicist's interest in the neural mechanisms of motion.

This chapter integrates what we know about the machinery of motion perception, emphasizing the contribution of psychophysical observations. Although there are obvious problems inherent in comparing results from psychophysics and physiology, we think that properly framed comparisons are not only possible but necessary to the full development of visual science. In fact, contrasts between the domain of psychophysics and the domain of physiology can be instructive whether the outcome be congruence or divergence between the two. We think it a healthy sign that many psychophysical experiments in motion perception draw their inspiration from physiologic observations (e.g. SEKULER and GANZ, 1963) and vice versa (e.g. MANDL, 1974). So throughout the chapter, where appropriate, we will juxtapose results from the two domains, psychophysics and physiology.

Before going on, we ought to consider what kinds of psychophysical experiments and stimuli are most likely to elucidate the mechanisms of motion. In general, the most informative observations are those that cannot be explained in terms of the proximal stimulus. Such observations highlight the idiosyncracies of the motion analyzing mechanisms themselves. The class of useful observations is further restricted because not all motion stimulation produces effects conveniently measurable by psychophysical techniques. For example, a solitary moving object has only a small, transitory effect on motion sensitive mechanisms. By contrast, repetitive stimulation has powerful and easily measured effects. This fact has been known and exploited since the early part of the nineteenth century. ADDAMS (1834) described one intriguing effect of prolonged, repetitive stimulation, a compelling illusion of motion that continues to attract attention to this day. After staring fixedly at a waterfall near Loch Ness in Scotland, ADDAMS turned his gaze to the rocks near the falls; the rocks appeared to drift upward, opposite the direction of the water's movement. Earlier, PURKINJE (1937) had reported a similar effect, the result of watching a parade of horseback riders for about an hour. The experience of illusory after-movement in the direction opposite the original inspection motion is called the motion after-effect or waterfall illusion. Though this effect has received much attention since the time of PURKINJE and ADDAMS, we now recognize that the motion after-effect is but one of the consequences of exposure to motion (SEKULER, 1975). In fact, among other effects, exposure to a moving pattern (1) alters the perceived speed of nearby moving patterns, (2) reduces the visibility of similar patterns seen subsequently, (3) alters the perceived speed and direction of subsequently seen moving patterns, and (4) causes subsequently seen stationary patterns to move.

Though modern research methods are more analytic than those of ADDAMS or PURKINJE, contemporary work is the direct descendant of the nineteenth century's pioneering efforts. Today, however, research on motion perception does not rely on naturally occurring repetitive stimuli, like parades or waterfalls; instead it relies heavily on electronically generated stimuli like gratings. Gratings are patterns of alternating parallel light and dark bars; they can be made to drift across the face of a cathode ray display at any desired rate and direction. Before turning to the substantive issues of the chapter we must consider two of the properties, contrast and spatial frequency, that determine pari passu a grating's visual effectiveness.

Contrast, or Michelson contrast, is given by the difference between the grating's maximum and minimum luminances divided by twice its average luminance. Contrast can assume a minimum value of 0.0 (a spatially uniform stimulus, with no difference between maximum and minimum luminance), and a maximum value of 1.0. In many of the studies we shall discuss, contrast thresholds are the dependent measure. Generally, stimulus contrast is varied while average luminance is held constant, until some criterion response is reached. The results are then expressed either in terms of the contrast that produced the criterion response or in terms of the reciprocal of that contrast, called sensitivity.

The spatial frequency of a periodic stimulus refers to the number of cycles of the stimulus that occupy one unit of distance. In vision research, cycles/degree of visual angle (abbreviated as c/°) is the most common unit of spatial frequency. When a stimulus contains appreciable amounts of several spatial frequencies (separated by more than an octave or so), the visual system seems to analyze the stimulus into those separate components, responding to each component as though the others were not even present (SEKULER, 1974).

The visual impact of a moving grating depends also upon its rate of movement, expressed in terms of either temporal frequency or velocity. We shall consider in detail the importance of drift rate later in the chapter.

As in any brief treatment of motion perception, limitations of space have required us to restrict the focus of this chapter. The studies discussed are ones we think most likely elucidate the physiologic basis of human motion perception. Because it did not meet this criterion, much classic work on motion perception has been ignored. Moreover since "motion" implies both a directional and a spatiotemporal component in the percept, we have emphasized studies which focus on these aspects.

B. Direction-Specificity in Human Vision

I. Direction-Specific Adaptation

Direction-specific elements exist in the human visual system. Their existence has been demonstrated in experiments showing *direction-specific adaptation,* the selective elevation of detection threshold for a stimulus moving in the same direction as a high-contrast adaptation stimulus.[1] Assume for the moment that human vision is *not* direction-selective; this means that a single mechanism

[1] In the following discussion we implicity assume that threshold elevation produced by adaptation varies directly with the detecting mechanism's sensitivity for the adaptation stimulus (i.e., that adaptation results from excitatory events). There is, however, considerable uncertainty as to the exact nature of the adaptation process, and it is even possible that threshold elevation is an after-effect of prolonged inhibition (see, for example, DEALY and TOLHURST, 1974; MAFFEI et al., 1973). In any case, only quantitative conclusions depend upon the validity of our assumption; inferences as to the existence of direction-specific mechanisms in human vision are largely independent of one's choice of model for the adaptation process. We have temporarily chosen an excitatory model for expository clarity.

detects gratings moving in opposite directions. This single mechanism must have the same sensitivity for rightward movement as for leftward (implied by the approximate equality of detection thresholds for opposite directions of motion; see LEVINSON and SEKULER, 1975b). Prolonged exposure to a grating moving to the right should elevate detection thresholds equally for rightward and for leftward movement, because only one mechanism is involved. Moreover, the threshold for detecting a rightward-moving test grating should be elevated as much by adaptation to a leftward as to a rightward grating. Now consider the alternative hypothesis, that elements highly sensitive to leftward or to rightward motion, but relatively insensitive to the opposite directions, populate the human visual system. Threshold elevation should then be greater when adaptation and test gratings move in the same direction than when they drift in opposite directions (i.e., direction-specific adaptation).

The latter alternative has received empirical support. SEKULER and GANZ (1963) reported that threshold for detecting a grating moving in one direction was higher following inspection of a grating moving in that same direction than after exposure to one moving in the opposite direction. Similarly, PANTLE and SEKULER (1969) found that a fixed direction of adapting motion produced more elevation of threshold for a same-directional than for an opposite-directional test grating (although some threshold elevation did occur in the opposite direction). Direction-specific adaptation has since been demonstrated many times, both psychophysically (SEKULER et al., 1968; TOLHURST, 1973; SHARPE and TOLHURST, 1973; LEVINSON and SEKULER, 1974) and electrophysiologically (CLARKE, 1974).

II. Contrast Response of Direction-Sensitive Mechanisms

Direction-specific adaptation procedures have been used in two psychophysical studies (PANTLE and SEKULER, 1969; PANTLE, 1973) in an attempt to specify the contrast response of human direction-sensitive mechanisms. PANTLE and SEKULER (1969) and PANTLE (1973) measured the amount of direction-specific adaptation (here defined as the difference between log threshold elevations for same and opposite directions) produced by adapting gratings of various contrasts. The adapting contrasts used in those studies are represented along the abscissa of Figure 1 where they are expressed as multiples of the threshold contrast. The relative magnitude of the adaptation effects obtained by PANTLE and SEKULER (1969) using square-wave adapting and test gratings (0.38 c/°) is shown by the crosses, the relative magnitude of those obtained by PANTLE (1973) using sinusoidal gratings (3.4 c/°) by the triangles. The adaptation effects have been normalized to give a maximum adaptation effect of 100% for each study.

KECK et al. (1976) used a slightly different response measure to specify the contrast response of direction-specific mechanisms. A number of researchers (SUTHERLAND, 1961; BARLOW and HILL, 1963a; SEKULER and PANTLE, 1967) have suggested that a moving adapting pattern gives rise to the well-known

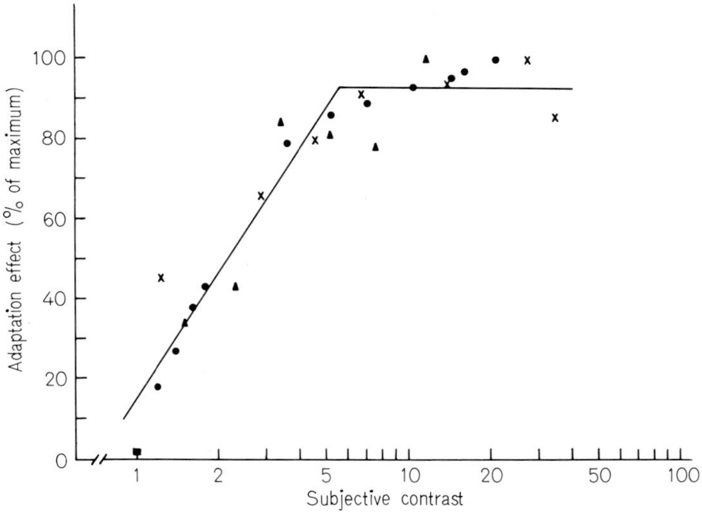

Fig. 1. Psychophysical measurements of contrast response of human direction-sensitive mechanisms. Crosses: direction-specific adaptation as function of contrast of square-wave adapting grating (0.38 c/°, threshold contrast = 2.4%; from PANTLE and SEKULER, 1969). Triangles: direction-specific adaptation as function of contrast of sinusoidal adapting grating (3.4 c/°, threshold contrast = 0.33%; from PANTLE, 1973). Filled circles: motion after-effect duration as function of contrast of sinusoidal adapting grating (4 c/°, threshold contrast = 0.5%; from KECK et al., in press)

motion after-effect by producing the aforementioned temporary imbalance in the responsiveness of mechanisms tuned to opposite directions of movement. On the assumption that motion after-effects would be longer when the imbalance was greater, KECK et al. (1976) measured the duration of after-effects to determine how effective gratings of different contrasts would be in producing differential adaptation of direction-specific mechanisms. Their results are also summarized in Figure 1 (filled circles). As with the studies of direction-specific adaptation, the abscissa gives the relative contrast of the adapting grating (sinusoidal, 4 c/°). After-effect duration, on the ordinate, was normalized so that the longest after-effect received the value 100%.

Despite differences in the stimuli and methods employed, the data obtained in the three studies summarized in Figure 1 are strikingly similar. Accordingly, we have fitted one function to all the data. The function is the best fitting pair of line segments determined by a method of least squares (BOGARTZ, 1968) with the single constraint that the right-hand segment have a zero slope. The function is an indirect measure of the contrast response of direction-specific mechanisms. The intersection of the two line segments provides an estimate of the point at which the response of direction-specific mechanisms saturates. As can be seen in the figure, the direction-specific mechanisms revealed by psychophysical adaptation have a very limited range of response to stimulus contrast. Their response increases linearly with the logarithm of stimulus contrast in the low contrast region, but it is essentially independent of stimulus contrast once the contrast exceeds threshold by more than a factor of 5–6.

Physiologic data on the contrast response of direction-specific neurons are sparse, but those available do resemble the psychophysical data. BARLOW and HILL (1963b) investigated the contrast response of a direction-specific cell of the rabbit retina. The stimulus was a 1° spot of variable luminance superimposed on a uniform background with a luminance of 0.2 mL. The minimum ratio of spot luminance to background luminance necessary to obtain a response from the cell was 1.2/l. For spot-to-background luminance ratios greater than 1.5/l the cell's response was found to be *independent* of stimulus contrast. GANZ and LANGE (1973) report that the responses of direction-sensitive cells in the cat cortex also saturate at a low contrast.

III. Independence of Direction-Specific Mechanisms

The existence of direction-specific mechanisms does not in itself imply that detection of moving stimuli is mediated by independent direction-specific detectors. The directionally selective elements revealed via adaptation experiments could represent early mechanisms for movement processing, mechanisms whose outputs are pooled by a unitary movement detector. Conversely, the presence of *some* threshold elevation for opposite-directional stimuli (PANTLE and SEKULER, 1969) does not necessarily mean that direction-selective channels have any sensitivity for their nonpreferred directions (e.g. see footnote 1). Any number of alternatives are compatible with the results of direction-specific adaptation experiments; such experiments can only demonstrate the *existence* of direction-specific mechanisms. To obtain directly the sensitivity of a directionally selective channel a rather different sort of manipulation is required: measurement of *summation* between stimuli moving in opposite directions.

LEVINSON and SEKULER (1973, 1975b) measured the contrast detection threshold for a grating moving in one direction to which had been linearly added a subthreshold grating moving in the opposite direction. Threshold was not changed by the addition of the subthreshold grating, a result which suggests that direction-specific mechanisms operate as independent contrast detectors. In a second experiment, LEVINSON and SEKULER compared the threshold for detecting a moving grating with that for detection of a grating flickering in counterphase. Figure 2 is a three-dimensional representation of the spatio temporal luminance profile for a counterphase flickering grating. The figure shows that a counterphase grating changes contrast and alternates in phase as a sinusoidal function of time; the counterphase grating does not physically drift in either direction.

A moving sinusoidal grating has a luminance profile which can be mathematically described by

$$L_m(x,t) = L_o\{1 + m \cdot \cos(fx \pm \omega t\} \tag{1}$$

where L_0 is the average luminance, m is contrast, $f/2\pi$ is the spatial frequency, x is position in the visual field, $\omega/2\pi$ is temporal frequency or drift rate, and t

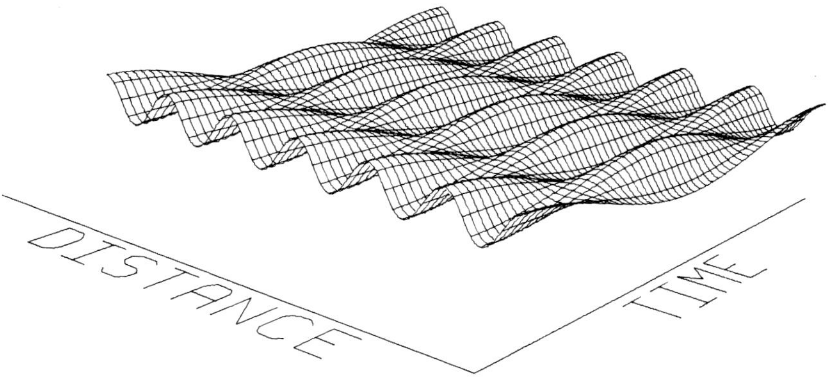

Fig. 2. Spatiotemporal luminance profile for counterphase flickering grating. Luminance axis is approximately parallel to plane of page. Six spatial cycles and one temporal cycle are shown

is time. The equation shows that the stimulus is really a grating which is continuously shifting in phase at rate ω; the sign of the phase shift ($\pm\omega t$) indicates one of the opposite directions of movement. A counterphase flickering grating has luminance profile

$$L_c(x,t) = L_o\{1 + m\cdot\cos(\omega t)\cdot\cos(fx)\} \tag{2}$$

Although it does not physically move as a whole, the counterphase grating can be trigonometrically decomposed into the sum of two half-contrast sinusoidal gratings moving in opposite directions:

$$L_c(x,t) = L_o\{1 + {}^1/_2 m\cdot\cos(fx\text{-}\omega t) + {}^1/_2 m\cdot\cos(fx + \omega t)\} \tag{3}$$

If direction-specific mechanisms in human vision are independent detectors, and if each detector has virtually no sensitivity to movement opposite its preferred direction, then threshold for a grating moving in one direction should be unaffected by the presence of contrast moving in the opposite direction. A counterphase grating might therefore be detected by one or the other direction-selective mechanism, whichever is momentarily the more sensitive. When a moving component of a counterphase grating is at threshold, the counterphase grating as a whole should be at threshold. Since the counterphase grating has twice the contrast of either of its moving parts, threshold for detecting the counterphase should be twice that for detecting a moving grating of the same spatial and temporal frequency. LEVINSON and SEKULER (1973, 1975b) found that detection thresholds for counterphase gratings were indeed two times greater than thresholds for the corresponding moving gratings; some of these measurements (plotted in terms of sensitivity, the reciprocal of threshold) are shown in Figure 3.

Some observations by COOPER and ROBSON (1968) of single cell responses in the cat visual cortex are relevant here. COOPER and ROBSON measured the

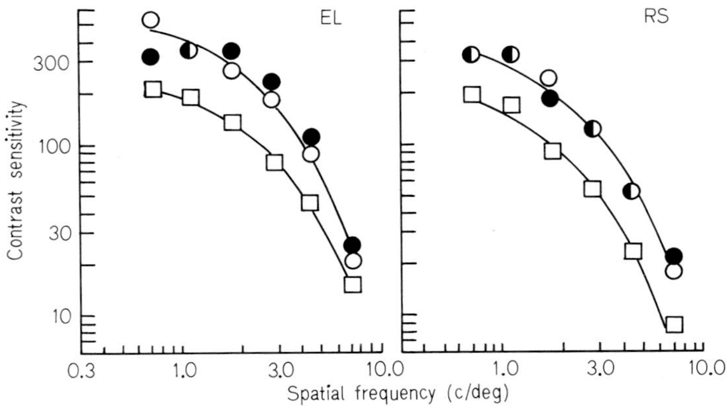

Fig. 3. Contrast sensitivities for rightward-moving gratings (open circles), leftward-moving gratings (*filled circles*), and counterphase gratings (*squares*). Curves are exponential functions; one function was fitted to counterphase sensitivities, other to sensitivities for both directions of movement. Temporal frequency was 4.0 Hz for EL, 7.9 Hz for RS

responses of directionally selective and nondirectionally selective neurons to moving or to counterphase gratings. Nondirection-specific cells responded as well to a counterphase stimulus as to a drifting grating of equal contrast. Direction-selective neurons, however, responded less than half as well to the counterphase grating. These observations are remarkably similar to the psychophysical findings.

IV. Inhibition Between Direction-Specific Mechanisms

Up to this point we have characterized direction-specific mechanisms in human vision as independent detectors with no sensitivity to their nonpreferred directions. This characterization has been drawn primarily from measurements made at threshold or near-threshold contrast levels. Measurements of interactions between moving stimuli at suprathreshold levels, however, have revealed *inhibition* between direction-selective channels. Inhibition between feature-selective channels in human vision is not a new phenomenon; experiments have shown inhibitory interactions for orientation channels (BLAKEMORE et al., 1970; CARPENTER and BLAKEMORE, 1973) and for spatial frequency channels (TOLHURST, 1972; STECHER et al., 1973). LEVINSON and SEKULER (1975a) used the composite adaptation technique devised by TOLHURST (1972) to measure inhibition between direction-specific mechanisms. They measured the threshold elevation for a rightward moving grating produced by adaptation to one of two kinds of stimulus: (1) a high-contrast rightward-moving grating, or (2) the same rightward grating plus an equal contrast of leftward-moving grating. If the leftward mechanism exerts inhibition on the rightward, *less* threshold elevation should occur when the leftward grating is present than when it is not. Typical results are given

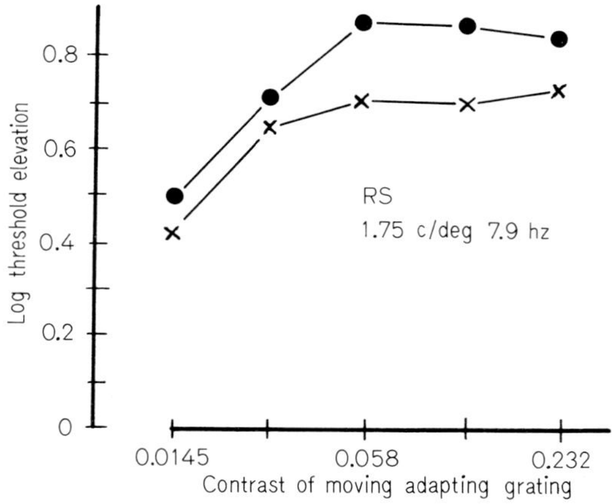

Fig. 4. Log threshold elevations for rightward-moving test grating as functions of rightward-moving adapting contrast. Adaptation was produced by rightward-moving grating (*filled circles*) or by rightward-moving grating plus equal-contrast leftward-moving grating (*crosses*). (From SEKULER and LEVINSON, 1974)

in Figure 4, as a function of the contrast of the rightward-moving component. The filled circles give threshold elevation produced by this rightward component alone; the crosses, elevation after exposure to the same rightward grating plus the equal-contrast leftward grating. The addition of the leftward component *does* reduce threshold elevation, an inhibitory interaction between the two moving adaptation gratings. LEVINSON and SEKULER also performed a disinhibition experiment which rules out physical characteristics of the composite waveform as an explanation for the difference in threshold elevation.

Although direct measurement of inhibition has thus far been achieved only at suprathreshold levels, it is possible that inhibitory processes may account for the operationally defined independence of direction-specific channels which we discussed in the preceding section. Indeed, the visual physiology of higher mammals suggests a prime role for inhibition in motion processing. Data supporting this position will be discussed later in this chapter.

C. Temporal Aspects of Motion Responses

I. Velocity Coding

While motion-sensitive mechanisms generally appear limited in ability to encode stimulus contrast, they do preserve information about stimulus velocity. In this section we will describe the responses of single motion-sensitive cells to stimuli moving at different speeds, and we will consider alternative ways in which such cells might abstract the property of stimulus speed.

Perhaps the simplest code for velocity would be one in which the output of single movement-sensitive cells increased as stimulus velocity increased, an additive model. In other words, high impulse rates would be associated with fast-moving stimuli; low rates, with slow-moving stimuli. In humans, subjective speed would be determined by the absolute level of the output of movement-sensitive cells. Studies by GRÜSSER and GRÜSSER-CORNEHLS (1973) on the frog retina reveal neurons which possess response characteristics of the type required by the additive model. They determined the relationship between the angular velocity of a stimulus and the average discharge rate of single optic nerve fibers. Nonperiodic stimuli were moved through the excitatory receptive field of each neuron and the impulse rate was measured during the traversal of the receptive field. The average discharge frequency of class 2 and class 3 neurons, those especially sensitive to movement (LETTVIN et al., 1961), increased with the angular velocity of the stimulus. The relationship between impulse frequency and angular velocity was described by a power function and it held over a range of 2–3 log units. The wide velocity range over which response rate increases would seem to provide an adequate physiologic mechanism for additive coding of velocity.

While the additive model is attractive because of its simplicity, and while it may describe velocity coding in the frog visual system, there are a number of experimental results which cast doubt on its validity for higher vertebrate systems. Unlike the movement-sensitive neurons of the frog, directionally-selective cells in the rabbit (BARLOW et al., 1964) and cat (HUBEL and WIESEL, 1965; PETTIGREW et al., 1968; GANZ and LANGE, 1973; MOVSHON, 1974) respond to a relatively narrow range of velocities. The responses are greatest at an intermediate velocity and less at both slower and faster velocities. Moreover, the optimal velocity for stimulating a cell varies from one cell to the next. As a consequence of their velocity tuning, the distribution of cells affected by a stimulus moving at one speed will be different than the distribution of cells affected by a stimulus moving at another speed. For example, a stimulus moving at 20°/s would maximally excite cells tuned to a stimulus velocity of 20°/s and cause little or no activity in cells tuned to a velocity of 1°/s. The reverse would be true for a stimulus moving at 1°/s. As stimulus speed is changed, the responses of cells substitute for those of other cells. Therefore, it is possible that perceived velocity depends upon the relative activities among velocity-tuned cells, much like perceived color depends upon the relative excitation of different cone systems. This substitutive model of velocity perception is consistent with the psychophysical experiment of PANTLE and SEKULER (1968b). They found that the amount of direction-specific adaptation that is produced by a moving grating depends upon how close the speed of the adapting stimulus is to the speed of the test stimulus. Direction-specific adaptation is greatest when the speeds of the adapting and test stimuli are similar. Comparable results have been reported by TOLHURST et al. (1973). It can be concluded that the human visual system contains different velocity-tuned mechanisms, that is, mechanisms which can be selectively adapted by a limited range of stimulus velocities.

II. The Spatiotemporal Response of Motion-Sensitive Mechanisms

At a given point on the retina the temporal rate of luminance modulation that is produced by a moving periodic stimulus is directly proportional to its velocity. In experiments with periodic stimuli it is important to be aware of this correlation because temporal frequency, rather than velocity per se, may be the critical variable governing the responses of motion-sensitive mechanisms. In order to disentangle the effects of velocity and temporal frequency, patterns with different spatial periods and velocities must be used in the same experiment. For a constant velocity (v), temporal frequency (ω) varies directly with the spatial frequency (f) of a periodic pattern, i.e. $\omega = v \mathrm{x} f$. For a constant temporal frequency, spatial frequency and velocity are inversely related; i.e. $v = \omega \times 1/f$.

With the above relationships in mind, GANZ and LANGE (1973) attempted to determine whether the responses of single motion-sensitive cells were controlled by the velocity of a drifting pattern or by its temporal frequency. They made recordings of the activity of directionally selective neurons in the cat cortex and found that the response of a single cell to a stimulus grating was an inverted U-shaped function of the rate of movement of the grating. More importantly, the optimal velocity for stimulating the cell was inversely related to the spatial frequency of the grating, whereas the optimal temporal frequency for stimulating the cell remained the same for gratings of different spatial frequencies. These findings suggest that the rate of movement of a periodic stimulus is analyzed in terms of its temporal frequency rather than its velocity. Each cell abstracted the property of temporal frequency independent of spatial frequency.

Human psychophysical studies in which periodic stimuli have been employed, point to a similar conclusion. Contrast sensitivity to a drifting sinusoidal grating with a spatial frequency less than 3 c/° is a U-shaped function of the velocity of the grating. The speed of the grating which results in maximum sensitivity (the optimal speed) varies inversely with the spatial frequency of the grating such that the optimal temporal frequency of stimulation (about 5 Hz) is approximately constant (WATANABE et al., 1968).

Further evidence that the responses of motion-sensitive mechanisms are governed by the temporal frequency of a periodic stimulus rather than its velocity is provided by a motion after-effect study by PANTLE (1974). PANTLE used the motion after-effect as a tool for isolating the responses of directionally selective mechanisms (see SEKULER and PANTLE, 1967). The relationship between after-effect magnitude and adapting velocity depended upon the spatial characteristics of the pattern used to generate the after-effect; the relationship between after-effect magnitude and temporal frequency, however, was invariant with changes (within limits) in spatial characteristics. In other words, as long as the temporal frequency of the adapting patterns was constant, neither a change of the spatial period of the patterns nor the reciprocal change of adapting velocity required to keep temporal frequency constant had an effect on after-effect magnitude.

In summary, existing evidence shows that the temporal frequency of a periodic pattern, not its velocity, is a basic determinant of the response of human motion-sensitive mechanisms. This general finding has a number of important consequences for the perception of complex patterns.

Consider the detection of a complex moving grating comprised of two sinusoidal components. Suppose that the spatial frequencies of the two components were f and $3f$. These components will normally be detected independently (GRAHAM and NACHMIAS, 1971). Both spatial components will move at the same velocity if they are phase-locked, but the temporal frequency of luminance modulation associated with each component will be different. If the critical variable that controlled the response of motion-sensitive mechanisms were velocity, then both spatial components ought to be maximally visible at the same optimal velocity. On the other hand, if temporal frequency is the critical variable, then one spatial component ought to be maximally visible at one velocity; and the other component, at a different velocity.

PANTLE (1970) conducted a selective adaptation experiment which demonstrated that the spatial components (Fourier components) of a low-frequency, square-wave grating were not all optimally visible at the same velocity. Luminance thresholds for the square-wave test grating (0.38 c/°) were measured after an observer viewed one of a number of adapting gratings of various spatial frequencies (0–23 c/°). When the test grating was moved at a fast speed (9–22°/s), its threshold was elevated only by adapting gratings in the vicinity of 0.35–0.70 c/°. This indicates that only the fundamental component of the fast-moving test grating mediated its detection at threshold. At a speed of 9–22°/s the temporal frequency associated with the drift of the fundamental component was in the optimal temporal frequency range, 3.6–8.8 Hz. All of the higher harmonic components would drift at rates of 10.8 Hz or greater. When the test grating was moved at a slow speed (0.5–2.5°/s), its threshold was elevated most by adapting gratings in the region of 1.4 c/°. Presumably the third harmonic of the test grating (1.2 c/° component) contributed most to its detection at the slow speed. At speeds of 0.5–2.5°/s, the temporal frequency of modulation associated with the drift of the third harmonic is less than optimal (only 0.6–3.0 Hz), but more nearly optimal than the temporal frequency of modulation associated with the fundamental component (0.2–1.0 Hz). At threshold, the spatial frequency components of complex periodic patterns which drift at rates near the optimal temporal frequency appear to be favored. Velocity is important only to the extent that it determines the temporal frequency of each component.

If the results of PANTLE (1970) can be generalized to suprathreshold stimuli, it may be possible to account for the changes of the subjective appearance of a complex pattern as it is moved at different speeds. BREITMEYER's studies (1973) lend credence to such a generalization. In one experiment, BREITMEYER had subjects adapt to a moving suprathreshold pattern with a random texture. The amplitude of the spectral components of the pattern in the range of 0.4–16.0 c/° varied by less than a factor of three. Contrast thresholds for stationary square-wave gratings ranging from 0.4–10.5 c/° were measured both before and after subjects had adapted to the random texture pattern moving at either 2.5 or 6.5°/s. After a subject adapted to the texture pattern moving at 2.5°/s, his threshold for a grating of 4.0 c/° was elevated more than that for the other test gratings. At 2.5°/s, the 4 c/° component of the texture pattern would produce a temporal luminance modulation of 10 Hz. It is interesting, then, that after a subject adapted to the texture pattern moving at 6.5°/s, his threshold for a grating of approximately 1.5 c/° was elevated most. At 6.5°/s, a 1.5 c/° component of the adapting pattern would drift at a rate of approximately 10 Hz. It can be concluded that the temporal rate of stimulation determined the magnitude of the threshold elevations produced by the various components of the texture pattern, the elevations being maximal for components drifting at 10 Hz. It seems likely that the spatial components which produced the largest adapting effects were also those which were most visible during the adapting period.

The psychophysical experiments reviewed in this section demonstrate that many aspects of the visual response to motion are determined by the temporal frequency of a moving pattern rather than its velocity. Flicker contrast sensitivity and various adapting effects remain at a maximum for temporal frequencies between 5–10 Hz even when stimulus velocity is changed. In addition, single movement cells in cats exhibit similar behavior.

D. Motion-Sensitive and Pattern-Sensitive Systems

The contrast detection thresholds measured in most of the experiments described earlier were "absolute" detection thresholds, usually defined as that contrast at which an observer can barely discriminate a stimulus from a uniform field of the same average luminance. Recent psychophysical experiments, however, show that two distinct contrast detection thresholds can be measured using the same spatiotemporal stimulus, one threshold for the recognition of spatial pattern and one for the detection of movement or flicker. At the "absolute" contrast detection threshold, an observer may see *either* a stationary pattern, or a moving, flickering stimulus of indistinct spatial structure. The contrast of the stimulus must be increased somewhat before the alternate aspect (movement or pattern) of the stimulus becomes visible (VAN NES et al., 1967; WATANABE et al., 1968; KULIKOWSKI, 1971). Figure 5a shows typical variations in sensitivity (reciprocal of threshold) for pattern recognition and for flicker detection as functions of spatial frequency, for a fixed temporal frequency. Figure 5b gives similar hypothetical functions of temporal frequency, with spatial frequency held constant (all curves are fashioned after the results of KULIKOWSKI and TOLHURST, 1973). Pattern recognition sensitivity is greatest when temporal frequency is low and when spatial frequency is moderately high; it declines gradually with increasing temporal frequency. Flicker or movement sensitivity is maximal for intermediate temporal frequencies and for low spatial frequencies. Each type of threshold can be independently elevated when observers are exposed to high-contrast adaptation stimuli (TOLHURST, 1973; TOLHURST et al., 1973; LEVINSON and SEKULER, 1974). Presumably the flicker and pattern

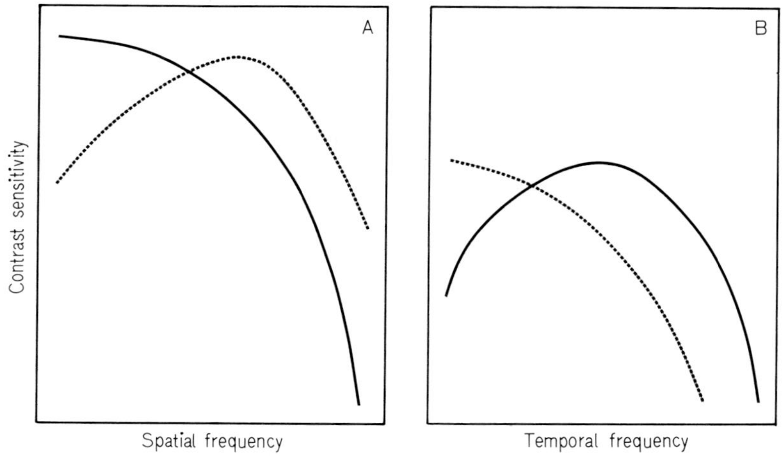

Fig. 5. Hypothetical contrast sensitivities of pattern-sensitive and movement-sensitive systems in human vision (based largely on data of KULIKOWSKI and TOLHURST, 1973). Solid curves represent sensitivities for detecting flicker or movement of grating; dashed curves are sensitivities for recognition of grating pattern. Panel A is at fixed temporal frequency, panel B at fixed spatial frequency. Axes are arbitrarily scaled, because positions of curves depend upon value of fixed frequency (spatial or temporal), as well as upon other parameters

thresholds represent activity in two parallel sets of visual mechanisms, a transient system sensitive to movement but with poor ability to resolve spatial detail, and a system designed for detailed pattern analysis over a range of temporal frequencies (KEESEY, 1972; KULIKOWSKI and TOLHURST, 1973).

Several aspects of the curves in Figure 5 are worth noting. The upper sensitivity envelopes of the functions give contrast sensitivity measured using "absolute" detection thresholds. These envelopes show no low temporal frequency or low spatial frequency declines in sensitivity; this is a typical finding when either spatial frequency or temporal frequency is moderate to high in value (ROBSON, 1966). The individual curves of Figure 5 are also not all single visual channels. TOLHURST (1973) has shown that both the motion and pattern curves in Figure 5a are envelopes for narrowly tuned spatial frequency-specific channels, similar to those originally found for stationary gratings by PANTLE and SEKULER (1968a) and by BLAKEMORE and CAMPBELL (1969). The movement-sensitive channels may be slightly less selective for spatial frequency than are the pattern detectors (GRAHAM, 1972; PANTLE, 1973; TOLHURST, 1973). In addition, the pattern system shows linear spatial summation, while the movement system sums very nonlinearly (KING-SMITH and KULIKOWSKI, 1975). Finally, TOLHURST et al. (1973) have extended the experiment of PANTLE and SEKULER (1968b) to show that the motion-sensitive system (Fig. 5b, solid curve) is composed of channels selective for temporal frequency;[2] the pattern system (dashed curve) has no such channels.

[2] Channels with moderately narrow bandwidth may be observed only when spatial modulation is present as well as temporal modulation (i.e., for gratings). When the stimuli are uniform flickering fields, several *broadly* tuned temporal frequency-specific channels are found (PANTLE, 1971; SMITH, 1971).

As potential neural correlates for these human motion and pattern systems, we may consider the X-type and Y-type retinal ganglion cells discovered electrophysiologically in cat by ENROTH-CUGELL and ROBSON (1966). The X-cells sum linearly over their receptive fields, while Y-cells are very nonlinear. When a stationary grating is presented in an X-cell's receptive field, it responds with a sustained, increased discharge, provided that the phase of the stimulus relative to the receptive field is optimal; Y-cells respond with transient increases in discharge rate at the onset and offset of a stationary stimulus, and these responses are relatively independent of phase. If the grating is made to drift, the discharge rate of either cell type is typically modulated by each bar of the grating as it passes over the receptive field. ENROTH-CUGELL and ROBSON also report measurements of contrast sensitivity as a function of spatial frequency for both types of neuron. The functions for X-cells generally show narrower tuning than those for Y-cells, and peak at higher spatial frequencies.

Unfortunately, the specification of a neural basis for the human motion and pattern systems has been hindered by the fact that different investigators classify cells using different criteria. ENROTH-CUGELL and ROBSON (1966) used linearity of spatial summation to group neurons as X- or Y-types. CLELAND et al. (1971), on the other hand, chose response dynamics as their criterion, classifying a cell as either "sustained" or "transient" depending upon the time course of its response to standing contrast. For retinal ganglion cells, under light-adapted conditions, these two classification schemes are roughly equivalent. Dark-adaptation, however, can change the responses of Y-type retinal ganglion cells from transient to sustained (ZACKS, 1975). Moreover, when the classification schemes are extended to neurons in the lateral geniculate nucleus (CLELAND et al., 1971), the alternative modes of classification differ significantly; there are transient X-cells and sustained Y-cells (SHAPLEY and HOCHSTEIN, 1975).

Adding to the confusion is a third classification criterion, axonal conduction velocity. CLELAND et al. (1971) and STONE and HOFFMANN (1971) report that transient neurons have faster conducting axons than do sustained cells, and that cells in the LGN are almost always driven by retinal ganglion cells of the same class. HOFFMANN and STONE (1971), using the "simple" versus "complex" classification scheme for cortical cells originally proposed by HUBEL and WIESEL (1962), have found many complex cells which are driven monosynaptically by rapidly conducting LGN afferents. Simple cells are not driven by fast axons, but some are clearly activated by slow-conducting afferents. This implies that simple cells may be part of the sustained system, while complex cells may belong to the transient system (STONE, 1972). It is tempting to compare this dichotomy with the X-Y distinction in the retina: simple cells frequently show linear spatial summation, whereas complex cells tend to sum nonlinearly (MAFFEI and FIORENTINI, 1973). IKEDA and WRIGHT (1974), however, provide evidence for sustained and transient cell types within the visual cortex, but these investigators claim that neurons of either type may be found among populations of both simple and complex cells.[3]

[3] A review of sustained-transient physiology may be found in HAMASAKI and WINTERS (1974) and in SEKULER (1974).

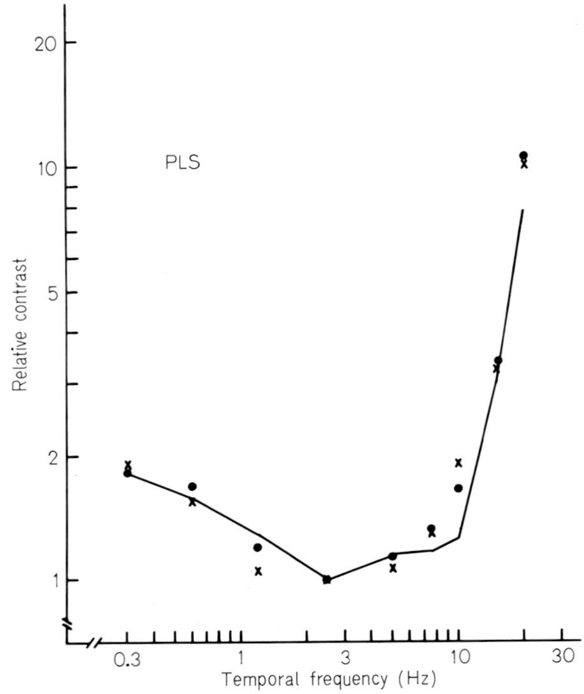

Fig. 6. Contrast thresholds for detecting flicker or movement at various temporal frequencies (*solid curve*) compared with response of direction-sensitive mechanisms, measured by motion after-effect cancellation technique (*data points*). All sets of data have been normalized to same minimum relative contrast

Recent psychophysical results deepen the mystery. The velocity or temporal frequency selectivity found psychophysically is most unlike that measured neurophysiologically. As we mentioned earlier, only the human movement-sensitive system contains channels narrowly tuned for drift rate; the pattern-sensitive system is a single channel with respect to temporal frequency (TOLHURST et al., 1973). In the cat visual cortex, however, both simple and complex cell types are selective for velocity (PETTIGREW et al., 1968; MOVSHON, 1974, 1975) and neurons classified independently as either sustained or transient may all show velocity-specific tuning (MOVSHON, 1975). Both simple and complex cell types in the cat cortex may also be directionally selective (PETTIGREW et al., 1968) as may be cortical neurons classified as sustained or transient (KELLY and VAN ESSEN, 1974; M. CYNADER, personal communication). In human vision, however, direction-specificity seems to be a property of the movement-detecting system alone. This assertion is supported by several experiments. PANTLE (in preparation) compared flicker or movement threshold at various temporal frequencies with a measure of the responsiveness of directionally selective mechanisms based on the motion after-effect. PANTLE devised a cancellation technique in which the observer acted as a null instrument. A motion after-effect was

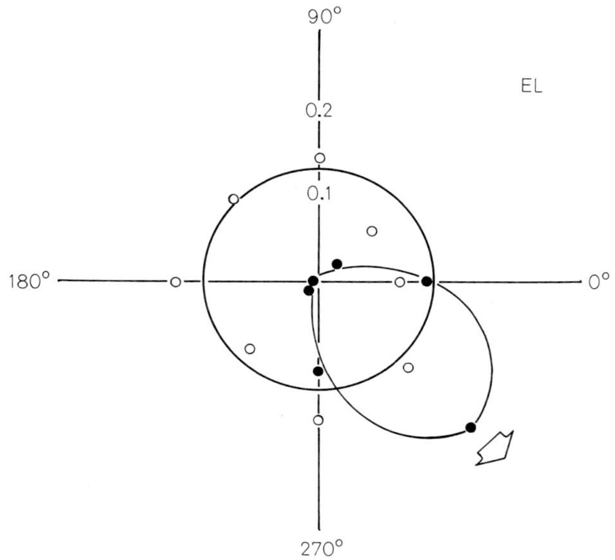

Fig. 7. Polar plot of log threshold elevation produced by adaptation to random dots drifting toward 315° (*arrow*). Test stimuli (also random dots) moved in various directions; threshold elevation for each test direction is represented by distance from origin (where threshold elevation is zero). Filled circles are measurements of motion detection, open circles of pattern recognition. (From LEVINSON and SEKULER, 1974)

generated by adaptation to a 1 c/° sinusoidal grating which moved rightward. A stationary test grating (1 c/°) that was presented afterward appeared to move to the left. The adapting and test patterns alternated, 8 s for the adapting stimulus and 2 s for the test stimulus. After the first few adapting-test cycles (trials), a second sinusoidal grating (also 1 c/°) was superimposed upon the rightward-moving *adapting* grating (R-G). The second adapting grating moved to the left (L-G) and the observer adjusted its contrast over a series of trials until it canceled the motion after-effect produced by R-G. For low contrasts of L-G, the after-effect generated by R-G was weakened; at high contrasts, the after-effect generated by R-G was overridden and reversed; and at some intermediate contrast, the after-effect generated by R-G was just canceled (i.e. the test pattern appeared stationary). The relative contrast of L-G required to *cancel* the after-effect generated by R-G is plotted (filled circles) as a function of the drift rate of L-G in Figure 6. The drift rate and contrast of R-G was constant for these measurements (5 Hz and 10 × threshold). As can be seen in Figure 6, the least contrast required for cancellation occurred when the drift rate of L-G was 2.5 Hz, and the data have been normalized to yield a cancellation contrast of one at 2.5 Hz. More importantly, the relative contrast required at various drift rates for L-G to cancel the after-effect produced by R-G is remarkably similar to the motion-sensitive system contrast thresholds obtained from the same observer (solid curve). A change of the drift rate of R-G from 5 to 1.25 Hz does not alter the relationship between relative contrast and tempo-

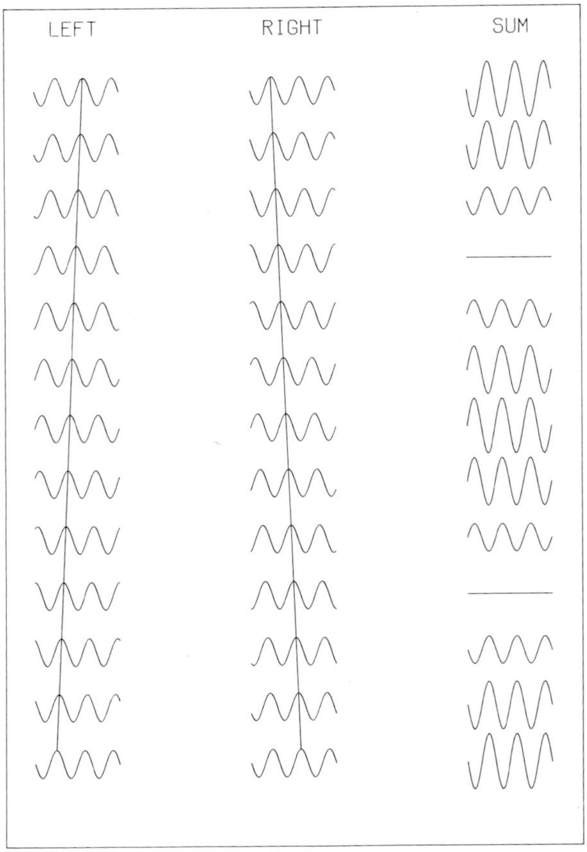

Fig. 8. Decomposition of counterphase flickering grating into two oppositely moving gratings. Column headed *left* shows luminance profile for sinusoidal grating drifting leftward at constant rate. Within column, each profile represents time sample, with successive samples separated by one-twelfth of temporal cycle. Lines joining peaks in successive time samples have been added to emphasize direction of grating movement. Column headed *right* shows corresponding time-sampled profiles for similar grating drifting rightward at same rate. Each profile in column headed *sum* is algebraic sum of other two profiles in same row. *Sum* profiles show grating undergoing phase reversals over time, counterphase grating. Starting from top, profiles in *sum* column undergo one complete cycle of phase alternation; note absence of lateral displacement in *sum* profile series. Peak-to-peak amplitude of top profile in *sum* column is twice amplitude of either of other profiles in that same row. This shows graphically that one can synthesize counterphase flickering grating of unit contrast from combination of two half-contrast moving gratings

ral frequency of L-G (crosses). The close correspondence between the cancellation and threshold data suggests that the direction-specific mechanisms assumed to underlie the motion after-effect are elements of the movement system.

LEVINSON and SEKULER (1974) have measured both flicker detection and pattern recognition thresholds for two-dimensional random dot patterns drifting at constant velocity in various directions. Their results are shown in Figure 7. Adaptation to a random dot pattern moving in one direction (*arrow* in Fig. 7)

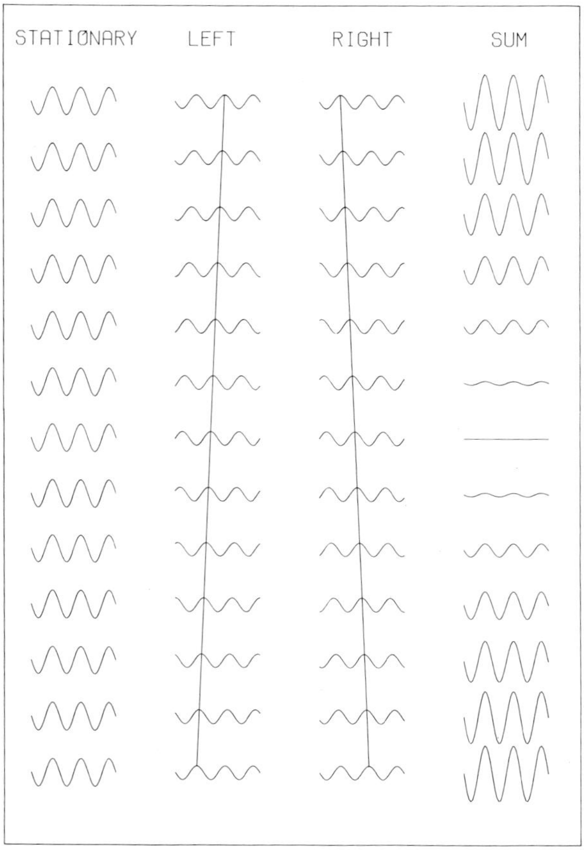

Fig. 9. Decomposition of on-off grating into two, oppositely moving gratings plus stationary grating. Time-sampled luminance profiles are shown for four types of grating: stationary grating, leftward moving grating (*left*), rightward moving grating (*right*) and on-off grating (*sum*). In any column, each profile represents time sample; successive profiles are separated by one-twelfth of temporal cycle. Each profile in *sum* column is algebraic sum of other three gratings in same row. *Sum* profiles represent grating that is slowly turned off and then back on. Peak-to-peak amplitude of top profile in *sum* column is 4 times amplitude of either moving profile and is twice amplitude of stationary grating. This shows graphically that one can synthesize on-off flickering grating of unit contrast from combination of two moving gratings of one-quarter contrast each plus stationary grating of one-half contrast

produces maximal elevation of *flicker* threshold (filled circles) when the test stimulus moves in the same direction, other test directions showing reduced amounts of elevation. Pattern recognition threshold (open circles), however, is uniformly elevated for *all* directions of test motion; adaptation for the pattern system appears to be *independent* of direction.

The pattern-sensitive system appears to respond to overall peak-to-trough stimulus contrast, regardless of direction. KULIKOWSKI and TOLHURST (1973) report comparisons of flicker detection and pattern recognition thresholds for gratings reversing in phase and gratings being turned on and off repetitively at the same rate. Although they used square-wave temporal modulation (introducing harmonics into the stimulus), we shall consider only the fundamental components. Figure 8 shows one mathematical decomposition of a phase-reversing (counterphase) grating of a given contrast; it is the sum of two half-contrast gratings drifting in opposite directions. The on-off grating of the same contrast (Fig. 9) is the sum of a half-contrast stationary grating, and two quarter-contrast gratings moving in opposite directions. Note that the composite gratings do not physically move. If the movement-detection system were responsive *only* to moving components, and if flicker thresholds depended upon one or the other moving component (stimulating independent direction-specific channels), then flicker sensitivity for the phase-reversing grating would be twice that for the on-off stimulus. KULIKOWSKI and TOLHURST (1973) found just such a difference.

On the other hand, if the pattern-recognition system were to *pool* all available contrast without regard for direction of movement then pattern recognition thresholds for the two stimulus types would be about the same. This is exactly what KULIKOWSKI and TOLHURST report.

Although the psychophysical results discussed above are perfectly consistent with previous psychophysical data and are intuitively sensible, they add considerably to the current electrophysiologic confusion. We conclude, then, that there are separate movement-sensitive and pattern-sensitive systems in human vision, but the neural correlates for these systems presently remain obscure.

E. Foundations of Direction-Selectivity

Much of this chapter has been concerned with the psychophysics of motion perception. Several times we have considered the consequences of the visual system's ability to extract directional information from a stimulus. Any treatment of motion perception would be incomplete without a discussion of the detailed structure of the mechanisms that actually extract the direction information. The next two sections of the chapter approach the structure of direction-selective mechanisms from different but complementary perspectives. First we shall consider what is known about the physiology of direction-selective mechanisms. Then we shall consider the general mathematical model that underlies such mechanisms. We should point out that there is nothing contradictory between these two perspectives, they are merely alternative ways of looking at the same thing.

I. Physiology of Direction-Selectivity

Upon mapping the receptive fields of cat simple cortical cells, HUBEL and WIESEL (1959) noted that a cell's directional preference often corresponded to its receptive field organization. Directional preference is derived, HUBEL and WIESEL suggested, from a spatially asymmetric synergistic interaction between adjacent areas of the receptive field.

This proposal has several implications that we should consider. First, a cell's direction-selectivity ought to vary depending upon *where* in the cell's receptive field you stimulate. Second, a cell which shows good selectivity when tested with large stimulus movements may not show any selectivity when tested with very small excursions. Several sets of observations contradict these implications (BARLOW and LEVICK, 1965; BISHOP et al., 1973; and MICHAEL, 1968). For example, BISHOP and his colleagues found that the directional selectivity of a simple cell in the cat cortex was fairly constant even though movements of the stimulating edge covered extremely small areas (less than 5′). Moreover, the cell's direction-selectivity was constant over the entire excitatory center of its receptive field; direction-selectivity does not require that the stimulus cross the boundary between on and off regions in the receptive field.

Alternative explanatory schemes account for direction-selectivity on the basis of inhibitory and disinhibitory interactions, either among direct, retinotopic inputs to a direction-specific neuron, or between directionally selective cells at the same level of processing (BARLOW and LEVICK, 1965; BISHOP et al., 1971). In the case of directional selectivity within the visual cortex (the case typical of higher mammals), it is likely that the inhibition is generated within the cortex as well. BENEVENTO et al. (1972) and CREUTZFELDT et al. (1974) have shown that trigger features, including direction and orientation preferences, may be shaped by the interplay of thalamic influences and intracortical inhibition. Intracellular recordings of responses to slowly moving stimuli reveal consistent and strong IPSP's to stimulation in the cell's nonpreferred direction. PETTIGREW and DANIELS (1973) have shown that responses of cortical neurons are affected by bicuculline, an antagonist of the inhibitory transmitter γ-aminobutyric acid. The direction-selectivity of many cells is often lost or the preferred direction altered. These findings have been confirmed in large part by ROSE and BLAKEMORE (1974) and by SILLITO (1974). Intracortical inhibition probably makes two slightly different sorts of contribution to the net directional selectivity of the visual cortex. Inhibition could sharpen the selectivity of cells that would be only weakly directionally selective without the inhibition. In addition, intracortical inhibition could give some selectivity to cells that otherwise could show none.

Computer simulations of self-organization in the striate cortex show how these intracortical influences may operate (MALSBURG, 1973 and personal communication; HOUCHIN, 1975). At the start of MALSBURG's simulations, some cortical cells showed selectivity simply because their receptive field structures allow synergy between adjacent areas. Other cortical cells, with symmetric receptive field areas, showed no direction-selectivity. As the simulation proceeded and intracortical influences operated, nearly all cells developed direction-selectivity. This development did not require any change in the receptive field organization of individuals cells. The change occurred because the cells were members of a cortical network "seeded" by a few directionally selective cells. It is possible that a similar situation holds in the mammalian visual cortex. Indeed, the recent work of PETTIGREW (1974) with visually deprived cats suggests that a coarse direction-specificity is an innate cortical property, a property that is sharpened considerably through visual experience. The same conclusion is supported by several other studies as well (TRETTER et al., 1975; VITAL-DURRAND and JEANNEROD, 1974a, 1974b).

II. Mathematical Structure of Direction-Selectivity

Let us turn now to a mathematical description of the physiologic models just described. To extract information about direction of motion a way must be found to convert changes in spatial position into information about temporal changes. All models of direction-specificity ultimately solve this problem in the same way: cross-correlation. Although the nuances vary from model to model, all reduce to same basic computational strategy. We should bear in mind that this same problem is faced by the nervous system in other situations, and that it may very well use the same strategies for solution. In fact, the following presentation owes much to CHERRY's (1961) treatment of the binaural fusion process.

Imagine that a retina is exposed to a pattern. The pattern has a luminance distribution that is some function of spatial position. If the pattern moves across the field, its effect on some retinal receptor R_a will change as a function of time, $f_a(t)$. A related function of time, $f_b(t)$, is produced at a neighboring retinal locus R_b. A neural element with access to the response of both receptors could recover the direction of motion by computing the cross correlation $\phi(\tau)$ between $f_a(t)$ and $f_b(t)$.[4] We can represent this formally by

$$\phi_{ab}(\tau) = \int_{-\infty}^{+\infty} f_a(t-\tau) \cdot f_b(t)\, dt \qquad (4)$$

where τ represents a "time lag" in the comparison of the two functions.

The shape of $\phi_{ab}(\tau)$ gives information about the phase relationships of functions $f_a(t)$ and $f_b(t)$. The model converts the relative spatial positions of two receptors into directional information (see Fig. 10). Logically, the spatial separation between the receptors acts as a kind of delay line in a comparator circuit. This property has been made explicit in several models of direction-selectivity (BARLOW and LEVICK, 1965; SCHOUTEN, 1967). The effect of the delay is to shape the cross-correlation function, giving it a peak at a specific value of τ, a value which represents direction and rate of stimulus motion. A negative

[4] We use concept of cross-correlation rather than autocorrelation to allow for the possibility that for identical inputs, the response of R_a may not be identical to R_b.

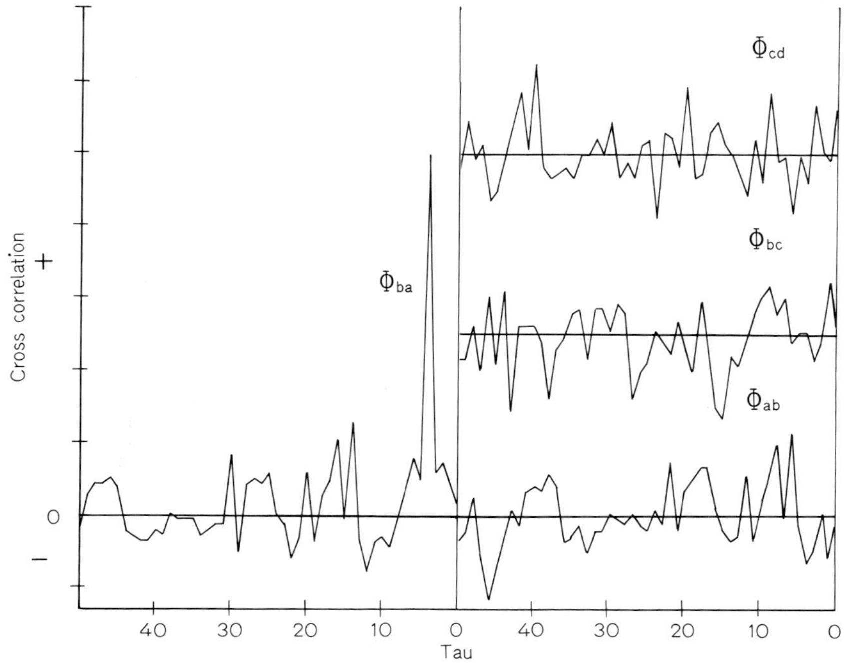

Fig. 10. Examples to illustrate basic cross-correlation model. Random pattern was created in large matrix. Each cell in matrix was randomly assigned either of two luminance levels. Higher luminance was designated as 1, lower as −1. We assume that pattern is imaged on highly simplified visual system with four receptors — A, B, C, and D. Each receptor has as its field of view square area precisely same size as any cell in pattern matrix. Receptive fields of A and B are separated by four pattern elements, with A's field being to left of B's field. Fields of C and D are midway along imaginary line connecting A and B. Field of receptor C lies *above* imaginary line, field of receptor D lies *below* line. Each pair of receptors is connected to one second-order element whose output is cross-correlation between its two inputs. We computed discrete cross-correlations that result from (1) moving pattern at uniform rate from left to right and (2) sampling correlation at fixed rate. Cross-correlations are shown for pairs B–A, C–D, B–C, and A–B in Fig. 10a–d. In each case response of first-named receptor is evaluated at various times, t, and cross-correlation shown between two receptors at various values of τ, ranging from 0–+50. Large peak in Fig. 10a at $\tau = 4$ reflects fact that response of receptor B at any time is strongly correlated with response of receptor A at four time samples earlier. In this case, our calculations assumed perfect correlation between two responses. But location of peak would be invariant even if responses at A and B were less than perfectly correlated. For example, if there were small random, imperfectly correlated fluctuations of each receptor's sensitivity, peak would be reduced, but its location unchanged. Cross-correlation between same two receptors, A and B, taken in other direction (Fig. 10d) shows no single strong peak like that in 10a. Reason is that events at receptor B are not correlated with *preceding* events at receptor A—at least for case of movement from left to right. Situation would be reversed in other direction of motion. Note absence of large peaks in Fig. 10b and 10c; this reminds us that only receptor pairs along path of motion contribute information from which direction can be extracted. This could account for various observed relationships between perceived direction of motion and orientation of moving elements (e.g. FRISBY, 1972). If each receptor had been allowed to "look at" more than single small element in field, location of peak cross-correlation would have been unaffected despite some smoothing and modulation of cross-correlation function

τ means one direction of motion, a positive value the opposite direction. A neural element specific for some value of τ would be directionally selective.

The possibility of implementing a cross-correlation within the limitations of any real nervous system has been discussed by CHERRY (1961), GABOR (1968), BORSELLINO and POGGIO (1972), REICHARDT (1961), and WIGHTMAN (1973). One obvious requirement is that the motion detector receive the value of $f_b(t)$ at some moment in time ("now") and cross-multiply that value with the current value of $f_a(t)$, past values of $f_a(t)$ and future values of $f_a(t)$. The system obviously couldn't know the future values. Also, it would not be useful for our second order unit to cross-correlate one receptor's *current* response with another receptor's most *ancient* responses. We've therefore adjusted the model to take account of these limitations. Following the lead of CHERRY (1961) and FOSTER (1971), equation (5) introduces a function, $W(t')$, which weights the cross-correlation for recency. It is convenient to assume that this weighting function has the form $W(t')=e^{-kt'}$ for t' greater than or equal to zero, and $W(t')=0$ for t' less than zero. FOSTER (1971) estimates the time constant, k, at about 0.3 s. (Note also that the limits of integration have been changed to reflect the system's inability to foretell the future; time t represents "now".)

$$\phi_{ab}(t,\tau)=\int_{-\infty}^{t} f_a(T-\tau)\cdot f_b(T)\cdot W(t-T)\,dT \tag{5}$$

Over what distances on the retina might this running cross-correlation be computed? Are there parallel sets of cells that derive their cross-correlations from receptors separated by different distances? FOSTER (1971) states that the human visual system behaves as if interactions leading to motion perception can take place between pairs of receptors separated by as little as 2 min of arc or by as much as 20 min of arc. These distances, and the running cross-correlation process discussed by FOSTER, are consistent with recent observations with random dot matrices (BRADDICK, 1974; LAPPIN and BELL, 1976).

Finally, what happens if we allow more than a single pair of receptors to influence each correlator unit? Fortunately, this doesn't add much complexity. POGGIO and REICHARDT (1973) have shown that any of a large set of motion detection models with n inputs and 1 output can be reduced to the sum of 2-input pairs, the case we have been considering here.

The process we're describing is sensitive to both spatial and temporal properties of the stimulus. As a result, any hardware realization of equation (5) must provide for the operation of both spatial and temporal forces. Either one alone is inadequate. This point brings us back to the first concern of this section, the physiology of movement perception. Either the physiology or its mathematical structure can be reduced to a common framework: an influence function defined along both spatial and temporal dimensions. In terms more common in physiology this influence function is some cell's spatio temporal weighting function or receptive field. So, although the anatomical details of various models of motion perception differ, we should bear in mind that they all share a common mathematical structure. We should also remember that the problem the nervous system solves in order to extract motion information from a visual stimulus is the same problem it solves in other modalities.

F. Unsolved Problems of Motion Perception

Though we know a good deal about the mechanisms of motion perception there are obvious and important gaps in our understanding. Some of these gaps have already been discussed. To identify others all we have to do is note how far we are from our goal: an explanation of everyday perception of motion. Without going into too much detail we will consider the general character of these gaps.

Much of the psychophysical work we have discussed has dealt with the mechanisms that govern a moving target's visibility. Such mechanisms determine whether a particular moving target is or is not detectable at some particular moment in time. Most studies of visibility ignore a more important, perceptual problem: the *appearance* of the target when it is clearly visible. Work on detectability does not automatically yield insights about the way moving targets look. A study by LEVINSON and SEKULER (1976) bridges this gap for at least one aspect of a moving target's appearance, its perceived direction of motion. LEVINSON and SEKULER reasoned that the selective desensitization which adaptation produces in direction-specific channels should also change the distribution of activity evoked among channels by a suprathreshold test stimulus drifting in a direction other than the adaptation direction. In particular, the central tendency of the response distribution should be shifted away from the channel that is normally most sensitive to the adapting direction. If the code for perceived direction involves direction-specific channels, then this adaptation-induced change in their pattern of responsiveness should alter the apparent direction of movement of the suprathreshold test stimulus. To verify this, LEVINSON and SEKULER measured the perceived direction of a suprathreshold sheet of moving dots after adaptation to another sheet of dots which moved either in that same direction or in some other direction. The results are shown in Figure 11. No change in perceived direction occurred when test and adapting directions were the same (zero normalized adaptation direction in Fig. 11). However, large shifts (10° or more) were observed for adaptation directions near the test direction ($\pm 30°$); the size of the perceived direction shift decreased as the adapting direction was made less similar to the test direction. Note that these shifts were always away from the adaptation direction. The existence and character of this perceived direction shift confirms the idea that perceived direction of motion depends upon the balance of activity in various direction-selective channels. Further work is needed to define the neural codes for other aspects of a moving target's appearance, for example its perceived speed.

There is another gap between everyday perception of motion and what we have learned from laboratory studies of motion. In the laboratory, stimuli are simple; they usually consist of contours all moving in the same direction and with the same speed. But outside the laboratory, at any one moment our visual field may contain many objects all moving in different directions and with different speeds. How can we use the laboratory results, with simple stimuli, to tell us about motion perception outside the laboratory with complex stimuli? For example, can we treat the response to a field of many complex

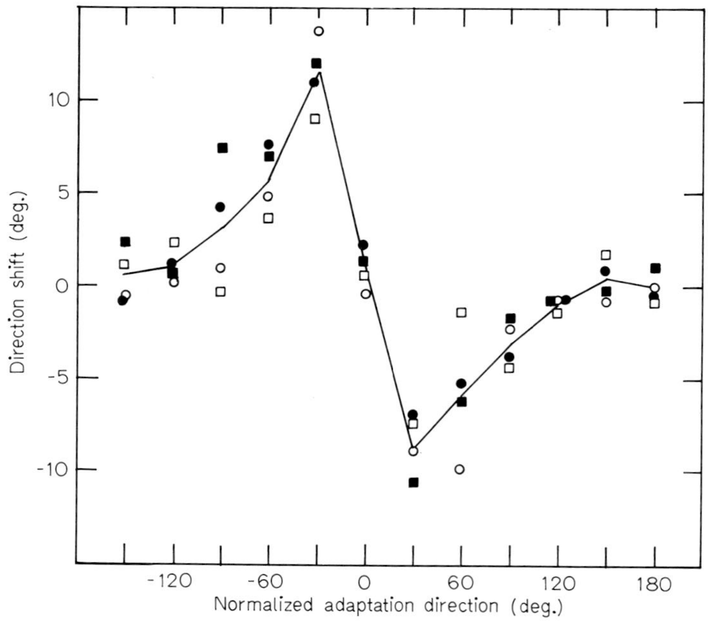

Fig. 11. Shift in perceived direction as function of direction of adapting movement. Adaptation directions have been adjusted such that zero normalized adaptation direction is point where test and adapting directions are same. Positive values are anticlockwise directions, negative values clockwise directions. Filled circles are for observer EL, test direction 0°; open circles for EL, test direction 90°; filled squares for oberserver RS, test direction 180°; open squares for RS, test direction 270°. Each point is based on six adjustments, and standard errors are generally less than 1°. Continuous curve shows mean of four data points at each normalized adaptation direction

motions as the sum of responses to the individual components of motion? Under some conditions we can. As we have already seen, when superimposed gratings of low contrast move at the same speed but in opposite directions, the visual system responds independently to each (LEVINSON and SEKULER, 1973, 1975b). But what of the more common everyday situation, different high contrast motion vectors in adjacent areas of the field? Both psychophysical and physiologic results suggest that the visual system under these circumstances may not respond to each motion component in an independent fashion. Some single neurons in the mammalian visual system respond to relative motion in their receptive fields in a manner not predictable from their responses to the separate components of that relative motion (MANDL, 1974; BRIDGEMAN, 1972). If such cells contribute to perception, they complicate the task of using psychophysical responses to simple motion to predict the psychophysical responses produced by relative motion. In fact, the little psychophysical work we already have on relative motion confirms the difficulty of such extrapolation. When moving targets of different speeds or direction are juxtaposed in the field, they influence each other's perceived speed and direction in rather complicated ways (HOLMGREN, 1974; LOOMIS and NAKAYAMA, 1973; TYNAN and SEKULER, 1975).

Psychophysical work with relative motion has really only just begun. In the past few years the partnership of psychophysics and physiology has given us a new understanding of how our brains analyze relatively simple kinds of motion. We will need a continuation of that partnership and a measure of progress equal to what we have already seen if we are truly to understand why moving things appear as they do.

Acknowledgement

The preparation of this chapter and some of the research described herein has been supported by Grant EY 00321 from the National Institutes of Health. This chapter was completed in July 1975.

References

Addams, R.: An account of a peculiar optical phaenomenon seen after looking at a moving body, etc. Lond. and Edinb. Philos. Mag. and Sci. (3rd series) **5**, 373–374 (1834).

Barlow, H.B., Hill, R.M.: Evidence for a physiological explanation of the waterfall phenomenon and figural aftereffects. Nature (Lond.) **200**, 1345–1347 (1963a).

Barlow, H.B., Hill, R.M.: Selective sensitivity to direction of movement in ganglion cells of the retina. Science **139**, 412–414 (1963b).

Barlow, H.B., Hill, R.M., Levick, W.R.: Retinal ganglion cells responding selectively to direction and speed of image motion in the rabbit. J. Physiol. (Lond.) **173**, 377–407 (1964).

Barlow, H.B., Levick, W.R.: The mechanism of directionally selective units in rabbit's retina. J. Physiol. (Lond.) **178**, 477–504 (1965).

Benevento, L.A., Creutzfeldt, O.D., Kuhnt, U.: Significance of intracortical inhibition in visual cortex. Nature (New Biol.) **238**, 124–126 (1972).

Bishop, P.O., Coombs, J.S., Henry, G.H.: Interaction effects of visual contours on the discharge frequency of simple striate neurones. J. Physiol. (Lond.) **219**, 659–687 (1971).

Bishop, P.O., Goodwin, A.W., Henry, G.H.: Direction selective subregions in striate simple cell receptive fields. J. Physiol. (Lond.) **238**, 25P (1973).

Blakemore, C., Campbell, F.W.: On the existence of neurones in the human visual system selectively sensitive to the orientation and size of retinal images. J. Physiol. (Lond.) **203**, 237–260 (1969).

Blakemore, C., Carpenter, R.H.S., Georgeson, M.A.: Lateral inhibition between orientation detectors in the human visual system. Nature (Lond.) **228**, 37–39 (1970).

Bogartz, R.: A least squares method for fitting intercepting line segments to a set of data points. Psychol. Bull. **70**, 749–755 (1968).

Borsellino, A., Poggio, T.: Holographic aspects of temporal memory and optomotor responses. Kybernetik **10**, 58–60 (1972).

Braddick, O.: A short-range process in apparent motion. Vision Res. **14**, 519–527 (1974).

Breitmeyer, B.G.: A relationship between the detection of size, rate, orientation and direction of motion in the human visual system. Vision Res. **13**, 41–58 (1973).

Bridgeman, B.: Visual receptive fields sensitive to absolute and relative motion during tracking. Science **178**, 1106–1108 (1972).

Carpenter, R.H.S., Blakemore, C.: Interactions between orientations in human vision. Exp. Brain Res. **18**, 287–303 (1973).

Cherry, C.: Two ears – but one world. In: Sensory Communication, Rosenblith, W.A. (ed.). pp. 99–117. Cambridge: M.I.T. Press, 1961.

Clarke, P.G.H.: Are visual evoked potentials to motion reversal produced by direction-sensitive brain mechanisms? Vision Res. **14**, 1281–1284 (1974).

Cleland, B.G., Dubin, M.W., Levick, W.R.: Sustained and transient neurones in the cat's retina and lateral geniculate nucleus. J. Physiol. (Lond.) **217**, 473–496 (1971).

Cooper, G.F., Robson, J.G.: Successive transformations of spatial information in the visual system. IEE/NPL Conference on Pattern Recognition, IEE Conference Publication **42**, 134–143 (1968).

Creutzfeldt, O.D., Kuhnt, U., Benevento, L.A.: An intracellular analysis of visual cortical neurones to moving stimuli: Responses in a co-operative neuronal network. Exp. Brain Res. **21**, 251–274 (1974).

Dealy, R.S., Tolhurst, D.J.: Is spatial adaptation an after-effect of prolonged inhibition? J. Physiol. (Lond.) **241**, 261–270 (1974).

Enroth-Cugell, Ch., Robson, J.G.: The contrast sensitivity of retinal ganglion cells of the cat. J. Physiol. (Lond.) **187**, 517–552 (1966).

Frisby, J.P.: The effect of stimulus orientation on the phi phenomenon. Vision Res. **12**, 1145–1166 (1972).

Foster, D.H.: A model of the human visual system in its response to certain classes of moving stimuli. Kybernetik **8**, 69–84 (1971).

Gabor, D.: Improved holographic model of temporal recall. Nature (Lond.) **217**, 1288–1289 (1968).

Ganz, L., Lange, A.: Changes in motion sensitivity of cat visual cortex neurons during the course of dark adaptation. Presented at the Spring Meeting of the Association for Research in Vision and Ophthalmology, Sarasota, Florida (1973).

Graham, N.: Spatial frequency channels in the human visual system: Effects of luminance and pattern drift rate. Vision Res. **12**, 53–68 (1972).

Graham, N., Nachmias, J.: Detection of grating patterns containing two spatial frequencies: A comparison of single-channel and multiple-channel models. Vision Res. **11**, 251–259 (1971).

Grüsser, O.J., Grüsser-Cornehls, U.: Neuronal mechanisms of movement perception and some psychophysical and behavioral correlations. In: Handbook of Sensory Physiology, Jung, R. (ed.). Vol. VII/3A, pp. 333–429. Berlin: Springer Verlag, 1973.

Hamasaki, D.I., Winters, R.W.: A review of the properties of sustained and transient retinal ganglion cells. Experientia (Basel) **30**, 713–719 (1974).

Hoffmann, K.-P., Stone, J.: Conduction velocity of afferents to cat visual cortex: a correlation with cortical receptive field properties. Brain Res. **32**, 460–466 (1971).

Holmgren, S.: On searching for Mach band type phenomena in the visual perception of spatial velocity distributions. Report 151, Dept. Psychol., Univ. Uppsala, Sweden (1974).

Houchin, J.: Direction specificity in cortical responses to moving stimuli—a simple model. J. Physiol. (Lond.) **249**, 7–9P (1975).

Hubel, D.H., Wiesel, T.N.: Receptive fields of single neurones in the cat's striate cortex. J. Physiol. (Lond.) **148**, 574–591 (1959).

Hubel, D.H., Wiesel, T.N.: Receptive fields, binocular interaction and functional architecture in the cat's visual cortex. J. Physiol. (Lond.) **160**, 106–154 (1962).

Hubel, D.H., Wiesel, T.N.: Receptive fields and functional architecture in two nonstriate visual areas (18 and 19) of the cat. J. Neurophysiol. **28**, 229–289 (1965).

Ikeda, H., Wright, M.J.: Evidence for "sustained" and "transient" neurones in the cat's visual cortex. Vision Res. **14**, 133–136 (1974).

Keck, M., Palella, T., Pantle, A.: Motion aftereffect as a function of the contrast of sinusoidal gratings. Vision Res. **16**, 187–192 (1976).

Keesey, U.T.: Flicker and pattern detection: A comparison of thresholds. J. opt. Soc. Amer. **62**, 446–448 (1972).

Kelly, J.P., van Essen, D.C.: Cell structure and function in the visual cortex of the cat. J. Physiol. (Lond.) **238**, 515–547 (1974).

King-Smith, P.E., Kulikowski, J.J.: Pattern and flicker detection analysed by subthreshold summation. J. Physiol. (Lond.) **249**, 519–548 (1975).

Kulikowski, J.J.: Effect of eye movements on the contrast sensitivity of spatio-temporal pattern. Vision Res. **11**, 261–273 (1971).

Kulikowski, J.J., Tolhurst, D.J.: Psychophysical evidence for sustained and transient detectors in human vision. J. Physiol. (Lond.) **232**, 149–162 (1973).

Lappin, J.S., Bell, H.H.: The detection of coherence in moving random-dot patterns. Vision Res. **16**, 161–168 (1976)

Lettvin, J., Maturana, H., Pitts, W., McCulloch, W.: Two remarks on the visual system of the frog. In: Sensory Communication, Rosenblith, W.A. (ed.). pp. 757–776. Cambridge: M.I.T. Press, 1961.

Levinson, E., Sekuler, R.: Spatio-temporal contrast sensitivities for moving and flickering stimuli. J. opt. Soc. Amer. **63**, 1296 (abstract) (1973).

Levinson, E., Sekuler, R.: Direction-specific adaptation in human vision: Measurements using isotropic random dot patterns. Presented at the meetings of the Psychonomic Society, Boston, Massachusetts (1974).

Levinson, E., Sekuler, R.: Inhibition and disinhibition of direction-specific mechanisms in human vision. Nature (Lond.) **254**, 692–694 (1975a).

Levinson, E., Sekuler, R.: The independence of channels in human vision selective for direction of movement. J. Physiol. (Lond.) **250**, 347–366 (1975b).

Levinson, E., Sekuler, R.: Adaptation alters perceived direction of motion. Vision Res. **16**, 779–781 (1976).

Loomis, J.M., Nakayama, K.: A velocity analogue of brightness contrast. Perception **2**, 425–428 (1973).

Maffei, L., Fiorentini, A.: The visual cortex as a spatial frequency analyser. Vision Res. **13**, 1255–1267 (1973).

Maffei, L., Fiorentini, A., Bisti, S.: Neural correlate of perceptual adaptation to gratings. Science **182**, 1036–1038 (1973).

Malsburg, C. v.d.: Self-organization of orientation sensitive cells in the striate cortex. Kybernetik **14**, 85–100 (1973).

Mandl, G.: The influence of visual pattern combination on responses of movement sensitive cells in the cat's superior colliculus. Brain Res. **75**, 215–240 (1974).

Michael, C.R.: Receptive fields of single optic nerve fibers in a mammal with an all-cone retina. II: Directionally selective units. J. Neurophysiol. **31**, 249–282 (1968).

Movshon, J.A.: Velocity preferences of simple and complex cells in the cat's striate cortex. J. Physiol. (Lond.) **242**, 121–123P (1974).

Movshon, J.A.: The velocity tuning of single units in cat striate cortex. J. Physiol. (Lond.) **249**, 445–468 (1975).

Nes, F.L. van, Koenderink, J.J., Nas, H., Bouman, M.A.: Spatiotemporal modulation transfer in the human eye. J. opt. Soc. Amer. **57**, 1082–1088 (1967).

Pantle, A.: Adaptation to pattern spatial frequency: Effects on visual movement sensitivity in humans. J. opt. Soc. Amer. **60**, 1120–1124 (1970).

Pantle, A.: Flicker adaptation. I. Effect on visual sensitivity to temporal fluctuations of light intensity. Vision Res. **11**, 943–952 (1971).

Pantle, A.: A look at spatial frequency interactions with moving gratings. Presented at the Spring Meeting of the Association for Research in Vision and Ophthalmology, Sarasota, Florida (1973).

Pantle, A.: Motion aftereffect magnitude as a measure of the spatio-temporal response properties of direction-sensitive analyzers. Vision Res. **14**, 1229–1236 (1974).

Pantle, A., Sekuler, R.: Size-detecting mechanisms in human vision. Science **162**, 1146–1148 (1968a).

Pantle, A., Sekuler, R.: Velocity-sensitive elements in human vision: Initial psychophysical evidence. Vision Res. **8**, 445–450 (1968b).

Pantle, A., Sekuler, R.: Contrast response of human visual mechanisms sensitive to orientation and direction of motion. Vision Res. **9**, 397–406 (1969).

Pettigrew, J.D.: The effect of visual experience on the development of stimulus specificity by kitten cortical neurones. J. Physiol. (Lond.) **237**, 49–74 (1974).

Pettigrew, J.D., Daniels, J.D.: Gamma-aminobutyric acid antagonism in visual cortex: Different effects on simple, complex and hypercomplex neurons. Science **182**, 81–83 (1973).

Pettigrew, J.D., Nikara, T., Bishop, P.O.: Responses to moving slits by single units in cat striate cortex. Exp. Brain Res. **6**, 373–390 (1968).

Poggio, T., Reichardt, W.: Considerations on models of movement detection. Kybernetik **13**, 223–227 (1973).

Purkinje, J.A.: Beiträge zur Nähren Kenntnis des Schwindels aus Heutognostischen Daten. In: Purkyne's sebrane spisy (opera omnia) Lhotak, K.J. (ed.). Vol. **2**, pp. 15–37. Prague, 1937.

Reichardt, W.: Autocorrelation, a principle for the evaluation of sensory information. In: Sensory Communication, Rosenblith, W.A. (ed.). pp. 303–317. Cambridge: M.I.T. Press, 1961.

Robson, J.G.: Spatial and temporal contrast-sensitivity functions of the visual system. J. opt. Soc. Amer. **56**, 1141–1142 (1966).

Rose, D., Blakemore, C.: Effects on bicuculline on functions of inhibition in visual cortex. Nature (Lond.) **249**, 375–377 (1974).

Schouten, J.F.: Subjective stroboscopy and a model of visual movement detectors. In: Models for the Perception of Speech and Visual Form, Wathen-Dunn, W. (ed.). pp. 44–55. Cambridge: M.I.T. press, 1967.

Sekuler, R.: Spatial vision. Ann. Rev. Psychol. **25**, 195–232 (1974).

Sekuler, R.: Visual motion perception. In: Handbook of Perception, Carterette, E.C., Friedman, M.P. (eds.), Vol. V, New York: Academic Press, 1975.

Sekuler, R., Ganz, L.: Aftereffect of seen motion with a stabilized retinal image. Science **139**, 419–420 (1963).

Sekuler, R., Levinson, E.: Mechanisms of motion perception. Psychologia (Kyoto) **17**, 38–49 (1974).

Sekuler, R., Pantle, A.: A model for the after-effects of seen movement. Vision Res. **7**, 427–439 (1967).

Sekuler, R., Rubin, E.L., Cushman, W.H.: Selectivities of human visual mechanisms for direction of movement and contour orientation. J. opt. Soc. Amer. **58**, 1146–1150 (1968).

Shapley, R., Hochstein, S.: Visual spatial summation in two classes of geniculate cells. Nature (Lond.) **256**, 411–413 (1975).

Sharpe, C.R., Tolhurst, D.J.: Orientation and spatial frequency channels in peripheral vision. Vision Res. **13**, 2103–2112 (1973).

Sillito, A.M.: Modification of receptive-field properties of neurons in visual-cortex by bicuculline, a GABA antagonist. J. Physiol. (Lond.) **239**, 36–37 (1974).

Smith, R.A.: Studies of temporal frequency adaptation in visual contrast sensitivity. J. Physiol. (Lond.) **216**, 531–552 (1971).

Stecher, S., Sigel, C., Lange, R.V.: Composite adaptation and spatial frequency interactions. Vision Res. **13**, 2527–2531 (1973).

Stone, J.: Morphology and physiology of the geniculocortical synapse in the cat: The question of parallel input to the striate cortex. Invest. Ophthal. **11**, 338–346 (1972).

Stone, J., Hoffman, K.-P.: Conduction velocity as a parameter in the organisation of the afferent relay in the cat's lateral geniculate nucleus. Brain Res. **32**, 454–459 (1971).

Sutherland, N.S.: Figural aftereffects and apparent size. Quart. J. exp. Psychol. **13**, 222–228 (1961).

Tolhurst, D.J.: Adaptation to square-wave gratings: Inhibition between spatial frequency channels in the human visual system. J. Physiol. (Lond.) **226**, 231–248 (1972).

Tolhurst, D.J.: Separate channels for the analysis of the shape and the movement of a moving visual stimulus. J. Physiol. (Lond.) **231**, 385–402 (1973).

Tolhurst, D.J., Sharpe, C.R., Hart, G.: The analysis of the drift rate of moving sinusoidal gratings. Vision Res. **13**, 2545–2555 (1973).

Tretter, F., Cynader, M., Singer, W.: Modification of direction selectivity of neurons in visual-cortex of kittens. Brain Res. **84**, 143–149 (1975).

Tynan, P., Sekuler, R.: Simultaneous motion contrast: Velocity, sensitivity and depth response. Vision Res. **15**, 1231–1238 (1975).

Vital-Durand, F., Jeannerod, M.: Role of visual experience in the development of optokinetic response in kitten. Exp. Brain Res. **20**, 297–302 (1974a).

Vital-Durand, F., Jeannerod, M.: Maturation of the optokinetic response: Genetic and environmental factors. Brain Res. **71**, 249–257 (1974b).

Watanabe, A., Mori, T., Nagata, S., Hiwatashi, K.: Spatial sine-wave responses of the human visual system. Vision Res. **8**, 1245–1263 (1968).

Wightman, F.: The pattern-transformation model of pitch. J. acoust. Soc. Amer. **54**, 407–416 (1973).

Zacks, J.L.: Changes in responses of X and Y type cat retinal ganglion cells produced by changes in background illumination. Presented at The Spring Meeting of The Association for Research in Vision and Ophthalmology, Sarasota, Florida (1975).

Chapter 4

Form-Color Aftereffects in Human Vision*

C.F. STROMEYER, Cambridge, Massachusetts (USA)

With 7 Figures

Contents

* This chapter was written at the laboratory of Professor KARL PRIBRAM at Stanford University and at the laboratory of Professor RICHARD JUNG at Freiburg University, where the author was an Alexander von Humboldt Fellow. Excellent comments on this chapter were made by Drs. BENJAMIN DAWSON, RICHARD HELD, NORVA HEPLER, STANLEY KLEIN, RICHARD E. KRONAUER, DONALD M. MACKAY, VALERIE MACKAY, LORRIN RIGGS, and KEITH WHITE, for which the author is most grateful.

A. Introduction

An engaging problem is how the visual system processes combinations of color and form. One logically possible view is that color and form are processed quite independently (at some level of the visual system). Thus, some mechanisms might respond selectively to form regardless of color and other mechanisms might respond to color regardless of form. Evidence for such form-selective mechanisms has been obtained (YUND et al., 1973; GOURAS and KRÜGER, in preparation) from microelectrode recordings of specific single cells in the visual cortex of rhesus monkey. These cells respond selectively to a specific form whether the form is portrayed by color gradients alone or by luminance gradients. Thus, although these mechanisms respond to color information, they do not convey specific information about color. The mechanisms are from-selective and not color-selective.

Another possibility is that there are mechanisms that respond selectively to specific combinations of color and form. The existence of such mechanisms is suggested by color aftereffects selective to form and the converse effects, form aftereffects selective to color.

The present chapter mainly examines the spatial properties of these form-color aftereffects in the hope that this information may eventually be related to physiologic findings. These spatial properties suggest that the aftereffects depend on the modification of relatively simple neural elements that respond to specific form-color combinations.

The chapter first examines color aftereffects selective to form and then form aftereffects selective to color. Next, two prominent features of the aftereffects are discussed: their longevity and tendency to be monocular. Finally, possible physiologic models of the aftereffects are examined. The question of whether the aftereffects are reflected in a change of threshold sensitivity for detecting patterns with color and spatial properties similar to the adapting patterns is discussed.

B. Color Aftereffects Dependent on Form

I. Spatial Selectivity

After viewing colored patterns, black and white patterns with spatial properties similar to the colored adapting patterns may appear colored. These color aftereffects can be made selective to the direction of edge contrast (edge polarity), line orientation, line width, and velocity. An examination of these spatial properties follows.

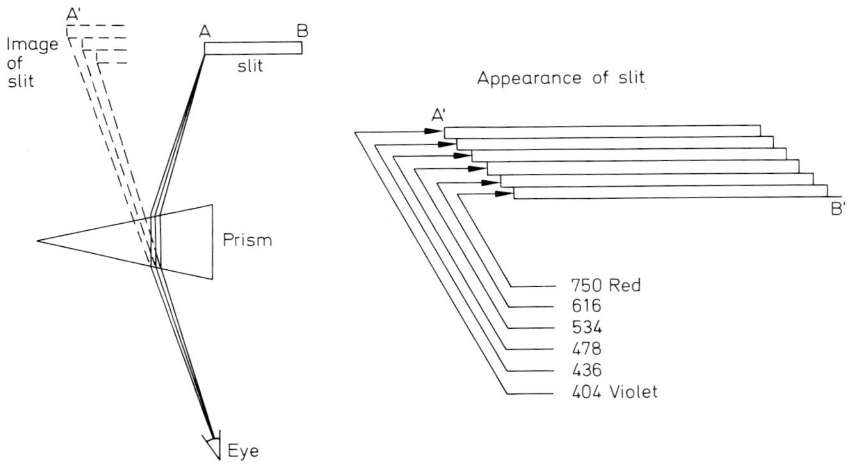

Fig. 1. Chromatic fringes formed by dispersion of the image of a light slit in a dark field. Blue-green and yellow-orange fringes, seen at the left and right edges respectively, are due to the half-spectra dispersed toward darker sides of slit edges. Wavelengths on the right were chosen so that, for a crown-glass prism, each image is shifted by an equal amount relative to the previous image. The images of the slit are separated vertically only for pictorial clarity. (Modified from BOUMA, 1971)

1. Direction of Edge Contrast (Polarity)

The first discovered color aftereffects selective to form are the phantom color fringes. McFARLAND (1883), an ophthalmologist, noted that the color fringes (bluish and yellowish) seen along edges while wearing strong prescription prisms diminished with time. GIBSON (1933) later observed that the fringes seen while wearing wedge prisms diminished over a 3-day period, and when the prisms were removed, complementary colored phantom fringes were seen along edges for several hours. These colored aftereffects are selective to the direction of edge contrast, e.g., left-vs, right-facing edges.

A wedge prism disperses light and produces half-spectrum color fringes along edges. For example, if a light vertical slit in a dark field is viewed through a prism whose base is toward the right, as in Figure 1, a blue-green half-spectrum will be seen at the left edge and a yellow-orange half-spectrum at the right edge (formed by the light dispersed on the darker sides of the edges). The vividness of these colored fringes increases with both the contrast and luminance of the slit, and the width of the fringes varies approximately with the sine of the angle between the slit orientation and the base-apex axis of the prism (HELD, 1954).

Two observations show that the phantom color fringes, seen as an aftereffect after wearing a wedge prism, are caused by neural and not dioptric mechanisms. First, the phantom fringes can be seen in monochromatic sodium light (KOHLER, 1951) and in deep-red light (HAY et al., 1963). Second, the curvature aftereffects and phantom fringes produced by the prisms may grow at different rates (KOHLER, 1951) and can be completely dissociated (HELD, 1962, 1978). Scanning a speckled surface through a prism in white illumination produces phantom fringes but no curvature aftereffects on a test grating (HELD, 1978), whereas scanning a grating through a prism in narrow-band green illumination produces curvature aftereffects but no phantom fringes on the test grating (HELD, 1962, 1978).

The phantom fringes might be caused by color adaptation of mechanisms sensitive to the direction of edge contrast. For example, mechanisms sensitive to left-facing edges may be adapted to give a bluish aftereffect and mechanisms sensitive to right-facing edges may be adapted to give a yellowish aftereffect. Similar colored aftereffects can be obtained with a pair of colored vertical gratings that have a sawtooth luminance profile (STROMEYER et al., 1973). The colored gratings have identical spatial frequency components and are distinguished by having left- or right-facing edges. Further evidence for edge-selective adaptation is provided by the observation that adapting to the Craik-Cornsweet edge illusion produces the greatest threshold rise for detecting a test pattern with the same edge polarity (TOLHURST, 1972).

HELD (1978) has suggested that such color aftereffects as the phantom fringes may serve to diminish the color effects of the eyes' chromatic aberration. This, however, does not imply that the aftereffects actually correct for or reduce the chromatic aberration. Several observations, indeed, suggest that chromatic aberration is not corrected by neural adaptation. For example, CAMPBELL and GUBISCH'S (1967) measurements of contrast sensitivity within the fovea show that the eye is strongly affected by chromatic aberration, and the results agree well with calculations based on diffraction. These investigators were led to conclude that the "neural antichromatic response" postulated by HARTRIDGE (1947) does not diminish chromatic aberration.

Studies of the color-stereo effect also indicate that the color aftereffects do not correct chromatic aberration. Different colored objects in one depth plane may appear at different depth planes when viewed binocularly. EINTHOVEN (1885) attributed this color-stereo effect to the fovea of each eye being disposed temporally with respect to the eyes' optic axes, which has the effect of a base nasal prism in each eye. The prisms disperse light and produce binocular disparities dependent on wavelength. (VOS, 1960; KISHTO, 1965, showed that other factors complicate this simple theory.) The color-stereo effect can be greatly enhanced by wearing base temporal prisms. HAJOS'S (1962) observers wore such prisms for 10 days. The color-stereo effect was measured by adjusting red and blue targets to appear in the same depth plane. The opposite sets of bluish and yellowish prism fringes in either eye adapted considerably, but there was not the slightest change in the magnitude of the color-stereo effect. The reduction of the fringes can indeed influence the hue seen along edges, but apparently this does not lead to a change in chromatic aberration as reflected in measures of contrast sensitivity or stereo vision.

2. Orientation

The phantom fringes, as suggested earlier, might result from color adaptation of mechanisms that are sensitive to the direction of edge contrast (polarity). Cells with nearly concentric receptive fields could give rise to the aftereffect, for if the on-area of the receptive field were displaced only slightly to the right of the center of the off-area, for example, the cell would respond slightly better to an edge that was light on the right and dark on the left than to an edge of opposite polarity. Such cells however would be very poorly tuned to line orientation, thus resembling the dipoles postulated by GIBSON and HARRIS (1968), discussed in section on Physiologic Models. Several studies on the orientation selectivity of the phantom fringes are *not* inconsistent with this neural model. KOHLER (1951) reports that after wearing prisms with a horizontal base-apex axis, the phantom fringes are seen on vertical and oblique edges but not on horizontal edges. The horizontal edges might stimulate *very broadly tuned* mechanisms to elicit *both* the yellow and the blue aftereffect; thus, no aftereffect would be seen on horizontal edges. The effects have been studied quantitatively by viewing light-dark test edges through a variable Risley prism that can be adjusted so that the real fringes produced by the prism and the phantom fringes just cancel (HAJOS, 1962). This technique is quite precise.

HELD (1978) notes that the S.D. of 10–20 settings may be only 0.1 prism diopter. The technique, however, has the disadvantage that the apparent strength of the *actual* prism fringes also varies when the luminance or contrast of the test pattern is varied, and thus little information can be gained about how these variables might affect the phantom fringes.

Using the compensation technique, HAJOS (1971) showed that the strength of the phantom fringes, at each orientation of the edges on the retina, is directly proportional to the original fringes. HELD (1978) obtained the same function after scanning a speckled surface through a prism in white illumination. All these studies, however, provide little information about the orientation selectivity of the mechanisms that underlie the aftereffects since the observers adapted to contours with *all* orientations.

MCCULLOUGH (1965) reasoned that if the phantom fringes were caused by color adaptation of edge detectors that were quite sensitive to orientation, then perhaps color aftereffects could be made dependent on grating orientation. She presented for *only* 2–4 min a pattern of vertical black and orange stripes alternating with a pattern of horizontal black and blue stripes. Achromatic test stripes with *retinal* orientations similar to the adapting patterns appeared tinted with colors complementary to the adapting patterns, *viz.*, vertical stripes appeared blue-green and horizontal stripes appeared orange, whereas 45° diagonal stripes appeared colorless. Color aftereffects could be seen on many patterns in the natural environment. ELLIS (1976) further showed that these aftereffects are related solely to the retinal orientations of the lines, for retinal orientation was found to govern accurately the strength of the aftereffects whether the observer adapted with either the head or the stripes tilted, and thus the *apparent* orientation of the stripes had no effect.

The different and striking aspect of MCCOLLOUGH's experiment was that vivid aftereffects could be generated with very brief adaptation (see section on Saturation for conditions that produce strong aftereffects). One possible reason why these effects are so strong is that the two orthogonal colored gratings adapt *independent* populations of mechanisms. This model would require that the mechanisms do not respond to lines tilted more than about 45° from the optimal axis. On the other hand, the aftereffects might be produced by dipole mechanisms, with extremely broad orientation sensitivity, that respond strongly, though not equally, to *all* orientations (HARRIS, 1969, 1972). In this case the vertical and horizontal adapting gratings might produce aftereffects that partially cancel each other. No aftereffects would be seen on 45° diagonal stripes simply because the dipoles that respond to this pattern had been adapted equally by the vertical and horizontal gratings of complementary colors.

If broadly tuned dipoles were responsible for the aftereffect, then a single, colored adapting grating might produce color aftereffects on test lines in any orientation. HAJOS (1973) reported that a *vertical* green grating produces a magenta aftereffect that is about half as strong on a *horizontal* test grating, as compared to the aftereffect seen on a vertical test grating. The aftereffects were quite weak, however, and perhaps they were difficult to judge on a single test grating without a second neutral, reference grating. LEPPMANN (1973) claims that after adapting several hundred seconds to a horizontal 5 c/° (cycles/degree) magenta grating alternating with a horizontal 10 c/° green grating, pink and green aftereffects are seen on various portions of a single test grid that varies in spatial frequency from 2–20 c/°, and the aftereffects are *equally* strong for both vertical and horizontal orientations of the test grid. STROMEYER et al. (in preparation), adapted 1 h to a vertical 2.5 c/° magenta grating alternating with a vertical 10 c/° green grating. Very *strong* green and pink aftereffects were seen on adjacent vertical test gratings of 2.5 and 10 c/° respectively, whereas *no* color at all was seen when both test gratings were oriented at 45° or horizontal. Also, adapting to an alternating vertical magenta grating and blank green field, produced a very strong green aftereffect on the vertical components of a checkerboard of vertical and 45° gratings. (Pink was seen on the 45° components due to simultaneous color contrast.) Checkerboards of horizontal and 45° gratings were essentially colorless. MACKAY and MACKAY (1977) have also observed that after adapting to a single colored grating, the color aftereffects were quite weak or absent on a single test grating tilted 45° from the adapting orientation. (Sometimes they observed that a very *weak* complementary color aftereffect was seen on a test grating tilted 90° from the adapting orientation. This might be caused either by a non-orientational McCollough effect or by a general negative afterimage of color, since the observers adapted to only *one* color and were tested 10 min after the adaption period.) MACKAY and MCKAY (1977) determined the strength of the aftereffects by adding colored light to the test grating to just cancel the aftereffects. The strength of the aftereffect fell to about half-strength when the test grating was tilted approximately 22° from the adapting orientation (chromaticity units were unspecified). Results for one observer are shown in Figure 2. The strength of the aftereffects is shown as a function of the orientation of a single test grating. Green aftereffects, produced by a single red, vertical adapting grating, are plotted above the horizontal line, and red aftereffects, produced by a single green, vertical grating, are plotted below the line.

Since aftereffects may be weak or absent on test gratings tilted 45° from the adaptation orientation, then two gratings separated in orientation by 45° might produce aftereffects as strong as those produced by gratings separated by 90°. Colorimetric measurements (FIDELL, 1970; MCCOLLOUGH and GERREIN, unpublished manuscript) tend to support this hypothesis although MACKAY and MACKAY (1977) observed a weak interaction. Many other visual effects also show that lines separated in orientation by 45° produce little if any interactions, *viz*., the tilt aftereffect (CULBERT, 1954; GILINSKY and MAYO, 1971), masking (SEKULER, 1965; CAMPBELL and KULIKOWSKI, 1966), and the contrast threshold and spatial frequency shift observed after adapting to a grating pattern (BLAKEMORE and NACHMIAS, 1971; KLEIN et al., 1974).

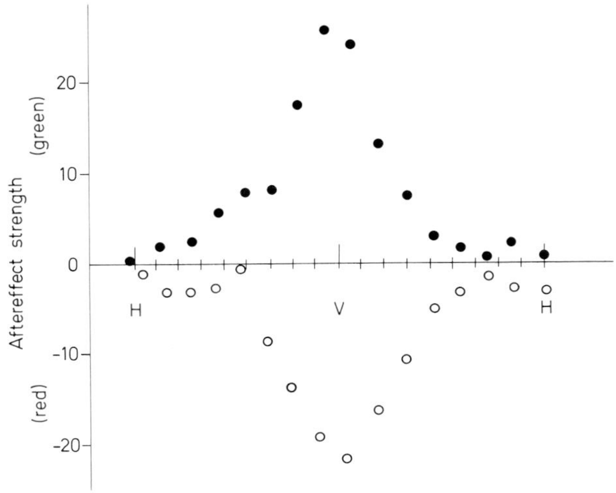

Fig. 2. Strength of color aftereffects as a function of the orientation of a single test grating (H—horizontal, V—vertical). Green aftereffects, produced by a single red, vertical adapting grating, are plotted above horizontal line; red aftereffects, produced by a single green, vertical grating, are plotted below line. Strength of aftereffect is determined by amount of colored light that must be added to test grating to just cancel aftereffect. Observer VM. (After MACKAY and MACKAY, 1977)

Several studies on orientation selectivity have employed two adapting gratings of different colors. FIDELL (1970) used a red grating and a green grating that were separated in orientation by various amounts and a test pattern that consisted of two adjacent gratings with the two adapting orientations. A chromatic cancellation technique indicated that no significant aftereffects were obtained with gratings separated by 11° or 22°, whereas gratings separated by 45° or 90° produced equally strong aftereffects. STROMEYER (1974a) observed that aftereffects can readily be obtained with adapting gratings separated by only 12° if the *test* patterns are separated by a considerably greater orientation. And MACKAY and MACKAY (1977) observed that adapting gratings separated by 11° produced aftereffects that were maximal on gratings separated by 40°, in accordance with a simple linear summation of the red and green aftereffects.

Several additional studies have employed alternating reddish vertical and greenish horizontal gratings or vice versa. As discussed above, two such gratings may produce aftereffects that are largely independent. HEPLER'S (1971) observers matched the color aftereffect seen on a single test grating of variable orientation. The purity of the matching light was decreased by a factor of two when the test grating was varied from vertical or horizontal to about 22° from vertical or horizontal. HAJOS (1973) obtained similar results in a very similar study. ELLIS and CASTELLAN (1975) observed that the excitation purity of the colored light that must be added to two adjacent, orthogonal test gratings to cancel the aftereffects decreased as a function of twice the cosine of the angle between the adapting and test orientations. When the adapting and test patterns were in the same orientations, the strength of the aftereffects increased *linearly* with *adapting* contrast. The investigators related these two functions by the equivalent contrast transformation of BLAKEMORE and NACHMIAS (1971) that allows one to estimate orientation bandwidths (half-bandwidths at half-amplitude) by determining the change in adapting orientation that reduces an aftereffect by the same amount as not changing the adapting orientation but reducing the adapting contrast to half value. Using this transformation, ELLIS and CASTELLAN (1975) conclude that the orientation function for the McCollough effect has a half-bandwidth, at half-amplitude, of about 26°.

The orientation tuning of these color aftereffects seems broader than the tuning observed in adaptation and masking studies where the threshold of the test grating is measured (CAMPBELL and KULIKOWSKI, 1966; BLAKEMORE and NACHMIAS, 1971). In the threshold detection tasks, the *most selective* mechanisms might be used to detect the test grating, for such mechanisms would be *least* affected by a masking grating of different orientation. However, mechanisms with *different* degrees of tuning might contribute to the color aftereffect (not just the most selective mechanisms), for the high-contrast test grating may stimulate all these mechanisms. Thus, the mechanisms underlying the masking effects might also contribute to the color aftereffect.

3. Size Tuning

The color aftereffects are selective to line orientation (the McCollough effect), the direction of edge contrast (the phantom fringes), and, as discussed here, to line width or spatial frequency.

This size selectivity was first shown by TEFT and CLARK (1968) who observed that test gratings could be rotated furthest from the adapting orientations without losing color when the spatial frequency of the adapting and test patterns matched. Also, different color aftereffects can readily be produced with a pair of vertical gratings that are separated in spatial frequency by one (LOVEGROVE and OVER, 1972) or two octaves (BREITMEYER and COOPER, 1972). Thus, for example, a green grating of thin stripes presented in alternation with a red grating of wide stripes will produce a pink aftereffect on thin test stripes and and a greenish effect on wide test stripes. The effects, however, are difficult to obtain with a half-octave separation (LOVEGROVE and OVER, 1972). Color aftereffects can also be made selective to the magnifications of random texture patterns (MACKAY and MACKAY, 1975b). HARRIS (1972), for example, showed that a random pattern of $^1/_4$° black squares on a red ground and $^1/_2$° squares on a green ground, produced a green aftereffect on test gratings with $^1/_4$° stripes and a pink effect on gratings with $^1/_2$° stripes. The effects were equally strong on vertical, horizontal, and diagonal gratings. (This does not show that the underlying mechanisms are not sharply tuned for orientation, for such mechanisms can be stimulated with spots and nonelongated stimuli.)

GREEN et al. (1976) produced color aftereffects selective to the size of squares of colored checkerboards. A checkerboard of, say, diagonal green and black squares produced a pink aftereffect on vertical rectilinear gratings of many spatial frequencies, although the aftereffect was strongest on a test grating that matched the fundamental frequency of the checkerboard. Using checkerboards with very large squares of 0.9°, MAY et al. (1976 and personal communication) found the aftereffects were strongest on test gratings oriented like the edges of the checks. Findings with checkerboards can be explained with simple line- and edge-sensitive mechanisms that resemble simple cells (KLEIN et al., in preparation).

The aftereffects depend strictly on the retinal size of the patterns and not on their perceived size. This was shown (HARRIS, 1970) by adapting to a vertical 5 c/° magenta grating and a vertical 10 c/° green grating and then adjusting the distance of a vertical test grating to appear neither pink nor green but neutral at some intermediate retinal size. Apparent size did not affect results.

This technique of locating the neutral point is quite sensitive, for a slight shift in the spatial frequency of the test grating can change the color seen on the pattern. The color can also be changed, not by an actual shift of the test pattern, but by the apparent spatial frequency shift of BLAKEMORE and SUTTON (1969). They showed that adapting to a grating causes gratings of neighboring spatial frequency to appear shifted away from the spatial frequency of the adapting pattern. This apparent shift can be used to shift the test pattern in a McCollough experiment away from the neutral point, thus making the grating appear colored by the pink or green aftereffect (STROMEYER, 1972a). WYATT (1974) has also shown that, if after viewing the pair of vertical, colored adapting gratings, the observer subsequently views tilted, achromatic gratings of different spatial frequencies, a final achromatic grating will appear both shifted in spatial frequency and colored depending on the physical tilt of this final grating. These effects can be explained by a one-stage model (WYATT, 1974) with mechanisms conjointly tuned to line orientation, color, and spatial frequency. The aftereffects can be made increasingly selective by successive exposure to various adapting patterns.

Are these color aftereffects selective to spatial frequency (periodicity) *or* to the width of either the black or light grating bars? In an attempt to answer this question, HARRIS (1971) used vertical, square-wave gratings of 4.5 and 9 c/°, presented in reddish and greenish illumination, and vertical test gratings with black to white bar width ratios of 1:3, 1:1, and 3:1. The neutral point (where the aftereffect appears neither pink nor green) depended on the spatial frequency (or periodicity) and not on the width of either the black or white bars. (Thus, the neutral point does not depend on the relative spatial phase of the higher harmonics.) UHLARIK and OSGOOD (1974), on the other hand, conclude that black bar width and not spatial frequency is important. The adapting and test patterns were low spatial frequency (1.1 to 3.6 c/°) vertical and horizontal rectangle-wave gratings with various light to dark width ratios. The aftereffects tended to be strongest when the black bars of the adapting and test patterns were similar in width; white bar width and also spatial frequency had less effect. OSGOOD (1974) showed that this result held over a range of spatial frequencies up to 16 c/°. The patterns consisted of all combinations of light and dark bar widths of 1, 2, 4, 6, and 8 thirty-seconds of a degree arc. This suggests that black bar width may *largely* control the size tuning of these color aftereffects. This could be accounted for by cells that are sensitive to black bar width and the chromatic nature of the surround (UHLARIK and OSGOOD, 1974). There was also a small tuning effect specific to the light bars.

Selectivity to black bar width might also explain the pink and green aftereffects (STROMEYER et al., 1973) obtained with identical, vertical first and second harmonic sine gratings summed in different quadrature phases (where peaks *or* troughs of the two gratings are aligned). One complex grating appears to have thin light stripes and wider dark stripes, and the other grating appears to have wide light stripes and thinner dark stripes.

OSGOOD (1974) also examined the influence of the black and white bar width of the *test* patterns *per se*. The color saturation of the aftereffects increased as the black bars became wider or the white bars became narrower. Thus, test gratings with wide black bars and thin white bars yield maximal color saturation.

When both the adapting and test patterns are square-wave gratings with the same spatial frequency, aftereffects are strongest near 5 c/° and fall off at lower and higher spatial frequencies (STROMEYER, 1972a; OSGOOD, 1974). The aftereffects appear difficult to obtain at low spatial frequencies (HAJOS, 1968; LOVEGROVE and OVER, 1972), but effects can definitely be obtained with large-field square-wave gratings of 0.5 and 2 c/° in green and magenta illumination (STROMEYER, 1974b). The weakness of the effects at low frequencies may be caused by the wide white test bars, since the saturation of the effects decreases as the white test bars become wider (OSGOOD, 1974). The decline in aftereffect strength at high spatial frequencies has been observed with gratings as high as 16 (OSGOOD, 1974) or 20 c/° (STROMEYER, 1972a).

4. Movement

Color aftereffects can also be made selective to the direction in which stripes move, and even to the velocity of stripes moving in one direction. HEPLER (1968) exposed observers for about $^1/_2$ h *each consecutive day* to horizontal stripes of 2.5 c/° moving at 2 °/s alternately upward in yellow-green illumination and downward in magenta illumination. Complementary-colored aftereffects were seen on the same black and white patterns after 135 min total adaptation. With 270 min cumulative adaptation, the effects were reported even 20 h after an adapting session. STROMEYER and MANSFIELD (1970) used two large patterns of 0.9 c/° horizontal stripes, placed either side of a fixation point. For 20 min the patterns moved at 4.2 °/s alternately upward in red illumination and downward in green illumination. The two patterns always moved in opposite directions, and thus, during the test phase the two black and white fields could be directly compared. The aftereffects could be seen best when the stripes reversed directions, and even days later the colors were sometimes seen as a faint flash at this transition point. Two conditions might promote seeing these aftereffects: eliciting both pink and green simultaneously in adjacent fields, and sharply alternating the direction of motion. The low spatial frequency and fast motion used by STROMEYER and MANSFIELD (1970) may also promote the aftereffects.

The aftereffects appear to be specific to the retinal direction of motion and not the perceived direction, for the aftereffects are seen when the eyes sweep over stationary stripes even though the stripes may appear stationary (STROMEYER and MANSFIELD, 1970). Retinal motion also governs the waterfall illusion (ANSTIS and GREGORY, 1965) for this aftereffect of seen motion can be induced by sweeping the eyes over stationary adapting stripes, but cannot be induced when the eyes track moving adapting stripes, in which case there is no retinal motion.

The color aftereffects also appear to be selective to the velocity of the moving stripes, as the effects are most saturated on test stripes that move at a velocity similar to or perhaps slightly faster than the adapting stripes (HEPLER, 1971; STROMEYER and MANSFIELD, 1970). HEPLER (1971) more conclusively showed this velocity selectivity by having observers adapt to stripes of 0.6 c/° moving downward at 1.8 and 3.1°/s in magenta and yellow-green illumination, respectively. Prolonged adaptation produced aftereffects that were most saturated on test stripes moving downward at the adapting velocities, and the saturation declined as the test velocity approached an intermediate velocity of 2.4°/s, where no colors were seen. HEPLER (1971) claims that velocity tuning curves cannot be obtained from these results, as broadly tuned aftereffects, of complementary colors, may simply cancel at an intermediate velocity, thus giving the false impression of sharp tuning. The observers were also tested with stripes moving upward and reported no aftereffects (HEPLER, personal communication). The aftereffects are thus selective to velocity, which being a vector, has a directional component. There is yet no evidence that color aftereffects can be made selective to the rate of temporal flicker of stationary stripes. Threshold measurements after adapting to various stimuli, however, reveal mechanisms that are selective to temporal flicker (PANTLE, 1971; SMITH, 1971), direction of motion (SEKULER and GANZ, 1963), and velocity (PANTLE and SEKULER, 1968b).

5. Selectivity to Retinal Position

The color aftereffects also appear to be quite specific to retinal position, since opposite pink and green aftereffects can be produced in adjacent retinal areas (HARRIS, 1969; STROMEYER, 1974a; MACKAY and MACKAY, 1974b; SIGEL and NACHMIAS, 1975). This effect is shown perhaps most strikingly (STROMEYER and DAWSON, 1978) by adapting to a pair of vertical 2 c/° gratings (of green and black stripes and magenta and black stripes) which are presented sequentially in counterphase retinal positions (the colored bars of each grating fall on the retinal areas occupied by the black bars of the other grating). A vertical 2 c/° test grating then appears pink when placed in the position occupied by the green grating (so that the black bars of the adapting and test gratings fall in the same positions), and the test grating appears green when placed in the position occupied by the magenta grating. A single vertical test grating when tilted slightly produces a MOIRÉ pattern of broad, alternating pink and green horizontal bands. Afterimages can be ruled out, for adapting to both gratings simultaneously (a grating of green and magenta stripes that are balanced for luminance) produces no effect. (Further examples of these effects are discussed in the section on Luminance and Contrast.)

Color aftereffects selective to motion are also highly selective to retinal position. HEPLER (1971) generated opposite sets of pink and green aftereffects on either side of a 3° diameter field that was retinally stabilized. STROMEYER and MANSFIELD (1970) observed that fixating a green square with red surround, centered on a moving spiral, produced an image of a pink square with green surround (on a black and white test spiral) that was motion-selective and that varied in size according to Emmert's law as viewing distance was varied.

The color aftereffects thus appear to be quite specific to retinal position. However, when viewing a large test pattern, an observer may be unable to report that the color of the aftereffect is confined strictly to the adapted area, for it is known that shallow color gradients may cause the perception of a homogeneous color expanse (KRAUSKOPF, 1967; LETTVIN, 1967). For example, MURCH (1969) reports that the McCollough aftereffect appears to spread *completely* over large test patterns that are considerably larger than the adapted area of the retina. (It should be noted, however, that no fixation point was used while viewing the test patterns and the observers were told to ignore colored patches that moved with the eyes.) STROMEYER (1972b), however, found that no color is seen when the test gratings are moved just off the adapted retinal area. Many other aftereffects are also highly localized, *viz.*, the apparent motion aftereffect (SEKULER and PANTLE, 1967; MASLAND, 1969; RICHARDS and SMITH, 1969), movement aftereffects selective to color (MURCH, 1974), figural aftereffects (KÖHLER and WALLACH, 1944; GANZ, 1966), and spatial frequency adaptation (BLAKEMORE et al., 1970; KLEIN et al., 1974).

6. Complex Patterns

The color aftereffects examined thus far can be explained by color adaptation of mechanisms tuned to line orientation, size, velocity, and retinal position. A single mechanism having only these simple properties will not respond selectively to more complex patterns and thus will not produce color aftereffects selective to these complex patterns. A simple conditioning theory might predict that color aftereffects can be made selective to any clearly discriminable stimuli (SNOW, 1966).

Recently, RIGGS (1973) and WHITE and RIGGS (1974a) produced aftereffects with curved lines or angles. The adapting patterns were gratings of arcs or angles—for example, gratings of horizontal lines with left and right-halves bent upward (concave up), or downward (concave down). One pattern was presented in reddish illumination and the other in green, and the observer typically scanned only along the *vertical midline* of each pattern. Test patterns with similar curves or angles then appeared colored complementary to the adapting patterns. WHITE and RIGGS (1974a) suggest that the effects may reflect adaptation of the lower-order hypercomplex cells that HUBEL and WIESEL (1965) showed respond to the direction of angles and curves.

Color adaptation of mechanisms selective to line orientation and retinal position might, however, explain some of these results, for these adapting patterns stimulate regions to the left of gaze with lines of given slope and color and regions to the right of gaze with just the opposite conditions. WHITE and RIGGS (1974a) present evidence that this explanation is insufficient to account for some their results. First (WHITE and RIGGS, 1974a, 1974b), have obtained weak but definitely present aftereffects when the adapting patterns moved relative to the retina so as to stimulate equally regions with all adapting line orientations in both adapting colors, which cancels aftereffects due simply to line orientation. Other investigators (STROMEYER, 1974a; MACKAY and MACKAY, 1974b; SIGEL and NACHMIAS, 1975; STROMEYER and DAWSON, in preparation), have not been able to obtain color aftereffects with this method, but perhaps the particular conditions used by WHITE and RIGGS were more effective. In related experiments, BLAKEMORE and OVER (1974) observed that the aftereffect of straight lines appearing curved in the direction opposite to previously viewed curved lines (GIBSON, 1933) does not occur when the observer scans along the chord of the adapting curves. They propose that curves are processed by orientation-selective mechanisms and not by curvature detectors.

RIGGS (1973) and WHITE and RIGGS (1974a) also observed that adapting to colored patterns with weak curvature or shallow angles (with the gaze on the vertical midline of each pattern) produced colored aftereffects that were most saturated on test patterns with considerably sharper curves or angles. For example (WHITE and RIGGS, 1974a) aftereffects tended to be maximal on test patterns with 90° angles. Aftereffects selective to line orientation, however, might qualitatively account for these results (STROMEYER, 1974a; MACKAY and MACKAY, 1974b; SIGEL and NACHMIAS, 1975; STROMEYER and DAWSON, in preparation). Alternating rectilinear red and green gratings, each tilted a small angle either side of horizontal, produce aftereffects that are strongest on gratings tilted considerably further from horizontal (STROMEYER, 1974a), although not as much as the gratings of the 90° test angles of WHITE and RIGGS (1974a). STROMEYER and DAWSON (in preparation) obtained similar aftereffects (according to rank ordering of saturation judgments) using either angle patterns *or* rectilinear gratings. Their results, however, differ considerably from the results obtained by WHITE and RIGGS (1974a) with angle patterns. The reason for this difference is presently unknown. SIGEL and NACHMIAS (1975) and CRASSINI and OVER (1975) showed that the saturation and hue of the aftereffects on different regions of test patterns of curves varied as might be expected on the basis of orientation-selective mechanisms.

It thus appears quite difficult to obtain color aftereffects that are selective to even relatively simple patterns like curves and angles. This strongly suggests that the diversity of the mechanisms underlying the form-color aftereffects may be quite limited, and the colored aftereffects may thus reflect a process of adaptation or conditioning of rather elementary visual units.

II. Color of the Aftereffects

1. Hue

The phantom color fringes are presumably complementary in hue to the original prism fringes, inasmuch as a variable prism can be adjusted so that the actual prism fringes and the phantom fringes just cancel. HAJOS (1971) reports that *both* the orange-yellow and the blue-green phantom fringes can be simultaneously cancelled by this method when a neutral test pattern is viewed in illumination that has a color temperature of 4500° K and that changing the color temperature by only 100° may upset this delicate balance.

The McCollough effect also appears to be complementary to the adapting hues, although red and green aftereffects are generated more readily than yellow and especially blue aftereffects. STROMEYER (1969) used a vertical adapting grating that was illuminated by a light that was passed through a narrow-band filter. The color varied from session to session, over the range 405–615 nm. The color aftereffects seen on a vertical test grating illuminated with light from a tungsten bulb were typically pink and green; adapting colors near blue occasionally produced weak yellowish aftereffects, but there was little evidence that yellow adapting colors produced blue aftereffects. This red and green predominance was also reported by HAJOS (1968) who used alternating vertical and horizontal adapting gratings illuminated with red, yellow, green, or blue light. The aftereffects seen on adjacent vertical and horizontal gratings in tungsten illumination were named mostly red and green, and very few yellow and blue effects were reported. It cannot be concluded, however, that the aftereffects are not complementary to the adapting colors, as successive and simultaneous color contrast will strongly affect the results (as seen in the next section). FIDELL (1968) also obtained few blue and yellow aftereffects with an alternating blue grating and yellow grating, whereas red and green aftereffects were readily obtained with an alternating reddish grating and green grating.

The tungsten light that is often used to illuminate the test pattern is quite deficient in the short-wave region of the spectrum, and this partially explains the infrequent reports of blue aftereffects. MCCOLLOUGH and CLARK (unpublished manuscript) observed that blue aftereffects were more readily seen when a very weak blue filter (Wratten 82a) was placed over the tungsten test illuminant. STROMEYER (1972a) observed that an orange adapting grating produced blue aftereffects on a test grating illuminated with white fluorescent light that was considerably more blue than tungsten light. PIEPER (1974) has shown by a color matching technique that the aftereffects produced by a single colored grating were approximately complementary in hue to the adapting colors, and blue effects were observed more often when the color temperature of the test illuminant was increased from 4000 to 6500 °K.

The McCollough effect is readily observed on test patterns in monochromatic light at photopic (MCCOLLOUGH, 1965; LEPPMANN and ALLEN, 1973; STROMEYER, 1969) and scotopic levels of illumination (STROMEYER, 1974b).

2. Simultaneous and Successive Contrast

Simultaneous color contrast may often modify the color aftereffects seen on various regions of the test patterns. For example, a vertical adapting grating can produce different colors on adjacent vertical and horizontal test gratings (STROMEYER, 1969). The color seen on the horizontal grating is apparently a contrast color induced by the aftereffect on the vertical grating. Adaptation to vertical green and horizontal red gratings will cause vertical and horizontal test gratings to appear pink and green, respectively, and 45° diagonal gratings will appear colorless. When these diagonal test gratings are placed adjacent to the vertical or horizontal test gratings, the diagonals will appear colored complementary to the aftereffects seen on the vertical or horizontal components (STROMEYER, 1971). Similar contrast effects are also seen with blue and orange aftereffects on test patterns viewed in Macbeth daylight (STROMEYER, unpublished observations). The blue aftereffects, in contrast to the green, pink and orange aftereffects, are nevertheless quite weak when viewed on a single test grating, but appear more saturated when the test grating is placed adjacent to a grating eliciting an orange aftereffect. Thus, the blue effects may be quite weak on patterns that are unaffected by simultaneous color contrast.

Successive color contrast also strongly affects the aftereffects. For example, alternating a green grating with a white grating causes the white grating to appear pink, due to successive contrast, and this pink grating generates a green McCollough effect (STROMEYER 1969; MURCH and HIRSCH, 1972; PIEPER, 1974). This suggests that there is a site of color adaptation (cones?) that precedes the site of the McCollough effect.

The effects of simultaneous and successive color contrast need to be controlled in order to determine the color of the aftereffect produced by a given adapting color. If the test pattern contains components with various orientations and spatial frequencies, contrast colors may possibly be seen on components that are very different from the adapting gratings, and thus no simple conclusion can be reached about the spatial tuning of the aftereffects.

3. Saturation

Although the aftereffects are quite striking, several colorimetric studies reveal that the excitation purity of light that matches the aftereffects is quite low (SNOW, 1966; MCCOLLOUGH and CLARK, unpublished manuscript; MCCOLLOUGH and GERREIN, unpublished manuscript; HEPLER, 1971; TIMNEY et al., 1974). HEPLER (1971, Fig. 9) provides a typical example. Long, spaced adaptation to both a vertical magenta and a horizontal yellow-green grating, yielded a greenish aftereffect on a single vertical grating which was matched with light with CIE chromaticity coordinates $x=0.388$, $y=0.403$; the coordinates of the reddish effect on a horizontal grating were $x=0.395$, $y=0.364$. HEPLER also showed that more specialized aftereffects were even weaker. The effects could be ordered from strongest to weakest: effects selective to line orientation, effects selective to the direction of motion of lines, and effects selective to the velocity of lines moving in one direction. The mechanisms underlying these effects may be progressively more specialized subsets of the population of elements all tuned to, say, horizontal lines. This view is also consistent with the weak saturation of the pink and green aftereffects produced with pairs of vertical gratings that differ only in the relative phase of their spatial harmonics (STROMEYER et al., 1973).

Special test conditions may increase the saturation of the aftereffects: for example, viewing the patterns at mesopic (STROMEYER, 1971) or even scotopic levels of illumination (STROMEYER, 1974c). The "dimming" effect of TROLAND (1917) may also be used to augment the effects. For example, STROMEYER (1971) observed that a relatively bright test pattern presented in a 0.2 s flash and followed by darkness produced colors that were more saturated than the most saturated red and green Munsell matte samples.

Very saturated aftereffects, however, can be obtained without these tactics. The conditions that the present author has found to be successful are: adapt to successively presented large-field vertical and horizontal, high-contrast square-wave gratings of 2–6 c/°, rear-projected on a diffusing screen. (WHITE and ELLIS, 1975, have shown that the alternation rate is not important over the range of one presentation per second to one presentation per minute; faster or slower rates produce weaker effects.) One grating is projected through a Wratten 34a magenta filter and the other through a Wratten 53 green filter, with the mean luminance at the screen set to about 200 cd/m^2. (RIGGS et al., 1974, recommend use of Wratten filters 32 and 53 for colorimetric work, because they are more nearly complementary in hue.) Test with a paper checkerboard pattern of vertical and horizontal, high-contrast square-wave gratings of 2–6 c/° in fluorescent illumination. Adaptation for 20 min will yield green and pink aftereffects equivalent in saturation to Munsell samples of chroma 4–7 at value 8. The results of OSGOOD (1974) suggest that the aftereffects will be even stronger if the *white test* bars are made very narrow ($^1/_{32}$°) and the black test bars are kept at the width suggested here. OSGOOD's observers reported that the aftereffects seen on such test gratings after adapting 20 min to alternating vertical green and horizontal magenta gratings were sometimes more saturated than Munsell samples RP 7/8 and GY 7/8.

III. Luminance and Contrast

The luminance and contrast of the patterns strongly affect the aftereffects. These factors are first considered for the adapting phase.

HARRIS and BARKOW (1969) showed that the McCollough effect can only be readily obtained with adapting patterns that contain luminance contrast. After adapting either to high-contrast gratings of alternating colored and black stripes or to gratings of colored and bright white stripes, aftereffects were seen on test patterns of black and white stripes. Adapting patterns with green stripes, for example, produced pink aftereffects. However, adapting patterns with the white stripes were less effective in producing the aftereffects than patterns containing black stripes. (It is surprising that a pattern of green and white stripes produces a pink aftereffect, for a green and white grating may be synthesized by a red and black grating superimposed on a homogeneous greenish field, and a red and black grating produces a green aftereffect—not a pink aftereffect.) Adapting patterns of colored and grey stripes which were balanced for luminance produced no aftereffects.

STROMEYER and DAWSON (1978) observed that, after adapting to low spatial frequency gratings either of colored and black stripes or of colored and bright white stripes that fell approximately in *one* retinal position, aftereffects were seen clearly on black and white test gratings only when the patterns were positioned on the retina so that the *local luminance contrast* of the adapting and test patterns matched. This is illustrated in Figure 3, which shows the retinal luminance profiles of adapting gratings of green and black or of white and darker green stripes. Imaginary vertical lines define identical retinal positions. As shown, a black and white test grating that matches the retinal contrast polarity of the adapting gratings elicits a pink aftereffect, whereas a test grating in antiphase

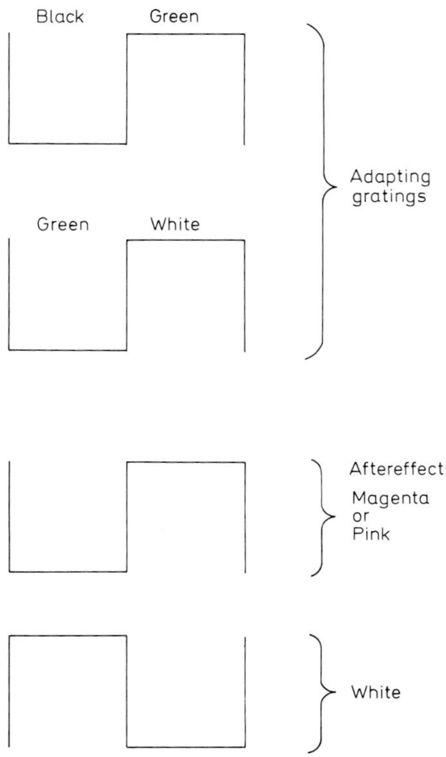

Fig. 3. Colored aftereffects selective to the polarity of luminance contrast. Upper part shows luminance profiles of adapting gratings of green and black stripes or of white and darker green stripes. Bottom part shows that a black and white test grating that has the same *retinal* contrast polarity as the adapting gratings elicits a pink aftereffect, whereas an antiphase test grating appears colorless. Imaginary vertical lines define identical retinal positions. (After STROMEYER and DAWSON, 1978)

appears essentially colorless. Afterimages cannot account for these effects, for the aftereffects clearly survived a nearly complete bleach of the cone pigments, and no aftereffects were produced by fixating simultaneously two adapting patterns which formed a pattern of alternating green and magenta stripes which were approximately balanced for luminance. Furthermore, a model based on afterimages predicts different color aftereffects from those observed (STROMEYER and DAWSON, 1978).

It thus appears that the adapting patterns must have luminance contrast to produce a definite MCCOLLOUGH effect. ELLIS and CASTELLAN (1975) and CASTELLAN (1975) observed that the strength of the aftereffect, as measured by the excitation purity of a colored light that just cancels the aftereffect, increases approximately in proportion to the adapting contrast, up to the highest values used, 45%.

The luminance contrast of the test patterns also strongly influences the color aftereffects. HAY et al. (1963) showed that the phantom color fringes become more vivid as the contrast of the test pattern is increased. KOHLER (1951) remarks that the phantom fringes are seen only on edges defined by luminance, edges defined by color differences alone being ineffective. The McCollough effect is also seen vividly on high-contrast test gratings, even though the edges are strongly blurred; the colors, however, become weak if the edges are kept sharp and the contrast is lowered (GIBSON and HARRIS, 1968). Colorimetric measurements by SNOW (1966) also show that the aftereffects become stronger as test contrast increases. POST and LODGE (1975) observed that color aftereffects selective to motion were strongest when the contrast of the adapting and test patterns was high as opposed to low. They argue against a simple learning model of the aftereffects, which predicts that aftereffects would be strongest on low-contrast test patterns following adaptation to low-contrast colored patterns (these patterns look similar). The aftereffects were stronger on high contrast test patterns after adapting to low-contrast colored patterns.

The absolute luminance level also influences the aftereffects. WHITE (1976a) showed that the strength of the McCollough aftereffect (indicated by the excitation purity of colored light that must be added to the test pattern to just cancel the aftereffect) increases with *higher* luminance (0.12, 12.7, and 103 cd/m^2) during the adapting phase and *lower* luminance (96, 12.0, and 0.12 cd/m^2) during the test phase. Colorimetric measurements by SNOW (1966) also suggest that the aftereffect is enhanced by weak test light (5 vs. 50 cd/m^2). The aftereffect may be seen at scotopic test levels (STROMEYER, 1974b). KOHLER (1951) observed that the phantom color fringes are also most vivid in dim illumination, but they apparently disappear at scotopic levels (KOHLER, 1951; HAY et al., 1963). HAY et al. (1963) concluded the strength of the phantom fringes is unaffected by different photopic levels of the test pattern. (However, they used a compensating prism to measure the phantom fringes. The vividness of the actual prism fringes used to cancel the phantom fringes may unfortunately also vary with illumination level.)

In summary, the color aftereffects appear more vivid as the luminance contrast increases in both the adapting and test phases, whereas higher absolute luminance within the adapting phase (within limits) and lower luminance in the test phase appear to enhance the aftereffects. Edges defined by color alone appear to be ineffective in both the adapting and test phases.

C. Form Aftereffects Dependent on Color

I. Orientation Aftereffects

Thus far color aftereffects dependent on form have been discussed. The present section discusses the converse aftereffects, *viz.*, form aftereffects dependent on color. After adapting to a colored pattern, a colored test pattern (or even a homogeneous colored field) may appear distorted along a given dimension depending on the color of the test stimulus.

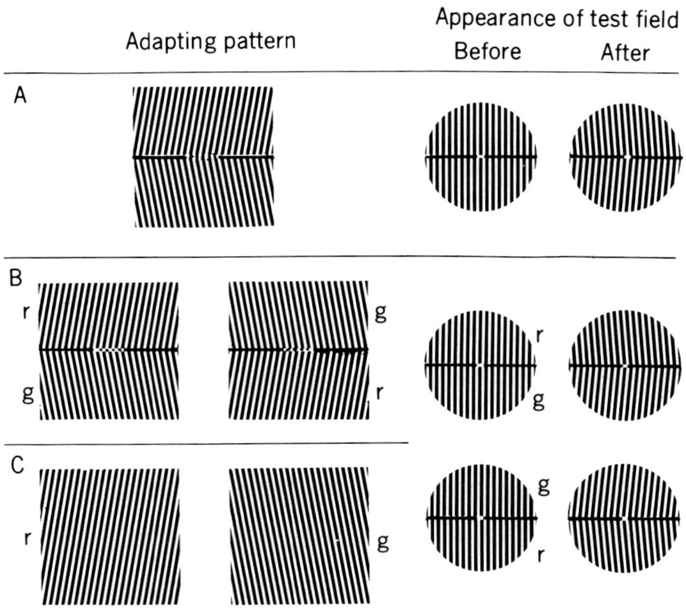

Fig. 4. Tilt aftereffects selective to luminance and color. Right half shows appearance of test patterns before and after exposure to adapting patterns shown on the left, which consist of achromatic (*top*) or red (*r*) and green (*g*) gratings. Tilt aftereffects selective to color are exaggerated here. (After HELD and SHATTUCK, 1971). Copyright 1971 by the American Association for the Advancement of Science

What conditions might give rise to these aftereffects? The perception of orientation, for example, may be determined by the central tendency of responses of mechanisms tuned to various orientations. After viewing a line of one orientation, a line of slightly different orientation will appear shifted away from the orientation of the first line. Adapting to the first line may skew the distribution of responses to the second line away from the orientation of the first line (OVER, 1971; COLTHEART, 1971). If there were partially independent populations of mechanisms predominantly sensitive to red *or* green lines, then this tilt aftereffect might be made selective to color. For example, adaptation may induce an imbalance in the green-sensitive elements, and this might give rise to a tilt effect selective to green.

HELD and SHATTUCK (1971) demonstrated a tilt effect selective to color by adapting, for example, for 10 min to a red grating tilted 10° one side of vertical and a green grating tilted 10° to the other side, as shown in Figure 4. Equal exposures to equal and opposite tilts presumably cancel the tilt effect due to luminance gradients alone, thus revealing only tilt effects selective to color. Test patterns were gratings that were approximately vertical and were green on the top half and red on the bottom, or vice versa (Fig. 4). The observer judged what slight tilt between the bottom and top halves appeared to form gratings of straight vertical lines. On the average a total tilt of 37′ was judged to be straight. The strength of the effect was also measured for various orientations of the adapting gratings. Maximal tilt effects occurred when the adapting gratings were 10–15° from vertical, and the effect fell off as the adapting gratings were rotated further from vertical, reaching zero strength at about 40°. This tuning function is very similar for tilt aftereffects that are not made selective to color (CULBERT, 1954; GILINSKY and MAYO, 1971).

The color-specific tilt effect is also selective to line width, and the size of the effect increases as spatial frequency increases at least up to 8 c/° (SHATTUCK and HELD, 1974) or 16 c/° (HELD, personal communication), the effect being generally strongest when the spatial frequency of the test gratings matches the adapting frequency (SHATTUCK and HELD, 1974). WARE and MITCHELL (1974) observed that tilt aftereffects that are not made selective to color are also selective to spatial frequency.

LOVEGROVE and OVER (1973) have also studied color-selective tilt effects. One eye was adapted to a *single*, colored grating. A strong tilt effect was seen when the test pattern presented to the adapted eye was the same color as the adapting pattern, but no effect was seen when the colors (red versus green) were different. This absence of effect is surprising, for luminance gradient of any color might be expected to produce tilt effects, especially in light of LOVEGROVE and OVER's observation that the interocular transfer of the tilt effect depends on luminance gradients alone and is not sensitive to color. BROERSE et al. (1975), however, observed monoptic tilt effects when the adapting and test colors were different, but the tilt effects were larger when the colors were the same.

II. Movement Aftereffects

HEPLER (1971) considered a model of cells sensitive to red stripes moving upward and other cells sensitive to red stripes moving downward and cells sensitive to green stripes moving upward and other cells sensitive to green stripes moving downward. Adaptation to red stripes moving upward changes the chromatic balance among populations of these cells. Thus black and white test stripes moving upward appear green, because the green cells will respond more strongly than the red cells to the upward motion. This model also predicted that stationary test stripes will appear to move in a direction that depends on the color of the test illuminant, for there is an imbalance between the red-up and red-down cells and between the green-up and green-down cells. This change of ratio may produce an aftereffect of apparent motion (SUTHERLAND, 1961).

Some of HEPLER's (1971) observers reported that after adapting to stripes moving in opposite directions in different colors, stationary stripes appeared to move slightly in the direction opposite to the adapting stripes when illuminated with the adapting colors. This aftereffect was also investigated with one observer using a retinally stabilized bipartite display in which the adapting stripes always moved in opposite directions on either side. Absolutely no aftereffect of seen motion was reported with this stimulus. HEPLER thus attributed the motion aftereffects observed in non-stabilized viewing to small eye movements. (MASLAND, 1969, however, has observed long-term movement aftereffects with an achromatic spiral that was optically stabilized.)

FAVREAU et al. (1972) and MAYHEW and ANSTIS (1972) demonstrated motion aftereffects selective to color, similar to the effects observed by HEPLER (1971) with nonstabilized images. After prolonged viewing of a spiral that rotated periodically in one direction in green illumination and the opposite direction in red, a stationary spiral appeared to move in directions opposite to the adapting conditions when illuminated red or green. The motion was weak and seen typically for only 1–2 s on each presentation of the spiral, but could be continually re-evoked even 1 day following adaptation. POTTS and HARRIS (1975) have shown that the motion aftereffects can also be made contingent on the color of the surround of a pattern.

MAYHEW and ANSTIS (1972) observed interesting color transposition effects. When the adapting colors were yellow and green or yellow and red, the yellow test illuminant evoked apparent motion the direction of which depended on the illuminant, red or green, that just preceded the yellow. For example, when the test illuminant was a sequence of red, yellow, and green, the direction of apparent motion elicited by yellow depended on whether red or green preceded the yellow. Successive contrast may account for this effect, for yellow will appear reddish with prior green stimulation and greenish with prior red stimulation. Transposition effects were also produced with the illuminant pair orange-red and yellow-green and the pair violet and yellow. The role of successive contrast with these colors is undoubtedly complicated and needs further study.

MAYHEW and ANTIS (1972) showed that the motion aftereffects were truly selective to color, for the effects did not change when the luminance of the colors was varied over a large range. They claim, however, that motion aftereffects can be made contingent on the brightness of achromatic displays. Observers adapted to stripes moving in opposite directions in white illumination, each direction paired with a different intensity. The aftereffects were generally seen well only when the test illumination was bright as opposed to dim. Motion aftereffects can also be made selective to the orientation and line width of achromatic stripes (MAYHEW and ANTIS, 1972), the magnification of two-dimensional textures (WALKER, 1972), and binocular disparities (ANSTIS and HARRIS, 1974).

LOVEGROVE et al. (1972) observed that after viewing either red or green moving stripes for 15 s, stationary red or green stripes appeared to move faster when the stripes were the same color as the adapting stripes. OVER and LOVEGROVE (1973) showed that a large surround pattern of moving red or green stripes causes a central area of stationary red or green stripes to appear to move in a direction opposite to the surround. The induced motion was larger when the center and surround were the same colors. The authors suggest that red or green movement-sensitive units in the surround inhibit units with similar color and motion sensitivity in the center, thus causing the center stripes to appear to move in the opposite direction.

The technique of adapting to a pair of colored patterns (for example, green stripes and red stripes moving in opposite directions) in order to eliminate aftereffects due to luminance gradients alone might reveal yet other form aftereffects selective to color. HOCHBERG and TRIEBEL (1955) observed that figural aftereffects produced by red or green annuli on a white ground were not selective to color (however, see HOCHBERG et al., 1960). The colored patterns, however, presumably also adapt luminance-selective mechanisms, which may obscure the observation of weak color-selective figural aftereffects. VIRSU and HAAPASALO (1973) and WYATT (1974) produced a color-selective figural aftereffect (the apparent spatial frequency shift of BLAKEMORE and SUTTON, 1969) by alternate exposures of a coarse grating in green illumination and a fine grating in red illumination. A grating of intermediate spatial frequency then appeared relatively finer in green illumination and relatively coarser in red illumination.

III. Monocular Rivalry

Monocular rivalry of patterns demonstrates many of the same form-color interactions as the form-color aftereffects, and thus, perhaps monocular rivalry may be regarded as a short-lived aftereffect that is partially dependent on color.

BREESE (1899) observed that when a grating of green and black stripes and a crossed grating of red and black stripes were viewed with one eye, one pattern was often seen more distinctly than the other and either pattern occasionally disappeared entirely. MCDOUGALL (1901) has noted similar rivalry effects. The rivalry is particularly strong with crossed sinusoidal gratings of low spatial frequencies (CAMPBELL and HOWELL, 1972). The rivalry is also promoted by having the gratings in different colors, rather than black and white (CAMPBELL and HOWELL, 1972). RAUSCHECKER et al. (1973) compared the rivalry rates (rivalry being indicated when one grating appeared dominant) for all pair combinations of red, green, blue, and yellow crossed sine gratings, plus a pair of white gratings. Rivalry was least for the white gratings and greatest for the pairs red-green and blue-yellow, which suggests that opponent-color mechanisms are involved.

The relative orientations of the two gratings is also important: no rivalry occurs until the gratings differ in orientation by 15–20° (CAMPBELL and HOWELL, 1972) and then rivalry increases until the difference reaches about 50° (CAMPBELL et al., 1973).

Little rivalry is seen when crossed square-wave gratings are substituted for the sine gratings. The apparent contrast of the square-wave gratings fluctuates, but neither grating disappears entirely (CAMPBELL and HOWELL, 1972). ATKINSON et al. (1973) observed decreased rivalry rates for crossed red and green sine gratings as the spatial frequency was increased from 0.5–15 c/°. Rivalry also decreased for 1 c/° sine gratings as the square-wave harmonics were successively added to the gratings; the rate of rivalry reached a low asymptote by the time the 7 c/° harmonic was added, so that adding higher harmonics had little effect. All the harmonics of either the vertical or the horizontal gratings would rival as a whole group. However, a pair of vertical red and green sine gratings may rival if two components are different in spatial frequency by at least one octave (CAMPBELL and HOWELL, 1972).

Changes in the eye's focus due to chromatic aberration cannot entirely account for the rivalry, for rivalry is readily observed with paralyzed accommodation (CAMPBEEL et al., 1973). Quasi-stabilized images, produced by moving the gaze along one bar of the crossed gratings, may cause one grating to fade. This, however, cannot wholly account for the rivalry, for rivalry is readily seen when the crossed gratings are viewed rotating on a disk. The speed of rotation does not affect the rivalry providing it is not fast enough to blur out the patterns (CAMPBELL et al., 1973). Rivalry can also be seen in an afterimage of the patterns (STROMEYER, unpublished observations).

Rivalry occurs only for gratings separated by sufficient orientation (15–20°) or spatial frequency (more than one octave), so that each pattern is processed by partially independent channels. These channels are not entirely independent, for rivalry shows that the channels interact (CAMPBELL and HOWELL, 1972).

IV. Color-Selective Subjective Images

After viewing colored gratings, neutral test gratings produce color sensations. DAWSON and STROMEYER (1978) observed the converse effect, *viz.*, after adapting to colored gratings, homogeneous colored test fields elicited subjective images of the adapting gratings. To produce this effect, green and magenta square-wave gratings of 1.5 c/° and 40% contrast were presented alternately in counterphase retinal positions for 10 min. For up to 2 h thereafter subjective gratings of dark bars were seen at the instant a homogeneous field shifted between green and magenta. The phase of these dark bars was reversed relative to the dark bars of the adapting gratings. Adapting to a single green or magenta grating alternating with a homogeneous field of complementary color also produced *both* subjective images (as though the observer had adapted to the two counterphase gratings), and thus an image was seen during *every* transition between the green and magenta test fields. Thus, presumably adapting to alternating vertical and horizontal gratings would produce subjective images of crossed gratings.

Two observations show that the aftereffect is not a simple afterimage. First, adapting to both vertical gratings simultaneously (a grating of green and magenta stripes of equal luminance) produced no effect, nor did this pattern neutralize the aftereffect generated with other patterns. Second, the aftereffect was also seen for about 2 h when the cone pigments were bleached out immediately following the adaptation period. Two conditions are apparently needed to produce the aftereffect: the luminance of the adapting patterns must be spatially modulated, and the colors must be temporally varied. The adapting patterns also produced McCollough color aftereffects on black and white gratings. It appears that conditions that do not produce the color aftereffects also do not produce the subjective images, and thus the two aftereffects appear to be related.

D. Monocularity and Binocularity of the Aftereffects

The form-color aftereffects appear to be largely monocular. HAJOS and RITTER (1965) observed that the phantom color fringes, induced by wearing prisms, are seen only with the adapted eye; opposite sets of phantom fringes can be induced simultaneously in separate eyes. Opposite sets of McCollough aftereffects can be induced in corresponding locations of the separate eyes using different pairs of orthogonal, colored gratings (MCCOLLOUGH, 1965). Upon adapting one eye, no color aftereffect is typically seen with the other eye (MURCH, 1972; STROMEYER et al., 1973; MACKAY and MACKAY, 1975b). The monocularity of the McCollough effect was further shown by WHITE and RIGGS (1975) who presented the adapting gratings to one eye and simultaneously presented a dynamic noise pattern to the other eye in order to produce strong binocular rivalry. The strength of the aftereffect depended only on the time the adapting patterns were present and not on the time they were seen.

The color-motion aftereffects are also monocular. Color aftereffects selective to motion (STROMEYER and MANSFIELD, 1970) and motion aftereffects selective to color (MAYHEW and ANSTIS, 1972) that are generated in one eye are not seen with the other eye, and opposite effects can readily be generated concomitantly in separate eyes. The color selectivity of the short-term motion aftereffect (LOVEGROVE et al., 1972) and simultaneously induced motion effect (OVER and LOVEGROVE, 1973) is also monocular, for the color selectivity disappears when the inducing pattern is presented to one eye and the test pattern to the other eye. However, it appears that these dichoptic effects are very weak compared to the monoptic effects, and thus the lack of color selectivity may be difficult to ascertain.

In contrast, visual aftereffects that are not made selective to color transfer to a large extent. This is true of the figural aftereffects (KÖHLER and WALLACH, 1944), the tilt aftereffect (CAMPBELL and MAFFEI, 1971), changes in contrast thresholds induced by adapting to a grating (BLAKEMORE and CAMPBELL, 1969), and the aftereffect of seen movement (WOHLGEMUTH, 1911). The mechanism of transfer of these latter two aftereffects (BLAKE and FOX, 1972; BARLOW and BRINDLEY, 1963) has been shown to be partially postretinal, for after an effect is induced in one eye, the effect is seen with the other eye after the adapted eye is made temporarily blind by pressure-blinding. Figural aftereffects (KÖHLER and EMERY, 1947) and the aftereffect of seen movement (PAPERT, 1964) have been shown to explicitly involve binocular mechanisms.

One figural aftereffect, the apparent spatial frequency shift (BLAKEMORE et al., 1970) transfers partially. As discussed earlier, the frequency shift can be used to modify the apparent spatial frequency of a test grating in the McCollough experiment, which may in turn change the color of the aftereffect seen on the test grating (STROMEYER, 1972a; WYATT, 1974). No color change is seen if the apparent frequency shift is induced in one eye, and the other eye views the test pattern to detect any change in color, although the frequency shift is clearly seen with either eye (STROMEYER, 1972a). This suggests that only the monocular component of the frequency shift can modify the color.

These studies on aftereffects suggest that binocular mechanisms may be insensitive to color. However, binocular disparity mechanisms have been shown to be somewhat sensitive to color. Simple line stereograms produce depth when portrayed by color differences alone (LU and FENDER, 1972). Also COMERFORD (1974) has shown that a colored spoke wheel pattern on a ground of a different color produces stereo depth when chromatic aberration is largely eliminated and the chromatic contours are equated in luminance by the minimally distinct border criterion (BOYNTON and KAISER, 1968), and varied in small steps above and below this criterion. Depth discrimination was better with a 30 min arc binocular disparity than with a 7 min arc disparity, and COMERFORD (1974) suggests that this may account for failures to obtain stereopsis with random dot stereograms portrayed with color differences alone (LU and FENDER, 1972). Although stereo mechanisms may be sensitive to color, attempts to generate McCollough effects selective to the binocular disparity of random dot patterns (OVER et al., 1973), gratings, and other patterns (STROMEYER et al., unpublished manuscript) have failed. Also OVER et al. (1973) observed that stereo depth-selective masking and induced displacements in depth are not selective to the colors red and green.

Some monocular information from the sites of the color aftereffects may, however, eventually converge upon binocular mechanisms. JULESZ and STROMEYER (JULESZ, 1971) investigated this problem by producing strong McCollough effects in order to subjectively color random line stereograms and thus produce sufficient stereo cues for the patterns to fuse and produce depth. The patterns did not originally fuse. The experiment failed. However, SHATTUCK and HELD (1975) caused a colored grating presented in the frontal plane to appear tilted in depth out of the plane, after inducing simultaneously or sequentially opposite color-selective tilt effects in either eye. The authors conclude that some information from the monocular sites of the color-selective tilt effects converges upon stereo mechanisms. Further evidence that this adaptation process occurs in monocular channels is shown by the fact that the color-selective tilt effects do not transfer interocularly, nor do opposite effects generated simultaneously in either eye cancel each other (SHATTUCK and HELD, 1975) or at all reduce each other (KAVADELLAS and HELD, 1977).

The previous studies have shown that the form-color aftereffects are largely monocular. Recently, however, MACKAY and MACKAY (1973, 1975b) demonstrated *weak* dichoptic effects that last as long as the McCollough effect (MACKAY and MACKAY, 1975b). One eye was exposed to alternating homogeneous red and green fields, while the other eye was simultaneously exposed to alternating orthogonal black and white gratings. One achromatic adapting grating was paired with red and the other with green. This produced an "anomalous" (positive colored) McCollough effect (rather than the usual complementary effect) in the eye that been exposed to the achromatic adapting gratings. The aftereffect in the other eye, which had been exposed just to color, was in the complementary hues—like the McCollough effect. These latter complementary effects were ambiguous in a few observers and generally somewhat weaker than the positive aftereffects in the other eye (MACKAY and MACKAY, 1973, 1975b). The strength of these dichoptic effects in either eye were about 0.1 to 0.3 times the strength of the regular McCollough effect produced with the same adapting duration. MURCH (1974) has also observed that when one eye is adapted to color and the other eye is simultaneously adapted to moving achromatic patterns, a color-selective motion aftereffect can be seen with the eye that had been exposed to color. MACKAY and MACKAY (1975b) argue that the dichoptic effects they observed may occur *entirely* within monocular channels.

WHITE (1976b and personal communication) obtained weak interocular transfer of the McCollough effect, as shown when each eye was separately examined with the colorimetric cancellation technique, after exposure of one eye to alternating green and magenta gratings while the other eye was simultaneously exposed to uniform fields of the same color as the gratings (e.g., left eye, green grating and simultaneously right eye, green uniform field). Transfer was not obtained when the adapting colors in the two eyes were in antiphase. WHITE (1976b) suggests that previous failures to obtain transfer may have been caused by binocular rivalry of blackness in one eye and the colored grating in the other eye during adaptation.

VIDYASAGAR (1976) demonstrated binocular color aftereffects by adapting both eyes simultaneously (binocular viewing) to a reddish vertical grating and a complementary, blue-green horizontal grating and by adapting concomitantly each eye separately (monocular viewing) for an equal time to the opposite condition (e.g., a blue-green vertical grating and reddish horizontal grating). A vertical test grating then appeared "bluish" when viewed by both eyes simultaneously, but "pinkish" when viewed with each eye separately. Similarly, a horizontal test grating appeared pinkish when viewed by both eyes, but bluish when viewed by each eye. *Both* aftereffects appear to require binocular mechanisms: The aftereffect produced by binocular viewing depends on a mechanism that is more strongly affected by a binocular stimulus than a monocular one; whereas the aftereffect produced by monocular viewing is facilitated by signals from the adapted eye and inhibited by signals from the other eye (VIDYASAGAR, 1976). The reason why monocular channels do not play a role is that each eye, considered separately, is adapted *equally* to gratings in the same orientation in complementary colors, which would produce little color-selective adaptation in monocular channels. The experiment does not show, however, that the typical McCollough effect does not depend *predominantly* on monocular mechanisms, for the experiment is explicitly designed so that such mechanisms would not be involved. The experiment has a remarkable implication: An aftereffect, for example, produced by exposure of the left eye to a reddish vertical grating and a blue-green horizontal grating, is more readily neutralized by adapting to the opposite condition when just the left eye is open than when both eyes are open (i.e., opening the right eye reduces the effect of the neutralizing gratings).

E. Time Course of the Aftereffects

The most striking feature of the form-color aftereffects is their persistency; they often last for days and perhaps weeks. The time course of various effects will be discussed here – the phantom color fringes, the McCollough effect, and movement aftereffects.

The phantom fringes reach about three-quarters of their maximal strength after wearing prisms in the natural environment for 2 days (HAY et al., 1963; HAJOS and RITTER, 1965). Significant aftereffects, however, can be produced in only 20–30 min by viewing a speckled surface through a prism or by viewing a grating with blue and yellow (HELD, 1954) or red and green materials (STROMEYER, 1968) affixed to left and right edges, respectively, and 30 min are sufficient to produce color aftereffects selective to the polarity of sawtooth gratings (STROMEYER et al., 1973).

GIBSON (1933) noted that the phantom fringes were visible for several hours after wearing prisms for several days. KOHLER (1951) observed vivid phantom fringes upon waking one morning after 16 days of adaptation, and after 50 days of adaptation, weak effects could be seen in dim illumination for many days. The compensation technique however shows that after wearing prisms for 10 days, there are no significant aftereffects even 1–2 days after the prisms are removed (HAJOS, 1962; HAY et al., 1963; HAJOS and RITTER, 1965).

MCCOLLOUGH (1965) observed that viewing orthogonal, colored gratings for 2–4 min produced aftereffects which persisted for more than 1 h. HEPLER (1971), by color matching, measured the CIE chromaticity coordinates of the aftereffects produced by adapting to orthogonal, colored gratings for 15 min on *each consecutive day*. For one observer the aftereffects reached maximal strength after 30 min of cumulative adaptation and for a second observer, after 120 min. After 6 h of cumulative adaptation, the aftereffects were undiminished for one observer 48 h after the last adapting session, and slightly diminished for the other observer.

RIGGS et al. (1974) and WHITE (1976b) investigated the build-up and the decay of the McCollough effect. The strength of the aftereffects was indicated by the colorimetric or excitation purity of the light that must be added to the test pattern to just cancel the aftereffect. The aftereffects increased with adapting time, up to 150 min (RIGGS et al., 1974). The aftereffects persisted in some cases for more than 7 days, and decayed following curves that were not quite straight either on log-log or semilog coordinates, although the investigators found the data could be partially fitted by the function $\Delta P = a - b \ln t$, where ΔP is the excitation or the colorimetric purity of the light used to cancel the aftereffects (relative to the pre-adaptation settings) and a is the strength of the aftereffects 1 min after adaptation (RIGGS et al., 1974; WHITE, 1976b). MACKAY and MACKAY (1974a, 1975a) obtained decay functions that were approximately linear on log-log coordinates, with a slope of $-{}^1/_3$, although such a function does not fit the data in MACKAY and MACKAY (1975c). (The units of the cancellation light were not specified by MACKAY and MACKAY.) KRONAUER and STROMEYER (unpublished) observed that the extensive data on decay obtained by WHITE (1976b) can be reasonably well fit by the function $(\Delta P_e)^{0.4} = -0.03 \ln(t/t_0)$, when the excitation purity, ΔP_e, of the light is greater than 0.01. The term t_0 is the extinction time of the aftereffect—the time at which the aftereffect reaches zero strength. For weaker aftereffects, where $P_e < 0.01$, the results are approximately fitted by $\Delta P_e \propto (t/t_0)^{-1/2}$. These functions are of the type $F(\Delta P_e) = \ln(t/t_0)$ and are invariant with translation in $\ln t$—thus they are not invariant with translation in t. The rate of decay is determined by the decay history and not solely by the present state of the aftereffect. There is no single time constant. Thus, in a given absolute time period, new aftereffects decay more than old aftereffects of the same strength (RIGGS et al., 1974; ELLIS and CASTELLAN, 1975; WHITE, 1976b).

What conditions cause the McCollough aftereffect to decay? Prolonged scanning of a black and white test grating may cause a strong aftereffect seen on the same grating to completely vanish (STROMEYER, 1972a). This suppression effect appears to be selective to the retinal area, bar width (STROMEYER, 1972a), and orientation (unpublished observations) of the test grating. SKOWBO et al. (1974) also showed that scanning achromatic gratings for 50 min will largely eliminate aftereffects that had been produced with similar gratings in colored light. However, they did not test whether this decay was temporary. GRAVES (1976) and WHITE and GRAVES (1976) showed the effect was not permanent, for the aftereffects *partially* regained strength with time after exposure to the achromatic patterns. It might be thought that the achromatic gratings, since they appear colored due to the McCollough effect, will generate in turn a complementary aftereffect that reduces the original McCollough effect. GRAVES (1976), however, has shown that the *strength* of the aftereffect seen on the achromatic gratings (which was varied by varying the time after chromatic adaptation) did not influence the suppression produced by the achromatic gratings. And WHITE and GRAVES (1976) have shown that *prolonged* viewing of achromatic gratings *before* the chromatic gratings will reduce the effectiveness of the chromatic gratings in producing a colored aftereffect.

JONES and HOLDING (1975) argue that the test measurements themselves will permanently reduce the aftereffects, for they observed that the aftereffects decayed little over a 5 day period following adaptation if *no* test pattern was viewed during this period. ELLIS, WHITE, and RIGGS (WHITE, 1976b), however, have compared decay functions obtained when each observer was repeatedly tested for the aftereffect or tested only after considerable delays following adaptation (from 1 h to several days), and they conclude that repeated testing has surprisingly little influence on assessed decay. The amount of total exposure to the test gratings was about an order magnitude less than the amount required for achromatic gratings to suppress the aftereffect, as observed in other experiments, discussed above (WHITE, 1976b).

MACKAY and MACKAY (1975a, 1975c) observed that although the aftereffects decayed by roughly equal, substantial amounts with *many hours'* exposure either to diffuse light or the natural environment, exposure of one eye to darkness produced *no* decay over the equivalent time period for the aftereffect in that eye. For example, one eye viewed colored gratings and was then occluded until the next day. The following day the other eye was exposed in the same manner to the colored gratings, and then the aftereffects were measured for both eyes over a long period and were found to be similar (MACKAY and MACKAY, 1975c). WHITE (1976b) found that the aftereffects for some observers decayed little when the eyes were occluded, whereas other observers experienced significant decay.

SIGEL and NACHMIAS (1975) attempted to neutralize aftereffects by adapting to the opposite of the original adaptation conditions. However, the original aftereffect often reappeared later. This effect was also observed by WHITE and HIRSCH (1975), MACKAY and MACKAY (1975c) and WHITE (1976b). If there were partially independent red and green systems, then the aftereffects might cancel at one point in time but not cancel at another, for the aftereffects decay at first more quickly and later more slowly than a simple exponential function (MACKAY and MACKAY, 1974a; RIGGS et al., 1974). WHITE (1976b) alternately adapted to opposite conditions (e.g., 45° magenta grating and 135°, green and then 45°, green and 135°, magenta) for as many as 27 reversals. The aftereffects got progressively *weaker*, which may be explained by both red and green aftereffects existing simultaneously at a given orientation, where the growth of each aftereffect follows a negatively accelerated function of chromatic exposure. This would suggest that the aftereffects are not neutralized by exposure to the opposite of the original adaptation conditions (WHITE, 1976b).

The aftereffects produced by moving colored patterns are particularly persistent. STROMEYER and MANSFIELD (1970) observed that 10–20 min adaptation produced colored aftereffects selective to the direction of motion that were seen for days and even weeks. Faint color flashes were seen when the contours sharply reversed direction. FAVREAU et al. (1972) found that the aftereffects increased over a 60-min adapting period and could be observed one day after adaptation. HEPLER (1971) had observers adapt for 15 min on *each consecutive* day. After as much as 6 h of cumulative adaptation, aftereffects were seen even 96 h after the last adapting session, as shown by colorimetric measurements.

The aftereffects of seen motion selective to color are likewise very persistent. A 10-min exposure (FAVREAU et al., 1972; MAYHEW and ANSTIS, 1972) can readily induce the aftereffect. FAVREAU et al. (1972) observed that the aftereffect was undiminished 1 day after 60 min of adaptation. MAYHEW and ANSTIS (1972) observed that with 10 min of adaptation the aftereffect lasts for hours and even days and is not neutralized by exposure to both the moving adapting patterns in black and white and homogeneous fields of the adapting colors.

Surprisingly this aftereffect of seen motion is often stronger when tested 30 min after adaptation rather than immediately following adaptation (MAYHEW and ANSTIS, 1972). FAVREAU (1976) has investigated this effect. Observers who adapted for 15 min to high-contrast patterns, reported no color-selective motion effects immediately after the adapting session but significant effects 7 min later. However, when the patterns contained alternating bands of different hues which were approximately balanced for luminance, the aftereffects were strongest immediately after the adapting session, and FAVREAU (1976) suggests that the presence of luminance contrast may typically interfere with the appearance of the motion effects immediately following the adapting session.

These motion aftereffects are persistent but are seen only transiently on each presentation of the test pattern (FAVREAU et al., 1972; MAYHEW and ANSTIS, 1972). MAYHEW (1972) has shown that the effects can be measured quantitatively by determining the duration of a motion aftereffect produced with a single colored pattern after having first adapted to patterns that produce contingent motion aftereffects, for apparently the contingent aftereffects control the duration.

F. Threshold Changes in Sensitivity

If the form-color aftereffects are caused by adaptation of mechanisms that are sensitive to color and form, then perhaps sensitivity changes might be reflected in a change of the threshold for detecting colored patterns similar to the adapting patterns. The findings on this issue are somewhat contradictory, although most studies show no threshold changes dependent on color.

In several studies the observer adapts to high-contrast colored gratings, and spatial sensitivity is then tested with a high-contrast colored grating with the mean luminance adjusted so that the grating is just visible (GENTRY and MORANT, 1972; TIMNEY et al., 1974; GENTRY et al., in preparation; TIMNEY et al., 1976). These studies reveal no color-selective adaptation. For example, in the study by TIMNEY et al. (1974), observers adapted for 90 min to vertical red and horizontal green gratings presented in alternation, and 30 min thereafter *luminance* thresholds were measured for the detection of high-contrast colored gratings presented either on a dark or white background. No threshold elevation due to adaptation was observed, although the McCollough aftereffect could be seen for at least one day. In the other studies by these investigators the test pattern was presented shortly after the adapting pattern. Large, orientation-selective threshold changes were obtained which were not selective to color.

In a similar study, however, MAUDARBOCUS and RUDDOCK (1974) observed that the luminance threshold for detecting a high-contrast red grating was raised following adaptation to a similar red grating but was not raised following adaptation to a blue grating. The threshold rise was spatial frequency-selective, as shown in Figure 5. This color-selectivity occurs only when the adapting and test patterns are presented to the same eye, for when the test pattern is presented to the nonadapted eye, the luminance threshold is elevated considerably regardless of the adapting colors (MAUDARBOCUS and RUDDOCK, 1973). The color-selectivity that they observed with monoptic viewing may be due to two factors: (1) the test pattern is presented for only 3 s immediately after the adapting pattern and (2) the adapting patterns are very bright, being 5 log units above the observer's threshold for detecting the high-contrast adapting patterns (approximately 10,000 trolands, RUDDOCK, personal communication). In the similar studies discussed above which did not find color selectivity, either the adapting luminance was considerably lower (TIMNEY et al., 1976) or the adapting and test patterns were separated by a longer interval (GENTRY et al., in preparation).

More recently, MAUDARBOCUS and RUDDOCK (in preparation) have argued that their effects are not caused by adaptation of color-selective spatial mechanisms. They observed that *neither* red nor blue adapting patterns elevated the threshold of the red test pattern superimposed on a *blue* ground, rather than on a dark ground. When the same red test pattern was superimposed on a *red* ground, then *both* the red and blue adapting patterns elevated the threshold for detecting the red test pattern. The same effects were obtained whether the adapting and test gratings were presented to the same eye or opposite eyes. Thus the investigators surmise that when an observer adapts to a very bright blue grating, a positive afterimage of the blue field results, and the red test grating is detected against this blue afterimage. No threshold rise occurs, just as in the case in which the red test grating is viewed against a real blue field. MAUDARBOCUS and RUDDOCK (in preparation) assume that color contrast mechanisms may be used to detect this grating of red and blue stripes, and these mechanisms are not well adapted by a grating of only blue color—thus

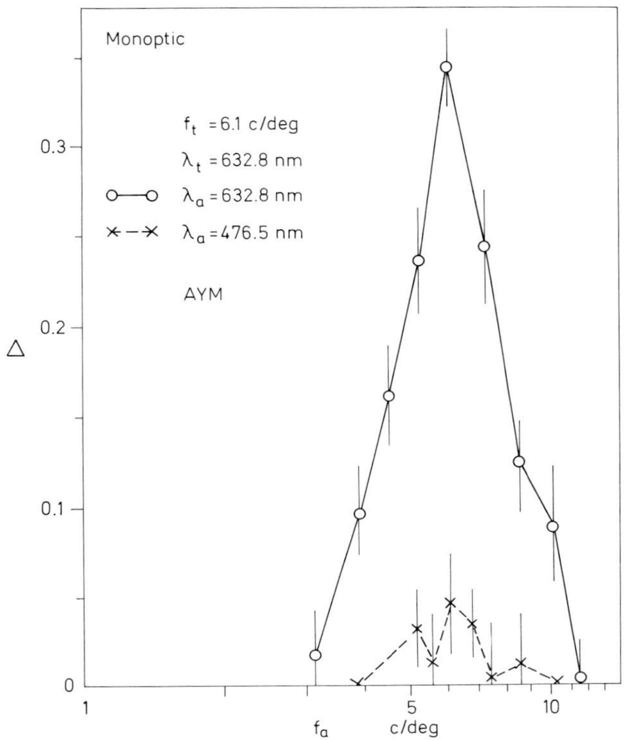

Fig. 5. Adaptation effect, Δ, for a red (632.8 nm) test grating of 6.1 c/° as a function of the spatial frequency of red (632.8 nm) and blue (476.5 nm) adapting gratings of approximately 10,000 trolands. All gratings were vertical, of unitary contrast, and viewed with the left eye. After 2 min initial exposure to adapting grating, adapting grating was presented for 20-s periods alternating with 3-s test periods, during which the observer adjusted illumination level of unitary contrast test grating so that stripes were just visible. Adaptation effect, Δ, is the logarithm of ratio of threshold just after adapting to a grating divided by threshold after adapting to a uniform field of the same color and illumination level as adapting grating. Observer AYM. (After MAUDARBOCUS and RUDDOCK, 1974)

there is little threshold rise. These color contrast mechanisms are presumably sensitive to only low spatial frequencies, for the color-selectivity of adaptation declines above about 6 c/° and disappears entirely at 16 c/° as shown in Figure 6.

HARRIS and KRAUSKOPF (1973) have attempted to obtain color-selective spatial adaptation with colored gratings that each stimulated only one Stiles π color mechanism. (Some of these π mechanisms have spectral sensitivities similar to the action spectra of individual cone pigments, and thus it is generally thought that these mechanisms occur quite early in the chain of visual processing, although see review by ENOCH, 1972, for evidence against this assumption.) HARRIS and KRAUSKOPF (1973) presented red or blue gratings on a large orange field which suppressed the green-sensitive π_4 mechanism, and the intensities of the blue and red gratings were chosen from incremental threshold curves (obtained with a large test spot rather than with gratings) so that the blue gratings presum-

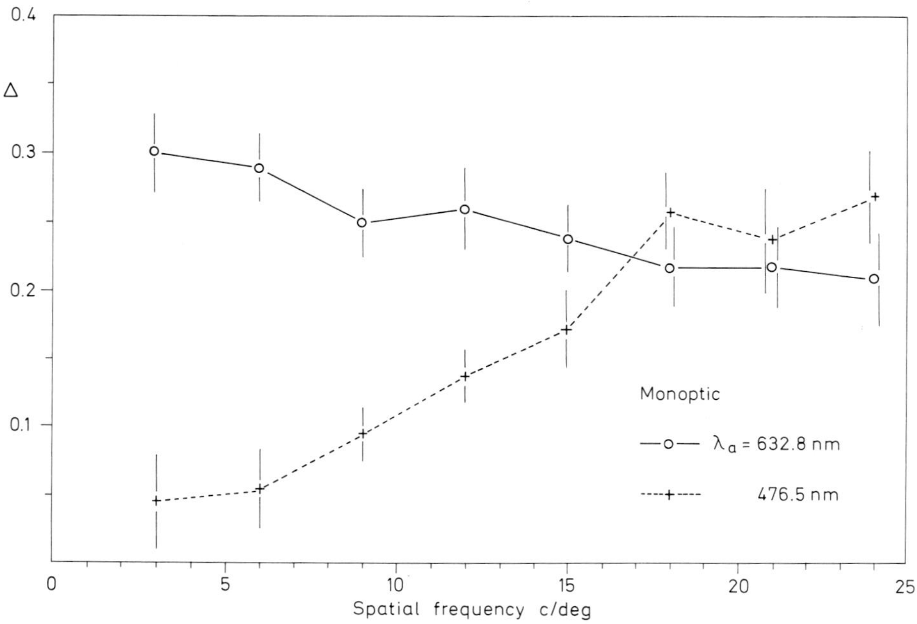

Fig. 6. Adaptation effect, Δ, for a red (632.8 nm) test grating produced by red (632.8 nm) and blue (476.5 nm) adapting gratings. All gratings were vertical and viewed by one eye. Test grating always had same spatial frequency as adapting grating—indicated on the abscissa. Observer AYM. Other details are given in the legend of Figure 5. (After MAUDARBOCUS and RUDDOCK, in preparation)

ably stimulated only the blue π mechanisms and the red gratings stimulated only the red-sensitive π_5 mechanism. Adaptation to either red or blue gratings was then shown to raise the threshold for detecting both red gratings and blue gratings. Thus, paradoxically, adapting to a blue grating that is presumably below the detection threshold for the π_5 mechanism will raise the threshold for detecting a red grating seen via the π_5 mechanism. This result led the authors to conclude that spatial adaptation occurs at a site where the outputs of the primary color mechanisms have combined and is not color-selective.

SHARPE (1974) has used a different strategy to isolate color mechanisms. He observed that adding red light to a low-contrast *bright,* blue grating and vice versa, did not change the threshold for detecting the grating until the added light reached a *critical level.* That is, red light below the critical level did not affect the threshold of the blue grating.

It is not clear what causes this critical level because the π_4 and π_5 mechanisms, that presumably detect the patterns, may be about equally sensitive to these high luminance gratings before the extra light is added, and thus adding light of any color would raise the threshold. The critical level observed with low spatial frequencies may perhaps reflect the response of opponent-color mechanisms. STROMEYER and STERNHEIM (in preparation) observed that under certain conditions the visibility of colored gratings of low spatial frequency may even be enhanced by adding light of a different color to the gratings, so that hue differences can be used to detect the patterns.

SHARPE assumed that any stimulus below the critical level would *not directly* stimulate the mechanism used to detect the original grating. However, when the added light was a grating pattern rather than a homogeneous field (for example, a red grating on a brighter blue field), then the grating produced adaptation that raised the threshold for detecting both blue gratings and red gratings, even though the adapting grating was always below the critical level.

There is an apparent conflict between some of the previous results. MAUDARBOCUS and RUDDOCK (in preparation) observed that adaptation produced little change in the threshold for detecting a colored grating on a background of a *different* color (red on blue), whereas HARRIS and KRAUSKOPF (1973) and SHARPE (1974) observed large threshold changes with similar test stimuli. This difference, however, may be due to the fact that MAUDARBOCUS and RUDDOCK used an adapting grating of *one* color, whereas the latter investigators used adapting gratings of contrasting colored stripes (for example, red gratings on a blue ground.) Also, MAUDARBOCUS and RUDDOCK used very bright adapting patterns.

The previous studies provide little evidence for color-selective spatial adaptation, except perhaps for the color contrast mechanisms postulated by MAUDARBOCUS and RUDDOCK. Two other studies have shown changes in sensitivity that appear to require spatially tuned color mechanisms. COSGROVE et al. (1974) showed that prolonged scanning of a red or green grating caused a retinally stabilized test line to fade most frequently when the color of the test line matched the color of the grating. MAYHEW (1973) has demonstrated threshold changes selective to color and motion. Observers adapted 5 min to a random texture that alternately rotated in one direction in red illumination and in the opposite direction in green illumination. The test stimuli were the same rotating patterns set at low luminance and superimposed on brighter backgrounds of the same colors. Even 20 min after adaptation one of two observers was less sensitive to the adapting color and motion conditions.

The positive results of several additional studies that attempt to show adaptation of spatially tuned color mechanisms can be largely explained on other grounds. MAY (1972) measured the threshold for detecting a 1 c/° red or green grating presented on a white ground before and after adapting to a red or green grating. Color-selective adaptation was found only when the adapting and test patterns were identical in spatial frequency and orientation, in which case gratings fell in *identical* retinal positions (a fixation point was used). MAY et al. (1974) have suggested that afterimages may largely account for these results. LOVEGROVE and OVER (1973) observed color selectivity in a forward masking paradigm in which a 10 ms colored test grating was flashed 10 ms after a 120 ms colored masking grating of the same spatial frequency and orientation. However, hue changes *alone* may possibly account for the reduced masking that occurs when the masking and test patterns are of different colors.

The masking and test patterns are presented so closely in time that perhaps only a single complex pattern is seen. When the two patterns are of different colors, there will be variations in the hue of the combined pattern that *depend on the relative spatial phase* of the two patterns, and these color changes may perhaps aid detection of the test pattern. When the two patterns are of the same color, then perhaps only variations in the apparent contrast of the combined pattern are used to detect the test pattern. Thus, spatially tuned color mechanisms may not be needed to explain these masking results. It remains to be seen what effects these cues play in the complicated binocular interactions investigated by BROERSE et al., 1975.

In summary, most of these studies on adaptation and masking provide little evidence for spatially tuned color mechanisms. However, it cannot thus be concluded that the form-color aftereffects are not caused by color adaptation of spatially tuned mechanisms, for it is possible that contours defined by luminance gradients (with light of any color) may typically be detected at threshold by mechanisms that respond to luminance and not to color. The luminances contributed by different colored lights appear to act additively in detection of fine spatial details (MYERS et al., 1973; GUTH and GRAHAM, 1975) and the apparent sharpness of a fine edge (BOYNTON and KAISER, 1968). LODGE (1976) showed luminance additivity in the detection of low spatial frequency sine gratings viewed on a *dark field*. For example, if a red grating and a green grating are individually set to threshold, and the luminance of each grating is then halved and the two gratings are summed in-phase, then the combined grating will also be just visible at threshold. This luminance additivity could be explained by linear physiologic summation within achromatic, black-white mechanisms (BOYNTON and KAISER, 1968), although LODGE (1976) showed how chromatic mechanisms may contribute to these detection tasks. Very similar results might also occur if the π_4 and π_5 mechanisms of Stiles were statistically *independent* detection mechanisms (IKEDA et al., 1970), and thus it is not clear if the results require physiologic summation within black-white mechanisms.

Thus, it is quite possible that luminance contrast is largely detected by black-white mechanisms or independent π mechanisms, the spectral sensitivities of which largely overlap. It is thus not surprising that adapting to a colored grating may elevate the threshold for detecting a grating regardless of the color. A different technique may be needed to probe only mechanisms that respond to particular form-color combinations in order to show that the form-color aftereffects are in fact paralleled by changes in sensitivity. Perhaps, adapting to a high-contrast colored grating would reduce sensitivity for *detecting* transient changes in the *color* of a high-contrast test grating with luminance and contrast held constant.

G. Physiologic Models

HARRIS (1978) discusses several models of the McCollough aftereffect, some of which are considered here.

I. Afterimages

The afterimage model attributes the aftereffect to adaptation of individual color receptors in the retina. Assume (GIBSON and HARRIS, 1968; STROMEYER,

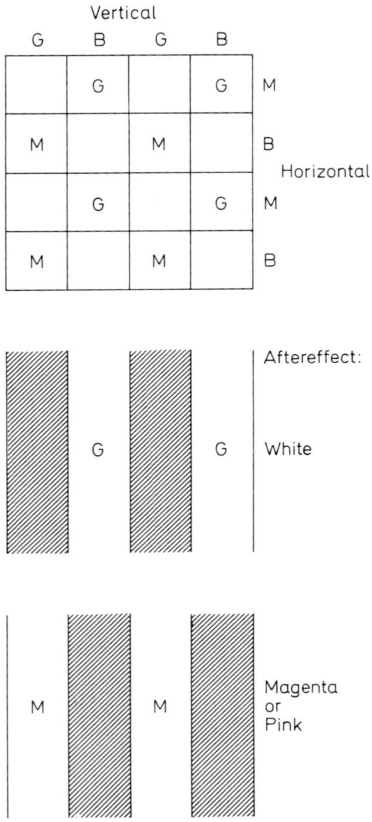

Fig. 7. Colors predicted by the afterimage model. Observer fixates a low spatial frequency, vertical grating of green (*G*) and black (*B*) stripes and a horizontal grating of magenta (*M*) and black stripes. Stripes are designated by the letters around top square. Square shows negative colored *afterimage* produced by the gratings. Black and white vertical test gratings of the same spatial frequency as adapting gratings would elicit the afterimages, shown on gratings below square. Imaginary vertical lines in the figure define constant retinal positions. The McCollough effect that is typically observed (once afterimages fade within several minutes of adapting) is indicated at the right. (After STROMEYER and DAWSON, 1978)

1968) that the observer tends to fixate the colored bars while viewing the alternating vertical and horizontal adapting gratings. This would produce a plaid afterimage. Complementary colors would then be seen on vertical and horizontal test gratings (with the same retinal spatial frequency as the adapting patterns) if the observer tended to fixate the white bars. The aftereffects, however, should reverse if the observer, instead, fixated the black bars of the test gratings, as shown in Figure 7. STROMEYER (1968) found that observers saw the color aftereffects when they fixated the center of the white test bars, but the colors did not reverse when the center of the black bars was fixated. STROMEYER and DAWSON (1978) also observed that the colored aftereffects produced by fixating gratings of colored and brighter white bars were seen well only when the black bars, rather than the white bars, of the test gratings fell on the retinal regions that had been stimulated by the colored adapting bars. This clearly contradicts the afterimage model. The afterimage model was conclusively disproved by HARRIS and GIBSON (1968) who presented each adapting pattern in 80 ms flashes randomly and equally in either of two counterphase retinal positions, in order to adapt all areas equally to both colors. The aftereffects grew with adaptation time, which shows that the last flash was irrelevant. STROMEYER and DAWSON (1974) also produced the aftereffect with orthogonal, colored sine gratings that were flashed in random positions for very brief periods.

HARRIS and BARKOW (1969) note that the afterimage model cannot explain their finding that the aftereffects can be produced with gratings of white and colored bars but cannot be produced with gratings of grey and colored bars that are balanced for luminance, for the model predicts that the aftereffects should be weaker as the luminance of the neutral bars is increased. Similarly, STROMEYER and DAWSON (1978) were unable to produce aftereffects by fixating a vertical grating of interlaced green and magenta bars of the same luminance but effects were readily obtained under similar conditions when the green and magenta bars were presented alternately in time (high-contrast gratings). The afterimage model predicts that both conditions will produce similar aftereffects. The model is further refuted by the observation that a green homogeneous field alternating with a black and white grating produces a green aftereffect; thus, a complementary afterimage (of the green field viewed on the adapting grating) produces a McCollough effect with color complementary to the afterimage (MURCH and HIRSCH, 1972). The McCollough aftereffect also clearly survives an almost complete bleach of the cone pigments with white light (STROMEYER and DAWSON, 1978).

Afterimages clearly do not explain the McCollough aftereffect, although they might play an uncontrolled role in some experiments.

II. Dipoles

GIBSON and HARRIS (1968) introduced the concept of dipoles as the simplest neural mechanism consistent with observation of the McCollough aftereffect. Dipoles are defined to receive inputs from two retinal loci. They respond when there is a luminance difference between the two loci, and they can be adapted to different regions of the color spectrum. Dipoles can be identified with the cells in the retina (of rhesus monkey) which have essentially concentric receptive fields (often slightly eccentric) or with similar, concentric cells at any level of the visual system (HARRIS, 1969). The dipole, thus conceived, responds to lines in all orientations, though not equally. Both vertical and horizontal gratings would adapt many of the same dipoles (HARRIS, 1969, 1972). Indeed, if the dipoles are quite concentric, each grating would adapt all the dipoles that the other grating adapts, though not equally. A single colored grating would thus produce color aftereffects on test gratings in all orientations. This does not occur, however, for vertical *or* horizontal adapting gratings produce only *very weak* aftereffects on 45° diagonal gratings (STROMEYER et al., in preparation).

III. Opponent-Color Mechanisms

McCollough (1965) ascribed her effect to "color adaptation of orientation-specific edge detectors." These mechanisms are presumably color-opponent cells, for the non-opponent cells are assumed to process luminance and not color information (de Valois, 1973).

The following considerations suggest that the aftereffect does not occur at a locus prior to the visual cortex. Most color-opponent retinal ganglion cells (Gouras, 1968; de Monasterio and Gouras, 1975) and lateral geniculate cells (LGN) (Wiesel and Hubel, 1966) in the rhesus monkey receive predominantly excitatory of inhibitory inputs from one cone type in the center of the receptive field and an antagonistic input from a different cone type in the surround, and possibly center (de Valois, 1973). The center and surround are typically concentrically arranged. These cells apparently do *not* have a spatially antagonistic center and surround mediated by cones of the same type, *viz.*, red-on center and red-off surround, and this feature of color-opponent cells apparently does not occur before the striate cortex (Gouras, 1974). The color-opponent cells of the retina (Gouras, 1968) and LGN (Wiesel and Hubel, 1966; de Valois and Pease, 1971; de Valois, 1972) fire well to *diffuse fields* of red or green. The cells also respond strongly to a *white* spot or bar that is wide enough to just fill the center of the receptive field (Wiesel and Hubel, 1966; de Valois, 1972; de Valois and de Valois, 1975). If these mechanisms underlie the McCollough effect, then adaptation to a low spatial frequency, colored grating, or to even a homogeneous colored field, ought to produce strong aftereffects on test gratings of high spatial frequencies.

Two types of color-selective cells are quite common in the region of macaque striate cortex subserving the fovea: Color-opponent cells without clear orientation selectivity and spectrally tuned or color-opponent cells with oriented receptive fields (Hubel and Wiesel, 1968; Dow and Gouras, 1973; Gouras, 1974; Michael, 1975; Poggio et al., 1975). The cells without orientation selectivity frequently have two spatially co-extensive receptive fields mediated by red and green cones respectively, which act antagonistically (Dow and Gouras, 1973; Poggio et al., 1975). Such cells typically respond weakly to white light (Poggio et al., 1975). (Thus, they would not respond well to a black and white test grating used to elicit a McCollough effect.)

The color-selective cells with oriented receptive fields typically are "simple" and "complex", as defined by Hubel and Wiesel (1968). Color-selective complex cells are more readily encountered than color-selective simple cells, although a larger proportion of simple cells appears to be color-selective (Gouras, 1974; Poggio et al., 1975). The complex cells typically respond best to moving bars of a given color and respond quite strongly to white bars (Poggio et al., 1975). All the simple cells studied by Poggio et al. (1975) were color-opponent, and the majority had a dual-opponent organization (e.g., green-on, red-off center and red-on, green-off surround) and generally responded poorly to white stimuli. However, it appears that many of the color-selective cells with oriented receptive fields studied by Dow and Gouras (1973) responded well to white bars and were of the simple type. Selective chromatic adaptation has shown (Dow and Gouras, 1973; Gouras, 1974) that many of these cells have a center-surround antagonism involving the *same* cone mechanism. For example, a cell might have a red-on line-shaped center with red-off and green-off inhibitory flanks (DOW and GOURAS, 1973). Such a cell would respond best to a red bar that filled the center of the receptive field, whereas a wide red bar that also encroached upon the red, antagonistic surround would produce little response. This type of cell is thus conjointly sensitive to *color* and *form*, unlike precortical color-opponent cells which respond well to diffuse colored light (GOURAS, 1974). The color-selective cortical cells are predominantly or exclusively driven only by one eye (HUBEL and WIESEL, 1968; DOW and GOURAS, 1973; GOURAS, 1974; POGGIO et al., 1975). Mechanisms that are conjointly selective to color and form, that respond well to achromatic patterns, and are largely monocular, may be responsible for the form-color aftereffects.

Color-opponent mechanisms might also explain the color aftereffects that can be seen on test patterns in scotopic illumination (STROMEYER, 1974b). It has been shown that many opponent-color cells in the LGN become nonopponent cells with the spectral sensitivity of the rod rhodopsin system at scotopic levels (DE VALOIS, 1965; WIESEL and HUBEL, 1966). JAMESON (1972) argues that a single cell by itself cannot thus signal color because the message changes radically with light versus dark adaptation. Stimulation of these cells at scotopic levels typically does not produce color sensations, which might be explained as follows. Diffuse light that just causes an LGN cell to fire at scotopic levels produces the same type of response as is produced by the center of the receptive field at photopic levels (WIESEL and HUBEL, 1966). Thus, the rod signals might equally affect cells with red centers and cells with green centers, and higher mechanisms would simply interpret this as achromatic. However, if the cortical cells are first biased by adapting to colored gratings, then colors might be seen on test gratings in scotopic illumination.

The facility with which red and green aftereffects are obtained compared to yellow and blue aftereffects may be accounted for by two properties of opponent-color cells. Red-green cells form the large majority of opponent cells in LGN (WIESEL and HUBEL, 1966) and striate cortex (GOURAS, 1974). And the response of the red-green cells is more radically affected by chromatic adaptation than the response of blue-yellow cells, as the spectral sensitivities of the cone inputs to the red-green cells largely overlap, and thus the opponent inputs are in a delicate balance across much of the spectrum (DE VALOIS, 1965).

IV. Associations

It has been argued that the form-color aftereffects may reflect a learning process, akin to classical conditioning (LEPPMANN, 1973; MAYHEW and ANSTIS, 1972; SKOWBO et al., 1974), or "associative habituation or synaptic couplings" (MACKAY and MACKAY, 1975a), or "central adaptability rather than sensory adaptation" (RIGGS et al., 1974). Two arguments have been advanced for this view. First, the aftereffects are very persistent, and thus probably not due to sensory adaptation alone (HARRIS, 1978; MAYHEW and ANSTIS, 1972; SKOWBO et al., 1974; Timney et al., 1974; MacKay and MacKay, 1975a; Riggs et al., 1974; Hepler, 1971). The second arguments (Harris, 1978) maintains that it is unparsimonious to ascribe each of the very many aftereffects to a specific type of neural mechanism. This argument is not very convincing, for only a very few simple stimuli may in fact produce selective aftereffects. Mayhew and Anstis (1972) remark that the only stimulus dimensions that produce contingent movement aftereffects also produce simple selective aftereffects. Thus, many distinctive stimuli, such as patterns defined by color contours alone, may generate no color aftereffects dependent on form. Learning models must also consider that most form-color aftereffects depend critically on the retinal and not the perceived dimensions of the stimuli (Harris, 1978). Such models are *unable* to predict almost all the properties of the aftereffects discussed in the present chapter.

H. Summary

The form-color aftereffects can readily be made selective to rather simple form properties, like the orientation, width, and velocity of lines. At present, it is questionable whether aftereffects can be made selective to more complex patterns. For example, it appears most difficult to obtain color aftereffects selective to the convexity, or curvature, of lines. The form-color aftereffects are largely monocular, and they appear to be strongly controlled by the luminance contrast of patterns. There is little evidence that patterns defined by color differences alone will produce any aftereffects. All these properties suggest that the form-color aftereffects depend on the modifications of relatively simple visual units that are driven by one eye. These modifications often last for hours and even days. Although their biological significance is unclear, they serve as a probe of mechanisms for processing combinations of form and motion with color.

References

Anstis, S.M., Gregory, R.L.: The after-effect of seen motion: The role of retinal stimulation and eye movements. Quart. J. exp. Psychol. **17**, 173–174 (1965).

Anstis, S.M., Harris, J.P.: Movement aftereffects contingent on binocular disparity. Perception **3**, 153–168 (1974).

Atkinson, J., Campbell, F.W., Fiorentini, A., Maffei, L.: The dependence of monocular rivalry on spatial frequency. Perception **2**, 127–133 (1973).

Barlow, H.B., Brindley, G.S.: Inter-ocular transfer of movement after-effects during pressure blinding of the stimulated eye. Nature (Lond.) **200**, 1347 (1963).

Blake, R., Fox, R.: Interocular transfer of adaptation to spatial frequency during retinal ischaemia. Nature (Lond.) **240**, 76–77 (1972).

Blakemore, C., Campbell, F.W.: On the existence of neurones in the human visual system selectively sensitive to the orientation and size of retinal images. J. Physiol. (Lond.) **203**, 237–260 (1969).

Blakemore, C., Nachmias, J.: The orientation specificity of two visual after-effects. J. Physiol. (Lond.) **213**, 157–174 (1971).

Blakemore, C., Nachmias, J., Sutton, P.: The perceived spatial frequency shift: Evidence for frequency-selective neurones in the human brain. J. Physiol. (Lond.) **210**, 727–750 (1970).

Blakemore, C., Over, R.: Curvature detectors in human vision? Perception **3**, 3–7 (1974).

Blakemore, C., Sutton, P.: Size adaptation: A new aftereffect. Science **166**, 245–247 (1969).

Bouma, P.J.: Physical aspects of colour. New York: St. Martin's Press, 1971.

Boynton, R.M., Kaiser, P.K.: Vision: The additivity law made to work for heterochromatic photometry with bipartite fields. Science **161**, 366–368 (1968).

Breese, B.B.: On inhibition. Psychol. Rev., Monogr. Suppl. **3** (1), 1–65 (1899).

Breitmeyer, B.G., Cooper, L.A.: Frequency-specific color adaptation in the human visual system. Percept. Psychophys. **11**, 95–96 (1972).

Broerse, J., Over, R., Lovegrove, W.: Loss of wavelength selectivity in contour masking and aftereffect following dichoptic adaptation. Percept. Psychophys. **17**, 333–336 (1975).

Campbell, F.W., Gilinsky, A.S., Howell, E.R., Riggs, L.A., Atkinson, J.: The dependence of monocular rivalry on orientation. Perception **2**, 123–125 (1973).

Campbell, F.W., Gubisch, R.W.: The effect of chromatic aberration on visual acuity. J. Physiol. (Lond.) **192**, 345–358 (1967).

Campbell, F.W., Howell, E.R.: Monocular alternation: A method for the investigation of pattern vision. J. Physiol. (Lond.) **225**, 19–21P (1972).

Campbell, F.W., Kulikowski, J.J.: Orientational selectivity of the human visual system. J. Physiol. (Lond.) **187**, 437–445 (1966).

Campbell, F.W., Maffei, L.: The tilt after-effect: A fresh look. Vision Res. **11**, 833–840 (1971).

Castellan, K.: The effect of inspection contrast on the McCollough effect. Sc.B. Thesis, Brown University, Providence, Rhode Island (1975).

Coltheart, M.: Visual feature analyzers and aftereffects of tilt and curvature. Psychol. Rev. **78**, 114–121 (1971).

Comerford, J.P.: Stereopsis with chromatic contours. Vision Res. **14**, 975–982 (1974).

Cosgrove, M.P., Kohl, G.A., Schmidt, M.J., Brown, D.R.: Chromatic substitution with stabilized images: Evidence for chromatic-specific pattern processing in the human visual system. Vision Res. **14**, 23–30 (1974).

Crassini, B., Over, R.: Curvature-specific color aftereffects. Percept. Psychophys. **17**, 398–404 (1975).

Culbert, S.S.: Directional after-effects following systematic distortion of the visual field. J. Psychol. **37**, 81–93 (1954).

Dawson, B.M., Stromeyer, C.F. III: Form aftereffect contingent upon a colour shift. *Perception* In press (1978).

De Monasterio, F.M., Gouras, P.: Functional properties of ganglion cells of the rhesus monkey retina. J. Physiol. (Lond.) **251**, 167–195 (1975).

DeValois, R.L.: Analysis and coding of color vision in the primate visual system. Cold Spr. Harb. Symp. quant. Biol. **30**, 567–579 (1965).

DeValois, R.L.: Processing of intensity and wavelength information by the visual system. Invest. Ophthal. **11**, 417–427 (1972).

DeValois, R.L.: Central mechanisms of color vision. In: Jung, R. (ed.): Handbook of Sensory Physiology, Vol. VII/3, Central Processing of Visual Information A: Integrative Functions and Comparative Data. Berlin-Heidelberg-New York: Springer-Verlag 1973.

DeValois, R.L., de Valois, K.K.: Neural coding of color. In: Carterette, E.C. and Freidman, M.P. (eds.): Handbook of Perception, Vol. V, Seeing. New York: Academic Press, 1975.

DeValois, R.L., Pease, P.L.: Contours and contrast: Responses of monkey lateral geniculate nucleus cells to luminance and color figures. Science **171**, 694–696 (1971).

Dow, B.M., Gouras, P.: Color and spatial specificity of single units in rhesus monkey foveal striate cortex. J. Neurophysiol. **36**, 79–100 (1973).

Einthoven, W.: Stereoscopie durch Farbendifferenz. Albrecht v. Graefes Arch. ophthal. **31**, part 3, 211–238 (1885).

Ellis, S.R.: Orientation constancy of the McCollough effect. Percept. Psychophys. **19**, 183–192 (1976).

Ellis, S.R., Castellan, K.: Orientation specificity of the McCollough effect: An equivalent contrast transformation. Paper presented to Meeting of Association for Research in Vision and Ophthalmology, 1975.

Enoch, J.M.: The two-color threshold technique of Stiles and derived component color mechanisms. In: Jameson, D., Hurvich, L. (eds.): Handbook of Sensory Physiology, Vol. VII/4, Visual psychophysics. Berlin-Heidelberg-New York: Springer-Verlag 1972.

Favreau, O.E.: Interference in colour-contingent motion after-effects. Quart. J. exp. Psychol. **28**, 553–560 (1976).

Favreau, O., Emerson, V.F., Corballis, M.C.: Motion perception: A color-contingent aftereffect. Science **176**, 78–79 (1972).

Fidell, L.K.S.: Pattern-specific complementary hue after-effects: More on the McCollough phenomenon. Doctoral dissertation. University of Michigan, Ann Arbor, Michigan (1968).

Fidell, L.S.: Orientation specificity in chromatic adaptation of human "edge-detectors." Percept. Psychophys. **8**, 235–237 (1970).

Ganz, L.: Mechanism of the figural aftereffect. Psychol. Rev. **73**, 128–150 (1966).

Gentry, T.A., Morant, R.B.: Orientation and chromatic adaptation effects in simultaneous visual masking. Paper presented to Meeting of Eastern Psychological Association, 1972.

Gentry, T.A., Timney, B.N., Skowbo, D., Morant, R.B.: Orientation-specific threshold elevation effects with chromatic gratings. (In preparation.)

Gibson, A.R., Harris, C.S.: The McCollough effect: Color adaptation of edge-detectors or negative afterimages? Paper presented to Meeting of Eastern Psychological Association, 1968.

Gibson, J.J.: Adaptation, after-effect and contrast in the perception of curved lines. J. exp. Psychol. **16**, 1–31 (1933).

Gilinsky, A.S., Mayo, T.H.: Inhibitory effects of orientation adaptation. J. opt. Soc. Amer. **61**, 1710–1714 (1971).

Gouras, P.: Identification of cone mechanisms in monkey ganglion cells. J. Physiol. (Lond.) **199**, 533–547 (1968).

Gouras, P.: Opponent-colour cells in different layers of foveal striate cortex. J. Physiol. (Lond.) **238**, 583–602 (1974).

Gouras, P., Krüger, J.: Responses of neurons in monkey visual cortex to successive colour and brightness contrast. (In preparation.)

Graves, A.L.: Influence of achromatic inspection on McCollough effects. Honors thesis. Brown University, Providence, Rhode Island (1976).

Green, M., Corwin, T., Zemon, V.: A comparison of Fourier analysis and feature analysis in pattern-specific color aftereffects. Science **192**, 147–148 (1976).

Guth, S.L., Donley, N.J., Marrocco, R.T.: On luminance additivity and related topics. Vision Res. **9**, 537–575 (1969).

Guth, S., Graham, B.V.: Heterochromatic additivity and the acuity response. Vision Res. **15**, 317–319 (1975).

Hajos, A.: Farbunterscheidung ohne „Farbigsehen". Naturwissenschaften **49**, 93–97 (1962).

Hajos, A.: Psychophysiologische Probleme bei „Farbkonturen" und „Konturfarben". Stud. psychol. (Praha) **10**, 254–266 (1968).

Hajos, A.: Sinnespsychologische Untersuchungen zur Invarianzbildung im visuellen System des Menschen. In: Zeichenerkennung durch biologische und technische Systeme. Berlin-Heidelberg-New York: Springer-Verlag, 1971. (Not in circulation.)

Hajos, A.: Experimente zur visuellen Wahrnehmung: Heterochrome und orthogonale Inhibition zwischen Balkensensoren. In: Reinert, G. (ed.): Bericht über den 27. Kongreß der Deutschen Gesellschaft für Psychologie in Kiel 1970. Göttingen: Hogrefe 1973.

Hajos, A., Ritter, M.: Experiments to the problem of interocular transfer. Acta psychol. **24**, 81–90 (1965).

Harris, C.S.: Retinal localization of orientation-specific color after-effects. J. opt. Soc. Amer. **59**, 504 (1969).

Harris, C.S.: Effect of viewing distance on a color aftereffect specific to spatial frequency. Paper presented to Meeting of Psychonomic Society, 1970. Abstract in Psychon. Sci. **21**, 350 (1970).

Harris, C.S.: Orientation-specific color after-effects dependent on retinal spatial frequency, rather than on stripe width. J. opt. Soc. Amer. **61**, 689 (1971).

Harris, C.S.: Color adaptation dependent on contours but not on orientation. Paper presented to Meeting of Association for Research in Vision and Ophthalmology, 1972.

Harris, C.S.: Insight or out of sight? Two examples of perceptual plasticity in the human adult. In: Visual Coding and Adaptability, C.S. Harris (ed.): Potomac, Maryland: Lawrence Erlbaum Assocs., 1978.

Harris, C.S., Barkow, B.: Color/white grids produce weaker orientation-specific color aftereffects than do color/black grids. Paper presented to Meeting of Psychonomic Society, 1969. Abstract in Psychon. Sci. **17**, 123 (1969).

Harris, C.S., Gibson, A.R.: Is orientation-specific color adaptation in human vision due to edge detectors, afterimages, or "dipoles"? Science **162**, 1506–1507 (1968).

Harris, C.S., Krauskopf, J.: Absence of color specificity in adapting to colored gratings. Paper presented to Meeting of Psychonomic Society, 1973. Abstract in Bull. Psychon. Soc. **2**, 235 (1973).

Hartridge, H.: The visual perception of fine detail. Phil. Trans. Roy. Soc., Series B **232**, 519–671 (1947).

Hay, J.C., Pick, H.L. Jr., Rosser, E.: Adaptation to chromatic aberration by the human visual system. Science **141**, 167–169 (1963).

Held, R.: Visual adaptation to chromatic dispersion. Paper presented to Meeting of Eastern Psychological Association, 1954.

Held, R.: Adaptation to rearrangement and visual-spatial aftereffects. Psychol. Beiträge **6**, 439–450 (1962).

Held, R.: The rediscovery of adaptability in the visual system: effects of extrinsic and intrinsic chromatic dispersion. In: Visual coding and adaptability, C.S. Harris (ed.): Potomac, Maryland: Lawrence Erlbaum Assocs., 1978.

Held, R., Shattuck, S.R.: Color- and edge-sensitive channels in the human visual system: Tuning for orientation. Science **174**, 314–316 (1971).

Hepler, N.: Color: A motion-contingent aftereffect. Science **162**, 376–377 (1968).

Hepler, N.K.: Motion-contingent color aftereffects: A lasting modification of perception. Doctoral dissertation. McGill University, Montreal, Canada (1971).

Hochberg, J.E., Day, R.H., Hardy, D.: Hue- and brightness-differences, contours, and figural after-effects. Amer. J. Psychol. **73**, 638–639 (1960).

Hochberg, J., Triebel, W.: Figural after-effects with colored stimuli. Amer. J. Psychol. **68**, 133–135 (1955).

Hubel, D.H., Wiesel, T.N.: Receptive fields and functional architecture in two nonstriate visual areas (18 and 19) of the cat. J. Neurophysiol. **28**, 229–289 (1965).

Hubel, D.H., Wiesel, T.N.: Receptive fields and functional architecture of monkey striate cortex. J. Physiol. (Lond.) **195**, 215–243 (1968).

Ikeda, M., Uetsuki, T., Stiles, W.S.: Interactions among Stiles π mechanisms. J. opt. Soc. Amer. **60**, 406–415 (1970).

Jameson, D.: Theoretical issues of color vision. In: Jameson, D., Hurvich, L. (eds.): Handbook of Sensory Physiology, Vol. VII/4. Visual Psychophysics. Berlin-Heidelberg-New York: Springer-Verlag, 1972.

Jones, P.D., Holding, D.H.: Extremely long-term persistence of the McCollough effect. J. exp. Psychol.: Human Perception and Performance **1**, 323–327 (1975).

Julesz, B.: Foundations of Cyclopean Perception. Chicago-London: University of Chicago Press 1971.

Kavadellas, A., Held, R.: Monocularity of color-contingent tilt aftereffect. Percept Psychophys. **21**, 12–14 (1977).

Kishto, B.N.: The colour stereoscopic effect. Vision Res. **5**, 313–329 (1965).

Klein, S., Kronauer, R.E., Stromeyer, C.F. III: Checkerboards and edge mechanisms. (In preparation.)

Klein, S., Stromeyer, C.F. III, Ganz, L.: The simultaneous spatial frequency shift: A dissociation between the detection and perception of gratings. Vision Res. **14**, 1421–1432 (1974).

Köhler, W., Emery, D.A.: Figural after-effects in the third dimension of visual space. Amer. J. Psychol. **60**, 159–201 (1947).

Köhler, W., Wallach, H.: Figural after-effects: An investigation of visual processes. Proc. Amer. phil. Soc. **88**, 269–357 (1944).

Kohler, I.: Über Aufbau und Wandlungen der Wahrnehmungswelt, insbesondere über „bedingte Empfindungen". Öst. Akad. Wiss. phil.-hist. Kl. **227**, 1–118 (1951).

Krauskopf, J.: Heterochromatic stabilized images: A classroom demonstration. Amer. J. Psychol. **80**, 634–637 (1967).

Leppmann, P.K.: Spatial frequency dependent chromatic after-effects. Nature (Lond.) **242**, 411–412 (1973).

Leppmann, P.K., Allen, D.B.: Further studies of form-specific chromatic aftereffects. J. opt. Soc. Amer. **63**, 1287 (1973).

Lettvin, J.Y.: The colors of colored things. Quart. Prog. Rep. Res. Lab. of Electronics, Massachusetts Institute of Technology **87**, 193–229 (1967).

Lodge, H.R.: Contrast additivity. An alternative approach. Vision Res. **16**, 263–268 (1976).

Lovegrove, W.J., Over, R.: Color adaptation of spatial frequency detectors in the human visual system. Science **176**, 541–543 (1972).

Lovegrove, W.J., Over, R.: Colour selectivity in orientation masking and aftereffect. Vision Res. **13**, 895–901 (1973).

Lovegrove, W.J., Over, R., Broerse, J.: Colour selectivity in motion after-effect. Nature (Lond.) **238**, 334–335 (1972).

Lu, C., Fender, D.R.: The interaction of color and luminance in stereoscopic vision. Invest. Ophthal. **11**, 482–490 (1972).

MacKay, D.M., MacKay, V.: Orientation-sensitive after-effects of dichoptically presented colour and form. Nature (Lond.) **242**, 477–479 (1973).

MacKay, D.M., MacKay, V.: The time course of the McCollough effect and its physiological implications. J. Physiol. (Lond.) **237**, 38–39P (1974a).

MacKay, D.M., MacKay, V.: Do curvature-contingent chromatic aftereffects require "detectors for curvature"? Vision Res. **14**, 1285–1288 (1974b).

MacKay, D.M., MacKay, V.: What causes decay of pattern-contingent chromatic aftereffects? Vision Res. **15**, 462–464 (1975a).

MacKay, D.M., MacKay, V.: Dichoptic induction of McCollough-type effects. Quart. J. exp. Psychol. **27**, 225–233 (1975b).

MacKay, D.M., MacKay, V.: Psychophysical evidence of neuronal plasticity in the primary visual system. Paper presented at I.U.P.S. Symposium on Brain and Behaviour, New Delhi, 1975c.

MacKay, V., MacKay, D.M.: Multiple orientation-contingent chromatic after-effects. Quart. J. exp. Psychol. **29**, 203–218 (1977).

Masland, R.H.: Visual motion perception: Experimental modification. Science **165**, 819–821 (1969).

Maudarbocus, A.Y., Ruddock, K.H.: The influence of wavelength on visual adaptation to spatially periodic stimuli. Vision Res. **13**, 993–998 (1973).

Maudarbocus, A.Y., Ruddock, K.H.: Comments on "Adaptation to pairs of coloured gratings: Inhibition between colour-specific spatial detectors in the human visual system?" Vision Res. **14**, 1485–1488 (1974).

Maudarbocus, A.Y., Ruddock, K.H.: The organisation of visual pathways as revealed by adaptation experiments with monochromatic linear gratings. (In preparation.)

May, J.G.: Chromatic adaptation of orientation- and size-specific visual processes in man. Vision Res. **12**, 1509–1517 (1972).

May, J.G., Agamy, G., Matteson, H.H.: The range of spatial frequency contingency color aftereffects. Paper presented to Meeting of Association for Research in Vision and Ophthalmology, 1976.

May, J.G., Leftwich, D.A., Aptaker, P.: Evoked potential correlates of adaptation to wavelength and orientation. Vision Res. **14**, 143–146 (1974).

Mayhew, J.E.W.: Directional asymmetry in the duration of simple movement aftereffects produced by movement aftereffects contingent on colour. Perception **1**, 453–457 (1972).

Mayhew, J.E.W.: Luminance thresholds for motion contingent on colour. Perception **2**, 41–51 (1973).

Mayhew, J.E.W., Anstis, S.M.: Movement aftereffects contingent on color, intensity, and pattern. Percept. Psychophys. **12**, 77–85 (1972).

McCollough, C.: Color adaptation of edge-detectors in the human visual system. Science **149**, 1115–1116 (1965).

McDougall, W.: IV—Some new observations in support of Thomas Young's theory of light- and colour-vision (II). Mind, N.S. **10**, 210–245 (1901).
McFarland, S.F.: A personal experience with prismatic glasses. Trans. Amer. ophthal. Soc. **3**, 479–480 (1883).
Michael, C.R.: Color-sensitive complex cells in primate striate cortex. Paper presented to Meeting of Association for Research in Vision and Ophthalmology, 1975.
Murch, G.M.: Size judgments of McCollough afterimages. J. exp. Psychol. **81**, 44–48 (1969).
Murch, G.M.: Binocular relationships in a size and color orientation specific aftereffect. J. exp. Psychol. **93**, 30–34 (1972).
Murch, G.M.: Color contingent motion aftereffects: Single or multiple levels of processing? Vision Res. **14**, 1181–1184 (1974).
Murch, G.M., Hirsch, J.: The McCollough effect created by complementary afterimages. Amer. J. Psychol. **85**, 241–247 (1972).
Myers, K.J., Ingling, C.R. Jr., Drum, B.A.: Brightness additivity for a grating target. Vision Res. **13**, 1165–1173 (1973).
Osgood, A.G.: The role of bar width, slit width and spatial frequency on an orientation contingent color aftereffect known as the McCollough effect. Doctoral dissertation. Kansas State University, Manhattan, Kansas (1974).
Over, R.: Comparison of normalization theory and neural enhancement explanation of negative aftereffects. Psychol. Bull. **75**, 225–243 (1971).
Over, R., Long, N., Lovegrove, W.: Absence of binocular interaction between spatial and color attributes of visual stimuli. Percept. Psychophys. **13**, 534–540 (1973).
Over, R., Lovegrove, W.: Color-selectivity in simultaneous motion contrast. Percept. Psychophys. **14**, 445–448 (1973).
Pantle, A.: Flicker adaptation-I. Effect on visual sensitivity to temporal fluctuations of light intensity. Vision Res. **11**, 943–952 (1971).
Pantle, A., Sekuler, R.: Size-detecting mechanisms in human vision. Science **162**, 1146–1148 (1968a).
Pantle, A.J., Sekuler, R.W.: Velocity-sensitive elements in human vision: Initial psychophysical evidence. Vision Res. **8**, 445–450 (1968b).
Papert, S.: Stereoscopic synthesis as a technique for localizing visual mechanisms. Quart. Prog. Rep. Lab. of Electronics, Massachusetts Institute of Technology **73**, 239–243 (1964).
Pieper, W.: Dynamische Filterprozesse im visuellen System des Menschen — Farbgesetzmäßigkeiten beim McCollough-Nacheffekt. Paper presented at Symposium Neuropsychologie der Wahrnehmung, Kongreß der Deutschen Gesellschaft für Psychologie, Salzburg, 1974.
Poggio, G.F., Baker, F.H., Mansfield, R.J.W., Sillito, A., Grigg, P.: Spatial and chromatic properties of neurons subserving foveal and parafoveal vision in rhesus monkey. Brain Res. **100**, 25–59 (1975).
Post, R.B., Lodge, H.R.: Effects of field structure and contrast on color-motion aftereffects. Paper presented to Meeting of Association for Research in Vision and Ophthalmology, 1975.
Potts, M.J., Harris, J.P.: Movement aftereffects contingent on the colour or pattern of a stationary surround. Vision Res. **15**, 1225–1230 (1975).
Rauschecker, J.P.J., Campbell, F.W., Atkinson, J.: Colour opponent neurones in the human visual system. Nature (Lond.) **245**, 42–43 (1973).
Richards, W., Smith, R.A.: Midbrain as a site for the motion after-effect. Nature (Lond.) **223**, 533–534 (1969).
Riggs, L.A.: Curvature as a feature of pattern vision. Science **181**, 1070–1072 (1973).
Riggs, L.A., White, K.D., Eimas, P.D.: Establishment and decay of orientation-contingent aftereffects of color. Percept. Psychophys. **16**, 535–542 (1974).
Sekuler, R.W.: Spatial and temporal determinants of visual backward masking. J. exp. Psychol. **70**, 401–406 (1965).
Sekuler, R.W., Ganz, L.: Aftereffect of seen motion with a stabilized retinal image. Science **139**, 419–420 (1963).
Sekuler, R., Pantle, A.: A model for after-effects of seen movement. Vision Res. **7**, 427–439 (1967).
Sharpe, C.R.: The colour specificity of spatial adaptation: Red-blue interactions. Vision Res. **14**, 41–51 (1974).
Shattuck, S.R., Held, R.: Color-contingent tilt aftereffect interacts with spatial frequency and also produces stereo depth. Paper presented to Meeting of Eastern Psychological Association, 1974.

Shattuck, S., Held, R.: Color and edge sensitive channels converge on stereo-depth analyzers. Vision Res. **15**, 309–311 (1975).

Sigel, C., Nachmias, J.: A re-evaluation of curvature-specific chromatic aftereffects. Vision Res. **15**, 829–836 (1975).

Skowbo, D., Gentry, T., Timney, B., Morant, R.B.: The McCollough effect: Influence of several kinds of visual stimulation on decay rate. Percept. Psychophys. **16**, 47–49 (1974).

Smith, R.A. Jr.: Studies of temporal frequency adaptation in visual contrast sensitivity. J. Physiol. (Lond.) **216**, 531–552 (1971).

Snow, C.E.: Edge-specific color aftereffect and phantom fringes as produced by the color adaptation of edge detector. A.B. thesis. Oberlin College, Oberlin, Ohio (1966).

Stromeyer, C.F. III: Colored aftereffects related to edges. Doctoral dissertation. Harvard University, Cambridge, Massachusetts (1968).

Stromeyer, C.F.: Further studies of the McCollough effect. Percept. Psychophys. **6**, 105–110 (1969).

Stromeyer, C.F. III: McCollough effect analogs of two-color projections. Vision Res. **11**, 969–978 (1971).

Stromeyer, C.F. III: Edge-contingent color after effects: Spatial frequency specificity. Vision Res. **12**, 717–733 (1972a).

Stromeyer, C.F. III: Contour-contingent color aftereffects: Retinal area specificity. Amer. J. Psychol. **85**, 227–235 (1972b).

Stromeyer, C.F. III: Curvature detectors in human vision? Science **184**, 1199–1200 (1974a).

Stromeyer, C.F. III: Form-specific colour after effects observed in scotopic illumination. Nature (Lond.) **250**, 266–268 (1974b).

Stromeyer, C.F. III: Rod signals in higher color mechanisms: The McCollough color aftereffect observed in scotopic illumination. In: Moskowitz, H., Scharf, B., Stevens, J.C. (eds.): Measurement and psychophysics: Papers in honor of S.S. Stevens. Dordrecht, Holland: Reidel 1974c.

Stromeyer, C.F. III, Dawson, B.M.: McCollough colour after effect. Nature (Lond.) **249**, 777–778 (1974).

Stromeyer, C.F. III, Dawson, B.M.: Color adaptation of convexity detectors in human vision. (In preparation.)

Stromeyer, C.F. III, Dawson, B.M.: Form-colour aftereffects: Selectivity to local luminance contrast. Perception. In press (1978).

Stromeyer, C.F. III, Dawson, B.M., Klein, S.: Orientation selectivity of contour dependent color aftereffects. McCollough effects. (In preparation.)

Stromeyer, C.F. III, Lange, A.F., Ganz, L.: Spatial frequency phase effects in human vision. Vision Res. **13**, 2345–2360 (1973).

Stromeyer, C.F. III, Mansfield, R.J.W.: Colored aftereffects produced with moving edges. Percept. Psychophys. **7**, 108–114 (1970).

Stromeyer, C.F. ·III, Sternheim, C.E.: The spectral sensitivity of Stiles's π_4 and π_5 mechanisms at various spatial frequencies (In preparation.)

Sutherland, N.S.: Figural after-effects and apparent size. Quart. J. exp. Psychol. **13**, 222–228 (1961).

Teft, L.W., Clark, F.T.: The effects of stimulus density on orientation specific aftereffects of color adaptation. Psychon. Sci. **11**, 265–266 (1968).

Timney, B.N., Gentry, T.A., Skowbo, D., Morant, R.B.: Chromatic grating thresholds and the McCollough effect. Vision Res. **14**, 1033–1036 (1974).

Timney, B.N., Gentry, T.A., Skowbo, D., Morant, R.B.: Threshold elevation following adaptation to coloured gratings. Vision Res. **16**, 601–607 (1976).

Tolhurst, D.J.: On the possible existence of edge detector neurones in the human visual system. Vision Res. **12**, 797–804 (1972).

Troland, L.T.: Preliminary note: The influence of changes of illumination upon after-images. Amer. J. Psychol. **28**, 497–503 (1917).

Uhlarik, J.J., Osgood, A.G.: The role of some spatial parameters of gratings on the McCollough effect. Percept. Psychophys. **15**, 524–528 (1974).

Vidyasagar, T.R.: Orientation specific colour adaptation at a binocular site. Nature (Lond.) **261**, 39–40 (1976).

Virsu, V., Haapasalo, S.: Relationships between channels for colour and spatial frequency in human vision. Perception **2**, 31–40 (1973).

Vos, J.J.: Some new aspects of color stereoscopy. J. opt. Soc. Amer. **50**, 785–790 (1960).

Walker, J.T.: A texture-contingent visual motion aftereffect. Psychon. Sci. **28**, 333–335 (1972).

Ware, C., Mitchell, D.E.: The spatial selectivity of the tilt aftereffect. Vision Res. **14**, 735–737 (1974).

White, K.D.: Luminance as a parameter in the establishment and testing of the McCollough effect. Vision Res. **16**, 297–302 (1976a).

White, K.D.: Studies of orientation-contingent color aftereffects. Doctoral dissertation. Brown University, Providence, Rhode Island (1976b).

White, K.D., Ellis, S.R.: McCollough effect: Pattern-alternation rate influences establishment. J. opt. Soc. Amer. **65**, 1200 (1975).

White, K.D., Graves, A.L.: Influence of achromatic inspection on McCollough effects. Paper presented to Meeting of Association for Research in Vision and Ophthalmology, 1976.

White, K.D., Hirsch, D.: Orientation-contingent color aftereffects: Time courses of decay following two inspection sessions. Paper presented to Meeting of Association for Research in Vision and Opthalmology, 1975.

White, K.D., Riggs, L.A.: Angle-contingent color aftereffects. Vision Res. **14**, 1147–1154 (1974a).

White, K.D., Riggs, L.A.: Angle- and curvature-contingent color aftereffects. Paper presented to Meeting of Association for Research in Vision and Ophthalmology, 1974b.

White, K.D., Riggs, L.A.: Binocular rivalry during establishment of the McCollough effect. J. opt. Soc. Amer. **65**, 1200 (1975).

Wiesel, T.N., Hubel, D.H.: Spatial and chromatic interactions in the lateral geniculate body of the rhesus monkey. J. Neurophysiol. **29**, 1115–1156 (1966).

Wohlgemuth, A.: On the after-effect of seen movement. Brit. J. Psychol. Monogr. Suppl. **1**, 1–117 (1911).

Wyatt, H.J.: Singly and doubly contingent after-effects involving color, orientation and spatial frequency. Vision Res. **14**, 1185–1193 (1974).

Yund, E.W., deValois, R.L., Hepler, N.K.: Where have all the colors gone? Paper presented to Meeting of Association for Research in Vision and Ophthalmology, 1973.

Chapter 5

Phonetic Perception

ALVIN M. LIBERMAN* and MICHAEL STUDDERT-KENNEDY,**
New Haven, Connecticut (USA)

With 6 Figures

Contents

To include a chapter on phonetic perception in a handbook like this is to assume that the process is not wholly accounted for by such principles as we might find in research on the perception of nonspeech sounds. It is appropriate, then, that we here offer support for that assumption. We will

---

* Also University of Connecticut and Yale University.
** Also Queens College and Graduate Center of the City University of New York.

not examine all relevant considerations, only those that bear most directly on the relation between the information in the acoustic signal and the listener's perceptual response to it; in our view, those are the most pertinent. Nor will we analyze such arguments as there are for the opposite assumption — namely, that auditory mechanisms are sufficient — though we will, as is proper, refer the reader to relevant papers[1].

Phonetic perception is what happens when, on hearing speech, a listener recovers the phonetic message. That message consists of the meaningless segments we perceive as consonants and vowels. These are ordered in strings, organized into larger units, and carried on a prosodic contour. The segments, both consonants and vowels, are called "phones"; among the larger units are syllables; the relevant aspects of prosody are stress and intonation. We must distinguish between the perceived phones and the more abstract phonologic forms that underlie them. Thus, the final segments in "cats" and "dogs" are different phones — voiceless [s] in "cats" and voiced [z] in "dogs" — yet at a more abstract phonologic (or morphophonemic) level they are the same. Our concern will be with the less abstract phones and their relation to the still less abstract sounds. Also, to keep our task within bounds, we will deal only with the segmental aspects of phonetic structure, including the organization of phones into syllables, though perception of prosody presents interesting, perhaps even similar, problems.

Students of language commonly assume a complex, grammatic relation between meaning and its phonetic vehicle, but often disregard the further complications that arise in the conversion to sound. They tend rather to suppose that the phonetic segments (or their constituent features) are represented discretely in the signal, as if by an acoustic alphabet. If that were so, perceiving phones would be like perceiving any other sounds; there would be no special problem of phonetic perception and no reason for this chapter. There is evidence, however, that the sounds of speech are not an alphabet on the phones, but a complex and grammatic code. In the first section of the paper we will place that code in the larger scheme of language and identify its important characteristics.

If it is true that the phones are linked to the sounds by a special code, we should suppose that extracting the phones from the sounds would require a correspondingly special decoder. In the second section we will give reasons for supposing that such a decoder may exist.

There is, of course, an alternative to grappling with the problems created by the peculiar relation between sound and phonetic message: We can try to evade them. Indeed, we might suppose that phonetic perception does not occur, that the segments of the phonetic level are mere fictions, invented by linguists for their convenience, with no functional significance in language or in its psychophysiology. In that view the listener would go directly from sound to some meaningful segment (for example, word), bypassing the phonetic and phonologic structure entirely. To justify our concern with phonetic perception, we will, in the third section, argue that phonetic (and phonologic) structure plays an important role in language and is, in fact, recovered by the listener when he comprehends what is said to him.

[1] For reviews of speech perception research from several points of view, see DARWIN, 1976; PISONI, in press; STEVENS and HOUSE, 1972.

A. Special Nature of the Speech Code: Function, Form, and Key

For anyone who would understand the perception of speech, the salient fact is that the perceived phones are related to the sounds by a peculiar grammatic code, one of several that link sound to meaning. To grasp the nature of that code, it is useful to view it as part of the larger grammar (see, for example, MATTINGLY and LIBERMAN, 1969; LIBERMAN, 1970). For that purpose, we will divide grammar — and language — in two. Making the cut at the phonetic level, we will look first toward meaning and then, in the other direction, toward sound.

I. Function of the Meaningless Phones and of the Grammatic Codes Linking Them to the Meaningful Message

To see what grammar accomplishes, and thus to appreciate the role of the meaningless phones, we should first consider the shortcomings of an agrammatic mode of communication (see LIBERMAN et al., 1972; LIBERMAN, in press). In that mode, there would be a straightforward connection between message and signal. Instead of grammatic rules like those that build longer and more complex structures (syllables and sentences, for example) out of shorter and simpler ones (phones and words), there would be only a list of all possible messages and their corresponding signals. Obviously, such a mode would work well enough if there were reasonable agreement in number between messages and signals. But, just as obviously, there is no such agreement: The number of messages we have to send is vastly greater than the number of holistically different signals we can efficiently produce and perceive, especially if we are committed to signaling with sound. In short, an agrammatic mode of communication would limit the number of possible messages to the small number of distinctively different sounds we can produce and perceive. The consequence would be that most of what we want to express with language would be inexpressible.

We should suppose, then, that one function of grammatic codes is to restructure the information in the messages so as to make it compatible with our sound-signaling ability, and thus to match the potentialities of the message-generating intellect to the limitations of the vocal tract and the ear. But why two grammars, syntax and phonology, and why the two kinds of segments, meaningful and meaningless, they govern? What is the function of this dual structure, characteristic of all languages, and especially of the meaningless, phonologic portion that concerns us in this chapter? Why not, in a simpler world, have only a syntax — rules that organize and reorganize segments (words, for example) that are meaningful? Such a language could, from a logical point of view, evade the limitations imposed by the paucity of different segments, since it would be possible, even with a small set, to construct an infinitude of messages. A phonology-free language would, of course, have to make do with a small vocabulary, but that is not, in logic, a devastating limitation. For to the extent that we can organize our semantic space by a hierarchy of features, a small vocabulary might nevertheless suffice for many of the things we want to talk about (OGDEN, 1967). But specifying a particular thing would, at best, take a lot of talking and listening, given the properties of vocal tracts and ears, and it would require, in addition, that one's mind work in ways that may be uncongenial to it.

At all events, no language does get along with a very small vocabulary. Vocabularies tend to be large and to grow ever larger (but see KLIMA, 1975, pp. 247–270). To achieve these large vocabularies, given the limited number of signals we can command, languages use a very few meaningless segments—two to three dozen, in most cases—to construct a large number of meaningful ones; hence, phonology. Taken together, then, syntax and phonology serve as a kind of interface, joining an intellect, which initiates, comprehends, and stores messages, to a vocal tract and ear, which produce and receive the sounds by which those messages are conveyed (MATTINGLY, 1972; LIBERMAN, 1974).

II. Function of the (Grammatic) Speech Code Linking Phonetic Message to Sound

Perhaps the need for grammatical recoding has ended with the production of the phonetic message. If so, the final link to speech could be agrammatic—a unit of sound for each segment of the message—and thus of no special interest to either the linguist or psychologist. But the phonetic message is only a stage in the grammatic process that connects meaning to sound. Further and still quite drastic restructuring is necessary. To see why, we need only put the most obvious requirements of phonetic communication against the capabilities of the ear and the vocal tract. Although that has been done in earlier publications (LIBERMAN et al., 1967; LIBERMAN et al., 1972; STUDDERT-KENNEDY, in press), we nevertheless offer a brief review here.

Two requirements of phonetic communication are of special interest: The phones must be communicated at a high rate, and their order must be properly apprehended by the listener. With regard to rate, it is obvious enough that language is more efficient the more rapidly it is communicated. It is only slightly less obvious that language is hard to understand when it is communicated too slowly. Slow communication can create difficulties because the meaning of the longer segments is distributed in complicated ways among the shorter segments they comprise. Hence full comprehension of a sentence, for example, must wait on completion of a structure that is formed by the words. The requirement about order follows from the use of a small number of phonetic segments. If we are to keep the number of segments per word within bounds, we must respect order: a word like "dam" must be distinguished from its mirror image, "mad".

It is plain that if the phonetic segments were transmitted agrammatically—that is, each phone by a discrete segment of sound—the requirements of phonetic communication would not be met. We could neither speak nor listen as fast as we need to—and, indeed, do—nor could the listener keep the segments in their proper order. Speaking rates vary considerably, but they reach 20–25 phones/s, at least for short stretches. Presumably, it would be impossible to speak that rapidly if, as in an agrammatic mode, the gestures were made discretely, one for every phone and each in its turn. And even if the speaker could articulate that fast, the listener could not resolve the sound segments that would result; at 20–25 acoustic segments/s, the units of sound (hence phones) would merge to produce, in perception, a buzz or pitch. Moreover, the listener would have difficulty identifying the order of such discrete sound units, even at rates low enough to permit him to resolve them. Given the results of research on nonspeech sounds (WARREN et al., 1969; 1976b), we should suppose that he could distinguish permutations of segments, but only on the basis of overall differences in the perceived pattern, not by assigning each segment to its own place in a sequence. Surely, then, the grammatic restructuring that makes communication distinctively linguistic cannot end with the production of the phonetic message. At least one more grammatic conversion is necessary if the message is to be transmitted and perceived efficiently.

III. Form of the (Grammatic) Speech Code Linking Phonetic Message to Sound; Fit of Form to Function

In the conversion of abstract phones to concrete sounds there is a restructuring of information, designed as if to match the requirements of phonetic communication to the properties of the vocal tract and the ear. Though much that is important about this conversion remains to be learned, enough is known to enable us to see some of its important characteristics. Thus, we know that the segments are first broken down into something like the well-known articulatory features of place of production, manner of production, and voicing[2] (for an explication, see, for example, LADEFOGED, 1971). As speech is produced, those separate features are assigned to the appropriate and more-or-less independent parts of the articulatory apparatus; the component gestures made by those parts are organized into preplanned coding units longer than a phonetic segment; and the organized complex of gestures, representing features of each of several successive phonetic segments, is produced simultaneously or with considerable overlap. The result is that the coding unit—roughly a syllable in many cases—comprises segments whose component gestures (features) are thoroughly interleaved (COOPER et al., 1952; FANT, 1962; LIBERMAN et al., 1967; COOPER,

[2] In the case of the consonants, place of production refers to where in the mouth—lips, alveolar ridge, or velum, for example—the consonant constriction is made; manner of production refers to an articulatory maneuver—velum closed or open, tract totally closed or only partly closed, for example—that is characteristic of phones with the same place of production; voicing distinguishes classes of phones having the same place and manner according to the state of the vocal cords—open or closed—at the beginning of the gesture.

1972; STEVENS and HOUSE, 1972; STUDDERT-KENNEDY, 1975a). We will call that arrangement by its common name, coarticulation.

Coarticulation enables a speaker to produce phonetic segments at rates considerably higher than the rates at which he must change the states of his articulatory muscles (COOPER, 1972). Thus, he speaks faster than he could if each phonetic segment were represented by a unit gesture, produced in its proper turn as one of a sequence of gestures. But coarticulation has consequences for perception as well, enabling the listener to evade just those limitations of the auditory system we referred to earlier. Consider, again, that if the phonetic message were transmitted agrammatically—that is, one acoustic segment for each phonetic segment—then the temporal resolving power of the ear would make it impossible to perceive speech at the rates that we do, in fact, commonly attain. But, as we have seen, the relation between phonetic message and sound is not agrammatic in that sense. Rather, coarticulation effectively folds information about several successive phonetic segments into a single stretch of sound. Moreover, the overlapped activity of several different articulators, e.g., lips and tongue, will often affect the same parameter of the sound, e.g., second formant[3]. At any chosen instant of time, therefore, each acoustic parameter is (commonly) carrying information about more than one phonetic segment. (For fuller discussion, see LIBERMAN et al., 1967.) That being so, the limit on rate of phonetic perception caused by the temporal resolving power of the ear is no longer set by the number of phonetic segments transmitted per unit time, but by the considerably smaller number of acoustic segments into which those phonetic segments have been encoded. Just how much saving is effected in this manner depends, of course, on the size of the encoding unit; and that will surely vary according to the nature of the contiguous phones in the string, rate of articulation, and other factors that we only dimly understand. But a significant amount of encoding will almost always occur—most obviously within the syllable—and it will, at every rate of articulation, effectively reduce the number of discrete acoustic segments that must be perceived.

Consider, now again, the difficulty the auditory system would have in identifying the order of phonetic segments at even moderate rates of speech if each phonetic segment were represented by an acoustic segment. But inasmuch as the phonetic segments are not so represented, the problem of identifying order of discrete acoustic segments does not arise (DAY, 1970; LIBERMAN et al., 1972; COLE and SCOTT, 1974; DORMAN et al., 1975a). Recall how successive phonetic segments are encoded into the same stretch of sound, and imagine, for example, simple cases like [ba] and [ab]. If these syllables are produced at moderately rapid rates of articulation, it will be true of both acoustic patterns that information about the consonant and the vowel is carried simultaneously from the beginning of the sound to its end. But given that the articulatory gestures have opposite directions in the two cases—from closed (consonant) to open (vowel) for [ba] and from open (vowel) to closed (consonant) in [ab]—the acoustic shapes of the two acoustic syllables will be different. Indeed, they will be

[3] A formant is a peak in the resonance curve of the vocal tract. The center value of this peak, specified in Hz, is called the formant frequency.

mirror images: For [ba] the formants will be rising throughout; for [ab] they will be falling. Thus, information about the order of phonetic segments is present in the acoustic signal, not as discrete events in ordered sequence, but as variations in shape or form (LIBERMAN, 1976).

IV. Key to the Speech Code

Suppose the speech code were entirely arbitrary. In that case, a perceiving device could only match the signal against a dictionary of auditory templates, just as if it were using a code book. Of course, the templates could not correspond to segments the size of phones but would, rather, have to be at least as large as the coding unit that encompasses the acoustic consequences of coarticulation. As we remarked earlier, we do not know exactly how large that unit is or how stable it might be in the face of variations in speaking rate, word and phrasal stress, and other conditions of articulation. We can only suppose that, at the smallest, the unit would have to be of approximately syllabic size, since there is normally so much coarticulation within syllable boundaries.

But the speech code is not arbitrary; there is a key that unlocks it. To see the nature of the key, and how it makes sense of the relation between message and signal, we need only remind ourselves that the peculiarities of the speech code are just those that are introduced by the speaker as he lends himself to the processes by which the message is encoded in the sound. When those processes are understood, their consequences can hardly appear arbitrary. Thus, the key to the code is in the manner of its production. We should remark parenthetically that in this respect speech is like the rest of language and different from most other processes: All the complications of language that the hearer must cope with are only those that, as speaker, he "knows" how to introduce; the complications of nonlinguistic perception, on the other hand, are typically not owing to the hearer (or viewer) but are, rather, external to him. At all events, the processes by which speech is produced make it possible to understand the relation between acoustic signal and phonetic message, however peculiar that relation might be.

Although knowing how speech is produced enables us to see why the complications of the code should be peculiar in the way they are, it does not provide an automatic decoding procedure. Thus, we now understand enough about the speech code to be able to synthesize speech by rule (INGEMANN, 1957; LIBERMAN et al., 1959; KELLY and GERSTMAN, 1961; KELLY and LOCHBAUM, 1962; COOPER, 1962; for a summary, see MATTINGLY, 1974). That is, we can build a mechanism that accepts as input a string of phonetic symbols and then, as output, delivers speech. Using rules for the conversion that can be either acoustic or articulatory, the synthesizer produces speech that is imperfect—reflecting our imperfect command of the code—but rather highly intelligible, nevertheless, and reasonably acceptable. Now if we could simply turn those rules around, we should have a working model for speech perception. Unfortunately, the rules for synthesis, like all grammatic rules, work in only one direction: downhill; they take us from message to signal but not the other way. Perhaps there are rules that go in either direction, but they have not yet been found. Thus, to suggest that a listener might use the rules as a key, is only to imply some kind of connection between perception and production, of which more later; the underlying mechanism is, at present, unknown.

B. Special Processes of Phonetic Perception

Surely the most parsimonious way to account for phonetic perception is to invoke only those mechanisms that are more or less common to mammalian (or primate) auditory systems (see MILLER, in press). Can we suppose, then, that such processes are sufficient, or must we look to specializations of various kinds? If specializations do exist, are they in the form of auditory devices that are tuned to respond to the phonetically relevant parts of the speech signal? Or are they more accurately characterized as integral parts of a system, more linguistic than auditory, that is specialized to deal with the peculiarities of grammatic codes? In this section we will consider whether both such types of specializations might exist — the one to deal with the purely acoustic characteristics of the perceptually important parts of the signal and the other to cope with the grammatic code relating the signal to the phonetic information it conveys.

I. Auditory Specializations for Extracting the Phonetically Relevant Information From the Speech Signal

Many important attributes of the speech signal, including some that carry a heavy load of phonetic information, are not physically salient. For example, although most of the linguistically important information is contained in the lowest three formants, the acoustic energy is not tightly concentrated there but is, rather, smeared diffusely over the entire speech spectrum. Or again, despite the fact that consonants carry a far heavier load of segmental phonetic information than do vowels, they are signaled by far less acoustically prominent portions of the spoken syllable. Thus, formant frequency shifts (transitions) that carry important, even essential, information about consonantal place of articulation often make excursions of hundreds of cycles in some 30–40 ms. Since humans seem to have no difficulty in extracting that information, one is led to wonder whether there may not be devices in the auditory system specialized for that purpose. These devices would be analogous, perhaps, to the feature detectors found in other species.

We have in mind the example of the cat, in which WHITFIELD and EVANS (1965) found single cells ("miaow" cells) responsive to the rate and direction of frequency change. WHITFIELD (1965) pointed out the possible relevance of this finding to the perception of formant transitions in speech when he suggested that such units might be ". . . a final link in the mechanism . . . by which speech-like and similar signals are processed (p. 247)." If WHITFIELD is correct, we would have, not an auditory specialization for language, but rather a general auditory device (perhaps typical of mammals) that is exploited by humans for linguistic purposes.

In fact, an auditory mechanism specialized for language may be difficult to demonstrate, since we obviously cannot apply to humans the electrophysiologic techniques that have been used on animals. It may, however, be possible to approach the matter indirectly, as, for example, by extending to speech, adaptation procedures originally developed in studies of vision. The first to do this were EIMAS and CORBIT (1973). With synthetic syllables (for example, [ba] vs. [pa]) ranging along an acoustic continuum, these investigators used the techniques of adaptation to produce shifts in the position of the perceptual boundary. The results led them to speculate that their procedures had affected a pair of binary phonetic feature detectors, and that adaptation or fatigue of one detector functionally sensitized its opponent. Subsequent work (see COOPER, 1975, for a review) demonstrated analogous effects for other consonantal feature oppositions. If these effects were truly on phonetic features, they would only provide additional evidence for the "reality" of such entities and offer still another method, though potentially a most useful one, for defining their boundaries.

More relevant to our concerns here, therefore, are adaptation studies like the one by BAILEY (1973), which showed that the effect decreased with a decrease in spectral overlap between adapting and test syllables. This suggests that if feature analyzing systems were indeed being isolated, the features were auditory rather than phonetic (for a relevant discussion, see ADES, in press). The finding by BAILEY assumes considerable importance from our point of view, because there is apparently no other kind of evidence for the existence of feature analyzing systems of an auditory sort. Unfortunately, the matter appears not so simple. Further investigation has shown that the degree of adaptation is contingent on so many other aspects of the synthetic continuum, including intensity (GANONG, 1976) and fundamental frequency (ADES, in press), that one may, in the end, be led to doubt the feature interpretation altogether. Perhaps, then, the achievement of the work on selective adaptation will have been to demonstrate the operation of distinct perceptual channels rather than the existence of feature detectors as such. Nevertheless, the investigators may have found a method for exposing processes that respond to linguistically significant parts of the speech signal, and thus to have made possible the discovery of auditory specializations for language.

II. Linguistic Specialization for Recovering the Phonetic Message

Even if auditory detectors of the kind just discussed do exist, they could do no more than extract from the acoustic signal those features that are phonetically relevant. They might thus solve problems created by the fact that speech is, in certain respects, a poor signal, but it would presumably remain to some other device, more phonetic than auditory, to deal with the different fact that speech is a special code. As we were at pains to point out earlier, the peculiar characteristics of the code arise from the way speech is produced, in particular, from coarticulation. We should suppose, then, that the distinguishing characteristic of the phonetic device would be that it somehow makes use of that circumstance (COOPER et al., 1952; LIBERMAN et al., 1952). For the present, the emphasis should be on the word "somehow"; we do not wish to speculate about the underlying mechanism, if only because we cannot offer relevant data. But if there is a device that behaves, by whatever means, as if it "understood" how speech is produced, then we should expect to find evidence for a link between perception and production. Indeed, it would be just such a linkage that would clearly characterize phonetic as against auditory perception (STUDDERT-KENNEDY, 1976; LIBERMAN and PISONI, in press).

In the sections that follow, we will identify several kinds of support for the assumption that there is a phonetic perceiving device and, correspondingly, a phonetic mode of perception. Some of that support is indirect in that it depends on our inability to account for certain phenomena of speech perception in terms of what we now know of how the ear works and what it commonly does; but some is more direct, being based on putative differences between auditory and phonetic perception and, in some cases, on the apparent links to production that characterize the phonetic mode.

1. Coping With the Segmentation

If there were an acoustic criterion that could directly divide the speech stream into segments corresponding in size to the phones, then we should see no need to invoke other-than-auditory processes. No matter how complex in structure the acoustic segments might be, we should suppose that correspondingly complex auditory processes would be equal to the job. As we have seen, however, one of the characteristics of the speech code is that the phonetic information is distributed in curious ways through the sound. This is the most striking disparity between acoustic signal and phonetic message and, from the standpoint of a perceiving device, the most troublesome. Indeed, the disparity is greater than our characterization of the speech code might have implied, since the sound segments do not map onto the phones either in the way they divide or in the way they group. Thus, rapid switches in sound source during the articulation of successive phones may spread the information about a single message segment through several acoustic segments (FANT, 1962, 1968), as when stop-consonant closure and release into a following vowel yield a brief silence, an explosive release, a period of aspirated noise, and a more-or-less abrupt voice onset. On the other hand, coarticulation may, as we have previously noted, cause the information about several message segments to be collapsed within a single segment of sound.

The severity of the problem is evidenced by the fact that it has resisted solution for many years, as much by those concerned with speech synthesis as by those working on automatic speech recognition. Both groups have been driven to acknowledge that segments the size of phones are not to be found *as segments* in the acoustic stream; the irreducible acoustic unit is of approximately syllabic dimensions, just as we would expect, given the very earliest result of research with synthetic speech (COOPER et al., 1952; LIBERMAN et al., 1952). In the first attempt to "synthesize" speech by commuting (and concatenating) segments of sound excised from prerecorded utterances, HARRIS (1953) found that the "building blocks" had to be larger than phones. Other investigators (PETERSON et al., 1958) later reported some success in producing speech by concatenating prerecorded segments, but the segments they required were a numerous and varied assortment of syllables and "phoneme dyads." Significant improvements in this method of synthesis have recently been made by FUJIMURA (1975, in press), though again the unit must be larger than the phone. And now, even in synthesis by rule, MATTINGLY (1976) has found it advantageous to preorganize the phonetic segments into syllables and then use those larger units as input to his synthesis program. As for the work on automatic speech recognition, it has long been plain that segmentation into phones by a straightforward acoustic criterion is hardly possible (HYDE, 1972), though segmentation into syllables can be done reasonably well (MERMELSTEIN, 1975).

The foregoing considerations and facts suggest that phones are not directly perceived but must rather be derived from a running analysis of the signal over stretches of at least syllable length. There is ample experimental evidence that this is so.

Consider, for example, the matter of segment duration and its role in the perception of phones. It is known that, in English, the contrast between voiced and voiceless stops in syllable-final position (e.g., [ab] vs. [ap]) can be determined by the duration of the preceding vowel (DENES, 1955; RAPHAEL, 1972). But what happens, then, if that vowel is itself preceded by the consonant-vowel transitions appropriate to, say, [b], as in [bab] vs. [bap]? Does the listener pay attention only to the duration of the preceding vowel? Presumably he cannot do that if, as we have suggested, the transition cues for the consonant simultaneously carry information about the vowel. And, indeed, he does not. According to recent experiments (Raphael et al., 1975), the duration used by the listener to determine voicing in the final segment includes all, or almost all, of the transition cues for the consonant in the initial segment.

Given only that result, we might suppose nevertheless that the listener takes one part of the acoustic signal as consonant and another part as vowel, provided we further suppose that the voicing of a syllable-final stop is determined by the sum of the durations of consonant plus vowel. At least two other experiments suggest, however, that the listener does not compute consonant and vowel durations on different parts of the syllable. In one of these experiments[4], listeners were asked to adjust the duration of a steady-state vowel to match the duration of the medial vowel in a stop-vowel-stop syllable whose formants had parabolic trajectories. As determined by that simple and direct technique, the perceived duration of the medial vowel was found to include a significant portion of the consonant-vowel transitions.

The other experiment dealt with duration as a cue for the perceived identity of a medial vowel and, simultaneously, with the voicing of a final stop, for example, [bɛt], [bæt], [bɛd], [bæd].[5] The results clearly imply that the listener did not assign one part of the syllable duration to the vowel and another part to the consonant. Rather, it was as if he used the whole duration of the syllable, but used it twice: once to determine the identity of the vowel and again to determine whether the syllable-final stop was voiced or voiceless.

That the information about the phonetic segments is spread through the syllable is indicated also by evidence that the flanking transitions in a CVC syllable are used to judge the identity of the medial vowel. For example, OCHIAI and FUJIMURA (1971) recorded natural, but distinctly articulated words and observed no errors of vowel identification. However, when they presented 50-ms portions gated from the vowel centers, listeners' judgments frequently shifted in directions that could be explained by contextual assimilation. Even more striking are the results of STRANGE et al. (1976). They recorded nine vowels spoken in isolation, and the same nine vowels spoken in various CVC frames. Despite the increased acoustic complexity introduced by a dynamic syllable structure, listeners correctly identified the vowels significantly more often when they were presented in a consonantal frame, even a variable one, than when they were presented in isolation. Thus, for the purpose of identifying the vowels, the perceiving system used those parts of the syllable that also contained information about the consonants. That is yet another reflection of the complex relation in segmentation between signal and message. But it also shows that though the perceptual target is a vowel, for which static formant frequencies are often assumed (PETERSON and BARNEY, 1952), the perceptual system nevertheless prefers the dynamic configuration of a syllable, perhaps because it can then take advantage of the many constraints inherent in the way the vocal apparatus works when it coarticulates.

Considering all that is known about the peculiar disparity in segmentation between perceived message and transmitted signal, we suppose that the appropriately segmented percept lies at some remove from the immediately given auditory pattern, and that it is recovered by processes different from those the auditory system is ordinarily called on to provide. As for the possibility that such special processes make reference to production, we can offer no direct evidence about segmentation as such, only the observation that to find the segments, it must help to understand where they were lost.

---

4 MERMELSTEIN, LIBERMAN, and FOWLER: personal communication.

5 MERMELSTEIN: personal communication.

2. Phonetic Interpretation of the Sounds of Speech

We should now look more directly at some phenomena of speech perception that depend, presumably, on the same decoding processes that perform the segmentation but pertain more closely to what those segments, once retrieved, sound like to a listener. Do they sound like other sounds or do they not? And when not, is there evidence of a link to production?

a) Impressions of the Difference Between Auditory and Phonetic Modes

To convey a feeling for what we mean by the suggestion that the sound of speech is different from the sound of nonspeech, it may be useful to describe several phenomena that are part of the experience of people who work with synthetic speech. One of these is reflected in an observation made by investigators who used the Pattern Playback, an early research synthesizer that converted handpainted spectrograms and other designs into sound (COOPER, 1950; COOPER et al., 1951). Having succeeded in constructing highly schematized spectrograms, like the one at the top of Figure 1, that nevertheless produced intelligible speech, the investigators thought to take advantage of the flexibility of the Playback in order to destroy the intelligibility of speech by a novel and, they assumed, uniquely effective procedure: Instead of drowning the speech in noise, which was the usual way, they would "mislead" the ear. To that end they added to the spectrogram "false" formants, always continuous with the "true" formants, that improperly connected and extended the proper components of the acoustic pattern. An example is shown in the middle and at the bottom of Figure 1. In fact, as the reader can see, the eye is misled. But the ear was not. When the altered pattern was converted to sound, the listener heard the original phonetic message against a loud background of variously pitched whistles. It was as if the perceptual machinery had separated the acoustic effects that a vocal tract can produce from those it cannot. At all events, the effect was of two qualitatively different kinds of perception—articulate, monotone speech in the one case, complex and very bad "music" in the other.

Much the same kind of phenomenon, though on a smaller scale, can be produced, not only on a device like the Pattern Playback, but also on the more modern parallel-resonance synthesizers now in common use. An example is seen in the contrast between the initial stop consonants of the syllables [ba] and [ga]. As shown in Figure 2, a sufficient acoustic cue is the direction of the second-formant transitions, rising for [b] and falling for [g]. Now, given our knowledge of psychoacoustics, we should suppose that those cues would sound like rising and falling glissandos or like chirps of different pitch, depending on how rapidly the formants moved on the frequency scale. And, in fact, when we present the formant-transition cues by themselves, as shown in the inset of Figure 2, that is exactly how they do sound (MATTINGLY et al., 1971; SHATTUCK and KLATT, 1976). But what do we say, then, about the fact that those same transitions are heard in the context of speech as the abstract linguistic events we can only describe as [b] and [g]? Of course, the transition cues are isolated in the one case but part of a larger, if otherwise constant, pattern

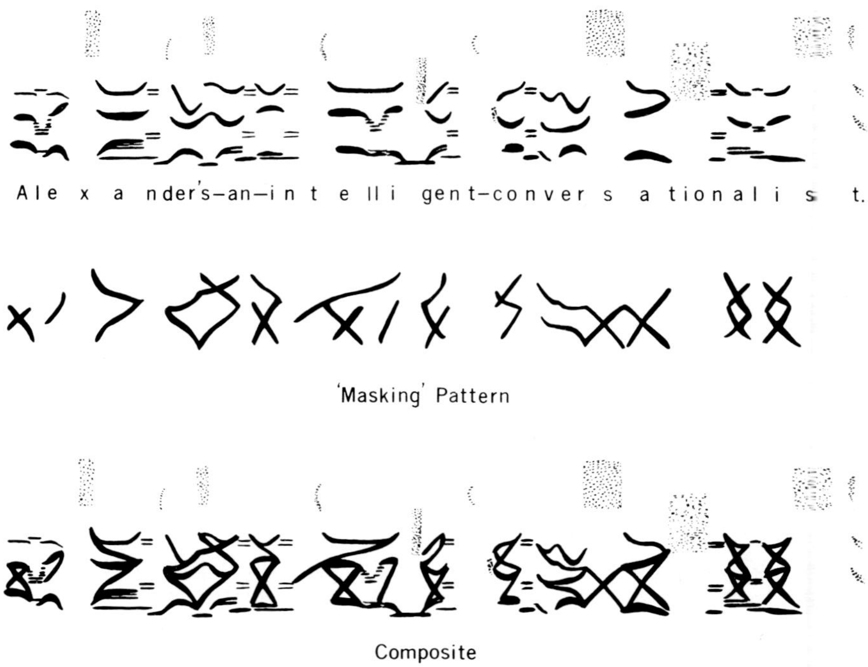

Fig. 1. At the top, a hand-drawn spectrogram appropriate for synthesis of a sentence; in the middle, a pattern intended to "mask" the sentence by "misleading" the ear; and, at the bottom, the composite of sentence and "mask", which produces, again, the perception of the sentence, plus a dissociated set of whistles and noises

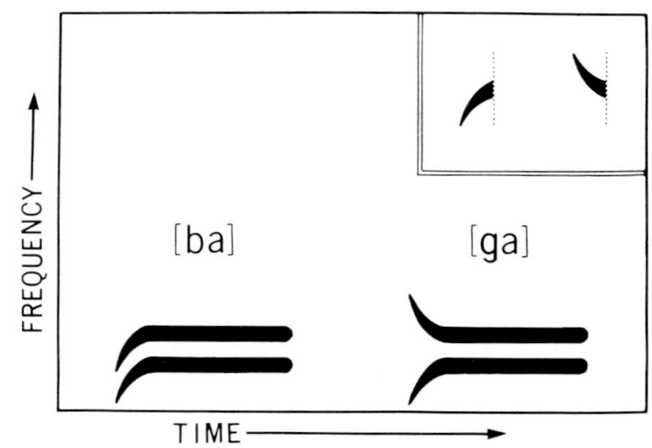

Fig. 2. Spectrographic patterns sufficient for synthesis of [ba] and [ga]. Inset: The second-formant transitions that cue the perceived difference between the syllables, but sound, in isolation, like chirps

in the other, so that we might attribute the difference in perception to some kind of auditory interaction.

But even when the transition cues are in exactly the same acoustic context, it is possible to hear them, simultaneously, as phonetic stops and auditory chirps. That effect was created by RAND (1974) in the following way. Into one ear he put all of the first formant and the steady-state parts of the second and third formants, while into the other ear he put just the transition cues (of the second and third formants) that distinguish [ba] and [ga], being careful to synchronize them properly with respect to the rest of the pattern. Though there is but one context—and indeed one brain—the formant transitions will, in this situation, often simultaneously produce two very different perceptions: the syllable [ba] (or [ga]) and a rising (or falling) chirp.

Essentially the same kind of effect has been created, though successively now instead of simultaneously, as part of an experiment designed by BAILEY et al. (1977) to permit comparison of speech and nonspeech perception. The stimulus patterns are similar to those commonly used in research with synthetic speech in that they contain transitions appropriate to several stop consonant-vowel combinations, followed by vowel steady-states; they differ from those normally used in that the formants are replaced by pure tones, one for each formant and set to its center of energy. On first being presented with such patterns, listeners hear them as a complex of tones, but after some time they begin to hear them as speech. We will not here presume to report on the results of the experimental comparisons that the study was designed to permit; we only remark the phenomenon, which is that there is a striking difference in subjective impression, depending on whether the listener is perceiving the stimulus patterns as tones or as speech; thus, it offers yet another way to gain a general appreciation of the perceptual differences between speech and nonspeech.

At all events, it is just such qualitative contrasts in perception as we have described here that can convey to a listener a direct impression of what we mean by the distinction between auditory and phonetic modes. We turn now to some relevant experimental observations.

b) Acoustic Cues as a Source of Information About What the Speaker's Vocal Tract Did

Those aspects of the speech signal that, when varied, cause phonetically significant changes in perception are known as "acoustic cues." It is to those cues that we should now look, because we find there the clearest evidence for the link between perception and production that characterizes perception in the phonetic mode. No single piece of evidence is, by itself, wholly convincing; it is only the pattern that tells. For when we view the data in the light of known or imaginable auditory processes, we see a number of unconnected facts that require, apparently, an equal number of ad hoc assumptions. If we apply Occam's razor, however, we find a more-or-less comfortable fit to the single assumption underlying this chapter: that the acoustic cues are processed, not only in the auditory system, but also at some more abstract, phonetic remove; there, an appropriately specialized device uses the articulatory information provided by those cues to shape the listener's perception of what the speaker said.

α) A Simple Example. To see how an acoustic cue—silence—might provide information about a phonetically important gesture, we should consider the fol-

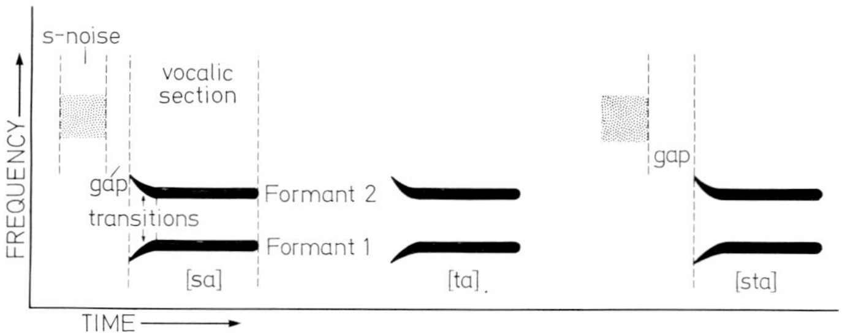

Fig. 3. Schematic spectrograms illustrating the importance of silence for the perception of a stop consonant: [sa] becomes [ta] when the noise is removed, or [sta] when a silent interval of appropriate length is introduced between the noise and the rest of the syllable

lowing facts about fricatives and stop consonants. A speaker cannot produce a stop consonant without closing his vocal tract for a brief period, and he cannot close his vocal tract without producing a period of silence. Hence, silence might be important to the perception of stop consonants, especially if the perceptual processes "know" that stops require closure and that closure results in silence. It is relevant, then, to discover that in the perception of stops silence is, in fact, an important condition.

Suppose, for example, we record the fricative-vowel syllable [sa]. As shown schematically in Figure 3, the acoustic pattern consists of a patch of noise, associated with the fricative, followed by a vocalic section. The vocalic section begins with the formant transitions characteristic of the fricative [s] when coarticulated with the vowel [a]; there follow, then, the steady-state formants characteristic of the (drawn-out) vowel [a]. It should be noted about the formant transitions at the beginning of the vocalic section that they are also appropriate, at least approximately, for the stop consonants [t] and [d], which have the same place of production as [s]. Now if we remove the patch of noise, listeners will commonly hear [ta], not [a]—that is, they will hear a stop consonant where none was before. If we now replace the s-noise in such a way as to create a silence of about 50 ms between it and the vocalic portion, listeners will again hear the stop, this time in [sta]. We should say, parenthetically, that the same kind of effect can be obtained starting with a stop-vowel syllable like [ta]. In that case, putting s-noise immediately in front of the syllable will cause the listener to hear [sa], not [sta]; if the listener to hear [sta], we must create a short period of silence between the s-noise and the vocalic section.

We see in this example that silence has just the sound we should expect it to have, given the assumption that it tells the listener whether or not the speaker closed his vocal tract long enough to have produced a stop consonant. But, surely, there might be other, perhaps more parsimonious, assumptions. We note in this connection that our examples conform to the paradigm for auditory forward masking, so we should take account of the possibility that the transition cues are simply being masked when the noise is too close to them; or we suppose, more vaguely, that there is some (not previously discovered) auditory interaction between silence and the transition cues which causes us to hear the peculiar sound of a stop consonant.

But there is considerable evidence that such alternative assumptions will not hold. Note, first, that in fricative-vowel syllables like the [sa] of our example, it has been found that the formant transitions contribute significantly to the perception of the fricative (HARRIS, 1958; DARWIN, 1971). We should suppose, therefore, that the transition cues are "getting through"—that is, they are not being masked by the s-noise. It is only their (phonetic) interpretation as fricative (when the silence is relatively short) or stop (when the silence is relatively long) that is affected.

More evidence of the same kind comes from a study of selective adaptation by GANONG (1975). There, the first step was to measure the shift in the (perceived) boundary between [b] and [d] caused by adaptation with the syllable [dε]. Then, a patch of s-noise was placed in front of the [dε] so that it sounded, as in our example, like [sε]. When that syllable ([sε]) was used as the adapter, the effect on the [b-d] boundary was found to be just as great as it had been with [dε]. From that it follows not only that the transition cues were getting through—that is, that they were not being blocked by the noise when they were perceived as [sε] rather than as [dε]—but that they were getting through in full strength.

A third kind of evidence comes from a comparison of how the transition cues are perceived when, in an acoustic context otherwise like that of our example, they are in or out of a proper syllable (DORMAN et al., 1975). The syllable consisted of a patch of s-noise followed by a vocalic portion that was either [pε] or [kε]. With the noise up close, listeners reported hearing [sε], not [spε] or [skε]; [spε] and [skε] were perceived only when there was an appropriate interval of silence between the noise and the rest of the syllable. In the other (nonsyllable, nonspeech) condition, the transition cues were isolated from the rest of the vocalic section, in which circumstance they sounded like chirps of different pitch and could easily be identified on that basis; then they were placed, as in the speech patterns, after the patch of s-noise. In that condition—that is, when heard as chirps—the transition cues were correctly identified even when there was no silent interval separating them from the noise. Thus, they were not significantly masked by the noise, but, just as important from our point of view, their perception was not changed in any qualitative way—that is, there was no apparent interaction among noise, silence, and transitions.

Much the same kind of result has been obtained with stops in syllable-final position (DORMAN et al., 1975). First, it was established that in the disyllables [bεb dε] and [bεg dε], listeners could correctly perceive the syllable-final stops [b] and [g] only if there was a sufficient period of silence (approximately 60 ms) between the syllables. Then, the second-formant transitions that were the only acoustic difference between the [b] and the [g] were isolated from the rest of the pattern of the first syllable, in which circumstance they were heard as two quite different chirps, and presented, as in the first condition, before the syllable [dɛ]. Listeners correctly identified the chirps most of the time, even when there was no silence at all between them and [dɛ]; the amount of masking was relatively slight, nothing at all like the total effect that had occurred in the case of the speech sounds, and there appeared, again, to be no interaction-caused change in the phenomenal "quality."

So much, then, for the possibility that silence is a necessary condition for perception of stops because it prevents masking of the transitions or because it collaborates in some auditory interaction with them. We turn now to the fact that in the absence of transitions and other stop-consonant cues, silence can be a more nearly *sufficient* condition for perception of a stop.

Suppose we insert the appropriate amount of silence between the noise of a fricative and a vocalic section so structured that no stop is heard when it is presented by itself. Begin, for example, with the syllable [lit], then put a patch of s-noise in front of it. In that case, the resulting syllable is perceived as [slit] if there is no silence between the noise and the vocalic section, but as [split] if the silence is increased sufficiently (DORMAN et al., 1976; ERICKSON et al., 1977). For a simpler example, consider that an appropriate amount of silence inserted between a patch of s-noise and the vowel [i] will produce [ski]; a similar arrangement with [u] will produce [spu] (SUMMERFIELD and BAILEY, 1977). Notice, too, in these last cases that silence is not only a sufficient cue for stop consonant manner but that the "place" of the perceived stop (whether [k] or [p]) is different, of which more later.

Silence has also been shown to be a sufficient condition for distinguishing fricative from affricate both in syllable-initial and syllable-final positions. Thus, one can record the word "say" and the word "shop" and then convert between "say shop" and "say chop" by varying the interval of silence between the two words (DORMAN et al., 1976). Or one can record "dish" and convert it to "ditch" by introducing an appropriate amount of silence between the vocalic part of the syllable and the fricative noise at the end.[6]

The foregoing considerations all imply that the perception of silence in our simple example is not only auditory but also phonetic. As a phonetic percept, it conforms to a fact about the speaker's production—namely, that a stop consonant cannot be produced without closing the vocal tract. Of course, such conformity could occur only if there were a phonetic perceiving device specialized to make use of the information about articulation, and if there were, correspondingly, a phonetic mode of perception.

β) Equivalence in phonetic perception of different acoustic cues produced by the same articulatory gesture. It is a commonplace of speech and speech perception that different acoustic cues may have equivalent effects in phonetic perception. That is of interest because the cues are often so different acoustically that it is hard to conceive how they might be related from an auditory point of view. The relevant facts fall into several classes; we will here offer samples of each.

Perhaps the simplest class comprises those ubiquitous cases in which there are multiple (and distributed) acoustic consequences of the same articulatory

---

[6] Raphael and Dorman: personal communication.

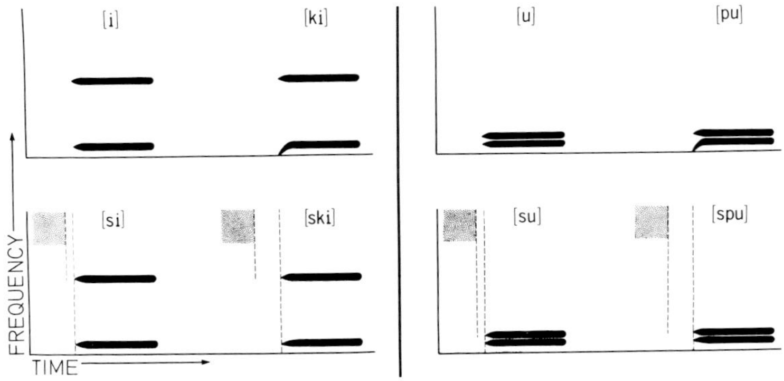

Fig. 4. Spectrographic patterns that illustrate how two very different acoustic cues—a transition of the first formant (top half) and an appropriate interval of silence (bottom half)—are phonetically equivalent in the perception of stop consonants

gesture. Consider again the example of the preceding section that is owed to SUMMERFIELD and BAILEY: An appropriate interval of silence between a patch of s-noise and the vowel [i] (or [u]) causes the listener to hear [k] in [ski] (or [p] in [spu]). We now represent that fact schematically in the top half of Figure 4. In the bottom half we represent the companion fact, discovered in earlier research on the "locus" of the stops, that a rising transition at the beginning of the first formant of [i] (or [u]) will also cause a listener to hear the stop [k] in [ki] or ([p] in [pu]) (DELATTRE, et al., 1955). Now we note the perceptual equivalence of about 60 ms of silence, which is the cue in the top half of the figure, and the rising frequency modulation at the beginning of the first formant, which is the cue in the bottom half, and we ask what that amount of silence and that kind of sound could possibly have in common. Nothing, we should think, when we consider them from an auditory point of view, but in articulation they have an obvious bond. To say [ski] (or [spu]), rather than [si] (or [su]), the speaker must close his vocal tract, which produces the silent interval; and then he must open it, which produces the rise in frequency of the first formant. Thus, the two very different cues are the distributed acoustic results of an essential component of the stop-consonant gesture. Given that they sound alike—either can produce the perception of stop consonant—we should suppose it is because they refer to the same articulation.

For this same example, it remains to take account of the fact that the perceived stops had two different places of production, velar in [ki] (or [ski]) and labial in [pu] (or [spu]). We note, first, that energy at frequency levels corresponding to the second-formant levels of [i] and [u] is appropriate for closure of the vocal tract at the velar and labial places, respectively. That helps us to understand why [i] becomes [ki] (or [ski]) and [u] becomes [pu] (or [spu]) when sufficient cues for the stop manner are added. But notice now a fact that is more relevant to our present purposes, which is that these differences in perception of place of production occur in the same way regardless of how the manner dimension was signaled. Thus, our two very different acoustic cues—silence and sound—are equivalent, not only in their ability to produce the perception of manner, but also in the way they combine with the other information in the signal to produce the perception of phonetic place.

Given our assumption of a link between production and perception, and given that a linguistically significant gesture almost always has multiple acoustic consequences, we should expect to find many other instances of phonetic-perceptual equivalence among cues that are very different in acoustic-auditory terms. Just how many must depend on how finely we dissect the acoustic signal into separate cues, and how often, in experiment, we play the cues off against each other. Relevant studies have already made an impressive record. It reaches back in time to an extension by LISKER (1957b) of an earlier study (LISKER, 1957a) on the voicing distinction in poststress position (as in "rabid" vs. "rapid"). Having determined in the earlier work that duration of intersyllabic silence is an important voicing cue, LISKER then found that specifiable amounts of that temporal cue could be traded for specifiable settings of spectral cues (extent of appropriate transitions of the first formant at the end of the first syllable and the beginning of the second). Now, in a recent experiment on the distinction between fricative-vowel and fricative-stop-vowel, SUMMERFIELD and BAILEY (1977) have established and precisely measured the equivalence of silence on the one hand, and, on the other, such spectral cues as the frequency at which the first formant starts and the extent of the first-formant transition.

There is also evidence of equivalence in phonetic perception among different kinds of temporal cues. Referring again to LISKER's experiment, we note his finding of an equivalence between duration of intersyllable silence and the duration of the first syllable of the word. In a recent experiment[7] referred to earlier, on the distinction between [dish] and [ditch], there is an equivalence between the duration of silence separating the vocalic position of the syllable from the noise and the duration of the noise portion of the fricative (or affricate). Also new is the discovery of a similar equivalence between duration of silence and duration of noise in the contrast between fricative-vowel and fricative-stop-vowel.[8] In all these cases time is traded for time; but in the one period of time there is silence, in the other sound.

In the spectral domain, too, equivalences among different cues are not hard to find. For example, an early paper (COOPER et al., 1952) presented preliminary evidence for the separate contributions of several acoustic cues to the perception of the [m−l] distinction, among others. Later, it was shown more clearly that in the perception of place of production in stops, second-and third-formant transitions made independent constribution (HARRIS et al., 1958; HOFFMAN, 1958). In the current literature is a particularly elegant study of the voicing distinction by SUMMERFIELD and HAGGARD (1977) that reports an equivalence between the starting point of the first formant and the variable known as "voice-onset-time" and shows explicitly how these acoustically disparate cues are related in articulation. A somewhat similar result with two voicing cues—fre-

---

[7] Raphael and Dorman: personal communication.
[8] Bailey, Summerfield and Dorman: personal communication.

quency of the fundamental frequency and voice-onset-time—has been found recently by MASSARO and COHEN (1976) [cf. HAGGARD et al. (1970)], though an articulatory basis was not made explicit.

Having offered several examples of the equivalences in phonetic perception between different acoustic cues that are the consequences of the same articulation, we should bring this section to a close. But not without first saying that it is hard to know where the list of relevant examples should end. Should we, for example, include the kind of equivalence that is found between spectral cues for syllable-initial consonants and the duration of the syllable[9], or between silence as a cue (for voicing, or place, or gemination) and the tempo of the surrounding speech (PICKETT and DECKER, 1960; PORT, 1976), or between the setting of the second-formant transition as a cue for the stops and the position of the first formant (RAND, 1971)?[10] It is when we try to answer that question, and thus to define the boundaries of the phenomenon we are here considering, that we see most clearly how unsatisfactory from a theoretical point of view is the notion of acoustic cue. We find it useful, even necessary, when we want to refer to those pieces of sound that an experimenter varied and found to be effective. But if the cues are to be fitted into a conceptual frame—as something other than items in a list—we should regard them as information about the behavior of a speaker's vocal tract.

So far, we have considered only those different acoustic cues that are phonetically equivalent because they are the common products of a single articulatory gesture. These are, perhaps, the least complex and most telling of the instances that imply a link between speech perception and speech production. But they are not the only ones. Equally numerous are the cases in which there is phonetic equivalence between acoustic cues that are very different because the phone they signal is produced in different contexts (LIBERMAN et al., 1967; but see STEVENS, 1975). In these cases, too, we suppose that a common articulation is responsible for that which is common in the perception. Of course, such articulations as these can hardly be identical in all particulars, since they are linked to the gestures for the surrounding phones, and these change, of course, with each new context; the commonality can only be seen in terms of shared components, whether end targets or inferred motor commands (for relevant discussion, see MACNEILAGE, 1970). But given such articulatory similarity as there may be, gross differences in acoustic signal can and often do arise with changes in context, primarily as a consequence of coarticulation. It is the more important, then, to give some attention to these context-conditioned variations in the cues because, as we said in an earlier section, coarticulation is the essence of the speech code.

To illustrate how acoustic cues that vary because of phonetic context are nevertheless equivalent in phonetic perception, we choose an example that shows two kinds of contextual effects—one that depends on variations in the identity of the phone following the target phone, and another having to do with variations in the position of the target phone in the syllable. The example is the pair

---

[9] SUMMERFIELD: personal communication; MILLER and LIBERMAN: personal communication.

[10] Also, BAILEY: personal communication.

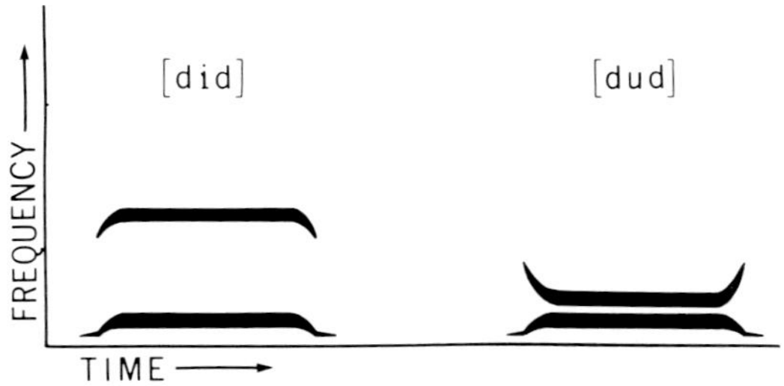

Fig. 5. Spectrograms sufficient to produce the syllables [did] and [dud], illustrating the variation in acoustic cues for the stop consonant [d] that can occur as a function of vowel context ([i] vs. [u]) and position in the syllable (initial vs. final)

of syllables [did] and [dud], shown schematically as two-formant approximations in Figure 5 and taken from the results of early experiments on the stops (DELATTRE et al., 1955). (These patterns are appropriate, and reasonably sufficient, for synthesizing the intended syllables.) Having noticed that the lower (first) formant is the same in the two cases, we fix attention on the higher (second) one. We see there that, as a consequence of coarticulation, a phonetic alteration limited to the middle (vowel) segment of a consonant-vowel-consonant syllable does not change only the middle portion of the sound; rather, it changes the entire second formant. The transition cues for [d] are therefore in very different positions in the spectrum, being relatively high in frequency for [did] and low for [dud]. Moreover, the transition cues for stops in corresponding positions in the syllable are opposite in direction—for [did] they are rising in initial position and falling in final position, but for [dud] they are falling in initial position and rising in final position. Of course, the inference we would draw from these cases is much the same as that we draw from those in which the context was fixed and the disparate acoustic cues were the products of exactly the same gesture: The cues are presumably interpreted by a phonetic device that acts as if it knew how they were produced. But if the device has that ability, then it can conceivably do more than just "hear through" the context-conditioned variation in the cues so as to arrive at the canonical form of the phonetic segment; it might also be able to take advantage of the fact that such variation produces a special kind of redundancy in the signal and provides important information about such aspects of the phonetic structure as sequential order, juncture, linguistic stress, and tempo. If so, then the acoustic variation that is produced by articulation (and coarticulation) in different contexts would not be an obstacle to perception but a considerable help and, correspondingly, a most important characteristic of the speech code.

γ) *Nonequivalence in phonetic perception of an acoustic cue produced by different vocal tracts: ecologic constraints of a phonetic sort.* Given that phonetic perception is somehow shaped by what a vocal tract does, as we have suggested it might be, we should ask: whose vocal tract? Common sense suggests that it can hardly be that of the listener, nor yet that of the speaker; most plausibly, it must be some abstract conception of vocal tracts in general. We should expect, then, that the phonetic device would behave as if it knew, for example, that two vocal tracts can do what one vocal tract cannot. In that case, acoustic cues might have one effect or another, depending on whether they were produced by one speaker or by two. That such ecologic considerations are important is indicated by experiments.

One experiment dealt with the perception of the syllable-final stop in the example of [εb dε] vs. [εg dε] that we described earlier. There, it will remembered, listeners could hear the [b] or [g] only if there was a sufficient interval of silence between the syllables, presumably because the phonetic perceiving device "knew" that the speaker could not have produced both stops without closing his vocal tract for a certain period of time. But two vocal tracts—one saying [εb] (or [εg]), the other [dε]—can produce the disyllable [εb dε] (or [εg dε]) with no silence at all between the two syllables. The experiment revealed that listeners behaved accordingly: When a single speaker produced both first and second syllables, a silent interval of some duration was necessary for perception of the syllable-final stops, but when one speaker produced the first syllable and another the second, listeners heard the syllable-final stops even when there was no intersyllabic silence at all (DORMAN et al., 1975b).

The other experiment dealt with the distinction between fricative and affricate (in "shop" vs. "chop") that we also described earlier. In that case, inserting a sufficient amount of silence between "say" and "shop" caused the listener to hear "chop." Our assumption was that this occurred because the silence informed the listener that the speaker had closed his vocal tract, as he must to produce the affricate. But two vocal tracts—one saying "now say" and the other "chop"—can produce "now say chop" with no silence at all between "say" and "chop." Thus, with two speakers, the size of the interval of silence provides no useful phonetic information. The results of the experiment suggested that the listeners' perceptions took account of that fact. Starting with "now say" and "shop", and given a silent interval appropriate for "chop," listeners did indeed hear "now say chop" if there was only one speaker; but if there were two, the listeners heard "now say shop" at all intervals of silence (RAPHAEL et al., 1975).

Those results imply that the vocal tract to which the perception is linked is a very abstract one indeed, as we should have expected. But they also provide additional support, of a rather different kind, for the hypothesis that some such link does indeed exist.

δ) Addition of equivalent acoustic cues: algebraic sums in the phonetic mode. The claim that two very different acoustic cues are equivalent in phonetic perception is largely based on the experimental demonstration of a trading relation between them. Thus, it has been determined that some number of milliseconds of a temporal cue is equal to some particular setting of a spectral cue. An implication is that the two cues together will summate algebraically to enhance or reduce the perceived phonetic contrast, depending on just how they are combined. We believe this to be worth remarking, because cues that are algebraically summed would have positive and negative signs only in the phonetic domain, or so it would seem. An example may show why.

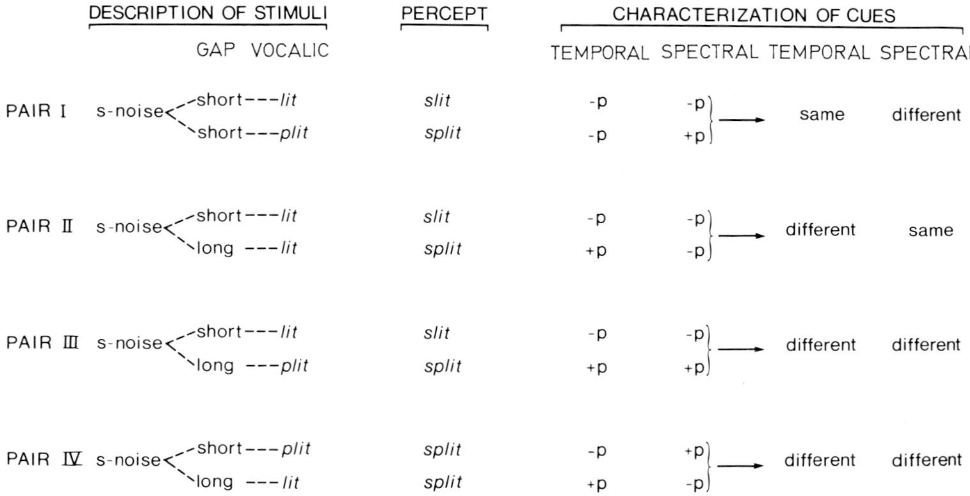

Fig. 6. Diagrams illustrating how spectral and temporal cues separately produce the same phonetic distinction (Pairs I and II) and how, taken together, they either enhance that distinction or reduce it (Pairs III and IV)

Recall the fact, described earlier, that an appropriate period of silence inserted between an s-noise and the syllable [lit] will produce [slit] if the interval is relatively short but [split] if it is sufficiently long. Given that we can, of course, also convert [lit] to [plit] by appropriately changing the spectrum at the beginning of the vocalic syllable—specifically, by altering the formant transitions—it follows that we can use the spectral maneuver to interconvert between [slit] and [split] while holding the temporal cue fixed (ERICKSON et al., 1977). Those facts are diagrammed in Figure 6 as Pairs I and II, where we characterize the cues as "minus p" or "plus p" to indicate the way they bias the perception. In this case, as in the others we described earlier, we see how a phonetic distinction can be produced by either of two cues, one spectral, the other temporal. In pairs III and IV, both the spectral and temporal cues differ between the members of the pair, but in different ways. In the one case (Pair III), the combination enhances the perceived difference, while in the other (pair IV), it permits the minus and plus biases to summate (algebraically) so as to produce two percepts (split) which are the same or very little different (LIBERMAN and PISONI, in press).

To appreciate the significance of the perceptual addition exemplified in Figure 6, we should think of it as a paradigm for comparative studies with nonhuman animals, a potentially enlightening endeavor because phonetic perception and the algebraic summation that goes with it exist presumably only in creatures that speak. Others would perceive the stimuli of Figure 6 in an auditory way. Hence, they should find the pairs that differ by two cues (III and IV) to be more discriminable that those (I and II) that differ only by one, and, further, the pairs with two-cue differences should be almost equally discriminable. Note, incidentally, how relatively easy it would be to test that hypothesis, not only with animals but with human infants: The measurement—relative difficulty of discrimination—is surely one of the easiest to make, and the order of difficulty to be expected from nonhuman animals is very different from that already obtained with us human beings.

ε) Nonequivalence in phonetic perception of the same or similar acoustic cues. Just as the processes of speech production cause different acoustic cues to be correlated in articulation and (hence) equivalent in perception, so also, if in a somewhat more complex way, do they sometimes cause the same cue to be uncorrelated in articulation and (hence) different in perception. An early instance of this was seen in the first "synthetic" experiment on the stops, where it was found that a burst centered at 1440 Hz was perceived differently in front of different vowels (LIBERMAN et al., 1952). Subsequently, much the same effect was found with real speech (SCHATZ, 1954). More recently, the general effect has been confirmed, though with better methods for controlling the stimuli, but now it is seen that the exact nature of the effect varies somewhat depending on just how much of the "real" burst is used and just where it is placed in time with reference to the vowel.[11]

Another example concerns silence, about which we have already heard so much. Having seen earlier that it is a cue for the perception of phonetic segments, we should note now that it is effective in regard to all three phonetic dimensions: manner, voicing, and place. In connection with manner, we should remember that an appropriate amount of silence, placed between the noise of a fricative and a vocalic piece of sound, will produce the perception of a stop consonant, the perceived "place" of the stop depending on the nature of the vocalic section. We should also remember that, in similar fashion, silence will produce the affricate manner when introduced appropriately between, for example, the word "say" and the word "shop." In regard to voicing, we saw earlier that variations in the duration of intersyllable silence will convert a poststress voiced stop (as in "rabid") into voiceless (as in "rapid"), and vice versa. Now we turn to the dimension of place, and point out, as we had not before, that in a disyllable like "rabid", reductions in the duration of intersyllable silence will cause the listener to hear "ratid"—that is, a stop with a different place of production (PORT, 1976). This perceptual change correlates—not accidentally, according to our hypothesis—with the fact that a speaker closes his vocal tract for a shorter time when he says "ratid" than when he says "rabid." Given the utterance "rabid" and an artificially shortened silence between the syllables, it is as if the listener heard "ratid" because his phonetic perceiver knows that the speaker could not have said "rabid" since he did not close his vocal tract long enough. In sum, then, a single acoustic dimension, duration of silence, produces contrasts on each of three phonetic and perceptual dimensions—manner, voicing, and place. That curious situation arises because the very different kinds of articulations—indeed, the different sets of muscles—that underlie the independence of those dimensions in the phonetic and perceptual domains happen to converge on a single acoustic dimension.

---

[11] RAPHAEL, DORMAN, and LIBERMAN: personal communication.

Perhaps the reader will have noticed that we did not specify the amounts of silence that are appropriate in the aforementioned cases, and he will quite naturally wonder if they are within the same ranges for the three phonetic and perceptual dimensions. We did not specify because the appropriate durations vary according to how the other relevant cues are set, and much of this remains to be worked out. It is reasonably clear, even now, that the durations of silence for manner and voicing overlap greatly. For place, there probably is some overlap with voicing, depending on just how the other cues are set, but at this moment the relevant data have not been gathered.

Since we have, up to this point, looked only at the segmental aspects of phonetic structure, it may seem inappropriate that we should now broaden our view to glimpse those other aspects that pertain to prosody and syntax. But the temptation to do so is great because there is, at just this juncture, a very natural and interesting connection. The point is that the duration of a syllable conveys information not only about the identity of the phonetic segments it comprises, as we have already seen, but also about the tempo (rate of articulation), degree of linguistic stress, and position in the syntactic frame. We do not know how the separate contributions to duration are sorted out in perception, but, as KLATT (1976) has pointed out, considerations of simple logic suggest that the perceiver can hardly arrive at his decisions in some particular order, one at a time, since each decision would appear to depend on every other one. In any case, it does appear that, in production, these several aspects of the message are encoded into the same aspect of the signal, and then, in perception, properly recovered.

C. Is Phonetic Perception Necessary?

So far we have assumed the perceptual reality of phone-size segments. In this final section we propose to justify that assumption.

I. Preliminary Remarks

No one, of course, doubts that linguistic utterances are perceived as sequences of wordlike, or morphemic, segments. But the processes by which these segments are extracted from the acoustic signal are far from certain. Do we, in perceiving speech, pass directly from the overall acoustic shape of the constituent morphemes to their syntactic and semantic attributes, or do we, rather, first analyze at least some portion of each utterance (with the possible exception of nonpropositional greetings, interjections, and expletives) into its phonologic components, and only then proceed to syntax and meaning? Certainly, the phonologic attributes of each morpheme are available to consciousness. But what is the form that gives access to the listener's lexicon? Is lexical storage analog and isomorphic with gross auditory shape, or is it digital and isomorphic with phonologic structure?

We should make clear from the outset that the precise form of any possible morphemic sound pattern is not our concern. We have spoken until now of phones, since we take a phonetic representation to be at the first remove from the auditory signal and to be perceptually available, even though not attended to in normal listening. However, for the present discussion, it is a matter of indifference whether the representation is assumed to be a feature matrix, a sequence of phones, or a sequence of more abstract phonologic segments. Our only concern is whether the form is segmented or unsegmented.

II. Evidence Against Segments Smaller Than Syllables

Consider, first, the grounds for believing the perceptual representation to be unsegmented. Foremost is the fact, to which we have repeatedly alluded, that phonetic segments are not discretely arrayed in time as are letters of the alphabet in space, but are, rather, transmitted simultaneously or with considerable shingling. This fact alone has led some students to abandon the phone as a perceptual unit in favor of the context-sensitive allophone (WICKELGREN, 1969; but see HALWES and JENKINS, 1971) or the syllable (MASSARO, 1972; WARREN, 1976a, 1976b).

A second line of argument draws on reaction-time studies, demonstrating that listeners, asked to monitor a word list or sentence, display successively shorter reaction times as the target item increases in duration from phone to syllable to word (SAVIN and BEVER, 1970) and even to sentence (BEVER, 1970), suggesting a perceptual progression from larger unit to smaller rather than the reverse. The solution to this paradox was provided by MCNEIL and LINDIG (1973), who showed that reaction times are, in fact, shortest for the items of which a list is composed or, in other words, for those items to which the experimental situation has drawn the listener's attention (see also FOSS and SWINNEY, 1973). RUBIN et al. (1976), have elaborated these conclusions, arguing that such monitoring experiments do not measure the time taken to process the targets perceptually, but rather the time taken to bring them into consciousness (cf. STUDDERT-KENNEDY, 1974, p. 2366). This does not, of course, preclude the possibility that normal processing entails unconscious access to the lexicon through phonologic analysis, since, in all likelihood, these experiments have no bearing on normal perceptual processes at all. However, it does invite the reflection that the several attributes of a morpheme—its phonologic components, syllabic structure, syntactic and semantic markers—may all be simultaneously available to the listener, once access to his lexicon has been granted by overall acoustic (or, in reading, visual) shape (WARREN, 1976b).

Finally, a broad line of argument springs from the suspicion that the study of speech perception has been tied to the isolated syllable and its components at the expense of attention to the overall acoustic pattern of running speech. This overall pattern, or prosody, certainly conveys important information. SVENSSON (1974), for example, has shown that the perceived form of hummed speech (that is, speech lacking all the acoustic cues for its phonetic segments) is often syntactically correct. MARTIN (1975) has argued that speech rhythm may enable listeners to predict upcoming stresses. And DARWIN (1975) has even induced listeners to reveal a preference in some circumstances for good prosody over good syntax and meaning. These and other studies (for example, COHEN and NOOTEBOOM, 1975, passim) do suggest that the role of prosody in speech perception may have been underestimated. In fact, if we combine these studies with recent work on possible invariant acoustic correlates of distinctive features in the speech stream (STEVENS, 1975), we may be tempted to propose once again the "novel theory of speech perception," first put forward by CHOMSKY and MILLER (1963, p. 311) and elaborated by CHOMSKY and HALLE (1968, p. 24), by which a few more-or-less invariant acoustic properties give the listener access to his lexicon and so precipitate a plausible syntactic and semantic analysis of an utterance.

In short, a fair body of evidence suggests that the acoustic structure of spoken utterances may be sufficient to gain access to the listener's lexicon, or at least his syllabary, without an intermediate stage of phonologic analysis. However, we do not believe that this view is correct and in the following sections we will try to explain why.

III. Evidence in Favor of Segments Smaller Than the Syllable

1. Experimental Evidence

There is a great weight of evidence for the psychological reality of every level of phonetic analysis, from feature to phone to syllable. We have reviewed much of this evidence elsewhere (STUDDERT-KENNEDY, 1976). Here we do no more than remark that studies of speaking errors (BOOMER and LAVER, 1968; FROMKIN, 1971), perceptual confusions (MILLER and NICELY, 1955; MITCHELL, 1973), synthetic speech continua (LIBERMAN et al., 1967), dichotic listening (SHANKWEILER and STUDDERT-KENNEDY, 1967; STUDDERT-KENNEDY and SHANKWEILER, 1970) and "verbal transformations" (GOLDSTEIN and LACKNER, 1973; WARREN, 1976a) leave little room for doubt that both phones and features have some form of psychological reality. To this experimental evidence we may add the testimony of linguistic analysis (for example, GLEASON, 1955), including studies of language change (for example, LEHMAN, 1975), not to mention the very existence of alphabetic writing.

2. Structure of the Syllable

As the etymology of its name implies, the syllable is a compound, the vehicle of a natural acoustic contrast between consonant constriction and vowel opening, a contrast frequently claimed as a phonologic universal (e.g., POSTAL, 1968). The contrast is clearly reflected in perception, as evidenced by a long series of studies over the past 15 years. These studies, employing a variety of experimental paradigms — identification and discrimination of synthetic speech sounds, short-term memory, reaction time, dichotic listening, backward masking and others — converge on the conclusion that consonants and vowels perform distinct perceptual functions. Once again, we have reviewed this matter elsewhere (STUDDERT-KENNEDY, 1975b, 1976) and will not do so here. We simply remark that none of the varied evidence for the perceptual contrast between consonants and vowels could exist if the syllable were not analyzed in perception.

We may note, in passing, one further point. In all languages, the syllable is the unit of poetic meter. Except where syllable and morpheme normally coincide (for example, Japanese haiku), metrical rules are specified in terms of syllables and their expected "length" or degree of stress. Of particular interest in the present context is the fact that length is frequently specified not by lexical form but by neighboring phonetic segments. In both Latin and ancient Greek verse, for example, the length assigned to a word-final CVC syllable varies as a function of the initial phone of the following word. Thus a famous ode of Horace (Book III, Ode XXVI) begins: "Vixi puellis nuper idoneus . . ." Here the third word scans as a trochee because the following word begins with a vowel, but would have scanned as a spondee had the following word begun with a consonant. This simple rule of ancient verse obviously required that the singer (and presumably the listener who could detect a singer's error) be aware of the phonologic structure of the syllable.

3. Perceptual Function of Phonologic Categories

A crucial process in the perception of fluent speech must be short-term storage of early portions of an utterance pending final interpretation. What is the form of this store? Clearly it cannot be simply auditory, since a precategorical auditory store (CROWDER and MORTON, 1969; CROWDER, 1972) is sensitive to overwriting from immediately following items (CROWDER, 1971). Nor, given our sensitivity to phonetic structure (most obviously in listening to poetry) can the store be purely functional or semantic, with all phonetic detail stripped away.

In fact, we wish to argue that, to fulfill this linguistic function, a general perceptual process is invoked, namely, division into "stages." Among the likely functions of "perceptual stages" — whether defined in time or in neural locus — is to isolate one process from another and to store energy or information for later use. We may see this most clearly at the periphery. Every sensory system integrates energy: If the system were infinitely damped, threshold for activation would never be reached. Accumulation of energy over some finite period permits the mechanical response of the ear, for example, to develop.

On the other hand, the period of integration must be finite to prevent physical destruction of the system: Mechanical energy becomes bioelectricity. Analogous cycles of integration and transformation presumably recur, as energy or information progresses through the system. Activity in afferent fibers gives rise to more central neural activity and, ultimately (jumping levels of discourse), to a preperceptual "image" (MASSARO, 1972). The image, in turn, must have some finite duration, long enough to institute further processing, short enough to prevent "babble."

Returning with this metaphor to language, we note that speech is arrayed in time, and that both syntax and meaning demand some minimum quantity of information before linguistic structure can emerge. The perceptual function of phonologic categories may then be, on the one hand, to forestall auditory babble, on the other, to store information derived from the signal until such time as it can be granted a linguistic interpretation. In other words, the perceptual function of phonologic categories is that of a buffer between acoustic signal and meaningful message.

4. Recovery of the Morpheme

We come, finally, to the phonologic function without which, we believe, linguistic communication would not be possible—namely, to provide a code for lexical storage.

Notice first that if lexical items are coded according to overall acoustic structure, the form must be sufficiently stylized, stripped of acoustic detail, for the word to be accessed despite a wide variety of surface forms. For example, the duration of a single monosyllabic word, spoken by a single speaker at a conversational rate in a random list or in a sentence, may vary by a factor of 2 to 1 (GAITENBY, 1965; KOZHEVNIKOV and CHISTOVICH, 1965; LACKNER and LEVINE, 1975), and yet be fully intelligible in both contexts. Furthermore, the durational variants are not related by a simple scale factor: Most of the variation occurs over the syllable nucleus rather than over its edges (GAITENBY, 1965; LEHISTE, 1970; HUGGINS, 1972), so that an algorithm for generalizing two extreme acoustic variants could hardly succeed without at least some analysis of the overall acoustic shape.

If we add to durational variations, other within-speaker variations in fundamental frequency (which, coupled with duration, is the primary acoustic correlate of variations in linguistic stress) and in formant structure (due to cross-morphemic effects of coarticulation in running speech), not to mention acoustically similar across-speaker variations due to age, sex, and dialect, we are confronted with a formidable array of acoustic forms each of which—if unanalyzed acoustic structure is to give access to the lexicon—will have to be reduced to canonical acoustic form.

Now, it is true that the invariance problem is scarcely less serious if the message units to be recovered from the signal are phonologic entities, such as features or phones, than if they are morphemes or words, and even a cursory survey of the literature of speech perception will show that, as in the earlier sections of our chapter, this is a recurrent preoccupation. However, we should note that the "audile" listener, consigned to lexical search with nothing but overall acoustic shape (and a few syntactic-semantic hints derived from prosody and context) to guide him, is deprived of at least one valuable aid, namely the systematic phonologic and phonotactic constraints of his language. He will not be permitted to resolve uncertainty by drawing on his knowledge that a particular portion of the acoustic pattern, or a particular sequence of acoustic segments, cannot occur in his language. Rather, every morphemic sound pattern will be distinct, and access to its semantic and syntactic attributes will be direct. In other words, the vast and subtle array of systematic phonology that linguistic studies have brought into view over the past 150 years will be no more than epiphenomenal froth, communicatively vacuous, at least for the listener, if not for the speaker.

Nonetheless, let us set the problem of invariance aside. Let us assume, for the moment, that it has been solved and that we are able to specify for every word or morpheme a unique canonical acoustic form apt for every context and every speaker. We shall then be confronted with the deeper problem of how the listener segments an utterance into its constituent morphemes or words.

The heart of the problem is simply that speakers freely coarticulate across word and morpheme boundaries. A consequence is that dividing the speech stream by use of an acoustic (or auditory) criterion will yield segments that bear a random relation (in size) to the words or morphemes. In that circumstance, the audile listener would have to store, not merely the 20,000–30,000 canonical auditory patterns that would represent the words in his vocabulary, but rather a number unimaginably greater than that (LIBERMAN and PISONI, in press). Even if he had a reliable acoustic criterion for dividing an utterance into syllables (see MERMELSTEIN, 1975), he would not be able to assign the syllables to their appropriate morphemes without analyzing them into their phonetic segments. For example, syllabification of the simple phrase, "He's a repeated offender," will yield eight CV syllables, four of which cross morpheme boundaries and two of which cross word boundaries. In other words, syllable boundaries in fluent speech are frequently random with respect to words or morphemes.

The problem is exacerbated for inflectional languages where changes in a single phoneme (initial, medial, or final) often suffice to signal changes in tense, mood, person, number, or case. Simple suffix changes, such as English plurals, might pose no problem for the audile listener, despite the lawful [s], [z] and [ǂz] alterations, and the absence of an acoustically marked morpheme boundary, for we need only suppose that the perceptual "morpheme detector" is automatically sprung as soon as a recognizable acoustic unit enters the system. We might even suppose that tense contrasts signaled by a change in medial vowel (as in "win"-"won") are learned as special cases. But we will find it a good deal more difficult to explain, for example, the formation of the Greek perfect tense by duplication of the initial consonant of the present, a fact presumably not lost on the listener. Indeed, as we multiply examples (and ad hoc solutions for the imaginary audile listener), we cannot but wonder why the various forms of a lexical item bear any relation to one another at all. Are we to suppose that these variations are lawful for the speaker, but merely adventitious for the listener?

Surely not. For, quite apart from the general lack of parsimony in positing totally independent input and output lexicons, we would be reduced to the absurdity of supposing that a listener consults a lexicon of auditory segments which bear no more than a random relation to the articulatory segments he deploys as a speaker. We are forced to conclude that only by extracting the phonetic segments—or, more properly, their underlying phonologic forms—can the listener discover most of what is said to him.

Acknowledgments

The preparation of this chapter was supported by a grant from the National Institute of Child Health and Human Development. Having freely borrowed the ideas of our colleagues at Haskins Laboratories, we are unable to say exactly which are owed to whom. We do especially acknowledge the contributions of QUENTIN SUMMERFIELD and PETER BAILEY, who were guests at the Laboratories while this chapter was being prepared, and we are indebted to Mark Liberman for valuable suggestions.

References

Ades, A.E.: Source assignment and feature extraction in speech. J. Exp. Psychol. [Human Percept.] (1977) (in press).

Ainsworth, W.A.: Automatic speech recognition. In: Mechanisms of Speech Recognition. Oxford: Pergamon Pr. 1976, pp. 104–119.

Bailey, P.J.: Perceptual adaptation for acoustical features in speech: Speech Perception. (Prog. Rep., Univ. Belfast) **2.2**, 29–34 (1973).

Bailey, P.J., Dorman, M.F., Summerfield, A.Q.: Identification of sine-wave analogues of CV syllables in speech and non-speech modes. J. Acoust. Soc. Am. **61** S(A) (1977).

• Bever, T.G.: The influence of speech performance on linguistic structure. In: Advances in Psycholinguistics. Flores D-Arcais, G.B., Levett, W.J.M., (eds.). Amsterdam: North Holland 1970.

Boomer, D.S., Laver, J.D.M.: Slips of the tongue. Br. J. Disord. Commun. **3**, 1–12 (1968).

• Chomsky, N., Halle, M.: The Sound Pattern of English. New York: Harper & Row 1968.

• Chomsky, N., Miller, G.A.: Introduction to the formal analysis of natural languages. In: Handbook of Mathematical Psychology. Luce, R.D., Bush, R.R., Galauker, E.E., (eds.). New York: Wiley 1963, Vol. I, pp. 269–321.

Cohen, A., Nooteboom, S.G., (eds.): Structure and Process in Speech Perception. New York: Springer-Verlag 1975.

• Cole, R.A., Scott, B.: Toward a theory of speech perception. Psychol. Rev. **81**, 348–374 (1974).

Cooper, F.S.: Spectrum analysis. J. Acoust. Soc. Am. **22**, 761–762 (1950).

Cooper, F.S.: Some instrumental aids to research on speech. In: Proceedings of the Fourth Annual Round Table Meeting on Linguistics and Language Teaching. Washington: Georgetown Univ. 1953, pp. 46–53.

• Cooper, F.S.: How is language conveyed by speech? In: Language by Ear and by Eye. Kavanagh, J.F., Mattingly, I.G., (eds.). Cambridge, Mass.: MIT Pr. 1972, pp. 25–45.

Cooper, F.S., Liberman, A.M., Borst, J.M.: The interconversion of audible and visible patterns as a basis for research in the perception of speech. Proc. Nat. Acad. Sci. USA **37**, 318–325 (1951).

Cooper, F.S., Delattre, P.C., Liberman, A.M., Borst, J.M., Gerstman, L.J.: Some experiments on the perception of synthetic speech sounds. J. Acoust Soc. Am. **24**, 597–606 (1952).

Cooper, W.E.: Selective adaptation to speech. In: Cognitive Theory. Restle, F., Shiffrin, R.M., Castellan, J.N., Lindman, H., Pisoni, D.B., (eds.). Hillsdale, N.J.: Erlbaum 1975, Vol. I, pp. 23–54.

Crowder, R.G.: Waiting for the stimulus suffix: decay, delay, rhythm and readvent in immediate memory. Q. J. Exp. Psychol. **23**, 324–340 (1971).

•Crowder, R.G.: Visual and auditory memory. In: Language by Ear and by Eye. Kavanagh, J.F., Mattingly, I.G., (eds.). Cambridge: MIT Pr. 1972.

•Crowder, R.G., Morton, J.: Precategorical acoustic storage (PAS). Percept. Psychophys. **5**, 365–373 (1969).

•Darwin, C.J.: Ear differences in the recall of fricatives and vowels. Q. J. Exp. Psychol. **23**, 46–62 (1971).

Darwin, C.J.: On the dynamic use of prosody in speech perception. In: Structure and Process in Speech Perception. Cohen, A., Nooteboom, J.G., (eds.). New York: Springer-Verlag 1975, pp. 178–194.

•Darwin, C.J.: The perception of speech. In: Handbook of Perception. Carterette, E., Friedman, M., (eds.). New York: Academic Pr. 1976, Vol. VII, pp. 175–226.

Day, R.S.: Temporal order perception of reversible phoneme cluster. J. Acoust. Soc. Am. **48**, 95(A) (1970).

Delattre, P.C., Liberman, A.M., Cooper, F.S.: Acoustic *loci* and transitional cues for consonants. J. Acoust. Soc. Am. **27**, 769–773 (1955).

Denes, P.B.: Effect of duration on the perception of voicing. J. Acoust. Soc. Am. **27**, 761–764 (1955).

Dorman, M., Cutting, J.E., Raphael, L.J.: Perception of temporal order in vowel sequences with and without formant transitions. J. Exp. Psychol. [Human Percept.] **104**, 121–129 (1975a).

Dorman, M.F., Raphael, L.J., Liberman, A.M., Repp, B.: Masking-like phenomena in speech perception. J. Acoust. Soc. Am. **57** (Suppl. 1) S48(A) (1975b). [Full text in Haskins Lab. Status Rep. Speech Res. 42/43, 265–276.]

Dorman, M.F., Raphael, L.J., Liberman, A.M.: Further observations on the role of silence in the perception of stop consonants. Haskins Lab. Status Rep. Speech Res. **48**, 199–207 (1976).

•Eimas, P.D., Corbit, J.D.: Selective adaptation of linguistic feature detectors. Cog. Psychol. **13**, 247–252 (1973).

Erickson, D.M., Fitch, H.L., Halwes, T.G., Liberman, A.M.: Trading relation in perception between silence and spectrum. J. Acoust. Soc. Am. **61**, S46(A) (1977).

Fant, C.G.M.: Descriptive analysis of the acoustic aspects of speech. Logos **5**, 3–17 (1962).

Fant, C.G.M.: Analysis and synthesis of speech processes. In: Manual of Phonetics. Malmberg, B., (eds.). Amsterdam: North-Holland 1968, pp. 173–277.

•Foss, D.J., Swinney, D.A.: On the psychological reality of the phoneme: perception, identification and consciousness. J. Verbal Learn. Verbal Behav. **12**, 246–257 (1973).

•Fromkin, V.A.: The non-anomalous nature of anomalous utterances. Language **47**, 27–52 (1971).

Fujimura, O.: Syllable as a unit of speech recognition. IEEE Trans. Acoust. Sp. Sig. Proc. **23**, 82–87 (1975).

Fujimura, O.: A look into the effects of context: some articulatory and perceptual findings. In: Proc. of VIIIth Int. Congr. of Phonetic Sciences, Leeds, 1975 (1977) (in press).

Gaitenby, J.H.: The elastic word. Haskins Lab. Status Rep. Speech Res. **2**, 3.4 (1965).

Ganong, W.F.: An experiment on "phonetic adaptation." Prog. Rep. (Res. Lab. Electr. MIT) **116**, 206–210 (1975).

Ganong, W.F.: Amplitude contingent selective adaptation to speech. J. Acoust. Soc. Am. **59** S(A) (1976).

Gleason, H.A., Jr.: Workbook in Descriptive Linguistics. New York: Holt, Rinehart & Winston 1955.

Goldstein, L.M., Lackner, J.R.: Alterations of the phonetic coding of speech sounds during repetition. Cognition **2**, 279–297 (1973).

Haggard, M.P., Ambler, S., Callow, M.: Pitch as a voicing cue. J. Acoust. Soc. Am. **47**, 613–617 (1970).

•Halwes, T., Jenkins, J.J.: Problem of serial order in behavior is not resolved by context-sensitive associative memory models. Psychol. Rev. **78**, 122–129 (1971).

Harris, C.M.: A study of the building blocks of speech. J. Acoust. Soc. Am. **25**, 962–969 (1953).

Harris, K.S.: Cues for the discrimination of American English fricatives in spoken syllables. Lang. Speech **1**, 1–7 (1958).

Harris, K.S., Hoffman, H.S., Liberman, A.M., Delattre, P.C., Cooper, F.S.: Effect of third-formant transitions on the perception of the voiced stop consonants. J. Acoust Soc. Am. **30**, 122–126 (1958).
Hoffman, H.S.: Study of some cues in the perception of the voiced stop consonants. J. Acoust. Soc. Am. **30**, 1035–1041 (1958).
Huggins, A.W.F.: On the perception of temporal phenomena in speech. J. Acoust. Soc. Am. **51**, 1279–1290 (1972).
Hyde, S.R.: Automatic speech recognition: a critical survey and discussion of the literature. In: Human Communication: A Unified View. David, E.E., Jr., Denes, P.B., (eds.). N.Y.: McGraw-Hill 1972, pp. 399–438.
Ingemann, F.: Speech synthesis by rule. J. Acoust. Soc. Am. **29**, 1255(A) (1957).
Kelly, J.L., Gerstman, L.J.: An artificial talker driven from a phonetic input. J. Acoust. Soc. Am. **33**, 835(A) (1961).
Kelly, J.L., Lochbaum, C.: Speech synthesis. Proc. of the Speech Commun. Sem., paper F7. Stockholm: Speech Transmission Lab. R. Inst. of Technology 1962.
Klatt, D.H.: Linguistic uses of segmental duration in English: acoustic and perceptual evidence. J. Acoust. Soc. Am. **59**, 1208–1221 (1976).
Klima, E.S.: Sound and its absence in the linguistic symbol. In: The Role of Speech in Language. Kavanagh, J.F., Cutting, J.E. (eds.). Cambridge: MIT Press 1975, pp. 247–270.
Kozhevnikov, V.A., Chistovich, L.A.: Rech' Artikuliatsia i Vospriatie. Moscow-Leningrad 1965 [Transl. as Speech: Articulation and Perception. Washington: Clearinghouse for Fed. Sci. and Techn. Inf. JPRS, 30]
Lackner, J.R., Levine, B.K.: Speech production: evidence for syntactically and phonologically determined units. Percept. Psychophys. **17**, 107–113 (1975).
Ladefoged, P.: Preliminaries to Linguistic Phonetics. Chicago: U. Chicago Pr. 1971.
Lehiste, I.: Suprasegmentals. Cambridge: MIT Pr. 1970.
Lehman, W.: Historical Linguistics, 2nd ed. New York: Holt, Rinehart & Winston 1975.
Liberman, A.M.: The grammars of speech and language. Cog. Psychol. **1**, 301–323 (1970).
Liberman, A.M.: The specialization of the language hemisphere. In: The Neurosciences: Third Study Program. Schmitt, F.O., Worden, F.G., (eds.). Cambridge, Mass.: MIT Pr. 1974, pp. 43–56.
Liberman, A.M.: How abstract must a motor theory of speech perception be? In: Proc. of the VIIIth Int. Congr. of Phonetic Sci., Leeds, England, 17–23 August, 1975. [Also in: Haskins Lab. Status Rep. on Speech Res. **44**, 1–15 (1975).]
Liberman, A.M.: Discussion paper. In: Origins and Evolution of Language and Speech. Harnad, S.R., Steklis, H.D., Lancaster, J., (eds.). New York: N.Y. Academy of Sci. 1976, pp. 718–724. [Annals of the New York Academy of Sciences **280**, 718–724 (1976).]
Liberman, A.M., Pisoni, D.B.: Evidence for a special speech-perceiving subsystem in the human. In: The Recognition of Complex Acoustic Signals. Bullock, T.H., (ed.). Berlin: Dahlem Konferenzen 1977 (in press).
Liberman, A.M., Delattre, P.C., Cooper, F.S.: The role of selected stimulus-variables in the perception of the unvoiced stop consonants. Am. J. Psychol. **55**, 497–516 (1952).
Liberman, A.M., Ingemann, F., Lisker, L., Delattre, P., Cooper, F.S.: Minimal rules for synthesizing speech. J. Acoust. Soc. Am. **31**, 1490–1499 (1959).
Liberman, A.M., Cooper, F.S., Shankweiler, D.P., Studdert-Kennedy, M.: The perception of the speech code. Psychol. Rev. **74**, 431–461 (1967).
Liberman, A.M., Mattingly, I.G., Turvey, M.T.: Language codes and memory codes. In: Coding Processes in Human Memory. Melton, A.W., Martin, E., (eds.). Washington, D.C.: V.H. Winston 1972, pp. 307–334.
Lisker, L.: Some cues to the voiced-voiceless distinction among the intervocalic stops in English. Haskins Lab. 24th Q. Prog. Rep., Appendix 5, 1957a.
Lisker, L.: Closure duration and the intervocalic voiced-voiceless distinction in English. Language **33**, 42–49 (1957b).
MacNeilage, P.F.: Motor control of serial ordering of speech. Psych. Rev. **77**, 182–196 (1970).
Martin, J.G.: Rhythmic expectancy in continuous speech preception. In: Stimulus and Process in Speech Perception. New York: Springer-Verlag 1975, pp. 161–177.

- Massaro, D.W.: Preperceptual images, processing time and perceptual units in auditory perception. Psych. Rev. **79**, 124–145 (1972).
- Massaro, D.W., Cohen, M.M.: The contribution of fundamental frequency and voice onset time to the /zi/-/si/ distinction. J. Acoust. Soc. Am. **60**, 704–717 (1976).
- Mattingly, I.G.: Speech cues and sign stimuli. Am. Sci. **60**, 327–337 (1972).
- Mattingly, I.G.: Speech synthesis for phonetic and phonological models. In: Current Trends in Linguistics, Vol. XII: Linguistics and Adjacent Arts and Sciences. Sebeok, T.A., (ed.). The Hague: Mouton 1974, pp. 2451–2488.
- Mattingly, I.G.: Syllable synthesis. J. Acoust. Soc. Am. **60**, S75(A) (1976). [Also in: Haskins Lab. Status Rep. on Speech Res. **49**, (1977).]
- Mattingly, I.G., Liberman, A.M.: The speech code and the physiology of language. In: Information Processing in the Nervous System. Leibovic, K.N., (ed.). New York: Springer-Verlag 1969, pp. 97–117.
- Mattingly, I.G., Liberman, A.M., Syndal, G.K., Halwes, T.: Discrimination in speech and nonspeech modes. Cog. Psychol. **2**, 131–157 (1971).
- McNeil, D., Lindig, L.: The perceptual reality of phonemes, syllables, words and sentences. J. Verbal Learn. Verbal Behav. **12**, 419–430 (1973).
- Mermelstein, P.: Automatic segmentation of speech into syllabic units. J. Acoust. Soc. Am. **58**, 880–883 (1975).
- Miller, G.A., Nicely, P.: An analysis of some perceptual confusions among some English consonants. J. Acoust. Soc. Am. **27**, 338–352 (1955).
- Miller, J.D.: Perception of speech sounds by animals: evidence for speech processing by mammalian auditory mechanisms. In: Recognition of Complex Acoustic Signals. Bullock, T.H., (ed.). Berlin: Dahlem Konferenzen 1977 (in press).
- Mitchell, P.D.: A test of differentiation of phonemic feature contrasts. Unpubl. Ph.D. thesis, City Univ. New York, 1973.
- Ochiai, K., Fujimura, O.: Vowel identification and phonetic contexts. Rep. Univ. Electro-Commun. (Chofu, Tokyo) **22-2**, 103–111 (1971).
- Ogden, C.K.: Opposition. Bloomington: Indiana U. Pr. 1967.
- Peterson, G.E., Barney, H.L.: Control methods used in a study of vowels. J. Acoust. Soc. Am. **24**, 175–184 (1952).
- Peterson, G.E., Wang, W.S.-Y., Sivertsen, E.: Segmentation techniques of speech synthesis. J. Acoust. Soc. Am. **30**, 739–742 (1958).
- Pickett, J.M., Decker, L.R.: Time factors in perception of a double consonant. Lang. Speech **3**, 11–17 (1960).
- Pisoni, D.B.: Speech perception. In: Handbook of Learning and Cognitive Processes. Estes, W., (ed.). Hillsdale, N.J.: Lawrence Erlbaum 1977, Vol. XVI (in press).
- Port, R.F.: The influence of speaking tempo on the duration of stressed vowel and medial stop in English trochee words. Unpubl. Ph.D. thesis, Univ. of Connecticut, 1967.
- Postal, M.: Aspects of Phonological Theory. New York: Harper & Row 1968.
- Rand, T.C.: Vocal tract size normalization in the perception of stop consonants. Haskins Lab. Status Rep. on Speech Res. **25/26**, 141–146 (1971).
- Rand, T.C.: Dichotic release from masking for speech. J. Acoust. Soc. Am. **55**, 678–680 (1974).
- Raphael, L.J.: Preceding vowel duration as a cue to the perception of voicing characteristic of word-final consonants in American English. J. Acoust. Soc. Am. **51**, 1296–1303 (1972).
- Raphael, L.J., Dorman, M.F., Liberman, A.M.: Perception of vowel and syllable duration in VC and CVC syllables. J. Acoust. Soc. Am. **58**, S57(A) (1975).
- Raphael, L.J., Dorman, M.F., Liberman, A.M.: Some ecological constraints on the perceptions of stops and affricates. J. Acoust. Soc. Am. **59**, Suppl. 1: S25(A) (1976).
- Rubin, P., Turvey, M.T., Gelder, P. van: Initial phonemes are detected faster in spoken words than in spoken nonwords. Percept. Psychophys. **19**, 394–398 (1976).
- Savin, H.B., Bever, T.G.: The non-perceptual reality of the phoneme. J. Verbal Learn. Verbal Behav. **9**, 295–302 (1970).
- Schatz, C.D.: The role of context in the perception of stops. Language **30**, 47–56 (1954).
- Shankweiler, D.P., Studdert-Kennedy, M.: Identification of consonants and vowels presented to left and right ears. Q. J. Exp. Psychol. **19**, 59–63 (1967).

Shattuck, S.R., Klatt, D.H.: The perceptual similarity of mirror-image acoustic patterns in speech. Percept. Psychophys. **20**, 470–474 (1976).

Stevens, K.N.: The potential role of property detectors in the perception of consonants. In: Auditory Analysis and Perception of Speech. Fant, C.G.M., Tatham, M.A.A., (eds.). New York: Academic Pr. 1975, pp. 303–330.

Stevens, K.N., House, A.S.: The perception of speech. In: Foundations of Modern Auditory Theory. Tobias, J., (ed.). New York: Academic Pr. 1972, pp. 3–62.

Strange, W., Verbrugge, R., Shankweiler, D.P., Edman, T.R.: Consonant environment specifies vowel identity. J. Acoust. Soc. Am. **60**, 198–212 (1976).

Studdert-Kennedy, M.: The perception of speech. In: Current Trends in Linguistics. Sebeok, T.A., (ed.). The Hague: Mouton 1974, Vol. XII (4), pp. 2349–2385.

Studdert-Kennedy, M.: From acoustic signal to phonetic message. J. Commun. Discord. **8**, 181–188 (1975a).

Studdert-Kennedy, M.: From continuous signal to discrete message: syllable to phoneme. In: The Role of Speech in Language. Kavanagh, J.F., Cutting, J.E., (eds.). Cambridge: MIT Pr. 1975b, pp. 113–125.

Studdert-Kennedy, M.: Speech perception. In: Contemporary Issues in Experimental Phonetics. Lass, N.J., (ed.). New York: Academic Pr. 1976, pp. 243–293.

Studdert-Kennedy, M.: Universals in phonetic structure and their role in linguistic communication. In: The Recognition of Complex Acoustic Signals. Bullock, T.H., (ed.). Berlin: Dahlem Konferenzen 1977 (in press).

Studdert-Kennedy, M., Shankweiler, D.P.: Hemispheric specialization for speech perception. J. Acoust. Soc. Am. **48**, 579–594 (1970).

Summerfield, A.Q., Bailey, P.J.: On the dissociation of spectral and temporal cues for stop consonant manner. J. Acoust. Soc. Am. **61**, S(A) (1977).

Summerfield, A.Q., Haggard, M.P.: On the dissociation of spectral and temporal cues to the voicing distinction in initial stop consonants. Haskins Lab. Status Rep. on Speech Res. **49** (1977) (in press).

Svennson, S.-G.: Prosody and grammar in speech perception. MILUS (Inst. of Linguistics, Univ. of Stockholm) **2** (1974).

Warren, R.M.: Auditory sequence and classification. In: Contemporary Issues in Experimental Phonetics. Lass, N.J., (ed.). New York: Academic Pr. 1976a, pp. 389–417.

Warren, R.M.: Auditory perception and speech evolution. In: Origins and Evolution of Language and Speech. Harnad, S.R., Steklis, H.D., Lancaster, J., (eds.). New York: Academy of Sci. 708–717 (1976b) [Ann. N.Y. Acad. Sci. **280**, 708–717].

Warren, R.M., Obusek, C.J., Farmer, R.M., Warren, R.P.: Auditory sequence: confusion of patterns other than speech and music. Science **164**, 568–587 (1969).

Whitfield, I.C.: 'Edges' in auditory information processing. In: Proc. of XXIIIrd Int. Congr. of Physiological Sci. Tokyo, September 1965, pp. 245–247.

Whitfield, I.C., Evans, E.F.: Responses of auditory cortical neurons to stimuli of changing frequency. J. Neurophysiol. **28**, 655–672 (1965).

Wickelgren, W.A.: Context-sensitive coding, associative memory and serial order in (speech) behavior. Psychol. Rev. **76**, 1–15 (1969).

B. Depth and Distance

Chapter 6

Primary Distance Perception

JOHN M. FOLEY, Santa Barbara, California (USA)

With 8 Figures

Contents

A. Introduction

Most of the time we do not bump into obstacles, fall into holes, or reach for objects well beyond our grasp. We are able to behave adaptively with respect to distances in our environment. It is common to interpret such behavior as the product of an input (perceptual) process and an output (motor) process, each of which may consist of several subprocesses. This chapter is concerned with the input process underlying distance-related behavior (distance perception).

In the typical experiment on distance perception, a human subject is given verbal instructions to indicate the perceived distances of objects (targets) from himself or from other objects. Perceived distance refers to how far away the target *appears* to be; it is not a judgment of physical distance. Verbal reports and manual pointing responses have been the most commonly used indices. The distances indicated in such experiments are usually called perceived distances, but there is a problem with this terminology in that different indices of the same perceived distance often do not completely agree. This problem will be considered below. In whatever way perceived distance is indicated, however, it is dependent on a large and as yet undetermined number of stimulus and non-stimulus variables.

This chapter is concerned primarily with one source of distance information, light vergence. This will be described in Section B, and variables will be defined in Section C. The special case of no distance information will be discussed in Section D. Section E will treat sensitivity to distance information. Section F will discuss the relation between relative distance and binocular disparity. Finally, Section G will present a theory of binocular distance perception.

B. Light Vergence as a Source of Distance Information

The pencil of rays reaching an observer from a luminous point in space contains information about the position of that point with respect to its distance, as well as its direction. In principle, any two rays emanating from a point are sufficient to determine its position. This information could, in principle, be extracted by using a lens to form an image of the point. Given the position of the image and the properties of the lens, the position of the object could be computed using optical laws. Alternatively, if two images of the object could be formed in different directions, either by two different optical systems or by one movable system, then the positions of the two images in relation to the nodal points are sufficient to determine the position of the object in space. In each of these cases the source of distance information is the same; it is the vergence of the pencil of rays at the point of measurement. The vergence of light from a point source at any point in space corresponds to the curvature of the wave front at that point. Quantitatively, light vergence is equal to the reciprocal of the distance in meters from the origin of the rays to the point of measurement (OGLE, 1968). It is measured in diopters. Six distance-related variables are considered in this chapter. Each is derived from light vergence and has a simple relation to it. The variables are monocular parallax, binocular parallax, motion parallax and their differences (disparities). These variables are essentially the same as those factors that HELMHOLTZ (1962, Chapter 30) distinguished as not depending on knowledge of the perceived object. Here they will be called *primary variables*. There has been considerable controversy over whether some of these variables are related to perceived distance at all. Present evidence indicates that they *are* related to perceived distance but that they interact strongly with other variables in ways that change these relations, sometimes masking or even reversing them. The emphasis of this chapter is on the relatively simple relations between these variables and perceived distance, relations which manifest themselves in situations in which the effects of other variables are minimized. These situations include those in which points of light are viewed in dark surroundings and those in which thin dark lines are viewed against a uniform illuminated background.

C. Definition of Variables

Any of several different sets of variables might be used to specify the visual stimulus and the perceptual response. Some authors describe the stimulus in terms of physical and psychological coordinates. Such description is possible for configurations of real objects in space. However, as will be seen, it is not possible for some laboratory stimuli for which one specifying variable is consistent with one distance, and another variable is consistent with another distance. Because we will consider such stimuli, specification will be in terms of the values of the relevant variables.

I. Stimulus Variables

Historically, the variables relevant to distance perception have been specified in several different ways. It now seems clear, however, that a polar coordinate system in which distances are expressed in terms of their reciprocals is highly advantageous. A number of different reference points have been employed within such a coordinate system. For example, visual angles have been specified with respect to entrance pupils, nodal points, or rotation centers. Directions have been specified with respect to the midpoint of one of these pairs, the midpoint of the arc of the Vieth-Mueller Circle between them, or an empirically determined egocenter. For the present purpose the difference between these is not significant. Stimulus variables of concern here are listed in Table 1. Horizontal direction and binocular parallax are illustrated in Figure 1. The distance variables are those which characterize the pencil of rays reaching the observer. Each ray has a direction. The relative direction of the rays which reach the observer from a luminous point (light vergence) stands in a fixed functional relation to the distance of the target. Light vergence is the only aspect of a visual stimulus which contains information sufficient to compute the distance from the object to the observer. Specification of the stimulus reaching the visual receptors

Table 1. Variables considered in this chapter[a]

Stimulus variables			
Horizontal direction	θ	Horizontal visual angle	$\Theta=\theta_i-\theta_j$
Light vergence	$\delta=\frac{1}{D}$	Light vergence disparity	$\Delta=\delta_i-\delta_j$
	(in diopters, where D is distance measured in meters)		
Binocular parallax	$\gamma=\frac{I}{D}\cos\theta$	Binocular disparity	$\Gamma=\gamma_i-\gamma_j$
	(in radians, where I is interpupillary distance)		
Perceptual variables			
Perceived horizontal direction	θ'	Perceived horizontal visual angle	$\Theta'=\theta'_i-\theta'_j$
Effective light vergence	$\delta'=\frac{1}{D'}$	Effective light vergence disparity	$\Delta'=\delta'_i-\delta'_j$
Effective binocular parallax[b]	$\gamma'=\frac{I}{D'}\cos\theta$	Effective binocular disparity	$\Gamma'=\gamma'_i-\gamma'_j$
Perceived egocentric radial distance	D'	Perceived depth	$d'=D'_i-D'_j$

[a] A complete specification of variables would include vertical direction. This is not needed here since all configurations considered are in or near the horizontal plane at eye level. $\theta=0$ corresponds to straight ahead.

[b] A more flexible definition of effective binocular parallax is $\gamma'=(I/D')\cos\theta'$, where in general $\theta'\neq\theta$, This definition may eventually prove more useful, but the definition proposed is adequate for the data under consideration here.

depends on whether one or two eyes are open and whether the head moves or remains fixed. At this level, three variables can be distinguished: monocular parallax[1], binocular parallax, and motion parallax. Each of these can be specified in diopters. However, in the binocular case it is common to specify distance in terms of binocular parallax, γ, which is sometimes called convergence angle. This is defined in Table 1 and illustrated in Figure 1. Note that for targets near the median plane and not too close to the observer, $\gamma \approx I/D$, where I is interpupillary distance, D is target distance and binocular parallax, γ, is measured in radians. Motion parallax is sometimes expressed as the rate of target direction change, $d\theta/dt$, as the subject moves his head laterally. However, for a constant rate of head movement and relatively small excursions, this variable also is approximately inversely proportional to distance. Thus each of these variables is a simple transformation of light vergence that takes relative eye position into account.

There are, however, two ways in which the three parallaxes can be varied independently. One way is to vary the conditions of viewing. By using a very

[1] The variable here called "monocular parallax" is more commonly called "accommodation" or "stimulus to accommodation." Since no role of accommodation in mediating discrimination of stimuli which differ on this dimension has been established, the term "monocular parallax" seems preferable.

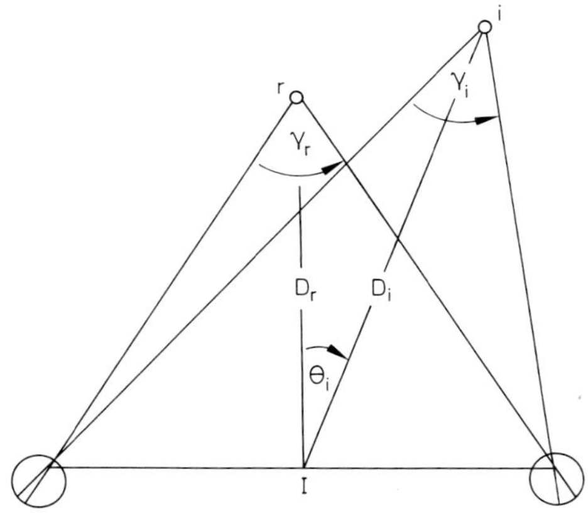

Fig. 1. Illustration of the stimulus variables horizontal direction, θ, and binocular parallax, γ, and their relation to binocular disparity. $\Gamma = \gamma_i - \gamma_j$

small pupil, occluding one eye, or fixing the head, monocular parallax, binocular parallax, and motion parallax, respectively, can be eliminated. In this sense, monocular parallax and motion parallax are subject to continuous variation because pupil size and the parameters of head movement are continuous variables. Such changes would be expected to affect discriminability of distance.

The second way in which the variables can be varied independently is to vary the direction of the rays that determine each variable. Monocular parallax can be varied by placing lenses in front of the eyes. Binocular parallax can be varied by means of prisms, or by telestereoscopic or stereoscopic presentation. Motion parallax can be varied by having the target move in synchrony with the head (concomitant motion). Thus it is possible to determine the effect of each variable in isolation and when paired with constant values of the other variables, as well as to determine the effect of two or all three of the variables varying in their normal relationship. Although these variables *can* be varied independently, in normal experience they are highly correlated.

II. Perceptual Variables

There are several dependent variables which are employed in studies of distance perception. In *discrimination paradigms*, the subject responds to each stimulus with one of two (or a few) responses, such as "nearer" or "farther." The dependent variables are the proportions of times each stimulus is associated with each response. If the differences between these proportions are statistically significant, then the stimuli are said to be discriminated. Closely related to discrimination paradigms are *matching paradigms*. In these an observer varies a physical extent so as to produce a perceptual match with a standard extent. The dependent variable is the physical stimulus selected to match the standard stimulus. In matching paradigms both stimuli are specified in terms of the physical variables described above. In neither discrimination nor matching paradigms is the subject required to indicate anything about how the stimuli appear to him, except that they look the same or, if they look different, the direction of their difference. There is a third class of paradigms called *subjective estimate paradigms* in which the subject indicates the perceptual magnitude of stimuli. These have played a very large role in the study of distance perception. Distance has often been indicated by means of a verbal report such as, "That target appears to be 1.5 m away." Manual indices, such as pointing at a target with an unseen hand or separating the unseen hands to indicate size, are also common. Such indices will be useful in understanding space perception only to the extent that they are closely and simply related to events in the perceptual system. No index or class of indices has established itself in this respect. Verbal reports rely on the observer's memory for the unit of measurement, which is likely to be imperfect and highly variable between subjects. GOGEL (1968, 1969) proposed that a transformation be applied to verbal reports of distance. This transformation is derived from reports made in a full-cue situation and it makes the transformed distances agree with physical distances in the full-cue situation. In practice this transformation has been found to correspond approximately to multiplication by 1.5. While this approach appears to be useful, it must be demonstrated that these transformed values are more closely and simply related to events in the perceptual system than are the reports themselves. In general, manual indices do not agree with verbal indices. When many cues are present, manual indices agree more closely with target distances than do verbal indices (FOLEY, 1977a). As in other domains of science, theoretical considerations may determine the choice of index. This possibility will be considered below.

The perceptual variables used in this chapter are designated in Table 1. The term "perceived" is reserved, as is conventional, for variables which describe the response made under instructions to indicate a perceived magnitude. There are two such variables: perceived horizontal direction, θ', and perceived distance, D'. Each may be specified with respect to the egocenter, which means that they are responses made under instructions to indicate perceived distance or direction from oneself. "Oneself" is sometimes specified further as the midpoint between one's eyes. Note that a distinction is made between "distance" which always refers to egocentric distance, and "depth," which is the difference between two distances.

Included among perceptual variables in Table 1 are two that do not qualify as perceived magnitudes. These are effective light vergence and effective binocular parallax. The observer does not report these directly; rather, they either represent transformations of distance-indicating responses or are inferred from experiments on relative distance with the aid of a theory. For this reason they are designated as effective magnitudes rather than perceived magnitudes. Each is computed by substituting perceived distance for physical distance in the definition of the corresponding physical variable. As with the physical variables, differences between perceptual variables are separately designated.

D. Perceived Distance in the Absence of Distance Information

It is possible to present a visual stimulus which provides no distance information to the observer. This can be achieved by viewing a luminous point in dark surroundings monocularly through a small artificial pupil. How far away does such a target appear to be? GOGEL (1972, Exp. II) had 24 observers view a point of light at 13.33 ft through a 1 mm artificial pupil. The median judged distance was 3.0 ft with a standard deviation of 4.8 ft. FOLEY (unpublished results) performed a similar experiment in which the optical distance of the target was varied over a wide range of distances by means of lenses, with targets viewed monocularly through a 1 mm pupil. Each of his six observers localized these targets between 0.7 and 2 m with no effect of target distance. It is of interest that, as luminance decreases, both accommodation (WALD and GRIFFIN, 1947; OTERO, 1951; and CAMPBELL, 1954) and convergence (IVANOFF, 1955) take on values corresponding to this same range of distances. RIPPS et al. (1962) have shown that for accommodation this same effect occurs with an artificial pupil. Recently OWENS (1974) has shown that the resting state of convergence is more closely related to perceived distance in the absence of information than is the state of accommodation. These findings suggest an interdependence between the depth signal in the absence of distance information and the oculomotor state, but the processes that would bring about this relation are not yet understood. Either might be the cause of the other, or both might constitute a joint effect of the visual stimulus. GOGEL (1969, 1972) has proposed that the distance at which a target is perceived in the absence of distance information be called the *specific distance*. He has hypothesized that when limited distance information is available, perceived distance will tend toward this specific distance, that is, perceived distance will generally lie intermediate between the target distance and the specific distance.

E. Primary Distance Discrimination

To say that a subject discriminates between two stimuli means simply that he can tell them apart. He demonstrates this by responding to them differently to an extent which is statistically significant. In a *simultaneous distance discrimination paradigm*, typically, two targets are presented simultaneously at different distances and in different directions. The subject indicates which of the two targets is perceived to be farther from himself. From trial to trial, the relation between direction and distance is varied randomly. In a *successive distance discrimination paradigm* the procedure is the same except that the stimuli are successive in time. They may be in the same or in different directions. In either case, if the proportion of correct responses is significantly different from chance, the subject is said to have discriminated the stimuli.

That two stimuli which differ only in distance are discriminable does not imply that they are perceived at different distances. Just as in scotopic vision differences in wavelength are manifested phenomenologically as differences in brightness rather than color, different physical distances may have as their perceptual correlates differences in apparent size, shape or motion. There is no established method for determining the *perceptual* basis for a discrimination. Generally, all that is offered by way of evidence is the subject's report that he saw the targets at the distances indicated, rather than inferring these distances in some way. The claim is more convincing if a consistent distance function is obtained, particularly if it is of a form which is not likely to be inferred, such as the nonmonotonic relation between perceived depth and disparity (FOLEY et al., 1975). Another approach is to use an indirect distance index such as the amount of perceived motion concomitant with head motion (GOGEL and TIETZ, 1973) or a difference in perceived size. Such evidence is not generally available, and the question of the perceptual basis of distance discrimination can often be answered only tentatively. It seems likely that experience may also play a role here. Targets which are at one time seen as different, but not at different distances, may, with experience, come to be seen at different distances.

I. Simultaneous Discrimination

Evidence with respect to simultaneous discrimination of monocular parallax is sparse. WUNDT (1862) obtained thresholds as low as 0.02 diopters for black threads seen against a white background at 2.5 m. Later studies produced a wide range of values for these thresholds, many of them higher than WUNDT's (LE GRAND, 1967). It is clear that some discrimination occurs under some conditions, but the phenomenon is not well described, nor are the processes by which this discrimination occurs understood.

If targets differing in binocular parallax are presented simultaneously so as to produce a binocular disparity, more than 95% of human observers show some capacity to discriminate them, even when there is no detectable difference in the monocular views (RICHARDS, 1970; JULESZ, 1971). Under optimal conditions disparities as small as 5″ of arc can be discriminated (BERRY, 1948; OGLE and WEIL, 1958; STIGMAR, 1970). The speed, reliability, and confidence of distance reports indicate that binocularly discriminated targets are not only discriminated, but they are also perceived at different distances. Discriminability (stereoacuity) has been shown to depend on the luminance, duration, and separation of the targets (OGLE, 1962).

Simultaneous differences in motion parallax also can be discriminated (TSCHERMAK-SEYSENEGG, 1939; FERRIS, 1972; ERIKSSON, 1972a; JOHANSSON, 1972). TSCHERMAK-SEYSENEGG used the method of adjustment and found the variability of settings to be about 4′ of arc for horizontal head movement and about 6′ of arc for vertical head movement. GRAHAM et al. (1948) and GIBSON et al. (1959) have employed paradigms in which the head remains fixed and the targets move with the same linear velocity, so that the stimulus at the eye is the same as if the head were moving at the target velocity. Although the authors refer to these experiments as experiments on motion parallax, neither motion parallax nor any primary variable in the sense of this chapter is involved. Nor is there any a priori justification for expecting discriminability to be the same when the targets, rather than the head, move. GIBSON et al. (1959, Exp. 1) found that 7 of 22 observers reported a spot with lower angular velocity in front of one with higher angular velocity (velocity ratio = 2). They concluded that this paradigm did not yield consistent space perception of any kind. However, GRAHAM et al. (1948), using thin vertical needles as stimuli, and the method of adjustment, measured angular velocity thresholds as low as 30″ of arc/second at a target velocity of about 5°/second. This study deserves careful consideration both because of the high sensitivity found and because it illustrates the basic and difficult problem of ascertaining the perceptual basis of a discrimination. Only 5 of the 10 observers in this experiment reported perceiving differences in distance. The others reported that they based their responses on perceived differences in the speed of the two needles as they moved across the field. The fact that thresholds for both groups were about the same suggests that the same process limits sensitivity for both. The thresholds found by GRAHAM et al. (1948) are sufficiently close to those of TSCHERMAK-SEYSENEGG (1939) to suggest that whether the head or the targets move, relative angular velocity is the critical variable. It is quite possible, however, given the variable velocity of head movements, that thresholds in the head movement task are not as low as GRAHAM et al. (1948) found. In most of the experiments on motion parallax, monocular parallax covaried with motion parallax. Thresholds obtained, however, are low compared with those for monocular parallax. Thus the conclusion appears justified that stimuli which differ only in motion parallax can be discriminated with considerable precision. The "no difference in distance" reports of GRAHAM et al. (1948) indicate that the discrimination is not always based on perceived distance. The paradoxical distance judgments obtained by GIBSON et al. (1959) remain unexplained. They may be related to the paradoxical distance judgments which frequently occur in successive discrimination paradigms (see below). Experiments by ERIKSSON (1972b, 1972c), which show that motion parallax does not determine depth when it is in opposition to height in field or relative size, suggest that the conditions under which lateral motion parallax is effective may be quite limited.

Motion of the eye toward or away from a target also provides a potential basis for determining the distance of a target. The relation between the excursion of the eye and either the change in light vergences or the change in visual angles is sufficient to compute target distances. ERIKSSON (1974) has demonstrated the existence of discrimination under these conditions.

II. Successive Discrimination

The question of whether or not successive stimuli which differ only with respect to the primary variables are discriminable *in distance* has long been controversial. That such stimuli are discriminable in size was reported by WHEATSTONE (1852) when binocular parallax alone is varied, and by BAPPERT (1922), when monocular parallax alone is varied. These results have since been confirmed by several investigators including HEINEMAN et al. (1959), GOGEL (1962a), BIERSDORF et al. (1963), BIERSDORF (1966), LEIBOWITZ and MOORE (1966), HARVEY and LEIBOWITZ (1967), WALLACH and FLOOR (1971), LEIBOWITZ et al. (1972), ONO et al. (1974), KOMODA and ONO (1974), and others. Discriminability of stimuli which differ only in binocular parallax is also indicated by the loss of position constancy when binocular parallax is put in conflict with motion parallax (HAY and SAWYER, 1969). It is also evident in the finding that as distance to a configuration changes, the pattern of disparities which produces a constant perceived three-dimensional shape also changes (FOLEY, 1966, 1967b).

1. Monocular Parallax

Tests of distance discrimination between successive stimuli which differ only in monocular parallax have yielded three kinds of results: (1) discrimination occurs with responses corresponding at least ordinally with target distances, (2) discrimination occurs, but the responses are reversed, i.e., the closer of two stimuli is called "farther" and vice versa, and (3) no discrimination occurs.

WUNDT (1862) was the first to report discrimination. An observer viewed a single thread against a bright background through a tube. He then looked aside while the distance of the thread was changed, then judged whether the second thread was nearer or farther than the first. After practice the observer had difference thresholds of 0.02 diopter at 2.5 m and 0.25 diopter at 0.4 m. Although comparable values have been obtained by some other investigators (LE GRAND, 1967), the specter of a possible artifact, such as would have arisen if the eye, tube and thread positions were not in alignment, has always hung over these results. Attempts to find distance discrimination with rods (BAPPERT, 1922) or circular disks (HEINEMAN et al., 1959) matched in visual angle and presented successively in the same direction, produced a preponderance of responses opposite to the actual change in target distance.

Other, slightly different experiments, however, have found discrimination with correct responses. According to WOODWORTH (1938), PETER did an experiment similar to BAPPERT's (1922) except that the targets were separated by 10°, and he obtained a significant proportion of correct responses for targets differing by 0.7 diopter or more (WOODWORTH, 1938). Likewise, in a paradigm in which the targets were presented one at a time with instructions to report the distance of the target, BIERSDORF (1966) found that six of his eight observers ordered the distances correctly although the range of reported distances was very much smaller than the range of target distances. FOLEY (1977a) fixed a single point of light at 50 cm and had observers both report the distance in inches (verbal) and reach out with an unseen hand and touch the bottom of a horizontal board just below where they perceived the target (manual). The simulated target (virtual image of the light) was displaced inward by negative ophthalmic lenses. Small changes in visual angle and retinal illuminance were

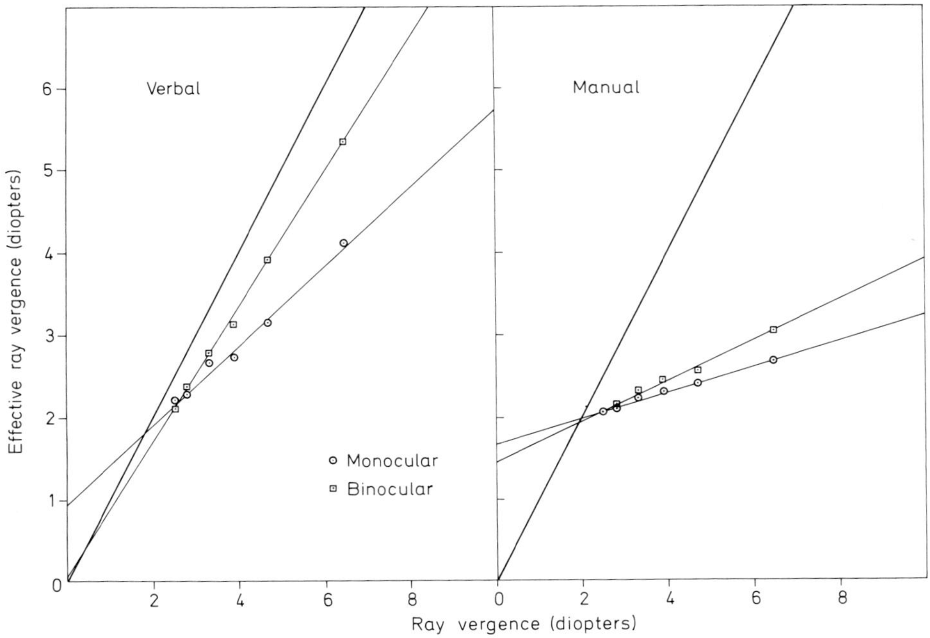

Fig. 2. Mean over six observers of effective ray vergence as a function of ray vergence for two stimulus conditions: monocular parallax varied, ⊙, and monocular and binocular parallax covaried, ⊡, data are replotted from FOLEY (1977a)

produced by the lenses, but any effect of these would have been in the direction opposite to monocular parallax. The results for two observers are shown in Figure 2. It is clear that there is discrimination on the basis of monocular parallax under these conditions. Manual distances are consistently greater than verbal ones, and for both indices the range of effective light vergence is only about one-fifth the physical range. The functions obtained were similar across subjects, indicating that the targets were not only discriminated, but also perceived at different distances. In a similar task, employing verbal reports only and stimulus distances up to 8.8 m, GOGEL and TIETZ (1973) obtained comparable results.

It is clear that the question of whether there is discrimination of stimuli differing only in monocular parallax is not one that can be given a simple yes or no answer. Clearly such discrimination is possible under some conditions. The problem is to specify what these conditions are. Research to date, the major results of which are summarized above, suggests that discrimination with correctly ordered responses is *least* likely to occur when the targets are identical in shape, color and luminance, when they are presented in the same direction closely adjacent in time, and when they are *not* very small (e.g., threads or points of light). Target identity might be expected to lead the observer to assume that the two targets are actually the same object or identical objects. If this were the case, then the observer would have to integrate the information from monocular parallax, e.g., that the object is now nearer, with the information that its retinal size has not changed. For an object of constant physical size, constant retinal size would indicate no distance change. Hence, the observer is confronted with conflicting evidence. Monocular parallax indicates that the object has moved in, while retinal size indicates that it has not moved. This might account for some of the failures of discrimination. Further, the oculomotor adjustment of the eyes to a nearer distance may reduce the *effective* visual angle of a target (micropsia). Although the actual visual angle in the eye increases about 2% (PASCAL, 1952), micropsia is evidenced by a reduction in judgment of angular size as accommodation and convergence increase (KOMODA and ONO, 1974). This means that, when target distance is decreased with visual angle constant, the signal sent to the CNS may correspond to a smaller visual angle. But decreasing the visual angle subtended by an object is known to increase perceived distance (EPSTEIN, 1967, Chapter 2). If this visual angle signal were to predominate over monocular parallax, then the paradoxical distance judgment would result. This hypothesis was proposed by ONO et al. (1974) and was confirmed by their finding that, if identical coins are used as stimuli, paradoxical distance judgment results; when different appearing coins are used, responses tend to be correct. It is as if the visual system cannot discriminate between a change in visual angle signal due to the stimulus and a change due to its own adjustments. It appears, however, that with targets, which are so small that effective angular size changes are indiscriminable, perceived distance is related to monocular parallax in a qualitatively appropriate, although not veridical, way. The hypothesis that *effective* visual angle varies with convergence has been proposed by MCCREADY (1965), RICHARDS (1967), KOMODA and ONO (1974), and ONO et al. (1974). A different interpretation of paradoxical distance involving the postulation of two processing stages has been proposed by GOGEL and STURM (1971) and GOGEL (1974).

2. Binocular Parallax

The story with respect to binocular parallax resembles that for monocular parallax. Although paradoxical distance responses are not common in binocular viewing, some studies have found discrimination and others have found none. Again the occurrence of discrimination appears to depend on the stimuli. It fails when the stimuli are such as to create the impression that the targets are physically identical. When they are in fact physically identical, discriminability is increased by presenting the stimuli in different directions and by using very small targets.

That stimuli differing only in binocular parallax are discriminable in distance was shown clearly by SWENSON (1932). Five observers viewed a circular disk of light presented binocularly in such a way that binocular parallax could be varied independently of monocular parallax, with visual angle and luminance held constant. Perceived distance was indicated by using a hand to place an unseen pointer directly below the perceived position of the target. Presumably at least several seconds intervened between successive stimuli. Target distances were 25, 30, and 40 cm. All five observers clearly discriminated these, and indicated distances corresponding very closely with target distances. In a similar experiment using points of light as targets, FOLEY and HELD (1972) confirmed this result, except that they found consistent overreaching of the targets. Figure 2 shows, in addition to the monocular parallax results discussed above, results from a condition in which binocular parallax and monocular parallax covaried in their normal relationship. The introduction of binocular parallax increases the slope by a factor of about 2. Distance discrimination of successive stimuli differing in binocular parallax has also been reported by GRANT (1942), GOGEL (1961, 1962a), LIE (1965), RICHARDS and MILLER (1969), ONO et al. (1971), and KOMODA and ONO (1974). Where discrimination occurs, subjects report that it is based on differences in perceived distance. There is also reasonably good agreement in the form of distance functions.

Given that man is sensitive to differences between successive values of binocular parallax, how sensitive is he? FOLEY (1976) measured the threshold for successive stereo discrimination as a function of the dark interval intervening between the two targets. The targets were luminous vertical lines, one above the other. The upper line came on first and the subject fixated the bottom of it. He was instructed to try to hold his fixation during the dark interval. The first line disappeared and, after an interval of 0–32 s, the second line appeared. The observer judged whether this second line was in front or behind the first. A forced-choice staircase technique was used to determine thresholds. The results for three observers are shown in Figure 3. Thresholds are about 1′ arc when the dark interval is 0 and increase to about 30′ arc when the dark interval is 32 s. In a somewhat similar experiment using points of light as stimuli and a single unspecified interstimulus interval, BOURDON (1902) concluded that at a distance of 1 m the threshold was 25′ of arc. He also found that this threshold decreased as distance increased.

Historically there has been much interest in the role of convergence in distance perception. The kinds of experiments done on this have been essentially experiments on binocular parallax with precautions taken to insure convergence on each target. This means each target is left on long enough to be fixated and instructions are given to fixate each. Neither was the case in the experiment of Figure 3. Although convergence movements may have been initiated, the second stimulus was terminated even before they could have begun. To see if fixating the target would improve performance, the experiment was repeated with the second stimulus left on for 1 s and the observer instructed to fixate it before responding. Within the range tested (3–32 s) all observers produced lower thresholds by an average of 10–20% in this condition. This improvement may have been due to convergence, increased duration, or both. In studies where binocular parallax varies over a wider range, it seems that convergence must have an even larger role because without eye movements perceived depth increases with disparity only up to 1–4° and becomes 0 at approximately 8° (FOLEY and RICHARDS, 1972; FOLEY et al., 1975).

Discrimination among successive targets which differ in depth by several degrees, such as those of FOLEY and HELD (1972), suggests that there is an extra-retinal signal related to the state of convergence which is combined with the retinal signal to determine the perception of depth. The mediation of these

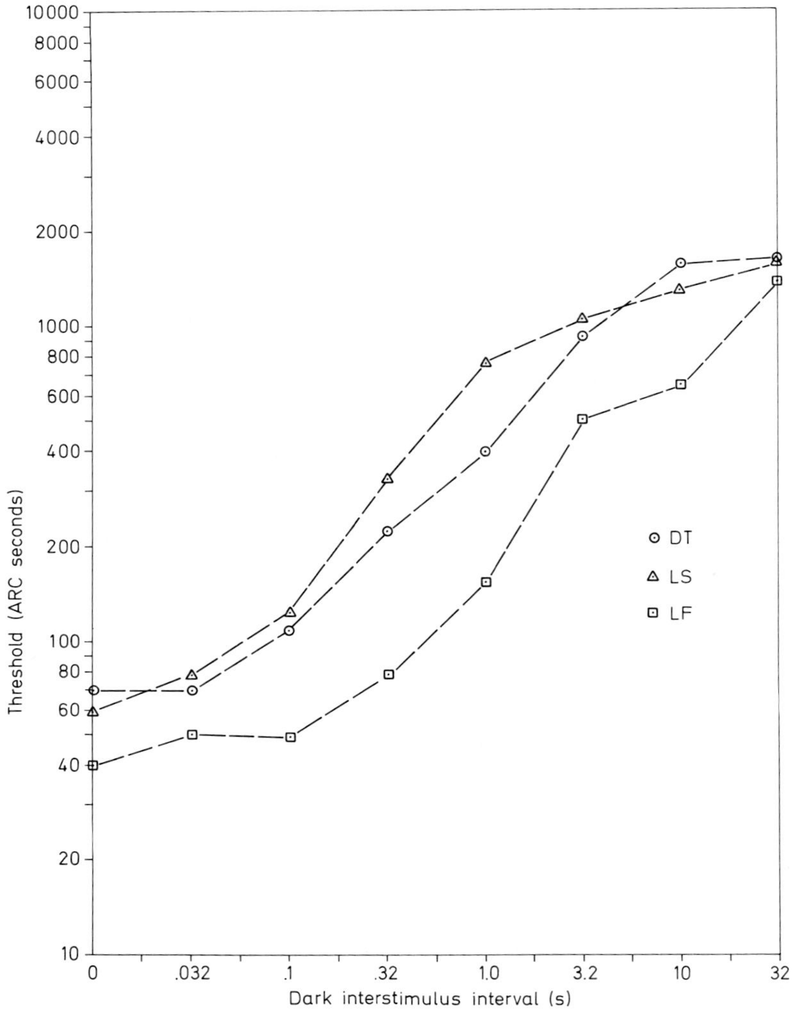

Fig. 3. Geometric mean threshold for successive discrimination of binocular parallax as a function of dark interstimulus interval. Each point represents the mean of 3–5 threshold determinations using a forced-choice staircase method (Data are replotted from FOLEY, 1976)

responses by an extraretinal signal is not established, however, since it cannot be claimed that the retinal stimuli were identical for targets at different distances. It is possible that slight differences in the retinal images with distance or differences in fixation disparity provide the basis for distance discrimination. This seems unlikely, however. Other issues related to extraretinal signals and the kinds of experiments needed to resolve them have been examined with respect to the closely related problem of the perception of direction by MATIN (1972) and MACKAY (1973). In the direction case there is evidence that perceived direction is related to an outflow signal from the CNS to the eye muscles. There is also some evidence for involvement of an inflow signal from the eye muscles (MATIN, 1972; SKAVENSKI, 1972). Vergence movements, however, are different from the conjugate movements under consideration in these papers. Vergence movements are much slower than saccades and can be modified by changes in disparity during their course (ALPERN, 1972). They may also bear different relationships to associated position signals (see Section 6).

3. Motion Parallax

ERIKSSON (1972a, Exp. 1) studied successive discrimination on the basis of motion parallax. He presented luminous squares one at a time at distances of 2 to 4 m. They were equal in visual angle and presumably in luminance. They were presented one at a time for 8 s. The observer moved his head left and right over a range of 55 cm while viewing the square monocularly. He then estimated the distance to the square. Monocular parallax covaried with motion parallax in this study, but a control condition showed it to be without effect at the relatively large distances involved. Reported distance increased with target distance and the change was statistically significant ($P<0.05$). ERIKSSON (1972a, Exp. 4) also confirmed this result using arrays of 20 squares as stimuli. In this latter case the range of reported distance was substantially less than the range of target distance. JOHANSSON (1972) studied motion parallax for configurations of light points at distances of 30–240 cm. He also found accurate discrimination and excellent correspondence between perceived and target distances. Evidence cited above would suggest that monocular parallax might have produced discrimination here. However, a control experiment indicated that it did not. Postexperimental reports by some subjects in these experiments suggest that the distances associated with the different stimuli may be inferred rather than directly perceived.

4. Combinations of Primary Variables

Very few studies have systematically examined the effect of two or three primary variables that either vary together in their normal relationship or vary independently. From Figure 2 it is clear that when monocular and binocular parallax are varied together, as compared to monocular parallax alone, not only is the range of perceived distance increased, but also there is closer correspondence with physical distance. This finding is consistent with GOGEL's (1969, 1972) hypothesis of a specific distance tendency, that is, a tendency for targets to be localized intermediate between their physical distance and the distance at which targets are localized in the absence of distance information. This effect is hypothesized to be most evident when distance information is limited and to diminish as cues are introduced. Other results consistent with the specific distance tendency are discussed by GOGEL (1972a).

SWENSON (1932) measured the effect of independent variation of monocular and binocular parallax on perceived distance. He found perceived distance to be intermediate between the distance corresponding to the binocular parallax and that corresponding to the monocular parallax, but nearer to the former. This suggests an averaging process in which binocular parallax is given a greater weight. It remains to be seen, however, whether the effects are completely additive and to what extent the weights may be dependent on experimental conditions. FREEMAN (1970) has proposed a general theory of space perception in which the weight for each variable is inversely proportional to the threshold for that variable and directly proportional to a quantity called "cue relevance" which depends on several nonstimulus factors such as past experience. This theory has not been tested for combinations of primary variables.

F. Relative Distance and Binocular Disparity

Research on how perceived distance is related to the primary variables is largely confined to binocular parallax. When targets are presented one at a time, perceived distance is a nonlinear, concave downward function of target distance. However, if the reciprocals of these distances, effective binocular parallax and binocular parallax, are plotted, their relation is approximately linear (Fig. 2).

What happens if two targets are presented simultaneously, thus introducing a binocular disparity? We might hope that the perceived distance to each target would be given by the function obtained by presenting targets one at a time. Such a hope is in vain. The perceived distance to each target depends markedly on its context, even if that context consists of just a single point of light. An experiment by FOLEY (1977b) illustrates this fact. Two points of light were presented within arm's reach. One was 3° above the other and they were separated by a constant disparity of 2.25°. The subject's task was to indicate the perceived distance to each target by pointing with his hand. The independent variable was the distance to the targets. The results for two subjects are presented in Figure 4. Pointed distance to each target is plotted against its physical distance. Squares represent the farther target; circles, the nearer target. Clearly the functions are different. The perceived distance of a target depends markedly on its position within the configuration.

Since the time of HELMHOLTZ (1962) and HERING (1942) considerable experimental and theoretical effort has been devoted to the relation between binocular disparity and perceived distance. Since disparity alone does not provide information about absolute distance from an observer, and the effectiveness of binocular parallax has only recently been recognized, many investigators have sought to find a relation between the perceived *relative* distance of targets, i.e., the ratio of their perceived distances, and their binocular disparity. There is something very curious in the history of this problem in that, although many experiments bear on it, their common bearing has not been generally recognized. This is particularly true of the work on the apparent fronto-parallel plane (see reviews by OGLE, 1950; 1962; SHIPLEY, 1959a). Consequently, very few explicit discussions of the general relation between depth and disparity are found in the literature. Three hypotheses, however, emerge from this literature.

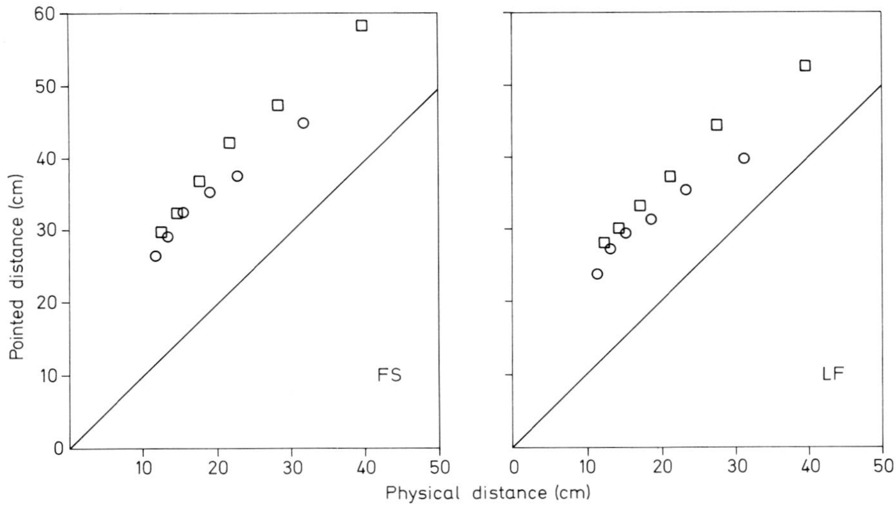

Fig. 4. Median pointed distance of a function of target distance for each point in a configuration of two points separated by a constant disparity of 2.25°, farther point, □; nearer point, △. Each panel gives the result for one subject. $n=6$. Data are from FOLEY (1977b)

The first hypothesis is that under primary conditions perceived depth has a fixed relation to disparity, a relation analogous to that between perceived size and visual angle when distance information is eliminated (HOLWAY and BORING, 1941). We might call this the *depth invariance hypothsis*. It is clearly rejected by an overwhelming body of evidence. For a constant disparity, perceived depth increases with perceived distance, which means that there is *some* degree of depth constancy in primary visual space. This is illustrated in Figure 4, and it had been shown previously by GOGEL (1961b), WALLACH and ZUCKERMAN (1963) and FOLEY (1967a).

The second hypothesis says that perceived relative distance depends on binocular disparity *independent* of the *distance of the targets*. This will be called the *relative distance invariance hypothesis*. According to it perceived depth depends on perceived distance, but relative distance does not depend on physical distance, only on disparity. The form of the function and what might determine it are left unspecified. This hypothesis had great appeal to investigators who believed that the visual system could not extract information about egocentric distance from binocular parallax. The hypothesis implies that transformations of the target configuration which preserve disparities will leave relative distances unchanged. It is a generalization of the hypothesis of HERING (1942) regarding the locus of the apparent fronto-parallel plane. It was assumed explicitly by BLANK (1953, 1958) in his modification of LUNEBURG's (1947) theory. The hypothesis is inconsistent with the results from relative distance tasks which will be considered below.

The third hypothesis says that the perceived depth interval between any two targets is equal to the physical depth interval which would produce their disparity, if it were located at the perceived egocentric distance of the targets. It is *as if* the relation between disparity, relative distance and egocentric distance is known to the observer, and he substitutes perceived distance for physical distance and solves for relative distance and depth. Using the concept of effective disparity (Table 1), this hypothesis can be expressed most succinctly as follows:

$$\Gamma' = \Gamma \tag{1}$$

where $\Gamma' = \gamma_i' - \gamma_j'$ and $\gamma' = \frac{I}{D'} \cos\theta$. It will be called the *effective-disparity invariance hypothesis*, since although the perceived distances associated with a constant disparity may vary, effective disparity does not. Using the approximation $\cos\theta \approx 1 - \frac{\theta^2}{2}$ (θ in radians), the left side of Equation 4 may be expressed as follows:

$$\frac{I}{D_i'} - \frac{I}{D_j'} - \frac{I}{D_i'}\frac{\theta_i^2}{2} + \frac{I}{D_j'}\frac{\theta_j^2}{2} = \Gamma. \tag{2}$$

For the special case where both targets are nearly straight ahead, i.e., θ_n, $\theta_f = 0$:

$$\frac{d'}{D_i'} = \frac{D_j'}{I}\Gamma, \qquad \text{and therefore } d' = \frac{D_i' D_j'}{I}\Gamma. \tag{3}$$

In this form the effective-disparity invariance hypothesis is most readily compared with the relative distance invariance hypothesis. It requires that perceived relative distance depend not only on disparity, but also on the perceived egocentric distance of one of the points (either one). The hypothesis does not specify how this egocentric distance is determined or how it is related to physical distance. The hypothesized relation (Eq. 2) is identical to the physical relation between binocular disparity and distance with perceived distance substituted for physical distance.

This hypothesis can be traced back to HELMHOLTZ (1962). Although he did not state the hypothesis explicitly, he applied it to his results on the apparent fronto-parallel plane. He found that the hypothesis required that perceived egocentric distance exceed physical distance by more than his own pointing experiments had shown. He suggested that this discrepancy was due to the absence of horizontal contours in his experiment. VON KRIES, in his notes in the HELMHOLTZ Handbook (HELMHOLTZ, 1962, Note 9 on Chapter 30), explicitly stated the hypothesis and wrote the equation for the special case of targets nearly straight ahead (Eq. 3). He did not associate this with the apparent fronto-parallel plane, but did point out the relevance to it of some other experiments on relative distance. At the time very little evidence was available, and he could only conclude that the hypothesis was a viable one. Since then considerable evidence has accumulated. This evidence rejects the relative distance invariance hypothesis and supports the effective-disparity invariance hypothesis.

Several paradigms have been employed in which an observer is required to set targets in some specified perceived distance relation. Three of these tasks are

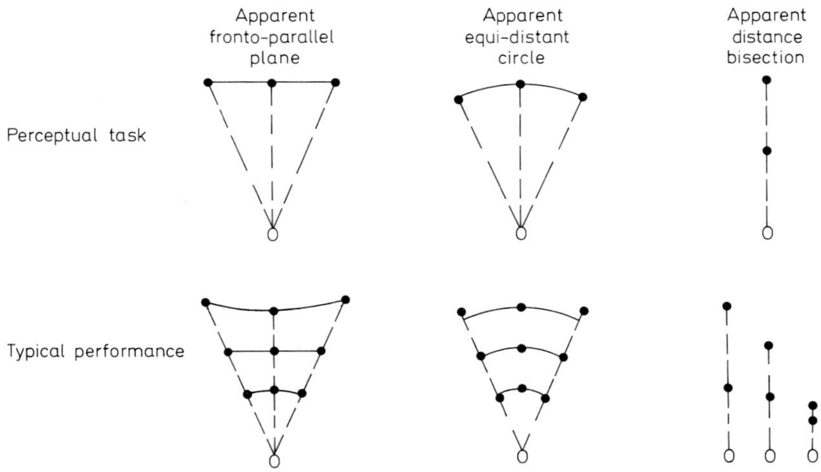

Fig. 5. Illustration of three relative distance tasks and typical performances on each (not to scale). The view is from above and the symbol 0 designates the position of the subject. The physical configuration coincides with the perceptual criterion only at one distance, generally found to be between 1 and 4 m

illustrated in Figure 5. In each task one target is fixed, usually in the median plane. The other target or targets are fixed in direction but variable in radial distance. The observer sets these (by remote control) in relation to the fixed target so as to satisfy some perceptual criterion. In Figure 5 the criteria illustrated are the apparent fronto-parallel plane (AFPP), the apparent equidistant circle (AEDC), and apparent distance bisection (one target half the perceived distance of the other). Performance in each of these tasks has been studied as a function of distance to the fixed target and typical performances are illustrated in the lower part of Figure 5. Although a few results are consistent with the hypothesis that a constant distance ratio corresponds to a constant disparity at different distances (HARDY et al., 1953; BLANK, 1953, 1958), in general this hypothesis clearly does not hold. In the AFPP (OGLE, 1962) and AEDC tasks (FOLEY, 1966), both disparities and changes in disparity with distance are small. Consequently, some investigators have tried in various ways to preserve the notion that relative distance depends only on disparity. When the distance bisection task is done over a sufficient range of binocular parallax, however, large disparity changes occur. These are approximately proportional to binocular parallax with constants of proportionality less than 1 (FOLEY, 1967b). Thus the relative distance invariance hypothesis is rejected.

A definitive test of the effective-disparity invariance hypothesis (Eq. 1) is not as readily achieved. The most direct tests require the measurement of perceived egocentric distance. For example, the hypothesis predicts that the disparity required for distance bisection be inversely proportional to the perceived distance of the far target (Eq. 3). But as VON KRIES (HELMHOLTZ, 1962) noted, perceived distances "can never be certainly and exactly told." FOLEY (1967a) and GOGEL (1972) made tests using verbal reports of distance. Although the data in both studies are limited, they indicate that perceived relative distance tends to be greater than required by Equation 3. FOLEY et al. (1975), using a manual index of distance and fixed eyes, obtained results consistent with the hypothesis at 0.5° disparity, which was the smallest they used. FOLEY (1977b) performed a more extensive study in which the targets were two points of light within arm's reach. These were simulated using the polarization technique so that they differed only in binocular parallax and direction. Both were in the median plane. One remained fixed at 25 cm; the other was located 3.5° below this and varied over a range of 12–38 cm. With free eye movement the subject indicated, both by means of verbal reports and manual pointing responses, the perceived distance of the two targets. These distances were used to compute the effective disparities, Γ'. These are plotted for two subjects in Figure 6. It can be seen that for the manual index effective disparity agrees well with physical disparity for disparities up to at least 2°, but that at large disparities the effective disparity falls increasingly below physical disparity. For the verbal index, effective disparity is larger than disparity at every point. Whether the effective-disparity invariance hypothesis is to be rejected, then, depends on what we take as an index of perceived distance. The close agreement between the manual index and the predictions of a plausible hypothesis provides, in itself, a reason for selecting this index[2]. Also if GOGEL's (1972) transformation (multiplication

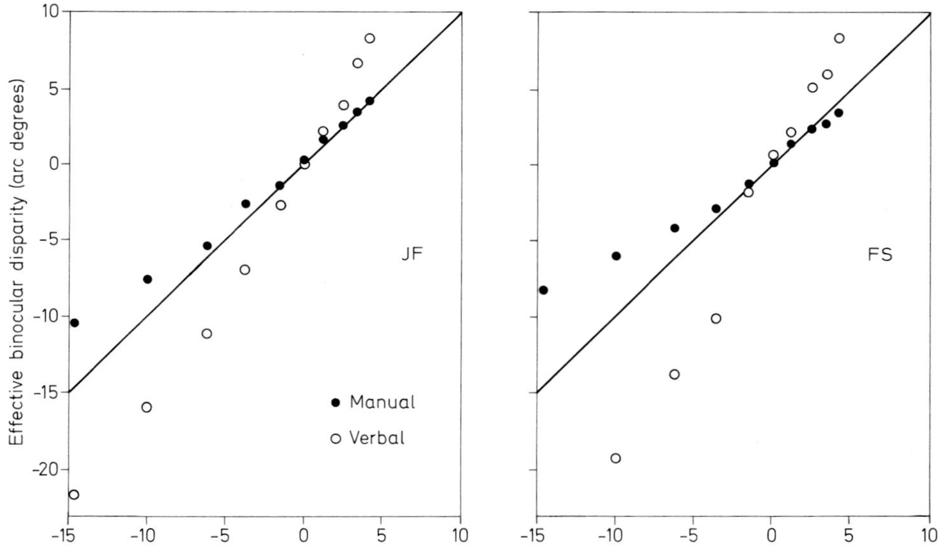

Fig. 6. Effective binocular disparity as a function of binocular disparity as indicated by both manual and verbal responses for two subjects. Manual responses agree with effective-disparity invariance hypothesis for small disparities. Data are from FOLEY (1977b)

[2] The good agreement between the manual responses and the hypothesis found for these two subjects does not hold for all subjects (FOLEY, 1977b). The more common outcome is for the manual function to have a slope less than 1. When this is the case we can define perceived distance as that transformation of either index which yields distances consistent with the effective disparity in-

by about 1.5) is applied to the verbal reports, the transformed values are close to the predictions of Equation 1. Clearly the effective-disparity invariance hypothesis remains viable for small disparities. It does not hold for disparities greater than 4°.

G. Binocular Distance Perception

I. Theory

FOLEY (1977b) has proposed a theory of binocular distance perception which incorporates the effective-disparity invariance hypothesis (Eq. 1) as one of two principal assumptions. For the purpose of describing the theory, it is convenient to rewrite Equation 1 as follows:

$$\gamma_i' = \gamma_r' + \Gamma_{ir}, \tag{4}$$

where i and r designate two targets and Γ_{ir}, their binocular disparity. The theory further assumes that for every configuration of targets there exists one point the effective binocular parallax of which is a linear function of its binocular parallax. This point is called the reference point and it is designated by r.

$$\gamma_r' = E + F\,\gamma_r \tag{5}$$

where E and F are constants. In many experiments the fixation point is the reference point (although exceptions to this will be considered below). The effective parallax of the reference point is assumed to have the same relation to its physical parallax as does a single point of light viewed binocularly in dark surroundings. The effective parallax of the reference point can be interpreted as the value of an extraretinal distance signal related to the vergence of the eyes (see Sect. G, VI). The effective parallax of any other point is simply the sum of the effective parallax of the reference point plus the disparity (Eq. 4). This relation can be rewritten:

$$\gamma_i' = \gamma_i + (\gamma_r' - \gamma_r). \tag{6}$$

This form of the equation makes explicit the fact that within a configuration all values of effective parallax differ from target parallax by a constant. All of the error in binocular distance perception is due to the misperception of the distance to the reference point. The two equations, 4 and 5, which have only two parameters, are able to predict the effective parallax of any point in any configuration, provided the disparities do not exceed 4°. Once effective parallaxes are determined, perceived distances are given by the following transfor-

---

variance hypothesis. Thus, the hypothesis is used to define the measure of perceived distance. This measure agrees well with measures derived from two quite different approaches (FOLEY, 1977b).

mation (from the definition of effective binocular parallax, Table 1):

$$D_i' = \frac{I}{\gamma_i'} \cos\theta. \tag{7}$$

The relative distance tasks (Fig. 5) provide an independent test of the theory. In each of these tasks the ratio d'/D_r' is a constant specified by the instructions. Therefore, Equation 2 allows one to compute effective binocular parallax γ' as a function of γ. Thus, if the theory holds, it should be possible to infer the effective binocular parallax and perceived distance of each point from the relative distance settings. Whether the inferred values of effective binocular parallax from different tasks agree with each other and with direct indices of perceived distance constitutes a test of the theory. Figure 7 shows the inferred function relating effective binocular parallax to binocular parallax for the assumed reference point in three different kinds of relative distance experiments (FOLEY, 1977b). Data from one manual pointing experiment are also shown for comparison. All the tasks yield approximately linear functions with slopes in the vicinity of 0.5 and intercepts of about 1°. Exact agreement among the functions would not be expected, since there were subject differences and differences in conditions.

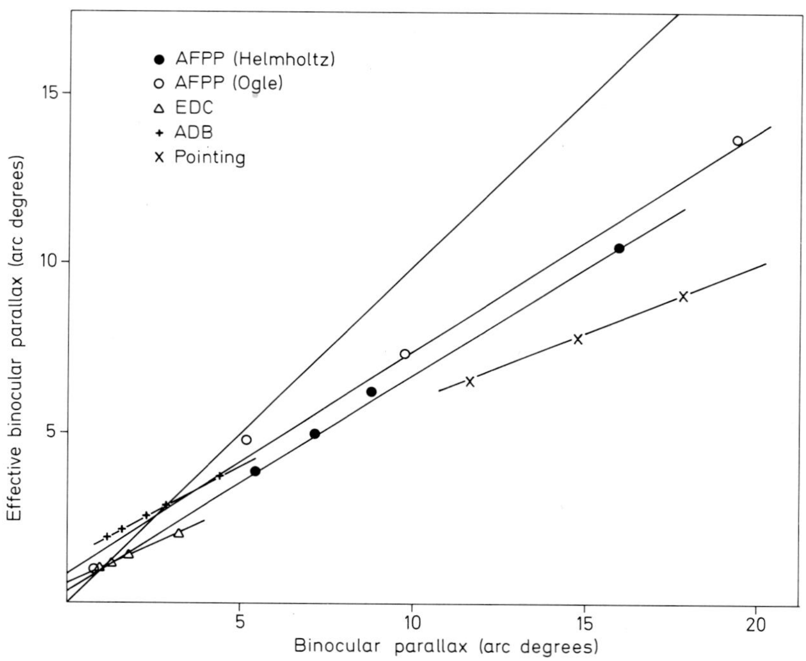

Fig. 7. Effective binocular parallax as a function of binocular parallax as determined by four different tasks. AFPP: apparent fronto-parallel plane (HELMHOLTZ, 1962; AMES et al., 1932); AEDC: apparent equidistant circle (FOLEY, 1966, Observer 9); DB: distance bisection (FOLEY, 1967b, Observer B); P: manual pointing (FOLEY and HELD, 1972, Observer JF)

II. Effect of Eye Movement

Up to this point we have not considered the role of eye movement with respect to the relation between perceived relative distance and binocular disparity. The basic test of the effective-disparity invariance hypothesis (Fig. 6) was done with free eye movement and with the observer looking at each light as he pointed to it. There is reason to believe, however, that with fixed eyes the results would be very similar for small disparities. SHIPLEY (1959b) and FOLEY and RICHARDS (1972) compared eye movement and no eye movement conditions in relative distance tasks. With disparities of less than 1°, effects were very small. In the FOLEY and RICHARDS (1972) study relative distance tended to be slightly greater with eye movement than without. In Figure 7 the bisection data and the equidistance data were obtained with eye movement; the apparent fronto-parallel plane data, with a fixation point. The comparison shows that the inferred effective parallax function for the reference point is linear and has similar parameters with and without eye movement. With eye movement the disparity invariance hypothesis holds only up to at least 2 or 3° of disparity. From the data of FOLEY and RICHARDS (1972) and FOLEY et al. (1975) it can be inferred that without eye movement this range is about 0.5 deg. When there are eye movements, as disparity gets large, perceived depth continues to increase monotonically. When there are no eye movements, after increasing for disparities up to 1–4°, perceived depth decreases to zero at disparities of 8–16 deg (FOLEY and RICHARDS, 1972; FOLEY et al., 1975). Thus, for large disparities eye movement has a very large effect.

The fact that the effective-disparity invariance hypothesis holds, even when the subject is fixating each point while indicating its perceived distance, means that, under these conditions, the momentary fixation point cannot be the reference point. The reason is that the effective parallax of the reference point changes at about half the rate of the actual parallax (Eq. 5 and Fig. 7). This means that the effective disparity between two reference points is about half the actual disparity. The fact that effective-disparity invariance holds in these experiments suggests that the reference point is determined by the configuration rather than the momentary state of convergence. It may represent a weighted average of the binocular parallaxes within the configuration.

III. Distance Constancy During Vergence Eye Movements

Such evidence as is available is consistent with the hypothesis that, at least for points and thin lines, perceived distances remain relatively constant during vergence movements. The evidence consists of reported impressions of constancy, not measurements made with different fixation points. There are no theories of distance constancy as such. However, the analogous problem of the constancy of perceived direction during conjugate eye movements has received considerable attention, and the hypotheses proposed are generalizable to distance. See chapters by MATIN (1972) in Volume VII/4 and MACKAY (1973) in Volume VII/3 of this handbook.

Independently, VON HOLST and MITTELSTAEDT (1950) and SPERRY (1950) proposed that when the eyes move, a signal related to the movement is generated and used to cancel out or subtract the effects of eye movement on the retinal signal. If the changes in the retinal signal are what would be expected on the basis of the eye movement, then perceived directions remain constant. MACKAY (1973) has called this view "subtractive theory." Subtractive theory is a special case of the more general hypothesis that perceived direction depends on the sum of a retinal signal and an extraretinal signal related to the position of the eyes. In the theory of distance perception presented above, the term effective binocular parallax can be interpreted as the sum of a retinal signal (disparity) and an extraretinal signal (the effective binocular parallax of the reference point). See Equation 4. Thus, subtractive theory might be generalized to distance constancy by interpreting the effective parallax of the reference point, γ_r', as the extraretinal signal. However, as has been shown above γ_r' does not vary with momentary convergence. Further, since the gain of γ_r' is only about half that of the vergence movements, if it did covary with them (which is equivalent to making the momentary fixation point the reference point), there would be a substantial lack of distance constancy. Thus, the most straightforward interpretation of the results would be that, although there is an extraretinal distance signal, it does not match the change in the retinal signal when the eyes move.

The eye movement signal of subtractive theory need not be interpreted as γ_r'. There may be a second extraretinal signal which perfectly matches the relatively short duration displacements of the eyes in scanning a configuration, but incompletely compensates for the long term displacements when the entire configuration is shifted in distance. A second extraretinal signal with these properties might be provided by the transient component of the response, the lower gain steady state of which is reflected in γ_r'. This possibility is consistent with an observation made by HELMHOLTZ (1962, Chapter 30). In pointing at a binocularly viewed thread, he found that overreaching was greatly reduced if he pointed immediately after opening his eyes, compared with pointing after a short period of looking steadily at the thread.

Where disparities exceed the range of the effective-disparity invariance hypothesis, however, subtractive theory encounters another problem. The obvious interpretation of the retinal signal is effective disparity. But in the absence of eye movements, this goes to 0 at large disparities. It follows that, when disparities are large, all targets should appear at the distance of the fixation point and vary as the fixation distance changes. That this does not happen suggests that perceived distance is not determined by the momentary sum of retinal and extraretinal signals, but that memory for position also plays a role. The hypothesis that memory plays a critical role in maintaining stability is incorporated in the "evaluative theory" which MACKAY (1973) has proposed as an alternative to subtractive theory. This theory states that, although information regarding eye movements is available to a sensory evaluator, it need not cancel retinal signals nor be subtracted from them. The theory holds, instead, that there is an internal representation of the environment ("map") which remains the same in the absence of evidence that it needs revision. Incoming sensory signals are compared against criteria to determine whether the map needs revision. The criteria are determined from moment to moment according to the course and goal of current motor activity and take into account the error variance of eye movement signals. This means that any difference between the retinal signal and the signal expected on the basis of eye movement information need not produce perceived motion. Perceived motion occurs only when this difference exceeds a criterion value. The facts of distance perception and distance stability during eye movements are consistent with this theory and specifically support the hypothesis that perceived position need not vary with momentary fluctuations in the sum of retinal and extraretinal signals.

IV. Perceived Distance of the Reference Point

The concept of the reference point was introduced to allow the general transformation between physical position and perceived distance to be specified by two parameters for each observer. The position of the reference point need not be occupied by any target, and it is not clear what functional role, if any, this point in space has in the processing of the configuration. What is distinctive about the reference point is that it is the one point in the configuration where effective binocular parallax and, therefore, its perceived egocentric distance, is independent of the configuration. When there is a fixation point, the hypothesis that the fixation point will be the reference point seems reasonable, but it has not been tested. In this case the extraretinal egocentric distance signal is likely to be a signal related to the vergence of the eyes. When free eye movements are permitted, this same relation does not hold, since the reference point remains constant while the eyes move. In an experiment with free eye movement, FOLEY (1969) measured the disparity required to produce a constant distance ratio between two points of light as a function of the distance of a third point. As the distance of the third point went from far to near, disparity needed to produce the constant ratio generally decreased, sometimes passing through a minimum and then increasing. This result indicated that under these conditions, the reference point is a joint function of the positions of all the points in the configuration. The fact that the effect was largest when the third point was farther than the others indicates that the farthest light had the greatest weight in determining the reference point.

The reference point can be determined directly by measuring the perceived distance of a single target and comparing this with the perceived distance of the same target when embedded in a configuration. The reference point is that point in the configuration for which the relation between perceived and physical distance is the same as for a single target. GOGEL (1961b, Exp. 4) measured distances with verbal judgments made with the aid of a monocular alley both for a single target and a configuration of three targets differing in binocular parallax. He found that the function relating perceived distance to binocular parallax for the single target lay between the functions for the middle and far points of the configuration. In a somewhat similar experiment, using only two points of light the perceived distances of which were reported for both single and simultaneous presentation, GOGEL (1972, Exp. 2) found the reference point to be between the two points, but nearer to the farther one.

V. The Domain of the Effective-Disparity Invariance Hypothesis

Although the effective-disparity invariance hypothesis was proposed for primary visual space and tested with only primary variables present, it may have much wider applicability. When nonprimary factors such as familiar distance, familiar size or relative size are introduced, relative perceived distance no longer depends on configuration distance or convergence of the eyes in the same way. Such changes may reflect changes in the extraretinal signal which determines the egocentric distance of the reference point. They need not be taken as invalidating the effective-disparity invariance hypothesis.

Two examples will be considered. FOLEY and RICHARDS (1972) found very little effect of convergence on relative distance judgments. However, their stimuli were presented against an illuminated screen which remained approximately the same angular size as convergence changed. Such conditions are of a kind that produce a very shallow distance function (KOMODA and ONO, 1974). GOGEL (1964) showed the converse, that is, that perceived distance and relative distance can be made to change by more than a factor of 2 while binocular parallax and presumably average convergence remain constant. Binocular targets were superimposed on a monocular alley which contained a striped vertical panel. The binocular targets appeared in front of the panel. When distance to the panel was increased, the perceived distance and relative distance of the binocular targets increased. Such results suggest that the extraretinal egocentric distance signal is not always closely related to the convergence of the eyes, but is subject to large influences by other factors. How these influences combine remains an unsolved problem.

There is another kind of result, however, which demonstrates a definite limit on the applicability of the effective-disparity invariance hypothesis. In certain binocular illusions the nearer of two targets appears farther away. This happens, for example, when a small-sized playing card is presented nearer than a normal one or when the small end of an AMES trapezoidal window is nearer than the large end. Such results are usually interpreted in terms of dominance of relative size over disparity. They are clearly inconsistent with the effective-disparity invariance hypothesis. However, GOGEL (1970) found that points of light adjacent to targets the depth relation of which is reversed are seen in the correct depth relation to an adjacent target. This means that effective-disparity invariance may hold locally, with different reference points in different parts of the field.

VI. Physiologic Considerations

Beginning with the work of BARLOW et al. (1967) and PETTIGREW et al. (1968), there is now a large body of evidence documenting the existence and properties of cortical cells which are tuned to specific disparities. The literature is reviewed in this handbook by BISHOP (1972). To date studies of these cells have not provided the basis for an adequate physiologic account of primary distance perception, nor does it seem likely that such an account can be based on the properties of these cells alone. The above analysis describes the relation between binocular disparity and perceived distance. Formally this relation can be expressed quite simply (Eq. 4). The extraretinal signal corresponding to the effective parallax of the reference point is added to the disparity. The reciprocal of this sum times the cosine of the direction angle is proportional to perceived distance. Neither depth nor relative distance are determined, even approximately, by disparity alone. Equation 3 shows that for targets near straight ahead perceived relative distance equals the product of an egocentric distance times disparity. Since in primary visual space egocentric distance varies by a factor of more than 10, the depth produced by a constant disparity will vary by a factor of more than 100. With more cues to egocentric distance, these factors will be larger. This extensive remapping of the relation between binocular disparity and perceived depth is a very salient fact that any satisfactory account of binocular depth perception must explain.

There may be some remapping produced by convergence through changes in the optics of the eye (SHIPLEY and RAWLINGS, 1970) and in the relative position of receptors (BLANK and ENOCH, 1973). Such changes, however, are both too small and of the wrong form to account for the change in the disparity-depth relation.

RICHARDS (1968) proposed that a remapping takes place at the level of the lateral geniculate nucleus. In RICHARDS' model each cortical binocular cell receives inputs from one position on the ipsilateral retina and several positions on the contralateral retina. These different mappings of the contralateral retina are mediated by different layers in the lateral geniculate nucleus. Only one layer is functional at a time, the functional layer being determined by the state of convergence. However, there is very little evidence for remapping at, or peripheral to, the disparity detectors. RICHARDS (1968) found that spontaneous activity of lateral geniculate cells is related to the state of convergence in the unanesthetized monkey. SPINELLI (1970) and MARG and ADAMS (1970) have reported the existence of cortical neurons which discharge in response to an object of a given size regardless of its distance, and, therefore, despite changes in retinal image size. However, this evidence is only fragmentary, and WURTZ (1969) found no effect of saccadic movements on the activity of cortical cells in awake monkeys. It seems more likely that the interaction of the extraretinal distance signal with the disparity signal occurs at a level of the nervous system central to the primary visual cortex.

The theory described in this chapter (Section G, I) is a formal one based on psychophysical findings and subject to test by psychophysical experiments. Figure 8 provides a summary of the formal operations of the model in a block

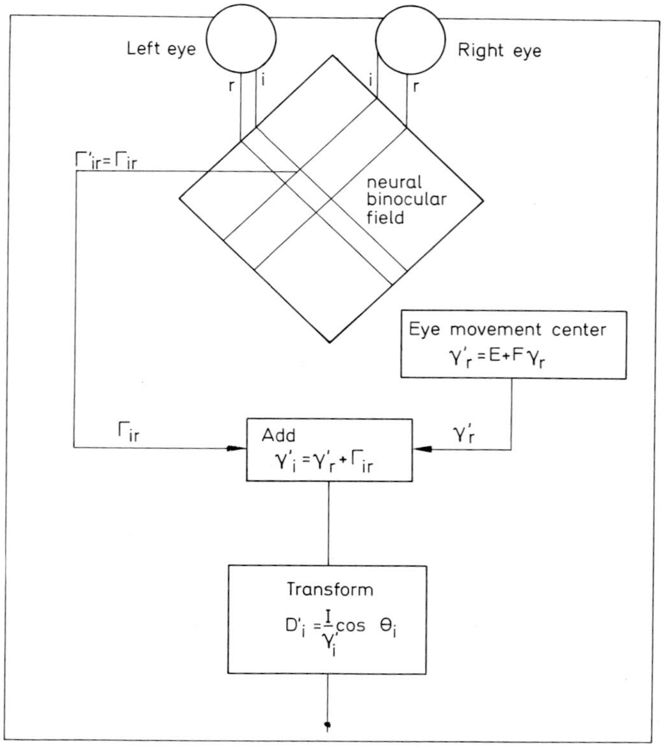

Fig. 8. A block diagram which suggests the elements of a physiologic model of binocular distance perception and their relationships

diagram that suggests some physiologic correlates. Although there are small changes in the retinal images and in fixation disparity as fixation distance changes, these appear both too small and too dependent on stimulus conditions to provide the basis for the relatively precise and reliable reference parallax signal. Consequently this signal is probably extraretinal. It is represented here as an outflow signal from an eye movement center. This is consistent with evidence for the existence of an outflow signal associated with saccadic eye movements (MATIN, 1972).

The effective disparity signal seems almost certain to be of retinal origin because a retinal binocular disparity is sufficient to produce stereoscopic depth independent of any oculomotor change. It is likely that the disparity detectors play a role in the generation of the effective disparity signal. It is clear, however, that there is more to the generation of this signal than the activation of a disparity detector by each pair of similar, horizontally disparate retinal images (JULESZ, 1971). The effective disparity signal is represented here as the output of a neural binocular field (SPERLING, 1970), leaving open the question of how it is generated. It is important to note that, since the model holds true even with free eye movement, the effective disparity signal is independent of the momentary fixation point. The effective binocular parallax of the reference point and the effective disparity combine additively to give the effective binocular parallax of any point in the configuration. Perceived distance is a simple transformation of this quantity.

H. Summary

The vergence of the light reaching an organism provides information as to the distance of the source. Depending on the conditions of viewing, distance is specified by the values of one or more of the following three primary variables: monocular parallax, binocular parallax, and motion parallax. There is evidence that human subjects can discriminate changes in each of these variables whether the values are presented simultaneously or successively. Although there is no good comparison of discriminability for the three variables in the literature, the evidence suggests that discrimination is best for binocular parallax. Under conditions where targets having different values of monocular or binocular parallax are discriminated, they are also perceived at different distances. It is not clear whether this is the case for motion parallax. If perceived distance is expressed as effective parallax, which is proportional to the reciprocal of perceived distance, then the relation between effective binocular parallax and binocular parallax is linear with intercept greater than zero and slope less than one. The function relating effective monocular parallax to monocular parallax is also linear with a greater intercept and lower slope.

Most studies of the relation between perceived depth magnitude and the primary variables have been concerned with binocular parallax. In general, the perceived distance of a target depends on the positions of other targets presented simultaneously and cannot be predicted from the function for targets presented one at a time. For disparities up to 4°, the relative distance of two targets as indicated by manual pointing responses is related to their binocular disparity according to the effective-disparity invariance hypothesis. This hypothesis says that the effective binocular disparity equals the actual binocular disparity. The effective-disparity invariance hypothesis and a linear function which gives the effective binocular parallax of a reference point in each configuration provide the basis of a theory of binocular distance perception. Experiments involving relative distance tasks such as the apparent frontoparallel plane, the apparent equidistant circle, and apparent distance bisection provide a test of this theory and determine its parameters. The effective binocular parallax of the reference point as inferred from these experiments is very similar to the effective binocular parallax of a single point of light determined directly by manual pointing. In each case the slope is in the vicinity of 0.5 and the intercept is in the range of 1–4°.

Although the perceived distance of the reference point is presumed to be determined by an extraretinal signal related to the vergence of the eyes, experiments with free eye movement show that the reference point is not the momentary fixation point. It is a point determined by the configuration as a whole, and it appears to be near the far point of the configuration. This finding is consistent with the view that distance constancy during vergence movements does not result from the cancellation of retinal signals by eye movement signals.

A physiologic interpretation of the theory is proposed, in which the effective binocular parallax is interpreted as an extraretinal signal from an eye movement control center and the effective binocular disparity is interpreted as the output of a neural binocular field. These two signals combine additively to give the effective binocular parallax of any target. Effective binocular parallax has a one-to-one relationship to indices of perceived distance.

References

Alpern, M.: Eye movements. In: Handbook of sensory physiology, VII/4, Visual psychophysics, Jameson, D., Hurvich, L. (Eds.) Berlin-Heidelberg-New York: Springer-Verlag 1972.

Ames, A., Ogle, K.N., Gliddon, G.H.: Corresponding retinal points, the horopter and the size and shape ocular images. J. Opt. Soc. Amer., **22**, 538–574, 575–631 (1932).

Bappert, J.: Neue Untersuchungen zum Problem des Verhältnisses von Akkommodation und Konvergenz zur Wahrnehmung der Tiefe. Z. Psychol. **90**, 167–203 (1922).

Barlow, H.B., Blakemore, C., Pettigrew, J.D.: The neural mechanism of binocular depth discrimination. J. Physiol. (Lond.) **193**, 327–342 (1967).

Berry, R.N.: Quantitive relations among vernier, real depth, and stereoscopic depth acuities. J. exp. Psychol. **38**, 708–721 (1948).

Biersdorf, W.R.: Convergence and apparent distance as correlates of size judgments at near distances. J. gen. Psychol. **75**, 249–264 (1966).

Biersdorf, W.R., Ohwaki, S., Kozil, D.J.: The effect of instructions and oculomotor adjustments on apparent size. Amer. J. Psychol. **76**, 1–17 (1963).

Bishop, P.O.: Neurophysiology of binocular single vision and stereopsis. In: Handbook of Sensory Physiology, VII/3A, Central Processing of Visual Information. Jung, R. (ed.) Berlin-Heidelberg-New York: Springer-Verlag 1973.

Blank, A.: The Luneburg theory of binocular space perception. J. opt. Soc. Amer. **43**, 717–727 (1953).

Blank, A.A.: Analysis of experiments in binocular space perception. J. opt. Soc. Amer. **48**, 911–925 (1958).

Blank, K., Enoch, J.M.: Monocular spatial distortions induced by marked accommodation. Science. **182**, 393–395 (1973).

Bourdon, B.: La Perception Visuelle d'Espace. Paris: Reinwald 1902.

Campbell, F.W.: The minimum quantity of light required to elicit the accommodation reflex in man. J. Physiol. (Lond.) **123**, 357–366 (1954).

Epstein, W.: Varieties of Perceptual Learning. New York: McGraw-Hill 1967.

Eriksson, E.S.: Movement parallax and distance perception. Report 117, Department of Psychology, University of Uppsala, Sweden (1972a).

Eriksson, E.S.: The effects of movement parallax on vertically separated stimuli at different distances. Report 119, Department of Psychology, University of Uppsala, Sweden (1972b).

Eriksson, E.S.: Movement parallax, anisotrophy, and relative size as determinants of space perception. Report 131, Department of Psychology, University of Uppsala, Sweden (1972c).

Eriksson, E.S.: Movement parallax during locomotion. Percept. Psychophys. **16**, 197–200 (1974).

Ferris, S.H.: Motion parallax and absolute distance. J. exp. Psychol. **95**, 258–263 (1972).

Foley, J.M.: Locus of perceived equidistance as a function of viewing distance. J. opt. Soc. Amer. **56**, 822–827 (1966).

Foley, J.M.: Binocular disparity and perceived relative distance: An examination of two hypotheses. Vision Res. **7**, 655–670 (1967a).

Foley, J.M.: Disparity increase with convergence for constant perceptual criteria. Percept. Psychophys. **2**, 605–608 (1967b).

Foley, J.M.: Distance in stereoscopic vision: The three-point problem. Vision Res. **9**, 1505–1521 (1969).

Foley, J.M.: The size-distance relation and intrinsic geometry of visual space: Implications for processing. Vision Res. **12**, 323–332 (1972a).

Foley, J.M.: Successive stereo and vernier discrimination as a function of dark interval. Vision Res., **16**, 1269–1273 (1976).

Foley, J.M.: Effect of distance information and range on two indices of visually perceived distance. Perception. **6**, (in press) (1977a).

Foley, J.M.: Binocular distance perception. (In preparation) (1977b).

Foley, J.M., Held, R.: Visually directed pointing as a function of target distance, direction, and available cues. Percept. Psychophys. **12**, 263–268 (1972).

Foley, J.M., Richards, W.: Effects of voluntary eye movement and convergence on the binocular appreciation of depth. Percept. Psychophys. **11**, 423–427 (1972).

Foley, J.M., Applebaum, T., Richards, W.: Stereopsis with large disparities: Discrimination and perceived depth. Vision Res. **15**, 417–421 (1975).

Freeman, R.B.: Theory of cues and the psychophysics of visual space perception. Psychon. Monogr. Suppl. **3**, No. 13, Whole No. 45, 171–181 (1970).

Gibson, E.J., Gibson, J.J., Smith, O.W., Flock, H.: Motion parallax as a determinant of perceived depth. J. exp. Psychol. **58**, 40–51 (1959).

Gogel, W.C.: Convergence as a cue to absolute distance. J. Psychol. **52**, 287–301 (1961a).

Gogel, W.C.: Convergence as a cue to the perceived distance of objects in a binocular configuration. J. Psychol. **52**, 303–315 (1961b).

Gogel, W.C.: Convergence as a determiner of perceived absolute size. J. Psychol. **53**, 475–489 (1962a).

Gogel, W.C.: The effect of convergence on perceived size and distance. J. Psychol. **53**, 475–489 (1962b).

Gogel, W.C.: Perception of depth from binocular disparity. J. exp. Psychol. **67**, 379–386 (1964).

Gogel, W.C.: The measurement of perceived size and distance. In: W.D. Neff (ed.) Contributions to Sensory Physiology. New York: Academic Press, 1968, Vol. III.

Gogel, W.C.: The sensing of retinal size. Vision Res. **9**, 3–24 (1969).

Gogel, W.C.: The adjacency principle and three-dimensional visual illusions. Psychon. Monogr. Suppl. **3**, No. 13, Whole No. 45, 153–219 (1970).

Gogel, W.C.: Scalar perceptions with binocular cues of distance. Amer. J. Psychol. **85**, 477–497 (1972).

Gogel, W.C.: Cognitive factors in spatial responses. Psychologia **17**, 213–225 (1974).

Gogel, W.C., Sturm, R.D.: Directional separation and the size cue to distance. Psychol. Forsch. **35**, 57–80 (1971).

Gogel, W.C., Tietz, J.D.: Absolute motion parallax and the specific distance tendency. Percept. Psychophys. **13**, 284–292 (1973).

Graham, C.H., Baker, K.E., Hecht, M., Lloyd, V.V.: Factors influencing thresholds for monocular movement parallax. J. exp. Psychol. **38**, 205–223 (1948).

Grant, V.W.: Accommodation and convergence in visual space perception. J. exp. Psychol. **31**, 89–104 (1942).

Hardy, L.H., Rand, G., Rittler, M.C., Blank, A.A., Boeder, P.: The Geometry of Binocular Space Perception. New York: Knapp Memorial Laboratories, Columbia University, College of Physicians and Surgeons 1953.

Harvey, L.O., Leibowitz, H.W.: Effects of exposure duration, cue reduction, and temporary monocularity on size matching at short distances. J. opt. Soc. Amer. **57**, 250–253 (1967).

Hay, J., Sawyer, S.: Position constancy and binocular convergence. Percept. Psychophys. **5**, 310–312 (1969).

Heinemann, E.G., Tulving, E., Nachmias, J.: The effect of oculomotor adjustments on apparent size. Amer. J. Psychol. **72**, 32–45 (1959).

Helmholtz, H.L.F. von: Treatise on physiological optics. Vol. 3, Southhall, J.P.C. (Trans.) New York: Dover 1962, Translation of 3rd German Edition of Handbuch der Physiologischen Optik, Hamburg: Voss (1910).

Hering, E.: Spatial Sense and Movements of the Eye. Radde, C.A. (Trans.) Baltimore: American Academy of Optometry, 1942, Translation of: Der Raumsinn und die Bewegungen des Auges. Leipzig: Vogel 1879.

Holst, E. von, Mittelstaedt, H.: Das Reafferenzprinzip. Naturwissenschaften **37**, 464–476 (1950).

Holway, A.H., Boring, E.G.: Determinants of apparent visual size with distance variant. Amer. J. Psychol. **54**, 21–37 (1941).

Ivanoff, A.: Night binocular convergence and night myopia. J. opt. Soc. Amer. **45**, 769–770 (1955).

Johansson, G.: Monocular movement parallax and near space perception. Report 132, Department of Psychology, University of Uppsala, Sweden (1972).

Julesz, B.: Foundations of Cyclopean Perception. Chicago: University of Chicago Press 1971.

Komoda, M.K., Ono, H.: Oculomotor adjustments and size-distance perception. Percept. Psychophys. **15**, 353–360 (1974).

Le Grand, Y.: Form and Space Vision. Millodot, M., Heath, G.G., (Trans.) Bloomington, Indiana: University of Indiana Press 1967.

Leibowitz, H., Moore, D.: Role of changes in accommodation and convergence in the perception of size. J. opt. Soc. Amer. **56**, 1120–1128 (1966).

Leibowitz, H.W., Shiina, K., Hennessy, R.T.: Oculomotor adjustments and size constancy. Percept. Psychophys. **12**, 497–500 (1972).

Lie, I.: Convergence as a cue to perceived size and distance. Scand. J. Psychol. **6**, 109–116 (1965).

Luneburg, R.: Mathematical Analysis of Binocular Vision. Princeton: Princeton University Press 1947.

McCready, D.W.: Size-distance perception and accommodation-convergence micropsia—A critique. Vision Res. **5**, 189–206 (1965).

Mackay, D.M.: Visual stability and voluntary eye movements. In: Handbook of Sensory Physiology, VII/3A, Central Processing of Visual Information, Jung, R. (ed.) Berlin-Heidelberg-New York: Springer-Verlag 1973.

Marg, E., Adams, J.E.: Evidence for a neurological zoom system in vision from angular changes in some receptive fields of single neurons with changes in fixation distance in the human visual cortex. Experientia (Basel) **26**, 270–271 (1970).

Matin, L.: Eye movements and perceived visual direction. In: Handbook of Sensory Physiology, VII/4, Visual Psychophysics, Jameson, D., Hurvich, L. (eds.) Berlin-Heidelberg-New York: Springer-Verlag 1972.

Ogle, K.N.: Analytical treatment of the longitudinal horopter; its measurement and application to related phenomena, especially to the relative size and shape of the ocular images. J. opt. Soc. Amer. **22**, 665–728 (1932).

Ogle, K.N.: Researches in Binocular Vision. Philadelphia: Saunders 1950.

Ogle, K.N.: The optical space sense. In: Davson, H. (ed.) The Eye. **4**, New York: Academic Press 1962.

Ogle, K.N.: Optics: An Introduction for Ophthalmologists. Springfield, Ill.: Charles C. Thomas 1968.

Ogle, K.N., Weil, M.P.: Stereoscopic vision and the duration of the stimulus. A.M.A. Arch. Ophthal. **59**, 4–17 (1958).

Ono, H., Mitson, L., Seabrook, K.: Changes in convergence and retinal disparities as an explanation for the wallpaper phenomenon. J. exp. Psychol. **91**, 1–10 (1971).

Ono, H., Muter, P., Mitson, L.: Size-distance paradox with accommodative micropsia. Percept. Psychophys. **15**, 301–307 (1974).

Otero, J.M.: Influence of the state of accommodation on the visual performance of the human eye. J. opt. Soc. Amer. **41**, 942–948 (1951).

Owens, D.A.: An investigation of the relationship between the specific distance tendency and the oculomotor system. Masters Thesis. Pennsylvania State University (1974).

Pascal, J.I.: Effect of accommodation on the retinal image. Brit. J. Ophthal. **32**, 676–678 (1952).

Pettigrew, J.D., Nikara, T., Bishop, P.: Binocular interaction on single units in cat striate cortex: Simultaneous stimulation by single moving slit with receptive fields in correspondence. Exp. Brain Res. **6**, 391–410 (1968).

Richards, W.: Apparent modifiability of receptive fields during accommodation and convergence and a model for size constancy. Neuropsychologia **5**, 63–72 (1967).

Richards, W.: Spatial remapping in the primate visual system. Kybernetik **4**, 146–156 (1968).

Richards, W.: Stereopsis and stereoblindness. Exp. Brain Res. **10**, 380–388 (1970).

Richards, W., Miller, J.F.: Convergence as a cue to depth. Percept. Psychophys. **5**, 317–320 (1969).

Ripps, H., Chin, N.B., Siegel, I.M., Breinin, G.M.: The effect of pupil size on accommodation, convergence, and the AC/A ratio. Invest. Ophthal. **1**, 127–135 (1962).

Shipley, T.: The frontal reference surfaces of visual space. Doc. Ophthalmol. **13**, 487–516 (1959a).

Shipley, T.: An experimental study of the frontal reference curves of binocular visual space. Doc. Ophthalmol. **15**, 321–350 (1959b).

Shipley, T., Rawlings, S.: The nonius horopter—II. An experimental report. Vision Res. **10**, 1263–1299 (1970).

Skavenski, A.A.: Inflow as a source of extraretinal eye position information. Vision Res. **12**, 221–229 (1972).

Sperling, G.: Binocular vision: A physical and a neural theory. Amer. J. Psychol. **83**, 461–534 (1970).

Sperry, R.W.: Neural basis of the spontaneous optokinetic response produced by inverted vision. J. comp. Physiol. Psychol. **43**, 482–489 (1950).

Spinelli, D.N.: Recognition of visual patterns. In: Perception and its Disorders, Hamburg, D.A., Pribram, K.H., Skunkard, A.J. (eds.) Baltimore: Williams and Wilkins 1970.

Stigmar, G.: Observations on vernier and stereo acuity with special reference to their relationship. Acta ophthal. (Kbh.) **48**, 979–998 (1970).

Swenson, H.A.: The relative influence of accommodation and convergence in the judgment of distance. J. gen. Psychol. **7**, 360-380 (1932).

Tschermak-Seysenegg, A.: Über Parallakotoskopie. Pflügers Arch. ges. Physiol. **241**, 454–469 (1939).

Wald, G., Griffin, D.R.: The change in refractive power of the human eye in dim and bright light. J. opt. Soc. Amer. **37**, 321–336 (1947).

Wallach, H., Zuckerman, C.: The constancy of stereoscopic depth. Amer. J. Psychol. **76**, 404–412 (1963).

Wallach, H., Floor, L.: The use of size matching to demonstrate the effectiveness of accommodation and convergence as cues for distance. Percept. Psychophys. **10**, 423–428 (1971).

Wheatstone, C.: On some remarkable, and hiterto unobserved phenomena of binocular vision. Part 2. Philos. Mag. **4**(3), 504–523 (1852).

Woodworth, R.S.: Experimental Psychology. New York: Holt 1938.

Wundt, W.: Beiträge zur Theorie der Sinneswahrnehmung. Leipzig: C.F. Winter'sche 1862.

Wurtz, R.H.: Comparison of effects of eye movements and stimulus movements on striate cortex neurons of the monkey. J. Neurophysiol. **32**, 987–994 (1969).

Chapter 7

Global Stereopsis: Cooperative Phenomena in Stereoscopic Depth Perception*

BELA JULESZ, Murray Hill, N.J. (USA)

With 26 Figures

Contents

A. Introduction

In the study of perceptual phenomena the *Gestalt* psychologists were the first to draw attention to those hierarchical systems for which the whole system is "more" than its constituent parts. By "more" one usually means the emergence of some system behavior that is qualitatively very different from the behavior of the constituent subsystems. In order to obtain such a metamorphosis at a certain hierarchical system level (global level), the subsystems of the previous stage (local level) cannot interact at random but must somehow *cooperate*.

There is a consensus that even the simplest cooperative system worth studying should exhibit: 1) *disorder-order transitions,* 2) *hysteresis,* and 3) *multiple stable states*. It should not be surprising that the human visual system—the most

* The red-green goggles supplied with this volume are to be used in viewing the stereo-pair illustrations marked with an asterisk. A short and much simpler version of this chapter exists with red-green anaglyph demonstrations (JULESZ, 1974) and might be read first.

Fig. 1. Disorder-order transition based on semantics. After scrutinizing the randomly appearing clusters, a camouflaged animal becomes visible (photographed by R.C. James, Carraher, and Thurston, 1966; reprinted by permission of Van Nostrand Reinhold)

Fig. 2. Ambiguous figure based on semantics, which can be seen as either a young girl or an old woman, demonstrates multiple-stable states in perceptual organization

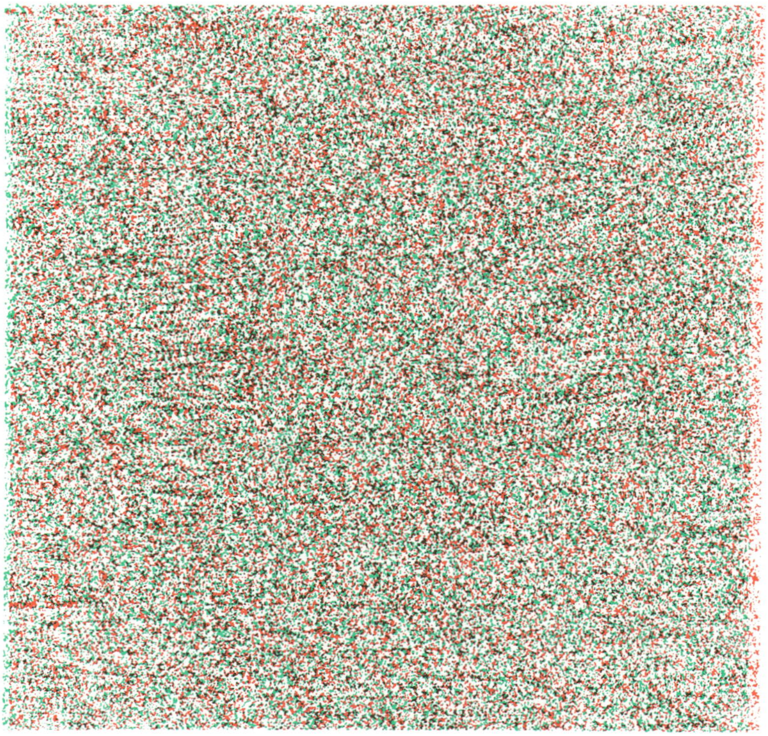

Fig. 3*. Complex random-dot stereogram portraying a hyperbolic paraboloid and a torus. Fusion takes several seconds the first time, but is much faster at repeated trials (JULESZ, 1971). Red filter of red-green goggles (supplied) should be over right eye.

intricate structure in the known universe—should show such cooperative phenomena. Gestaltist psychologists and their followers demonstrated many such phenomena. For instance, a *disorder-order transition* can be experienced when viewing Figure 1: it takes some time before the random speckles suddenly form a familiar image. Usually, after such an image is recognized (i.e., after the transition to an ordered mental state did occur), it is almost impossible to get rid of it; and this then illustrates *hysteresis*—a lag between cause and effect. It takes a great effort to switch to a certain perceptual state, but after this state is obtained, great effort is again required to switch back to the former state. Finally, Figure 2 illustrates the existence of *multiple-stable states* in visual perception. In this famous ambiguous figure whether the young girl or the old woman is seen first, it requires considerable effort to destroy one perceptual organization and obtain the other.

In the demonstrations of Figures 1 and 2, and in most of the other examples used by the Gestaltist school, the cooperative phenomena are the result of highly intricate processes based on "semantics"—familiarity with shapes in our environment (e.g., dalmatian dogs and human faces). Without the enigmatic problems of semantics being first understood, these examples seem to be far too complicated for scientific scrutiny. Indeed, the insurmountable problems

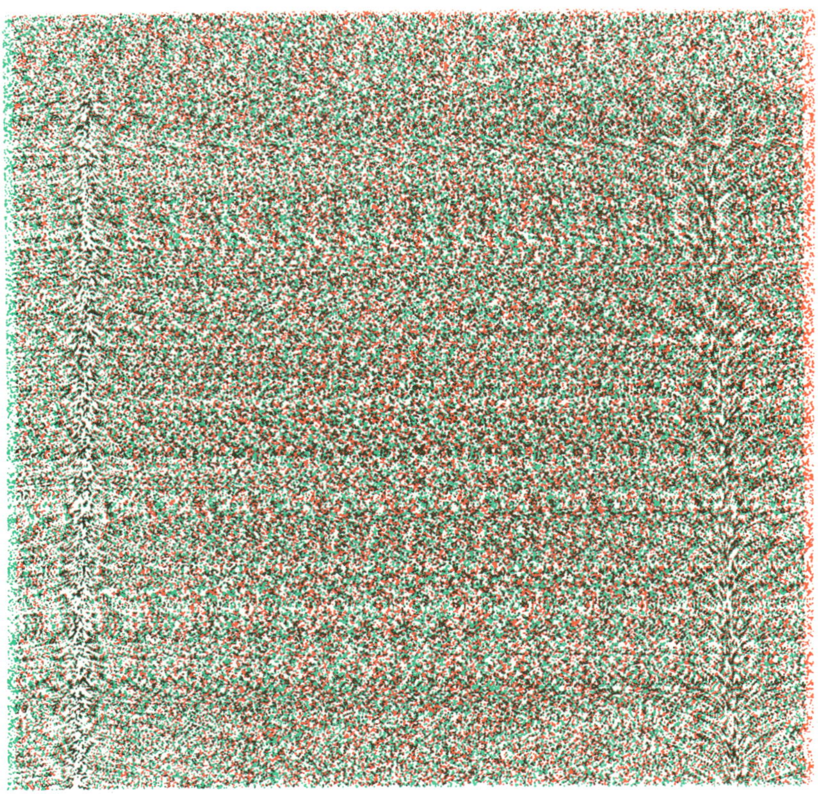

Fig. 4*. Ambiguous random-dot stereograms portraying two global organizations (hyper-globality), with an upper and lower unambiguous margin (JULESZ and JOHNSON, 1968)

of semantics hindered the development of visual perception in the same way as that of linguistics. In 1959, about the time Noam Chomsky set himself to the task of studying how far one could explore rules of grammar ignoring semantics, the technique of random-dot stereograms was introduced in psychology. These random-dot stereograms (JULESZ, 1960) were computer generated without involving familiarity with objects in our environment. Developments since have shown that without semantics even the simplest linguistic problems cannot be solved, and one is unable to resolve ambiguities (WINOGRAD, 1972). On the other hand, as this review might prove to the reader, the method of familiarity deprivation in visual perception still retains spatial-temporal continuity of objects that in turn permit us to resolve ambiguities and clarify the cooperative processes of binocular depth perception. Thus, stereoscopic depth perception (stereopsis) of random-dot stereograms (to be called *global stereopsis*) might serve as a model system for studying cooperative phenomena in visual perception by providing insights that could be useful in other areas of psychology too.

Before we go into details, let us demonstrate that random-dot stereograms—devoid of all monocularly perceivable familiarity cues—exhibit the cooperative phenomena of disorder-order transitions, hysteresis, and multiple stable states. When Figure 3 is stereoscopically fused (printed here only in its anaglyph version Figure 3* to be viewed with the red-green goggles provided with the handbook) for a few seconds the impression is a disordered state of many random dots in binocular rivalry. But then suddenly an order transition takes place and the hidden binocular correlation emerges and complex surfaces appear in vivid depth. After the disorder-order transition, this ordered state prevails. Even after a long interruption, a second attempt at fusion occurs much faster than the first time. This is a good example of hysteresis. Finally, when Figure 4 is stereoscopically fused (in Figure 4* anaglyph version using the red-green goggles) one can either perceive a plane hovering in front of the surround, or a wedge being depressed behind the surround, respectively. Usually one of these percepts prevails, and it is not easy to switch between these two stable perceptual states (if one covers the upper and lower unambiguous margins).

B. Ambiguities in Stereopsis

It had been known since Wheatstone invented the stereoscope in 1838 that the basis of *stereopsis* (stereoscopic depth perception) was *binocular disparity* due to the horizontal parallax shift between *corresponding points* that were cast on the left and right retinae. Of course, without being able to identify these corresponding points, the problem of stereopsis is *ambiguous*, as illustrated in Figure 5. Here four targets (which fall on the same horizontal line) cast their projections on each retina, and without knowing which of the projections belong to which target, 16 localizations are possible, out of which only four are real, while the remaining 12 are phantom targets.

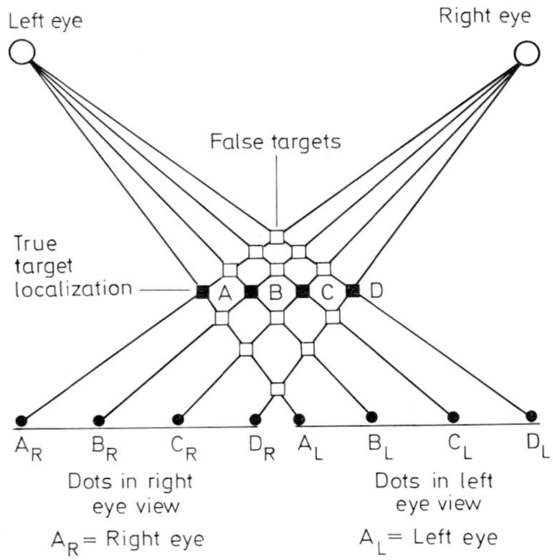

Fig. 5. Illustration of how ambiguous depth localizations arise in global stereopsis (JULESZ, 1971)

With many targets, such as points in a dense surface or faces in a crowd, the ratio of possible incorrect binocular localizations (N^2-N) to the correct ones (N) increases endlessly. How does then the visual system resolve ambiguities? The prevalent view has been that it does so by *monocular form recognition*. It was tacitly assumed that, in the case of a large crowd, for example, mechanisms in both the left and right channels performed face recognition, and in this way the correspondence between two similar faces in the two retinal projections could be established and hence binocular disparity determined. Thus, even in stereopsis it was assumed that semantics was essential to resolve ambiguities.

Such monocular form recognition prior to stereopsis seemed, however, unlikely. First, stereopsis appears to be a relatively simple process—one that takes place rather quickly, usually faster than the recognition of form. Second, and more important, camouflage experts were well aware that in aerial reconnaissance a monocularly viewed camouflaged target would jump out in vivid depth when stereoscopically viewed. Of course, no real-life scene is perfectly camouflaged, and after the binocularly fused target in a stereophotograph was perceived, the target could be faintly detected in the separate left and right images.

ASCHENBRENNER (1954) made some improved camouflaged stereograms by photographing from different angles a random texture over which another similarly textured area had been placed. Even in these stereograms some faint monocular cues could be distinguished—such as speckles cut in half by the edge of the camouflaged area. The remarkable thing, however, is that these camouflaged stereograms were regarded only as curiosities, and their implication to stereopsis was overlooked by psychologists.

The introduction into psychology by JULESZ (1960) of the first computer-generated *random-dot stereograms* (to be abbreviated as RDS) had two objectives. First, it provided stereograms in which the monocular information was *completely* absent. But even more importantly, in these stereograms all the statistical and geometrical properties were perfectly *controlled* in space and time, thus enabling researchers to tackle the problem of how stereopsis resolves ambiguous depth localization.

Figure 3 shows a complex RDS. In Figure 6 a similar, but much simpler RDS, is demonstrated. This stereogram is not simpler because it only consists of a 100×100 array of randomly selected black and white cells (instead of the 1000×1000 cells array of Figure 3), but rather because the correlated areas have only two binocular disparity values (instead of about 100, as in Figure 3). The left and right arrays are identical in Figure 6, except for a diamond-shaped area which is also identically textured in both images, but which in one image is horizontally shifted by one or more entire cells with respect to the other image, as if it were a solid sheet. Because of this shift, some areas become uncovered that are seen only by one eye, and in these areas a similar random texture is inserted. When the images of Figure 6 are viewed separately, they appear as completely random textures, and that is what they are. Yet when they are stereoscopically fused, a diamond-shaped area in the center jumps out in vivid depth (or the diamond recedes if one reverses the red-green goggles, since instead of a nasal binocular disparity shift this produces a temporalward shift).

The main implication of this demonstration is that stereopsis can occur in the absence of any monocular form or other depth cues. For complex random-dot stereograms, such as Figure 3, the disorder-order transition between the

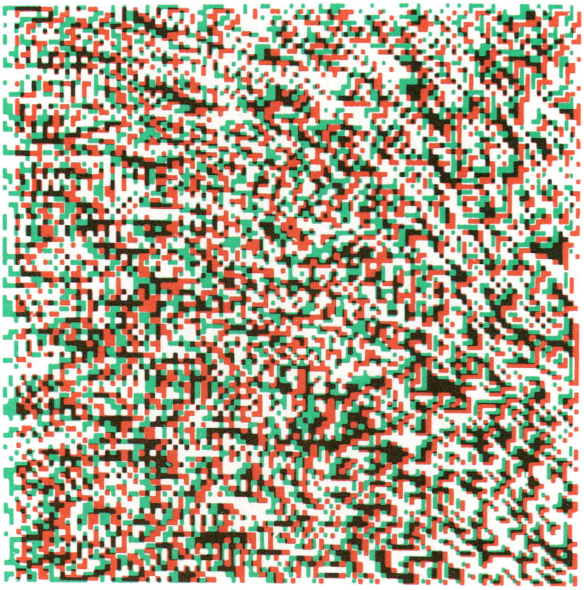

Fig. 6*. Random-dot stereogram which, when monocularly viewed, appears as a random array, but after binocular fusion portrays a diamond in vivid depth hovering over the background (JULESZ, 1960, 1971)

nonfused and fused state occurs without intricate semantic information. Even a person who has never seen a hyperbolic paraboloid will be able to perceive this surface in depth. The only "semantics" is the requirement of searching (without conscious effort) for a *dense* surface.

Indeed, when a stereogram with an equal number of black and white random dots, such as Figure 6, is fused, there is a 0.5 probability that at zero binocular disparity the corresponding left and right points that belong to the diamond-shaped retinal areas are identically black or white. Thus, at a depth plane corresponding to zero disparity, a lacelike surface consisting of half the points is already fused by chance alone. If the left and right image is horizontally shifted by one picture element, or any multiple of it in the nasal (or temporal) direction, again half of all points are identical in the left and right retinal projections. Thus, one can easily imagine a lacy background in front of (or behind) which another (or several adjacent) lacy surface(s) hovers. The visual system, however, does not select nearby lacy planes, but instead searches for large disparities necessary to obtain *dense* surfaces. This search for a unique solution that yields the densest (maximum) correlation in certain areas is the essence of global stereopsis.

It should be stressed that it is not the large binocular disparity shifts (instead of some small shifts in a local neighborhood) that make this search process global. After all, in classical stereograms the corresponding elements (i.e., a few dots or line segments) can binocularly interact at very large disparities, as measured by RICHARDS (1971) and reported earlier by OGLE (1962). This maximum binocular disparity limit that still yields some stereopsis can be even larger than it is for RDS (TYLER and JULESZ, 1976b). However, for classical stereograms—either with a few elements or monocular labels—there is *no* ambiguity which of the dots and line segments in the left and right retinal projections correspond to each other. Such a process of unambiguous depth localization will be called *local stereopsis,* regardless of the amount of binocular disparity of corresponding elements.

On the other hand, if there is the slightest ambiguity as to which elements in the two eyes' view correspond to each other, we have to evoke the workings of *global stereopsis*. Indeed, no corresponding element pair *alone* can resolve the many phantom localizations in Figure 5. A global process is needed that evaluates different sets of corresponding element pairings (local stereopsis) and selects one set of pairings that lie densest on some three-dimensional surface (and inhibits all the other phantom localizations that fall on the same *line of sight* in Figure 5).

C. Local, Global, Coarse, and Fine Stereopsis

In the previous section local stereopsis was defined as depth localization (using binocular disparity as the single depth cue) of *elements* whose correspondence (and thus the binocular disparity between them) could be unambiguously

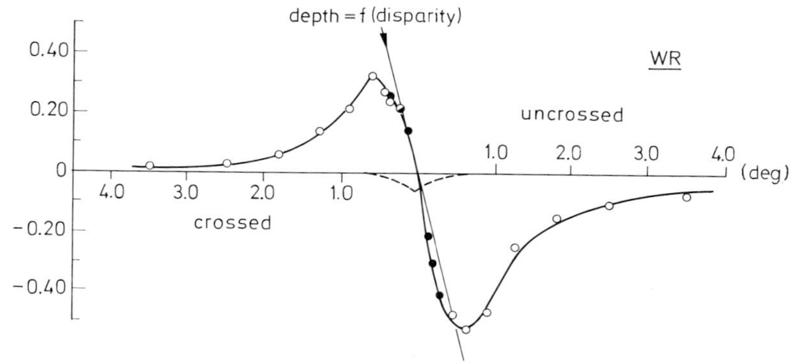

Fig. 7. Relative perceived depth in local stereopsis as a function of binocular disparity (RICHARDS, 1971). For definition of regions of fusion, patent stereopsis, and qualitative stereopsis, see text

established. Global stereopsis referred to the finding of a preferred *set* of local depth localizations among many other sets. Since some workers use these terms differently—in a sense which should be called rather "fine" and "coarse" stereopsis—in order to clarify these distinctions, some facts about local stereopsis are briefly reviewed below.

When a vertical line is stereoscopically viewed by each eye, one can plot perceived depth as a function of binocular disparity (with respect to a fused marker). Such a typical plot is shown in Figure 7 as measured by RICHARDS (1971). The curve shows three interesting regions. There is an initial region where perceived depth is monotonically increasing with increasing disparity, which will be called the region of *patent stereopsis.* Within this region (at smaller disparities) the filled circle indicate disparity values that yield a single fused percept of a vertical line in depth. This will be called the *fusional region* or *Panum's fusional area,* and outside it the line appears as *double.* With further increase of disparity the perceived depth decreases until it disappears. This is called the region of *qualitative stereopsis.* This definition is similar, but more precise than that introduced by OGLE (1962). The quantitative dependence of perceived depth on binocular disparity is a function of the stimulus size. For instance, in Figure 8, as measured by RICHARDS and KAYE (1974) a 3 min arc wide vertical bar (of a 0.5 deg arc fixed height) yields a limit of patent stereopsis at about 0.5 deg arc, while a 0.8 deg arc wide bar yields a patent stereopsis limit of 2 deg arc. (The limits for qualitative stereopsis are 2 deg arc and 8 deg arc, respectively.) The stereopsis of narrow bars (or small dots) will be called *fine stereopsis,* while stereopsis of wide bars (or large dots) will be called *coarse stereopsis.* These notions will be revisited when the role of spatial-frequency channels in stereopsis is discussed.

Here it should suffice to note that fine stereopsis is carried by the high spatial-frequency disparity detectors, while coarse stereopsis by the low spatial-frequency disparity detectors. Obviously, one can have a few unambiguous elements in a stereogram that are either narrow or wide, and these would result in a *fine local stereopsis,* or a *coarse local stereopsis.* Similarly, several elements in a stereogram that result in ambiguous correspondence between

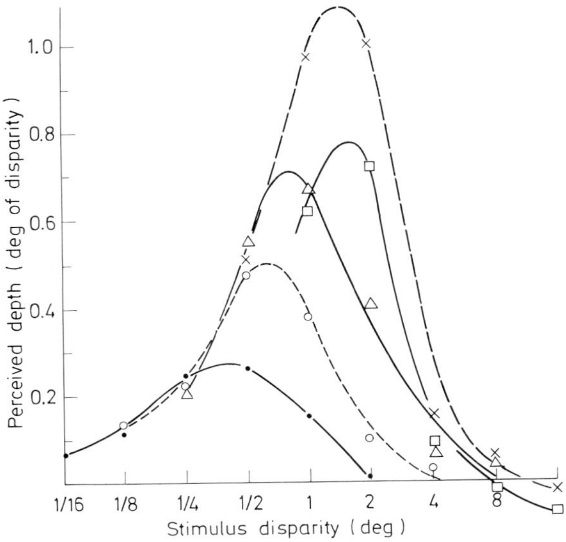

Fig. 8. Relative perceived depth in local stereopsis for the function of binocular disparity (RICHARDS and KAYE, 1974). Crossed (convergence) disparity only. Each curve represents a separate bar width: dots, 3 min arc; open circles, 6 min arc; triangle, 12 min arc; cross, 24 min arc; square, 48 min arc; bar height of stimulus was fixed at 30 min arc

elements can have narrow or wide elements, which in turn elicit the operation of *fine global stereopsis* or *coarse global stereopsis,* respectively.

From this definition one can see that even a stereoimage having many elements can be regarded as being processed by the local stereopsis mechanism, provided the correspondence between elements is unambiguous. For instance, in Figure 9 only one dot falls on the same horizontal line in the left and right retinal projections, and neighboring dots on adjacent horizontal lines are outside the limits of adequate binocular interactions (e.g., the limits of fusion, or patent stereopsis). However, it is not such a simple question whether the binocular fusion of Figure 10 should be regarded as local or global stereopsis. Here there are several elements within Panum's fusional area, yet there is no ambiguity, since here each point belongs to a unique characteristic micropattern (e.g., a line segment of a distinct orientation, length, width, or color). Should this case be regarded as local stereopsis or not? Since the correspondence between micropatterns can be locally determined—because binocular disparity units with simple receptive fields tuned to similar orientation, length, width, and color (BARLOW et al., 1967; PETTIGREW et al., 1968a, b; HENRY et al., 1969; HUBEL and WIESEL, 1970) resolve ambiguous depth localization—one could regard this case as belonging to local stereopsis. This, however, raises the question that by *extending* the complexity of feature extractors would not all elements have neighborhoods that are adequately unique to be fused by local stereopsis!

We have already discussed that this complexity of feature extractors that could label a local neighborhood cannot be as complex as form recognition, since random-dot stereograms are devoid of recognizable forms. The essence

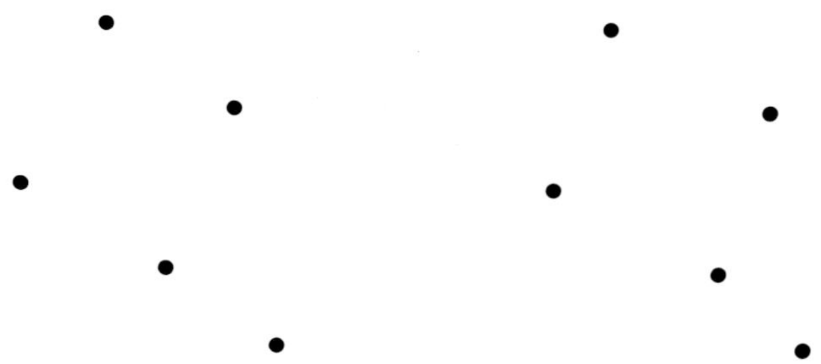

Fig. 9. Illustration of local stereopsis. In this stereogram only one point falls on a horizontal line, and no two neighboring points are permitted to fall within the region of binocular interaction (e.g., Panum's area, or the limit of patent stereopsis, depending on the perceptual task)

Fig. 10. Illustration of local stereopsis. In this stereogram more than one point falls within Panum's area (or that of patent stereopsis), but each point is labeled by a characteristic micropattern

of random-dot stereograms, or random-line stereograms, is the selection of identical elements of similar size, shape, and color. This prevents simple binocular disparity units from resolving ambiguities. However, there might exist a gamut of hypercomplex binocular disparity units (not yet found by neurophysiologists) that are selectively tuned to any combination of line segments that fell on their extended receptive fields in the two retinae. Thus, for instance, in the case of Figure 11, where the stereogram is composed of identical line segments in random orientations, one could assume that a hypercomplex binocular disparity unit were to detect the various orientations of say, only four line segments. Furthermore, if the discrimination in orientation were only in 30-deg steps (i.e., six orientations), the number of possible hypercomplex units would amount to $6^4 = 1296$. This means that in addition to having disparity detectors for all possible disparity values (in a few sec of arc steps) and retinal positions (in min arc steps), this vast number of detectors had to be multiplied by at least three orders of magnitude in order to enable local stereopsis to function. This seems a highly improbable solution.

Furthermore, one can extend the idea of random dot (and line) stereograms based on black and white dots (or line segments with two different orientations) to include increasingly more complex feature dichotomies. For instance, if one were to believe that hypercomplex binocular disparity units might exist that can distinguish between the various orientations of four adjacent line segments, then one could construct a stereogram consisting of two types of "elements" composed of four adjacent line segments in some specific orientations. Element A might have three horizontal and one vertical line segments. While B might consist of two horizontal line segments and two vertical ones. A random selection of these two elements would still result in a fusible stereogram, yet the postulated hypercomplex disparity units would not be able to resolve the ambiguities locally.

While theoretically one could postulate monocular receptive field properties of local disparity units of increasing complexity, the other solution, a binocular global process, is a more parsimonious way to resolve ambiguities with a reasonable neural machinery size. Here binocular disparity detectors that are tuned to the same disparity values are pooled and have their receptive fields (of the simple type) fall on different retinal positions. Furthermore, one has to evoke the existence of a second type of global units composed of simple disparity detectors tuned to different disparity values but inspecting the same retinal location. Such global stereo units have not been found yet by neurophysiologists. However, this review—based on a very large amount of psychophysical evidence—will end with a proposed model that delineates the required properties of such global detectors. Regardless of how the detailed structure of global stereopsis might turn out, one can study the psychophysics of global stereopsis and point out where it differs from local stereopsis.

Fig. 11*. Random-line stereogram, portraining a center square in depth. Corresponding line segments differ by plus or minus 15 deg orientation, chosen at random. After MARLOWE (JULESZ, 1971)

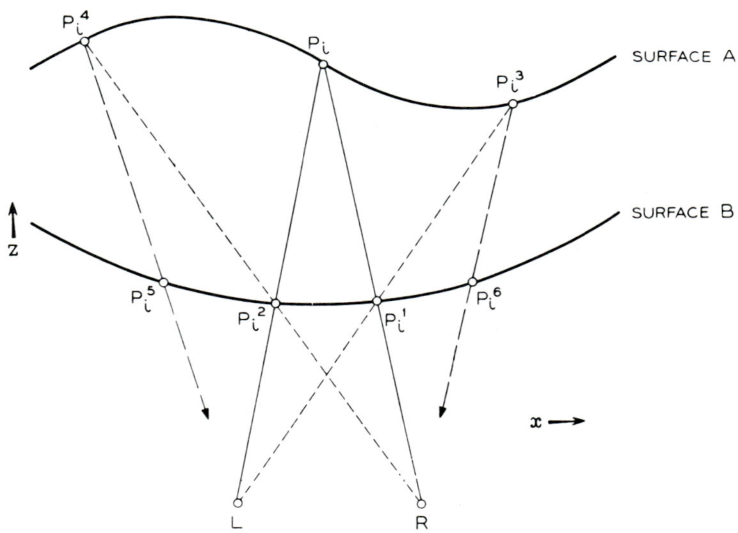

Fig. 12. Illustration of how hyper-global, random-dot stereograms are generated (JULESZ and JOHNSON, 1968 b)

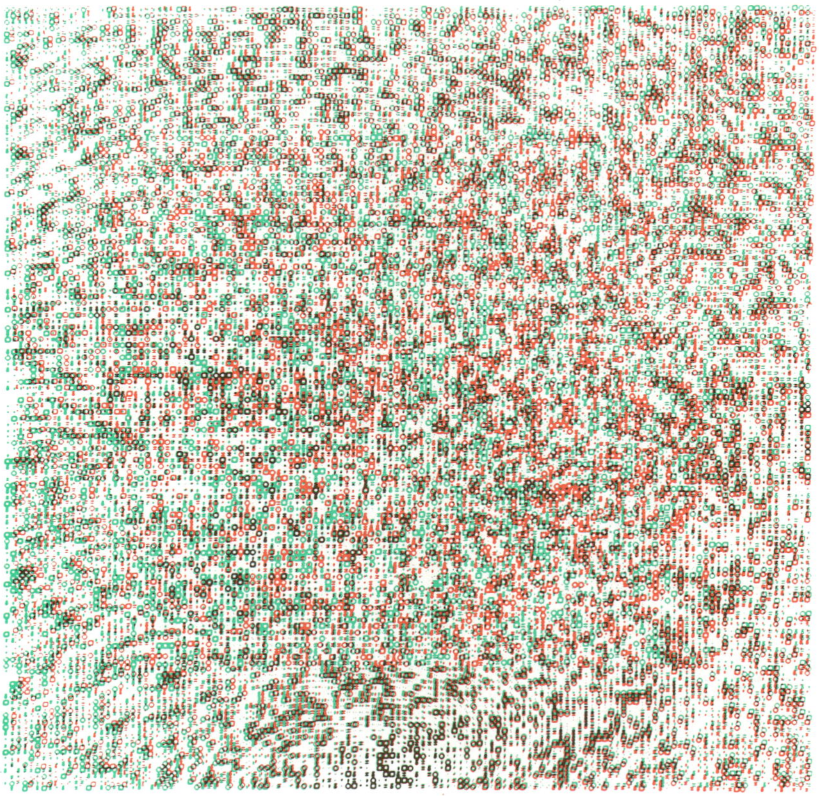

Fig. 13*. Unambiguous random-dot stereogram portraying an ascending pyramidal staircase. If the viewer is reversed so that the red filter is over the left eye, the staircase is descending (JULESZ and JOHNSON, 1968 b)

Throughout this chapter, the notion of *cyclopean* targets, cyclopean perception, and cyclopean retina will also be used in place of RDS targets, global stereopsis, and the processing site of depth for RDS, respectively. "Cyclopean" is used for stereopsis without monocular form or depth cues (JULESZ, 1971), and so a cyclopean target is a target in depth hovering over its surround that can be seen only when stereoscopically viewed.

D. Multiple Stable States (Hyperglobality)

Classical stereograms exhibit little, if any, evidence of disorder-order transitions and multiple stable states. While the binocular fusion of a simple line target is a sort of transition from its earlier nonfused state, it is not a disorder-order transition, since the target is already perceivable prior to fusion. However,

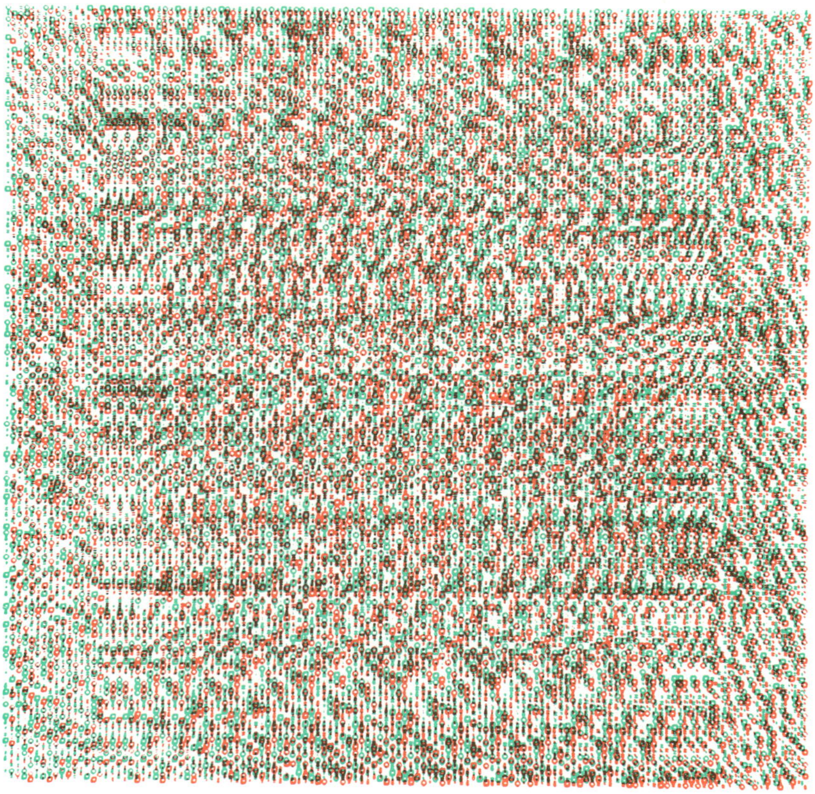

Fig. 14*. Ambiguous random-dot stereogram portraying a pyramidal staircase that ascends or descends at the observer's will. Observers with a strong bias will see the same depth organization regardless of whether the viewer is reversed or not (JULESZ and JOHNSON, 1968b)

in the complex RDS of Figure 3, it takes several seconds until the random aggregates of dots are suddenly perceived as a hyperbolic paraboloid and a torus. Even a simple RDS, such as Figure 6, requires about 50 msec perception time (Julesz, 1964; Uttal et al., 1974; Julesz and Chang, 1976). On the other hand, the perception time of classical stereograms (with some monocular form cues) is usually much briefer than it is for RDS (Julesz et al., 1976a).

While this disorder-order transition of RDS requires considerable processing effort by the global stereopsis mechanism in order to resolve the many local ambiguities and find one global organization, there is even more processing involved when a stereogram contains multiple global states. Such multiple stable states of stereopsis can be obtained by ambiguous RDS, such as Figure 4, when presented in a tachistoscopic flash (Julesz, 1964). These stereograms are the extension of the classical wallpaper effect (at which periodic structures can be fused at multiple disparity values). However, for the classic wallpaper effect the global stereopsis mechanism is not needed, since the convergence movement of the eyes can bring the stereograms in near alignment at various disparities that are multiples of the periodicity in the image and after such near alignment the local stereopsis mechanism can operate. The fact that in the Julesz (1964) demonstration ambiguous depth percepts can be obtained in a brief flash indicates the workings of a global neural process that can distinguish between multiple stable states. These multiple stable neural states will be called *hyper-globality* to distinguish them from the simpler disorder-order transitions, which were called globality.

Particularly compelling hyper-global states can be obtained by the extension of the RDS techniques (Julesz and Johnson, 1968). In these ambiguous RDS, the two or more global percepts are not restricted to parallel planes (as in the wallpaper effect) but can be surfaces of any shape. The basic idea is explained by Figure 12. Here A and B represent two cylindrical surfaces (for easier portrayal) that are perpendicular to the printed page. In order to be seen, a mathematically given surface such as A must be speckled with colored dots. For a single surface, one can choose the color of the speckles completely freely (keeping the neighboring dots about 1 min of arc apart, the limit of human visual resolution), and their geometric projections of the left and right retinae will evoke the fused percept of surface A. This was the technique of producing Figures 3 and 6. However, if we also demand that the *same* random-dot stereogram portray both surfaces A and B, the coloring of the surfaces cannot be freely chosen. One can see how the selection of black for P_i^1 forces P_i^2, P_i^3, P_i^4, etc. to be black also.

In Figure 13, we show an unambiguous organization of a pyramidal staircase that ascends in depth (with the red filter over the right eye) or descends (with the red filter over the left eye). In Figure 14, however, both the ascending and descending pyramidal stariracses are simultaneously portrayed, and it requires considerable time to learn how to perceive both organizations at will. Even those who can easily master this switch in mental organization usually have to destroy the prevailing state by blinking or by waiting some time for neural adaptation.

Those observers who have no time to learn to shift their perceptual organization can still appreciate the stability of being locked in one organization. Whichever way they happen to perceive Figure 14, switching the red-green viewer will *not* reverse depth (unlike Figure 13). Regardless of nasal or temporal disparity, observers will always perceive their preferred organization. It requires considerable effort to learn to suppress the dominant percept in order to obtain the other one. This dominance is similar to the young girl/old woman picture in Figure 2 (p. 216), but note that here we have an example of multiple stable states without semantics or other cognitive bias. It is interesting to observe that to perceive even the preferred state in Figure 14 takes longer than to perceive the disorder-order transition in Figure 13. Thus, there is a hierarchy in processing efforts: local stereopsis, global stereopsis, and hyper-global stereopsis.

In all these examples, the disparity between the multiple depth organization was relatively large, and only one of these could be perceived at a given time. However, with very small disparity differences it is possible to perceive simultaneously more than one depth surface.

E. Plasticity in Stereopsis

Before turning our attention to some dynamic aspects of stereopsis we review the plastic phenomena that are exhibited in stereopsis. For instance, in Figure 15 the left and right image of a RDS differ by 15% in linear size, and still fusion is easily obtained. Similarly, in Figure 11 the corresponding line segments differ by plus or minus 15 deg orientation, chosen at random, yet global stereopsis is easily obtained.

Another plastic phenomenon is exhibited by single-line and multiple random-line stereograms (RLS). MITCHELL and O'HAGAN (1972) investigated stereoacuity with horizontal and vertical single lines that were orthogonal and disparate in the two eyes' views. They noted that with increased line length perceived

Fig. 15. Random-dot stereograms in which one of the images is 15% expanded (JULESZ, 1971)

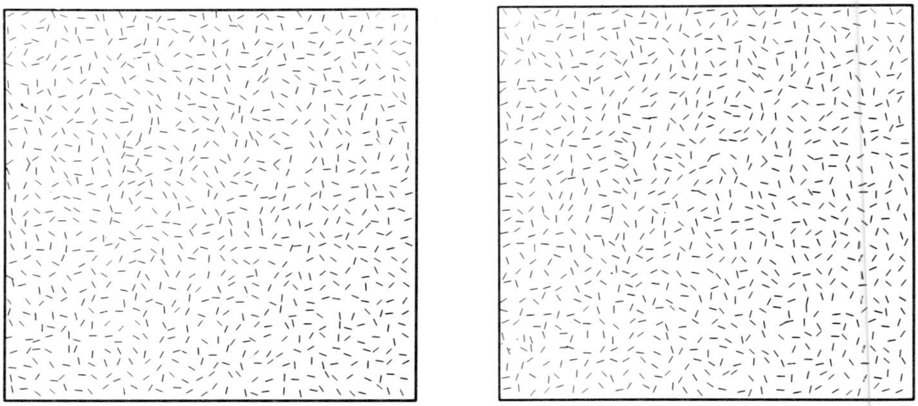

Fig. 16. Random-line stereograms (RLS) in which the corresponding line segments are orthogonal to each other. Stereopsis can still be obtained, but with increased line segment length the perceived depth is reduced (FRISBY and JULESZ, 1975a)

depth changed and was smaller (or larger), although binocular disparity between the centers of the orthogonal lines was kept constant. FRISBY and JULESZ (1975) used RLS [the kind studied by MARLOWE (1969)], where corresponding line segments were orthogonal, as shown in Figure 16, and observed decreased depth with increased line length. This plasticity of perceived depth has very different reasons for single-line and multiple-line stereograms, as FRISBY and JULESZ (1976) have pointed out in a second study. The increase and decrease of depth in the MITCHELL and O'HAGAN study is always half the line length and can be simply explained by assuming that the endpoints of the line segments tend to be aligned, forming a ∟ or ⊢ percept. However, for multi-line stereograms that contain many lines in all possible orientations, no such local fusional behavior can account for the decrease of depth with increased mismatch of length. It will be shown how the spring-coupled dipole model of global stereopsis (JULESZ, 1971) can easily account for this perceived depth reduction. Here it should be noted that no existing neurophysiological finding can explain such behavior, since these are based on local (single) binocular disparity detectors, and only some neural interaction between these local detectors (globality) can exhibit a plasticity of depth.

F. Hysteresis as a Function of the Number of Elements

All the previously reviewed phenomena were static, except for some notes on perception times. In this section the simplest dynamics of the global stereopsis mechanism is reviewed. FENDER and JULESZ (1967) presented retinally stabilized RDS for both eyes (using close-fitting contact lenses with a mirror mounted on them), and showed another dramatic difference between local and global

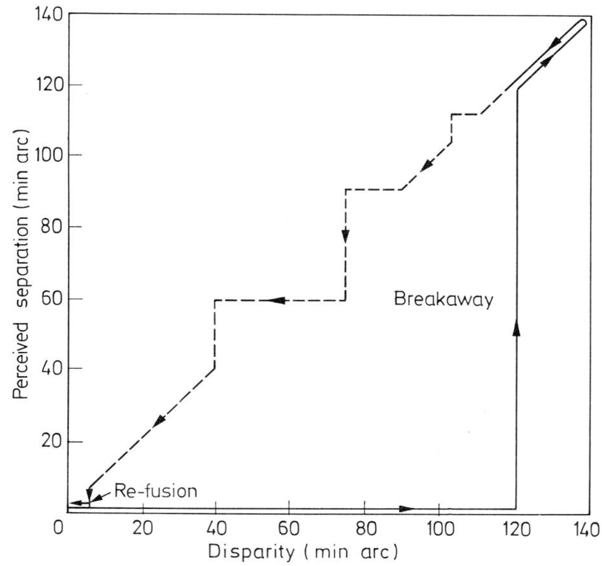

Fig. 17. Hysteresis effect for random-dot stereograms (FENDER and JULESZ, 1967)

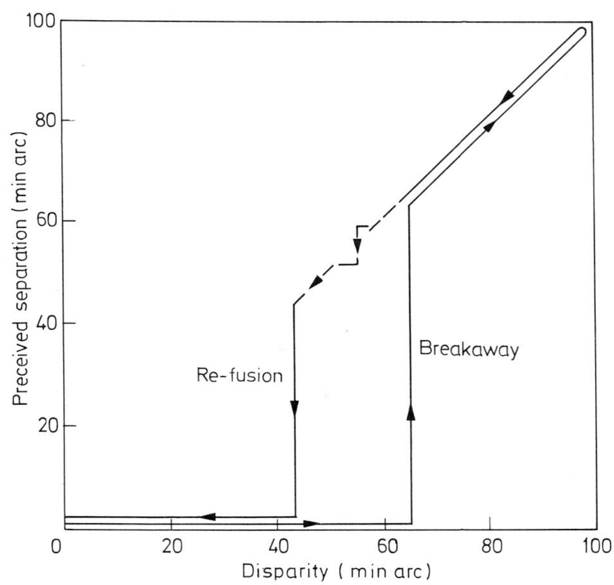

Fig. 18. Hysteresis effect for a vertical line target (FENDER and JULESZ, 1967)

stereopsis. They observed that a RDS of foveal size has to be brought within 6 min arc alignment for binocular fusion but after fusion can be slowly pulled apart on the retinae by as much as 120 min arc without breaking fusion. With more pulling the image suddenly breaks in two and must be brought within 6 min arc alignment for re-fusion. Also, pulling faster than a critical speed results in a break of fusion. This hysteresis effect for RDS is shown in Figure 17. On the other hand, for a single vertical line target this hysteresis is greatly reduced. Fusion and re-fusion can be obtained at a 42 min arc disparity, while the limit of pulling (breakaway point) is only 30% more as shown in Figure 18. The difference between 2000% and 30% hysteresis shows clearly that stereopsis is a cooperative phenomenon. In cooperative phenomena hysteresis is always exhibited and increases with the amount of participating elements.

These experiments clearly show that Panum's fusional limit is a plastic threshold, and whether two points are "corresponding" or not depends on the past history of the stimulation (already fused or not), the complexity of the stimulus (is the point pair a member of a RDS, or of a stereogram with only a few elements), and the amount and speed of pulling.

G. Dynamic Random-Dot Stereograms

The RDS in Figures 3, 4, 6, 13, and 14 are static. One can generate dynamic RDS such that different static RDS are presented in temporal succession at best stroboscopic movement rates, but such that the global organization is the same or slowly changing while each successive RDS is portrayed by new random-dot textures (PAPERT, 1964; JULESZ and PAYNE, 1968; JULESZ, 1971). Such dynamic RDS, when viewed by one eye, appear as whirling dots in Brownian motion, yet when stereoscopically fused appear to segregate into discrete surfaces at various depth.

Quite recently, dynamic RDS can be produced in real-time on digital com-

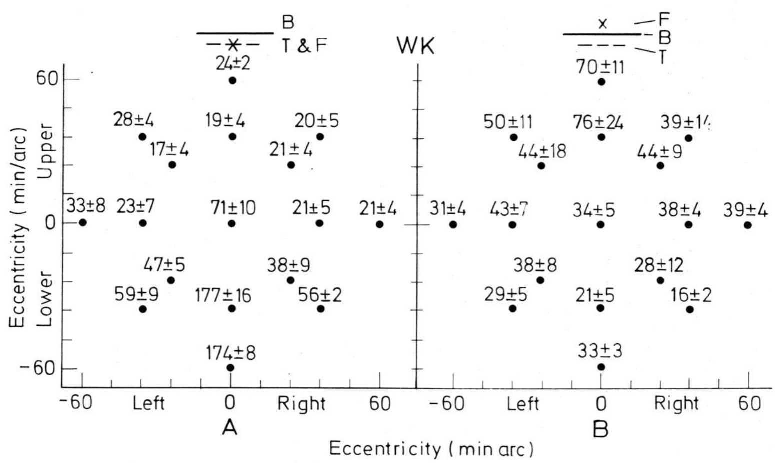

Fig. 19. Duration thresholds (means and standard deviations in msec) for detecting a 24′ × 24′ cyclopean test target centered at the points shown (for a typical subject). The fixation marker is at the center of gaze (0′, 0′), and the abscissa and ordinate designate visual field eccentricities in 12 min arc units. A) fixation marker with 6′ crossed disparity. B) fixation marker with 6′ uncrossed disparity (BREITMEYER et al., 1975)

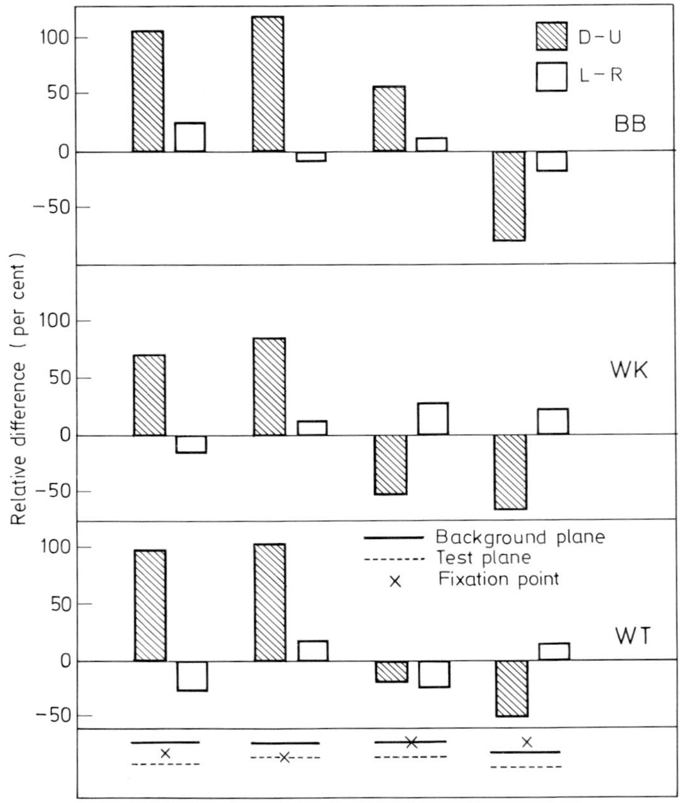

Fig. 20. Percent relative differences between mean duration thresholds of lower and upper hemifields (diagonalized bar) and left and right hemifield (blank bar) at four different viewing conditions (shown along the bottom of figure) for three typical subjects (BREITMEYER et al., 1975)

puters that directly control video monitors (JULESZ, 1971; ROSS and HOGBEN, 1974; UTTAL, 1974). With such on-line generation of dynamic RDS, it is now possible to apply psychophysical techniques in the study of global stereopsis. In a typical study (BREITMEYER et al., 1975; JULESZ et al., 1976a) dynamic RDS were generated of 50 × 50 dots-array size at 5 msec rates. The global organization, say, a narrow bar or a small square (e.g., of 24 × 24 min arc size), can be presented for a brief duration hovering over the background. One can easily change the target size, location, duration, and disparity and determine the perception thresholds. A typical finding for an observer is given in Figure 19. The fixation marker was located at the center of gaze, and the horizontal and visual field eccentricities were graduated in units of 12 min arc. The background plane had a 6 min arc temporalward (uncrossed) disparity with respect to the fixation marker, which the target had a 6 min arc nasal (crossed) disparity. One can see from Figure 19 (left image) that duration thresholds (and standard deviations) are distributed isotropically between the left and right visual hemifields: however, an unexpectedly large anisotropy exists between the upper and lower hemifields. As the fixation mark has a 6 min arc nasal disparity (i.e.,

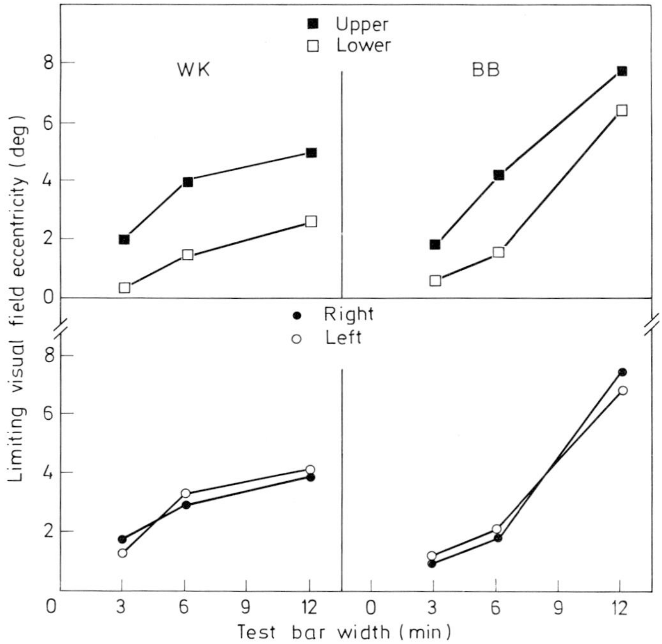

Fig. 21. Limiting visual field eccentricities (in deg) at which a test bar of given width (in min arc) and of 500 msec duration can just be detected (JULESZ et al., 1976a)

in front of the surround), the upper and lower hemifield anisotropy reverses, as shown in Figure 19 (right image). This disparity-dependent up-down anisotropy and left-right isotropy is shown for three observers in Figure 20. This "cyclopean horopter"—the locale of small cyclopean (1) targets with the same temporal thresholds—defines a tilted surface. This surface is tilted behind the midline for points above the midline and tilted in front for points below the midline. Such an arrangement might be of value for lemurs and monkeys with visual systems in which stereopsis did evolve. The same up-down hemifield anisotropy and left-right isotropy holds also for spatial resolution as shown in Figure 21.

The results clearly show that binocular disparity detectors tuned to crossed disparities have different distribution (or time constants) from those tuned to uncrossed disparities. RICHARDS (1973) suggested that some people might have missing crossed or uncrossed binocular disparity detectors, respectively. The results by BREITMEYER et al. (1975) indicate a much more complex picture. For instance, in Figure 19 (left) observer WK showed a large cyclopean scotoma in the lower hemifield for uncrossed disparities, which, however, disappears for crossed disparities (Fig. 19, right). Since convergence movements can quickly change the fixation point, in everyday life such cyclopean scotomas are not often experienced. Furthermore, the slightest monocular cue improves the temporal and spatial acuities (thresholds) manifold (JULESZ et al., 1976a), so common targets with monocular cues will not provide such drastic anisotropies of performance.

The finding that no hemispheric superiority exists for global stereopsis is at odds with earlier claims by CARMON and BECHTOLDT (1969) and DURNFORD and KIMURA (1971), who used static RDS. CARMON and BECHTOLDT presented RDS to patients with hemispheric lesions and found significantly slower responses in pointing to the cyclopean target when the lesions resided in the right hemisphere. On the other hand, they found isotropic responses for left-right hemifield stimulation. These two findings together indicate, however, that the superiority of the right hemisphere probably has nothing to do with stereopsis, but rather with locating the position of the cyclopean target. DURNFORD and KIMURA used normal subjects but asked them to identify on each trial one of several cyclopean geometrical figures portrayed by the static RDS. This added the task of geometric pattern recognition or categorization to the task of perceiving depth; and consequently any left-right difference in depth perception may have been totally or partially confounded with known left-field (right hemisphere) superiority in recognition of geometric patterns (NEBES, 1974).

Another type of dynamic RDS portrays a single dot at a given instant but randomly scanned at rapid rates. Corresponding points in the left and right arrays can be portrayed in brief succession or after a variable delay (ROSS and HOGBEN, 1974). In spite of random scanning, dots within a 120–140 msec interval appear to form a uniform texture, such that dots plotted at the beginning of this interval appear of the same brightness as dots plotted later. It seems as if the dots were stored in a buffer that keeps their brightness for about 120 msec in a sliding temporal interval. However, when ROSS and HOGBEN introduced delays between corresponding dots, global stereopsis rapidly decayed when the delay exceeded 50–70 msec. This finding might suggest that the fine positional information disappears sooner than the brightness information, and stereopsis ceases above 70 msec delays. However, ROSS (1974) discovered a novel depth effect (based on binocular temporal delays, but differing from the Pulfrich effect) that starts in the 50–70 msec delay range and dominates stereopsis beyond. Therefore, the 70 msec delay limit might also be explained by the Ross phenomenon suppressing stereopsis. In order to check the assumption that the fine positional information decays beyond 50–70 msec, HOGBEN et al. (1976) replaced stereopsis with symmetry perception such that a constant delay was introduced between each point and its symmetric companion. Since in symmetry perception no other phenomenon enters at delays beyond 50 msec, and yet the perception of symmetry rapidly decayed when the delay exceeded 50–90 msec, it is most likely that both effects are due to the loss of fine positional information.

Of course, one can delay (in multiples of a frame period) a dynamic RDS generated frame-by-frame, as shown in the study (confirming the delay-line hypothesis of the Pulfrich-effect) by JULESZ and WHITE (1969). With a new hardware development by KROPFL (reviewed in BREITMEYER et al., 1975), computers can be speeded up by 16–36 times (depending on the number of bits in a word) and can be displayed at any position on TV monitors with electrostatic deflection. As a result, the number of dots in a frame and the frame duration can be varied in a wide range. However, the Ross-method permits greater flexibility in studies where the continuous variation of delay times is important.

Let us briefly return to the Ross phenomenon, since it permits an easy perceptual demonstration of dynamic RDS-like phenomena, as pointed out by TYLER (1974). He produced dynamic noise ("snow") by tuning his TV set to a channel without broadcast, and viewed this noise binocularly with a neutral density filter covering one eye. Under such viewing conditions the noise seems to form layers in depth. The front layers move horizontally in one direction while the background layers appear to move in reverse. R.S. Mackay also noted this effect in 1960 (JULESZ, 1961, p. 222).

In addition to measuring detection thresholds under cyclopean conditions, dynamic RDS can be used also to elicit tracking eye-movements to moving cyclopean targets and to measure the eye-movement latency (RT). For example, JULESZ and OSWALD (1977) found a 100–150 msec longer RT when observers tracked suddenly moving cyclopean bars than when they tracked similar bars with 30% monocular density difference with respect to the background. They also noticed that a bar with a 4% monocular density cue could not be tracked if it had no binocular disparity, while the same 4% density cue lowered the RT by 15% for targets with disparity when compared to the zero density difference (cyclopean) condition. Thus the cyclopean retina can utilize weak contour cues that are monocularly subliminal.

Finally, cyclopean targets pulsating in depth—portrayed by dynamic RDS—can elicit visual evoked responses (VER) on the human scalp (LEHMANN and JULESZ, 1978). This VER is of larger amplitude on the hemisphere that is contralateral to the stimulated hemifield. Thus, this VER is not generated by "counting" the periodic reappearance of the cyclopean target (which is probably a highly central process), but is elicited by pools of binocular disparity detectors in the cortex that receive their input from the contralateral visual hemifields.

H. Spatial Frequency Channels in Stereopsis

The fine and coarse spatial (positional) information brings us to the problem of spatial-frequency channels in stereopsis. It is known that early color photography (based on randomly speckled visible grains of various colors) yields stereograms that can be fused in spite of the fact that the color grains in the left and right images are obviously uncorrelated and are rivalrous. While the high-frequency information yields rivalry, the low-spatial frequency information (large areas of similar average brightness and color) are correlated and result in binocular fusion. Similar observations can be made with RDS (JULESZ, 1961), as shown in Figure 22. Here the left and right fields are almost identical except in the left image where the diagonal connectivities are broken up. Whenever three adjacent dots along the $+$ or $-45°$ diagonal arc of the same color, the middle dot is complemented (i.e., black is changed to white or vice versa). This complementation changes 16% of the dots, while 84% stay correlated in the two images. The monocular appearance of the two images is very different, since complementation radically changes the high spatial frequency spectrum of the left image, yet binocular fusion can easily be obtained. This is not surprising, since strong blurring of both images of Figure 22 reveals that the low-spatial frequency spectra are very similar.

These findings were extended and quantified by JULESZ and MILLER (1975) who used two-dimensional spatial-frequency filtered stereograms and masking noise. They showed that if the stereogram was low-pass filtered (or high-pass filtered) and the masking noise spectrum was two octaves distant from the stereogram spectrum, then in spite of the large binocular rivalry due to the masking noise, the stereogram could still be fused. However, if the same effective masking noise energy fell in a spectrum that was adjacent to the stereogram spectrum, only binocular rivalry could be experienced. [The interested reader can verify these demonstrations in the special stereo (anaglyph) issue in which the JULESZ and MILLER (1975) paper appeared.] These demonstrations suggest that stereopsis utilizes spatial-frequency-tuned channels and, therefore, these channels are before or at the site of global stereopsis.

While these low- and high-spatial frequency channels are probably the same as the ones found in monocular adaptation studies (BLAKEMORE and CAMPBELL, 1969; PANTLE and SEKULER, 1969) and monocular masking studies (STROMEYER and JULESZ, 1971; HARMON and JULESZ, 1972), the interactions between the left and right low-frequency channels (coarse stereopsis) and between the left and right high-frequency channels (fine stereopsis) are novel effects. Furthermore, MAYHEW and FRISBY (personal communication) extended the JULESZ and MILLER masking method by using elongated (instead of circular) spectra, and found that the spatial-frequency-channels utilized by global stereopsis are *not* orientationally sensitive.

I. Binocular Fusion and Rivalry

It has been known since Panum's (1858) original studies that binocular rivalry can occur between discrepant images to the two eyes. There is a long-standing controversy between two camps who attributed single vision either to binocular fusion or suppression during rivalry, respectively (reviewed, for example, by KAUFMAN, 1975). The demonstrations of low- or high-spatial frequency channels being simultaneously in fusion and rivalry (JULESZ and MILLER, 1975) does not settle the question of whether only one of these two mechanisms participates in stereopsis and which one. However, quite recently, JULESZ and TYLER (1976) have found some evidence that both fusion and rivalry may simultaneously participate in a binocular perception task and in a complementary fashion. They generated dynamic RDS for which the left and right arrays were either identical (100% correlation), or uncorrelated (0% correlation), or the complements of each other (−100% correlation). Any two of these three states of correlation were presented in succession, and duration thresholds for detecting these transitions were measured. The duration threshold for detecting a transition from the correlated state to the uncorrelated state was much shorter than vice versa. In order to explain the detection thresholds for the various transitions, a model based on the notion of an entropy-like measure (called neurontropy) has been proposed. It was assumed that in binocular vision both a fusional and rivalry process operate simultaneously but in a dual fashion. Thus the correlated state would be regarded the same way by the fusional process as the complemented state by the rivalry process. It was found that transitions from the uncorrelated to the complemented state (and vice versa) were the most difficult to detect, but surprisingly could be detected. Since RDS with zero correlation obviously cannot be fused, and RDS with -1 correlation cannot be fused either (JULESZ, 1960), therefore the detection of transients between these two states could be accomplished only by the rivalry process. The basis for this accomplishment was some perceptual change in the granularity of the dynamic noise. The other transients (between correlation and the rest) involved the fusion mechanism as well, and it was much easier to perceive some changes in depth. The large difference in the detection thresholds indicate that the rivalry process is much less efficient than the fusional process.

The neurontropy model was tested by TYLER and JULESZ (1976) for many other cross-correlation states between 1 and -1, and the results support the prediction. It was found that even a 1% change in correlation can be detected, and the duration threshold from correlation to uncorrelation can be as low as 2 msec. These values can be obtained only with large fields containing a thousand or more dots. The duration threshold decreases linearly with the linear stimulus size, but reaches an asymptote at 2.5×2.5 degrees (TYLER and JULESZ, 1978).

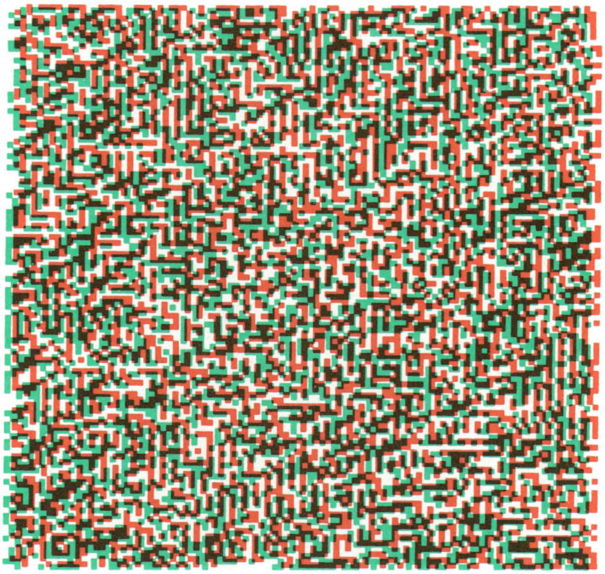

Fig. 22*. Random-dot stereogram in which the diagonal connectivity in the left image is broken, with 84% of the dots remaining identical, thus only the high spatial frequencies are different in the left and right arrays (JULESZ, 1961)

The neurontropy model is too new for the detailed inclusion in a review. Here it should suffice to note that in the model the rivalry process seems to inhibit fusion. The strength of the rivalry process seems to vary greatly between observers from zero to −0.14 weight.

J. Interactions Between Pools of Disparity Detectors

When an ambiguous RDS, similar to Figure 4* but with a square in front or behind, is briefly presented (while the observer is fixating on a marker in the depth plane of the surround) the stereogram is perceived at only one depth at a time, dictated by the natural bias of the observer (JULESZ, 1964). However, when a slight bias is introduced by inserting a few unambiguous dots in the ambiguous center (whose disparity is equal with one of the ambiguous organization), a 4% physical bias is adequate to overcome the natural bias

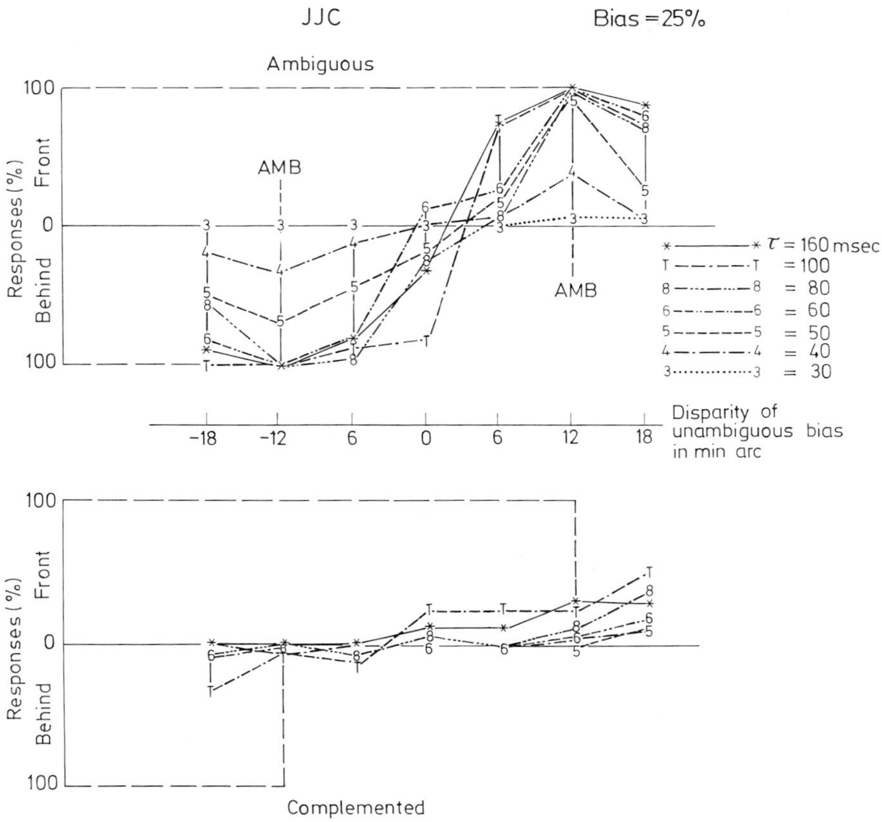

Fig. 23. Pulling effect for a typical subject with 25% bias as a function of stimulus duration. The lower graph is a control test for which the ambiguous area is substituted for a nonfusible area (the left area is the complement of the right) (JULESZ and CHANG, 1976)

of the observer. This finding that 100% stimulation in one depth organization can dominate over 92% stimulation in the other depth organization (which corresponded to the natural bias of the observer) strongly indicates that stereopsis must be a parallel process rather than a serial one (JULESZ, 1964, 1971). (The reader who wants to know why the bias is 92% instead of 96% is referred to JULESZ and CHANG, 1976.) Indeed, if one were to assume that the neural bias is due to a serial process that always starts with the favored organization, then a 92% correlation would appear an excellent fit, making unnecessary the search for other depth organizations. On the other hand, a parallel model can easily explain why, when there are two (or more) possible depth organizations, the one with maximum correlation prevails.

Recently, JULESZ and CHANG (1976) investigated with the use of on-line generated dynamic RDS this pulling effect by a few unambiguous dots on an ambiguous area, when the two had different disparities. They found that the unambiguous bias carried that depth percept whose disparity was nearest to the disparity of the bias. The closer the disparities were to each other the stronger the pulling effect that was observed. A typical result is shown in Figure 23. Here the two ambiguous depth states are at +12 or −12 min arc disparity value, when observer fixates at 0 disparity, and the abscissa gives the disparity values of the unambiguous bias. Here the bias was 25%, while the duration τ of the stimulus was varied. The stimulus duration had to be over 50 msec to provide a strong pulling effect. In all experiments the stimulus duration was 160 msec or shorter, indicating that the pulling effect was the product of neural interactions, rather than convergence movement of the eyes. The strongest pulling effect was obtained when the bias covered the ambiguous area. However, when the bias surrounded the ambiguous area the pulling effect was still strong.

The pulling effect amounts to a sort of "neural amplification" where a few percent of disparity detectors can influence the firing of all other units to which they are coupled. This gives a sensitive method of studying the cooperativity of global stereopsis. Findings indicate that pools of binocular disparity detectors in the cortex facilitate each other if they get their stimulation from adjacent or overlapping retinal areas and are tuned to the same or adjacent disparity values. However, pools of disparity detectors that are tuned to remote disparity values act to inhibit each other. (Indeed, in Figure 14* only one of the multiple depth organizations prevails, while the others are inhibited.) This technique permits the study of how these waves of facilitation and inhibition spread between the pools, by presenting the bias and the ambiguous organization with various time delays and spatial distances between each other.

K. Neurophysiological Considerations

Up to this point, the only neurophysiological references were the binocular disparity detectors in the visual cortex of the cat and monkey. Since all the neurophysiological facts known to the author are related to local stereopsis, this review of global stereopsis emphasizes the psychophysical facts and tries to bring all these facts together in a heuristic model, that in turn might guide the neurophysiologist in search of global stereopsis mechanisms.

Two recent books written by psychologists – one by KAUFMAN (1974) and one by GULICK and LAWSON (1976) – try to evaluate the implications of random-dot stereograms in experimental psychology and might be of interest to the reader. For an up-to-date review of the neurophysiology and psychology of local stereopsis, the reader is referred to the chapter by BISHOP (1973) in the VII/3A volume of this Handbook of Sensory Physiology series. An earlier review article by BISHOP and HENRY (1971) also gives an excellent overview.

There are several sources that review neurophysiological findings of binocular disparity detectors and their possible role in global stereopsis. The book by JULESZ (1971) contains several chapters devoted to these problems. The monograph by SPERLING (1970) also outlines a neural hypothesis of global stereopsis. In addition to these references, a recent article by NELSON (1974) is devoted entirely to problems of globality in stereoscopic fusion and binocular vision.

With the existing neurophysiological facts on stereopsis and their relevance to the psychophysics collected on humans, one has to be very careful. The pioneering studies by BARLOW et al. (1967), PETTIGREW et al. (1968), JOSHUA and BISHOP (1969), and BLAKEMORE (1969) on stereopsis were restricted to the cat. HUBEL and WIESEL (1970) could not find binocular disparity detectors prior to Area 18 in the macaque monkey, while in the cat many such units were reported in Area 17, however, very recently POGGIO and FISCHER (1977) found disparity detectors, both with sharp and broad tuning characteristics, in Area 17 of behaving monkeys. Binocular disparity detectors were also found in the wulst (a cortical analog) of the owl (PETTIGREW and KONISHI, 1976).

The binocular disparity detectors in the macaque monkey (HUBEL and WIESEL, 1970) and psychophysical evidence that macaque monkeys can perceive depth in static RDS (BOUGH, 1970; COWEY et al., 1975) finally brought the psychophysical evidence of stereopsis in humans and the first neurophysiological evidence of local stereopsis detectors together, since it is likely that human stereopsis is very similar to that of the monkey. COWEY et al. (1975) showed that monkeys could perceive depth in RDS presented as anaglyphs when disparity was 30–55 min arc. SARMIENTO (1975) showed that stereoacuity of the monkey can be as good as 2.5 sec arc, which is the threshold for humans too.

Only studies with RDS yield an unfakeable test for stereopsis, and earlier studies with classical targets do not rule out the use of some other monocular depth cues. While static RDS require elaborate testing, dynamic RDS permit fast determination of stereopsis. JULESZ et al. (1976b) could elicit bar pressing to sudden depth changes (portrayed by dynamic RDS) in macaque monkeys, that were trained to press for luminance changes, after one session. With dynamic RDS global stereopsis was shown to exist in the cat (LEHMKUHLE et al., 1977), and the falcon (FOX et al., 1977). It is also easy to train animals to track moving cyclopean targets. However, it remains to be seen whether moving cyclopean gratings can elicit optokinetic nystagmus in animals and human infants.

Evidence for the existence of global stereopsis detectors (a pool of adjacent disparity detectors tuned to the same binocular disparity) comes from psychological adaptation studies (BLAKEMORE and JULESZ, 1970). When a RDS is presented at a given binocular disparity for 2 min, then a similar test target at the same retinal location and disparity when presented in brief succession appears to be seen at different depth than prior to adaptation.

It is interesting that TYLER (1975) was able to obtain a cyclopean frequency-shift aftereffect when adapting to a sinusoidal depth grating (a rippled surface portrayed by a RDS). This seems to suggest the existence of cyclopean spatial-frequency analyzers. TYLER (1974) also found that the upper limit of cyclopean spatial-frequency perception is 3 cyc/deg. Since luminance gratings can be detected up to 60 cyc/deg the smallest global stereo detector appears to be about 20 times larger than the smallest contrast detector.

L. Learning in Stereopsis and Convergence Movements

The main role of convergence movements of the eyes in stereopsis is to bring corresponding points into Panum's area. Without monocular cues this alignment by the convergence mechanism is greatly handicapped. This explains why stereopsis of RDS with large disparities (in excess of Panum's area), such as demonstrated in Figure 3, requires such a long time at the first trial. It takes great effort—owing to chance alone—to converge on the cyclopean target. However, the hysteresis phenomenon (FENDER and JULESZ, 1967) permits a 2 deg arc disparity change after fusion—without losing fusion—provided this change occurs slowly. Probably the learning effect in large-disparity RDS is related to an improved strategy of finding where to converge in order to fuse the hidden cyclopean target, and then to change convergence back to the surround, but slowly so as not to break fusion. That this learning is primarily due to convergence movements has been demonstrated by SAGE and FRISBY (1975), who showed that latency for large-disparity (1 deg, 17 min arc) RDS is considerably reduced when conspicuous monocular features are added. Even with these monocular features perception times are greatly reduced in successive trials. The stronger these monocular cues the less learning occurs, since strong monocular cues make it unnecessary to improve convergence movements. For small-disparity (5 min arc) RDS the convergence mechanism plays no role, as observed by SAGE and FRISBY, who found no significant difference in obtaining stereopsis for these stimuli whether monocular cues were added or not.

The measured latency times of stereopsis in the SAGE and FRISBY study (using static RDS) are in seconds, even for small-disparity RDS. With refined techniques, using dynamic RDS, one can show that critical duration times for perceiving small-disparity RDS drops from 15–100 msec below 2 msec when monocular cues are added (JULESZ et al., 1976a). Thus, even the global stereopsis mechanism benefits from monocular cues. That the global stereopsis mechanism can also perform learning has been shown by RAMACHANDRAN and BRADDICK (1973), who used static small-disparity RLS. They found that this learning effect is specific to stimulus orientation and retinal position. However, for observers with good stereopsis, this learning effect is small compared to the learning of convergence movements in large-disparity RDS.

It should be stressed that these reported learning effects, particularly those of RAMACHANDRAN and BRADDICK, are very short term. The problem why the successful fusion of a large-disparity complex RDS, such as Figure 3, reduces perception time when viewed the second time after years is still most likely explained by remembering (unconsciously) the proper convergence-divergence strategies. It seems that the latency time of fusion and the accompanying long-term learning effect are not related to the simplicity/complexity of the surface shapes, but *only* to the amount of the largest binocular disparity changes in a RDS. Thus, the complex stereogram of Figure 3, when decreased in binocular disparity to be within Panum's area, can be perceived effortlessly in a brief flash (see anaglyph Figure 5.4-2* in the book by JULESZ, 1971), but the simple RDS of Figure 6, when increased in disparity (so as to exceed Panum's limit, but stay within the extended fusional limit of FENDER and JULESZ, 1967) does require many seconds for fusion. Using binocular retinal stabilization to prevent vergence, in a pilot study at Fender's laboratory in the first quarter of 1977, D. DINER, R. WILLIAMS, and the author showed that it is easy to fuse RDS of foveal size (such as Figure 6) with 6 min arc disparity. However, a similar RDS with 18 min arc disparity could not be fused in 40 min (the maximum time permitted with close-fitting contact lenses). This indicates the importance of vergence movements for the fusion of large-disparity RDS. That the long-term learning is most likely related to the remembering of improved vergence strategies can be concluded from a recent study of MACCRACKEN et al. (1977) who quantified the learning effect using the RDS of Figure 3. They found both short-term learning in consecutive trials in a single session—as FRISBY and CLATWORTHY (1975) found earlier—and long-term learning between two sessions separated by 48 hours. The long-term learning was not complete at the start of the trials 2 days after the first session, and continued in repeated trials. Indeed, if vergence movements play a significant role, it might be that the qualitative aspects of an improved eye-movement strategy are remembered but the exact amount of disparity might be forgotten and would have to be re-learned.

M. A Cooperative Model of Global Stereopsis

A model of stereopsis has to explain all the static and dynamic phenomena reported in the previous sections, particularly the many manifestations of cooperativity and plasticity. The model of global stereopsis as reviewed here (JULESZ and CHANG, 1976) is an improved version of the spring-coupled magnetic dipole model of JULESZ (1971). The neurophysiologic implications of the model are of a global nature, far more complicated than the local binocular disparity detectors discovered by the neurophysiologists. Since a model should be more than merely an isomorphism to the observed facts, but should be matched to some human heuristics, therefore familiar entities were selected, such as rotating dipoles, spring couplings, and magnetic interactions, whose workings can be easily comprehended by most people. However, this phenomenological model has some obvious neurophysiologic analogies that will be stressed. The model serves three purposes: 1) it is a convenient mnemotechnics, since it organizes the many seemingly ad hoc facts of stereopsis in a coherent entity; 2) it is a research tool for the psychologist, since it provides some predictions of psychophysical phenomena to be explored; 3) its structure implies some explicit principles of neural organization that might guide the neurophysiologist in search for global structure.

There are a few other models of stereopsis. SPERLING (1970) postulated an energy-well model in which marbles roll in a bowl filled with viscous fluid, and the shape of the energy well can be modified by disparity and vergence. For a critique of this model the reader is referred to KAUFMAN (1974). While the model has a dynamic character and can illuminate several processes of local stereopsis, it lacks cooperativity and cannot explain how ambiguities are resolved in global stereopsis. Sperling's treatise contains a second part in which he outlines a neurophysiologic theory of binocular vision. This theory is not detailed enough to be called a model but has a few important cooperative notions. Once binocular disparity detectors obtain a certain activity they start to inhibit other units that are tuned to different binocular disparities. He also postulates different disparity detectors for fine and coarse stereopsis, the first being utilized in pattern vision, while the second is primarily concerned with the convergence system. Some of these notions were incorporated in a neural model of global stereopsis by NELSON (1974), using spreading inhibition between disparity detectors of different disparities and facilitation between disparity detectors tuned to the same disparities. DEV (1974) tested an almost identical model by computer algorithms. As NELSON himself points out, his model is very similar to the spring-coupled dipole model of JULESZ (1971). Nelson and Dev models have a parallel structure—similar to the Automap-1 model of JULESZ (1962)—the JULESZ (1971) model is serial, and it was already discussed that global stereopsis is a parallel process. On the other hand, the Nelson and Dev models do not give a direct grasp of their workings, while the dipole model of JULESZ (1971) does. Therefore, this model was improved (JULESZ and CHANG, 1976) so that it has a parallel structure but retains the conceptual simplicity of the earlier dipole mode.

After this chapter was written, MARR and POGGIO (1976) published a cooperative, nonlinear, iterative algorithm that resembles Dev's, but differs from it in some important aspects. In this algorithm each disparity detector is facilitated by neighbors tuned to similar disparities, and inhibited by disparity detectors tuned to different disparities that fall on the same lines of sight (in Fig. 5). While the MARR and POGGIO algorithm incorporates these two basic ideas

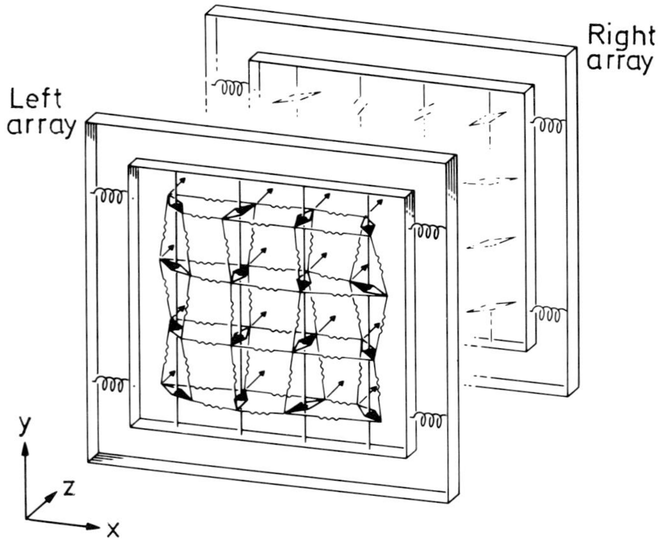

Fig. 24. Spring-coupled dipole model in which the dipole arrays are in spring-suspended frames (JULESZ, 1971)

of the spring-coupled dipole model of JULESZ (1971), it cannot cope with hysteresis and plastic phenomena of stereopsis in its present form, while the spring-coupled dipole model easily accounts for them. In spite of the greater generality of the analog spring-coupled dipole model and its heuristic appeal, the computer algorithm of MARR and POGGIO is quite robust, and convergences in a few iterations (if the constants of excitations and inhibitions are properly chosen), and so it permits quantitative analysis of several problems.

Before the parallel dipole model is explained, the simpler spring-coupled dipole model will be reviewed briefly, since the basic idea is incorporated in both models, but it is easier to grasp in the original version. For details of this earlier model the reader might consult JULESZ 1971, Chapt. 6, or JULESZ (1974). The reader should imagine that many magnetic dipoles (electromagnets) are mounted in ball-joint bearings and can rotate in any direction (see Fig. 24). These magnetic dipoles are the cortical representations of the stimuli cast on the retinae. Local stereopsis corresponds to the amount of horizontal rotation of a given dipole. If a retinal element in one of the eyes receives a white dot, its corresponding dipole electromagnet is magnetized with a certain polarity, while for a black dot the polarity becomes reversed. The black and white random-dot array on the left and right retinae therefore corresponds to two dipole arrays facing each other with similarly ordered north and south poles (see Fig. 24).

Thus, the ordering of dipole polarities is forced on the system, while the "order parameter" is the number of *locked* dipoles between the left and right dipole arrays that correspond to binocular fusion. An essential feature of the model is the coupling of the dipoles to their adjacent neighbors (both horizontally

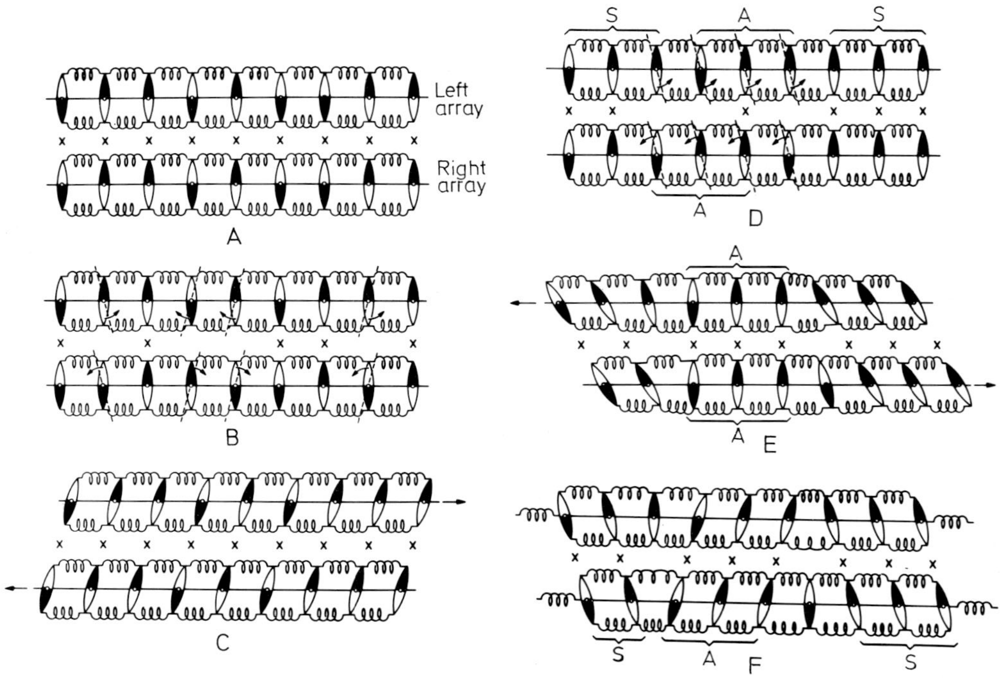

Fig. 25. Spring-coupled dipole model (in one dimension) under various conditions as explained in text (JULESZ, 1971)

and vertically) by mechanical springs. The two ordered and coupled dipole arrays should be imagined in close proximity sliding over each other, as shown in Figure 24. If the patterns on the retinae are identical and the two dipole arrays overlap (i.e., are within Panum's fusional area) then the south and north poles of corresponding dipoles interlock. Identical arrays of interlocked dipoles in one dimension are shown in Figure 25A.

When a RDS is presented (such as Fig. 6), then before the arrays are shifted in near alignment, by chance 50% of the dipoles become interlocked. Because of spring coupling, the other 50% are forced to face corresponding dipoles with identical polarities in the other array. This is shown in Figure 25B, where half of the dipoles attract each other, and the other half repel each other making the global attraction force between the arrays zero. Because there is no attraction, the arrays can easily slide into any other position. However, in a totally interlocked array, the pulling of the two arrays causes the dipoles to turn together as illustrated in Figure 25C.

In order to fuse the arrays of Figure 6, the background areas are first aligned. This shift, when it is larger than Panum's fusional limit, is achieved by vergence movements of the eyes; within Panum's limit the shifts are neurally executed. In the model the arrays are physically moved with respect to each other in the horizontal direction. Thus, when the two arrays come in near alignment (within the near-interaction field of magnetic dipoles) the corresponding dipoles in the background area (with zero disparity) will interlock. Once interlocked—owing to the coupling—they act as a global dipole and turn together, thus exerting a large force of attraction on each other.

The center area, however, with nonzero disparity, contains dipoles that partly attract and partly repel each other (Fig. 25D). When, as a second step, the center area is shifted into alignment, the magnets of the center area will interlock; however—and this is the crucial aspect of the model—the already interlocked dipoles of the background turn, while remaining interlocked (Fig. 25E). If finally, the two dipole arrays are assumed to be suspended in a spring-loaded frame (as shown in Fig. 25F), the two arrays are interlocked they will be in equilibrium position.

It should be noted again that sensing the degree of rotation in the horizontal direction of an interlocked dipole pair corresponds to local stereopsis. The dipoles, of course, can also turn in the vertical direction, but this rotation is not sensed. The limit of horizontal rotation that still gives rise to stereopsis is the limit of patent stereopsis.

In order to incorporate the spatial-frequency dependency of stereopsis (as discussed in Sect. H), the dipole arrays should not correspond to the patterns cast on the retinae but rather to a spatial-frequency-filtered retinal pattern. In its simplest version only one spatial filtering is performed that emulates the modulation transfer function of vision. A more complex model can use several dipole arrays that correspond to various spatial frequency filtering of the retinal pattern, respectively. In Sect. N it will be shown how such separate dipole arrays can be coupled together.

N. Explanations and Predictions by the Model

Already this simple model can explain many plastic and cooperative phenomena of stereopsis, including the hysteresis effect of Fender and Julesz (1967). For instance, if we expand one array by 10% or rotate it by 6 deg with respect to the other, the dipoles in this array will turn on their ball joints and try to face their corresponding dipoles. In case of the hysteresis effect, after the dipole arrays become interlocked they exert a great force that overcomes the force of the springs in Figure 25F (at least for displacements less than 120 min arc)—but only if the pulling is slow. When the pulling of the stimuli proceeds at a fast rate, the inertia of the springs will cause the arrays to move away from each other, and after a critical distance is reached, the dipoles become unlocked. With proper masses attributed to the dipoles, spring constants, and frictions, this model can be regarded as an analog computer.

The model can account for the fact that fusion and breakaway disparities are different for simple vertical lines and RDS in the Fender and Julesz study, if one assumes that the dipoles correspond to simple cortical features extractors that are tuned mainly for spatially changing patterns and ignore homogeneous retinal areas. (This can be easily achieved, if the spatial frequency filter acting on the retinal input strongly attenuates the low spatial frequencies.) When the stereograms are fine random-dot textures, the rapidly changing dipole polarities cancel any far interaction, and the left and right dipole arrays interact only when brought into close alignment. On the other hand, a vertical line target in a homogeneous surround corresponds to a few polarized dipoles (surrounded by an array of unpolarized dipoles), and therefore they can interact with each other from a large distance. Conversely, breakaway occurs at lesser pulling distance than for RDS.

Similarly, the model can easily account for fine and coarse stereopsis. For instance, a narrow vertical line corresponds to a few dipoles and the left and right dipole arrays have to be close to each other to interlock (fine stereopsis). Wide bars, however, correspond to many adjacent dipoles (or a double layer of dipoles at the left and right boundaries) that can interlock at larger distances (coarse stereopsis). Interestingly, this fine and coarse stereopsis dichotomy is explained by the simple model with only one spatial frequency filter. With several dipole arrays, corresponding to low- and high-spatial-frequency filtering, respectively, the coarse and fine stereopsis phenomena can be even better described.

The model could explain and even predict several strange psychological phenomena that were not considered or even known at the time the model was constructed. For instance, if a narrow white (or black) horizontal stripe is laid over a RDS such that the background and the center square in depth are cut in half, portions of the stripe (adjacent to the square) are carried by the square and are seen at the same depth (SHIPLEY, 1965). Obviously, if the width of the stripe is small, the vertical spring coupling can pull these undetermined areas in the same depth plane where the adjacent interlocked dipole subarrays lie.

The spring-coupling can also explain the depth reduction in the FRISBY and JULESZ (1975) study. When the corresponding orthogonal line segments in Figure 16 have increased length, the interlocking of the dipole arrays (belonging to the center area in depth) is weakened and the pulling of adjacent dipoles (that belong to the background) by their spring coupling can reduce the turning of the dipoles—and thus result in a reduced sensation of depth.

O. A Parallel Cooperative Model of Stereopsis

While the serial cooperative model of stereopsis can explain several static and dynamic phenomena of global stereopsis, it has several imperfections. As was noted before, the findings of JULESZ (1964) and JULESZ and CHANG (1976)—that a slight bias can overcome the natural bias in an ambiguous stereogram—in-

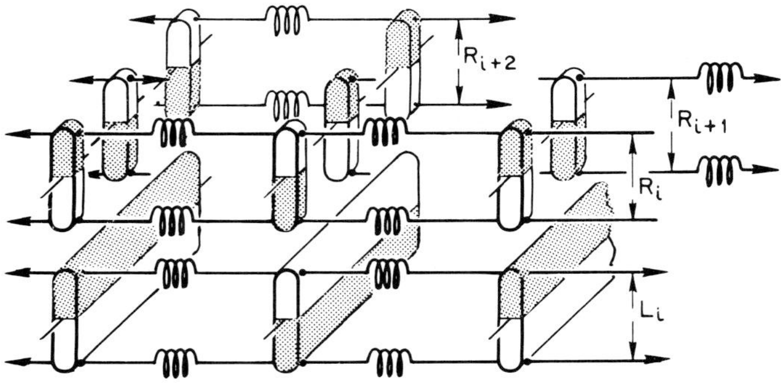

Fig. 26. Improved "parallel" spring-coupled dipole model of global stereopsis (JULESZ and CHANG, 1976)

dicate a parallel process at work. Furthermore, the back and forth shifts in the serial model have a certain "deus ex machina" character (although if one adds to the small shifts by the cortical mechanism the larger shifts owing to convergence eye-movements, the model's serialness has some merits). The improved model of stereopsis retains the cooperativity and plasticity of the previous model, yet has a parallel structure and does not require a series of nasal and temporal shifts.

The new model is similar to the previous model, except that instead of shifting the dipole arrays in time, the dipoles in the left array, interact (in parallel) with several dipoles of the right array as shown in Figure 26. In one representation of the model, there is only a single left dipole array that simultaneously interacts with several right dipole arrays. Each right dipole arrays is similarly polarized but is shifted by one element in the horizontal direction with respect to its adjacent dipole array. Thus, a certain dipole array exists which corresponds to the right image; the array behind it has a dipole polarization pattern that is shifted temporally by one dipole. The next array behind this one is shifted again, etc., while the right dipole arrays above that array are shifted in the nasal direction by one dipole steps. These stacked dipole arrays thus correspond to different disparity values, where the center array corresponds to zero disparity (depth of fixation), and each stacked array has an increased disparity value by one unit. [This feature of the model is similar to that of the Automap-1 model of JULESZ (1963), where each stacked array differed from its neighbor by a disparity value of, say, 4 sec arc, representing the limit of stereo resolution.]

Figure 27A schematically illustrates what happens when a random-dot stereogram is presented with a center square in front of the surround. The illustration portrays only one row of the dipole array, and only three dipole arrays of the right field are shown (R_0, R_1, R_2), corresponding to 0, 1, and 2 dot disparities, respectively. For easier illustration, these three arrays are shown on top of each other, instead of being stacked behind each other.

In the initiation phase dipoles of the background are interlocked, belonging to the left array and the array of R_0, as underlined in Figure 27A. The center square with 2 dots disparity corresponds to the interlocked dipoles belonging

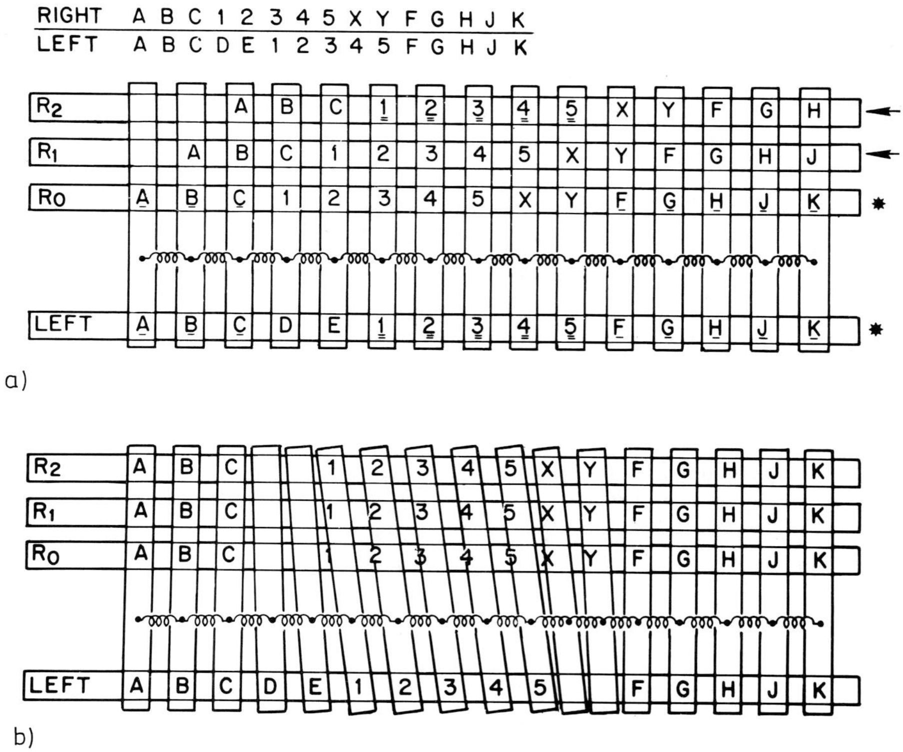

Fig. 27. Schematic illustrations of the workings of the parallel model as described in the text: a) interlocking phase, b) readout phase (JULESZ and CHANG, 1976)

to the left array and the array of R_2. In the R_1 array only 50% of the dipoles are interlocked, by chance alone, with dipoles in the left array, while the other 50% repel each other. In the second or readout phase, one should imagine that all the R_0, R_1, R_2... dipole arrays are shifted to the left so that they become left justified with the R_0 array as illustrated in Figure 27B. This process is equivalent to waves of spreading inhibition. Indeed, when the dipole arrays of R_1, R_2, etc. are shifted to the left, they can carry with them those dipoles that are interlocked. For instance, as R_2 is shifted to the left, all dipoles that belong to R_2 and are interlocked with the left dipole array (i.e., the center square) will remain interlocked but turn (as shown in Fig. 27B). Since in R_0 and R_1, only 50% of the dipoles are interlocked in the area that corresponds to the center square (and 50% repel each other) no force in the R_0 and R_1 arrays can counteract the pull exerted by the 100% interlocked dipoles in R_2. Similarly, dipoles in R_0 that are interlocked (i.e., correspond to areas of the background) will remain interlocked and resist turning as arrays of R_1 and R_2 are pushed to the left.

In this model if a subdomain of the left dipole array is interlocked with more than one right dipole array (ambiguous stereograms), then the shifting of the arrays will only result in turning a dipole subarray when one of the right arrays has more interlocked dipoles than the other arrays. Thus, the model explains why in a 94% versus a 100% correlated ambiguous organization, the latter organization prevails. In a concrete example the two depth organizations have a plus or minus 2 unit disparity. Here the left dipole array corresponding to the ambiguous center square is interlocked with equal number of dipoles in R_2 and R_{-2}. So after these arrays are shifted in alignment with R_0, that organization would prevail (i.e., that dipole array would remain interlocked) which exerted bigger pulling force owing to some natural bias. However, owing to the vertical spring coupling, the pulling force of dipoles in R_2 might pull the dipoles of the ambiguous center square in the nasal direction, thus overcoming the natural bias. After subdomains of the coupled dipoles turn—being carried by one of the moving dipole arrays—an avalanche effect takes place, since the left-justified dipole arrays become all identical and the same subdomains of dipoles in each dipole array interlock with the corresponding dipoles in the left array as shown in Figure 27b.

Even when the bias is not in R_2 (or R_{-2}, i.e., one of the ambiguous disparity values), owing to the spring coupling, the interlocked dipoles in adjacent arrays (of near disparity values) can pull the dipoles in R_2 with adequate force to overcome the natural bias.

P. Neurophysiological Implications of the Model

Each dipole as it turns corresponds to a gamut of disparity detectors tuned to different disparities but surveying the same retinal position. Thus, each dipole is a global (highly complex) neural unit of stereopsis. All the adjacent dipoles that turned together (owing to their spring couplings) correspond to a gamut of disparity detectors tuned to the same disparity but surveying different retinal positions in a given neighborhood. Thus, a second class of global stereo units might be hypothesized.

The spring coupling between adjacent dipoles corresponds to the facilitation between disparity units that are tuned to the same disparity. The interlocking phase of the dipoles corresponds to the spreading of facilitation between these units. The readout phase corresponds to a spreading inhibition between units that are tuned to different disparities. In case of ambiguities, a dipole can take only one rotational angle, thus any other depth organization becomes suppressed. The shifting of the various arrays might correspond to some temporal dispersion of neural activity (inhibition). Here "left justification" simply corresponds to a pool of disparity detectors identifying their disparity values. This identification signal is also sent as inhibition to other pools of disparity detectors. Thus "left justification" does not refer to some anisotropy in the spreading of activity. There are many other ways one can implement a "readout" mechanism that does not involve anisotropies.

Both the serial and parallel models proposed here can account for the hysteresis phenomena of FENDER and JULESZ, but only the parallel model is compatible with the JULESZ and CHANG findings. Indeed, no serial scanning (performed cortically) could explain how in the fovea a 4% bias from a distance of ± 18 min arc binocular disparity could suppress competing depth localizations; and the brief exposure excludes the serial vergence movements of the eyes. This area of interaction between binocular disparity detectors in the fovea (where this area of interaction is the smallest, and visual acuity the largest) is large enough to permit the coexistence of many independent dots which can elicit hundreds of false targets. The cooperative models can easily suppress these false targets and find a unique, continuous surface in depth. The same models perform well even for large-disparity RDS, in which the number of false targets increases astronomically as the eyes converge or diverge. While one can invent simpler models (based on a large number of binocular-disparity-tuned *local* feature analyser types), such models require a *memory buffer* coupled to the vergence mechanism of the eyes. In contrast, the cooperative models do not require complex memory, only hysteresis, and still can explain, and even predict, the rich phenomena of global stereopsis. However, model building at present is and will remain a "metascientific" activity until psychological and neurophysiological advances will enable us to discriminate between competing models.

Q. Conclusions

In this chapter emphasis was given to the great progress that resulted when local and global problems of stereopsis were separated. It seems that global stereopsis is simpler than some of the form perception problems in monocular vision. This relative simplicity persuaded many neurophysiologists to first study binocular vision. On the other hand, global stereopsis, in spite of its simplicity, exhibits many cooperative and plastic phenomena that could give insight into higher mental functions.

The reason why so much effort was spent on describing a model of stereopsis is that present neurophysiology has only local neural elements, while the proposed model has a global structure and might guide neurophysiologists in their further search. It was also intentional to build an analog instead of an algorithmic model. In cognition, where serial processes dominate, computer algorithms (run on the ubiquitous serial computers) might be good simulations of some thought processes. However, in perception, and particularly in global stereopsis where thousands of local processes influence each other simultaneously in a cooperative manner, simulation of parallel computation by step-by-step performed serial computations tends to disguise the real structure of the system.

Because of the easy grasp of the working of the model, the model can serve as an intermediary language between psychologic facts and possible (though hypothetical) neurophysiologic mechanisms. If one understood that, for instance, a rotating dipole is equivalent to a pool of disparity detectors connected to the same retinal location but tuned to various binocular disparities, then it is quite natural to "translate" neuron pools into dipoles, solve the problem in the spring-coupled magnetic dipole domain by *direct insight* (or in complex cases by computer simulation) and translate back the solution into neuron pools and spreading waves of facilitation and inhibition.

With the help of the model several problems of stereopsis can be clarified and summarized: Obviously a few distant dots or lines will correspond to the polarization of a few remote dipoles that are too far from each other for any spring coupling and interact only through the far magnetic field. This then corresponds to *local stereopsis*.

With increased dot or line density in the stereograms, the corresponding polarized dipoles start to exert force on each other through the springs. This cooperativity is gradual, but beyond a certain element density the coupling between adjacent dipoles becomes so strong that its effects are as important as the magnetic interaction between the corresponding dipoles. When the coupling between dipoles (i.e., facilitation and inhibition between pools) becomes the dominant factor, the phenomena of *global stereopsis* manifest themselves. When the left and right arrays of a stereogram are identical—except for rigid horizontal shifts of some subarrays—the corresponding interlocked dipoles have to rotate only horizontally in their ball joints. This can be called *point-to-point* matching. When the left and right arrays also differ in size or shape, the corresponding interlocked dipoles have to rotate both horizontally and vertically. This corresponds to a *plasticity* of matching. The problems of *fine* and *coarse* stereopsis were already discussed in Sect. N.

Only time can tell whether these distinctions serve a useful purpose. At present one can only hope that in the framework of global stereopsis, these distinctions will clarify certain problems and will generate new experiments.

In this review the only material included was related to stereopsis per se, and RDS were regarded merely as a tool for studying stereopsis. However, the technique of RDS goes beyond this goal and permits the tracing of the information flow in the CNS, which has been called "psychoanatomy" by JULESZ (1971). Most perceptual phenomena can be studied by stimuli in which the luminance gradients are replaced by binocular disparity gradients. For instance, most optical illusions remain the same under cyclopean portrayal (JULESZ, 1971). This means that the processes responsible for the illusions must be central, since RDS operationally skip all the earlier processing stages before the cyclopean retina. Another example is the finding by JULESZ and OSWALD (1978) that the RT of tracking eye-movements is 100–150 msec longer when the monocular contour cues are absent. This increase in the latency of tracking is about the same in monkeys after their superior colliculus is ablated (WURTZ and GOLDBERG, 1972). Whether this is just a coincidence, and the cyclopean targets require more cortical processing time, or whether the increase in latency is the result of making the superior colliculus inoperative by removing all monocular contour cues, remains to be seen.

Similarly, the finding of LU and FENDER (1972), confirmed recently by GREGORY (1977), that isoluminant colored RDS (e.g., red and green randomly selected cells with matched luminance values) do not yield depth perception, while isoluminant colored classical stereograms do yield depth, has an important psychoanatomic implication. The cyclopean retina seems to be "colorblind".

Let us end this review by noting that global stereopsis elicited by RDS might be of importance even to the neurophysiologist who is not interested in stereopsis per se, but who probes the visual cortex with microelectrodes to elucidate other functions. Cortical neurons represent at least five or six interneuron levels from the retinal receptor stage on, and at each interneuron level the complexity of the neural net increases exponentially, at least for the processing of luminance patterns cast on the retinae. However, for binocular correlation, the same cortical neurons (if tuned to binocular disparity detection) become first-order interneurons and the complexity of the neural net is greatly reduced. Whether such cortical units will be found that respond to cyclopean targets alone, remains to be seen.

Acknowledgements: Author thanks Dr. C. WILLIAM TYLER for his many suggestions and careful reading of the first draft of the manuscript, and Mrs. DOROTHY CAIVANO for her patience in learning to use a computer-editing system and in typing the many changes.

References

Aschenbrenner, C.M.: Problems in getting information into and out of air photographs. Photogramm. Eng. **20** (**3**), 398–401 (1954).

Barlow, H.B., Blakemore, C., Pettigrew, J.D.: The neural mechanism of binocular depth discrimination. J. Physiol. **193**, 327–342 (1967).

Bishop, P.O.: Neurophysiology of binocular single vision and stereopsis. In: Handbook of sensory physiology, Jung, R. (ed.). **VII/3**, 256–305. Berlin: Springer, 1973.

Bishop, P.O., Henry, G.H.: Spatial vision. Ann. Rev. Psychol. **22**, 119–160 (1971).

Blakemore, C., Campbell, F.W.: On the existence of neurones in the human visual system selectively sensitive to the orientation and size of retinal images. J. Physiol. **203**, 237–260 (1969).

Bough, E.W.: Stereoscopic depth aftereffect produced without monocular cues. Nature **225**, 41–42 (1970).

Breitmeyer, B., Julesz, B., Kropfl, W.: Dynamic randomdot stereograms reveal an up-down anisotropy and a leftright isotropy between cortical hemifields. Sci. **187**, 269–270 (1975).

Carmon, A., Bechtoldt, H.P.: Dominance of the right cerebral hemisphere for stereopsis. Neuropsychol. **7**, 29–39 (1969).

Cowey, A., Parkinson, A.M., Warnick, L.: Global stereopsis in rhesus monkeys. Quart. J. Exp. Psychol. **27**, 93–109 (1975).

Dev, P.: Segmentation processes in visual perception: a cooperative neural model. COINS Techn. Report 74C-5. Amherst, Mass.: Computer and Information Sciences, Univ. of Mass., 1974.

Durnford, M., Kimura, D.: Right hemisphere specialization for depth perception reflected in visual field difference. Nature (Lond.) **231**, 394–395 (1971).

Fender, D.H., Julesz, B.: Extension of Panum's fusional area in binocularly stabilized vision. J. Opt. Soc. Am. **57**, 819–830 (1967).

Fox, R., Lehmkuhle, S.W., Bush, R.C.: Stereopsis in the falcon. Science **197**, 79–81 (1977).

Frisby, J.P., Clatworthy, J.L.: Learning to see complex random-dot stereograms. Perception **4**, 173–178 (1975).

Frisby, J.P., Julesz, B.: Depth reduction effects in random line stereograms. Perception **4**, 151–158 (1975).

Frisby, J.P., Julesz, B.: The effect of length differences between corresponding lines on stereopsis from single-line and multiline stimuli. Vision Res. **16**, 83–87 (1976).

Gregory, R.: Vision with isoluminant colour contrast: 1. A projection technique and observations. Perception **6**, 113–119 (1977).

Gulick, W.L., Lawson, R.B.: Human Stereopsis: A Psychophysical Approach. New York: Oxford University Press, 1976.

• Harmon, L.D., Julesz, B.: Masking in visual recognition: effects of two dimensional filtered noise. Sci. **180**, 1194–1197 (1973).

Henry, G.H., Bishop, P.O., Coombs, J.S.: Inhibitory and subliminal excitatory receptive fields of simple units in cat striate cortex. Vision Res. **9**, 1289–1296 (1969).

Hogben, J.H., Julesz, B., Ross, J.: Short-term memory for symmetry. Vision Res. **16** (1976).

• Hubel, D.H., Wiesel, T.N.: Stereoscopic vision in macaque monkey. Nature **225**, 41–42 (1970).

Joshua, D.E., Bishop, P.O.: Binocular single vision and depth discrimination: Receptive field disparities for central and peripheral vision and binocular interaction on peripheral single units in cat striate cortex. Exp. Brain Res. **10**, 389–416 (1970).

Julesz, B.: Binocular depth perception of computer-generated patterns. Bell System Techn. J. **39**, 1125–1162 (1960).

Julesz, B.: Binocular depth perception and pattern recognition. Information Theory, Fourth London Symposium, 1960, E.C. Cherry. London: Butterworth 1961.

Julesz, B.: Stereopsis and binocular rivalry of contours. J. Opt. Soc. Am. **53**, 994–999 (1963).

• Julesz, B.: Binocular depth perception without familiarity cues. Sci. **145**, 356–362 (1964).

Julesz, B.: Binocular disappearance of monocular symmetry. Sci. **153**, 657–658 (1966).

• Julesz, B.: Foundations of Cyclopean Perception. Chicago: University of Chicago Press, 1971.

Julesz, B.: Cooperative model of stereoscopic depth perception. In: Synergetics: Cooperative phenomena in multi-component systems. Haken, H. (ed.). Proc. of the Symposium on Synergetics, 1973.

• Julesz, B.: Cooperative phenomena in binocular depth perception. Amer. Sci. **62**, 32–43 (1974). Reprinted in: Current trends in psychology: Readings from American Scientist. (Ed. Janis, I.L.) Los Altos, California: W. Kaufmann Inc. 1977.

Julesz, B., Breitmeyer, B., Kropfl, W.: Spatio-temporal left-right hemifield isotropy and upper-lower hemifield anisotropy in cyclopean vision. Perception **5**, 129–141 (1976a).

Julesz, B., Chang, J.J.: Interaction between pools of binocular disparity detectors tuned to different disparities. Biol. Cybernetics **22**, 107–119 (1976).

Julesz, B., Johnson, S.C.: Stereograms portraying ambiguously perceivable surfaces. Proc. Natl. Acad. Sci. **61**, 437–441 (1968a).

Julesz, B., Johnson, S.C.: Mental Holography. Stereograms portraying ambiguously perceivable surfaces. Bell System Tech. J. **49**, 2075–2083 (1968b).

Julesz, B., Miller, J.E.: Independent spatial-frequency-tuned channels in binocular fusion and rivalry. Perception **4**, 125–143 (1975).

Julesz, B., Oswald, H.: Binocular utilization of monocular cues that are undetectable monocularly. Perception **7**, No. 3 (1978)

Julesz, B., Petrig, B., Büttner, U.: Fast determination of stereopsis in rhesus monkey using dynamic random dot stereograms, J. Opt. Soc. Am. **66**, 1090 (1976b).

Julesz, B., Payne, R.A.: Differences between monocular and binocular stroboscopic movement perception. Vision Res. **8**, 433–444 (1968).

Julesz, B., Tyler, C.W.: Neurontropy, an entropy-like measure of neural correlation in binocular fusion and rivalry. Biol. Cybernetics **22**, 107–119 (1976).

Julesz, B., White, B.W.: Short-term visual memory and the Pulfrich Phenomenon. Nature **22**, 639–641 (1969).

• Kaufman, L.: Sight and mind, An introduction to visual perception. New York: Oxford University Press, 1974.

Lehmann, D., Julesz, B.: Lateralized cortical potentials evoked in humans by dynamic random-dot stereograms. Vision Res. in press (1978).

Lehmkuhle, S., Fox, R., Bush, R.C.: Global stereopsis in the cat. ARVO meeting, Sarasota, Apr. 25–29, 1977.

Lu, C., Fender, D.H.: The interaction of color and luminance in stereoscopic vision. Invest. Ophthalm. **11**, 482–490 (1972).

MacCracken, P.J., Bourne, J.A., Hayes, W.N.: Experience and latency to achieve stereopsis: a replication. Perceptual and Motor Skills, **45**, 261–262 (1977).

Marlowe, L.H.: Orientation of contours and binocular depth perception. Ph. D. thesis, Dept. of Psychology, Brown University, Rhode Island (1969).
Marr, D., Poggio, T.: Cooperative computation of stereo disparity. Science, 194, 283–287 (1976).
Mitchell, D.E., O'Hagan, S.: Accuracy of stereoscopic localisation of small line segments that differ in size or orientation in the two eyes. Vision Res. **12**, 437–454 (1972).
Nebes, R.D.: Hemisphere specialization in commissurotomized man. Psychol. Bull. **81**, 1–14 (1974).
Nelson, J.I.: Globality and stereoscopic fusion in binocular vision. J. Theoretical Biol. **49** (**1**) (1975).
Ogle, K.N.: The optical space sense. The Eye (Ed. H. Davson). New York: Academic Press, Vol. 4, 211–432 (1962).
Pantle, A., Sekuler, R.W.: Contrast response of human visual mechanisms sensitive to orientation and direction of motion. Vision Res. **9**, 397–406 (1969).
Panum, P.L.: Physiologische Untersuchungen über das Sehen mit zwei Augen. Kiel: Schwers, 1858.
Papert, S.: Stereoscopic synthesis as a technique for localizing visual mechanisms. M.I.T. Quart. Progr. Rep. **73**, 239–243 (1964).
Pettigrew, J.D., Konishi, M.: Neurons selective for orientation and binocular disparity in the visual wulst of the barn owl (Tyto Alba). Science **193**, 675–678 (1976).
Pettigrew, J.D., Nikara, T., Bishop, P.O.: Binocular interaction on single units in cat striate cortex: Simultaneous stimulation by single moving slit with receptive fields in correspondence. Exp. Brain Res. **6**, 391–410 (1968).
Poggio, G.F., Fischer, B.: Binocular interaction and depth sensitivity of striate and prestriate cortical neurons of behaving rhesus monkeys. J. Neurophysiol. **40** (1977).
Pulfrich, C.: Die Stereoskopie im Dienste der isochromen und heterochromen Photometrie. Naturwissenschaften **10**, 533–564, 569–601, 714–722, 735–743, 751–761 (1922).
Ramachandran, V.S., Braddick, O.: Orientation specific learning in stereopsis. Perception **2**, 371–376 (1973).
Richards, W.: Anomalous stereoscopic depth perception. J. Opt. Soc. Am. **61**, 410–414 (1971).
Richards, W.: Factors affecting depth perception. AFOSR-TR-73-0439 Final Report, Air Force Office of Sci. Res. and MIT, Mass. (1973).
Richards, W., Kaye, M.G.: Local versus global stereopsis: two mechanisms? Vision Res. **14**, 1345–1347 (1974).
Ross, J.: Stereopsis by binocular delay. Nature **248**, 363 (1974).
Ross, J., Hogben, J.H.: Short-term memory in stereopsis. Vision Res. **14**, 1195–1201 (1974).
Sage, A., Frisby, J.P.: The role of monocularly conspicuous features in facilitating stereopsis from random-dot stereograms. Perception **4**, 159–171 (1975).
Sarmiento, R.F. The stereoacuity of macaque monkey. Vision Res. **15**, 493–498 (1975).
Shipley, T.: Visual contours in homogeneous space. Sci. **150**, 348–350 (1965).
Sperling, G.: Binocular vision: A physical and neural theory. J. Am. Psychol. **83**, 461–534 (1970).
Stromeyer, C.F., III, Julesz, B.: Spatial frequency masking in vision: Critical bands and spread of masking. J. Opt. Soc. Am. **62**, 1221–1232 (1972).
Tyler, C.W.: Depth perception in disparity gratings. Nature **251**, 140–142 (1974).
Tyler, C.W.: Stereopsis in dynamic visual noise. Nature, **250**, 781–782 (1974).
Tyler, C.W.: Stereoscopic tilt and size aftereffects. Perception **4**, 187–192 (1975).
Tyler, C.W., Julesz, B.: The neural transfer characteristic (Neurontropy) for binocular stochastic stimulation. Biol. Cybernetics **23**, 33–37 (1976a).
Tyler, C.W., Julesz, B.: On the depth of the cyclopean retina (to be published) (1976b).
Tyler, C.W., Julesz, B.: Binocular cross-correlation in time and space. Vision Res. **18**, 101–105 (1978).
Uttal, W.R., Fitzgerald, J., Eskin, T.E.: Parameters of tachistoscopic stereopsis. Vision Res. **15**, 705–712 (1975).
Wheatstone, C.: On some remarkable and hitherto unobserved phenomena of binocular vision. Philosphical Trans., Royal Soc. (London) 128: 371–394. Reprinted in Visual perception: The nineteenth century. Dember, W. (ed.). New York: Wiley, 1964, pp. 371–377, 286–287.
Winograd, T.: Understanding natural language. New York: Academic Press, 1972.
Wurtz, R.H., Goldberg, M.E.: Activity of superior colliculus in behaving monkey. IV Effects of lesions on eye-movements. J. Neurophysiol. **35**, 587–596 (1972).

C. Developmental Processes and Species Comparison

Chapter 8

Mechanisms of Shape-Recognition Among Vertebrates

D. INGLE,* Belmont, Massachusetts (USA)

With 12 Figures

Contents

A. Introduction

This chapter reviews data concerning the abilities of various vertebrates to recognize visual shapes. In the earlier decades of this century, many psychologists and zoologists were curious as to whether lower vertebrates with relatively simple brains (such as the fishes) possessed abilities to "abstract" visual shapes or to perceive similarities among visual forms. These questions were influenced

* The author was supported by a N.I.M.H. Career Scientist Award (KO 2 13, 175) during preparation of this chapter.

by the proposal of Gestalt psychology that the essential character of a visual shape was a direct and unlearned percept which lower animals might share with man. Some of these earlier attempts to evaluate the abilities of animals to generalize their training to "similar" sets of shapes are reviewed by HERTER (1953), and by SUTHERLAND (1961a). Further comparative studies of shape discrimination were resumed in the 1950's and 1960's, allied with neurophysiological data which promised new insight into underlying analytic mechanisms. Although we have continued to add new experiments on shape recognition, the exact relationship between brain evolution and the presumed improvements in shape vision remain unclear. Because comparative studies have once more been stimulated by a recent renaissance in comparative neuroanatomy, a review of the main facts and hypotheses of shape recognition seems timely indeed.

In addition to reviewing the usual discrimination-learning studies, (bread and butter for the experimental psychologist), I have included selected studies of natural discrimination-abilities. Usually the laboratory-oriented student of vision pays little attention to the means by which animals search their environment for food, predators, social rivals, hiding places, etc. Yet, for many species, there are high correlations between particular stimulus configurations and the exact pattern of response elicited: pecking, biting, threatening, ducking, grasping, etc. Such natural experiments have two considerable advantages for comparative neurobehavioral studies. First, one can frequently collect large amounts of data without taking the time to train animals into new habits. Secondly, a consistent behavioral discrimination among visual stimuli reflects an evolutionary priority upon a particular class of neural analyzers. It seems likely that prior knowledge of "optimal stimulus configurations" in behavior will help the neurophysiologist search for the most important afferent filters. In reviewing abilities of non-mammalian vertebrates, I have attempted a tentative synthesis of discrimination-training experiments, (largely with fish), and natural shape recognition abilities, (largely with amphibians), and found that the "fit" is surprisingly good. Whether or not similar methods can be applied to mammalian (and indeed to human) vision is one of the lingering questions that I would hope to leave in the mind of the reader.

B. Natural Uses of Vision

I. Releasers of Prey-Catching: Stimulus Size and Configuration

The physiological studies of BARLOW (1953) and of LETTVIN et al. (1959) indicate that the frog retina contains a class of ganglion cells specifically sensitive to small "bug-like" objects. Quantitative studies in both frogs (BUTENANDT and GRÜSSER, 1968) and toads (EWERT and HOCK, 1972) confirm the impression that optimal discharge of these units is produced by objects about 4° in size. Furthermore, behavioral studies indicate that frogs (INGLE, 1968) and toads (EWERT, 1968) orient most frequently towards objects of just this size. Although there is considerable evidence that size-preferences of frogs and toads can change during shifts of motivation (EWERT, 1970, 1974, 1975; INGLE, 1971b, 1973a, 1976b), we emphasize that the normative size-selection mechanism provides a good basis for noticing corners and protuberances of larger objects. Indeed, a hungry toad or frog will sometimes snap at the leading corner of a slowly moving diamond shape or the arm of a cross, as if these features are especially "bitable."

EWERT (1968) has shown that the elongation of a prey object along its axis of motion can enhance its value as food. However, this effect critically depends upon stimulus size and figure-ground relations. The effect of elongation is strong for a 2° high object, but much weaker for a 4° object; and it applies strongly to black spots but weakly to white spots. While this facilitation effect is interesting in its own right, we cannot conclude that "configuration *per se*" is abstracted by the toad. Similar conclusions follow from a recent study by INGLE and MCKINLEY, 1977, who studied the response of toads toward double-stimuli composed of a linked pair of small worm-like rectangles. When these objects were only 7° apart, the toad oriented or snapped at the "head" end (judged relative to the direction of motion) but when separated by 21° or more they snapped nearly as often at the tail end. As we shall see below in considering shape recognition in fishes, the ability of an animal to "perceptually integrate" disparate parts of a shape may critically depend upon their separation distance. For this reason, larger shapes may not always be encoded in the same way as smaller stimuli.

Finally, we note some interesting data concerning spontaneous preferences of animals for feeding on particular shapes on the basis of their inherent configuration. Using the pecking behavior of newly hatched chicks, FANTZ (1957) as well as GOODWIN and HESS (1966) report that chicks consistently prefer small circles to triangles of the same size. This preference occurs within different size ranges, but size is prepotent over shape when a smaller circle competes with a larger triangle. Other less extensive experiments seem to show that the same perference appears in distantly related species as well: goldfish (INGLE, 1971c); frogs (PASCHE, 1932); and lizards (EHRENHARDT, 1937). It would be useful, of course, to extend this type of feeding test to a variety of visual shapes and to assess the role of visual experience in the selection. The study by FANTZ (1957) did conclude that the circle preference of chicks was displayed immediately upon testing, where no prior pecking experience was available. We must conclude that a chick (and perhaps many other species) brings an intrinsic bias for noticing particular shapes into its first learning experience.

II. Selective Behaviors Toward Stationary Objects

Although most studies of frog visual behavior have focussed upon feeding activity, the ability of frogs to respond adaptively to stationary objects also deserves detailed study. In earlier reviews, (INGLE, 1970, 1971b) we offered qualitative observations on detour behavior of frogs and toads. In an analytical study of this ability (INGLE, 1971a) we found that frogs were much better at avoiding a wide grid barrier when stripes were oriented vertically than when they were horizontal. We might suppose that frogs do not easily detect horizontal edges, but more recently it was found that frogs prefer to jump down upon horizontal stripes in preference to vertical stripes (INGLE, 1976a). For *Rana pipiens*, at least, it appears that vertical edges more easily evoke detours *around*, but horizontal edges invite stepping *upon*. We do not know whether or not these specific behavioral tendencies reflect a hard-wiring from visual to motor systems, or whether the meaning of horizontal and vertical edges is learned. It is interesting that a study by WIENS (1972) shows that the larval frog's tendency to approach vertical stripes viewed in the water depends upon experience with that stimulus. Further studies using such natural behaviors might reveal how sharply these preferences are tuned, and therefore would help us infer the kind of visual filter required.

Because of the frog's selective behavior to edge-orientation, we wondered whether frogs might also show preferences for the shape of apertures providing an escape route from noxious stimulation. When we varied both size and height of apertures in a dark box, we found that frogs consistently preferred to escape via horizontal rather than vertical apertures (INGLE, 1973b). One might have predicted this result on the teleological ground that a jumping frog's body is wider in the horizontal axis. The underlying mechanism may depend upon either (a) the greater salience of vertical edges in inhibiting a jump toward a vertical aperture, or (b) a stronger summation mechanism between vertical edges than between horizontal edges. In either case, we stress that certain pairs of shapes can be discriminated by frogs using mechanisms that subserve basic visuomotor behaviors. Such behaviors can be rather sharply tuned, as we found when measuring the effect of aperture width on the frog's willingness to jump between two vertical barriers set directly in front (INGLE and COOK, 1977). As this width approaches the frog's own head size, a change of only 3° visual angle suddenly reduces the straight-ahead direction from 75% to 25% frequency.

These experiments suggest that barrier-tests may provide a useful tool for species comparisons and for approaching physiological mechanisms of vision. A series of studies on fishes, amphibians, reptiles and mammals would prove useful for two reasons. First, a better appreciation of adaptations of various species to their ecological niche (especially arboreal species) could be obtained by testing abilities to jump around and onto various objects and surfaces. But secondly, we should consider the possibility that abilities of animals to discriminate shapes in a learning test are based partially upon the inherent visual analyzers already required to move about in a complex visual world. We have made a first test of this idea by testing goldfish in a simple apparatus (Fig. 1) which is similar to that used by MACKINTOSH and SUTHERLAND (1963) to study abilities of goldfish to discriminate between rectangles of various orientations. We placed small black shapes (vertical, horizontal or diagonal) upon a glass barrier inserted behind one or the other hole, and simply observed reliability

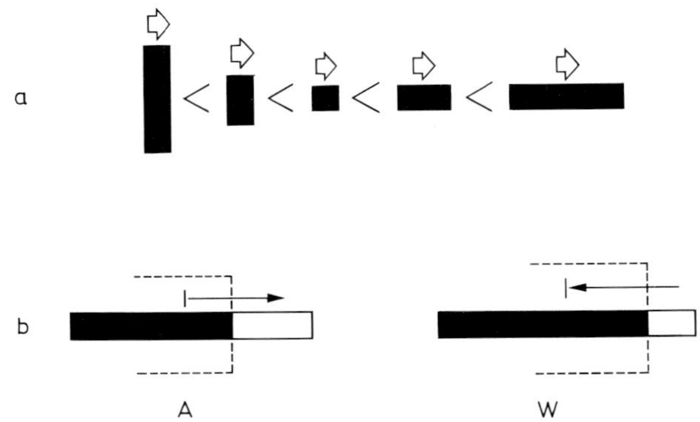

Fig. 1a and b. Configurational determinants of optimal prey stimuli for frogs and toads. In (a) an experiment of EWERT (1968), using continuously moving shapes as prey stimuli for toads, is summarized. For a black object moving horizontally, elongation along axis of movement enhances toad's response, but elongation in vertical dimension strongly diminishes potency of stimulus as prey. In (b) studies of INGLE (1968) are summarized, which show that an advancing edge of a black rectangle *A* is less effective as a prey-stimulus than is a withdrawing edge of a similar object. Same outcome was obtained using white rectangles on a dark background, or using stimuli or various lengths. In contrast to EWERT's method, stimuli used by INGLE were created by moving a black card behind a slit in a white wall

of barrier-detection. Surprisingly, goldfish performed at 90% accuracy with horizontal or diagonal bars, but only with 60% avoidance of the vertical shapes. This asymmetry in detection behavior might reflect an asymmetry in visual edge detectors, or it might result from the side-to-side swimming of fish toward the targets. What is important for our discussion of shape analyzing behavior, is that goldfish do not regard horizontal and vertical bars as equally "salient."

C. Physiological Correlates of Feeding and Barrier Selection

In our review of the natural "shape discrimination" abilities shown by fishes and amphibians, we have treated feeding and barrier detection as two quite different classes of behavior. While this must be true in some sense, it does not follow that different afferent pathways must be used in primary encoding of the various relevant stimuli. For example, it is generally assumed that a human observer uses his geniculostriate system for scanning food objects or for evaluating a picket fence. However, recent ablation studies in the frog (INGLE, 1973f) do seem to justify a fundamental neurological distinction between the two kinds of vision. When the optic tectum is ablated, frogs are totally unresponsive to moving prey-objects (although they may eat worms that touch the snout) but retain the ability to detour around a barrier or orient towards an aperture while escaping noxious stimulation. Following unilateral tectum ablations, the cut optic fibers often regenerate to the ipsilateral optic tectum, where they induce the frog to orient in the wrong direction in response to prey. Nevertheless, the same frog orients realistically when confronted with a barrier. Thus we must conclude that two relatively independent afferent systems mediate prey-catching and barrier-avoidance. It is assumed that the retinal projection to the caudal thalamus mediates the second class of behavior since (a) large pretectal lesions can abolish barrier-avoidance without interfering with prey-catching (INGLE – unpublished data); (b) single neurons sensitive to large stationary edges can be recorded in the posterior thalamus (INGLE – unpublished data) but not in the deeper layers of the tectum.

No detailed analysis of barrier-detection abilities are reported for fish following ablation of the tectum, but our unpublished studies indicate that blindness to food objects does follow tectum removal in the goldfish as well as in the frog. Furthermore, regeneration of the optic nerve to the ipsilateral tectum is accompanied by wrong-way orientations to food, as in the frog. The fish tectum does seem to harbor some visual units that are sensitive to edge-orientation, unlike the frog tectum. For example, WESTERMAN (1966) reported that units taken to be intrinsic neurons often had elongated receptive fields, and responded optimally to edges oriented parallel to the long axis of this field. The tuning curves for edge-orientation may not be as sharp as those reported for mammalian striate cortex neurons. However, a recent report by ZENKIN and PIGAREV (1969) does report neurons within the tectum of the pike, which are sharply tuned to horizontal edges. The functional significance of such horizontal selectivity is not at all obvious, but its existence may have implications for shape recognition. It should be mentioned that GRAEBER et al. (1972) have found that the ability to discriminate horizontal from vertical stripes remains following tectum ablation in the shark. Such abilities are naturally referred to the retinothalamic projection. It is interesting that these discrimanda resemble the grid barriers used to test frogs with the tectum ablated (INGLE, 1973f), since a thalamic edge-orientation sensitivity is implied by both types of study.

In summary, we conclude that both the tectum and the thalamus have specific kinds of visual sensitivities potentially useful in shape recognition, although quantitative studies are still necessary to show how these "filters" may be related to overt discrimination behavior. In thinking about these possibilities, and in designing relevant recording studies, we should also remember that the tectum and the thalamus may interact to produce still more specific filter properties. For one thing, tectal neuron responses are modified by focal lesions within the posterior thalamus (INGLE, 1973e) and posterior thalamic neurons are strikingly modified by lesions in the tectum (BROWN and INGLE, 1973). Secondly, these two retinofugal targets each project to other areas – such as the midbrain tegmentum – where other interactions may occur. Thus far physiologic and ablation studies confirm the existence of at least two distinct neural systems for shape discrimination in lower vertebrates, but give us little hint as to the complexity of processing inherent in these "simpler" brains.

D. Shape-Recognition Studies with Fish

I. Problems and Methods

Among the many shape-recognition studies performed during the last 50 years, two main concerns are dominant. First, experimenters have tried to identify cues that fishes use to discriminate among shapes of the same size and luminance. One approach involves comparison of learning rates with a pair of discriminations—e.g., A vs. B on the one hand, and C vs. D on the other. For example, HAGER (1938) found that a discrimination of 3 vs. 4 stripes was learned better by minnows when the pair were each vertically oriented, than when each stimulus consisted of horizontal contours. This suggests that they can "count" stripes more easily while scanning in the horizontal direction.

A second method involves setting one cue against another to determine the relative salience of the two. SAXENA (1966) found that fish learning a stripe-number discrimination ignore a change in the positive stimulus from horizontal to vertical and continue to select stimuli on the basis of stripe number. On the other hand, when stripe numbers are equal, fish are quite capable of making a horizontal vs. vertical discrimination (INGLE, 1968b). When a fish responds selectively to but one set of cues during a conflict test of this kind, he does not necessarily "ignore" the subordinate cues. Indeed INGLE (1966) found that when color and pattern cues learned together by goldfish were intentionally set in conflict, such that the pattern differences dominated the behavior, a generalization test via the "untrained" eye showed that the color discrimination was now retained.

The second approach to analysis of shape-recognition processes involves tests of "transposition" abilities: i.e., choosing between novel stimuli (C vs. D) on the basis of cues learned in an earlier discrimination (A vs. B). For one thing, the transposition method has been used to explore questions of shape-invariance during transformations of size or orientation, where the essential configuration is preserved. For example, can a fish recognize a triangle vs. circle pair when both are rotated or reduced in size? Do fish recognize "configurational" properties of such shapes or do they select elementary parts of a given shape as the predominant cue?

II. Directional and Orientational Biases in Fish Vision

In the last section we noted evidence of HAGER (1938) that fish may scan a row of stripes more effectively along the horizontal axis. An experiment by MEESTERS (1940) makes a similar point: fish trained on large vs. small squares transfer their habit to a long vs. short discrimination better to a pair of horizontal rectangles than to vertically elongated shapes. Such a bias to scan shapes along the horizontal axis might favor distinction between shapes

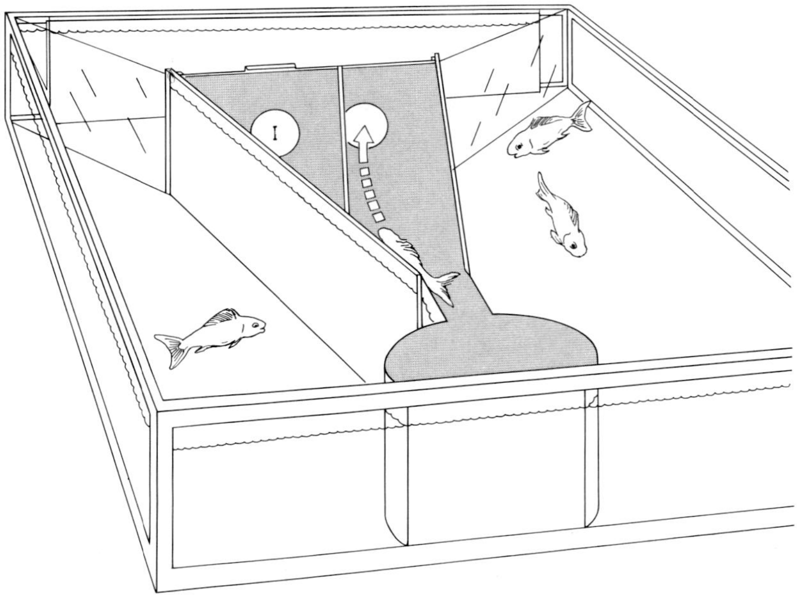

Fig. 2. Shape detection test used by INGLE (1971c) with goldfish. Subjects learn to swim directly out of dark box through open window, since small dark shape is mounted upon a glass barrier. Detectability of these shapes as "barriers" can be compared in terms of percent choice of open aperture when paired against small rectangles set in vertical, horizontal, or diagonal orientations. In this paradigm, four fish were tested intermittently within a given session. Stimulus arrangement was intended to resemble that used by MACKINTOSH and SUTHERLAND (1963) who used dark rectangles as discriminanda in a food-rewarded task

with different horizontal extents, regardless of other properties. Such a suggestion fits with the finding of MACKINTOSH and SUTHERLAND (1963) that goldfish more readily learn a discrimination between horizontal and vertical bars than between the same shapes oriented diagonally at 45° vs. 135° angles. This idea is consistent with a further result of this study: goldfish treat an oblique rectangle at 35° like a vertical shape, and generalize from a 55° rectangle to a horizontal shape. Furthermore, in the detection tests of INGLE (1971c), goldfish avoided the vertical rectangles very poorly, and these shapes had a slight horizontal extent. However, in further experiments goldfish discriminated either diagonal vs. vertical or diagonal vs. horizontal much more readily than they discriminated mirror-image diagonals (Fig. 3). That finding supports the suggestion of MACKINTOSH and SUTHERLAND (1963) that goldfish scan shapes along both horizontal and vertical axes. The relative extent of scanning along each axis may depend upon the exact manner in which stimuli are presented. When fish swim toward a shape (in an appetitive task), their side-to-side oscillations impart greater horizontal motion to the retinal image, and may favor the comparison of horizontal extents. However, where each stimulus is given a circular motion (INGLE, 1971c), and the fish does not approach the stimulus, the two extents may each be well discriminated.

Another directional bias has been well documented by SUTHERLAND and BOWMAN (1969): the tendency of goldfish to notice differences in features at

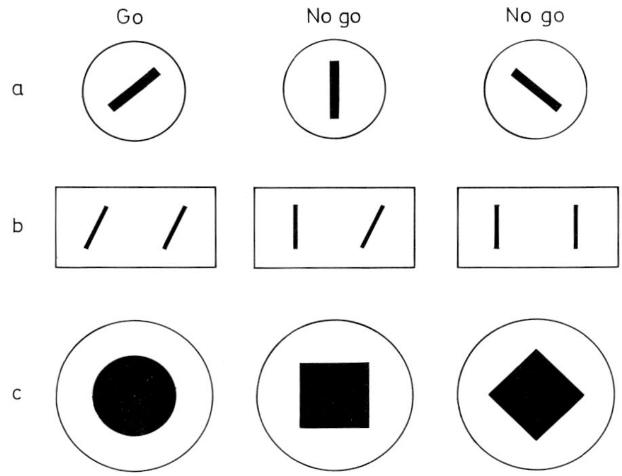

Fig. 3. Three sets of stimuli, as used in tests of "relative difficulty" by INGLE (1971c). Goldfish learn first to make a conditioned avoidance response (see Fig. 8 for view of apparatus) in response to one of the "Go" stimuli shown on left hand of each row. Subsequently fish view the "No go" pair within same row, but with escape door locked in order to discourage attempts to escape starting box. Relative number of learning errors by each "No go" stimulus provides a measure of the discriminability of each in respect to the left-hand stimulus of that set. All fish tested (during three separate experiments) easily discriminated middle stimulus from respective "Go" stimulus, but confused right and left hand shapes. In test *a*, one half of test group had a horizontal rather than vertical bar as the first "No go" stimulus, but this still proved more discriminable from left side oblique than did mirror-image oblique on right side

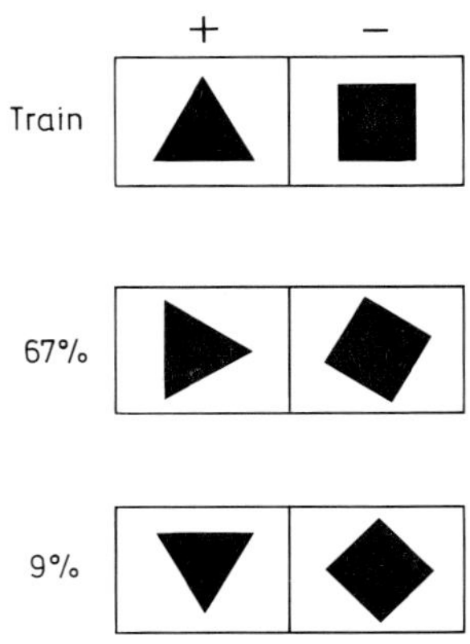

Fig. 4. An example of disruptive effect of shape rotation on a learned discrimination, from MEESTERS (1940). Fish trained to approach triangle (+) for food reward, are less accurate in this habit when both stimuli are rotated by 30° (second pair) and actually reverse choice when triangle is rotated by 60° and opposing square by 45° to become a diamond. These fish apparently approached the stimulus with a point at the top

the tops of shapes. For example a small knob or indentation on the top half of a square or diamond shape will permit the fish to recognize that shape rotated by 45°. Yet fish do not utilize knobs at the bottoms during equivalent generalization tests. MEESTERS (1940) similarly showed that fish trained to choose an upright triangle vs. a square would then select a diamond over an inverted

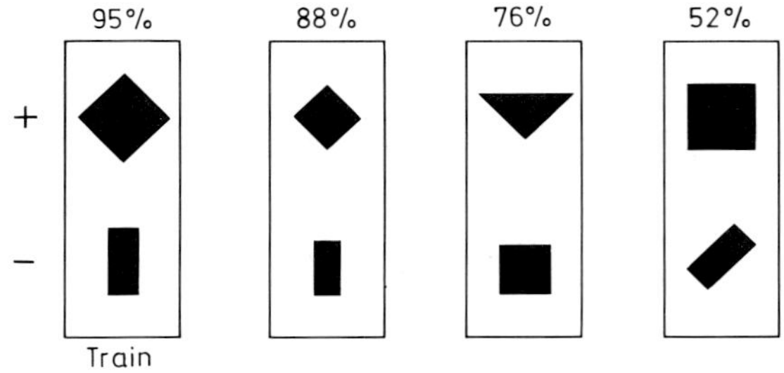

Fig. 5. An experiment from a study by SCHULTE (1957) in which carp were trained to choose between two shapes vertically aligned. Again, a 45° rotation (pair on right side) disrupts discrimination habit. A 50% size reduction does not significantly reduce discrimination scores, but cutting shapes in half does reduce score noticeably. In this test (second from right) fish seem to be guided by point at bottom of triangle. In this figure average test scores for 8 or more subjects are given

triangle—presumably on the basis of the features at the tops (Fig. 4). Fish do not always attend to the *tops*, however. SCHULTE (1957) presented vertically-offset shapes to carp and found that the bottom half of the top figure could guide recognition during generalization tests (Fig. 5). From these limited data it appears that the tendency of fish to notice parts of a figure conflicts with classification in terms of total configuration. Whether or not this result would still be obtained with much smaller shapes is an important but unanswered question.

III. Studies of the Circle-Square Discrimination

Since changes in either size or orientation of stimuli do not change the geometrical distinctions between circles and squares, one might expect that fish would classify a square as a form with corners or with straight edges. Fish can detect both protuberences (BOWMAN and SUTHERLAND, 1970) and orientation of straight edges (INGLE, 1968b). However, these are not likely to be the dominant cues, since SUTHERLAND and BOWMAN (1969) found that fish show negligible transfer from a circle-square problem to a circle-diamond pair. Using a 3 stimulus paradigm, INGLE (1971c) further showed that goldfish view a circle as more similar to a diamond than to a square. Both studies show that the square and the diamond must be distinguished by goldfish on some basis other than the presence of corners or straight edges. The situation is still more complicated since goldfish failed to transfer between large (14°) and small (7°) circle vs. square problems according to INGLE (1971c). Thus, the coding of critical differences between circles and squares may reflect two different sets of rules, each applicable to a different range of stimulus size.

One intuitive hypothesis holds that circles and diamonds resemble one another in that their left and right sides are bowed in opposite directions, unlike the parallel sides of a square. This "parallel vs. nonparallel" rule seems reasonable for an organism which scans a shape along vertical or horizontal (but not diagonal) axes. This hypothesis is in line with the reported difficulty of mirror-image oblique rectangle discrimination for goldfish, as described above.

Furthermore, the present idea was put to a direct test (INGLE, 1971c) by comparing the relative distinctiveness of stimuli composed of parallel or nonparallel lines. In this study, all fish failed to distinguish the two sets of parallel lines (see Fig. 3), while they easily discriminated the parallel from the nonparallel set. These line-pairs were about 15° apart, which was the width of the circles and squares used in the same study. However, we know nothing as yet about the ability of goldfish to make the parallel-nonparallel distinction with still smaller configuration—i.e., it is uncertain whether this rule would help for discrimination of smaller circles and squares. Our current hypothesis is that the "parallelness" rule would apply only to larger shapes, and that lack of generalization to small circles and squares is thus explained. This hypothesis predicts that transposition would occur between small squares and small diamonds; as yet that experiment has not been carried out.

While we have presented data which suggest that goldfish do not "abstract" their recognition of circles and squares, it might seem that the "parallelness" rule of recognition is somewhat abstract. However, there is one simple cue available for this discrimination: the unequal distances between the tops and bottoms of the nonparallel lines. That lower vertebrates could use such information seems plausible in light of the natural discriminations of toads, who discriminate separations between pairs of moving prey (EWERT et al., 1970), or those of frogs, who discriminate separations of stationary edges during barrier avoidance (INGLE and COOK, 1977). We conclude with the cautionary advice that behaviors which at first suggest a "complex" discrimination rule may be carried out using much simpler types of information processing. In fact, it requires quite a long series of experiments to prove the abilities of animals to recognize shape by abstract rules, and few authors have had this exemplary patience.

IV. Other Studies of Rotational Invariance

MEESTERS (1940) has described the failure of fish to discriminate between outline squares and triangles, following rotations of 45°. As the triangle is inverted, and the square becomes a diamond, the point vs. edge cues are thus reversed (Fig. 4). Furthermore, SCHULTE (1957) found no rotational invariance when a rectangle vs. diamond problem was presented with shapes rotated by 45°, as seen in Figure 5. On the other hand, SAXENA (1966) found that a square-cross discrimination was successfully transposed by trout to a diamond-X discrimination (Fig. 6). The basis of classification may not have been configurational at all, but topological—i.e., a distinction between open vs. closed figures. It was interesting to note that this cross-diamond discrimination broke down when the shapes were reduced in size, but not when test stimuli were enlarged. Perhaps the open figure was seen as a "hole", and the salience of this cue was much reduced by minification of the shape. This datum reinforces the idea that coding rules for shape recognition by fishes are often size-dependent.

In another transposition test by SAXENA (1966), fish failed to use orientation cues in grouping dots. As Figure 7 shows, when a vertical row of 3 dots was

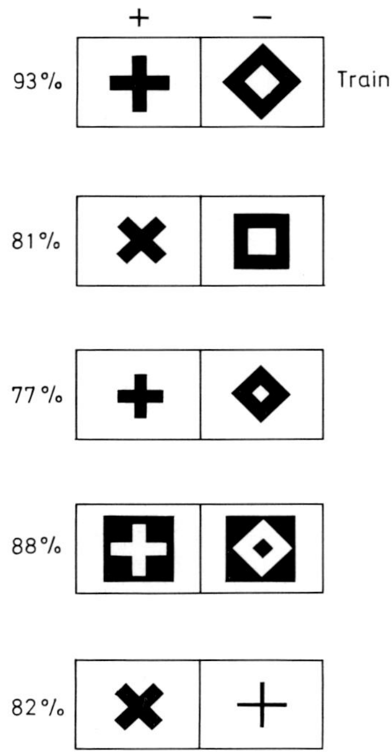

Fig. 6. In a study of SAXENA (1966) trout were trained to discriminate between a cross and an open diamond. This habit did transfer well when shapes were rotated by 45°, reduced to half size, or when brightness contrast was reversed. However, the final test depicted shows that "shape" of cross was not perceptually dominant when thickness of arms was reduced. Unfortunately a test using thin-cross *vs.* thin-lined diamond was not carried out

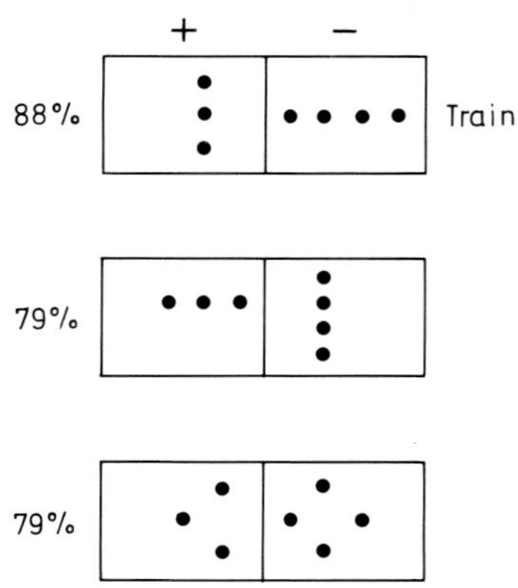

Fig. 7. Another discrimination series from SAXENA (1966) shows that trout attend more easily to number of dots, associated with food, than to the orientation of row of dots. Even when dot configuration is changed (3rd set), fish continue to compare number of dots on the two sides. These data were obtained from repeated tests with two subjects

rewarded, in distinction to a horizontal row of 4 dots, the fish easily transposed the problem on the basis of *number* of dots, rather than according to their mutual *orientation*. Choice of dot-number remained when the total size of both stimuli was reduced, and when dots were grouped into triangle vs. diamond configurations. We conclude that fish show little evidence for abstract configurational perception or even the ability to group small dots into linear configurations. These are, of course, processes which Gestalt psychologists have attributed to human vision, and suspected of being primitive biological adaptations.

We conclude that the various transposition studies provide little evidence for either an "abstract" basis for shape recognition, or operations of typical Gestalt processes attributed to human vision.

E. Interocular Transfer Abilities

I. Limits of Perceptual Equivalence Between Opposite Brain-Halves

Studies of "generalization" of discrimination learning from eye to eye in teleost fishes began with the report of SPERRY and CLARK (1949) who trained subjects to reverse a preference for approaching the lower of two vertically aligned stimuli. Since most of their subjects reverted to their natural bias during interocular transfer tests, these results suggested a limited "perceptual equivalence" between the two brain-halves of fish. However, a study of carp, highly trained to discriminate visual shapes via one eye, revealed good transfer with most problems when stimuli are presented via the opposite "untrained" eye (SCHULTE, 1957). SCHULTE did observe that transfer was typically poor (compared to retention via the training eye) if the visual patterns were distorted in some way. These results may indicate some limit on the capacity of the commissural system to transmit *all* relevant visual information to the second brain-half.

Studies undertaken by INGLE (1968b) showed that a visual memory could remain confined to one brain-half. Goldfish trained to discriminate a striped disc set at either 52° or vertical, showed interocular transfer at a high level even when test stimuli presented contralaterally were "vertical vs. 38°" stripes. On the other hand, fish trained with the "vertical vs. 23°" problem showed no signs of transfer, when the "vertical vs. 38°" test was used via the second eye. Since the difference in transfer outcomes could not be attributed to the "difficulty" of the test problem, the transfer failure presumably reflects an inherent limitation in the "orientation resolution" capacity of the commissural system. However, the negative transfer data should not overshadow the conclusion that the "vertical vs. 52°" discrimination did transfer consistently. The data from these experiments, therefore, show that fish commissural systems encode some cues that fish utilize for shape recognition. For this reason, a physiological study of the commissures would be of great importance in understanding the neural basis of shape analysis in the fish brain.

II. The Problem of Interocular Equivalence of Mirror-Image Shapes

Although SUTHERLAND (1961) had already pointed out the special problem of mirror-image shape recognition in various animals, the relevance of this problem for studies of interocular transfer was ignored until the publications of MELLO (1965, 1966a, 1966b) concerning the pigeon. When pigeons were monocularly trained to peck at an arrowhead pointing to the left (for example) but not at the mirror-image version, transfer tests using the "untrained eye" revealed a predominant response towards the arrowhead pointing to the right. These results have been replicated by others in the pigeon (CORBALLIS and BEALE, 1970) and in the split-chiasm monkey (NOBLE, 1968; HAMILTON and TIEMAN, 1973). In these cases, a sufficient explanation of so-called "mirror-image reversal" effects may derive from an experimental artifact: the pigeon or monkey notices mainly the part of the shape not occluded by the beak or by the hemianopia. However, the problem is more complicated than this when examined in the fish. In seeking to replicate MELLO's results, INGLE (1967) made the surprising observation that goldfish could show two modes of interocular transfer, depending upon the particular discriminanda used. Figure 8 illustrates the essential problem in predicting mirror-image transfer on the basis of MELLO's term "veridical transfer." Are lateral field stimuli judged equivalent if both arrowheads point forward in space? Or are they equivalent after being moved into a common binocular zone? When fish were tested with oblique line pairs, or with arrowheads (as in Fig. 8), transfer was unequivocally made on the basis of the "left-right equivalence." However, when larger shapes were used as discriminanda, fish transferred according to the rule of "front-back equivalence." INGLE suggested that larger shapes were perceptually "fragmented" into two portions, such that the spatial location of each part was emphasized. The absolute spatial locations of each part would be remembered—in this case—rather than their mutual relationships.

The suggestion that the two types of interocular transfer were related to the size of the discriminanda was directly confirmed by studies of CAMPBELL (1971, 1975) using both goldfish and cichlid fishes. For each individual fish, small stimuli were associated with "left-right" transfer and large versions of the same stimuli produced "front-back" equivalence. Further generalization tests with the larger shapes (CAMPBELL, 1975) showed that the fish were guided mainly by the front half of the shape. As with studies of pigeons and monkeys, it appears that "paradoxical" transfer may depend upon greater attention being paid to one portion of the shape. CAMPBELL's data therefore suggest that the paradoxical transfer in fish has nothing to do with encoding of directional

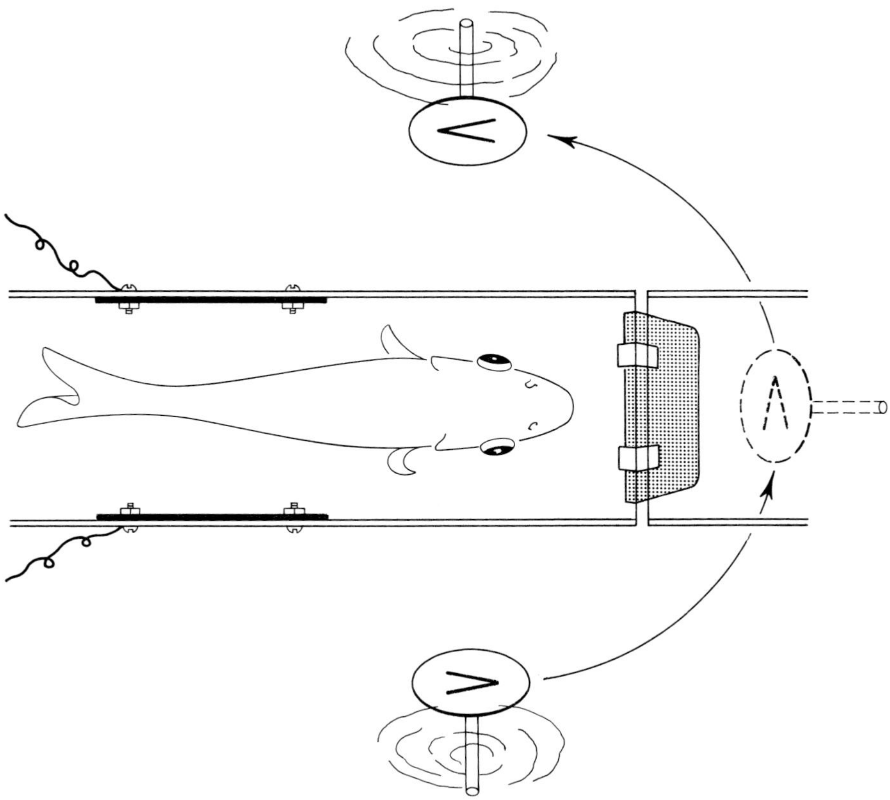

Fig. 8. Top view of goldfish in discrimination-training box, viewing "arrowhead" stimuli in training and testing locations via opposite eyes. When these stimuli subtend 8° or less angular size, fish show a "veridical" mode of transfer from training via right eye to testing via right eye. Arrowhead seen on fish's right side is thus "perceptually equivalent" to the stimulus shown here on fish's left side. The first stimulus would in fact be transformed into the second if it were moved circumferentially around fish in horizontal plane. Either stimulus moved to frontal (binocular) field would point toward fish's left, as shown by dashed image. Thus, demonstrated mode of interocular equivalence (for smaller shapes) would meet needs of binocular vision

relationships, but rather depends upon the breakdown of such relationships where larger shapes are used. This conclusion reinforces the reviewer's earlier suggestion that size can be a critical factor in shape recognition for fishes.

F. Comparison of Learned and Unlearned Discrimination Cues

Table 1 summarizes some of the visual cues shown to be important for discrimination learning of fishes, and these are set in apposition with those cues found to be effective in guiding feeding and barrier avoidance behaviors of fishes or of Anuran amphibians. Two major classes of discrimination cues are distinguished within each behavioral realm: the analysis of *local features* and the measurement of *spatial relationships*. This dichotomy is not equivalent to the earlier distinction between "localizing" and "identifying" modes of vision as postulated by SCHNEIDER (1967), HELD (1968), and TREVARTHEN (1968). Actually, fish and frogs make orienting movements guided by both classes of object and fish (at least) learn to identify stimuli within both classes.

Table 1

Discrimination tests	Natural behavior
1. Small Shapes	
Selection of points, dots, or irregularities	Localization or biting small food objects
Rules for distinguishing small circles from squares	Spontaneous feeding preference for circles
2. Larger Shapes	
Primacy of horizontal or vertical extents	Avoidance bias for vertical grid or stepping bias towards horizontal grid
Difficulty of mirror-image diagonals compared with horizontals vs. vertical	Differences in horizontal and vertical bars as barrier
Open vs. closed shapes	Go through vs. go around
"Parallelness" as a clue	Sensitivity to inter-edge distance for jumping between
Invariance of recognition with direction of brightness contrast	Discrimination of either black or white areas as apertures

The fact that goldfish readily localize small irregularities for identification of shapes (BOWMAN and SUTHERLAND, 1970) fits well with the very general tendency of fish, amphibians, reptiles and birds to localize small objects as food or as living prey. Hungry frogs or toads will readily snap at the corner of a large moving object, and occasionally at protuberances from a slowly moving object. Furthermore, fish are quite sensitive to the number of small objects (spots as in SAXENA's experiments or protuberances as noted by BOWMAN and SUTHERLAND), and this ability to isolate each feature as an independent entity may be related to the ability of fish or toads to bite selectively at one prey within a group. Finally, one may see more than coincidence in the idea that smaller circles and squares are distinguished by rules different from those used for larger shapes (INGLE, 1971c) and the finding that small circles and squares (or triangles) are spontaneously discriminated as food objects. Further experiments would be required to make these comparisons more specific. For example, the findings that toads strongly prefer white prey to black (EWERT, 1968) and that frogs have the opposite preference (INGLE, 1976b) suggest that the invariance of shape recognition with changes in figure-ground contrast might not hold true for small circles and triangles as it does for larger shapes. Secondly, if the close similarity in pecking rate of chicks for squares and diamonds (GOODWIN and HESS, 1966) were duplicated for goldfish, then one might predict that a circle-square discrimination with small shapes would generalize to a circle-diamond problem, unlike results reported above with larger shapes.

The representation of shapes as potential barriers would fit with a good deal of data. The predominant analysis of shapes by goldfish (and others) in terms of their horizontal and vertical extents, fits with (1) the salience of horizontal or of vertical edges for guiding particular reponses, such as jumping onto surfaces or sidestepping barriers, (2) the differential detectability of horizontal and vertical bars as barriers, and (3) the preference differences of frogs for jumping towards horizontal (rather than vertical) apertures. Since the locomotor movement of goldfish and frogs involve horizontal and vertical (but not diagonal) directions, a diagonal edge might be viewed as ambivalent in suggesting alternative detour directions.

The distinctiveness of open and closed shapes can be viewed as an analog of the distinction between entering an aperture vs. detouring around a solid object. Brightness reversal of figure-ground is not important here (for large shapes) because animals select apertures either darker or lighter than background. The discrimination of parallel vs. nonparallel lines (INGLE, 1971c) by fish can be seen in terms of the sensitivity of animals to aperture width (INGLE and COOK, 1977): nonparallel edges direct the animal towards top or bottom, but with either parallel set there is no "tension", since any point of entry is equally negotiable.

Finally, the food vs. barrier distinction has an anatomical correlate in the frog, at least: *tectum* vs. posterior *thalamus*. The total apprehension of shape may therefore involve interaction of thalamic and tectal filters, so that small features are perceived within a framework provided by orientation, width, symmetry etc., just as a prey-object is embedded within a world of stationary objects and surfaces. This hypothesis is also supported by data from goldfish interocular transfer studies (INGLE and CAMPBELL, 1977) in which a direct tecto-thalamic connection (post-optic commissure) was implicated in transfer of shape recognition between brain-halves.

G. Shape Transposition Abilities of Mammals

I. Generalization Studies in the White Rat

Studies of visual discrimination and generalization by the white rat provide a data base for comparisons with data summarized for fishes. Figure 9 gives typical examples of shape-transposition tendencies found for the rat by LASHLEY (1938): the rat utilizes the bottom of the stimulus as a dominant cue, and fails (like the fish) to recognize the same form following inversion. Indeed, FIELDS (1932) found that even 30° stimulus rotations disturbed the rat's discrimination of circle vs. triangle. Although rats could relearn each new triangle vs. circle problem, they did not generalize after a further 30° rotation. At

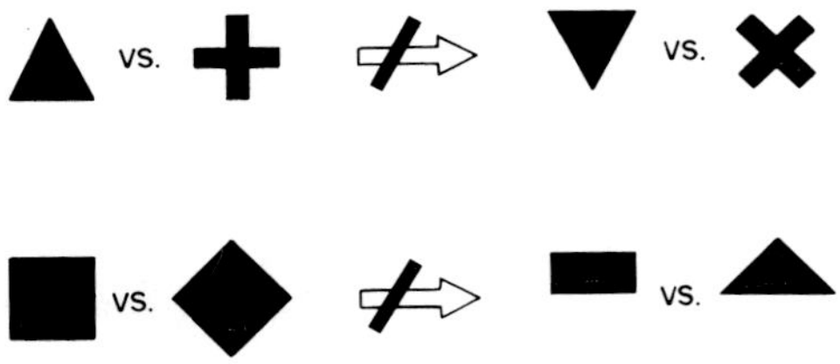

Fig. 9. Two examples of successful generalization of shape recognition by rats (LASHLEY, 1938). In first example (*top*), a discrimination between "H" and "X" was retained despite rotation of these figures by 90° and by 45° respectively. In the second case (*bottom*), the rats were able to "group" the dot-pairs into diagonal vs. vertical classes, as inferred from transfer to the corresponding rectangles

the end of a long training period, the rats studied by FIELDS could recognize any triangle as a rewarded stimulus, as if they had memorized each example independently. As we shall see below, failure of generalization (i.e., abstraction) is quite compatible with learning to treat all triangles differently from all circles when time is allowed to master each version of the problem.

In light of the striking failure that LASHLEY observed in most tests of "rotation invariance" with rats, it is interesting that rats were successful on the test in Figure 10A. When an H vs. X pair is rotated by 90°, the rats are able to select the sidewards H as the positive stimulus. But since fish are able to discriminate 3 vs. 4 dots in a group (SAXENA, 1966), we must ask whether LASHLEY's rats were responding on the basis of such differences: either 3 vs. 2 lines, or 2 vs. 1 intersections. Further generalization tests would be necessary to conclude whether "form" or "number of parts" are the critical cues which allow generalization to transcend rotation. The success of transposition from diagonal vs. vertical dot pairs to diagonal vs. vertical rectangles (Fig. 10B) is another interesting example of successful transposition by LASHLEY's rats. At first thought, it might appear that the rats show a "gestalt" tendency to group dots into rows, while fish do not. However, the experiments are different in one critical respect. SAXENA (1966) presented fish with a conflicting set of cues: number vs. row-orientation (Fig. 7) where the first cue dominated. That does not mean that row-orientation was not noticed: the fish might have generalized quite well to horizontal vs. vertical rectangles. Indeed, using color vs. pattern conflict with fish, INGLE (1965) showed that pattern dominance via the trained eye has not prevented color differences from being simultaneously learned, as tests via the opposite eye demonstrated. LASHLEY also demonstrated that rats could transfer from solid rectangles to rows of squares set in horizontal vs. vertical directions. This ability could actually be aided by the relatively poor acuity of the white rat, since one improves his impression of the "grouping" simply by defocussing. When a more complicated "grouping" is presented—e.g., a cross—the rats do not generalize from solid to dot-figures. Such generalization failure may be seen with other mammals and with birds, as reviewed below. The fact that rats show dot-grouping tendencies with simple linear arrays does not prove their visual form perception to be more complex

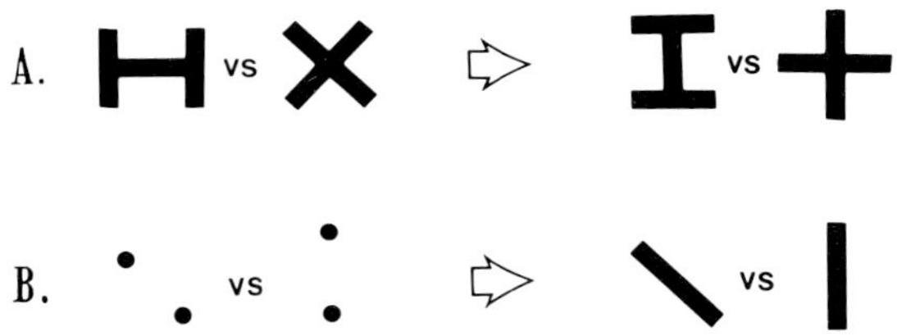

Fig. 10. Two examples of generalization failure by rats (LASHLEY, 1938). In first instance (*top row*) figural rotation disrupts easily learned discrimination between triangle and cross. This result can be explained by the assumption that rats attend chiefly to lower portions of these figures. In agreement with this notion, LASHLEY found that removal of lower halves of each stimulus would disrupt a square vs. diamond discrimination

than that shown by fish. However, it would be important to conduct LASHLEY'S tests with fish as well, before concluding that there are no significant differences.

Further studies of shape transposition in domestic rats by SUTHERLAND and CARR (1964) have confirmed the conclusion of LASHLEY that the bottoms of shapes are of particular importance in recognition tests. For example, an upright triangle resembles a square more than it resembles a diamond. On the other hand, an inverted triangle resembles more nearly the diamond than the square, since the apex of the first two shapes are on the lower side. When a rat is trained on a thin vertical rectangle as the positive stimulus, and an equal size horizontal rectangle as the negative discriminandum, rats will generalize with 70% frequency to a square set below the center mark than to a square set above (Fig. 11 A), presumably due to their greater awareness of the lower part of the vertical shape (SUTHERLAND, 1961 b).

SUTHERLAND and CARR also showed that rats fail to generalize from horizontal to vertical rectangles when these are each opposed to a (negative) square. Rats seem to discriminate the greater height of the vertical rectangle as compared to the square, and thus regard the horizontal rectangle as a still more "squat" kind of square. Whether the rat's visual system measures total amount of vertical contours or the absolute distance between top and bottom is not known, but clearly the animal is not basing its choice on "configuration". As Figure 11 B shows, rats in this experiment would not generalize from the familiar vertical rectangle to a smaller version (during single stimulus tests) but did well transposing to a larger version. This outcome is predicted by the "absolute height" rule, since the small vertical shape is the same height as the square. When SUTHERLAND (1961 b) trained rats on a vertical vs. horizontal discrimination, then rats did transfer to shapes reduced by half in length, in agreement with the fact that the small vertical is still taller than the original negative shape. Making these shapes larger improves generalization, presumably by enhancing the vertical differences. If the rat selects the easiest solution to the training problem, it is not surprising that he would ignore potential "form-specific" rules during transposition tests. Unfortunately, the possibility that a rat could eventually learn to select any rectangle and reject all squares has not been explored.

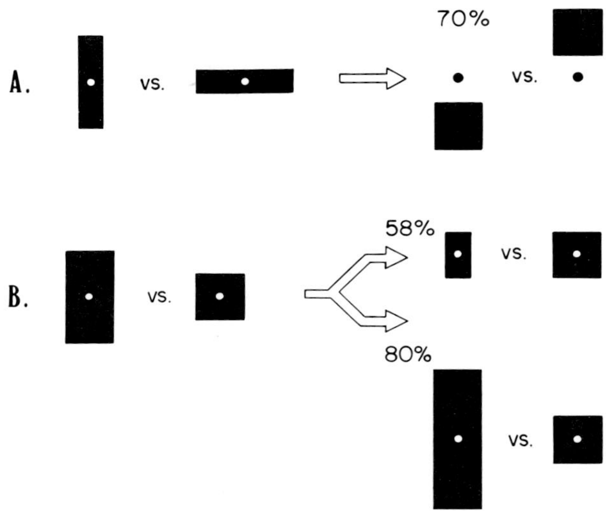

Fig. 11. In the top row (A) SUTHERLAND (1961 b) showed that one difference noticed by rats when discriminating vertical from horizontal rectangles is downward extension of vertical shape. This discrimination habit transferred at a 70% level to square placed below drinking-tube (small circles). In another series of tests with rats, SUTHERLAND and CARR (1964) found that rats notice greater vertical *extent* of first rectangle rather than its *shape*. Thus rats do not generalize to a smaller vertical rectangle whose height is equal to the square, but they easily discriminate the still larger vertical rectangle

During the training phase, LASHLEY noticed that his rats tended to jump more often towards horizontal than towards vertical stripes: over half of the group actually chose horizontal on all 20 initial trials. This result strikingly resembles the behavior of frogs on a jumping stand (INGLE, 1976a). Whether or not the preferences reflect prior experience, these data put rats and frogs on a common basis in that orientation of edges has a strong salience, even prior to explicit discrimination training. DODWELL (1961) has argued that the horizontal preference observed by LASHLEY might have reflected pretraining experience in jumping toward the horizontal base of an open door. In his own study, DODWELL trained some rats to jump toward vertical stripes rather than toward horizontal, and the others to make the reverse choice. On training day 1, there was a slight preference (64%) for horizontal by the rats trained toward that stimulus, but no preference by the other group. For 4 days, each group made steady progress in choosing its appropriate stimulus, but thereafter the vertical-positive group learned much faster. These results are compatible with the idea that vertical stripes have greater salience, such that rats are at first more afraid to jump towards them, but later find it easier to orient toward the more conspicuous cue. In unrewarded frog tests (INGLE, 1976a) a strong aversion was found for vertical stripes when paired with a random speckled surface, and no preference for the horizontal stripes over the random surface. Although the ecological significance of "vertical edge" for frog and rat may not be equivalent, the data indicate that mammals may also bring innate types of visual orientation bias into a training situation.

II. Generalization Studies in the Cat

Cats are generally thought to have a sophisticated visual system, capable of high levels of perceptual generalization. A study by SMITH (1934) is usually quoted as proof of the cat's ability to discriminate "form per se". For example, after training on a circle vs. triangle problem, his subject (unlike rats) did show transfer to inverted figures. But there is reason to believe that the cats were chiefly guided by the negative circle: i.e., low transfer was obtained on a triangle vs. square test. Since these cats could transfer to circle-triangle pairs despite size reduction, brightness reversal, figural distortion and reduction to outline figures, SMITH concluded that the cat can abstract the essential character of these forms. Unfortunately a procedural error renders this conclusion suspect: cats were to some extent reinforced during the generalization tests, receiving food on correct choices and finding the negative door locked. It is difficult to know how quickly the cats could utilize the differential reinforcement to sharpen up their initial generalization tendencies to familiar shapes. No data were presented to show that initial choices were consistently for the "similar" stimulus, as a strong generalization hypothesis would predict. Although cats may not develop rapid "learning sets" for quite disparate sets of objects, the situation may be different where some familiar cues overlap between successive 20-trial tests. That is, the cat may not be able to uniquely identify a set of cues that specifies all triangles, but some individual cues which will be familiar (points, brightness, asymmetry) can quickly be switched-in after the first couple of reinforcements. Since unreinforced generalization tests were not given, (as in fish, rat and bird studies), no estimates of the cat's alleged superiority in abstraction can be made from SMITH's data. More promising in indicating potentialities of carnivores is the limited data of FIELDS (1936), showing that racoons can generalize from a triangle-circle task to inverted triangle vs. square.

Other studies indicate, contrary to SMITH's impressions, that cats may fare very badly on generalization tests. For example, WINANS (1971) found that local brightness cues were so strong as to disrupt shape generalization in her cats. These animals did not manage figure-ground reversal and showed low transfer when the position of the figure was shifted on the response panel. While these data apply to the initial confrontation of the cat with a new stimulus configuration DOTY (1971) has clearly shown that cats can overcome these "errors" and learn to choose a triangle over a circle despite regular variation in size, position, orientation, or brightness. However this ability may derive from the ability of cats to remember a number of individual stimulus examples, rather than reflect an abstraction of "triangularity". Indeed, DOTY reports that two of three normal cats transferred poorly from initial practice to series B and series C, although they mastered each series. DOTY's training method is excellent for evaluation of neocortical lesions, since it prevents cats from falling back on simple rules for discriminating shapes. But it does not directly answer the question as to whether a highly differentiated visual cortex necessarily guarantees a mammal with ability to abstract "form" from a series of particular examples.

III. Generalization Abilities of Primates

Among psychologists there has been little doubt that monkeys or the apes can recognize "form per se". Certainly, the studies of GELLERMAN (1933) with two chimps and two young children demonstrated a persistent selection of triangles over other shapes despite variations of size, orientation, and brightness reversal. For example, the chimps immediately generalize from an isosceles triangle vs. circle to a right triangle vs. trapezoid. It was interesting to note that both chimp and child spontaneously turned their heads to inspect the rotated triangles on first encounter. This does indicate that some confirmation was needed in respect to spatial relationships. Unfortunately, no data have been collected with chimps with rotations of other types of shapes, or under conditions where time for head rotation is eliminated.

The extensive experiments of ANDREW and HARLOW (1948) are also quoted as evidence that rhesus monkeys share such abilities with their ape cousins. However, these authors emphasize that monkeys transpose the circle-triangle problem rather poorly on initial tests. The great improvements shown on tests within a second series was taken as evidence of "learning to classify on the basis of form". Although the authors may be correct, two problems prevent a definite conclusion from these data. First, there was much overlap in individual shapes from the set for "concept formation training" and the final generalization series, even though specific pairings were not repeated. The data were not presented in such a way as to prove that shapes in the final series were correctly classified despite their not having been seen before. While it seems probable that monkeys did develop some "sophistication" by the end of the experiment, it remains unclear just how much memorization of a few specific stimuli contributed to test performance. A second problem of interpretation was highlighted by further tests in which monkeys overgeneralized to nontriangular shapes on the basis of "pointedness". Such a test is required to prove that the "concept" which an organism may develop from experience with variations of a particular form is actually restricted to that class of forms. Can a monkey learn to choose triangles without points and also ignore non-triangles with points? If monkeys simply learn to notice points, this may reflect "perceptual learning" but does not necessarily represent a concept of "form".

IV. Concept Formation by Pigeons

One interesting approach to shape classification is exemplified by two studies of "concept formation" in pigeons. It should be first noted that pigeons fail transposition tests (e.g., triangle vs. square) where stimuli are rotated or are reduced to sets of corner-dots (TOWE, 1954), and thus might be thought unable to discriminate "form per se." However, HERRNSTEIN and LOVELAND (1964) had no difficulty training pigeons to consistently select a "human figure" as a positive stimulus appearing within a long series of projected slides. They concluded that pigeons must here form a "complex concept" because of the variations in size and completeness of the human form. The basic finding has been since replicated by SIEGEL and HONIG (1970), who attempted to match critical tests such that all elements of natural scenes were identical except presence of a human figure. Nonetheless, it is not clear from the general description of stimuli used whether or not the birds could have learned a small family of typical human (or animal) shapes based on unique cues (faces, heads, pairs of legs). It is also not clear whether pigeons would have overgeneralized to dogs, squirrels, or bears on the basis of head, eyes, arms, etc. It may be, however, that visual systems more easily classify and generalize ecologically significant stimuli (animals recognizing other animals) than the geometrical artifacts favored by visual psychologists.

In extending the "naturalistic" approach to visual learning, a recent summary by HERRNSTEIN et al. (1976) has added to the "human figure" class of readily identifiable slide projections two more categories: "bodies of water" and, appropriately for birds, "trees". Following training to discriminate many positive examples of these classes from numerous negative instances, the pigeons were able to immediately classify new slides as containing or not containing relevant configurations. The authors note that none of the plausible cues for "tree" are consistently present: greenness, woodiness, leafiness, branches, trunks or verticality; but they do not provide evidence as to whether pigeons may identify an appropriate scene as containing any two or three of these cues. This experiment seems to demonstrate that some very salient cues were available to the birds, but not that they had developed an "abstract" description of "trees".

Along the same lines, CERELLA (1975) demonstrated that pigeons familiar with one oak leaf example (vs. 40 other leaf patterns) can immediately generalize with good accuracy to other oak leaves where size, orientation and number of lobes varies. These studies do not offer insight into the actual basis of this generalization: it seems plausible that pigeons could discriminate oak leaves on the basis of lobes of a certain size and degree of curvature. Pigeons can doubtless detect similarities among various sets of configurations, as CERELLA also shows with a discrimination of polar projections of "cubes vs. irregular quadrilaterals". Here pigeons might identify the occurrence of a central "Y" in the cube projection which has left and right edges *parallel* to the stem of the Y. As we have argued above, using the goldfish as a subject, the detection of parallel lines is not necessarily an abstract visual process; it may in fact be rather primitive. The new attempts to identify natural classes of objects call attention to the need to identify new sets of cues, but they do not answer the question as to whether some combinations of cues are "innately" more salient for a given species.

H. Concluding Remarks

From this selected review we may draw three general conclusions. First, the recognition rules that may be inferred from tests of lower vertebrates roughly correspond to discriminations made during various types of natural behavior.

Second, we find little evidence that fish, birds and rodents classify simple planometric figures as if they were perceiving "form per se". Third, some suggestive evidence exists that carnivores, monkeys and possibly birds do exhibit "abstract" classifications of visual forms after training with several variations of the form-class. However, methodologic problems with the latter studies do not yet permit a firm conclusion that any species other than man and the great apes exhibit recognition of "form per se".

Although these generalizations emerge from a large volume of data, we should not feel secure with these tentative conclusions. For example, fish, birds, or rats might overcome their rather stereotyped discrimination habits if given prolonged training with variants of critical shapes, as was done with cats and monkeys. It is not surprising that animals would utilize the simplest basis for discrimination when they are rewarded for finding the first workable rule. Even the cat appears to use very simple rules during early shape-discrimination training when its habits are easily upset by changes in position of stimuli or reversal of figure-ground relations (Winans, 1971). More comparable test procedures for highly visual representatives of teleost, avian, rodent, carnivore, and primate groups are thus required to make the important decision as to whether any particular type of visual system can be associated with special abilities to abstract visual forms.

A second class of questions concerns the adequacy of the particular tests traditionally employed (granting that they could be more "fairly" administered). We should guard against premature conclusions from transposition failures which may be limited to a narrow class of stimuli, such as circle-triangle or square-diamond problems. Some species may be adapted to use their abilities for abstracting visual forms with specific configurations but not with others. For example, recognition of elongated "wormlike" forms, regardless of orientation or distance, might be important for certain birds. For animals which grasp objects in their mouth or by hand, a narrow rectangle has a "prehensile" significance, regardless of its orientation, which a square-like object does not have. Gull chicks do in fact learn to twist their heads to efficiently grasp the parent's bill while food-begging (Hailman, 1967), and lizards may be observed turning their heads to fit the mouth to the angle of a proffered mealworm (Ingle, unpublished data.) Primates are likely to discriminate the size and shape of objects preparatory to shaping their hand for grasping them. Since the forearm rotates easily, the grasp may have some rotational invariant properties depending upon shape of the target. Generalization tests with squares and rectangles might thus have more ecological significance for certain species than circles and triangles. Similarly, the problem of size-invariance is also unsolved—largely because most tests involve movement of the animal toward the stimuli, and inevitable experience with a wide range of retinal-image sizes. Detailed information on actual distances over which animals identify visual shapes during natural conditions would be useful. It seems likely that "identification zones" are much deeper for some mammals and birds than for any fish or amphibians.

While we must make more strenuous efforts to look for instances in which shapes can be recognized despite rotational and size transformations, we should at the same time be prepared to sacrifice our assumptions that object recognition among mammals is typically based upon such "abstract descriptions" of form.

Resolution of these questions has neurophysiological implications: i.e., the type of lateral intracortical connections required to assemble information for identification of forms, rather than simply noting their parts. One theoretical approach (POLLEN and RONNER, 1975) finds the Fourier-transform model of shape description an attractive possibility since the problems of size- and orientation-invariance would be automatically solved if the basic assumptions for such a system could be substantiated through physiological studies. But, at present, we have good reason to question the belief that the cat's behavior demands a mechanism for computing invariant descriptions of particular shapes. One alternative hypothesis of visual cortical function involves the switching of attention to particular features of a stimulus when simpler rules do not predict behavioral outcomes. Another hypothesis is that visual cortex represents an evolutionary improvement over subcortical functions, by virtue of holding more detailed visual traces for longer periods. Animals with visual cortices would thus have the opportunity to scan short-term visual memory and confirm hypotheses as to what was seen. No "abstract description" of shapes would automatically emerge from this particular cortical mechanism. Thus, the differences in visual intelligence between species might not reflect the "abstract" encoding capacities of any particular visual center, but the capacities of other brain structures to use a standard visual code within a richer context.

The very fact that we have attained new detailed knowledge of microstructure of visual components and have described the rich interconnections between centers and subcenters, highlights our embarrassment in drawing conclusions about the behavioral functions of the "higher" visual centers. Indeed, the cherished belief that the geniculostriate system is the sole gateway to "perception" has fallen victim to new comparative studies of non-primates: the pathway to the extra-striate cortex from the tecto-pulvinar system mediates some significant mode of pattern recognition. On the other hand, shape discrimination eventually recovers following ablation of most extra-striate visual cortex. More definitive knowledge of the form-recognition capacities of various species is obviously required to design appropriate tests which may distinguish functions of each visual cortical entity. It remains puzzling to comparative neuropsychologists that students of cat or of monkey vision usually limit their evaluations of cortical damage to discrimination tests easily solved by teleost fishes, who have not yet discovered the advantages of the neocortex. In the light of these major obstacles to a physiological view of perception, the needs for a truly comparative analysis of behavior, and for a detailed appreciation of the natural uses of vision by particular species, are not contradictory, but complementary, sources of insight for fundamental solutions.

References

Andrew, G., Harlow, H.F.: Performance of Macaque monkeys on a test of concept of generalized triangularity. Comp. Psychol. Monogr. **19**, 1–20 (1948).

•Barlow, H.B.: Summation and inhibition in the frog's retina. J. Physiol. (Lond.) **119**, 69–88 (1953).

Bowman, R., Sutherland, N.S.: The discrimination of "W" and "V" shapes by goldfish. Quart. J. exp. Psychol. **21**, 69–76 (1969).

Bowman, R., Sutherland, N.S.: Shape discrimination by goldfish: coding of irregularities. J. comp. physiol. Psychol. **72**, 90–97 (1970).

Brown, W.T., Ingle, D.: Receptive field changes produced in frog thalamic units by lesions of the optic tectum. Brain Res. **69**, 405–409 (1973).

Butenandt, E., Grüsser, O.-J.: The effect of stimulus areas on the response of movement detecting neurons in the frog's retina. Pflügers Archiv ges. Physiol. **298**, 283–293 (1968).

Campbell, A.: Interocular transfer of mirror-images by goldfish. Brain Res. **33**, 482–485 (1971).

Campbell, A.: Paradoxical interocular transfer of mirror images: Selective attention. In: New approaches to the study of vision in fishes. (ed. M.A. Ali). New York, Plenum Press 1975.

Cerella, J.: "Studies of Pattern Perception in Pigeons", Unpublished Ph. D. Thesis, Harvard University Department of Psychology (1975).

Corballis, M.C., Beale, I.L.: Bilateral symmetry and behaviour. Psychol. Rev. **17**, 451–464 (1970).

Cronly-Dillon, J.R.: Units sensitive to direction of motion in goldfish optic tectum. Nature (Lond.) **203**, 214–215 (1964).

Cronly-Dillon, J.R., Sutherland, N.S., Wolfe, J.: Intraretinal transfer of a learned visual shape discrimination in goldfish after section and regeneration of the optic nerve branchia. Exp. Neurol. **15**, 455–462 (1966).

Dodwell, P.C.: Visual orientation preferences in the rat. Quart. J. exp. Psychol. **13**, 40–47 (1961).

Doty, R.W.: Survival of pattern vision after removal of striate cortex in the adult cat. J. comp. Neurol. **143**, 341–370 (1971).

Ehrenhardt, H.: Formensehen und Sehschärfebestimmungen bei Eidechsen. Z. vergl. Physiol. **24**, 258–304 (1937).

Ebbesson, S.O.E., Jane, J.A., Schroeder, D.M.: On the organization of central visual pathways in vertebrates. Brain Behav. Evol. **3**, 178–194 (1970).

Ewert, J.-P.: Der Einfluß von Zwischenhirndefekten auf die Visuomotorik im Beute- und -Fluchtverhalten der Erdkröte. Z. vergl. Physiol. **61**, 41–70 (1968).

Ewert, J.-P.: Neural mechanisms of prey-catching and avoidance behavior in the toad (*Bufo bufo* L.). Brain Behav. Evol. **3**, 36–56 (1970).

Ewert, J.-P.: The neural basis of visually guided behavior. Sci. Amer. **230**, 33–42 (1974).

Ewert, J.-P.: "The Visual System of the Toad: Behavioral and Physiological Studies on a Pattern Recognition System". In: *The Amphibian Visual System: A Multidisciplinary Approach* (K. Fite, Ed.). New York: Academic Press 1976.

Ewert, J.-P., Börchers, H.-W.: Reaktionscharakteristik von Neuronen aus dem Tectum opticum und Subtectum der Erdkröte. Z. vergl. Physiol. **71**, 165–189 (1971).

Ewert, J.-P., Gebauer, L.: Größenkonstanzphänomene im Beutefangverhalten der Erdkröte (*Bufo bufo* L.). J. comp. Physiol. **85**, 303–315 (1973).

Ewert, J.-P., Hock, F.: Movement-sensitive neurones in the toad's retina. Exp. Brain Res. **16**, 41–59 (1972).

Ewert, J.-P., Ingle, D.: Excitatory effects following habituation of prey catching activity in frogs and toads. J. comp. physiol. Psychol. **77**, 369–374 (1971).

Ewert, J.-P., Rehn, B.: Quantitative Analyse der Reiz-Reaktionsbeziehungen bei visuellem Auslösen des Fluchtverhaltens der Wechselkröte. Behaviour **35**, 212–234 (1969).

Ewert, J.-P., Speckhardt, I., Amelang, W.: Visuelle Inhibition und Exzitation im Beutefangverhalten der Erdkröte. Z. vergl. Physiol. **68**, 84–110 (1970).

Fantz, R.L.: Form preferences in newly hatched chicks. J. comp. physiol. Psychol. **50**, 422–430 (1957).

Fields, P.E.: Studies in concept formation. 1. The development of the concept of triangularity by the white rat. Comp. Psychol. Monogr. **9**, 1–70 (1932).

Fields, P.E.: Studies in concept formation: IV. A comparison of white rats and raccoons with respect to their visual discrimination of certain geometrical figures. J. comp. Psychol. **21**, 341–355 (1936).

Fite, K.: The visual fields of the frog and toad: A comparative study. Behav. Biol. **9**, 1–12 (1973).

Gellerman, L.W.: Form discrimination in chimpanzees and two-year-old children: 1. Form (triangularity) per se. J. genet. Psychol. **42**, 2–27 (1933).

Goodwin, E.B., Hess, E.H.: Innate visual form preferences in the pecking behavior of young chicks. Behaviour **34**, 223–237 (1966).

Graeber, R.C., Ebbesson, S.O.E., Jane, J.J.: Visual discrimination in sharks without optic tectum. Science **110**, 413–415 (1972).

Grüsser, O.-J., Grüsser-Cornehls, U.: Neurophysiologische Grundlagen visueller angeborener Auslösemechanismen. Z. vergl. Physiol. **59**, 1–24 (1968).

Hager, H.J.: Untersuchungen über das optische Differenzierungsvermögen der Fische. Z. vergl. Physiol. **26**, 282–302 (1938).

Hailman, J.P.: The ontogeny of an instinct. The pecking response in chicks of the laughing gull (*Larus atricilla* L.) and related species. Behaviour, Suppl. 15 (1967).

Hamilton, C.R., Tieman, S.B.: Interocular transfer of mirror image discriminations by chiasm-sectioned monkeys. Brain Res. **64**, 241–255 (1973).

Held, R.: Dissociation of visual functions by deprivation and rearrangement. Psychol. Forsch. **31**, 338–348 (1968).

Herrnstein, R.J., Loveland, B.H.: Complex visual concept in the pigeon. Science **146**, 549–551 (1964).

Herter, K.: Die Fischdressuren und ihre sinnesphysiologischen Grundlagen. Berlin: Akademie Verlag (1953).

Hosch, L.: Untersuchungen über Großhirnfunktionen der Elritze (*Phoxinus laevis*) und des Gründlings (*Gobio fluviatilis*). Zool. Jb., Abt. allg. Zool. Physiol. Tiere **57**, 57–98 (1936).

Ingle, D.: Limits of visual transfer in goldfish. Unpublished Ph.D. thesis, University of Chicago, 1963.

Ingle, D.: Interocular transfer in goldfish: color easier than pattern. Science **149**, 1000–1002 (1965).

Ingle, D.: Effect of direction on movement detection by goldfish. Proc. Amer. psychol. Ass. **2**, 151–152 (1966).

Ingle, D.: Two visual mechanisms underlying the behavior of fish. Psychol. Forsch. **31**, 44–51 (1967).

Ingle, D.: Visual releasers of prey catching behavior in frogs and toads. Brain Behav. Evol. **1**, 500–518 (1968a).

Ingle, D.: Interocular integration of visual learning by goldfish. Brain Behav. Evol. **1**, 58–85 (1968b).

Ingle, D.: Visuomotor functions of the frog optic tectum. Brain Behav. Evol. **3**, 57–71 (1970).

Ingle, D.: Discrimination of edge-orientation by frogs. Vision Res. **11**, 1365–1367 (1971a).

Ingle, D.: Prey catching behavior of Anurans toward moving and stationary objects. Vision Res. Suppl. **3**, 447–456 (1971b).

Ingle, D.: The experimental analysis of visual behavior. In: Fish Physiology, W.S. Hoar and D.J. Randall (eds.) **5**, 59–71 (1971c). New York: Academic Press.

Ingle, D.: Size-preference for prey catching in frogs: relationship to motivational state. Behav. Biol. **9**, 485–491 (1973a).

Ingle, D.: Selective choice between double prey objects by frogs. Brain Behav. Evol. **7**, 127–144 (1973b).

Ingle, D.: Evolutionary perspectives on the function of the optic tectum. Brain Behav. Evol. **8**, 211–237 (1973c).

Ingle, D.: Spontaneous shape discrimination by frogs during unconditioned escape behavior. Physiol. Psychol. **1**, 71–73 (1973d).

Ingle, D.: Disinhibition of tectal neurons by pretectal lesions in the frog. Science **180**, 422–424 (1973e).

Ingle, D.: Two visual systems in the frog. Science **181**, 1053–1055 (1973f).

Ingle, D.: Spatial vision in anurans. In: *The Amphibian Visual System: A Multidisciplinary Approach* (K. Fite, Ed.), Academic Press, New York, 1976a.

Ingle, D.: Central visual mechanisms in Anurans. In: R. Llinas and W. Precht (eds.). Neurobiology of the Frog. Berlin: Springer Verlag 1976b.

Ingle, D.: Detection of stationary objects by frogs following tectum ablation. J. comp. physiol. Psychol. **91**, 1359–1364 (1977)

Ingle, D., Campbell, A.: Interocular transfer of visual discriminations by goldfish with selective commissure lesions. J. comp. physiol. Psychol. **91**, 327–335 (1977).

Ingle, D., Cook, J.: The effect of viewing distance upon size preference of frogs for prey. Vision Res. **17**, 1009–1019 (1977).

Ingle, D., McKinley: Some effects of stimulus configuration on prey cat ching behavior by the toad, *Bufo marinus*. Animal Behavior (1978), in press.

Ingle, D., Sprague, J.M.: "Sensorimotor Function of the Midbrain Tectum". In: Neurosci. Res Prog. Bull. **13**, No. 2, May, 1975.

Jacobson, M.: Physiology of fish vision. In: The Central Nervous System and Fish Behavior (D. Ingle, ed.), pp. 17–24. Univ. of Chicago Press, Chicago, Illinois 1968.

Jacobson, M., Gaze, R.M.: Types of visual response from single units in the optic tectum and optic nerve of the goldfish. Quart. J. exp. Physiol. **49**, 199–209 (1964).

Janzen, W.: Untersuchungen über Großhirnfunktionen des Goldfisches (*Carassius auratus*). Zool Jb. Abt. allg. Zool. Physiol. Tiere **52**, 591–628 (1933).

Lashley, K.S.: The Mechanism of vision: XV. Preliminary studies of the rat's capacity for detail vision. J. gen. Psychol. **18**, 123–193 (1938).

Lee, D.N.: Visual information during locomotion. In: Studies in perception: essays in honor of J.J. Gibson. Ithaca, N.Y.: Cornell University Press (1975).

Lettvin, J.Y., Maturana, H.R., McCulloch, W.S., Pitts, W.H.: What the frog's eye tells the frog's brain. Proc. IRE **47**, 1940–1951 (1959).

Lettvin, J.Y., Maturana, H.R., McCulloch, W.S., Pitts, W.H.: Two remarks on the visual systems of the frog. In: Sensory Communication, 757–776, W. Rosenblith (ed.), M.I.T. Press, Cambridge Mass. (1971).

Mackintosh, N.J., Sutherland, N.S.: Visual discrimination by goldfish: The orientation of rectangles. Animal Behav. **11**, 135–141 (1963).

McCleary, R.A.: Type of response as a factor in interocular transfer in the fish. J. comp. physiol. Psychol. **53**, 311–321 (1960).

Meesters, A.: Über die Organisation des Gesichtsfeldes der Fische. Z. Tierpsychol. **4**, 84–149 (1940).

Mello, N.K.: Interhemispheric reversal of mirror-image oblique lines following monocular training in pigeons. Science **148**, 252–254 (1965).

Mello, N.K.: Concerning the inter-hemispheric transfer of mirror-image patterns in pigeon. Physiol. Behav. **1**, 293–300 (1966a).

Mello, N.K.: Interocular generalization: a study of mirror-image reversal following monocular discrimination training in pigeon. J. exp. anal. Behav. **9**, 11–16 (1966b).

Noble, J.: Paradoxical interocular transfer of mirror-image discriminations in the optic chiasm sectioned monkey. Brain Res. **10**, 127–151 (1968).

Nolte, W.: Experimentelle Untersuchungen zum Problem der Lokalisation des Assoziationsvermögens im Fischgehirn. Z. vergl. Physiol. **18**, 255–279 (1933).

Parriss, J.R.: Retention of shape discrimination after regeneration of the optic nerves in the toad Quart. J. exp. Psychol. **15**, 22–26 (1963).

Pasche, J.: Formensehen bei Fröschen. Z. vergl. Physiol. **17**, 423–463 (1932).

Pollen, D.A., Ronner, S.F.: Periodic excitability changes across the receptive fields of complex cells in the striate and parastriate cortex of the cat. J. Physiol. (Lond.) **245**, 667–697 (1975).

Savage, G.E.: Some preliminary observations on the role of the telencephalon in food-reinforced behavior in the goldfish, *Carassius auratus*. Animal Behav. **17**, 760–772 (1969).

Saxena, A.: Lernkapazität, Gedächtnis und Transpositionsvermögen bei Forellen. Zool. Jb., Abt allg. Zool. Physiol. Tiere **69**, 63–94 (1966).

Schipperheyn, J.J.: Respiratory eye movements and perception of stationary objects in the frog Acta physiol. pharmacol. neerl. **12**, 157–159 (1963).

Schneider, D.: Das Gesichtsfeld und der Fixiervorgang bei einheimischen Anuren. Z. vergl. Physiol **36**, 147–164 (1954).

Schneider, G.E.: Contrasting visuomotor functions of tectum and cortex in the Golden Hamster Psychol. Forsch. **31**, 52–62 (1967).

Schulte, A.: Transfer- und Transpositionsversuche mit monokulardressierten Fischen. Z. vergleich Physiol. **38**, 432–476 (1957).

Siegel, R.K., Honig, W.K.: Pigeon concept formation: Successive and simultaneous acquisition J. exp. anal. Behav. **13**, 385–390 (1970).

Smith, K.U.: Visual discrimination in the cat: II. A further study of the capacity of the cat for visual figure discrimination. J. genet. Psychol. **45**, 336–357 (1934).

Sperry, R.W., Clark, E.: Interocular transfer of visual discrimination habits in a teleost fish. Physiol. Zool. **22**, 372–378 (1949).

Sutherland, N.S.: The methods and findings of experiments on the visual discrimination of shape by animals. Quart. J. exp. Psychol. Monogr. No. 1, 1–68 (1961).

Sutherland, N.S.: Outlines of a theory of pattern recognition in animals and man. Proc. roy. Soc. B. **171**, 297–317 (1968).

Sutherland, N.S., Bowman, R.: Discrimination of circles and squares with and without knobs by goldfish. Quart. J. exp. Psychol. **21**, 330–338 (1969).

Sutherland, N.S., Carr, A.E.: Shape discrimination by rats: Squares and rectangles. Brit. J. Psychol. **55**, 39–48 (1964).

Towe, A.L.: A study of figural equivalence in the pigeon. J. comp. physiol. Psychol. **47**, 283–287 (1954).

Trevarthen, C.B.: Two mechanisms of vision in primates. Psychol. Forsch. **31**, 299–337 (1968).

Westerman, R.A.: Specificity in regeneration of optic and olfactory pathways in teleost fish. In: Studies in Physiology (D.R. Curtis and A.K. McIntyre, eds.). New York: Springer 1965.

Wiens, J.A.: Anuran habitat selection: early experience and substrate selection in *Rana cascadae* tadpoles. Animal Behav. **20**, 218–220 (1972).

Winans, S.S.: Visual cues used by normal and visual-decorticate cats to discriminate figures of equal luminous flux. J. comp. physiol. Psychol. **74**, 167–178 (1971).

Zenkin, G.M., Pigarev, I.N.: Detector properties of the ganglion cells of the pike retina. Biofizika **14**, 722–730 (1969).

Zusne, L.: Visual perception of form. New York: Academic Press 1970.

Chapter 9

Ethological Aspects of Auditory Pattern Recognition

MASAKAZU KONISHI, Pasadena, California (USA)

With 8 Figures

Contents

A. Introduction

Ethological studies of animal signals and their functions have opened a new avenue for the study of sensory and perceptual mechanisms. Animals in their natural environments do not react to every potential stimulus, but are highly selective as to which stimuli they accept. The sense organs and nervous system of each species are the products of evolution; their structure and function are adapted to the life style of the species and designed to ensure its survival. In the environment of each species there are things and events to which the species attributes special meanings such as predator, prey, mate, and offspring. The same things and events may not be perceived, or are perceived differently, by other species; therefore, each species can be said to have a unique perceptual world, as UEXKÜLL (1909) originally conceived it.

The ethological approach has certain advantages over the traditional methods of training animals for recognizing biologically neutral or irrelevant stimuli. A study of perception that ignores the nature of the animal's own perceptual world can yield misleading conclusions. For example, it would be impossible to train a female cricket to distinguish the song of its own species from that of another by using food reinforcement, while it can easily discriminate between them without any reward during a certain phase of its reproductive period. In the female cricket's perceptual world the male's calling song does not mean food but a mate. The use of biologically significant stimuli can reveal perceptual phenomena which could otherwise never be uncovered.

Ethology contains a strong element of evolutionary and comparative zoology. Understanding of certain phenomena in one species may be facilitated by comparison with other species. The use of animals other than those commonly used in physiological and psychological laboratories can be revealing. For example, in animals like bats, electric fish, and owls, which have extraordinary modes of life, sense organs of one kind or another and their central projections are highly developed, offering unique opportunities to study some basic principles of perceptual processes to which "ordinary" animals do not provide easy access. The main aim of this chapter is to sho how an animal's natural behavior can be exploited to study auditory pattern recognition in various species.

B. Recognition of Biologically Significant Sounds

Many animals use sound to recognize their mates, different individuals, offspring, prey, and predators. Various acoustic signals have evolved for communication within a species. Signals used for mate recognition tend to be species-specific; each species has a unique signal. The uniqueness is coded in the acoustic properties of the signal. Many attempts have been made to discover the rules of coding. Potential rules are predictable on purely physical bases. Frequency, amplitude, and time are the variables that can be used singly or in various combinations to produce different sounds. The methods used in elucidating the rules of coding, manipulate those variables either by modifying animal sounds or by synthesizing signals with known physical structure. The criteria for recognition are territorial behavior (including vocal reply), sexual and filial approach, and evasive behavior in response to test signals. A few representative examples suffice to illustrate the above points.

WALKER (1957) used natural and electronically generated songs to discover the cues used for species recognition in tree crickets. A female tree cricket approaches a loudspeaker which emits the calling song of her own species. The song is a series of narrow-band pulses separated by regular silent intervals. The cricket distinguishes the species' own signal from the songs of other species primarily by the number of pulses per unit time, which is called the pulse rate. Changing the carrier frequency of the pulses alone does not affect the cricket's response so long as the frequency is within its audible range. Some species of tree crickets emit pulses in groups (chirps), producing two types of pattern in time: interpulse and interchirp intervals. In these species the pulse rate is still the primary species cue, but the chirp rate also seems to play some role in species recognition.

All insects, mostly crickets and grasshoppers, that have been studied so far use the pattern of amplitude modulation both for species recognition and for coding other messages for intraspecific communication. The frequency aspects of sound do not seem to be used for coding acoustic signals among these insects. This is perhaps due to the insect's inability to discriminate frequencies, although neurophysiological studies show the presence of auditory neurons responding to different frequency ranges in the locust (MICHELSEN, 1971).

Some insects use the same principle of acoustic communication for the detection of predators. Noctuid moths show evasive behavior upon hearing the echolocating cries of their enemy, bats. Although the moth's ear responds to a continuous tone within the bat's vocal frequency range, only a small proportion of wild moths respond to such a signal, whereas the same tone delivered as brief pulses similar to the bat cries elicits vigorous escape responses in a much larger proportion of moths (ROEDER, 1966a). Thus, the pattern of amplitude modulation in the bat's cries is a crucial cue for detecting the predator by the moths. In this case also the frequency aspect of the bat cries is significant only insofar as the signal must be within the moth's audible frequency range, which coincides with the frequency range of the bat's echolocating cries.

Frequency discrimination has been demonstrated behaviorally in several major vertebrate groups including fish, reptiles (turtles), birds and mammals (POPPER and FAY, 1973, PATTERSON, 1966, TRAINER, 1946, MASTERTON et al., 1969). Frequency discrimination is the most important prerequisite for coding messages in the frequency domain of sound. In frogs the power spectrum (distribution of sound energy in different frequencies) of the species' mating call is usually species-specific, i.e., each species has a unique tonal quality in its mating call. Male bullfrogs call back in response to the croaking of other males. They do not react to the calls of other frog species. CAPRANICA (1965) tested the response of male bullfrogs to synthesized calls in order to determine which acoustic components are used by the frog for species recognition. Acoustic energy in the bullfrog's call is concentrated in two frequency ranges, 200–300 Hz and 1400–1500 Hz, which are separated by a low energy band of 500–700 Hz. The male bullfrog responds best when both the low and the high frequency peaks are present. Spectral patterns different from the normal one elicit fewer responses (Fig. 1).

An interesting example of auditory pattern recognition is provided by the cricket frog, *Acris crepitans*, the mating call of which shows geographic variations. Field behavioral experiments demonstrated that female cricket frogs prefer the song of their own area to those of other regions (CAPRANICA et al., 1973). Songs from various areas differ from one another not only in power spectrum but also in temporal pattern. The cricket frog uses both of these differences for the recognition of the song pattern from its own area. For example, the female cricket frog ceases to respond to the local song "if the spectral peak is shifted by as small as 500 Hz either above or below the average for the local population."

Birdsong is also used in species recognition. Birds produce various brief sounds, which are known as calls. Singing is usually associated with territorial advertisement by the male during the breeding season. Song is generally more complex and longer than calls. Also, it is distinguished from other vocalizations by accompanying behavior such as the particular posture during singing.

The effects of altering song on the response of territorial males have been studied quantitatively in four species: European robins, *Erithacus rubecula*

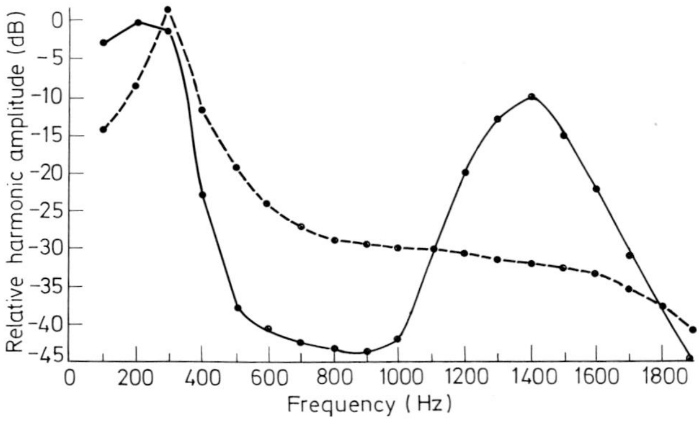

Fig. 1. Relationship between call power spectra and evoked responses in the bullfrog. Spectral pattern shown in solid line is a synthesized version of normal call and evoked 100% reaction. Deviation from this pattern such as shown in dashed line caused fewer responses, 78%. (After CAPRANICA, 1965)

(BREMOND, 1967), indigo buntings, *Passerina cyanea* (EMLEN, 1972), ovenbirds, *Seiurus aurocapillus* (FALL, 1963), and white-throated sparrows, *Zonotrichia albicollis* (FALLS, 1963). Different sets of results were obtained in different species, however, some general patterns seem to emerge from these studies. The songs of different birds belonging to a species contain both uniform and individually variable properties. In all cases, the properties necessary for species recognition are the uniform ones. However, the converse is not always true; there are uniform attributes that are not used for specific recognition. Furthermore, there is redundancy in encoding species distinctiveness in song.

In the three North American species listed above, the silent intervals between the component notes in song exhibit but small individual variation and are very important in species recognition (Fig. 2). In addition to the temporal pattern, the structure or quality of the notes seems to play a significant role. The song of the white-throated sparrow reduces its stimulatory effects when its pure-tone notes are altered either through replacement by frequency-modulated notes or by addition of a harmonic frequency.

In the indigo bunting, changing the sequence in which different notes occur within the song does not reduce its effectiveness in eliciting territorial responses. On the other hand, alternation of low- and high-frequency components in the robin's song is essential for species recognition. Despite these leading studies the analysis of coding in birdsong has been restricted either to simple song patterns or to crude modification of complex songs. Some of the differences in results may be due to different methods of playback and scoring responses.

Birdsong is used not only for species identification but also for individual recognition. Individual variations in song are often in the fine structure of its component notes. These differences offer natural tests for the extent to which birds can detect slight variations in complex acoustical patterns. Male ovenbirds and indigo buntings can distinguish the songs of their immediate neighbours from those of distant and strange individuals (WEEDEN and FALLS, 1959; EMLEN, 1971).

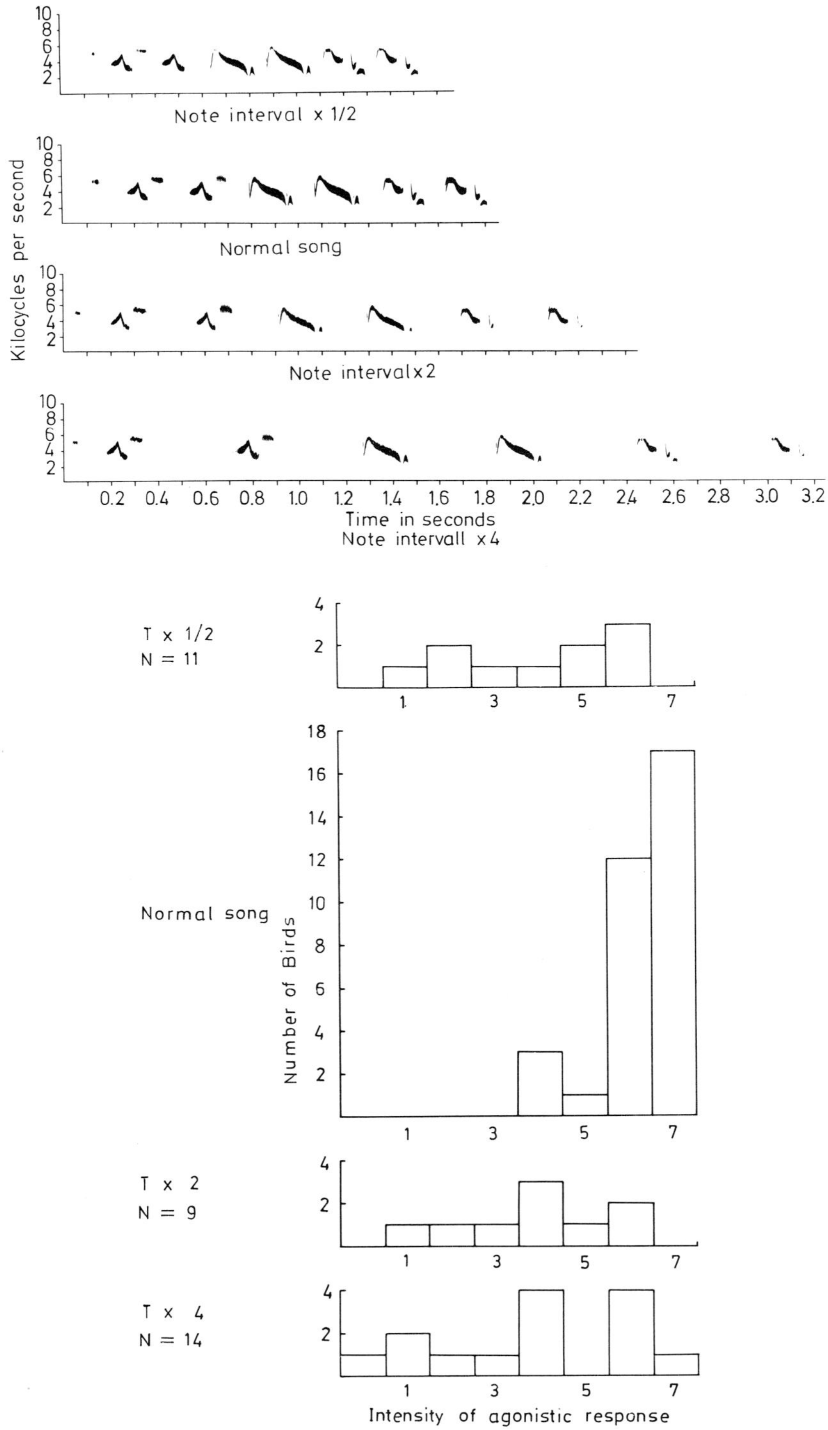

Fig. 2. Effects of altering song internote intervals on territorial behavior in male indigo buntings. Shortening internote intervals by one-half and lengthening by factors of two and four reduced intensity of agonistic responses, which are graded from 0 to 7 based on behavioral observation. (From EMLEN, 1972)

Acoustic signals facilitate individual recognition between parents and young in some birds. In the guillemot, which is a sea bird, each pair raises one chick at a time. Parents utter a special call to attract their chicks for feeding and protection. There are individual differences in this call. Field and laboratory playback experiments demonstrated that a newly hatched guillemot could recognize the individual characteristics of the calls of both parents (TSCHANZ, 1968). Parents can also distinguish their own chick from others by voice. A considerable amount of vocal-auditory interaction takes place between parents and chicks during a period of 2–3 days before the chicks hatch out of the egg. Both parents and chicks mutually learn the characteristics of their calls during this period. It is interesting to note that chicks hatched in an incubator can distinguish the attracting call from other calls. The attracting call contains species-specific properties which naive chicks can recognize.

A unique form of individual recognition by sound is used by some birds that live in dense tropical bushes where visual contact between paired birds is difficult to maintain. In these species "male and female use different notes and sing alternately, often with marked precision in timing," which is called duetting (HOOKER and HOOKER, 1969). Duetting occurs only between paired male and female partners. The follower in a duet sequence must recognize the individual vocal characteristics of its partner. In some cases the follower selects a particular note from its repertoire to go with a specific note delivered by its partner. Another aspects of duetting that bears on auditory pattern recognition is the speed and accuracy with which the follower bird responds to the leader. Mean intervals of 120–150 ms between the onset of the leader song and that of the follower have been reported (THORPE, 1963).

C. Vocal Learning in Songbirds

Both conventional laboratory methods and the ethological observations mentioned so far, reveal only whether or not an animal can distinguish one acoustic pattern from another and—at best—what cues are used for recognition. This is far from knowing how an animal "perceives" auditory patterns. Vocal learning in songbirds presents a unique case in which the animal subject can "tell" the human observer how it perceives complex sound patterns because the bird translates the auditory patterns into the corresponding vocal outputs. In a sense birds can tell more about their auditory pattern perception than human subjects, who need a considerable amount of musical training to describe their perception of complex sound patterns.

The aim of this section is to discuss the main attributes of vocal learning in birds as they relate to the problem of auditory pattern recognition; no complete review of the literature in this field is intended. The case of the

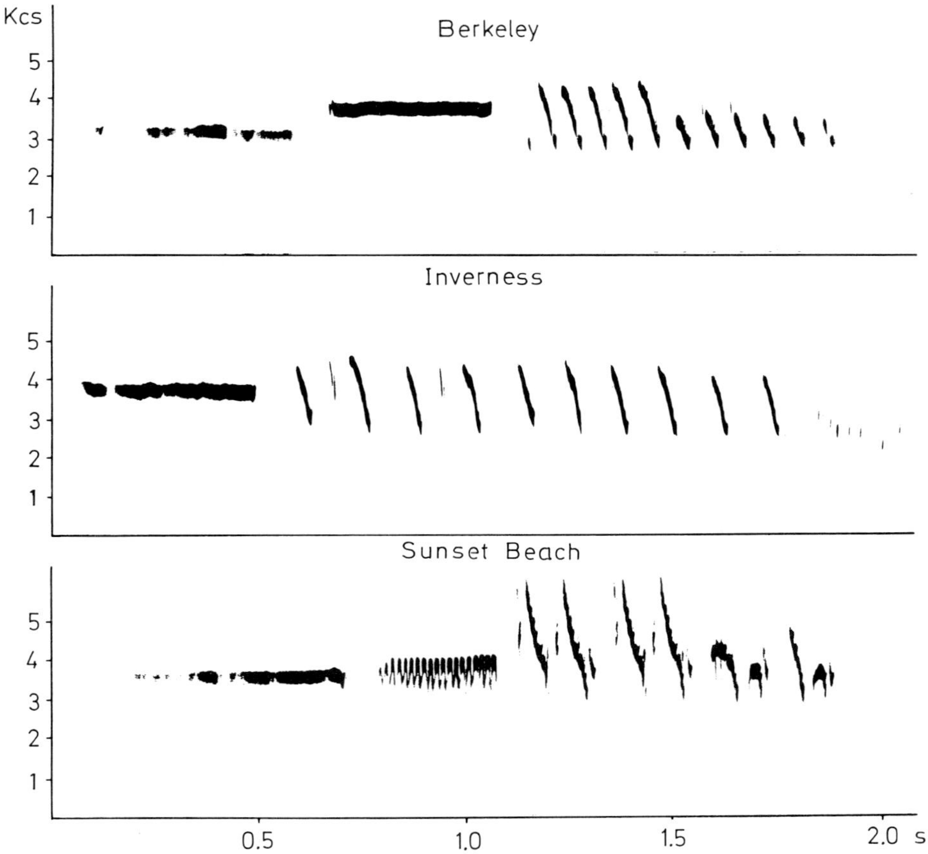

Fig. 3. Song dialects in white-crowned sparrow. There are properties common to all dialects such as the introductory whistle shown as a thick horizontal bar on the sound spectrogram. Different dialects vary most in the fine structure of the notes in the trill part of the song. Dialects are maintained from generation to generation through learning of adult song by young birds. Berkeley, Inverness, and Sunset Beach are coastal locations in Northern California

white-crowned sparrow, *Zonotrichia leucophrys* should suffice to illustrate most of the major characteristics of song learning in passerines. Other examples will be used to complement the white-crown results.

The song of the white-crowned sparrow exhibits geographic variations (Fig. 3) (MARLER and TAMURA, 1962). These variants are akin to dialects in human speech, since they are transmitted from generation to generation through copying of adult birds by young individuals. The bird not only learns to sing the song of its birthplace, but also can distinguish it from other dialects as demonstrated by field playback experiments (MILLIGAN and VERNER, 1971).

If a 5–6 day old nestling is removed from its parents and raised in acoustic isolation, it will develop a type of song which is never found in the natural population of the white-crowned sparrow (Fig. 4). On the other hand, a 2–3-month-old fledgling caught in the wild and raised in a sound-proof room will

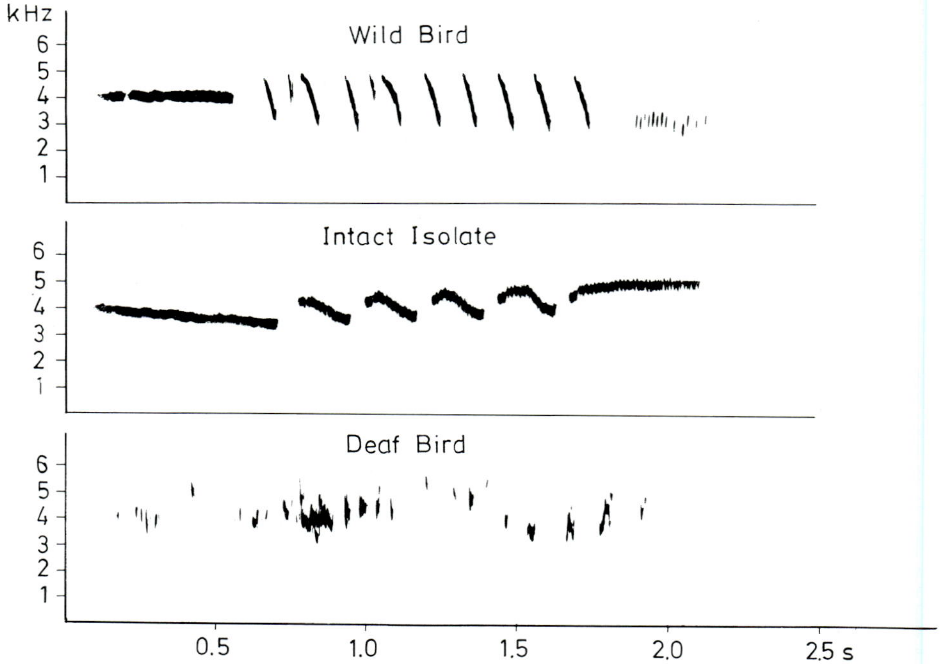

Fig. 4. Sound spectrograms of wild, intact isolate, and deaf white-crowned sparrows

develop a good copy of the dialect of its birthplace (MARLER and TAMURA, 1964).

There is a "critical period" of song learning which lasts from about 14 to 50 days after hatching (MARLER, 1970). If a bird fails to hear a "proper" song during this period, it will develop an abnormal song. The failure cannot be corrected by subsequent exposure to a normal song. Young white-crowned sparrows do not sing during this period but only hear and remember the dialect of their birthplace. Vocal reproduction of the learned model song takes place later as the birds become sexually mature. Several months can elapse between the time of exposure to the model song and the onset of singing.

Young white-crowned sparrows do not learn the songs of other species living and singing in the same habitat. If a young bird is exposed to playback of both the species' own and alien songs, it will copy the species' song. An alien song presented alone is rejected and the bird develops an abnormal song as if it had been raised in total sound isolation. However, there is no preference for a particular dialect; all wild-type song patterns are acceptable. If two dialects are offered, the bird develops a pattern somewhat intermediate between the two. These results suggest that the white-crowned sparrow has a predisposition to learn the species' own song. It is still not known what acoustic properties a song must possess for acceptance by the white-crowned sparrow.

In order to analyze these properties systematically birds have been tutored with computer-synthesized songs. A song containing a simple outline of the wild-type song turned out to be acceptable as a model. The natural introductory whistles which are narrow-band noises could be substituted for by pure tone notes. Simple FM notes have been used to replace the elaborate natural trill notes (KONISHI, unpublished data).

For the white-crowned sparrow, it is the acoustic structure of song that determines whether or not the song is copied. In some species social relationships between birds determine the selection of model song. Young zebra finches, *Taeniopygia guttata*, learn song exclusively from their fathers. If young zebra finches are raised by Bengalese finch parents, then they learn the song of the foster father, even when they can hear adult zebra finches singing in the same aviary.

Even in this case the structure of song is important for learning. This was shown in the following experiment. If two female Bengalese finches that do not sing raise young zebra finches in a room where the songs of both species can be heard, the zebra finches select the species' own song to copy (IMMELMANN, 1969). The Bengalese song differs sufficiently from the zebra finch song. However, it is not known how much the song of the foster father can depart from the zebra finch song before it is rejected by young zebra finches.

Birdsong develops gradually under normal circumstances; early utterances and occasional juvenile twittering all seem to contribute to the development of song. These vocalizations are gradually sorted out, rearranged, and combined with new elements to produce final full song as sexual maturity approaches. During the vocal reproduction of the learned song, the white-crowned sparrow faces a unique problem of auditory pattern recognition in which the bird must evaluate its own vocal output. The white-crowned sparrow need not hear the model song from any external source again during its vocal reproduction. The memory of the model song alone can guide the development of song. Should a white-crown that has learned a model song become deaf before the onset of singing, it can no longer translate the memory of the model into the corresponding vocal pattern (KONISHI, 1965). During song development the bird must hear its own voice and modify it until there is no more difference between the song memory and vocal output. The song memory serves as a "template" with which the bird must match its vocal output. Since deaf birds cannot compare their voice with the song template, they lose control of the vocal motor mechanism, which itself does not seem to possess pattern-generating capability as evinced by the structureless song of the deaf bird (Fig. 4).

The song of a deaf white-crowned sparrow differs from that of an intact bird raised in isolation. This difference has a significant theoretical implication. There may be a song template that is not acquired but innate. Song development is steered not according to the memory of an external model but to an internal one. The song of the isolate contained some traces of the wild-type song of the species, whereas the deaf bird sang a song completely devoid of the species attributes. The intact isolate could compare its vocal output with the innate song template, whereas the deaf bird could not.

The innate song template of the white-crowned sparrow is not sufficient to produce wild-type song. The extent to which the innate template can guide

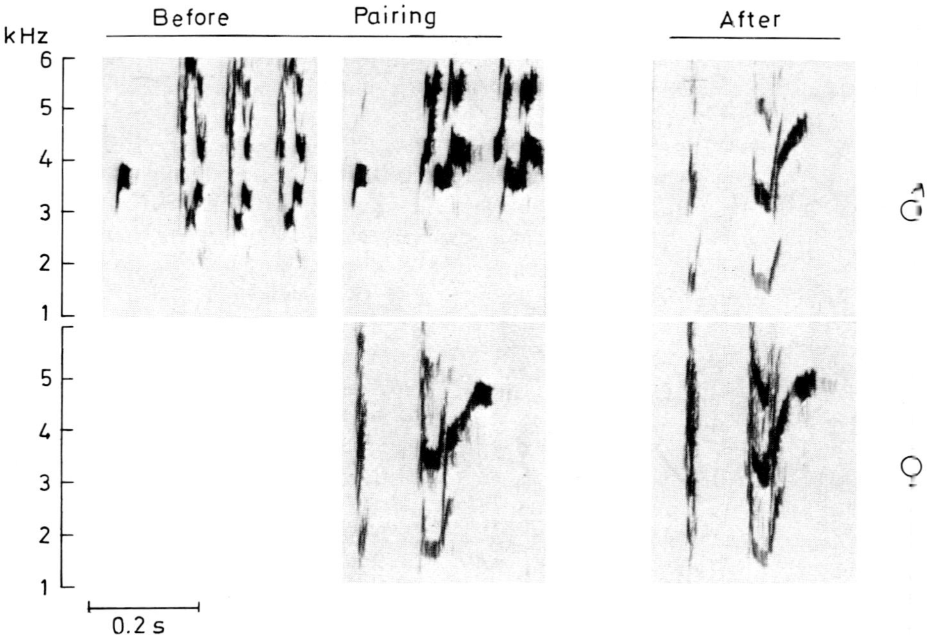

Fig. 5. Imitation of flight call in siskin. After pairing male added to his repertoire of flight calls one closely resembling female's flight call. (From MUNDINGER, 1970)

normal song development varies from species to species. The song sparrow, *Melospiza melodia,* seems to possess an innate song template good enough to guide the development of the species song with complex acoustic properties. Birds hatched and raised by canary foster parents in a sound-proof room developed relatively normal songs along with some abnormal songs, whereas a deaf song sparrow produced an extremely abnormal song (MULLIGAN, 1966; KROODSMA, 1977). Therefore, when a naive song sparrow hears its own voice, it "knows" what acoustical properties the species song should contain.

In most species song development is irreversible; i.e., once a song motor pattern is "crystallized" it cannot be altered by later experience, nor can a new pattern be added to the bird's repertoire of songs. It was long thought that calls are not learned even in those species which learn song. Recent studies show that some birds can modify call notes by imitation from other individuals throughout their lifetime (MUNDINGER, 1970). Some of the cardueline finches such as American goldfinch, *Cardeulis tristis*, pine siskin, *C. pinus*, and European siskin, *C. spinus* utter a particular call on the wing known as the flight call. There are individual differences in this call. When male and female pair up, one bird copies the other's flight call. Either sex may imitate. The accuracy of copying is rather remarkable (Fig. 5). A new pair might also produce a new sound pattern made up of contributions from both sexes. Paired birds apparently recognize each other by exchanging their identical calls as demonstrated by field playback experiments.

D. Neuroethological Correlates of Auditory Pattern Recognition

Early ethologists explained an animal's ability to recognize biologically significant stimuli by postulating perceptual mechanisms which process stimuli by matching them with built-in neural criteria in the central nervous system (LORENZ, 1935). It is unlikely that a single process can explain auditory pattern recognition in all animals for the following reasons: behavioral studies show that different animals may use different rules of coding acoustic signals, and processing of an acoustic stimulus does not occur in one step but involves several stages that can vary from animal group to animal group.

A minimum strategy of study which is applicable to all animals is a systematic investigation of the input-output function of each of the stages involved in signal processing starting from the eardrum or its functional equivalent.

In some animals the ear itself is structurally highly specialized for the reception of biologically significant sounds. Thus, the tympanum of the cricket, *Teleogryllus commodus*, has a resonance frequency of 4 kHz, which is the frequency of the species' acoustic signals (JOHNSTONE et al., 1970). Similarly, the noctuid moth's ear is mechanically tuned to the frequency range of the bat's cries (ADAMS, 1970).

It was mentioned that the power spectrum of the mating call is important for species recognition in some frogs. There is no indication that the frog's eardrum is tuned to its mating call.

Discrimination of acoustic power spectra must be based on the ability of the frog's inner ear to perform frequency analysis of complex sound. There is neurophysiological evidence that the inner ear of all vertebrate groups can perform frequency analysis of complex sound, though to varying degrees. In some frogs the inner ear is "tuned" to the power spectrum of the species' mating call. This was demonstrated by recording single neurons in the auditory nerve or cochlear nucleus. The response of an auditory neuron is a function of sound frequency and intensity; the frequency to which a neuron exhibits the lowest threshold of response is called the best frequency of that cell. Different auditory neurons have different best frequencies.

If primary auditory neurons of the bullfrog are classified according to their best frequencies, they exhibit a trimodal distribution peaking at 250 Hz, 700 Hz and 1400 Hz (Fig. 6, top). If the mid-frequency sensitive neurons between 500 Hz and 800 Hz are ignored, the remaining distribution roughly resembles the power spectrum of the bullfrog's mating call (Fig. 6, bottom). Thus most units are tuned to the frequency ranges in which the acoustic energy of the call is concentrated.

Furthermore, the response of a low-frequency unit can be suppressed by a second tone. This inhibitory effect depends on the frequency and relative amplitude of the second tone. "In general, the best inhibitory frequencies for these low-frequency units occur about 300 to 600 Hz above their best excitatory frequencies" (FENG et al., 1975). The range of best inhibitory frequencies roughly corresponds to the mid-frequency area in the call spectrum. An increase in energy in this range exceeding the amplitude of the low peak reduces the frog's

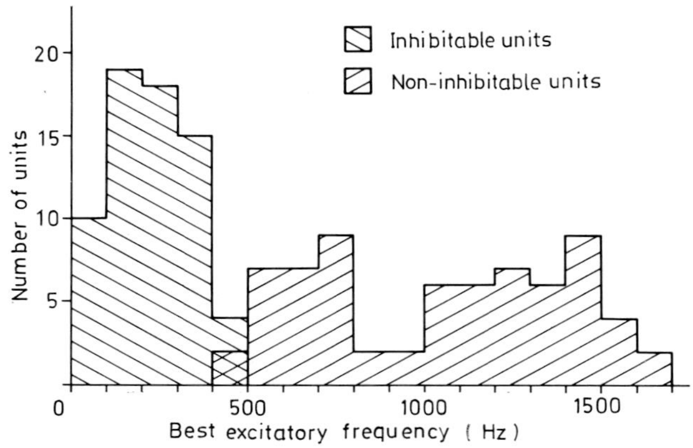

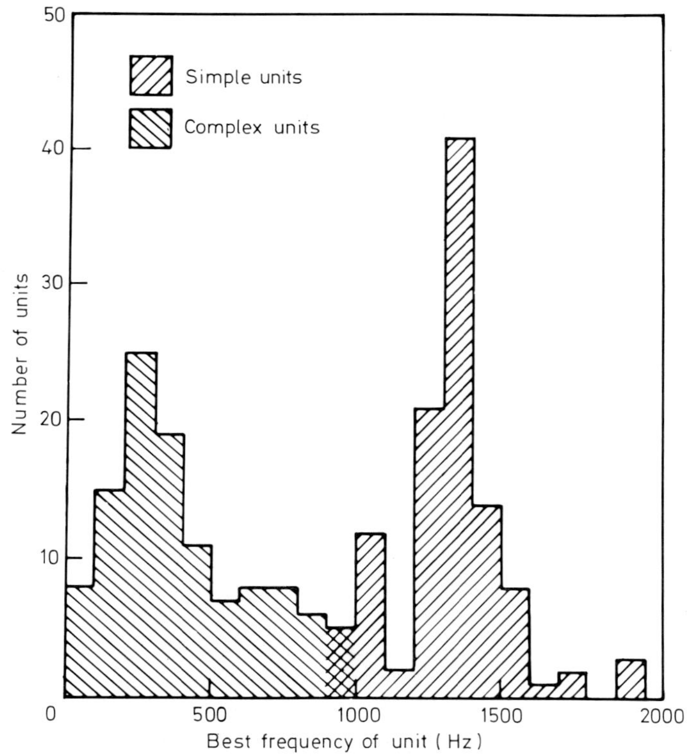

Fig. 6. Comparison of number of auditory fibers (*top*) and vocal energy distribution (*bottom*) in the bullfrog. There are three groups of fibers; the low- and middle-frequency (250 Hz and 700 Hz) units innervate the amphibian papilla and the high-frequency (1 400 Hz) cells the basilar papilla. The response of a low-frequency neuron can be inhibited by a second tone. (From FENG et al., 1975)

response to the call. The inhibitory and excitatory effects of activating the neurons in the mid-frequency area may be balanced to determine the behavioral outcome.

It is interesting to note that there are two separate sensory organs in the frog's inner ear: the amphibian papilla innervated by low- and mid-frequency sensitive fibers and the basilar papilla giving rise to high-frequency neurons. The bullfrog's mating call contains low- and high-frequency components which stimulate respectively the amphibian and basilar papillae to evoke a maximum response. In this respect, the bullfrog seems to be exceptional.

In other frog species the number of auditory neurons matches with the call spectrum only for the high-frequency units innervating the basilar papilla. Their calls lack a low-frequency component to stimulate the low frequency neurons from the amphibian papilla (LOFTUS-HILLS and JOHNSTONE, 1971; CAPRANICA and MOFFAT, 1975).

The geographic variations in the song of the cricket frog have also been studied from the neuroethological point of view (CAPRANICA et al., 1973). These call variants have different spectral peaks, which are matched by parallel shifts in the distribution of high-frequency neurons in different frequency ranges. For example, in New Jersey both the call spectral peak and the cellular distribution peak occur at 3550 Hz in contrast with 2900 Hz in North Dakota. The call lacks low-frequency components, and the low-frequency-sensitive fibers do not show any geographic variation.

It appears as though the characteristics of the vocal and auditory systems may be determined by the same set of genes. This speculation has received additional support from recent work on hybrid frogs of another genus. The hybrid's auditory nerve is tuned (in the sense used above) to the power spectrum of its own mating call, which is intermediate between the parental calls (CAPRANICA, personal communication). In crickets it has been shown that hybrid females orient toward the hybrid calling song in preference to either of the parental songs.

The above observation led HOY and PAUL (1973) to the hypothesis that the same "template" may be used both to recognize and to produce song. This theory does not apply to the hybrid between the grasshopper species *Chorthippus biguttulus* and *C. mollis* (VON HELVERSEN and VON HELVERSEN, 1975). Most hybrid females preferred the song of one or the other parental species to those of their hybrid brothers. Moreover, female grasshoppers sing in response to the song of the male, and the song patterns to which females responded best differed from their own songs. Those hybrids that chose one parental song were shown to respond best to the same temporal pattern of sound that the same parental species preferred most. Some hybrid females responded to both parental songs. When these hybrids were tested with synthetic songs the temporal pattern of which varied systematically from the one parental form to the other, they showed two peak responses corresponding to the two parental patterns. This result suggests that these hybrids were endowed with the neural substrates for song recognition of both parental species instead of an intermediate mechanism.

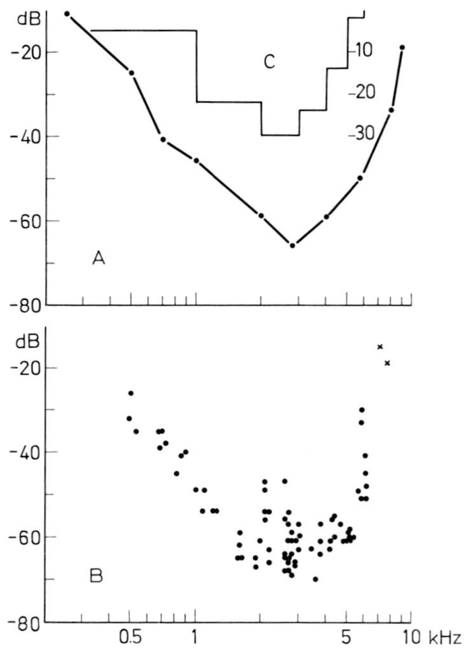

Fig. 7. Behavioral auditory curve, single unit thresholds and numbers in the canary. (A) Behavioral audiometric curve (from DOOLING, 1969). (B) Distribution of thresholds of single units at their best frequencies in one individual. (C) Numbers of units classified according to their best frequencies from another bird. dB re: 1 dyne cm^{-2}. (From KONISHI, 1970)

There is another aspect of hearing in which single neuron and behavior data can be correlated. The auditory threshold of a whole animal is a function of sound frequency and intensity. The relationship between single unit and behavioral threshold has been studied in birds (KONISHI, 1970). The behavioral auditory threshold curve of a bird corresponds to the lower envelope of its single unit threshold at their best frequencies. That is, the most sensitive unit in each frequency band determines the behavioral threshold of the whole animal at that frequency (Fig. 7).

Furthermore, the number of neurons in the bird's cochlear nucleus, as classified according to their best frequencies, is inversely proportional to the threshold of hearing (Fig. 7). The largest number of neurons occur in the frequency range of the lowest auditory threshold, while the least number of units is found near the low and high frequency limits of hearing. The number of neurons in each frequency band perhaps reflects the need to convey to higher centers other types of information within that band such as the fine details of spectral distribution. It is noteworthy that neurons in the highest auditory nucleus, Field L of the avian forebrain, exhibit the same relationships among the three parameters, number and threshold of units and behavioral sensitivity (LEPPELSACK, 1974). This means that the higher auditory nuclei do not bias the frequency-intensity function of hearing, which is determined most likely in the inner ear.

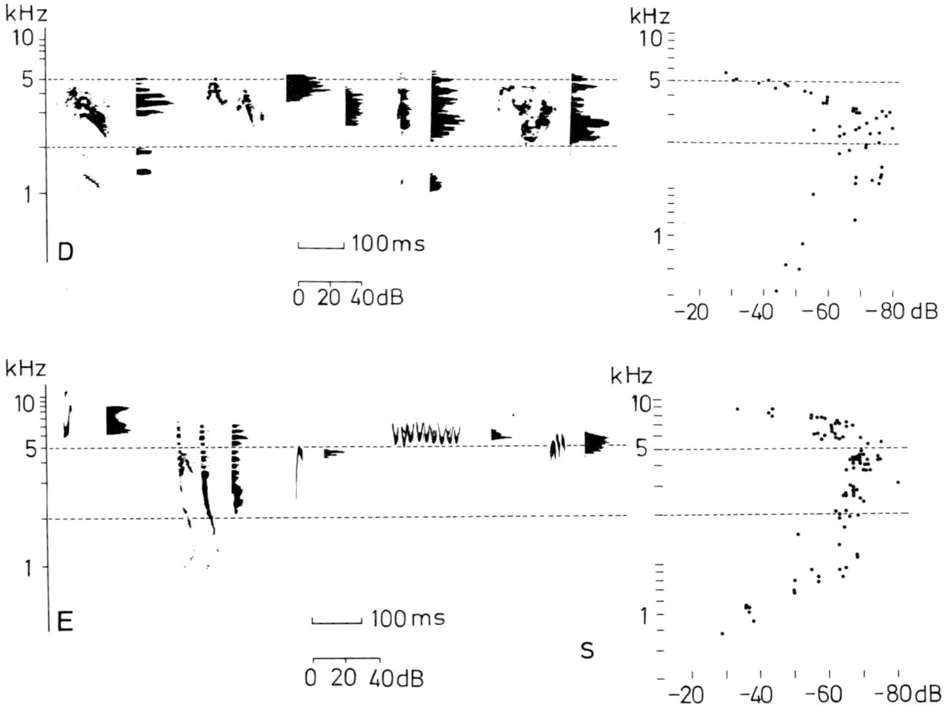

Fig. 8. Single-unit thresholds and vocalizations for (*D*) house sparrow and (*E*) slate-colored junco. Narrow-band time-frequency sound spectrograms of vocalizations and their frequency-amplitude profiles are compared with single unit thresholds from one individual of each species, *S* denotes typical sound component in species song. Sound frequencies are shown in logarithmic scale. All decibel values with a negative sign refer to 1 dyne cm^{-2}. Time scale is for time-frequency spectrograms, and bar scale in decibels is for frequency-amplitude profiles. (From KONISHI, 1970)

There is some correlation between hearing and vocalization in birds; the highest audible frequency of a songbird is usually close to the maximum vocal frequency of that species. The frequency range of peak sensitivity is loosely correlated with that of dominant vocal frequencies. There is no vocal-auditory correlation in the lower part of audible frequencies; all birds studied so far can hear low frequencies well below the lowest vocal frequency (Fig. 8).

Extreme specialization of the ear for reception of biologically significant sounds seems to be lacking among normal birds and mammals. Peripheral specialization saves the brain the trouble of dealing with unprocessed sensory data, therefore it is suited for animals with small brains. However, it is not necessarily restricted to lower animals; for example among the bats that emit a constant frequency sound for echolocation, the ears are sharply tuned to that frequency (POLLAK et al., 1972).

The specialization of the ear and auditory nerve for communication tends to be associated with the frequency aspect of acoustic signals rather than with the temporal feature. As mentioned earlier, crickets use different patterns of amplitude modulation to code different messages for intraspecific communication. The frogs that use the power spectrum of their call for species recognition must also discriminate between different calls having similar spectra for intra-species communication. These calls have different temporal patterns (CAPRANICA, 1968). For some birds, the temporal pattern of song is important for species recognition.

There are many reports of auditory neurons which selectively respond to particular temporal parameters such as on and off time. For example, the auditory neurons of the noctuid moths translate the temporal aspect of the signal into a pattern of impulse discharge from which the central nervous system can obtain information about the time and amplitude characterstics of the signal both of which are important for recognition of the bat. Within the thoracic nerve cord of the moths are interneurons which further process the information conveyed by the auditory fibers. One type of interneurons called the pulse markers fires once only upon "the arrival of three or four sensory impulses separated by sufficiently short intervals.". Another interneuron fires continuously during the train of bat's cries and is called the train marker (ROEDER, 1966b).

However, these interneuron types are by no means unique to the noctuid moths; pulse and train-marker type units are found in the cricket thoracic nerve cord (ZARETSKY, 1972). It may well be that differences between species lie in the manner of integrating the output of various interneuron types, although no higher-order interneurons to process the information conveyed by the pulse and train markers are known.

In the vertebrate auditory system also, interneurons which respond to specific temporal aspects of stimuli occur in higher stations. For example, the midbrain and forebrain auditory areas of birds and mammals and the midbrain nuclei of frogs and alligators all have "on-units," which fire once or twice at the onset of sound like the moth's pulse markers (KATSUKI et al., 1959; LEPPELSACK, 1974; MANLEY, 1971; POTTER, 1965). This type of unit seldom occurs among lower-order interneurons in the cochlear nucleus.

Auditory pattern recognition which involves complex combinations of signal parameters has received increasing attention in recent years. Auditory pattern recognition in the noctuid moths is relatively simple because their central auditory system has to deal with only two aspects of the signal, amplitude and its changes in time, while the frequency parameters do not enter the central nervous system. In some frogs and birds both the temporal and spectral characteristics of calls are important for communication. Their ears and auditory nerves can translate simultaneously both of these parameters into spatial and temporal patterns of discharge. The spatial aspect here is due to the frequency-specific projection of the inner ear onto the central auditory pathway, i.e. the tonotopic arrangement of neurons, although such an arrangement is not known in frogs. Primary auditory neurons have a simple V-shaped frequency threshold function. Convergence of these units on higher-order neurons in various configurations involving both excitatory and inhibitory interactions is thought to give rise to interneurons with stimulus requirements and response characteristics unknown among lower-order neurons (SUGA, 1972).

SUGA (1972) points out that most animal sounds are composed of three basic elements, pure tone, frequency-modulated sound, and noise. In the inferior colliculus and auditory cortex of bats he found neurons which responded "either to only one of the three elements, to two of the three or to all of three." These units are perhaps not unique to bats; for example, they have been found in the cat's auditory cortex and Field L, the forebrain auditory area, of a bird. Furthermore, the proportion of various neuron types, as determined by a standard set of stimuli such as FM signals and tone and noise bursts, does not seem to differ between the cat cortex and the avian Field L (GOLDSTEIN et al. 1968: LEPPELSACK, 1974).

This lack of specificity in neuron types may be construed as an indication either of methodological shortcomings resulting from the use of biologically irrelevant stimuli or of the manner in which the nervous system of different animals use the same "modular" circuits of neurons. It can be argued that different species possess the same types of auditory interneurons because they have to process the same basic acoustic elements. SUGA's hierarchical scheme of auditory "feature detection" implies that the outputs of these interneurons converge on even higher-order neurons that respond exclusively to biologically significant sounds.

Are there call or song detector neurons? EVANS (1974) supports continued search for such neurons by pointing out studies demonstrating auditory neurons responding to particular aspects of complex acoustic signals and the failure to discriminate complex auditory patterns after ablation of the auditory cortex in cats and monkeys.

Direct attempts to discover call detector neurons have been made in several recent studies. WINTER and FUNKENSTEIN (1972) used the animal's natural vocalizations to study the response characteristics of neurons in the auditory cortex of the squirrel monkey *Saimiri sciureus*. Of 283 units studied, about 3.5% of the cells responded exclusively to one call type or to calls with similar acoustic properties. Similar results were reported by WOLLBERG and NEWMAN (1972). However, according to a later study by these authors neurons that selectively responded to one call type were extremely rare (NEWMAN and WOLLBERG, 1973). Of 83 units, 89% responded to more than half of the 12 different calls tested. Only one unit was said to have responded exclusively to one call, the isolation peep. This unit, however, could be excited by tone bursts, as long as their carrier frequency was within the major band of acoustic energy in the call. This is not a complex unit but a pure tone unit responding to that frequency component in the call.

All the above authors have not explicitly answered the fundamental question, that is, whether or not the response of a call-specific neuron can be predicted from its response to pure tones. SOVIJÄRVI (1973) addressed himself to this question in his analysis of the responses of the cat's cortical units to pure tones and complex sounds including the vocalizations of the cat and other animals. In 68% of 100 units studied, their responses to complex sounds could be predicted from their reactions to pure tones, namely tuning curves. The responses of the remaining 32 units to complex sounds could not be predicted from their tuning curves. However, it is noteworthy that many of these units responded to FM components and transients in the complex sounds.

Similarly, LEPPELSACK (1976) found in the forebrain auditory nucleus of the starling, *Sturnus vulgaris* a small number of units that responded to complex natural vocalizations lacking acoustic energy within the frequency ranges bounded by their excitatory tuning curves.

From all these studies the following generalizations can be made: (1) There are neurons in which responses to complex natural vocalizations cannot be predicted from their response to pure tones. (2) The discharge of "complex units" often does not follow any temporal features of complex sounds. (3) "Complex units" tend to lack spontaneous discharge.

However, the results of studies using tape recorded natural vocalizations must be evaluated with caution. They all suffer from several methodological shortcomings. For example, the recordings used may not be "clean," i.e., they contain undesirable noises. The loudspeaker may not be "flat" over the frequency range of vocalizations. Room acoustics may be very complex because of various objects in it, even if it attenuates sound transmission from outside. If neuronal responses depend on the direction of sound propagation, complex room acoustics alone can introduce significant variation in neuronal response characteristics. It is difficult to measure the intensity of a complex sound with fast amplitude and frequency modulation. The peak amplitudes given in all these reports do not reflect the total energy contained in complex sounds, so that some of the results may be simply explained on the basis of different amounts of energy transmitted by different calls. This also makes it hard to compensate for an energy loss when a call is partially deleted or filtered.

There is a more serious methodological shortcoming. Responses to pure tones are by no means simple. Neurons in higher auditory nuclei can have complex tuning curves consisting of excitatory and inhibitory components. The excitatory tuning curve of a unit may not predict its response to complex sounds. Quite complex response patterns of a unit can be predicted when both its excitatory and inhibitory tuning curves are considered together (SUGA, 1973).

While natural vocalizations may help discover "complex units," the step beyond this level of analysis is bound to be difficult. The structure of sound essential for eliciting responses in these units can be determined only by testing with synthetic sounds. There is already a movement in this direction (SCHEICH, 1977).

In this respect the advantage of using animals with simple signals is obvious. The echolocating cry of the moustache bat *Pteronotus parnellii rubiginosus* consists of a constant frequency (CF) and an FM segments. The main sound energy of the CF part is concentrated at 61 kHz. A relative movement between acoustic emitter and receiver causes a Doppler shift. The moustache bat can detect a Doppler shift as small as $\pm 0.01\%$ and adjust the CF segment such that the frequency of its echo remains unchanged at 61 kHz.

The cochlea as well as the auditory cortex of this species is specialized for receiving this particular frequency. For the purpose of this section we will discuss only the auditory cortex. This exhibits tonotopic arrangements of neurons and 30% of the cortical area is occupied by units tuned to 61–63 kHz. Units tuned to the frequency range of the FM segments do not occur along the tonotopic gradient of the above area but occupy another relatively large zone, as if different cortical regions are allocated to the processing of the two signal components separately (SUGA and JEN, 1976). Along the margin of the tonotopically organized area are neurons that respond exclusively to the whole bat cry containing both the CF and FM components in the normal temporal sequence. The cells cease to respond when the two components are separated by a silent interval (SUGA, 1977).

All previous attempts to discover call detector neurons used random probing of auditory nuclei without reference to their internal structure. It is naive to assume that highly specialized units are randomly distributed in the nuclei. In this respect the spatial arrangement of different neuron types in the bat auditory cortex is revealing.

Do call detector neurons serve the purpose for which they are supposed to exist? The presence of special neurons does not necessarily mean they are used by the animal for the function that they are supposed to serve. Perhaps the most conspicious shortcoming in the search for call detector neurons is the lack of systematic investigation of each station in the ascending auditory pathway. It is premature to assign higher order functions to higher relay stations without studying lower stations. Some of the neuronal response properties may be relayed unchanged to higher centers from lower stages. At present the input-output relationship between any two successive stations is neither known nor predictable a priori.

References

Adams, W.B.: Mechanical tuning of the acoustic receptor organ of the noctuid moth. 79th Meet. Amer. acoust. Soc. Abstr. 27 (1970).

Brémond, J.C.: Reconnaissance de schémas réactogènes liés à l'information continue dans le chant territorial du Rouge-gorge (*Erithacus rubecula*). Proc. 14th Int. Ornith. Congr. Oxford, 1967, pp. 217–226.

Bullock, T.H.: Recognition of Complex Acoustic Signals. T.H. Bullock (ed.). Berlin: Abakon Verlagsgesellschaft (1977)

•Capranica, R.R.: The evoked vocal response of the bullfrog. Cambridge, Mass.: M.I.T. Press, 1965.

Capranica, R.R.: The vocal repertoire of the bullfrog. Behaviour **16**, 302–325 (1968).

Capranica, R.R., Frishkopf, L.S., Nevo, E.: Endocing of geographical dialects in the auditory system of the cricket frog. Science **182**, 1292–1295 (1973).

Capranica, R.R., Moffat, A.J.M.: Selectivity of the peripheral auditory system of spadefoot toads (*Scaphiopus conchi*) for sounds of biological significance. J. comp. Physiol. **100**, 231–249 (1975).

Dooling, R.J.: An audibility curve for the common canary as determined by instrumental avoidance conditioning. Master's thesis, St. Louis University (1969).

Emlen, S.T.: An experimental analysis of the parameters of bird song eliciting species recognition. Behaviour **20**, 130–171 (1971).

Emlen, S.T.: The note of song in individual recognition in the indigo bunting. Z. f. Tierpsychol. 28, 241–46 (1971).

•Evans, E.G.: Neural processes for the detection of acoustic patterns and for sound localization. In: Neuroscience: Third Study Program, Cambridge, Mass., M.I.T. Press, 1974, pp. 131–145.

Falls, J.B.: Properties of bird song eliciting responses from territorial males. Proc. Int. Ornith. Congr. **1**, 259–271 (1963).

Feng, A.S., Narins, P.M., Capranica, R.R.: Three populations of primary auditory fibers in the bullfrog (*Rana catesbeiana*): Their peripheral origins and frequency sensitivity. J. comp. Physiol. **100**, 221–229 (1975).

Frishkopf, L.S., Capranica, R.R., Goldstein, M.H. Jr.: Neural coding in the bullfrog's auditory system—a teleological approach. Proc. Inst. Elect. Electron. Eng. **56**, 969–980 (1968).

Goldstein, M.H. Jr., Hall, J.L. II, Butterfield, B.O.: Single-unit activity in the primary auditory cortex of unanesthetized cats. J. acoust. Soc. Amer. **43**, 444–455 (1968).
Helversen, D. von, Helversen, O. von: Verhaltensgenetische Untersuchungen am akustischen Kommunikationssystem der Feldheuschrecken (Orthoptera, Acrididae). II. Das Lautschema von Artbastarden zwischen *Chorthippus biguttulus* und *Ch. mollis*. J. comp. Physiol. **104**, 301–323 (1975).
Hooker, T., Hooker, B.I.: Duetting, In: Bird vocalizations. Hinde, R.A. (ed.), Cambridge: Cambridge Univ. Press 1969.
Hoy, R.R., Paul, R.C.: Genetic control of song specificity in crickets. Science **180**, 82–83 (1973).
Immelmann, K.: Song development in the zebra finch and other estrildid finches. In: Bird voalizations. Hinde, R.A. (ed.), Cambridge: Cambridge Univ. Press 1969.
Johnstone, B.M., Saunders, J.C., Johnstone, J.R.: Tympanic membrane response in the cricket. Nature (Lond.) **227**, 625–626 (1970).
Katsuki, Y., Watanabe, T., Maruyama, N.: Activity of auditory neurons in upper levels of brain of cat. J. Neurophysiol. **22**, 343–359 (1959).
Konishi, M.: The role of auditory feedback in the control of vocalization in the white-crowned sparrow. Z. Tierpsychol. **22**, 770–783 (1965).
Konishi, M.: Comparative neurophysiological studies of hearing and vocalization in songbirds. Z. vergl. Physiol. **66**, 257–272 (1970).
Kroodsma, D.E.: A re-evaluation of song development in the song sparrow. Anim. Behav. **25**, 390–399 (1977).
Leppelsack, H.J.: Funktionelle Eigenschaften der Höhrbahn in Feld L des Neostriatum caudale des Staren (*Sturnus vulgaris* L., Aves). J. comp. Physiol. **88**, 271–320 (1974).
Leppelsack, H.J., Vogt, M.: Responses of auditory neurons in the forebrain of a songbird to stimulation with species-specific sounds. J. comp. Physiol. **107**, 263–274 (1976).
Loftus-Hills, J.J., Johnstone, B.M.: Auditory function, communication, and the brain-evoked response in anuran amphibians. J. acoust. Soc. Amer. **47**, 1131–1138 (1971).
Lorenz, K.: Der Kumpan in der Umwelt des Vogels. J. Ornithol. **83**, 137–413 (1935).
Manley, J.A.: Single unit studies in the midbrain auditory area of Caiman. Z. vergl. Physiol., **71**, 255–261 (1971).
Marler, P.: A comparative approach to vocal learning: Song development in white-crowned sparrows. J. comp. physiol. Psychol. Monogr. Vol. 71, No. 2, Part 2, p. 1–25 (1970).
Marler, P., Tamura, M.: Song dialects in three populations of white-crowned sparrows. Condor. **64**, 368–377 (1962).
Marler, P., Tamura, M.: Culturally transmitted patterns of vocal behavior in sparrows. Science, **146**, 1483–1486 (1964).
Masterton, B., Heftner, H., Ruvizza, R.: The evolution of human hearing. J. acoust. Soc. Amer. **45**, 966–985 (1969).
Michelsen, A.: The physiology of the locust ear (I–III). Z. vergl. Physiol. **71**, 49–128 (1971).
Milligan, M.M., Verner, J.: Inter-populational song dialect discrimination in the white-crowned sparrow. Condor. **73**, 208–213 (1971).
Mundinger, P.C.: Vocal imitation and individual recognition of finch calls. Science, **168**, 480–482 (1970).
Mulligan, J.A.: Singing behavior and its development in the song sparrow *Melospiza melodia*. Univ. Calif. Pub. Zool. **81**, 1–76 (1966).
Newman, J.D., Wollberg, Z.: 1975 Multiple coding of species-specific vocalizations in the auditory cortex of squirrel monkeys. Brain Res., **54**, 287–304 (1973).
Patterson, W.C.: Hearing in the turtle. J. Aud. Res. **6**, 453–464 (1966).
Pollak, G., Henson, O.W., Novik, A.: Cochlear microphonic audiograms in the "pure tone" bat *Chilonycteris parnellii parnellii*. Science **196**, 66–68 (1972).
Popper, A.N., Fay, R.R.: Sound detection and processing by teleost fishes: a critical review. J. acoust. Soc. Amer. **53**, 1515–1529 (1973).
Potter, H.D.: Patterns of acoustically evoked discharges of neurons in the mesencephalon of the bullfrog. J. Neurophysiol. **28**, 1155–1184 (1965).
Roeder, K.D.: Auditory system of noctuid moths. Science **154**, 1515–1521 (1966a).
Roeder, K.D.: Interneurons of the thoracic nerve cord activated by tympanic nerve fibers in noctuid moths. J. Insect Physiol. **12**, 1227–1244 (1966b).

Scheich, H.: Central processing of complex sounds and feature analysis. In: Recognition of Complex Acoustic Signals (T.H. Bullock, ed.). Berlin: Abakon Verlagsgesellschaft (1977)

Suga, N.: Analysis of information-bearing elements in complex sounds by auditory neurons of bats. Audiology, **11**, 58–72 (1972).

Suga, N.: Feature extraction in the auditory system of bats. In: Basic mechanisms in hearing. Møller, A.R. (ed.): New York and London: Academic Press 1973.

Suga, N.: Amplitude spectrum representation in the Doppler-shifted-CF processing area of the auditory context of the mustache bat. Science **196**, 64–67 (1977)

Suga, N., Jen, P.H.-S.: Disproportionate tonotopic representation for processing CF-FM sonar signals in the mustache bat auditory cortex. Science **194**, 542–544 (1976).

Thorpe, W.H.: Antiphonal singing in birds as evidence for avian auditory reaction time. Nature (Lond.) **197**, 774–776 (1963).

Trainer, J.E.: The auditory acuity of certain birds, Ph.D. Thesis, Cornell University (1946).

Tschanz, B.: Trottellummen. Beiheft 4 zur Z. Tierpsychol. Berlin-Hamburg, Paul Parey (1968).

Uexküll, J. von: Umwelt und Innenwelt der Tiere. Berlin: Springer-Verlag 1909.

Walker, T.J.: Specificity in the response of female tree cricket (Orthoptera, Gryllidae, Oecanthinae) to calling songs of the males. Ann. entomol. Soc. Amer. **50**, 626–636 (1957).

Weeden, J.S., Falls, J.B.: Differential responses of male ovenbirds to recorded songs of neighboring and more distant individuals. Auk, **76**, 343–351 (1959).

Winter, P., Funkenstein, H.H.: The effect of species-specific vocalization on the discharge of auditory cortical cells in the awake squirrel monkey (*Saimiri sciurens*). Exp. Brain Res., **18**, 489–504 (1972).

Wollberg, Z., Newman, J.D.: Auditory cortex of squirrel monkey: response patterns of single cells to species-specific vocalizations. Science 175, 212–214 (1975).

Zaretsky, M.D.: The neurophysiological and behavioral mechanisms of the response to intraspecific acoustical signal in crickets. Ph.D. dissertation, Univ. of Calif., Berkeley (1972).

Chapter 10

Visual Competence in Early Infancy

MARSHALL M. HAITH [1], Denver, Colorado (USA)

With 9 Figures

Contents

---

[1] The research reported here is the result of the cooperation and help of many people. I am grateful to the staff and administration of the Cambridge Hospital for providing space and facilities to us for this work. Dr. Phil Porter, Chief of Pediatrics and Ms. Mildred Howard, head nurse, were especially supportive of our work. Robert Lentz made invaluable contributions to technological development. Henry Gerbrands and Fred Morrison helped in the early stages of setting up laboratories. Tina Turner, Gail Brent, Diane Lusk, Joy Corsi, Terry Bergman, Leah Mann, Morton Mendelson, and Karen Cohen all helped in the running of subjects and/or the reduction of data. Many of these people have also helped in the development of the conceptualizations and I also owe thanks to Jerome Kagan, William Kessen, Phil Salapatek, and Arnold Sameroff for their counsel over the years as this research developed. Bennett Bertenthal, Karen Cohen, Kurt Fischer, Patricia Goldman, Jerome Kagan, Kathy Lochridge, Morton Mendelson and Sandra Pipp commented on an earlier version of this manuscript and Bruce Platt read several versions. All made many helpful suggestions. Finally, I am grateful to Betty Richardson for her help in preparing the manuscript and for her substantive suggestions.

The research reported here was supported by National Institutes of Mental Health Grants #MH22020 and MH23412.

An earlier form of the ideas proposed here was presented at the Regional Meetings of the Society for Research in Child Development, Clark University, 1968, and at Meetings of the Committee for Research in Infancy, Washington, 1971.

"If any sort of instinctive cognizance were inborn," maintained HELMHOLTZ in support of his *Empirical Theory of Perception,* "one would expect that it would have to be first of all in the recognition of the maternal breast and the knowledge of those movements by which [the newborn] could turn toward this visual image. But such a cognizance is quite obviously missing. One sees that the child...turns away from the breast just as often as towards it, even though it can see it freely. Apparently, it is unable to interpret the visual image or the direction of its movements.

"Just as often one sees that a child of one or two weeks, in front of whom one holds a burning candle, becomes restless and moves his eyes back and forth...at first the child does not yet know how to reach a flame with his gaze.

"From this I conclude that the interpretation even of some of the simplest, and, for the human child, most important visual images must be translated by him, and are not given in advance by inherent organization without preceding experience" (WARREN and WARREN, 1968, p. 253).

Such pivotal importance to theories of perception and knowledge has maintained interest in newborn visual competence throughout the history of philosophical and psychological inquiry. Indeed, compelling reasons are needed to sustain research on visual organization in an organism from which verbal report is unavailable, discriminative response indicators are severely limited, and direct neuroanatomical investigation is impossible. Even so, research on visual perception in the early weeks of life has made both methodologic and conceptual progress, and is one of the most active fields in developmental psychology.

This chapter will review research and thinking about visual competence in early infancy. Following a brief review of general theoretical attitudes toward perceptual development, I will review research on the status of various anatomical and neurophysiologic components of the human visual system at birth and shortly thereafter. Reference will also be made to nonhuman research where applicable. After establishing that significant visual sensory competence exists at birth, I will discuss the major conceptions which have guided research on how this competence is deployed. The bulk of research and theory has depended on the assumption that infant visual activity can best be described in terms of preference behavior. I take issue with this approach and suggest a new orientation which places emphasis on how sensory capacity is utilized through congenitally organized "rules" for seeking visual information. This reorientation brings together recent work on visual neurophysiology and infant visual scanning patterns. My conclusion is that organized visual-information acquisition strategies are present at birth, but that the structure of the perceptual system is, in large part, shaped by experience: and that HELMHOLTZ was probably not far off the mark.

A. Background

Apart from its importance for grand epistemic theories, why select the methodologically intractable infant for study? A variety of reasons comes to mind. For a complete understanding of perceptual and cognitive development, and of how the infant acquires information about his world, the ontogenetic course of man's most important sense must be understood. Additionally, a better understanding of adult perceptual functioning could result from an analysis of its developmental course. As compelling as any other reason, special intrigue accompanies the attempt to represent the perceptual world of an organism whose status we once shared, but no longer can remember, whose impressions of the visual world must, in some sense, be like our own, yet still quite different.

It has been said that science progresses through cycles of discrete breakthroughs followed by gradual assimilation and elaboration of the new trend. No characterization better captures the attempts in the last 15 years to understand the organization and development of visual functioning in the young infant. From a standing start in 1960, the field took a great leap forward, and has enjoyed continued momentum to the present. Of considerable relevance to later discussion, a parallel surge in research activity has taken place in the related fields of early visual deprivation and neurophysiologic recording from single cells in the visual system.

Advances before 1960 were certainly not retarded by lack of interest. To the contrary, valid information about perceptual organization in infancy could have played a crucial role in the conflict between various post-Helmholtzian accounts of perceptual development, especially those about nature versus nurture. Even though these theories may not have dealt directly with the infant, their implications for infant perception were obvious. On the side of nature, for example, Gestalt theory maintained that form perception was governed by the inborn organization of brain fields (KOFFKA, 1935; WERTHEIMER, 1923). These neural fields favored some visual stimulus organizations over others, and permitted certain configurational forces to exert systematic influence on perception. Thus, for the Gestaltists, the requisite brain organization for form perception was either available to the infant at birth or became available through maturation. Experience played no role.

Learning theorists, on the other hand, yielded little to the gifts of nature. Actually, perception in the traditional sense of the term occupied little of the learning theorists' efforts because internal events were not of concern unless they could be directly tied to environmental events or behavioral observables. The traditional behavioral analysis equated perception and discrimination; the primary concern was how the internal response, corresponding to the percept, was formed or enhanced through association with environmental contingencies. Thus, for example, the discrimination of two faces could be enhanced by reinforcing the differential naming of each. GIBSON and GIBSON (1955) referred to this model of perceptual development as an enrichment theory, because it held that the percept was enriched by the addition of cues through conditioning.

As with many major controversies, the apologists for the Gestalt and Behaviorist theories were addressing different issues. The Gestaltists were interested in the percept itself (or why a tree looks like a tree, as DODWELL [1970] put it) as reflected by their concern with nonveridicality between stimulus and percept. The learning theorists ignored stimulus-percept relations and concentrated on discrimination between stimuli as reflected in performance on learning tasks. Using the examples of space perception and form perception, HERSHENSON (1970) noted there is no reason to assume that *all* visual perception will necessarily obey the same ontogenetic principles. Thus, structures required for space perception, for example, could develop without experience, whereas those required for form perception could be more sensitive to specific environmental variation. (Judging from the amount of space he devoted to the issue, HELMHOLTZ found the nativist theory of space perception the most difficult to disprove.) Recent evidence from studies of form perception supports the thesis of environmental impact on neural structure and perception (see GOLDMAN, in press 1976, for a review of this work.)

The controversy between Gestalt and Behaviorist theories did highlight two major recurring themes in discussions of perceptual development: (1) the issue of the relative contributions of nature and nurture to perception; (2) the question of emphasis on the receptive characteristics of the organism as opposed to his active involvement in the perceptual act.

These themes are identifiable in the modern polarity that exists between the constructivist and the differentiation accounts of perceptual development. HEBB (1949), assuming the clearest constructivist position, held that neural organization in the visual cortex resulted from visual experience mediated by explicit eye movement activity. The neural organization ("phase sequence") representing a whole form, e.g., a triangle, is constructed from sequential firing of smaller nets (cell assemblies). The cell assemblies are initially activated through visual fixation of the elements, lines and angles, in turn. HEBB's position is quite consonant with Russian motor-copy theory which also requires detailed sequential fixation of visual elements of a form for eventual unitary perception of it.

NEISSER (1967) also takes the constructivist position. Though he largely ignores the developmental aspect of perception, his microgenetic analysis of adult visual perception can be extended to ontogenesis. Thus, since an adult identifies a form through analysis of hierarchically organized form operators, one might expect that successively more sophisticated operators are established through experience. NEISSER places less emphasis on eye movements in form recognition than does HEBB: such movements are only necessary for fine analysis by foveation when less detailed peripheral vision cannot perform the task. However, since NEISSER was more concerned with form recognition than acquisition of form perception, perhaps eye movements were stressed less.

The GIBSON'S, on the other hand, have maintained that "construction" of objects in the world by the child is not necessary. All of the visual information is available in the input; development consists of learning to deal with that information. Thus, the structure is available in the stimulus and the organism "resonates" to it (GIBSON, 1966). E.J. GIBSON (1969) argues that form features are only important in differentiating one object from another and it is only in this respect that eye movements are important, i.e., for finding the differentiating features.

As with the controversy between Gestalt theory and Learning theory, the constructivist and differentiation positions attempt to explain different phenomena and thus are less contradictory than it appears. HEBB and NEISSER are concerned with perceptual *identification,* essentially the aim of the Gestaltists, whereas E.J. GIBSON is concerned with perceptual *differentiation.* Their positions with regard to the nature-nurture issue seem less clear. HEBB is clearly an extreme environmentalist, admitting only figure-ground segregation at birth, whereas J.J. GIBSON argues that all information, in theory, is available to the organism at birth and could be detected. For both, then, the receptive apparatus is present at birth. For both, learning does take place in the form of discovery of features which distinguish one form, pattern or figure from another. Yet, they do differ, the constructivist position emphasizing activity both in the form of eye movements and in synthesis of figural elements, the Gibsonian position emphasizing receptivity and the primacy of stimulus structure.

Despite these theoretical controversies, only recently has it been possible to address questions about perceptual development in the first half-year of life. The breakthrough was methodologic rather than conceptual. FANTZ'S reports in the late 50's and early 60's (1956, 1958, 1961) broke a virtual silence of over two decades. FANTZ suggested that a variety of questions about visual discrimination and preference could be asked simply by observing the corneal reflection of what a baby prefers to look at. The procedure has been adopted by a large majority of investigators in studies of infant vision and has established that babies can detect pattern at birth (defined in terms of nonhomogeneity); a host of related findings will be discussed later.

Since comprehensive reviews of infant visual perception have appeared in recent years (BOND, 1972; HERSHENSON, 1967; KESSEN et al., 1970), the present review will not be exhaustive. Rather, I will selectively review what is known about structural and functional characteristics of the visual system at birth, and the current thinking about infant visual behavior. Then I shall present some new data, and suggest a somewhat different way of thinking about newborn visual activity.

I. Visual Sensory Capacity

Agreement that the newborn has sufficient sensory capacity to provide the "blooming, buzzing confusion" with which JAMES (1890) endowed him, is lacking. NELSON's textbook of pediatrics (1964) ascribes no more to the newborn than light sensitivity (p. 1482) and MANN (1964) and DUKE-ELDER and COOK (1963) appear to agree, stating that the immaturity of the macula is responsible for the inability of the newborn to fixate. Research findings suggest that the newborn's visual experience lies somewhere between the bountiful sensory attack which JAMES surmised and the varying shades of gray suggested by these later writers.

The whole human visual system is relatively advanced at birth in comparison either to the visual status of other newborn mammals or to other newborn human systems. Comparative analysis suggests that with increasing organismic complexity there is a fairly regular increase in maturity of the visual system at birth as indicated by retinal histology (ORDY et al., 1965), cortical electrophysiology (ELLINGSON, 1964; ROSE and ELLINGSON, 1970; WIESEL and HUBEL, 1974), cortical neurogenesis (RAKIC, 1974), and visual behavior (ROSE, 1971). This comparative trend will be referred to later in drawing inferences about the human newborn. Embryologically, components of the visual system are among the first established (DUKE-ELDER and COOK, 1963; MANN, 1964) following a general trend for development to proceed in a cephalocaudal direction. This relative maturity of the eye is seen in area-to-weight comparisons between the adult and newborn for the eye and for the body; the approximate adult-newborn ratios are 1.8:1 for the eye and 21:1 for the whole body (MANN, 1964).

The rest of this section reviews research concerning visual sensory competence of the human newborn. Related nonhuman research is also included. Anatomical, neurophysiologic, and behavioral evidence is adduced to make inferences about the functional integrity of specific systems involved in visual processing. The order of discussion of these systems corresponds roughly to the direction of the light path, and to the sequence of activity that light gives rise to. Reports of integrated functioning in discrimination studies are then discussed. The general conclusion of this section is that, although significant postnatal development occurs, the newborn visual system is surprisingly mature, the evidence suggesting that all aspects of the primary visual pathways are functional, visual acuity is good, eye movements are for the most part coordinated, and at least some pattern perception is present.

1. Pupillary Activity

Although DUKE-ELDER and COOK (1963) hold that the dilatory muscle of the iris is not functional at birth, (p. 305) there is broad agreement that the pupillary reflex, though sluggish, is present and adaptable to the level of light intensity even in premature infants (BEASLEY, 1933b; GENZMER, 1882; GUERNSEY, 1929; KRONER, 1881; KUSSMAUL, 1859; SHERMAN et al., 1936). Some of the disagreement may reflect difficulty in studying newborns over a wide variation of light conditions, because they tend to close their eyes even under mild illumination (HAITH, 1968; KESSEN and HERSHENSON, 1963). However, infrared television now permits recording of visual behavior even in absolute darkness (HAITH, 1969) and has provided unmistakable evidence of substantial pupillary constriction in light and dilation in darkness.

2. The Lens

Little work has been carried out on newborns' ability to accommodate adaptively, and the existing data are not totally consistent. On the one hand, FANTZ et al. (1962) studied visual orientation in newborns to various grating patterns which were paired with a homogeneous pattern. Preference relations did not vary over distances of 5, 10, and 20 in. suggesting that the newborn may be able to accommodate to stimuli presented at varying distances. However, HAYNES et al. (1965), studied accommodation by dynamic retinoscopy, and concluded just the opposite—the newborn is not capable of variable accommodation. The lens appeared to be fixed at a median accommodative distance (across subjects) of about 19 cm and gradually became increasingly more adaptable over the first four months of life. Figure 1 displays the error of accommodation as a function of target distance for infants from birth to four months of age. The figure indicates that the error of accommodation was closely related to the distance of the object from an optimal position for the youngest infants. For the oldest infants, error of accommodation did not vary with object distance. Evidence was offered that the newborn lens is capable of some variation; accommodative distance during wakefulness was different from that during sleep.

HERSHENSON (1967) questioned the HAYNES et al. data on the basis that the object for fixation may have been insufficiently attractive to produce radial tracking in the younger infants. An additional problem is that accommodative readings can be taken only when the eye is still; newborns normally move their eyes at least twice per second when they are in an alert state (HAITH, 1968). The readings may have been made when the younger infants were in a momentary open-eyed trance and, therefore, not actively fixating. However, it is difficult by either of these interpretations to account for the developmental regularity in the HAYNES et al. findings.

Even if the data do reflect accommodative fixity, the newborn can attain a focused retinal image for stimuli presented at one particular distance. The minimal separable angle at this distance has been estimated at from 7.5′ to 40′ based on the optokinetic response and visual orienting (DAYTON et al., 1964a; FANTZ et al., 1962; GORMAN et al., 1957). These figures correspond to visual acuity of 20/150 to 20/800, or a discrimination of a line separation of 1/60 in. to 1/12 in. at a distance of $7^1/_2$ in. Closer or farther stimuli would become increasingly more defocused as the distance from the ideal focal plane increases, but as stimuli are placed successively farther in front of or behind this plane, they would not suddenly "vanish" for the newborn, as has been frequently assumed.

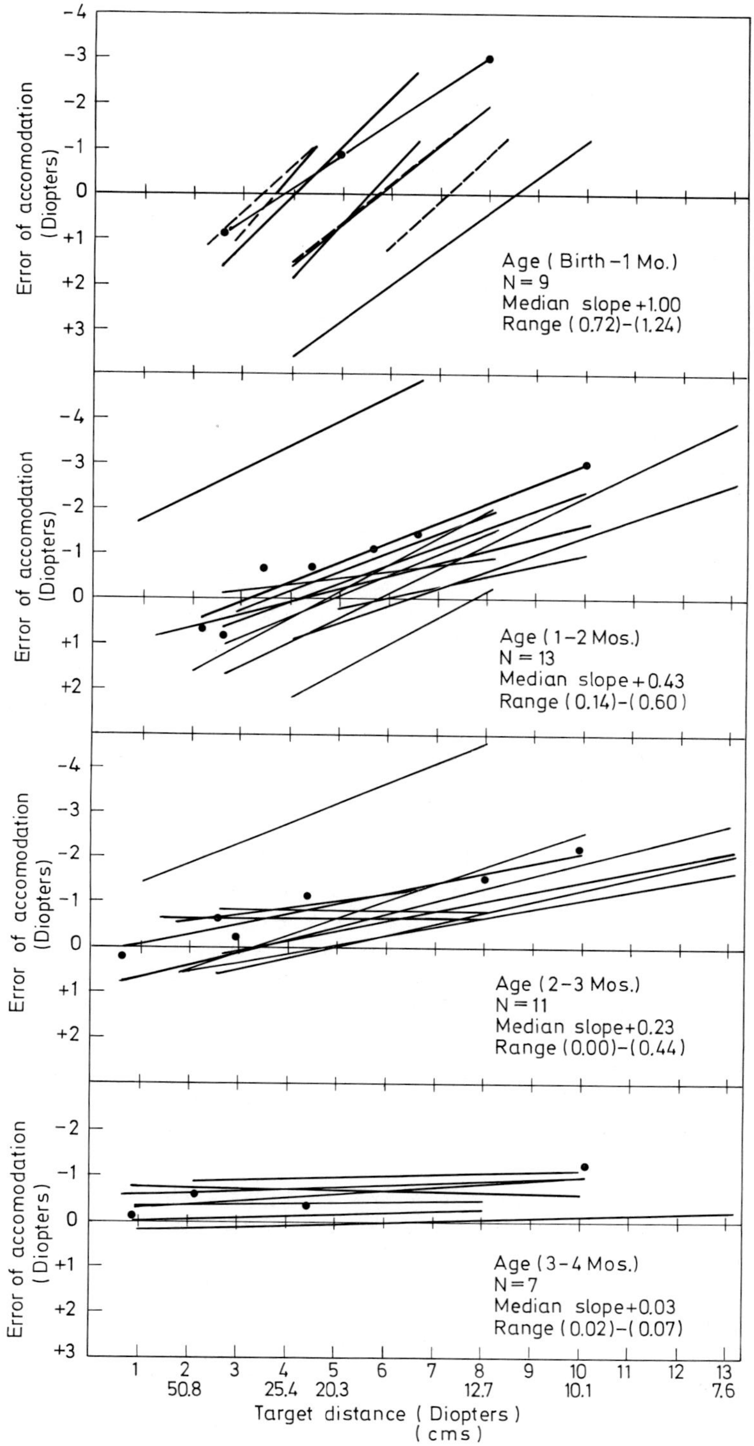

Fig. 1. Change with age in error of accommodation as target distance varies. Decrease in slope with age indicates more adaptive lens adjustment for varying distance for older infants. (From HAYNES et al., 1965, p. 528. Copyright 1965 by the American Association for the Advancement of Science)

3. The Retina

There is substantial disagreement and inconsistency about some aspects of the newborn retina. Traditionally, the foveal area has been thought to be nonfunctional. However, recent research on monkeys and man has cast doubt on this assumption.

Relative agreement exists on the state of peripheral and paramacular regions (DUKE-ELDER and COOK, 1963; MANN, 1964). The rods and cones are differentiated, and their outer segments discernible. The shape of the newborn's rod cells is similar to that of the adult's, whereas the cones are much stubbier. Less agreement is found for the macular area. Authoritative references in the field of retinal embryology maintain that the macular region is more developed than the peripheral regions through the first trimester of fetal life (DUKE-ELDER and COOK, 1963). After that period, the peripheral regions of the retina develop more rapidly and reach a fairly complete stage of development by birth. The macular region, however, is believed to continue developing through at least the first four months of postnatal life (DUKE-ELDER and COOK, 1963; MANN, 1964). These sources hold that, at birth, the ganglion cells, approximately one layer thick, and bipolar cells, approximately four layers thick, have not yet been displaced from in front of the macular area and, thus, still lie in the path of light. Only one cone-nucleus layer is held to exist at birth and "the cones themselves are short and ill-developed, a circumstance which helps to explain the absence of fixation at birth" (DUKE-ELDER and COOK, 1963). MANN concurs that the cone nuclei form a single row at the center of the fovea "but have increased to two and sometimes three rows at the periphery of the macula. The cones themselves do not yet appear any longer than their fellows in the paracentral regions. This arrangement demonstrates the anatomical reason for the well-known clinical fact that the power of central fixation is not present at birth" (MANN, 1964, p. 115).

Early research on retinal voltage changes to light stimulation, using the technique of electroretinography (ERG), confirmed the idea that the newborn macula was nonfunctional (ZETTERSTRÖM, 1951, 1955). In the mature human, flashes of white light normally produce a short-latency, negative *a*-wave followed by a longer-latency, positive *b*-wave. The *a*-wave is related to photopic vision, mediated by cones, whereas the *b*-wave is related to scotopic vision, mediated by rods. Newborn ERG's were characterized by the existence of only the scotopic *b*-wave and absence of a photopic *a*-wave (ZETTERSTRÖM, 1951, 1955). DUKE-ELDER and COOK (1963) place great emphasis on this deficit in newborns, relating it to macular immaturity. From these arguments the newborn visual system has been widely assumed to be substantially immature, or certainly limited (e.g., BRONSON, 1974).

An examination of the data from which MANN makes her inferences raises doubts about its validity; apparently, many of DUKE-ELDER and COOK's comments depend on the same data base. The histologic evidence for the assumptions about retinal development can be traced back to BACH and SEEFELDER (1911–1914). Their work, in turn, was based on a few newborn babies who died for unknown reasons. There is thus no assurance that these babies developed normally; development may very well have been retarded thereby yielding an impression that the retina is less developed at birth than it really is.

Ordy et al. (1975) carried out a remarkable study of retinal development in rhesus monkeys from birth, using the techniques of electroretinography, fundus photography, histology, electron microscopy, and behavioral tests for visual acuity. Anatomically, the rhesus visual system is quite similar to man's and has comparable resolution and electrophysiologic characteristics. The macula of newborn rhesus retinas showed clear evidence of advanced thinning of the ganglion and bipolar layers and several layers of cone nuclei rather than only one as reported for the human by Mann and Duke-Elder and Cook. Although the outer segments of rods and cones were held to be the last elements to differentiate sometime after birth (Mann, 1964), electron microscopy revealed well differentiated inner and outer rod and cone segments, and well developed lamellar bimembraneous folding sacs.

Histological examination of the postnatal maturational changes in the retina [of rhesus] revealed advanced development of the cones, rods, their inner and outer segments, separation of the internal and external granular layers, as well as a foveal depression, at birth (p. 685).

Consequently, it seems most likely that in newborn primates, in addition to various postnatal changes in the dioptrical image-forming mechanisms... the most directly relevant changes for postnatal increases in visual acuity and spectral sensitivity at the retinal level may be related more directly to fixed changes in visual pigment concentration in the outer segments (p. 684).

Of course, these data could be challenged as not definitive for inferences about the human. However, the newborn monkey's stage of visual development is similar to that of the human newborn; acuity lies in the same range as determined by the same techniques used with human newborns, the ERG and visual evoked response (VER) are similar and the retinal cone cells are described as stubby but differentiated. Judging from a wide variety of measures of visual function such as the ERG (Horsten and Winkelman, 1962, 1964; Ordy et al., 1965), visual evoked response (Ellingson, 1964), single-cell electrophysiology (Wiesel and Hubel, 1974), eye opening (Rose and Ellingson, 1970), retinal development (Horsten and Winkelman, 1962, 1964; Ordy et al., 1965), and date of cell birth of presumptive cortical cells (Rakic, 1974), visual system maturity at birth in mammals increases with phylogenetic complexity. Thus, if anything, the rhesus retina should be less well developed at birth than the human retina.

These inferences are strengthened by research with newborn humans. Horsten and Winkelman (1964) reported a limited amount of histologic data on the newborn human retina. Even though the reason for infant death was not given, again leaving open the possibility that the specimens were taken from babies who did not develop normally, Horsten and Winkelman also found several cone cell layers at the macula, in accord with Ordy et al. Thus, it seems likely that the data used by Mann, for whatever reason, are not completely dependable.

The electrophysiologic findings which appeared to support Mann's thesis have also been challenged. Horsten and Winkelman (1962, 1964) reported the presence of both the *a*-wave and the *b*-wave of the ERG in the human newborn through the use of brighter light flashes than used by Zetterström, and also of dark adaptation. Additionally, the x-wave component of the ERG, a response to colored light, mediated only by the photopic system, has been demonstrated in newborns (BARNET et al., 1965). Additional evidence of cone functioning is offered by data on photic following at rates of up to 72 flashes per second (HORSTEN and WINKELMAN, 1964), thought to be too fast for scotopic vision. Thus, there is good reason to believe that photopic vision is functional at birth at least to some degree. Since cone cells do exist outside the macular region, these data do not necessarily indicate macular functioning. On the other hand, there is no convincing indication that the fovea is nonfunctional; to infer this, simply because postnatal development of the foveal area is greater than for the peripheral area, is clearly indefensible (HORSTEN and WINKELMAN, 1964).

Since development of the visual system proceeds from inside out with the end organs the last to develop (DUKE-ELDER and COOK, 1963), evidence of some maturity of all components of the retina suggest that components further along the line should also be fairly well developed. The physiologic data support this interpretation. In the kitten, for example, before the eyes normally open and the VER can be obtained from retinal stimulation, thalamocortical activity can be detected through direct stimulation of the optical pathways (PURPURA, 1971).

4. The Retino-Geniculate and Thalamocortical Pathways

Little evidence regarding functioning of pathways from retina to cortex exists except by inference from cortical activity to be discussed below. Embryologically, the ganglion cells grow from the retina toward the thalamus, but myelination proceeds in the opposite direction. The fibers of the optic tract, from geniculate to optic chiasma, are fully myelinated at birth (DUKE-ELDER and COOK, 1963, pp. 118–119).

The lateral geniculate body is the first of the thalamic nuclei to appear, the laminae becoming evident at six months gestational age (DUKE-ELDER and COOK, 1963). Although the fiber tracts are established at birth the optic radiations are not fully myelinated. Myelination proceeds centrifugally and is reported by DUKE-ELDER and COOK not to be complete until the fourth month after birth. However, CONEL (1939) reported evidence of some myelination just below the sixth lamina of the visual cortex at birth.

5. The Striate Cortex

Anatomical, electrophysiologic, and behavioral evidence indicate that the newborn visual cortex is functional at birth. The target first-order projection sites of geniculostriate fibers in primates are cortical layers IVa, IVb, and IVc (HUBEL and WIESEL, 1968). Embryologically, these layers are formed quite early.

In an elegant study, RAKIC (1974) used radioactive tagging of brain cells to determine when cells of various cortical strata arise in the rhesus monkey.

He demonstrated that cells which later constitute the deeper layers of the neocortex arise earlier prenatally than those which will form the more superficial layers. The deposition of cells in all layers of the rhesus monkey visual cortex was virtually completed by about two months before birth. In the rodent and kitten, neurogenesis and deposition of neurons in cortical layers often is not completed until much later, sometimes not until after birth.

The VER provides another line of evidence in support of cortical integrity of the newborn. Studies of the VER in humans have established that all principal electrophysiologic components are present at birth (ELLINGSON, 1964). Monkeys, kittens, and rabbits, respectively, develop a full VER somewhat later (ELLINGSON, 1964). ROSE and LINDSLEY (1968) have presented strong evidence suggesting that two components of the early VER reflect cortical activity arising from afferents in two different pathways. In kittens, a long-latency negative component appears in the first 10–12 days (ELLINGSON, 1964; ROSE and ELLINGSON, 1970). This wave, which is relatively diffusely distributed cortically, probably reflects the stimulation of afferents arising from the superior colliculus and terminating in dendrites in the superficial layers of the cortex (ANOHKIN, 1961; PURPURA, 1971; ROSE and LINDSLEY, 1968; SCHEIBEL and SCHEIBEL, 1961; SCHEIBEL, 1962). ANOHKIN (1961) has argued that this long-latency negative wave is phylogenetically older, and matures earlier, than other components of the VER.

A second, later-appearing component, has been associated with the thalamocortical pathways. This negative-positive short-latency wave appears in the kitten at around 14 days, is more specific, and is thought to be phylogenetically more recent. PURPURA (1971) and ANOHKIN (1961) point out that the development of axosomatic synapses in the deeper layers of the cortex precede the appearance of this component and suggest that the VER positivity reflects the activity of these axosomatic synapses. SCHEIBEL and SCHEIBEL (1961) and SCHEIBEL (1962) emphasize the development of these connections in layer IV, the layer receiving specific thalamocortical afferent impulses, as being responsible for the short-latency, negative-positive component. ROSE and LINDSLEY (1968) corroborated the interpretations of a thalamocortical basis for the short-latency component and collicular basis for the long-latency component by eliminating selectively each VER component through lesioning of the geniculostriate and retinotectal paths in rats.

Behavioral evidence provides still a third line of support for cortical functioning. ROSE and ELLINGSON (1970) described the relation between the development of behavior and physiologic and anatomical data in the kitten:

> Initially, when apical axodendritic connections are developing, only a long-latency negative wave is present, and there is no visual behavioral activity in the kitten; the eyes first open at 10 to 12 days of age. During the second 10 days, when the basilar dendrites and axosomatic connections mature and the shorter latency positive-negative component develops, the kitten manifests initial following (at 14 days—approximately 2 to 4 days after the eyes open). Between 9 and 15 days, electrocortical sensory arousal first appears (p. 429).

By ROSE and ELLINGSON's argument, since the VER in the human at birth contains both the short-latency, positive-negative component, and the longer-latency negative component, electrocortical sensory arousal and visual following should also be observable. They are (BARTON et al., 1971; BLANTON, 1917; DAYTON et al., 1964b; ELLINGSON, 1964; HAITH, 1966). Compared to the kitten, the newborn human's visual apparatus seems quite sophisticated. If considerations regarding the anatomical and physiologic underpinnings of the VER are correct, and these same considerations apply to humans,[2] then the widely accepted notion that the newborn is totally decorticate is puzzling indeed. RAKIC's data on early neurogenesis of cortical cell components in primates, CONEL's classic studies, and the electrophysiologic and behavioral data all indicate at least some cortical activity at birth.

Given that there is cortical activity, at a minimum, the primary receptive sites of geniculate fibers in layer IV of the visual cortex should be operative. CONEL (1939) reported poor development of cells in areas 18 and 19, so it is unlikely that areas outside of 17 are functional. Although the status of visual analyzers at birth is an open question, primate cells in layer IV of area 17 are typically simple cells (HUBEL and WIESEL, 1968).

HUBEL and WIESEL (1963) studied kittens at 8, 16, 19, and 20 days using single unit recording techniques in area 17, and found responses comparable to adult cat recordings. Simple- and complex-cell activity was obtained in these kittens but with two major deviations from adult recordings. Newborn cells were more tolerant of rotation of bar slits and edges off the optimal axis, and the general response of cells was much less brisk and more fatiguable than in the adult cat. However, eye dominance patterns, the columnar organization of receptive fields, motion selectivity, and binocular receptivity of cells were all found to be similar to that of the adult. BARLOW and PETTIGREW (1971) and PETTIGREW (1974) also recorded single-unit responses in visually inexperienced kittens in the first week of life, and confirmed the motion-direction selectivity and binocular responsivity of single cells. However, selectivity for line orientation was much more diffuse than HUBEL and WIESEL reported, as was selectivity for binocular disparity. WIESEL and HUBEL (1974) recently reported a study of single cells in the visual cortex of newborn rhesus monkeys. They found adult-like columnar organization of eye dominance and orientation patterns, and cell responsiveness which was much more brisk than that recorded in newborn kittens. Given the greater maturity of the human newborn visual system than the kitten's or primate's at birth, it is reasonable to assume that at least simple cells are operative at birth in the human.

To summarize, there is reason to believe that anatomical and physiologic components of the visual system necessary for activity of at least simple cells

[2] Aside from the difficulty of generalizing across species, there is noncordance in some aspects of the features of the long-latency component in newborn kittens and humans which suggest caution. The principle difference is that the later component, in the kitten, is recordable outside the region of the scalp over the visual cortex suggesting a diffuse collicular projection system. However, in human newborns, the late component is recordable only over the occipital cortex, which could be interpreted as indicating a different neurophysiologic basis. It is more likely that the late component reflects the operation of a diffuse collicular projection system for the newborn baby, as for the kitten, but that cortical areas outside area 17 have not attained sufficient maturity to produce a synchronized recordable response. Since studies on premature human newborns have revealed an earlier onset of the long-latency negative component as is the case for the kitten, it seems reasonable to assume comparable neurologic underpinnings of these components.

in the visual cortex—rods and cones, the lateral geniculate body, cells in layer IV of the visual cortex—are functionally adequate at some level in the normal human newborn.

6. Other Pathways

Much less can be deduced about the other major visual pathways which make use of the superior colliculus, the pulvinar, and diffuse projections to the cortex. The presence of the late component of the VER even in premature humans suggests that at least some aspects of this projection are functional.

II. Visual Discrimination, Acuity, and Convergence

Studies of integrated visual functioning in the newborn provide evidence in accord with the neurophysiologic work. Substantial sensory and discriminatory capacity is indicated as well as considerable oculomotor capability.

Reports suggest that the newborn discriminates varying light intensities (HERSHENSON, 1964), can detect minimal separable angles of 7.5′ (DAYTON et al., 1964a; estimates vary from 7.5′ to 40′), is sensitive to visual movement (BEASLEY, 1933a; BLANTON, 1917; HAITH, 1966; TAUBER and KOFFLER, 1966; WICKELGREN, 1969), and will track a moving stimulus, although somewhat jerkily (DAYTON et al., 1964b).

The ability of young infants to discriminate color has been studied by several investigators (e.g., CHASE, 1937; PRATT et al., 1930; SPEARS, 1964; STAPLES, 1931, 1932; STIRNIMANN, 1944; VALENTINE, 1913–1914). Unfortunately, it has not been possible to insure that intensity levels of different hues were equivalent for the infant even when intensities of different hues were matched for the adult eye, because the infant's corneal, intraocular (fluid and lens), and receptive structures may differ from the adult's in spectral transmissivity and reception characteristics. BORNSTEIN (1975) has developed a procedure which capitalizes on infant preference for colors which fall squarely within adult-judged pure-color boundaries over those located between boundaries; it would be difficult to attribute this preference across the color spectrum to specific intensity differences. Unfortunately, no infants under four months of age have yet been tested.

The literature is no clearer on very early form perception. FANTZ (1963) showed quite early that newborns will look at nonhomogeneous fields more than homogeneous ones; but little more can be said than that even now. Every other study that has shown differential responsiveness to form is subject to a frustrating range of alternative interpretations; discrimination of the forms may have been based, as intended, on the whole form; or on only one of a large number of possible elements which differentiate the forms (HAITH, 1968; KESSEN and HERSHENSON, 1963; SALAPATEK and KESSEN, 1966); or on contour density (KARMEL, 1969b; MCCALL and KAGAN, 1967; MCCALL and MELSON, 1970; SALAPATEK, 1973). Unfortunately, these problems of interpretation also hold for most of the work done with infants at older ages. Thus, it is possible to conclude that newborns respond to light, differential light intensities, movement, inhomogeneity in the visual field and perhaps some, presently unspecifiable, elements of form, and possibly color. On the basis of current knowledge, there is no reason to assume that newborns perceive forms wholistically.

The data on development of the ability of the newborn to converge the two eyes on a single object are not clear. DUKE-ELDER and COOK maintain that "...initially the movements of the eyes are independent, irregular and nonconjugated...conjugate fixation does not become accurate until the age of six months by which time convergence is firmly established..." (p. 305). It is not clear what the data bases for these observations were. However, DAYTON et al. (1964b), using electrooculography, showed that the large majority of eye movements are indeed conjugate; and ASLIN and SALAPATEK (1973) confirmed these observations with one- and two-month-olds. However, it is not logically necessary that, because the eyes move together, they converge on the same point in space. On the basis of a small sample of data, HERSHENSON (1964) concluded that convergence is the rule in newborns. On a larger sample of data, however, WICKELGREN (1967, 1969) concluded that deconvergence was the rule. The problem is a difficult one, because a discrepancy between the visual axes of the two eyes of only 10′ or so typically prevents fusion, and current methods for determining fixation location in infants are not capable of even approaching that degree of precision. It is unlikely that sustained convergence is present at birth, but at what age it does occur, and whether the newborn experiences double images, suppresses one image, or alternates images will probably not be determined for some time.

III. Visual Preference and Attention: One Conception of Visual Activity in Early Infancy

The preceding section established the fact of considerable sensory competence in the newborn. This section concerns attempts by researchers to arrive at a conceptualization of how this competence is used—how the infant employs his perceptual capacity to learn about his visual world, and by what mechanisms perceptual growth occurs. Virtually all of the extant conceptualizations may be cast into a preference model of visual behavior. I conclude this section by arguing that these conceptions have been shaped less by consideration of what the infant is up to, than by the available research methodologies. In brief, the prevalent use of a preference methodology has resulted in a conception of the infant as a preference creature. In the section following this, I outline an alternative conception.

BERLYNE (1960) captured the rising interest of psychologists in human and nonhuman activities that could not be easily subsumed under the traditional rubric of learning theory. Among other topics, BERLYNE reviewed research on attention, orientation, curiosity, search, and arousal which could be roughly categorized as important in the *acquisition* of information about the environment rather than in *reaction* to it. Whether because of BERLYNE's book, or the Zeitgeist it captured, the implications of this theme could hardly be lost on researchers who were familiar with the behavior of the young immobile infant. The young infant spends many hours each day looking about, while the older mobile infant's total existence, virtually, apart from eating and sleeping, is spent in exploratory activity—looking, grasping, mouthing, and manipulating.

FANTZ's reintroduction of a paradigm (1956, 1958, 1961), first used by STIRNIMANN (1944), for studying visual attention was welcomed by investigators who needed a method to exploit BERLYNE's message in work with infants even as young as the newborn. Typically, the infant is presented two stimulus patterns side by side, and the frequency and duration of fixation of each is recorded by an observer. The observer indicates that one of the stimuli is fixated when the corneal reflection of that stimulus is judged to be near the center of the pupil. The stimulus the infant views first, the greatest number of times, or longest, is said to be preferred or selectively attended in that particular two-stimulus set. A variant of this procedure employs stimuli presented singly, in sequence; relative "preference" is then determined by how long each stimulus is fixated in comparison to all stimuli in the set. This paradigm, surprisingly powerful, straightforward, and adaptable for research with infants at any age, has profoundly affected research and thinking. Whereas the dominant concern in infant visual research had been what the infant could see, it was now directed toward the question of what the infant chose to look at.

Early work was not theoretically motivated, and resists easy summary, except that it served to establish that the newborn looks at patterned surface in preference to homogeneous surfaces (FANTZ, 1958, 1961, 1963, 1965). Although the search for which dimensions and forms maximize attention in the infant has been the dominant theme, this paradigm has also been employed to explore a broad range of questions about newborn and older infant vision—questions about habituation of attention (see JEFFREY and COHEN, 1971; KESSEN et al., 1970, for review), depth perception (FANTZ, 1966, 1967; JONES-MOLFESE, 1972), size constancy (MCKENZIE and DAY, 1972), perception of motion (SILFEN and AMES, 1964), visual memory (COHEN and GELBER, 1975; FAGAN, 1970), object orientation (MCGURK, 1970), and discrimination (SAAYMAN et al., 1964).

However, this section will be concerned with the conceptualizations which have guided research on visual attention and preference. Although some of the conceptual work has been based on research with older infants, sharp age distinctions have typically not been made; and, by extrapolation, it has been used to account for newborn visual activity also. Three basic theoretical schemes have been put forth to account for visual attention or preference and perceptual development in early infancy: species-specific sign stimuli, complexity/contour density, and discrepancy.

1. Species-Specific Sign Stimuli

It could be argued that, through evolution, selection pressures have favored organisms who attend to adaptively significant environmental features. The face would be an obvious candidate for such a role (FANTZ, 1961; GIBSON,

1969), and was at one time held to be favored by the newborn. However, research on infants under five months of age has produced contradictory results (HAAF and BELL, 1967; WILCOX, 1969; see BOND, 1972, and GIBSON, 1969 for reviews); the earlier-reported findings of face preference in young infants can probably be explained in terms of preference for more definable structural aspects of the face, such as symmetry or complexity. It should be noted that with few exceptions (CARPENTER et al., 1970; CARPENTER, 1974; SPITZ and WOLF, 1946), investigators have not used real 3-dimensional faces; rather, the baby has typically been presented with 2-dimensional schematic drawings, photographs, or 3-D clay models (e.g., BOND, 1972; CARON et al., 1973; GIBSON, 1969; KAGAN, 1971). However, when babies are given the opportunity to scan their mother's real face, significant scanning of the face does not occur until seven weeks of age (BERGMAN et al., 1971).

There are several reports of attention by newborns to particular levels of stimulus dimensions which could be thought of in terms of their adaptive significance, including attention to movement (HAITH, 1966; HAITH et al., 1969; SILFEN and AMES, 1964), to intermediate levels of brightness (HERSHENSON, 1964) to particular colors (STIRNIMANN, 1944) (but see problems discussed earlier regarding color perception), and to curvilinear contours after two months of age (FANTZ, 1958, 1967; FANTZ and NEVIS, 1967). However, researchers responsible for these findings have not emphasized the ethological framework, perhaps because the specific adaptive importance of some of the preferences is difficult to justify.

One thing we know for sure is that infants do change and develop perceptually. Yet, ethologically oriented work suggests no mechanism by which such change occurs. The fixity of preference implied by the sign stimulus notion also seems questionable in light of recent work on the neurophysiologic and behavioral demonstrations of plasticity of visual perception in mammals (BARLOW et al., 1972; GANZ, 1974; GOLDMAN, 1975). For example, visual cortical cells of kittens raised in a vertical or horizontally striped environment respond almost exclusively to a stimulus orientation similar to their rearing condition; in contrast, cortical cells in kittens normally raised respond equally well to stimulus orientation all axes (BLAKEMORE and COOPER, 1970; HIRSCH and SPINELLI, 1970). This effect can be demonstrated even when the vertical-horizontal manipulation is carried out in the two eyes of the same animal (HIRSCH and SPINELLI, 1970). Additionally, cortical receptive fields can be produced through altered experience, which are never seen in nature (e.g., PETTIGREW and FREEMAN, 1973). Recent reports have established that plasticity in receptive fields of humans may also be affected by early visual experience (ANNIS and FROST, 1973; FREEMAN et al., 1972; FREEMAN and THIBOS, 1973).

Of course, the alterability of perceptual mechanisms does not necessarily imply a perceptual tabula rasa at birth; however, any theoretical mechanisms put forth to account for early perceptual biases must also provide for change with experience. Provisions that have been built into traditional ethological theory for establishment of preferences have a "one-shot" character (e.g., in the case of imprinting) which does not fit with the more gradually occurring neurologic and behavioral changes that have been reported.

2. Visual Complexity and Contour Density

Several studies followed the suggestion of DEMBER and EARL (1957) and BERLYNE (1960) that attentional preference of organisms for stimuli depends on the relations between the informational complexity of the stimulus and the processing capabilities of the organism. Complexity is variously defined in terms of number of stimulus elements, number of angles, number of non-redundant elements, and so on, all of which refer to the degree of unpredictability in a form or a stimulus set (BERLYNE, 1960; HAITH et al., 1969; HERSHENSON et al., 1965). This conception assumes that the infant enters the world with a certain stimulus-processing capability. This organismic level determines the level of complexity he prefers; presumably he prefers a level that is just beyond his current processing capabilities which he then "processes" until that level can be managed. Increments in the complexity of the individual are a result of interaction with "pacer" stimuli. Each increment further increases the informational level or stimulus complexity that the subject can manage. In contrast to the ethological approach, this approach is clearly concerned with perceptual growth.

Some investigators have found evidence of stimulus preference which correlates with their interpretation of complexity (BERLYNE, 1958; BRENNAN et al., 1966; COHEN, 1969; GREENBERG and O'DONNELL, 1972; HERSHENSON, 1964; HERSHENSON et al., 1965; THOMAS, 1965) and others have even found preference for increasing complexity with age (BRENNAN et al., 1966). But, on the whole, the concept of complexity has not been fruitful. Definitions of complexity differ strikingly from one study to the next (see KESSEN et al., 1970, for a complete discussion), and physical parameters such as area of the figure, length of contour, angularity, and brightness have sometimes been hopelessly confounded with manipulations of "complexity" (KARMEL, 1969a, b; MCCALL and KAGAN, 1967; MCCALL and MELSON, 1970). A study by HAITH et al. (1969) manipulated only predictability—an agreed-upon interpretation of complexity—of a sequence of events, while rigorously controlling all other factors. A response-complexity function was found which was precisely opposite to prediction; least "attention" was elicited by the intermediate level of complexity.

An untangling of the factors involved in typical variations of "Complexity" indicates that contour density, defined as the ratio of the "...sum of the lengths of all black-white transitions" to the area (KARMEL, 1973, p. 3), seems to account best for infant preferences and their change with age. KARMEL (1969b) presented 13- and 20-week-old infants with regular and irregular checkerboards of four different densities within each category. Attentional preferences were orderable on the density dimension, but not on the regularity, or complexity, dimension. KARMEL found that his own data and those of other investigators (BRENNAN et al., 1966; HERSHENSON, 1964) could be organized by assuming that preference is an inverted-U function of the square root of contour density, with peak preference occurring at increasing density levels with increasing age. Data collected since 1969 have also been incorporated into this scheme (COHEN, 1972; GREENBERG and O'DONNEL, 1972; KARMEL, 1974; KARMEL and MAISEL,

1975). KARMEL accounts for increasing preferences by positing a decrease with age in receptive field size; elements of high density displays fall below the receptive-field sizes of retinal receptors in younger infants, and are not detected. In short, then, infants prefer the maximal detectable density. SALAPATEK has accepted this position and the potential power of its explanatory value, "... virtually all early pattern preferences may be explained as a preference by the infant for the pattern with the most contour density, given the pattern is a certain distance above his visual pattern-acuity threshold" (SALAPATEK, 1973, p. 23).

It should be pointed out that KARMEL feels his scheme holds clearly only for infants older than six weeks of age (KARMEL and MAISEL, 1975), so the applicability of the contour density dimension as KARMEL defines it (i.e., in terms of the whole stimulus rather than in terms of local regions) to newborn looking may be limited. However, I will argue later that local contour density plays a major role in newborn scanning.

3. Discrepancy

Still a third position, whose main proponent is KAGAN (1970a, b), emphasizes discrepancy as the key dimension controlling infant attention beyond two months of age. This approach agrees with the premise of complexity theory that the current psychological status of the infant is important, but the operative dimension is held to be the degree of psychological discrepancy of the input from one of the infant's stored schemas rather than the distance along a physical dimension. Presumably, the infant, through experience with systematic inputs, develops representations or schemas of these inputs. Current stimuli attract the infant to the extent that they optimally engage him in attempts to fit the input to a familiar schema. If the input is too familiar, it will quickly be fitted into the schema, and then ignored. If it is too discrepant from any stored schema, then the infant will not attend. Thus, discrepancy theory predicts an inverted-U relation between amount of discrepancy of a stimulus from the stored schema and the infant's attention to it. KAGAN does not maintain that discrepancy becomes important for the infant until two months of age; before this time he emphasizes the attractiveness of color, contrast and movement, and accepts the operation of a "rule system" proposed by HAITH (1968).

A substantial set of studies on older infants appears to fit this characterization of infant attention (summarized in KAGAN, 1970a, b). However, as currently formulated, this conceptualization faces several difficulties. There are no set provisions for how a schema is established or why an infant shifts modes from the rule system operative at birth. The thesis that stimuli which can not be matched to schemas will be ignored poses a serious logical problem, because, by this principle, new schemas would never be developed. (In principle, newborns starting with no schemas would never develop any.) Also, there is no way to determine which schema an infant is using as his reference point to "assimilate" a new stimulus. Finally, even if the relevant schema were known and the infant did respond to the present stimulus in terms of some cognitive distance from it, no objective basis exists for determining the degree of discrepancy between that stimulus and the operative schema. WELCH (1974), who did not confirm the prediction of a curvilinear relation between looking time and the difference between an adapted and probe stimulus, accepted the idea that perhaps she did not sample points extreme enough on the discrepancy dimension. However, as she notes, "Such an argument unfortunately reveals a fundamental weakness of the discrepancy hypothesis...It is incapable of disproof" (p. 349). This is true, of course, for any model which predicts behavior to be a U-shaped function of an undefinable dimension. In a recent study, ZELAZO et al. (1974) used a procedure to establish a dimensional basis for discrepancy that may hold promise for dealing with this problem.

Other objections to discrepancy theory involve the analogy of the infant's cognitive system to a rigid pigeonhole categorizing operation. However, viewed as a whole, KAGAN's three-factor theory (at around eight months of age infants are held to enter a third phase in which attention is attracted to stimuli that elicit hypotheses) permits more developmental flexibility than either of the other two positions, and is alone in acknowledging that different principles may be operative at different times in the first year of life.

4. Comment

Early research treated the young infant as if he were a passive sensory surface, the principle concern being what dimensions of stimuli he could sense. Contemporary research in the attention-preference tradition acknowledges that the infant can control his sensory apparatus; even at birth he has the sensory-motor competence to select from among the available inputs. The question shifted from what visual dimensions a baby senses to what dimensions he prefers.

Although the more modern emphasis on attention and preference is held to reflect the active dynamic volitional character of infant perception, the accommodation of research and thinking has been more apparent than real. The guiding principle or principles of visual perception are still sought exclusively in the stimulus and the baby's experience with it. The world of the infant is portrayed as a multiple-choice set, and the infant as a whole-stimulus selector. Whether complexity, contour density or discrepancy is the dimension under study the baby, like Goldilocks, tries to find the alternative which is "just right." THOMAS (1973) captured the prevalent conceptualization in a recent remark "...the author has long believed that an understanding of the infant's responses to visual stimuli could best be approached through a theory of choice. Thus, the position taken here is that the baby's looking behavior belongs to a theory of preferential choice behavior" (p. 468). Thus, the modern accommodation has consisted of an appreciation that the infant is not perceptually "slaved" to the onset and offset of a single stimulus; he may choose to look at another stimulus or to look at nothing at all. However, in releasing him from single-stimulus bondage, the modern approach has only mildly increased his degrees of freedom.

The attention-preference paradigm has been a powerful tool for studying some aspects of visual discrimination, e.g., memory, sensory competence, and habituation in babies. But it has practical limitations for the exploration of perceptual activity, and these limitations have had conceptual consequences. The greatest practical limitation of the technique is lack of precision; one can only determine when the baby looks at stimulus A, stimulus B or neither. Given this limitation, concern with stimulus preference is understandable. But in their concern with preference, investigators have given scant consideration to what a baby is doing while he looks at a "preferred" stimulus, and no attention at all to the details of processing when he is looking at a nonpreferred stimulus (an important matter since there is often less than 10% looking time difference between the two and at times, less than 2% [Ruff and Birch, 1974]). To take the point a little further, consider a typical experiment in which stimulus B is nonpreferred in an A–B pairing, but preferred in a B–C pairing. The practice of considering the response to B as qualitatively different under these two conditions seems unreasonable.

A conceptual consequence of the limitation on precision is that investigators have assumed that the stimulus is "grasped" as a whole. Every major conceptualization of stimulus preference implicitly assumes that stimuli are seen wholistically. Only rarely do investigators appreciate that stimulus components, rather than the "stimulus" per se, may govern behavior. An important developmental difference in looking behavior has possibly been misinterpreted because of this assumption. The younger infant often "stares" longer at a single stimulus before looking away and frequently looks at only one member of a paired-stimulus array. The interpretation is that the infant under two months is "captured" by the stimulus, a victim of "obligatory attention", rather than being capable of "capturing" the stimulus as is the older infant (Ames and Silfen, 1965; Bond, 1972; Hershenson, 1967; Kessen et al., 1970; Salapatek, 1973; Stechler and Latz, 1966). One can ask what the stimulus is for the baby; if ach component of stimulus A is a "stimulus" for the young infant, then careful analysis of his visual activity might show that he is no more paralyzed than is a three-year-old first examining the crystal structure of one snowflake among many. The age discrepancy in viewing-time between younger and older infants makes sense if we do not assume, as many have, that the infant's visual behavior is as grossly organized as the methods used to measure it. In fact, infants under two months of age, including newborns, move their eyes virtually every half second when looking at relatively simple displays (Haith, 1968; Kessen et al., 1972; Salapatek, 1968, 1969, 1973; Salapatek and Kessen, 1966).

The key point is that the preference paradigm has been so useful for research that thinking about infant visual behavior has been implicitly conditioned; the paradigm has become a conceptual as well as a methodologic tool. The next section suggests an alternative conception.

B. An Alternative Conception of Visual Activity in Early Infancy

I. Introduction

The following sections discuss several "rules" that appear to guide visual activity in newborns. These rules are based on findings from studies to be described. The findings indicate that the prevalent conceptualization of the infant as a multiple-choice stimulus selector is artificial and inadequate. Before describing this research, I will elaborate the considerations leading to a rejection of the preference approach, and sketch out the rationale for and the form of a reconceptualization.

Apart from newborn sensory competence, there are several basic considerations that must be accommodated by any theory of visual behavior at birth. First, babies are born into a tremendously broad range of visual environments. It seems maladaptive for them to have a fixed set of visual preferences, but very adaptive for them to possess behavioral dispositions that bring them into contact with highly informative aspects of their visual world. In brief, the *form* of perceiving activity could be prespecified; but the *content* of perception, and the neurologic structure of the sensory system is probably malleable. Second, humans move their eyes very frequently under typical conditions. Estimates for frequency of adult eye movements typically range from three to four times a second. Newborns typically move their eyes at least twice each second. A conceptualization of visual perception in terms of preference simply does not deal with this "microprocessing" activity on the proper scale. Nor does the derivative conceptualization of serial habituation (JEFFREY, 1968), which appreciates the fact that stimuli may be treated by the baby in terms of subcomponents, but depends on habituation processes which require many seconds of interaction. "Preference" is really only a derivative of the extent of microprocessing activity, and a full understanding of visual behavior awaits a description and theory of this activity. Third, eye movement activity occurs whenever the organism is awake, independent of whether "preferred" stimuli are available or even, in the case of absolute darkness, when no stimuli are available. Fourth, ultimately, the most powerful theory will make neurologic sense. This is not to take a reductionist position, but to emphasize the point that the task is to describe a biological system that is an entity, no matter what different tools we, as scientists, use to understand it. Advances in the neurophysiology of vision in the last 15 years have been staggering, and we would be foolish to ignore the possibility of clues to an understanding of infant vision from this work.

These considerations guided the studies to be described. I have turned my attention away from the search for evidence of pretuning for particular stimulus dimensions, and have rejected a conceptualization which leans on the notion of preference and the discrete stimulus control it implies. I have looked, instead, for very general "rules" of visual behavior in the newborn, assuming that if such rules or regularities do exist, they would be adaptive in the sense of optimizing exposure to highly informative aspects of the visual world, and in providing necessary stimulation for the growth and shape of the visual system.

The result has been the formulation of a set of ordered rules that describe the visual behavior of the newborn in varying visual circumstances. These rules also make neurophysiologic sense, and appear to be derived from one basic principle: "Keep the firing rate of neurons in the visual cortex at a maximal level." (Actually, I assume that the function relating behavior and firing rate is asymptotic, so that firing beyond a certain level has no further behavioral effect.) Two eye-movement control routines implement this rule. The first routine is responsible for finding portions of the visual field, such as contours, which can be scanned with the eyes to increase firing rate, and is called the Ambient Scan Routine (ASR). The second is responsible for detailed inspection, and is called the Inspection Scan Routine (ISR); an example of the operation of the ISR is repeated edge crossing achieved by eye movements once the edge is located. The ASR is assumed to be constantly active, but suppressed to the degree that the ISR keeps firing rate high; thus, the baby might move his eye away from a visual location in which the ISR can produce high firing rates (and thereby locate an area of even higher firing-rate potential), but he would be less likely to do so than if he were scanning an area of low firing-rate potential. We shall see that this reconceptualization can handle virtually everything we know about visual scanning in newborns and, in addition, can account for the development of binocular convergence and accommodation. Further, it brings the work on newborn vision squarely into contact with recent neurophysiologic findings in nonhuman animals, and proposes that the content of visual perception and the structure of the neural receptive system may very well be shaped by experience much as it has been shown to be in deprivation research on young animals (GOLDMAN, 1976) and in "natural" experiments in humans (ANNIS and FROST, 1973; FREEMAN and THIBOS, 1973).

The results of several studies will now be described in the context of the rules that appear to be operative at birth for guiding visual search activity.

Rule 1. If awake and alert and light not too bright, open eyes. It seems obvious enough that the newborn must open his eyes to facilitate visual search. The appreciation of this fact impugns the popular idea that newborn visual activity is totally reflexive, by implying that he has at least some control over his visual experience. And there are some subleties. I demonstrated (HAITH, 1968) that newborns judge light levels through their eyelids by showing that offset of a moderately bright light produces instantaneous opening in an alert closed-eyed baby. By finding that eye-opening to sound depends on ambient light, KEARSLEY (1971) challenged the traditional report that sound produces an auropalpebral response or eye-clamping response in newborns (KESSEN et al., 1970; PRATT, 1954). KEARSLEY found that eye-widening in response to sound becomes increasingly more likely with decreasing ambient light levels.

Rule 2. If darkness is found, initiate an intensive controlled search (presumably for shadows or dimly illuminated objects).

Rule 3. If light is found, but no edges, engage in a broad, sometimes uncontrolled, search. Rules 2 and 3 were derived from two studies in which newborns were exposed to complete darkness and to homogeneous light fields while the image of their right eye was recorded by an infrared camera onto videotape. The recording procedure is shown in Figure 2. The baby lay supine on a padded holder with a restraining head rest. A vertically mounted T.V. camera, sur-

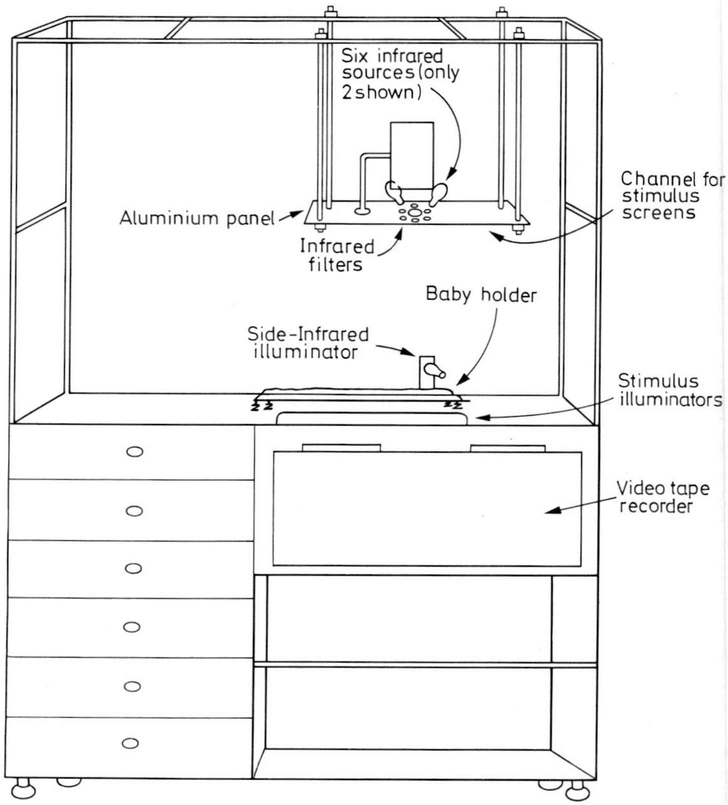

Fig. 2. Illustration of apparatus used in all studies reported. Infrared lights provide illumination for recording of image of the eye via Infrared TV Camera onto videotape. Stimulus Illuminators light Stimulus Screen above Baby Holder so that a baby, lying supine in the holder, only sees screen and stimulus spray painted on it. TV camera records through screen

rounded by infrared light sources, recorded the image of the right eye and the reflections of the light sources. A side illuminator enhanced pupil-iris contrast for later measurement of eye position. Finally, a screen painted either black or white and covering a visual field of $95° \times 95°$ was placed in channels just below the camera during the light conditions. The baby could see only the screen when the stimulus illuminators were on, and nothing behind the screen. When the stimulus illuminators were off the room was completely dark.

Figure 3 schematizes one stimulus-order condition in each study. In Study 1, darkness and light conditions were presented for 120 s each and occurred through gradual transitions to eliminate orienting responses. A black screen or a white screen was used during the light condition. In Study 2, only a white screen was used, transitions were abrupt or gradual, and alternating light and dark periods were 30 s in duration.

The differences between studies did not affect the findings of primary concern. Newborns opened their eyes widely in darkness and scanned actively. In comparison to the homogeneous light conditions, in darkness the newborn

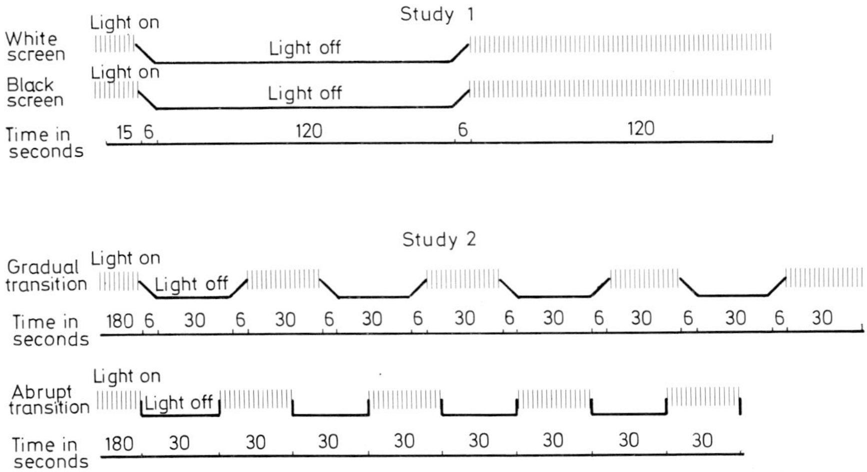

Fig. 3. Timing diagram for one sequence group in each condition of the light-dark studies

opened his eyes more widely, more frequently maintained eye control, made more smooth as opposed to jerky eye movements, and made more small eye movements. These findings were obtained by highly reliable judgments (89% or better perfect agreement for all scales) made from the videotape record. In addition, they replicated between studies, and were statistically stable. The data for the two studies are shown in Table 1 for the eye-opening, eye-control, eye-movement type, and eye-movement size measures, respectively.

Table 1. Eye activity measures in light and dark studies[a]

Measure	Category	Darkness		Light	
		Study 1	Study 2	Study 1	Study 2
Degree of eye-opening	1 	4	14	19	28
	2 	11	10	22	17
	3 	30	20	41	43
	4 	56	56	17	12
Degree of control	In-control	92	81	63	54
	Out-of-control	1	0	23	12
	Not observable	7	19	14	34
Type of movement	Jerky	40	19	70	50
	Smooth	29	60	10	31
	Drift	31	22	20	19
Size of movement	Small	57	81	50	58
	Large	21	12	32	30
	No movement	22	7	18	12

[a] Numbers indicate the % of 2.5 s periods assigned to each category.

Two findings deserve discussion. For the eye-opening measure, category 4 indicated eye opening to the point of strain with sclera frequently visible above and below the extreme upper and lower borders of the iris. Unexpectedly, babies earned many more category 4 judgments in darkness than in light. Greater eye opening in darkness was not simply attributable to an inverse relation between brightness level and degree of opening, because there were virtually no differences observed between subjects who were presented a black screen (0.07 Footlamberts) as opposed to a white screen (0.9 Footlamberts) in the light condition. This measure probably reflects qualitatively different activity in light and darkness.

The second unexpected result was the striking difference in visual control in light and dark. Out-of-control nystagmus newborn (repetitive alternation between fast jerk and slow drift eye-moment at the nasal or temporal edges of the eye socket) occurred in fewer than 1% of the judgments in dark whereas it occurred in 18–27% in light. This result is especially notable, because in neither condition did the newborn have anything to look at.

In addition to the repeatability of these findings in the two studies reported, the same observations in darkness (MENDELSON and HAITH, 1976) and in unpatterned light (KESSEN et al., 1972; SALAPATEK, 1968; SALAPATEK and KESSEN, 1966) have been replicated in several additional studies, so we may be confident of their stability. The general picture that emerges is that the alert newborn when placed in darkness engages in a vigilant, active, and controlled scan of his "visual field." This behavior might serve the function of optimizing detection of shadows of objects or subtle reflections from objects. When placed in light, the baby continues to scan, but in broader horizontal sweeps and, frequently, in an out-of-control fashion. In combination with findings which I shall report below, this behavior appears to reflect a search for contours, and extends so broadly along the horizontal axis that the eye reaches extreme positions where control is difficult. Since control is maintained in darkness, we may conclude that the newborn possesses an eye-movement system which can operate under endogenous control. In light, however, the scanning system appears to relinquish control, in part, to exogenous input. When there is nothing to scan, the eye may extend beyond boundaries in which control is possible.

Thus, the newborn possesses mechanisms to control scanning which enable him to find visual information. The discovery of active scanning in complete absence of light further dishonors the popular notion that the newborn is solely a reflex organism whose visual activity is stereotypically linked to light. It also points up a weakness in preference conceptualizations because they do not provide for ongoing visual behavior in the absence of stimuli.

Rule 4. If an edge is found, stay near the edge and attempt to cross it. KESSEN et al. (1972) presented vertical and horizontal edges formed by black and white hemi-fields to newborns. The vertical edge was highly attractive whether placed to the left or right of field center, as reflected both in average fixation location and in the number of times the edge region was crossed. However, the same babies who found the vertical edge so attractive behaved no differently when an above- or below-center horizontal edge was presented than they did when a blank field was presented.

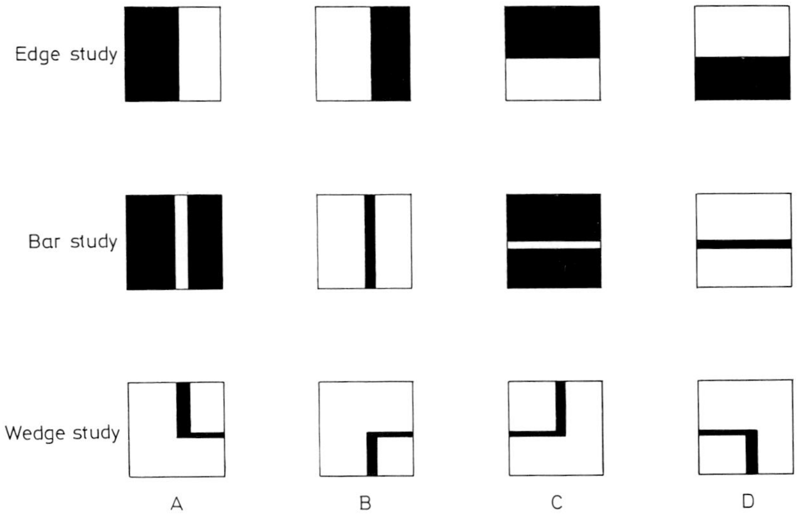

Fig. 4. Illustrations of edge, bar, and angle stimulus screens used. Subjects were presented either Stimuli *A* and *C* or *B* and *D* in each study

These results provided an important clue to the principle underlying scan activity in newborns. The most obvious, but probably wrong, interpretation emphasizes the fact that newborns uniformly show far greater mobility in horizontal eye movements than vertical eye movements. Since the edges were 17° above, below, right, or left of center, discovery of the vertical edges may have been more likely than discovery of the horizontal edges. This interpretation is discredited by the finding that virtually all babies crossed or fixated very near the horizontal edges at some time, but failed to stay near them.

The second interpretation, which is supported by data to be reported, is that babies *detected* all the edges but could not *cross* the horizontal edges easily because, at that distance from center, vertical mobility was especially limited. Because the edge was not crossable, they scanned elsewhere. One effect of crossing an edge should be increased cortical firing. Thus, if it could be demonstrated that the attractiveness of an edge were a function of its crossability, it would suggest that the baby's visual activity may be governed by his success at increasing cortical firing rate. This notion was tested further.

Newborns were shown edges in one study and bars in a second, as illustrated in the first two rows of Figure 4. Each baby saw a vertical and a horizontal stimulus for 60 s in alternation with 30 s blank control fields, but a particular baby saw only one field-brightness. The placement of the edges and the center of the bars coincided with the predicted (based on earlier data) resting location of the eye, presumably where horizontal as well as vertical eye-movement mobility would be greatest. Eye-movement records were obtained as in the light-dark studies, but precise fixation determinations were made each 0.5 s as illustrated in Figure 5 (see HAITH, 1969, for details). Video records were stored on a videodisc which "froze" the image of the eye and the reflected infrared dots.

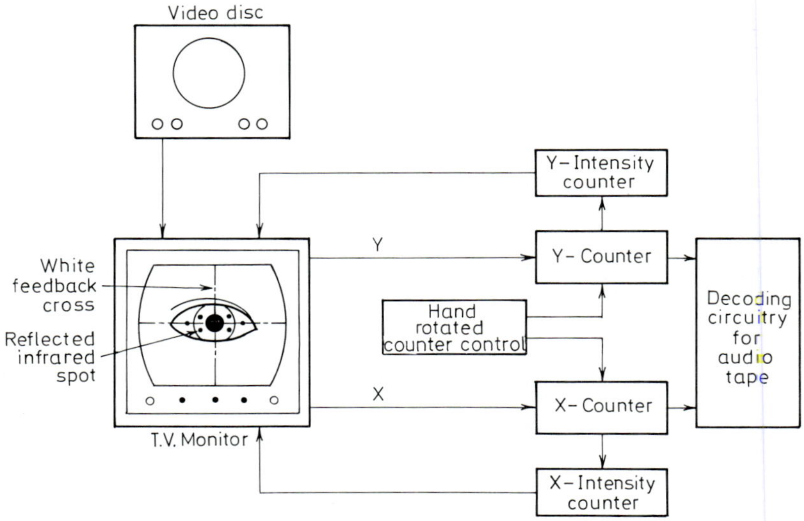

Fig. 5. Illustration of method for measuring eye location. Video Disk displayed a single video frame permitting measurement of Cartesian coordinate of pupil center and one Infrared Light Spot from which fixation position could be determined. Hand Rotated Counter Controls were adjusted until intersection of White Cross was positioned at point of interest. Contents of X and Y counters were recorded onto audiotape

The positions of white X, Y crosshairs were adjusted until they coincided first with the center of the pupil and then with an infrared light. For each measurement the contents of an X counter and a Y counter, which denoted the locations of the vertical and horizontal crosshairs respectively, were recorded onto audiotape (LENTZ and HAITH, 1969) for later playback into a computer. Graphic displays and statistical analyses of eye movements were then provided by the computer.

The major results were quite clear (see Table 2). Vertical and horizontal edges and vertical and horizontal bars all attracted fixations; the average fixation position was reliably closer to the stimulus area during experimental than during control trials for all of these stimuli. Also, edge-boundary crossings were greater

Table 2. Average distance from the edge or center of bar and percent of movements crossing contours for the edge and bar studies

Orientation period	Edge study				Bar study			
	Vertical		Horizontal		Vertical		Horizontal	
	Exp	Con	Exp	Con	Exp	Con	Exp	Con
Average fixation distance (from edge or bar center)	0.95[a]	2.37	0.85	1.36	0.71	1.71	1.19	1.76
Average percent of crosses (of edges or bar sides)	21	11	26	20	37	25	29	24

[a] Numbers in inches.

for all experimental periods. Thus, horizontal edges can affect scanning if they are placed close to the natural resting location of the eye. The fact that horizontal edges are attractive only when they are placed close to the natural resting location is consistent with the interpretation that horizontal edges were unattractive in the previous study because they could not be easily crossed.

Stronger evidence of the importance of edge crossing is provided by the reliable increase in edge-crossing frequency during experimental periods. However, inference based on the observed increase in edge crossing could be challenged. The observed increase in frequency of edge crossing in experimental over control periods could have resulted simply from the tendency for newborns to stay near the edge location in experimental periods. Edge crossing, therefore, could have been an artifact of average proximity to an edge combined with natural "random-walk" scan activity. Further analysis disconfirmed this interpretation. The size of eye movements that crossed the edge location, as compared to those that did not, were analyzed separately for control and experimental periods. As shown in Table 3, movements which crossed a contour location were much larger (13–25%) for each of the four comparisons when the contour was there than when it was not. Importantly, the size of noncross eye movements was virtually identical across conditions, thereby denying an interpretation that the cross-movement finding could be attributed to generalized "excitement" from the presence of the edge and bar patterns.

This replicated interaction not only denies a random-walk interpretation of newborn scanning of patterns, it also implies rudimentary intentionality. This is true because the terminus of a saccadic eye movement is determined *before* the eye moves and cannot be changed in flight as a function of, for example, the crossing of a black-white border (ALPERN, 1969; FUCHS, 1971; KOMODA et al., 1973; STARK, 1971).

One additional replicated finding supports the idea that newborns actively tried to cross edges, and further supports the idea that horizontal edges pose special difficulty. Recall that blank field scanning ranges broadly along the horizontal axis. Even though this observation was repeated in these two studies,

Table 3. Size of eye-movement of edge or bar location crosses and noncrosses during experimental and control periods[a]

Orientation	Condition	Stimulus			
		Edge		Bar	
		Type of eye-movement			
		Cross	No-cross	Cross	No-cross
Vertical	Experimental	2.40	1.19	1.66	0.82
	Control	1.92	1.25	1.47	0.86
Horizontal	Experimental	2.08	1.24	1.77	1.05
	Control	1.80	1.20	1.46	0.92

[a] Numbers in inches.

the horizontal distribution of fixations was still larger during horizontal-stimulus experimental periods; the increase was 70% for the edge, and 80% for the bar. Further, the increase was manifested principally in the horizontal component of eye movement, i.e., parallel to the bar. No effect of vertical bars on dispersion was found. Empirical evidence suggests that newborns have difficulty in producing eye movements with a high vertical slope, a condition which has its base both in anatomic and neurophysiologic fact.[3] Apparently, they "solve" this problem with horizontal edges by generating eye movements with a shallow vertical component and increased horizontal component, which increases the likelihood of horizontal edge crossing.

The results of these studies are consistent with the notion that newborns find linear edges and actively engage in scan activity that maximizes the likelihood of crossing contours.

Rule 5. Stay near areas of maximum contour density; scan broadly near areas of low density, and narrowly near areas of high density. If a principle such as "keep cortical firing rate high" guides scanning activity, then there should be some relation between the firing-rate potential of a stimulus and how a baby scans it. Depending on the firing rate produced by a stimulus, the scanning strategy should vary the likelihood of discovering more optimal stimuli (assuming the current stimulus to be less than asymptotically high). For example, one would expect stimuli with low firing-rate potentials to be scanned more broadly than those with high firing-rate potential.

SALAPATEK and KESSEN (1966) and SALAPATEK (1968) reported that fixation dispersion was reduced when forms were presented to newborns in comparison to blank fields. The first study reported profound clustering of fixations around a single angle of an equilateral triangle. This finding has typically been interpreted as angle attractiveness which, if true, suggests that rules and assumptions are needed which provide for element or form attractiveness. However, local edge or contour density is also greatest near an angle. Since contour density could affect cortical firing, it may be that the constraint on scanning was produced by this density, not by angularity. This interpretation is also consistent with reports that smaller stimuli (with closer sides, and hence more contour density) produce reduced dispersion (SALAPATEK, 1968), and that the simple

[3] A substantial angle exists between the vertical meridian of the eye and the vector of motion produced by contraction of the superior and inferior rectus muscles. Thus, a pure vertical movement, even when the eye is at midline, requires active changes in contraction of all the eye muscles. This is not the case for horizontal eye movements, because virtually no angle exists between the horizontal meridian of the eye and the lateral and medial rectus muscles (ALPERN, 1969). Aside from oculomotor complexity, neurophysiologic evidence suggests that activation of the vertical eye-movement muscles is neurally more complex than activation of the horizontal muscles. Though little of a definitive nature can be stated from the confusing literature on higher control centers for eye movement in subhumans, (see, for example, PASIK and PASIK, 1964), one consistent finding is that conjugate horizontal deviation of the eyes can easily be produced by unilateral stimulation of eye-movement centers, whereas vertical movement of the eyes virtually always requires bilateral stimulation (PASIK and PASIK, 1964; BENDER and SHANZER, 1964; CROSBY et al., 1952; see also papers in BACH-Y-RITA, 1971). Vertical eye movements are more vulnerable to state changes; i.e., they drop out earlier than horizontal movements under the effects of anesthesia (WAGMAN, 1964). Finally, JONES (1926) and BEASLEY (1933a, 1933b) reported that horizontal tracking preceded vertical tracking of moving stimuli in human infants.

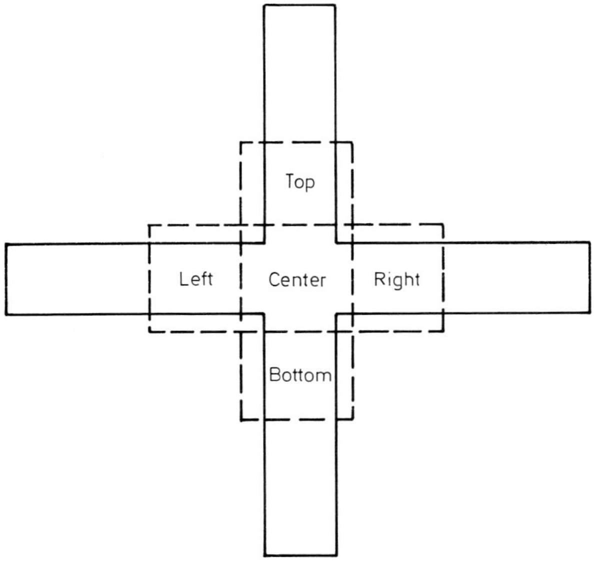

Fig. 6. Prototype used to define regions for calculation of fixation distributions in angle study. For all stimuli, Center region was relevant, but for any one stimulus only one vertically adjacent and one horizontally adjacent region were relevant

vertical bars and edges used in the previous studies (KESSEN et al., 1972, and the two studies reported above) did not affect dispersion. The increase in fixation dispersion with horizontal edges which we reported above appears to be a special case reflecting the only option that the newborn had for contour crossing.

I tested the attractiveness of angles as opposed to bars by presenting newborns the stimuli shown in the third row of Figure 4. These contained a vertical bar, a horizontal bar, an internal and an external right angle. The data were analyzed simply by counting the number of fixations in each of three relevant $17° \times 17°$ regions (see the prototype used for analysis in Fig. 6) for control and experimental periods. These forms were strikingly attractive, the three relevant regions commanding 73% of fixations in experimental periods as opposed to 38% in control periods. However, an examination of the distribution of fixations revealed that the angle region had no special attractiveness; in fact, when present in experimental periods, the left region attracted fixations away from the angle area (in terms of expectations based on control period distribution). Surprisingly, but in line with our interpretation regarding the limited horizontal window within which newborn scanning is effective, horizontal elements were much more attractive than vertical ones. This finding supports the idea that the newborn does not maintain fixations on stimuli which are above or below 8° from his resting location.

This study suggests that angles have no special attractiveness for the newborn. Figure 7 indicates why, on the basis of contour proximity alone, acute angles might be specially attractive, but not right angles. A baby trying to fixate

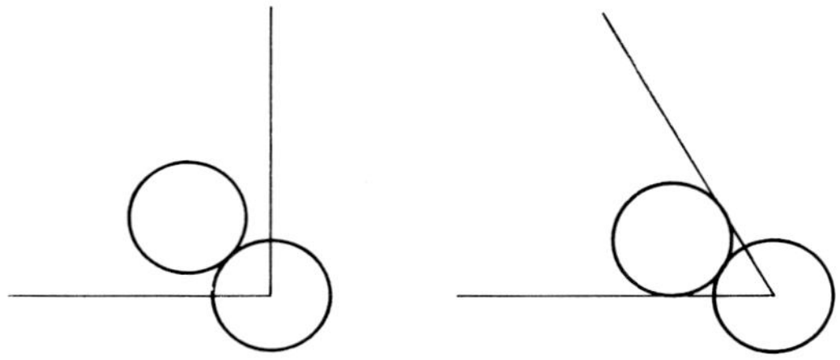

Fig. 7. Illustration of effect of fixating two points near an acute and a 90° angle. A fixation at the intercept of either angle results in a foveal projection (indicated by circle) of both angle sides. However, a fixation equidistant from intercept and from sides results in a foveal projection of both sides only for the acute angle

near regions in which contour density is high, can fixate in more areas in which two contours are near the fovea with an acute angle than with a right angle.

II. A Single Principle Underlying Newborn Scanning

This section further articulates the concepts which I feel control newborn scanning and relates them to the findings described above. I proposed earlier that the principle of maximizing visual cortical firing-rate (VCFR) during wakefulness could account for what we know about newborn visual activity. Two scan routines were also introduced by which the newborn varies firing-rate—an Ambient Scan Routine (ASR) and an Inspection Scan Routine (ISR). The ASR facilitates detection of visual stimuli. The ISR operates when a stimulus is detected, and generates eye movements which maximize VCFR. To the extent that the ISR maintains firing-rates at an acceptable level, the ASR is suppressed (but not inhibited). Now I will discuss what we know about newborn scanning and related nonhuman neurophysiologic work.

1. Scanning in Darkness and in a Formless Light Field

In unpatterned fields VCFR should be low. HUBEL and WIESEL (1959) reported no change in ambient VCFR in cats even when light levels were varied over several log units. Thus contour appears to be necessary for heightened VCFR. With low VCFR the ASR should produce an active broad-based scan, as is observed in darkness and unpatterned light.

2. Fixation of Edges and Bars

The issue of why a newborn fixates a stimulus in the first place has never been treated satisfactorily, but is manageable under the present scheme.

The fovea, as compared to nonfoveal areas, enjoys a greater concentration of cells, a higher ratio of ganglion afferents, smaller receptive fields, and a larger proportional representation in all visual parts of the brain (POLYAK, 1957; TRUEX and CARPENTER, 1969). Therefore, a stimulus falling on the foveal region would generate higher VCFR than stimuli located anywhere else on the retina. Black–white edges and bars have been found to be especially effective in producing firing activity in animals (BARLOW et al., 1972; HUBEL and WIESEL, 1959, 1962, 1963). Such firing would be especially salient for the young organism, because the immature cortex manifests relatively less ambient VCFR (is "quiet"), high fatiguability, and a relatively brief train of pulses to a single stimulus (HUBEL and WIESEL, 1963; HUTTENLOCHER, 1967; PURPURA, 1971; ROSE and ELLINGSON, 1970). As the newborn fixates closer to an edge, VCFR should increase and, as he moves away, it should decrease. This analysis clearly predicts that the newborn should tend to fixate near an edge, as demonstrated in the studies reported.

3. Crossing of Edges

Why does the newborn attempt to cross back and forth over edges rather than simply remain near them? First of all, VCFR is enhanced by relocation of edges on the retina, because cells are maximally stimulated when an edge first falls within their receptive field. Figure 8 shows records of cell firing rates from studies by HUBEL and WIESEL that illustrate this effect. HARTLINE (1969) maintained that the initial burst of firing followed by a lower maintained rate reflects a lower latency for processes of facilitation than inhibition. Movement of the eye, producing a relocation of the stimulus onto new receptive fields, would produce not only a fresh onset response, but also an offset response (increased firing) in cells no longer inhibited (HARTLINE, 1969). HUBEL and Wiesel speculated that stimulus movement is especially effective in increasing the firing rate of a cell "... because of the synergistic effects of leaving an inhibitory area and simultaneously entering an excitatory area" (HUBEL and WIESEL, 1962, p. 112). And, "...sequential activation of the afferents by movement of a line across the field is generally a very powerful stimulus, perhaps partly because none of the antecedent cells has time to adapt" (HUBEL and WIESEL, 1965, p. 282). They further suggest that eye movements can perform a similar function to stimulus movement: "A given line or border would move back and forth over a small retinal region; in the cortex this would sequentially activate many cells with simple fields" (HUBEL and WIESEL, 1962, p. 147).

Although this reasoning accounts for efforts by the newborn to relocate an edge on the retina, we have not yet accounted for why he should sequentially locate it on alternate sides of the fovea (i.e., cross the contour). By our reasoning the infant should attempt to keep the stimulus near the fovea at the end of each eye movement in order to produce the highest rate of firing. To reach an area near the fovea but furthest from the present site, the best compromise is to cross the edge and relocate it on the other side. A move some distance from the current location might produce a maximum effect for several reasons. If the image were not perfectly sharp, receptive fields were relatively large (KARMEL and MAISEL, in press, 1975), or a gradient of cell fatigue exists, cells with receptive fields near those maximally stimulated would be preadapted,

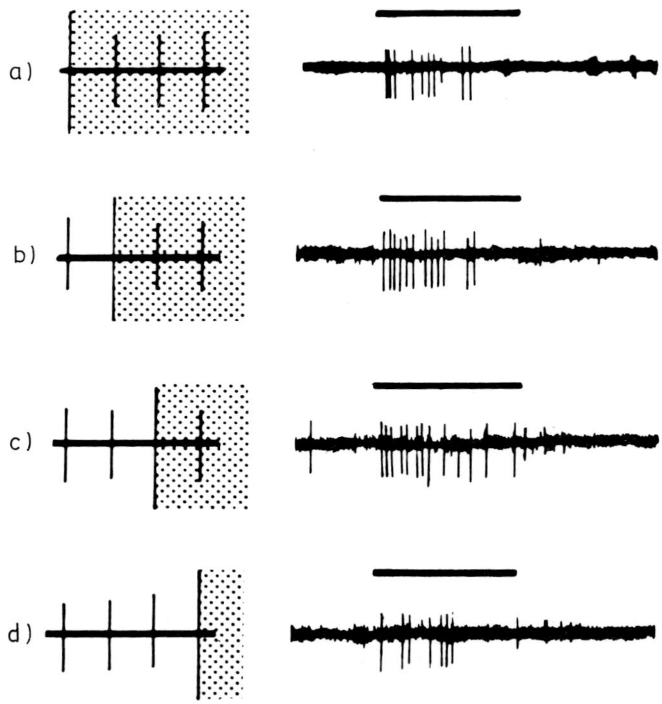

Fig. 8. Cortical firing rate in a single cell in cat visual cortex. Left portion of figure indicates position of an edge in receptive field. Right portion of figure indicates firing activity of cell (lower record of each lettered section) and onset and offset of stimulus (smooth horizontal bar above each record). Firing rate is maximum at stimulus onset and then declines. (From HUBEL and WIESEL, 1962, p. 119)

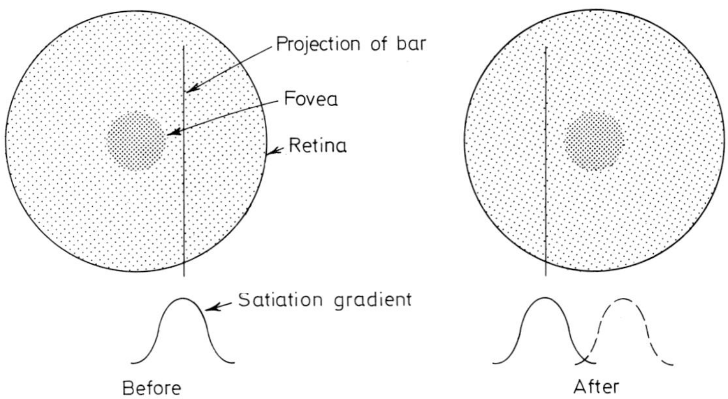

Fig. 9. Model of neural activity before and after an edge cross. Large circular zones represent retina and central circular zone, fovea. Normal curves (bottom) indicate hypothesized gradient of adaptation of cells. An eye movement which produces a relocation of projection of edge on opposite side of fovea results in least overlap between cells comprising the two gradients. At the same time projected edge remains near cell-rich fovea

and produce a smaller increment in firing than those further away. Figure 9 illustrates the proposed effect. Another interpretation is also possible. When an edge is crossed the projection of that edge falls on the opposite side of the vertical meridian of the retina, thereby activating cells in the opposite hemisphere. Since area 18 is quite poorly developed in the newborn (CONEL, 1939), cross-hemispheric interaction is unlikely; an edge-cross strategy, therefore, would clearly activate a fresh pool of cortical receptors. Actually, since there is probably dual representation of about 1° around the vertical meridian of the macula (at least for the monkey; STONE et al., 1973) the infant might attempt to keep the edge projections just outside this region, and therefore make somewhat longer eye-movements than necessary to cross the edge—an interpretation which accounts for the relatively large eye-movements made in edge crossing.

4. Scanning of Stimuli With Varying Edge Density

It is not difficult to understand how increasing edge density would magnify the effects described. The greater the number of edges, the more receptive fields affected, and the higher the VCFR. The closer the edges are, the more likely they could be projected reasonably close to the fovea, as long as they are not so close that the activated receptive fields overlap (KARMEL, 1969b). The assumption that the ASR is increasingly suppressed as the VCFR increases accounts for findings of increased fixation clustering with increasing edge density.

An implication of this assumption is that a newborn may not locate the highest density portion of a visual display. If he were first to scan an area of high firing rate potential, the ASR might be too greatly suppressed for detection of other stimuli. Thus, the newborn might not look at both stimuli in a paired-stimulus paradigm if the first member selected had sufficient edge density to reduce the scan range below what is necessary to find the other member, thereby giving the appearance of obligatory attention.

Summation and extension. The ideas proposed here account for most of what we know about visual behavior of the newborn and perhaps the infant up to six to eight weeks of age:

1. Why he searches when no stimuli are available.
2. Why he looks at a brightness transition (edge).
3. Why he scans the transition by crossing over it.
4. Why fixation distribution is constrained as nonhorizontal edge density increases.

Does this analysis lend itself to explanation of any other visual phenomena?

Two important visual developments have not been adequately explained in the literature—improvement of visual accommodation and binocular convergence. The principles of visual investigation I have proposed suggest how this improvement occurs.

5. How Appropriate Accommodation May Be Achieved

Although the data have been challenged, the best information available suggests that newborns do not possess the ability to accommodate to stimuli at varying distances (HAYNES et al., 1965; see Fig. 1). Rather, they tend to accommodate at a distance of around 19 cm and only acquire full accommodative flexibility at around 4 months of age.

As the distance of an object from the plane of accommodation increases, so does retinal blur. This blur produces less definite lateral inhibition in the retina and, consequently, lower VCFR. Blur, in the extreme, becomes a homogeneously illuminated field which results in low ambient VCFR. HUBEL and WIESEL (1962) accidentally observed the effect of blur on firing rate of a single cell. After encountering difficulty in obtaining any response from a cell to a projected vertical black-white edge, they placed a piece of black tape on a white background (producing a sharper retinal image than the projected stimulus) in the cell's field and obtained vigorous firing activity. Apparently, the projected image produced light scatter and reduced edge sharpness below firing threshold for that cell. In a similar fashion, but more dramatically, blur produced by poor accommodation could make an edge an ineffective stimulus for some cells. As accommodation becomes more adaptive, the edge image sharpens, and more cells should be excited, at higher firing rates. If, as I have suggested, the newborn attempts to increase VCFR, he should learn to accomodate as the neurologic and muscular mechanisms mature. (Although I did not discuss this point earlier, the dioptrical light-forming system of the newborn is probably not perfect even for the optimal distance. The occurrence of retinal blur or light gradient across a relatively large number of receptive fields would increase the relative attractiveness for very sharp bright edges.)

6. Binocular Convergence

Little convincing evidence exists on how much deconvergence is present at birth, and at what age the baby achieves convergence. As I stated earlier the eyes are not uncoordinated; they move together in majority but do not appear to focus on the same object (WICKELGREN, 1969).

The common notion is that the infant's motivation for learning to converge is to reduce the number of images in his visual field. This idea is questionable because it presumes true knowledge of the number of objects in the visual field. Moreover, chronic deconvergence in adults results in suppression of one image, rather than an impression of double images.

The cortical-firing hypothesis suggests another explanation. Repeated demonstrations have been offered of the binocular influence on firing-rate of single cortical cells (BISHOP, 1970; HUBEL and WIESEL, 1962). A particular cell will fire to a particular stimulus orientation in a particular location whether the stimulus is presented to the right eye or left, although one eye will usually have a dominant influence reflected by a higher firing rate. When the stimulus is presented to both eyes, in register, firing-rate more than doubles over that for the single eye alone (e.g., HUBEL and WIESEL, 1959, 1962). If the same image is out of register in the two eyes, a suppression of firing occurs. (These relations hold for the cat for all types of cells, but for the primate, simple cells in layer IV are monocular, and only higher-level cells binocular [HUBEL and WIESEL, 1968].) The difference in firing rates produced by the two conditions (slight nonregistration producing suppression, and registration producing synergistic enhancement) would be quite striking, and could serve to induce the young infant to engage in neuromusculatur activities that produce convergence.

III. Beyond the Early Weeks

This chapter has focused principally on the early weeks of infancy. But I should comment briefly on some related research and conception with older infants.

Several investigators have suggested that an important reorganization in behavior occurs at around two months of age (BERGMAN et al., 1971; EMDE et al., 1976; JEFFREY and COHEN, 1971; KARMEL and MAISEL, 1975; KESSEN et al., 1970; PARMALEE, 1973; SALAPATEK, 1969) and I suspect that the rules we have outlined are inapplicable or in need of extension beyond that time. Some of the changes include clearer differences in EEG patterns with state changes, disappearance of some reflexes, occurrence of more adult-like sleep patterns, onset of smiling, and an increase in conditionality and ability to habituate. Changes in visual behavior include onset of eye contact (BERGMAN et al., 1971), response to internal aspects of displays (SALAPATEK, 1969), a reversal of the early preference of a checkerboard over a bull's-eye (FANTZ and NEVIS, 1967), and a suggestion that visual organization becomes important (RUFF and BIRCH, 1974). KAGAN (1970a, b) holds that discrepancy also becomes important around this time, and KARMEL and his colleagues that contour density assumes primary importance (KARMEL and MAISEL, 1975). Babies at this age are also more likely to look at both patterns in a paired-comparison set. Straightforward modifications of the principal components – VCFR, ISR, ASR – of the scheme we have outlined are possible to account for some of these changes. For example, one could argue that, with development, a given level of suppression of the ASR requires increasingly high VCFR. This assumption could handle the finding of increased likelihood of fixation of both stimuli in a paired-comparison set by older infants and the finding of more extensive scanning of components of forms by older than younger infants (SALAPATEK, 1973).

Or, one could argue that development is accompanied by changes in what controls VCFR. For example, the activity of single cells might define VCFR at birth, but as increasingly more complex cells are brought into play, they could take precedence (when stimulus displays permit) over lower-level cells. However, a principle of net VCFR begins to lose meaning at this point because, if true, the implication is that patterns of firing become more important than simple net firing-rate. These considerations are prompted by several suggestions that organization of visual stimuli assumes increasing importance with age. We have shown that a striking increase in babies' scanning of the eye area of an adult face occurs between five and seven weeks of age, which we interpreted as indicative of the appreciation of the organization of facial components (BERGMAN et al., 1971). SALAPATEK (1969) reported that only after one month of age are internal as well as external aspects of a display requiring some visual organization appreciated. Visual organization is also implied by the finding that early preference for a checkerboard, which has high contour density, yields to preference at around two months for a bull's-eye, which has a focal point and a configural arrangement (FANTZ, 1958, 1967; FANTZ and NEVIS, 1967). Finally, GIBSON (1969) has impressively documented the increase in configural responding of infants to facial features. It is interesting to note that KARMEL and MAISEL (1975) argue that the dimension of contour density most powerfully accounts for visual preference beyond the age at which I have maintained that it should exert powerful control over scanning range. Some clarification is in order.

In a set of important papers, KARMEL (1969a, 1969b, 1973; KARMEL and MAISEL, 1975) demonstrated that a wide set of data on infant preference could be summarized by assuming that preference for visual stimuli is an inverted U function of the square root of amount of contour, with the peak preference increasing with age. Contour preference is assumed to be controlled by the amount of cortical firing produced by a pattern. With little contour density, relatively low cell-firing occurs. Low firing rates would result also from very high densities, because edge separations would not be resolved. Thus, intermediate densities should be preferred, and are. Age-shifts in peak preference for increasing density is accounted for by assuming that receptive field size of cells decreases with age, permitting resolution of increasingly higher densities. (As we noted earlier, increasing accommodative ability would produce the same effect.) The neural activity interpretation of the preference effect has been documented through recording of the VER to patterns containing varying amounts of contour in different age infants; stimuli producing peak VER's for a particular age group were also those most preferred. However, the relation did not hold well for infants under six weeks of age.[4]

First, I should reiterate that the scheme proposed in the preceding section was not developed to account for infant preference. Second, KARMEL's definition of contour density, the sum of the lengths of all the black-white edges divided by the area (standardized for distance), is really a description of relative contour *amount*, not density as we have used the term here. Imagine a white square outlined by a ribbon of black; such a stimulus would not provide the same firing-rate potential as the same amount of contour arranged in four parallel strips alternated with thin strips of white, because only the latter could all be positioned near the cell-rich fovea. We have preferred to use the term local contour density in our scheme, thereby not making the assumption that the infant can sum input across a broad range of his visual field. Thus, I predict that stimuli with high local contour density will be scanned more narrowly than stimuli with low local contour density (up to an asymptotic limit, declining as the limits of resolution are reached). A preference measure would indicate longer "looking time" at the higher-density, more narrowly-scanned stimulus for infants under 6 weeks of age.

[4] KARMEL and MAISEL (1975) reported findings from an unpublished dissertation by Hoffman that the late component of the VER was related to infant preference before 5 weeks of age; the early component has been the principle focus of KARMEL's laboratory in the search for brain-behavior relations in older subjects. Insufficient detail of the results for younger subjects was reported for inclusion here.

Additionally, contour arrangement in some orientations may affect scanning differently from arrangements in other orientations, because of the neuromuscular limits on vertical scansion; contour relocation on the retina is produced by eye-movements principally along an axis perpendicular to stimulus orientation. Thus, vertical contour should be scanned more narrowly than nonvertical contour. It is not known when facility in vertical scanning appears, but PIPP (1975) found extensive vertical scanning in 8-week-olds, elicited by vertical bars possessing depth at their edges.

Thus, although older infants may be able to "compute" an average density from the whole stimulus, younger infants should respond most to local contour density in an orientation which will optimize VCFR, given the constraints on their eye-movement capacity. However, the evidence is fairly clear that contour, per se, plays a decreasing role in visual activity beyond early infancy, with visual meaning and organization assuming increasing importance. At that time, firing patterns may become more important than firing rates, higher contour density being preferred when lower density is the only alternative.

C. Summary

The major accomplishments of early visual behavior can be explained by the idea that the newborn human possesses the competence and the motivation to maintain VCFR at a high level. A virtue of this approach is that it is exceptionally straightforward and testable, and that it brings conceptualization about infant vision into correspondence with the productive research on nonhuman animals. Probably more importantly, it emphasizes that visual exploration begins in the infant rather than in the stimulus. This approach recognizes that babies must be able to adapt to an enormous range of possible visual worlds. It would make little sense for them to come into that world with a fixed set of preferences for particular stimuli. Conversely, it makes a great deal of sense for them to enter the world with systematic tendencies for *acquiring* visual information, and for that information to then structure or tune the neurologic system so that it is especially sensitive to environmentally frequent visual elements and configurations. The demonstration of plasticity of cortical analyzers in nonhumans and humans suggests that, even if the system is partially pretuned (WIESEL and HUBEL, 1974), information-acquisition tendencies are necessary for *maintenance* of the environmentally relevant aspects.

The principle of scanning in a fashion which keeps VCFR high also seems sensible, both from an adaptive viewpoint and from what we know about visual information processing. The literature on visual deprivation points to the importance of activity in the neural pathways for growth and maintenance (HUBEL and WIESEL, 1963; RIESEN, 1961; WIESEL and HUBEL, 1974); thus, scanning which keeps cortical firing-rate high is important for maintenance of neural integrity. Additionally, theorists agree that information lies at edges, not in the homogeneous interspaces between edges (J. GIBSON, 1966). Thus, by maintaining a high firing rate, the newborn scans near the most informative areas of a stimulus.

Where does this position take us with regard to the basis themes on which traditional conceptualizations of perceptual development have been ordered? On the nature-nurture issue, I obviously believe that information-acquisition strategies or rules are available at birth. These strategies probably change with age and experience, but their presence at birth can hardly be denied. Whether even primitive organization of visual input beyond contour-orientation sensitivity is present is a moot question at this time. But, once again, the literature clearly implies strong effects of experience on perceptual structures. Thus, it seems likely that the form of information-aquisition strategies are well-organized at birth but the *content* of perception is not.

My position on the receptive versus active aspects of perception should be clear. To some extent the controversy in the past could be relegated to semantics, because it concerned the language to be used to describe only internal, unobservable processes. The present approach emphasizes organismic activity (eye-movements) in perceptual development in a concrete fashion. Thus, my position on this question depends, to some extent, on whether visual information-acquisition activities are included in one's definition of "perception" along with the more traditional conception of this construct as representing the interpretation of sensory experience. I believe these two aspects of visual perception are too interdependent in the "perceptual act" to be separated.

Apparently HELMHOLTZ would agree.

> We are not simply passive to the impressions that are urged upon us, but we *observe*, that is, we adjust our organs in those conditions that enable them to distinguish the impressions most accurately. Thus, in considering an involved object, we accommodate both eyes as well as we can, and turn them to focus steadily the precise point on which our attention is fixed, that is, so as to get an image of it in the fovea of each eye; and then we let our eyes traverse all the noteworthy points of the object one after another" (WARREN and WARREN, 1968, p. 183).

The scheme outlined here used a minimum of assumptions to account for what we know about the newborn. Hopefully, it will provide a core orientation that can be added to as knowledge about the newborn accumulates. And perhaps it can even be extended to account meaningfully for much of the research on older infants. Whatever the case, I do hope that the suggestion of an approach which emphasizes organismically defined rules for acquiring information from the world will be explored more fully in attempts to account for perceptual development.

References

Alpern, M.: Part I; Movements of the eyes. In: H. Davson (ed.), The eye (Vol. 3), pp. 1–214. New York: Academic Press 1969.

Ames, E.W., Silfen, C.K.: Methodological issues in the study of age differences in infant's attention to stimuli varying in movement and complexity. Paper read at meetings of Society for Research in Child Development, Minneapolis, March 1965.

Annis, R.C., Frost, B.: Human visual ecology and orientation anistropies in acuity. Science **182**, 729–731 (1973).

Anohkin, P.K.: The multiple ascending influences of the subcortical centers on the cerebral cortex. In: M.A.B. Brazier (ed.), Brain and behavior: Proceeding, 139–170. New York: Stechert 1961.

Aslin, R.M., Salapatek, P.: Saccadic localization of visual targets by the very young human infant. Paper read at meetings of the Psychonomic Society, St. Louis, 1973.

Bach, L., Seefelder, R.: Atlas zur Entwicklungsgeschichte des menschlichen Auges. Parts I, II, III. Leipzig 1911, 1912, 1914.

Bach-y-Rita, P.: The control of eye movements. New York: Academic Press 1971.

Barlow, H.B., Narasimhan, R., Rosenfeld, A.: Visual pattern analysis in machines and animals. Science **177**, 567–575 (1972).

Barlow, H.G., Pettigrew, J.D.: Lack of specificity of neurons in the visual cortex of young kittens. J. Physiol. (Lond.) **218**, 98–100 (1971).

Barnet, A.B., Lodge, A., Armington, J.C.: Electroretinogram in newborn human infants. Science **148**, 651–654 (1965).

Barton, S., Birns, B., Ronch, J.: Individual differences in the visual pursuit behavior of neonates. Child Develpm. **42**, 313–319 (1971).

Beasley, W.C.: Visual pursuit in 109 white and 142 Negro newborn infants. Child Developm. **4**, 106–120 (1933a).

Beasley, W.C.: An investigation of related problems in the vision of newborn infants. Psychol. Bull. **30**, 626 (1933b).

Bender, M.B., Shanzer, S.: Oculomotor pathways defined by electric stimulation and lesions in the brainstem of the monkey. In: M.B. Bender (ed.), The oculomotor system, 81–140. New York: Harper & Row 1964.

Bergman, T., Haith, M.M., Mann, L.: Development of eye contact and facial scanning in infants. Paper presented at the meetings of the Society for Research in Child Development. Minneapolis 1971.

Berlyne, D.E.: The influence of the albedo and complexity of stimuli on visual fixation in the human infant. Brit. J. Psychol. **49**, 315–318 (1958).

Berlyne, D.E.: Conflict, arousal, and curiosity. New York: McGraw-Hill 1960.

Bishop, P.O.: Beginning of form vision and binocular depth discrimination in cortex. In: The neurosciences second study program, 471–485. New York: Rockefeller 1970.

Blakemore, C., Cooper, G.F.: Development of the brain depends on visual environment. Nature (Lond.) **228**, 472–478 (1970).

Blanton, M.G.: The behavior of the human infant during the first thirty days of life. Psychol. Rev. **24**, 456–483 (1917).

Bond, E.: Form perception in the infant. Psychol. Bull. **77**, 225–245 (1972).

Bornstein, M.H.: Qualities of color vision in infancy. J. Exp. Child Psychol. **19**, 401–419 (1975).

Brennan, W., Ames, E.W., Moore, R.W.: Age differences in infants' attention to patterns of different complexities. Science **151**, 354–356 (1966).

Bronson, G.: The postnatal growth of visual capacity. Child Develpm. **45**, 873–890 (1974).

Caron, A.J., Caron, R.F., Caldwell, R.C., Weiss, S.J.: Infant perception of the structural properties of the face. Develop. Psychol. **9**, 385–399 (1973).

Carpenter, G.C., Tecce, J.J., Stechler, G., Friedman, S.: Differential visual behavior to human and humanoid faces in early infancy. Merrill-Palmer Quart. **16**, 91–108 (1970).

Carpenter, G.C.: Visual regard of moving and stationary faces in early infancy. Merrill-Palmer Quart. **20**, 181–194 (1974).

Chase, W.P.: Color vision in infants. J. exp. Psychol. **20**, 203–222 (1937).

Cohen, L.B.: Observing responses, visual preferences, and habituation to visual stimuli in infants. J. exp. Child Psychol. **7**, 419–433 (1969).

Cohen, L.B.: Attention-getting and attention-holding processes in infant visual preferences. Child Develpm. **43**, 869–879 (1972).

Cohen, L.B., Gelber, E.R.: Infant visual memory. In: L. Cohen and P. Salapatek (eds.), Infant perception. New York: Academic Press 1975, 347–403.

Conel, J.L.: The postnatal development of the human cerebral cortex. In: The cortex of the newborn (Vol. I). Cambridge, Mass.: Harvard University Press 1939.

Crosby, E.C., Foss, R.E., Henderson, J.W.: The mammalian midbrain and isthmus regions. J. comp. Neurol. **97**, 357–383 (1952).

Dayton, G.O., Jr., Jones, M.H., Aiu, P., Rawson, R.A., Steele, B., Rose, M.: Developmental study of coordinated eye movement in the human infant. I. Visual acuity in the newborn human: a study based on induced optokinetic nystagmus recorded by electrography. Arch. Ophthal. **71**, 865–870 (1964a).

Dayton, G.O., Jr., Jones, M.H., Steele, B., Rose, M.: Developmental study of coordinated eye movements in the human infant. II. An electrooculographic study of the fixation reflex in the newborn. Arch. Ophthal. (Chicago) **71**, 871–875 (1964b).

Dember, W.N., Earl, R.W.: Analysis of exploratory, manipulatory, and curiosity behaviors. Psychol. Rev. **64**, 91–96 (1957).

Dodwell, P.C.: Visual pattern recognition. New York: Holt, Rinehart, and Winston 1970.

Duke-Elder, S., Cook, C.: System of ophthalmology (Vol. III). St. Louis: Mosby 1963.

Ellingson, R.J.: Cerebral electrical responses to auditory and visual stimuli in the infant (human and subhuman studies). In: P. Kellaway and I. Petersen (eds.), Neurologic and electroencephalographic correlative studies in infancy, 78–116. New York: Grune & Stratton, Inc. 1964.

Emde, R.N., Gaensbauer, T.J., Harmon, R.J.: Emotional expression in infancy: A biobehavioral study. Psychol. Issues, (Vol. 10), No. 37. New York: International Universities Press, 1976.

Fagan, J.F. III.: Memory in the infant. J. exp. Child Psychol. **9**, 217–226 (1970).

Fantz, R.L.: A method for studying early visual development. Percept. Mot. Skills **6**, 13–15 (1956).

Fantz, R.L.: Pattern vision in young infants. Psychol. Rec. **8**, 43–47 (1958).

Fantz, R.L.: The origin of form perception. Sci. Amer. **204**, 66–72 (1961).

Fantz, R.L.: Pattern vision in newborn infants. Science **140**, 296–297 (1963).

Fantz, R.L.: Visual perception from birth as shown by pattern selectivity. Ann. N.Y. Acad. Sci. **118**, 793–814 (1965).

Fantz, R.L.: Pattern discrimination and selective attention as determinants of perceptual development from birth. In: A.H. Kidd and J.L. Rivoire (eds.), Perceptual development in children. New York: International University Press 1966.

Fantz, R.L.: Visual perception and experience in early infancy: A look at the hidden side of behavior development. In: H.W. Stevenson, E.H. Hess, and H.L. Rheingold (eds.), Early behavior: Comparative and developmental approaches. New York: Wiley 1967.

Fantz, R.L., Nevis, S.: Pattern preferences and perceptual-cognitive development in early infancy. Merrill-Palmer Quart. **13**, 77–108 (1967).

Fantz, R.L., Ordy, J.M., Udelf, M.S.: Maturation of pattern vision in infants during the first six months. J. comp. physiol. Psychol. **55**, 907–917 (1962).

Freeman, R.D., Mitchell, D.E., Millodot, M.: A neural effect of partial visual deprivation in humans. Science **175**, 1384–1386 (1972).

Freeman, R.D., Thibos, L.W.: Electrophysiological evidence that abnormal early visual experience can modify the human brain. Science **180**, 876–878 (1973).

Fuchs, A.F.: The saccadic system. In: P. Bach-y-Rita and C.C. Collins (eds.), The control of eye movement, 343–362. New York: Academic Press 1971.

Ganz, L.: Conjunctive neural gating as a mechanism mediating the development of object recognition. Paper read at the Minnesota Symposium in Child Psychology, Minneapolis, 1974.

Genzmer, A.: Untersuchungen über die Sinneswahrnehmungen des neugeborenen Menschen. Halle: Max Niemeyer 1882.

Gibson, E.J.: Principles of perceptual learning and development. New York: Appleton-Century-Crofts 1969.

Gibson, J.J.: The senses considered as perceptual systems. Boston: Houghton-Mifflin 1966.

Gibson, J.J., Gibson, E.J.: Perceptual learning: Differentiation or enrichment? Psychol. Rev. **62**, 32–41 (1955).

Goldman, P.I.: Maturation of the mammalian nervous system and the ontogeny of behavior. In: R.A. Hinde, J. Rosenblatt, and E. Shaw (eds.), Advances in the study of behavior (Vol. 7). New York: Academic Press, in press (1976).

Gorman, J.J., Cogan, D.G., Gellis, S.S.: An apparatus for grading the visual acuity of infants on the basis of opticokinetic nystagmus. Pediatrics **19**, 1088–1092 (1957).

Greenberg, D.J., O'Donnell, W.J.: Infancy and the optimal level of stimulation. Child Develpm. **43**, 639–645 (1972).

Guernsey, M.: A quantitative study of the eye reflexes in infants. Psychol. Bull. **26**, 160–161 (1929).
Haaf, R.A., Bell, R.Q.: A facial dimension in visual discrimination by human infants. Child Develpm. **38**, 893–899 (1967).
Haith, M.M.: The response of the human newborn to visual movement. J. exp. Child Psychol. **3**, 235–243 (1966).
Haith, M.M.: Visual scanning in infants. Paper presented at the regional meetings of the Society for Research in Child Development, Clark University, 1968. Published in: L.J. Stone, H.T. Smith, and R.B. Murphy (eds.), The competent infant: A handbook of readings. New York: Basic Books 1973.
Haith, M.M.: Infrared television recording and measurement of ocular behavior in the human infant. Amer. Psychol. **24**, 279–283 (1969).
Haith, M.M., Kessen, W., Collins, D.: Response of the human infant to level of complexity of intermittent visual movement. J. exp. Child Psychol. **7**, 52–69 (1969).
Hartline, H.K.: Visual receptors and retinal interaction. Science **164**, 270–278 (1969).
Haynes, H., White, B.L., Held, R.: Visual accommodation in human infants. Science **148**, 528–530 (1965).
Hebb, D.O.: Organization of behavior. New York: Wiley 1949.
Hershenson, M.: Visual discrimination in the human newborn. J. comp. physiol. Psychol. **58**, 270–276 (1964).
Hershenson, M.: Development of the perception of form. Psychol. Bull. **58**, 326–336 (1967).
Hershenson, M.: The development of visual perceptual systems. In: H. Moltz (ed.), The ontogeny of vertebrate behavior. New York: Academic Press 1970.
Hershenson, M., Munsinger, H., Kessen, W.: Preference for shapes of intermediate variability in the newborn human. Science **147**, 630–631 (1965).
Hirsch, H., Spinelli, N.: Distribution of receptive field orientation: Modification contingent on conditions of visual experience. Science **168**, 869–871 (1970).
Horsten, G.P., Winkelman, J.E.: Electrical activity of the retina in relation to histological differentiation in infants born prematurely and at full term. Vision Res. **2**, 269–276 (1962).
Horsten, G.P., Winkelman, J.E.: Electroretinographic critical fusion frequencies of the retina in relation to the histological development in man and animals. Ophthalmologica **18**, 515–521 (1964).
Hubel, D.H., Wiesel, T.N.: Receptive fields of single neurons in the cat's striate cortex. J. Physiol. (Lond.) **148**, 574–591 (1959).
Hubel, D.H., Wiesel, T.N.: Receptive fields, binocular interaction and functional architecture in the cat's visual cortex. J. Physiol. (Lond.) **160**, 106–154 (1962).
Hubel, D.H., Wiesel, T.N.: Receptive fields of cells in striate cortex of very young visually inexperienced kittens. J. Neurophysiol. **26**, 944–1002 (1963).
Hubel, D.H., Wiesel, T.N.: Receptive fields and functional architecture in two non-striate visual areas (18 and 19) of the cat. J. Neurophysiol. **28**, 229–289 (1965).
Hubel, D.H., Wiesel, T.N.: Receptive fields and functional architecture of monkey striate cortex. J. Physiol. (Lond.) **195**, 215–243 (1968).
Huttenlocher, P.R.: Development of cortical neuronal activity in the neonatal cat. Exp. Neurol. **17**, 247–262 (1967).
James, W.: The principles of psychology. New York: Henry Holt, 1890.
Jeffrey, W.E.: The orienting reflex and attention in cognitive development. Psychol. Rev. **75**, 323–334 (1968).
Jeffrey, W.E., Cohen, L.: Habituation in the human infant. In: H. Reese (ed.), Advances in child development and behavior (Vol. 6), 63–97. New York: Academic Press 1971.
Jones, M.C.: The development of early behavior patterns in young children. Pediat. Sem. **33**, 537–585 (1926).
Jones-Molfese, V.: Individual differences in neonatal preferences for planometric and stereometric visual pattern. Child Develpm. **43**, 1289–1296 (1972).
Kagan, J.: Attention and psychological change in the young child. Science **170**, 826–832 (1970a).
Kagan, J.: The distribution of attention in infancy. In: D.H. Hamburg (ed.), Perception and its disorders. Res. pub. ARNMD (Vol. 48), 214–237. Baltimore: Williams & Wilkins 1970b.
Kagan, J.: Change and continuity in infancy. New York: Wiley, 1971.

Karmel, B.Z.: Complexity, amount of contour, and visually dependent preference behavior in hooded rats, domestic chicks, and human infants. J. comp. physiol. Psychol. **69**, 649–657 (1969a).

Karmel, B.Z.: The effects of age, complexity, and amount of contour on pattern preferences in human infants. J. exp. Child Psychol. **7**, 339–354 (1969b).

Karmel, B.Z.: Brain mechanisms involved in early visual perception. Paper presented at the meetings of the Society for Research in Child Development, Philadelphia, 1973.

Karmel, B.Z.: Contour effects and pattern preferences in infants: A reply to Greenberg and O'Donnell. Child Develpm. **45**, 196–199 (1974).

Karmel, B.Z., Maisel, E.G.: A neuronal activity model for infant visual attention. In: L.B. Cohen and P. Salapatek (eds.), Infant perception from sensation to cognition, Part 1. Basic visual processes (Vol. 1). New York: Academic Press 1975, 78–131.

Kearsley, R.B.: Neonatal response to auditory stimulation: A demonstration of orienting behavior. Unpublished doctoral dissertation, Harvard University, 1971.

Kessen, W., Hershenson, M.: Ocular orientation in the human newborn infant. Paper read at the meetings of the American Psychological Association, Philadelphia, August 1963.

Kessen, W., Haith, M.M., Salapatek, P.: Human infancy: A bibliography and guide. In: P. Mussen (ed.), Carmichael's manual of child psychology, 287–444. New York: Wiley 1970.

Kessen, W., Salapatek, P., Haith, M.M.: The visual response of the newborn to linear contour. J. exp. Child Psychol. **13**, 9–20 (1972).

Koffka, K.: Principles of Gestalt psychology. New York: Harcourt, Brace & World 1935.

Komoda, M.K., Festinger, L., Phillips, L.J., Duckman, R.H., Young, R.A.: Some observations concerning saccadic eye movements. Vision Res. **13**, 1009–1020 (1973).

Kroner, T.: Ueber die Sinnesempfindungen der Neugeborenen. Breslau: Grass, Barth 1881.

Kussmaul, A.: Untersuchungen über das Seelenleben des Neugeborenen. Tübingen: Moser 1859.

Lentz, R., Haith, M.M.: Audio tape storage of experimental data: An application to tachistoscopic research with children. Behav. Res. Meth. Instr. **1**, 273–275 (1969).

Mann, I.: The development of the human eye. London: British Medical Assoc. 1964.

McCall, R.B., Kagan, J.: Attention in the infant: Effects of complexity, contour, perimeter, and familiarity. Child Develpm. **38**, 939–952 (1967).

McCall, R.B., Melson, W.H.: Complexity, contour, and area as determinants of attention in infants. Develop. Psychol. **3**, 343–349 (1970).

McGurk, H.: The role of object orientation in infant perception. J. exp. Child Psychol. **9**, 363–373 (1970).

McKenzie, B.E., Day, R.H.: Object distance as a determinant of visual fixation in early infancy. Science **178**, 1108–1110 (1972).

Mendelson, M.J. and Haith, M.M.: The relation between audition and vision in the human newborn. Monographs of the Society for Research in Child Development, 1976, **41** (4, serial No. 167).

Neisser, U.: Cognitive psychology. New York: Appleton-Century-Crofts 1967.

Nelson, W.E.: Textbook of pediatrics. Philadelphia: Saunders 1964.

Ordy, J.M., Samorajski, T., Collins, R.L., Nagy, A.R.: Postnatal development of vision in a subhuman primate (Macacca Mulatta). Arch. Opthal. (Chicago) **73**, 674–686 (1965).

Parmalee, A.H.: The ontogeny of sleep patterns and associated periodities in infants. In: Prenatal and postnatal development of the human brain. S. Karger, Basel 1973.

Pasik, P., Pasik, T.: Oculomotor functions in monkeys with lesions of the cerebrum and the superior colliculi. In: M.B. Bender (ed.), The oculomotor system. New York: Harper & Row 1964, 40–80.

Pettigrew, J.D., Freeman, R.D.: Visual experience without lines: Effect on developing cortical neurons. Science **182**, 599–601 (1973).

Pettigrew, J.D.: The effect of visual experience on the development of stimulus specificity by kitten cortical neurons. J. Physiol. (Lond.) **237**, 49–74 (1974).

Pipp, S.: Infant visual scanning patterns of depth and contrast. Paper presented at the meetings of the Society for Research in Child Development, Denver, April 1975.

Polyak, S.: The vertebrate visual system. H. Klüver (ed.). Chicago: University of Chicago Press 1957.

Pratt, K.C., Nelson, A.K., Sun, K.H.: The behavior of the newborn infant. Ohio St. Univ. Stud. Contr. Psychol. 1930, No. 10.

Pratt, K.C.: The neonate. In: L. Carmichael (ed.), Manual of Child Psychology, 215–291. New York: Wiley 1954.
Purpura, D.P., Synaptogenesis in mammalian cortex: Problems and perspectives. In: M.B. Sterman, D.J. McGinty, and A.M. Adinolfi (eds.), Brain development and behavior, 23–41. New York: Academic Press 1971.
Rakic, P.: Neurons in rhesus monkey visual cortex: Systematic relation between time of origin and eventual disposition. Science **183**, 425–427 (1974).
Riesen, A.H.: Stimulation as requirement for growth and function in behavioral development. In: D.W. Fiske and S.R. Maddi (eds.), Functions of varied experience, 57–105. Homewood, Ill.: Dorsey 1961.
Rose, G.H.: Relationship of electrophysiological and behavioral indices of visual development of mammals. In: M.B. Sterman, D.J. McGinty, and A.M. Adinolfi (eds.), Brain development and behavior, 145–183. New York: Academic Press 1971.
Rose, G., Ellingson, R.J.: Ontogenesis of evoked potentials. In: W.A. Himwich (ed.), Developmental neurobiology, 393–440. Springfield, Ill.: 1970.
Rose, G.H., Lindsley, D.B.: Development of visually evoked potentials in kittens: Specific and non-specific responses. J. Neurophysiol. **31**, 607–623 (1968).
Ruff, H.A., Birch, H.G.: Infant visual fixation: The effect of concentricity, curvilinearity, and number of directions. J. exp. Child Psychol. **17**, 460–473 (1974).
Saayman, G., Ames, E.W., Moffett, A.: Response to novelty as an indicator of visual discrimination in the human infant. J. exp. Child Psychol. **1**, 189–198 (1964).
Salapatek, P.: Visual scanning of geometric figures by the human newborn. J. comp. physiol. Psychol. **66**, 247–258 (1968).
Salapatek, P.: The visual investigation of geometric patterns by the one- and two-month-old infant. Paper presented at meetings of AAAS, Boston, 1969.
Salapatek, P.: Visual investigation of geometric pattern by the human infant. Paper presented at the meetings of the Society for Research in Child Development, Philadelphia, 1973.
Salapatek, P., Kessen, W.: Visual scanning of triangles by the human newborn. J. exp. Child Psychol. **3**, 155–167 (1966).
Scheibel, A.B.: Neural correlates of psychophysiological development in the young organism. In J. Wortis (ed.), Recent advances in biological psychiatry (Vol. 4), 313–325. New York: Plenum 1962.
Scheibel, M.E., Scheibel, A.B.: Neural correlates of psychophysiological development in the young organism. Anat. Rec. **139**, 319–320 (1961).
Sherman, M., Sherman, I., Flory, C.D.: Infant behavior. Comp. Psychol. Mongr. **12** (1936).
Silfen, C.K., Ames, E.W.: Visual movement preferences in the human infant. Paper presented at the meetings of the Eastern Psychological Association, Philadelphia, April 1964.
Spears, W.C.: Assessment of visual preference and discrimination in the four-month-old infant. J. comp. Physiol. Psychol. **57**, 381–386 (1964).
Spitz, R.A., Wolf, K.M.: The smiling response: A contribution to the ontogenesis of social relations. Genet. Psychol. Mongr. **34**, 57–125 (1946).
Staples, R.: Color vision and color preference in infancy and childhood. Psychol. Bull. **28**, 297–308 (1931).
Staples, R.: The responses of infants to color. J. exp. Psychol. **15**, 119–141 (1932).
Stark, L.: The control system for versional eye movements. In: P. Bach-y-Rita and C.C. Collins (eds.), The control of eye movements, 363–428. New York: Academic Press 1971.
Stechler, G., Latz, E.: Some observations on attention and arousal in the human infant. J. Amer. Acad. Child Psychiat. **5**, 517–525 (1966).
Stirnimann, F.: Über das Farbempfinden Neugeborener. Ann. Paediat. **163**, 1–25 (1944).
Stone, J., Leicester, J., Sherman, S.M.: The naso-temporal division of the monkey's retina. J. comp. Neurol. **150**, 333–348 (1973).
Tauber, E.S., Koffler, S.: Optomotor response in human infants to apparent motion: Evidence of innateness. Science **152**, 382–383 (1966).
Thomas, H.: Visual-fixation responses of infants to stimuli of varying complexity. Child Develpm. **36**, 629–638 (1965).
Thomas, H.: Infant's selection of visual stimuli. Psychol. Rev. **80**, 468–488 (1973).

Truex, R.C., Carpenter, M.B.: Human neuroanatomy. Baltimore: Williams & Wilkins 1969.

Valentine, C.W.: The colour perception and colour preferences of an infant during its fourth and eighth months. Brit. J. Psychol. **6**, 363–386 (1913–1914).

Wagman, S.H.: Eye movements induced by electric stimulation of cerebrum in monkeys and their relationship to bodily movements. In: M.B. Bender (ed.), The oculomotor system, 18–39. New York: Harper & Row 1964.

Warren, R.M., Warren, R.P.: Helmholtz on perception: Its physiology and development. New York: Wiley 1968.

Welch, M.J.: Infant's visual attention to varying degrees of novelty. Child Develpm. **45**, 344–350 (1974).

Wertheimer, M.: Untersuchungen zur Lehre von der Gestalt: II. Psychologische Forschung **4**, 301–350 (1923). Abridged translation by M. Wertheimer. Principles of perceptual organization. In: D. Beardslee and M. Wertheimer (eds.), Readings in perception. Princeton, N.J.: Von Nostrand 1958.

Wickelgren, L.W.: Convergence in the human newborn. J. exp. Child Psychol. **5**, 74–85 (1967).

Wickelgren, L.W.: The ocular response of human newborns to intermittent visual movement. J. exp. Child Psychol. **8**, 469–482 (1969).

Wiesel, T.N., Hubel, D.H.: Ordered arrangement of orientation columns in monkeys lacking visual experience. J. comp. Neurol. **158**, 307–318 (1974).

Wilcox, B.M.: Visual preferences of human infants for representations of the human face. J. exp. Child Psychol. **7**, 10–20 (1969).

Zelazo, P., Hopkins, R., Jacobson, S., Kagan, J.: Psychological reactivity to discrepant events. Int. J. cogn. Psychol. **2**, 385–393 (1974).

Zetterström, B.: The clinical electroretinogram: IV. The electroretinogram in children during the first year of life. Acta ophthal. (Kbh.) **29**, 295–304 (1951).

Zetterström, B.: Flicker electroretinography in newborn infants. Acta ophthal. (Kbh.) **33**, 157–166 (1955).

Chapter 11

Developmental Aspects of Speech Perception[1]

P.D. EIMAS, Providence (USA)

Contents

In order to comprehend and speak a human language, an individual must be capable of abstracting the many levels of linguistic information from the acoustic signal, and of performing the necessary mental and motoric activities for the transformation of highly abstract semantic intentions into an understandable physical event. When one considers the full extent of the linguistic knowledge and competence that must be available in order to be a fully competent member of a language community, and the speed and ease with which normal children acquire language, it becomes evident that the child brings to the language acquisition task some very special, perhaps species-specific, abilities to assist and hasten the learning process (cf., CHOMSKY, 1965; LENNEBERG, 1967).

The intention of this chapter is to describe some of the perceptual abilities that the very young human infant uses in the processing of speech signals, well before he is able to articulate even the most elementary sounds of language. It is of course obvious that the language-processing abilities of the infant are severely limited. There is, not unexpectedly, no evidence for any responsiveness on the part of the infant to variations in linguistic information of a syntactic or semantic nature. However, as this chapter will attempt to demonstrate, the

[1] The preparation of this report, which was completed in 1974, and the author's research reported herein was supported by HD 05331 from the National Institute of Child Health and Human Development. I wish to express my appreciation to Dr. FRANKLIN S. COOPER, who has very generously made available the facilities of the Haskins Laboratories.

infant does have the capacity to process speech as speech, that is to say, as a class of sounds that are different from nonspeech acoustic signals, and to extract from this form of processing a phonetic message that can be represented by a set of distinctive features (cf., JAKOBSON et al., 1963; HALLE, 1964).[2] Indeed, it appears that the infant's ability to perceive distinctions among the sounds of speech is governed to a larger extent by phonetic differences than by acoustic differences. In addition to presenting the evidence for the phonetic (that is, linguistic) processing of speech by infants, recent experimental findings will be described which indicate that the extraction of the phonetic feature message during the perception of speech is accomplished by specialized feature-detector systems.

Before consideration of the speech-perception data, however, the infant's capability for processing nonspeech sounds will be examined. Inasmuch as speech and nonspeech sounds undergo considerable common processing by means of the same receptors, neural pathways, subcortical areas, and perhaps cortical areas, all of which transform and encode acoustic information, some knowledge of the general auditory functioning of the human infant would seem in order. A review of the nonspeech literature is also instructive in that it reveals, by contrast, the highly developed and sophisticated nature of the speech processing mechanisms in the infant.[3]

A. Perception of Nonspeech Signals

A number of researchers (e.g., EISENBERG et al., 1964) have demonstrated that the neonate is sensitive to a wide variety of sounds including whistles, tuning forks, brief clicks, and music, and that the continuous presentation of acoustic stimulation often results in a general quieting of the infant (e.g., BRACKBILL et al., 1966). Demonstrations of this nature have, after more than 100 years, put to rest the proposition that the human neonate is deaf (see PEIPER, 1963, for a review of this long controversy). In addition to being respon-

[2] According to STUDDERT-KENNEDY (1974), it is helpful to view the transformation from acoustic signal to linguistic message as a series of stages, even though the actual analysis most likely does not proceed in accord with a strict serial model (WOOD, 1973). These stages of analysis would include at least the following: (1) auditory, (2) phonetic, (3) phonologic, and (4) lexical, syntactic, and semantic. The present chapter is concerned with the first two stages: the initial representation of the acoustic waveform and the transformation of this auditory analysis into a phonetic message of distinctive features.

[3] In fairness, it should be noted that the majority of research on the perception of nonspeech sounds has used neonates and has often been conducted with intentions other than mapping the sensitivity of the infant auditory system. There are, for example, numerous studies which used acoustic stimuli to study the processes of habituation and dishabituation (GRAHAM and JACKSON, 1970). Thus, it is possible that the general auditory system of the human infant is more highly developed than the present data indicate.

sive to sound, neonates and young infants have been found to habituate to a wide range of sounds as measured by a number of components of the orientation reaction. For example, BARTOSHUK (1962a, b) and BRIDGER (1962), have used the cardiac response to show both habituation and dishabituation to sound stimuli. The latter finding is particularly important in that it provides a methodology for assessing discriminative capacities along the many dimensions of sound. For researchers concerned with the early detection of developmental abnormalities, EISENBERG et al. (1966) have shown that developmentally "suspect" and high-risk infants take longer to habituate to sound than developmentally normal infants.

Research related to estimating the absolute and differential sensitivity of the infant to the basic dimensions of sound (for example, intensity and frequency) has not been extensively undertaken, and as a result there is a lack of reliable information. Intensity differences can be discriminated by infants as young as a few days of age (BARNET and GOODWIN, 1965; STEINSCHNEIDER et al., 1966; STUBBS, 1934), and indeed, BARTOSHUK (1964) was able to demonstrate STEVENS' power law in the neonate: the logarithm of the cardiac response was linearly related to intensity, measured in decibels. The absolute threshold, while not as yet specifically defined, does appear to be significantly higher than that of the normal hearing adult (HECOX, 1975). The difference threshold has also not been determined, although BARTOSHUK (1962b) found that the neonate can discriminate a difference of 11 dB, which may be a reasonable first approximation.

The evidence on frequency discrimination by neonates and young infants is, if anything, even more meager, and marked by inconsistent findings. What does appear to be true is that infants between a few days and five months are capable of discriminating frequency changes (e.g., BRIDGER, 1962). Indeed, BRIDGER found that one neonate was able to discriminate a difference of 50 Hz. BARTOSHUK (1962b), MCCALL and MELSON (1970) and MELSON and MCCALL (1970) have also obtained evidence that infants are sensitive to changes in a tonal pattern. It may well be that failures to find evidence for frequency discrimination (e.g., TREHUB, 1973a) are more a function of procedural factors than of sensory capacities.

The apparently reduced sensitivity of the infant to such characteristics of sound as intensity, frequency, and, most probably, location (see LEVENTHAL and LIPSITT, 1964; TURKEWITZ et al., 1966) may be reflecting the immaturity of the auditory nervous system, particularly the auditory cortex (HECOX, 1975). If, however, the relative insensitivity of the infant to nonspeech acoustic input were solely a function of the immaturity of the auditory nervous system, particularly the auditory cortex, infants would most likely be unable to differentiate the basic sounds of speech, since they vary along more complex acoustic dimensions than either frequency or intensity. The low estimates of sensitivity may be, in part, a consequence of less than optimal testing procedures and, more importantly, of using stimuli that have little in the way of special significance for the organism. Such stimuli for the human species are obviously those which convey linguistic information (cf., MATTINGLY, 1972). Regardless of the explanation for the apparent reduced processing capacity for the simple dimensions of sound, the infant does bring to the task of speech perception at least the abilities to discriminate variations in frequency, frequency patterns, and intensity (cf., MORSE, 1974, for a more extensive review of this literature).

B. Perception of Speech

A major conclusion of the research on the perception of speech over the past 20 years is that adult listeners perceive speech in a very different manner from that in which they perceive nonspeech signals. The claim has been made that speech is processed in a linguistic mode in contrast to an auditory mode, the latter of which serves the perception of nonspeech signals, including those of considerable complexity (EIMAS, 1974, 1975a; LIBERMAN et al., 1967; LIBERMAN, 1970; STUDDERT-KENNEDY, 1974). Evidence for this conclusion comes from a large number of studies of dichotic listening, electrophysiologic activity associated with the processing of speech and nonspeech sounds, and adult listeners' ability to identify and discriminate series of synthetic speech stimuli.

The dichotic listening studies have consistently shown that speech, including real and synthetic nonsense syllables, is better perceived when the sound arrives at the right ear than when the speech signal is presented to the left ear, whereas the converse is true for acoustic events without linguistic significance (see, for example, KIMURA, 1961, 1964; STUDDERT-KENNEDY and SHANKWEILER, 1970). Electrophysiologic studies, which have measured the average evoked potential to sound, have confirmed very nicely the separate processing of speech and nonspeech events. WOOD et al. (1971) and MOLFESE (1972), to cite but two studies, have found greater electrical activity in the left hemisphere than in the right hemisphere when speech is processed, whereas, at least in case of the MOLFESE study, the converse was true when nonspeech sounds were processed by the same subjects. MOLFESE, most interestingly, found this to be the case for infants as young as one week of age. Finally, adult listeners have typically been found to be quite consistent in their ability to assign synthetic speech patterns, which vary continuously along some acoustic dimension, to phonetic categories. Of greater importance, however, was the finding that the ability of these same individuals to discriminate stimulus pairs was strongly influenced by the phonetic categories to which the stimuli had been assigned. Two stimuli that were acoustic variations of the same phonetic category or critical distinctive phonetic feature were discriminated only slightly better than would be expected by chance, whereas two stimuli, separated by the same acoustic difference, but being exemplars of different phonetic categories or features, were highly discriminable. This categorical form of perception is particularly characteristic of the acoustic dimensions which are sufficient to differentiate the stop consonants (for representative studies, see EIMAS, 1963; LIBERMAN et al., 1957; MAT-

TINGLY et al., 1971; PISONI, 1973; and for general reviews of the categorical perception of speech, see LIBERMAN et al., 1967; STUDDERT-KENNEDY et al., 1970). Categorical-like perception has also been obtained with young school-aged children (WOLF, 1973) and with consonants other than the stops (MIYAWAKI et al., 1975). It has also been obtained to some extent with vowel stimuli under rather restricted conditions (FUJISAKI and KAWASHIMA, 1969; PISONI, 1973). It is of particular importance to note that when the variations in the acoustic dimensions that distinguish among the stop consonants and the [r]–[l] contrast are presented in a nonspeech context for purposes of discrimination, perception is no longer categorical. MATTINGLY et al. (1971) and MIYAWAKI et al. (1975) did not find the peaks and near-chance throughs, which are characteristic of synthetic speech discrimination functions, when the same variations were presented in contexts that listeners perceived as nonspeech sound patterns.

These findings on the perception of speech are taken to reflect, at least in part, the special mechanisms that serve the processing of speech. At the phonetic level, EIMAS (1974), among others, has assumed that the speech-analyzing mechanisms extract a phonetic message from the auditory representation. It is this process of feature extraction, most probably localized in the left hemisphere, that transforms the continuous variations in the acoustic-auditory information into a set of discontinuous phonetic feature values. Additional, higher-level integrative mechanisms are most likely needed to arrive at a percept, that is, the experience of hearing a particular phone or set of phones as well as to extract the syntactic and semantic content of the message.

C. Infant Perception of Voicing and Place Contrasts

Although MOFFITT (1971) and MORSE (1972) have shown that infants between 2 and 6 months of age were able to distinguish between two stop consonants with different values of the phonetic feature "place of articulation", they did not demonstrate in a compelling manner that the perception (discrimination) of these contrasts was linguistic in nature. It could as readily have been the case that the infants were responding solely to differences in the acoustic waveform rather than to differences in the phonetic feature structure of the two signals. In order to determine whether infants perceive the sounds of speech in a linguistically relevant manner, that is, in accord with the phonetic message, EIMAS et al. (1971) selected the dimension of voice onset time (VOT) for investigation. The reasons for initiating research with this particular dimension have been spelled out in the original report. They compared the discriminability of an identical (20 ms) difference in VOT under two conditions: (1) When the two stimuli to be discriminated were each an exemplar of one of the two voicing contrasts found in English (that is, the voiced and voiceless stops), and (2) when the two stimuli were both representatives of the same voicing contrast, that is, they were either both voiced or both voiceless stops. These conditions will be referred to hereafter as Group D and Group S, respectively. Greater discriminability in the former condition would be evidence for categorical-like perception, and presumably for perception in a speech mode, that is, for perception in accord with a phonetic feature code.

The VOT continuum was defined by LISKER and ABRAMSON (1964) as the time between the release burst and the onset of laryngeal pulsing or voicing. The research of LISKER and ABRAMSON (ABRAMSON and LISKER, 1970, 1972; LISKER and ABRAMSON, 1964, 1967, 1970) has established that variations in VOT are sufficient for the perceived distinctions among the voicing contrasts of English and other languages. Variations in VOT can be realized acoustically and incorporated into synthetic speech. Identification functions for a series of synthetic speech that vary in VOT only from adult listeners have indicated that for the bilabial stops, which were used in the EIMAS et al. study, delays in the onset of voicing of less than 25 ms duration are almost invariably perceived as the voiced stop [b], whereas delays longer than 25 ms are perceived as the voiceless stop [p]. Consequently, for the first condition, EIMAS et al. selected stimuli with VOT delays (values) of +20 and +40 ms, while for the second condition, the stimuli had VOT delays (values) of +60 and +80 ms or 0 and −20 ms. The minus sign indicates that the onset of voicing occurred before the release burst. Three of the stimuli were, thus, perceived by adult listeners as [b] (VOT values equal to −20, 0, and +20) and three as [p] (VOT values equal to +40, +60, and +80).

The procedure used by EIMAS and by almost all of the subsequent infant speech perception research to be reported below was a modification of the conjugate reinforcement methodology, whereby each criterion response, a high-amplitude, nonnutritive sucking response, was reinforced with the presentation of a synthetic speech pattern.[4] After the infant is placed in a reclining seat and presented with a blind nipple to suck, the amplitude criterion and baseline rate of sucking are established. Immediately thereafter, each criterion sucking response is reinforced. The infant typically discovers the contingency within a few minutes and the rate of sucking increases. After an asymptotic rate of sucking is attained, the rate declines with continued presentation of the same reinforcing sound pattern, presumably as a consequence of the one novel stimulus losing its reinforcing properties as it becomes increasingly familiar. After a two-minute period of response decrement, the satiation period, the second stimulus is presented without interruption and again contingent on high-amplitude sucking for four minutes. Control infants are treated in exactly the same manner, with the critical exception that after the initial period of response decrement, no change is made in the auditory stimulus, that its, the first and second stimuli are acoustically identical. Either an increase in response rate associated with the stimulus change greater than that demonstrated by the

[4] In the EIMAS et al. (1971) experiment, it was actually the intensity of the reinforcing event that was contingent upon the rate of sucking. A sucking rate of two responses per second maintained the reinforcing stimulus at maximum intensity. All subsequent experiments have used the procedure described above, with little, if any, difference in the overall pattern of results.

control infants, or a decrement less than that of the controls, is taken as inferential evidence that the infants perceived a difference between the two auditory patterns. For a more detailed explication of the procedure and its rationale, the reader is referred to EIMAS et al. (1971) and EIMAS (1974, 1975a).

The results of the EIMAS et al. study are shown in Table 1. The mean change in response rate (that is, the mean rate of sucking during the four minutes of postshift stimulation minus the mean rate during the two minutes of satiation immediately prior to the stimulus shift) is shown, averaged across age groups, individuals, and minutes. Analyses of these data revealed a significant overall effect due to treatments, and individual comparisons showed Group D to be reliably different from the remaining two groups ($p < 0.01$, for each comparison), which in turn did not differ statistically from one another. In a replication study with two- and three-month-old infants, EIMAS (1975a) used a larger difference in VOT (50 ms) and synthetic speech patterns representing the alveolar voiced- and voiceless-stop consonants, [d] and [t]. The same pattern of results was obtained, as shown in Table 1. Group D showed a reliable recovery during the postshift period, whereas Group S showed a continued decrement in the rate of responding. The difference between the groups was highly reliable ($p < 0.01$).

Table 1. Mean recovery data for the voiced-voiceless distinctions, [b]–[p] and [d]–[t], during the four minutes of postshift stimulation. From EIMAS et al. (1971) and EIMAS (1975a)

Phonetic distinction	Experimental conditions		
	Group D	Group S	Group C
[b]–[p]	+8.5	−2.9	−8.6
[d]–[t]	+9.7	−7.3	

It is possible to argue that a failure to obtain evidence of discriminability for Group S in the satiation, release-from-satiation paradigm used by EIMAS et al. (1971) and others, is not conclusive evidence that the two stimuli are not discriminated by infants. It may be the case that the second stimulus, although discriminably different from the first, is not sufficiently motivating or reinforcing. Consequently, there is no increment in the response rate to obtain the stimulus. However, a consistent pattern of failure to find recovery for all acoustic variations of the same phonetic feature category would, of course, still provide important information about the speech processing abilities of the human infant, particularly given consistent evidence of discriminability, that is, recovery, when the two stimuli were from different phonetic categories. Be that as it may, a recent study by LASKY et al. (1975) has provided at least somewhat more convincing evidence that the failure to show a recovery of the sucking response by infant listeners who received variations of the same phonetic feature represents a failure to discriminate the stimuli. They used a measure of cardiac deceleration in a habituation–dishabituation paradigm to assess the discriminability of 40 ms differences in VOT in four- to six-month-old infants from a Spanish-speaking environment. They found dishabituation, but only when the two stimuli represented different values of the phonetic feature of voicing, either prevoiced vs. voiced or voiced vs. voiceless. While it is still possible to argue that the failure to find dishabituation to within-category variations of a phonetic feature represents a lack of attention to the second stimulus rather than a failure to discriminate, such an argument demands an explanation of why attentional failures occur only in the within-category condition. (Such an explanation is, of course, also needed for the high-amplitude sucking paradigm.) Given the absense of such an explanation, it is our belief, based on the available data, that the failure to recover or dishabituate to the stimuli of Group S represents a failure to discriminate what are in fact identical stimuli when described in terms of phonetic features. Whether other paradigms can be employed to demonstrate that, under certain conditions, within-category acoustic information is available for response decisions by infants, as it is for adult listeners (PISONI and TASH, 1974), remains an interesting empirical problem.

With regard to the discrimination of voicing contrasts, the data clearly indicate that infants during the first few months of life are able to make very fine distinctions in voice onset time, and that the manner in which these distinctions are perceived is linguistic in nature. Indeed, EIMAS (1975a) has presented evidence that the discrimination of voicing contrasts by young infants is virtually entirely controlled by phonetic, as opposed to acoustic, differences. There is likewise evidence from investigations of the discrimination of phonetic distinctions based on place of articulation that infants may be even more constrained at times by phonetic considerations than are adult listeners (EIMAS, 1974).

Research with adult listeners on the perception of phonetic contrasts that are distinguished by place of articulation has revealed a number of sufficient cues for the perceived distinctions among the voiced- and voiceless-stop consonants. Two of these cues are variations in the starting frequency and direction of the second- and third-formant transitions together, and variations in the second-formant transition alone. Their perception, as mentioned, is very nearly categorical (e.g., LIBERMAN et al., 1957; MATTINGLY et al., 1971). Earlier research by MOFFITT (1971) and MORSE (1972) demonstrated that infants were able to distinguish between speech sounds that varied in place of articulation. More recently, EIMAS (1974, Experiment 1) compared the discriminability of three-formant synthetic speech patterns by two- and three-month-old infants when the stimuli represented the same or different values of the phonetic feature "place." The acoustic difference between stimuli was, as nearly as possible, the same for both conditions. The data, in terms of the mean recovery scores during the postshift period, are presented in Table 2.

As was true for the discrimination of differences in VOT, analyses of the data revealed that Group D differed significantly from Groups S and C ($p < 0.025$ in each instance), which in turn were not reliably different from each other. Thus, the manner in which the cues for place of articulation are perceived is linguistic, which is to say that disrimination is constrained by the phonetic distinctive feature structure of the signal.

In a second study with the same population of infants, EIMAS (1974, Experiment 2) compared the ability to discriminate acoustic cues for place of articu-

Table 2. Mean recovery data during the four minutes of postshift stimulation for phonetic distinctions based on place articulation. From EIMAS (1974)

	Experimental conditions		
	Group D	Group S	Group C
Experiment I	+4.1	−6.1	−4.8
Experiment II			
Speech	+8.5	−4.6	−1.2
Nonspeech	+4.0[a]	+7.9	+0.6

[a] A mean change of +7.3 responses was obtained in a replication of this condition.

lation when these cues were presented in a speech context, as was the case in Experiment 1, and when the same cues were presented in a nonspeech context, as in the MATTINGLY et al. (1971) series of experiments. The speech stimuli were two-formant synthetic patterns rather than the three-formant patterns of the first experiment, and varied only in the starting frequency and direction of the second-formant transition. The nonspeech stimuli, which were perceived by adult listeners as bird-like chirps, were simply the very brief (40 ms) second-formant transitions. No other acoustic energy was present. Within each class of stimuli there were three groups, D, S, and C. The acoustic differences between the two stimuli for Groups D and S were very nearly the same, and inasmuch as the nonspeech formant transitions were exactly the same as those of the speech patterns, the speech and nonspeech stimuli were completely comparable with respect to acoustic differences. The results of this experiment are also found in Table 2. Statistical analysis confirmed that the speech stimuli were again perceived in a categorical manner: Group D differed significantly from Groups S and C. The nonspeech stimuli, on the other hand, were perceived in a continuous manner, in that Groups D and S did not differ significantly from each other. Indeed, in the original experiment, the recovery score for Group S was greater than that for Group D. However, as indicated in Table 2, a replication of the nonspeech Group D yielded a recovery score very close to that of Group S. A groups (D versus S) by type of stimulus (speech versus nonspeech) analysis of variance revealed a highly significant interaction between these variables ($p < 0.001$): Group S, which received speech stimuli, recovered significantly less than the remaining three groups, which did not differ reliably from one another. From these data, EIMAS concluded that "...the results of these two experiments indicate that infants are capable of categorizing continuous variations in the acoustic dimensions that signal phonetic distinctions corresponding to place of articulation. Moreover, the manner in which this categorization takes place agrees perfectly with the three major, and possibly universal, phonetic distinctions based on place of articulation. Finally, the processing system that subserves perception of the phonetic feature of place differs from the system that is capable of processing the same acoustic information in a nonspeech context" [p. 513].

D. Perception of the [r]–[l] Distinction

In a recent study, MIYAWAKI et al. (1975) investigated the perception of variations in the starting frequency of the initial steady-state portion of the third formant which are in effect variations in the starting frequency of the third-formant transition. In the appropriate acoustic setting, these variations are effective in signaling the perceived distinctions between [r] and [l]. The perception of these cues in a speech context was very nearly categorical, whereas in a nonspeech setting, the perception was continuous. The perception of these same stimuli by two- and three-month-old infants was recently investigated by the author (EIMAS, 1975b). The procedure and paradigm were the same as in the previous studies of infant speech perception, except that there were now two within-category conditions for the speech and nonspeech patterns: one within-category condition represented acoustic variations of [r] ($S_{[r]}$), and the other, the acoustic variations of [l] ($S_{[l]}$). The reason for this addition was that MIYAWAKI et al. found that the acoustic variations of [r] were considerably less discriminable than equivalent variations of [l]. The same trend was, to a lesser extent, obtained with the nonspeech patterns. The additional within-category groups permit determination of whether or not infants are also differentially sensitive to equivalent variations in the third-formant transition at different points along the continuum.

The infant discrimination data are shown in Table 3 along with the adult discriminability levels for the same pairs of stimuli. The latter were obtained from the study by MIYAWAKI et al. (1975). In terms of overall trends, the two sets of data are remarkable similar. The infants perceived the speech stimuli in a nearly categorical manner, and they found the acoustic variations of [l] to be somewhat more discriminable than the variations of [r], just as adult listeners did. Group D differed from Group $S_{[r]}$ at the 0.025 level of significance, and from Group C at the same level of significance, but Group D differed from Group $S_{[l]}$ at only the 0.06 level. The nonspeech stimuli, in contrast, were perceived in a more nearly continuous fashion, in that the differences between the three nonspeech experimental groups were not statistically reliable ($p > 0.30$ for each comparison).

Table 3. Mean recovery data during the four minutes of postshift stimulation for the [r–l] distinction

	Experimental conditions			
	Group D	Group $S_{[r]}$	Group $S_{[l]}$	Group C
Speech	11.3 (79%)[a]	−2.3 (44%)	3.4 (57%)	−1.6
Nonspeech	5.6 (85%)	4.2 (70%)	5.9 (75%)	−0.9

[a] The numbers in parentheses represent the percentages of correct discriminations (chance equals 33%) for adult American English-speakers (from MIYAWAKI et al., 1975). Within each experimental condition the stimulus pairs were the same for the infant and adult subjects.

As was found earlier in the studies of the discriminability of the cues for place of articulation, infants were able to process the acoustic information in two modes: the linguistic and the auditory. In addition, there was evidence in this study that during the processing of speech patterns infants were able to use acoustic information in addition to the distinctive feature structure of the patterns. This was evidenced by the finding that Group $S_{[l]}$ showed a greater level of recovery than Groups C and $S_{[r]}$, although the differences failed to reach the 0.05 level of statistical significance.

It is of interest to note that adult Japanese speakers, for whom the [r]–[l] distinction is not phonemic or allophonic (i.e., context conditioned) had considerable difficulty in discriminating variations in the third-formant transition in a speech context and showed no evidence for the categorical perception of these sounds (MIYAWAKI et al., 1975). Japanese listeners were, however, able to discriminate the identical acoustic information in a nonspeech setting. In fact, the discriminability function for the nonspeech sounds was virtually the same as that for American speakers. It would be of considerable value to investigate the ability of Japanese infants to perceive these same speech and nonspeech sounds. The outcome would have special relevance for estimations of the role of receptive linguistic experience on speech perception, a topic to be considered next.

E. Infant Speech Perception and the Linguistic Environment

A number of studies of infant speech perception have been directed toward determining the role of the infant's linguistic environment on his ability to perceive speech. These studies have addressed themselves specifically to the question of whether or not it is necessary for the infant to have had receptive experience with a particular phonetic contrast before it is discriminable. Thus, these experiments have tested young infants, usually between two and six months of age, on phonetic contrasts that are not phonemic or allophonic in the parental language. It is recognized, of course, that even if a language fails to use a contrast phonemically or allophonically the young infant may still have had some, although very limited, exposure to this contrast. For example, as mentioned above, there exists a third mode of voicing found in many languages, of which Thai is one (LISKER and ABRAMSON, 1964), produced with a relatively long voicing lead. Although this prevoiced stop is not phonemic in English, it is still quite possible through normal variation or errors in articulation for infants from English speaking environments to have experienced stop consonants with substantial amounts of prevoicing. Despite the fact that it may be virtually impossible to completely isolate an infant from speech sounds that are not normally a part of the linguistic environment, research of this nature can still provide at least some indication of the influence of perceptual experience on discriminative capacity.

With regard to the perception of prevoicing, EIMAS (1975) and MOFFITT and PANKHURST (1973), using the conditioned sucking paradigm, have presented evidence that American and Canadian infants are able to discriminate prevoiced from voiced stops, and moreover, are able to do so in very nearly a categorical manner. Of particular interest to the perception of voicing stops is the LASKY et al. (1975) study. They found that infants from a Spanish-speaking environment categorically perceived the three voicing contrasts—prevoiced, voiced, and voiceless—despite the fact that Spanish uses only two contrasts. Moreover, no evidence was obtained for the discrimination of the two values of VOT that, according to ABRAMSON and LISKER (1972), cross the single Spanish phonetic boundary. On the basis of these data and the evidence from EIMAS, and MOFFITT and PANKHURST, it is possible to conclude, as do LASKY et al., that infants are predisposed to perceive three voicing categories with VOT boundary values situated approximately between −60 and −20 ms and between +20 and +60 ms. These studies on the perception of voicing, and particularly of the prevoiced mode, reveal that the linguistic environment has played a relatively small role in determining the discriminative capacities of the infant. Indeed, the specific phonetic environment of the infant appears to be relatively independent of the infant's ability to perceive speech in a liguistic mode, as well as to be at times independent of the phonetic boundary values obtained with infant listeners (cf., LASKY et al., 1975).

TREHUB (1973b) has investigated the perception of two phonetic contrasts that are not phonemic in English. She found that an oral/nasal vowel distinction [a] versus [ã] which occurs in French and Polish (JAKOBSON, 1968) and a stridency contrast [ʒa] versus [řa], of which the second sound occurs in Czech but not in English (CHOMSKY and HALLE, 1968), were both discriminated by young infants from English-speaking environments. Furthermore, TREHUB has noted that adult listeners have "extreme difficulty in differentiating [ʒa] from [řa]," just as adult English-speaking listeners have great difficulty in discriminating prevoiced- from voiced-stop consonants, if indeed they can discriminate the latter contrast at all. Evidence of this nature indicates that linguistic experience eventually operates on speech perception at the phonetic level to eliminate discriminative abilities that were originally present in the infant, rather than to build in discriminative abilities that were not originally present. However, when and exactly how this occurs is not known. Nor do we know the extent to which the apparent loss of discriminative ability is permanent. (But see EIMAS, 1975, for some speculations on these matters.)

F. Summary of Infant Speech Perception

The evidence has clearly indicated that very young infants are able to distinguish a large number of phonetic contrasts, which are often differentiated by very fine variations in complex acoustic dimensions. Furthermore, when the appropriate experimental conditions have been employed, the evidence has supported the contention that infants are capable of perceiving speech in accord with the phonetic structure of the sound, and hence in a linguistic mode. Finally, it is important to note that this form of behavior occurs after relatively limited exposure to speech in general, and often with virtually no receptive experience with particular phonetic contrasts. Inasmuch as linguistically relevant perception occurs without any apparent reinforcement or active tuition, this capability would appear to be part of the biology of the infant. The next section describes mechanisms of a biological nature that might well serve the perception of speech in infant and adult listeners.

G. Theoretical Mechanisms of Speech Perception

In a recent series of papers, EIMAS, CORBIT, and COOPER (EIMAS and CORBIT, 1973; EIMAS et al., 1973; COOPER, 1974a) have presented evidence for the existence of feature detectors that are especially tuned to restricted ranges of complex acoustic information, and serve to extract discrete phonetic feature information from the continuous acoustic–auditory input. The experimental data supported the contention of at least two detectors for the voicing contrasts of English and many other languages, and three detectors for the corresponding major values of place of articulation. Whether there also exists a detector system for the prevoicing contrast remains to be determined. EIMAS and CORBIT (1973) and EIMAS (1975a) have spelled out the necessary assumptions in order that a feature detector model may be able to accommodate the infant speech perception data and much of the adult discrimination and identification findings. However, before considering the utility of this model of speech perception and the properties of feature detectors, the evidence for the inferred existence of phonetic feature detectors will be examined.

All of the studies purporting to demonstrate the presence of detector systems at the level of phonetic perception have used a selective adaptation procedure. In essence, identification functions for series of synthetic speech stimuli, varying in VOT or the starting frequency and direction of the second- and third-formant transitions were obtained initially with adult listeners in an unadapted state. Next, identification functions were obtained for the same series of stimuli after adaptation, which was accomplished by the repeated presentation of a speech stimulus with the particular phonetic feature value under investigation. It was assumed that prolonged repetition of a feature value would fatigue the appropriate detector and lessen its sensitivity. As a consequence, the assignment of a series of stimuli to phonetic categories would be altered: more stimuli would be assigned to the unadapted category. That was exactly the effect of selective adaptation: after adaptation with the voiceless stop [p], for example, more stimuli varying in VOT alone were assigned to the voiced category [b], resulting in a marked shift in the category boundary toward the adapting stimulus. Moreover, the effect occurred when the adapting stimulus was from a different series from the identification series. Thus, adaptation with [t] produced almost as large an effect as adaptation with [p], as measured by identification of a bilabial series. This latter finding argues against the hypothesis that the adapting unit was the entire phone or syllable, and that the shift in the boundary was a result of response contrast or decision factors. SAWUSCH and PISONI (1973) and SAWUSCH et al. (1974) have also presented data supporting a sensory explanation of the selective adaptation effect as opposed to response decision explanations.

Similar effects have been obtained for the three values of place of articulation. COOPER (1974a) found that adaptation with [b] altered the [b]–[d] boundary, whereas adaptation with [g] altered the [d]–[g] boundary, both shifts occurring in the expected directions. Adaptation with [d] resulted in shifts in the two boundaries, both of which were in the directions predicted by the assumption that what in fact adapted was the detector underlying the perception of the alveolar value of place. COOPER (1974a) concluded that there exist three separate and independent modes of analysis for the feature place, one of which, the labial mode, has been shown to be dependent on manner distinctions (COOPER and BLUMSTEIN, 1974). There would seem to be no doubt that the selective adaptation procedure alters the identification function by lessening the sensitivity of detectors to those features that the adapting stimulus and identification series have in common.

A number of the properties of phonetic feature detectors have recently been determined: (1) The primary locus of the detector systems is central, as evidenced by the fact that most of the selective adaptation effect occurs after binaural fusion (ADES, 1974a; EIMAS et al., 1973). The monaural component, although reliable, is quite small (ADES, 1974a). (2) Both auditory and phonetic components contribute to the effect (see COOPER, 1975, for a review of the data related to this issue). (3) The stimuli to which detectors are sensitive are complex and at times contingently arranged, as is often the case in the visual system of man (e.g., MCCOLLOUGH, 1965; RIGGS, 1973). COOPER (1974b) has found that the analysis of voicing in stop consonants is accomplished, at least in part, with respect to the vowel environment and ADES (1974b) has shown that place information is contingent on the locus of the consonant within the syllable.

In summary, the evidence supports the existence of analyzing systems that are analogous to the feature-detector systems of other sensory modalities, and that extract the phonetic feature message from the acoustic signal. Although a beginning has been made toward the delineation of the properties of phonetic feature detectors, considerably more information is needed before a precise model of their structure and operation can by constructed. For example, greater detail is needed concerning the specific acoustic cues for place, voicing, and other manner distinctions. In addition, the relationships between auditory property detectors (cf., STEVENS, 1973) and phonetic feature detectors needs to be elaborated, as well as the extent to which the speech signal must be normalized in order to eliminate acoustic variations in speech due to coarticulation and individual differences in the size and sharpe of the articulatory apparatus.

A feature-detector model of speech perception offers a number of advantages. In the first place, it can explain the infant speech data (EIMAS, 1974, 1975a) without recourse to complex motor theories of speech perception (cf., LIBERMAN et al., 1967; STEVENS and HOUSE, 1972). Secondly, a feature-detector model of speech analysis at the phonetic level provides the infant with the automatic and unconscious means for the recognition and special processing of speech. It also provides the infant with a mechanism whereby a continuous stream of acoustic input can be segmented into the very building blocks of language—the distinctive phonetic features. Undoubtedly the acquisition of language would be seriously extended, and perhaps impossible, if it were necessary for the human infant to learn the special nature of speech and its manner of processing.

Finally, this form of model can also accommodate the apparently close relationship between the processes of speech production and speech perception (COOPER, 1975; EIMAS et al., 1973; LIBERMAN et al., 1967; STEVENS, 1972), by assuming that the speech-analyzing system evolved in relation to the restraints imposed by the mechanisms of speech production, and conversely. According to this view, the relationship between perception and production is a product of evolutionary development, and not ontogenetic development, as is assumed with most models of speech perception. Given the enormous adaptive value of speech and language, selection pressures would have operated to produce a communication system in which an efficient and specialized means of transmission is matched by an equally efficient and specialized means of reception (cf., LIEBERMAN, 1970, 1973; STEVENS, 1972). Highly specialized, species-specific communication systems are not uncommon (see, for example, the research of CAPRANICA, 1965, on the bullfrog; of CAPRANICA et al., 1973, on the cricket frog; of HOY and PAUL, 1973, on the cricket; and of WINTER and FUNKENSTEIN, 1973, and WOLLBERG and NEWMAN, 1972, on the squirrel monkey) and there is no reason to believe that a similar evolutionary pattern did not occur in man.

A feature-detector model of this nature implies an element of genetic control over the processes of transmission and reception, although it by no means excludes the possibility of experiential modification (e.g., CAPRANICA et al., 1973). Evidence for the genetic control of communication has been obtained by HOY and PAUL (1973), and with respect to human speech such evidence may be inferred from the nearly universal modes of voicing and place distinction, as well as the ability of young inarticulate infants to perceive speech in accord with these same distinctions. It is, we believe, by means of these biologically determined perceptual structures that the infant is able to perceive speech in a linguistic manner, and thereby to initiate the important task of acquiring language.

References

Abramson, A.S., Lisker, L.: Discriminability along the voicing continuum: cross-language tests. In Proceedings of the Sixth International Congress of Phonetic Sciences, Prague, 1967, 569–573. Prague: Academia 1970.

Abramson, A.S., Lisker, L.: Voice-timing perception in Spanish word initial stops. In: Status Report on Speech Perception *SR-29/30*, New Haven, Conn, 15–25. Haskins Laboratories 1972.

Ades, A.E.: Bilateral component in speech perception? J. acoust. Soc. Amer. **56**, 610–617 (1974a).

Ades, A.E.: How phonetic is selective adaptation? Experiments on syllable position and vowel environment. Percept. Psychophys. **16**, 61–67 (1974b).

Barnet, A.G., Goodwin, A.M.: Average evoked electroencephalographic responses to clicks in the human newborn. Electroenceph. clin. Neurophysiol. **18**, 441–450 (1965).

Bartoshuk, A.K.: Response decrement with repeated elicitation of human neonatal cardiac acceleration to sound. J. comp. physiol. Psychol. **55**, 9–13 (1962a).

Bartoshuk, A.K.: Human neonatal cardiac acceleration to sound: Habituation and dishabituation. Percept. Mot. Skills **15**, 15–27 (1962b).

Bartoshuk, A.K.: Human neonatal cardiac responses to sound: A power function. Psychon. Sci. **1**, 151–152 (1964).

Brackbill, Y., Adams, G., Crowell, D.H., Gray, M.L.: Arousal level in neonates and preschool children under continuous auditory stimulation. J. exp. Child Psychol. **4**, 178–188 (1966).

Bridger, W.H.: Sensory discrimination and autonomic function in the newborn. J. Amer. Acad. Child Psychiat. **1**, 67–82 (1962).

Capranica, R.R.: The evoked vocal response of the bullfrog. Cambridge, Mass.: Research Monograph 33, M.I.T. Press 1965.

Capranica, R.R., Frishkopf, L.S., Nevo, E.: Encoding of geographical dialects in the auditory system of the cricket frog. Science **182**, 1272–1274 (1973).

Chomsky, N.: Aspects of the theory of syntax. Cambridge, Mass.: M.I.T. Press 1965.

Chomsky, N., Halle, M.: The sound pattern of English. New York: Harper and Row 1968.

Cooper, W.E.: Adaptation of phonetic feature analyzers for place of articulation. J. acoust. Soc. Amer. **56**, 617–628 (1974a).

Cooper, W.E.: Contingent feature analysis in speech perception. Percept. Psychophys. **16**, 201–204 (1974b).

Cooper, W.E.: Selective adaptation to speech. In: Shiffrin, R.M., Castellani, N.J., Lindman, H., Pisoni, D.B. (eds.), Cognitive theory. Potomac, Maryland: Erlbaum, 23–54 (1975).

Cooper, W.E., Blumstein, S.E.: A 'labial' feature analyzer in speech perception. Percept. Psychophys. **15**, 591–600 (1974).

Eimas, P.D.: The relation between identification and discrimination along speech and nonspeech continua. Lang. Speech **6**, 206–217 (1963).

Eimas, P.D.: Auditory and linguistic processing of cues for place of articulation by infants. Percept. Psychophys. **16**, 513–521 (1974).

Eimas, P.D.: Speech perception in early infancy. In: Cohen, L.B., Salapatek, P. (eds.), Infant perception: Vol. 2, 193–231. New York: Academic Press (1975a).

Eimas, P.D.: Auditory and phonetic coding of the cues for speech: Discrimination of the [r–l] distinction by young infants. Percept. Psychophys. **18**, 341–347 (1975b).

Eimas, P.D., Cooper, W.E., Corbit, J.D.: Some properties of linguistic feature detectors. Percept. Psychophys. **13**, 247–252 (1973).

Eimas, P.D., Corbit, J.D.: Selective adaptation of linguistic feature detectors. Cogn. Psychol. **4**, 99–109 (1973).

Eimas, P.D., Siqueland, E.R., Jusczyk, P., Vigorito, J.: Speech perception in infants. Science **171**, 303–306 (1971).

Eisenberg, R.B., Coursin, D.B., Rupp, N.R.: Habituation to an acoustic pattern as an index of differences among human neonates. J. Aud. Res. **6**, 239—248 (1966).

Eisenberg, R.B., Griffin, E.J., Coursin, D.B., Hunter, M.A.: Auditory behavior in the human neonate: A preliminary report. J. Speech Hear. Res. **7**, 245—269 (1964).

Fujisaki, H., Kawashima, T.: On the modes and mechanisms of speech perception. Annual Report of the Engineering Research Institute **28**, 67–73, Faculty of Engineering, University of Tokyo, Tokyo, 1969.

Graham, F.K., Jackson, J.C.: Arousal systems and infant heart rate responses. In: Reese, H.W., Lipsitt, L.P. (eds.), Advances in Child Development and Behavior **5**, 60–117. New York: Academic Press 1970.

Halle, M.: On the basis of phonology. In: Fodor, J.A., Katz, J.J. (eds.). The structure of language, 324–333, Englewood Cliffs, New Jersey: Prentice Hall 1964.

Hecox, K.: Electrophysiological correlates of human auditory development. In: Cohen, L.B., Salapatek, P. (eds.), Infant Perception. Vol. 2, 151–191. New York: Academic Press (1975).

Hoy, R.R., Paul, R.C.: Genetic control of song specificity in crickets. Science **180**, 82–83 (1973).

Jakobson, R.: Child language, aphasia, and phonological universals (tr. A. Keiler). The Hague: Mouton 1968.

Jakobson, R., Fant, C.G.M., Halle, M.: Preliminaries to speech analysis. Cambridge, Mass.: M.I.T. Press 1963.

Kimura, D.: Cerebral dominance and the perception of verbal stimuli. Canad. J. Psychol. **15**, 166–171 (1961).

Kimura, D.: Left-right differences in the perception of melodies. Quart. J. exp. Psychol. **16**, 355–358 (1964).

Lasky, R.E., Syrdal-Lasky, A., Klein, R.E.: VOT discrimination by four- to six-and-a-half-month-old infants from Spanish environments. J. exp. Child Psychol. **20**, 215–225 (1975).

Lenneberg, E.H.: Biological foundations of language. New York: John Wiley & Sons 1967.

Leventhal, A.S., Lipsitt, L.P.: Adaptation, pitch discrimination, and sound localization in the neonate. Child Develpm. **35**, 759–767 (1964).

Liberman, A.M.: The grammars of speech and language. Cogn. Psychol. **1**, 301–323 (1970).

Liberman, A.M., Cooper, F.S., Shankweiler, D.P., Studdert-Kennedy, M.: Perception of the speech code. Psychol. Rev. **74**, 431–461 (1967).

Liberman, A.M., Harris, K.S., Hoffman, H.S., Griffith, B.C.: The discrimination of speech sounds within and across phoneme boundaries. J. exp. Psychol. **54**, 358–368 (1957).

Lieberman, P.: Towards a unified phonetic theory. Linguistic Inquiry **1**, 307–322 (1970).

Lieberman, P.: On the evolution of language: A unified view. Cognition **2**, 59–94 (1973).

Lisker, L., Abramson, A.S.: A cross-language study of voicing in initial stops: acoustical measurements. Word **20**, 384–422 (1964).

Lisker, L., Abramson, A.S.: Some effects of context on voice onset time in English stops. Lang. Speech **10**, 1–28 (1967).

Lisker, L., Abramson, A.S.: The voicing dimension: some experiments in comparative phonetics. In: Proceedings of the Sixth International Congress of Phonetic Sciences, Prague, 1967, 563–567. Prague: Academia 1970.

Mattingly, I.G.: Speech cues and sign stimuli. Amer. Sci. **60**, 327–337 (1972).

Mattingly, I.G., Liberman, A.M., Syrdal, A.K., Halwes, T.: Discrimination in speech and nonspeech modes. Cogn. Psychol. **2**, 131–157 (1971).

McCall, R.B., Melson, W.H.: Amount of short-term familiarization and the response to auditory discrepancies. Child Develpm. **41**, 861–869 (1970).

McCollough, C.: Color adaptation of edge-detectors in the human visual system. Science **149**, 1115–1116 (1965).

Melson, W.H., McCall, R.B.: Attentional responses of five-month girls to discrepant auditory stimuli, Child Develpm. **41**, 1159–1171 (1970).

Miyawaki, K., Strange, W., Verbrugge, R., Liberman, A.M., Jenkins, J.J., Fujimura, O.: An effect of linguistic experience: The discrimination of [r] and [l] by native speakers of Japanese and English. Percept. Psychophys. **18**, 331–340 (1975).

Moffitt, A.R.: Consonant cue perception by twenty- to twenty-four-week-old infants. Child Develpm. **42**, 717–731 (1971).

Moffitt, A.R., Pankhurst, D.J.: Speech perception during infancy. Unpublished manuscript, Carleton University, Ottawa, Canada (1973).

Molfese, D.L.: Cerebral asymmetry in infants, children and adults: Auditory evoked responses to speech and noise stimuli. Unpublished Doctoral Dissertation, The Pennsylvania State University, College Park, Pennsylvania (1972).

Morse, P.A.: The discrimination of speech and nonspeech stimuli in early infancy. J. exp. Child Psychol. **14**, 477–492 (1972).

Morse, P.A.: Infant speech perception: A preliminary model and review of the literature. In: Schiefelbusch, R.L., Lloyd, L.L. (eds.), Language perspectives—acquisition, retardation, and intervention, 19–53. Baltimore, Maryland: University Park Press 1974.

Peiper, A.: Cerebral function in infancy. (Tr. B. Nagler and H. Nagler.) New York: Consultants Bureau 1963.

Pisoni, D.B.: Auditory and phonetic memory codes in the discrimination of consonants and vowels. Percept. Psychophys. **13**, 253–260 (1973).

Pisoni, D.B., Tash, J.: Reaction times to comparisons within and across phonetic categories. Percept. Psychophys. **15**, 285–290 (1974).

Riggs, L.A.: Curvature as a feature of pattern vision. Science **181**, 1070–1072 (1973).

Sawusch, J.R., Pisoni, D.B.: Category boundaries for linguistic and nonlinguistic dimensions of the same stimuli. Paper presented at the 86th Meeting of the Acoustical Society of America, Los Angeles, California (November, 1973).

Sawusch, J.R., Pisoni, D.B., Cutting, J.E.: Category boundaries for linguistic and nonlinguistic dimensions of the same stimuli. Paper presented at the 87th Meeting of the Acoustical Society of America, New York, New York (April, 1974).

Steinschneider, A., Lipton, E.L., Richmond, J.B.: Auditory sensitivity in the infant: Effect of intensity on cardiac and motor responsivity. Child Develpm. **37**, 233–252 (1966).

Stevens, K.N.: The quantal nature of speech: Evidence from articulatory-acoustic data. In: David, E.E., Jr., Denes, P.B. (eds.), Human communication: A unified view, 51–66. New York: McGraw-Hill 1972.

Stevens, K.N.: The potential role of property detectors in the perception of consonants. Paper presented at the Symposium on Auditory Analysis and Perception of Speech, Leningrad, USSR (August 1973).

Stevens, K.N., House, A.S.: Speech perception. In: Tobias, J. (ed.), Foundations of modern auditory theory, II, 3–62. New York: Academic Press 1972.

Stubbs, E.M.: The effect of the factors of duration, intensity, and pitch of sound stimuli on the responses of newborn infants. Univ. Iowa Stud. Child Welfare **9**, No. 4, 75–135 (1934).

Studdert-Kennedy, M.: The perception of Speech. In: Sebeok, T.A. (ed.), Current trends in linguistics, XII. The Hague: Mouton 1974.

Studdert-Kennedy, M., Liberman, A.M., Harris, K.S., Cooper, F.S.: Motor theory of speech perception: A reply to Lane's critical review. Psychol. Rev. **77**, 234–249 (1970).

Studdert-Kennedy, M., Shankweiler, D.P.: Hemispheric specialization for speech perception. J. acoust. Soc. Amer. **48**, 579–594 (1970).

Trehub, S.E.: Infants' sensitivity to vowel and tonal contrasts. Develop. Psychol. **9**, 91–96 (1973a).

Trehub, S.E.: Auditory-linguistic sensitivity in infants. Unpublished Doctoral Dissertation, McGill University, Montreal, Canada (1973b).

Turkewitz, G., Birch, H.B., Moreau, T., Levy, L., Cornwell, A.C.: Effect of intensity of auditory stimulation on directional eye movements in the human neonate. Anim. Behav. **14**, 93–101 (1966).

Winter, P., Funkenstein, H.H.: The effect of species-specific vocalization on the discharge of auditory cortical cells in the awake squirrel monkey *(Saimiri sciureus)*. Exp. Brain Res. **18**, 489–504 (1973).

Wolf, C.G.: The perception of stop consonants by children. J. exp. Child Psychol. **16**, 318–331 (1973).

Wollberg, Z., Newman, J.D.: Auditory cortex of squirrel monkey: Response patterns of single cells to species-specific vocalizations. Science **175**, 212–214 (1972).

Wood, C.C.: Parallel processing of auditory and phonetic information in speech perception. In: Status Report on Speech Perception *SR-35/36*, 39–53. New Haven, Conn.: Haskins Laboratories 1973.

Wood, C.C., Goff, W.P., Day, R.S.: Auditory evoked potentials during speech perception. Science **173**, 1248–1252 (1971).

D. Effects of Deprivation

Chapter 12

Maturation and Modification in the Developing Visual System

COLIN BLAKEMORE, Cambridge (England)

With 17 Figures

Contents

A. Introduction

The idea that the sense-data received by an animal or a man, especially when young, might alter the way that it perceives and reacts to events later in life is not a new one. The debate about Nature and Nurture is as old as philosophy. But is has received an empirical shot in the arm (like many other areas of psychology) with the advent of electrophysiological methods for studying the actual neural substrate of perception—the sensory pathways of the brain. Important arguments, which used to depend for their evidence on the often incomplete accounts of visual perception after recovery from blindness, on simple description of the behaviour of infants, and even on the introspection of the protagonists, can now rely on formulated experiments. This is however a difficult time at which to write a review of the field, partly because of the remarkable speed with which new results are being published, and partly because of the differences in observations and interpretations that still divide the subject into camps, despite the replacement of introspection by experiment.

I shall concentrate on the visual system because it is there that most experimental effort has been expended. Experiments involving rigorous deprivation or carefully controlled regulation of the sensory environment are more difficult in other sensory systems, but there have been a few such studies and I shall mention them first.

I. Auditory System

In the auditory system, MOORE and AITKIN (1975) have at least demonstrated that intermittent exposure of kittens to a tone of one frequency, with normal auditory experience for the rest of the time, does not lead to any selective change in the representation of that frequency amongst neurones of the inferior colliculus. On the other hand, there is evidence that cells in many nuclei of the auditory system are not fully developed in very young animals and that they only gradually achieve their adult properties (PUJOL, 1972; KÖNIG et al., 1972). The recent discovery of feature-selective neurones of remarkable specificity in the squirrel monkey's auditory cortex—cells that respond optimally to species-specific vocalizations—raises the possibility that the emergence of such cells might depend on the animals' auditory experience (NEWMAN and WOLLBERG, 1973; WINTER and FUNKENSTEIN, 1974).

II. Olfactory System

If much more were known of the functional organization of the normal adult olfactory system, that sensory pathway might be a good candidate for experiments on the influences of sensory experience, since the olfactory environment of an animal can be quite rigorously controlled. In this respect it is fascinating to learn that prolonged exposure of infant rats to a single odour, such as camphor, benzene or pyridine, causes *degenerative* changes amongst the mitral cells of the olfactory bulb. The exact pattern of degeneration seems to be different for each class of odorous compound (PINCHING and DØVING, 1974).

III. Somatic Sensory System

The somatic sensory cortex of the newborn kitten is, in most respects so far investigated, very similar in its organization to that of the adult (RUBEL, 1971). In the rat S1, cells do not become responsive until 7 days of age, but at that stage the somato-topic map is normal, most cells sensitive to vibrissa movement are direction selective and neurones are organized into discrete clusters according to the positions of their receptive fields. Those receptive fields are, however, much larger than in the adult (perhaps because of the absence of inhibitory surrounds), spontaneous activity is much lower and the cells cannot follow repetitive mechanical stimulation (ARMSTRONG-JAMES, 1975).

Again, selective restriction of somatic sensory experience is virtually impossible, but there have been some remarkable studies on the effects of partial de-afferentation. In the mouse somatic sensory cortex, each individual vibrissa is represented by a distinct macroscopic assemblage of cells called a "barrel" (WOOLSEY and VAN DER LOOS, 1970). If vibrissae are removed early in life their particular barrels cannot be found in the cortex (VAN DER LOOS and WOOLSEY, 1973). It is not yet clear whether this effect is essentially a degenerative one or whether it reflects an adaptive developmental strategy. Even more surprising are the experiments of WALL and his colleagues on the somatic pathway in adult mammals. Removing the rat's nucleus gracilis, and hence depriving the thalamic nucleus ventralis postero-lateralis of input from the hind limb, causes, within a few days, an orderly expansion there of the representation of the upper limb, which actually takes over thalamic neurones previously concerned with the hind limb (WALL and EGGER, 1971). In the dorsal horn of the spinal cord of the adult cat, severing several dorsal roots in the lumbar region totally de-afferents that part the cord, but within a short time the neurones there have gained receptive fields on the neighbouring areas of the body from input that must arrive in distant dorsal roots (BASBAUM and WALL, 1976). WALL suggests that these experiments reveal the strengthening of previously "silent" synaptic input to neurones in the somatic sensory pathway, from regions of the skin that normally do not contribute to their receptive fields (MERRILL and WALL, 1972; WALL and WERMAN, 1976). Such a mechanism, if it is a general feature of the nervous system, may be the cause of many important developmental processes.

B. Visual System

Studies of the developing visual system fall into two main areas: 1. observation of the natural maturation of various neuronal structures and the effects of partial or total deprivation of visual experience; and 2. study of the influence of specially controlled visual environments.

I. Natural Maturation in the Visual Pathway

a) Cats

Until quite recently the primary visual cortex of the kitten has been the subject of most studies of the natural development of the visual system and the effects of deprivation. In 1963, HUBEL and WIESEL, after their classic description of the organization of area 17 in the adult cat (1962), published a brief report of experiments in some young kittens. Although their sample was very small (17 neurones from two totally inexperienced animals, 8 and 16 days old), their conclusions were substantial. The cells were less responsive and perhaps less selective in their properties, but they shared two important characteristics with cortical neurones in adult cats: they could nearly all be influenced from both eyes and they responded best to moving edges of a particular orientation. Selectivity for orientation is the distinctive property of almost all cells in the adult cat's visual cortex: here was striking evidence that this property is created by a mechanism that is inherently present in the genetically programmed synaptic input to the cortex.

Even the spatial distribution of orientation selective cells in the immature kitten's cortex seemed similar to that in the adult: neighbouring neurones preferred similar orientations, with sudden shifts from place to place during the penetration (Fig. 1). This pattern has been taken to represent a mosaic of columns or sheets (HUBEL and WIESEL, 1974a) in which orientation is mapped across the surface of the cortex. It is quite remarkable that such an apparently perfect organization could exist at the age of 8 days, when afferent fibres

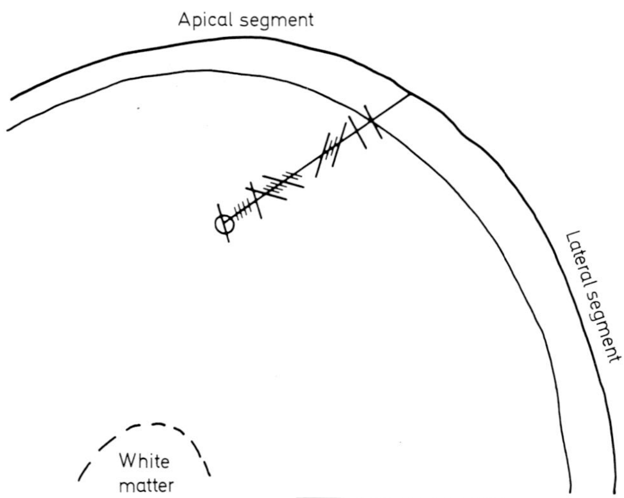

Fig. 1. Reconstruction of a microelectrode penetration through the visual cortex of a visually inexperienced, 16-day-old kitten. Each well-isolated cortical cell is represented by a long line, whose angle shows the preferred orientation (perpendicular to the track indicating vertical in space). The shorter lines show regions in which there was unresolved background activity. The circle represents a lesion at the end of the track. The scale is 0.5 mm. Note the grouping of cells with similar orientational preference. (From HUBEL and WIESEL, 1963)

are only just contacting cells in the deeper layers of the cortex (ANKER and CRAGG, 1974), the number of synapses per neurone is only 1.5% of that in the adult and dendritic spines are hardly present at all (CRAGG, 1972, 1975).

Because of the somewhat greater technical problems in recording in very young kittens and the possibility that slow but passive maturation may occur, an alternative approach to the investigation of purely innate factors in the construction of the visual cortex is to deprive animals of visual experience in some way and to record from them when they are assumed to have reached physiological maturity. (The strategy of observing visual behaviour after a long period of deprivation has been a popular tool in the study of visual development, with studies ranging from RIESEN'S, 1958, original experiments on dark-reared monkeys to the age-old observations on blind humans who have had their sight restored late in life—see VON SENDEN, 1960; ACKROYD et al., 1974). Unfortunately such a procedure confounds any genuine maturational improvements with possible degradation in the system that might result from a lack of adequate stimulation. Certainly when WIESEL and HUBEL (1965a) did record from the cortex in cats that had been deprived for several months after birth by suturing the eyelids closed, they found about one quarter of all neurones to be entirely unselective for the orientation of a moving edge and even more to be altogether unresponsive to visual stimulation. But almost half of their sample, in animals deprived for $2^1/_2$ to $4^1/_2$ months, were apparently orientation selective to some degree.

This general finding, that the organization of the visual cortex is entirely pre-specified and that prolonged deprivation leads to only slight degenerative changes, was challenged by BARLOW and PETTIGREW (1971) and PETTIGREW (1974). They recorded from the cortex in binocularly deprived and normal kittens of various ages and were initially interested in the disparity-detecting properties of immature cortical cells. (In the adult, binocularly driven neurones are often extremely sensitive to the retinal disparity of stimuli presented to both eyes and the optimal disparity varies from cell to cell—see BARLOW et al., 1967.) Their interest soon shifted to the fundamental question of whether orientation selectivity itself is really genetically pre-specified. At first they could find no cells at all in deprived animals that satisfied more rigid criteria for orientation selectivity than HUBEL and WIESEL (1963) had originally employed, though PETTIGREW (1974) did report two such neurones in his entire sample from inexperienced kittens. BARLOW and PETTIGREW'S main impression was that, while inexperienced cortical cells (whatever the age of the kitten) usually have input from both eyes and sometimes have an intrinsic selectivity for the direction or axis of movement of stimuli (see Fig. 2), they are almost never truly orientation selective or selective for the disparity of a binocularly presented stimulus. PETTIGREW (1974) compared his results from binocularly deprived kittens with those from normal animals of similar age. In fact there were no obvious differences until 4 weeks of age, after which the normal animals showed a rapid improvement in all aspects of stimulus specificity. What was emphasized, then, was the remarkable lack of organization in the immature cortex and the fundamental importance of visual stimulation in promoting the emergence of normal degrees of specificity. IMBERT and BUISSERET (1975a) seemed in broad agreement with this attitude;

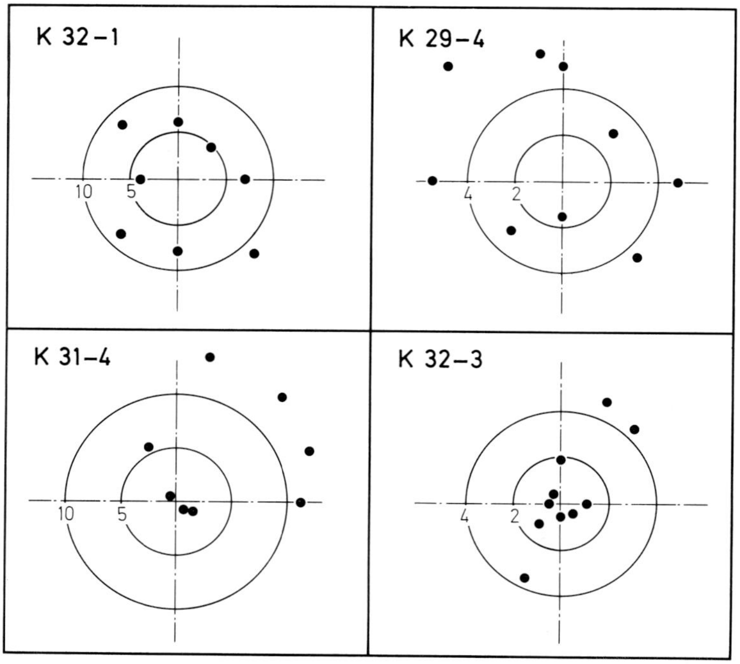

Fig. 2. Polar graphs, plotting the number of impulses for each sweep of a 0.5° diameter spot in the directions indicated. All kittens were visually inexperienced: K 29, 14 days; K 31, 16 days; K 32, 28 days. Unit K 31-4 shows clear direction selectivity, K 29-4 and K 32-3 have a preference for one axis of movement and K 32-1 has, at most, only a vague directional bias. (From PETTIGREW, 1974)

indeed they found cells to have no stimulus specificity at all in dark-reared kittens, 5–6 weeks of age.

Reconciling these two extreme views seems improbable but BLAKEMORE and VAN SLUYTERS (1975) have tried. They studied qualitatively 397 cells in normal kittens, from 9 days of age, and kittens deprived of visual experience by various methods. Learning from BARLOW and PETTIGREW (1971) the importance of distinguishing direction and orientation selectivity they divided cortical cells in the animals into five classes:

1. Visually unresponsive.

2. Non-oriented; responding equally to movement in any direction.

3. Pure direction selective; responding to stimuli of any kind moving in one direction.

4. Orientational bias; having a preferred axis of motion but often not preferring a moving line to a moving spot and even responding appreciably to movement along the orthogonal axis.

5. Orientation selective; of the simple, complex and hypercomplex types discovered by HUBEL and WIESEL (1962, 1965a).

They did find some truly orientation selective cells, by the strictest criteria, in animals with no visual experience, particularly in the younger animals (see Fig. 3). These cells were nearly all of the simple type (having separate, spatially summating ON and OFF areas in the receptive field), were commonly monocularly driven and were found mainly in deeper cortical layers. The remainder of cortical cells in deprived animals were of the less specific classes, though it must be said that both orientational bias and pure direction selective cells have a "preferred" orientation when tested only with a moving bar. It is possible that HUBEL and WIESEL (1963) were, in part, describing cells of these types—somewhat different from the majority of neurones in the adult but genetically gifted with a considerable degree of stimulus specificity. BLAKEMORE and VAN SLUYTERS (1975) also reported that there was indeed a rudimentary columnar arrangement present in the inexperienced cortex, in that neighbouring orientation selective and orientational bias cells tended to have quite similar preferred orientations.

Visual experience produced a definite increase in the fraction of truly orientation selective cells, even before three weeks of age (see Fig. 4) and many of these neurones were of the complex type (having receptive fields somewhat larger on average than simple cells and responding in the same way to stationary stimuli flashed anywhere in the receptive field).

BLAKEMORE and VAN SLUYTERS (1975) have suggested that largely prespecified simple cells may, by the action of a simple neuronal algorithm, impose similar orientation selectivity on the less specific cells in the radial block of cortical tissue in which they lie. Thus simple and complex cells in the same column should ultimately gain virtually identical preferred orientations, even though they may receive some of their afferent inputs from independent direct signals from the lateral geniculate body (HOFFMANN and STONE, 1971; TOYAMA et al., 1974; SINGER et al., 1975).

Ample confirmation of most of these observations comes in a recent quantitative study by BUISSERET and IMBERT (1976), which again suggests that about 25% of cells are "specified" in very young, inexperienced kittens; the proportion decreases without experience but increases rapidly if there is visual experience. It is an indication of the speed with which normal vision can promote the maturation of the cortex that if binocularly deprived kittens of 4 weeks of age are given just 6 hours of experience they have a considerable improvement in the proportion of orientation selective cells (IMBERT and BUISSERET, 1975a, b; PECK and BLAKEMORE, 1975).

Recent work by WIESEL and HUBEL (1974) themselves and SHERK and STRYKER (1976) has emphasized the existence of stimulus specificity in young inexperienced kittens. Indeed the latter authors, recording from 22–29 day old deprived kittens, found that over 90% of the "responsive" units in both areas 17 and 18 responded selectively to the orientation of a moving bar (although their responses were often weak and variable) and most of them passed stringent tests to distinguish genuine orientation selectivity from preference for direction or axis of motion. However SHERK and STRYKER (1976) excluded from analysis all cells which did not respond "reliably enough to determine receptive field location", so their data cannot be taken as definitive estimates of the proportion of selective cells. They have, however, fully confirmed that orientation selectivity is present without patterned visual experience. They even demonstrated that

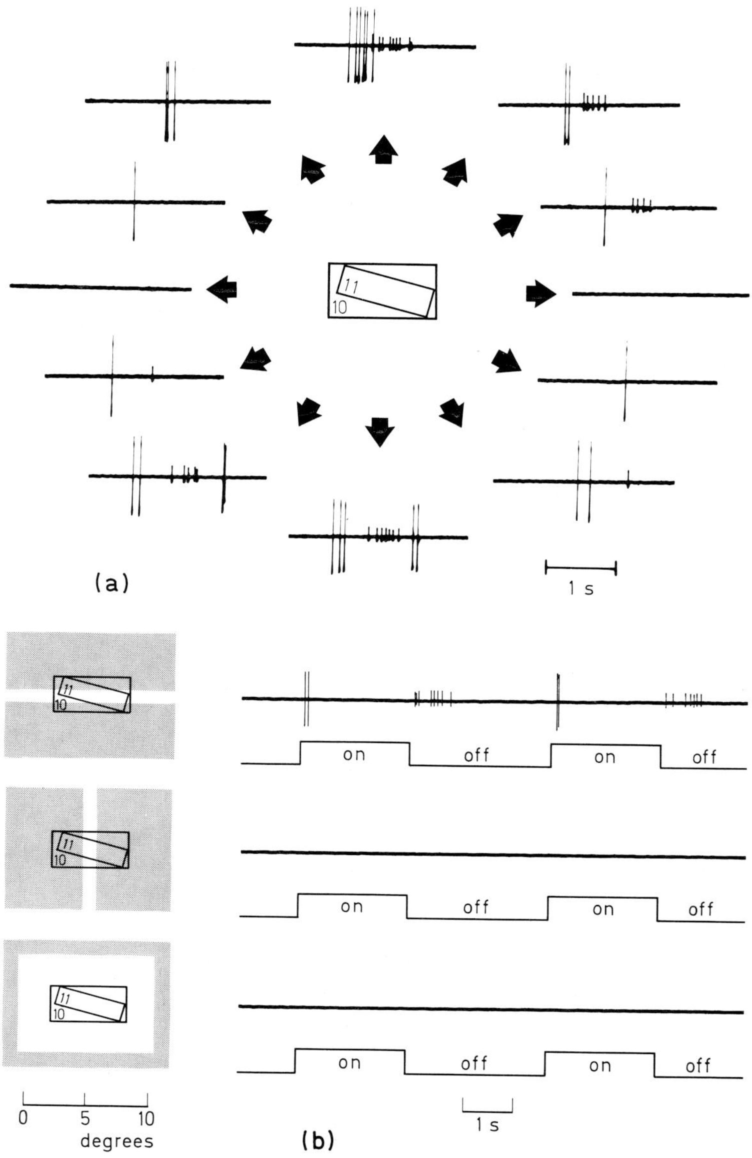

Fig. 3a and b. Responses from two, simultaneously-recorded, truly orientation selective cells from a 9-day-old kitten whose lids had not opened until the time of the experiment. (a) A $3 \times 16°$ light bar is swept across the two receptive fields (labelled "10" for the unit producing the large action potential and "11" for the cell with the small spike) in the directions indicated by the arrows. Neither cell responds to a vertical bar moved horizontally. (b) Responses to stationary, flashed stimuli. Both cells respond to a horizontal bright bar, unit 10 at ON, unit 11 at OFF. Neither cell responds to a vertical bar nor to whole field illumination. (From BLAKEMORE and VAN SLUYTERS, 1975)

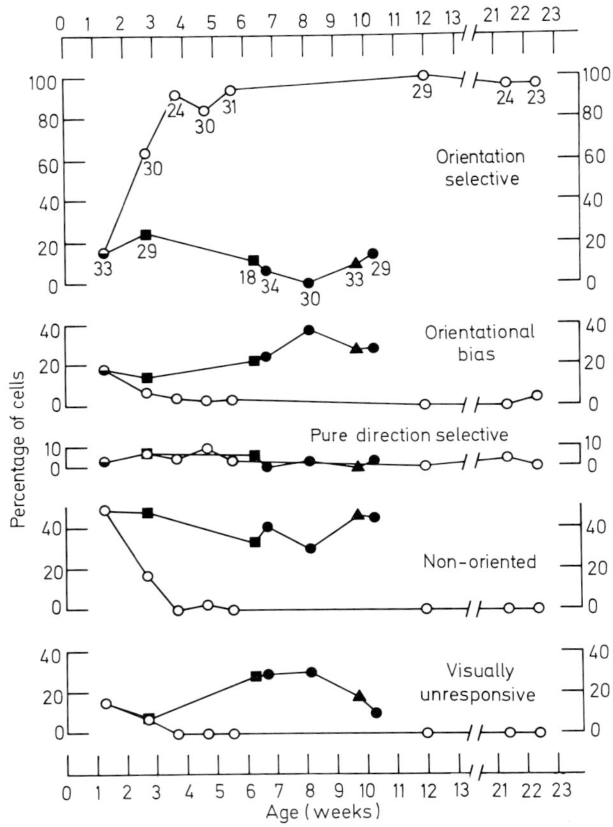

Fig. 4. Comparison of the effects on the kitten's visual cortex of binocular deprivation and normal visual experience. The five pairs of curves show the percentages of the types of receptive fields (defined in the text) for 397 cells from seven normal kittens (unfilled circles) and six binocularly deprived kittens (filled symbols: lid suture = circles; dark rearing = squares; nictitating membrane sutured across the eye = triangle). In each case the two curves originate from a point representing the data for a 9-day-old kitten recorded at the time of natural lid opening. The numbers beneath the data points for the top pair of curves indicate the total number of cells recorded in each animal. (From BLAKEMORE and VAN SLUYTERS, 1975)

the angular specificity of orientation tuning is often not abnormally poor by comparison with adult cats. And they confirmed that there is sometimes columnar grouping of cells according to preferred orientation: Figure 5A shows some of the sequences of preferred orientation found by SHERK and STRYKER (1976), plotted in the graphical form used by HUBEL and WIESEL (1974a). Two of these (from their animals K23 and K22), have some regional groupings at least as impressive as those previously described by HUBEL and WIESEL (1963) and BLAKEMORE and VAN SLUYTERS (1975). However their data for K28, while apparently showing a striking sequential progression of orientation preference, in fact represent a random distribution. The same results are replotted in Figure 5B, but each data point is now drawn at *every* possible location on the

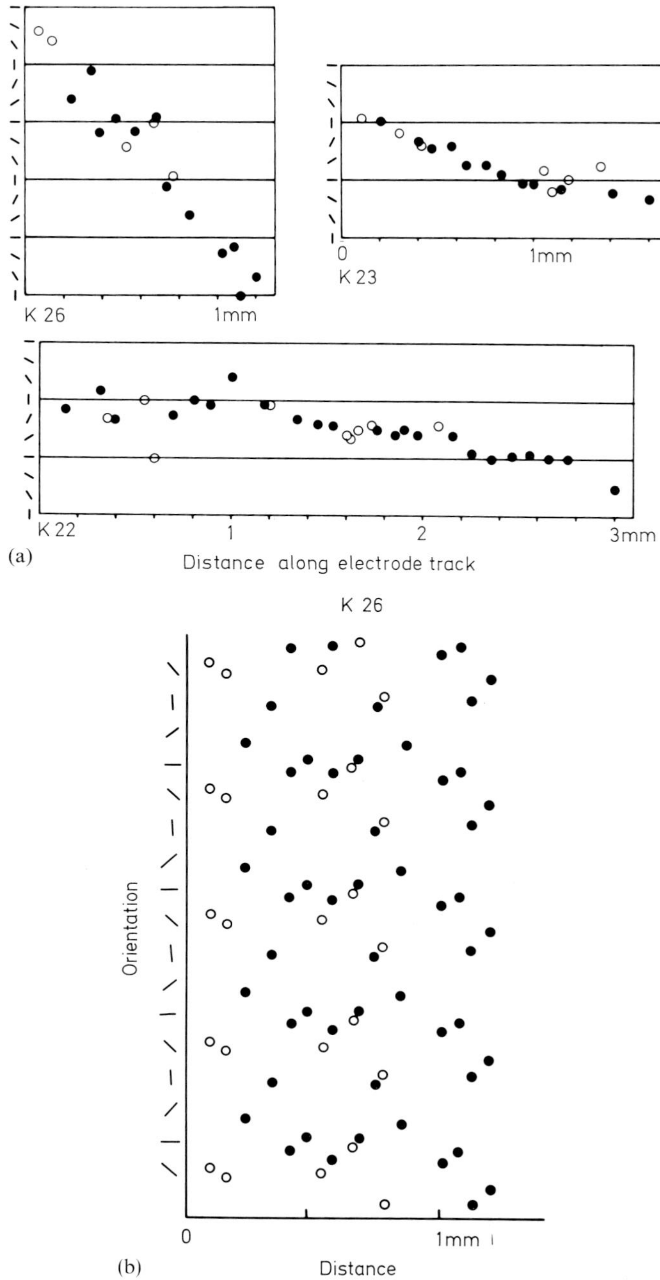

Fig. 5a and b. Reconstructions of penetrations in young visually inexperienced kittens, chosen to show "systematic and progressive change in preferred orientation through the cortex" (SHERK and STRYKER, 1976). (a) The abscissae show the location of each recording site along the penetration and the ordinates indicate the optimal orientation for each single unit (filled circles) or multiunit site (open circles). (b) For kitten K 26, exactly the same data are replotted, but with each point shown within *every* possible period of the orientation scale on the ordinate, rather than within arbitrarily selected periods. Any true sequential trend should still be apparent as a closely-spaced diagonal row of points, but none is evident. The sequence of orientations is essentially random. The same may be true of the data for the early part of the penetration for K 22, but the rest of the results for K 22 and K 23 show clearly segregated sequences when plotted in this manner orientation ordinate. (Since this axis is a cyclical dimension there is no *a priori* reason why any point should be plotted solely within one particular period of the scale.) Any genuine progressive trend should still be apparent as well-separated, parallel, diagonal lines of closely-spaced points, but none is visible in Figure 5B. (This is a matter of general concern, because it shows the danger associated with plotting data on a compressed, repetitive, periodic co-ordinate, such as orientation.) A detailed comparison with the precision of "columnar" sequences in adult cats (ALBUS, 1975a), or better still in visually experienced kittens of the same age, will be needed before we can be certain that the mapping of orientation is as exact in deprived kittens as it is in normal animals.

WIESEL and HUBEL (1974) and SHERK and STRYKER (1976) remain convinced that the contribution of visual experience in normal kittens is negligible, but that the passive maturational process assumed to underlie all cortical development is disrupted by binocular deprivation, because this intervention in itself leads to degenerative changes. (The results of reverse suturing—*vide infra*—however, provide virtually unequivocal evidence that visual experience can be responsible for the *re-establishment* of effective and specified input to the cortex.)

Recently SINGER and TRETTER (1976) have confirmed that long-term binocular deprivation causes gross abnormality in the visual cortex: only about one-third of cells recorded in area 17 and fewer than half in area 18 were visually responsive and a small fraction showed orientation or direction selectivity, usually with broad tuning and weak responsiveness. However the basic pattern of afferent and efferent connectivity, judged by orthodromic and antidromic responses to electrical stimulation of input and output pathways, remained quite normal. The main deficits were in the synaptic security of afferent input and the strength of intracortically-generated inhibition.

Less work has been done on structures other than the visual cortex. Despite the slightly abnormal electroretinogram from a deprived eye in the cat (HAMASAKI and POLLACK, 1972), the properties of individual ganglion cells, and the proportions of the different types, seem quite undisturbed (SHERMAN and STONE, 1973).

In the cat's lateral geniculate nucleus, there are physiological effects of deprivation, but they are subtle. Receptive fields are still of the basic ON- or OFF-centre concentric types but the responses from cells driven by a deprived eye are somewhat sluggish and the centres are unusually large (WIESEL and HUBEL, 1963a). This early study was made before it was realised that ganglion cells and geniculate cells in the cat fall into two main classes, Y and X, having rapidly and slowly conducting axons respectively and different kinds of concentric receptive field organization (ENROTH-CUGELL and ROBSON, 1966; CLELAND et al., 1971; STONE and DREHER, 1973). A third class of ganglion cells, W cells, with very slowly conducting fibres and often with complicated receptive fields, project mainly to the midbrain but partly to the lateral geniculate nucleus, especially the C laminae (STONE and HOFFMANN, 1972; CLELAND et al., 1975; WILSON and STONE, 1975; CLELAND et al., 1976). It seems that visual deprivation, especially monocular deprivation, causes a specific reduction in the proportion of Y cells that can be recorded in the deprived geniculate laminae (SHERMAN et al., 1972; SHERMAN and STONE, 1973; HOFFMANN and CYNADER, 1977). Since

Y cells are assumed to have large cell bodies, the dramatic average "shrinkage" of cells in the deprived laminae of the lateral geniculate nucleus of monocularly deprived cats (WIESEL and HUBEL, 1963a; GUILLERY, 1972; GAREY et al., 1973) could be due to a selective failure of growth of these large Y cells, and this has recently been confirmed anatomically (GAREY and BLAKEMORE, 1977a, b; LEVAY and FERSTER, 1977). Because of the varied sampling properties of different microelectrodes, the virtual absence of Y cells amongst units recorded in the deprived geniculate may merely reflect such a change in soma dimensions—the true proportion of functional Y cells might be quite normal; higher impedance microelectrodes should detect them. Indeed, recordings from the *axons* of deprived LGN cells, in the optic radiation, produce a more normal fraction of Y cells (EYSEL, GRÜSSER and HOFFMANN, personal communication, 1976). There is now evidence that monocular deprivation (MAFFEI and FIORENTINI, 1976a) leads to a failure of cells in the deprived laminae of the cat's lateral geniculate nucleus to respond to high spatial frequencies, which can be looked on as a deficiency in the higher resolution X cells. Preliminary observations on axons of the optic tract suggested that this effect may even occur in the retina itself.

In the kitten's superior colliculus, the natural development of receptive field properties and the effects of deprivation can be taken to reflect those in the visual cortex, since, in the adult cat, input from the cortex seems fundamentally important in contributing to the binocularity and direction selectivity of collicular neurones (WICKELGREN and STERLING, 1969a; ROSENQUIST and PALMER, 1971). Collicular cells in the deep layers can respond to touch and sound in the first few days of life, but visual responsiveness in all layers is not observed until about one week of age (STEIN et al., 1973; NORTON, 1974). Binocularity and direction selectivity first appear at about 2 weeks and the proportion of directional cells increases with age: the colliculus is not completely adult in its properties until about 7 weeks. The general changes in collicular properties seem well correlated with the slow development of visuomotor behaviour in the young kitten.

Long-term binocular deprivation, which reduces if not abolishes stimulus specificity in the cortex, is similar to removal of the cortex in its effects on collicular cells: they are rarely binocularly driven or direction selective (WICKELGREN-GORDON, 1972; DEC et al., 1976).

b) Primates

The deep motivation behind much of this work on the developing visual system is surely the hope of gaining greater insight into visual development and its disorder in human infants. In that respect WIESEL and HUBEL's (1974) work on baby monkeys is both elegant and significant. They recorded from the visual cortex in one 2-day old monkey and three animals that had been deprived binocularly from shortly after birth—in fact in one case the baby was delivered by Caesarian section and the lids sutured immediately. They found most cells to have entirely normal orientation selectivity and to be arranged in the very orderly columnar progressions found in the adult monkey (Fig. 6). In the deprived animals binocularity was much reduced (*vide infra*)

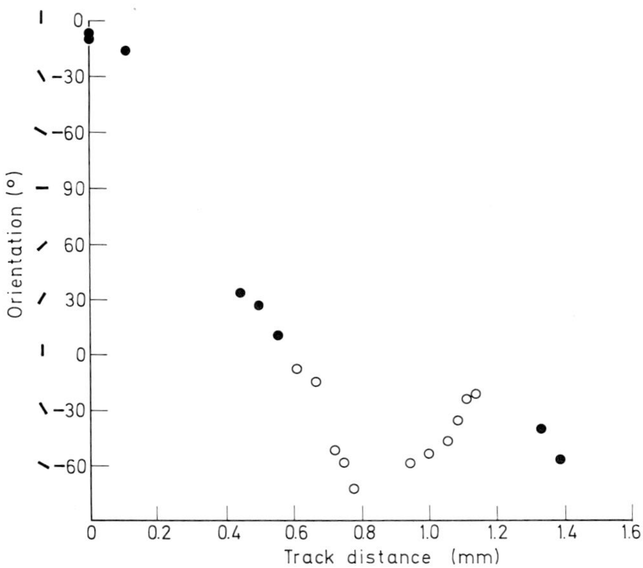

Fig. 6. A graph of preferred orientation versus penetration distance for a penetration in the striate cortex of a baby monkey who was delivered by Caesarian section and whose lids were sutured immediately. Recording was on the 13th day. Open circles = activity plotted through the contralateral (left) eye. Filled circles = ipsilateral eye. (From WIESEL and HUBEL, 1974)

and 10–15% of cells were unusally sluggish or non-oriented. These latter observations they attribute to degenerative changes.

It is very likely that the structure and function of visual cortical areas, despite superficial similarities, are somewhat different in adult cats and monkeys. It is possible then that they also have different degrees of dependence on innate and environmental factors. Nevertheless, there is excellent evidence that both binocular function and pattern perception in *humans* are rapidly and dramatically influenced by abnormal early visual experience (AWAYA et al., 1973; VON NOORDEN, 1973). In monkeys, too, the binocularity of cortical cells can certainly be changed by experimental manipulation, so we should not consider the question of environmental influences on the *normal* development of the primate visual cortex to be closed by these important experiments of WIESEL and HUBEL (1974).

c) Other Animals

The only other mammal whose developmental physiology has been extensively investigated is the rabbit, which has panoramic vision, very little binocular field and much more complicated retinal processing than cat or monkey (retinal ganglion cells themselves can be orientation selective, preferring horizontal or vertical orientations – LEVICK, 1967). The available evidence suggests that the development of receptive field properties in both the visual cortex (MATHERS et al., 1974) and the superior colliculus (SPEAR et al., 1972) proceeds gradually over the first 2–3 weeks of life. In the colliculus, examples of all types of receptive fields found in the adult are present before natural lid-opening (9 days) but the proportion of more complicated cells increases dramatically after lid-opening. In the cortex receptive fields cannot be defined before the time of lid-opening and the first to appear are the "symmetrical" types. The "asymmetrical" fields (including orientation selective) do not occur until about 13 days of age. However, these developments do not seem to depend on visual experience, since all cell types are found in deprived animals (CHOW and SPEAR, 1974), although their maturation is delayed by deprivation (GROBSTEIN and CHOW, 1975). Also, in the small binocular segment of the rabbit cortex, monocular deprivation causes an increase in the number of cells with mismatched receptive field properties in the two eyes (VAN SLUYTERS and STEWART, 1974), though not a dramatic change in ocular dominance (*vide infra*).

A very recent report on the second visual cortical area of the lamb (RAMACHANDRAN et al., 1977) suggests that visual experience, as in the kitten, is not needed for the emergence of orientation selectivity. Also receptive field disparity, a prominent feature of area V2 in the adult sheep (CLARKE et al., 1976), seems to be present immediately after birth: indeed the range of disparities may be even larger than in the adult. One feature that is very different in binocularly deprived lambs is that neurones can usually be activated separately through either eye and do not exhibit strong binocular summation, whereas in the adult's V2 many cells only respond when stimulated, at the correct disparity, through both eyes simultaneously.

In the rat (YINON et al., 1975a), where there is very little binocular interaction in the cortex, long term monocular deprivation caused, in the hemisphere contralateral to the deprived eye, a reduction in the proportion of visually responsive cells and a specific fall in the fraction of units responding to circumscribed stimuli such as moving lines or spots. No orientation selective cells were found, but they are not very common in the normal rat cortex.

II. The Development of Visual Behaviour

The question of perceptual development and the behavioural consequences of deprivation are reviewed in detail by GANZ in this volume. I shall only mention here some studies of the natural development of visual ability because they are relevant to the question of the influence of visual experience on visual perception.

In kittens the gradual improvement in visuomotor performance is not, apparently, limited by motor development, since various kinds of responses to auditory stimuli first occur reliably in advance of the age at which the same responses can be elicited by visual stimuli (NORTON, 1974). Visual orienting and following reactions to moving objects first appear at 15–25 days; perception of depth, as judged by the avoidance of a drop on the visual cliff, occurs at 25–35 days, together with the visual placing reaction; "guided" visual placing of the paws towards a small pronged surface (HEIN and HELD, 1967) does not

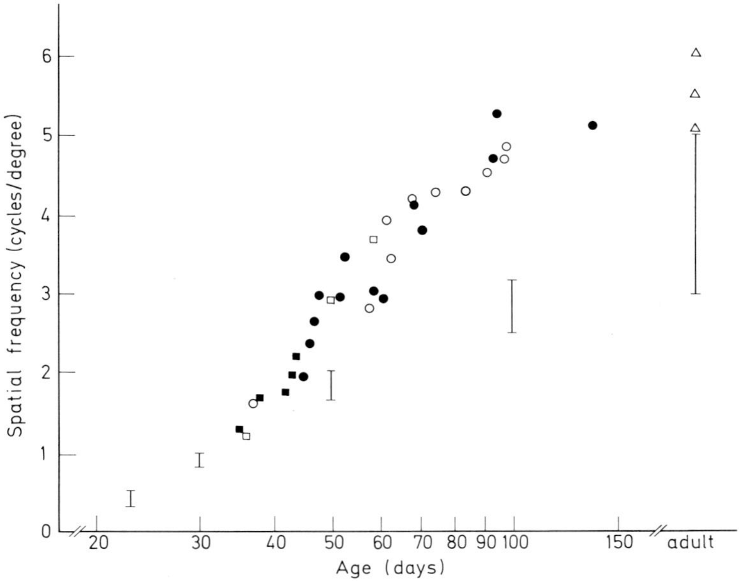

Fig. 7. The visual acuity (defined as the spatial frequency for 70% correct performance in a stripes *versus* grey field discrimination) for 4 kittens (open and filled squares and circles) as a function of age (data of MITCHELL et al., 1976). For comparison, the results for 3 adult cats (open triangles) are shown, together with FREEMAN and MARG's (1975) estimates of the probable range of acuity (vertical bars) derived from measurements of cortical potentials evoked by moving gratings. (From MITCHELL et al., 1976b)

appear until about 30–35 days. It is something of a puzzle that dark-reared kittens will first begin to work in order to receive diffuse light stimulation only at about 60 days of age, long past the age at which visual experience is normally needed to promote or maintain the development of receptive field properties in the visual cortex (DODWELL et al., 1976).

HELD and HEIN (1963), in a classic experiment, showed that the development of simple visuomotor reactions depends not just on visual experience, but on the visual feedback of self-produced movements: a kitten held in such a way that it receives "passive", not self-induced, experience of movement of the visual field does not develop such behaviours at the same age as an "active", normally moving colleague (see HEIN, this volume). (Interestingly, IMBERT and BUISSERET, 1975b, have recently reported that the restraint of such a "passive" kitten does *not* prevent the rapid improvement in the specificity of cortical cells produced by brief exposure to a moving visual scene, although total paralysis does.) HELD (1970) has produced a cogent argument (or perhaps more a warning about interpretation) that most perceptual defects apparently caused by effects of deprivation on parts of the visual pathway may be due, at least in part, to failures of visuomotor development, because of the lack of feedback of self-induced movement. It is important to keep HELD's proposition in mind, but such visuomotor failures are unlikely to be the most important source

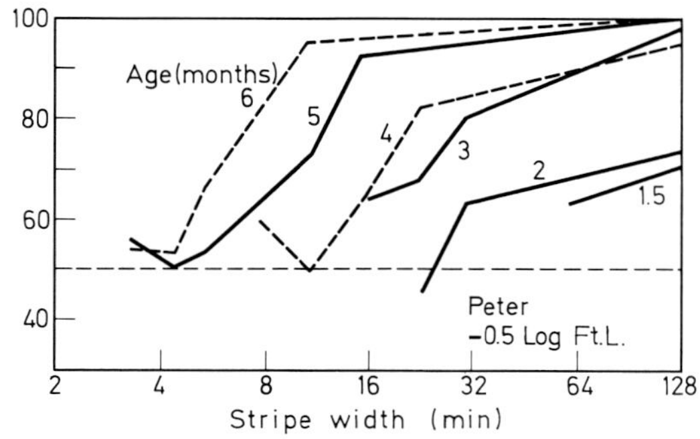

Fig. 8. Results from a longitudinal study of visual acuity, using a preferential looking technique, on one human infant (Peter). The ordinate shows the percentage of time spent staring at a striped field in preference to a grey one. The age of the child at each determination of acuity is shown next to each curve. The data were indistinguishable for vertical and diagonal stripes and have therefore been combined. (From TELLER et al., 1974)

of disability in previously monocularly or binocularly deprived cats, since they recover quite slowly compared with the improvement of a "passive" kitten when allowed to have normal active visual experience.

As well as visuomotor co-ordination, visual acuity itself improves very gradually in kittens, monkeys and human infants. FREEMAN and MARG (1975) measured pattern-evoked potentials from the occipital cortex of kittens to discover the maximum spatial frequency of a high-contrast alternating grating which produced a just detectable evoked potential (see CAMPBELL et al., this volume). They found a slow increase in this physiologically-determined cut-off spatial frequency between 3 and 14 weeks of age. A fortuitous rediscovery of KARL LASHLEY's jumping stand enabled MITCHELL et al. (1976b, 1977b) to measure grating resolution behaviourally even in very young kittens, and they report the same gradual improvement (see Fig. 7), although at all ages above about 5 weeks the acuity was better than that predicted from the evoked potential measurements. No doubt the cloudy optics of the kitten's eye (and its smaller size) are partly responsible for low acuity in very young animals, but it is extremely unlikely that changes in optical quality account entirely for these changes (BONDS and FREEMAN, 1976): a kitten's eye seems beautifully clear by about 5 weeks of age and is unlikely to limit acuity to the 1 c/° or so that is found at that age.

Even stronger evidence against optical explanations for the slow improvement in kitten vision is the fact that visual acuity *also* improves very gradually with age in infant monkeys (ORDY et al., 1965) and humans (ATKINSON et al., 1974; TELLER et al., 1974; LEEHEY et al., 1975; BANKS and SALAPATEK, 1976; HARRIS et al., 1976; MARG et al., 1976), up to six months, at least—see Figure 8. Baby humans and monkeys are born with open eyes and apparently perfectly clear optics. This tedious improvement in visual resolution must surely be accepted as a strong argument in favour of a possible role for visual experience in the development of primate visual perception.

III. Binocular Plasticity

a) Monocular Deprivation

It is now established beyond any doubt that cortical cells in very young kittens and baby monkeys often have input from both eyes, without prior visual experience. Binocular deprivation has been reported to cause a reduction in the proportion of binocularly driven cortical cells both in kittens (KRATZ and SPEAR, 1976) and monkeys (WIESEL and HUBEL, 1974), but many workers have found the effects on binocularity, especially in kittens, to be small or even undetectable (WIESEL and HUBEL, 1965a; PETTIGREW, 1974; CRAWFORD et al., 1975; BLAKEMORE and VAN SLUYTERS, 1975; LEVENTHAL and HIRSCH, 1977). On the other hand, in both species, deprivation of one eye alone causes a remarkably rapid reorganization (see Fig. 12): virtually all cells become dominated by the experienced eye (WIESEL and HUBEL, 1963b; HUBEL and WIESEL, 1970a; BAKER et al., 1974; CRAWFORD et al., 1975).

In normal adult monkeys, and less spectacularly in cats, the cortex is arranged into what HUBEL and WIESEL (1974b) have called "hypercolumns". The relative dominance of the two eyes varies gradually from one region to another (ocular dominance columns) as does the preferred orientation of the cells (orientation columns). The hypothetical block of tissue in which there is one full cycle of ocular dominance (from dominance by one eye through dominance by the other), and that in which there is a full cycle of all orientations, is a pair of "hypercolumns". Recently WIESEL et al. (1974) and LEVAY et al. (1975) have demonstrated that axons from the right-eye and left-eye geniculate laminae, terminate in alternating "stripes" in layer IV of the monkey's cortex. Presumably these stripes represent one axis of the hypercolumns – the alternating ocular dominance of cortical cells. The "duty cycle" of these stripes is changed by prolonged monocular deprivation; the zones of termination representing the deprived eye shrink in relation to those of the experienced eye (HUBEL et al., 1977). In kittens there is physiological evidence for contraction of the appropriate set of ocular dominance columns during even a brief period of monocular deprivation (MOVSHON and DÜRSTELER, 1977), and THORPE and BLAKEMORE (1975) report some anatomical results which suggest that axons from the deprived laminae of the lateral geniculate nucleus have a less extensive distribution in the visual cortex after long-term monocular deprivation. The inexcitability of cortical cells in monocularly deprived cats even for electrical stimulation of the optic nerve of the deprived eye (BLAKEMORE and HILLMAN, 1977) can also be interpreted in terms of literal withdrawal from cortical synapses of the afferent axons of deprived geniculate neurones.

While changes in ocular dominance might therefore, in some cases, represent an actual redistribution of afferent axons within the cortex, there may be some more subtle synaptic changes that have the same physiological expression. PETTIGREW et al. (1973a), found convincing but not persistent, changes in the ocular dominance of a few individual cells in the anaesthetized kitten's cortex if they were simply repetitively stimulated through one eye alone for several minutes; and KASAMATSU (1976) has argued that after recovery from brief local anaesthesia of one optic nerve, during a similar acute experiment, there is a persistent shift in cortical ocular dominance, presumably caused by the temporary abolition of signals from one eye. PETTIGREW and GAREY (1974) exposed anaesthetized, paralysed kittens to a moving pattern of stripes seen only by one eye and found much more pronounced effects on ocular dominance when recording from the cortex the next day. PECK and BLAKEMORE (1975) and SCHECHTER and MURPHY (1976) reported considerable overall shifts in ocular dominance in 4 week old binocularly deprived kittens allowed just a few hours of visual experience through one eye (though again there was some evidence that a few hours of "consolidation" were needed between exposure and recording). The time course of shifts in ocular dominance produced by brief monocular deprivation in normal kittens has been studied by OLSON and FREEMAN (1975) and by MOVSHON and DÜRSTELER (1977): they are agreed that, in one month-old kittens, clear changes can be detected after about a day of deprivation. The speed of the effects of short-term deprivation makes it a little unlikely that they represent, at least initially, a gross redistribution of axon terminals in the cortex, although in the long run some kind of functional modification of geniculo-cortical synapses may result in changes in the actual pattern of axonal termination. Also, monocular deprivation may have quite different effects on first-order geniculo-cortical synapses and on the terminals of intrinsic excitatory cortical interneurones, which relay information to other cortical cells.

In view of the different effects on cortical ocular dominance of binocular and monocular deprivation, WIESEL and HUBEL (1965a) proposed that at some stage, perhaps the geniculo-cortical synapse itself, there must be binocular competition for synaptic space between axons from the two eyes' pathways. The more active axons take over from the less active ones. During binocular deprivation (in kittens, at least) the spontaneous activity in the two pathways may be adequately balanced to prevent the loss of input from one eye to the other.

Support for the hypothesis of competition comes from GUILLERY and STELZNER's (1970) measurements of cell growth in the lateral geniculate nucleus of monocularly deprived cats. Within the portion of the nucleus representing the binocular part of the visual field, cells in the deprived principal lamina (A or A1) are relatively shrunken compared with those in the corresponding section of the "experienced" lamina. But on the side where layer A receives input from the (contralateral) deprived eye, the cells in the extreme lateral "monocular segment" of the lamina, representing the monocular crescent of the visual field, are not detectably shrunken. In this region of the visual field there is no possibility of binocular competition between signals from the two eyes. The decreased recordability of Y cells in the deprived laminae of the geniculate, discussed above, is also limited to the binocular segment of the nucleus (SHERMAN et al., 1972).

An elegant set of experiments by GUILLERY and his colleagues (see SHERMAN et al., 1974) has shown that competition, not simply differences in the eccentricity in the visual field, is responsible for the sparing of the peripheral field representation from the effects of monocular deprivation. An artificial monocular segment—a critical segment—can be created within the central part of the visual field by placing a retinal lesion in the open eye. Within the part of the deprived geniculate lamina corresponding to this critical segment, cells do not undergo shrinkage and Y cells can be recorded. Even in the visual cortex cells can often be driven from the deprived eye within the critical segment although they behave as if they have been binocularly deprived, usually having no stimulus selectivity.

Finally KRATZ and SPEAR (1976) have shown that the loss of stimulus specificity in the cortex caused by bilateral lid suture is somewhat less marked if one of the eyes is removed at birth. So it seems that at a cortical level there are two processes set up by deprivation — a passive loss of, or failure to develop, stimulus specificity, combined with a competitive interaction which depends on the relative strength of inputs from the two eyes and which therefore produces the much more dramatic effects when only one eye is closed rather than both.

It seems clear that the loss in cortical input that results from suturing the lids of one eye depends on the absence of patterned images in that eye, not just the reduction in illumination. Covering one eye with a transparent neutral density filter certainly does not abolish its input to the cortex (CYNADER and CHERNENKO, 1976; BLAKEMORE, 1976), while putting a translucent diffuser over one eye (with a neutral density filter over the other, giving matched attenuation) causes the full-blown effect (BLAKEMORE, 1976).

In the cat's superior colliculus, the changes produced by monocular deprivation again seem to reflect modification of the cortical input to this structure (HOFFMANN and SHERMAN, 1974): cells become dominated by the experienced eye, but less powerfully so than in the cortex (WICKELGREN and STERLING, 1969b; HOFFMANN and SHERMAN, 1974); and the effects are much more pronounced on the side ipsilateral to the deprived eye, since the colliculus receives its major ipsilateral input via a projection from the visual cortex (HOFFMANN and CYNADER, 1977). In the colliculus contralateral to the deprived eye (which provides most of the direct retino-tectal projection), removal of the visual cortex causes an immediate shift in the ocular dominance of cells — they suddenly become dominated by the deprived eye alone, perhaps because the direct retinal input is held in some kind of inhibitory check by the cortico-tectal input (BERMAN and STERLING, 1976).

Mice have a considerable binocular representation in the visual cortex and DRÄGER (1975) has reported that monocular deprivation results in shifts in cortical ocular dominance, but perhaps not quite as total as in the cat or monkey. A recent report (PETTIGREW and KONISHI, 1976) has shown that even owls (which have orientation selective, disparity-selective binocular units in an area of the forebrain called the visual Wulst) lose input from an eye that has been deprived early in life. Except for the very weak effects in rabbits (VAN SLUYTERS and STEWART, 1974), then, monocular deprivation has been found to cause gross shifts in ocular dominance in all animals that normally have binocular cortical units.

b) *Strabismus, Alternating Monocular Occlusion and Ocular Immobilization*

In human infants, early strabismus (failure of the two eyes to be converged at the correct angle) causes anomalies in binocular vision and often a reduction of acuity in the squinting eye (amblyopia). HUBEL and WIESEL (1965b) demon-

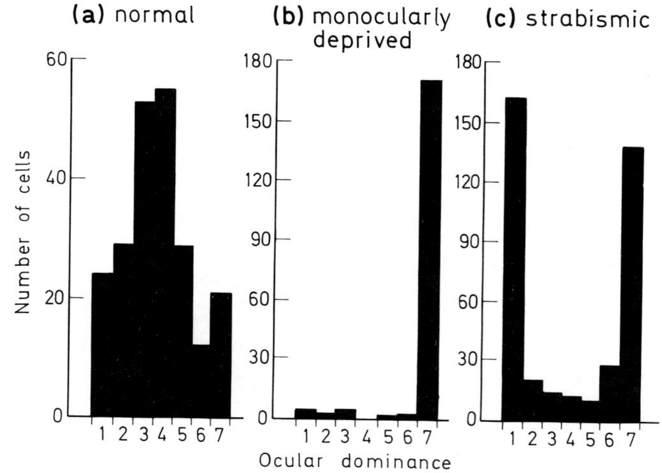

Fig. 9. Classification of ocular dominance for 224 cortical neurones from normal cats. (A: data of HUBEL and WIESEL, 1965a), 184 cells from kittens reared with the contralateral eye occluded (B: data of WIESEL and HUBEL, 1965a) and 384 cells from animals reared with artificial exotropia (C: data of HUBEL and WIESEL, 1965b). Cells are classified into seven groups according to the relative influence of the two eyes: *1*, monocularly driven by contralateral eye; *2* and *3*, binocularly driven with contralateral eye much stronger and slightly stronger respectively; *4*, equal input; *5* and *6*, ipsilateral eye slightly stronger and much stronger respectively; *7*, monocularly driven by ipsilateral eye

strated that a divergent artificial squint in a kitten (produced by sectioning the medial rectus muscle), or alternate covering of the two eyes, produces a very exaggerated pattern of ocular dominance columns in the cortex. Most neurones are not binocularly driven and an electrode passing through the cortex encounters successive groups of monocularly dominated cells. This led them to the hypothesis that the maintenance of binocular connections in the cortex depends on simultaneous and congruent activation of the two inputs. This idea is supported by BLAKEMORE and VAN SLUYTERS' (1974a) and VAN SLUYTERS and BLAKEMORE's (1973a) observation that kittens with artificial squint do not always lose their cortical binocularity if they are reared exclusively in an environment of repetitive stripes all of the same orientation (ensuring that the two eyes always see roughly the same kind of pattern, whatever the angle of convergence).

Simultaneous exposure of the two eyes to different orientations (HIRSCH and SPINELLI, 1970; BLAKEMORE, 1976), or alternating exposure to an identical pattern of stripes (BLAKEMORE, 1976) causes a breakdown in binocularity, in the same way as strabismus. Even simple attenuation of the intensity in one eye, by 1–2 log units, induces a similar increase in monocularity, without a selective loss of representation of the eye with the dimmer image (CYNADER and CHERNENKO, 1976; BLAKEMORE, 1976). Since a 2 log unit fall in retinal illumination produces only about a 12 msec increase in latency (ENROTH-CUGELL and LENNIE, 1975), and the bursts of activity set up at the cortical cell by a stimulus crossing the receptive field last much longer than this, it is unlikely that the breakdown in binocularity is caused solely by the small disparity in *timing* of messages from the two eyes. It is more likely to be due to differences in the frequency of impulses in the bursts from the two eyes or to synergistic effects of a number of factors (BLAKEMORE, 1976).

Immobilization of one eye in *adult* cats (by surgical transsection of the nerve supply to the extraocular muscles) was found by BUCHTEL et al. (1975) to cause a reduction in the proportion of binocular units in the cortex, and receptive fields in the immobile eye were sometimes abnormally large. FIORENTINI and MAFFEI (1974) report that the decrease in binocularity occurs within a week of immobilization and is restricted to simple cells (HUBEL and WIESEL, 1962). Indeed MAFFEI and FIORENTINI (1976b) have even reported that the same changes take place if the animal is kept in total darkness, and that they do not happen if *both* eyes are immobilized (whether the animal is subsequently in the light or the dark). They argue that the effects may be due to discrepancy in afferent signals from the extra-ocular muscles of the two eyes. If this is true it raises a great complication for the simple interpretation of the effects of early strabismus, since muscle section also causes a degree of immobility. Indeed MAFFEI and BISTI (1976) have reported that if kittens are kept in total darkness after the simple induction of a unilateral divergent squint, cortical binocularity is also lost. They again interpret this in terms of changes in proprioceptive signals from the eye muscles.

These new results on ocular immobilization and on the possible role of extra-ocular receptors in maintaining cortical binocularity are fascinating, but much more work is needed to establish their generality. A word or two of caution is in order. For instance ALBUS (1975b) has shown that simple cells, even in normal adult cats, are predominantly monocularly driven, in the central 5 deg or so of the visual field representation: great care is therefore needed in matching the retinal eccentricity of the receptive fields and the proportions of various cell types in experimental and control animals. And KRATZ and SPEAR (1976) have suggested that binocularity can be reduced by binocular deprivation alone, as it is in monkeys (WIESEL and HUBEL, 1974).

Evidence that immobility of one eye is certainly not the sole factor in causing the cortical consequences of squint comes from YINON (1976) and VAN SLUYTERS (1977) who have demonstrated that the effects of both divergent and convergent strabismus are confined to a sensitive period (*vide infra*) very similar to that for monocular deprivation, and that squint after about 3–4 months of age has no effect on binocularity (unlike the reported effects of oculomotor denervation in adult cats). And VAN SLUYTERS (1977) has found that simple prismatic deviation of the visual axis (without any surgical intervention at all) is just as potent in reducing cortical binocularity as is extra-ocular muscle transsection.

Artificial strabismus in monkeys produces a similar gross reduction in the binocularity of cortical neurones (BAKER et al., 1974) and in the case of convergent squint there can be reduced visual acuity (strabismus amblyopia) in the squinting eye, if the monkey has adopted the strategy of consistently fixating with its non-squinting eye (VON NOORDEN and DOWLING, 1970; VON NOORDEN,

1973). BAKER et al. (1974) recorded from squinting monkeys whose acuity had been measured behaviourally. Exotropic (divergent) animals never developed amblyopia, presumably because they alternately fixated with the two eyes; and some esotropic (convergent) animals were also alternators. In these animals, although cortical binocularity was always reduced, neither eye had predominant control. In some esotropes, however, a deep amblyopia, even to the level of light perception alone, developed in the deviating eye and ocular dominance in the cortex seemed to reflect this "suppression" of the squinting eye: most cells were monocularly driven by the normal eye. In cats too some authors have reported a *slight* preponderance of cortical cells dominated by the non-squinting eye (WICKELGREN-GORDON, 1972; GORDON and GUMMOW, 1975; YINON et al., 1975b) although others have denied this (e.g. HUBEL and WIESEL, 1965b; BLAKEMORE, 1976); the difficulty of establishing small differences between the two eyes is immense, because of the general dominance by the contralateral eye (HUBEL and WIESEL, 1962) and the arrangement of cells into ocular dominance columnar groups (HUBEL and WIESEL, 1965b).

In any case, a small difference in the *number* of cortical cells responding to each eye is hardly a powerful explanation for a gross difference in visual acuity between the two eyes. Acuity is presumably limited by the ability of neurones to resolve (by their pattern of firing) spatial detail on the retinal image. IKEDA and WRIGHT (1976) have tested the spatial resolution of neurones in the cat's lateral geniculate nucleus, using striped grating patterns drifting across the receptive field. The spatial threshold of each neurone was measured by increasing the spatial frequency of the grating until the cell no longer responded to it. In animals with paralytic convergent squint the spatial resolution was much lower for cells in the laminae receiving from the squinting eye, within the area centralis representation. This result seems a much better analogue to human amblyopia. IKEDA and WRIGHT (1976) argue that their result might be due to the fact that, since the squinting eye is not directed at the object of fixation but its accommodative state is matched to that of the other eye, it will from time to time receive a defocused retinal image. Cells with preferences for high spatial frequencies will thus occasionally be deprived of adequate stimulation and hence may deteriorate in their properties. Indeed *gross* unilateral or bilateral defocus during development in kittens has been shown to produce changes in spatial resolution at both the geniculate (IKEDA and TREMAIN, 1978) and the cortical level (EGGERS and BLAKEMORE, 1978), in accordance with psychophysical observations on human anisometropic amblyopes (e.g. LEVI and HARWERTH, 1977). However, BLAKEMORE and EGGERS (1978) have not seen changes in resolving power for cortical neurones in kittens with either divergent or convergent squint produced by disinsertion of a single muscle. Since IKEDA and WRIGHT (1976) produced their convergent squints by section of oblique muscles as well as lateral rectus, removal of connective tissue from the lateral part of the orbit and removal of the nictitating membrane, it is possible that their neuronal effects are caused at least in part by more nearly total immobility of the eye.

IKEDA and WRIGHT'S (1976) work has drawn attention to the fact that perceptual anomalies produced by developmental disorders are best studied not simply in terms of the number of neurones with particular properties, but by a detailed examination of the sensitivity and resolution of those cells. Many workers in this field, myself included, have been guilty of arguing too loosely from mere changes in the proportions of different kinds of cells in animals to perceptual deficits in humans, which presumably depend on the *performance* of neurones rather than on their *numbers*.

In the kitten superior colliculus, convergent squint or section of both medial and lateral rectus muscle has much less effect than in the cortex (WICKELGREN-GORDON, 1972; GORDON and GUMMOW, 1975). In the colliculus ipsilateral to the normal eye binocularity is only marginally changed, and on the other side there is a bias towards the contralateral, non-squinting eye, which may be more exaggerated at a year of age than at 3 months.

c) Rotation of One Eye

Recently BLAKEMORE et al. (1975) and YINON (1975) have developed a method of rotating the kitten's eye. If this is done unilaterally in a young kitten, the binocularity of cortical cells is reduced, as expected. These animals have remark-

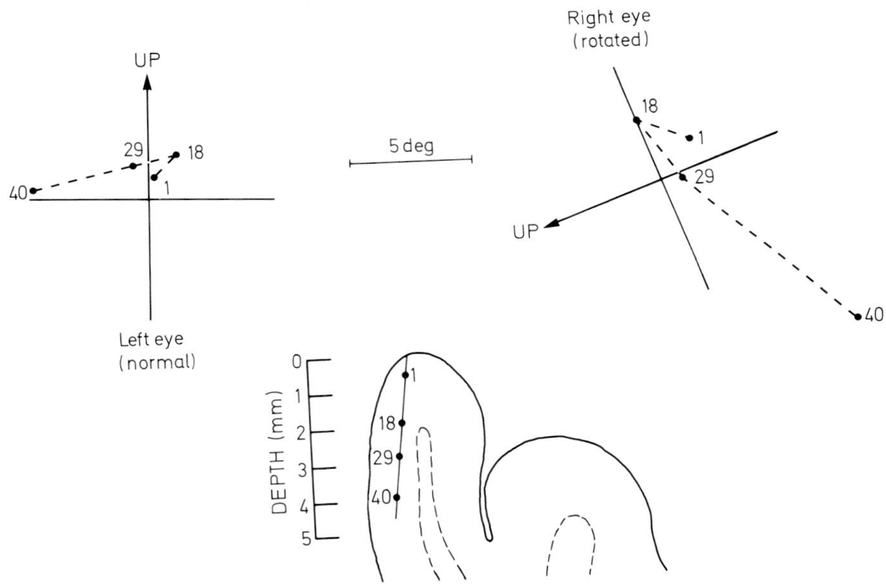

Fig. 10. Preservation of approximately normal retinotopic projection to the visual cortex in a kitten whose right eye had been artificially intorted by 109°. The electrode penetration is reconstructed in the lower half and the locations of four binocularly driven cells are marked on the track. Above are diagrams of the positions of the receptive fields of these cells as they appeared on the screen in front of the animal. The centre of each field is plotted as a circle and they are joined with interrupted lines, in sequence. The projections in space of the true retinal vertical and horizontal meridians are drawn as solid lines, intersecting at the approximate projection of the area centralis. The upper visual field of each eye (the field of the inferior retina) is marked "UP". The sequence of the receptive fields, in both eyes, moves from the retinal vertical midline, slightly into the field of the contralateral hemiretina, and then far out into the field of the ipsilateral hemiretina, typical of a penetration that starts in area 18 and moves deep into area 17. (From BLAKEMORE et al., 1975)

ably good visuomotor co-ordination when using the rotated eye alone and certainly achieve some degree of adaptation to the rotation, at least as far as the localization of objects in space is concerned (BLAKEMORE et al., 1975; PECK and CREWTHER, 1975). However, this perceptual compensation cannot be explained by any reorganization of the retinotopic map in the visual cortex, which remains unaltered (see Fig. 10). Not only do these animals localize well in space, through the rotated eye, but they apparently also judge the orientations of lines to be the same through the two eyes: when trained to make horizontal-vertical discrimination with the normal eye alone, cats with 90° eye rotation show perfect interocular transfer and respond to the same stimulus when seen through the rotated eye (MITCHELL et al., 1976a). Here then is extraordinary perceptual compensation for a grossly distorted sensory input without any obvious physiological correlate.

Eye rotation in adults does not disrupt binocularity and, for binocular units, preferred orientations and directions of movement in the two eyes remain well-matched, on retinal coordinates (BLAKEMORE et al., 1975; YINON, 1977). In kittens, on the other hand, those binocular neurones that persist, after rotation of one eye by more than a few degrees, have a wide range of interocular differences in preferred orientation (*vide infra*).

d) The Sensitive Period

Gross changes in the binocularity of cortical cells only seem to take place after deprivation within a "sensitive period" that runs from about three weeks to about three months of age in kittens (HUBEL and WIESEL, 1970) and from birth to about two months (BAKER et al., 1974; VON NOORDEN, 1973) or perhaps more than a year (HUBEL and WIESEL, unpublished observations) in monkeys. Artificial strabismus in kittens seems to be effective in reducing cortical binocularity during roughly the same sensitive period as for the effects of monocular deprivation (YINON, 1976; VAN SLUYTERS, 1977).

The discovery of this sensitive period for effects on cortical binocularity has enormous relevance to human developmental disorders, for it has long been known that (unlike most kinds of brain damage) disruptions of visual input by such problems as squint, aniseikonia and anisometropia (differences in magnification and power in the two eyes) have much more striking and permanent consequences if they occur in early infancy than if they happen later in life. Several clinical studies confirm the existence of such a period of high susceptibility to binocular disorders early in life. For instance, AWAYA et al. (1973) studied fifteen children who had had one eye occluded for about a week, at different ages. All of them were suffering from so-called "stimulus deprivation amblyopia" in the deprived eye but acuity was improved to some extent by pleioptic treatment, especially when the initial deprivation took place after the age of one year. In monkeys, early occlusion of one eye is known to cause dramatic reduction of acuity in the deprived eye (VON NOORDEN et al., 1970; VON NOORDEN, 1973).

Several recent experiments have utilized the interocular transfer of certain perceptual after-effects to analyse disorders of binocular vision. In normal humans, the so-called figural after-effects (see OYAMA, this volume) transfer be-

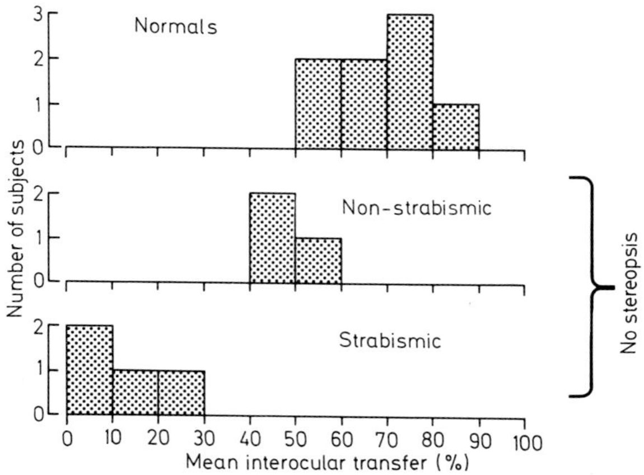

Fig. 11. Measurements of the degree of interocular transfer of the tilt after-effect in normal humans and those who failed conventional tests of stereoscopic vision, either without or with a manifest strabismus or record of squint. The after-effect was induced by adaptation to a grating tilted 10° off vertical, seen in one eye only, and the subject used the other eye to judge the apparent tilt of a vertical grating falling on the corresponding retinal area. The transferred effect was expressed as a percentage of that produced by adapting and testing through the same eye. The histograms plot the mean interocular transfer from right eye to left and vice versa. It is somewhat reduced in non-strabismic observers without normal stereopsis and is even more dramatically reduced in strabismic subjects. (From MOVSHON et al., 1972)

tween the two eyes. Viewing an adaptation or inspection figure with one eye will alter the threshold or appearance of patterns subsequently seen through the other eye. GIBSON's (1933) tilt after-effect and the well-known movement after-effect both transfer at about 70% of the strength found by testing in the adapted eye. However, in humans with reduced stereoscopic acuity, whether manifesting a strabismus or not, the transfer of the after-effect is drastically reduced (MOVSHON et al., 1972; MITCHELL and WARE, 1974; MITCHELL et al., 1975)—see Figure 11. Presumably this loss of binocular transfer reflects the reduction in binocularity of cortical cells caused by some early anomaly. HOHMANN and CREUTZFELDT (1975) have extended these observations on the tilt after-effect to generate new information about the human sensitive period. They measured the transferred after-effect in nine children who had corrected squints (strabismus concomitans convergens), which originally appeared at various ages. The transferred after effect was normal in magnitude for children in whom the strabismus did not start until after the ages of 2–3 years but was much reduced in children with earlier onset of strabismus. BANKS et al. (1975) have very similar results.

e) Recovery from Monocular Deprivation

Simply opening an eye that has been monocularly deprived causes the behavioural ability of the animal when using its deprived eye to improve considerably (GANZ and FITCH, 1968; DEWS and WIESEL, 1970; MITCHELL et al., 1977a;

GANZ, this volume) and this renewed capacity for visual discrimination does seem to depend on the cortex, since learning after monocular deprivation is abolished by gross cortical lesions (SPEAR and GANZ, 1975). The perceptual improvement may be accompanied by only a slight increase in the proportion of cells influenced by the re-opened eye (WIESEL and HUBEL, 1965b; GANZ et al., 1968), although MITCHELL et al. (1977a) found considerable new representation of the deprived eye after re-opening it at 45 days.

An intuitively stronger method of forcing recovery on a deprived eye (similar to the technique of patching that is commonly used in the treatment of human amblyopia) is to close the initially experienced eye when the deprived one is re-opened. This procedure of reverse suturing certainly helps a kitten to gain perceptually from a deprived eye, but if the reverse suturing takes place after the end of the classical sensitive period there is little (CHOW and STEWART, 1972) or no (HUBEL and WIESEL, 1970a) improvement in the influence of the deprived eye on cortical cells.

Early evidence for the apparent irreversibility of the effects of monocular deprivation led HUBEL and WIESEL to propose that the initial changes in ocular dominance represent essentially degenerative effects, rather than a kind of synaptic plasticity that might have an important formative function. However, it is now clear that reverse suturing within the sensitive period can even cause total reversal in the pattern of ocular dominance. BLAKEMORE and VAN SLUYTERS (1974b) deprived kittens in one eye from the time of natural eye opening and, at some time later (5, 6, 8, 10 or 14 weeks), opened the deprived eye and closed the other one for a period of 9 more weeks before recording. In the animals reverse sutured early in the sensitive period there was a complete or partial switch in ocular dominance in favour of the newly opened eye. The later the age of reverse suturing, the less the change in dominance, providing further evidence for the time-scale of the sensitive period, but showing it to be a period of synaptic *lability*, not just of a capacity for selective degeneration. The fact that electrode penetrations in reverse sutured, and indeed in monocularly deprived, kittens are just as rich as normal in their yield of recorded units provides evidence that these results do represent changes in the properties of individual neurones, not just changes in the "recordability" of cells with different but fixed ocular dominance. Figure 12 compares HUBEL and WIESEL's original data, defining the sensitive period, with the reversibility of ocular dominance demonstrated by BLAKEMORE and VAN SLUYTERS.

More recently MOVSHON and BLAKEMORE (1974) and MOVSHON (1976a) have examined in some detail the speed with which the reversal in ocular dominance can take place. Reverse suturing at 4 weeks causes almost complete reversal in ocular dominance within a week; at 5 weeks the process is half finished in a week (see Fig. 13). There is just sufficient time within the sensitive period to turn off the input from one eye by depriving it, to switch it on again by reverse suturing and then to remove it a second time by reverse suturing once again (MOVSHON, 1976a)!

In reverse sutured animals the behavioural capacity of each eye, judged by simple tests of visuomotor behaviour, seems to match, roughly, the state of ocular dominance in the visual cortex (BLAKEMORE and VAN SLUYTERS, 1974; MOVSHON, 1976b). MITCHELL et al. (1977a) have confirmed that reverse suturing

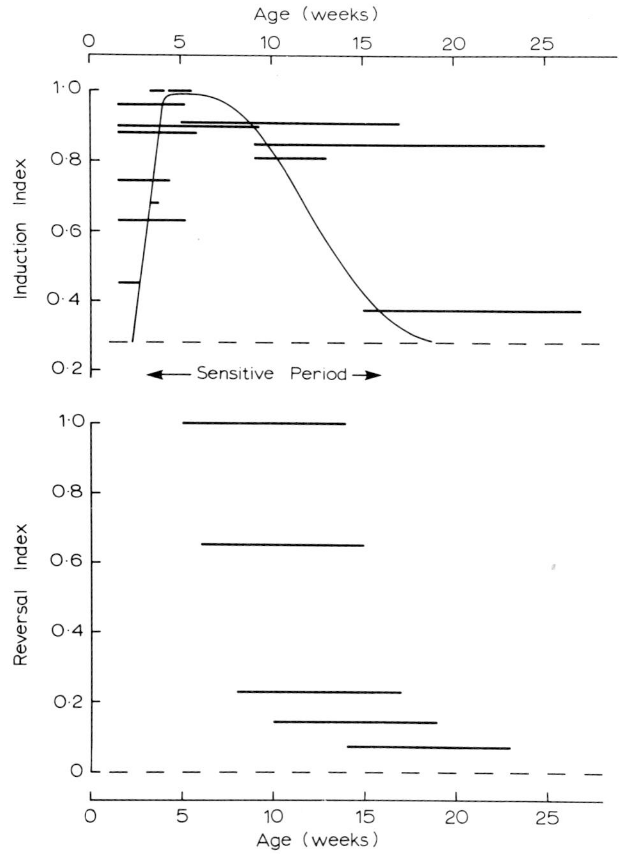

Fig. 12. Two graphical representations of the sensitive period for the induction of the effects of monocular deprivation and the reversal of those effects. In the upper graph (data of HUBEL and WIESEL, 1963, 1970a; WIESEL and HUBEL, 1965a) each horizontal bar represents one kitten whose contralateral eye was occluded for the period of time covered by the bar on the abscissa. The induction index is the proportion of cortical cells dominated by the open eye (groups 5, 6, and 7). The interrupted line plots this index for normal cats, calculated from the data of Fig. 8A. In the lower graph (data of BLAKEMORE and VAN SLUYTERS, 1974b) each bar again represents a kitten whose ipsilateral eye was occluded until it was re-opened at a certain age (the beginning of the bar) and the contralateral eye was then closed for a further 9 weeks (the length of the bar). The reversal index is the proportion of cortical cells dominated by the newly-opened ipsilateral eye (groups 5, 6 and 7). The interrupted line plots this index for a sample of cells from a control animal that was monocularly deprived in the ipsilateral eye until the age of 5 weeks. The smooth curve fitted by eye in the upper graph shows the approximate shape of the sensitivity change during the first few weeks of life. The latter half of this curve matches quite well the general trend in the data of the lower graph. (From BLAKEMORE et al., 1976)

is more potent than simply reopening a deprived eye in re-establishing input to the cortex but that the actual level of visual acuity achieved by the deprived eye is not very different in the two cases.

In general, reverse sutured animals never go through a stage at which cortical cells are highly binocular (see Fig. 13): at the intermediate stages there are predominantly two groups of monocularly dominated neurones. These are very

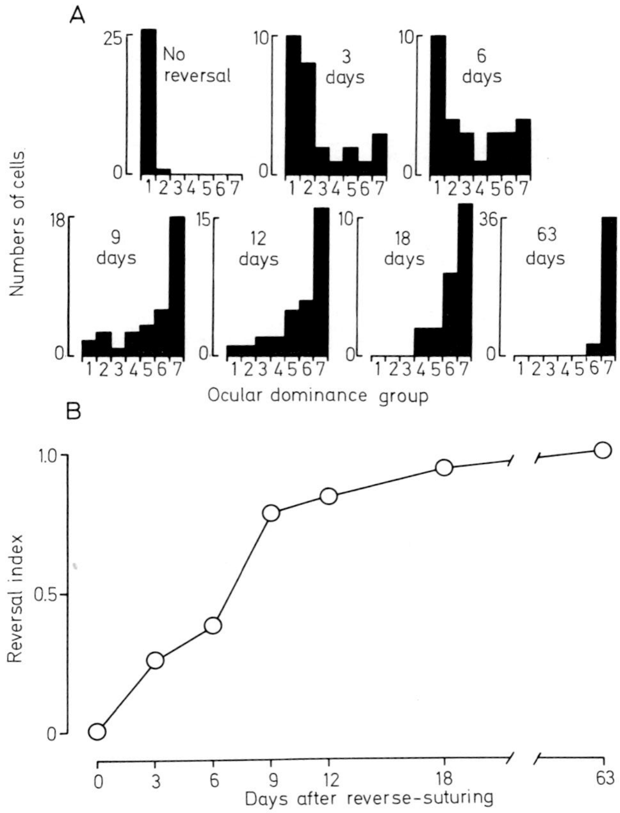

Fig. 13. The rapid shift in ocular dominance in the visual cortex of reverse sutured kittens. The ocular dominance histograms are all from animals that had the ipsilateral eye occluded until 5 weeks of age. The first animal was recorded at that age but the others were reverse sutured then and recorded some time later, as indicated. The graph below plots the reversal index, the proportion of cells dominated by the newly-opened eye, for these same animals. (From MOVSHON and BLAKEMORE, 1974)

clearly clustered together in exaggerated ocular dominance columns (BLAKEMORE and VAN SLUYTERS, 1974b; MOVSHON and BLAKEMORE, 1974; MOVSHON, 1976a; MITCHELL et al., 1977a), whose relative dimensions reflect the *overall* domination of the cortex by one eye or the other. So it is as if the changes following reverse suturing represented the appearance of tiny areas dominated by the "new" eye, which gradually expand and (if the reverse suturing is done early enough) ultimately take over the whole cortex (MOVSHON, 1976a; BLAKEMORE et al., 1976). Such an orderly pattern might result from the actual growth and invasion of the terminal arborizations of afferent fibres, especially since these distributions correlate so well with the ocular dominance columns in the normal monkey. Anatomical work is needed here to establish this point: if the changes in ocular dominance columns after reverse suturing *do* derive from axonal sprouting then that growth must be occurring at an unprecedented speed—up to about 100 μm per day (BLAKEMORE et al., 1976).

Preliminary work on reverse sutured monkeys (BLAKEMORE et al., 1978) has produced results very similar to those obtained in kittens. Ocular dominance can be totally reversed by reverse suture at $5^1/_2$ weeks of age; reversal at 8–9 weeks causes partial re-capture of cortical cells by the originally deprived eye; reverse suturing at a much later age has no effect. Even amongst the monocularly driven, non oriented units of layer IVc there is physiological evidence of partial "re-expansion" of the formerly shrunken ocular dominance columns, after early reverse suture. On the basis of anatomical and physiological observations on fetal and infant monkeys, RAKIC (1977) and HUBEL et al. (1977) have found that the patterns of termination of afferent axons within layer IVc are not strictly segregated in monkeys at birth, as they are in the adult. There is considerable intermixing of right-eye and left-eye territories, and binocularly driven cells can be recorded within layer IVc. They propose that during the first few weeks of life axonal segregation may be perfected by competitive rejection of the "weaker" input to any region. In normal animals this would lead to the formation of ocular dominance bands of equal size for the two eyes: but in monocularly deprived monkeys the experienced eye should be at a competitive advantage over a much wider fraction of layer IVc, and hence its columns should appear to expand. This hypothesis is elegant because it would explain, purely on the basis of competitive *rejection*, the duration of the sensitive period: that would be the time during which the normal sorting-out process is taking place. However, the physiological results on reverse suturing in monkeys seem to provide a little evidence that, upon re-stimulation, deprived afferent axons may be able partly to reinvade territory within layer IVc from which they had been functionally (though not necessarily structurally) excluded. Anatomical work may clarify this question.

IV. Malleability of Feature Detection

a) Retinal Disparity

The experiments on monocular deprivation and reverse suturing establish beyond doubt that one system of hypercolumns—ocular dominance—is totally plastic. Such an extraordinary phenomenon, restricted as it is within a fairly well-defined period early in life, must surely serve some fundamental biological purpose. Gross changes in cortical ocular dominance have so far been induced in cats, monkeys, mice and owls—all animals with large binocular visual fields—but not in the small binocular cortical segment of the rabbit (VAN SLUYTERS and STEWART, 1974), an animal that seems basically dependent on separate monocular vision. One might suspect, therefore, that binocular plasticity is particularly important in animals that rely heavily on binocular vision, perhaps for stereoscopic depth perception (see BARLOW et al., 1967; BISHOP, 1973).

At first it seems odd that binocularity, a property that everyone agrees is innately present in the cortex, is most obviously under the influence of visual experience. But the ocular dominance histogram, which is simply an estimate of the independent relative effects of the two inputs, provides no information about the *interaction* of those two synaptic inputs on individual cells. In adult cats (BARLOW et al., 1967; PETTIGREW et al., 1968) and monkeys (HUBEL and WIESEL, 1970b), and sheep (CLARKE et al., 1976) many cortical neurones show powerful excitatory and inhibitory interaction between signals from the two eyes, depending on the retinal disparity of the simultaneously presented images. These neurones can, by virtue of these interactions, be "depth-selective", and variation in optimal disparity from one cell to another creates a mechanism for the interpretation of the relative distances of objects—in a word, stereopsis. There is evidence that binocular plasticity, revealed in its grossest form by monocular deprivation, artificial strabismus and so on, is normally involved in creating this exquisite neural mechanism. It is difficult to imagine that genetic information alone could be precise enough to specify the relation between signals from the two eyes with the accuracy necessary for stereoscopic vision (BARLOW, 1975).

PETTIGREW (1974) examined the way that cortical cells add together stimulation from the two eyes in kittens with or without previous visual experience. Neurones in young inexperienced animals or binocularly deprived kittens never showed the narrow disparity selectivity typical of those in adult cats. They simply seemed to sum responses from the rather diffuse receptive fields in the two eyes and did not show the usual profound occlusion at inappropriate disparities. PETTIGREW (1974) interprets this result as an indication that the influence of visual experience is principally on *inhibitory* mechanisms in the cortex, which are presumed to assist in the refinement of many aspects of stimulus specificity. This conclusion is supported by SINGER and TRETTER's (1976) description of the weakness of intracortical inhibition in binocularly deprived cats.

If correlated visual experience (through both eyes at the same time) is responsible for chiselling out sharp optimal disparities from the granite of genetic instructions, then can the actual disparity selected be influenced by visual experience? PETTIGREW et al. (1973a) did report ephemeral shifts in optimal disparity after stimulating cortical cells simultaneously through both eyes at a particular retinal disparity, during an acute recording experiment. The effects were, however, unimpressive, perhaps because of the absence of a "consolidation" period, which may be important in producing synaptic changes (*vide infra*). However, SHLAER (1971) has demonstrated somewhat more convincing shifts in the average disparity of cortical cells by rearing kittens wearing small-angle prisms, base-up in front of one eye and base-down in front of the other, thus introducing a permanent vertical misalignment of the retinal images. Cells in the cortex remained mainly binocularly driven (unlike those in animals with much larger misalignments produced by artificial strabismus) but the receptive fields on average became vertically misaligned on the retinae in the direction of the prismatic disparity. Perhaps, then, subtle changes in binocular integration are normally going on early in development to match receptive field disparities to the binocular convergence angle of the eyes, which may be changing during the first weeks of life (SHERMAN, 1972). A breakdown in binocularity might represent the failure of this delicate adaptive mechanism. The diffuseness of receptive fields for many cortical cells in binocularly deprived cats (PETTIGREW, 1974; SINGER and

TRETTER, 1976) may also reflect some indeterminacy in retinotopic projection to the cortex.

BUCHTEL et al. (1975) have reported an extraordinary phenomenon, similar to that described by SHLAER (1971), but in adult cats with one eye immobilized. Preliminary electrophysiological results suggested that for those cats who consistently adopted their mobile eye as the behaviourally dominant one and "suppressed" information from the immobilized one, cortical cells did not so clearly lose binocularity and the receptive fields were topographical shifted in disparity, as if to make them aligned in space for a straight-ahead viewing position for the normal eye.

To add further confusion to the situation VAN SLUYTERS (1977) has recently failed to confirm SHLAER's (1971) observation that there is a partially compensatory shift in receptive field disparity after kittens are reared wearing small-angle prisms. Binocularity was found to break down even for the smallest prismatic deviation used unless the animal could make a disjunctive eye movement to overcome it.

b) *Orientation Selectivity*

In 1970 two independent reports appeared that suggested that orientation selectivity itself, in kittens, might be influenced by visual experience. HIRSCH and SPINELLI (1970, 1971) reared kittens in the dark except for daily exposure wearing goggles that presented a pattern of three vertical bars to one eye and three horizontal bars to the other. They recorded from the cortex using a somewhat unconventional, but at least objective, method of judging the selectivity of neurones. Quantitative analysis of responses to a small moving spot was used to map out the shape of the receptive field. This method would probably fail to predict the preferred orientation of most complex cells but would be useful in assessing the preferred orientation of simple cells with elongated spatially-summating areas. In fact they found that about half the cells had "diffuse" receptive fields (which this plotting method also finds in the normal cat's cortex), but of the 23 cells with obviously elongated receptive fields, 21 were monocularly driven and all but one had a receptive field orientation closely matching the experience of its eye. Some receptive fields seemed even more remarkably reminiscent of the exposure pattern; they had elongated patches of sensitivity, whose orientation, size and spacing fitted those of the stripes shown to that eye.

This result is unexpected, according to WIESEL and HUBEL's (1965a) description of binocular deprived kittens, because about half of the cortical cells in such animals were said to retain normal orientation selectivity as well as binocularity. Therefore HIRSCH and SPINELLI's cats might have been expected to have many normal, binocularly driven cells tuned to orientations other than vertical and horizontal.

BLAKEMORE and COOPER (1970) used a slightly different procedure: they simply exposed each kitten to horizontal or vertical lines displayed on the inside of a large cylindrical chamber in which the kitten could walk about on a glass platform suspended in the middle of the striped environment. It wore a ruff around its neck to prevent it from viewing its own body. Visual experience was thus more or less restricted to lines of one orientation. After several hundred hours of such exposure the animals were brought, for a total of about 20 hours, into a normal, lighted room. Their initial virtual blindness soon disappeared but was replaced by an unwillingness or inability to respond to stimuli of the orientation that they had not seen early in life. For example they would only orient to a moving stick if it was held at the appropriate angle. (These simple behavioural observations have been confirmed by MUIR and MITCHELL, 1975, who showed, however, that there is gradual recovery of response to the wrong orientation.)

Of the 125 neurones recorded in the cortex of the first two such kittens, all but one were selective for the orientation of a moving bar and their preferred orientations were biased towards that of the stripes seen by the animal. No cells were found with preferences within 20° of the opposite orientation. In general, the width of tuning for orientation was much narrower for cells sensitive to angles very close to the experienced orientation and broader for cells optimally sensitive to disparate orientations. The fact that (as in monocularly deprived kittens) there were no obvious regions of "silent" cortex suggested to BLAKEMORE and COOPER (1970) that the overall changes in orientation selectivity might be due to positive modification rather than simply to degenerative loss.

Apparently these changes can occur quite quickly. PETTIGREW et al. (1973a) occasionally saw transient enhancements and shifts of orientation selectivity after exposing deprived kitten cortical neurones to stripes during an actual recording experiment, and this has also been reported by IMBERT and BUISSERET (1975a) who, however, only saw such effects in kittens that had had previous visual experience. Somewhat more compelling results were produced by BLAKEMORE and MITCHELL (1973) using the method of exposure in a vertically striped cylinder: even one hour of experience was thought to be enough to make cortical cells normally responsive and orientation selective, with preferred orientations biased toward vertical (see Fig. 14). PETTIGREW and GAREY (1974), using a computer-controlled, quantitative method of analysis (GAREY, personal communication), confirmed the effects of brief exposure to stripes and demonstrated the crucial importance of a period of *consolidation*, without further visual stimulation, between exposure and recording. They exposed anaesthetized, paralysed kittens to moving vertical stripes restricted to one hemifield of one eye, thus leaving one cortical hemisphere unstimulated. They then compared the properties of cortical cells in the experienced and deprived hemispheres. Immediately after exposure there were no differences—both hemispheres were immature in their properties—but on the next day most cells in the stimulated hemisphere were monocularly driven and sensitive to vertical orientations. In electronmicrographs of the visual cortex from the same animals there were striking differences in the density of synaptic vesicles in the two hemispheres (GAREY and PETTIGREW, 1974). Rapid biasing of preferred orientation after 3 hours of exposure to stripes (but quantitatively less striking than BLAKEMORE and MITCHELL's, 1973, results) has been confirmed by TRETTER et al. (1975).

The possibility of a sensitive period for the effects of exposure to stripes has been investigated by BLAKEMORE (1974, and unpublished observations).

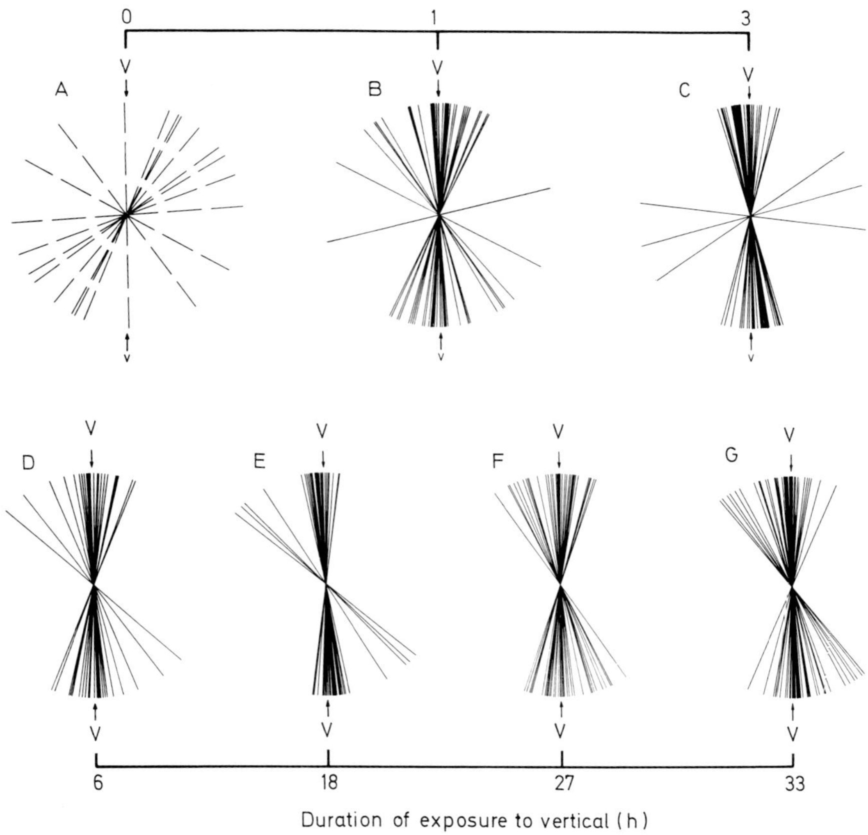

Fig. 14. Effects on preferred orientation of cortical cells in kittens reared in the dark except for a brief exposure to vertical contours in a striped chamber at about 4 weeks of age, with recording at 6 weeks. The animals were exposed for the number of hours shown on the abscissae. Each line plots the preferred orientation for one cortical cell. The control animal (A) was totally binocularly deprived and the interrupted lines show the infantile orientational preferences for the cells with an "orientation bias". No genuinely orientation selective cells were recorded in this animal. (From BLAKEMORE and MITCHELL, 1973)

Among more than twenty kittens exposed to stripes for at least a few hours at various times during life, a strong bias towards the experienced orientation was only ever found in animals that had their visual experience between about 3 and 14 weeks of age. Thus there might be a sensitive period for this phenomenon which coincides closely with that for effects on binocularity.

There are reasons however, for interpreting cautiously these results on the sensitive period: the immobility and perpetual sleepiness of very young kittens makes it difficult to guarantee adequate exposure; and animals older than about 2 months are extremely mobile and sometimes boisterous, so that their constant head rotation and so on would cause much more variation in the retinal orientation of the stripes in their fields. Certainly we have noticed consistently in this laboratory that animals exposed long into the second and third month, whether exposed before that or not, tend to have much broader distributions of preferred orientation.

(Interesting results from Creutzfeldt and Heggelund, 1975, suggest that prolonged exposure of *adult* cats to high contrast stipes actually *reduces* the proportion of recorded cells responding to that orientation. Such effects might be due to prolonged "fatigue" of adult cortical neurones of the type described by Maffei et al., 1973, and this view is strengthened by the impression that this effect declines throughout the recording session—Creutzfeldt, personal communication.)

Quite recently Spencer (1974) has confirmed the electro-physiological observations on stripe-reared cats and Spencer and Coleman (1974) have also presented evidence for a morphological change that might explain those results. They measured the shapes of the tangentially-distributed dendritic trees of stellate and pyramidal cells, visible in Golgi-impregnated sections of layer IV of the cortex. In dark-reared kittens the trees tended to be circular, in normal cats they were elongated, with a length to width ratio of about 2, and in long-term stripe-reared kittens they were even more obviously oval in shape. More spectacular still was the observation that the orientation of the oval dendritic tree, relative to the retinotopic map in the cortex, closely matched the orientation seen early in life. They proposed that the orientations of the receptive fields of cortical cells are largely determined by the shape of their dendrites, picking off from a retinotopic matrix of incoming fibres. Such an idea is in many ways attractive and has been proposed before for invertebrates (Young, 1960) as well as for the cat (Colonnier, 1964). However it is unlikely to be the whole story. Undoubtedly intracortical inhibition is important in determining orientation tuning if not preferred orientation (Blakemore and Tobin, 1972; Creutzfeldt et al., 1974). Also, the occurrence (*vide infra*) in some animals of cells with markedly different preferred orientations in the two eyes (even though each cell has only one set of dendrites) makes it less plausible that elongation of the dendritic tree is the only factor involved in determining receptive field orientation. More subtle changes in the efficiency of synapses, as proposed by Blakemore and Van Sluyters (1975) and suggested by the anatomical results of Garey and Pettigrew (1974), seem a more likely explanation of at least the effects of brief exposure. Perhaps, as with the consequences of monocular deprivation, we should expect to find more than one morphological correlate—changes in synaptic efficiency, possibly followed by axonal or dendritic growth.

A number of recent studies (Spinelli and Hirsch, 1971; Pettigrew and Freeman, 1973; Van Sluyters and Blakemore, 1973b; Blakemore and Van Sluyters, 1975) have investigated the effects of rearing kittens in environments of small spots, in which the animal is not deprived of patterned contrast in the image but is prevented from seeing elongated contours. Cortical neurones in animals exposed only to very small spots have two interesting properties: 1. though the cells are thoroughly mature in responsiveness and lack of habituation, only a small minority of them show any degree of selectivity for orientation or direction; 2. most cells have a most unusual form of size-selectivity making them optimally responsive to small moving spots of the angular size that they experienced. The failure of small spots (about 2 deg in diameter) to encourage a wholesale increase in the proportion of orientation selective cells, but the relative success of larger spots (about 5 deg in diameter) in doing so (some 60% of cells become genuinely orientation selective), has led BLAKEMORE and VAN SLUYTERS (1975) to propose that elongated contour in the retinal image is the necessary condition for the refinement (or maintenance) of stimulus specificity in the kitten's cortex. It has even been suggested that kitten cortical cells may become differentially sensitive to much more complicated stimuli, such as two dimensional moving shapes (ŻERNICKI and MICHASLKI, 1974).

c) "Meridional Amblyopia" and Natural Meridional Variations in Acuity

It is well known that humans are generally better at resolving patterns of vertical or horizontal contours than of diagonal ones. In fact both contrast sensitivity and cut-off spatial frequency are usually lower for diagonal gratings than for vertical and horizontal. Optical factors cannot explain this anisotropy, since it persists if the gratings used to measure the threshold are created inside the eye by an ingenious method utilizing the interference of coherent light (CAMPBELL et al., 1966; MITCHELL et al., 1967). Nor is it explained by the mosaic of retinal receptors (POLYAK, 1941); indeed the electroretinogram produced by rapid displacement of a grating from side to side is equal in amplitude whatever the orientation of the grating (MAFFEI and CAMPBELL, 1970). The visual evoked response from the occipital cortex for such a stimulus is, however, similarly anisotropic in amplitude as a function of orientation, and there seems to be a close relationship between the amplitude of the cortical potential evoked by a grating and its psychophysical visibility (MAFFEI and CAMPBELL, 1970; CAMPBELL et al., this volume). This has led many to propose that the hypothetical population of orientation selective cells in the human head is, in some way, more sensitive for vertical and horizontal than for diagonal, either because there are more cells tuned to those orientations or because such cells are more absolutely sensitive than cells selective for diagonal contours. (In fact, not enough thought has been given to the question of what actual neuronal properties might determine meridional variations in sensitivity: as in the question of amblyopia, the spatial resolving power of neurones, not just their numbers, must be considered.)

To the hard-nosed Empiricist, these variations in acuity with orientation can be blamed directly on small variations in the probabilty of seeing various contours in our visual environments. The argument goes that we live in an angular, carpentered world in which horizontal and vertical orientations predominate (but see MAYER and SWITKES, 1977, for a cautionary note); therefore we become more sensitive to them. The demonstrations of the modifiability of orientation selectivity in kittens have been taken as evidence for this hypothesis. However there has been no convincing demonstration that merely increasing slightly the *proportion* of certain contours in a kitten's environment produces a bias in the distribution of preferred orientations towards those contours. What may be most effective is the exclusion of every other kind of contour, and that certainly does not happen to diagonal contours in normal human vision.

The equally adamant Nativist would reply that normal meridional variations in acuity must reflect some inherent over-sensitivity or over-representation of vertical and horizontal detectors—perhaps some non-linearity in the pattern of orientation columns in each hypercolumn. (Keep in mind that the rabbit's retina has orientation selective ganglion cells, and they all prefer horizontal or vertical: LEVICK, 1967.)

In fact there are reports of small differences in the numbers of neurones preferring horizontal and vertical, compared with those favouring diagonals, in cats (HENRY et al., 1974; SPENCER, 1974; LEVENTHAL and HIRSCH, 1977) and in the foveal representation of the monkey cortex (MANSFIELD, 1974), though this anisotropy is not consistently reported (WATKINS and BERKLEY, 1974; ROSE and BLAKEMORE, 1974; HUBEL and WIESEL, 1968).

There is a little evidence for some influence of visual experience in the establishment of natural meridional anisotropies. ANNIS and FROST (1973), for instance, found a slightly reduced meridional anisotropy in Cree Indians, who live in a somewhat less perpendicularly-dominated environment. On the other hand, TIMNEY and MUIR (1976) discovered that urban Chinese have a much less exaggerated orientational anisotropy than Euro-Canadians with no apparent difference in the degree of "carpentering" in their environments.

TELLER et al. (1974) measured cut-off spatial frequency in human babies by using the preferential looking technique: the baby was confronted with a vertical or diagonal grating and a similarly-shaped blank grey field, side by side, and its ability to discriminate between them was judged by whether the baby spent more than half its time looking at the stripes (since infants are known to prefer looking at contours rather than at blank fields). The experiment, as well as showing that acuity improves only very slowly up to at least six months (Fig. 8), failed to reveal any difference in the actual acuity for diagonal and vertical gratings. TELLER et al. (1974) point out that the interpretation of this result is not straightforward since even adult humans do not show differences in contrast sensitivity for oblique and vertical gratings low enough in spatial frequency for these young babies to resolve them (CAMPBELL et al., 1966). The results could be taken to mean that meridional anisotropies develop only very slowly in response to visual experience, but equally it could be said that babies can hardly be expected to have meridional variations in resolution until they can see spatial frequencies high enough to reveal the differences in adults! Evidence in favour of extremely slow appearance of the anisotropy comes from MAYER's (1977) failure to detect it at all in five year olds, though it was present reliably at about the age of ten years.

On the other hand, contradictory evidence comes from LEEHEY et al. (1975), who have repeated TELLER et al. (1974) study using what is presumably a more sensitive method for detecting small anisotropies. They presented babies simultaneously with vertical (or horizontal) and oblique gratings of identical contrast and found that with patterns just lower than the presumed cut-off spatial frequency babies spent more time looking at the vertical (or horizontal) pattern than at the diagonal. They argue that this must be due to greater apparent contrast in gratings at the principal orientations (implying greater contrast sensitivity for them). A kind of "cognitive preference" for vertical (or horizontal) versus diagonal, even though both might be equally visible, is almost ruled out by their observation that the babies do *not* prefer vertical (or horizontal) gratings to oblique if the spatial frequency is even lower and therefore both are clearly visible. It remains only to say that it is perhaps rather surprising to find these anisotropies in human babies at spatial frequencies lower than those at which they occur in adults. The fact that they can even be found, though less pronounced, in infants only 2 weeks old (HELD, personal communication) makes it unlikely that they are imposed by experience (but one should keep in mind that the monkey's critical period for effects on binocularity probably peaks in the first two weeks of life).

But if we conclude provisionally that natural meridional anisotropies in resolution are due at least in part to some innate component in the make-up of the cortex, it is surprising to discover that environmentally-imposed differences in the contrast of different orientations on the retina during early development can indubitably induce *unnatural* meridional variations in acuity in both cats and people. MUIR and MITCHELL (1975) used behavioural methods to measure the cut-off spatial frequency for gratings of different orientations in normal cats and those that had been reared in striped environments like BLAKEMORE and COOPER's (1970). The former had roughly the same acuity for all orientations while the latter had reduced acuity (by a factor of up to 2) for the "deprived" orientation. (It is not yet clear whether the acuity of stripe-reared cats is actually better than normal for gratings of the experienced orientation, but it seems unlikely from available data.) Perplexingly, the ability to discriminate orientation is only slightly influenced by environmental modification of the kitten's visual cortex. HIRSCH (1972) found only a 3–4% difference in angular discrimination thresholds for lines near the experienced and inexperienced orientations in his animals exposed to stripes in goggles.

Nature has provided a remarkable developmental experiment in certain humans who have, in effect, been relatively deprived of high spatial frequency content for one range of orientations early in life. These are individuals who have suffered from astigmatism of high power, causing one meridian of the retinal image to be relatively defocused compared with the orthogonal. (The absolute degree of defocusing of each meridian is, of course, influenced by the accommodative state of the observer and the viewing distance, but in the case of hypermetropic astigmatism, the meridian of greatest defocus can be entirely beyond the accommodative capacity of the subject, and under any conditions the other meridian will have higher contrast on the retina. In myopic or mixed astigmats the situation is more complicated, but it seems likely that they adopt the most convenient meridian for the habitual control of their accommodative response—MITCHELL et al., 1973; FREEMAN, 1975a). So, an infant with high astigmatic error will habitually have been exposed to contours of higher contrast on the retina in one orientation than in the opposite.

The mere optical error of an astigmatic eye can, of course, be corrected with a cylindrical lens but MARTIN (1890) noticed that, even after apparently ideal correction, many adult astigmats still have an "amblyopie astigmatique" or "meridional amblyopia"—a reduced resolving power for the contours that were most defocused by the uncorrected astigmatism. This observation was

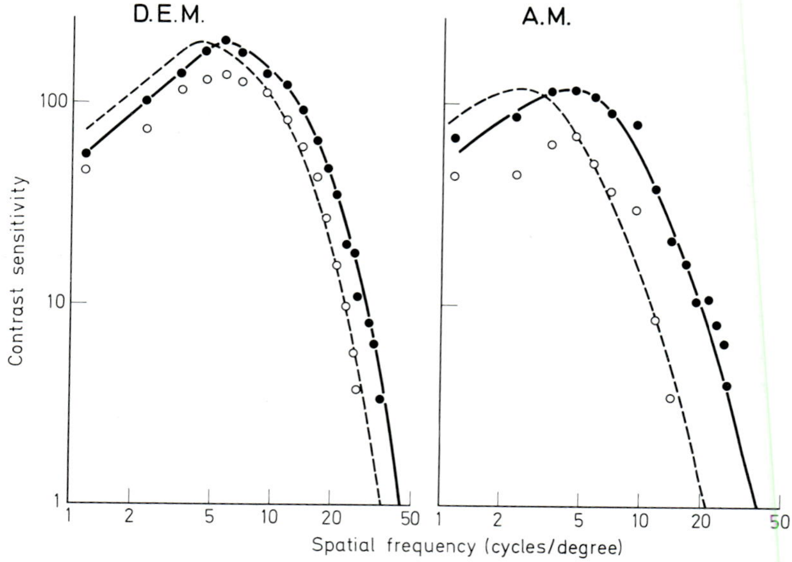

Fig. 15. Measurements of contrast sensitivity as a function of spatial frequency for vertical (filled circles) and horizontal (open circles) gratings for subject DEM, and for 75° (filled) and 165° (open) gratings for AM. Both subjects are astigmatic and have, at all spatial frequencies, lower contrast sensitivity for horizontal, or near horizontal, gratings than for vertical, or near vertical, gratings. The solid curves are fitted by eye to the filled circles and the interrupted lines are the same curves simply shifted to the left, giving a fair fit to the open circles at the high frequency end but not at the low. (From MITCHELL and WILKINSON, 1974)

not generally known but, in their intended study of normal meridional variations in acuity, MITCHELL et al. (1967) found one subject (MITCHELL himself) who could resolve vertical gratings much better than horizontal, even when those patterns were produced by interference directly inside the eye, virtually by-passing all effects from the optics. Subject D.E.M. is highly astigmatic with vertical as the preferred orientation of focus. Still this finding remained just an interesting anomaly until its possible relationship to the developmental experiments on environmental influences in the kitten cortex was noticed. Since then, thorough study has shown that almost all humans who have had uncorrected early astigmatism suffer some degree of meridional amblyopia (MITCHELL et al., 1973; MITCHELL and WILKINSON, 1974; FREEMAN and THIBOS, 1975a). The effect cannot be explained by errors in optical correction during the experiment, because it persists in the optical by-pass method and, in any case, contrast sensitivity is not uniformly reduced at all spatial frequencies above about 5 c/° as would be expected if it were due to defocus. Actually, though the reduction in contrast sensitivity declines at low spatial frequencies, it is still present at frequencies as low as 1 c/° (see Fig. 15), where the original astigmatic error itself would have had negligible effect on the relative contrast of different orientations, and where normal observers do not have any clear difference in sensitivity for vertical and oblique.

The analogy seems obvious between these results and those on orientation modification in the kitten's cortex and the effects of that modification on the kitten's visual acuity (with the reservations already expressed about the possible over-simplification of correlating differences in acuity with differences in the numbers of cortical cells). Further evidence that meridional amblyopia stems from some neural anisotropy of representation in the human visual cortex comes from the report by FREEMAN and THIBOS (1975b), that the occipital potential of fully corrected astigmats is decreased in amplitude for gratings of the least resolvable orientation, in a manner that matches the acuity of the observer (see CAMPBELL et al., this volume).

The argument about the relationship between orientational biasing in the kitten's cortex and meridional amblyopia caused by astigmatism comes full circle with the experiment of FREEMAN and PETTIGREW (1973), who reared kittens in a relatively normal environment but wearing powerful cylindrical lenses that produced artificial astigmatism. Subsequent recording from the cortex showed a slight but obvious bias in the proportion of neurones favouring the orientation that was originally clearly in focus on the retina.

d) The Reproducibility and Validity of Orientational Modification

Within the last few years, the apparently secure and internally consistent story about early environmental influences on orientation selectivity has been questioned by a number of workers. MAFFEI and FIORENTINI (1974) reared kittens for long periods in an environment of vertical stripes of a single spatial frequency (most of the original stripe-rearing experiments had used bars of many different widths). They reported that recordings of the massed activity of the lateral geniculate body and the cortical evoked potential both showed a *reduction* in response for gratings, whatever their orientation, at the experienced spatial frequency. A few geniculate single neurones and cortical complex cells showed dips in sensitivity at that frequency in their individual contrast sensitivity functions. Moreover (see the footnote in their paper), a small sample of cortical cells had no bias in their preferred orientations. BLAKEMORE, MOVSHON and VAN SLUYTERS (1978) have performed a similar experiment but with conditions more like those used in earlier work – shorter exposure, a larger field of view covered by the stripes and, it must be said, less precise control of the range of spatial frequencies experienced by the kittens. Using quantitative methods they found no decrease in the fraction of cortical and geniculate neurones "tuned" to the experienced frequency, no reduction in their sensitivity at that frequency, no decrease in the amplitude of the cortical evoked potential for that frequency, a clear difference in amplitude of the potential for vertical and horizontal gratings and a significant bias in the distribution of preferred orientations towards vertical. PETTIGREW and GAREY (1974) and TRETTER et al. (1975) also used stripes of a single spatial frequency and obtained positive modification of preferred orientation after brief exposure. In this case, then, it appears that the differences in results may be attributable to differences in the duration and control of the exposure.

No such simple argument can however be mobilized to account for the negative results of STRYKER and SHERK (1975), who reared kittens in conditions extremely similar to those used by BLAKEMORE and COOPER (1970), BLAKEMORE and MITCHELL (1973), MUIR and MITCHELL (1975) and many other workers.

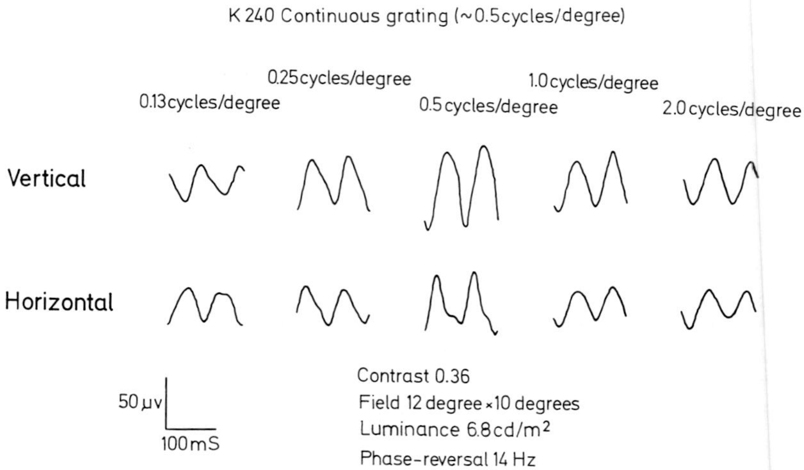

Fig. 16. Occipital potentials evoked by phase-shifting gratings viewed by a kitten that had been exposed when young to an environment consisting of a regular vertical grating of about 0.5 c/°. The top row is for vertical gratings, the bottom for horizontal. Each record is the average of 400 sweeps, each sweep including one complete cycle (two phase shifts). The records were collected in an irregular sequence. At all spatial frequencies except the lowest, the amplitude of potential for the vertical grating is almost twice that for the horizontal. (BLAKEMORE, MOVSHON and VAN SLUYTERS, 1978)

In what is arguably the most rigorously controlled and careful study so far STRYKER and SHERK obtained negative results. All animals had orientation preferences distributed all around the clock. Small biases in the expected direction in some animals were no more common than slight biases in the wrong direction in others. The orientation columnar sequences seemed entirely undisturbed, with regular progressions in preferred orientation from one group of cells to the next.

STRYKER and SHERK employed a much more objective technique of analysis to obtain a thoroughly reliable sample of cortical cells. 1. They recorded from animals according to a "blind" schedule in which the experimenters did not know the rearing history of the animals. 2. They plotted orientational tuning curves with a randomly presented series of moving lines, under computer control. 3. They sampled single cells or multi-unit activity at roughly 100 µm intervals during long diagonal penetrations, in order to survey at regular increments the orientation columnar sequence, and thus they avoided paying undue attention to areas in which cells might happen to have been easy to record.

They suggested that one or all of these three objective procedures might account for the difference between their findings and the previously reported results. I shall attempt to answer each of these points but there is no doubt that more work is needed to settle this important debate.

First, the question of sampling method is a crucial one with many pitfalls for the experimenter (see BLAKEMORE and VAN SLUYTERS, 1975). The very arrangement of cells into columnar clusters makes a small sample from a limited region almost certain to be biased in orientation. On the other hand, it seems wrong to prolong experiments beyond a few hours in young kittens, when previous reports suggest that many properties of their neurones might be modified by stimulation during the experiment itself (PETTIGREW et al., 1973a; IMBERT and BUISSERET, 1975a; OLSON and FREEMAN, 1975; KASAMATSU, 1976). However there is no possible reason for a bias produced by inadequate samples to be in any particular direction, unless literally some preliminary search was carried out to find an appropriate area to record from. Certainly in every published report on orientational modification from this laboratory the majority of each sample of neurones has come from the very first penetration with the first and only electrode used in the whole recording experiment. However, cells tuned to angles very close to the experienced orientation do tend to be more responsive and more precisely tuned, and to occur in areas of somewhat richer yield than poorly specified cells or those tuned to rather disparate orientations (BLAKEMORE and MITCHELL, 1973; PETTIGREW and GAREY, 1974; BLASDEL et al., 1977). This might explain why conventional penetrations, in which every isolated single cell is studied, reveal relatively more of these well-specified, approprimately oriented units. But no simple selection from a sample can turn a highly biased one into a uniform one.

The question of the use of a "blind" procedure implies a much more serious criticism of previous work, because it suggests that what may be biased is the opinion of the experimenter rather than the cortical cells of his kitten. However, the basic phenomenon of orientational modification has now been demonstrated independently in nine separate laboratories (HIRSCH and SPINELLI, 1970, 1971; BLAKEMORE and COOPER, 1970; BLAKEMORE and MITCHELL, 1973; PETTIGREW et al., 1973a, b; MIZE and MURPHY, 1973—see footnote; FREEMAN and PETTIGREW, 1973; PETTIGREW and GAREY, 1974; SPENCER, 1974; TRETTER et al., 1975; CYNADER et al., 1975; IMBERT and BUISSERET, 1975a, b; TURKEL et al., 1975). It is difficult to believe that observer bias could account for all of these positive results. In any case, PETTIGREW et al. (1973b) and SPENCER (1974) did use "blind" recording procedures and obtained positive results. Also, BLASDEL et al. (1977) have very recently completed a series of "blind" experiments involving stripe-reared animals (whose acuity had already been measured behaviourally) and normal controls, shipped from Nova Scotia to California for recording, and the results are impressively positive. Their technique of analysis used a computer-controlled, randomly presented display: quantitative methods of some kind were also used in the experiments of HIRSCH and SPINELLI (1970, 1971); PETTIGREW et al. (1973a, b); PETTIGREW and GAREY (1974); TRETTER et al. (1975); IMBERT and BUISSERET (1975a).

The fact that the occipital evoked potential is reliably greater for gratings of the experienced orientation than for the orthogonal, in both stripe-reared kittens (see Fig. 15) and humans with meridional amblyopia (FREEMAN and THIBOS, 1975b), provides further objective evidence, without sampling bias, that there has been some genuine change in the population of cortical cells, though not necessarily a gross redistribution of preferred orientations.

Finally, a very complete recent study on reverse sutured kittens (MOVSHON, 1976a) suggests that, as a deprived eye "re-maps" into the visual cortex, it lays down its own orderly orientation columnar array which can be partly

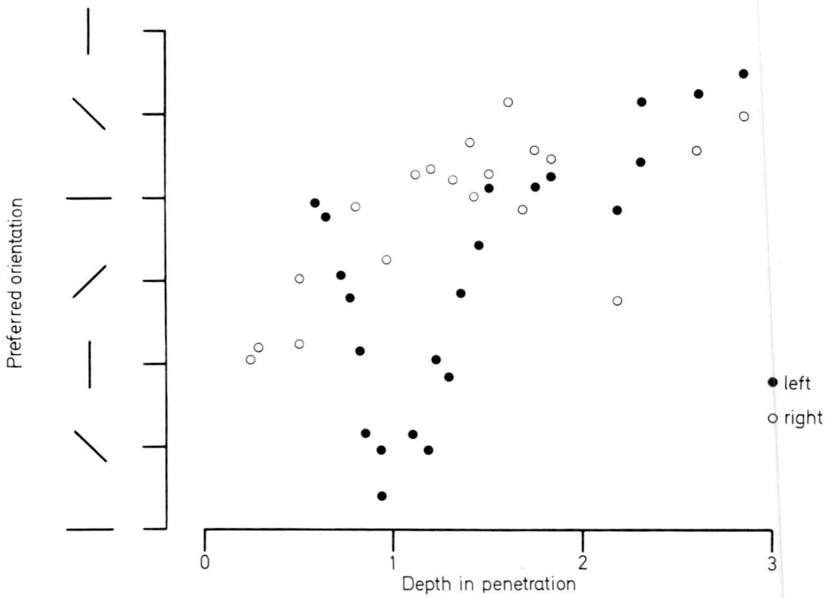

Fig. 17. Sequences of preferred orientation (like those of Fig. 5) for cortical cells in a kitten deprived by occluding the right eye until 6 weeks of age, then reverse sutured for a further 6 days, allowing the right eye to re-gain influence over some cells. The receptive fields were analysed separately in the two eyes and the preferred orientations are plotted separately even for the few binocularly driven cells. Both eyes show progressive shifts in preferred orientation, clearer for the left eye than the right, but they are not in register with each other. Each eye apparently lays down its own set of orientation columns in the absence of simultaneous binocular vision. (From MOVSHON, 1976a)

independent of that belonging to the retreating input from the originally experienced eye. Long penetrations through the cortex of reverse sutured animals, at intermediate stages of "re-capture", reveal columnar progressions of preferred orientation for the receptive fields in both eyes; but the two sequences can be almost entirely out of register (see Fig. 17). This explains why the few binocularly driven cells in such an animal (which are shared by both columnar sequences) can have different preferred orientations in the two eyes, differing by up to 90° (*vide infra*). Here is powerful evidence that visual experience is capable not only of generating orientation selectivity but also that preferred orientation and even its columnar distribution can fall under environmental control.

Why then did STRYKER and SHERK (1975), MAFFEI and FIORENTINI (1974), DAW and WYATT (1976) and BERMAN and DAW (1977) not obtain positive results with stripe rearing? We might hope that the differences in results stem from an interesting uncontrolled variable which could influence the sensitivity of the cortex to modification. Recent results from KASAMATSU and PETTIGREW (1976) suggest that the ascending noradrenergic projection to the cortex from the locus coeruleus might play a crucial role in the response of the cortex to monocular deprivation. So perhaps some subtle motivation or reward process is involved in modification and this factor was deficient in STRYKER and SHERK's procedure. However, a much more mundane but virtually certain source of variability is the problem of adequately controlling the retinal stimulus, as already discussed. Certainly the definite presence of orientation selective cells and the probable existence of some kind of orientation columnar sequence in totally inexperienced animals (BLAKEMORE and VAN SLUYTERS, 1975; SHERK and STRYKER, 1976), makes it doubly important to emphasize that stripe-rearing depends on rigorous *deprivation* for certain contours, rather than on a slight predominance of one particular orientation in the environment. In this laboratory, some experiments on animals exposed for a lengthy period to stripes in a cylinder have also produced no bias at all, though if ever there was a statistically significant anisotropy it was always in the correct direction. The most economical explanation seems to be that the experimenter can never completely guarantee the elimination of unwanted contours in a striped drum, and even if he could, the variation in the mobility of individual kittens would introduce unexpected and uncontrollable variations in the range of exposure in different animals.

Encouraging support for this possible explanation comes from STRYKER, SHERK, HIRSCH and LEVENTHAL (note added in proof in STRYKER and SHERK, 1975) who have now succeeded in observing *positive* biasing of orientation, using their objective methods, in animals reared with stripes in goggles, in the style of HIRSCH and SPINELLI (1970). This method of exposure eliminates unwanted features and restricts the range of retinal orientation more exactly than simple exposure in a striped drum, but it also introduces conflict between signals from the two eyes, since they view orthogonally orientated contours. The biased distribution of orientation preference is not, however, dependent on the presence of interocular conflict since STRYKER et al. (1976) are now able to obtain a clear bias amongst orientation selective cells in cats reared wearing goggles in which the two eyes view the *same* orientation.

There seems now, then, to be less debate about the existence of the orientational biasing phenomenon, although the question of interpretation is far from settled. In their recent work using exposure with goggles STRYKER et al. (1976) have found large numbers of cells to be visually unresponsive or non oriented, as in long-term deprived cats. With orthogonal exposure to the two eyes only about half of all cells were orientational. And a much smaller fraction were oriented after exposure to the same orientation in the two eyes. Obviously the most conservative explanation of these results is that the bias amongst the orientation selective cells is due only to a kind of selective *functional validation*. Those cells that should respond to other orientations, and hence remain unstimulated early in life, undergo the same kind of degenerative changes that occur during binocular deprivation.

A similar interpretation can be put on recent results from SINGER (1976), in kittens, and WIESEL and HUBEL, in monkeys (WIESEL, personal communication, 1977). They arranged for the animals to receive visual experience restricted to lines of a single orientation, through one eye alone. Cortical cells driven exclusively by the experienced eye had their preferences biased towards that orientation, but (although the overall ocular dominance distribution was weighted towards the experienced eye) the other eye dominated some cells, with a bias of orientation orthogonal to that actually seen by the experienced eye (although many of these cells were non oriented in the cat). This could be explained than by the kind of interocular competitive effect that is thought to account for the results of straightforward monocular deprivation (WIESEL and HUBEL, 1965a). The stimulated eye could have expanded its representation, but only amongst those orientation columns in which its experience of stripes gave it a competitive advantage, The other eye retains control of unstimulated orientation columns within its territory. These interesting observations also support the idea that the neural site of at least some component of the competitive interaction in monocular deprivation is at the visual cortex itself, not just at the level of the lateral geniculate nucleus.

The interesting question remains whether environmental modification of orientational preferences is merely due to selective functional validation, or whether some cells might actually change their innate predispositions or indeed have no such pre-program and be entirely dependent on the pattern of stimulation for the determination of their receptive field properties. There seem, at the moment, to be only two possible approaches to this fundamental issue. The first involves attempts to modify the response properties of individual cells by stimulation during an acute recording experiment. The results of such studies are, however, rather weak and far from conclusive (PETTIGREW et al., 1973a; IMBERT and BUISSERET, 1975a), not necessarily because there is no such plasticity but because of the possible need, already discussed, for a period of consolidation (e.g. PETTIGREW and GAREY, 1974).

The second strategy involves the interpretation of the sequential distribution of cell types during individual penetrations in which orientation preference has, overall, been biased by experience. Here the results are equivocal. HIRSCH and SPINELLI (1970, 1971) and STRYKER et al. (1976) found small clusters of oriented cells at intervals during each penetration whereas other cells were visually unresponsive, non-oriented or only crudely selective. On the other hand, PETTIGREW et al. (1973b), also recording from animals reared by HIRSCH and using a "blind" experimental procedure, came to exactly the opposite conclusion: reconstructions of the penetrations showed no large regions of neurones with "deprived" properties, yet the entire sample was highly biased in orientation preference. Similar conclusions were reached by BLAKEMORE and COOPER (1970) and BLAKEMORE and MITCHELL (1973)—as long as the exposure exceeded a few hours. In their recent study, where most of the kittens were restrained inside a striped cylinder and therefore the retinal stimulus was more exactly controlled, BLASDEL et al. (1977) also describe some extremely long penetrations with little or no variation in orientation preference (although it must be said that about 25% of all the neurones they recorded were unresponsive, non oriented or so unreliable that they could not be analysed quantitatively, and the proportion was lower in normal than in stripe reared animals). I have recently completed a new study, using an entirely objective procedure of analysis, of animals that were monocularly exposed to stripes in goggles (BLAKEMORE, 1977). Although many cells were extremely sluggish and often poorly tuned, only 7.6% were actually non-oriented or unresponsive, and the remainder had their preferred orientations highly biased. Reconstructions of individual penetrations showed unusually long stretches in which orientation preference did not drift from cell to cell in the manner found in normal cats.

The whole problem of interpreting samples of cells gained with a microelectrode is pointed up by STONE's (1973) observations on the enormously different proportions of X, Y and W cells recorded in the retina with different types of electrode. And even in monocularly deprived animals, where it had been universally accepted that only a tiny fraction of cortical cells retain input from the deprived eye, STRYKER and SHATZ (1976), using high impedance electrodes, have now discovered small nests of neurones in layer IV, dominated by the deprived eye, in accordance with the pattern of termination of geniculate axons.

The possibility, then, that cells can shrink and become virtually unrecordable, yet remain functional, makes the assessment of different theories of the mechanism of orientation modification a formidable prospect. Much more work is undoubtedly needed before this interesting question can finally be settled. At the moment the most parsimonious account of the results is that based on the idea of functional validation of stimulated neurones. From the point of view of the Empiricist-Nativist debate, however, the mechanism by which the environment might have its effects on sensory systems is relatively unimportant. The fact is that, as meridional amblyopia so aptly demonstrates, restricted visual experience can alter perceptual capacity, whether due to active modification or functional validation.

The interesting report by TURKEL et al. (1975), that exposure to horizontal or vertical contours in a striped drum produces strong modification of orientation preference amongst cortical cells, but exposure to diagonals does not, may conceivably be explained by differences in control of the retinal orientation of the stimulus. To be anthropomorphic for a moment, it is tempting to think that kittens might tilt their heads much more often when confronted with oblique stripes (to bring them to a principal meridian on the retina, perhaps to facilitate exploratory eye movements) than when faced with vertical or horizontal.

However, LEVENTHAL and HIRSCH (1975) have also reported that the bias of preferred orientations is much broader (with the range actually including vertical and horizontal) after exposure to diagonal lines in goggles worn by the kittens than after exposure to horizontal and vertical. Movements of the animal are unlikely to affect the retinal orientation very much under these conditions. LEVENTHAL and HIRSCH (1977) have also found that orientation selective neurones in totally deprived animals are often monocularly driven, confirming the results of BLAKEMORE and VAN SLUYTERS (1975), and usually have horizontal or vertical preferred orientations without any experience of those contours. They argue that cells can only develop oblique preferences on the basis of visual experience but can retain a preference for horizontal or vertical without experience. Such an argument alone, however, cannot explain the virtual absence of horizontal preferences amongst cells driven monocularly by an eye that has experienced only vertical contours.

e) "Binocular Matching": a Possible Adaptive Value of Environmental Modification

In kittens, visual experience is apparently needed to match the properties of binocularly driven cells in the two eyes, as well as to refine their actual disparity selectivity. If an animal has received uncorrelated visual experience in the two eyes, any binocular cells that it still possesses are likely to have mismatched receptive fields, such as an orientation selective field in one eye and a non-oriented field in the other, or even grossly different preferred orientations on the two retinae.

Even in the binocularly deprived cat, SINGER and TRETTER (1976) have described cells with dissimilar receptive field properties in the two eyes; and those binocular cells that have some degree of orientation selectivity can have preferred orientations differing by as much as 50° in the two eyes (BLAKEMORE and VAN SLUYTERS, 1975). The great breadth of tuning of many cells in the deprived cortex makes this finding statistically somewhat insecure, but differences of even 15° are very rare in the normal adult (BLAKEMORE et al., 1972; NELSON et al., 1977). Reverse sutured animals that have never had simultaneous binocular vision, and eye-rotated animals, can have even greater variation, some cells having almost orthogonally oriented, finely tuned orientation selective receptive fields in the two eyes (BLAKEMORE and VAN SLUYTERS, 1974b; BLAKEMORE et al., 1975; MOVSHON, 1976a).

On the other hand VAN SLUYTERS (see BLAKEMORE et al., 1976) has shown that if kittens are allowed normal binocular vision before a period of monocular deprivation and then are reverse sutured, any neurones that regain binocular input have closely similar preferred orientations in the two eyes. The initial period of binocular vision is apparently enough to match the properties of the inputs and, though temporarily removed by monocular deprivation, exactly the same receptive field characteristics reappear after reverse suturing.

Even in the situations where the distributions of interocular differences in preferred orientation are very wide, the mode of the distribution is always near zero—so there is some modal tendency for cells to adopt similar preferences on the two retinae. Visual experience seems, however, to narrow the range to its normal value and may even be capable of shifting the mean to some extent. SHINKMAN and BRUCE (1977) reared animals wearing prisms that rotated the view of one eye relative to the other by 16°. There was no massive loss of binocularity (presumably for cells with receptive fields near the axis of rotation of the prism) and, for binocular cells, the mean interocular difference in receptive field orientation was close to the angular disparity introduced by the prisms. Exposure of animals to gratings differing in orientation in the two eyes by 45° did produce a disruption of binocularity (SHINKMAN et al., 1977).

BLAKEMORE and VAN SLUYTERS (1975) have proposed that there is a broad genetic predisposition towards a particular orientation in kitten cortical cells but that normal correlated binocular visual experience utilizes the inevitable similarity of the two retinal images to "program" increasing identity of preferred orientation in the two eyes. Indeed the real biological value of environmental modification of orientation preference may be the matching of binocular properties, and is unlikely to be the optimizing of the population's detection properties to the predominance of features in the visual world. Such close similarity of feature selectivity in the two eyes is an essential requirement for the proposed role of binocular driven cells in stereoscopic analysis and is a property of such high informational content that it is difficult to conceive of genetic instructions being adequate to prespecify it completely.

We know less about the binocular matching of receptive field properties in the inexperienced monkey's cortex but it is probable that they are much more accurately genetically determined than in the cat, since orientation selectivity seems much more wholly preprogrammed in monkeys than in cats. And even in lambs the preliminary account of area V2 by RAMACHANDRAN et al. (1977) suggests that binocular units have well-matched orientations without visual experience.

f) Movement and its Direction

There is evidence that motion of the retinal image is essential for the maturation of cortical cells and that the preferred directions of direction selective neurones can be modified by experience. CYNADER et al. (1973) and OLSON and PETTIGREW (1974) kept kittens in environments illuminated only by low frequency, very brief, stroboscopic flashes of light. They found that orientation selectivity and particularly direction selectivity are much less common in the cortex of these animals than in normals, that the tuning of these cells is often very broad and that some cells respond well or even exclusively to stroboscopic flashes of light. FLANDRIN et al. (1976) found direction selectivity and binocularity to be enormously reduced in the superior colliculus of such animals, much as if the visual cortex had been removed.

If the full development of stimulus specificity depends on experience of a moving retinal image, restriction of movement to one direction might be expected to bias the preferred directions of kitten cortical cells towards that direction. TRETTER et al. (1975) exposed restrained kittens to vertical stripes moving to the right at 15°/s. After 3 hours of exposure the preferred orientations of subsequently recorded cortical cells were biased towards vertical (with a few orientations close to horizontal and almost none near diagonal, as described by PETTIGREW and GAREY, 1974). Six hours of exposure were needed, however, to produce an obvious change in the distribution of preferred directions, which became biased towards rightward motion. This modification of preferred direction has been confirmed by DAW and WYATT (1976), using a "blind" recording procedure. They found no consistent bias in the preferred orientations of non-directional cells. However their environment did not exclude horizontal contours completely; and since their definition of orientation selectivity involved differential response to stationary flashed bars (mainly applicable to simple cells) but the velocity of the conditioning stimulus was 30°/s (beyond the range of response of almost all simple cells: MOVSHON, 1975), perhaps this result is not surprising. On the contrary, CYNADER et al. (1975) actually produced a strong bias of preferred orientations towards vertical (as well as modification of preferred directions) in kittens exposed not to stripes but simply to large light blobs moving sideways in one direction at 9–36°/s, where the vertical contours in the pattern would carry the principal component of movement. SINGER (1976) has confirmed the modification of both orientation and direction preferences in kittens exposed to moving vertical stripes.

Interestingly, the sensitive period for changes of direction selectivity may be a little different from that for modification of binocularity and orientation. DAW and WYATT (1976) examined this question with a procedure like the reverse suturing method of BLAKEMORE and VAN SLUYTERS (1974b). They exposed kittens for a time to stripes moving in one direction and then, later, to movement in the opposite direction. The results suggest that the sensitive period for reversing directional modification declines earlier in life than that for inducing and reversing ocular dominance changes (see Fig. 12). The general shape of the function is, however, very similar. The difference in the sensitive period for modification of direction selectivity and binocularity has been confirmed by BERMAN and DAW (1977) who made a direct comparison between reverse sutured kittens and animals with a reversal of the experienced direction of movement. A general decline of sensitivity after the fourth week does however seem to apply to modification of binocularity, orientation and direction even if the exact time courses are not identical.

The cat's superior colliculus normally contains a majority of direction selective cells usually preferring centrifugal movement, away from the area centralis. Attempts to modify this distribution have produced, to say the least, mixed results. VITAL-DURAND and JEANNEROD (1974), who reared cats in an environment of vertical stripes moving in one direction at 60°/s, found that following responses and optokinetic nystagmus were subsequently more easily induced by motion in that direction, but that a sample of collicular cells had their preferred directions biased, if anything, in the opposite direction. On the other hand, FLANDRIN and JEANNEROD (1975) repeated the experiment, using rightward moving stripes (20°/s) and found a preference for rightward movement in the left colliculus (as in normal cat). Activity in the right colliculus seemed generally poor, but, of the eight directional cells recorded, none responded best to leftward movement as would be found in a normal cat. However, to add to the contradiction, CYNADER et al. (1975) found little or no change in the pattern of preferred directions in the superior colliculus in their animals exposed to moving blobs. The question of collicular plasticity must be considered to be unanswered!

g) Failure of all Procedures in the Rabbit

Rabbits, it seems, are almost totally uninfluenced by their early visual experience. The development of all kinds of cortical cells in deprived rabbits (CHOW and SPEAR, 1974; GROBSTEIN and CHOW, 1975) has already been mentioned, as well as the marginal effects of monocular deprivation on ocular dominance in the binocular segment (VAN SLUYTERS and STEWART, 1974), although receptive fields of binocular cells do become increasingly mismatched.

Rearing in restricted environments also produces negative results. Exposure to stripes moving in one direction influences neither the direction selectivity nor the orientation selectivity of rabbit retinal ganglion cells (DAW and WYATT, 1974) and ordinary stripe rearing has no effect on preferred orientations in the cortex (MIZE and MURPHY, 1973), though the same authors did confirm modification in kittens, using similar methods.

h) Qualifications about the Sensitive Period

Though the evidence remains clear that the original sensitive period for the kitten defined by HUBEL and WIESEL (1970a) is the time of maximum cortical plasticity, the period may literally have no clear beginning and no end: sensitivity may simply be much heightened from 3 weeks to 3 months. There is evidence that monocular deprivation before 3 weeks can alter the relative sizes of geniculate cells (GAREY et al., 1973) and that artificial strabismus during the same period reduces binocularity in the cortex (VAN SLUYTERS, 1977).

Also, there are many reports of slight modifying effects of visual experience after the end of the sensitive period. CHOW and STEWART (1972) found some increase in the proportion of cortical cells driven by the originally deprived eye after very prolonged reverse suture starting late in life. SPINELLI et al. (1972) reported an increase in the proportion of binocularly driven cells (but not a reduction in the bias of elongated fields) in animals allowed a long period of "recovery" after rearing with oppositely oriented lines in front of the two eyes. As already mentioned, BUCHTEL et al. (1975) found a decrease in the binocularity of cortical cells in adult cats in which one eye was immobilized by section of the nerves to the extra-ocular muscles and FIORENTINI and MAFFEI (1974) have reported that this unexpected increase in monocularity applies principally to simple cells and occurs within a week of immobilization even without visual experience (MAFFEI and FIORENTINI, 1976b).

Even in monocularly deprived cats, enucleation of the experienced eye long after the critical period is reported to increase immediately the proportion of cells that can be actively excited from the deprived eye in the visual cortex (KRATZ et al., 1976). Some 30% of neurones recorded in the cortex either immediately after enucleation, or some time later, could be driven by the deprived eye, although it had received no visual experience before the time of recording. The responses were however weak and the cells were rarely selective for orientation. Another study of the same phenomenon (HOFFMANN and CYNADER, 1977) produced a much lower yield of units driven by the deprived eye; in some penetrations none were found at all and when they did occur they were in small isolated clusters. Obviously the problems of searching for a representative sample of units in the cortex are not trivial when the experienced eye has been removed (KRATZ et al., 1976), especially in view of STRYKER and SHATZ's (1976) finding that small clusters of units driven exclusively by the deprived eye do survive in monocularly deprived cats but are more difficult to record. The principle question raised by KRATZ et al's (1976) study is whether any responsive cells which become detectable after enucleation of the good eye are in fact neurones that used to be dominated by the experienced eye. If so, then the conclusion must be that activity originating in the normal eye holds in check by inhibition, perhaps pre-synaptic, the input from the deprived eye. BLAKEMORE and HILLMAN (1977) have, however, examined the effects in a long-term monocularly deprived cat of switching off signals from the experienced eye by reversible pressure-blinding, thus allowing a study of the consequences on individual units of removing activity. In no case did a cell develop a responsiveness to the deprived eye, at least not within the few minutes that the other eye was blinded. The conclusion from this study is that KRATZ et al's (1976) effect may not be due to a change in the properties of individual cells that are normally dominated by the experienced eye, but could be caused by the simple increased detectability of other surviving units dominated by the deprived eye when the massive cortical activity originating in the normal eye is absent.

On the other hand there is support for the notion of active inhibition from the normal eye's pathway upon the deprived eye's from an experiment by DUFFY et al. (1976). They found that intravenous administration of the drug bicuculline (which is known to antagonize intracortical inhibition mediated by γ-amino butyric acid) caused a considerable fraction of cells dominated completely by the normal eye, in long-term monocularly deprived cats, to regain a similarly orientated receptive field in the deprived eye. A word of caution is needed about this interesting result: first, unlike the cats of KRATZ et al. (1976), their animals had had a 2 week period of normal binocular vision before the eye was closed; and second, any actions caused by intravenous administration of the drug might be attributable to changes occurring more peripherally in the visual pathway than the cortex, to changes in reticular activation or even to variations in blood pressure.

There is certainly evidence that visual experience can cause gradual changes in neuronal properties after the end of the classical sensitive period. Cats that have been binocularly deprived right through the sensitive period and have little or no stimulus selectivity in cortex or colliculus show a rapid improvement in the proportions of orientation and direction selective cells if the eyes are opened (BERMAN et al. 1974; CYNADER et al., 1974).

Even experience with clinical developmental disorders points to a "sensitivity gradient" rather than a finite sensitive period, for amblyopia discovered even late in life can be greatly improved by remedial training. So we cannot look upon the sensitive period as having a beginning or an end. It is, rather, a time of heightened sensitivity to the influence of the environment when the first really clear images are reaching the retina and when, in kittens, *both* eyes can be guaranteed to have opened (BLAKEMORE and CUMMINGS, 1975). That sensitivity to plastic change ought to decline is obvious: continuous variability in the properties of cortical cells throughout life would impose a ridiculous unpredictability on the coding properties of the output of the visual cortex, which would surely make its signals difficult to interpret.

C. Conclusions

Fifteen years have produced a flood of new data, many of them exciting and remarkable (though perhaps no more surprising than many of the incredible properties of developing tissue discovered by experimental embryologists). If any criticism can be levelled it is that many communications have been too brief or the studies themselves too restricted to allow comparison with other results and to guarantee ready reproducibility. But that is, no doubt, one of the inevitable disadvantages of a burgeoning field of research, one in which the positive excitement of rapid progress is bound to produce quickly changing concepts.

One thing remains certain—the ancient and basic argument about Nature and Nurture is not finally resolved by any or all of the new discoveries. What emerges is an inevitable compromise, with differences of emphasis between cats and monkeys, toads and rabbits. Perhaps the visual cortex of a kitten behaves in some sense like the Empiricists' *tabula rasa*, but genetic instruction has, at the very least, put together the wax tablet and ruled the lines on which experience writes its message, and, at the most, may have done everything except dotting the i's and crossing the t's.

References

•Ackroyd, C., Humphrey, N.K., Warrington, E.K.: Lasting effects of early blindness. A case study. Q. Jl. exp. Psychol. **26**, 114–124 (1974).

Albus, K.: A quantitative study of the projection area of the central and the paracentral visual field in area 17 of the cat. II. The spatial organization of the orientation domain. Expl Brain Res. **24**, 181–202 (1975a).

Albus, K.: Predominance of monocularly driven cells in the projection area of the central visual field in cat's striate cortex. Brain Res. **89**, 341–347 (1975b).

Anker, R.L., Cragg, B.G.: Development of the extrinsic connections of the visual cortex in the cat. J. comp. Neurol **154**, 29–41 (1974).

Annis, R.C., Frost, B.: Human visual ecology and orientation anisotropies in acuity. Science **182**, 729–731 (1973).

Armstrong-James, M.: The functional status and columnar organization of single cells responding to cutaneous stimulation in neonatal rat somatosensory cortex S1. J. Physiol. **246**, 501–538 (1975).

Atkinson, J., Braddick, O., Braddick, F.: Acuity and contrast sensitivity of infant vision. Nature **247**, 403–404 (1974).

Awaya, S., Miyake, Y., Imaizumi, Y., Shiose, Y., Kanda, T., Komuro, K.: Amblyopia in man, suggestive of stimulus deprivation amblyopia. Jap. J. Ophthal. **17**, 69–82 (1973).

Baker, F.H., Grigg, P., von Noorden, G.K.: Effects of visual deprivation and strabismus on the responses of neurons in the visual cortex of the monkey, including studies on the striate and prestriate cortex in the normal animal. Brain Res. **66**, 185–208 (1974).

•Banks, M.S., Aslin, R.N., Letson, R.D.: Sensitive period for the development of human binocular vision. Science **190**, 675–677 (1975).

Banks, M.S., Salapatek, P.: Contrast sensitivity function of the infant visual system. Vision Res. **16**, 867–869 (1976).

•Barlow, H.B.: Visual experience and cortical development. Nature **258**, 199–204 (1975).

•Barlow, H.B., Blakemore, C., Pettigrew, J.D.: The neural mechanism of binocular depth discrimination. J. Physiol. **193**, 327–342 (1967).

•Barlow, H.B., Pettigrew, J.D.: Lack of specificity of neurones in the visual cortex of young kittens. J. Physiol. **218**, 98–100P (1971).

Basbaum, A.I., Wall, P.D.: Chronic changes in the response of cells in adult cat dorsal horn following partial deafferentation: the appearance of responding cells in a previously non-responsive region. Brain Res. **116**, 181–204 (1976).

Berman, N., Cynader, M., Hein, A.: Recovery of function in cat superior colliculus following prolonged pattern deprivation. Talk to Association for Research in Vision and Ophthalmology, Sarasota, Florida (1974).

Berman, N., Daw, N.W.: Comparison of the critical periods for monocular and directional deprivation in cats. J. Physiol **265**, 249–259 (1977).

Berman, N., Sterling, P.: Cortical suppression of the retino-collicular pathway in the monocularly deprived cat. J. Physiol. **255**: 263–273 (1976).

Bishop, P.O.: Neurophysiology of binocular single vision and stereopsis. In: Handbook of Sensory Physiology. Vol VII/3 Part A. Ed. Jung, R. Berlin: Springer Verlag, pp. 255–305, 1973.

Blakemore, C.: Developmental factors in the formation of feature extracting neurons. In: The Neurosciences Third Study Program. Eds. Schmitt, F.O., Worden, F.G. Cambridge, Mass: M.I.T. Press, pp. 105–113, 1974.

Blakemore, C.: The conditions required for the maintenance of binocularity in the kitten's visual cortex. J. Physiol. **261**, 423–444 (1976).

Blakemore, C.: Genetic instructions and developmental plasticity in the kitten's visual cortex. Phil. Trans. Roy. Soc. **B 278**, 425–434 (1977).

Blakemore, C., Cooper, G.F.: Development of the brain depends on the visual environment. Nature **228**: 477–478 (1970).

Blakemore, C., Cummings, R.M.: Eye-opening in kittens. Vision Res. **15**, 1417–1418 (1975).

Blakemore, C., Eggers, H.M.: Animal models for human visual development. In *Vision: 1977*, A Dedicatory Symposium for the College of Optometry, University of Houston (in the press).

Blakemore, C., Fiorentini, A., Maffei, L.: A second neural mechanism of binocular depth discrimination. J. Physiol. **226**, 725–749 (1972).

Blakemore, C., Garey, L.J., Vital-Durand, F.: Reversal of physiological effects of monocular deprivation in monkeys. J. Physiol. (in the press) (1978).

Blakemore, C., Hillman, P.: An attempt to assess the effects of monocular deprivation and strabismus on synaptic efficiency in the kitten's visual cortex. Expl Brain Res. **30**, 187–202 (1977).

Blakemore, C., Mitchell, D.E.: Environmental modification of the visual cortex and the neural basis of learning and memory. Nature **241**, 467–468 (1973).

Blakemore, C., Movshon, J.A., Van Sluyters, R.C.: Modification of the kitten's visual cortex by exposure to spatially periodic patterns. Expl Brain Res. (in the press) (1978).

Blakemore, C., Tobin, E.A.: Lateral inhibition between orientation detectors in the cat's visual cortex. Expl Brain Res. **15**, 439–440 (1972).

Blakemore, C., Van Sluyters, R.C.: Experimental analysis of amblyopia and strabismus. Brit. J. Ophthal. **58**, 176–182 (1974a).

Blakemore, C., Van Sluyters, R.C.: Reversal of the physiological effects of monocular deprivation in kittens: further evidence for a sensitive period. J. Physiol. **237**, 195–216 (1974b).

Blakemore, C., Van Sluyters, R.C.: Innate and environmental factors in the development of the kitten's visual cortex. J. Physiol. **248**, 663–716 (1975).

Blakemore, C., Van Sluyters, R.C., Movshon, J.A.: Synaptic competition in the kitten's visual cortex. Cold Spring Harbor Symp. Quant. Biol. **40**, 601–609 (1976).

Blakemore, C.,Van Sluyters, R.C., Peck, C.K., Hein, A.: Development of cat visual cortex following rotation of one eye. Nature **257**, 584–586 (1975).

Blasdel, G.G., Mitchell, D.E., Muir, D.W., Pettigrew, J.D.: A physiological and behavioural study in cats of the effect of early visual experience with contours of a single orientation. J. Physiol. **265**, 615–636 (1977).

Bonds, A.B., Freeman, R.D.: Development of optical quality in the kitten eye. Talk to the Association for Research in Vision and Ophthalmology, Sarasota, Florida (1976).

Buchtel, H.A., Berlucchi, G., Mascetti, G.G.: Behavioural and electrophysiological analysis of strabismus in cats. In Aspects of Neural Plasticity. Ed. F. Vital-Durand and M. Jeannerod. (Les Colloques de l'Institut National de la Santé et de la Recherche Médicale) (1975).

Buisseret, P., Imbert, M.: Visual cortical cells: their developmental properties in normal and dark reared kittens. J. Physiol. **255**, 511–525 (1976).

Campbell, F.W., Kulikowski, J.J., Levinson, J.: The effect of orientation on the visual resolution of gratings. J. Physiol. **187**, 427–436 (1966).

Chow, K.L., Spear, P.D.: Morphological and functional effects of visual deprivation on the rabbit visual system. Expl Neurol. **42**, 429–447 (1974).

Chow, K.L., Stewart, D.L.: Reversal of structural and functional effects of long-term visual deprivation in cats. Expl Neurol. **34**: 409–433 (1972).

Clarke, P.G.H, Donaldson, I.M.L., Whitteridge, D.: Binocular visual mechanisms in cortical areas I and II of the sheep. J. Physiol. **256**, 509–526 (1976).

Cleland, B.G., Dubin, M.W., Levick, W.R.: Sustained and transient neurones in the cat's retina and lateral geniculate nucleus. J. Physiol. **217**, 473–496 (1971).

Cleland, B.G., Levick. W.R., Morstyn, R., Wagner, H.G.: Lateral geniculate relay of slowly conducting retinal afferents to cat visual cortex. J. Physiol. **255**, 299–320 (1976).

Cleland, B.G., Morstyn, R., Wagner, H.G., Levick, W.R.: Long-latency retinal input to lateral geniculate neurones of the cat. Brain Res. **91**, 306–310 (1975).

Colonnier, M.: The tangential organisation of the visual cortex. J. Anat. **98**, 327–344 (1964).

Cragg, B.G.: The development of synapses in cat visual cortex. Investig. Ophthal. **11**, 377–385 (1972).

Cragg, B.G.: The development of synapses in the visual system of the cat. J. comp. Neurol. **160**, 147–166 (1975).

Crawford, M.L.J., Blake, R., Cool. S.J., von Noorden, G.K.: Physiological consequences of unilateral and bilateral eye closure in macaque monkeys: some further observations. Brain Res. **84**, 150–154 (1975).

Creutzfeldt, O.D., Heggelund, P.: Neural plasticity in visual cortex of adult cats after exposure to visual patterns. Science **188**, 1025–1027 (1975).

Creutzfeldt, O.D., Kuhnt, U., Benevento, L.A.: An intracellular analysis of visual cortical neurones to moving stimuli: responses in a co-operative neuronal network. Expl. Brain Res. **21**, 251–274 (1974).

Cynader, M., Berman, N., Hein, A.: Cats reared in stroboscopic illumination: effects on receptive fields in visual cortex. Proc. Nat. Acad. Sci. U.S.A. **70**, 1353–1354 (1973).

Cynader, M., Berman, N., Hein, A.: Recovery of function in the cat visual cortex following prolonged pattern deprivation. Talk to Association for Research in Vision and Ophthalmology, Sarasota, Florida (1974).

Cynader, M., Berman, N., Hein, A.: Cats raised in a one-directional world: effects on receptive fields in visual cortex and superior colliculus. Expl Brain Res. **22**, 267–280 (1975).

Cynader, M., Chernenko, G.: Some factors influencing the development of ocular dominance in cat striate cortex. Talk to Association for Research in Vision and Ophthalmology. Sarasota, Florida (1976).

Daw, N.W., Wyatt, H.J.: Raising rabbits in a moving visual environment: an attempt to modify direction sensitivity in the retina. J. Physiol. **240**, 309–330 (1974).

Daw, N.W., Wyatt, H.J.: Kittens reared in a unidirectional environment: evidence for a critical period. J. Physiol. **257**, 155–170 (1976).

Dec, K., Sarna, M., Tarnecki, R., Żernicki, B.: Effects of binocular deprivation of pattern vision on single unit responses in the cat superior colliculus. Acta Neurobiol Exp. **36**, 687–692 (1976).

Dews, P.B., Wiesel, T.N.: Consequences of monocular deprivation on visual behaviour in kittens. J. Physiol. **206**, 437–455 (1970).

Dodwell, P.C., Timney, B.N., Emerson, V.F.: Development of visual stimulus-seeking in dark-reared kittens. Nature **260**, 777–778 (1976).

Dräger, U.C.: Extent of plasticity of connections in visual cortex and tectum of normal and retinal-dystrophic mice. Talk to Association for Research in Vision and Ophthalmology. Sarasota, Florida (1975).

Duffy, F.H., Snodgrass, S.R., Burchfiel, J.L., Conway, J.L.: Bicuculline reversal of deprivation amblyopia in the cat. Nature **260**, 256–257 (1976).

Eggers, H.M., Blakemore, C.: Physiological basis of anisometropic amblyopia. Science (in the press) (1978).

Enroth-Cugell, C., Lennie, P.: The control of retinal ganglion cell discharge by receptive field surrounds. J. Physiol. **247**, 551–578 (1975).

Enroth-Cugell, C., Robson, J.G.: The contrast sensitivity of retinal ganglion cells of the cat. J. Physiol. **187**, 517–552 (1966).

Fiorentini, A., Maffei, L.: Change of binocular properties of the simple cells of the cortex in adult cats following immobilization of one eye. Vision Res. **14**, 217–218 (1974).

Flandrin, J.M, Jeannerod, M.: Superior colliculus: environmental influences on the development of directional responses in the kitten. Brain Res. **89**, 348–352 (1975).

Flandrin, J.M., Kennedy, H., Amblard, B.: Effects of stroboscopic rearing on the binocularity and directionality of cat superior colliculus neurons. Brain Res. **101**, 576–581 (1976).

Freeman, D.N., Marg, E.: Visual acuity development coincides with the sensitive period in kittens. Nature **254**, 614–615 (1975).

Freeman, R.D.: Asymmetries in human accommodation and visual experience. Vision Res. **15**, 483–492 (1975).

Freeman, R.D., Pettigrew, J.D.: Alterations of visual cortex from environmental asymmetries. Nature **246**, 359–360 (1973).

Freeman, R.D., Thibos, L.N.: Contrast sensitivity in humans with abnormal visual experience. J. Physiol. **247**, 687–710 (1975a).

Freeman, R.D., Thibos, L.N.: Visual evoked responses in humans with abnormal visual experience. J. Physiol. **247**, 711–724 (1975b).

Ganz, L., Fitch, M.: The effect of visual deprivation on perceptual behavior. Expl Neurol. **22**, 638–660 (1968).

Ganz, L., Fitch, M., Satterberg, J.A.: The selective effect of visual deprivation on receptive field shape determined neurophysiologically. Expl Neurol. **22**, 614–637 (1968).

Garey, L.J., Blakemore, C.: Monocular deprivation: morphological effects on different classes of neurons in the lateral geniculate nucleus. Science **195**, 414–416 (1977a).

Garey, L.J., Blakemore, C.: The effects of monocular deprivation on different neuronal classes in the lateral geniculate nuclous of the cat. Expl Brain Res. **28**, 259–278 (1977b).

Garey, L., Fisken, R.A., Powell, T.P.S.: Effects of experimental deafferentation on cells in the lateral geniculate nucleus of the cat. Brain Res. **52**, 363–369 (1973).

Garey, L.J., Pettigrew, J.D.: Ultrastructural changes in kitten visual cortex after environmental modification. Brain Res. **66**, 165–172 (1974).

Gibson, J.J.: Adaptation, after-effect and contrast in the perception of curved lines. J. exp. Psychol. **16**, 1–31 (1933).

Gordon, B., Gummow, L.: Effects of extraocular muscle section on receptive fields in cat superior colliculus. Vision Res. **15**, 1011–1019 (1975).

•Grobstein, P., Chow, K.L.: Receptive field development and individual experience. Science **190**, 352–358 (1975).

Guillery, R.W.: Binocular competition in the control of geniculate cell growth. J. comp. Neurol. **144**, 117–129 (1972).

Guillery, R.W., Stelzner, D.J.: The differential effects of unilateral lid closure upon the monocular and binocular segments of the dorsal lateral geniculate nucleus in the cat. J. comp. Neurol. **139**, 413–422 (1970).

Hamasaki, D.I., Pollack, J.G.: Depression of the late receptor potential and the ERG by light deprivation in cats. Vision Res. **12**, 835–842 (1972).

Harris, L., Atkinson, J., Braddick, O.: Visual contrast sensitivity of a 6-month old infant measured by the evoked potential. Nature **264**, 570–571 (1976).

Hein, A., Held, R.: Dissociation of the visual placing response into elicited and guided components. Science N.Y. **158**, 390–392 (1967).

Held, R.: Two modes of processing spatially distributed visual stimulation. In: The Neurosciences Second Study Program. Ed. Schmitt, F.O. New York: Rockefeller Univ. Press, pp. 317–324, 1970.

•Held, R., Hein, A.: Movement-produced stimulation in the development of visually guided behavior. J. comp. Physiol. Psychol. **56**, 872–876 (1963).

Henry, G.H., Dreher, B., Bishop, P.O.: Orientation specificity of cells in cat striate cortex. J. Neurophysiol. **37**, 1394–1409 (1974).

Hirsch, H.V.B: Visual perception in cats after environmental surgery. Expl Brain Res. **15**, 405–423 (1972).

•Hirsch, H.V.B., Spinelli, D.N.: Visual experience modifies distribution of horizontally and vertically oriented receptive fields in cats. Science **168**, 869–871 (1970).

Hirsch, H.V.B., Spinelli, D.N.: Modification of the distribution of receptive field orientation in cats by selective visual exposure during development. Expl Brain Res. **13**, 509–527 (1971).

Hoffmann, K-P., Cynader, M.: Functional aspects of plasticity in the visual system of adult cats after early monocular deprivation. Phil. Trans. Roy. Soc. B. **278**, 411–424 (1977).

Hoffmann, K-P., Sherman, S.M.: Effects of early monocular deprivation of visual input to cat superior colliculus. J. Neurophysiol. **37**, 1276–1286 (1974).

Hoffmann, K-P., Stone, J.: Conduction velocity of afferents to cat visual cortex: a correlation with cortical receptive field properties. Brain Res. **32**, 460–466 (1971).

Hohmann, A., Creutzfeldt, O.D.: Squint and the development of binocularity in humans. Nature **254**, 613–614 (1975).

•Hubel, D.H., Wiesel, T.N.: Receptive fields, binocular interaction and functional architecture in the cat's visual cortex. J. Physiol. **160**, 106–154 (1962).

•Hubel, D.H., Wiesel, T.N.: Receptive fields of cells in striate cortex of very young, visually inexperienced kittens. J. Neurophysiol. **26**, 994–1002 (1963).

Hubel, D.H., Wiesel, T.N.: Receptive fields and functional architecture in two non-striate visual areas (18 and 19) of the cat J. Neurophysiol. **28**, 229–289 (1965a).

•Hubel, D.H., Wiesel, T.N.: Binocular interaction in striate cortex of kittens reared with artificial squint. J. Neurophysiol. **28**, 1041–1059 (1965b).

Hubel, D.H., Wiesel, T.N.: Receptive fields and functional architecture of monkey striate cortex. J. Physiol. **195**, 215–243 (1968).

Hubel, D.H., Wiesel, T.N.: The period of susceptibility to the physiological effects of unilateral eye closure in kittens. J. Physiol. **206**, 419–436 (1970a).

•Hubel, D.H., Wiesel, T.N.: Cells sensitive to binocular depth in area 18 of the macaque monkey cortex. Nature, Lond. **225**, 41–42 (1970b).

Hubel, D.H., Wiesel, T.N.: Sequence regularity and geometry of orientation columns in the monkey striate cortex. J. comp. Neurol. **158**, 267–293 (1974a).

Hubel, D.H., Wiesel, T.N.: Uniformity of monkey striate cortex: a parallel relationship between field size, scatter, and magnification factor. J. comp. Neurol. **158**, 295–305 (1974b).

Hubel, D.H., Wiesel, T.N., Levay, S.: Plasticity of ocular dominance columns in monkey striate cortex. Phil. Trans. Roy. Soc. **B. 278**, 377–409 (1977).

Ikeda, H., Tremain, K.T.: Amblyopic LGN cells in kittens raised with 'penalisation' of one or both eyes. J. metabolic Ophthalmol. (in the press) (1978).

Ikeda, H., Wright, M.J.: Properties of LGN cells in kittens reared with convergent squint: a neurophysiological demonstration of amblyopia. Expl Brain Res. **25**, 63–77 (1976).

Imbert, M., Buisseret, P.: Receptive field characteristics and plastic properties of visual cortical cells in kittens reared with or without visual experience. Expl Brain Res. **22**, 25–36 (1975a).

Imbert, M., Buisseret, P.: The cortical organisation and the visual experience. Talk at the 1st European Neurosciences Meeting, Munich, September, 1975. (Expl Brain Res. **23**, Suppl 98, 1975b).

Kasamatsu, T.: A long-lasting change in ocular dominance of kitten striate neurons induced by reversible unilateral blockade of tonic retinal discharges. Expl Brain Res. **26**, 487–494 (1976).

Kasamatsu, T., Pettigrew, J.D.: Depletion of brain catecholamines: failure of ocular dominance shift after monocular occlusion in kittens. Science **194**, 206–209 (1976).

König, N., Pujol, R., Marty, R.: A laminar study of evoked potentials and unit responses in the auditory cortex of the postnatal cat. Brain Res. **36**, 469–473 (1972).

Kratz, K.E., Spear, P.D.: Effects of visual deprivation and alteration in binocular competition on responses of striate cortex neurons in the cat. J. comp. Neurol. **170**, 141–152 (1976).

Kratz, K.E., Spear, P.D., Smith, D.C.: Postcritical-period reversal of effects of monocular deprivation on striate cortex cells in the cat. J. Neurophysiol. **39**, 501–511 (1976).

•Leehey, S.C., Moskowitz-Cook, A., Brill, S., Held, R.: Orientational anisotropy in infant vision. Science N.Y. **190**, 900–902 (1975).

Levay, S., Ferster, D.: Relay cell classes in the lateral geniculate nucleus of the cat and the effects of visual deprivation. J. comp. Neurol. **172**, 563–584 (1977).

•Leventhal, A.G., Hirsch, H.V.B.: Cortical effect of early selective exposure to diagonal lines. Science **190**, 902–904 (1975).

Leventhal, A.G., Hirsch, H.V.B.: Effects of early visual experience upon orientation sensitivity and binocularity of neurons in visual cortex of cats. Proc. Nat. Acad. Sci. **74**, 1272–1276 (1977).

Levi, D.M., Harwerth, R.S.: Spatio-temporal interactions in anisometropic and strabismic amblyopia. Investig. Ophthalmol. **16**, 90–95 (1977).

Levick, W.R.: Receptive fields and trigger features of ganglion cells in the visual streak of the rabbit's retina. J. Physiol. **188**, 285–307 (1967).

Maffei, L., Bisti, S.: Binocular interaction in strabismic kittens deprived of vision. Science **191**, 579–580 (1976).

Maffei, L., Campbell, F.W.: Neurophysiological localization of the vertical and horizontal visual co-ordinates in man. Science **167**, 386–387 (1970).

Maffei, L., Fiorentini, A.: Geniculate neural plasticity in kittens after exposure to periodic gratings. Science **186**, 447–449 (1974).

Maffei, L., Fiorentini, A.: Monocular deprivation in kittens impairs the spatial resolution of geniculate neurones. Nature **264**, 754–755 (1976a).

Maffei, L., Fiorentini, A.: Asymmetry of motility of the eyes and change of binocular properties of cortical cells in adult cats. Brain Res. **105**, 73–78 (1976b).

Maffei, L., Fiorentini, A., Bisti, S.: Neural correlate of perceptual adaptation to gratings. Science **182**, 1036–1038 (1973).

Mansfield, R.J.W.: Neural basis of orientation perception in primate vision. Science **186**, 1133–1135 (1974).

Marg, E., Freeman, D.N., Peltzman, P., Goldstein, P.J.: Visual acuity development in human infants: evoked potential measurements. Investig. Ophthalmol. **15**, 150–153 (1976).

Martin, G.: Théorie et clinique de l'amblyopie astigmatique. Annals Oculist **104**, 101–138 (1890).

Mathers, L.H., Chow, K.L., Spear, P.D., Grobstein, P.: Ontogenesis of receptive fields in the rabbit striate cortex. Expl Brain Res. **19**, 20–35 (1974).

Mayer, M.J.: Development of anisotropy in late childhood. Vision Res. **17**, 703–710 (1977).

Mayer, M.J., Switkes, E.: Harmonic analysis of the visual environment: visual anisotropy and carpentered environments. Talk to Association for Research in Vision and Ophthalmology. Sarasota, Florida (1977).

Merrill, E.G., Wall, P.D.: Factors forming the edge of a receptive field: the presence of relatively ineffective afferent terminals. J. Physiol. **226**, 825–846 (1972).

Mitchell, D.E., Cynader, M., Movshon, J.A.: Recovery from the effects of monocular deprivation in kittens. J. comp. Neurol. **176**, 53–64 (1977a).

Mitchell, D.E., Freeman, R.D., Millodot, M., Haegerstrom, G.: Meridional amblyopia: evidence for modification of the human visual system by early visual experience. Vision Res. **13**, 535–558 (1973).

Mitchell, D.E., Freeman, R.D., Westheimer, G.: Effects of orientation on the modulation sensitivity for interference fringes on the retina. J. opt. Soc. Am. **57**, 246–249 (1967).

Mitchell, D.E., Giffin, F., Muir, D., Blakemore, C., Van Sluyters, R.C.: Behavioural compensation of cats to early rotation of one eye. Expl Brain Res. **25**, 109–113 (1976a).

Mitchell, D.E., Giffin, F., Timney, B.: A behavioural technique for the rapid assessment of the visual capabilities of kittens. Perception **6**, 181–193 (1977b).

Mitchell, D.E., Giffin, F., Wilkinson, F., Anderson, P., Smith, M.L.: Visual resolution in young kittens. Vision Res. **16**, 363–366 (1976b).

Mitchell, D.E., Reardon, J., Muir, D.W.: Interocular transfer of the motion after-effect in normal and stereoblind observers. Expl Brain Res. **22**, 163–173 (1975).

Mitchell, D.E., Ware, C.: Interocular transfer of a visual after-effect in normal and stereoblind humans. J. Physiol. **236**, 707–721 (1974).

Mitchell, D.E., Wilkinson, F.: The effect of early astigmatism on the visual resolution of gratings. J. Physiol. **243**, 739–756 (1974).

Mize, R.R., Murphy, E.H.: Selective visual experience fails to modify receptive field properties of rabbit striate cortex neurones. Science **180**, 320–323 (1973).

Moore, D.R., Aitkin, L.M.: Rearing in an acoustically unusual environment—effects on neural auditory responses. Neuroscience Letters **1**, 29–34 (1975).

Movshon, J.A.: The velocity tuning of single units in cat striate cortex. J. Physiol. **249**, 445–468 (1975).

Movshon, J.A.: Reversal of the physiological effects of monocular deprivation in the kittens's visual cortex. J. Physiol. **261**, 125–174 (1976a).

Movshon, J.A.: Reversal of the behavioural effects of monocular deprivation in the kitten. J. Physiol. **261**, 175–187 (1976b).

Movshon, J.A., Blakemore, C.: Functional reinnervation in kitten visual cortex. Nature **251**, 504–505 (1974).

Movshon, J.A., Chambers, B.E.I., Blakemore, C.: Interocular transfer in normal humans, and those who lack stereopsis. Perception **1**, 483–490 (1972).

Movshon, J.A., Dürsteler, M.: The effects of brief periods of unilateral eye closure on the kitten's visual system. J. Neurophysiol. (in the press) (1977).

Muir, D.W., Mitchell, D.E.: Behavioral deficits in cats following early selected visual exposure to contours of a single orientation. Brain Res. **85**, 459–477 (1975).

Nelson, J.I., Kato, H., Bishop, P.O.: Discrimination of orientation and postition disparities by binocularly activated neurons in cat striate cortex. J. Neurophysiol. **40,** 260–283 (1977).

Newman, J.D., Wollberg, Z.: Multiple coding of species-specific vocalizations in the auditory cortex of squirrel monkeys. Brain Res. **54**, 287–304 (1973).

Von Noorden, G.K.: Experimental amblyopia in monkeys. Further behavioral observations and clinical correlations. Investig. Ophthal. **12**, 721–726 (1973).

Von Noorden, G.K. Dowling, J.E.: Experimental amblyopia in monkeys. II. Behavioral studies in strabismic amblyopia. Arch. Ophthal. **84**, 215–220 (1970).

Von Noorden, G.K., Dowling. J.E., Ferguson, D.C.: Experimental amblyopia in monkeys. I. Behavioral studies of stimulus deprivation amblyopia. Arch. Ophthal. **84**, 206–214 (1970).

Norton, T.T.: Receptive field properties of superior colliculus cells and development of visual behavior in kittens. J. Neurophysiol. **37**, 674–690 (1974).

Olson, C.R., Freeman, R.D.: Progressive changes in kitten striate cortex during monocular vision, J. Neurophysiol. **38**, 26–32 (1975).

Olson, C.R., Pettigrew, J.D.: Single units in visual cortex of kittens reared in stroboscopic illumination. Brain Res. **70**, 189–204 (1974).

Ordy, J.M., Samorajski, T., Collins, R.L., Nagy, M.S.: Postnatal development of vision in a subhuman primate (Macaca mulatta) Arch. Ophthal. **73**, 674–686 (1965).

Peck, C.K., Blakemore, C.: Modification of single neurons in the kitten's visual cortex after brief periods of monocular visual experience. Expl Brain Res. **22**, 57–68 (1975).

Peck, C.K., Crewther, S.G.: Perceptual effects of surgical rotation of the eye in kittens. Brain Res. **99**, 213–219 (1975).

Pettigrew, J.D.: The effect of visual experience on the development of stimulus specificity by kitten cortical neurones. J. Physiol. **237**, 49–74 (1974).

Pettigrew, J.D., Freeman, R.D.: Visual experience without lines: effect on developing cortical neurons. Science **182**, 599–601 (1973).

Pettigrew, J.D., Garey, L.J.: Selective modification of single neuron properties in the visual cortex of kittens. Brain Res. **66**, 160–164 (1974).

Pettigrew, J.D., Konishi, M.: Effect of monocular deprivation on binocular neurones in the owl's visual Wulst. Nature **264**, 753–754 (1976).

• Pettigrew, J.D., Nikara, T., Bishop, P.O.: Binocular interaction on single units in cat striate cortex: simultaneous stimulation by single moving slit with receptive fields in correspondence. Expl Brain Res. **6**, 391–410 (1968).

Pettigrew, J.D., Olson, C., Barlow, H.B.: Kitten visual cortex: short-term, stimulus induced changes in connectivity. Science **180**, 1202–1203 (1973a).

Pettigrew, J.D., Olson, C., Hirsch, H.V.B.: Cortical effect of selective visual experience: degeneration or reorganization? Brain Res. **51**, 345–351 (1973b).

Pinching, A.J., Døving, K.B.: Selective degeneration in the rat olfactory bulb following exposure to different odours. Brain Res. **82**, 195–204 (1974).

Polyak, S.L.: The Retina. Chicago, University of Chicago Press, 1941.

Pujol, R.: Development of tone-burst responses along the auditory pathway in the cat. Acta oto-lar. Stockh. **74**, 383–391 (1972).

Rakic, P.: Prenatal development of the visual system in the rhesus monkey. Phil. Trans. Roy. Soc. **B**. **278**, 245–260 (1977).

Ramachandran, V.S., Clarke, P.G.H., Whitteridge, D.: Cells selective to binocular disparity in the cortex of newborn lambs. Nature **268**, 333–335 (1977).

• Riesen, A.H.: Plasticity of behaviour: Psychological aspects. In: Biological and Biochemical Bases of Behavior, Eds. Harlow, H.F., Woolsey, C.N. Madison, Wisconsin, Univ. of Wisconsin Press, pp. 425–450, 1958.

Rose, D., Blakemore, C.: An analysis of orientation selectivity in the cat's visual cortex. Expl Brain Res. **20**, 1–17 (1974).

Rosenquist, A.C., Palmer, L.A.: Visual receptive field properties of cells in the superior colliculus after cortical lesions in the cat. Expl Neurol. **33**, 629–652 (1971).

Rubel, E.W.: A comparison of somatotopic organization in sensory neocortex of newborn kittens and adult cats. J. comp. Neurol. **143**, 447–480 (1971).

Schechter, P.B., Murphy, E.H.: Brief monocular visual experience and kitten cortical binocularity. Brain Res. **109**, 165–168 (1976).

Von Senden, M.: Space and Sight. London: Methuen, 1960.

Sherk, H., Strykner, M.: Quantitative study of cortical orientation selectivity in visually inexperienced kitten. J. Neurophysiol. **39**, 63–70 (1976).

Sherman, S.M.: Development of interocular alignment in cats. Brain Res. **37**, 187–203 (1972).

Sherman, S.M., Guillery, R.W., Kaas, J.H., Sanderson, K.J.: Behavioral, electrophysiological and morphological studies of binocular competition in the development of the geniculo-cortical pathways of cats. J. comp. Neurol. **158**, 1–18 (1974).

Sherman, S.M., Hoffmann, K-P., Stone, J.: Loss of a specific cell type from dorsal lateral geniculate nucleus in visually deprived cats. J. Neurophysiol. **35**, 532–541 (1972).

Sherman, S.M., Stone, J.: Physiological normality of the retina in visually deprived cats. Brain Res. **60**, 224–230 (1973).

Shinkman, P.G., Bruce, C.J.: Binocular differences in cortical receptive fields of kittens after rotationally disparate binocular experience. Science **197**, 285–287 (1977).

Shinkman, P.G., Bruce, C.J., Isley, M.R.: Effects of rotated visual inputs on the development of binocularity and interocular matching in cortical units' receptive fields. Talk to XXVIIth International Congress of Physiological Sciences. Paris, 1977.

Shlaer, R.: Shift in binocular disparity causes compensatory changes in the cortical stucture of kittens. Science **173**, 638–641 (1971).

Singer, W.: Modification of orientation and direction selectivity of cortical cells in kittens with monocular vision. Brain Res. **118**, 460–468 (1976).

Singer, W., Tretter, F.: Receptive-field properties and neuronal connectivity in striate and parastriate cortex of contour-deprived cats. J. Neurophysiol. **39**, 613–630 (1976).

Singer, W., Tretter, F., Cynader, M.: Organization of cat striate cortex: a correlation of receptive field properties with afferent and efferent connections. J. Neurophysiol. **38**, 1080–1098 (1975).

Spear, P.D., Chow, K.L., Masland, R.H., Murphy, E.H.: Ontogenesis of receptive field characteristics of superior colliculus neurons in the rabbit. Brain Res. **45**, 67–86 (1972).

Spear, P.D., Ganz, L.: Effects of visual cortex lesions following recovery from monocular deprivation in the cat. Expl Brain Res. **23**, 181–201 (1975).

Spencer, R.F.: Influence of selective visual experience upon the post-natal maturation of the visual cortex of the cat. PhD thesis. The University of Rochester (1974).

Spencer, R.F., Coleman, P.D.: Influence of selective visual experience upon the morphological maturation of the visual cortex. Anat. Rec. **178**, 469 (1974).

Spinelli, D.N., Hirsch, H.V.B.: Genesis of receptive field shapes in single units of cat's visual cortex. Fed. Proc. **30**, 615 (1971).

Spinelli, D.N., Hirsch, H.V.B., Phelps, J., Metzler, J.: Visual experience as a determinant of the response characteristics of cortical receptive fields in cats. Expl Brain Res. **15**, 289–304 (1972).

Stein, B.E., Labos, E., Kruger, L.: Sequence of changes in properties of neurons of superior colliculus of the kitten during maturation. J. Neurophysiol. **36**, 667–679 (1973).

Stone, J.: Sampling properties of microelectrodes assessed in the cat's retina. J. Neurophysiol. **36**, 1071–1079 (1973).

Stone, J., Dreher, B.: Projection of X- and Y-cells of the cat's lateral geniculate nucleus to areas 17 and 18 of visual cortex. J. Neurophysiol. **36**, 551–567 (1973).

Stone, J., Hoffmann, K-P.: Very slow-conducting ganglion cells in the cat's retina: a major new functional group? Brain Res. **43**, 610–616 (1972).

Stryker, M.P., Hirsch, H.V.B., Sherk, H., Leventhal, A.G.: Orientation selectivity in cat visual cortex following selective orientation deprivation using goggles. Talk to Association for Research in Vision and Ophthalmology. Sarasota, Florida (1976).

Stryker, M.P., Shatz, C.J.: Ocular dominance in layer IV of the normal and deprived cat's visual cortex. Neuroscience Abstracts **2**, 1137 (1976).

Stryker, M.P., Sherk, H.: Modification of cortical orientation selectivity in the cat by restricted visual experience: a reexamination. Science **190**, 904–906 (1975).

Teller, D.Y., Morse, R., Borton, R., Regal, D.: Visual acuity for vertical and diagonal gratings in human infants. Vision Res. **14**, 1433–1439 (1974).

Thorpe, P.A., Blakemore, C.: Evidence for a loss of afferent axons in the visual cortex of monocularly deprived cats. Neuroscience Letters, **1**, 271–276 (1975).

Timney, B.N., Muir, D.W.: Orientation anisotropy: incidence and magnitude in Caucasian and Chinese subjects. Science **193**, 699–701 (1976).

Toyama, K., Matsunami, K., Ohno, T., Tokashiki, S.: An intracellular study of neuronal organization in the visual cortex. Expl Brain Res. **21**, 45–66 (1974).

Tretter, F., Cynader, M., Singer, W.: Modification of direction selectivity of neurons in the visual cortex of kittens. Brain Res. **84**, 143–149 (1975).

Turkel, J., Gijsbers, K., Pritchard, R.M.: Environmental modification of oculomotor and neural function in cats. Talk to Association for Research in Vision and Ophthalmology, Sarasota, Florida (1975).

Van der Loos, H., Woolsey, T.H.: Somatosensory cortex: structural alterations following early injury to sense organ. Science **179**, 395–398 (1973).

Van Sluyters, R.C.: Artificial strabismus in the kitten. Talk to Association for Research in Vision and Ophthalmology, Sarasota, Florida (1977).

Van Sluyters, R.C., Blakemore, C.: A procedure for the maintenance of cortical binocularity in kittens reared with divergent strabismus. Talk to Association for Research in Vision and Ophthalmology, Sarasota, Florida (1973a).

Van Sluyters, R.C., Blakemore, C.: Experimental creation of unusual neuronal properties in visual cortex of kittens. Nature **246**, 506–508 (1973b).

Van Sluyters, R.C., Stewart, D.L.: Bincoular neurons of the rabbit's visual cortex: effects of monocular sensory deprivation. Expl Brain Res. **19**, 196–204 (1974).

Vital-Durand, F., Jeannerod, M.: Maturation of the optokinetic response: genetic and environmental factors. Brain Res. **71**, 249–257 (1974).

Wall, P.D., Egger, M.D.: Formation of new connexions in adult rat brains after partial deafferentation. Nature **232**, 542–545 (1971).

Wall, P.D., Werman, R.: The physiology and anatomy of long ranging afferent fibres within the spinal cord. J. Physiol. **255**, 321–334 (1976).

Watkins, D.W., Berkley, M.A.: The orientation selectivity of single neurons in cat striate cortex. Expl Brain Res. **19**, 433–446 (1974).

Wickelgren, B.G., Sterling, P.: Influence of visual cortex on receptive fields in the superior colliculus of the cat. J. Neurophysiol. **32**, 16–23 (1969a).

Wickelgren, B.G., Sterling, P.: Effect on the superior colliculus of cortical removal in visually deprived cats. Nature **224**, 1032–1033 (1969b).

Wickelgren-Gordon, B.: Some effects of visual deprivation on the cat superior colliculus. Investig. Ophthal. **11**, 460–467 (1972).

Wiesel, T.N., Hubel, D.H.: Effects of visual deprivation on morphology and physiology of cells in the cat's lateral geniculate body. J. Neurophysiol. **26**, 978–993 (1963a).

Wiesel, T.N., Hubel, D.H.: Single-cell responses in striate cortex of kittens deprived of vision in one eye. J. Neurophysiol. **26**, 1003–1017 (1963b).

Wiesel, T.N., Hubel, D.H.: Comparison of the effects of unilateral and bilateral eye closure on cortical unit responses in kittens. J. Neurophysiol. **28**, 1029–1040 (1965a).

Wiesel, T.N., Hubel, D.H.: Extent of recovery from the effects of visual deprivation in kittens. J. Neurophysiol. **28**, 1060–1072 (1965b).

Wiesel, T.N., Hubel, D.H.: Ordered arrangement of orientation columns in monkeys lacking visual experience. J. comp. Neurol. **158**, 307–318 (1974).

Wiesel, T.N., Hubel, D.H., Lam, D.M.K.: Autoradiographic demonstration of ocular-dominance columns in the monkey striate cortex by means of transneuronal transport. Brain Res. **79**, 273–279 (1974).

Wilson, P.D., Stone, J.: Evidence of W-cell input to the cat's visual cortex via the C laminae of the lateral geniculate nucleus. Brain Res. **92**, 472–478 (1975).

Winter, P., Funkenstein, H.H.: The effect of species-specific vocalization on the discharge of auditory cortical cells in the awake squirrel monkey (*Saimiri sciureus*). Expl Brain Res. **18**, 489–504 (1974).

Woolsey, T.A., Van der Loos, H.: The structural organization of layer IV in the somatosensory region (S1) of mouse cerebral cortex. Brain Res. **17**, 205–242 (1970).

Yinon, U.: Eye rotation in developing kittens: the effect on ocular dominance and receptive field organization of cortical cells. Expl Brain Res. **24**, 215–218 (1975).

Yinon, U.: Age dependence of the effect of squint on cells in kittens' visual cortex. Expl Brain Res. **26**, 151–157 (1976).

Yinon, U.: Inverted vision in adult cats: preservation of unidirectionality in cortical neurons. Brain Res. **120**, 164–166 (1977).

Yinon, U., Shaw, C., Auerbach, E.: Retinal and cortical changes in the visual system of pattern-deprived rats. In Sensory Physiology and Behavior. Ed. R. Galun, P. Hillman, I. Parnas and R. Werman. New York: Plenum. pp. 41–53 (1975a).

Yinon, U., Auerbach, E., Blank, M., Friesenhausen, J.: The ocular dominance of cortical neurons in cats developed with divergent and convergent squint. Vision Res. **15**, 1251–1256 (1975b).

Young, J.Z.: Regularities in the retina and optic lobes of Octopus in relation to form discrimination. Nature **186**, 836–839 (1960).

Żernicki, B., Michalski, A.: Single-unit responses to natural objects in visual areas 17 and 18 of cats reared under different visual experiences. Acta Neurobiol. Exp. **34**, 697–712 (1974).

Chapter 13

Innate and Environmental Factors in the Development of Visual Form Perception

LEO GANZ, Stanford, Calif. (USA)

With 12 Figures

Contents

Is the perception of form innate? Since the analysis of the question by LOCKE in his *Essay Concerning Human Understanding* (1690) and by BERKELEY in his *Essay Towards a New Theory of Vision* (1709), it has been widely assumed that the perception of primitive sensations such as color or light intensity is innate, but that form perception is acquired slowly through visual experience.

It was recognized, first, that the retinal image represents a two-dimensional projection of a three-dimensional world, and hence could supply information from which the third dimension had to be inferred. Secondly, it was understood that any object of stimulation had a nonunique relationship to any retinal image, since conditions of illumination, distance of the object, and the orientation of the receptor organ (e.g., eye and head movements) were constantly changing. It was thought likely that considerable experience was required to discover the underlying invariances inherent in what WILLIAM JAMES called the booming, buzzing confusion of stimulation projected onto the proximal receptor surface. The perception of a line, given a projected linear array of light dots projected onto the retina, was for empiricists not a simple, innately given competence. Rather, they believed an organism had to experience those light dots simultaneously so that associations could form between the neural representatives of those light dots. Empiricism has retained its theoretical vigor, especially following HEBB's neurophysiological formalization of its principles (1949). The present chapter, BLAKEMORE's (this volume), and HAITH's (this volume) document the continuing wealth of behavioral and neurophysiological research which Empiricism has stimulated.

Nativism postulates that many structural properties of perception are innate. It has an equally venerable pedigree, going back to DESCARTES' belief in innate ideas (e.g., the ideas of space, time, and motion) (1637) and Kant's a priori synthetic judgments (1781), e.g., visual space perception (VON KRIES, 1910). HOCHBERG (1962) has written an excellent history of the Nativism-Empiricism controversy. More recently, Nativism has been integrated into the phenomenology of Gestalt psychology, and most recently the doctrine has stimulated a plethora of behavioral and neurophysiological observations on neonates of diverse species, some of which we will describe below.

Perhaps the most powerful argument for the existence of innate perceptual processing machinery is HÖFFDING's principle (1887), cited and further elaborated by KÖHLER (1940). When something is learned on trial 1 and tested on trial 2, the knowledge thus acquired can only be useful to the organism if the stimulus conditions during trial 2 contact the memory traces laid down in the earlier trial. But, under natural environmental conditions, there will be many changes in the stimulus as it is projected onto the receptor mosaic (such as the retina), because of changes in illumination, in receptor organ orientation, in object distance, and the like. Using current terminology, we would say that there must be an extensive pattern-recognition apparatus which processes the sensory image to a canonic form before the stimulus on trial 2 can contact the memory trace laid down on trial 1. In a word, since some degree of perception is required for the acquisition of knowledge, all of our perceptual abilities cannot themselves depend on that acquisition.

While initially a philosophic issue, nativism-empiricism was gradually recognized to be also a question of fact: What precisely are the perceptual abilities of organisms of various species prior to sensory experience and how does subsequent experience affect it? A visual deprivation experiment by SPALDING (1873) yielded the first scientific evidence. He observed that newly hatched chicks were too helpless immediately upon hatching to provide a fair test of their perceptual abilities. Accordingly, just as the chicks began to break out of their eggs, he drew over each of their heads a hood, fitting closely around their necks so that no normal pattern vision was possible. Some wore opaque hoods; others wore translucent hoods allowing homogeneous light but no patterned light. After 1–3 days, he removed the hoods and noted their behavior immediately thereafter. He observed head- and eye-movements following an object, a successful sequence consisting of a snap-seize-swallow of a fly which was flying near the chick's neck, a leap over a small obstacle. His observations on 20 visually deprived chicks convinced him they had a sense of visual direction, could move their head and eyes in the direction of moving objects, could peck at small objects and therefore, could both estimate distance and translate that estimate into appropriate action, and could direct themselves toward goals without hitting intervening obstacles, again demonstrating a competence for perceptual-motor coordination and depth estimation.

SPALDING's study shows us that an experiment which involves congenital visual deprivation addresses itself to the classic problem of innate perceptual competence. Are there specific perceptual abilities which organisms manifest prior to exposure to visual stimuli? Ideally, innate competence should be examined in neonates. Unfortunately, this proves unfeasible in organisms which are embryologically immature at birth. Deprivation is then used to postpone the critical first test until a level of maturity is reached which permits a fairer test of visual competence. Since sensory deprivation, especially in neonates, atrophies neural structures (see CHOW, Vol. *VII/3A* and BLAKEMORE, this volume), this procedure has technical weaknesses. One is left wondering whether deprivation destroyed abilities present at birth, or whether visual experience was needed to develop them, or some combination of the two.

A second issue to which sensory deprivation experiments can contribute is the question of sustenance and development: What is the essential visual environment—in a nurturing sense—that is needed to maintain and sustain innate competences? Closely related is the question of perceptual learning. To what extent does sensory experience perfect, sharpen, and tune innate competences? To what extent does the sensory environment play a *constructive* role in the development of sensory systems? A selective sensory deprivation experiment, by removing one or another aspect from an organism's environment, can isolate the essential sensory nutrients, so to speak.

Lastly, because sensory deprivation can destroy both neural structures and perceptual behavior in a selective way, it can be used as a tool of functional anatomy, to analyze structure-function relationships. Some of these relationships are explored below (see also BLAKEMORE, this volume).

There have been a number of recent reviews covering various aspects of visual deprivation: anatomic (GLOBUS, 1975; CHOW, 1973; FIFKOVA, 1974); neurochemical (WALKER et al., 1975); neurophysiologic (BLAKEMORE, this volume; RIESEN, 1975; GROBSTEIN and CHOW, 1975; BARLOW, 1975). The effect of visual deprivation on perceptual-motor coordination in space has also been recently reviewed (GANZ, 1975); there have also been reviews of general behavioral effects of visual deprivation (TEES, 1976) as well as deprivation in other modalities (RIESEN and ZILBERT, 1975). The present chapter addresses itself specifically to the effects of various forms of visual deprivation on form vision and on the neural structures presumed to mediate form vision.

Before considering the effects of deprived visual experience on the development of perception, we turn to a logically antecedent question:

A. What is Known About Visual Perception in Neonates Prior to Experience or Deprivation?

I. Studies of Human Neonates

Observations on neonates suggest that some ability to analyze visual forms in the environment is genetically programmed.

Inferences about form discrimination capabilities of neonates have been derived from the analysis of eye movements—especially fixation preferences (see HAITH, this volume; see also SALAPATEK, 1975; FANZ et al., 1975). In one such study, pairs of figures were presented to human infants ranging in age from 1 week–6 months (FANTZ, 1961). They fixated a bull's-eye pattern for a longer period than a red square, by a ratio of 18:10, a checkerboard pattern longer than a red square, by a ratio of 17:7. The preference for a checkerboard was already present before they were 2 days old (FANTZ, 1965). A schematic face was very much preferred over other stimuli before 5 days of age (FANTZ, 1965). However, a "face" the components of which were thoroughly disjointed and haphazardly rearranged evoked just as long a fixation as a more traditional rendition (see also FANTZ and NEVIS, 1967; KAGAN, 1970; WILCOX, 1969; FANTZ et al., 1975; SALAPATEK, 1975).

Skepticism and caution are advisable in deducing innate visual abilities from such studies of fixation time. First of all, little can be said about the recognition capacities of these infants. The fact that a jumbled array is as attractive as a face means that object recognition is probably not involved, although selective responsiveness to simple features is present. The experiments of KARMEL (1969a, 1969b; KARMEL and MAISEL, 1975) support the hypothesis that fairly basic sensory mechanisms are responsible for controlling infant fixation preferences. He suggests that the main variable in these situations is not shape as such but rather the amount of visual contour. He measured visual preferences in infant rats, chicks, and humans. The stimuli consisted of regular or irregular checkerboard patterns. The results indicated that the disposition of the squares in the pattern was not a significant variable. The predictive variable was the quantity of linear contour. A curvilinear relationship was obtained; there was an optimal amount of contour for visual fixation. Above or below this quantity, visual preference was reduced. This experiment suggests that what attracts the infant's fixation is not related to form recognition, but rather to simpler factors, such as the amount of transient activity aroused in the infant's visual system, which in turn attracts his gaze. SALAPATEK (1975) has carried out a parametric series of fixation preference studies and has also concluded that contour density is the main variable attracting infant gaze before they are 2 months old, whereas form characteristics are not. If a very young infant is shown a circle (1° visual angle in size) embedded in a matrix of "X"s or squares, its gaze is not drawn to the anomalous shape. An older child will turn immediately to the anomaly. SALAPATEK is impressed with the essentially passive reflexlike locking of gaze onto the outside of a complex form by one-month-olds. Active exploration with eye movements emerges at about 8–10 weeks. He concludes that the perception of very young infants is the perception of parts, rather than wholes, with the configurational properties of the stimulus exerting little influence. One exception to this conclusion is the possible discrimination of curves from straight lines as demonstrated by fixation preferences (FANTZ et al., 1975).

To date, visual preference studies offer no evidence for object recognition in human neonates. In fact, the available evidence suggests that there is little recognition in very young infants. For example, FANTZ and NEVIS (1967) have shown that older infants tend to prefer novel patterns. They tend not to fixate patterns shown repeatedly, a finding that suggests object recognition is present in the older infants. In contrast, infants younger than 2 months do not fixate constant patterns differently from variable ones. Hence the neonates do not seem to recognize objects as exemplars of samples shown in previous trials like the older infants. Instead they respond preferentially to subfeatures of those objects such as pieces of contour, or as SALAPATEK and KESSEN (1966, 1973; SALAPATEK, 1975) have shown, to the vertices of an equilateral triangle.

Motion as an elementary feature is particularly important in drawing an infant's gaze. For example, WILCOX and CLAYTON (1968) utilized motion pictures of live models to study visual preference of 5-month-old infants. They found that facial expression was a weak variable, while moving vs. nonmoving models was a very potent variable. Similarly, WOLFF (1963) concluded from his studies on elicitation of smiling in infants that motion appeared to be the crucial factor in drawing attention to a face in infants younger than 2 months. These observations are particularly interesting in light of the neurophysiologic studies on neonate animals, discussed further below, in which motion is found to be a potent stimulus parameter for neurons of neonatal kittens (HUBEL and WIESEL, 1963; PETTIGREW, 1974).

In reviewing the literature on the development of perception of the human face in human infants, GIBSON (1969) concluded that there is a developmental progression in the sensitivity of the infant to facial features. She cites SALZEN (1963) who reported that smiling can be elicited in infants 7–8 weeks old by a moving human face, but also by almost any change in brightness, flickering lamps, an oscillating cardboard disc with black sectors, etc. She cites similar findings by AHRENS (1954) who found that dot patterns were more effective in eliciting smiling than a realistic human face in very young infants. Only at 3–4 months did realistic face patterns become more effective than the abstract features. Familiar faces evoked a different response than unfamiliar faces reportedly at the age of about 6 months.

To summarize, development in human infants seems to proceed from reaction to simple contours (especially contours in motion), to differentiated form features, and later to recognition of configurations of features.

II. Selective Response of Neonatal Birds to Visual Features

Because birds are so precocious at birth, studying them has produced some of our best information on the processing of form information in neonates. For example, herring gull chicks, taken from their nest on the morning after hatching, peck at models of the parents' bills (TINBERGEN and PERDECK, 1950). They peck most at models which are in motion, slender, elongated, pointed down, and have a small red spot. What is particularly interesting about this experiment, from the vantage point of our interest in neonatal pattern recognition, is that synthetic stimuli can be prepared which maximize these features, and that the neonatal gulls peck more frequently at the synthetic models than at naturalistic ones. A thin rod with a few spots on it elicits considerably more pecking than a full recreation of the head of the mother gull. Each rod comprises a "supernormal" stimulus. What is intriguing—in the light of current neurophysiologic discoveries of feature analyzers—is that the supernormal stimulus *must* mean that the birds are responding in an *isolated manner* to a few abstract features: motion, an elongated form, a red spot, etc. The arrangement of these features in the supernormal stimulus is not natural. Yet that stimulus evokes more responses than the fully natural model. Hence, the natural disposition of the features is not an essential attribute. Furthermore, one or another feature will elicit the pecking response without the presence of the others, in a quasi-additive fashion. Therefore, it seems unlikely that the birds are responding to the arrangement of features at birth. Similarly, presenting multiple identical features simultaneously (e.g., three red dots) is supernormal, though this is counter to the configuration of the natural figure. Therefore, it would appear that the birds are capable of abstracting or feature-analyzing from the moment they leave the egg. These features control behavior in a quasi-additive manner not sensitive to the configuration of those features.

Evidence of the same sort derives from a study on neonatal chicks. When newly hatched chicks are given a wide range of small forms to peck at, they show definite preferences for round and elliptical forms over triangular and square shapes. They peck as much as ten times more frequently at the round or elliptical forms (FANTZ, 1957). Again, such abilities imply sophisticated visual analyzers in birds ready to work from the moment they hatch, enabling them to perceive form features.

III. Selective Response of Young Monkeys to Visual Features

In the monkey, ZIMMERMAN (1961) administered discrimination training beginning only hours after birth. On a problem involving discrimination of horizontal from vertical stripes, the animals required 18 days to reach criterion; on a triangle-vs.-circle discrimination they required 25 days to reach that same level. We can conclude that in the monkey form-discrimination abilities are present soon after birth.

Transposition tests applied to form-discrimination tasks provide further insight. If innate feature-analyzing mechanisms are present, then we would expect innate stimulus generalization along a dimension processed by that mechanism. For example, if a monkey has a visual mechanism which extracts only contour information, and disregards the insides of forms, then it is to be expected that an infant monkey will generalize a response trained to a solid figure to a contour-only representation of the same figure. The evidence is positive: Monkeys seem to transpose beyond the range of their experience. In one study, infant monkeys 11–29 days old at the start of training were trained to discriminate solid triangles from circles. They generalized at very high levels to an up-down transposition of the triangle, to outline figures, to black-white reversal of the figure, and to outline figures with fragmented contours (ZIMMERMAN, 1962). Evidently, some feature-analytic mechanisms are present by the time a monkey is several weeks old. Of course, some doubt still remains as to whether these few weeks of visual experience were sufficient to provide the requisite range of experience necessary to build up the needed neural networks. This doubt is particularly germane now that we know that as little as a few hours of visual experience has a definite trophic effect on the visual system (HUBEL and WIESEL, 1970; PETTIGREW et al., 1973; BLAKEMORE and MITCHELL, 1973; PETTIGREW and GAREY, 1974).

B. Simple Intensity and Form Perception in Binocularly Deprived Organisms

One way of experimentally controlling visual form experience is by binocular congenital visual deprivation (BD). In practice, a wide variety of stratagems has been explored to deprive organisms of visual form experience, such as rearing in total darkness, eyelid suturing, cloth masks, and translucent contact lenses. If interested, the reader should consult the individual studies for the procedural details of these techniques.

I. Luminance and Luminous Flux Discrimination

There is good consensus that organisms reared from birth in an environment of darkness with 1 h diffuse light daily for several months can learn a visual intensity discrimination as readily as nondeprived controls. Evidence reported for the rat (Tees, 1968a), cat (Riesen and Aarons, 1959; Riesen, 1965a, 1965b), and monkey (Wilson and Riesen, 1966) is shown in Figure 1. Cats reared completely in darkness (Aarons et al., 1963) also demonstrate this ability. Such studies suggest that an innate competence for intensity discriminations is present in many mammals.

The absence of any effect of visual deprivation on intensity discriminations cannot simply be attributed to the task being too simple. Dark- and light-reared rats have been compared on a difficult discrimination utilizing a small difference in intensity (Tees, 1968a). The problem was difficult enough to require many more trials until acquisition by the control group. Nevertheless, dark-reared and normal controls were not found to differ in learning speed. These results have a methodologic implication. It is clear that visually deprived animals do not suffer a general intellectual, motivational, or visuomotor deficit so debilitating that they cannot learn to discriminate any visual maze tasks, as has been suggested (Meyers and McCleary, 1964; Wertheimer, 1951). Nor does it seem to be the case that BD organisms have generalized and long-lasting deficits

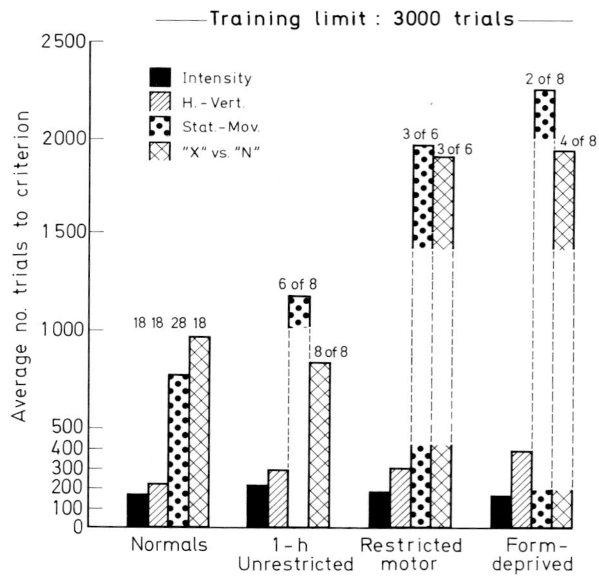

Fig. 1. Visual discrimination learning by cats after various conditions of deprivation (from Riesen, 1965a). The form-deprived group was given diffuse light for 1 h; the restricted motor group was given 1 h of visual experience along with limited locomotion; and the unrestricted group was given 1 h of visual experience and unlimited locomotion. Otherwise, the three experimental groups were in darkness. Training was begun after about 8 weeks. The numbers in the bar graphs refer to the proportion of animals learning the particular discrimination to criterion. All the normal animals acquired all the discriminations

in making associations between any visual stimuli and motor responses (ZUCKERMAN and ROCK, 1957).

It is true, however, that the *basis* for the intensity discrimination has been found to be different in the two groups (TEES, 1971). When both brightness cues (differences in flux per stimulus area) and luminous flux cues (differences in total flux) are available, light-reared rats use significantly more brightness cues while dark-reared rats make greater use of total flux cues. When only brightness cues are available, dark-reared rats do worse than light-reared controls (though the difference between groups is not large). It might be noted that while a luminous flux discrimination can be learned on the basis of stimulus intensity alone, brightness discrimination requires the integration of stimulus intensity and stimulus area. An analysis of performance on stimulus equivalence trials shows that while dark-reared rats use total-flux cues more often than brightness cues, almost all animals use both cues at some time. Therefore, the difference between groups is one of *cue preference* rather than total incompetence on the part of the dark-reared group. As TEES (1971) points out, dark-rearing causes a change in the hierarchy of cues used by the animal. Although regrettably nebulous, the concept of selective attention must be invoked. Visual deprivation affects the readiness with which organisms attend to different features of their environment, features which we know they are capable of perceiving.

Three months of dark-rearing starting at the age of 90 days does not induce such changes in cue hierarchy (BLAND and COOPER, 1970). Hence, these shifts in readiness to use cues occur at a critical period when the organism is most susceptible to environmental manipulation of that readiness.

II. Form Discrimination

It is not generally realized that BD organisms having undergone moderately long periods of sensory deprivation, typically have moderately good albeit deficient acuity, can learn *simple* form discriminations surprisingly well, and can generalize what they have learned to a large variety of situations, i.e., they can transpose. Regarding acuity, RIESEN et al. (1964) reared rhesus infants from birth for 20–60 days with a combination of dark-rearing and pattern deprivation. Their optokinetic nystagmus was measured with targets of varying width, and an estimate of their acuity was derived. Initial differences between deprived and control animals had disappeared by the second day of testing. A second study, using somewhat more extensive deprivation — 3–6 months total dark-rearing of pigtail macaques — and a fixation preference technique (REGAL, BOOTHE, TELLER, and SACKETT, personal communication), reports acuities between 2.5–7.5 c/° in the dark-reared groups and 15 c/° in control animals.

Regarding form discrimination, HEBB (1937) reared rats in complete darkness from a few days of age to maturity. Some were then trained in a fully lighted room, while the others were trained completely in the dark except for exposure to the discriminanda. The results clearly show that dark-reared rats can readily learn a horizontal vs. vertical grating discrimination. Moreover, many can generalize to smaller-sized figures and to outlines. Such generalization must mean that the rats do not respond to tiny dots within the figure, but rather to features such as the orientation of contours in the figure. Nor do the rats respond to the geometric figure as a whole but rather to certain constituents of the figure. For example, when rats were trained with a positive stimulus consisting of three horizontal bars, they generalized the response to a vertical rectangle which was made up of numerous small horizontal constituents. In other words, they were responding to the small local horizontal contour feature, rather than to the overall shape of the figure. The ability of these visually naive rats to respond to such medium-sized perceptual units implies the existence of feature-processing mechanisms within the almost visually naive nervous system of the rat which are accessible to the animal without extensive learning. Either no visual experience is necessary, or at most the visual experience with the training figures themselves is sufficient.

Another clear indication of simple form discrimination in BD groups is found in a study in which chimpanzees were raised in darkness for $7^1/_2$ months, receiving 90 min diffuse light each day while held supine on a table (Riesen, 1958, 1965b). Such animals learned to discriminate large striped plaques with different orientations as quickly and as readily as control animals who daily received active patterned light. Similar findings were obtained in yet another study in which cats reared until the age of 8 weeks in total darkness except for 1 h of diffuse light each day learned a horizontal-vertical discrimination almost as readily as a group with 1 h unrestricted patterned light (Riesen, 1965b). The results obtained from the form-deprived group show this in Figure 1.

In a recent study (Ganz et al., 1972) four BD cats (deprived until $3^1/_2$ months old) learned a horizontal-vertical discrimination quite readily and not significantly slower than nondeprived controls. Two studies on BD rats (Woodruff and Wickens, 1951; Tees, 1968b) also showed that the experimental group learned a contour orientation task as readily as normals.

One current study (Zablocka et al., 1975) did however find some deficiencies. Kittens were reared with binocular visual deprivation for their initial 4–6 months. They showed severe deficiencies in acquiring a circle vs. cross discrimination, which however, proved transitory. After some further training on a very easy visual task (stimulus vs. no stimulus) the cats were reintroduced to the form discrimination, which they now solved relatively quickly. Their results suggest that visual deprivation had induced a general neglect of visual forms. Pretraining was essential to induce a new cognitive *set,* namely the use of visual cues in general, for problem solving. Their abilities to discriminate simple forms were not deficient.

This repeated finding—namely, that BD groups are quite as good as normals in developing simple form discriminations—allows us to draw three conclusions: (1) Many species—from rats to chimpanzees—can process visual contour information of an elementary sort, with at most brief visual experience; the processing mechanism are either present in the CNS innately or are quickly gained. This represents an innate perceptual competence. (2) Some of these contour-processing mechanisms clearly survice even after $7^1/_2$ months dark-rearing. (3) Visuomotor deficiencies associated with the visual deprivation treatment, which are present initially, effectively disappear (to the extent that the maze-discrimination skills require them) once pretraining is completed. This is important methodologically (WERTHEIMER, 1951; ZUCKERMAN and ROCK, 1957).

C. Closer Examination of Innate vs. Experiential Factors

I. Oculomotor Commands and Innate (Simple) Form Perception

As an alternative to the hypothesis that there are visual form-processing mechanisms functional at birth, HEBB (1949) suggested that animals can make and transpose simple form discriminations innately, because they follow the edges of a form with their eyes (see also RIZZOLATI and TRADARDI, 1971). This might have the effect of reducing a complicated stimulus pattern such as a triangle or a rectangle into a temporal oculomotor command pattern of successively fixated, foveally centered edges. Conceivably, such processing could account for the BD animals' ability to generalize to stimuli of other sizes, from solid figures to outlines, etc. It should be noted that this theory invokes an innate visual form-processing mechanism, but places it in the oculomotor system.

A number of theorists have postulated that there is a strong oculomotor involvement in the encoding of visual percepts (HEBB, 1949; FESTINGER et al., 1967; HOCHBERG, 1970; NOTON and STARK, 1971). They argue that a form on the retina sets up a series of sequential visuomotor expectancies to fixate its various parts using a sequence of saccades: "... it is the plan for such active looking-and-testing that is stored over successive fixations, not the myriad details that are glimpsed with each independent fixation ..." (HOCHBERG, 1970, p. 114). It is clear that adults can recognize forms with very brief exposures, not allowing scanning of the stimulus. But perhaps such scanning is essential only in the initial development of these percepts. How would the perception of form be affected if an animal were prevented, since birth, from ever scanning a form with successive eye fixations?

In order to test this theory directly, an experiment was conducted on young BD monkeys using an adaptation of the Riggs-Ditchburn stabilized-image apparatus which permitted the placement of training stimuli on the retina independent of eye movements. (For details of apparatus see GANZ and WILSON, 1967). The subjects were trained to discriminate a vertical from a horizontal rectangle. They then generalized that discrimination to smaller, fragmented, or retinally displaced versions of those stimuli, all without being able to follow the edges of the figures with their eyes. The results are shown in Figure 2. Evidently,

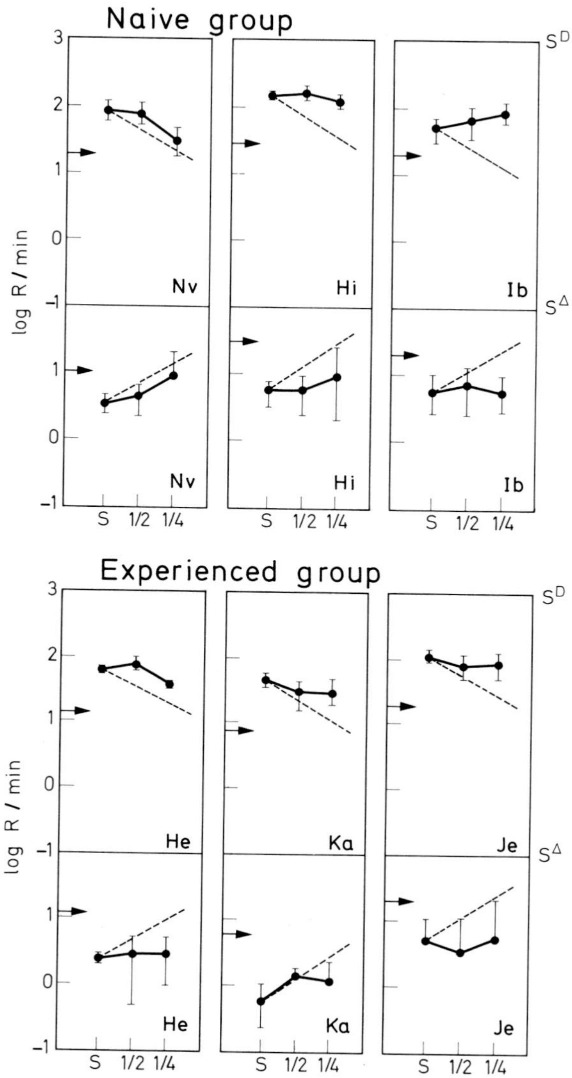

Fig. 2. Generalization of an operant response in a group of visually naive and a group of visually experienced monkeys (from GANZ and WILSON, 1967). The monkeys learned to press a bar in the presence of S^{D} to obtain food reinforcement and to suppress pressing the bar in the presence of S^{Δ}. The stimuli were a vertical and a horizontal rectangle. They were presented in a manner which made contouring eye movements ineffective. The figure shows the results of generalization tests applied to fragmentations of the training figure up to one-half and one-quarter the original area. The solid line depicts observed values and the dashed line predicted values (see GANZ and WILSON, 1967 for details). Horizontal stems are placed 1 sd from the mean. Note that the monkeys respond more than predicted to the fragmented versions of the S^{D} and less than predicted to fragmented versions of the S^{Δ}. This indicates a recognition of the oriented contour even when presented in fragmented version. This is true for both the visually naive and the experienced animals. (The *arrow* indicates a false-alarm rate estimate: the level of performance when the training stimuli are omitted entirely)

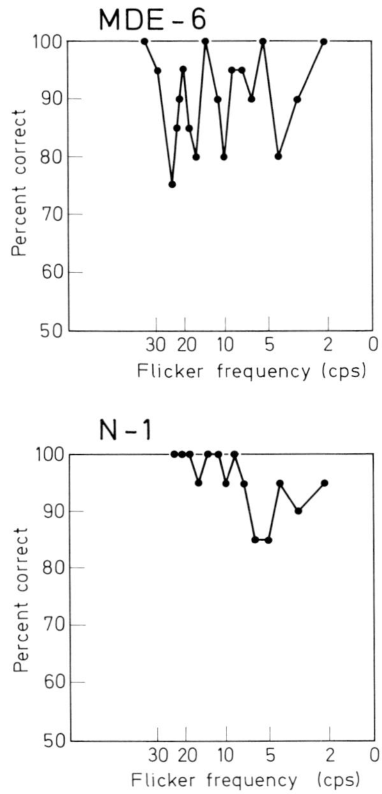

Fig. 3. Transfer of a horizontal vs. vertical grid discrimination in two animals (from GANZ et al., 1972). MDE-6 is a monocularly deprived and N-1 is a normally reared cat. After the discrimination had been acquired, the stimulus windows holding the translucent stimuli, illuminated from behind, were now illuminated by strobe flashes. Each flash lasted 10 μs. The transfer tests were begun with strobe stimulation at 30/s. Then the rate of flicker was gradually brought down to 2 c/s on succeeding days. Note that discrimination performance, though variable, does not break down at lower flash rates

visually naive monkeys could readily generalize from a vertical rectangle S+ to a vertical array of three dots or to a rectangle one-quarter the original size. It seemed clear that from their first exposure to visual forms, horizontal and vertical rectangles or horizontal and vertical arrays of dots were not responded to as aggregates of numerous independent subunits, but as chunks of contour lines or edges. In other words, the monkeys were utilizing their contour-orientation selective mechanisms to make the discrimination; the mechanism was not oculomotor. Moreover, very little visual experience was required to develop these mechanisms, although it cannot be concluded that no experience was needed.

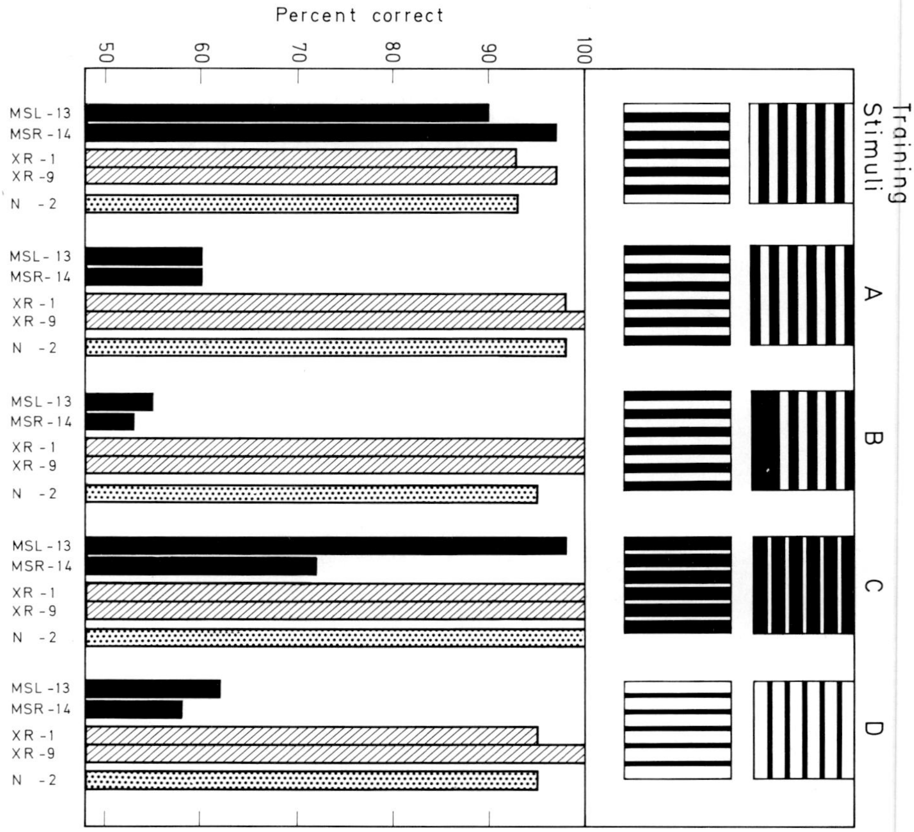

Fig. 4. Transposition tests of an orientation discrimination (horizontal vs. vertical stripes) in monocularly reared and control animals (from GANZ and HAFFNER, 1974). The histograms depict mean percent correct performance of the training pair and four transposition pairs. In the discrimination apparatus, the two stimuli were shown side by side horizontally, and not vertically as in the figure. Animals labeled MSR and MSL are monocularly deprived animals and their results are shown with *dark-shaded* bars. XR (*medium shaded bars*) labels those monocularly deprived animals which were subsequently reverse sutured (deprived eye opened and experienced eye closed). N (*lightest-shaded bars*) labels a visually nondeprived cat. Note that the orientation discrimination of the simple monocular deprived animals breaks down on many transposition tests, suggesting that the basis of the discrimination for them involves not orientation of contours but specific space-localized differences in flux. The XR animals given monocular deprivation and then cross-suture treatment perform successfully on the four transposition tests

The monkeys in the GANZ and WILSON experiment were never given the opportunity to set up normal sequences of looking and testing, since visual forms were only presented retinally stabilized. Therefore, form perception should have been grossly deficient if such active visuomotor explorations were essential. The experiment indicated that perception, at least of simple horizontal and vertical rectangles, was not grossly deficient. However, such strategies might be required for more complicated visual forms; we have no evidence either way at this time.

Another indication that these simple form discriminations in BD animals are not dependent on following the contours of the form with eye movements or head movements comes from a study by GANZ et al. (1972). Deprived cats learned a horizontal *vs.* vertical grating discrimination quite readily. Did the cats learn so well because they moved their heads or eyes, as observed by RIZZOLATI and TRADARDI (1971), and thereby changed the nature of the task? For example, the cats might move their head up and down when faced with the grid. Such a movement would create more transient neural activity in the visual system when the cat faced a horizontal grid than when it faced a vertical grid. The deprived cat might then use such a difference, or one analogous to it, as a basis for discrimination. To test this hypothesis, extremely brief flashes of both stimuli were introduced. At first the flicker rates were well above flicker fusion, so that the display appeared steadily illuminated, and then the rate of flicker was gradually lowered. As shown in Figure 3, discrimination performance was maintained throughout. Therefore it is not possible that the animals were solving the task by monitoring *on*- or *off*-activity resulting from eye or head movements. Most likely, they were making a true contour orientation discrimination. This is also the conclusion of a more recent study (GANZ and HAFFNER, 1974). Deprived organisms acquired a vertical-horizontal discrimination and were then tested with a wide variety of transpositions in which the total luminous flux reaching the animal from the two stimuli was varied. The results depicted in Figure 4 show that deprived animals with cross-suture treatment could learn a true contour orientation discrimination, independent of flux specifics.

II. Binocular Deprivation and Interocular Transfer

The interocular transfer paradigm provides another approach to the question of innate competence for form perception. MEYERS and MCCLEARY (1964) reared BD cats in darkness with 1 h of binocular diffuse light per day. When 7 weeks old the cats were administered a form-discrimination task with one eye open. The cats were taught to flex a limb when a cross was presented and not to flex that limb when a circle was presented to avoid electric shock punishment. Between training periods, they were kept in total darkness. Two of the five animals transferred perfectly when the occluder was switched to the training eye, one animal transferred poorly, and two animals did not transfer at all. Note that to show positive transfer it was necessary for the naive eye's central afferent connections to process the incoming form information in such a manner that contact could be made with the memory traces laid down through the eye that was exposed during training. Therefore, positive transfer implies that the totally visually naive eye did have access to some form-processing neural networks, independent of experience. Several other studies have also shown moderate amounts of interocular transfer in binocularly deprived animals (GANZ et al., 1972; Ganz and Haffner, 1974). Since negative results in interocular transfer tests can be caused by many different factors, studies that have failed to demonstrate interocular transfer are less conclusive than those that have. At any rate, the evidence thus far suggests that visual form experience is not an essential precondition for the interocular transfer of a simple form discrimination.

III. Discrimination of More Complex Figures by Visually Deprived Organisms

One obvious experimental strategy for discovering the aspects of visual form perception requiring visual experience is to find tasks which visually deprived organisms learn more poorly than visually experienced controls. Where visual experience is essential (whether to develop or to maintain the necessary neural structures), the two groups will differ greatly. A noteworthy aspect of the literature on visual deprivation is the consistent and dramatic difference between two sets of visual discrimination tasks. In the last section, we have seen that where the task involves the detection of some visual feature (such as contour orientation), the two groups, deprived and experienced, perform comparably. Therefore, we concluded that some simple feature detection is relatively independent of visual experience. In the present section we review studies where the discrimination tasks involve the recognition of a particular relationship between two or more features. Here the deprived organism does dramatically worse. We show, moreover, that this finding cannot be attributed simply to differences in task difficulty and infer that visual experience develops neural structures which permit a selective response to relationships between features.

In the rat, poor performance on a triangle vs. circle discrimination has been obtained in binocularly deprived animals (Michels et al., 1958) and on an "N" vs. "X" discrimination (Tees, 1968b). Similarly, BD $7^1/_2$-month-old chimpanzees require many more trials to learn to discriminate a square from a circle than controls (Riesen, 1965a). The fact that controls learn the task quickly indicates that it is a simple visual task for a visually experienced animal. Nor were the BD chimps simply blind, since they had previously learned the stripe-orientation problem readily.

In a different experiment (Riesen, 1965a) BD cats were reared with 1 h diffuse light and 23 h darkness from birth to 8 weeks (the results are shown in Fig. 1). Many could not learn an "X" vs. "N" discrimination or a very slow movement discrimination. They failed even after extensive prior training on brightness and orientation problems in which they were as competent as normal animals. When one recalls that experimental cats were equal to controls in their ability to learn brightness and contour orientation problems, the great differences on a more complicated form discrimination are even more striking. Again, since the "X" and "N" are comparable in visual angle to the stripes and the striped discrimination was learned readily, the form deficiency is not attributable simply to a loss in acuity.

Our own observations have yielded similar results (GANZ et al., 1972). BD cats reared $3^1/_2$ months in continuous diffuse light were equivalent to normal animals in learning a contour-orientation problem. However, on an upright *vs.* inverted triangle discrimination, the BD cats were much poorer than controls. In another study (MEYERS and MCCLEARY, 1964) similar deficiencies in learning a form discrimination were present when an indicator response was used requiring little visuomotor coordination. Cats that were dark-reared and then taught a simple limb-flexion response to one visual form (a cross) and not to another (a circle) required twice as much training as controls.

Therefore, it cannot be argued that the BD group can recognize visual forms but is deficient in associating forms with locations in space. In the MEYERS and MCCLEARY study, only a *go* versus *no go* task was involved, and yet BD groups still showed deficiencies. The animals appear to have a true visual deficiency which is confined to more complicated forms.

TEES (1968a, b) performed an experiment to find out if problem difficulty per se is a critical factor in determining the effect of visual deprivation on subsequent discrimination learning. He compared light- and dark-reared rats on a pattern discrimination ("X" vs. "N") with performance on a variety of angular orientation problems graded in difficulty. The results are shown in Table 1. On the three contour-orientation problems, shown in rows 1, 2, and 3, the dark-reared and light-reared groups were comparable. Only on pattern discrimination (row 4) was the dark-reared group more deficient than the light-reared group. Only this latter comparison yielded a statistically significant difference ($p < 0.001$). Note particularly that the vertical *vs.* oblique discrimination (row 2) is of comparable difficulty to the pattern discrimination (row 4) for the light-reared group. Yet, on this fairly difficult vertical *vs.* oblique discrimination (row 2), the light-reared and dark-reared groups are quite comparable. Hence, problem difficulty per se does not explain why the visually deprived organisms perform poorly on the pattern discrimination, since there are some difficult discriminations on which they perform comparably. Clearly, there is something inherent in a pattern discrimination of the "N" vs. "X" type, something presumably related to the fact that the critical cue resides in a relationship among feature parts, rather than the existence vs. nonexistence of some feature.

Table 1. Trials to criterion for normally reared and visually deprived rats on visual discrimination problems (from TEES, 1968b). ($N = 12$ for each group)

Problem	Rearing condition	Mean	Standard deviation
Horizontal vs. vertical	Light	144.17	42.71
	Dark	168.33	38.04
Vertical vs. oblique	Light	314.17	81.28
	Dark	318.33	85.81
Oblique vs. oblique	Light	250.83	77.27
	Dark	293.33	121.78
Pattern ("N" vs. "X")	Light	261.67	121.98
	Dark	420.00	244.64

In another experiment (GANZ and HAFFNER, 1974) we have employed transposition tests to analyze the cues that visually naive cats use once they learn a discrimination involving a relationship between features. Cats were reared for several months first with one eye sutured closed. Later, the deprived eye was opened, and then the other eye sutured closed for an equivalent period of time. Thus we could examine how discriminations were acquired by the two eyes separately, each animal serving as its own control. As a test task, we used an upright vs. inverted triangle discrimination, a task in which S^+ and S^- have the same features, but in which the geographic interrelationship of the parts differs. The transposition results are shown in Figure 5. When either total luminous flux of parts of the figure was manipulated (tests D and E) or the figures were presented as white-black reversals (test F), cats transposed successfully when viewing the display with their initially experienced eye. But when viewing the display through their initially deprived eye, every cat dropped to near chance levels. This suggests that the cats learned the discriminations with their initially deprived eye by responding to local flux differences between the two stimuli. For example, a white-outlined, upright triangle has more flux near the bottom of the display window than the same triangle in an inverted position. Therefore, the same animal responds to configurational cues with its experienced eye and finds it impossible to recognize configurational cues with its deprived eye. Incidentally, the same cats could learn a stripe-orientation problem independently of local luminous flux. In other words, they could perceive and utilize contour-orientation information with their deprived eye. Without visual experience during their infancy, these animals cannot recognize features presented in relationships, although they can recognize the features themselves. From this group of results we infer that *one of the effects of visual experience is to develop neural structures which permit the organism to extract configurational cues and thus to recognize objects in the visual world even when they change in absolute size and luminous flux*. Phrased slightly differently, objects moving in the real world present a bewildering array of features which change as a result of changes in illumination, orientation, and distance. However, certain ratios of properties remain fairly constant. If the organism, through visual experience, develops neural structures which respond to these ratios or relationships, then it can recognize objects despite changes in the constituents.

In a later section we discuss some of the possible characteristics of these neural structures.

Fig. 5. Transposition tests of a form discrimination (upright vs. inverted triangle). The *bars* depict ▷ mean percent correct performance to the training stimulus pair and six transposition pairs, as in the previous figure (from GANZ and HAFFNER, 1974). *Darker-shaded bars* represent results from monocularly reared cats, given cross-suture treatment, and performing with their initially deprived eye. *Lighter-shaded bars* represent results from cats using their initially experienced eye. Two animals, XL-10 and XR-5 were tested at different times with their initially deprived and with their initially experienced eyes. Tests B and C show that all the cats, with either eye, responded primarily to the bottom half of the figure. Performance is clearly poorer with the initially deprived eye when spatially-localized flux cues are manipulated, as in pair D where the horizontal bar is thin while the inverted apex is thick or as in pair E where the horizontal bar is thick while the apex is thin, or as in pair F where the entire training figure is shown with black-white relationships

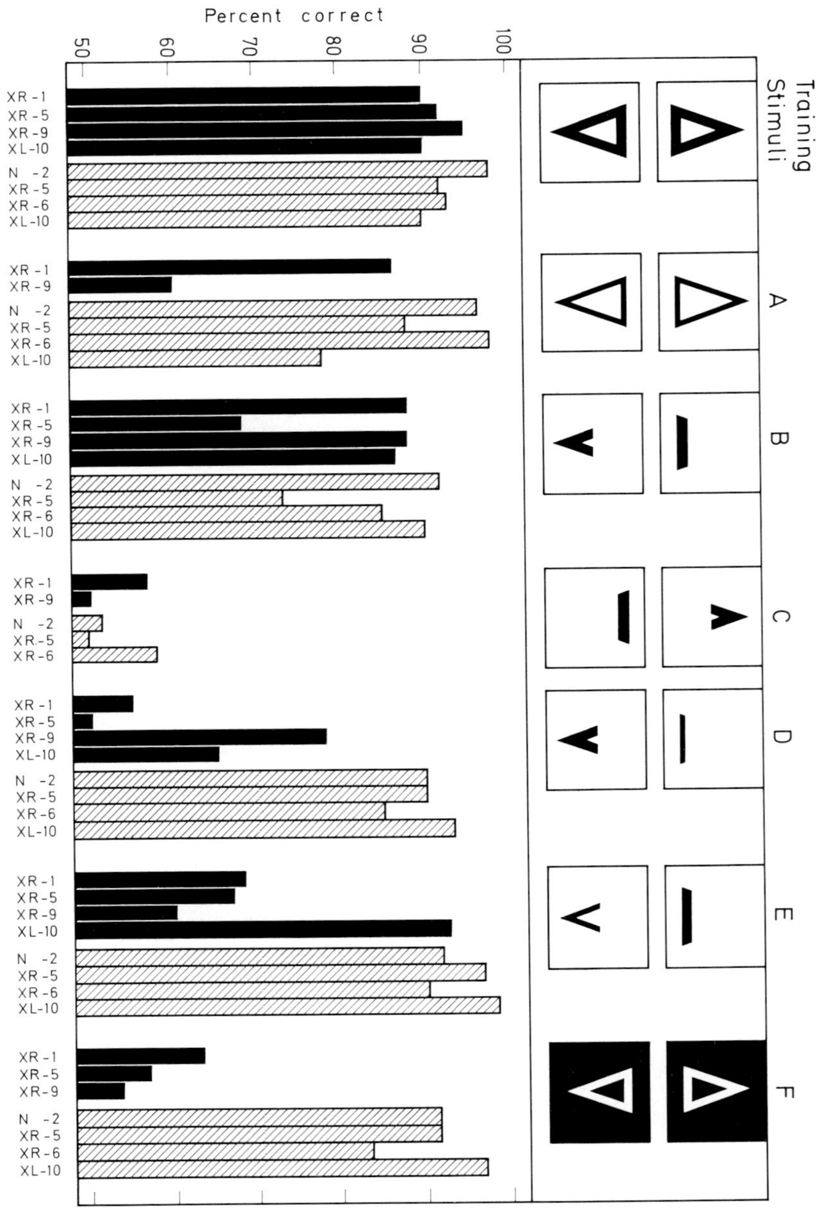

reversed. These results suggest that the monocularly deprived cats given recovery treatment under cross-suture conditions are unable to acquire a form discrimination such as this one on a true form basis, but are forced to depend on spatially-localized flux cues. Note, in this regard, that cats XR-5 and XL-10 have learned the identical discrimination quite differently, depending on which eye is open during training and testing

IV. Specificity in the Vertebrate Visual System without Visual Experience

We have reviewed evidence which indicates that whereas perceptual recognition of an elementary sort, such as the discrimination of contours with different orientations, is for the most part independent of visual experience, perceptual recognition which involves the extraction of feature relationships appears to require visual experience. Which aspects of the visual system's capabilities are provided genetically and which aspects are developed through an interaction between visual experience and the neural structures provided genetically?

The evidence thus far indicates that the potential physiologic basis for certain aspects of perceptual organization—local sign, contour orientation and position, movement, binocular integration, and crude stereopsis—is genetically specified and provided at birth.

Some of the first evidence for such physiologic structures comes from experimental embryology. If the optic nerve of a teleost or amphibian is cut, the regenerating retinal ganglion axons find their way back to their original terminations in the optic tectum. Moreover, a frog with such a regenerated optic nerve orients in visual space veridically, (MATTHEY, 1926; STONE and USSHER, 1927; SPERRY, 1942). It has also been shown (BEERS, 1929; STONE and COLE, 1943; SPERRY, 1943, 1951) that this accomplishment is not dependent on practice, because if the eye is rotated 180° in its socket at the time that the optic nerve is cut the original connections are still reestablished although they have become maladaptive. Such an animal makes snapping movements temporally and downwards to a lure that is presented nasally and in the upper visual field. As far as we know, this maladaptive behavior remains permanently and is not altered by subsequent visual experience. These experiments imply that the topographic organization of the visual system is genetically determined. In turn, this organization establishes an innate framework of connections for acts requiring visuomotor coordination in frogs and fish. According to more recent work (GAZE et al., 1965), it appears that the genome specifies a spatial *gradient* of retino-tectal connections; only the relative positions of the connections are specified.

The advent of microelectrode recording techniques has permitted a much more precise functional look at innate structures. In the frog, there is indeed—as the experiments just described implied—a one-to-one mapping of the retina onto the tectum (JACOBSON, 1969). Furthermore, ganglion cells seem to divide into functional classes—for example, one class of cells is most responsive to large moving edges in the frog's visual field; another class is most responsive to small objects, and so on. The axons of each class of retinal ganglion cells terminate at a different layer of the optic tectum (MATURANA et al., 1960). There is good reason to believe that this stratified organization is also genetically determined, because when the optic nerve is cut, the regenerating axon returns not only to the appropriate topographic location, but also in depth to a layer within the optic tectum appropriate to its functional class (MATURANA et al., 1959).

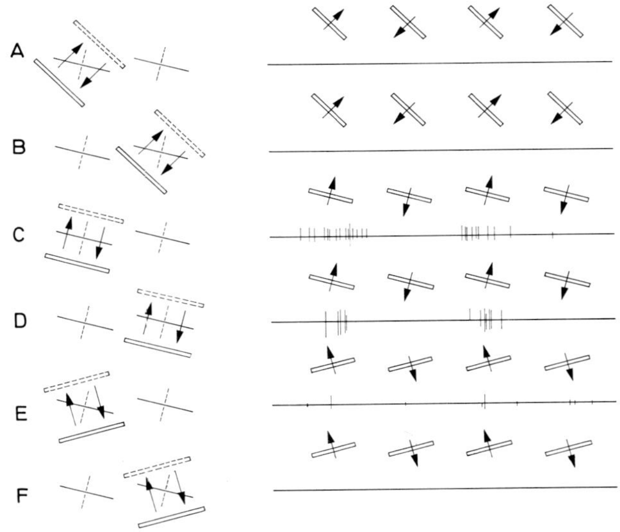

Fig. 6. Simultaneous recording from two visual cortex neurons taken from a 19-day-old kitten whose right eye had been covered from the time of normal eye opening by a translucent occluder (from HUBEL and WIESEL, 1963). The *small and large hatch marks* in the records at the right represent the action potentials of these two neurons. The *rectangles* in the *columns* on the *left* indicate stimulation of the left eye (e.g., row A) or stimulation of the right eye (e.g., row B), etc. Each eye was stimulated separately by a slit 0.5°×0.4°, moved across the receptive field at a velocity of about 1°/s. Time calibration = 1 s

More recent studies have shown that such innate structures are not restricted to amphibia, but are also an essential aspect of the mammalian visual system. Using microelectrodes HUBEL and WIESEL (1963) recorded the activity of neurons in the visual cortex of visually naive kittens 8 and 16 days old. They reported that the cells discharged most when stimulated by elongated stimuli presented at specific orientations and moving in particular directions. Some cells were selectively sensitive only to particular directions of motion. Diffuse light was much less effective as a stimulus than bits of contour or edges. Most of the units could be stimulated by either eye and showed binocular integration. An illustration of recordings from two such neurons is given in Figure 6. Furthermore, it was found that an electrode which penetrated the visual cortex normal to the surface recorded long sequences of cells with receptive fields of the same direction of motion, whereas an oblique penetration uncovered many more shifts in orientation. This last observation suggested that the neurons might be organized in columns of cells of similar orientation or at least of similar directions of motion selectivity. The number of cells recorded, however, was too small to be certain of this point. All of these observations reflect an organization found in visually experienced adult animals. The visual cortex neurons of neonatal kittens differed from those of adult visually experienced cats in having less selectivity with regard to orientation, responding less briskly, and habituating more rapidly.

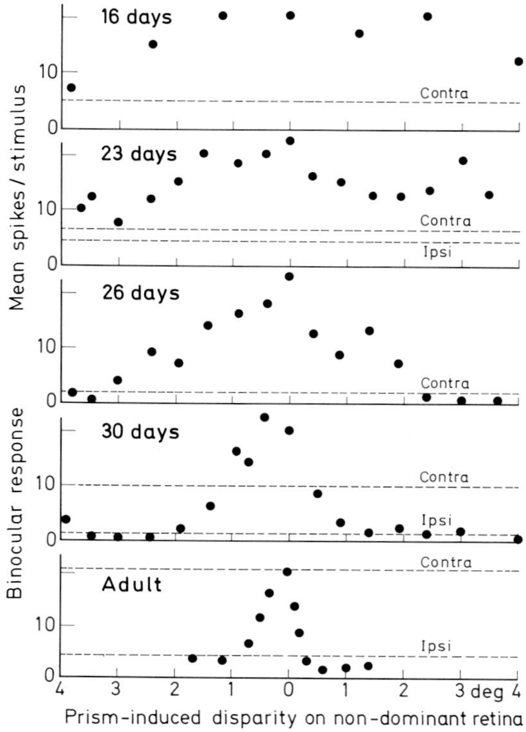

Fig. 7. Binocular responses as a function of disparity in visual cortex of *normal* kittens of various ages (from PETTIGREW, 1974). Each record depicts the most selective neuron recorded from at that age level. Each point represents the mean number of spikes elicited by movement of the preferred stimulus during the entire traverse of the stimulus across the cell's receptive field. The horizontal axis represents different binocular disparities of the stimulus presented to the nondominant retina. Note that immature neurons are characterized by binocular facilitation which is relatively insensitive to changes in the retinal disparity of stimuli presented to both eyes. With increasing age and visual experience, narrower limits are placed on the zone of facilitation, the binocular response actually being depressed below monocular levels unless the receptive fields are exactly aligned in the plane of stimulation

Additional neurophysiologic analysis of single neurons in the visual cortex of visually inexperienced kittens studied during the first few weeks of life has been reported (BARLOW and PETTIGREW, 1971; PETTIGREW, 1974). Movement-direction selectivity and binocular convergence in single neurons of visually inexperienced kittens were again reported, however, with some new observations on binocular disparity. The development of disparity specificity in kittens reared without visual deprivation can be seen in Figure 7. Note that the immature neuron (i.e., from animals 23 days or younger) shows binocular facilitation over wide ranges of binocular disparity, but the binocular response is never less than the monocular response. After 30 days the response to binocular stimulation has become weaker than the monocular response at all but a narrow range of disparities, where facilitation is shown. This change in pattern is presumed by PETTIGREW to follow the development of inhibitory flanks in a neuron's receptive field. The growth of selectivity to a narrow range of binocular disparities is thought to follow the development of these inhibitory flanks.

In order to separate visual experience factors from maturational factors occurring at this time (CRAGG, 1975), PETTIGREW examined BD kittens at the same ages (2–6 weeks). He reported that the BD kittens did not show any sharply tuned disparity functions at 4–6 weeks, when the visually experienced kittens were developing selective binocular disparity functions. Even the older lid-sutured kittens, continued to give nonselective disparity functions like the 16-day-old kitten neuron illustrated at the top of Figure 7.

In order to estimate the orientation selectivity of neurons in visually naive kittens, the response to a moving dot was compared with the response to a moving bar (BARLOW and PETTIGREW, 1971; PETTIGREW, 1974). In normally reared adult cats, the orientation specificity for a bar was found to be much sharper than for a dot. In contrast, they claimed that a young kitten (4 weeks or younger) shows the same orientation-selectivity to both. This finding implied that line-orientation selectivity required normal visual experience, but recent studies contradict this conclusion.

With regard to the specific question of *orientation-selectivity of cortical neurons in totally visually deprived organisms,* the most recent evidence indicates that it is innately determined. BUISSERET and IMBERT (1975) have reported that about 25% of visual cortex cells are selective to orientation in congenitally dark-reared kittens as well as in normal, visually experienced kittens of the same age. BLAKEMORE and VAN SLUYTERS (1975) reared kittens congenitally in the dark. They observed that in two very young kittens (9 and 19 days old) where deprivation had been quite brief, 15–20% of the cells showed definite orientation selectivity. These cells responded more strongly to lines than to dots, showing that they manifested linear summation. Since they responded selectively to *static* lines presented at various orientations, the selectivity was independent of motion. Moreover, flashed spots of light revealed specific *on* and *off* regions and antagonistic flanks quite characteristic of simple cells. LEVENTHAL and HIRSCH's report (1975) of neurons sensitive to vertical orientations in goggle-reared kittens exposed only to oblique lines (see below) also argues for some innate organization of line-orientation sensitive neurons. Along a similar vein, STRYKER and SHERK (1975) exposed kittens to a circular drum with either vertical stripes or horizontal stripes (otherwise they were in darkness). Nevertheless, a full complement of neurons showing orientation selectivity and an orderly progression of orientation preferences was found (see below). More directly, SHERK and STRYKER (1976) have shown that in the visual cortex of kittens binocularly deprived since birth a substantial proportion of neurons are selectively sensitive to the orientation of a moving line. The selectivity is almost as high as in adult visually experienced cats (see Fig. 8). These neurons respond more vigorously to a line than to a dot, exhibiting linear summation. Their orientation preferences are similarly aligned along perpendicular columns. Furthermore, tangential descents of the microelectrode reveal stepwise changes in optimal orientation. Therefore, all seems to corroborate HUBEL and WIESEL's original conclusion (1963) that many aspects of the organization of the cat's visual cortex are innately determined.

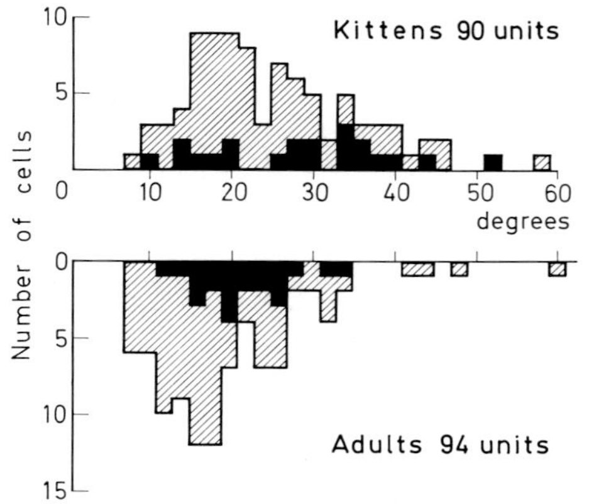

Fig. 8. A comparison of the distribution of orientation tuning widths in visually inexperienced kittens and in adult cats (from SHERK and STRYKER, 1976). To obtain the orientation tuning width of a particular neuron, a Gaussian function was fit to the response histogram obtained from moving bar stimuli presented at various orientations. The tuning width is given by the standard deviation of that function. The distribution of standard deviations for the two groups is also depicted. *Hatched regions* indicate cells in area 17; *filled regions* indicate cells in area 18. Height of each bin indicates the total number of cells with a particular tuning width

In the rabbit, there appears to be a lack of orientation-selective cells at birth; they develop after about 10–25 days (MATHERS et al., 1974). This development is largely maturational, since visually deprived rabbits have a proportion of orientation-selective cells equivalent to visually experienced rabbits.

In the monkey, WIESEL and HUBEL (1974) have observed neurons with normal orientation selectivity in two neonates with only binocular diffuse vision and in a normally reared 2-day-old neonate. Furthermore, the systematic progression of line orientation preferences that one finds in normal visually experienced monkeys is also found in young visually inexperienced monkeys. Thus, the systematic organization of line-orientation sensitivity into slabs of identical orientation, the slabs arranged in systematic order, is genetically determined.

While powerful genetic organizational factors are undoubtedly present, many studies on young cats and monkey (BARLOW and PETTIGREW, 1971; PETTIGREW, 1974; BUISSERET and IMBERT, 1975; BLAKEMORE and VAN SLUYTERS, 1975; WIESEL and HUBEL, 1974) are also in agreement that dark-rearing or binocular diffuse light-rearing diminishes the proportion of orientation-selective neurons and increases the proportion of visually unresponsive neurons. In the cat and monkey, we can conclude that the visual environment plays a *sustaining* role, since the proportion of innately orientation-selective neurons diminishes with progressive deprivation. It also plays a *constructive* role, since the proportion of selectively oriented neurons increases with progressive visual experience (PETTIGREW, 1974; IMBERT and BUISSERET, 1975; BLAKEMORE and VAN SLUYTERS, 1975; MOVSHON, 1976) relative to the proportion found in neonates.

V. Some Speculations Regarding the Constructive Effects of Visual Experience

PETTIGREW (1974) has suggested that it is predominantly the inhibitory connections which develop as a function of experience. Two examples of this can be cited. Regarding visual orientation, it appears that an orientation-selective neuron does not become more responsive to a particular orientation as a result of visual experience. Rather, a neuron *loses*, almost totally, responsiveness to the outside range of orientations to which it had responded suboptimally before. With regard to binocular disparity selectivity the same principle holds. Prior to visual experience, neurons respond to a wide variety of binocular disparities; furthermore, no disparity inhibits responsiveness below spontaneous activity levels. After visual experience, neurons lose sensitivity to the outside range of disparities and respond at levels below spontaneous rates when suboptimal disparities are presented. These observations strongly suggest that one effect of visual experience is the development (or potentiation) of inhibitory connections. This hypothesis receives further support from anatomic studies using electron microscopy to examine the development of synapses of the rat's visual system. In the superior colliculus it is particularly the endings presumed to represent inhibitory synapses (viz, axon terminals containing flat vesicles) which develop less fully if the animal is deprived (LUND and LUND, 1972).

This hypothesis of the effects of visual experience on the development of inhibitory connections is most germane to the present discussion, because it is precisely an inhibitory connection which transforms an *or* gate network into an *and* gate type and an *and-not* gate type (BARLOW and LEVICK, 1965). For a neuron to be selectively sensitive to a particular configuration of feature values, that neuron must be inhibited when stimuli are presented at other values. As BARLOW and LEVICK phrased it, there must be *veto-power* exerted by suboptimal feature values. Thus, inhibitory flanks confer configurational specificity onto visual cortex neurons.

The fact that the kittens in the GANZ and HAFFNER experiment cannot solve the configurational discrimination problem leads us to the following inference: it is the neurons which have veto-properties (because of the development of inhibitory connections through experience) that mediate configurational discriminations. For example, if a cat is to respond consistently to an upright triangle, some mechanism must respond to a horizontal line, but that mechanism must be vetoed by the presence of the triangle's apex when that apex appears below the horizontal.

Binocular visual deprivation experiments have yielded a set of parallel observations at the behavioral and neurophysiologic level, of significance for the ontogeny of visual form perception. We have seen that binocularly deprived organisms can solve visual discrimination problems dependent on the presence or absence of a feature on an innate basis, but not configurational problems. Similarly, kittens with extensive binocular deprivation have neurons in their visual cortex which are sensitive to the orientation of movement and show binocular convergence, but lack neurons that are selective to the orientation of contour and to binocular disparity. These neurons are characterized as lacking veto-power by suboptimal versions of the features to which they respond and operate like *or gates*. Thus both the perceptual behavior and neural behavior of binocularly deprived cats, are characterized by the law of heterogeneous summation, which states that if a complex stimulus releasing a response is fragmented into parts, the total number of responses released by the parts in isolation is the same as the number of responses released by the whole when the parts are presented simultaneously. The law has been shown to be valid in explaining instinctive behavior in a variety of nonhuman species (KLOPFER, 1962). In reviewing the evidence from a comparative viewpoint, KLOPFER has concluded that there is a shift in evolution from the law of heterogeneous summation to the operation of configurational principles of stimulus organization. When configurational principles operate, a stimulus fragment is insufficient to elicit behavior unless the other fragments are also present and optimally arrayed and interrelated. There is also an ontogenetic progression. BOWER (1966) has shown that human infants' responsiveness to stimuli obeys heterogeneous summation until about 12 weeks of age and then shifts to configurational principles. The literature on binocular deprivation, cited above, demonstrates that lack of visual experience causes a particular deficiency in discrimination problems whose solution is contingent solely on configurational cues. Conversely, one of the effects of visual experience is to develop the ability to solve configurational perceptual tasks.

Because of the vagaries of the stimulating environment, perceptual recognition based on simple flux or simple orientation cues is necessarily much more fragile and is easily disrupted when the conditions of illumination are altered. This is precisely what is found in generalization experiments on visually deprived organisms (GANZ, 1968; GANZ and HAFFNER, 1974). Analogous clinical observations are reported in humans whose congenital cataracts were later removed (SENDEN, 1932; see especially the cases of UHTHOFF, of HOME, and of HIRSCHBERG on pp. 151–153).

PETTIGREW's results (1974) suggest that visual experience develops the inhibitory flanks of cortical neurons. One *constructive* aspect of visual experience may be to change the gating action of these neurons from an *or* gate to an *and-not* gate, in which suboptimal features exert considerable inhibition. Thus, suboptimal features come to exert a veto-power (BARLOW and LEVICK, 1965). Presumably this renders the neuron configurationally selective and in turn permits organisms to respond selectively to configurations.

D. Postnatal Changes

I. Meridional Visual Deprivation and Enrichment

Although a preliminary framework of perceptual organization is evidently provided at birth, it is also known that the organism undergoes a period of structural plasticity postnatally. During this limited period (which starts at about

4 weeks and continues to approximately 14 weeks in the cat: BLAKEMORE and VAN SLUYTERS, 1974; HUBEL and WIESEL, 1970; WIESEL and HUBEL, 1963, 1965a, 1965b), the environment as it impinges on the organism's sensory receptors seems to refine, to sharpen the tuning, to enhance the operating efficiency of the system.

We know from developmental studies that although a full complement of neurons is present at birth in the visual system of cat or monkey, neuronal dendrification undergoes extensive development postnatally (GLOBUS and SCHEIBEL, 1967; SCHEIBEL and SCHEIBEL, 1964; CRAGG, 1975). Visual deprivation studies have shown that this period of intensive development corresponds to a period of environmental susceptibility during which sensory deprivation can have stimulus-specific trophic effects on the organization of neural networks.

In a study by HIRSCH and SPINELLI (1970, 1971) kittens (3 weeks old) were reared with goggles which exposed one eye to a vertical grid and the other eye to a horizontal grid for 8 h a day; the remaining hours were spent without goggles and in darkness. At 12 weeks, single units were recorded from the visual cortex. Of 40 cells whose receptive fields were mapped, half were optimally responsive to elongated stimuli. Normally, these elongated receptive fields manifest many different optimal orientations. But, in this experiment, only two orientations were found: vertical and horizontal. Moreover, 95% of the cells with elongated receptive fields were found to be oriented in accordance with the orientation to which that eye had been exposed, e.g., the eye that had seen a vertical grid now elicited activity with elongated receptive fields practically only in the vertical direction.

There was further evidence of remarkable isomorphism between the receptive fields and the grating patterns to which the kittens had been exposed. Fourteen of the units found had two or more elongated, parallel, excitatory regions within the receptive field. Moreover, the spacing of these parallel regions was comparable in visual angle of separation to the spacing of the bars in the stimuli. In other words, the excitatory receptive fields had a remarkable similarity to the configuration of the stimuli mounted in the masks. Two such neurons are illustrated in Figure 9. A change in connectivity had presumably occurred so that neurons responsive to subfeatures which were activated simultaneously retained or even enhanced their convergence on higher order cells. Presumably, subfeatures not activated together either failed to gain connections or actually lost connections, in converging on higher order cells. In this way, neurons of a higher order developed sensitivity to the overall pattern to which they were exposed, very much as HEBB anticipated (1949).

The results of HIRSCH and SPINELLI (1970, 1971) were confirmed by BLAKEMORE and COOPER (1970) in a very similar experiment (differing, however, in some important details). Kittens were reared in the dark except for a few hours of binocular exposure each day in a black and white striped cylindrical chamber. All neurons sampled were reported to have an orientation selectivity within 20° of the orientation to which the kittens had been exposed. STRYKER and SHERK (1975) have attempted to replicate BLAKEMORE and COOPER's experiment, using additional controls and computer-controlled techniques of receptive field mapping. They failed. They have, however, successfully replicated the HIRSCH and SPINELLI experiment, in which the selective exposure is monocular

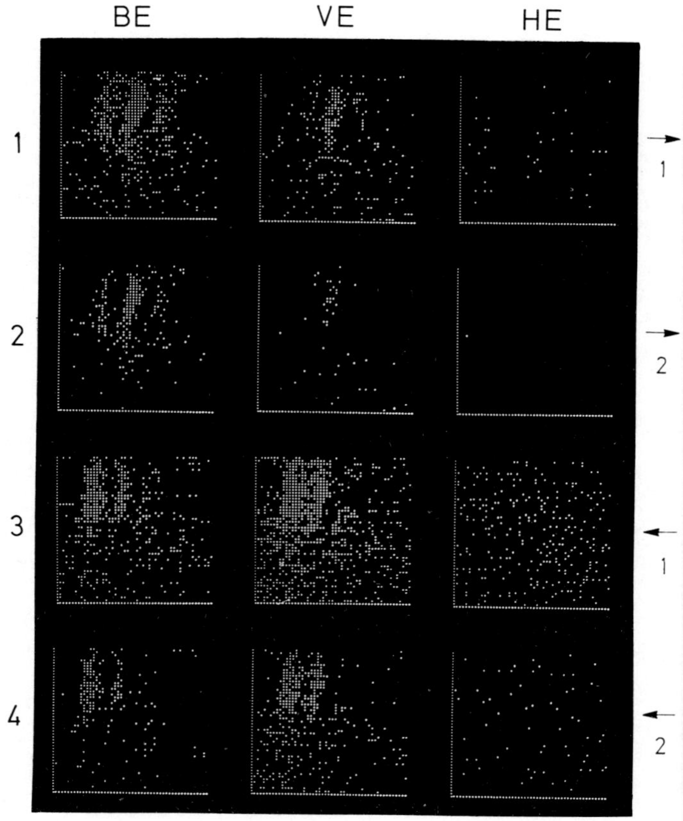

Fig. 9. Cortical neurons the receptive fields of which mimic the three bars viewed during development (from SPINELLI et al., 1972). A black spot some 2° in diameter moves across successive portions of a 25° × 25° field. When the neuron fires above a certain level, a point is displayed at the corresponding region of the rasters shown above. Thus, the white portions of the diagrams represent regions of *ON*-excitation and the dark portions regions of *ON*-inhibition. *BE, VE,* and *HE* represent stimulation with both eyes open, the vertical-stripe reared eye open, and the horizontal-stripe reared eye open respectively, during recording. Rows 1 and 2 were taken from one neuron, and rows 3 and 4 from another. Two levels of spike rate are shown for each cell. In rows 1 and 2 the stimulating dot moved right and in rows 3 and 4, left, these being the preferred directions of motion for the two neurons. Notice in both units the presence of three parallel excitatory bars

and in which the stripes are presented on a pair of goggles. BLAKEMORE (this volume) analyzes some of the possible causes for the failure to replicate BLAKEMORE and COOPER's study and cites a number of recent experiments where positive results using the cylindrical chamber have been obtained.

A study by LEVENTHAL and HIRSCH (1975), using the goggle-rearing technique, demonstrates an interesting interaction between genetic and experiential determinants of orientation selectivity. Kittens are exposed to horizontal lines in one eye and vertical lines in the other eye; later they undergo microelectrode analysis of their visual cortex. The results replicate the earlier finding (HIRSCH and SPINELLI, 1970, 1971): the vertical-line-exposed eye activates almost exclusively vertically oriented receptive fields, etc. However, if kittens are exposed to diagonal lines—45° upper-right obliques to the left eye and 45° upper-left obliques to the right eye—then horizontal and vertically oriented receptive fields are still obtained in substantial proportion, in addition to oblique receptive fields at the angle corresponding to the obliques to which that eye was exposed. This effect suggests a special genetic status for the cortical neurons with vertical and horizontal receptive fields. They are, for whatever reason, more resistant to environmental modification.

To summarize, the experiments on the effect of meridional visual experience on neural circuitry have demonstrated three somewhat different effects. The first is that experience enhances selectivity (HUBEL and WIESEL, 1963; PETTIGREW, 1974; IMBERT and BUISSERET, 1975; BLAKEMORE and VAN SLUYTERS, 1975). The visual cortex of the neonatal, visually naive kitten has a large proportion of neurons which are deficient in selectivity with regard to orientation and binocular disparity when compared to a normal adult cat (STRYKER and SHERK, 1975). Visual experience sharpens the receptive field to make it responsive only to a narrow range of values. This may be accomplished by the growth of inhibitory connections or by the potentiation of initially latent inhibitory connections. A second effect concerns the distribution of receptive field orientations. If the kitten's visual world is biased, such that only certain orientations predominate (HIRSCH and SPINELLI, 1970, 1971) then the receptive field distribution among visual cortex neurons will shift in the direction of that bias. A third effect was demonstrated by HIRSCH and SPINELLI (1970, 1971). In addition to an enhancement of selectivity, visual experience was also found to change the pattern of convergence, of what appear to be simple cells onto superordinate cells, in such a manner as to resemble the configurational feature-concomitances to which the organism was exposed. A similar result is apparent after rearing in an environment with randomly arranged dots (PETTIGREW and FREEMAN, 1973; BLAKEMORE and VAN SLUYTERS, 1975). Neurons are found to be unresponsive to lines, but to fields of dots. Again, a striking resemblance is observed between the details of the stimulating environment and the shape of the resultant receptive fields. Also related is CYNADER et al.' report (1973) that rearing kittens in a stroboscopically illuminated environment increases the proportion of neurons responsive to strobed stimuli. These studies suggest a constructive role of visual experience on superordinate receptive field neurons so as to mimic the concomitances of their visual experiences.

II. Perceptual Changes Following Meridional Visual Deprivation

When kittens were first removed from their striped cylinders and allowed to ambulate in a normal visual environment, BLAKEMORE and COOPER (1970) noted that the kittens were extremely inept, showed no visual placing when brought to the surface of a table top, and no startle response, observations reminiscent of many other visual deprivation experiments (Riesen and Mellinger, 1956; Baxter, 1966; Held and Hein, 1963; Wiesel and Hubel, 1963; Ganz and Fitch, 1968). Some effects however were characteristic for the meridional deprivation treatment. Blakemore and Cooper (1970) report that the kittens were virtually blind to contours perpendicular to the orientation they had been exposed to. For example, they showed no startle response to an approaching set of patterns whose lines were all perpendicular to the stripe orientation they had experienced. They showed visual placing only if the lines composing the landing surface were similar in orientation to the ones experienced in the striped cylinder. Muir and Mitchell (1973, 1975) report similar observations: Meridionally reared kittens do not follow well contours placed at 90° to the orientation to which they were exposed during rearing. Recovery measurements on these specific deficiencies in performance are not reported.

Hirsch (1972) has carried out some systematic measurements on form discrimination abilities in meridionally deprived cats. First the cats learned a form discrimination, such as a square vs. "X" discrimination, though just a bit more slowly than normals. Next they were exposed to equivalence testing. Presumably a cat would transfer well with its horizontal-stripes-reared eye (HE) to a horizontal lines vs. "X" test, but poorly to a vertical lines vs. "X" test. The reverse was expected when the cat was using its vertical-stripes-reared eye (VE). In fact, no differences were observed. It was also surprising to find that these cats showed fairly good interocular transfer between VE and HE. If for the experimental animals the visual world really looked different through the two eyes one would have expected poor transfer. Perhaps the most consistent differences were found in a line-orientation task. The cats were slightly poorer in discriminating line orientations at 90° angles from those they experienced during the deprivation period. The most plausible explanation for the small behavioral effects is that some recovery had occurred by the time the discrimination tests were completed. Blakemore and Mitchell (1973) have reported that one can virtually reverse the effects of meridional deprivation by placing a kitten in a striped cylinder with an orientation perpendicular to that used in the initial deprivation, as long as the second treatment is administered while the kitten is still in the period of environmental susceptibility (see also Blakemore and Van Sluyters, 1974; Movshon, 1976). Spinelli et al. (1972) have reported extensive changes following a recovery treatment administered over an even more extended period of time. The development of 53% binocular cells after recovery from an initial 0% immediately after the deprivation period suggests that certain aspects of cortical plasticity are prolonged. The development of a small number of neurons with more normal receptive field properties during the period of behavioral testing in Hirsch's study would probably have markedly reduced any perceptual manifestations. We know from ablation experiments that dramatic losses in simple form-discrimination tasks are obtained only when the last few percents of visual cortex are removed (Galambos et al., 1967; Chow, 1968).

Perceptual effects of meridional deprivation do show up, however, when more sensitive measures are employed. Grating resolution is one such measure. Muir and Mitchell (1973, 1975) reared cats in the same fashion as in Blake-

MORE and COOPER's experiment. The kittens received visual experience in a striped drum from 20 days–5 months of age. Some kittens received binocular vertical and others binocular horizontal stripe experience followed by normal visual experience from 3–6 months. The kittens were then trained to discriminate a square wave grating from a grey square. Their acuity measured 2.7–3.2 cycles/degree when the gratings were oriented along the meridian to which they had been exposed and 1.7–2.5 cycles/degree when the grating was oriented along the meridion they had not experienced. There is, therefore, a sizeable loss of meridian-specific acuity resulting from the deprivation period, though not as dramatic as the neurophysiologic effects. These deficiencies were still present after the cats had been in a normal visual environment for 30 months.

FREEMAN et al. (1972) have found comparable effects in human subjects. Astigmatism is a condition in which the eye's resolving power differs for the various meridians. Thus when a distant vertical grating is in focus, the horizontal one might become blurred. If this condition is left uncorrected in infancy and early childhood, such a person might be exposed more frequently to sharp contours of one direction than another as in the Hirsch-Spinelli and Blakemore-Cooper experiments. FREEMAN et al.' results are shown in Figure 10. In each frame the ordinate represents the highest spatial frequency resolved by the subject, while the abscissa represents the meridian of the grating. Frame A shows measurements from normal subjects, i.e., without astigmatism. There is no significant difference in resolution between the vertical and horizontal meridian, but as is commonly reported, resolution along the oblique is poorer. The astigmatics whose astigmatism was optically corrected (frames B and C) still showed residual resolution losses of 30 – 50%. Frames D and E (*dashed lines, empty circles*) show the results of an experiment in which gratings were generated directly on the retina of astigmatic subjects using laser-generated interference fringes. These gratings bypassed the optics of the subjects' eyes completely, yet similar meridionally specific resolution losses were still present. Hence, meridionally specific acuity losses of a nonoptical type are present in subjects who had astigmatic errors in refraction in their infancy. These striking losses of residual acuity are presumably caused by neural changes resembling the effects obtained by HIRSCH and SPINELLI and by BLAKEMORE and COOPER.

We see therefore from the effects measured by MUIR and MITCHELL (1973) and by FREEMAN et al. (1972) that meridional visual deprivation is associated with permanent losses in visual acuity. Indirectly, they provide further support for the presence of neural modifications of the type first measured by HIRSCH and SPINELLI and by BLAKEMORE and COOPER which result from meridional biases in visual experience early in life.

It has been repeatedly observed that human visual acuity is significantly worse for oblique contour orientations as compared to vertical or horizontal contours, the *oblique effect* (APELLE, 1972). The meridional deprivation effects just described might be thought an excellent explanation for the oblique effect, if our environment provides us with a preponderance of vertical and horizontal contours. LEEHEY et al. (1975) have measured infant acuity, using a two-alternative preferential looking technique (TELLER et al., 1974). They found a preferential fixation of vertical and horizontal gratings over obliques. This preference is

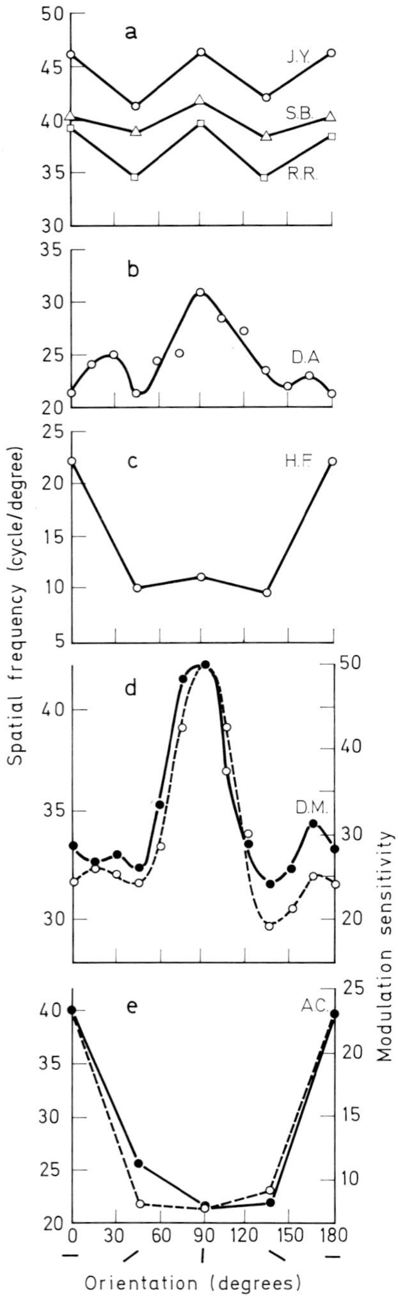

Fig. 10. Visual resolution of high-contrast sinusoidal or square-wave gratings that have different orientation (from FREEMAN et al., 1972). The vertical axis depicts grating sensitivity in terms of the maximum number of cycles per degree of visual angle that can just be resolved. *A*. Subjects with negligible refractive error show the typical resolution decrement of obliquely oriented gratings but insignificant differences between horizontal and vertical gratings. *B–E*. Highly astigmatic subjects whose refractive error is corrected still show a markedly different resolution for vertical and horizontal gratings. In *D* and *E*, the gratings are created directly on the retina using the sinusoidal interference fringes created by a beam of coherent light. The fact that the differences between vertical and horizontal grating resolution is similar between *B* and *D*, and between *C* and *E*, respectively, is conclusive evidence that the resolution differences cannot be ascribed to optical factors. The residual meridionally-selective resolution loss is presumed to be due to neural factors

found with broad gratings in the youngest infants (6 weeks) and progressively finer gratings in older infants, suggesting it reflects an acuity deficiency for obliques. Therefore, even the youngest infants show enhanced resolution of verticals and horizontals. It is unlikely that environmental effects cause the oblique effect in such young infants, since they spend so much of their time in supine positions. Thus, the oblique effect may have a genetic basis, as suggested by recent neurophysiologic analysis (LEVENTHAL and HIRSCH, 1975).

III. Perceptual Changes Following Deprivation of Binocular Synergy

HUBEL and WIESEL (1965) produced a divergent strabismus by cutting one of the extraocular muscles, the medial rectus, in newborn kittens. The kittens were reared with this condition for several months. Such treatment exposes both eyes to a normal visual environment with the only exception that there is little binocular correspondence. Subsequent casual observation of open field behavior did not reveal any perceptual-motor deficiencies. Neurophysiologic recording showed that the neurons were normal with respect to the shape and selectiveness of their receptive fields and normally responsive to visual stimuli. However, instead of the usual 80% of neurons with binocular convergence found in normal adult cats, only 20% were found. In this same study a group of cats were reared with alternate monocular deprivation. Only one eye was open one day, the other eye the next and so on, giving each eye extensive visual experience but without simultaneous experience with both eyes. This group showed even more drastic reduction in the number of neurons with binocular convergence than the strabismic group. Alternate monocularly reared kittens have been tested for interocular transfer of a luminous flux, a horizontal vs. vertical stripe, or an upright vs. inverted triangle discrimination (GANZ et al., 1972). They showed virtually perfect interocular transfer comparable to normal controls. SHERMAN (1971) reared cats with an experimentally induced strabismus and found substantial though not perfect transfer. Therefore, when simple discrimination tasks are used to estimate the transfer of visual information, extensive neurophysiologic deficiencies in binocular convergence are found to coexist with substantial transfer of visual information across the two retinogeniculate-striate mnemonic systems.

When the visual tests are less dependent on memory trace arousal and more dependent on binocular primary visual cortex function, then real deficiencies in the integration of the two eyes become apparent. MITCHELL and WARE (1974) have made use of the fact that many orientation-specific aftereffects caused by adaptation to gratings are transferred from one eye to the other in normal subjects (GIBSON and RADNER, 1937; GILINSKY and DOHERTY, 1969; BLAKEMORE and CAMPBELL, 1969; OYAMA, this volume). For example, a grating tilted slightly off the vertical clockwise appears less tilted after continued viewing. After such habituation, a vertical grating will even appear to be tilted counterclockwise. Both these aftereffects transfer interocularly to a substantial degree.

Presumably this transfer occurs in a normal subject because of the presence of neurons with binocular convergence. Were such binocular convergence to be missing or deficient, one might expect interocular transfer of adaptation effects to be weaker. MOVSHON et al. (1972) have reported that strabismic human subjects, who do not show stereopsis, also show a dramatic reduction in the interocular transfer of tilt aftereffects. Using a similar strategy, MITCHELL and WARE (1974) compared normal groups with those having poor stereoacuity (a measure of the resolution with which binocular disparity cues are used for depth information) and with a third, stereo-blind group. The latter group was unable to utilize binocular disparity information for depth perception. They found that the stereo-weak group had weak interocular transfer of tilt aftereffect, while the stereo-blind group had virtually no interocular transfer. There was a correlation of +0.86 between stereoacuity and the extent of interocular transfer of the tilt aftereffect. Thus, the proportion of neurons with binocular convergence controls the interocular transfer of habituation effects and, more importantly, the resolving power of binocular disparity for depth.

What is the critical period in the development of the human visual system, during which strabismus can cause a loss of stereopsis? BANKS et al. (1975) examined subjects who had had a convergent strabismus during different periods of their lives, followed by surgical correction. Interocular transfer of the tilt aftereffect was used to assess the degree of binocularity in their visual system. They found that strabismus begins to effect binocularity at the age of about 4 months. This period of susceptibility to environmental influence then peaks at about 20 months and decays exponentially thereafter until about 6 years. HOHMAN and CREUTZFELDT (1975) used a similar technique. They concluded that the sensitive period for the development of binocular neurons extends at least to the third year. Such sensory deprivation research tends to reinforce the inference of clinical research that in cases of congenital strabismus, early corrective surgery is essential for the development of normal or near-normal acuity and stereopsis (ING et al., 1966; KLEIFELD et al., 1974; TAYLOR, 1974). For example, TAYLOR (1974) reports that the deleterious effects of congenital esotropia (an inward deviation of one eye) on stereopsis can be eliminated completely if corrective surgery of the extraocular muscles is carried out during the first 2 months of life. If treatment is delayed beyond the period of plasticity, attainment of normal stereopsis is impossible.

Stereoacuity in the normal human adult, the binocular-disparity measure of resolution, is equal in magnitude to vernier acuity, viz., about of visual angle (RIGGS, 1965). Thus, stereo vision is so precise that it is only limited by the monocular resolution of the system. The fact that this is of the same order of magnitude as the diameter of a single foveal cone (POLYAK, 1957), attests to the degree of precision retained in the projection of spatial information from retina to visual cortex. It is not surprising that stereo vision proves very sensitive to even short periods of deprivation of binocular convergence. Normal visual experience is apparently essential in order to tune the visual system to its peak stereoacuity. At the neuron level, this probably involves not only a sharpening of disparity selectivity, as shown in Figure 7, but also a shaping of the receptive fields of the two eyes so that they are similar in orientation

(BLAKEMORE and VAN SLUYTERS, 1975). This may well be the major constructive effect on the visual system during the period of environmental susceptibility. If true, we might expect organisms without such extensive and acute stereovision to show much less environmental plasticity. For example, the rabbit which has a much smaller region of visual field with binocular overlap and therefore much more limited capacity for binocular disparity analysis has consistently demonstrated much less plasticity to a variety of deprivation treatments (MATHERS et al., 1974; CHOW and SPEAR, 1974; MIZE and MURPHY, 1973; GROBSTEIN and CHOW, 1975; VAN SLUYTERS and STEWART, 1974). Deprivation experiments among a wider range of mammals will reveal whether this relationship between extent and precision of stereoacuity on the one hand and degree of visual system plasticity on the other has general significance.

IV. Monocular Deprivation and the Problem of Visual Neglect

The evidence reviewed in this section demonstrates that monocular deprivation of visual patterns impairs all types of visual discriminations through the deprived eye: brightness, orientation, acuity, and geometric form. Monocular rearing also impairs interocular transfer of discriminations learned with one eye and tested with the other eye. If an animal is raised partly in total darkness and partly with monocular exposure, the larger the ratio of monocular exposure/binocular exposure, the greater the impairment in discrimination learning and interocular transfer. In an early review of the behavioral effects of visual deprivation (GANZ, 1968), we concluded that deprivation, in addition to its variegated sensory effects, also induces neglect of stimulus cues with a loss in the stimulus control of behavior. This is evidenced, for example, by a tendency to obtain shallow stimulus-generalization gradients following undiscriminated operant-response training. Later discrimination training establishes that the animals can learn to respond to the cue dimension in question. Therefore, one infers that initially the deprived animals paid less attention to an aspect of their environment, although capable of so doing. A loss in selective attention to visual cues, or visual neglect, is a recurrent theme in the behavioral effects of monocular visual deprivation. We conclude this from the following considerations: (1) The behavioral losses are more severe and dramatic than would be expected from the neurophysiologic effects. (2) Severe perceptual deficiencies are found in virtually all visual tasks employed, which in turn implies a suprasensory effect, in addition to the sensory deficiencies. (3) Forced use of the monocularly deprived eye reverses some of these perceptual deficiences without comparable changes at the neurophysiologic level, at least not at primary visual cortex.

1. Brightness Discrimination

Having gathered evidence that brightness discrimination is an innate ability and that it is impervious to binocular deprivation, one expects little effect from monocular deprivation (MD). Therefore it comes as a surprise that monocularly reared animals learn brightness discriminations with their deprived eye quite slowly (RIESEN et al., 1953; GANZ et al., 1972). Moreover, when monocularly reared animals are trained with one eye, they show only partial transfer of training to the other eye, whether from experienced to naive eye, or from naive to experienced eye. Indeed, some MD animals show no transfer. In contrast, normal controls, alternate monocular animals, and many binocularly deprived animals show essentially perfect transfer.

2. Form Discrimination

MD groups—including chimpanzees, monkeys, and cats—learn all varieties of visual form discriminations much more slowly with their deprived eye than with their experienced eye (CHOW and NISSEN, 1955; GANZ and FITCH, 1968; DEWS and WIESEL, 1970; VON NOORDEN et al., 1970; GANZ et al., 1972). An MD animal using its deprived eye on a visual form discrimination is inferior to a BD animal using its deprived eye. MD subjects learn even line orientation problems much more slowly than normals (RIESEN et al., 1953; RIESEN and MELLINGER, 1956; GANZ et al., 1972) while BD subjects, we have noted, learn these simple problems with little or no deficiency. In one study in which MD cats were trained on a horizontal-vertical discrimination, with their experienced eye alternating with their deprived eye on successive days, they still failed to acquire the discrimination with their deprived eye a thousand trials after they had acquired the discrimination with their experienced eye (GANZ and FITCH, 1968). This implies a greater dissociation between the geniculostriate-mnemonic systems of the two eyes than is found in either normals or binocularly deprived. The interocular transfer data discussed further below proves the two eye-systems are not totally dissociated however. We have found (GANZ et al., 1972) that after cross-suture treatment forcing use of the deprived eye, MD cats can learn a horizontal vs. vertical grid discrimination, but with great difficulty. In contrast, they are totally unable to acquire a configurational discrimination such as an upright vs. inverted black-outline triangle discrimination.

3. Amount of Monocular Exposure

In two studies (HUBEL and WIESEL, 1970; DEWS and WIESEL, 1970), the effect of varying the amount of monocular visual deprivation has been carefully evaluated both neurophysiologically and behaviorally. During the perinatal period when kittens are most susceptible to visual deprivation—approximately at 4 weeks—6 days of monocular deprivation is measurably detrimental to the pattern of binocular synergy of visual cortex cells and as little as 1 h will reduce binocular convergence (PETTIGREW, 1974; BLAKEMORE and MITCHELL, 1973). More monocular deprivation induces more deterioration, both neurophysiologically and behaviorally. For example, in a cat reared monocularly for $3^1/_2$ months (HUBEL and WIESEL, 1970, Fig. 9A) only 21% of the cells could be activated by the deprived eye, of which only 9% showed normal orientation and movement selectivity and scarcely any binocular cells remained. Such a cat could not learn a form discrimination and showed severe visuomotor deficiencies (Dews and Wiesel, 1970, cat #10). By contrast, in a cat given $5^1/_2$ weeks of monocular deprivation (Hubel and Wiesel, 1970, Fig. 7B) 39% of the cells could be activated by the deprived eye, 38% of which showed normal selectivity and a substantial number of cells showed binocular synergy. This cat (Dews and Wiesel, 1970, cat #13) could solve all visual problems presented, including the discrimination of a 1.5-mm gap, although not quite as well as with its normal eye.

Therefore the severity of behavioral deficiencies is monotonically related to the magnitude of the ratio: amount of monocular experience/amount of binocular experience. This strongly implies that the exposure of the experienced eye is somehow responsible for many of the behavioral deficiencies that the deprived eye shows, somehow inhibiting the input of the deprived eye.

The order of severity of deficiencies is paralleled quite closely on the neurophysiologic level. Monocular deprivation induces strikingly more severe losses in the ability of the deprived eye to elicit cortical activity than does binocular deprivation (Wiesel and Hubel, 1965a; Ganz et al., 1968). However, both BD and MD treatments have a deleterious effect on the orientation selectivity of cortical neurons (Imbert and Buisseret, 1975; Blakemore and Van Sluyters, 1975).

These dramatic effects of experimental monocular deprivation also have their parallel in the literature of clinical ophthalmology, the so-called *occlusion amblyopia* or *stimulus deprivation amblyopia*. Burian (1966) occluded the normal left eye of a 3-year-old boy for about 3 months as part of a treatment plan to force use of the (right) amblyopic eye. When the left eye was uncovered, it was found to be amblyopic (acuity = 6/60) and strabismic. Awaya et al. (1973) reported on 15 young children who underwent unilateral occlusion of the normal eye for approximately *1 week*, as treatment for palpebral entropion (an inversion of the edge of an eyelid). Fivefold losses in acuity, low amplitude visual evoked potentials (cortical leads), and marked exotropia were found in the previously covered eye. These reports suggest that the human visual system also undergoes a period of marked environmental susceptibility early in life. Monocular occlusion during the plastic period of the human visual system—the first 3 or more years (Banks et al., 1975)—is likely to be quite harmful both to monocular visual acuity and stereoacuity.

4. Monocular Deprivation and Interocular Transfer

How well do MD cats transfer a form discrimination learned with one eye to the other eye? In one study (Riesen et al., 1953) kittens were reared in total darkness. At 14 weeks a daily 30-min period of monocular patterned light was added. Monocular training of the experienced eye was begun at 17 weeks. Some subjects were trained on a brightness discrimination and others on a form problem. In a second study (Riesen and Mellinger, 1956) kittens were reared in darkness for 3 weeks and thereafter given 2 h daily monocular experience. At 3 months monocular training with the experienced eye was begun on a triangle vs. circle discrimination. They failed to transfer. On the initial interocular transfer trials the following observation was made: "[the monocular deprived experimental] ... animals showed disturbances in general visual behavior when use of the second eye was begun. They bumped into the partition or walls of the box, moved slowly, sometimes with long pauses ..." (RIESEN and MELLINGER, 1956, p. 168). Thus, failure to transfer visuomotor coordination was demonstrated. Of course, this complicates the interpretation of the transfer study, because even if recognition of the positive stimulus had occurred without visuomotor coordination through the deprived eye, that positive stimulus could not be used to guide behavior in the box. This criticism of the choice of an indicator response (MEYERS and MCCLEARY, 1964) is justified to a degree, but is not sufficient by itself to fully account for the lack of transfer. In a study on MD-reared chimpanzees (CHOW and NISSEN, 1955) (BD up to 6 weeks; then 22.5 h BD, 1.5 h MD up to 6–17 weeks) an approach response to the positive stimulus plaque was reinforced with food and any approach responses to the negative stimulus plaque were suppressed by association with shock. At various phases in the training, color, horizontal vs. vertical, and circle vs. triangle discriminanda were used. There was no substantial interocular transfer on initial testing when the discrimination was learned by the experienced eye and tested with the deprived eye, nor was there substantial transfer to the experienced eye of a problem learned by the deprived eye. However, the problems were always eventually acquired by the deprived eye with considerable savings. At least two conclusions can be drawn: (1) The absence of immediate interocular transfer in MD groups is not simply attributable to spatiomotor difficulties, because the Chow and Nissen study used a *go–no go* procedure in which different spatial locations were not involved. (2) The absence of immediate interocular transfer cannot be simply attributed to deficiencies of the deprived eye (for example, poor resolution, nystagmus, etc.), since transfer was lacking even when the deprived eye had learned the problem first. Presumably, the chimpanzee had overcome these sensory deficiencies by the time it had acquired the discrimination with its deprived eye. Therefore, the lack of interocular transfer must be due to some central deficiency involving binocular convergence. Furthermore, the absence of interocular transfer can not be attributed to simple degenerative effects of prolonged dark-rearing per se. This is because BD groups (see above) and AMD groups (see below) received equivalent *amounts* of deprivation but did show interocular transfer.

Twenty-five kittens were raised in one study entirely monocularly, up to the age of $3^1/_2$ months, the eyelids of one eye being sutured closed (GANZ and FITCH, 1968). Several aspects of perception were examined, including form discrimination in a Grice discrimination apparatus. The stimuli were a horizontal and a vertical rectangle 7° by 0.8° in visual angle, a size more than 10 times greater than the resolving power of the deprived eye as measured by an optokinetic technique in that same study. The kittens were run using only their experienced eye on one day, only their deprived eye on the following day, etc. With their deprived eye, they were still at chance level after 2000 trials. These results suggest deficiencies in interocular transfer more profound than in animals reared with 1–2 h per day of monocular experience.

In a subsequent series (GANZ et al., 1972), cats were again reared in an exclusively monocular environment for $3^1/_2$ months. The animals were then given pretraining on a brightness discrimination. MDE animals learned the discrimination to criterion first with their deprived eye and then learned the same discrimination with their experienced eye. MED animals were administered the problem in the reverse order. For present purposes, this brightness discrimination can be considered pretraining in which they learned to negotiate the discrimination box and to learn discrimination techniques with each eye separately. Then they were given the horizontal-vertical discrimination training monocularly and were tested for interocular transfer when criterion level performance was attained. The results are shown in Table 2. We see once more that the monocularly deprived animals learning with their deprived eye are considerably slower than equivalently deprived animals learning the task with their experienced eye.

Evidence for partial interocular transfer was also found. If we compare the MDE group learning with its experienced eye with the MED group learning with its experienced eye, it is clear that the MDE group is superior ($p<0.01$). Presumably, the MDE group has benefitted from having learned a line-orientation task with its deprived eye, prior to learning with the experienced eye. Since this represented the second discrimination task for each eye, all animals were proficient with general aspects of the Grice-box situation. Therefore, the transfer must involve quite specific visual form information. Similarly with the deprived eye, animals MED-1 and MED-10 achieve criterion in 60–80 trials with their deprived eye, whereas the MDE group requires 432.5 trials. Hence, in the MED group, the deprived eye benefits from the animals' previous training experience through the experienced eye. A later study (GANZ and HAFFNER, 1974) also provides definite evidence of interocular transfer, albeit not substantial transfer. The two retinogeniculate-striate mnemonic systems are dissociated, but not completely.

The presence of definite interocular transfer in animals with visual cortex neurons with virtually no binocular synergy may mean that the interocular transfer of information in a discrimination task can occur at levels beyond the primary visual cortex.

Table 2. Average number of trials to criterion on a grating orientation-discrimination in animals reared in various conditions of deprivation. (Task is administered first to one eye and then to the other) (from GANZ et al., 1972; Table III)

Deprivation group	N	First training eye		Second training eye	
(MDE) Monocularly	4	D:	432.5	E:	7.5
(MED) Monocularly	4	E:	42.5	D:	600.0
Binocularly	4	D:	95.0	D:	5.0
Alternating monocular	4	D and E:	82.5	D and E:	0
Alternating binocular	1	D and E:	70.0	D and E:	0
Undeprived control	1	E:	90.0	E:	0

D = initially deprived eye; E = initially experienced eye.

5. Proportion of Neurons With Binocular Convergence and Degree of Interocular Transfer After Monocular Deprivation

Evidence seems quite compelling (see Ganz et al., 1972) that for simple visual discrimination tasks, the amount of interocular transfer is *not* proportional to the number of binocular striate cortex neurons that can be visually activated. Note, in Table 2, for example, that the alternate monocular animals showed nearly perfect interocular transfer. Yet we know from other experiments (Hubel and Wiesel, 1965) that such treatment leads to tenfold reduction in the proportion of neurons with binocular convergence. The alternate monocular group has about the same proportion of neurons with binocular convergence as the monocularly deprived animals. Wiesel and Hubel (1965b) report that 9 of 199 recorded cells in MD cats showed some degree of binocularity (4.5%); Ganz et al. (1968) counted 11 of 83 cells (13%) with binocular convergence in MD cats. In alternate monocular animals, Hubel and Wiesel observed that 18 of 194 (9%) of the recorded cells had some degree of binocularity. Interocular transfer, however, is present, but very weak in MD cats while almost perfect interocular transfer is typically shown by alternate monocular animals. These results are consistent with those of Sherman (1971) who showed that strabismic cats—deficient in binocularly activated cells to an extent approximately equal to the groups just cited above—show good though not perfect transfer.

Therefore, the sheer number of neurons with binocular convergence is not a good predictor of interocular transfer. Approximately 10% is enough to mediate the perceptually rather simple, impoverished stimulating conditions that a psychologist typically administers in a discrimination task.

Why then does the monocularly deprived animal show poorer transfer than the alternate monocular animal both from deprived to experienced eye and from experienced eye to deprived eye? One reason may be that the alternate monocular cat's neurons with binocular convergence all have receptive fields which are fairly normal and similar in shape through the two eyes. By way of contrast, the monocularly deprived animal has binocular convergence neurons which are activated in a normal fashion by the nondeprived eye with elongated, discrete receptive fields, and by the deprived eye with diffuse, circular receptive fields. Since the shapes of the receptive fields are in effect the encoders of an organism's memory traces, if the shapes of receptive fields are different in the two eyes there will be no single S^+ which when presented to the transfer eye would unequivocably activate the memory traces laid down during training. This *scrambling of the codes* would then account for the weakened interocular transfer in MD cats in both directions (experienced to deprived and vice versa).

That monocularly deprived animals do in fact encode their visual world in a qualitatively different way in their two eyes has been shown (Ganz and Haffner, 1974). Kittens were reared with several months of monocular deprivation and then given a cross-suture treatment of equal duration to force them to use the initially deprived eye to its utmost. After training on a brightness discrimination and a stripe orientation problem, the cats were administered an upright vs. inverted triangle discrimination task. Each eye was given equivalence tests so as to analyze the cues used in the discrimination. The results are shown in Figure 5. Transposition tests B and C indicate that all the cats, normal controls, and deprived, were attending mostly to the bottom half of the figures. Transposition tests D, E, and F separated the initially experienced eye's performance from the initially deprived eye's performance. By manipulating local flux cues, GANZ and HAFFNER showed that for the experienced eye, form is the essential cue, whereas for the deprived eye, a geographic flux cue is the essential cue. Note in this regard that XL-10 and XR-5 have learned the identical discrimination quite differently, depending on which eye is used.

6. Analysis of Recovery in Monocularly Deprived Animals

An analysis of *recovery* from deprivation provides evidence that deprivation affects a selective attention mechanism. In one study (GANZ and FITCH, 1968) MD groups were split into two groups: a binocular recovery group and a reverse-suture recovery group. The binocular recovery group was given many months of experience with both eyes open. According to the selective-attention hypothesis, binocular experience should have relatively little effect on recovery. During binocular exposure the selective attention mechanism presumably continues to facilitate experienced eye-connected neurons. Since it is perfectly adaptive for the animal, there need be no switch to a facilitation of some deprived eye-activated neurons. In contrast, the afferent hypothesis states that only afferent stimulation is required for recovery of function. Hence, we would expect this group to improve since its deprived eye is open throughout the recovery period. In the reverse-suture recovery group, the experienced eye was covered and the deprived eye opened. According to the selective-attention hypothesis, this should cause the animal to start facilitating deprived eye analyzers if at all possible, since it is the only adaptive course available. The afferent hypothesis would also predict recovery in the reverse-suture group. Significant enhancement of the optokinetic response to fine lines was found only after forced use of the deprived eye and not when both eyes were left open for a period of time.

Binocular and cross-suture recovery treatments in monocularly deprived cats were compared using the optokinetic response (GANZ and FITCH, 1968). Lines of various thickness were moved in front of a kitten and its tendency to follow that line with slow ocular pursuit movements was measured as a function of line thickness. Figure 11 shows the acuity estimates for the deprived and experienced eye of 11 kittens. The optokinetic index, a measure of the kitten's tendency to follow a line in the direction of movement, is lower when the deprived eye is used. But note that for the deprived eye this index is lower by the same amount for all three line widths used: 143′, 9.3′, and 1.3′ arc. Therefore, deprivation has made the kittens less prone to follow objects with the deprived eye, whatever their width. It seems reasonable to classify this as visual inattention, at least in part, rather than a simple loss in visual resolution. Additional evidence supporting the visual inattention hypothesis derives from a comparison of the effects of binocular and cross-suture recovery treatments in that same study. In the binocular recovery group both eyes were left open during the

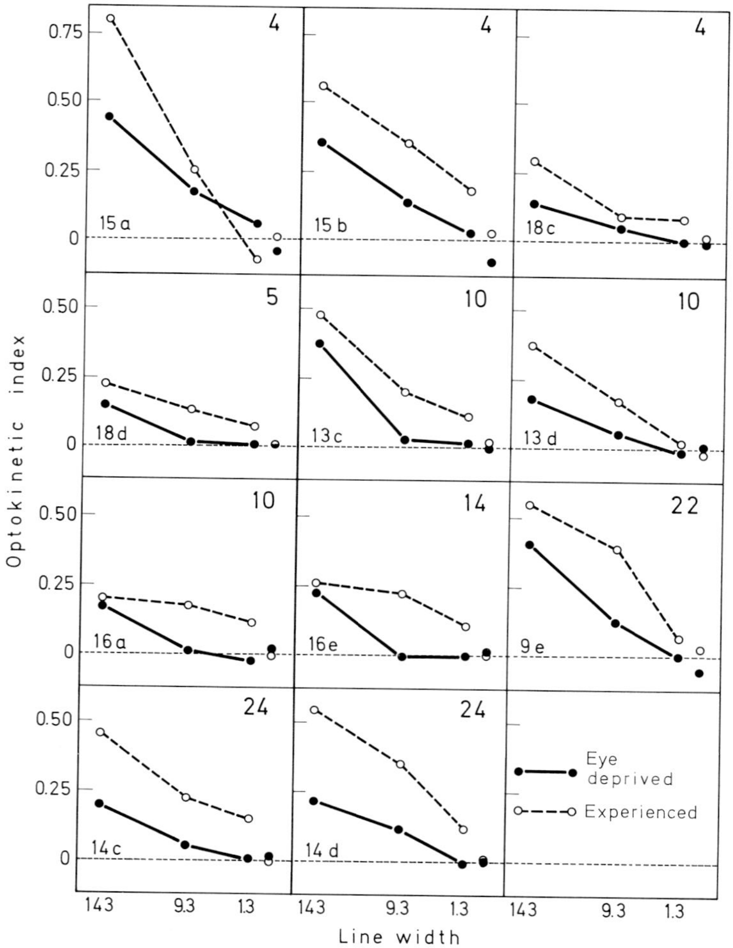

Fig. 11. Visual acuity in eleven-monocularly reared cats as measured by the optokinetic response (from GANZ and FITCH, 1968). The vertical axis represents a measure of the cat's tendency to follow slowly moving lines with its eyes (see GANZ and FITCH, 1968, for details). The horizontal axis represents the width of the line in minutes of arc. The *filled circles* and *unfilled circles* represent data from deprived and experienced eyes, respectively. Note that the tendency to pursue a moving object is weaker in the deprived eye for all stripe widths. The number in the upper-right corner of each frame refers to the number of weeks of the deprivation treatment

interval between the first and second optokinetic tests. The optokinetic index of the deprived eye was still inferior after the recovery treatment. In other words, the binocular recovery treatment was not effective.

Figure 12 shows that after cross-suture treatment the two eyes produce equivalent optokinetic indices. For animal 16e, the index improved in the deprived eye for all three line widths. The fact that the binocular recovery

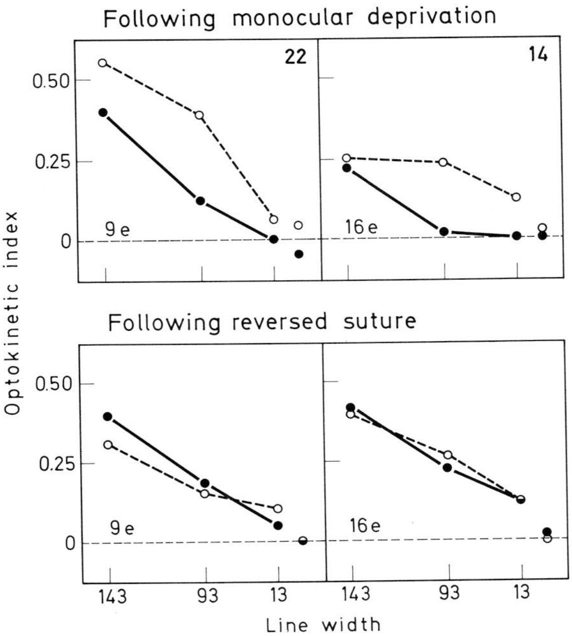

Fig. 12. Visual acuity in two monocularly reared cats as measured by the optokinetic response (from GANZ and FITCH, 1968). Figure legend as in Figure 11. Note that the recovery treatment involves cross-suturing. Following cross-suture treatment, the two eyes are more comparable in optokinetic index, the deprived eye having improved in four of the five measurements taken

treatment is much less effective than the cross-suture recovery treatment supports a stimulus-inattention explanation of the effects of monocular deprivation.

Another study (GANZ and HAFFNER, 1974) explores the effects of binocular vs. cross-suture recovery treatment on form discriminations. In this study both the cross-suture animals and the simple monoculars (given binocular recovery treatment) learned intensity and form-orientation discriminations at the same rate. However, when transposition tests were applied, obvious differences emerged in the way each group interacted with its visual environment. The stimulus training and the transposition stimuli are shown in Figure 4 along with the results obtained. Note that for stimulus pair A, in which merely the white and black stripes were interchanged, the performance of the two binocular recovery animals falls almost to chance levels, whereas the cross-suture recovery animals transpose perfectly. Similarly, with stimulus pair B, in which one white stripe was removed from the bottom of the horizontal grating, the binocular recovery group falls to chance, whereas the cross-suture recovery group transposes successfully, and so on, identically for most of the other transposition tests (the results of five more transposition tests are given in GANZ and HAFFNER, 1974). The performance of the cross-suture animals never falls below 95% on any of the transposition tests. These tests show that when monocularly deprived animals are given a simple binocular recovery treatment, they learn to solve the horizontal vs. vertical grating problem by responding to geographically localized light intensity cues and not to contour orientation per se. In contrast, monocularly deprived cats given cross-suture recovery treatment learn that discrimination by using actual contour orientations. CHOW and STUART (1972) have also observed form-discrimination abilities in cats given even longer deprivation treatments followed by cross-suture recovery. We interpret these results as indicating that cross-suture treatment is effective in forcing the animals to use the deprived eye connected neurons which are still left in their visual cortex. A monocular deprivation study by SPEAR and GANZ (1975) involving visual cortex ablation has established that the cross-suture cats are indeed using visual cortex for these discriminations. By implication, monocularly reared cats not forced to use their deprived eye, neglect the input of these neurons of which they have an equivalent number. So again, we are forced to postulate visual neglect as a major determinant of the perceptual effects of visual deprivation.

Further corroboration comes from studies (HUBEL and WIESEL, 1970; DEWS and WIESEL, 1970) in which pairs of cats were reared for comparable periods of monocular deprivation. One of the pair was tested for recovery with both eyes left open, while the second had its normal eye sutured closed during the recovery period. For example, cat #10 (DEWS and WIESEL, 1970) was first deprived monocularly for 4 months and then had both eyes open during an extended recovery period (testing of course was monocular). Severe losses in form discrimination and visuomotor coordination were evident when the deprived eye was tested. Neurophysiologically, as already noted above, the deprived eye, could activate only 21% of the visual cortex cells, only 9% of which showed normal orientation and movement sensitivity. Cat #1 was deprived 3 months and then the normal eye was closed throughout a recovery period that lasted over a year. This animal using its initially deprived eye showed excellent discrimination abilities and excellent visuomotor coordination. The animal discriminated a break in a 1.5 mm line. Of great interest is the fact that *cat #1, though it showed dramatic improvement in behavior evidenced no improvement in the neurophysiologic deficiencies:* the deprived eye could activate only 11% of the cells in the visual cortex, only 7% of which showed normal selectivity to orientation and movement. Thus, we see once more that:

1. Cats can perform complicated visual discriminations having only a small percent of their orientation selective neurons.

2. Binocular stimulation during the recovery period leads to minimal improvement in visual capacity by the deprived eye. This must mean that afferent stimulation of those selective neurons by visual forms is not sufficient to ensure their use by the organism.

3. Stimulation of only the deprived eye during the recovery period leads to high levels of behavioral recovery, evidence that the animal, *when it is forced to use its deprived eye for the solution of everyday visual tasks, makes a central contribution ("attending") to the activity of the neurons that are still present.* This central contribution spells the difference between functional utilization and functional neglect. Concerning the ability to solve visual discrimination problems—comparing DEWS and WIESEL's cats #1 and #10—it appears that this central contribution is in fact as potent a variable as the losses in orientation

selective neurons. An analysis of stimulus generalization behavior in stimulus deprived subjects further supports the issue of a central facilitating variable (GANZ, 1968).

What is the neurophysiologic basis of this central "visual neglect"? Direct evidence that the experienced eye is responsible for the tonic inhibition of the deprived eye in an MD cat is provided by KRATZ et al. (1976). In an MD cat, only about 10% of the neurons can be stimulated visually through the deprived eye. After the experienced eye was enucleated this proportion increases to 17–45%, within at most 12 h following the enucleation. This effect lasts over a 3–15 month period. Presumably, a larger proportion of neurons can be stimulated visually through the deprived eye following enucleation of the experienced eye, because the deprived eye is now released from inhibition. These results suggest that while not the only factor it is, nevertheless, a very potent factor. DUFFY et al. (1976) have obtained similar recovery effects in monocularly deprived cats after intravenous infusion of bicuculline, an GABA antagonist (GABA is a putative inhibitory neurotransmitter in the cerebral cortex).

7. Summary of the Effects of Monocular Deprivation

1. MD causes deficiencies in all aspects of visual performance — brightness, orientation, and form discrimination — as well as perceptual-motor orientation in visual space.

2. Interocular transfer of discriminations is much poorer in the monocularly deprived than in controls, but not entirely absent.

3. Performance on all these tasks is typically much worse in MD subjects than in subjects given binocular deprivation from birth. This suggests that it is the exposure of the *experienced eye* to visual patterns that is somehow responsible for many of the behavioral deficits that the deprived eye shows.

4. There are some striking discrepancies between the neurophysiologic and behavioral effects of monocular deprivation. For example, alternating monocular deprivation (AMD) induces about the same loss of binocular convergence as monocular deprivation (MD). About 10% of the neurons can be operated by either eye; 90% can be operated by only one eye. Yet, interocular transfer is virtually perfect in AMD and quite poor in MD groups.

5. The MD cats' surprisingly poor interocular transfer may be attributable to the fact that their visual cortex binocular convergence neurons exhibit different receptive field shapes, depending on which eye is stimulated. In effect, this would cause the wrong memory traces to be activated on an interocular transfer trial.

6. Two recovery treatments following monocular deprivation have been employed: (a) a binocular treatment in which both eyes are left open (b) a cross-suture treatment in which the deprived eye is opened and the experienced eye is closed. Several studies have shown extensive recovery of visual discrimination abilities after cross-suture treatment. However, stimulus equivalence testing demonstrates that abstract form perception is still absent. In other words, the cross-suture treatment teaches the animal to use the residual capacities it has more efficiently. These include visual resolution of thin lines, contour orienta-

tion, and some perceptual-motor spatial orientation. However, the animals remain unable to *recognize* visual forms in moderately altered contexts.

7. The greater efficacy of cross-suture compared with binocular recovery treatment implies that prior to recovery monocularly deprived animals neglect visual input to their amblyopic eye. This neglect, in addition to their visual form agnosia is reversible.

8. The neurophysiologic basis of visual neglect of the input to the amblyopic eye may involve inhibition of deprived eye-connected neurons by experienced eye-connected neurons.

E. General Conclusions

1. The perception of fairly simple visual form characteristics, such as the orientation of a rectangle or the brightness of a surface, is innate; it appears to be independent of experience in numerous species. Such perception need not be dependent on encoding of percepts into eye-tracking scan paths.

2. The perception of the configuration of a set of contours requires visual experience.

3. Striate cortex of cat and monkey contains a group of neurons showing true orientation selectivity and binocularity which is genetically determined. These neurons are innately organized into columns of similar orientation preference arrayed systematically along an orientation domain.

4. Normal visual experience during an organism's period of plasticity plays a *constructive* role by sharpening the orientation selectivity of striate cortex neurons as well as the sharpness of binocular disparity tuning. The accurate alignment of the orientations of these receptive fields the two eyes' neurons with binocular convergence is another important constructive role of visual experience. These effects in turn enhance vernier and stereoacuity.

5. Normal visual experience *constructs* superordinate neurons in the striate cortex and possibly other loci. These superordinate neurons may develop a receptive field geometry through visual experience which reflects the concomitances to which the organism is exposed. Behavioral observations in deprived organisms suggest that without such neurons, configurational perception is probably impossible.

6. Visual experience also plays a *sustaining* role, helping neurons mature according to their genetic determinants.

7. A genetic basis for a privileged status of neurons may exist, the receptive fields of which are oriented vertically or horizontally over oblique orientations. This may account for the so-called oblique-effect found psychophysically even in very young infants.

8. Monocular deprivation, over and beyond the sensory deficiencies it induces, causes organisms to underutilize their remaining deprived eye activated striate cortex neurons.

References

Aarons, L., Halasz, H.K., Risen, A.H.: Interocular transfer of visual intensity discrimination after ablation of striate cortex in dark reared kittens. J. Comp. Physiol. Psychol. **56**, 196–199 (1963).

Ahrens, R.: Beiträge zur Entwicklung des Physiognomie- und Mimikerkennens. Z. f. Exp. Angew. Psychol. **2**, 599–633 (1954).

•Apelle, S.: Perception and discrimination as a function of stimulus orientation: the "oblique effect" in man and animals. Psychol. Bull. **78**, 266–278 (1972).

Awaya, S., Miyake, Y., Imaizaki, Y., Shiose, Y., Kanda, T., Komuno, K.: Amblyopia in man suggestive of stimulus deprivation amblyopia. Jpn. J. Ophthalmol. **17**, 69–82 (1973).

Banks, M.S., Aslin, R.N., Letson, R.D.: Sensitive period for the development of human binocular vision. Science **190**, 675–677 (1975).

•Barlow, H.B.: Visual experience and cortical development. Nature **258**, 199–204 (1975).

Barlow, H.B., Levick, W.R.: The mechanism of directionally sensitive units in rabbit's retina. J. Physiol. **178**, 477–504 (1965)

Barlow, H.B., Pettigrew, J.D.: Lack of specificity of neurons in the visual cortex of young kittens. J. Physiol. **218**, 98P–100P (1971)

Baxter, B.L.: Effect of visual deprivation during postnatal maturation on the electroencephalogram of the cat. Exp. Neurol. **14**, 224–237 (1966)

Beers, D.: Return of vision and other observations in transplanted amphibian eyes. Proc. Soc. Exp. Biol. **26**, 447–479 (1929).

Berkeley, G.: Essay towards a new theory of vision. In: Selections from Berkeley. Fraser, A.C., (ed.), 6th ed. Oxford: Clarenden 1910.

Blakemore, C., Campbell, F.W.: On the existence of neurones in the human visual system selectively sensitive to orientation and size of retinal images. J. Physiol. **203**, 237–260 (1969)

•Blakemore, C., Cooper, G.F.: Development of the brain depends on visual environment. Nature **228**, 477–478 (1970)

•Blakemore, C., Mitchell, D.E.: Environmental modification of the visual cortex and the neural basis of learning and memory. Nature **241**, 467–468 (1973).

Blakemore, C., Sluyters, R.C. Van: Reversal of the physiological effects of monocular deprivation in kittens: further evidence for a sensitive period. J. Physiol. **237**, 195–216 (1974)

Blakemore, C., Sluyters, R.C. Van: Innate and environmental factors in the development of the kitten's visual cortex. J. Physiol. **248**, 663–716 (1975).

Bland, B.H., Cooper, R.M.: Experience in vision of the posterior neodecorticate rat. Physiol. Behav. **5**, 211–214 (1970).

Bower, T.G.R.: Heterogeneous summation in human infants. Anim. Behav. **14**, 395–398 (1966).

Buisseret, P., Imbert, M.: Responses of neurones in the striate cortex observed in normal and dark-reared kittens during post-natal life. J. Physiol. **246**, 98P–99P (1975).

Burian, H.M.: Occlusion amblyopia and the development of eccentric fixation in occluded eyes. Am. J. Ophthalmol. **62**, 853–856 (1966)

Chow, K.L.: Visual discrimination after extensive ablation of optic tract and visual cortex in cats. Brain Res. **9**, 363–366 (1968)

Chow, K.L.: Neuronal changes in the visual system following deprivation. In: Handbook of Sensory Physiology. Jung, R. (ed.). Berlin: Springer-Verlag 1973 Vol. VII/3A, pp. 559–630.

Chow, K.L., Nissen, H.W.: Interocular transfer of learning in visually naive and experienced chimpanzees. J. Comp. Physiol. Psychol. **48**, 229–237 (1955).

Chow, K.L., Spear, P.D.: Morphological and functional effects of visual deprivation on the rabbit visual system. Exp. Neurol. **42**, 429–447 (1974).

Chow, K.L., Stewart, D.L.: Reversal of structural and functional effects of long-term visual deprivation in cats. Exp. Neurol. **34**, 409–433 (1972).

Cragg, B.G.: The development of synapses in the visual system of the cat. J. Comp. Neurol. **160**, 147–166 (1975).

Cynader, M., Berman, N., Hein, A.: Cats reared in stroboscopic illumination: effects on receptive fields in cats visual cortex. Proc. Nat. Acad. Sci. USA **70**, 1353–1354 (1973).

•Descartes, R.: Discourse on the method of rightly conducting the reason, (1637). See Haldane and Ross.

Dews, P.B., Wiesel, T.N.: Consequences of monocular deprivation on visual behavior in kittens. J. Physiol. **206**, 437–455 (1970)

Duffy, F.H., Snodgrass, S.R., Burchfiel, J.L., Conway, J.L.: Bicuculline reversal of deprivation amblyopia in the cat. Nature **260**, 256–257 (1976).

Fantz, R.L.: Form preferences in newly hatched chicks. J. Comp. Physiol. Psychol. **59**, 422–430 (1957).

• Fantz, R.L.: The origin of form perception. Sci. Am. **204**, 66–72 (1961).

Fantz, R.L.: Ontogeny of perception. In: Behavior of Non-Human Primates: Modern Research Trends. Schrier, A.M., Harlow, H.F., Stollnitz, F. (eds.). New York: Academic Press 1965.

Fantz, R.L., Nevis, S.: Pattern preferences in perceptual cognitive development in early infancy. Merrill-Palmer Q. **13**, 77–108 (1967).

Fantz, R.L., Fagan, III, J.F., Miranda, S.B.: Early visual selectivity. In: Infant Perception: From Sensation to Cognition. Cohen, L.B., Salapatek, P. (eds.). New York: Academic Press 1975, pp. 249–345.

Festinger, L., Burnham, C.A., Ono, H., Bamber, D.: Efference and the conscious experience of perception. J. Exp. Psychol. Monogr. **74**, (4, no. 637) (1967).

Fifkova, E.: Plastic and degenerative changes in visual centers. In: Advances in Psychobiology. Newton, G., Riesen, A.H. (eds.). New York: Wiley 1974 Chap. 2, Vol. II, pp. 59–122.

• Freeman, R.D., Mitchell, D.E., Millodot, M.: A neural effect of partial visual deprivation in humans. Science **175**, 1384–1386 (1972).

Galambos, R., Norton, T.T., Frommer, G.P.: Optic tract lesions sparing pattern vision in cats. Exp. Neurol. **18**, 8–25 (1967)

Ganz, L.: An analysis of generalization behavior in the stimulus-deprived organism. In: Early Experience and Behavior. Newton, G., Levine, S. (eds.). Springfield, Ill.: C.C. Thomas 1968.

Ganz, L.: Orientation in visual space by neonates and its modification by visual deprivation. In: The Developmental Neuropsychology of Sensory Deprivation. Riesen, A.H. (ed.). New York: Academic Press 1975, p. 171–210.

Ganz, L., Fitch, M.: The effect of visual deprivation on perceptual behavior. Exp. Neurol. **22**, 638–660 (1968).

Ganz, L., Haffner, M.E.: Permanent perceptual and neurophysiological effects of visual deprivation in the cat. Exp. Brain Res. **20**, 67–87 (1974).

Ganz, L., Wilson, P.: Innate generalization of a form discrimination without contouring eye movements. J. Comp. Physiol. Psychol. **63**, 258–269 (1967).

Ganz, L., Fitch, M., Satterberg, J.A.: The selective effect of visual deprivation on receptive field shape determined neurophysiologically. Exp. Neurol. **22**, 614–637 (1968).

Ganz, L., Hirsch, H.V.B., Tieman, S.B.: The nature of perceptual deficits in visually deprived cats. Brain Res. **44**, 547–568 (1972).

Gaze, R.M., Jacobson, M., Székely, G.: On the formation of connections by compound eyes in Xenopus. J. Physiol. **176**, 409–417 (1965).

• Gibson, E.J.: Principles of Perceptual Learning and Development. New York: Appleton-Century Crofts 1969.

Gibson, J.J., Radner, M.: Adaptation, after-effect and contrast in the perception of tilted lines. I. Qualitative studies. J. Exp. Psychol. **20**, 453–467 (1937).

Gilinsky, A.S., Doherty, R.S.: Interocular transfer of orientational effects. Science **164**, 454–455 (1969).

Globus, A.: Brain morphology as a function of presynaptic morphology and activity. In: The Developmental Neuropsychology of Sensory Deprivation. Riesen, A.H. (ed.). New York: Academic Press 1975, Chap. 2, pp. 9–91.

Globus, A., Scheibel, A.B.: The effect of visual deprivation on cortical neurons. Exp. Neurol. **19**, 331–345 (1967).

Grobstein, P., Chow, K.L.: Receptive field development and individual experience. Science **190**, 352–358 (1975).

• Haldane, E.S., Ross, G.R.T. (translators). The philosophical works of Descartes. 2 Vols. New York: Dover 1955.

Hebb, D.O.: The innate organization of visual activity: I. Perception of figures by rats reared in total darkness. J. Gen. Psychol. **51**, 101–126 (1937).

Hebb, D.O.: The Organization of Behavior. New York: Wiley 1949.

• Held, R., Hein, A.: Movement-produced stimulation in the development of visually guided behavior. J. Comp. Physiol. Psychol. **56**, 872–876 (1963).

Hirsch, H.V.B.: Visual perception in cats after environmental surgery. Exp. Brain Res. **15**, 405–423 (1972).

• Hirsch, H.V.B., Spinelli, N.: Distribution of recptive field orientation: modification contingent on conditions of visual experience. Science **168**, 869–871 (1970).

Hirsch, H.V.B., Spinelli, D.N.: Modification of the distribution of receptive field orientation in cats by selective visual exposure during development. Exp. Brain Res. **13**, 509–527 (1971).

• Hochberg, J.: Attention, organization and consciousness. In: Attention: Contemporary Theory and Analysis. Mostofsky, D. (ed.). New York: Appleton 1970, pp. 99–124.

• Hochberg, J.E.: Nativism and empiricism in perception. In: Psychology in the making (L. Postman Ed.). New York: Knopf 1962, pp. 255–330.

Hohmann, A., Creutzfeldt, O.D.: Squint and the development of binocularity in humans. Nature **254**, 613–614 (1975).

• Hubel, D.H., Wiesel, T.N.: Receptive fields of cells in striate cortex of very young, visually inexperienced kittens. J. Neurophysiol. **26**, 994–1002 (1963).

• Hubel, D.H., Wiesel, T.N.: Binocular interaction in striate cortex of kittens reared with artificial squint. J. Neurophysiol. **28**, 1041–1059 (1965).

Hubel, D.H., Wiesel, T.N.: The period of susceptibility to the physiological effects of unilateral eye closure in kittens. J. Physiol. **206**, 419–436 (1970).

Imbert, M., Buisseret, P.: Receptive field characteristics and plastic properties of visual cortical cells in kittens reared with or without visual experience. Exp. Brain Res. **22**, 25–36 (1975).

Ing, M., Costenbader, F.D., Parks, M.M., Albert, D.G.: Early surgery for congenital esotropia. Am. J. Ophthalmol. **61**, 1419–1427 (1966).

Jacobson, M.: Development of specific neuronal connections. Science **163**, 543–547 (1969).

Kagan, J.: Attention and psychological change in the young child. Science **170**, 826–832 (1970).

Karmel, B.Z.: Complexity, amount of contour and visually dependent behavior in hooded rats, domestic chicks, and human infants. J. Comp. Physiol. Psychol. **69**, 649–657 (1969a).

Karmel, B.Z.: The effect of age, complexity, and amount of contour on pattern preferences in human infants. J. Exp. Child Psychol. **7**, 339–354 (1969b).

Karmel, B.Z., Maisel, E.B.: A neuronal activity model for infant visual attention. In: Infant Perception: From Sensation to Cognition. Cohen, L.B., Salapatek, P. (eds.). New York: Academic Press 1975, pp. 78–131.

Kleifeld, O., Fink, H., Schubach-Erz, E.: Ergebnisse der Schieloperation bei Kindern in Abhängigkeit vom Alter der Kinder bei Schielbeginn, der Dauer des Schielens und der Schielart. Albrecht von Graefes Arch. Klin. Ophthalmol. **189**, 165–170 (1974).

Klopfer, P.: Behavior and Ecology. New York: Prentice Hall 1962.

Köhler, W.: Dynamics in Psychology. New York: Liveright 1940, pp. 125–144.

Kratz, K.E., Spear, P.D.: Effects of visual deprivation and alterations in binocular competition on responses of striate cortex neurons in the cat. J. comp. Neurol. **170**, 141–152 (1976).

Kries, J. von: Empiricism and nativism. Appendix Section 6 (pp. 607–625) in Southall, J.P.C. (Ed.) Helmholtz Treatise on Physiological Optics. Vol. III. Optical Society of America, 1925. Translated from H. von Helmholtz Handbuch der Physiologischenoptik, Vol. III. Hamburg and Leipzig: Leopold Voss, 1910.

Lashley, K.S.: Persistent problems in the evolution of mind. Q. Rev. Biol. **24**, 28–42 (1949).

Leehey, S.C., Moskowitz-Cook, A., Brill, S., Held, R.: Orientational anisotropy in infant vision. Science **190**, 900–902 (1975).

Leventhal, A.G., Hirsch, H.V.B.: Cortical effect of early selective exposure to diagonal lines. Science **190**, 902–904 (1975).

Locke, J.: Essay Concerning Human Understanding. Philadelphia: Troutman & Hays 1853.

Lund, J.S., Lund, R.D.: The effects of varying periods of visual deprivation on synaptogenesis in the superior colliculus of the rat. Brain Res. **42**, 21–32 (1972).

Mathers, L.H., Chow, K.L., Spear, P.D., Grobstein, P.: Ontogenesis of receptive fields in the rabbit striate cortex. Exp. Brain Res. **19**, 20–35 (1974).

Matthey, R.: Récupération de la vue après greffe de l'oeil chez le triton adulte. C.R. Soc. Biol. (Paris) **94**, 4–5 (1926).

Maturana, H.R., Lettvin, J.Y., McCulloch, W.S., Pitts, W.H.: Evidence that cut optic nerve fibers in a frog regenerate to their proper places in the tectum. Science **130**, 1709–1710 (1959).

Maturana, H., Lettvin, J.Y., McCulloch, W.S., Pitts, W.H.: Anatomy and physiology of vision in the frog (*Rana pipiens*). J. Gen. Physiol. **43** (6/2), 129–177 (1960).

Meyers, B., McCleary, R.: Interocular transfer of a pattern discrimination in pattern deprived cats. J. Comp. Physiol. Psychol. **57**, 16–21 (1964).

Michels, K., Beven, W., Strassel, H.: Discrimination learning and interdimensional transfer under conditions of controlled visual experience. J. Comp. Physiol. Psychol. **51**, 778–781 (1958).

Mitchell, D.E., Ware, C.: Interocular transfer of a visual after-effect in normal and stereo-blind humans. J. Physiol. **236**, 707–721 (1974).

Mize, R.R., Murphy, E.H.: Selective visual experience fails to modify receptive field properties of rabbit striate cortex neurons. Science **180**, 320–323 (1973).

Movshon, J.A.: Reversal of the physiological effects of monocular deprivation in the kitten's visual cortex. J. Physiol. **261**, 125–174 (1976).

Movshon, J.A., Chambers, B.E.I., Blakemore, C.: Interocular transfer in normal humans and those who lack stereopsis. Perception **1**, 483–490 (1972).

Muir, D.W., Mitchell, D.E.: Visual resolution and experience: acuity deficits in cats following early selective visual deprivation. Science **180**, 420–422 (1973).

Muir, D.W., Mitchell, D.E.: Behavioral deficits in cats following early selected visual exposure to contours of a single orientation. Brain Res. **85**, 459–477 (1975).

Noorden, C.K. von, Dowling, J.E., Ferguson, D.C.: Experimental amblyopia in monkeys. I. Behavioral studies on stimulation deprivation amblyopia. Arch. Ophthalmol. **84**, 206–214 (1970).

Noton, E., Stark, L.: Scanpaths in eye movements during pattern perception. Science **171**, 308–311 (1971).

Pettigrew, J.D.: The effect of visual experience on the development of stimulus specifity by kitten cortical neurones. J. Physiol. **237**, 49–74 (1974).

Pettigrew, J.D., Freeman, R.D.: Visual experience without lines: effect on developing cortical neurons. Science **182**, 599–601 (1973).

Pettigrew, J.D., Garey, L.J.: Selective modification of single neuron properties in the visual cortex of kittens. Brain Res. **66**, 160–164 (1974).

Pettigrew, J., Olson, C., Barlow, H.B.: Kitten visual cortex: short-term stimulus-induced changes in connectivity. Science **180**, 1202–1203 (1973).

Polyak, S.: The vertebrate visual system. Chicago: Univ. Chicago Press 1957.

Regal, D.M., Boothe, R., Teller, D.Y., Sackett, G.P.: Visual acuity and visual responsiveness in dark reared monkeys (personal communication).

Riesen, A.H.: Plasticity of behavior: psychological aspects. In: Biological and Biochemical Bases of Behavior. Harlow, H.F., Woolsey, C.N. (eds.). Madison, Wisconsin: U. Wisconsin Pr. 1958.

Riesen, A.H.: Effects of early deprivation of photic stimulation. In: The Biosocial Basis of Mental Retardation. Osler, S.F., Cooke, R.E. (eds.). Baltimore: Johns Hopkins Press 1965a.

Riesen, A.H.: Effects of visual deprivation on perceptual function and the neural substrate. In: Symposium Bel Air-Désafférentation Experimentale et Clinique. Ajuriaguerra, J. (ed.). Geneva: George 1965b, pp. 47–66.

Riesen, A.H.: Electrophysiological changes after sensory deprivation. In: The Developmental Neuropsychology of Sensory Deprivation. Riesen, A.H. (ed.). New York: Academic Press 1975, pp. 153–170.

Riesen, A.H., Aarons, L.: Visual movement and intensity discrimination in cats after early deprivation of pattern vision. J. Comp. Physiol. Psychol. **52**, 142–149 (1959).

Riesen, A.H., Mellinger, J.C.: Interocular transfer of habits in cats after alternating monocular visual experience. J. Comp. Physiol. Psychol. **49**, 516–520 (1956).

Riesen, A.H., Zilbert, D.E.: Behavioral consequences of variations in early sensory environments. In: The Developmental Neuropsychology of Sensory Deprivation. Riesen, A.H. (ed.). New York: Academic Press 1975, pp. 211–252.

Riesen, A.H., Kurke, M.I., Mellinger, J.C.: Interocular transfer of habits learned monocularly in visually naive and visually experienced cats. J. Comp. Physiol. Psychol. **46**, 166–172 (1953).

Riesen, A.H., Ramsey, R., Wilson, P.: Development of visual acuity in rhesus monkeys deprived of patterned light during early infancy. Psychonom. Sci. **1**, 33–34 (1964).

Riggs, L.A.: Visual acuity. In: Vision and Visual Perception. Graham, C.H. (ed.). New York: Wiley 1965.

Rizzolati, F., Tradardi, V.: Pattern discrimination in monocularly reared cats. Exp. Neurol. **33**, 181–194 (1971).

Salapatek, P.: Pattern perception in early infancy. In: Infant Perception: From Sensation to Cognition. Cohen, L.B., Salapatek, P. (eds.). New York: Academic Press 1975, pp. 133–248.

Salapatek, P., Kessen, W.: Visual scanning of triangles by the human newborn. J. Exp. Child Psychol. **3**, 155–167 (1966).

Salapatek, P., Kessen, W.: Prolonged investigation of a plane geometric triangle by the human newborn. J. Exp. Child Psychol. **15**, 22–29 (1973).

Salzen, E.A.: Visual stimuli eliciting the smiling response in the human infant. J. Genet. Psychol. **102**, 51–54 (1963).

Scheibel, M., Scheibel, A.: Some structural and functional substrates of development in young cats. Prog. Brain Res. **9**, 6–25 (1964).

Senden, M. von: Raum- und Gestaltauffassung bei Operierten Blindgeborenen vor und nach der Operation. Leipzig: Barth 1932. Space and Sight. Heath, P. (transl.) Glencoe, Ill.: Free Press 1960.

Sherk, H., Stryker, M.P.: Quantitative study of cortical orientation selectivity in visually inexperienced kitten. J. Neurophysiol. **39**, 63–70 (1976).

Sherman, S.M.: Role of the visual cortex in interocular transfer in the cat. Exp. Neurol. **30**, 34–45 (1971).

Sluyters, R.C. van, Stewart, D.L.: Binocular neurons of the rabbit's visual cortex: effects of monocular sensory deprivation. Exp. Brain Res. **19**, 196–204 (1974).

Spalding, D.A.: Instinct, with original observations on young animals. Macmillan's Magazine **27**, 282–293 (1873) [Reprinted in Br. J. Anim. Behavior **2**, 2–11 (1954).

Spear, P.D., Ganz, L.: Effects of visual cortex lesions following recovery from monocular deprivation in the cat. Exp. Brain Res. **23**, 181–201 (1975).

Sperry, R.W.: Reestablishment of visuomotor coordinations by optic nerve regeneration. Anat. Rec. **84**, 470 (1942).

Sperry, R.W.: Effect of 180 degree rotation of the retinal field on visuomotor coordination. J. Exp. Zool. **92**, 263–279 (1943).

Sperry, R.W.: Mechanisms of neural maturation. In: Handbook of Experimental Psychology. Stevens, S.S. (ed.). New York: Wiley 1951.

Spinelli, D.N., Hirsch, H.V.B., Phelps, R.W., Metzler, J.: Visual experience as a determinant of the response characteristics of cortical receptive fields in cats. Exp. Brain Res. **15**, 289–304 (1972).

Stone, L.S., Cole, C.H.: Grafted eyes of young and old adult salamanders (*Amblystoma punctatus*) showing return of vision. Yale J. Biol. Med. **15**, 735–754 (1943).

Stone, L.S., Ussher, N.T.: Return of vision and other observations in replanted amphibian eyes. Proc. Soc. Exp. Biol. Med. **25**, 213–215 (1927).

Stryker, M.P., Sherk, H.: Modification of cortical orientation selectivity in the cat by restricted visual experience: a reexamination. Science **190**, 904–906 (1975).

Taylor, D.M.: Is congenital esotropia functionally curable? J. Pediatr. Ophthalmol. **11**, 3–35 (1974).

Tees, R.C.: Effect of early visual restriction on later visual intensity discrimination in rats. J. Comp. Physiol. Psychol. **66**, 224–227 (1968a).

Tees, R.C.: Effect of early restriction on later form discrimination in the rat. Can. J. Psychol. **22**, 294–301 (1968b).

Tees, R.C.: Luminance and luminous flux discrimination in rats after early visual deprivation. J. Comp. Physiol. Psychol. **74**, 292–297 (1971).

Tees, R.C.: Perceptual development in mammals. In: Studies on the Development of Behavior and the Nervous System. Vol. III. Neural and behavioral specificity. Gottlieb, G. (ed.). New York: Academic Press 1976, pp. 282–331.

Teller, D.Y., Morse, R., Borton, E., Regal, D.: Visual acuity for vertical and diagonal gratings in human infants. Vision Res. **14**, 1433–1439 (1974).

Tinbergen, N., Perdeck, A.C.: On the stimulus situation releasing the begging response in the newly hatched Herring Gull chick (*Larus a. argentatus*). Behaviour **3**, 1–9 (1950).

Walker, J.P., Walker, J.B., Kelley, R.L., Riesen, A.H.: Neurochemical correlates of sensory deprivation. In: The Developmental Neuropsychology of Sensory Deprivation. Riesen, A.H. (ed.). New York: Academic Press 1975, pp. 93–124.

Wertheimer, M.: Hebb and Senden on the role of learning in perception. Am. J. Psychol. **64**, 133–137 (1951).

Wiesel, T.N., Hubel, D.H.: Single-celled responses in striate cortex of kittens deprived of vision in one eye. J. Neurophysiol. **26**, 1003–1017 (1963).

Wiesel, T.N., Hubel, D.H.: Comparison of the effects of unilateral and bilateral eye closure on cortical unit responses in kittens. J. Neurophysiol. **28**, 1029–1040 (1965a).

Wiesel, T.N., Hubel, D.H.: Extent of recovery from the effects of visual deprivation in kittens. J. Neurophysiol. **28**, 1060–1072 (1965b).

Wiesel, T.N., Hubel, D.H.: Ordered arrangement of orientation columns in monkeys lacking visual experience. J. Comp. Neurol. **158**, 307–318 (1974).

Wilcox, B.M.: Visual preferences of human infants for representations of the human face. J. Exp. Child Psychol. **7**, 10–20 (1969).

Wilcox, B.M., Clayton, F.L.: Infant visual fixation on motion pictures of the human face. J. Exp. Child Psychol. **6**, 22–32 (1968).

Wilson, P.D., Riesen, A.H.: Visual development in rhesus monkeys neonatally deprived of patterned light. J. Comp. Physiol. Psychol. **61**, 87–95 (1966).

Wolff, P.: Observations on the early development of smiling. In: Determinants of Infant Behavior II. Second Tavistock Seminar on Mother-Infant Interaction, London, 1961. Foss, B.M. (ed.). New York: Wiley 1963.

Woodruff, A.B., Wickens, D.D.: The effect of severe restriction of visual experience on form perception in the white rat. Am. Psychologist **6**, 291 (1951).

Zablocka, T., Konorski, J., Zernicki, B.: Visual discrimination learning in cats with different early visual experiences. Acta Neurobiol. Exp. **35**, 389–398 (1975).

Zimmerman, R.R.: Analysis of discrimination learning capacities in the infant rhesus monkey. J. Comp. Physiol. Psychol. **54**, 1–10 (1961).

Zimmerman, R.R.: Form generalization in the infant monkey. J. Comp. Physiol. Psychol. **55**, 918–923 (1962).

Zuckerman, C.B., Rock, I.: A reappraisal of the role of past experience and innate organizing processes in visual perception. Psychol. Bull. **54**, 269–296 (1957)

Chapter 14

Form Perception and Related Issues in Blind Humans

YVETTE HATWELL, Grenoble (France)

With 3 Figures

Contents

A. Introduction

Experimental research with the blind is relatively scarce. While philosophers and psychologists have often speculated on the nature of the world of the congenitally blind, few systematic studies are based upon a coherent theoretic framework. Furthermore, it is often difficult to compare one study with another, due to the heterogeneity of the population samples studied. Blindness is a rare disorder in our geographic area. Consequently, the available subjects may vary in their chronological age, age at onset of blindness, duration of blindness, etiology, intellectual and socioeconomic status, education, etc. Even the degree of residual vision is variable, since "legal blindness" permits a level of visual functioning that allows some form perception (1/10th or 1/20th).

The most interesting theoretical problems deal with the analysis of form perception in totally blind subjects who can use only pure tactile perceptions, and in sighted subjects who use both visual and tactual information. For this reason the present paper will only be concerned with "true blindness," defined as total lack of vision or vision not exceeding light perception.

I. Visual Versus Tactile Perception

From the evolutionary point of view, tactile sensitivity is very primitive. Unlike all the other sense organs, which are located only in the head, tactile receptors are distributed throughout the surface of the body, and their density varies from one zone to another. The main characteristic of tactile receptors is that they are contact receptors and not distance receptors as is the case for vision. Consequently, the tactile perceptual field is much more limited than the visual field, and exploratory movements are necessary to increase it. Thanks to their mobility and their highly differentiated structure, the hands of primates, especially humans, are the main organs that enable the tactile exploration of the physical world.

It follows that in "active touch," kinesthetic components are always associated with purely tactile perception resulting from the contact of the skin with external objects, and this active tactile-kinesthetic process has been called "haptic perception" by REVESZ (1950). These kinesthetic components are absent in "passive touch," that is, in passive stimulation of the skin of a motionless observer.

At first glance, the visual and tactile modalities appear very different in their nature and in the kind of information they convey. It is therefore of great epistemological and psychological interest to know whether they are nonetheless governed by the same laws and whether they lead to the same spatial constructs.

These problems have been discussed by philosophers and psychologists for a long time. Are the spatial concepts of congenitally blind subjects the same as those of sighted subjects? To what extent do haptic perceptions contribute to the visual perception of space in sighted persons? Is there an autonomous haptic perceptual system, or is such a system always subordinate to the visual one?

A systematic comparison between haptics and vision is needed to answer these questions. Although the problem is an old one, such a systematic analysis has only recently taken place. The most comprehensive contributions in this field are those of REVESZ and of the GIBSONS and they will be briefly outlined to stress their originality and their differences.

In the early 1930s, REVESZ published a book that has had an important impact on tactile perception theory after being translated into English some twenty years later (REVESZ, 1950). Some of the main lines of his position are the following:

From a phenomenological point of view, the specific visual sensory world has nothing in common with the specific haptic sensory world, and no transition can exist between them. But vision and haptics are both spatial-perceptual systems. Even though in sighted humans the haptic system always seems to be dominated by the visual one, this haptic system is autonomous and is governed by its own laws. "Haptics creates its world through its own activity and its own laws, irrespective of whether in this process it makes use of the aid of the sense of vision." Thus, REVESZ's conception assumes that each sensory system is autonomous and that it may have original modes of functioning, as well as laws in common with other systems. If haptics is shown to function according to the same principles and laws as vision, it is not because vision transfers to it, but because some common principles govern this kind of partial perception. Of course, this does not exclude intersensory coordination and interaction, but for REVESZ, the widespread assumption that visual laws can be generalized to haptics without verification is highly questionable, since each system has to work with different sensory materials.

According to REVESZ, the main difference between vision and haptics is that vision is the realm of simultaneity while haptics is the realm of successivity. Visual perception is of the "immediate type" and an analytic process must occur further to attain the "structure" of the figure, that is, in REVESZ's language, the relationships among its elements. On the contrary, haptic perception begins with this analytic process, and only after successive explorations can the subject achieve a global perception of the object. These differences will lead to differences in perceptual modes of functioning. Haptic perception will be mainly *metric* since the relationships (position, distance, proportions, etc.) of the different elements can be grasped only by an active process of successive comparisons, and measurement is facilitated by using the fingers as units. On the contrary, these relationships may be apprehended in "one immediate act" in visual perception. For the same reasons, haptic perception will tend to establish types and schemata and will therefore have a "cognitive nature," while visual perception leads to a greater individualization of the objects perceived. Clearly, REVESZ's conception was influenced by the Gestalt psychology of visual perception of his time, to which he adds his own analysis of haptic perception.

The assumption that vision and haptics differ because the former is primarily simultaneous and the latter is sequential has been denied by GIBSON (1966). Like REVESZ, he recognizes that visual and haptic *sensations* are different, but since he does not regard sensations as the raw material leading to *perception,* these differences are not pertinent to the study of perceptual processes. Moreover, his analysis of the information available in visual stimulation has shown that the main higher-order variables are the invariant relationships that are conserved under specific transformations of the stimulus array (by movements of the objects or of the observer), and these transformations necessarily involve a temporal process. The visual stimulation concerned by an "immediate act of perception" lacks these main ordinal patterns and as a result does not carry all the spatial information available in a complete active perception. Therefore, active visual processes and haptic processes are both temporal.

Like Revesz, the Gibsons also assume a kind of autonomy of each perceptual system, but this autonomy does not imply any kind of modality-specific laws. Perceptual laws are the same in all senses and basically consist of invariances extraction, and differentiation of distinctive features of the stimulation (Gibson, 1962). Autonomy means only that the information carried by different kinds of stimulus energies (ambient light or mechanical energy) is equivalent. It is not necessary that one sense be validated by another, nor is it required that one sense derive meaning from another. Therefore, no channel of information is intrinsically more trustworthy than another, and generally, redundant information is provided by the perceptual systems when they are simultaneously in action.

The Gibsons' assumption of analogous perceptual processes (though sensations are different) in all modalities is clearly related to their general conception of a "primitive unity of senses" at birth, which evolves towards a greater differentiation among modalities during childhood (Gibson, 1969). Such a theoretic position has been greatly supported in recent years by the experimental work of Bower (1974) and other psychologists working on the perceptual behavior of newborn or very young infants.

Though the theoretic and experimental implications of Revesz's and the Gibsons' theories are relatively clear when applied to the study of tactile perception in the blind, few experiments have explicitly tested these hypotheses, and those that have, were all oriented toward the Gibsonian perspective.

Thus, the aim of this paper is to review the current literature on this topic while stressing the weakness of our knowledge with respect to crucial points.

II. Shortening of the Study

The present analysis will not cover the entire field of tactile and kinesthetic perception in the blind. It will be limited to what was earlier defined as active touch or haptics, that is, the tactile-kinesthetic process. Except for incidental reports, passive touch and pure kinesthetic perception that is not combined with an exteroceptive tactile contact will be excluded.

Form perception is usually distinguished from localization processes in the analysis of spatial behavior. This old distinction between the perception of objects and the perception of the place they occupy in the space has recently gained new support from contemporary research in neuropsychology, since form perception has been shown to function under cortical control while localization seems to be subcortically controlled (Schneider, 1967, 1969; Ingle, 1967; Trevarthen, 1968; Held, 1968; Paillard, 1974). As the title of this paper suggests, only form perception will be considered here, excluding all problems dealing with tactile localization and geographic orientation in the blind.

III. Major Topics in Research on Form Perception in the Blind

Contemporary studies have been designed primarily to answer the following basic questions:

1. Is there a direct and unlearned correlation between visual and haptic perception of shapes? Schematically, this refers to the controversy between the empiricist point of view of an acquired correlation between separate and independent sensory modalities, and the more nativistic conception of a primitive unity of senses which ensures immediate transfer of information from one modality to another. Applied to research on the blind, this problem has been approached by observing the behavior of congenitally blind subjects whose visual functions have been restored surgically after prolonged blindness.

2. Is there a tactile perceptual enhancement in congenitally blind (CB) subjects due to their prolonged practice with the haptic modality ("sensory compensation" and effect of training)? Or, on the contrary, is the haptic perception of the late blind (LB) and of the blindfolded sighted (BS) superior to that of the CB due to their previous visual experience (effects of "visualization")?

3. Are the spatial percepts of the CB similar to those of the normally sighted subjects (NS) using their visual perceptions? This question is related to the general problem of equivalence of information carried by the visual and the haptic modalities.

4. What are the major determinants of haptic form perception in the blind? In addition to the factors already mentioned, different aspects have been investigated, such as the role of perceptual exploration and scanning, memory factors, cognitive and developmental factors, etc.

The studies reviewed in this paper deal with these different problems and will be presented in the following classification. The first part of the chapter is devoted to the analysis of research concerning the general characteristics of form perception in the blind with special emphasis given to the above-mentioned questions 1, 2, and 3. The second part will discuss the role of some basic determinants (scanning, memory, cognition) that must necessarily be considered today in order to understand the nature of the perceptual processes in the haptic modality.

Since some critical reviews of the classic studies on the blind are already available (Axelrod, 1959; Hatwell, 1966), the present paper will be confined mainly to recent research.

B. Characteristics of Form Perception in Blind Children and Adults

The problem of the innate or acquired correlation between visual and tactile sensory information will first be discussed with the observations of some cases of CB subjects whose visual functions have been restored. Following the basic work of VON SENDEN (1932 and 1960), new data are now available and will be analyzed.

In spite of their considerable theoretical and practical interest, these studies can hardly lead to unquestionable conclusions, since methodological controls are often lacking. The main set of experimental research on the blind concerns, therefore, the haptic form perception of nonoperated subjects. As will be clear later, the observed results are often specific to the type of experimental situation used and the type of dependent variable measured. Consequently, the findings will be classified here according to the research material and procedures used (stationary versus rotating patterns, recognition versus reproduction methods, etc.) to avoid unwarranted generalizations.

I. Visual Restoration After Prolonged Blindness

What is the visual world of a congenitally blind person suddenly recovering sight at an adult age like? Is it possible for her to identify at first sight objects that she has known by touch only? To this famous question raised by Molyneux in the 18th century, the improvement of surgical ophthalmology and experimentation with animals have produced some answers. VON SENDEN (1960) has systematically analyzed the clinical observations of 32 cases of successfully operated blind adolescents or adults, and his conclusions are by now well known. The first visual impressions are "amorphous," that is, these patients cannot name or differentiate simple visual shapes, nor can they perceive their size, distance, number, etc. Only the distinction between figure and background seems possible at first. The general reaction is, to quote Pokrovskii (LONDON, 1960), "I see something but I don't know what." Moreover, the restored visual function requires a long and difficult training to be effective; sometimes, no improvement is observed even many years after successful surgical treatment.

More recent observations have confirmed these results (LONDON, 1960; VALVO, 1968; ACKROYD et al., 1974). Only GREGORY's patient (GREGORY and WALLACE, 1963) managed rapidly to transfer some elements from the tactile modality to the visual modality. Forty-eight days after a corneal graft, he was able to identify visually the capital letters of the alphabet, which he had previously learned to identify by touch. This case seems exceptional in the existing literature with respect to such an early intermodal transfer. ACKROYD et al. (1974) assume that this may be due to the high intellectual level of GREGORY's patient. However, one of the subjects that they themselves observed was also intellectually above average and was highly motivated. Furthermore, his blindness occurred at age 3, a condition which constituted a good prognosis for readaptation. Nevertheless, the visual training of this patient failed completely. According to the authors, this case confirms the importance of early visual stimulation on which HEBB (1949) has insisted. The results of recent neurophysiological work are also related to these observations, since they stress the need for early visual stimulation in order to maintain the integrity of the optical pathways and to allow the development of the specific feature analyzers in the visual cortex (HUBEL and WIESEL, 1970). While these latter studies only bear on animals, there is good reason to assume that they are relevant to humans, too.

If visual learning in the CB operated on after childhood is so difficult, it may be because the visual structures of the cortex, which render the perception of the spatial characteristics of objects possible, have not developed during the critical period, because some of the necessary sensory stimulation was lacking. This is what JEANNEROD (1975) concludes from an analysis of some of the observations of VON SENDEN and their relation to the available findings in current research on early visual deprivation in animals.

II. Haptic Perception of Stationary Patterns in the Blind

a) Sensory Discrimination and the Capacity of the Channel

The study of tactile discrimination thresholds in the blind and the sighted is directly linked to the old problem of sensory compensation. A popular belief holds that the systematic training of the tactile modality in the CB enhances their sensory acuity. In fact, despite some contradictory results (due to differences in method and population) experimentation has shown that, in most cases, there is no difference in tactile discrimination thresholds in the blind and the sighted (SEASHORE and LING, 1918; HAYES, 1934; AXELROD, 1959, though AXELROD's results are not totally clear on that point). Today, interest is concentrated much more on the information transmission capacity of the tactile channel. To what extent can the blind subject perceive and simultaneously process several tactile stimulations?

LAPPIN and FOULKE (1973) have attempted to answer this question by studying the processing of information arriving through one or more fingers. They asked subjects to explore 32 patterns each containing one or two raised dots and to discover as rapidly as possible the one-dot patterns. Different experimental conditions and different spatial arrangements of the patterns allowed for the comparison of the performances when using one, two, or four fingers simultaneously and when using one or both hands at the same time. The study involved only eight subjects (four LB and four BS, all adults). The results show that the one-dot patterns are more rapidly recognized in the "two fingers and two hands" situation, i.e., when both index fingers (or both major fingers) are simultaneously in use, whereas the performance is not as good in the situation "two fingers and one hand" (index and major fingers of the same hand used at the same time). The authors assume that the difficulty in processing simultaneous information deriving from the same hand comes from interferences and competition between nerve pathways ending in the same hemisphere, whereas in the "two fingers and two hands" situation, both hemispheres function separately as two independent centers.

This study shows some of the limitations of the tactile channel. Other recent research stresses the fact that this system may have capacities superior to those classically attributed to it. Thanks to the progress of modern technology, stimuli emitted by computers (very precisely controlled duration, position, intensity, etc.) are being used more and more frequently. Although some of the results obtained remain only indicative because of the small samples, the perspectives they open for further research are of great interest.

For example, BLISS and CRANE (1969) studied the span of immediate memory of the position and the number of stimulations applied on the hand. Using the partial report method, they found better immediate recall in one CB adult (8 points recalled out of 12) compared to 3 BS and 1 LB (4 points recalled). The authors observed that a tactile sensory register of the eidetic type exists (similar to the visual register). The capacity of this tactile register is 50% superior to that of the corresponding immediate recall, and decay occurs within 1.3 s. Thus, the capacity and duration of the tactile storage are inferior to those of the visual system, but the authors conclude that "they are impressed by the considerable potential of the tactile channel with regard to information processing."

We shall discuss further the astonishing results WHITE et al. (1970) obtained with the "tactile-vision-substitution-system," a sensory prosthesis that transforms the visual image of an object (explored by a TV camera) into a corresponding pattern of tactile stimulations. These tactile stimulations are received by the subject on his back through a cluster of 400 vibrotactors. Whereas the dorsal area is generally known to have poor tactile resolution, it appears that under certain conditions (when the subject himself can orient and move the camera and thus actively transform the stimulation), the resulting identification of this very complex tactile pattern is possible, in CB, LB, and BS subjects. Thus, the capacity of the tactile system, while more limited than that of the visual one, may be markedly superior to that attributed to it in the past.

b) Geometric Illusions

The existence of tactile illusions corresponding to the visual illusions is well known (BEAN, 1938; REVESZ, 1934), but a systematic analysis of them is more recent. Unfortunately, in most of the work, the CB and the LB subjects have not been differentiated, which greatly hampers the interpretation of the results.

Several authors have reported the Muller-Lyer illusion in the blind. HATWELL (1960a) notes the presence of this illusion in blind subjects (CB and LB mixed) aged 8–17 years, but the magnitude of the illusion is less than the corresponding one in the sighted. However, the distortion does not appear in the "dumbbell" variant (□ — □). TSAI (1967) also notes this Muller-Lyer illusion in blind (CB and LB mixed) subjects of 14–46 years and in equivalent BS subjects; in both groups, the extent of the tactile illusion is inferior to the visual illusion, but the error made by the blind is greater than that of the BS.

PATTERSON and DEFFENBACHER (1972) compared 10 CB (mean age 36 years), 10 LB (mean age 42 years), 10 BS (mean age 22 years), and 10 NS (mean age 22 years) and found the Muller-Lyer illusion in all groups. The authors confirm TSAI's finding that the error is lower in the BS than in the NS, but here, no difference appears between CB, LB, and NS groups.

Other illusions have also been observed in the blind. HATWELL (1960a) finds an overestimation of the vertical compared to the horizontal in the inverted T figure, a null illusion in the L figure, and an inverse illusion (overestimation of the horizontal) in the ⊢ figure in blind subjects (CB and LB mixed) age 8–17. The factor responsible for the illusion seems to be the position of the intersection points in this case, the horizontal being overestimated when compared to the vertical. PASNAK and AHR (1970) have found the Poggendorf illusion in the blind (no indication of age at onset of blindness) and in the BS, and here too, its magnitude is less than in the NS. On the other hand, HATWELL (1960a) does not find the Delboeuf illusion in a group of mixed CB and LB age 8–16.

The interest of these studies lies in the doubt they cast on the purely retinal or peripheral theories of visual illusions. Since the same distortions are observed in the tactile field, the origin of the error must be attributable in part to central processes. For TSAI, the blind, just as the NS, manage to get a "global impression" of the figure, while the BS use only the index of their preferred hand and consequently have a truly sequential apprehension of the figure. This would explain the smaller magnitude of the error in the BS. This hypothesis is taken up by PATTERSON and DEFFENBACHER who stress that the differences in the type of exploration between the blind and the BS stems from their different experience of the use of tactile stimulation. HATWELL proposes a similar interpretation, showing an increase in the vertical-horizontal illusion when the blind are asked to explore with the index finger only. She emphasizes the capacity of the tactile system to isolate some critical elements of the figure. This capacity to analyze and therefore to minimize the field effects would account for the reduction of the tactile illusion as compared to the visual one and would also explain the absence of the Delboeuf illusion in the blind.

It has been noted that the aforementioned studies rarely dissociate the CB from the LB. Such a distinction is, however, absolutely necessary if the validity of the "perspective theory" proposed by GREGORY (1963) is to be tested. Nevertheless, it should be noted that PATTERSON and DEFFENBACHER (1972) have found the Muller-Lyer illusion in the CB. This illusion is one that GREGORY attributes to the "constancy scaling factor" and to the projection in perspective of tridimensional space. This interpretation must, therefore, be partly reformulated, since it appears inappropriate in the case of the CB.

c) Haptic Form Recognition

Effects of visual experience on haptic perception. A large number of studies compare blind subjects (CB and LB) and BS subjects in tactile recognition of simple geometric shapes. When these shapes are tridimensional and/or relatively small, there is some concordance in the results: there is no difference between the groups studied for subjects ranging from age 8 years to adulthood (WORCHEL, 1951; HATWELL, 1959; EWART and CARP, 1963). With shapes of larger size and drawn in Braille relief, HATWELL (1959) finds a slight superiority of the blind over the BS, but the results of the CB and the LB are mixed. No difference appears between CB and LB (age 7–17) in a task of embedded figures of the Gottschaldt type, nor in the reconstitution of an incomplete figure cut out of cardboard (HATWELL, 1960b). GOTTESMAN's work (1971) is interesting because it concerns very young blind subjects, an age group rarely studied. He compares 15 CB and 15 BS aged 2–8 years in the recognition of familiar objects, of "topological figures" and of "euclidian figures" inspired by the work of Piaget and Inhelder (1947) and replicated by Page (1959). Here again, no difference appears between the groups. However, Gottesman stresses that his sample of blind subjects has been very severely selected and consequently, it cannot be representative of the total population of CB children.

With the complex tridimensional stimuli used by Gibson in 1962, Davidson et al. (1974) also find that CB and BS subjects aged 15–17 years are equally adept at a task of matching a standard to three comparison stimuli. However, the CB group performs better than the BS group when the comparison array contains five stimuli instead of three. According to the authors, these results show that an increase in task memory demand affects the BS, who are unpractised with haptic perception, more than the highly trained CB subjects.

Thus, no clear differences appear in the ability to recognize simple shapes in the CB, LB, and BS groups. Juurmaa (1973) hypothesizes that with very complex and unusual shapes, the BS will be inferior to the CB, because they are hampered by their lack of training in the tactile modality. For simple and ordinary shapes, the effects of their previous visual experience would compensate for their handicap on the practical level. This suggestion seems in line with Davidson and Whitson's results (1974).

The only field where a superiority of the blind appears clearly is in the perception of straightness. This was found by Hunter (1954) with a group of 20 blind subjects (CB and LB mixed) age 13–18, and has been confirmed by Davidson (1972) in an experiment more satisfying from a methodologic point of view—a group of 16 CB age 18 years gives estimations significantly more correct than those given by a group of 16 BS in the task first used by Hunter.

Comparison between visual and haptic recognition of forms. In the blind, just as in the BS, the tactile recognition of shapes is far more difficult than the visual recognition of the same shapes by the sighted using their eyes (NS subjects). The difference seems so obvious that there is relatively little work directly comparing visual perception and tactile perception. Hatwell (1959) finds that the visual performance of the 7-year-old NS subjects is superior to that of the BS and CB aged 12–14 in a task of simple shape recognition. Similarly, at age 7, the embedded shape task (Hatwell, 1960b) is successfully performed by 78% of the NS and only 27% of the blind (CB and LB mixed). Martinez (1971) also notes an important difference between CB, BS, and NS children in the identification of symmetrical figures.

Once this important quantitative difference in performance is recognized, it is necessary to discover whether fundamental qualitative differences exist between visual and tactile perception in the processing of information. Unfortunately, work in this area is rare and much remains to be done. Two pieces of research may, however, be quoted.

Pick et al. (1966) asked CB (aged 7–19 years) and BS (aged 4 years to adulthood) to judge if meaningless geometric shapes drawn in relief were "the right way up" or "upside down." Contrary to what Ghent (1961) found in visual perception using the same shapes, neither the CB nor the BS showed any systematic preference in the identification of the "upside down" shapes, and their choices were not different from those effected randomly. This would tend to show that, on this point, the tactile organization of shapes has different characteristics as compared to the visual one. However, in the same research, a group of blindfolded partially sighted subjects (age 6–21) showed the same preferences as the sighted subject of GHENT. The interpretation of this result is not clear.

Another research of PICK and PICK (1966) will be more thoroughly analyzed. In a Gibsonian perspective, these authors studied the differentiation of stimulus dimensions in the tactile field. They compared 37 CB aged 7–17 years, and 48 BS aged 6 years to adulthood in the task of letter-like form discrimination taken from the GIBSON et al. study (1962). In the PICKS' research, a standard form (raised metal lines) is presented simultaneously with the comparison form, and the subject is asked to judge haptically whether the two forms are the same or different. Each standard is paired with five comparison stimuli which are themselves constructed by introducing five types of transformations of the standard: line-to-curve changes, rotations and reversals, perspective transformations, size changes, and break-and-close changes. The main results concerning the CB and BS subjects are as follows:

In the CB and the BS groups, tactile discrimination is much more difficult than the corresponding visual discrimination observed in GIBSON's study. Adult BS subjects still make errors, whereas the visual task was successfully performed at age 8. This result corresponds with what has previously been said about the superiority of visual as compared to tactile performance.

The unique difference appearing between CB and BS in the relative difficulty of the five transformations is in the line-to-curve changes, which are easy for the CB while they present an intermediate level of difficulty for the BS. The authors judged this result to be unclear. It can now be related to the superiority of the CB in the perception of straightness noted by HUNTER and confirmed by DAVIDSON (1972).

When comparing the relative difficulty of the five transformations in the tactile performances of the CB and BS (in the PICKS' study) with the visual performances of the NS Ss (in GIBSON's study), rotation/reversals appear easier to detect tactually than visually, a result quite similar to that recently observed by O'CONNOR and HERMELIN in a somewhat different task (1975).

An interesting finding concerns the perspective transformation, which is the most difficult one for all groups, both tactually and visually. The PICKS do not comment on this result, although it does not seem fully compatible with GIBSON's original hypotheses. In effect, the aim of GIBSON was to analyze how the distinctive features of *graphemes* are learned by the child. Consequently, she has used "letter-like-forms" as standards and a set of transformations of these standards, some of them being meaningful and others not meaningful in our graphic system. For example, the rotation/reversal changes are transformations which modify the value of some graphemes (b and d) while perspective transformations never do so (A and A). GIBSON has found that rotation/reversals are differentiated at 5–7 years, whereas 60% errors are still observed at age

8 in the perspective transformations. She attributes this result to reading training, which renders the child sensitive to the pertinent transformations and not to the other ones.

This assumption is highly plausible. But if it is correct, what would be the predicted results in the tactile performance of CB subjects? The Braille raised-dots alphabet and the Braille graphic system of writing are quite different from ours. Practically, they exclude the mere possibility for the writer to introduce perspective transformations of a grapheme, since each letter is composed of a pattern strictly determined as to the number and position of its dots. Subjects exclusively trained in Braille reading and writing (as the CB are) should therefore be more sensitive than the NS to perspective transformations, which are "abnormal" in Braille, while they often occur in our writing and are to be neglected. Nevertheless, perspective transformations are found to be the most difficult for the CB as well as for the NS, and this is not easy to interpret in the Gibsonian perspective of perceptual learning of distinctive features of the graphemes.

However, a serious objection can be raised to these remarks. The PICKS have used the same standard forms as GIBSON, permitting a direct comparison between visual and tactile performances on the same material. But the mere significance of GIBSON's study is lost in the tactile transposition, since the tactile standards and their transformations are no more "letter-like-forms" for the blind and therefore are not comparable to "graphemes," so that any interpretation on this aspect is probably unjustified. It would be interesting to test GIBSON's hypotheses in the tactile perception of the CB with standards made of raised-dots patterns, which would be "Braille-letter-like-forms," paired with transformations that are meaningful or not meaningful in the Braille alphabet.

d) Form Reproduction and Reconstruction

This technique is more rarely used because of physical difficulties with its application. There are no (or very few) devices that enable the blind to draw directly in relief and, in any case, drawing is not a familiar activity for the blind. WORCHEL (1951) had blind subjects draw with an ordinary pencil but this technique is very questionable, since the subject has no means of perceptually controlling his graphic end-product. Even in using the Sewell Raised Line Drawing Kit, a device that enables the subject to directly draw raised lines with a ball-point pen, MILLAR (1975) has shown that the drawings of the CB are very different from those of the NS or the BS children of the same ages. These differences are explained by the failure of the CB to use the "translation rules" (or conventional symbolic equivalences), which the sighted learn very early when they have to draw (and thus to project) three-dimensional solid objects in a two-dimensional plane.

Consequently, the use of pegs and pegboards with blind subjects is more satisfying (DREVER, 1955) as well as the use of sticks or rods or other shapes to assemble or reconstruct (WORCHEL, 1951; HATWELL, 1959; O'CONNOR and HERMELIN, 1975; ROBIN and PECHEUX, 1976).

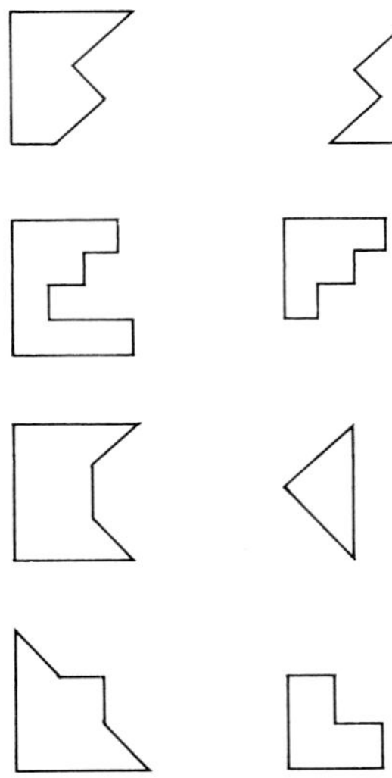

Fig. 1. Examples of shapes used in the O'CONNOR and HERMELIN study (adapted from: O'CONNOR and HERMELIN, Modality-specific spatial coordinates, Perception and Psychophysics, **17**, pp. 213–216, 1975)

With these various methods and with the use of simple patterns or of more complex ones to reproduce or assemble, the results are as follows:

α) Effect of visual experience on haptic performance. WORCHEL (1951), using a drawing and assembling method; DREVER (1955), using pegboards; and HATWELL (1959), using sticks, have found a clear superiority of the LB and the BS over the CB. In reviewing current research on the blind, WARREN et al. (1973) also stress the advantage that LB subjects seem to have in these tasks as compared to the CB. Nevertheless, the results of O'CONNOR and HERMELIN (1975) do not totally correspond with this assertion. In a task taken from Thurstone's P.M.A. test, the subject had to judge whether a cut-out shape placed at the right side of a piece of cardboard can or cannot fit into the gaps of a larger shape (a square with missing parts) presented on the left side. In some cases, the cut-out sections fit directly into the incomplete square; in other cases, it has to be mentally rotated 180° to fit into the square. No difference is observed in the total error scores of CB and BS subjects aged 13–14 years, and in both groups, the effect of rotated or unrotated presentations of the cut-out section is not significant (Fig. 1).

According to the authors, the disagreement of their results with those of WORCHEL in a similar task stems from the complexity of the shapes used here, whereas those of WORCHEL were simple and well-known geometric shapes. Moreover, it appears from these results that "the hand is less liable to take orientation into account as a crucial feature" since rotated presentations are not more difficult than unrotated ones.

In a second experiment, which was designed to study figure orientation only, independently from its shape component, the subject is presented a plastic hand in different orientations and in different axial rotations, and is asked to say whether it is a right or a left hand. O'CONNOR and HERMELIN find now that the BS are significantly superior to the CB, and conclude that when the task emphasizes spatial orientation and minimizes shape aspects, integration of the tactile input with a visual spatial reference system takes place in the BS and gives them the advantage, while a modality-specific coding is adopted when shape is salient.

In summary, the various studies have shown a superiority of the LB and the BS over the CB or, more rarely, equal performances. Let us note that nobody has ever reported better performance by CB subjects as compared to LB or BS in these tasks.

When superiority is observed, resulting from previous visual experience in haptic perception, it is generally explained by the possibility that these subjects have to "visualize," that is, to translate their fragmentary and successive haptic impressions into synthetic and well-organized visual images (WORCHEL, 1951). Visual imagery, in the strict definition of the term, certainly figures in the case of the BS, but its role in the case of the LB is more doubtful, some of them having lost their sight at a very early age (about 4 years). This point will be discussed further.

β) Comparison between visual and haptic performance. As in the form recognition research, visual performance is always superior to tactile performance. This appears, for example, in HATWELL (1959) and more recently in O'CONNOR and HERMELIN (1975), who note that NS groups are superior to both CB and BS groups in the shape-composition task as well as in the orientation task. A similar tendency is observed by ROBIN and PECHEUX (1975), but this research cannot be clearly interpreted, since the blind sample is composed of 18 "legally blind" subjects thus including a proportion (not specified by the authors) of partially sighted children.

Is there some qualitative differences between the visual performances of the NS and the tactile performances of the CB? It is generally found that the types of errors are approximately the same, except in some particular aspects. For example, in the O'CONNOR shape experiment, NS subjects make more errors when the shape has to be mentally rotated to fit into its complement than when it is in the same orientation, whereas CB and BS do equally well in the two situations. This observation could be related to PICK's result that rotation/reversal transformations are easier to detect in tactile than in visual performance.

III. Haptic Form Perception and Representation of Moving Patterns

In the situations now studied, subjects have to imagine the spatial position of a pattern in the course of its displacement in a defined direction or when it has stopped moving.

a) Effects of Visual Experience on Haptic Performances

Early versus late blindness. CB appear generally inferior to LB in these tasks again. That is what DREVER (1955) finds in a situation in which a pegboard containing patterns of two, three, or four pegs is rotated 180° in the horizontal plane, and the subject is then asked to replace the pegs in the holes they occupied before rotation (mean age of the subjects 14 years). A similar handicap of a group of eight CB (aged 8–11) as compared to age-matched LB, is observed by HATWELL (1966). In this research, the subject had to represent the relative position of three tied pegs differing in shape (and symbolizing "a train") when moving along a circular trajectory in the horizontal plane.

One result recently obtained by MILLAR (1976) is, nevertheless, not exactly in agreement with these findings. Her stimulus material consists of a transparent Perspex square bisected by a straight slot from the top to the base. The square is presented with the slot in the sagittal plane (0° position) and while the subject is handling the square, it is rotated clockwise in six different positions (45°, 90°, 135°, etc.). The child must then draw a raised line (recall method) corresponding to what he thinks is now the orientation of the slot after rotation of the square. In this task, no difference appears between five CB and five LB aged 10 years, while both groups make more errors in the oblique orientations of the slot than in the orthogonal ones.

CB versus BS subjects. In his rotating pegboard experiment, DREVER (1955) found no differences between CB and BS groups (aged 14 years). In a similar task, however, HUNTER (1964) noted different results: the scores of a CB group (aged 12–18 years) are significantly inferior to those of an equivalent BS group. The differences between CB and BS are also very marked in HATWELL's research (1966): a group of 24 CB aged 10–11 years gave scores inferior to those of 15 BS aged 7 years in the task where the subjects had to reconstruct the position of three tied pegs moving along a circular trajectory (Fig. 2).

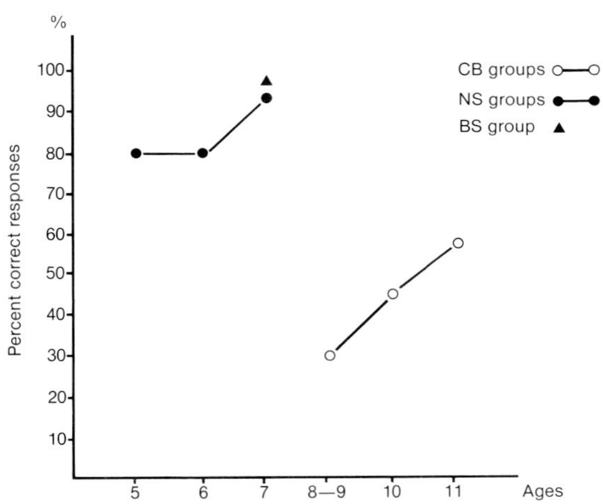

Fig. 2. Performances of CB, NS and BS children in a task of representation of the displacement of a pattern of three tied pegs moving along a circular trajectory (Adapted from: HATWELL, Y., Privation sensorielle et Intelligence, Paris, Presses Universitaires de France, 1966)

b) Comparison Between Visual and Haptic Performances

As in the case of form recognition and reconstruction of stationary patterns, visual performance is always highly superior to tactile performance. This clearly appears in Hatwell (1966); the scores of CB aged 11 years are approximately the same as those of NS aged 5–6 years (Fig. 2). Similarly, O'Connor and Hermelin (1975) find that the NS group score better than both the CB and the BS groups in the two experiments related, which also involve a kind of mental representation of moving patterns.

In summary, these data tend to emphasize the advantage given by visual spatial frame of reference in tactile perception and representation of displacements. Tactile perception, which is a contact perception, seems particularly ill-adapted to apprehend moving objects and consequently, the representation of the spatial transformations linked to displacement is generally much slower to develop in the CB than in the BS and in the NS.

C. Other Determinants of Haptic Form Perception

In the preceding section, it has been shown that the haptic perception of form in the blind is less efficient than the visual perception of the sighted subject and that, in some cases, it also differs from the haptic perception of the blindfolded sighted subjects. These facts need to be analyzed further to try to clarify the psychological mechanisms underlying these differences.

To understand the relative inefficiency of haptics, it is necessary to keep in mind the contact reception character of the tactile-kinesthetic system as opposed to the telereception of vision. In 1906, Sherrington assumed that the phylogenetic and ontogenetic evolution of organisms is marked by a primitive predominance of contact or proximal receptors, while distant receptors predominate in higher and in older organisms because of their considerably wider possibilities for conveying information about the external world. These assumptions are still present in some current research on sensory dominance in animals and humans, and hence they put special emphasis on the assertion that the main limits of haptic perception are related to its poor perceptual span.

Therefore, in analyzing the psychological consequences of the restricted field covered by tactile apprehension, some comprehensive data may be found to explain the performances observed in CB subjects. Contemporary research is mainly oriented toward the study of scanning strategies (since exploratory movements are the only way to enlarge the tactile perceptual field), and in the study of memory factors (since memory demands seem greater in the successive tactile perception than in the visual one). Finally, the influence of the cognitivist views in psychology has led several researchers to study the effects of cognitive factors on form perception and, more generally, on the spatial behavior of the CB subjects, assuming that perception is more or less dependent on cognition. These different directions of research will be outlined below:

I. Tactile Perceptual Exploration

Perceptual exploration holds a special place in contemporary psychology considering that scanning strategies provide two types of information. First, they indicate how the subject "interrogates" the stimulus and this interrogation itself reflects the focusing of his attention to some more or less critical properties of a given object; consequently, it gives some indication of how the subject understands and evaluates the task and its requisites. Secondly, the analysis of scanning strategies allows an approach to information processing, since the subject does not use all the data he collects or he does not use it correctly.

Most of the current research on scanning concerns visual perception, but after the impulse given by the Soviet psychologists and by the GIBSONS (1962, 1966, 1969) the interest was also directed toward tactile perceptual exploration.

The way in which tactile shapes are explored differently by the CB and the BS has often been observed. For example, this factor is quoted by some authors to explain the differences appearing in the magnitude of geometric illusions in CB, BS, and NS subjects. In the same manner, HATWELL (1959, 1960a) notes that the BS tend to use only the index finger of their preferred hand to explore raised-line shapes, while the CB use several fingers and both hands simultaneously.

But these were only informal and noncontrolled observations. More systematic data are now available, which unfortunately concern the BS more often than the blind. To our knowledge, the only experimental studies in this field are those of DAVIDSON (DAVIDSON, 1972; DAVIDSON and WHITSON, 1974; DAVIDSON, 1976) using film records of exploratory movements. His first research has already been cited and concerns the perception of straightness by CB and BS subjects aged 18 years. The stimulus consisted of a 19 mm-high, thick plastic strip cemented to a curve (or to a straight) edge of a heavy plastic base. The subject's task was to categorize five stimuli as "concave," "convex," or "straight." DAVIDSON outlines five classes of exploratory behavior: "grip" (curling three or four fingers over the front edge of the stimulus), "pinch" (holding the stimulus edge in a pincer between the thumb and another finger), "fingertip sweep" (placing one or more fingers held straight out on the top edge of the curve and sweeping back and forth), "span" (spanning the stimulus with the whole hand, with fingers spread out) and "trace" (holding one or two fingers perpendicular to the table and scanning across the front edge or the back edge of the curve) (Fig. 3).

The analysis of the results shows that the two groups do not use the same methods. CB subjects significantly exceed BS in the frequency of their use of the "grip" (60% for the CB and 25% for the BS), and the CB use four fingers significantly more often than the BS, whose exploration is generally limited to the use of two fingers. It has already been mentioned that in this task, CB performed better than BS subjects. Therefore, differences in the exploratory strategies are linked here to differences in the accuracy of perceptual judgments.

In another study, DAVIDSON and WHITSON (1974) find that CB subjects are more accurate than the BS as task difficulty increases and that marked

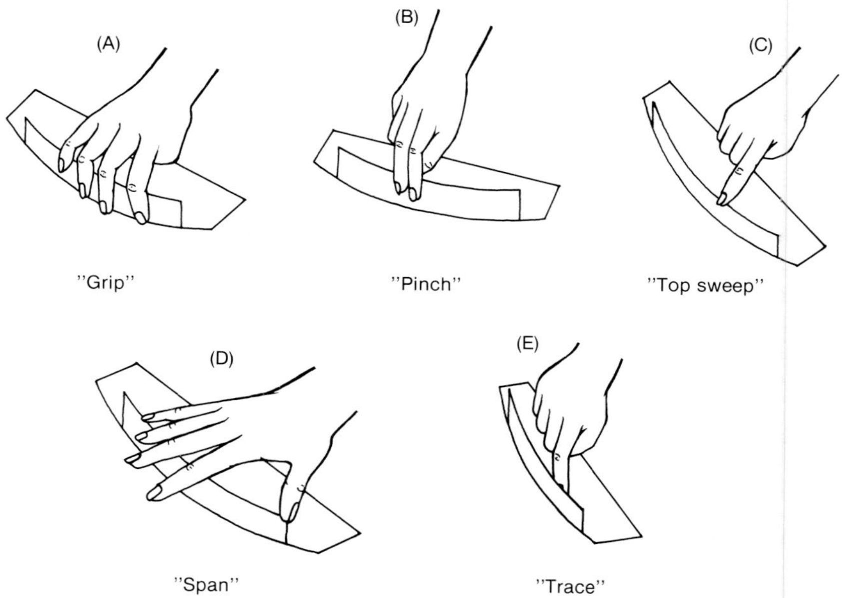

Fig. 3. Classes of scanning in Davidson's study (from: Davidson, P.W., Haptic judgments of curvature in blind an sighted humans, Journal of Experimental Psychology, 93, pp. 43–55, 1972)

differences in exploratory search exist between the two groups. Moreover, when the BS are restricted to use the blind's characteristic search strategy ("gripping"), improvement of their performance is observed.

Thus, the filmed analysis of the CB and BS explorations confirm the qualitative observations made previously. It seems, therefore, that the ability to simultaneously treat several pieces of information is less developed in the BS than in the CB, and that is why the BS prefer to use only one or two fingers to "trace" the contours of the object. The intense exercising of the tactile modality in congenital blindness improves scanning strategies and improves the ability to process information impinging simultaneously on several tactile receptors. However, except for the task of perception of straightness, the BS generally perform as well or even better than the CB. The advantage given by their previous visual experience seems, therefore, to compensate for their handicap in the simultaneous processing of tactile information.

These findings concern manual active exploration of a two- or three-dimensional stationary object. In a somewhat different perspective, the research of White et al. (1970) stresses, from an original point of view, the old distinction between active and passive touch. These authors have worked with a vision substitution display that converts a visual image into a tactile one. It consists of a TV camera acting as a sensory device, and a commutator that transforms the visual image of the camera into electric impulses activating a set of vibrotactors. The 400 vibrotactors are placed on the observer's back. Like the visual image from which it is generated, the converted tactile image is a two-dimensional projection of a three-dimensional physical object, and any movement of the camera over the stimulus modifies the number and the position of the vibrotactors in action. Such a system preserves, in the tactile stimulation, the spatial and temporal adjacencies that are, in GIBSON's view, the main higher-order variables of visual stimulation.

The first experiments with this apparatus have been classically oriented: the subjects (CB and BS adults) were shown one of three solid shapes (a circle, a triangle, and a square) in a stationary array (motionless camera) and were asked to identify which shape was present. The rate of error was very high. In further experiments, accuracy improved consistently and reached 100% after some trials when the subject himself was allowed to move the camera over the stimulus by means of a lever.

The importance of self-generated scanning movements of the camera is one of the most striking findings of that research. When the subjects could actively explore with the camera the objects to be identified, the CB performed as well as the BS and both groups rapidly reached high levels of accuracy in geometric form discrimination, slant perception, identification of complex common objects (a telephone, a model car). One subject, blind from the age of 4, exclaimed his surprise when he suddenly understood the visual concept of size constancy. Another observation is reported by the authors although the tactile stimulation with the motionless camera was localized by the subjects to their back, the same subjects exploring actively, localized the stimulation in front of themselves.

Concerning this last point, a further invaluable document is now available. GUARNIERO (1974) is an adult CB who served as a subject and has reported his perception experience with the Tactile-Vision-Substitution System and the main steps of his training on this device. Concerning localization of the stimulation, he notes that, even when moving the camera himself, sensations were first located by him on his back. Later, after prolonged practice, the objects "seen" with the TVSS "come to have a top and a bottom, a right and a left side, but no depth; they existed in an ordered bidimensional space, the precise location of which has not yet been determined."

According to WHITE et al. the observations they made support the Gibsonian view of perceptual learning which predict that when the tactile array contains the same ordinal patterns as the optic array, learning to respond to higher-order invariants in such tactile stimulation will be possible.

It must be noted that the role of active self-generated movements in the development of spatial perceptions has been stressed by HELD and HEIN (1963) in the visual modality. The performances of the CB and BS subjects with the TVSS bring considerable support to their conception of a correlation between afferences and efferences in perceptual processes.

Earlier in this paper, the limited capacity of the tactile channel has been maintained. From that study, it now appears that the ability to process multiple information simultaneously is considerably improved under conditions of active transformation of the stimulus array. This fact is indirectly confirmed by the work of BEAUCHAMPS et al. (1971). It does not concern blind observers, but the results obtained by BS subjects with the TVSS lead to a better understanding of the nature of tactile information processing. The aim of this study was to compare the effects on pattern recognition of two methods of exploring the stimulus—horizontal panning of the TV camera across static figures (geometric forms and block letters) and drawing the figure with a moving dot in the camera's field. For practical reasons of standardization of the tactile input, the panning and drawing procedures were both controlled by the experimenter; thus, the correlation between the self-generated sensor (camera) movements and the changes in the stimulus array was eliminated.

The results show that in BS adults, the drawing procedure produces fewer errors than the panning one. This means that when active exploration is not allowed, the sequential tactile information that is conveyed by the drawing procedure, is better handled than the simultaneous information conveyed by the panning method, a result often found in classic studies of tactile perception in the BS.

Again, using a motionless camera and different modes of presentation of capital letters, LOOMIS (1974) found also that spatial patterns that are sequentially traced or scanned by a linear slot are more recognizable by CB and BS adults than patterns that move themselves as a whole in the full field of the camera.

II. Memory Factors

The hypothesis that the relative inefficiency of haptics stems from the memory requisites linked to its sequential nature is an old one, but only recently has experimental research been carried out to test it, and the studies first concerned pure kinesthetic perception and not the tactile perception of form. These will, nevertheless, be briefly outlined here, since the hypotheses on which they rest have been extended to form perception.

POSNER (1967) has asked if the visual and kinesthetic short-term memory codes are of the same nature, that is, if they have the same central processing requirements. Consequently, he compared BS and NS adults in a task involving the retention of blind positioning movements. The results show that in the NS, reproduction of visually guided movements is accurate in a 20 s unfilled delay condition, while forgetting is greatly increased when an attention-demanding task is interpolated. On the contrary, no difference appears in the BS between the forgetting of blind movements in the unfilled delay condition and in the attention-demanding interpolated task condition. POSNER concludes that since the kinesthetic code seems unaffected by an interference task, it is probably not centrally processed.

The aim of SHAGAN and GOODNOW (1973) was to test POSNER's hypotheses. These authors assumed that the results observed by POSNER in the BS were due to the lack of practice of these subjects, and that the kinesthetic information in the CB, who are highly trained, will have the same coding properties as the visual-kinesthetic information of the NS. They tested 32 CB and 32 BS aged 17 years with the apparatus used by POSNER and the results support their hypotheses: CB subjects are sensitive to interference effects of the attention-demanding task, whereas the BS, as in POSNER's study, are not sensitive to this effect. Hence, SHAGAN and GOODNOW conclude that kinesthetic information is centrally processed in the experienced CB subjects, as the visual-kinesthetic information is centrally processed in the NS subjects.

Turning now to the effects of memory factors in form perception, the role of experience with haptic perception is also stressed by DAVIDSON et al. (1974). Studying the effect of increasing memory demand on haptic matching of shapes, these authors found that CB and BS adolescents perform equally well when the comparison array contains three objects (the standard plus two others) successively presented to the subject, while CB show significantly better scores with five comparison objects. The authors assume that in the CB, the perceptual experience of gathering information by hand improves scanning strategies and, incidentally, also improves memory encoding and storage.

Tactile memory encoding processes have also been studied by MILLAR (1974). She compared CB and BS children aged 9–10 years and 6 years in a task of nonsense shape comparison with four delays of retention and four activity intervals: unfilled delay, rehearsal by tracing shapes with the finger during delay, verbal distractor (counting backward) and movement distractor (fixing and nesting a series of differently sized barrels). The results show that in the two age groups, CB are faster (lower response latencies) and less accurate (more errors) than BS subjects. But both verbal and movement distractors have significant effects, and these effects appear in the CB as well as in the BS. Thus, the hypothesis that tactile retention is not centrally processed is not supported even in the BS. Experimental data also counterindicate a hypothesis of a modality-specific coding: Performance under movement rehearsal is not better than under unfilled delay and, moreover, verbal distractors are more effective than movement distractors. This shows that response deficits are due to central attentional demands rather than to movement demands. In conclusion, the fact that there is no interaction between previous visual experience and distractor effects suggests that tactile shape recognition processes do not differ substantially between CB and BS, even when they are young. The speed-accuracy trade-off found in the CB is interpreted by the author as a difference more in response strategy than in retention, since "sacrificing some accuracy for speed is more economical when dealing permanently with relatively slow inputs."

In summary, recent research on memory encoding and retrieval of tactile-kinesthetic perception tends to show that tactile training generally improves retention capacities and that tactile memory seems centrally processed and not modality-specific

III. Intelligence and Cognitive Development

In nearly all the studies reviewed here, mentally retarded subjects have been eliminated from the experimental samples on the basis of a verbal I.Q. Under this condition, correlation between haptic performances of the blind and their I.Q. is not significant (WORCHEL, 1951). Otherwise, it is generally admitted that congenital blindness, when it is not associated with other sensory (or motor) impairment or with brain damage, does not by itself affect the intellectual level as measured by classic verbal tests (HAYES, 1941).

Nevertheless, some studies have shown that, in fact, abstract functioning is often impaired in CB with normal I.Q. The handicap is very marked in spatial tasks using PIAGET's theoretic framework. This appears in HATWELL (1966) and more recently in MILLAR (1976), who adapted PIAGET's perspective task and found that the performances of CB aged 6, 8, and 10 years are lower than those of equivalent BS subjects.

Other studies have also shown that conservation achievement (substance, weight, number, etc.) is delayed in CB children when compared to NS (HATWELL, 1966; TOBIN, 1972; GOTTESMAN, 1973; DOHERTY, 1973) and when compared to BS children (GOTTESMAN, 1973; DOHERTY, 1973). Only CROMER (1973) found no difference in substance conservation in three matched groups of CB, BS, and NS children (12 subjects in each group, whose age range is 5;7 to 9;6). Commenting on the difference between his results and those of HATWELL (1966), CROMER stresses the effect of his matching procedure, which controls more variables than did HATWELL's one and especially the rural/urban status of the subjects. Nevertheless, citing TOBIN (1972), he recognizes that with a larger number of CB Ss and with a better age range (the age range of the 12 subjects of CROMER's study is manifestly too wide), "the achievement of full conservation might be delayed for the blind due to their impoverished perceptual schemes," while the onset of operational thinking may be the same.

CB children are also inferior to LB and BS children in classification tasks involving generalization and transfer (AXELROD, 1959). HATWELL (1966) observed also that CB children aged 6–10 years are inferior to NS in classification and seriation tasks using concrete material, while the level of the blind appears quite similar to that of the NS in some logical verbal tasks having the same formal structure as the concrete classifications and seriations in which the blind fail. Thus, in HATWELL's study, important discrepancies appear in the cognitive performances of CB children as compared to NS: They are seriously handicapped in spatial and conservation concepts, they have a more moderate impairment in logical tasks involving manipulation of concrete material, and they have quite similar performances to NS subjects in purely verbal logical tasks.

Other studies suggest that even in verbal tasks (Similarities and Vocabulary subtests of the W.I.S.C.), blind children appear to function at a more concrete level of conceptualization than the sighted (ZWEIBELSON and BERG, 1967).

When this cognitive development lag is observed, it is most often attributed to restrictions in the number and the quality of blind children's experiences and consequently to poorer interactions with the environment (AXELROD, 1959; HATWELL, 1966; DOHERTY, 1973). To what extent are some of the cognitive difficulties of CB subjects related to their haptic perceptions? It could hardly be assumed, especially in children, that perceptual and cognitive development are fully independent, but different explanations of the observed coincidence between perceptual and cognitive retardation could be given. For example, it could be argued that perceptual development is subordinate to cognitive development (PIAGET, 1961); hence the poor perceptual efficiency of CB children could be the result of their relatively poor cognitive efficiency. But, of course, the problem would remain, in this case, to explain the origin of such a cognitive impairment in the blind.

A counter hypothesis is assumed by HATWELL (1966), who considers that the perceptual impairment of the CB (and more generally the sensory and cultural deprivation that accompanies blindness), is responsible for their late achievement of PIAGET's stage of concrete operations. Her arguments are mainly based on the comparison of the results of the CB in the different Piagetian tasks she used, and on the fact that early blindness does not affect to the same extent these sets of cognitive areas (spatial, physical, concrete logical, and verbal logical operations), because perceptual and "figurative" components are differently involved in each one.

On the other hand, in spite of the fact that the GIBSONS have never been directly concerned with the problem of cognitive development in childhood, it could be hypothesized within their theoretical framework that the extraction of higher-order invariances in tactile stimulation is more difficult for the CB because of their restricted perceptual experience; consequently, their cognitive functioning will be further impaired to the extent that they lack elementary perceptual knowledge on physical objects' properties.

The discussion of this question clearly goes beyond the scope of this chapter. But whatever it may be, a systematic analysis of the relations between perception and cognition in blindness appears necessary for an understanding of the characteristics of form perception in blind subjects.

D. Discussion and Conclusion

The aim of this chapter is to analyze the findings that now seem well established on haptic form perception in the blind, and also to stress the inadequacy of our knowledge on some points. After having reviewed the literature available today, the two main directions in which the studies have been oriented will be considered separately.

I. Effects of Previous Visual Experience on Haptic Perception

It has been shown that CB children and adolescents very often appear impaired as compared to LB or BS, especially in spatial behavior. This point stresses the enhancement that previous visual experience brings to haptic perceptual organization.

To qualify the nature of this aid, it has generally been argued that an intersensory transfer takes place in LB and BS subjects, and this transfer has been described as "visualization" (WORCHEL, 1951; REVESZ, 1950). Visualization is the mental transformation of tactile data into visual images. Since visual imagery is richer and better organized than tactile imagery, the subjects who have the opportunity to realize such a transformation are at an advantage when compared to those who cannot.

That a tactile-visual intersensory transfer occurs in BS subjects is obvious. Several studies in sensory conflicts have shown the high dominance of the visual system in humans and its tendency to "capture" and even to bias all other perceptual data. The problem is, therefore, not to contest the validity of this explanation, but to analyze the psychological processes involved in it.

It must be remembered first, that subjects are generally classified as LB if their blindness has occurred after age 3 or 4. It is then doubtful that an 18-year-old person who has been blind since age 4 is still able to "visualize," because with time her visual imagery has become too poor to be useful in a pure translation process. Nevertheless, LB performances are generally superior to that of CB and do not differ basically from those of BS subjects. Hence, the psychological explanation must at least account for these two established points: 1) visual experience intervenes in the process of haptic perception in the LB and the BS and gives them an advantage as compared to the CB; 2) the aid given by the visual experience takes place early in infancy and is maintained further even if total blindness occurs at the end of this infancy period, thus excluding true visualization in adulthood. Let us examine these two points.

1. If it is not only an image-translation process, what is the mechanism underlying the action of vision on haptics? Psychologists do not fully agree today on the nature of intersensory relations in childhood. GIBSON (1969) and BOWER (1974) assume that progressive differentiation between modalities occurs from an initial undifferentiated state. On the contrary, according to PIAGET (1935), there is a progressive coordination between sensory spheres that are at first dissociated. For GIBSON, the main aspects of perceptual processes in both modalities (visual and haptic) are invariance extraction and progressive differentiation of the distinctive features of the stimulation, while for PIAGET (1961), richer and more coordinated perceptual schemes are formed as a result of progressive perceptual activities of exploration and comparison. In spite of these differences, it is assumed in both conceptions that the perceptual processes in the haptic modality and in the visual one are governed by the same laws, and thus have a common mode of functioning.

It could, therefore, be assumed that a general higher-order perceptual polysensorial system is constituted in normal children and that it functions as a totality. Each modality that participates in it will improve with any progress of the entire system and also with the progress of any other modality with which it is combined. The refined invariance extraction that visual stimulation allows may affect the tactile perceptual process in improving the active exploration of the tactile stimulus array in search of the corresponding invariants or distinctive features. A similar statement could be made in PIAGET's vocabulary (enhancement of the capacity of decentration and perceptual activities, etc.). This would mean that haptic perception benefits from all the perceptual learning that occurs in the visual sphere and reciprocally, that visual perception owes considerable improvement to its combination with haptics in early development, a point stressed by contemporary Soviet psychologists (ZAPOROZHETS, 1965). These gains then, concern the higher-order functioning of the perceptual system as well as the local translation processes, and these advantages would be lacking in congenital blindness.

2. Whatever it may be, the importance of early development in subsequent perceptual and cognitive development is stressed by the experimental results described in this chapter, and this leads us to the second point of our analysis. If early blindness is considered as a form of sensory deprivation, then the comparison between CB and LB clearly supports HEBB's view (1949) on that topic. The crucial role of infancy is also stressed by PIAGET (1935) for whom the early sensorimotor schemes that are constructed during this period constitute the true foundation of all further representational knowledge.

Is it then possible to say that the LB are advantaged, because they have had the opportunity in infancy to normally build up and coordinate these basic schemes, and that this advantage will permanently aid them when they have to build further, on a solely haptic basis, the conceptual knowledge of the physical world?

From the above review of research, it is clear that no answer can be given to this question, since no pertinent experimental work is available. The reader will certainly have noticed the total lack of studies dealing with haptic perception in blind babies, as well as those dealing with their cognitive development from a Piagetian point of view. The main general study of infant and preschool blind children is that of NORRIS et al. (1957), but it has been conducted from a different perspective (application of GESELL's Baby tests and Social Maturity scales). In fact, the striking progress of our knowledge about the perception of normal neonates and infants has not been accompanied by similar improvement in the study of congenitally blind babies. Only FRAIBERG (FRAIBERG et al., 1966; FRAIBERG, 1968) has given some fascinating and promising observations on the role of sound in object permanence and search behavior in some CB babies studied longitudinally.

Our conclusion will be therefore, that no serious interpretation of the differences observed between CB and LB children and adolescents could be given as long as the perceptual and cognitive development of CB babies remains so largely unknown.

II. Do Visual and Haptic Modalities Convey Equivalent Information?

Despite the great number of studies reviewed, a clear-cut answer cannot be given. To clarify the problem, a distinction has to be made between the quantitative aspects of modality equivalence, i.e., the absolute amount of information carried and processed by each modality, and the qualitative aspects, i.e., the nature of the information conveyed and that of the perceptual processes involved in each case.

From a *quantitative* point of view, vision obviously appears richer than haptics. What can be grasped in a few visual glances is in no way comparable to what can be gained in some similar "haptic glances." This impoverished contact with the environment could then explain why the haptic perception of the CB is always found to be markedly poorer than the visual perception of normally sighted subjects. But, as it has been stressed earlier, an intersensory process takes place early in life and consequently the visual perception of NS subjects, when studied separately, has itself already been considerably transformed and improved by its previous coordination with haptics. In fact, it is impossible to find any "true visual perceiver" similar to the "true haptic perceiver" as represented by the congenitally blind.

Hence, the comparison between the visual perception of the NS and the haptic perception of the CB is always a comparison between a complete and integrated polysensorial system and an incomplete and impoverished one.

With these methodological restrictions in mind, the analysis of the nature of the information carried by each modality (that is, the *qualitative* comparison between modalities) certainly remains a fundamental question. Of the two different conceptions evoked in the introduction of this chapter, that of REVESZ (autonomy and possibility of specific laws in each modality) and that of GIBSON (equivalence of the processes and of the information carried by each modality), which one is best supported by the experimental findings available?

Clearly, the original modes of functioning that REVESZ attributed to haptics have never been experimentally tested in modern psychologic research. Though REVESZ is often cited in bibliographic references, none of the reviewed authors has explicitly designed his experiments to validate or confirm REVESZ's conception, perhaps because REVESZ's analysis of visual perception seems outdated now.

Nevertheless, if one considers the data available today on haptic perception in the blind, the similarities with the known visual processes appear more numerous than the differences. Though haptic pattern perception in the blind is slower to develop than visual perception in the sighted, it has generally been found to follow the same lines of development. This appears, for example, in the analysis of the types of errors made by the CB in the different experimental situations. Of course, the similarities observed do not definitely confirm REVESZ's conception. Since most of the experiments have been planned to test quantitative differences and not structural differences between vision and haptics, it is not surprising that only quantitative differences have effectively been observed.

Moreover, it remains theoretically possible that perceptual processes that are different in nature have, nevertheless, some similar expressions in overt behavior. But from the above review of the contemporary research, we may at least conclude that except in some minor specific features, no fundamental argument has been found to validate the idea of specific laws governing each modality, vision and haptics.

On the contrary, consistent data seem to support the Gibsonian view of modality equivalence and central processing of higher-order variables. Obviously, the most striking of these data is the work of WHITE et al. (1970) and BACH Y RITA (1972) with the tactile-vision-substitution-system (TVSS). This research is so important that it needs a special discussion to outline its implications and its limits.

It has been said that the results obtained with the TVSS lead to the conclusion that in visual as well as in tactile stimulation, invariance extraction is possible if there is a continuous transformation of the stimulus array by an active perceiver. Under these conditions, when the same higher-order variables are conveyed by the stimulation, the same spatial information is picked up by the subject, either visually or tactually. Hence, spatial perception appears to be relatively independent of the specific sensory receptors involved in each modality.

But is it justifiable to conclude that the experiments with the TVSS have established the complete equivalence of the perceptual processes in vision and haptics? Commenting on the work of WHITE and BACH-Y-RITA, BRESSON (1972) seems tempted to answer affirmatively to this question, though he does not really do so. Actually, such an affirmative answer would go beyond the facts and would neglect an essential aspect of the data.

In effect, it is important to remember that the TVSS is a display, as its name suggests, that is substituted for the impaired visual system. The principles governing it lead to an area of the skin being transformed into a "pseudoretina" that receives stimuli analogous to the optic rays, which normally excite the retina cells. Consequently, the tactile stimulation transmitted by the vibrotactors applied on the back of the observer are, as has been emphasized, a two-dimensional projection of three-dimensional physical objects. The main contribution of WHITE and BACH Y RITA et al. is to show that when an area of the skin is treated as a retina, that is, when it receives plane projections of a three-dimensional world, the spatial information extracted from this tactile stimulation is exactly the same as that extracted from the visual one, provided that the same conditions of active transformation of the stimulus array are allowed.

But evidently, the kind of tactile stimulation used here is a very unusual one, since normal skin perception is in no way of the projective type. Hence, it cannot be stated that in habitual manual haptic perception, the processes and spatial information at work are the same as those evidenced with the TVSS.

A supplementary argument that the TVSS gives us more insights into the visual processes than into the usual haptic processes is GUARNIERO's report (1974) of his own experience during his training on that device. Acting as a subject, this CB adult has stressed the extreme novelty of his sensory impressions. He writes:

> It is impossible to pass over in silence the dramatic impact of gaining access to a whole new world of sensory experience ... Although the somatocortex only was involved, nevertheless, the experienced quality of the sensations was nothing like that perceived by touch. Rather than coining a new word, or using "touch" or "feel", I shall use the word "see" to describe what I experienced.

More important, perhaps, than these subjective impressions of sensory qualities is the following observation. When learning object recognition, GUARNIERO has never been able to recognize any object when presented for the first time in the TVSS. Only when he was allowed to touch it before or after its presentation in the device could he recognize it.

> I never discovered any correlation between how something "looked" and how it felt, either at this point or later. Since I could not recognize the objects which I "saw" as the same as those I knew by touch, it took some time for me to associate their names and their "appearances."

This means that no direct intersensory transfer occurred between the known and familiar haptic perception of these objects and the tactile two-dimensional image projected on the back of the subject, and that the correlation between them could be established only after practice. Of course, this observation is consistent with the classic or more recent reports on the behavior of CB subjects, whose visual functions were surgically restored.

If we now turn back to the more classic comparative studies of form perception in CB and NS subjects, some support is found for the modality equivalence concept. In spite of minor structural differences, such as in the perception of symmetrical or rotated figures, it appears from most of the experimental research that some common mechanisms seem to be involved in vision and haptics, and that the differences between the haptic perception of the CB and the visual perception of the NS are more quantitative than qualitative. For example, it has been noted that tactile information processing appears very similar to visual information processing (sensory register, immediate memory, delay of storage, central processing, etc.), and that the differences between the two systems lie more in the efficiency and capacity of storage and processing than in the nature of the perceptual treatment. Other common general processes may explain why the same geometric illusions are found in the blind and the sighted, or why the perceptual and cognitive development of the CB appear to be only slowed down and not structurally modified in comparison to the sighted. Nevertheless, some methodological restrictions are again to be made here, which minimize the validity of these conclusions.

The first one concerns the stimulus used. In a great number of studies, the analysis of the kind of spatial relations to be tested in haptic perception has not explicitly been made and the experimental stimuli consisted of "euclidian" simple shapes currently used in visual perception experiments (square, circle, etc.) or of random shapes. Is this material the most suitable to examine the geometry to which vision and haptics lead? In choosing systematically euclidian relations, which are known to be well-adapted to visual perception, it is implicitly assumed that these situations are equally well-adapted to haptic perception, and thus, that euclidian geometry is relevant for both. To really know if the spatial constructs formed by vision and haptics are of the same nature, it would be useful to systematically compare CB and NS subjects in the perception of shape properties and of spatial transformations belonging to different geometries (and especially the topologic one), and not only to euclidian geometry. Only in these conditions would structural differences appear, if they actually exist.

A final methodological observation concerns another aspect of the stimulus material used. Many of the studies cited have been carried out with plane-contour-raised-line forms. After having used such material myself, I wonder if it is suitable. A contour-raised-line form has no "ecologic" significance to the CB subject, especially when young, whereas it may be an adequate haptic substitute of familiar visual drawings to the BS. This observation is confirmed by MILLAR (1975). The Gibsonian criticisms of the impoverishment in the classic visual perception laboratory experiments could be applied to several studies of haptic perception in the blind. Except in applied research, as for example, studies concerning training the blind in the use of raised-line geographic maps, three-dimensional forms should be preferred and the emphasis be put on the search for the higher-order variables of haptic stimulation in everday life conditions of the blind.

A quotation from WHITE et al. (1970) in the conclusion of their analysis of the results with the TVSS is particularly suggestive:

> "The perceptual systems of living organisms are the most remarkable information-reduction machines known. They are not seriously embarrassed in situations where an enormous proportion of the input must be filtered or ignored, but they are invariably handicapped when the input is drastically curtailed or artificially encoded."

Perhaps WHITE's remarks will be helpful to make a critical analysis of the work already achieved and to renew experimental research on the blind.

References

•Ackroyd, C., Humphrey, N.K., Warrington, E.K.: Lasting effects of early blindness: a case study. Q. J. Exp. Psychol. **26**, 114–124 (1974).

Attneave, P., Benson, B.: Spatial coding of tactual stimulation. J. exp. psychol. **81**, 216–222 (1969).

Axelrod, S.: Effects of Early Blindness. New York: American Foundation for the Blind, 1959.

Bach Y Rita, P.: Brain Mechanisms in Sensory Substitution. New York: Academic Press 1972.

Bean, C.H.: The blind have "optical" illusions. J. exp. Psychol. **22**, 283–289 (1938).

Beauchamps, K.L., Scadden, L.A., Matheson, D.W.: Effect of stimulus-change method on tactile-image recognition. Percept. Mot. Skills **33**, 1067–1070 (1971).

Bliss, J.C., Crane, H.D.: Tactile perception. Research Bulletin (A.F.B.) n° 19, 205–230 (1969).

•Bower, T.G.R.: Development in infancy. San Francisco: Freeman and C° 1974.

Bresson, F.: Aspects génétiques de la perception. In: Neuropsychologie de la perception visuelle. Hecaen, H., (ed.). Paris: Masson 1972.

•Cromer, R.F.: Conservation by the congenitally blind. Br. J. Psychol. **64**, 241–250 (1973).

Davidson, P.W.: Haptic judgments of curvature by the blind and sighted humans. J. exp. Psychol. **93**, 43–55 (1972).

Davidson, P.W.: Some functions of active handling: studies with blinded humans. The New Outlook, 198–200 (1976).

Davidson, P.W., Whitson, T.T.: Haptic equivalence matching of curvature by blind and sighted humans. J. exp. Psychol. **102**, 687–690 (1974).

Davidson, P.W., Barnes, J.K., Mullen, G.: Differential effects of task memory demand on haptic matching of shape by blind and sighted humans, Neuropsychologia **12**, 395–397 (1974).

Doherty, P.J.: Conservation in visually handicapped. Paper presented at the 4th Annual Australian Conference on Cognitive Development, Canberra 1973.

Drever, J.: Early learning and the perception of space. Am. J. Psychol. **68**, 605–614 (1955).

Ewart, A.G., Carp, F.M.: Recognition of tactual forms by sighted and blind subjects. Am. J. Psychol. **75**, 488–491 (1963).

Fraiberg, S.: Parallel and divergent patterns in blind and sighted infants, Psychoanal. Study Child **33**, 264–299 (1968).

Fraiberg, S., Barry, L., Siegel, M.D., Gibson, R.: The role of sound in the search behavior of a blind infant. Psychoanal. Study Child **21**, 327–357 (1966).

Ghent, L.: Form and its orientation: A child's eye view. Am. J. Psychol. **74**, 177–190 (1961).
Gibson, E.J.: Principles of perceptual learning and development. New York: Appleton-Century-Crofts 1969.
Gibson, E.J., Gibson, J.J., Pick, A.D., Osser, H.: A developmental study of the discrimination of letter-like forms. J. Comp. Physiol. Psychol. **55**, 897–906 (1962).
Gibson, J.J.: Observations on active touch. Psychol. Rev. **69**, 477–491 (1962).
Gibson, J.J.: The senses considered as perceptual systems. Boston: Houghton Mifflin 1966.
Gottesman, S.: A comparative study of Piaget's developmental schema of sighted children with that of blind children. Child Dev. **42**, 573–580 (1971).
Gottesman, S.: Conservation development in blind children. Child Dev. **44**, 824–827 (1973).
Gregory, R.L.: Eye and Brain. London: Weidenfeld and Nicolson 1963.
Gregory, R.L., Wallace, J.G.: Recovery From Early Blindness: a Case Study. Monograph Supplement 2. Experimental Psychological Society, Cambridge (England): Heffers 1963.
Gregory, R.L., Wallace, J.G.: Perceptual implications of recovery from blindness in man. In: The Function of Gaze. Dubois-Poulsen, A., Lairy, G.C., Remond, A., (eds.). Paris: Inserm 1971.
Guarniero, G.: Experience of tactile vision. Perception **3**, 101–104 (1974).
Hatwell, Y.: Perception tactile des formes et organisation spatiale tactile. J. de Psychol. **56**, 187–204 (1959).
Hatwell, Y.: Etude de quelques illusions géométriques tactiles chez les aveugles. Annee Psychol. **60**, 11–27 (1960a).
Hatwell, Y.: La perception tactile des formes: perception et activité perceptive tactile. J. de Psychol. **57**, 165–176 (1960b).
Hatwell, Y.: Privation sensorielle et intelligence. Paris: Presses Universitaires de France 1966.
Hayes, S.P.: Sensory compensation and the vicariate of the senses. Outlook for the Blind **28**, 7–12, and **36**, 67–71 and 122–129 (1934).
Hayes, S.P.: Contributions to a Psychology of Blindness. New York: American Foundation for the Blind 1941.
Hebb, D.O.: The Organization of Behavior. New York: Wiley and C° 1949.
Held, R.: Dissociation of visual functions by deprivation and rearrangement. Psychologische Forschung **31**, 339–348 (1968).
Held, R., Hein, A.: Movement produced stimulation in the development of visually-guided behavior. J. Comp. Physiol. Psychol. **56**, 872–876 (1963).
Hubel, D.H., Wiesel, T.N.: The period of susceptibility to the physiological effects of unilateral eye closure in kittens. J. Physiol. (Lond.) **206**, 419–436 (1970).
Hunter, I.M.L.: Tactile kinesthetic perception of straightness in blind and sighted humans. Quart. J. Psychol. **6**, 149–154 (1954).
Hunter, I.M.L.: An analysis of space perception in congenitally blind and sighted individuals. J. Gen. Psychol. **70**, 325–329 (1964).
Ingle, D.: Two visual mechanisms underlying the behavior of fish. Psychologische Forschung **31**, 44–51 (1967).
Jeannerod, M.: Déficit visuel persistant ches les aveugles-nés: données cliniques et experimentales. Annee Psychol. **75**, 169–196 (1975).
Juurmaa, J.: Transposition in mental spatial manipulation: a theoretical analysis. Research Bulletin (A.F.B.) N° 26, 87–134 (1973).
Lappin, J.S., Foulke, E.: Expanding the tactual field of view. Percept. Psychophys. **14**, 237–241 (1973).
London, I.D.: A Russian report on the postoperative newly seeing. Am. J. Psychol. **73**, 478–482 (1960).
Loomis, J.M.: Tactile letter recognition under different modes of stimulus presentation. Percept. Psychophys. **16**, 401–408 (1974).
Martinez, F.: Comparison of two types of tactile exploration in a task of mirror-image recognition. Psycho. Sci. **22**, 124–125 (1971).
Millar, S.: Tactile short-term memory by blind and sighted children. Br. J. Psychol. **65**, 253–263 (1974).
Millar, S.: Visual experience or translation rules? Drawing the human figure by blind and sighted children. Perception **4**, 363–371 (1975).

Millar, S.: Spatial representation by blind and sighted children. J. Exp. Child Psychol. **21**, 460–479 (1976).
Norris, M., Brodie, F.H., Spaulding, P.: Blindness in Children. Chicago: University of Chicago Press 1957.
O'Connor, N., Hermelin, B., Modality-specific spatial coordinates. Percept. Psychophys. **17**, 213–216 (1975).
Page, E.I.: Haptic perception. Educ. Rev. **11**, 115–124 (1959).
Paillard, J.: Le traitement des informations spatiales, in: De l'Espace corporel à l'espace écologique (Symposium de l'Association de Psychologie Scientifique de Langue Française). Paris: Presses Universitaires de France 1974.
Pasnak, R., Ahr, P.: Tactual Poggendorf illusion in blind and blindfolded subjects. Percept. Mot. Skills **31**, 151–154 (1970).
Patterson, J., Deffenbacher, K.: Haptic perception of the Muller-Lyer illusion by the blind. Percept. Mot. Skills **35**, 819–834 (1972).
Piaget, J.: La Naissance de l'intelligence chez l'enfant. Neuchatel: Delachaux et Niestlé 1935.
Piaget, J.: Les Mécanismes perceptifs. Paris: Presses Universitaires de France 1961.
Piaget, J., Inhelder, B.: La Représentation de l'espace chez l'enfant. Paris: Presses Universitaires de France 1947.
Pick, A.D., Pick, H.L.: A developmental study of tactual discrimination in blind and sighted children and adults. Psycho. Sci. **6**, 367–368 (1966).
Pick, H.L., Klein, R.E., Pick, A.D.: Visual and tactual identification of form orientation. J. Exp. Child Psychol. **4**, 391–397 (1966).
Posner, M.I.: Characteristics of visual and kinesthetic memory codes. J. exp. Psychol. **75**, 103–107 (1967).
Revesz, G.: Psychology and art of the blind. New York: Longmens, Green and C° 1950 (Translated from: Die Formenwelt des Tastsinnes. The Hague: Martinus Nijhoff 1933).
Revesz, G.: System der optischen und haptischen Raumtäuschungen. Z. Psychol. Physiol. **131**, 296–375 (1934).
Robin, M., Pecheux, M.G.: Problèmes posés par la reproduction de modèles spatiaux chez des enfants aveugles: une étude expérimentale. Perception **5**, 39–49 (1976).
Schneider, G.E.: Contrasting visuomotor functions of tectum and cortex in the Golden Hamster. Psychol. Forsch. 31, 52–62 (1967).
Schneider, G.E.: Two visual systems. Science **163**, 895–902 (1969).
Seashore, C.E., Ling, T.L.: A comparative study of sensitiveness of the blind and seeing persons. Psychol. Monogr. **25**, n° 108 (1918).
Shagan, J., Goodnow, J.J.: Recall of haptic information by blind and sighted individuals. J. exp. Psychol. **101**, 221–226 (1973).
Senden, M., von: Raum- und Gestaltauffassung bei operierten Blindgeborenen, 1932.
Senden, M., von: Space and Sight. Glencoe, Illinois: The Free Press 1960.
Sherrington, C.S.: The integrative action of the nervous system. New Haven: Yale University Press 1906.
Tobin, M.J.: Conservation of substance in the blind and partially sighted. Br. J. Educ. Psychol. **42**, 192–197 (1972).
Trevarthen, C.B.: Two mechanisms of vision in Primates. Psychol. Forsch. **31**, 299–337 (1968).
Tsai, L.S.: Müller-Lyer illusion by the blind. Percept. Mot. Skills **25**, 641–644 (1967).
Valvo, A.: Behavior patterns and visual rehabilition after early and long lasting blindness. Am. J. Ophtalmol. **65**, 19–23 (1968).
Warren, D.H., Anooshian, L.J., Bollinger, J.G.: Early versus late blindness: the role of early vision in spatial behavior. Research Bulletin (American Foundation for the Blind) n° 26, 151–170 (1973).
White, B.W., Saunders, F.A., Scadden, L., Bach Y Rita, P., Collins, C.C.: Seeing with the skin. Percept. Psychophys. **7**, 23–27 (1970).
Worchel, P.: Space perception and orientation in the blind. Psychol. Monogr. **65**, n° 15 (1951).
Zaporozhets, A.W.: The development of perception in preschool child. Monogr. Soc. Res. Child Dev. **30**, 82–101 (1965).
Zweibelson, I., Barg, C.F.: Concept development in blind children. New Outlook for the Blind 62, 218–222 (1967).

II. Complex Aspects of Perception

A. Spatially Distributed Patterns

Chapter 15

Human Pattern and Object Perception

PETER C. DODWELL, Kingston, Ontario, Canada

With 8 Figures

Contents

A. Introduction

Sensation and perception have traditionally been separated and contrasted with one another in the development of experimental psychology (BORING, 1942). The division has frequently been challenged and there is no agreement on how it can best be made. Most psychologists would now agree that a sharp boundary should not be drawn; nevertheless the distinction is to some degree valid, and on introducing the topic of Human Pattern Perception in a *Handbook of Sensory Physiology* one should try to show what significance, if any, the boundary has for the study of sensory systems. Most of what I have to say will concern the visual system, but is applicable in large measure to other modalities as well.

Modern work in psychology has attempted to understand the visual system in three ways, or at three levels:

1. As the detector of signals in a normally "noisy" ambient stimulus environment
2. As the organizer or integrator of information contained in optical arrays
3. As the user of visual information for cognitive ends

There would probably be little disagreement with the assertion that most work in sensory physiology is at level one, and at this level psychologists too have made major contributions, particularly in the areas of sensory scaling, threshold measurement and the theory of signal detectability (JAMESON and HURVICH, 1976). The really significant achievement in the latter case has been to find methods of separating measures of pure sensitivity from contaminating factors such as response bias due to set, expectation, rewards or personal values. Psychologists thus have procedures which allow them to carry out investigations at level one which are not burdened by problems of interpretation at higher levels. It seems that level one corresponds quite well with the traditional psychological field of enquiry which is called sensation. Substantial advances have been made using the new scaling and signal detection methodologies, but these are reviewed in other parts of this Handbook, as well as in books by GREEN and SWETS (1966) and by KLING and RIGGS (1971), among others.

Basic and important though the laws of psychophysics may be, they deal in the main with fairly elementary sensory dimensions and response functions, such as the relationship of judged intensity to variation on a simple physical dimension like pitch or luminance. As soon as one enquires about the organization or integration of sensory information, which has been characterized above as level two, a new range of questions and problems arises. These are concerned with such things as the division of figure from background in a patterned display, simultaneous and successive brightness and color contrast, visual constancies, illusions and the question of orientation and stability of the three-dimensional visual world. Although not so closely bound to our knowledge of physics and sensory physiology as the major portion of psychophysics, many of these questions of organization nevertheless invite physiological explanation, or at least our understanding of them may be colored by the present state of physiological knowledge (DODWELL, 1970). It is here that the psychologist's penchant for speculative physiologising is given freest rein. However, explanations about perceptual organization usually need to be tempered by other considerations of a cognitive nature. One of the more difficult aspects of the study of perception (as compared to sensation) is that investigation and understanding at any one level seldom can proceed far without impinging on facts or theories that seem to be more relevant to other levels.

Organization and integration are thought of here as forms of perceptual processing which are more or less automatic in character. To understand the uses of perceived patterns in our commerce with the world forces one to look at visual perception in its cognitive aspect: that is, at level three. At this level our understanding of perception cannot proceed far without taking account of classification and categorization as fundamental operations of the mature perceiving organism (BRUNER, 1957; ROSCH, 1973). Language is a major tool for classifying and communicating, so its possible relevance to perception cannot be ignored, and memory also plays a fundamental role (e.g. OLDFIELD, 1954; POSNER, 1969).

What I have characterized as levels two and three in understanding the nature of the visual system are the areas traditionally called the Psychology of Perception; they have to do with complex events, but are not specified simply in terms of complexity. Rather, it is the different functions of the visual (or other) system that serve to differentiate them. For example the ability to discriminate between different two-dimensional shapes (such as squares, circles, and triangles) may seem a simple matter, yet it cannot be understood in terms of an ordered set of physical parameters: the perceiving system itself must impose order where none is intrinsic to the stimulation—or not obviously so. Similarly, categorization (e.g., by language) can be simple or complex, but again implies the active engagement of the organism in the perceptual process, not simply a passive recording of sensory change. The levels of functioning and understanding are not independent of one another of course; the question of how the different levels are related to one another deserves more attention.

Psychological research usually proceeds on the assumption that "reduction" is a good thing, i.e., that a phenomenon should be explained at as low a level as may be: for example, if explanation in terms of the functioning of a sensory organ is possible why look further? This is the normal use of Occam's razor. However, one needs to ensure that the razor is wielded with as much discretion as zeal, that a reductionist explanation is adequate and does full justice to the facts. Most theoretical disputes in psychology turn on the antipathy between those who seek to understand perception reductively in terms of its primitive—which generally means its physiological—substratum, and those who regard the only adequate explanations as teleological, that is, ones which take into account the cognitive ends which perception serves. Each point of view has had its illustrious protagonists, both historically and on the contemporary scientific scene. Perhaps the most celebrated of the former were HERING and HELMHOLTZ in their disputes over the nativistic or empiristic basis of perception. Although many of their detailed arguments might seem archaic today, the principles from which they argued still lie at the heart of much of our scientific debate about perception (HOCHBERG, 1962; DODWELL, 1975).

In the following sections I shall outline some of the recent advances in the understanding of human pattern and object perception, relate these to the concept of levels already discussed, then proceed to a consideration of how the different levels of research and understanding bear on each other.

B. Perceptual Organization

A most basic and salient fact about human perception—not clearly appreciated by the nineteenth century sensory physiologists and experimental psychologists of the early twentieth—is the fact that normal adult perception is wholistic perception. It is characteristic for us to see (or hear, feel, etc.) objects and events, rather than agglomerations of discrete sensations. Our perceptions have an organized configurational quality which is obvious, once it has been pointed out. Figure 1 gives some of the classical examples of apparently automatic, or at least natural, organization in visual patterns.

Pointing to this compelling property does nothing to explain it however. Gestalt theory identified the configurational properties with organizational

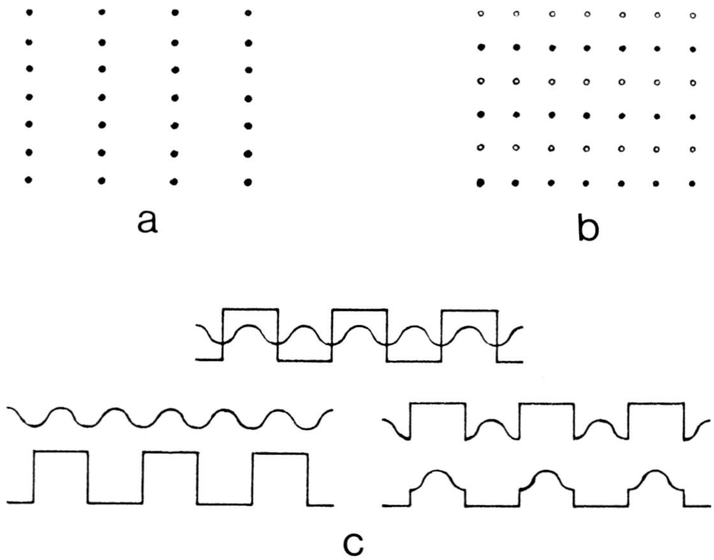

Fig. 1a–c. Some examples of "natural" organization; (a) by proximity, (b) by similarity, and (c) by continuity

"forces" in the cerebral cortex which determined the perceived attributes of objects and patterns. Although the crude physiological speculations of Gestalt theory have long been discredited, no fully satisfactory substitute has been found. It has been shown that "organization" is subject to change in the light of experience, and/or context (e.g., Bruner and Minturn, 1955; Rock and Kremen, 1957), so cannot be a straightforward innate processing mode. On the other hand there are many characteristics of visual pattern recognition which are most readily explained in terms of such processing.

This second point is well illustrated by recent discoveries in the field of stereopsis. Figure 2 shows one of the now celebrated random dot stereograms first studied by Julesz (1960). Each half consists of a random pattern of black and white square dots. The two are identical except that a square area in the center of one (about one-quarter of the total area) has been displaced laterally with respect to the rest of the pattern. When the two patterns are brought into registry, or fused, by the eyes, the phase shift between the central square and the rest of the two fused patterns is detected and seen as stereoscopic depth. As there are no monocular cues to this central square, and it is difficult to see how its appearance can be influenced by specific experience with other sorts of depth cue, such as perspective or motion parallax, an explanation in terms of physiologically based data processing seems most natural. This is reinforced by the fact that cortical units tuned to detect retinal disparities have been found in mammalian cortexes, first by Barlow et al (1967), which have at least some of the properties needed to extract this "pure" stereodepth information.

Fig. 2. Julesz random dot stereogram. When viewed stereoscopically a pattern emerges which is not to be found in either half on its own (see text for explanation)

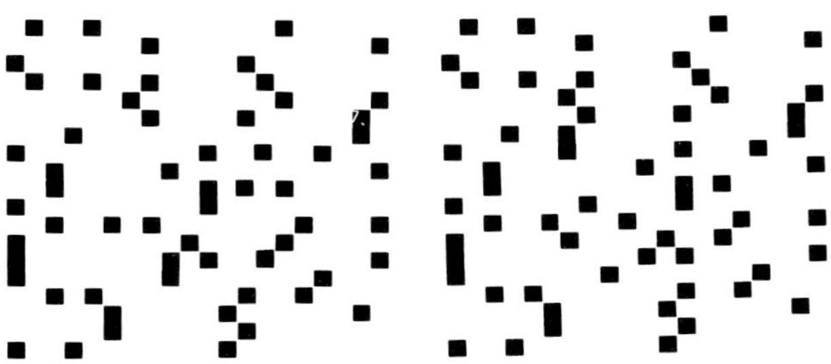

Fig. 3. Reduced random dot stereogram which does not produce stereoscopic subjective contours

An interesting but as yet little-explored facet of stereodepth processing concerns the conditions under which it breaks down as the density of points in the Julesz fields is reduced. The "subjective contours" of the stereoscopically produced central square of Figure 2 are very clear, and remain so in a stereogram in which the density of black points is reduced by half, for example. But if the density is much reduced, as in Figure 3, the figure-forming characteristic is lost, as are the subjective contours, and what one sees is a set of separate small black squares in depth, rather than the single central square defined by the whole set of out-of-phase elements. Whatever the explanation for the breakdown of the figure-forming process may be in this case, it certainly seems that it will be found at the second level of visual functioning, characterized above as "perceptual organization" rather than at the higher, interpretative level.

A somewhat different but equally interesting phenomenon is illustrated in Figure 4 taken from Kanizsa (1955). In this case a pronounced set of contours is apparent which gives the appearance of a white equilateral triangle overlying

Fig. 4. "Subjective," or gradient-free contours produced by a complex display

other figural elements. GREGORY (1972) calls these "cognitive contours," because the most natural explanation seems to be that the display is interpreted in terms of superposition. However, this label assumes the explanation is valid. Others have called them "subjective," "anomalous," "virtual," and "gradient-free" contours, the latter being perhaps the most appropriate term. (It should be noted that the Julesz stereograms also exhibit contours without gradients; COREN [1972] has argued that the two sets of phenomena are related.) Another possible explanation is that the displays which generate such contours activate, minimally, a set of feature detectors like the line and edge detectors of HUBEL and WIESEL (1962, 1968). The findings and theories on gradient-free contours have been summarized usefully by KANIZSA (1974). So far there is no compelling experimental evidence to decide between different models, but the various possibilities illustrate the general problem of the preferred level of explanation for perceptual phenomena which was pointed out earlier.

Ambiguous figures such as the famous "wife/mother-in-law" picture (BORING, 1930) pose another sort of problem for understanding perceptual organization. This particular picture is shown in Figure 5a and seems rather obviously to invite a level-3 explanation: It is the interpretation of the elements of the picture that is important, and that fluctuates over time. It seems clear that this is a cognitive process in which prior experience and the ability to label correctly are involved; different individuals "see" one or other of the possible scenes with varying facility. Yet this is not true of all ambiguous figures. Figure 5b shows the equally famous Necker cube, in which the ambiguous perception seems to be of a different order. Reversals of the apparent orientation of the cube have a more involuntary or automatic character than changes in the appearance of the wife/mother-in-law. This is akin to the perceptual organization of Figure 4, and the level at which explanation should be sought is likewise ambiguous. On the one hand interpretation of the cube's orientation seems to be an elaborate cognitive operation, which includes an understanding of the two-dimensional representation of three-dimensional objects, but on the other hand it could be that the reversals are caused by fatiguing of neuronal edge or line detectors. This would fit well with the finding that reversals are often spontaneous and not fully under voluntary (or cognitive) control, and that the particular projection of the cube which is viewed affects the rate of

(a)

(b)

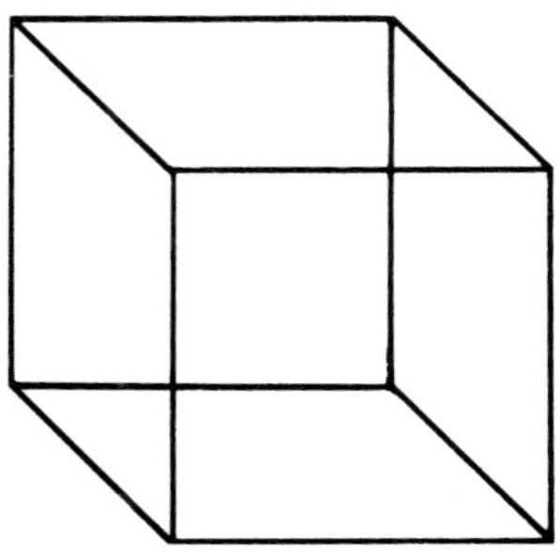

Fig. 5. (a) The "wife/mother-in-law" ambiguous picture. Both ladies can be seen (but not simultaneously) if this picture is viewed for some seconds. (b) The Necker cube. A different sort of reversal occurs here with continued fixation

alternation. Another beautiful example of an ambiguous figure with ambiguities also in the explanatory domain is shown in Figure 6—a sort of doubly ambiguous picture.

We hesitate to ascribe changes in the appearance of some ambiguous figures definitely to level 2 or level 3. In fact it may well be that no exhaustive explanation at one level is possible. Most of the difficulties in understanding pattern and object perception lie just in the fact that to understand perceptual organization requires comprehension of processes which occur concurrently at different levels. The tendency, still rather common amongst psychologists, to believe that a single model or level of explanation can successfully account for perceptual phenomena needs careful scrutiny; in many cases it is misguided.

A modern twist was given to the study of figure-forming processes by the introduction of "impossible objects" as items worthy of serious scientific investi-

Fig. 6. A picture displaying double ambiguity. One of a famous series of prints by the Dutch artist M. Escher

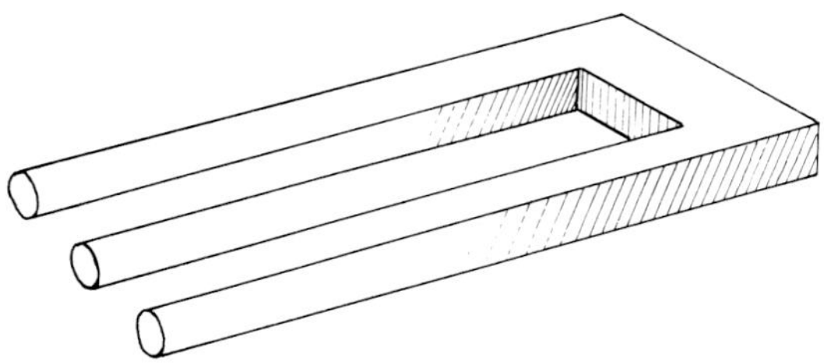

Fig. 7. The Devil's Trident (or tuning fork). An example of an "impossible" object

gation. One of the best of these is illustrated in Figure 7. Although the pattern has a certain coherence, and even suggests solidity through the conventions of two-dimensional representation of three-dimensional objects, the set of edges and implied surfaces obviously do not correspond to any physically realizable object. How, on the one hand, can we be so deceived, yet on the other be able to detect, quite readily, the impossibility?

HOCHBERG (1968) has studied this matter by presenting versions of such figures with different degrees of temporal or spatial separation between the distinguishing features of the impossible object. For example, it could be viewed through a "window" which allowed only one critical feature at a time to

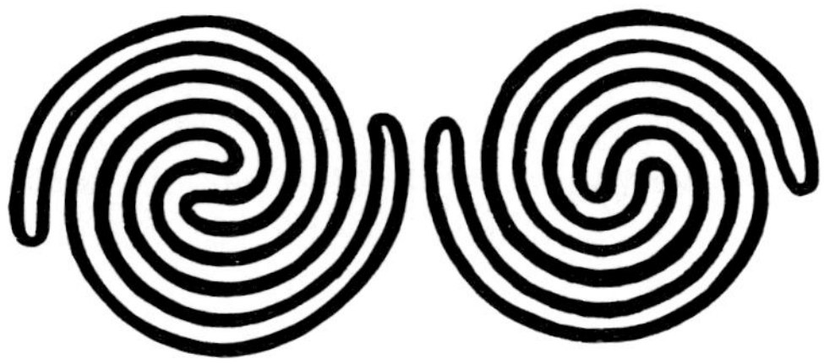

a b

Fig. 8. Two different patterns which are nearly indistinguishable because they lack "distinctive features" (see text for explanation)

be seen, in which case the "impossibility" of the object is not detectable, or it could be viewed as a whole, but with the "prongs" much extended to provide spatial separation. In this case the detection of impossibility, or ambiguity, is a direct function of the separation. A very good question here is: what constitute "critical features" in such impossible objects? Intuition suggests that corners, sharp curves or other areas of "high information content" (see next section) are critical, and experiment confirms this. HOCHBERG espouses a theory of perceptual organization which is in fact a modernized version of a very old idea, namely that the perception of patterns and objects is a constructive process. The elements, or building blocks, are held to be largely innately determined, if not completely so, and the integration of these elements into coherent patterns is thought to arise from active interplay of the perceiver with the stimuli impinging on him from the environment. Thus the impossibility of a representation is only discovered as the schematic map is carefully analyzed. The plausibility of an impossible object arises from the initially plausible agglomeration of familiar critical features.

Many other psychologists have argued along similar lines, most noteably HEBB (1949), and the very same idea turns up in the field of Artifical Intelligence, where "scene analysis", as it is called, basically consists of parsing agglomerations of features (lines, intersections, etc.) into "units" (objects) which are, in fact, an interpretation of the features (GUZMAN, 1970; MINSKY, 1969).

The fact that coherent pattern analysis breaks down in the absence of such critical features is well illustrated in Figure 8. It is not possible to tell by inspection of these shapes that they are not mirror images of each other. In fact their topologies are different, as can be verified by tracing along each of them with a pencil.

It is noteworthy that the critical features chosen for parsing in Artificial Intelligence turn out to be very much like the critical features found to be important for human perceivers. In itself this is hardly surprising because of course the "critical elements" for the computerized scene analysis were chosen rationally by human perceivers. Nevertheless it is encouraging to find that experimental evidence (from research on impossible objects for example) and simulation findings are quite congruent. That is to say, the Artificial Intelligence seems to operate perceptually in somewhat the same manner as the intelligent human.

There is good evidence, then, that pattern and object recognition are not just passive processes, in which the observer simply classifies sets of inputs in a particular way. What was characterised above as the "figure-forming" process is in some sense an active process. Yet there are cases, such as the JULESZ stereograms described earlier, where the processing of pattern information does take on a sort of automatic character. We are left again with the fact that perceptual phenomena are diverse, and require explanation at several different levels.

Although not very much of a definite and detailed nature is known about the organizational processes (see, e.g., HOWARD, 1974) they can to some degree be mimicked by computer simulation, and this gives one cause to hope that improved understanding of them can be a realistic and not-too-distant objective. Some of the current models in psychology concerned with figural synthesis are discussed in a later section.

C. Statistical Treatment

One way to try to understand pattern perception is to discover unusual sorts of patterns, present them to human (or subhuman) observers, and see what they make of them. This has been the strategy of much human perceptual research, including that described in the previous section. Another approach is to attempt to quantify pattern in some way, and to construct artificial patterns so that the dimensions of quantification can be related, as independent variables, to the discriminative behavior of organisms. In this manner what ATTNEAVE (1954) described as a "psychophysics of form" might be developed.

The earliest work of this genre was heavily influenced by the concepts and methods of information theory. By equating the Gestalt notion of "goodness of form" with the informational concept of redundancy, the attempt was made to reduce the former somewhat intuitive notion to a quantitative basis (ATTNEAVE and ARNOULT, 1956; GARNER, 1962). To take a simple example: a circle has good Gestalt, and is redundant in the sense of being regular, highly predictable from a partial view of it, and hence of low "surprise" value (i.e., low information content). More generally, any pattern or form which by empirical investigation is found to have this quality of predictability also tends to have strong figural properties. Many experimental investigations have shown this to be true, and in large measure the discrimination and categorization of artificially constructed (nonsense) patterns can be understood in terms of their informational content.

One may ask what features of a pattern contribute distinctiveness, or—an equivalent question—which features carry most information. A large number of physical characteristics have been studied, including number of elements in dot patterns, number of lines and angles, texture, and ratio of perimeter to area. Generally speaking, features of high information content are similar to the critical elements discussed in the previous section (angles, points, of intersection or high curvature, etc.). It should be pointed out that structured patterns are not merely agglomerations of features. One must still ask how the features are related to one another to form a true pattern (GRIMSDALE et al., 1959; REED, 1973). That aspect of the problem of form recognition has received too little attention from most workers in this line of investigation. The early work is well summarized by ATTNEAVE and ARNOULT (1956).

A related, but distinct, approach is to generate large numbers of nonsense shapes with statistically defined parameters, (rather than fully specified features), to assess relative discriminability behaviorally, and to look for underlying order in terms of commonalities revealed by factor analysis (BROWN and OWEN, 1967). With stimuli of this sort an attempt can be made to solve the difficult problem of generality: given a particular organism and a particular discrimination it can make, is it possible to say anything about the classes of pattern it can learn to discriminate? If the basic dimensions of form discrimination were revealed by factor analysis in terms of the statistically defined parameters, the question might be answerable in principle, and there is some evidence that human discriminative performance is related to dimensions such as "compactness," "jaggedness," "skewness," and "dominant axis" as these are revealed by factor analysis (ANDREWS and BROWN, 1967). Another related approach is to have observers rate patterns in terms of judged similarity, complexity or preference, to measure the proximity of each pattern to every other one in terms of the ratings, and by the method of multidimensional scaling to look for the underlying "psychological space."

These lines of research on the quantification of pattern have generated a large literature, reviewed by ZUSNE (1970), and have produced some results of interest, which can be characterized as being at level two. Statistical description and manipulation of patterns certainly adds to our knowledge about how abstract shapes can be categorized, and is compatible with some developments in Artificial Intelligence concerned with the organization and interpretion of pattern information (see HUNT, 1975). One may ask how much such studies have contributed to a fundamental understanding of human pattern and object recognition. Organizational principles revealed in very constrained laboratory situations may have limited relevance to more usual types of perceptual classification; at least the relevance remains to be demonstrated. Experiments on "natural categories" (ROSCH et al., 1976) suggest that the normal level of perceptual categorization for humans is level three. The experiments with artificially generated two-dimensional shapes tell little, if anything, about the cognitive uses of pattern recognition. Nevertheless, it is possible that there is some important connection between the way such shapes are categorized and human object recognition in more naturalistic settings.

Perhaps the most serious questioning of the validity of the statistical approach to pattern recognition, as well as more technical criticisms aimed specifically at the information-theoretic point of view, is to be found in GREEN and COURTIS (1966); see also CORCORAN (1971) and ROCK (1973). Recently GARNER (1974) has summarized and reviewed his own major contributions to the study of pattern recognition which are in the information-theoretic tradition, and his book is probably the best and most convincing single introduction to this type of research.

D. Formal Models and Physiological Hypotheses

A quite different way to approach questions about pattern and object perception is to ask if our knowledge of visual physiology can suggest explanations, or lead to fruitful lines of experimental work. Many psychologists have tried this approach, and with some success. It is usually limited by the current state of physiological knowledge, but on occasion psychologists have taken the lead in fostering understanding of neurophysiology. One outstanding example is to be found, of course, in color vision, where the fit between psychophysical and physiological findings is quite remarkable. Here the psychophysical knowledge of three primaries, and of opponent processes, certainly guided the search for the physiological substrates. In the field of pattern perception the best individual example is perhaps K.S. LASHLEY, whose behavioral and physiological researches remain classics in the field (e.g., LASHLEY, 1952). An attempt to demonstrate how close the relations are between physiological findings and behavioral theory and experiment in the field of pattern recognition can be found in DODWELL (1971a). While most of this work has been done with infrahuman subjects, there is good reason to believe that many results can be extrapolated to human vision. Indeed, at the human psychophysical level a rich interplay between psychological fact and physiological hypothesis is evidenced by several of the other chapters in this volume.

LASHLEY's work on equipotentiality and the admittedly vague theory of interference patterns which he used to explain stimulus equivalence (LASHLEY, 1952) laid the groundwork for later more sophisticated models to explain how specific patterns can be recognized despite variation in size, location, contrast and orientation. The problem is to find a mechanism for mapping a highly variable stimulus input into a relatively much smaller set of categories which we call different patterns. Salient among the models which address this problem are the network model of PITTS and MCCULLOCH (1947), and DEUTSCH's model of pattern coding (1955). PITTS and MCCULLOCH proposed formal logic networks which could compute specific functions of their inputs. This led to a much sharper concept of pattern invariance than was previously available, and their ideas were fundamental to VON NEUMANN's development of automata theory, leading eventually to computers. However, their model did not open up a new line of empirical research on pattern recognition. DEUTSCH's model, although originally less tied to a neurophysiological substrate, postulates a remarkably simple but powerful information-processing system for the coding of shape, and some developments from it closely anticipate the findings of HUBEL and WIESEL (1962) on the neurophysiological coding of contour. These matters are discussed in detail in DODWELL (1970).

HUBEL and WIESEL's discoveries about the coding of line segments by individual cells of the visual cortex are, without doubt, the single most influential factor in the recent development of ideas about how pattern recognition works. Their early results (1962) on cells with simple and complex retinal receptive fields gave promise of the discovery of the basic, innately programed detection system for elements of pattern, and of a built-in system for generalization.

Cells with complex fields code line elements and are specific as to orientation, but not position; even at this level some generalizing of the code seems to be present. The subsequent discovery of hypercomplex cell types (HUBEL and WIESEL, 1968) suggested both hierarchical organization within the system and more sophisticated forms of abstraction.

Theorists were soon predicting the imminent revelation of the true neurophysiological basis of pattern recognition, and even a detailed account of its mechanism. In the event, these predictions have not been borne out, for at least two reasons, one of them empirical, one conceptual. One factual obstacle to such a breakthrough was the finding by ENROTH-CUGELL, ROBSON, CAMPBELL and others of a different basis for spatial information coding at the single unit level. They found evidence to suggest that spatial frequency, orientation and movement are the primary parameters of coding, rather than the line segment system of HUBEL and WIESEL (see CAMPBELL, 1974; ROBSON, 1975, for reviews of this work). Thus there is disagreement about what the neurophysiological code for pattern elements actually is (let alone for patterns themselves). Conceptually, it became clear that single unit recording in itself would probably not yield the desired information on pattern classification because it is *a priori* very improbable that single cells exist in the cortex that are "square detectors", let alone "mother-in-law" detectors (e.g., DODWELL, 1970, Chap. V). The strongest case for the "single unit" point of view has been put by KONORSKI (1967) in the theory of gnostic units, and by BARLOW (1972) in his Neuron Doctrine. An alternative postulate is that the primary elements coded in the visual system (line segments, if HUBEL and WIESEL's results are so interpreted) become integrated by some other process, namely an organizational process at level two, according to the scheme suggested earlier.

Several integrative schemes have been suggested, including those of HEBB (1949) and HOCHBERG (1968) mentioned earlier. HEBB's theory, perhaps the most celebrated in neuropsychology over the past few decades, claims that the integrative process is one of simple association of networks by contiguous activity in space and time, the primary network elements (pattern elements) being given innately. Thus, through a process of perceptual learning, individual patterns are represented by extended neural networks rather than by individual cells. HEBB's original postulates have been updated and elaborated on in various ways, and have spawned a vast literature on perceptual (and cognitive) development. An attempt to reconcile those postulates with the neurophysiological discoveries of the 1960s was made by DODWELL (1964, 1970) and, from the Artificial Intelligence viewpoint, by SUTHERLAND (1968). See also BARLOW et al. (1972).

HOCHBERG's (1968) theory of "schematic maps" shares some features with HEBB's theory. Pattern recognition is postulated to be a cognitive activity in which the schematic map is put together piecewise by scanning over complex patterns to detect their elements and how they fit together. Unlike HEBB, HOCHBERG does not give a developmental account of the acquisition of pattern recognition, although his ideas are not incompatible with the Hebbian point of view. Both theories postulate an important role for eye movements in pattern recognition, a notion which has found widespread acceptance (NOTON and STARK, 1971). Both of these theories are quite informal, although rather more than just commonsense notions about how integration might occur. Somewhat more formal are models of figural synthesis on the basis of some type of automatic processing. Probably the best-known example of these is the currently fashionable notion that, if individual cells of the visual cortex code for spatial frequency in a specific orientation, the visual nervous system must use this information to perform a basic Fourier analysis on the inputs (see ROBSON, 1975, or SEKULER, 1974, for evaluations of this idea). The frequency components are then automatically synthesized into a new but abstract representation of the input pattern. Another example of automatic processing is found in the model of POLLEN et al. (1971) who propose that HUBEL and WIESEL-type cells in many different orientations perform a brightness analysis on the input pattern. That pattern is then reconstructed from the individual cell outputs in a manner analogous to the "strip integration" technique used in radio astronomy to reconstruct patterns of celestial radiation.

Perhaps the most formal of the integrative models is HOFFMAN's theory of Lie Transformation Groups in Neuropsychology (LTG/NP) (HOFFMAN, 1966, 1968). This theory proposes that synthesis occurs through the activity of mathematical operators called "Lie Group Germs," or "Lie Derivatives," which act integratively (in the mathematical sense) to form Lie Transformation Groups; these in turn cover the visual manifold (visual cortical field). Although such operators act locally—in fact are postulated to be embodied in individual cells of the visual cortex—their effective action is global because of the relation holding between (infinitesimal) Group Germs and (finite) Group Transformations. The relation is specified in the mathematical theory: the Lie Group Germs are the infinitesimal generators of finite transformations along specifiable orbits, or trajectories, over the whole visual manifold. The theory is too complex, and too deep, to describe in detail. It has, however, the following important properties:

1. It relates the "global" visual field to the "molecular" basis of vision in single cell activity. The individual cell outputs à la HUBEL and WIESEL are local vectors; acting together they form a vector field on which patterns are generated and specified.

2. It yields explanations of many basic perceptual phenomena such as constancies, illusions, and visual aftereffects, as direct consequences of mathematical properties of the Lie Transformation Groups.

3. It yields a consistent account of the development of visual perception from certain primitive elements, represented in the elementary Lie Group germs, to a fully mature operational system which, again, follows naturally from the mathematical theory.

4. It yields a form of pattern synthesis which takes full account of the geometrical, structural character of the visual field.

No other theory is quite so consistent, or coherent, as LTG/NP, and no other theory approaches it in the depth of its mathematical treatment. It is, therefore, surprising that the theory has had so little impact on research in pattern recognition—a situation which will probably change in due course (CAELLI, 1975; DODWELL, 1977).

In summary, we may say that the various models for integration of visual patterns, or figural synthesis as it was earlier termed, are definitely level-2 proposals. There is no agreement on which model is most nearly correct, nor are the different models necessarily incompatible with one another. Clearly physiological discoveries have influenced them, and will continue to do so, but equally clearly it seems unlikely that the problems addressed at this level will be solved with present physiological methods. This remark applies even more strongly when we consider problems at our third level, namely problems about object recognition, and the cognitive uses to which perceptual information is put. While the relevance of the models described in this section to human object recognition might be questioned (just as in the earlier instance of statistical models) the fact that they seek to relate organizational principles to physiological processes as well as to behavioral evidence on pattern recognition suggests a rather central role for them in any comprehensive theory of perception.

E. Spatial Framework

Normal visual perception occurs within a stable frame of reference. Objects are seen in a particular visual direction, and we relate our own movements, as well as those of external entities, to the frame. The nature of that framework, how it arises, what contributes to its maintenance, are questions on which psychologists have concentrated their attention. The work of LOTZE, and of HERING (1864) was basic to the development of the notions of "visual direction" and "local sign" on the retina. Each point on the retina (of a single eye) was held to have an intrinsic visual direction associated with it, thus allowing one to map visual field coordinates into retinal coordinates. Inter-ocular distance and convergence angle allow one to specify a unique mapping of the three-dimensional visual world on to the pair of two-dimensional surfaces which are the retinas.

LUNEBURG (1947) showed that such a mapping implies that the space of binocular vision is non-Euclidean, and in fact is a space of constant negative curvature. Experimental support for this model of visual space comes from the so-called BLUMENFELD alley experiments (BLANK, 1958, 1961; ZAJACZKOWSKA, 1956), in which subjects in an otherwise dark environment set small lights in straight rows receding from them. Under one condition the lights are set in parallel rows, in another they are set in equidistant rows. In an Euclidean environment these two criteria would lead to identical settings. In fact there are systematic differences in the settings which are consistent with the LUNEBURG model. Particularly in the near visual space there are distortions, so that apparently straight rows of lights are not physically collinear, and there are discrepancies between physical and psychological (apparent) distances. It should be noted, however, that such experiments are carried out in a highly artificial visual environment; there are no external cues, apart from the test lights, and the observer is entirely dependent on these, as well as information from accommodation and convergence of the eyes, in making perceptual judgements. It is consistent with the LUNEBURG theory that this should be so, yet in other ways it is clear that, given a normal visual environment and a rich variety of spatial cues, the visual world appears to be four-square Euclidean. But this also is not exactly true either, as we shall see.

A "perceptual space" is inferred from the judgements that observers make about sizes, distances, and orientations. The above example of a difference between the LUNEBURG visual space and "normal" visual space is a particular example of the general principle that perceptual judgements are determined in part by the context in which they are made. Since the properties of perceptual space are inferred from such judgements, there can be no one perceptual space that is pure and immutable. No unitary comprehensive theory of perceptual space is thus possible. This principle is most clearly evident in the investigation of perceptual constancies.

"Perceptual constancy" refers to the fact that variation in a perceived attribute such as shape, size or color differs from (is less than) what knowledge of the proximal (retinal) stimulus leads one to expect. So, for example, object colors are judged to be remarkably constant under changes of illumination, and the judged size or shape of objects certainly varies much less than the geometry of retinal projection would predict. The constancies have been known about for a long time, but were first studied experimentally in this century; the classic work was done by THOULESS (1931) and BRUNSWIK (1944), and they were the focus of much interest in the forties and fifties. The most obvious of constancies is size constancy. The optics of retinal projection lead one to expect that if an object's distance from the observer is doubled its size should be halved, since the retinal image's linear dimensions diminish by half. This does not happen; there is an antithesis between one's knowledge of the physical attributes of objects such as size and shape, which do not vary with the observer's point of view, and the proximal effects on the receptors. This conflict is typically resolved by a compromise between the two sorts of information, which THOULESS called "phenomenal regression to the real object." While we generally judge the size of an object to remain constant as its distance changes, this judgement is not made independently of retinal subtense. The compromise is not rational, although practically universal, and is usually measured by a ratio suggested by BRUNSWIK (1929) for size, with similar interpretations for other constancies.

$$\text{BRUNSWIK ratio} = P - R/C - R$$

where R = retinal size, C = constant (physical) size, P = perceived or judged size.

The ratio has the property of being zero when no constancy is shown, i.e., when judgements are made purely in terms of retinal size, and is one when constancy is perfect, that is, when judgements of size are independent of viewing distance. The general upshot of research on the constancies has been that the more information the observer has, the more closely will his judgements be based on physical attributes of the object. Thus, if judgements of size are made under "reduced" conditions such as monocular vision in dim illumination and with few other cues to distance, poor constancy is shown. If the judgements are made binocularly, with free head movement and under good illumination in a natural setting, constancy is almost perfect (HOLWAY and BORING, 1941). It has also been found that the manipulation of context affects perceived size (e.g., BECK and GIBSON, 1955) as does training and induced set (e.g., THOULESS, 1932). There are also conditions such as convergence micropsia and macropsia (GRANT, 1942; VON HOLST and MITTELSTAEDT, 1950) which affect perceived size and which appear to be due to direct physiological processing. Thus there is a variety of factors which are known to affect judgements of size, distance, etc., and they are of rather different sorts. Emphasizing one set of factors leads one sort of theorist to think of the constancies as essentially cognitive in nature, and as resulting from an active "construction" of visual space (e.g., ITTELSON, 1952), but others have argued that perception, including the perception of the constancies, is just a matter of learning to discriminate the relevant properties of a stimulus array (GIBSON, 1966) or even that physiological processing arrangements guarantee a degree of constancy in perception (VON HOLST and MITTELSTAEDT, 1950).

The proponents of each point of view can marshall striking—even compelling—evidence which supports their favored explanatory schema. When all the evidence is considered, however, no single explanation is satisfactory. The study of perceptual constancy reveals once again the problems facing the theorist in perception: An apparently unitary perceptual phenomenon (or category of phenomena) may have a multiplicity of causes or contributing factors.

F. Stability, Clarity, and Anisotropy

A major characteristic of the human visual framework is its stability. This is true of other modalities, and of other species too. The question of its genesis, of what allows one to distinguish the three-dimensional spatial framework from oneself, and from objects that exist and move in it, has exercised philosophers and scientists for two thousand years and more. It was the question of major concern to Bishop BERKELEY in developing his New Theory of Vision (1709). The modern scientific approach to the question probably began with STRATTON'S experiments on adaptation to the effects of wearing spectacles which invert the visual field (STRATTON, 1897). The first precise and viable theory was propounded by VON HOLST and MITTELSTAEDT in their paper on the "Principle of Reafference" (VON HOLST and MITTELSTAEDT, 1950). The principle, which follows from HELMHOLTZ'S motor outflow theory, states that a corollary discharge or "efference copy" accompanies every motor command in the CNS. When the resulting movements cause a change in sensory input—as when the eyes are moved—the consequent change in sensory stimulation is compared to the efference copy. Changes of input which are entirely a result of self-produced movement are defined as reafference, other changes of stimulation are termed exafference. If the sensory input exactly matches the efference copy, then no external movement is detected; in the case of vision, movement of the retinal image is in some sense cancelled out, so that the visual frame of reference remains stable. Retinal stimulation which does not match the efference copy, however, results in the perception of externally moving objects. This is a powerful model with many applications, and some evidence to support it. Although the physiological detection of the efference copy is elusive (see, however, NODA et al., 1972) and the matching operation difficult to specify in detail, there seems little doubt that this mechanism is one possible basis for achieving perceptual stability. It cannot account for all of it, however; stability of the visual world does not break down when an observer is moved through his visual environment, for example in an automobile. When the relationship between motor command and visual sensory input is broken artifically, as in riding a bicycle, there is no perceptual breakdown. So, a simple form of the principle cannot account for all the data, even on a casual and commonsense view of the matter. It has been argued by MACKAY (1957, 1973) that the concept of elimination of a reafferent signal by the efference copy is unnecessary; the central nervous system has to *evaluate* sensory reafference, not cancel it. Correct evaluation of reafference would offer positive evidence of the stability of the world, but this would occur in a central information and control system rather than as a peripheral signal processing event. In MACKAY's model the importance of reafferent signals is not disputed, but a different function within the CNS is postulated for them. The question of the relationship between reafferent signals, stability and internal representation of the environment is discussed in detail in a joint publication by MACKAY and MITTELSTAEDT (1973).

The philosophical problem of spatial perception which BERKELEY tackled has another important facet, and this has to do with the relationship between touch and vision. In BERKELEY's view touch was the modality to reveal the stable three-dimensional nature of space, to which the less reliable visual information has to be subordinated. There is a long line of research on the question of whether touch educates vision, or vice versa (see, e.g., HARRIS, 1965) and the experimental evidence is somewhat conflicting. Most of the evidence on human neonates (e.g., WHITE, 1971; YONAS and PICK, 1975) and recent careful work on recovery from blindness (GREGORY and WALLACE, 1963; ACKROYD et al., 1974) indicates the importance of tactile exploration for visual-spatial development. An intriguing question here is whether humans undergo anything like the critical period for visual-spatial development now known to occur in cats (HUBEL and WIESEL, 1970; BLAKEMORE and VAN SLUYTERS, 1975) and almost certainly in other mammals too. So far there is no firm experimental evidence on this point, but a strong suggestion, particularly from clinical findings, that such a period may occur in the first two years of life for the human infant (VAN NORDEN, 1973).

Closely related to stability and visual orientation is the fact of perceptual clarity. The human eye has evolved as an instrument which can detect extremely small changes in its adequate stimulus, and important for this is its ability to integrate information over time (see, e.g., CORNSWEET, 1970). A different characteristic with obvious survival value for a distance receptor is the ability to reorientate rapidly and fixate accurately, something which the human eye does superbly. The fact that the eye not only integrates over time—and "perceptual persistence" can be directly measured (HABER and STANDING, 1969)—but can also move and process fine details very rapidly, as in reading (see Chap. X), seems to pose a contradiction. Visual storage can last for several hundred milliseconds at least, yet the eyes move and can read symbols clearly at rates which suggest there should be considerable interference between "old" information and "new" on the retina. In addition the eye is subject to involuntary eye movements, including rapid physiological nystagmus (tremor) at low amplitude (RATLIFF and RIGGS, 1950) induced by the antagonistic action of the powerful extrinsic eye muscles. The retinal image, then, even under the best conditions, contains a good deal of visual noise. The puzzle is to know how clear vision is possible.

If all movement of the retinal image is stopped either optically or mechanically (RATLIFF et al., 1952; DITCHBURN and GINSBORG, 1952) detail vision fades quite rapidly and may disappear completely (BARLOW, 1963; YARBUS, 1967). Image motion is a necessary condition of maintained clear vision, although it does not greatly affect acuity thresholds. Until fading occurs, they are somewhat lower under stabilized than unstabilized conditions. The amplitude of involuntary eye movements, however, may exceed by a factor of 100 the fineness with which detail can be detected, especially in stereovision.

These facts together suggest that there must be a special mechanism for extracting visual information from noise, including that produced by various types of eye movement. Some of these, such as the saccadic shifts of fixation which occur during reading and other types of visual scanning, might be eliminated by the cancellation of reafferent signals as explained earlier, but the reafference principle will not explain the ability to extract signals from random noise, to process rapidly, or to attain acuities which are much finer than the amplitude of retinal shift. The appropriate mechanism may be one which cross-correlates succesive time samples of the visual input with each other and stores a pattern correlation function which is continually "updated" (DODWELL, 1971b). Although direct evidence for this mechanism is lacking so far, its power to explain these otherwise puzzling problems is sufficient to render the mechanism highly plausible. It can account for extraction of signal from noise, statistical smoothing and high visual acuity in the presence of perturbations, the need for retinal motion in maintaining clear vision, and the ability of the visual system to integrate information over time. The time-sampling hypothesis is supported by evidence that psychological time is quantized into "moments" of about 50 ms (STROUD, 1955; KRISTOFFERSON, 1967). Such a correlational mechanism—at levels one (detection) and two (organization)—cannot, however, explain all that is known about acuity and clear vision. Once again set, experience, and motivation can be shown to be relevant, at least in some situations.

The human visual system has certain well-known anisotropies so far as pattern detection is concerned. The principle axes of the visual field—horizontal and vertical—have some special characteristics. Judgements of horizontality and verticality are much more accurately made than judgements of other orientations (JASTROW, 1893), lines in these orientations are more readily detected, and so on. The facts have recently been summarized by APPELLE (1972). In typical fashion, two sorts of explanation have been put forward; one claims that there is an inbuilt superiority for horizontal and vertical detection because of superior physiological equipment, such as more, or more refined, receptive field units for these orientations; the other claims that experience accounts for the anisotropies, as horizontal and vertical contours are more frequently encountered than others, and are more important for the maintaining of spatial orientation. Through a combination of neurophysiological and behavioral analysis, the correct explanation appears to have been found and it is neither purely environmental nor simply nativistic. As a matter of fact it is a good object lesson in the futility of espousing just one of these viewpoints to the exclusion of the other. Hereditarily endowed capacities interact with experienced stimulation to create a viable visual system. HUBEL and WIESEL's early discoveries about receptive field organization and contour coding (1962, 1963) suggested that the system was largely prewired, but it was subsequently shown that it could be heavily biased by selective exposure. The best-known example of this is BLAKEMORE and COOPER's experiment (1970) in which cats exposed only to contours in one orientation developed the detectors for that orientation but not others, and the appropriate discriminative capacities. The process of "tuning" to an imposed stimulus has even been observed directly in very young kittens by PETTIGREW et al. (1973). MITCHELL and his associates have demonstrated the effect of selective rearing of this sort on psychophysical thresholds in the cat, and (at least by implication) in humans with severe astigmatic abnormalities (MUIR and MITCHELL, 1973; MITCHELL et al., 1973). Evidence of threshold bias in humans with normal eyesight but reared in a "noncarpentered" environment has also been obtained (ANNIS and FROST, 1973) although there is some conflicting evidence (TIMNEY and MUIR, 1976). It seems probable that the orientational anisotropies develop—or can develop—as a result of the type of environment to which an organism is exposed. However, they only develop because the organism has a particular type of inbuilt retinal receptive field organization with its own particular geniculo-striate connections, which is susceptible to tuning by imposed stimulation in a particular way. Further evidence on this point is provided by LEVENTHAL and HIRSCH (1975) who showed that orientational tuning by selective exposure (in cats) is sharp when the exposed orientations are horizontal or vertical, but essentially non-existent if the exposure is to diagonally oriented contours.

It should perhaps be emphasized that the anisotropic effects, though real in human pattern vision, are relatively slight and probably do not significantly affect object recognition and organization. Attempts to show differences cross-culturally in spatial organization, such as in distance judgements and susceptibility to illusion, have generally shown rather slight (although statistically reliable) effects of a few percent (e.g., SEGALL et al., 1966).

G. Conclusion

There are many facets to the study of human pattern and object perception, and the present review is far from exhaustive. Two fields in particular that have scarcely been touched on are concerned with the biasing effects of set, motivation, and instruction on perceptual reports, and the application of information-processing notions to perception. The first of these two has had an active life but is perhaps now past its prime. There is no doubt that such factors as interest and attention affect the way we perceive things, and in particular the way we report them, and much ingenuity has been expended in trying to separate these two aspects of the problem (see, e.g., DIXON, 1971).

The effects are at level 3, i.e., cognitive, but tell us relatively little about the nature of perceptual processing per se. The information-processing approach to pattern recognition on the other hand, which can be distinguished from the statistical treatment of form in terms of information theory which was discussed earlier, is an active contemporary field. Its contribution has mainly been in terms of the systematic analysis of the ways in which symbols (letters, digits, words) are observed, remembered, and reproduced. Borrowing heavily from the fields of systems engineering and computer science it can be regarded as the most recent—and rather successful—attempt to enlist the latest in technological developments as an aid to understanding perception. It is perhaps too early to assess its lasting contribution to the field, except in matters to do with reading, and this is covered in another chapter (Chap. X).

The various contributions to understanding human pattern and object perception which have been discussed have brought to light the fact that most of the phenomena are complex in the sense that many factors seem to bear on them. Explanations, if they are tight and tidy, always seem to be incomplete. Where a physiological process is known to be relevant, as in the orientation of form for example, it cannot provide the explanation if cognitive factors such as the free assignment of the "up-down" orientation of the form are operative (ROCK, 1973). Yet the latter cannot exhaustively account for things if they ignore physiological functioning. Most of the theoretical disputes about pattern and object perception (and about perception generally) have been disputes between those who favor "basic", or nativistic physiological explanations, and those who prefer cognitive, empiricist, functional explanations. I have argued elsewhere (DODWELL, 1974) that the dichotomy is a false one, despite its long and distinguished history in experimental psychology (BORING, 1942). It is false because it is wrong to suppose that a perceptual phenomenon must have just one explanation, and this can be seen by comparing perception with other psychological activities like speaking a language or playing chess. This is not the place to give the arguments in detail (see DODWELL, 1975); however, by giving their outline one can get an idea of how the three levels of functioning referred to continually in this chapter can be related to three levels of explanation. These levels are not independent of one another, but their dependence is of a particular sort.

In learning a spoken language there are certain physically necessary conditions which can be studied in their own right, such as the ability of the learner to hear and reproduce a particular sound. These are empirically necessary for the segmentation of a sound stream into syllables, words, and phrases, but certainly not sufficient to explain the latter. The study of syntax and semantics likewise presupposes word and phrase structure, but syntax and semantics are not explained by them. The cognitive uses—the purpose—of language cannot be discovered or explained by the study of single words, yet the study of word formation is a perfectly legitimate scientific activity in its own right. Similarly, the acquisition of language is studied by psychologists, and many arresting and insightful things have been discovered; yet the study of language acquisition does not itself say anything about the nature of language and the role it plays in human life. For this a different sort of conceptual, cognitive, analysis is required. It only makes sense, for instance, to study the "language" of chimpanzees if one already knows what language is. Such research may reveal much about chimpanzees, and even perhaps about how language is acquired. It will not, and cannot, reveal anything about the nature of language.

Chess playing has recently been studied by psychologists, and with some success (e.g., CHASE and SIMON, 1972). Discovering what psychological processes are necessary conditions for chess mastery may reveal a great deal about what makes a good chess player, but does not explain what the point of chess is as an intellectual pursuit. By studying the behavior of chess Masters much can be learned about how to become a good player, but it only makes sense to do this if one already has a good understanding of what chess is all about, and this is obtained by conceptual more than experimental investigation. When psychologists investigate chess playing they study the perceptual and other processes which are needed to develop that skill, but this does not lead to a simple, exhaustive, explanation of chess. The investigation itself presupposes a great deal of understanding of the nature of games, controlled competition, rule-following behavior and its rewards, and so on.

It is just so with the study of perception too. Studying reading or perceptual constancy, for instance, only makes sense if one tacitly acknowledges many basic qualities of the world and the language we use to describe it; it also presupposes certain forms of visual detection and organization which are themselves worthy objects of independent study. These in turn are based on physiological processes which are to be studied by yet a different set of techniques.

Sensory physiologists study processes which are necessary conditions for perception to occur; although many correlations emerge between sensory functioning and perceptual behavior of various kinds, the one is not explained by the other, just as, in our examples of chess playing and language, events at one level could not explain those at another. The same sort of relationship holds between the different levels of functioning studied by psychologists. Investigations aimed at processes of detection are clearly relevant to perceptual organization, for the latter cannot occur without the former: yet detection is not organization, and statements about detection do not necessarily imply anything about organization. Similarly organization in perception can be studied in its own right and by itself entails nothing about cognition, or the recognition of objects, people, events, etc. It is sometimes difficult to separate the study of organization from cognitive judgement (a classical mistake of Gestalt psychology) but that is another matter. My conclusion, then, is that the proper objective of psychological investigation in general, and particularly in the fields of pattern and object perception, is to study processes within a multistage system which itself can only be understood if a number of different explanatory schemas and models of the world are invoked. Explanations of process are different from explanations of purpose, yet clearly both are necessary to the understanding of object perception. The fact that one cannot be *derived* from the other does not detract from the importance of either.

One can now see why certain theoretical disputes have survived so long in the psychology of perception. Arguments over nativism and empiricism persist for example, although no longer in their crass and simple form. They will continue to be with us, not because no one has discovered how to solve them, but rather because they are in principle insoluble. Rather than pose nativism and empiricism as alternative explanatory principles, they should be recognized as complementary. Inborn properties of the visual system provide the necessary conditions for experiential factors to interact with, and so on. This is just one example of how the tendency to seek all-embracing explanations in psychology has been misguided. When it is recognized that the objectives of experimental psychology are limited in the ways described in this section, one comes to see why on the one hand no spectacular theoretical breakthroughs in understanding the nature of perception are likely to occur, and why the study of human pattern and object perception holds little promise of fundamentally affecting the way we see the world around us on the other.

Acknowledgement

This paper was written while the author held a research grant from the National Research Council of Canada, (AOA44), and during tenure of a Leave Fellowship from the Canada Council. Both sources of support are gratefully acknowledged.

References

Ackroyd, C., Humphrey, N.K., Warrington, E.K.: Lasting effects of early blindness. A case study. Q. J. Exp. Psychol. **26**, 114–124 (1974)

Andrews, M.H., Brown, D.R.: A multidimensional analysis of visual shape discrimination. Paper presented at Midwestern Psychological Association, Chicago, May, 1967

Annis, R.C., Frost, B.J.: Human visual ecology and orientation anisotropies in acuity. Science **182**, 729–731 (1973)

Appelle, S.: Perception and discrimination as a function of stimulus orientation: the "oblique effect" in man and animals. Psychol. Bull. **78**, 266–278 (1972)

Attneave, F.: Some informational aspects of visual perception. Psychol. Rev. **61**, 183–193 (1954)

Attneave, F., Arnoult, M.D.: The quantitative study of shape and pattern perception. Psychol. Bull. **53**, 452–471 (1956)

Barlow, H.B.: Slippage of contact lenses and other artifacts in relation to fading and regeneration of supposedly stable retinal images. Q. J. Exp. Psychol. **15**, 36–51 (1963)

Barlow, H.B.: Single units and sensation: a neuron doctrine for perceptual psychology? Perception **1**, 371–394 (1972)

Barlow, H.B.: Visual experience and cortical development. Nature **285**, 199–204 (1975)

Barlow, H.B., Blakemore, C., Pettigrew, J.D.: The neural mechanism of binocular depth discrimination. J. Physiol. **193**, 327–342 (1967)

Barlow, H.B., Narasimhan, R., Rosenfeld, A.: Visual pattern analysis in machines and animals. Science **177**, 567–575 (1972)

Beck, J., Gibson, J.J.: The relation of apparent shape to apparent slant in the perception of objects. J. Exp. Psychol. **50**, 125–133 (1955)

Berkeley, G.: A New Theory of Vision. (Original, 1709). London: Dent. 1910

Blakemore, C., Cooper, G.F.: Development of the brain depends on visual environment. Nature **228**, 477–478 (1970)

Blakemore, C., Van Sluyters, R.C.: Innate and environmental factors in the development of the kitten's visual cortex. J. Physiol. **248**, 663–716 (1975)

Blank, A.A.: Analysis of experiments in binocular space perception. J. Opt. Soc. Am. **48**, 911–925 (1958)

Blank, A.A.: Curvature of visual space. An experiment. J. Opt. Soc. Am. **51**, 335–339 (1961)

Brown, D.R., Owen, D.H.: The metrics of visual form: methodological dyspepsia. Psychol. Bull. **68**, 243–259 (1967)

Boring, E.G.: A new ambiguous picture. Am. J. Psychol. **42**, 444–445 (1930)

Boring, E.G.: Sensation and Perception in the History of Experimental Psychology. New York-London: Appleton-Century-Crofts 1942

Bruner, J.S.: Neural mechanisms in perception. Psychol. Rev. **64**, 340–358 (1957)

Bruner, J.S., Minturn, A.L.: Perceptual identification and perceptual organization. J. Gen. Psychol. **53**, 21–28 (1955)

Brunswik, E.: Zur Entwicklung der Albedowahrnehmung. Z. Psychol. **109**, 40–115 (1929)

Brunswik, E.: Distal focusing of perception: size constancy in a representative sample of situations. Psychol. Monographs. **254** (1944)

Caelli, T.M.: The prediction of interactions between visual forms by products of Lie operators. Math. Biosci. 1975

Campbell, F.W.: The transmission of spatial information through the visual system. Neurosciences. Third Study Program. Cambridge: M.I.T. Press 1974

Chase, W.G., Simon, H.A.: Perception in chess. Cognitive Psychology **4**, 55–81 (1972)

Corcoran, D.W.J.: Pattern Recognition. Harmondsworth Baltimore: Penguin Books 1971

Coren, S.: Subjective contours and apparent depth. Psychol. Rev. **79**, 359–367 (1972)

Cornsweet, T.N.: Visual Perception. New York: Academic Press 1970

Deutsch, J.A.: A theory of shape recognition. Brit. J. Psychol. **46**, 30–37 (1955)

Ditchburn, R.W., Ginsborg, B.L.: Vision with a stabilized retinal image. Nature **170**, 36–37 (1952)

Dixon, N.F.: Subliminal Perception: The Nature of a Controversy. London: McGraw-Hill 1971

Dodwell, P.C.: A coupled system for coding and learning. Psychol. Rev. **71**, 148–159 (1964)

Dodwell, P.C.: Visual Pattern Recognition. New York: Holt, Rinehart and Winston 1970

Dodwell, P.C.: Perceptual Processing: Stimulus Equivalence and Pattern Recognition. New York: Appleton-Century-Crofts 1971a

Dodwell, P.C.: On perceptual clarity. Psychol. Rev. **78**, 275–289 (1971b)

Dodwell, P.C.: Contemporary theoretical problems in seeing. Handbook of Perception. E.C. Carterette, M. Friedman (eds.). New York: Academic Press 1975, Vol. V

Dodwell, P.C.: Criteria for a neuropsychological theory of perception. Cah. Psychologie (1977 in press)

Garner, W.R.: Uncertainty and Structure as Psychological Concepts. New York: Wiley 1962

Garner, W.R.: The Processing of Information and Structure. Potomac: Erlbaum 1974

Gibson, J.J.: The Senses Considered as Perceptual Systems. Boston: Houghton-Mifflin 1966

Grant, V.W.: Accommodation and convergence in visual space perception. J. Exp. Psychol. **31**, 89–104 (1942)

Green, D.M., Swets, J.A.: Signal Detection Theory and Psychophysics. New York: Wiley 1966

Green, R.J., Courtis, M.C.: Information theory and figure perception: the metaphor that failed. Acta Psychol. **25**, 12–26 (1966)

Gregory, R.L.: Cognitive contours. Nature **238**, 51–52 (1972)

Gregory, R.L., Wallace, J.G.: Recovery from early blindness. Exp. Psychol. Soc. Monogr. **2**, (1963)

Grimsdale, R.L., Sumner, F.H., Tunis, C.J., Kilburn, T.: A system for the automatic recognition of patterns. Proc. Inst. Electrical Engineers, **106**, 210–221 (1959)

Guzman, A.: Decomposition of a visual scene into bodies. Joint Computer Conference Proc. Washington: Thompson Book Co. 1968

Haber, R.N., Standing, L.G.: Direct measures of short-term visual storage. Q. J. Exp. Psychol. **21**, 43–54 (1969)

Harris, C.S.: Perceptual adaptation to inverted, reversed and displaced vision. Psychol. Rev. **72**, (1965)

Hebb, D.O.: The Organization of Behavior. New York: Wiley 1949

Hering, E.: Beiträge zur Physiologie. Leipzig: Engelmann 1864

Hochberg, J.: Nativism and empiricism in perception. In: Psychology in the Making. Postman, L. (ed.). New York: Knopf 1962

Hochberg, J.: In the mind's eye. In: Contemporary Theory and Research in Visual Perception. Haber, R.N. (ed.). New York: Holt, Rinehart and Winston 1968

Hoffman, W.C.: The Lie algebra of visual perception. J. Math. Psychol. **3**, 65–98 (1966)

Hoffman, W.C.: The neuron as a Lie group germ and a Lie product. Q. J. Appl. Math. **26**, 423–440 (1968)

Holway, A.H., Boring, E.G.: Determinants of apparent visual size with distance invariant. Am. J. Psychol. **54**, 21–37 (1941)

Howard, I.B.: Proposals for the study of anomalous perceptual schemata. Perception. **3**, 497–513 (1974)

Hubel, D.H., Wiesel, T.N.: Receptive fields, binocular interaction and functional architecture in the cat's visual cortex. J. Physiol. **160**, 106–154 (1962)

Hubel, D.H., Wiesel, T.N.: Receptive fields of cells in striate cortex of very young visually inexperienced kittens. J. Neurophys. **26**, 994–1002 (1963)

Hubel, D.H., Wiesel, T.N.: Receptive fields and functional architecture of monkey striate cortex. J. Physiol. **195**, 215–243 (1968)

Hubel, D.H., Wiesel, T.N.: The period of susceptibility to the physiological effects of unilateral eye closure in kittens. J. Physiol. **906**, 419–436 (1970)

Hunt, E.B.: Artifical Intelligence. New York: Academic Press 1975

Ittelson, W.H.: The constancies in perceptual theory. In: Human Behavior From the Transactional Point of View. Kilpatrick, F.R. (ed.). Hannover: Inst. for Assoc. Res. 1952

Jameson, D.A., Hurvich, L.M. (eds.): Visual Psychophysics. In: Handbook of Sensory Physiology. New York: Springer-Verlag 1972, Vol. VII/4

Jastrow, J.: On the judgement of horizontal, vertical and oblique positions of lines. Am. J. Psychol. **5**, 220–223 (1893)

Julesz, B.: Binocular depth perception of computer-generated patterns. Bell System Technical Journal **39**, 1125–1162 (1960)

Kanizsa, G.: Margini quasi-percettivi in campi con stimolazione omogenea. Riv. Psicol. **49**, 7–30 (1955)

Kanizsa, G.: Contours without gradients, or cognitive contours? Ital. J. Psychol. **1**, 93–112 (1974)

Kling, J.W., Riggs, L.A.: Woodworth and Schlosberg's Experimental Psychology. 3rd ed. New York: Holt, Rinehart and Winston 1971

Konorski, J.: Integrative Activities of the Brain: An Inter-Disciplinary Approach. Chicago: U. Pr. 1967

Kristofferson, A.B.: Attention and psychological time. Acta Psychol. **27**, 93–100 (1967)

Lashley, K.S.: The problem of cerebral organization in vision. Biol. Symposia **7**, 301–322 (1942)

Lashley, K.S.: Functional interpretation of anatomic patterns. In: Patterns of Organization in the Central Nervous System. Proceedings of the Association for research on nervous and mental diseases, 1952

Leventhal, A.G., Hirsch, H.V.: Cortical effect of early exposure to diagonal lines. Science **90**, 902–904 (1975)

Luneburg, R.K.: Mathematical Analysis of Binocular Vision. Princeton: Princeton U. Pr. 1947

MacKay, D.M.: The stabilization of perception during voluntary activity. Proceedings of the 15th International Congress of Psychology. Amsterdam: North Holland Publishing 1957

MacKay, D.M.: Visual stability and voluntary eye movement. In: Handbook of Sensory physiology. Jung, R. (ed.). Heidelberg-New York: Springer-Verlag 1973, Vol. VII/3

MacKay, D.M., Mittelstaedt, H.: Visual stability and motor control (reafference revisited). Cybernetics and Bionics. Munich-Vienna: Oldenburg 1974

Mitchell, D.E., Freeman, R.D., Millodot, M., Haegerstrom, G.: Meridional amblyopia: evidence for modification of the human visual system by early visual experience. Vision Res. **13**, 535–558 (1973)

Minsky, M.: Semantic Information Processing. Cambridge: M.I.T. Press 1969
Muir, D.A., Mitchell, D.E.: Visual resolution and experience: acuity deficits in cats following early selective visual deprivation. Science **180**, 420–422 (1973)
Noda, H., Freeman, R.B., Creutzfeldt, O.D.: Neuronal correlates of eye movements in the visual cortex of cat. Science **175**, 661–663 (1972)
• Noton, D., Stark, L.: Scan paths in eye movements during pattern recognition. Science **171**, 308–357 (1971)
• Oldfield, R.C.: Memory mechanisms and the theory of schemata. Br. J. Psychol. **45**, 14–23 (1954)
Pettigrew, W.J., Olson, C., Barlow, H.B.: Kitten visual cortex: short-term stimulus-induced changes in connectivity. Science **180**, 1202–1203 (1973)
• Pitts, W., McCulloch, W.S.: How we know universals: The perception of auditory and visual forms. Bull. Math. Biophysics. **9**, 127–147 (1947)
Pollen, D.A., Lee, J.R., Taylor, J.H.: How does the striate cortex begin the reconstruction of the visual world? Science **173**, 74–77 (1971)
• Posner, M.I.: Abstraction and the process of recognition. In: Bower, G.H., Spence, J.T. (eds.). Psychology of Learning and Motivation. New York: Academic Press 1969
Ratliff, F., Riggs, L.A.: Involuntary movements of the eye during monocular fixation. J. Exp. Psychol. **40**, 687–700 (1950)
Reed, S.K.: Psychological Processes in Pattern Recognition. New York: Academic Press 1973
• Riggs, L.A., Ratliff, F., Cornsweet, J.C., Cornsweet, T.N.: The disappearance of steadily-fixated visual test objects. J. Opt. Soc. Am. **43**, 495–501 (1953)
• Robson, J.G.: Receptive fields: neural representation of the spatial and intensive attributes of the visual image. In: Handbook of Perception. Carterette, E.C., Friedman, M. (eds.). New York: Academic Press 1975, Vol. V
Rock, I.: Orientation and Form. New York: Academic Press 1973
Rock, I., Kremen, I.: A re-examination of Rubin's figural after-effect. J. Exp. Psychol. **53**, 23–30 (1957)
• Rosch, E.: Natural categories. Cognitive Psychology **4**, 328–350 (1973)
• Rosch, E., Mervis, C.B., Gray, W.D., Johnson, D.M., Boyes-Braem, D.: Basic objects in natural categories. Cognitive Psychology **8**, 382–439 (1976)
Segall, M.H., Campbell, D.T., Herskovitz, M.J.: The Influence of Culture on Visual Perception. Indianapolis: Bobbs-Merrill 1966
• Sekuler, R.: Spatial vision. In: Annu. Rev. Psychol. **25**, 195–232 (1974)
Stevens, S.S. (ed.): Handbook of Experimental Psychology. New York: Wiley 1951
Stratton, G.M.: Vision without inversion of the retinal image. Psychol. Rev. **4**, 341–360, 463–481 (1897)
Stroud, J.: The fine structure of psychological time. In: Information Theory in Psychology. Quastler, H. (ed.). Glencoe: Free Press 1955
Sutherland, N.S.: Outlines of a theory of pattern recognition in animals and man. Proc. R. Soc. Lond. [Biol.] **171**, 297–317 (1968)
Thouless, R.H.: Phenomenal regression to the real object I. Br. J. Psychol. **21**, 339–359 (1931)
Thouless, R.H.: Individual differences in phenomenal regression. Br. J. Psychol. **22**, 216–241 (1932)
Timney, B., Muir, D.W.: Orientation anisotropy: incidence and magnitude in Caucasian and Chinese subjects. Science **193**, 699–701 (1976)
• Uhr, L.: Pattern Recognition. New York: Wiley 1966
Von Holst, E., Mittelstaedt, H.: Das Reafferenprinzip. Die Naturwissenschaften **37**, 464–476 (1950)
• Von Holst, E., Mittelstaedt, H.: The Principle of Reafference. In: Perceptual Processing. Dodwell, P.C. (ed.). New York: Appleton-Century-Crofts 1971
Von Norden, G.K.: Experimental amblyopia in monkeys. Further behavioral observations and clinical correlations. Invest. Ophtalmology **12**, 721–738 (1973)
White, B.L., Human Infants. New York: Prentice-Hall 1971
Yarbus, A.L.: Eye Movements and Vision. New York: Plenum 1967
Yonas, A., Pick, H.R.: An approach to the study of infant space perception. In: Infant Perception. Cohen, L., Salapatek, P. (eds.). New York: Academic Press 1975
Zajaczowska, A.: Experimental test of Luneburg's theory. Horopter and alley experiments. J. Opt. Soc. Am. **46**, 514–527 (1956)
Zusne, L.: Visual perception of form. New York: Academic Press 1970

Chapter 16

Visual Illusions

S. Coren, Vancouver (Canada) and J.S. Girgus, New York (USA)

With 7 Figures and 1 Table

Contents

Frequently, when an observer views a simple pattern and is asked to describe his conscious visual percept, his subjective assessment of stimulus relations, including the size, shape, or direction of pattern components, differs from what might be expected on the basis of direct physical measurements of the stimulus array. Configurations which reliably elicit such discrepant judgments are generally called visual-geometric illusions. Several hundred different illusion configurations have been catalogued since Oppel published the first formal investigations of these phenomena in 1854–1855.

Both the variety and strength of these distortions is quite striking. Consider, for instance, the set of configurations shown in Figure 1. Figure 1a is the well-known Mueller-Lyer illusion, in which the left half of the horizontal shaft is seen as longer than the right, despite the fact that they are physically equal. The magnitude of this distortions is quite large, resulting in a relative overestimation and underestimation of shaft length of 25–30%. Figure 1b shows a distortion of direction known as the Poggendorff illusion. In this configuration, the segments of the transversal are colinear, although the segment on the right appears to be too high relative to the segment on the left. Figure 1c is the Zoellner illusion in which the vertical lines are parallel but look as if they are not. Figure 1d is an illusion of shape first introduced by Hering in 1861. Here the horizontal lines are, in fact, straight, but appear bowed in opposite directions. Figure 1e is the Ponzo illusion where the upper horizontal line is apparently longer than the lower. In Figure 1f, the vertical line appears longer than the horizontal. Figure 1g shows the Oppel-Kundt illusion in which the

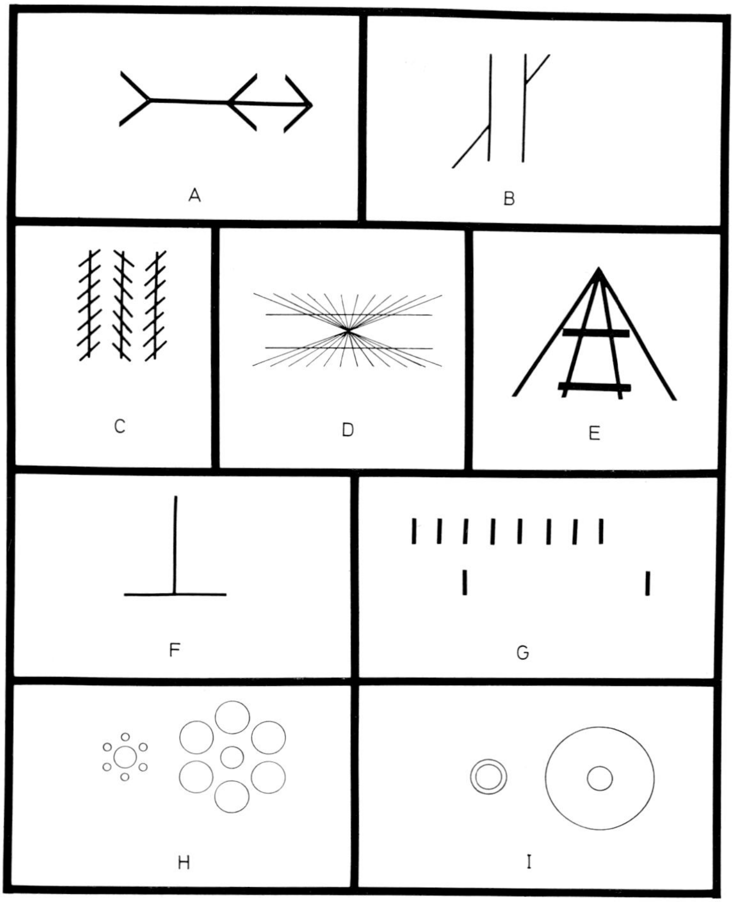

Fig. 1a–i. Variety of illusion configurations (see text for explanation)

divided extent appears longer than the undivided extent. Figure 1h is the Ebbinghaus illusion in which the two central circles are the same size, although the one surrounded by the larger circles appears considerably smaller than the one surrounded by smaller circles. Figure 1i shows a similar size distortion known as the Delboeuf illusion.

The many different varieties of visual distortion which have been found make it unlikely that we are dealing with any single distorting mechanism. The available evidence seems to indicate that these distortions represent contributions from many sources, including the dioptrics of the eye and peripheral and central neural interactions. In addition there are cognitive or judgmental processes which may add to the illusory effect. Thus, in order to understand these common perceptual distortions, it is necessary to consider a number of different mechanisms and levels of visual processing (COREN and GIRGUS, 1973a, 1974; GIRGUS and COREN, 1973a; GIRGUS et al., 1973).

A. Optical Components in Visual Illusions

It is clear that the first interface between the visual system and the external environment is the dioptric system of the eye. If interaction between the stimulus and the cornea, crystalline lens, or optic media leads to changes in the relationships among stimulus elements, the distribution of light that falls on the retina will also be affected. In some cases (where changes are large and systematic), an illusory distortion in the percept may result.

It is universally agreed that the quality of the image is altered as the light passes through the cornea, pupillary aperture, and crystalline lens. Even a perfect optical instrument of the size and shape of the eye would theoretically image a point source of light as a distribution in the form of the familiar diffraction pattern. The resultant image would then be a bell-shaped distribution of light about 1.5 min of arc in diameter, or more, depending upon the pupil size (HELMHOLTZ, 1886; FRY, 1955; WESTHEIMER, 1963). The eye, of course, is not a perfect optical system. To begin with, the surfaces of the cornea and lens deviate from perfect sphericity (AMES and PROCTOR, 1924). This *spherical aberration* further spreads and blurs the image (KOOMEN et al., 1949; WESTHEIMER, 1963). In addition, optically the eye acts as if it were composed of a single substance with refractive properties which approximate that of water, thus the short wave lengths of light are more sharply refracted, hence come to a focus in front of the longer. This implies that if the eye is accommodated for red, blue will be out of focus. This effect corresponds to approximately two diopters of refractive difference between the ends of the visible spectrum (SCHOBER and WITTMAN, 1938; SHEARD, 1926). Thus, for any point of white light, this *chromatic aberration* will increase the blur of the retinal image. In addition to spherical and chromatic aberrations, the image on the retina is degraded by light scattering from opacities in the optic media and some defocusing which occurs when the image passes through the overlying neural tissue on its way to the photosensitive receptors. The total effect of these sources of image degradation is a significant smearing of the retinal image.

KRAUSKOPF (1962) and WESTHEIMER and CAMPBELL (1962) have directly measured this blur or "line spread function" in intact human eyes. They utilized a technique in which they measured the energy distribution of a bright line which was imaged on the retina and then reflected back along virtually the same path as the one by which it entered. Figure 2a shows the measured spread obtained for a bright line viewed through a 6 mm pupil at best focus (KRAUSKOPF, 1962). Since the image of any object may be thought of as being made up of a series of points, each of which leads to such a spread function by the time it reaches the retina, the resultant retinal image for any external stimulus should be a blurred representation of the original. It is clear, however, that we do not consciously register this retinal blur. It has been generally assumed that the sharpness of the conscious percept results from the fact that the brain assumes the point of maximal excitation represents the locus of contour (GANZ, 1964; RATLIFF, 1965).

Figure 2b shows two distributions that correspond to the retinal images

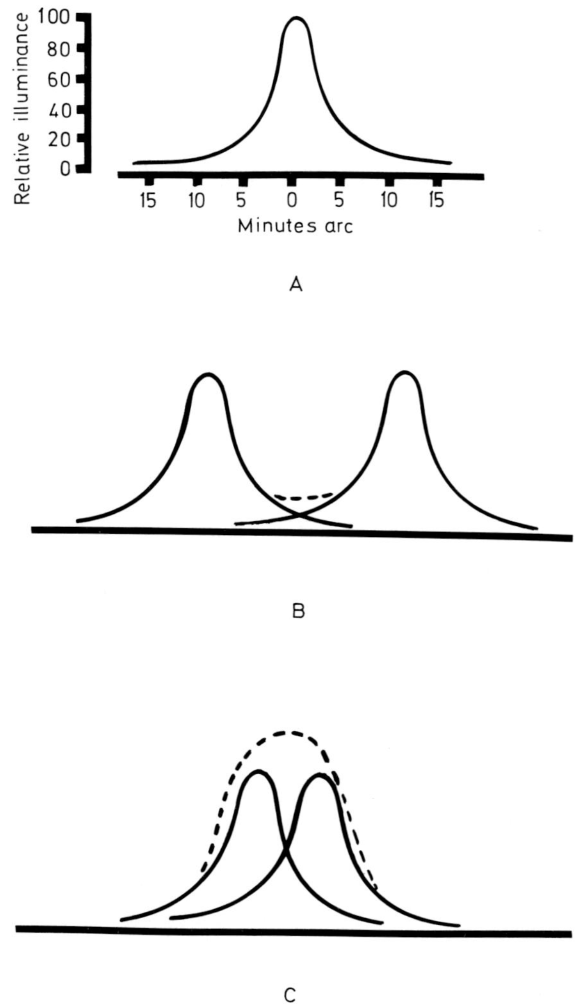

Fig. 2. (a) Measured distribution of light on retina for bright line viewed through 6 mm pupil at best focus (KRAUSKOPF, 1962). (b) Hypothetical distribution for two lines on retina some distance apart. (c) Hypothetical distribution for two close lines on retina. Dotted curve shows summed distribution

of two points of light. If the brain designates the locus of contours by identifying the most active regions in the pattern of retinal stimulation, this input will result in the perception of the two points. However, if the points are now moved closer to one another, as in Figure 2c, the summed distribution *(dotted curve)* will not be distinguishable from the distribution associated with a single point whose locus lies between the two distributions. Consider the effect of such summation of blur on two intersecting lines which form an angle. When the lines are far apart as in 2b, we would expect little or no effect on the

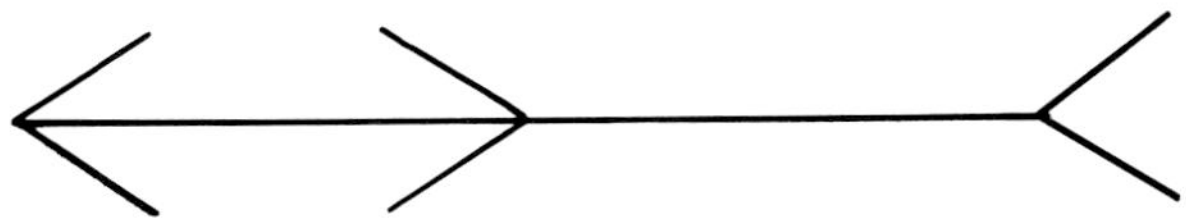

A

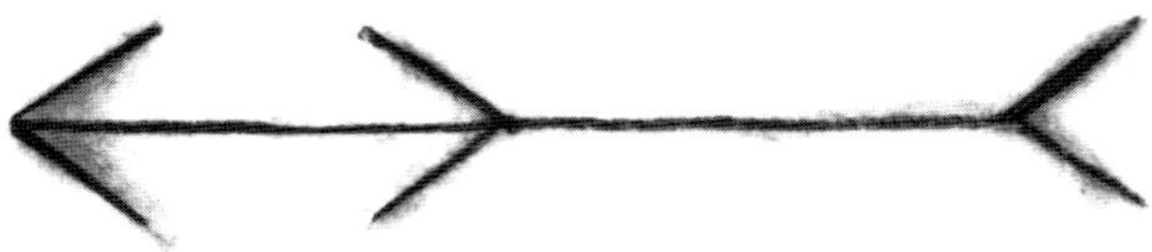

B

C

Fig. 3. Effect of progressive blurring on intersecting line illusion, showing how increases in blur lead to increases in apparent size of illusion

resulting percept. As the lines draw closer together, however, they begin to approximate a situation analogous to that shown in Figure 2c. Here we would expect a very definite effect on perception. Under these circumstances, the apparent locus of the vertex of the angle should be displaced into the body of the angle. There should also be a concomitant shift in the locus and tilt of the sides, making the angle appear more obtuse than it actually is.

Such contour shifts may be used to explain many observed illusions which contain intersecting line elements (EINTHOVEN, 1898; CHAING, 1968). For example, in the Mueller-Lyer illusion (Fig. 1a), the shift of the apparent locus of the vertex into the angle would result in the left half of the figure being seen as longer than the right. This may be crudely demonstrated by considering Figure 3. Figure 3a shows the Brentano form of the Mueller-Lyer illusion. Figure 3b artificially blurs this configuration by defocusing the image. This represents a more extreme version of what the eye does to a sharp external contour.

Note that in Figure 3b the apparent maxima have shifted in a manner which accentuates the distortion, and in Figure 3c, where the blur is even greater, the difference in apparent distance between the loci of the vertices is even more accentuated. CHAING (1968) has attempted to apply a version of this theoretical approach to a number of intersecting line illusions, including the Poggendorff (1b), Zoellner (1c), Mueller-Lyer (1a), and Hering (1d) illusions. In each instance, the direction of distortion predicted by the recombination of degraded optical images is consonant with the observed illusory effect.

COREN (1969) manipulated the quality of the image on the retina directly and, in this way, tested the contribution of optical image degradation in the formation of the Poggendorff illusion (1b). The amount and sources of image spread associated with normal viewing through a 4 mm pupil is shown in the first column of Table 1. Since chromatic aberration depends upon a mixture of wavelengths in the stimulus, this source of blur is easily reduced by viewing through a narrow band interference filter. Since spherical aberration is due to deviations from ideal curvature of the surface of the cornea and lens, it may be eliminated by using a small artificial pupil, thus restricting the input to central, relatively undeviated rays. This artificial pupil also eliminates any residual refractive error (AMES and PROCTOR, 1921; LUDVIGH, 1953). It should be noted that an artificial pupil does tend to increase the light spread due to diffraction. This increase in blur, for a 1 mm pupil, however, is considerably smaller than the decrease obtained by correcting the other sources of image degradation. The blur diameters for the specific combination of narrow band chromatic filter and 1 mm artificial pupil used by COREN (1969) are shown in the second column of Table 1. When subjects are tested on the Poggendorff illusion under the two viewing conditions shown in Table 1, a reduction in illusion magnitude is observed under the low blur as predicted by the theory.

However, the magnitude of the reduction in illusions is considerably less than the theoretical prediction. If we assume a symmetrical distribution of energy on the retina and then reduce its spread to 1/N of the original spread of energy, it is easy to calculate, or demonstrate geometrically along the lines suggested by CHAING (1968) and PRESSEY and den HEYER (1968), that the magnitude of the illusion should be reduced to 1/Nth of its original size. In the condition where the illusion is viewed with the filter and artificial pupil, the blur is reduced to one-fourth of its original size if total blur is the determining

Table 1. Appropriate computed diameters of the blur disc measured in seconds of arc. (After COREN, 1969)

Sources of blur	4-mm pupil	1-mm pupil with 18 mm band width chromatic filter
Chromatic aberration	216	13
Spherical aberration	432	30
Diffraction	34	126
Assumed uncorrected refractive error of 0.0625D	54	13
Total	736	182

factor, and to approximately three-tenths of its original size if the largest single blur circle is the most relevant measure. This calculation would lead us to expect a 70–75% reduction in illusion. However, the obtained illusion reduction was only 22%. Thus, while optical aberrations may play a significant role in the formation of some visual geometric illusions involving intersecting line elements, they are definitely not the whole answer, nor even the major source of distortion.

B. Retinal Components in Visual Illusions

Since the retina may be viewed as an extended photosensitive surface upon which the dioptric system forms an image, it has often been compared to the film in a camera. The mass of evidence, however, indicates that the retina does not simply passively convert patterns of light into corresponding patterns of neural impulses.

For example, one phenomenon that has been frequently reported is that of spatial summation. A point of light which is too weak to be seen alone may become visible when a second point of light (also too weak to be seen alone) is imaged on an adjacent spot on the retina (GRAHAM, 1934). ADRIAN and MATTHEWS (1928), using the conger eel; HARTLINE (1940a), using the frog; and GRANIT (1947), KUFFLER (1952), and BARLOW et al. (1957), using the cat have shown this neural pooling or summation to be retinal in origin. Basically, the findings of these researchers indicate spatial summation on the retina by demonstrating that impulses in the optic nerve are more readily produced by a large patch of light than by small ones of the same luminance.

The results are generally explained in terms of the neural convergence that occur as the impulses are transmitted from the receptors to succeeding neural levels in the visual system. Alternatively they may be seen as consistent with the concept of the neural receptive field, defined as including all those receptors capable of producing a response in any given optic nerve fibril or retinal ganglion cell (HARTLINE, 1940b; KUFFLER, 1953).

It should be noted that the summation effects found by the investigators listed above produce shifts in contour locus which are similar to the effects that would be predicted on the basis of optical blur. These experiments usually utilize paradigms in which the stimulus input is passed through the optical components of the eye, often with accommodation relaxed and the pupil dilated. Thus, we should probably be cautious about assuming a neural basis for these summation effects. It should be noted, however, that spatial summation does manifest itself in neural responses recorded directly from both retinal ganglion cells and other cells higher in the visual system (BARLOW, 1953; KUFFLER, 1953).

There is another form of spatial interaction of the retina which is clearly of neural origin. This is the mutual inhibition of spatially adjacent neural units.

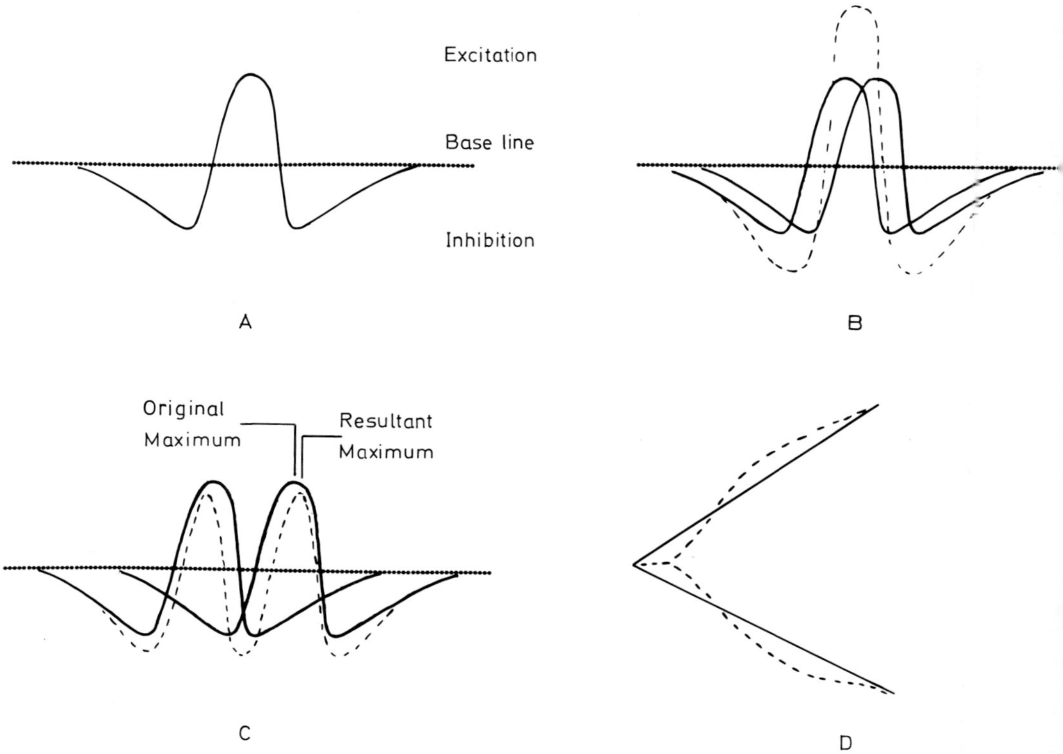

Fig. 4. (a) Distribution of neural activity resulting from point of light imaged on retina. (b) Distributions of neural activity resulting from two points of light imaged close together on retina. Dotted line shows how two distributions will sum under these circumstances. (c) Distributions of two points of light imaged somewhat further away from each other on retina. Dotted line again shows summed distributions. (d) Physical loci of two intersecting lines (solid lines) and predicted ridges of neural activity dotted lines)

The original physiologic demonstration of this effect stems from the work of Hartline (1940), which has been replicated many times using the eye of the horseshoe crab *Limulus* to demonstrate the existance of lateral inhibitory interactions (Hartline et al., 1956). In general, such investigations find that neural response to a spot of light was dramatically depressed by the presence of another spot of light imaged on a neighboring region of the retina. These inhibitory effects are rather broad in their spatial extent and have been used to explain a number of brightness phenomena including Mach bands (Ratliff, 1965), and brightness contrast (Diamond, 1960). It should be pointed out that this inhibitory process serves to sharpen the neural output, restoring some of the high frequency components lost through the blurring of the image in its passage through the optic system.

If we combine both of these mechanisms, each point of retinal stimulation may be analyzed as having both a spread of excitation and a spread of inhibition. Figure 4a shows the distribution of neural activity resulting from an incoming point of light. Suppose that we have two points of light imaged on the retina. If the points are close enough to each other, the two excitatory spreads will sum as shown by the dotted line in Figure 4b. Notice that the dotted line in Figure 4b shows a distribution of activity identical with the distribution that would be expected from a single spot of light. Figure 4c shows the predicted interaction if the spots are somewhat farther apart. If the inhibitory flank of the distribution from one spot affects the spread of excitation of nearby points, there will be some reduction in activity. Figure 4c shows how this reduction may be asymmetrical. Such an asymmetrical reduction in activity should lead to a shift in the position of the two maxima of excitation such that they are farther away from each other. To the extent that the visual system interprets the locus of contours on the basis of the local maxima of neural activity, such neural interaction should lead to a perceived contour repulsion for stimuli separated by appropriate distances. In support of this, DAY (1962), GANZ (1964), and POLLACK (1958) have all shown that contours simultaneously imaged on the same retina tend to appear displaced away from each other.

BÉKÉSY (1967) and GANZ (1966) have analyzed the possible consequences of this contour repulsion for the perception of illusion configurations containing converging and intersecting lines. They basically predict that these inhibitory mechanisms will lead to the apparent opening up of acute angles, with the maximum of activity which corresponds to the vertex moving into the body of the angle and the sides tending to flare out slightly. Figure 4d shows the physical loci of the image of two intersecting lines on the retina as solid lines and the predicted ridges of neural activity as dotted lines. It is easy to see that this type of interaction can be used to account for the illusory effects observed in the MUELLER-LYER (1a), the POGGENDORFF (1b), the ZOELLNER (1c), the HERING (1d), and many other illusions involving intersecting lines. It is interesting to note that this neural effect on the contours making up the angle similar in general conformation to the effects expected on the basis of the optical effects discussed in the preceding section.

It should be clear that the major stimulus requirement for the operation of this neural mechanism is converging lines on the same retina. Probably the most direct means of analyzing the contribution of these effects involves presenting some of the elements of the illusion pattern to one eye, and the remainder of the elements to the other, with no angles present in either monocular view. When this is done with the Poggendorff illusion (1b), the transversals are presented to one eye and the verticals to the other. If there are adequate cues for fusion, the observer will see the normal Poggendorff configuration when the two views are combined stereoscopically. Figure 5 shows three stereoscopic arrays with their final fused illusions configurations. Note that this method of stimulus presentation completely eliminates any optical or neural interactions which stem from the presence of angles on any one retina. This technique has been used by OHWAKI (1960), DAY (1961), SPRINGBETT (1961), and SCHILLER and WIENER (1962) to circumvent the possibility of retinal interactions. The same basic finding emerged from all of these studies. Significant illusory effects remain when configurations are tested under stereoscopic conditions, but the strength of the distortion is much less than it is under normal

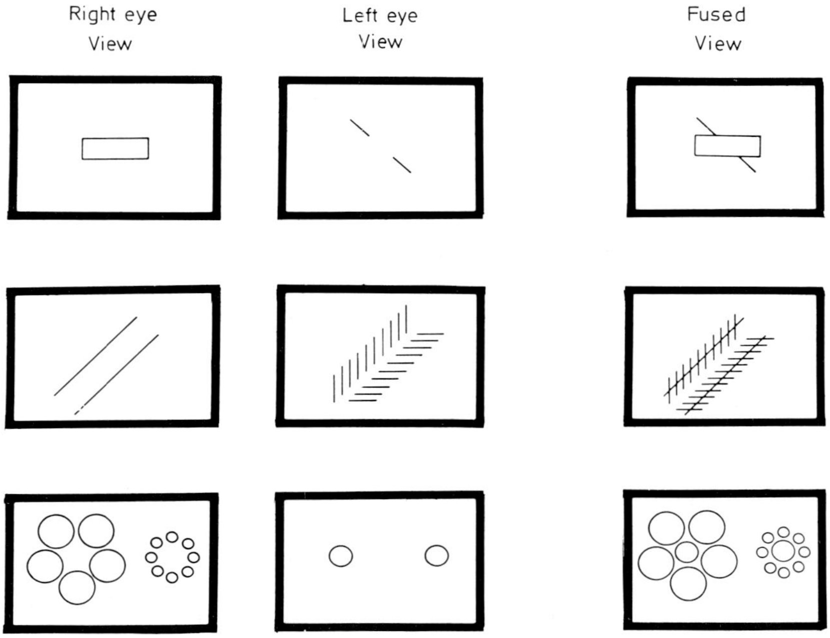

Fig. 5. Stimuli for stereoscopic presentation of Poggendorff, Zoellner, and Ebbinghaus illusions

viewing conditions. This reduced effect would seem to imply a retinal component in intersecting line illusions. It should be remembered, however, that, under these conditions, any reduction in illusion magnitude due to the elimination of retinal interactions may be confounded with binocular rivalry effects which tend to cause apparent suppression of parts of the figures as well as general instability and fluctuation in the fused array. In addition, it should be remembered that these arrays remove the effects of the optical interactions described in the previous section as well as the effects of the retinal neural interactions presumably being tested in these experiments.

C. Cortical Components in Visual Illusions

At least two investigators have raised the possibility of cortical involvement in visual illusions (Coltheart, 1971; Köhler and Wallach, 1944). Köhler and Wallach based their reasoning about illusions on data gathered on figural aftereffects which are contour displacements occurring on subsequently viewed stimuli following steady fixation of certain patterns. Their explanations of both figural after-effects and illusions rested on a model of brain tissue operation which assumed mass action of cortical fields. Although this model of the brain has been largely discredited (LASHLEY et al., 1951), the predictions that derive from it regarding illusions are identical to those derived from more recent models of the operation of the post-geniculate visual system (COLTHEART, 1971). Thus, the cortical satiation model proposed by KÖHLER and WALLACH is still worthy of description.

KÖHLER and WALLACH contended that, if a specific cortical locus is continuously stimulated, the neural tissue involved eventually becomes "fatigued" or "satiated" and thus becomes more difficult to activate. This fatigue presumably spreads out spatially to include nearby neural units. If a test line is now presented so that its spread of excitation overlaps the fatigued or satiated region, the response to this new stimulus should be asymmetrically reduced. This should cause an apparent shift of the test line in the direction away from the locus of the initially viewed stimulus.

In order to use this mechanism to explain illusions containing intersecting line elements, one must simply posit that these satiation effects can occur very quickly. This would cause two simultaneously present lines to be repulsed away from each other. This would lead to an apparent overestimation of acute angles similar to that which is predicted by optical aberrations or lateral inhibition on the retina. In addition, similar effects could be predicted from a model positing lateral inhibitory interactions between adjacent cortical sites (BLAKEMORE et al., 1970).

BURNS and PRITCHARD (1971), using microelectrode recording techniques, have directly mapped the effect of both a single line and and angle pattern on the cortex of the cat. They found that the locus of maximal response for points in close spatial proximity were shifted toward each other, while the maximal response loci for points which are more widely separated were displaced away from each other. In sum, the resultant pattern of cortical activity when viewing an angle apparently closely resembles that shown in Figure 4a, which was derived solely from retinal interactions. Unfortunately, this finding need not be interpreted as resulting from any cortical involvement. Since the image has passed through the peripheral optical and neural systems before reaching the cortex, the contour shifts observed in the cortex of the cat may simply be an accurate topologic representation of distortions already present before the image reached the cortex. This same confounding of retinal and central factors can be found in other psychophysical attempts to assess cortical contributions to illusions (BLAKEMORE et al., 1970). It is thus critical to screen out opportunity for peripheral interactions before ascribing distortion to a more central process. The most effective technique used so far to accomplish this is the one described above, in which some of the elements are presented to one eye while the remainder are presented to the other eye in such a way that no converging or intersecting lines are present on a single retina (DAY, 1961; OHWAKI, 1960; SCHILLER and WEINER, 1962; SPRINGBETT, 1961). Problems associated with this technique have already been pointed out. The major difficulties involve the presence of binocular rivalry and suppression for contours of different orientations imaged on corresponding points on the two retinas. This fault in the technique has been successfully circumvented by JULESZ (1971) and PAPERT (1961) who presented illusion configurations using random dot stereograms. In these stimuli, each monocular view presents a random texture of elements containing no hint of the illusory configuration. Binocular disparity cues are introduced into a subset of the textural units. In the resulting fused array, observers see the illusory configurations separated from the background in depth. Since there are no monocular contours to interact and no rivalrous elements to confuse the observation, this technique effectively removes all peripheral optical and neural effects. Thus, for this technique, the first site of contour interaction must occur *after* binocular fusion has taken place. The available data indicate that binocular fusion most probably occurs beyond the lateral geniculate bodies and possibly even beyond area 17. These data come from the work of HUBEL and WIESEL (1961, 1962) who found no binocularly driven units on the lateral geniculate bodies of the cat. BISHOP et al. (1959) reported finding some binocular driven cells in this same species, although the percentage is quite low, amounting only to 8.5%. DEVALOIS (1960) was unable to find any binocular units in the lateral geniculate nuclei of the monkey. This picture changes higher up in the system. HUBEL and WIESEL (1962, 1968) report a large number of binocularly driven cells in area 17 of the cortex of the cat but few such cells in area 17 of the monkey cortex. A later study (HUBEL and WIESEL, 1970) indicates a preponderance of binocularly driven cells in area 18 of the cortex of the macaque monkey. Taken together, these data seem to suggest that any illusory effects obtained in humans using random dot stereograms are at least post-geniculate in origin and possibly occur beyond area 17 of the cortex.

JULESZ (1971) reports that most of the classical illusions still appear to be present using random dot stereogram presentations. Unfortunately, no one has managed to measure the magnitudes of illusions under these conditions. JULESZ (1971) has anecdotally reported that some illusory effects appear to be considerably weakened under these conditions.

There are two techniques which may completely eliminate lateral cortical interactions as well as peripheral optical and neural effects. These techniques involve the removal of all binocular and monocular intersecting and converging lines from the array. For example, COREN (1970a, 1970b) removed all the line elements in three intersecting line illusions and replaced them with dots marking the line ends and vertices. Figures 6a and 6b show the normal form and the dot form of the Mueller-Lyer illusion; Figures 6c and 6d show the normal form and the dot form of the Poggendorff illusion; and Figures 6e and 6f show the normal form and the dot form of the Hering illusion. Presumably the dot forms of these illusion configurations remove all opportunities for contour displacements due to optical and neural interactions. COREN (1970a, b) found that this manipulation significantly reduced the magnitude of the observed distortion in all three illusions. Nonetheless, significant distortion in the classically observed directions remained in all three dot configurations.

Another method which seems to eliminate most contour interactions, including those in the cortex, involves using subjective contour forms of the illusions configurations. COREN (1972) has suggested a number of principles that facilitate

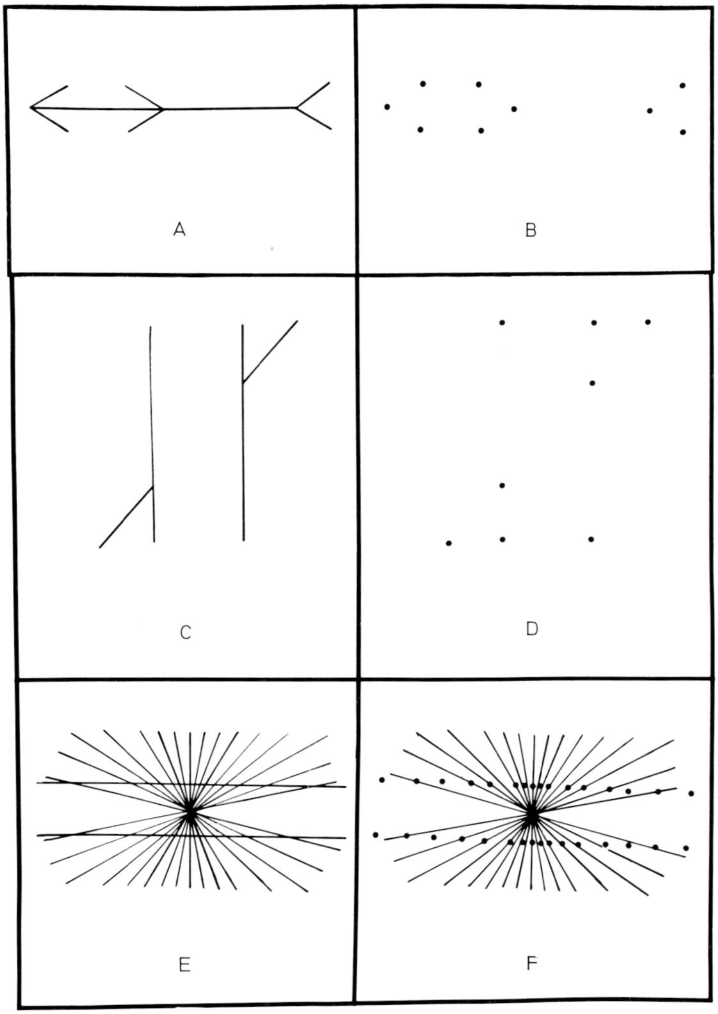

Fig. 6. Standard form and dot form of Mueller-Lyer (A, B), Poggendorff (C, D) and Hering (E, F) illusions

the production of such apparent contours which may be produced in the absence of any physical brightness gradients in the stimulus. GOLDSTEIN and WEINTRAUB (1973) have shown that, when the Poggendorff illusion (Figure 1 b) is presented using an array of this type, the strength of the illusion is significantly reduced. A significant amount of illusion is, however, still present under these conditions.

It is, of course, possible that, although both the dot forms and the subjective contour forms of the illusions lack actual contours, they nonetheless contain enough implicit stimulus information to excite cortical orientation analyzers. These units may then interact laterally in the manner described above, or in the manner suggested by COLTHEART (1971). There is, however, nothing in the literature to suggest that cortical orientation receptors are, in fact, stimulated by such arrays. It is somewhat more reasonable at this point to assume that there are some cognitive judgmental processes, with unknown physiologic underpinnings, which contribute to the observed illusion effects. A number of such mechanisms have been suggested and it may be helpful to describe some of the major theoretical positions that fall into this category.

D. Cognitive Mechanisms in Illusions

Cognitive mechanisms refer to the ways in which the organism interprets incoming visual information based upon his experiences, hypotheses, and strategies of judgment. There are at least three major cognitive theories that have been proposed to explain visual illusions. One of these is usually called *misapplied constancy scaling*. Looking at the Ponzo illusion shown in Figure 1e, it is easy to imagine that we are looking at a crude two-dimensional representation of a three-dimensional scene in which the converging lines are perspective cues (e.g., a road or railroad tracks receding into the distance). It is clear from Figure 1e that the upper horizontal line appears to be larger than the lower. Although both are the same physical size. One proposed explanation for this phenomenon takes the following form: Both lines subtend the same visual angle since they are, in fact, the same length and at the same distance from the observer. However, the upper line is seen as farther away because of the perspective cues provided by the converging lines. Under these circumstances, the upper line is now perceived as larger since, according to the mechanism of size constancy, when two objects are at different distances and subtend the same visual angle, the further object must be physically larger. This explanation has been used by a number of investigators (DAY, 1972; GILLAM, 1971; GREGORY, 1968; LEIBOWITZ et al., 1969; THIERY, 1896) to explain many of the illusion configurations shown in Figure 1.

A second judgmental factor that has been proposed to explain visual illusions involves *size contrast* (or the process of emphasizing clearly seen differences). This is the same process that makes a sports announcer look small when interviewing basketball players, but tall when interviewing race horse jockeys. The Ebbinghaus illusion (1h) has frequently been explained in this way (COREN and MILLER, 1974).

A third proposal for a cognitive factor suggests that the observer confuses the test elements with the inducing elements when making his judgment. Thus, ERLEBACHER and SEKULER (1969) have suggested that the observer confuses the extents between the wing tips with the test shaft length in the Mueller-Lyer illusion. Such confusion could lead to the observed distortion. This theory is supported by the fact that the magnitude of the illusion is reduced if we emphasize the difference between the test line and the inducing elements by coloring the wings differently from the test shaft or by verbally directing the observer's attention away from the wings and toward the shaft (COREN and GIRGUS, 1973b).

It would be helpful if an experimental technique could be found that could separate these cognitive-judgmental components from the non-cognitive contributions of the optical and neural systems and thus, more accurately assess the contribution of the physiologic components described above. Fortunately, a technique exists whereby this separation may be accomplished.

As early as 1896, HEYMANS noticed that the perceived magnitude of the Mueller-Lyer illusion will diminish after it is scanned with free eye movements for a few minutes. Since this initial observation, the phenomenon of illusion decrement has been frequently demonstrated for the Mueller-Lyer illusion (BURNHAM, 1968; COREN and GIRGUS, 1973b; DEWAR, 1968; FESTINGER et al., 1969; JUDD, 1902; KOEHLER and FISHBACK, 1950; MOUNTJOY, 1959; and PARKER and NEWBIGGING, 1963). In addition, illusion decrement has been shown in the Poggendorff, Zoellner, Hering, and Oppel-Kundt illusions (COREN and GIRGUS, 1972; COREN and HOENIG, 1972). The available evidence seems to indicate a cognitive processing basis for the illusion reduction found under these conditions. For example, the rate of illusion decrement varies as a function of traditional learning variables such as spacing of trials (DREWAR, 1969; MOUNTJOY, 1958); it persists over days and weeks (JUDD, 1902; GIRGUS and COREN, 1973b); and it generalizes on the basis of perceived similarity between configurations rather than on the basis of structural or contour similarities (COREN and GIRGUS, 1974).

It should be noted that some investigators have posited cortical fatigue or satiation of specific feature detectors as an explanation for this diminution in illusion magnitude during inspection (COLTHEART, 1971; KOHLER and FISHBACK, 1950). However, if the observed illusion decrement were due to satiation of either the cortex or specific kinds of feature analyzers in the cortex, then steady fixation of the stimulus should provide the maximum amount of decrement. Yet it has been frequently demonstrated that fixation leads to considerably less decrement than systematic scanning of the illusion pattern (COREN and HOENIG, 1972; FESTINGER et al., 1968). Satiation theories would additionally predict more decrement for configurations with more intersecting and converging line elements since the satiation presumably has its primary effect on angles. Yet GIRGUS et al. (1973) have shown that the rate and magnitude of illusion decrement is independent of the number of converging and intersecting line elements in the configuration. In fact, a dot form of the Mueller-Lyer illusion such as that shown in Figure 6b (which contains no intersecting lines to set up asymmetrical patterns of satiation and which contains no contours to excite feature analyzers) shows the same rate of decrement as the normal form of the stimulus (Fig. 6a).

Taken together, these data seem to indicate that illusion decrement is due to some sort of cognitive-judgmental reorganization. To the extent that this is the case, illusion decrement becomes a useful tool in assessing the contribution of optical and neural interactions to illusions. It is highly unlikely that a few

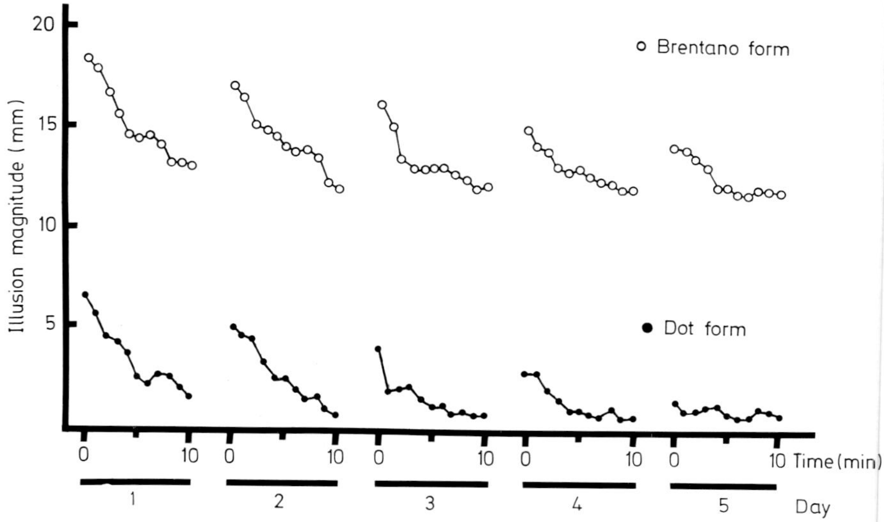

Fig. 7. Changes in magnitude of Brentano form and dot form of Mueller-Lyer illusion over 5 days of testing

minutes of inspection of any pattern will result in any alteration of the gain of lateral inhibition or of the extent of retinal blur. Thus, if we allow an illusion to decrement until asymptote, the residual effect should represent the noncognitive contribution to the illusory effect.

We may easily assess the validity of such a suggestion by considering the two forms of the Mueller-Lyer illusion shown in Figures 5a and 6b. In the normal configuration (6a), we would expect cognitive, optical, and neural factors all to contribute to the observed distortion since there are converging lines in the stimulus. For the dot form of the illusion (6b), we would expect little or no optical and neural interactions, since all converging lines have been eliminated. With prolonged inspection, we would expect the asymptotic level of 6a to be significantly greater than zero, indicating residual optical and neural effects, while 6b should almost completely disappear because of the absence of these sources of distortion. GIRGUS et al. (1975) asked ten observers to inspect each of these two configurations for 10 min a day for 5 days. Tests of illusion magnitude were taken at 1 min intervals.

The data from this experiment are shown in Figure 7. Note that within each day there is a reduction in illusion magnitude. This is the normally observed illusion decrement. In addition, there is a cumulative effect over days for the initial illusion magnitude. The observer apparently begins each day with less distortion. Note, however, that the asymptotic level for each figure is virtually unchanged over days. This asymptote presumably represents the residual illusory effect due to the optical and neural factors which are unchanged by the process of pattern inspection. As predicted for the form of the illusion containing coverging lines, a significant amount of illusion still remains. In fact, the diminution in illusion magnitude represents only about 35% of the illusion effect first observed, indicating that the remaining 65% is probably due to noncognitive factors. The initial magnitude of the dot form of the illusion is considerably less than that of the standard configuration. This is presumably due to the absence of optical and neural effects in this form of the illusion. The obtained illusion decrement for the dot form represents 88% of the initial illusion magnitude for this form. This may imply that 12% of the illusion observed for this figure is due to cognitive factors which are insensitive to the processing that occurs during inspection, to cortical interactions evoked by this degraded stimulus, or to, as yet undiscovered, optical and neural factors. It should be noted, however, that the amount of illusion remaining after inspection in the dot form was not significantly different from zero for the sample of obervers tested in this study.

E. Multiple Causation and Visual Illusions

The evidence presented above seems to indicate that most visual illusions are multiply caused. The final distorted percept results from optical factors arising from the dioptric limitations of the eye, from neural interactions on the retina and perhaps in the cortex, and from some sort of cognitive-judgmental overlay. Thus, to talk of *the* cause for visual illusions, of a single mechanism, or even of a single level of visual processing to explain illusory effects seems somewhat misguided.

Using the kinds of data presented above, we may demonstrate the contributions of several levels of visual processing to any given illusory distortion. Let us consider the Poggendorff illusion (1b) as an example. From COREN's (1969) direct manipulations of blur, we may derive a contribution of about 22% from optical factors. Using the data from COREN's (1970a) dot forms and GOLDSTEIN and WEINTRAUB's (1973) subjective contour forms, both of which ought to eliminate optical and neural interactions completely, we find a reduction in illusion magnitude of about 40%. Since optical factors account for 22% of the effect, 18% of the effect must be due to neural interactive effects at either retinal or cortical levels. We may assess the cognitive-judgmental contribution to the distortion by considering decrement data. COREN and GIRGUS (1972) report that 5 min of inspection leads to a 39% reduction in the initial strength of the Poggendorff illusion. This leaves 21% of the observed distortion unaccounted for. Some of this residual illusion might disappear during a longer inspection period, since 5 min is probably not long enough for an asymptote to have been reached. Thus, this 21% presumably represents a mixture of cognitive-judgmental effects which would disappear with additional inspection and nonplastic cognitive-judgmental effects which would not. In addition, it is possible that this residual illusion may contain the results of higher level interactions evoked by the excitation of orientation specific units in the cortex.

This analysis should make it clear that, despite the apparent simplicity of a stimulus, such as the Poggendorff configuration, the perceptual effect is really a summed distortion resulting from several sources. It should also be apparent that an approach of this kind is required for most, if not all illusion configurations. In addition, this kind of analysis demonstrates how illusions may be used as a tool for isolating the contributions of various levels of processing in the visual system to the final conscious percept.

It is important to note that visual illusions are not special cases of perceptual aberration. Rather, illusions are manifestations of the normal processing in the visual system which happens to result in a final percept which does not directly reflect the physical stimulus relations in the visual array and thus results in a phenomal impression that is at variance with the physical reality. One wonders, in fact, if anything which is as much a permanent and universal experience as the perceptual distortions observed in the configurations shown in Figure 1 can justly be called illusions, unless all perceptions may rightfully be called illusions.

References

Adrian, E.D., Matthews, R.: The action of light on the eye: III. The interaction of retinal neurones. J. Physiol. (Lond.) **65**, 273–298 (1928).

Ames, A., Proctor, C.A.: Dioptrics of the eye. J. opt. Soc. Amer. **5**, 22–35 (1921).

Barlow, H.B.: Summation and inhibition in the frog's retina. J. Physiol. (Lond.) **119**, 69–88 (1953).

Barlow, H.B., Fitz Hugh, R., Kuffler, S.W.: Change of organization in the receptive folds of the cat's retina during dark adaptation. J. Physiol. (Lond.) **137**, 327–337 (1957).

Bekesy, G. von: Sensory Inhibition. Princeton, N.J.: Princeton University Press, 1967.

Blakemore, C., Carpenter, R.H.S., Georgeson, M.A.: Lateral inhibitor between orientation detectors in the human visual system. Nature (Lond.) **228**, 37–39 (1970).

Bishop, P.O., Burke, W., Davis, R.: Activation of single lateral geniculate cells by stimulation of either optic nerve. Science **130**, 506–507 (1959).

Burnham, C.A.: Decrement in the Mueller-Lyer illusion with saccadic and tracking eye movements. Percept. Psychophys. **3**, 424–426 (1968).

Burns, B.D., Pritchard, R.: Geometrical illusions and the response of neurones in the cat's visual cortex to angle patterns. J. Physiol. (Lond.) **213**, 599–616 (1971).

Chaing, C.: A new theory to explain geometrical illusions produced by crossing lines. Percept. Psychophys. **3**, 174–176 (1968).

Coltheart, M.: Visual feature—analyzers and after-effects of tilt and curvature. Psychol. Rev. **78**, 114–121 (1971).

Coren, S.: The influence of optical aberrations on the magnitude of the Poggendorff illusion. Percept. Psychophys. **6**, 185–186 (1969).

Coren, S.: Lateral inhibition and geometric illusions. Quart. J. exp. Psychol. **22**, 274–278 (1970a).

Coren, S.: Lateral inhibition and the Wundt-Hering illusions. Psychon. Sci. **18**, 341 (1970b).

Coren, S.: Subjective contour and apparent depth. Psychol. Rev. **79**, 359–367 (1972).

Coren, S., Girgus, J.S.: Illusion decrement in intersecting line figures. Psychon. Sci. **26**, 108–110 (1972).

Coren, S., Girgus, J.S.: Visual spatial illusions: many explanations. Science **179**, 503–504 (1973a).

Coren, S., Girgus, J.S.: Differentiation and decrement in the Mueller-Lyer illusion. Percept. Psychophys. **12**, 466–470 (1973b).

Coren, S., Girgus, J.S.: Transfer of illusion decrement as a function of perceived similarity. J. exp. Psychol. **102**, 881–887 (1974).

Coren, S., Hoenig, P.: Eye movements and decrement in the Oppel-Kundt illusion. Percept. Psychophys. **12**, 224–225 (1972).

Coren, S., Miller, J.: Size contrast as a function of figural similarity. Percept. Psychophys. **16**, 355–357 (1974).

Day, R.H.: On the stereoscopic observation of geometric illusions. Percept. Motor Skills **13**, 247–258 (1961).

Day, R.H.: Excitory and inhibitory processes as the basis of contour shift and negative after-effect. Psychologia **5**, 185–193 (1962).

Day, R.H.: Visual spatial illusions: a general explanation. Science **175**, 1335–1340 (1972).

DeValois, R.: Color vision mechanisms in the monkey. J. gen. Physiol. **43** (supplement part 2), 115–128 (1960).

Dewar, R.E.: Distribution of practice and the Muller-Lyer illusion. Perception and Psychophysics **3**, 246–248 (1968).

Diamond, A.L.: A theory of depression and enhancement in the brightness response. Psychol. Rev. **67**, 168–199 (1960).

Einthoven, W.: Eine einfache physiologische Erklärung für verschiedene geometrisch-optische Täuschungen. Pflüger's Arch. ges. Physiol. **71**, 1–43 (1898).

Erlebacher, A., Sekuler, R.: Explanation of the Muller-Lyer illusion: Confusion theory examined. J. exp. Psychol. **80**, 462–467 (1969).

Festinger, L., White, C.W., Allyn, M.R.: Eye movements and decrement in the Mueller-Lyer illusion. Percept. Psychophys. **3**, 376–382 (1968).

Fry, G.A.: Blur of the retinal image. Columbus, Ohio: Ohio State University Press, 1955.

Ganz, L.: Lateral inhibition and the location of visual contours: An analysis of figural after-effects. Vision Res. **4**, 465–481 (1964).

Ganz, L.: Mechanism of the figural after-effects. Psychol. Rev. **73**, 128–150 (1966).

Gillam, B.: A depth processing theory of the Poggendorff illusion. Percept. Psychophys. **10**, 211–216 (1971).

Girgus, J.S., Coren, S.: Peripheral and central components in the formation of visual illusions. Amer. J. Optom. **50**, 533–540 (1973).

Girgus, J.S., Coren, S., Durant, M., Porac, C.: The assessment of components involved in illusion formation using a long term decrement procedure. Percept. Psychophys. **2**, 144–148 (1975)

Girgus, J.S., Coren, S., Horowitz, L.: Peripheral and central components in variants of the Mueller-Lyer illusion. Percept. Psychophys. **13**, 157–160 (1973).

Goldstein, M.B., Weintraub, D.J.: The parallel-less Poggendorff: Virtual contours put the illusion down but not out. Percept. Psychophys. **11**, 353, 354 (1973).

Graham, C.H.: Vision: III. Some neural correlations. In: Handbook of general experimental psychology. Murchison, C. (ed.). Worcester, Mass.: Clark University Press, 829–879, 1934.

Gregory, R.L.: Perceptual illusion and brain models. Proc. roy. Soc., Section B, **171**, 279–296 (1968).

Hartline, H.K.: The response of single optic nerve fibers of the vertebrate eye to illumination of the retina. American J. Physiol. (Lond.) **121**, 400–415 (1938).

Hartline, H.K.: The receptive fields of optic nerve fibers. Amer. J. Physiol. **130**, 690–699 (1940).

Hartline, H.K., Wagner, H.G., Ratliff, F.: Inhibition in the eye of limulus. J. gen. Physiol. **39**, 651–673 (1956).

Helmholtz, H. von: Handbuch der physiologischen Optik. Hamburg and Leipzig: Voss, 1886. (Translated as Helmholtz's Treatise on Physiological Optics, J.P.C. Southall ed.). New York: Dover, 1962.)

Heymans, G.: Quantitative Untersuchungen über das „optischen Paradoxen“. Z. Psychol. **9**, 221–255 (1896).

Hubel, D.H., Wiesel, T.N.: Integrative action in the cat's lateral geniculate body. J. Physiol. (Lond.) **155**, 385–398 (1961).

Hubel, D.H., Wiesel, T.N.: Receptive fields, binocular interaction and functional architecture in the cat's visual cortex. J. Physiol. **160**, 106–154 (1962).

Hubel, D.H., Wiesel, T.N.: Receptive fields and functional architecture of monkey striate cortex. J. Physiol. **195**, 215–243 (1968).

Hubel, D.H., Wiesel, T.N.: Stereoscopic vision in macaque monkey. Nature (Lond.) **225**, 41–42 (1970).

Judd, C.H.: Practice and its effects on the geometrical illusions. Psychol. Rev. **9**, 27–39 (1920).
Julesz, B.: Foundations of cyclopean perception. Chicago: University of Chicago Press, 1971.
Koehler, W., Fishback, J.: The destruction of the Mueller-Lyer illusion in repeated trials: I. An examination of two theories. J. exp. Psychol. **40**, 267–281 (1950).
Koehler, W., Wallach, H.: Figural after-effects: On investigation of visual processes. Proc. Amer. phil. Soc. **88**, 269–357 (1944).
Koomen, M., Tousey, R., Scolnik, R.: Spherical aberration of the eye. J. opt. Soc. Amer. **39**, 370–376 (1949).
Krauskopf, J.: Light distribution in human retinal images. J. opt. Soc. Amer. **52**, 1046–1050 (1962).
Kuffler, S.W.: Neurons in the retina: Organization, inhibition and excitation problems. Cold Spr. Harb. Symp. quant. Biol. **17**, 281–292 (1952).
Kuffler, S.W.: Discharge patterns and functional organization of mammalion retina. J. Neurophysiol. **16**, 37–68 (1953).
Lashley, K.S., Chow, K., Semmes, J.: An examination of the electrical field theory of cerebral integration. Psychol. Rev. **58**, 123–136 (1951).
Leibowitz, H., Brislin, R., Perlmutter, L., Hennessy, R.: Ponzo perspective illusion as a manifestation of space perception. Science **1966**, 1174–1176 (1969).
Ludvigh, E.: Perception and contour. U.S. Nav. Sch. Med. Project No. NM 001 075.01-04, Report No. 4., 1953.
Mountjoy, P.T.: Effects of exposure time and intertrial interval upon decrement to the Mueller-Lyer illusion. J. exp. Psychol. 97–102 (1958).
Ohwaki, S.: On the destruction of geometrical illusions in stereoscopic observation. Tôhuku Psychol. Folin. **29**, 24–36 (1960).
Oppel, J.J.: Über geometrisch-optische Täuschungen. Jahresbericht des Frankfurter Vereins **55**, 37–47 (1854–1855).
Papert, S.: Centrally produced geometrical illusions. Nature (Lond.) **191**, 733 (1961).
Parker, N., Newbigging, P.L.: Magnitude and decrement of the Mueller-Lyer illusion as a function of pretraining. Canad. J. Psychol. **17**, 134–140 (1963).
Pollack, R.H.: Figural after-effects: Quantitative studies of displacement. Aust. J. Psychol. **10**, 269–277 (1958).
Pressey, A.W., den Heyer, K.: Observations on Chaing's "new" theory of geometrical illusions. Percept. Psychophys. **4**, 313–314 (1968).
Ratliff, F.: Mach bands: Quantitative studies on neural networks in the retina. New York: Holden-Day, 1965.
Schiller, P., Wiener, M.: Binocular and stereoscopic viewing of geometric illusions. Percept. Motor Skills **15**, 739–747 (1962).
Schober, H., Wittmann, K.: Untersuchungen über die Sehschärfe bei verschiedenfarbigen Licht. Das Licht: Z. praktische Leucht- u. Beleuchtungs-Aufnahmen **8**, 199–201 (1938).
Sheard, C.S.: The chromatic aberration of the eye: The chromatic variations in the interval of the sturm and allied phenomena as determined by the subjective method of skiascopy. J. opt. Soc. Amer. **12**, 79–82 (1926).
Springbett, B.M.: Some stereoscopic phenomena and their implications. Brit. J. Psychol. **52**, 105–109 (1961).
Thiéry, A.: Über geometrisch-optische Täuschungen. Phil. Stud. **12**, 67–126 (1896).
Westheimer, G., Campbell, F.W.: Light distribution in the image formed by the living human eye. J. opt. Soc. Amer. **52**, 1040–1045 (1962).
Westheimer, G.: Optical and motor factors in the formation of the retinal image. J. opt. Soc. Amer. **62**, 86–93 (1963).

Chapter 17

Figural Aftereffects*

TADASU OYAMA, Chiba (Japan)

With 13 Figures

Contents

---

* In this chapter, an overall review of the literature was not intended. Reviews by BONNET (1963), MCEWEN (1958), SAGARA and OYAMA (1957), and MALHOTRA (1966) will be useful for that purpose.

A. Introduction

I. GIBSON's Discoveries

The phenomenon which has lately been considered an example of figural aftereffects was discovered quite incidentally by GIBSON in 1929 at the end of an experiment which, in the tradition of STRATTON's (1897) famous research, was concerned with the formation of new space habits during a period of wearing glasses which distorted the visual world (GIBSON, 1933). From his experimental results, GIBSON formulated as follows:

> A curved line, when perceived for any considerable period of time, becomes phenomenally less curved than it was at the beginning of the period, and at the end of the period an objectively straight line will seem curved in the opposite direction. This fact holds whether the curvature is actually in the object, or is induced by the distorting effect of prisms (GIBSON, 1933; pp. 10–11).

He also concluded that adaptation (the former effect) and aftereffect (the latter effect) are different aspects of the same process. VERHOEFF (1925), GIBSON (1933, 1937), and GIBSON and RADNER (1937) found that fixation of the apex of an obtuse angle, or fixation of a straight line tilted somewhat from the vertical or the horizontal, produces a similar adaptation and aftereffect. These phenomena produced by three different stimulus objects are called "curved," "bent," and "tilted" line effects, respectively. GIBSON (1933, 1937) found two tendencies in each of these effects, the areal localization of the aftereffect (the aftereffect was markedly reduced when the test line was presented with a separation of several degrees from the place of the inspection line) and the interocular transfer of the aftereffect (the aftereffect was reduced to nearly half of the aftereffect obtained by the same eye).

GIBSON (1937) developed a theory to explain the adaptation and aftereffect of the tilted line. A tilted line deviates from the vertical to the right or to the left. Variously tilted lines and the vertical line constitute a "sensory continuum." According to GIBSON's theory, a sensory continuum generally consists of a central norm or standard between opposite qualities. The opposite qualities might be designated as plus and minus, the norm as zero. Such a sensory continuum usually corresponds to a stimulus continuum as shown by the solid lines in Figure 1. From this point of view, the tilt adaptation may be regarded as a process in which the correspondence between the stimulus continuum and the sensory continuum is altered throughout in such a way as to reduce the discrepancy between the actual stimulus and the perceptual norm. The actual stimulus is now correlated with a perceptual quality nearer its norm (adaptation), and this perceptual norm is now correlated with a stimulus value closer to that of the actual stimulus (aftereffect) as shown by the broken lines in Figure 1. It is clear that very similar explanations can also be applied to the adaptation and aftereffects of the curved and bent lines, in both of which the straight line corresponds to the norm and the convexity and concavity constitute two opposite qualities.

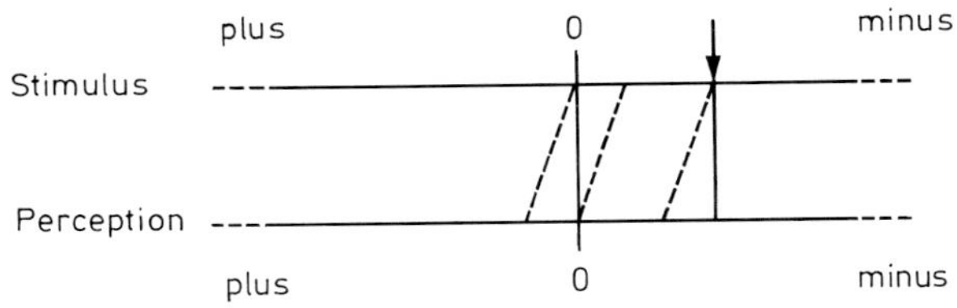

Fig. 1. Diagram of the relationship between the stimulus continuum and the sensory continuum before and after a period of tilt adaptation. The arrow indicates a prolonged stimulus presentation. The solid lines indicate the correspondence between retinal and tilt seen at the beginning, and the dotted lines at the end of the adaptation period. (From GIBSON, 1937.) Copyright 1937 by American Psychological Association. Printed by permission

II. KÖHLER and WALLACH's Studies

On the basis of his hypothetic model of central visual processes, KÖHLER (1940) expected that a prolonged inspection of any figure produces gradual changes in the corresponding cortical area and results in perceptual changes of this figure or a test figure subsequently presented in the same area. KÖHLER (1940) and KÖHLER and WALLACH (1944) conducted many experiments to test these expections. Their experiments generally showed apparent shrinkage or growth of test figures in size, as well as apparent paling in color and recession in depth. KÖHLER and WALLACH named these effects "figural after-effects." The paling of the outline of a T object (test object) and its recession in the third dimension are generally more distinct when the T object concides with the area previously occupied by the I object (inspection object) than when the T object lies in the interior of the area of the I object. However, the shrinkage of a T object is more conspicuous when the T object is surrounded by the outline of the I object than when both coincide.

Many observations of KÖHLER and WALLACH indicated that the color of a T object is more strongly affected when the outline of the T object approaches the outline of the I object more closely and that the same holds for the depth effect. These tendencies suggested that "satiation" (the alternation of the hypothetic cortical medium produced by the continued occurrence of a figure process) decreases when the distance from the outline of the I object increases. However, the amount of size effect does not simply depend upon the degree of satiation at the place of the T object. When the outline of the T object is removed from the region of the maximum satiation, the color and depth effects are weakened, but the size effect grows within a certain limit. Such a paradoxical nature of the figural aftereffects was called "distance paradox."

According to KÖHLER and WALLACH's point of view, the shrinkage and growth of T objects as well as the changes in their locations follow only one principle: the T object as a body or its outline recedes from the region in which a high degree of satiation has been established. When the whole body of the T object is located outside of a satiated area, the recession of the T object as a body from that area will be observed. I objects, as shown in Figure 2, produce such an aftereffect that two T objects placed horizontally in line

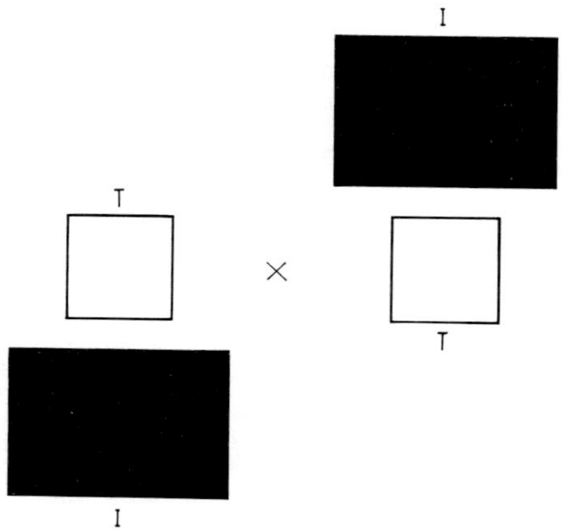

Fig. 2. A stimulus pattern used by KÖHLER and WALLACH (1944). After inspection of I rectangles, the right T square appears to move downward and the left, upward. (From KÖHLER and WALLACH, 1944)

with the fixation mark appear to move in opposite directions, the right T object downward and the left, upward. When the I object is presented on one side only, the displacement of the T object occurs only on that side, but any difference in size between the two T objects is hardly noticeable. If the T object is surrounded by a zone of intense satiation, the recession of its outline away from the affected region will necessarily make the T object shrink. On the other hand, if the outline of the T object surrounds a zone of satiation, the recession of its outline will result in the growth of the T object. Thus, all of these aftereffects can be explained by one principle: "displacement."

After establishing the principles of displacement and distance paradox, KÖHLER and WALLACH tried to apply these principles to GIBSON's discoveries. For example, in the tilted line effect, the T line is generally expected to move away from the I line, and each end of the T line placed furthest from each side of the I line is displaced most in the direction opposite to the I line, while the middle point of the T line coinciding to the middle point of the I line does not move in any direction. The continuous variation of the distance between the I and T lines on each side of the middle point produces a continuous variation in the amount of displacement at various points of the T line. Thus the T line is turned.

In some situations, the predictions based on GIBSON's theory contradict those based on KÖHLER and WALLACH's theory. KÖHLER and WALLACH's theory predicts that the turning of the T line will occur in any orientation of the I and T lines when these two lines form a small angle, while GIBSON's theory predicts that the turning of the T line will occur only near the vertical or horizontal axis when the I line deviates slightly from such an axis. KÖHLER and WALLACH confirmed their prediction in one of their experiments.

On the basis of many experimental results, KÖHLER and WALLACH concluded that displacement is a more general principle than GIBSON's concept of adaptation to the norm and that GIBSON's discoveries (curved, bent, and tilted line effects) are examples of figural aftereffects.

B. Temporal Factors

I. Development and Decay of Figural Aftereffects

HAMMER (1949) studied two temporal aspects of the displacement effect: (1) its developmental aspect as dependent on the duration of the inspection period and (2) its decay after the inspection period. Figures 3 and 4 show the results of her study. The aftereffect (displacement) obtained "immediately" after the inspection period increased with an increase in the duration of the inspection period to a maximum at approximately 1 minute. After an inspection

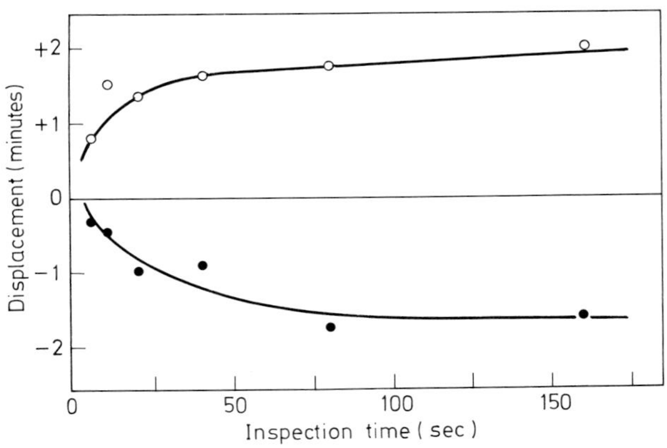

Fig. 3. The developmental course of displacement effect. Positive displacements are to the subject's right of the zero point; negative, to the left. The open circles indicate the data obtained when the I line was presented to the left of the T line; the solid circles, the data obtained when the I line was presented to the right. (From HAMMER, 1949)

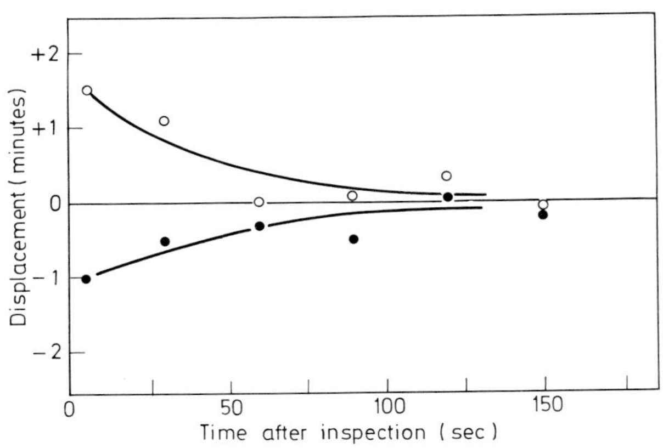

Fig. 4. The decay course of displacement effect. Signs of displacement and symbols have the same meanings as in Figure 3. (From HAMMER, 1949)

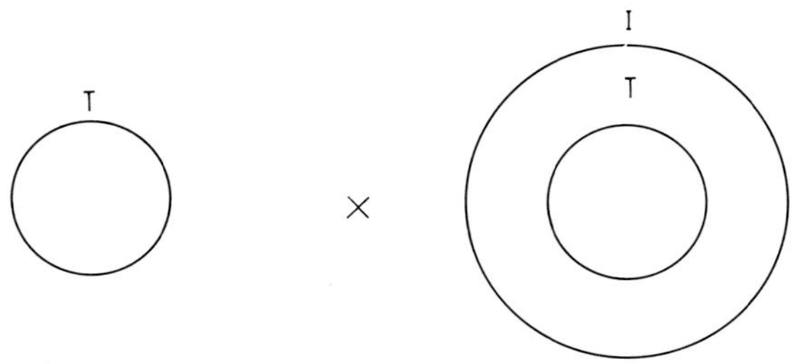

Fig. 5. A typical stimulus pattern used by Japanese investigators

period of constant duration (60 s), the aftereffect was "immediately" maximum and decreased rapidly with an increase in time, reaching zero at approximately 90 s. Similar results were obtained by GIBSON and RADNER (1937) in the development of the tilted line effect, by BALES and FOLLANSBEE (1935) in the decay of the curved line effect, and by NOZAWA (1953) in the development and decay of the curved line effect.

These investigators measured aftereffect by the adjustment method, which required several seconds for one setting. Consequently, the aftereffect, recorded as "immediately after the inspection," was actually measured several seconds later. OYAMA (1953) pointed this out and tried to measure the aftereffect *immediately*, in a more exact sense of the word, after the inspection period by a very simplified form of the constant method. He used an I circle placed to the right of the fixation mark and two T circles placed to the right and left of the fixation mark, as shown in Figure 5. The right T circle was always concentric with the I circle and constant in diameter, while the left T circle varied in diameter from T figure to T figure. Only one T figure was presented after each inspection period, and the subject was to report whether the left T circle appeared larger or smaller than the right T circle at the moment immediately after the inspection. His results showed that a 1-s inspection was long enough to produce a considerable aftereffect (shrinkage) while a longer inspection hardly increased the aftereffect.

OYAMA also obtained the decay curves of aftereffects for various inspection durations. All of these curves showed that the aftereffect always started from almost the same level and decreased with negative acceleration to reach zero. Their qualitative characteristics were similar to each other and to those of HAMMER's decay curve shown in Figure 4, but the rates of decay were different among the curves; the longer the inspection period was, the slower the rate of decay. OYAMA stated that previous investigators who used the adjustment method were concerned with the lower points of decay curves in their studies on the development of aftereffects, while he compared the curves at their starting points. When the data obtained 5 s after the inspection period were plotted against the inspection duration, a gradually increasing curve very similar to HAMMER's developmental curve shown in Figure 3 resulted.

IKEDA and OBONAI (1953) performed essentially the same experiment as OYAMA (1953). Figure 6 shows their results. The curves represent decay courses of aftereffects for seven different inspection durations of 1–240 s, respectively.

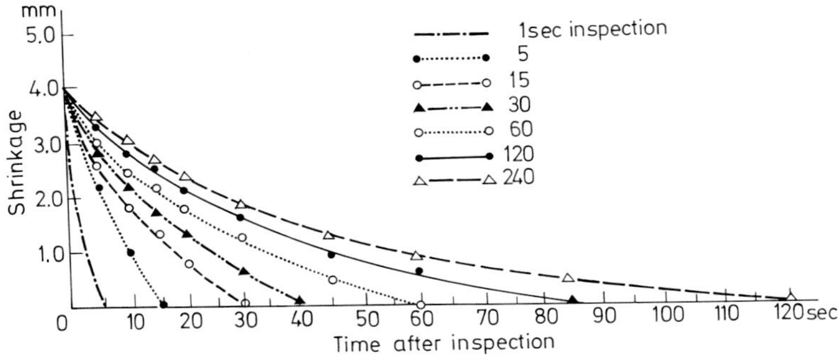

Fig. 6. Decay courses of shrinking effect after various inspection periods. (From IKEDA and OBONAI, 1953)

These curves start at almost identical levels, and the longer the inspection period is, the smaller the rate of decay. These results reconfirmed OYAMA's findings more systematically and quantitatively. IKEDA and OBONAI also studied the same problem concerning the growth of a T circle produced by a smaller I circle and the curved line effect and reached the same conclusion.

II. Mathematical Representation of Decay Process

OYAMA (1953) and IKEDA and OBONAI (1953) independently proposed the same exponential function for the decay of aftereffect on the basis of experimental data

$$A = A_0 e^{-\lambda t} \tag{1}$$

in which A indicates the magnitude of the aftereffect, A_0 the initial magnitude of the aftereffect, λ a parameter representing the rate of decay, and t the time interval between the inspection and test periods. This equation is essentially the same as that of MUELLER (1949), who used HAMMER's (1949) data, except that λ is a parameter which varies as a function of inspection duration and not a constant as in MUELLER's equation.

OBONAI (1962) found it possible to relate the half-decay time (τ) determined from IKEDA and OBONAI's data to the inspection duration (i) by a power function

$$\tau = k\, i^{\alpha} \tag{2}$$

where the constant α was 0.387 and 0.300 in their two experimental series (shrinkage and growth), respectively, and the constant k was 2.5 in common. The half-decay time (τ) is defined as the time in which the aftereffect is reduced to one-half of its initial value and is inversely related to λ.

$$\tau = 0.693/\lambda \tag{3}$$

It is very easy to relate Equation 1 to Equation 2 by Equation 3. TAYLOR (1962, 1966) proposed 0.5 as a general value for α on the basis of the results of seven experiments on figural aftereffects made by GIBSON and RADNER (1937), HAMMER (1949), NOZAWA (1953), OYAMA (1953), and IKEDA and OBONAI (1953).

III. Tachistoscopic Experiments

Some microscopic aspects of the temporal processes have been studied with tachistoscopes, which presented I and T figures very briefly. FARNÈ (1965) found that aftereffects were clearly observable even after a 40-ms inspection, but the aftereffects continued to increase for at least 5 s.

IKEDA and OBONAI (1955a) showed in their tachistoscopic study that the aftereffect increased to a maximum at an interval of 60 ms after the presentation of an I object, and then decreased as the interval increased. FEHRER and GANCHROW (1963) and FARNÉ (1965) obtained similar inverted U-shaped curves with a maximum at an interval of 35–160 ms. These results indicate that the exponential function proposed by MUELLER (1949), OYAMA (1953), and IKEDA and OBONAI (1953) shows only a macroscopic structure of decay process.

KRAUSKOPF (1954), PARDUCCI and BROOKSHIRE (1956), and FARNÈ (1965) found that aftereffects decreased with the increase of test duration in a range of 40 ms–5 s.

IV. Retroactive Effect

IKEDA and OBONAI (1955b) reversed the time order of the presentation of I and T circles and found a retroactive effect of the I circle. The spatial arrangement of I and T figures and experimental method were very similar to their studies on usual figural aftereffects. I and T figures were presented by means of tachistoscope for 100–500 ms. They found that the effect of the size ratio of I to T circles was very similar to that in figural aftereffects shown in Figure 8, but the magnitude of effect, growth, or shrinkage of T circle was generally smaller and that the maximum retroactive effect occurred with a time interval of about 60 ms when the durations of I and T presentations were both 100 ms.

C. Spatial Factors

I. Experimental Examinations of "Displacement" and "Distance Paradox"

Figure 7 shows the results of FOX (1951), OYAMA (1956a), and POLLACK (1958) who measured the displacement of T objects as a function of the spatial separation between the I and T objects. Displacements always occurred in the

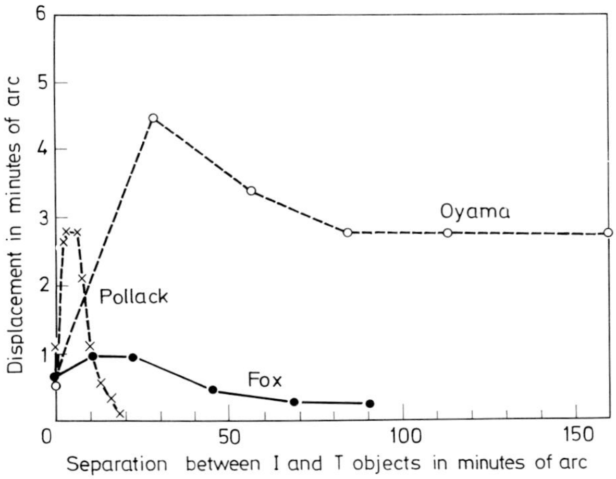

Fig. 7. Displacements as a function of spatial separation between I and T objects. (REDRAWN from FOX, 1951; OYAMA, 1956a; POLLACK, 1958.) Fox's curve: copyright 1951 by American Psychological Association. Reprinted by permission. POLLACK's curve: from POLLACK, R.H. Figural aftereffects: quantitative studies of displacement. Australian Journal of Psychology **10**, 273, 1958. By courtesy of the author

direction away from the I object, and the displacement increased as the separation increased to reach a maximum and then gradually decreased. In this sense, KÖHLER and WALLACH's principles of displacement and distance paradox were confirmed. However, the distance for the maximum displacement was different among the three investigators, from approximately 5 min of arc in POLLACK's work to 30 min in OYAMA's.

YOSHIDA (1953) and KOGISO (1956) indicated that T dots not only receded from the area occupied by the I object, as predicted by the principle of displacement, but sometimes were also attracted to the area. GANZ (1964) and GANZ and DAY (1965) found that the direction of displacement depended upon the separation and the luminace of the I object. Attractions occurred with small separations (0–12 min of arc) and high luminances.

II. Experiments with Concentric I and T Circles

In the stimulus situation shown in Figure 5, OYAMA (1954), IKEDA (1951), IKEDA and OBONAI (1955a), and KOGISO (1957) measured the amount of growth and shrinkage of the T circle, varying the size of the I circle from much smaller to much larger than the T circle. Some of these results are illustrated in Figure 8 in which the abscissa represents the relative size of the I circle to the T circle, while the ordinate represents the relative amount of the aftereffect. These curves, as well as those not quoted here, have essentially the same shape in spite of the large variety of experimental conditions, such as the absolute size of the T circle, the observation distance, the method of measurement, the inspection duration, etc.

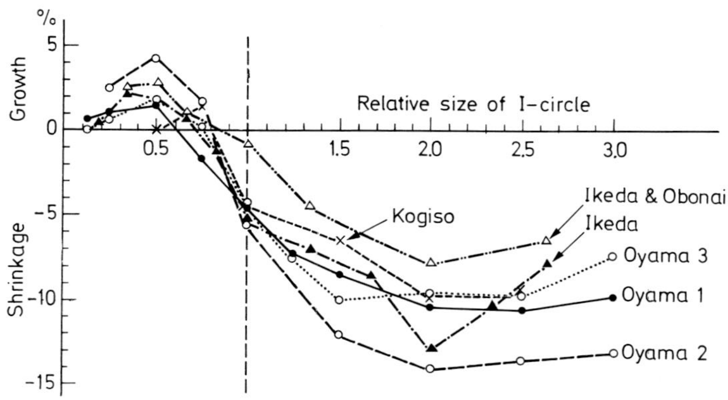

Fig. 8. Figural aftereffects as a function of the size ratio of I circle to T circle. The results obtained by IKEDA (1951), IKEDA and OBONAI (1955a), KOGISO (1957), and OYAMA (1954). (From OYAMA, 1956)

OYAMA (1956b) and SAGARA and OYAMA (1957) discussed these results with the following conclusions:

1. The T circle grows when it is larger than the I circle and shrinks when it is smaller. This fact agrees exactly with the displacement principle.

2. If the size of the T circle is equal to that of the I circle and coincides with it, according to the displacement principle, neither growth nor shrinkage should occur. On the contrary, Figure 8 indicates that it shrinks under such conditions. KÖHLER and WALLACH previously recognized this fact and presented an additional hypothesis to explain it. However, HEBB (1949) and SMITH (1948) objected that the additional hypothesis was ad hoc.

3. The amount of shrinkage, in general, is greater than the amount of growth. This is not derivable from the simple displacement principle.

4. In almost all curves in Figure 8 the maximum growth occurs when the diameter of the I circle is one-half that of the T circle, and the maximum shrinkage occurs when the I circle is twice as large as the T circle. This rule holds regardless of the absolute size of the T circle. It means that the optimum condition for displacement, or the limit of distance paradox, is not determined by the absolute distance between the outlines of I and T circles but by the relative size of the I circle to the T circle. Similar facts were discovered by OGASAWARA (1952) concerning simultaneous illusion of concentric circles (Delboeuf illusion) in which the maximum attraction effect occurred when the size ratio of the two circles was 2:3 or 3:2 (OYAMA, 1960a). In this illusion, the direction of displacement and the numerical values of the ratio at which the maximum effects are obtained are different from those of figural aftereffects. In spite of these differences, the fact that the principle of ratio relation applies adequately to both phenomena strongly suggests that there is a fundamental similarity between the two phenomena.

Some additional experimental evidence has been reported since these statements were made. Concerning the second statement, DUNCAN (1960) measured the change in the apparent size of a continuously inspected outline circle, which corresponds to the aftereffect with identical and coincident I and T circles, and found a significant shrinkage in the inspected circle in a great number of subjects. Relating to the fourth statement, FREEMAN (1964) measured the aftereffect (mainly growth) as a function of the size ratio of I to T circles, varying the ratio from 1:1 to 1:2.4. In addition, the size of the I circle was varied over three levels, and the I circle was presented with five different eccentricities. The curves obtained for the relationship between the aftereffect and the size ratio of T to I circles were always in the same shape, and the maximum growth always occurred when the size ratio of I to T circles was roughly 1:2, under all conditions of absolute size and eccentricity. Concerning the simultaneous illusion of concentric circles, WEINTRAUB et al. (1969) reconfirmed that the maximum attraction occurs near the size ratio of 2:3 or 3:2 under various conditions of stimulus lines.

In a paper entitled "Unsolved Problems in the Field of Figural After-Effects," KÖHLER (1965) discussed five important criticisms presented to him. Three of them are related to the above-mentioned statements 1, 2, and 4. He tried to reply to these criticisms from his point of view.

The close relationship between the figural aftereffect and the simultaneous illusion of concentric circles suggested in statement 4, was supported by the experimental results of IKEDA and OBONAI (1955a). They discovered the continuous transition of results from one to the other of these two phenomena, as shown in Figure 9, when they varied the temporal interval of presentation of the two circles gradually from simultaneity to succession by means of a tachistoscope. The curves obtained under simultaneous presentation are similar to OGASAWARA's curve on the illusion of concentric circles, and those under successive presentations are like those in Figure 8. The process of gradual shift from the former to the latter is observed under intermediate asynchronies.

Using a pair of concentric I and T circles with a constant size ratio of 2:1, MEYER et al. (1960) found that the aftereffect increased when the location of the I and T objects was displaced to the periphery in a range of 2–6 degrees from the fovea.

OYAMA (1954, 1956b) found that the aftereffect decreased slightly when the eccentricity increased, but occurred even when the I circle was located completely outside of the T circle. FREEMAN (1964) showed that the aftereffect (growth in most cases) gradually decreased when the eccentricity increased and changed from growth to shrinkage when the I circle was placed outside of the T circle.

CRABUS and STADLER (1971) and STADLER (1972) studied the effect of the shift of gaze between the inspection and test periods. They found fairly large aftereffects even when the T circle was presented in a physically (and phenomenally) identical but retinally different position from the I circle and asserted the importance of phenomenal or egocentric position in figural aftereffects. HOWARD (1973) and YOSHIDA (1974) replicated some of their experiments but could not achieve the same results. SHIGERU ICHIHARA of Tokyo Metropolitan University also replicated CRABUS and STADLER's experiment and found the same tendency in a few of his subjects but not in the rest of his subjects (personal communication, 1974).

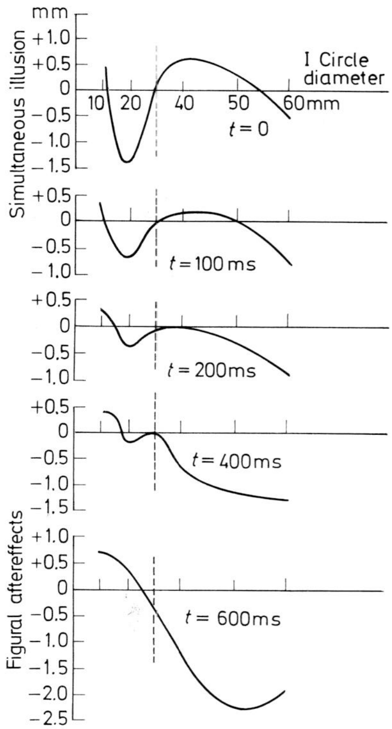

Fig. 9. Figural aftereffects as a function of the size of the I circle at each stage of asynchronism of presentation of I and T figures. Exposure time of both I and T figures is 500 ms. The delay of the start of exposure of the T figure to that of the I figure is indicated by *t*. (Redrawn from IKEDA and OBONAI, 1955a)

III. Retinal Size Versus Apparent Size

When the I and T objects are presented at different distances from the subjects, the following question will arise. Which is the determining factor of aftereffects, the retinal size or the apparent size? This problem was first presented by PRENTICE (1947, 1950) and then studied by many investigators. OYAMA and ICHIHARA (1973) conducted the most systematic study on this problem, using a special tachistoscope which can present stimuli at two different distances, 115 and 230 cm. Aftereffects of I circles of various sizes on a T circle of a constant size (1 degree) were measured by the transposition method (OYAMA, 1959) for five subjects under four distance conditions of I and T circles, near-near, far-near, far-far, and near-far. A white card with a fixation mark was presented for 1 s at the same distance as the T figure between the I and T periods to make the subjects' eyes ready to fixate the T figure. Constancy measurements made with the same subjects in the same experimental situation indicated strong tendencies to size constancy. The results of the four conditions

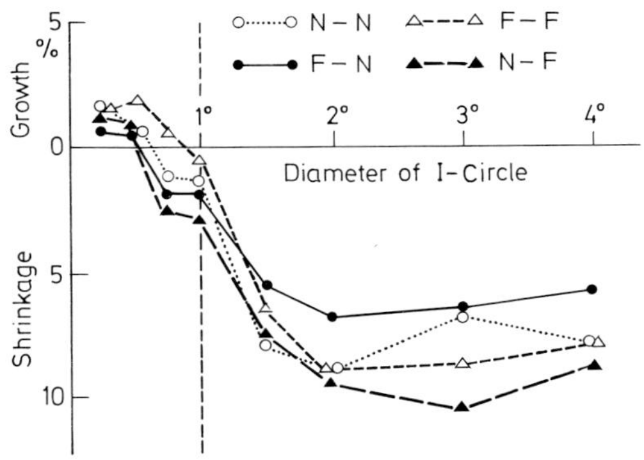

Fig. 10. Figural aftereffects as a function of the retinal size of the I circle. The I and T circles were presented at the same distance (115 or 230 cm) in each of series N-N and F-F, and at different distances (115 and 230 cm or 230 and 115 cm) in series N-F and F-N. The diameter of the T circle was always 1 degree in visual angle. Four curves obtained in these four series are very similar, irrespective of differences in the presentation distances. (From OYAMA and ICHIHARA, 1973)

were very similar when represented as a function of the retinal-size ratio of the I to T circle, as shown in Figure 10, but were quite different when represented as a function of the apparent-size ratio. It was concluded that the retinal size determines figural aftereffects. However, this conclusion does not mean that figural aftereffects are based on a retinal interaction process. WALKER and KRUGER (1972) used random dot stereograms which produced no retinal contours but central or cyclopean contours and found figural aftereffects of the same magnitude as in ordinary solid figures.

IV. Normalization Versus Displacement

While GIBSON (1933) used only a straight line as the T object in his study on the curved-line effect, NOZAWA (1953), CARLSON (1963), and WILSON (1965) also used curved lines as T objects and measured the aftereffects of various I curves on various T curves. Their results showed that the T curve frequently decreased its apparent curvature even when its physical curvature was greater than the I curve and its apparent curvature was expected to increase according to KÖHLER and WALLACH's theory. Figure 11 shows the results obtained by WILSON (1965) who used every combination between eight I curves and five T curves (including a straight T line). The abscissa represents the curvature of the I curve and the ordinate represents the average curvature of the comparison stimulus, which was presented on the other side of the T curve and adjusted to match the T curve in apparent curvature after inspection. WILSON stated:

The curves show that both the adaptation effect and the repulsion effect are present. If only adaptation were acting, inspection of a straight line would produce no after-effect, and the plotted curves would pass through the points marked by triangles. But each of the curves passes the corresponding triangle on the side remote from origin, showing that apparent curvature of T

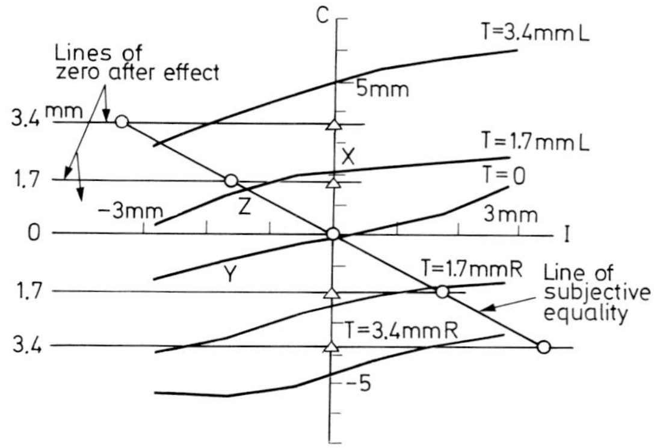

Fig. 11. Apparent curvature of various T curves after inspection of various I curves. The abscissa indicates the curvature of the I curve represented by the physical displacement of its ends from the straight, and the ordinate, the apparent curvature of the T line. Five curves show the results of five T-curves having different curvatures and directions. (From WILSON, 1965.) Reprinted with permision from Quarterly Journal of Experimental Psychology **17**, 6 (1965)

has been increased and therefore that the repulsion effect is acting. If only repulsion were acting, there would be no after-effect when I and T coincide, and the curves would therefore pass through the points marked with circles. Instead they pass closer to the origin, showing an adaptation effect (pp. 5–6).

In another experiment, WILSON (1965) showed that the aftereffect rises rapidly to a maximum when the difference in curvature between the I curve and T line increases in either direction and thereafter falls slowly with increasing difference between I and T objects. NOZAWA (1965) measured the aftereffects of an I curve on a T line in various orientations and found that the aftereffects are minimum when presented in a vertical or horizontal direction and maximum when tilted 45° from these axes. It might be related to the anisotropy found in optical illusions and some other phenomena (OYAMA, 1960a; TAYLOR, 1963).

MORANT and HARRIS (1965) conducted two experiments concerning the tilted line effect. In their first experiment, the subject was asked to adjust a luminous T line in a dark room to appear vertical or horizontal after a 2 min inspection of a variously tilted luminous I line. The difference between the two curves shown in Figure 12 indicates the difference between the direct effects of I lines tilted from the vertical (or horizontal) axis on the T line placed in the vertical (or horizontal) axis and their indirect effects on the T line placed in the horizontal (or vertical) axis. These curves showed that the direct effect was always greater than the indirect effect, as already shown by GIBSON and RADNER (1937), and that a small aftereffect was found even when the I line was placed at a 45° angle to both the vertical and horizontal axes, and consequently no adaptation was expected from GIBSON's theory.

In the second experiment of MORANT and HARRIS (1965), a variously tilted I line was presented to the left of the fixation point for a period of 1 min and then a vertical T line and a comparison line were presented to the left and right of the fixation point. They were all luminous lines in a dark room. The results of this experiment gives an inverted U-shaped curve shown in Figure 13. This is similar to the distance paradox curves shown in Figure 7. The

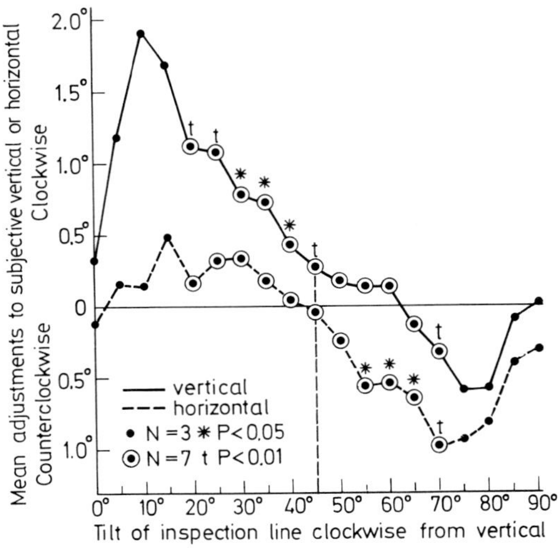

Fig. 12. Subjective vertical or horizontal after inspection of variously tilted I lines. The solid line represents the subjective vertical, and the broken line, the subjective horizontal. (From MORANT and HARRIS, 1965)

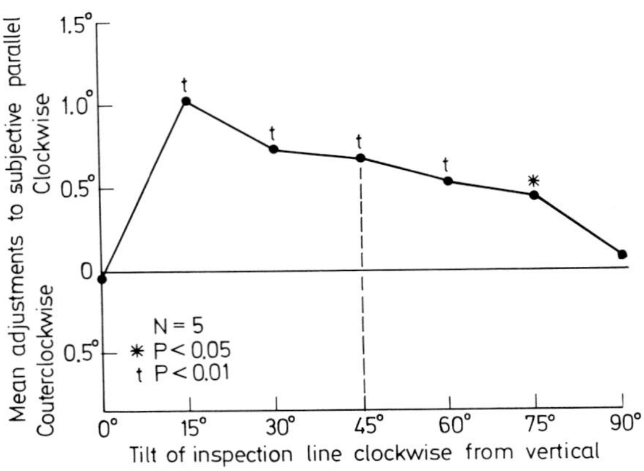

Fig. 13. Apparent tilt of the vertical T line after inspection of variously tilted I lines. (from MORANT and HARRIS, 1965)

effect reaches a maximum when the I line forms an angle of 15° with the T line and then gradually declines to zero as the angle increases further, but never crosses the zero line. A considerable aftereffect was obtained again when the I line was placed at a 45° angle to both axes. On the basis of the results of these two experiments, MORANT and HARRIS concluded that two factors produce the tilted line effect: a localized process resembling KÖHLER and WALLACH's "satiation" and a nonlocalized process resembling GIBSON's "normalization." When the I and T lines are in the same area of the visual field, these two factors summate algebraically. If a comparison figure on the different side of the visual field is used, only the satiation-like process can be shown.

D. The Effects of Contrast, Luminance, Hue, and Width of Outline

I. Contrast

POLLACK (1958), YOSHIDA (1960), and GRAHAM (1961) indicated that aftereffects increased when the luminance contrast of I objects with their background increased. NOZAWA (1953), GIBB et al. (1966), and ADAM and RING (1968) reconfirmed this tendency and also found that the aftereffects decreased when the contrast of T objects increased. These findings agree with what OYAMA (1962) found in optical illusions.

II. Luminance

GRAHAM (1961) varied the luminance on I and T figures over a wide range (from just above foveal threshold to 532 millilamberts), keeping the contrast constant, but found no significant change in aftereffects.

III. Hue

KÖHLER (1951) observed some aftereffects even when the I object and its background had the same luminance and differed only in hue. HOCHBERG et al. (1960) studied this problem under two levels of illuminance and concluded that aftereffects appear whenever clear contours are visible, even if no luminance difference exists between figure and ground.

CRAWFORD and KLINGAMAN (1966) found statistically significant differences in aftereffects, with the increasing order from gray to orange to blue I objects, whereas OYAMA (1960b) could not find any significant difference among I objects of different hues.

IV. Width of Outline

OYAMA (1954) found that aftereffects increased when the width of the outline increased from 0.3 min to 4.6 min in visual angle, but GRAHAM (1961) could not find any significant difference among widths of 5.8–46 min.

E. Related Phenomena

Figural aftereffects have been studied in relation to many other phenomena. Most of these studies were suggested by KÖHLER and WALLACH's satiation theory or other theoretical models of figural aftereffects.

I. Visual Sensitivities

Changes of visual threshold and of CFF were measured at various points around the retinal place, where the I objects had been presented, to map the field of satiation (NOZAWA, 1956, 1958; SPIGEL, 1964; GANZ, 1964; GANZ and DAY, 1965). MOTOKAWA's electric sensitivity method was also used to map the field of retinal induction (MOTOKAWA et al., 1957).

II. Reversible Patterns

Reversible patterns were used as T objects to measure the aftereffect of I objects which correspond to parts of reversible patterns. The appearance of the corresponding area in the T patterns was inhibited after inspection (HOCHBERG, 1950; OYAMA, 1952; CARLSON, 1953).

III. Motion Perception

Stroboscopic movement and autokinetic movement were also used to test the aftereffect of inspection of some objects (DEATHERAGE, 1954; CONKLIN, 1957). Sometimes, stroboscopic movements were used as I objects (TRAIN and WALTHALL, 1958; KUBOSAKI, 1968).

IV. Optical Illusions

Relations between figural aftereffects and optical illusions, discussed briefly in an earlier part of this chapter, were studied experimentally by SUMMERFIELD and MILLER (1955) and MORINAGA and NOGUCHI (1961) and discussed theoretically by GANZ (1966a, b) and HOWARD (1971). KÖHLER and FISHBACK (1950a, 1950b) asserted that the decrement of the Müller-Lyer illusion during repeated adjustments is caused by the same neural process as figural aftereffects, satiation. However, their assertion has been criticized by many investigators (AZUMA, 1952; DAY, 1962; MOED, 1959; MOUNTJOY, 1960, 1966).

V. Aftereffects in the Third Dimension

KÖHLER and EMERY (1947) extended the study of figural aftereffects into the third dimension of visual space—depth. They found aftereffects caused by inspection of tilted, obtusely angled, and curved surfaces on the appearance of frontal parallel planes. These were analogous to GIBSON's tilted line, bent line, and curved line effects, respectively. They also demonstrated the displacement effects in depth, apparent advancement, and recession of the T object. They showed that these aftereffects in the third dimension, in general, cannot be reduced to two dimensional figural aftereffects in the two monocular fields. BERGMAN and GIBSON (1959) found adaptation and negative aftereffects in the third dimension, even when they used coarsely textured surfaces and neither contour nor figure was visible. They thought that this evidence negated KÖHLER and EMERY's view. BLAKEMORE and JULESZ (1971) used random dot stereograms lacking monocular contours and found clear three-dimensional aftereffects. They showed that this aftereffect occurs after stereopsis and that the neural mechanisms responsible for this aftereffect are central.

VI. Kinesthetic Aftereffects

GIBSON (1933) already discovered a kinesthetic phenomenon similar to the curved line effect in vision. He asked blindfolded subjects to repeatedly move their fingers along a curved edge for 3 min. When they moved their fingers afterward along a straight edge, this edge appeared curved in the opposite direction. KÖHLER and DINNERSTEIN (1947) demonstrated that kinesthetic judgment of a width can also be distorted by prior experience with a different width. Their results showed that T objects, which were narrower than the I objects, appeared to shrink, and wider T objects appeared to expand, just as in visual figural aftereffects. These kinesthetic aftereffects have been studied by many other investigators.

F. Physiologic Models

I. MOTOKAWA's Retinal Induction Model

MOTOKAWA developed a physiologic model based on the assumption that figural aftereffects are caused by a kind of retinal induction, the induced change of excitability in the retinal level, which can be measured with the phosphene threshold after the presentation of a patch at various parts around a T figure (MOTOKAWA et al. 1957; MOTOKAWA, 1970). In general, the induction fields of a T figure measured by this method are distorted by the preceding presentation of an I figure in such a way that the induction field recedes from the I contour. When the I and T contours are adjacent or largely separated, the distortion of the induction field is very small. But at intermediate separations, the distortions are considerably great. These physiologic facts agree well with the psychological principles of displacement and distance paradox.

II. OSGOOD and HEYER's Excitation Distribution Model

OSGOOD and HEYER (1952) presented another physiological model suggested by MARSHALL and TALBOT's (1942) model for contour resolution, in which stimulation of a fine line was assumed to produce a Gaussian distribution of cortical excitation, due to spatial dispersion in visual pathways and physiologic nystagmus of the eyes. OSGOOD and HEYER assumed that the apparent localization of a contour in subjective visual space coincides with the location of maximum excitation of the Gaussian distribution and that the locus of the maximum excitation representing a T contour can be shifted by differential inhibition induced by preceding excitation of the same type of distribution produced by an I contour.

III. Lateral Inhibition Models

GANZ (1964, 1966a, 1966b) presented the view that a figural aftereffect is not really an aftereffect but a simultaneous illusion. GANZ suggested that all of the contour displacements correspond to the shifts of the maximum excitations caused by lateral inhibitions produced by afterimages of I objects. As evidence supporting his model, GANZ (1966b) offered the following: (1) varying the intensity of the inducing or inspection figure affects the simultaneous illusion and figural aftereffect in similar ways, (2) temporal characteristics of afterimages and figural aftereffects are very similar, (3) an interocular presentation of the inspection and test objects, which was once considered by KÖHLER and WALLACH a method to eliminate the role of afterimages in figural aftereffects, can not really eliminate the influence of afterimages occurring in the visual cortex. However, GANZ's model can be criticized on the basis of already mentioned differences in the direction of displacements and the optimum separation for the maximum displacement. HOWARD (1971) modified GANZ's model, adding an extra area of excitation outside of lateral inhibition.

DEUTSCH (1964) assumed the following: (1) an I contour produces distributions of excitation and lateral inhibition, (2) its removal brings about a postexcitatory depression and postinhibitory rebound in the corresponding areas, (3) the apparent distance between two points is generally measured in the nervous system by the sum of the excitability of the elements between them, (4) apparent displacement in figural aftereffects is produced by the change of the excitability between two points corresponding to I and T contours.

IV. Feature-Analyzer Models

COLTHEART (1971) developed a physiological model of the tilted line effect on the basis of HUBEL and WIESEL's (1962, 1968) findings on orientation-specific cortical units. He assumed that units having preferred orientations which exactly or nearly correspond to the orientation of an I line will adapt during inspection and become less sensitive in different degrees inversely depending on the difference between the unit's preferred orientation and the stimulus orientation. Such a distribution of reduced sensitivity among the population of orientation-specific units will produce a biased distribution of excitation to the subsequently presented T line and apparent shift of its orientation in a way similar to OSGOOD and HEYER's model in which a distribution of reduced sensitivity in position-detecting mechanisms produces apparent shift of a T contour. However, in Coltheart's model, nystagmus was not considered a cause of the dispersion of excitation as in OSGOOD and HEYER's model, and the perceived orientation was assumed to be determined by the weighted average rather than the peak of excitation.

BLAKEMORE and SUTTON (1969) found a new aftereffect. After inspection of a grating, the spatial frequency of another grating is overestimated when it is higher than that of the inspection grating and underestimated when it is lower. They suggested that this new aftereffect is due to differential sensitivity reduction of size-detecting mechanisms and that a large component of classical figural aftereffects is explicable on the basis of sensitivity reduction of size-detecting rather than position-detecting mechanisms. Their suggestion is very important especially because it offers a possible explanation of the fact that the growth and shrinkage of T circles are determined by the size ratio of I and T circles rather than the spatial separation between the I and T contours (see p. 578). This fact cannot be explained by any other model presented so far. If we also hypothesize logarithmic changes of the distribution and tuning characteristics of the size-detecting mechanisms, we can explain the size-ratio principle, as pointed out by OYAMA (1977). Simple apparent displacements can also be explained by the same generalized model of sensitivity reduction if we apply it the position-detecting mechanisms.

References

Adam, J., Ring, M.: Investigation of interactions of luminance contrast and temporal factors in figural aftereffects. Percept. mot. Skills **27**, 287–291 (1968).

Azuma, H.: The effect of experience on the amount of the Müller-Lyer illusion. Jap. J. Psychol. **22**, 111–123 (Japanese text with English summary) (1952).

Bales, J.F., Follansbee, G.L.: The after-effect of the perception of curved lines. J. exp. Psychol. **18**, 499–503 (1935).

Bergman, R., Gibson, J.J.: The negative after-effect of the perception of a surface slanted in the third dimension. Amer. J. Psychol. **72**, 364–374 (1959).

Blakemore, C., Julesz, B.: Stereoscopic depth aftereffect produced without monocular cues. Science **171**, 286–288 (1971).

Blakemore, C., Sutton, P.: Size adaptation, a new aftereffect. Science **166**, 245–247 (1969).

Bonnet, C.: Les effets consécutifs figuraux. L'Année Psychol. **63**, 359–393 (1963).

Carlson, V.R.: Satiation in a reversible perspective figure. J. exp. Psychol. **45**, 442–448 (1953).

Carlson, V.R.: The generality of negative aftereffect following adaptation to curvature. Scand. J. Psychol. **4**, 129–133 (1963).

Coltheart, M.: Visual feature-analyzers and aftereffect of tilt and curvature. Psychol. Rev. **78**, 114–121 (1971).

Conklin, J.E.: The influence of figural inspection on the autokinetic illusion. Amer. J. Psychol. **70**, 395–402 (1957).

Crabus, H., Stadler, M.: Über Wahrnehmungsprozesse in den Koordinaten der Netzhaut und des anschaulichen Raumes. Psychol. Forsch. **34**, 325–342 (1971).

Crawford, F.T., Klingaman, R.L.: Figural aftereffect as a function of hue. J. exp. Psychol. **72**, 916–918 (1966).

Day, R.H.: The effects of repeated trials and prolonged fixation on error in the Müller-Lyer figure. Psychol. Monogr. Gen. Appl. **76**, No. 14 (1962).

Deatherage, B.H.: Figural aftereffects and stroboscopic movement. Amer. J. Psychol. **67**, 259–267 (1954).

Deutsch, J.A.: Neurophysiological contrast phenomena and figural aftereffects. Psychol. Rev. **71**, 19–26 (1964).

Duncan, C.P.: Effect of self-satiation on perceived size of a visual figure. J. exp. Psychol. **60**, 120–136 (1960).

Farnè, M.: Figural after-effects with short exposure-time. An interpretation of the so-called "subliminal perception." Psychol. Forsch. **28**, 519–534 (1965).

Fehrer, E., Ganchrow, D.: Effects of exposure variables on figural aftereffects under tachistoscopic presentation. J. exp. Psychol. **66**, 506–513 (1963).

Fox, B.H.: Figural after-effects: "satiation" and adaptation. J. exp. Psychol. **42**, 317–326 (1951).

Freeman, Jr., R.B.: Figural after-effects: displacement or contrast? Amer. J. Psychol. **77**, 607–613 (1964).

Ganz, L.: Lateral inhibition and the location of visual contours: an analysis of figural after-effects. Vision Res. **4**, 465–581 (1964).

*Ganz, L.: The mechanism of the figural aftereffect. Psychol. Rev. **73**, 128–150 (1966a).

Ganz, L.: Is the figural aftereffect an aftereffect? A review of intensity, onset, decay, and transfer characteristics. Psychol. Bull. **66**, 151–165 (1966b).

Ganz, L., Day, R.H.: An analysis of the satiation-fatigue mechanism of figural after-effects. Amer. J. Psychol. **78**, 345–361 (1965).

Gibb, M., Freeman, I., Adam, J.: Effects of luminance contrast factors upon figural aftereffects induced by short fixation periods. Percept. mot. Skills **22**, 535–541 (1966).

Gibson, J.J.: Adaptation, after-effect, and contrast in the perception of curved lines. J. exp. Psychol. **16**, 1–31 (1933).

Gibson, J.J.: Adaptation, after-effect, and contrast in the perception of tilted lines. II. Simultaneous contrast and the areal restriction of the after-effect. J. exp. Psychol. **20**, 553–569 (1937).

Gibson, J.J., Radner, M.: Adaptation, after-effect, and contrast in the perception of tilted lines. I. Quantitative studies. J. exp. Psychol. **20**, 453–467 (1937).

Graham, E.H.: Figural after-effects as functions of contrast, area, and luminance of the inspection-figure. Psychologia (Kyoto) **4**, 201–108 (1961).

Hammer, E.R.: Temporal factors in figural after-effects. Amer. J. Psychol. **62**, 337–354 (1949).

Hebb, D.O.: The organization of behavior. New York: Wiley 1949.

Hochberg, J.E.: Figure-ground reversal as a function of visual satiation. J. exp. Psychol. **40**, 682–686 (1950).

Hochberg, J.E., Day, R.H., Hardy, D.: Hue- and brightness-differences, contours, and figural after-effects. Amer. J. Psychol. **73**, 638–639 (1960).

Howard, R.B.: Neurophysiological models of figural aftereffects and visual illusions. Psychonomic Monograph Supplements **4**, 57–72 (1971).

Howard, R.B.: Figural aftereffects as optical illusions? Failure to replicate two results. Bull. Psychon. Soc. **2**, 392–394 (1973).

Hubel, D.H., Wiesel, T.N.: Receptive fields, binocular interaction and functional architecture in the cat's visual cortex. J. Physiol. **160**, 106–154 (1962).

Hubel, D.H., Wiesel, T.N.: Receptive fields and functional architecture of monkey striate cortex. J. Physiol. **195**, 215–243 (1968).

Ikeda, H.: Studies on figural after-effects. (in Japanese). Tokyo Bunrika University Dissertation, 1951.

Ikeda, H., Obonai, T.: The quantitative analysis of figural after-effects. I. The process of growth and decay of figural after-effects. Jap. J. Psychol. **23**, 246–260; **24**, 59–66 (Japanese text), 84–85 (English summary) (1953).

Ikeda, H.,Obonai, T.: Studies in figural after-effects. IV. The contrast-confluence illusion of concentric circles and the figural after-effect. Jap. psychol. Res. 1. No. **2**, 17–23 (1955a).

Ikeda, H., Obonai, T.: Figural after-effect, retroactive-effect and simultaneous illusion. Jap. J. Psychol. **26**, 235–246 (Japanese text), 290–291 (English summary) (1955b).

Kogiso, I.: An experiment on the displacement in figural aftereffects. Jap. J. Psychol. **26**, 405–407 (in Japanese) (1956).

Kogiso, I.: The structure of the field of visual perception. (in Japanese). Masters thesis, University of Tokyo, 1957.

Köhler, W.: Dynamics in psychology. New York: Liveright 1940.

Köhler, W.: Relational determination in perception. In: Cerebral mechanisms in behavior. Jeffress, L.A. (ed). New York: Wiley 1951, pp. 200–243.

Köhler, W.: Unsolved problems in the field of figural after-effects. Psychol. Rec. **15**, 63–83 (1965).

Köhler, W., Dinnerstein, D.: Figural after-effects in kinesthesis. In: Miscellanea psychologica. Michotte, A. (ed.). Louvan: Institut Supérieur de Philosophie 1947, pp. 196–220.

Köhler, W., Emery, D.: Figural after-effects in the third dimension of visual space. Amer. J. Psychol. **60**, 159–201 (1947).

Köhler, W., Fishback, J.: The destruction of the Müller-Lyer illusion in repeated trials. I. An examination of two theories. J. exp. Psychol. **40**, 267–281 (1950a).

Köhler, W., Fishback, J.: The destruction of the Müller-Lyer illusion in repeated trials. II. Satiation patterns and memory traces. J. exp. Psychol. **40**, 398–410 (1950b).

Köhler, W., Wallach, H.: Figural after-effects: an investigation of visual processes. Proc. Amer. philos. Soc. **88**, 269–357 (1944).

Krauskopf, J.: The magnitude of figural after-effects as a function of the duration of the test-period. Amer. J. Psychol. **67**, 684–690 (1954).

Kubosaki, H.: A comparison between apparent and real visual movement. Jap. J. Psychol. **39**, 262–265 (in Japanese) (1968).

Malhotra, M.K.: Figurale Nachwirkungen: Sammelbericht. Psychol. Forsch. **30**, 1–101 (1966).

Marshall, W.H., Talbot, S.A.: Recent evidence for neural mechanisms in vision leading to a general theory of sensory acuity. In: Visual mechanisms. Klüver, H. (ed.). Biol. Sympos. **7**, 117–164 (1944).

McEwen, P.: Figural after-effects. Brit. J. Psychol. Monogr. Suppl. 31 (1958).

Meyer, D.R., Sukemune, S., Myers, R.: Local variations in the magnitude of a figural aftereffect. J. exp. Psychol. **60**, 314–317 (1960).

Moed, G.: Satiation-theory and the Müller-Lyer illusion. Amer. J. Psychol. **72**, 609–611 (1959).

Morant, R.B., Harris, J.R.: Two different after-effects of exposure to visual tilts. Amer. J. Psychol. **78**, 218–226 (1965).

Morinaga, S., Noguchi, K.: Immediate illusions and figural after-effects in the perception of curved and tilted lines. J. Coll. Arts Sci., Chiba Univ. **3**, 295–302 (1961).

Motokawa, K.: Physiology of color and pattern vision. Tokyo: Igaku Shoin 1970.

Motokawa, K., Nakagawa, D., Kohata, T.: Figural after-effects and retinal induction. J. gen. Psychol. **57**, 121–135 (1957).

Mountjoy, P.T.: Fixation and decrement to the Müller-Lyer figure. Psychol. Rec. **10**, 219–223 (1960).

Mountjoy, P.T.: New illusory effect of the Müller-Lyer figure. J. exp. Psychol. **71**, 119–123 (1966).

Mueller, C.G.: Numerical transformations in the analysis of experimental data. Psychol. Bull. **46**, 198–223 (1949).
Nozawa, S.: Prolonged inspection of a figure and the after-effect there-of. Jap. J. Psychol. **23**, 217–234; **24**, 47–58 (Japanese text), 85–87 (English summary) (1953).
Nozawa, S.: An experimental study on figural after-effect by the measurement of field strength. Jap. psychol. Res. **1**, No. 3, 15–24 (1956).
Nozawa, S.: An experimental study on figural after-effect by the measurement of field strength. II. Jap. psychol. Res. **1**, No. 5, 22–27 (1958).
Nozawa, S.: Factors of comparison in figural after-effects. In: Yuki Kinichi Sensei Taikan Kinen Shinrigaku Ronbunshu. Umeoka, Y., Oyama, T. (eds.). (in Japanese). Sapporo: Department of Psychology, Hokkaido University 1965, pp. 15–22.
Obonai, T.: Some analytical studies of the induction field. Psychol. Beitr. **6**, 620–629 (1962).
Ogasawara, J.: Displacement-effect of concentric circles. Jap. J. Psychol. **22**, 224–234 (Japanese text with English summary) (1952).
Osgood, C.E., Heyer, A.W., Jr.: A new interpretation of figural after-effects. Psychol. Rev. **59**, 98–118 (1952).
Oyama, T.: Figural after-effects and reversible figure. In: Chiwa Sensei Kanreki Kinen Ronbunshu. (in Japanese). Tokyo: Department of Psychology, University of Tokyo 1952, pp. 47–55.
Oyama, T.: Experimental studies of figural after-effects I. Temporal factors. Jap. J. Psychol. **23**, 239–245 (Japanese text), 288–289 (English summary) (1953).
Oyama, T.: Experimental studies of figural after-effects. II. Spatial factors. Jap. J. Psychol. **25**, 195–206 (Japanese text), 223–224 (English summary) (1954).
Oyama, T.: Experimental studies of figural after-effects III. Displacement effect. Jap. J. Psychol. **26**, 365–375 (Japanese text), 462 (English summary) (1956a).
Oyama, T.: Temporal and spatial factors in figural after-effects. Jap. psychol. Res. **1**, No. 3, 25–36 (1956b).
Oyama, T.: A new psychophysical method: method of transposition or equal-appearing relations. Psychol. Bull. **56**, 74–79 (1959).
Oyama, T.: Japanese studies on the so-called geometrical-optical illusions. Psychologia (Kyoto) **3**, 7–20 (1960a).
Oyama, T.: Figural after-effects as a function of hue and brightness. Jap. psychol. Res. **2**, 74–80 (1960b).
Oyama, T.: The effect of hue and brightness on the size-illusion of concentric circles. Amer. J. Psychol. **75**, 45–55 (1962).
Oyama, T.: Feature analysers, optical illusions, and figural aftereffects. Perception **6**, 401–406 (1977).
Oyama, T., Ichihara, S.: Which determines figural after-effect, retinal size or apparent size? Jap. psychol Res. **15**, 92–98 (1973).
Parducci, A., Brookshire, K.: Figural after-effects with tachistoscopic presentation. Amer. J. Psychol. **69**, 635–639 (1956).
Pollack, R.H.: Figural after-effects: quantitative studies of displacement. Austral. J. Psychol. **10**, 269–277 (1958).
Prentice, W.C.H.: The relation of distance to the apparent size of figural after-effects. Amer. J. Psychol. **60**, 617–623 (1947).
Prentice, W.C.H.: On the size of the figural after-effect with varying distances. Amer. J. Psychol. **63**, 589–593 (1950).
Sagara, M., Oyama, T.: Experimental studies on figural aftereffects in Japan. Psychol. Bull. **54**, 327–338 (1957).
Smith, K.R.: The satiational theory of the figural after-effect. Amer. J. Psychol. **61**, 281–286 (1948).
Spigel, I.M.: Spatio-temporal relations in the after-effects of an I-figure on the critical flicker-frequency. Amer. J. Psychol. **77**, 264–269 (1964).
Stadler, M.: Figural aftereffects as optical illusions? Amer. J. Psychol. **85**, 351–376 (1972).
Stratton, G.M.: Vision without inversion of the retinal image. Psychol. Rev. **4**, 341–360; 463–481 (1897).
Summerfield, A., Miller, K.M.: Visual illusion and figural after-effect, with and without fixation. Quart. J. exp. Psychol. **7**, 149–158 (1955).

Taylor, M.M.: Figural after-effects: a psychophysical theory of the displacement effect. Canad. J. Psychol. **16**, 247–277 (1962).

Taylor, M.M.: Visual discrimination and orientation. J. opt. Soc. Amer. **53**, 763–765 (1963).

Taylor, M.M.: The effect of the square root of time on continuing perceptual tasks. Percept. Psychophysics **1**, 113–119 (1966).

Train, L.E., Walthall, W.J., Jr.: A comparison of figural after-effects from the perception of real and of apparent movement. J. gen. Psychol. **59**, 157–166 (1958).

Verhoeff, F.H.: A theory of binocular perspective. Amer. J. Physiol. Opt. **6**, 416–448 (1925).

Vernon, M.D.: The perception of inclined lines. Brit. J. Psychol. **25**, 186–196 (1934).

Walker, J.T., Kruger, M.W.: Figural aftereffects in random-dot stereograms without monocular contours. Perception **1**, 187–192 (1972).

Weintraub, D.J., Wilson, B.A., Green, R.D., Palmquist, M.J.: Delboeuf illusion: displacement versus diameter, arc delections, and brightness contrast. J. exp. Psychol. **80**, 505–511 (1969).

Wilson, J.: Adaptation and repulsion in the figural after-effect. Quart. J. exp. Psychol. **17**, 1–13 (1965).

Yoshida, T.: An experimental study of figural after-effect. Jap. J. Psychol. **23**, 235–238 (Japanese test), 287–288 (English summary) (1953).

Yoshida, T.: Figural after-effect as a function of the brightness ratio between the inspection figure and its surrounding field. In: Studies in psychology in commemoration of Prof. Matsusaburo Yokoyama's 71st Birthday. (in Japanese), Tokyo: Department of Psychology, Keio University 1960, pp. 99–114.

Yoshida, T.: An experiment on figural after-effects. The Proceedings of the 38th Annual Convention of Japanese Psychological Association, Hiroshima University, 320–321 (in Japanese) (1974).

Chapter 18

Face Perception: A Review of Experiments with Infants, Normal Adults, and Brain-Injured Persons

R.K. YIN, Washington, D.C. (USA)

Contents

Two everyday observations about human behavior suggest that the human face may be a special visual object. First, the average person can discriminate and remember hundreds of faces in spite of the fact that, by any objective measure, faces are highly similar objects.[1] This talent is not merely a marginal perceptual skill, for the ability to distinguish two faces as different and the same face as the same is often powerful enough to overcome changes due to cosmetics, dress, eyeglasses, and beards, and even the effects of age. Second, the average person uses the face as a source of a great amount of information about other individuals. Identification is but one aspect of this information; faces also serve as the basis for inferences about character and personality, mood, and the specific feelings being expressed by another person.

These same two observations can be made of few, if any, other visual objects. In some cases, as in distinguishing among different types of flowers or automobiles, the objects may be quite similar and require subtle discrimination, but the inferences made about these objects are not as varied or complex as those made about faces. In other cases, as in interpreting a work of art, the inferences may be varied and complex, but the objects are not so physically alike as to require acute discriminatory abilities. The potential uniqueness of face perception, in short, is that people derive a great deal of information from the face on the basis of very slight physical differences. The question of how people perform this task has stimulated considerable research to learn more about the face recognition process.

---

[1] Among experimental psychologists, GALTON (1883) was among the earliest to observe the paradox and to attempt new experiments on face recognition.

A. Early Research: Focus on Judgments and Judges

Early investigators attempted to deal with the problem mainly by examining: (1) the actual judgments of human character made from the face, (2) the specific portions of the face related to different kinds of judgments, and (3) the characteristics of good and poor judges of facial attributes. These investigators may have been indirectly influenced by the pseudoscience of *physiognomy*, which thrived in the United States at the turn of the 20th century and which attempted to relate facial characteristics to the lasting attributes of human character.[2] The investigations covered such topics[3] as:

- the accuracy of judging personality, intelligence, or occupation from faces (DUNLAP, 1927a; PINTNER, 1918; ANDERSON, 1921; LAIRD and REMMERS, 1924; GASKILL et al., 1972; GURNEE, 1934; CHILD, 1936; COOK, 1939);
- the relative importance of the upper and lower or right and left halves of the face in bearing judgmental information (DUNLAP, 1927b; WOLFF, 1933; MCCURDY, 1949; LINDZEY et al., 1952);
- the effects on judgments of altering various facial features (SANDER, 1928, as cited by GOMBRICH, 1968; WHITE and LANDIS, 1930; IRWIN, 1932; BRUNSWIK and REITER, 1937; SAMUELS, 1939; STRITCH and SECORD, 1956; and BRUNSWIK, 1956); and
- the personality correlates of judges with good and poor abilities in remembering faces (JONES, 1935; HOWELLS, 1938; SECORD and MUTHARD, 1955; KAESS and WITRYOL, 1955; KESSEN, 1957; MESSICK and DAMARIN, 1964).

Most of this research has revealed few regularities in judgmental accuracy or in the important characteristics of the judgmental process. In spite of this lack of progress, there have still been sporadic attempts to focus on other attributes of individual differences, such as the sex or race of the judge in relation to the sex or race of the stimulus face (MALPASS and KRAVITZ, 1969; and CROSS et al., 1971). Although certain facial features such as a broad forehead have been associated with certain judgments such as the perception of "babyishness" (HÜCKSTEDT, 1965; GARDNER and WALLACH, 1965; GRONER, 1967; BRADSHAW, 1969), the major conclusion from all of this research is nevertheless that specific judgments are simultaneously a function of the stimulus used (which may be a photo or a schematic face), the characteristics of the judge, the specific judgmental situation and instructions, and the tests and measures being used. Since the methods have varied widely and relied heavily on verbal responses that may be ambiguous in their meaning, little has been learned about face perception through this approach.

---

[2] Physiognomy has a Chinese counterpart that has existed for thousands of years. The Chinese study of the face purports not merely to provide judgments of character, but also to serve as the basis for telling one's fortune (MAR, 1974).

[3] Much research has been conducted on a related matter, the interpretation of facial expressions. There are several available reviews of this literature (e.g., JENNESS, 1932; WOLFF, 1943; WOODWORTH and SCHLOSBERG, 1954; DAVITZ, 1964; EKMAN, 1973). Since the problem deals more with producing and perceiving emotional behavior than with the recognition of different faces, no further coverage of this matter seems warranted in our discussion.

An alternative way of studying face perception has been to examine its salient characteristics in comparison to the perception of other visual objects. The notion is that if face perception involves a unique skill, then face recognition should be different from object recognition under at least three major conditions. First, infants should have some predisposition for attending to and recognizing facial configurations in order to facilitate later differentiation among faces of different people. Second, normal adults, and children above a certain age, should show an ability to remember faces that is unmatched by their ability to remember other visual objects. Third, selective brain injuries should impair face recognition, but not recognition of other objects.

Instead of studying the judgments about the face, in other words, the alternative approach merely calls for a comparison of face and object recognition in different situations. Presumably, such a comparison would ultimately indicate the unique aspects of face recognition, and these would then form the basis for further direct inquiry about the face recognition process. Thus far, the research has only slowly converged on a satisfactory set of comparisons, with the result that there is still only partial evidence regarding the nature of face perception.

B. Development of Face Perception in Infants

For infant perception, three types of evidence would support the notion of a special ability to recognize faces:

- first, that attraction to a facial stimulus (but not other visual objects) occurs very early in life, preferably close to birth and before any intensive exposure to the face;[4]
- second, that the attraction to faces follows a developmental course different from that for other visual objects (and that all other objects tend to follow the same course); and
- third, that appreciation of differences between faces or facial features occurs earlier and is more acute than that of differences among other visual objects.

By these criteria, studies of infant perception have yielded positive but not yet conclusive evidence for a special face perception ability.

Most of the research has concentrated on testing whether infants are especially attracted to the face. The well known experiments by SPITZ and WOLF (1946) followed earlier work by KAILA (1932) and showed that a facial stimulus elicited a smiling response that peaked in the infant's 20th week of life. The investigators also showed that the adequate stimulus was not necessarily a real human face, but any slightly moving round shape with two spots for

[4] For instance, SPITZ and WOLF (1946) argue that, especially during breast feeding, the infant's main attention is on the mother's face, and that this early and frequent exposure could account for later sensitivity to the face.

eyes. Later work by AMBROSE (1961) showed that home-reared infants, unlike the institution raised infants who were the subjects of the SPITZ and WOLF experiments, exhibited the peak of smiling response at 14 weeks, and most subsequent experiments have verified the peaking of the smiling response to faces somewhere between the 14th and 20th weeks of life.

FANTZ (1961) made it possible to test the reactions of younger infants by measuring visual fixation time in response to various objects, and he used a schematic face to show that the peak fixation time to the face occurred when an infant was about ten weeks old. Although FANTZ (1966) later modified his claims about the significance of the facial stimulus, his research generated further interest in face perception because he used a scrambled face (in which the same features for the schematic face were rearranged) among his comparison stimuli, and there was slightly less fixation in response to the scrambled face than to the regular face.

Neither SPITZ and WOLF nor FANTZ really attempted to determine whether other stimulus properties such as complexity or symmetry could explain the differential response to the facial stimulus. As a result, other experiments have been designed to make comparisons among different objects. Of additional concern has been the variation of response measures, to ensure that the results are not an artifact of a specific response.[5] For instance, KAGAN et al. (1966) presented four month old infants with four models of faces (a regular face, a scrambled face, a face with no eyes, and a blank face) and assessed the smiling response and fixation time as reactions to these faces. The results confirmed SPITZ's findings, as there were smiling preferences for the regular face, but did not confirm FANTZ's findings, as there were no fixation differences among the stimuli. The research also left open the possibility that the preferential response to the face was really a response to a stimulus varying along a complexity dimension.

HAAF and BELL (1967) subsequently designed four schematic pictures so that their rank order in terms of complexity was different from their rank order in terms of resemblance to a real face. Testing four month old infants for total fixation time, the investigators found that the preferential ordering of stimuli followed the face dimension, and not the complexity one. At the same time, several investigators have failed to find any differential responses to facial as opposed to non-facial pictures (THOMAS, 1965; KOOPMAN and AMES, 1968; and WILCOX, 1969). In one case (THOMAS, 1965), the results actually showed increasing preferences for four patterns (stripes, checkers, full face, and full figure), and the investigator concluded that complexity rather than faceness was the more important dimension.

The most comprehensive series of experiments, however, has reaffirmed the original findings of HAAF and BELL. In this series, LEWIS (1969) compared the responses of infants to four facial configurations: a scrambled cartoon

[5] As a rule, an adequate test of infants' visual preferences must employ two or more response measures (LEWIS et al., 1966). Also, certain methodologic pitfalls must be avoided. For instance, one question is the distance at which the stimulus is placed. HAYNES et al. (1965) showed that, at ages less than one month, the infant's accommodative response appears to be locked at a single focal distance, about 19 cm.

face, a realistic cartoon face, a scrambled face photograph, and a real face photograph. There were four response measures—the duration of the first fixation, the amount of smiling, the amount of vocalization, and the amount of fretting/crying—and different infants were tested at 12, 24, 36, and 57 weeks of age. The magnitude of three of the responses was consistently greatest for the real face photograph, followed by the cartoon face, the scrambled face photograph, and the scrambled cartoon face. The fourth response, the amount of fretting/crying, showed no stimulus differences. The results indicated that infants responded along the predicted stimulus dimension, i.e., the degree of resemblance to a real face, with the scrambled faces serving as a control for stimulus complexity.

Although this line of research does suggest that infants are especially attracted to the face, the problem of controlling for the effects of complexity, contrast, symmetry, or any other stimulus property has been difficult to resolve. This is because the investigator usually makes an a priori choice in ranking a series of stimuli according to complexity or to the degree of resemblance to a real face, and one cannot be sure that the infant would exercise the same choice. A different approach for studying infants' preferences for faces has been made where an upside-down face is used as the comparison pattern. Such a comparison automatically equates complexity, contrast, and other stimulus properties other than orientation itself, and the comparison also eliminates the effects of extraneous cues perhaps unnoticed by the investigator.

The research on upright and inverted faces has shown that the upright face may be especially attractive to infants. WATSON (1966) showed faces at four different orientations (0°, 90°, 180°, and 270°), and found that both the smiling response and fixation time for the upright face peaked prominently at 14 weeks, and that no such peaks occurred for the disoriented faces. In a second set of experiments, FAGAN (1972) showed that five- to six-month infants gave differential fixation responses to a novel and familiar pair of upright faces, but not to a similar pair of inverted faces. FAGAN also showed that although male and female infants varied in the age at which they could first make such apparent discriminations between upright faces, whenever the ability first emerged no similar ability to discriminate between inverted faces was found. Whereas WATSON's research reinforces the notion of a critical period at the infant's third or fourth month during which the face appears to have a special attraction, FAGAN's research suggests that infants are able to discriminate between two different faces at five to six months of age. In both cases, the use of the inverted face precludes an explanation of these findings on the basis of other stimulus properties, with the exception of the orientation factor. Further research should therefore be designed to show whether disorientation has similar effects on other typically mono-oriented objects.

In contrast to this research on the differential attraction of the full face, there has been less attention to the role played by the facial features. The common notion is that the upper half of the face contains more important features (AHRENS, 1954). One investigation (CARON et al., 1973) used a habituation paradigm to test GIBSON's view (1969) that appreciation for the features occurs before an appreciation for the full face. The experiment examined the importance of all the facial features and found support for GIBSON's view by showing that four-month infants could especially discriminate eye-like configurations but not whole faces. However, further replication with other procedures is needed to determine those features, if any, that are of special attraction, and whether discrimination of these features is particularly linked to a characteristic of faces and not merely to some general characteristic of visual acuity.

In summary, the research on infants' perception is just beginning to show the possibility of a special ability for recognizing faces. The most solid evidence comes from tests of older infants, which have shown a consistent peaking of response to the full face, occurring somewhere between the 14th and 20th weeks, and seemingly not easily explained by any other stimulus characteristic. This peaking may be related to the infant's social development, so that at about the fifth month of life the face becomes the basis for beginning to distinguish one person from another.

C. Face Perception by Normal Adults and Children

If there is a special ability to distinguish one face from another, normal adults should perform well in a laboratory test of this task, and the talent should be dissociable from other visual perception skills. Moreover, if normal adults do perform exceptionally well, then there remains the question of determining when such skills develop in childhood, and whether the developmental course can yield clues about the nature of the face perception process.

Unfortunately, only a few investigators have compared face with object perception by normal adults or children, perhaps due to the inconclusive evidence from the earlier studies of face judgments. In addition, the studies of normal adults also contain many suggestive but potentially misleading insights about face recognition. HARMON (1973), for instance, showed that computer-controlled degradation of a face pattern did not prevent its identification even after the individual facial features had been severely blurred. Other distortions, however, such as the use of photographic negatives (GALPER, 1970; GALPER and HOCHBERG, 1971; PHILLIPS, 1972) or the inversion of a face photograph (HOCHBERG and GALPER, 1967; ROCK, 1974) appear to make face recognition extremely difficult. The general problem with many of these studies, as well as with others in which face pictures have been used to study nonverbal memory or communication (e.g., YARMEY, 1970; SMITH and NIELSEN, 1970; BUGENTAL et al., 1971; HILLIARD, 1973; and WARRINGTON and TAYLOR, 1973), is that the face pattern was the only nonverbal pattern used in the study. The absence of comparisons with other patterns makes it difficult to attribute the results to a peculiarity of faces, and the results need to be interpreted with this reservation.

The few studies that have compared face with object recognition have shown that face recognition may involve different recognition strategies. One series of experiments compared face recognition with recognition of other mono-oriented objects (e.g., arrays of houses, airplanes, or stick figures) when twenty pictures of each type of object had to be remembered: (1) in the upright orientation, and (2) in the inverted orientation (YIN, 1969). Although recognition for all objects was more difficult when inverted, face recognition was disproportionately affected. The results have been confirmed with other experiments using pictures of dogs, other houses, and famous as well as unknown faces (SCAPINELLO and YARMEY, 1970; YARMEY, 1971). Similarly disproportionate declines in face recognition occur when face pictures are presented for a 100 ms exposure, or when they must be matched to subjects' own written descriptions (YIN, 1970a). Whatever the "distortion" (i.e., inversion, brief exposure, or verbal description), recognition of the normally oriented face is superior but recognition under distorted conditions is inferior in comparison to other meaningful objects of the same class.

These experiments also suggested that subjects used a special strategy for remembering the normally presented face, that this strategy was not used for remembering other objects, and that it was difficult to use for looking at and remembering "distorted" faces. Under the distorted conditions, subjects typically complained that all the faces looked alike. The special strategy appeared to involve an appreciation of the whole face as a single object, and the coding of this face according to some aspect of the subject's social experiences (e.g., "the face looks like Jack Benny"). With other objects, such a strategy was occasionally attempted, but a more common strategy was simply to select and remember a distinctive feature.

Research with normal children aged 6 to 16 years has further explored the possible distinction between these two recognition strategies. In two experiments, CAREY and DIAMOND (1977) initially showed that children's ability to remember normally presented faces appeared to rise sharply around the 10th year, even though memory for other objects, including inverted faces, only improved slightly.[6] The investigators then showed that the improved face recognition performance could be attributed to the older children paying more attention to the whole face and its expression, and ignoring less relevant features such as type of headwear, beards, or eyeglasses. On the one hand, children 10 years or younger were easily misled by changes in such features in matching two different face pictures of the same person, and performance was not any better even when the pictures had the same expression. The older children, on the other hand, were successfully able to ignore the feature differences and more easily matched the correct face pictures. Similar results were obtained whether the procedure called for simple matching of pictures or for matching from memory.

The potential existence of two different strategies appears to be a promising lead for future research. The fact that normal adults may attend to the whole

[6] The effects of disorientation had previously been shown when children were presented with inverted faces and later tested for memory of these faces (GOLDSTEIN, 1965). Different results occur, however, if children are required to make a mental inversion, i.e., presented with upright faces but tested with inverted faces (BROOKS and GOLDSTEIN, 1963). Our discussion does not deal with any of the latter type of study, where mental inversions or recombinations are required.

face as well as code the face according to some social experience would certainly establish face recognition as a different process. When adults are denied the ability to use this wholistic-social strategy, they may have to fall back on the more common strategy for remembering other objects, i.e., a feature analysis. However, when the feature analysis is applied to faces, memory is much worse, as isolated facial features do not differ sufficiently to enable the coding of many different faces. Future research should be carried out with one note of caution: if schematic or artificial reproductions of the face are used, and if only the facial features are varied, the results are likely to show that subjects used a feature strategy in remembering the faces (e.g., BRADSHAW and WALLACE, 1971). This is because such schematic faces are an inadequate stimulus for relating to the subject's social experience, and the subject is automatically forced to rely on a feature analysis.

D. Abnormal Deficits in Face Perception

Just as faces may be especially attractive to infants and may play a special role in normal adult life, clinical investigations have revealed a perceptual deficit that may be specific to faces. The investigations have centered on two types of patients: those who spontaneously report a difficulty in identifying familiar people on the basis of the face, and those who make disproportionately more errors in face recognition tests. In either case, the prime question has been the degree to which a face recognition deficit actually exists. Only secondarily have investigators probed the question of whether the deficit is specific to faces or merely symptomatic of a more general perceptual deficiency.

Spontaneous Face Recognition Difficulties. "Prosopagnosia" is the term used to label the deficit in which patients have spontaneous difficulties in recognizing faces.[7] Cases of prosopagnosia occur rarely, with only some seventy-five cases having been reported over the last fifty years (HÉCAEN et al., 1957; HÉCAEN and ANGELERGUES, 1962; BEYN and KNYAZEVA, 1962; RONDOT and TZAVARAS, 1969). The major symptom is that the patient is unable to recognize individual faces, even though he can describe all the features of the face. The defect can exist in varying degrees, and is detected by the patient's reports of failure to identify persons previously familiar to him (sometimes including his own mirror image), and his inability to recognize photos of familiar or famous people. The patient may also appear to have a particular difficulty in fixing on or interpreting the occular region of the face (AHRENS, 1955; GLONING and QUATEMBER, 1966; and GLONING et al., 1966).

Beyond these observations, the clinical picture becomes very diverse. Among the more severe cases, PALLIS (1955) reported a patient who saw distortions of shading ("all the men appear unshaved"); the patient of BEYN and KNYAZEVA

[7] The term was coined by BODAMER (1947), 'prosopon' being the Greek term for face.

(1962) could not appreciate the sex or age of a face; and COLE and PEREZ-CRUET'S patient (1964) had difficulty distinguishing white from black people as well as men from women. Among less severe cases, the deficit can have a more transient nature, and not be accompanied by any other defects (e.g., BORNSTEIN and KIDRON, 1959; HÉCAEN and ANGELERGUES, 1962).

Except for these mild or transient cases, the patient who cannot recognize faces usually suffers from other defects. Although the reports are not consistent, the patients appear to share three symptoms in common: (1) a visual field defect, with a general tendency for it to be on the left side and in the upper quadrant of the field; (2) an inability to recognize specific places on the basis of visual cues, similar to the impairment with faces; and (3) a difficulty in drawing from memory. This last symptom may have more to do with a difficulty in revisualizing, i.e., creating an image in one's mind, than with motor coordination in drawing, since the patients are usually able to copy pictures in front of them. Other associated symptoms that have been less consistently reported include problems in object and animal recognition, color recognition, and general memory and mental functioning.

In short, the existing studies do not yet provide evidence for a face-specific deficit. Although the less severe cases do appear to involve only a face deficit, faces may merely be serving as a very difficult material, and the face recognition deficit may still be symptomatic of a more general recognition deficit. In the more severe cases, although there is little agreement over the associated symptoms, face recognition deficits have nevertheless always been accompanied by some other visual recognition problem.

The site of the injury that causes prosopagnosia is also an unanswered question. Because of the visual field defects that usually accompany prosopagnosia, the posterior portions of the brain are more suspect than the anterior ones. However, no evidence exists for the degree of lateralization, with some investigators claiming the importance of bilateral injuries and others suggesting that the right hemisphere may be the more important for recognizing faces. Bilateral involvement has been suspected if only on the basis of the small number of cases that have been reported. The reasoning is that if a unilateral injury were sufficient to produce the deficit, there would have been more cases of prosopagnosia (RITCHIE RUSSELL, as quoted by BORNSTEIN and KIDRON, 1959). In addition, the one necropsy report from a prosopagnosic case revealed two lesions, one in the region of the left angular gyrus and the second in the region of the lower lip of the right calcerine fissure (PEVZNER et al., 1962). The evidence for a right hemisphere involvement alone, on the other hand, comes from investigations in which patients had less severe face recognition deficits (HÉCAEN and ANGELERGUES, 1962; DERENZI and SPINNLER, 1966; and BORNSTEIN et al., 1969).

Difficulties on Face Recognition Tests. Over the last ten years, clinical investigations have uncovered more subtle face recognition deficits than those spontaneously reported by prosopagnosic patients. These more subtle deficits take the form of exceptionally poor performances on face recognition tests, although the patients do not have any notable difficulties in identifying faces of personally familiar people. Moreover, most of the research has consistently shown that patients with right hemisphere injuries have the most difficulty in recognizing faces, whether the tests involve memory (e.g., MILNER, 1968) or merely call for patients to match various face pictures (e.g., BENTON and VAN ALLEN, 1968). Patients with right-sided injuries and visual field defects appear to be the most deficient, thereby suggesting that right posterior injuries are the most relevant to the face recognition deficit (DERENZI and SPINNLER, 1966; DERENZI et al., 1968).

The existence of larger numbers of patients with these subtle deficits has enabled investigators to compare face recognition with other visual tasks. This has allowed more frequent examination of the potential face-specificity of the deficit than has been possible with prosopagnosic patients. On the surface, the comparisons between recognition of face and other objects have produced mixed results. In some studies, deficient face recognition has been associated with deficient abilities in discriminating colors (DERENZI et al., 1969), brightness patterns (BENTON and GORDON, 1971), and abstract figures (DERENZI and SPINNLER, 1966). These results therefore suggest that there is no face-specific deficit.

In contrast, other studies have repeatedly dissociated deficient face recognition from recognition of comparison pictures, including arrays of chairs, houses, cups, and other meaningful objects of the same class (DERENZI and SPINNLER, 1966; YIN, 1970b; and TZAVARAS et al., 1970). These results therefore lend some support to a face-specific deficit, and they also may be the basis for rejecting a hypothesis by FAUST (1947) that the face recognition deficit represents a more general inability to discriminate individual objects of the same class. Furthermore, the face-specific evidence also challenges the argument that faces are so familiar, and require such subtle discriminations, that few comparable tests of object recognition exist: In one study, right posterior patients were deficient in remembering faces, but *superior* to other patients with unilateral injuries in remembering a second group of face pictures when presented upside-down, thus providing strong evidence of a deficit specific to recognizing normally presented faces (YIN, 1970b).

A possible reason for these contrary results is that investigators have used considerably different face recognition tests. Some studies only require the subject to match similar faces (e.g., BENTON and VAN ALLEN, 1968; BENTON and GORDON, 1971). Other studies require the subject to examine a single face, and then from immediate memory to select the single face from an array of new faces (e.g., DERENZI and SPINNLER, 1966). Yet other studies require the subject to examine faces individually but nevertheless to remember a large group of faces (e.g., YIN, 1970b). These variations are important because the unique aspect of face recognition may be the ability to remember and discriminate many different faces. Those situations that merely require matching or memorization of a single face may not tap the unique face recognition skill, and hence performance on these tests is not likely to be dissociated from performance in recognizing other objects. In fact, there has been a tendency for those studies with such "weak" face tests to show no face-specific deficit, and for those studies with "strong" face tests to arrive at the opposite conclusion.

A similar problem arises in those few studies that have tried to relate prosopagnosia to poor performance on face recognition tests. Several investigators

(HÉCAEN and TZAVARAS, 1968–1969; ASSAL, 1969; BENTON and VAN ALLEN, 1972), for instance, have shown that prosopagnosic patients performed normally on face recognition tests, but the tests in these studies only employed a matching procedure. WARRINGTON and JAMES (1967) suggested that whereas the prosopagnosic patient was deficient in recognizing familiar and well known faces, the less severe deficit involved tests with unknown faces. They therefore compared performance on tests of famous and unknown faces and found that right hemisphere patients were worse on both, but that performance on the two tests was not correlated. Their conclusions about the apparent lack of association must again be tempered by the observation that the two tests had different procedures, and that the unknown face recognition test only involved memory for a single face at a time and not a group of faces. In contrast, the prosopagnosic patient examined be DERENZI et al. (1968) had deficiencies on a face recognition test that did involve memory for a group of faces.

In summary, studies of abnormal deficiencies in face perception have shown that persons with injuries to the right hemisphere have difficulty recognizing faces. This deficiency appears particularly to be one of not being able to remember a group of faces, a task that may require both the ability to appreciate facial differences and to encode those differences into memory. The deficiency as thus defined appears to be dissociable from deficiencies in recognizing other visual objects. However, the relationship between this face recognition deficit and cases of prosopagnosia where patients spontaneously report face recognition deficits is unclear. Furthermore, there is little evidence regarding the site of injury for these prosopagnosic patients.

E. Summary: How Might Faces Be Special?

Even though a compelling case cannot yet be made, the experimental evidence may gradually be converging to give sufficient demonstration of a face-specific recognition process that enables people to discriminate and remember a large number of faces. If one entertains the possibility of a face-specific process, how might such a process be characterized? We shall close our discussion with a few speculations that in turn may suggest the possible lines for future research.

One way of characterizing a face-specific process would be by its development over the course of individual growth. Studies of very young infants would have to show that the infant's special attraction to the face is attributable to the organic development of a face schema, reflected by a predisposition to perceive whole faces in the visual environment. The studies would simultaneously have to demonstrate the lack of such a predisposition for any other visual object, with the latter perhaps being perceived on the basis of some sort of feature analysis not applicable to face recognition. Anecdotal evidence in support of the existence of a face schema might be the predisposition of adults to perceive faces in inanimate patterns, such as faces in fires, cars, or houses where a facial image is inappropriately perceived. In the infant, the role of the face schema would be to alert the infant to the faces in the environment, in order to help the infant attend to the differences among these faces.

In the normal child, the major development in the face recognition process would be the development of a social code, to facilitate memory for different faces. The code would link the wholistic pattern of each face to some aspect of the individual's social experience, which would include emotional behavior, differentiation of people as unique individuals, and even possibly the differentiation of people according to various social roles. The routine functioning of the social code is suggested by another piece of anecdotal evidence from normal adults: people easily remember the face of those whom they "get to know," but do not remember the faces of anonymous persons, as seen for instance in a crowded bus or subway; furthermore, adults often remember faces of people within the context of certain social roles (e.g., the teller at the bank), but when such faces are seen out of context, there lingers an embarrassing ambiguity that the face is familiar but not quite identifiable.

If such a social code facilitates memory for faces, then one important hypothesis for laboratory studies of face recognition (where, typically, a group of unknown faces is shown to the subject) is that a subject given a face recognition task applies the social code in relation to a face picture, much as he might if meeting a new acquaintance in person. If the subject cannot use the social code, either in the laboratory or in the real life situation, his memory will be deficient. Moreover, individual differences among adults might occur as a result of differences in social experiences, and hence of the richness of their social codes. Finally, the fact that each individual's social code is unique to his own experience might help to explain the difficulties encountered by studies of judgments of the face, for the substance of the judgments need not be verbal nor uniform from one individual to another.

As for the deficits in normal face recognition, these could occur either as a result of difficulties in viewing the whole face or in using the social code. The studies of brain-injured patients have not yet distinguished between these two deficiencies, but it may very well be that prosopagnosic patients tend to suffer from the former, while patients with more subtle face recognition problems tend to suffer from the latter. In either situation, however, the deficit would be the result of an injury implicating a face-specific process, and not visual recognition or memory in general. Which brings us to one final question: Why should the nervous system preserve a special subsystem for recognizing faces?

The answer must lie in man's diverse social nature and the role of faces in interpersonal relations. Unlike other personal attributes such as voices, which, while distinctive, are not always reliable grounds for identifying people (who may choose to remain silent), the face is a readily observable part of the social environment. Because of man's diverse social relationships, it is incumbent to have a readily accessible object such as the face for identifying different people and inferring their expression, mood, and intentions. Without the ability to distinguish among faces, people would be unable to sustain meaningful social relationships. On this ground alone, specialization by the nervous system to recognize faces would be as important as specialization for man's dominant mode of communication, which is his production and perception of speech.

References

Ahrens, R.: Beitrag zur Entwicklung des Physiognomie- und Mimikerkennens. Z. exp. angew. Psychol. **2**, 412–454 (1954).

Ahrens, R.: Beitrag zur Frage der Prosopagnosie. Schweiz. Arch. Neurol. Psychiat. **75**, 4 (1955).

Ambrose, J.A.: The development of the smiling response in early infancy. In B. Foss (ed.), Determinants of Infant Behaviour. Vol. I, 179–201. London: Methuen, 1961.

Anderson, L.D.: Estimating intelligence by means of printed photographs. J. appl. Psychol. **5**, 152–155 (1921).

Assal, G.: Régression des troubles de la reconnaissance des physionomies et de la mémoire topographique chez un malade opéré d'un hématome intracérébral pariéto-temporal droit. Rev. neurol. **121**, 184–185 (1969).

Benton, A.L., Gordon, M.C.: Correlates of face recognition. Trans. Amer. neurol. Ass., Vol. 96, 1971.

Benton, A.L., Van Allen, M.W.: Impairment in facial recognition in patients with cerebral disease. Cortex **4**, 344–358 (1968).

Benton, A.L., Van Allen, M.W.: Prosopagnosia and facial discrimination. J. neurol. Sci. **15**, 167–172 (1972).

Beyn, E.S., Knyazeva, G.R.: The problem of prosopagnosia. J. Neurol. Neurosurg. Psychiat. **25**, 154–158 (1962).

Bodamer, J.: Die Prosop-Agnosie. Arch. Psychiat. Nervenkr. **179**, 6–53 (1947).

Bornstein, B., Kidron, D.P.: Prosopagnosia. J. Neurol. Neurosurg. Psychiat. **22**, 124–131 (1959).

Bornstein, B., Sroka, H., Munitz, M.: Prosopagnosia with animal face agnosia. Cortex **5**, 164–169 (1969).

Bradshaw, J.L.: The information conveyed by varying the dimensions of features in human outlines faces. Percept. Psychophys. **6**, 5–9 (1969).

Bradshaw, L.J., Wallace, G.: Models for the processing and identification of faces. Percept. Psychophys. **9**, 443–448 (1971).

Brooks, R.M., Goldstein, A.G.: Recognition by children of inverted photographs of faces. Child Develpm. **34**, 1033–1044 (1963).

Brunswik, E.: Perception and the Representative Design of Psychological Experiments. Berkeley: University of California, 1956.

Brunswik, E., Reiter, L.: Eindrucks-Charactere schematisierter Gesichter. Z. Psychol. **142**, 67–134 (1937).

Bugental, D., Love, L., Gianetto, R.: Perfidious feminine faces. J. Pers. soc. Psychol. **17**, 314–318 (1971).

Carey, S., Diamond, R.: From piecemeal to configurational representation of faces. Science **195**, 312–313 (January 1977).

Caron, A.J., Caron, R.F., Caldwell, R.C., Weiss, S.J.: Infant perception of the structural properties of the face. Develop. Psychol. **9**, 385–399 (1973).

Child, I.: The judging of occupations from printed photographs. J. soc. Psychol. **7**, 117–118 (1936).

Cole, M., Perez-Cruet, J.: Prosopagnosia. Neuropsychologia **2**, 237–246 (1964).

Cook, S.W.: The judgment of intelligence from photographs. J. abnorm. soc. Psychol. **34**, 384–389 (1939).

Cross, J.F., Cross, J., Daly, J.: Sex, race, age, and beauty as factors in recognition of faces. Percept. Psychophys. **10**, 393–396 (1971).

Davitz, J.R.: The Communication of Emotional Meaning, chapter 2. New York: McGraw-Hill, 1964.

DeRenzi, E., Spinnler, H.: Facial recognition in brain-damaged patients. Neurology (Minneap.) **16**, 145–152 (1966).

DeRenzi, E., Scotti, G., Spinnler, H.: Perceptual and associative disorders of visual recognition. Neurology (Minneap.) **19**, 634–642 (1969).

DeRenzi, E., Faglioni, P., Spinnler, M.: The performance of patients with unilateral brain damage on face recognition tests. Cortex **4**, 17–34 (1968).

Dunlap, K.: A project for investigating the facial signs of personality. Amer. J. Psychol. **39**, 158–161 (1927a).

Dunlap, K.: The role of eye-muscles and mouth-muscles in the expression of emotion. Genet. Psychol. Monogr. **2**, 197–233 (1927b).

• Ekman, P. (ed.): Darwin and Facial Expression. New York: Academic Press, 1973.

Fagan, J.F.: Infants' recognition memory for faces. J. exp. Child Psychol. **14**, 453–476 (1972).

Faust, C.: Partielle Seelenblindheit nach Occipitalhirnverletzungen mit besonderer Beeinträchtigung des Physiognomie-Erkennens. Nervenarzt **18**, 294–297 (1947).

• Fantz, R.L.: The origin of form perception. Sci. Amer. **204(5)**, 66–72 (1961).

Fantz, R.L.: Pattern discrimination and selective attention as determinants of perceptual development from birth. In: A.H. Kidd and J.L. Rivoire (eds.), Perceptual Development in Children, 143–173. New York: International Universities Press, 1966.

Galper, R.E.: Recognition of faces in photographic negative. Psychon. Sci. **19**, 207–208 (1970).

Galper, R.E., Hochberg, J.: Recognition memory for photographs of faces. Amer. J. Psychol. **84**, 351–354 (1971).

Galton, F.: Inquiries into Human Faculty and Development. New York: Macmillan 1883.

Gardner, B., Wallach, L.: Shapes of figures identified as a baby's head. Percept. Mot. Skills **20**, 135–142 (1965).

Gaskill, P.C., Fenton, N., Porter, J.P.: Judging the intelligence of boys from their photographs. J. appl. Psychol. **11**, 394–403 (1927).

• Gibson, E.: Principles of Perceptual Learning and Development. New York: Appleton-Century-Crofts 1969.

Gloning, K., Quatember, R.: Methodischer Beitrag zur Untersuchung der Prosopagnosie. Neuropsychologia **4**, 133–141 (1966).

Gloning, I., Gloning, K., Moff, H., Tschabitscher, H.: Zur Prosopagnosie. Neuropsychologia **4**, 113–132 (1966).

Goldstein, A.G.: Learning of inverted and normally oriented faces in children and adults. Psychon. Sci. **3**, 447–448 (1965).

Gombrich, E.H.: Meditations on a hobby horse or the roots of artistic form. In L.L. Whyte (ed.), Aspects of Form: 2nd edition, 209–224. London: Lund Humphries, 1968.

Groner, R.: Dimensionen der Wahrnehmung von Gesichtern. Z. exp. angew. Psychol. **14**, 135–154 (1967).

Gurnee, H.: An analysis of the perception of intelligence in the face. J. soc. Psychol. **5**, 82–89 (1934).

Haaf, R.A., Bell, R.Q.: A facial dimension in visual discrimination by human infants. Child Develpm. **38**, 893–899 (1967).

• Harmon, L.D.: The recognition of faces. Sci. Amer. **229**, 71–82 (November 1973).

• Haynes, H., White, B., Held, R.: Visual accommodation in human infants. Science **148**, 528–530 (April 1965).

Hécaen, H., Angelergues, R.: Agnosia for faces (prosopagnosia). Arch. Neurol. (Paris) **7**, 92–100 (1962).

Hécaen, H., Tzavaras, A.: Etude neuropsychologique des troubles de la reconnaissance des visages humains. Bull. Psychol. **22**, 754–762 (1968–1969).

Hécaen, H., Angelergues, R., Bernhardt, C., Chiarelli, J.: Essai de distinction des modalites cliniques de l'agnosie des physiognomies. Rev. neurol. **96**, 125–144 (1957).

Hilliard, R.D.: Hemispheric laterality effects on a facial recognition task in normal subjects. Cortex **9**, 246–258 (1973).

Hochberg, J., Galper, R.E.: Recognition of faces: An exploratory study. Psychon. Sci. **9**, 619–620 (1967).

Howells, T.H.: A study of ability to recognize faces. J. abnorm. soc. Psychol. **33**, 124–127 (1938).
Hückstedt, B.: Experimentelle Untersuchungen zum „Kindchenschema". Z. exp. angew. Psychol. **12**, 421–450 (1965).
Irwin, F.W.: Thresholds for the perception of difference in facial expression and its elements. Amer. J. Psychol. **44**, 1–17 (1932).
Jenness, A.: The recognition of facial expressions of emotion. Psychol. Bull. **29**, 324–350 (1932).
Jones, L.: Memory for faces and memory for names. Charact. Person **4**, 115–119 (1935).
Kaess, W.A., Witryol, S.L.: Memory for names and faces: A characteristic of social intelligence. J. appl. Psychol. **39**, 457–462 (1955).
Kagan, J., Henker, B., Hen-Tov, A., Levine, J., Lewis, M.: Infants' differential reactions to familiar and distorted faces. Child Develpm. **37**, 519–532 (1966).
Kaila, E.: Die Reaktionen des Säuglings auf das menschliche Gesicht. Ann. Univ. Aboensis **17**, 1–114 (1932).
Kessen, W.: The role of experience in judging children's photographs. J. abnorm. soc. Psychol. **54**, 375–379 (1957).
Koopman, P., Ames, E.W.: Infant's preferences for facial arrangements: A failure to replicate. Child Develpm. **39**, 481–487 (1968).
Laird, D.A., Remmers, H.: A study of estimates of intelligence from photographs. J. exp. Psychol. **7**, 429–446 (1924).
Lewis, M.: Infants' responses to facial stimuli during the first year of life. Develop. Psychol. **1**, 75–86 (1969).
Lewis, M., Kagan, J., Kalafat, J.: Patterns of fixation in the young infant. Child Develpm. **37**, 331–341 (1966).
Lindzey, G., Prince, B., Wright, H.K.: A study of facial asymmetry. J. Personality **22**, 68–84 (1952).
Malpass, R.S., Kravitz, J.: Recognition of faces of own and other race. J. Pers. soc. Psychol. **13**, 330–334 (1969).
Mar, T.: Face Reading. New York: Signet Books, 1975.
McCurdy, H.G.: Experimental notes on the asymmetry of the human face. J. abnorm. soc. Psychol. **44**, 553–555 (1949).
Messick, S., Damarin, F.: Cognitive style and memory for faces. J. abnorm. soc. Psychol. **69**, 313–318 (1964).
Milner, B.: Visual recognition and recall after right temporal-lobe excision in man. Neuropsychologia **6**, 191–209 (1968).
Pallis, C.A.: Impaired identification of faces and places with agnosia for colours. J. Neurol. Neurosurg. Psychiat. **18**, 218–224 (1955).
Pevzner, S., Bornstein, B., Loewenthal, M.: Prosopagnosia. J. Neurol. Neurosurg. Psychiat. **25**, 336–338 (1962).
Phillips, R.J.: Why are faces hard to recognize in photographic negative? Percept. Psychophys. **12**, 425–426 (1972).
Pintner, R.: Intelligence as estimated from photographs. Psychol. Rev. **25**, 286–296 (1918).
Rock, I.: The perception of disoriented figures. Sci. Amer. **230**, 78–85 (January 1974).
Rondot, P., Tzavaras, A.: La prosopagnosie après vingt années d'études cliniques et neuropsychologiques. J. Psychol. norm. Path. **2**, 133–165 (April-June 1969).
Samuels, M.R.: Judgments of faces. Charact. Pers. **8**, 18–27 (1939).
Scapinello, K.F., Yarmey, A.D.: The role of familiarity and orientation in immediate and delayed recognition of pictorial stimuli. Psychon. Sci. **2**, 329–331 (1970).
Secord, P.F., Muthard, J.E.: Individual differences in the perception of women's faces. J. abnorm. soc. Psychol. **50**, 238–242 (1955).
Smith, E.E., Nielsen, G.D.: Representations and retrieval processes in short-term memory. J. exp. Psychol. **85**, 397–405 (1970).
Spitz, R.A., Wolf, K.M.: The smiling response: A contribution to the ontogenesis of social relations. Genet. Psychol. Monogr. **34**, 57–125 (1946).
Stritch, T.M., Secord, P.F.: Interaction effects in the perception of faces. J. Personality **24**, 270–284 (1956).
Thomas, H.: Visual-fixation responses of infants to stimuli of varying complexity. Child Develpm. **36**, 629–638 (1965).

Tzavaras, A., Hécaen, H., Le Bras, H.: Le problème de la spécificité du déficit de la reconnaissance du visage humain lors des lésions hémisphériques unilaterales. Neuropsychologia **8**, 403–416 (1970).
Warrington, E.K., James, M.: An experimental investigation of facial recognition in patients with unilateral cerebral lesions. Cortex **3**, 317–326 (1967).
Warrington, E.K., Taylor, A.M.: Immediate memory for faces: Long- or short-term memory? Quart. J. exp. Psychol. **25**, 316–322 (1973).
Watson, J.S.: Perception of object orientation in infants. Merrill-Palmer Quart. **12**, 73–94 (1966).
White, R.K., Landis, C.: Perception of silhouettes. Amer. J. Psychol. **42**, 431–435 (1930).
Wilcox, B.M.: Visual preferences of human infants for representations of the human face. J. exp. Child Psychol. **7**, 10–20 (1969).
Wolff, W.: The experimental study of forms of expression. Charact. Pers. **2**, 168–176 (1933).
Wolff, W.: The Expression of Personality: Experimental Depth Psychology. New York: Harper 1943.
Woodworth, R.S., Schlosberg, H.: Experimental Psychology, chapter 5. New York: Holt 1954.
Yarmey, A.D.: The effect of mnemonic instructions on paired-associates recognition memory for faces or names. Canad. J. behav. Sci. **2**, 181–190 (1970).
Yarmey, A.D.: Recognition memory for familiar "public" faces: Effects of orientation and delay. Psychon. Sci. **24**, 286–288 (1971).
Yin, R.K.: Face recognition: A special process? Unpublished doctoral dissertation, Dept. of Psychology, M.I.T., Cambridge (1970a).
Yin, R.K.: Face recognition by brain-injured patients: A dissociable ability? Neuropsychologia **8**, 395–402 (1970b).
Yin, R.K.: Looking at upside-down faces. J. exp. Psychol. **81**, 141–145 (1969).

B. Temporal Patterns

1. Speech Perception

Chapter 19

Word and Sentence Perception

M.F. GARRETT, Cambridge, Mass. USA

Contents

A. Introduction

In what follows we will be concerned broadly with questions of language comprehension, and specifically, with the perception of words in sentences. I emphasize, however, that in every case the motivation for considering results of research on word perception is their relevance to language comprehension processes at least at the level of sentence analysis.

Two terminological matters need brief mention before proceeding further: the notion of word or sentence *perception* on the one hand and the notion of sentence or language *comprehension* on the other.

In broaching a discussion of *speech* perception one is seldom inclined to terminological preambles. Everyone seems prepared to think comfortably of the assigment of acoustic outputs of the human vocal tract to one or another category of speech *sounds* as an instance of a specifically perceptual process. Similarly, psychologists are wont to speak of "word perception" with no apparent conflict of definition and intuition. But when the notion of *sentence* perception is raised, psychological brows sometimes wrinkle; intuitions about what counts as a sentence do not include it as a perceptual object. That arises in part from a limited view about sentences: namely, that they are (just) a temporal succession of discrete perceptual entities (speech sounds, or at best words). If one broadens one's view to include the notion of a *structural analysis* associated with each such succession of speech sounds, the reasonableness of thinking of sentences as percepts becomes more apparent. Nothing could be clearer than that the notion of perception must subsume decision processes on temporally as well as spatially distributed sensory arrays. Given that, there is no natural dividing line which separates the perception of crosses, circles and squares from that of beagles, brass bands, and brocaded tapestries; and similarly for a distinction between the perception of sounds, syllables, words, phrases and sentences. What is really at issue in deciding whether one wishes to exercise the word "perceptual" to describe a particular human performance is whether there exists for that case a well-defined (for the organism) construct which can be identified as the object of perception, and whether the elaboration of that construct (or the assignment of some sensory array to it) depends on a more-or-less continuous sensory input. Both these criteria are satisfied for sentences: the relevant sorts of constructs are the "structural descriptions" associated with sentences by an adequate grammar (see, e.g., CHOMSKY, 1965; FODOR et al., 1974, especially Chap. 1–3).

Although one should acknowledge that it is not clear precisely what information is to be included in a perceptually relevant structural description for a sentence, we will not try to deal with such issues here. We will simply distinguish between those on-line perceptual processes that yield a structure capable of supporting inference, and the results of such inferential processes, e.g., those that allow us to answer questions, paraphrase remarks, evaluate the truth of statements, and in general to act appropriately upon the results of our analysis of language inputs. For current purposes we will adopt a "minimum requirements" approach to the question of what must be in a perceptually relevant structural description. Those minimum requirements are that the structural description include 1. a specification of the lexical and grammatical formatives included in a candidate string (roughly a segmentation of the string at the "word" level), 2. a specification of the grammatical relations that hold among the lexical formatives, and 3. a specification of the grammatical relations that hold among the elementary sentences (sentoids) which comprise the surface sentence. The assignment of a structure that captures at least these properties will be treated as a perceptual problem in what follows, and it is left an open question both how the results of specifically inferential processes may affect such perceptual analyses, and vice versa.

The position just sketched is, of course, not a theoretically neutral characterization of language processing; in particular, it assumes that such processing can be thought of in terms of "levels" of description which correspond to the structural types of formal linguistic analysis (e.g., sound structure and one or more levels of syntax). That assumption could prove to be false (cf. SCHANK, 1973). Two points are relevant. First, should the assumption prove false, it would require some other explanation for the numerous findings that show a correspondence between linguistic structural descriptions and performance on a variety of experimental tasks (see, e.g., FODOR et al., 1974, Chap. 5). Second, if the assumption is false, one should fail to find evidence for *independent* psychological processing systems which correspond to linguistic types; but as we shall observe, there is evidence that the contribution which certain lexical and syntactic properties of sentences make to their computational difficulty is unrelated to their semantic burden.

Note, finally, that the "levels" assumption is not equivalent to one of sequentially ordered *stages* of processing. In particular, it is quite conceivable that a level of description corresponding, e.g., to syntactic structures could be the target of a quasi-independent processing system without at the same time its being necessary that all "semantic" or interpretive processes be wholly dependent on (i.e. temporally delayed until) the availability of such a description. Equally obvious is that by "independent" here I do not mean that there is no interaction between levels—only that such interaction is restricted to the *outputs* of the processing levels. To state the matter in terms of an example, it is to claim that the *syntactic* analysis of two instances of a given sentence type is carried out in the same manner, regardless of differences in their meaning—in particular, it is to claim that the presence of semantic information which contrains interpretation of a sentence does not render its syntactic analysis simpler or irrelevant. We will return to this point in the context of a discussion of several experimental findings.

B. Word Perception: Effects of Form

Questions about how words are perceived have been raised in a variety of experimental contexts—from past concerns with "semantic generalization" (e.g., RAZRAN, 1947) and intelligibility in speech communication (e.g., RUBENSTEIN and ABORN, 1960) to more recent preoccupations with character recognition, lexical structure, and sentence processing. Fundamentally, we are interested in the perception of words as it relates to the analysis of larger linguistic structures—sentences. This is so whether the modality is visual or auditory (listening to speech), and we will consider research from both areas (bearing in mind the possible effects of modality specific factors) with an eye to what we may learn about sentence perception. We note in passing that there is some evidence that the representations used in recognition of both visual and acoustic presentations of words are similar (e.g., RUBENSTEIN et al., 1971; MEYER et al., 1972). That is, the lexical access system we exploit for hearing and for reading systems may have most of its significant features in common. This does not, however, tell us anything about the organization of that system other than that such parameters of word form as are relevant will be specified in terms of some sort of "sound spelling."

What might the relevant parameters for word recognition be? Words are related to each other in virtue of their *form,* their *distribution* (syntax) and their *meaning*. Perceptually relevant similarities of form might include phonetic sequence, length, syllable structure, stress pattern, and morphological decomposition. Similarities based on distribution include major grammatical categories (e.g., noun, verb, adverb, etc.) and subcategorization by phrasal environments (e.g., distinctions among verbs in terms of whether they require or prohibit an object NP or among adverbs in terms of whether they modify sentences or are parts of verb phrases, etc.). Similarities based on meaning might include reference, association, affective tone, hierarchical relation (subordinate/superordinate) synonymy, antonymy, etc. There is a plethora of evidence attesting to the existence of these sorts of relations among words, but their interpretation in the context of word recognition and sentence perception processes is not transparent.

We know, a priori, that there must be *some* manner in which lexical entries can be determined solely from information about their form, for we can interpret both words and sentences in isolation and in "nonsensical" combinations; similarly, there is some manner in which lexical entries can be chosen solely from information about their meaning, for we can *produce* sentences which correspond to meanings inherent in nonlinguistic percepts. What is not clear is what relation these two capacities bear to the way in which we normally understand sentences. Are the component lexical and grammatical elements of a sentence located without recourse to features of their syntactic and semantic classification, or is the character of lexical access processes crucially dependent on semantic "directions" derived both from situational (nonlinguistic) context and from linguistic context of the preceding sentence or portion of a sentence? The natural response to such a question is, of course, to claim a central role for semantic factors in our lexical access processes. Nothing could seem more intuitively reasonable than that our recognition of the word "water" is facilitated by the preceding context:

> He lifted the dipper from the pail and
> took a cool drink of ___.

But when the effects of poststimulus guessing are controlled for, such effects are much less compelling, and it becomes extraordinarily difficult to say what the locus of our intuition is, e.g., lexical lookup or "confirmation of sentence interpretation." There are, moreover, a number of experimental findings that do not fit this intuitive picture. Before turning to those findings, let us first establish some of the parameters of word form which seem related to lexical access.

The initial phonetic elements of words have long been regarded as having greater significance for the individuation of lexical items than do the medial or final phonetic elements. Distributional facts seem to bear this out and certainly no one who has attempted a crossword puzzle can escape the conclusion that initial sounds suggest candidate words more readily than do sounds from other word positions. Two similar recent experiments provide relevant evidence. If one assumes that in order to utter a word one must locate its representation in one's mental inventory of word forms (see FORSTER and CHAMBERS, 1973 for some support for this assumption), an experiment by ERICKSEN and ERICKSEN (1974) provides evidence for the pre-eminent perceptual role of word initial elements as does an experiment by FORSTER (1974). In both these experiments words were visually presented with one or more of the letters of the array delayed in its appearance (relative to the rest of the array) by varying intervals (e.g., 40–100 ms). ERICKSEN and ERICKSEN, for a naming task (subject simply reads the word aloud) found greater interference with performance when the initial letter was delayed. FORSTER, for a lexical decision task (subject indicates whether the array spells a real word or a nonword) found that delay of word initial and word final elements interfered more than delay of medial elements. FORSTER's findings suggest that the observed effects are indeed related to the lexical access process, for if something like "scan order" (for pronunciation rather than for lexical lookup) were the primary determinant of such effects, it is hard to see why word final elements should have greater effects than medial ones, and hard to see why the effect should hold strongly (as it does) for short words as well as for relatively long ones.

These, of course, are arguments about the interpretation of visual effects as dependent on scan order. However, in the auditory domain, even scan order makes sense as a basis for an access system, since there is a significant (relative to total access time performances) deployment of the phonetic information across time. Hence, a real time auditory word recognition system might reasonably be expected to exploit that time rather than delay all decision until the full input of a word is achieved. Evidence from shadowing experiments by MARSLEN-WILSON (1975) confirms this expectation. Subjects in a close shadowing task (shadowing latencies on the order of 500–1000 ms) are more likely to "restore"' a distorted nonword target item to a real lexical entry dictated by context when the distortion is medial or final than when it is initial.

Two other types of evidence bear on this issue if we set aside (for the moment) the problem of relating properties of production processes to recognition processes. These are the regularities of "tip-of-the-tongue" (TOT) states and certain types of speech errors. BROWN and MCNEIL (1966) reported that subjects in a (self-determined) TOT state were more likely to correctly identify the initial sound elements of the target word (while still being unable to produce—presumably, to locate—the word in question) than any of the other parts of the phonetic array. They also found that length in syllables and stress patterns of trial candidates and the target item showed a greater than chance correspondence.

The directly relevant data from speech errors concerns the patterns of relations between intended words and those erroneously produced by a speaker. For example,

1. "There are a lot of words that one never hears spoken but sees read." (intended: "written").

2. "I'm chronically on the fringe of ..., on the verge of making a break."

3. "I thought when you called him the other day he didn't want to take his car ... his bicycle to school.

4. "It's a little colloquium." (intended: "colloquial").

5. "When you get done with one of those bodies ... one of those bottles, give it to me."

6. "You mean *one* conductor could play a symphony, and a different conductor can get a different interpretation of that same sympathy?" (intended: "symphony").

A number of investigators have commented on various aspects of such errors (e.g., FROMKIN, 1971; MACKAY, 1972), but the most interesting possibility about such errors for our purposes is that they may be dissociated into types arising from errors in a semantic search and those arising from errors in a search based on properties of form (e.g., 1–3 vs. 4–6).

The interest of this distinction is that it may implicate the relation between sentence production systems and sentence comprehension systems. FAY and CUTLER (1975), and GARRETT (1976) report that word substitution errors which do *not* have any obvious semantic relations (e.g., 4–6 above) turn out to be phonetically very similar and, in particular, similar in their initial portions. For errors that are apparently semantically based (e.g., 1–3 above), there is little indication of phonetic similarity. Whether there is also a contribution of similarity of form to the semantically based errors is a complicated question, and the available facts do not indicate a clear answer. For our purposes, however, the most significant point is the correspondence between the nature of the phonetic overlap in the nonsemantic word substitution errors and the several previously cited diverse lines of evidence indicating that lexical access processes are heavily determined by the initial elements of a word. Further, in these errors, as in the TOT status, there is a correspondence between the syllable length and the stress patterns of target and intruding words.

If one takes these errors and those in the TOT experiment together they indicate a system organized by at least initial phonetic elements, syllable length and stress pattern. But these two "tasks" are primarily production tasks and it is not at all clear why production processes should show errors dependent on form. After all, the production system must presumably establish a correspondence between the meaning of some message and the assembly of lexical items to be uttered. Thus, lexical errors which substitute items closely related in meaning are understandable from this perspective, while those which substitute items closely related in form are not. Two (at least) explanations suggest themselves. The first is simply that we have what amounts to two lexical lists in our heads; one organized by meaning relations and the other by relations of word form, the former primarily used for production and the latter for comprehension. Such a proposal does not explain the TOT or speech error results that depend on form without an appeal to some mechanism relating production processes to the recognition system. This might be done in terms of an error checking or monitoring function, since it is clear that we do monitor our own speech output, and that this monitoring plays an important role in controlling production processes. But it is not immediately obvious how such a connection between production and comprehension processes could yield the sort of error in examples 1–3. A simpler solution in some respects is to assume a single lexical listing organized by form. *Recognition* processes are assumed to require a search, but production can use direct access (see FAY and CUTLER, 1975). This requires that the meaning-related errors and the form-related errors occur at quite different processing levels. In meaning-related errors one must assume a failure of semantic specification followed by an *accurate* search through the word-form list; in the form-related errors, there must be accurate semantic specification followed by a failure of the presumed direct accessing system. Whatever account one provides, however, the evidence for a convergence of production and recognition tasks at the lexical level is strong.

We may take it that the evidence from lexical decision tasks, speech errors and TOT states all suggest an organization in terms of initial (and possibly final) sound elements, syllable structure and stress pattern (and possibly grammatical category). There is one further aspect of the form of words which may serve as a basis for their organization in a mental lexicon, namely, their morphemic structure. This is, in some measure, also a classification by meaning, since morphemic structure is intended to reflect the decomposition of words into elements which have uniform semantic consequences. However, that decomposition also has a more or less uniform phonetic reflection. Thus, the role of semantics in morphemic analysis is one of individuation of sound sequences, not a cross-classification (e.g., as is one in terms of the abstract semantic parameters assumed in a componential analysis of meaning (e.g., KATZ, 1974).

A number of investigations provide evidence for effects of some types of morphemic analysis on lexical access (e.g., MACKAY, 1974; TAFT and FORSTER, 1975), while others report little effect of morpheme structure and related processes (e.g., OSGOOD and HOOSAIN, 1974; JARVELLA and SNODGRASS, 1974) on word recognition. TAFT and FORSTER argue on grounds of a series of lexical decision experiments that affixal elements, especially prefixes, are separated from their stems during the lexical access process. Basically their argument rests on the finding that nonwords like "juvenate" are identified (as nonwords) less rapidly than nonwords like "pertoire" (frequency of the source words "rejuvenate" and "repertoire" is equated). They argue that this difference arises because of interference from a morphemic entry (e.g., "juvenate") encountered during the lexical decision process. MACKAY found that derivational complexity predicted reaction time performance in a task requiring subjects to produce nominalizations of verb stems (e.g., decide→decision). From these studies it is argued that subjects are accessing a mental lexicon organized around underived forms—hence really a lexicon of morphemes rather than one of words.

On the other hand, JARVELLA and SNODGRASS (1974) in a reaction time task found no evidence of derivational effects, and OSGOOD and HOOSAIN (1974) in a series of tachistoscopic recognition experiments found that surface *word* forms predicted performance rather than decomposition into morphemic elements. This is at best a vexed issue given the current findings, although there may be relatively low-level methodological and task differences which would rationalize the varying outcomes. But the most interesting possibility is that one should distinguish two components of the lexical access process: 1. the computation of a search code (based presumably on such parameters as initial phonetic elements, length, etc.), and 2. the checking of the results of the search (i.e., evaluation of "candidate analyses") against some record of the input (see RUBENSTEIN et al., 1970; FORSTER and BEDNALL, 1975). If one assumes, for example, that the task OSGOOD and HOOSAINS' subjects were performing was primarily dependent on decision processes dictated by word form, while those of MACKAY, and of TAFT and FORSTER were primarily influenced by the search processes attendant on the form of lexical entries, the difference in their results may be resolved. There are a number of reasons for adopting such a distinction in addition to the conflict of results just cited. In particular, some results in the study of lexical ambiguities which we will soon take up seem to require such a "decomposition" of the access process.

In sum, though it is not presently clear how morphological structure relates to lexical access processes, there does seem fairly good grounds for assuming that initial phonetic elements, length in syllables, and stress patterns are important. Moreover, some of the performances that indicate the importance of these parameters of form also show a very strong effect of major syntactic categories. The role of such variables and their possible relations to those we have been discussing will be considered in the next section.

C. Word Perception in Sentences

When the question of lexical access in sentences was initially broached in this paper, it was assumed that the fundamental problem is to say how the several sorts of properties of the vocabulary items of a language interact during the perceptual processing of a sentence. One way of approaching that problem is to ask how sentence context modifies the perception of words relative to their recognition in isolation. From that standpoint, we may say with certainty that sentence context facilitates word recognition. The numerous past tests of intelligibility carried out with phonetically balanced word lists were designed, in fact, to reduce the problem of communicative success to its most elemental dependence on phonetic form. When the organization imposed by language structure at higher levels is allowed to intrude on such tasks, performance levels rise dramatically. That this rise is not due to a simple reduction in the number of lexical alternatives which must be considered at any given point in a message was demonstrated by MILLER's "summer project" experiment (1962) in which a hardy band of volunteers committed a list of 25 monosyllabic words firmly to memory and then undertook perceptual tests with five-word strings constructed from those lists. When the strings were syntactically organized there was facilitation of performance—*provided presentation rates approximated normal conversational rates*. This shows that it is perceptual processing, not "guessing," that accounts for enhanced performance with sentences. Note: It is "postsentence" guessing that is ruled out—not lexical search. In this experiment there was a demonstrable effect of vocabulary size on performance that could not account for the sentence facilitation effects since there was a dissociation of the sentences and nonsentences for equal vocabulary sizes at the conversational rate, but not at the slower rate which permitted guessing. It is *not* that "a reduction in the number of alternatives" at each sentence slot may not, in some sense, arise from the syntactic/semantic organization of the word strings; but that is not quite the way to talk about the facilitation—it makes the operation look more like a guessing game than a computational process. If it *is* a guessing game, it is an unconscious, on-line, sophisticated guessing game, not a series of quick post hoc stabs; such a guessing game might as well be called perception.

The example of sentence context facilitation from MILLER's work is one of many that could be given in both visual and auditory sentence processing. There seem to be two candidates for the extra information that might explain the superior performance: 1. that it is a consequence of the syntactic organization of the sentence, and 2. that it is a consequence of the semantic interpretation of the sentence. Evidence exists for both of these, but as we shall see, there is some reason to suppose that the semantic effects, at least, do not affect the lexical lookup processes directly, although they must certainly affect the decision processes which follow.

Let us first briefly consider the potential role of syntactic classifications of words. There are two principal sorts of distinctions that seem relevant: on the one hand, there are the various major and minor grammatical categories (noun, verb, adjective, proposition, determiner, etc.), and on the other the broader contrast between open and closed class elements (roughly, "content" words and "function" words). The evidence for perceptual effects of both types of classifications is indirect but abundant. Of the two types of distinction, that between open- and closed-class items seems most likely to be directly related to word recognition procedures. In particular, it seems likely that closed-class items may be separately stored from open-class items and that their access is based upon different principles than that of open-class elements. There are a number of reasons for supposing this might be true, the most obvious being the central role closed-class items play in providing a basis for syntactic inference, including the assignment of open-class items to major grammatical categories. Quite apart from obvious structural reasons for this, there are other computationally relevant differences between open- and closed-class items: the latter is a relatively small, fixed set of short, very high frequency elements, often of distinctive phonetic character, which are rarely ambigous as to specific category membership. The former is a very large, open set of elements, ranging greatly in length and frequency for which ambiguity of category membership (especially noun or verb) is the norm rather than the exception. It seems likely that the mechanism by which assignment of open class word forms to grammatical categories presupposes the identification of closed-class items and subsequent determination of open-class elements, e.g., in terms of sequencing constraints on open- and closed-class morphemes. Thus, it would seem that the most plausible psychological models will assign a distinct computational role to open- and closed-class vocabulary elements, just as do most parsing systems that have been developed for the computer analysis of natural languages.

There is ample behavioral evidence, most of it well known, for some such distinction in psychological models of sentence processing even if the precise character of that processing is obscure. Developmentally, the closed-class grammatical words generally appear later than the open-class words; the so-called telegraphic stage of childrens speech is the most striking example of this. In memory and learning tasks different syntactic categories provide striking differences in performance. For example, GLANZER's (1962) early finding that closed class words (like "and," "by," "or," etc.) and open class words interacted very differently with nonsense syllable learning in paired associate lists was the first of many subsequent experiments showing a facilitation of recall for nonsense lists when constituent structure is imposed on them by the use of closed-class words (e.g., EPSTEIN, 1966). I have argued elsewhere (GARRETT, 1975) that certain types of speech errors (primarily those involving the complete interchange of any two segments of the intended output, e.g., "That's just a *back truck*ing out," and those involving the shift of a single bound or free morpheme, e.g., "We've just *here* been once") show very distinct patterns for open- and closed-class items.

Though these sorts of findings support the view that open- and closed-class elements play quite different roles in sentence processing, there really is no clear indication of what the nature of that difference is. However, one very interesting possibility that I have already mentioned is that assignment of open-class elements to their appropriate grammatical category is a function of the identification and ordering of closed-class items. This would, if correct, imply that open-class items *could* be accessed in sentences in terms of their syntactic class; this contrasts with the situation for isolated words where such a cross-classification would not be usable, and hence is a candidate for an account of the superior word recognition performance in sentences. Note in this connection that such superiority is mostly accounted for by better recovery of nouns and verbs. What evidence do we have for such a cross-classification? Once again we may appeal to certain regularities of speech errors. The word-substitution errors of examples 1–6 are, as was earlier remarked, apparently of at least two sorts, those which relate intended target words and intruding words in terms of sound similarity and those which relate them in terms of meaning similarity. But both types of errors are further constrained by syntactic category—virtually without exception nouns substitute for nouns, verbs for verbs, and adjectives for adjectives; these are by far the most frequent classes (and nouns the most frequent of these) to be involved in word substitutions, but where other types are involved, they too respect grammatical category. This evidence of a powerful influence of major syntactic classes goes beyond just an effect on word substitutions for specifically production processes (see GARRETT, 1975), but for our purposes, it is enough to note the indication that the word storage system is cross-classified by syntactic category.

The attribution of sentence facilitation of word recognition at least partly to a syntactically based lookup procedure is, at present, speculative. There are several lines of evidence for a difference in the role of open- and closed-class words in sentence processing, and it is possible that one consequence of that difference might be to provide a basis for the grammatical classification of open-class items *prior* to lexical lookup. Given the independent evidence (from word substitution errors in production) that the lexicon is cross-classified by such categories, it is least possible that this will account for superior word recognition in sentences. It is also possible that the production errors do not reflect an aspect of the access system used during recognition processes. A direct experimental resolution of these possibilities is not yet available, however.

The remaining candidate for explaining the word superiority in sentences is, of course, "semantic" relations among words. That such relations can affect lexical access processes is clear since we can select words to convey a linguistic message under the control of nonlinguistic perceptions. There is also experimental evidence, such as that of MEYER et al. (1972), that meaning relations between the members of simultaneously presented word pairs can facilitate lexical decision $\left(\text{e.g., } \genfrac{}{}{0pt}{}{\text{cat}}{\text{dog}} \text{ versus } \genfrac{}{}{0pt}{}{\text{cat}}{\text{hog}}\right)$, in which the former pair would be faster than the latter. The question is whether such information influences the process of initial lookup for words, or whether it has its influence in post-lookup decision processes.

Consider first the parallel question to the one raised in connection with the open-versus closed-class distinction for syntactic cross-classification: how can such information be available in sentences *prior* to lexical lookup? Two approximate sources seem possible: nonlinguistic situational constraints, and the influence of already interpreted preceding linguistic context. For a single sentence, assuming generally left-to-right processing, that would mean that only late-occurring words would have reasonably specific semantic constraints available. We should note, however, that in contrast to the detailed information about the syntactic class of particular phonetic strings to be derived from an analysis of closed-class items, all these sources of semantic constraint can exert only an approximate selection for any particular word.

The most directly relevant evidence comes from the study of the effects of lexical ambiguity during sentence processing. Research with a variety of experimental paradigms indicates that the presence of a lexically ambiguous item increases the difficulty of sentence perception. But, surprisingly, given the plausibility of the view that semantic constraints affect lexical lookup, there are also several different studies that show that the difficulty associated with such ambiguity is intractable: providing prior semantic constraints which disambiguate apparently does *not* eliminate the processing difficulty.

Given this pattern, we should examine the evidence for a processing difference between ambiguous and unambiguous words. Two aspects of that difference are of paramount importance. First, the difficulty engendered by the presence of ambiguous lexical items must arise *immediately* during sentence processing, not sometime afterwards as is the case with "garden-path" sentences (e.g., "the old man searched for his glasses and found them on the window ledge filled with sherry"). If the difficulty from ambiguity arises only from a mismatch between early *decisions* and later interpretive constraints, there are no grounds for relating the findings to lexical access processes. Second, we need evidence that multiple readings of a given lexical item are retrieved during sentence perception. Evidence for both these points is available. MacKay (1974) has argued for on-line difficulties of lexical ambiguity in sentence completion tasks. Foss (1970, 1971) in a series of studies has provided evidence that lexical ambiguity interferes with performance of an on-line monitor task (e.g., phoneme detection). Cairns and Kammerman (1975), using the phoneme monitor task, have recently reported findings that show the effect of lexical ambiguities is transient, apparently disappearing after about two succeeding words of the sentence have been input. Holmes et al. (1976) have found that both rapid visual presentation ("RSVP"; see Forster, 1970) and sentence classification tasks show effects of lexical ambiguities, and that these effects are primarily localized in report of the ambiguous lexical item. Chodorow (1975) has also found poorer performance on sentences with ambiguous lexical items using time-compressed speech. Note that, in nearly all of these experimental tasks, the sentences used were *not* garden-path types of sentences, and in many instances quite the contrary—the "preferred" interpretation of the ambiguity was the one required by sentence context.

On the second point, LACKNER and GARRETT have reported findings which indicate the computation of both readings of ambiguous words during sentence processing. They presented ambiguous sentences (e.g., The spy put out the torch which ...) and disambiguating context sentences (e.g., The spy extinguished the torch ...) dichotically. Subjects were instructed to attend to the channel which carried the ambiguous message. Relative to base frequency of the alternative interpretations of the ambiguous items, the biasing contexts determined which of the readings was assigned to the ambiguity, even though subjects could not later report the content of the disambiguating channel and were quite unaware of the ambiguous nature of the attended channel. LACKNER and GARRETT argue that this could only have occurred if both readings of the ambiguous items were present during sentence processing.

In sum, there seem to be good grounds for applying the results of the ambiguity research to questions about lexical access during sentences. What then are the effects of semantic context on this process? If the difficulty occasioned by the presence of an ambiguous lexical item arises from the access of two or more of the multiple lexical entries associated with a given phonetic form, then the *failure* of semantic contexts to eliminate ambiguity effects (i.e., to select antecedently the semantically dictated entry) constitutes a prima facie case for the existence of an independent lexical access system whose search processes depend on form, and perhaps on syntactic category, but not on meaning. Note that this is not to claim that there is no system for locating specific lexical entries as a function of semantic parameters; it is only to suggest that such a system is not generally available for recognition lookup.

For experiments that have tried to find an effect of semantic constraints on lexical ambiguity, the results are, at this point, fairly uniform—the lexical ambiguity effect occurs in *both* "neutral" and biasing contexts. For example, FOSS and JENKINS (1973) presented sentences with an ambiguous word like "stock" preceded by either the word "rancher" (biasing context), or "man" (neutral context) and tested with phoneme monitor on the word immediately following, e.g., "The rancher purchased the stock to *b*uild up his herd" (monitor target italic). Reaction times for the monitor were longer for ambiguous than for unambiguous control words in both sentence contexts. CUTLER and FOSS (1974), also using the phoneme monitor task, have similarly failed to eliminate the lexical ambiguity effect using even stronger contexts. CONRAD's (1974) findings (using an interference task based on color naming) are similar. It should be noted in this connection that the sort of biasing contexts used in these experiments are very similar to those which experimenters like MEYER et al., *have* found effective in the lexical decision task with word pairs. So, clearly, it is not that one is using constraints too weak to affect a semantically organized access system.

HOLMES et al. have found similar results using a quite different paradigm, the "sentence classification task." Subjects are visually presented with a word string and are required to judge whether it is or is not a sentence. For sentences containing a lexically ambiguous word, sentence classification times were longer than for those with an unambiguous control word, and this was true for conditions with a neutral context and with a biasing context. (The biasing contexts were independently tested in written tests and shown to influence strongly the selection of an interpretation for the ambiguous items.) HOLMES et al. also found the same pattern of results using a rapid, word-by-word visual presentation of sentences ("RSVP"); accuracy was poorer for ambiguous items in biased as well as unbiased contexts.

Assuming these results to be representative, it would appear then that the constraining effect of semantic context does not affect the initial lexical lookup that results in the retrieval of two or more meanings for an ambiguous word.

At this point we seem to have ruled out the effects of semantic constraints on lexical access procedures as an account of the superior recognition performance for words in sentence contexts. That conclusion is perhaps too strong. Earlier a distinction was made between procedures of lookup based on form (and perhaps syntactic class), and the decision procedures that ensue upon location of a lexical entry. It is the former of these that seems independent of semantic bias. We cannot ignore the likelihood that the decision procedures attendant upon the location of a lexical entry play a role in the facilitation of word recognition as a function of sentence context. After all, the recognition of words in isolation may *also* require that some semantic criterion be satisfied. Recognition of words in isolation is not the norm, but the exception, and it would not be unreasonable to imagine that the constraints of "normal" word encounters would be imposed on performance with words in isolation. If so, the *absence* of a semantic context to provide some decision criterion might well prove debilitating.

D. Summarizing Remarks

We have reviewed various sorts of evidence which bear on the role of aspects of word form in lexical lookup and on the role of semantic and syntactic contexts for lexical lookup in sentences. The position that seems provisionally acceptable is that it is primarily aspects of form and perhaps of syntactic context that dictate the initial entry into the mental lexicon, and that semantic constraints operate after that lookup process is completed. Though the evidence cited certainly does not dictate this particular interpretation, it seems the most plausible account of the presently available information.

The broader issue that these particular sentence processing problems are related to can best be described in terms of a decomposition of sentence processing activity into quasi-independent subsystems, where each subsystem is directed at the recovery of particular *types* of linguistic facts that bear upon the ultimate interpretation of a sentence. The evidence discussed here indicates that for the particular area of lexical content, there is some reason to continue working on the hypothesis that there is a separable subsystem for lexical lookup.

The same sort of question can be raised with respect to syntactic processing. Is there a separate, quasi-independent subsystem in the sentence processing system which governs syntactic processing? The discussion presented above does not directly address that question, but the indications that open and closed class lexical items are computationally distinct may be seen as a manifestation of such an independent syntactic processing system. Indeed, one can cay that the operation of sequencing constraints on closed-class elements just *is* a minimal independent syntactic processor. How much further the independent activities of such a processing system might be extended is not clear. But FORSTER (1974) has argued persuasively for a separation of lexical, semantic, and syntactic processing on the basis of a series of experiments which looked for an interaction between semantic constraints and relative levels of syntactic difficulty in processing.

For example, FORSTER and OLBREI (1973) used the much investigated case of active versus passive sentence types to assess the influence of semantic factors on syntactic analysis. Conventional views of that matter have been that passive sentences will present greater processing difficulty for listeners just in case there are no semantic constraints which dictate the logical object and subject functions of the NPs in the sentence. FORSTER and OLBREI argue convincingly that previous experimental demonstrations of this interaction used inappropriate processing measures, or confounded other variables with sentence type and semantic constant. They present evidence, using two distinct experimental paradigms (RSVP and sentence classification), of an active/passive difference in semantically constrained (e.g., "The doctor treated the patient") and semantically unconstrained sentences (e.g., "The doctor talked to the nurse"). FORSTER and RYDER (1971) report a similar lack of interaction between semantic constraints and syntactic difficulty. They found correlated complexity orderings for two sets of sentences matched for syntactic type but differing greatly in their semantic difficulty. The semantically simpler sentences showed the same complexity ordering as the difficult ones. If semantic constraints *do* affect syntactic processing, this lack of apparent interaction is remarkable.

This is essentially the same sort of argument we have applied to the case of semantic constraints on processing difficulty for ambiguous words, and it has yielded the same sort of conclusion.

These issues are issues of extraordinary complexity, and it would be foolhardy to treat the position indicated by the research reviewed here as decisive. It would, however, seem equally unreasonable to continue to cling to the assumption of "maximal interaction" that is so intuitively appealing. For after all, evidence of interaction is easy to come by and tells us mostly what we know — there is interaction at *some* level; evidence for independence is difficult to get — but it tells us much more about the system.

References

Broerse, A.C., Zwaan, E.J.: The information value of initial letters in the identification of words. JVLVB, **5**, 441–446 (1966).

Brown, R., McNeill, D.: The tip of the tongue phenomenon. JVLVB **5**, 325–337 (1966).

Cairns, H.S., Kammerman, J.: Lexical information processing during sentence comprehension. JVLVB, **14**, 170–179 (1975).

Chodorow, M.: Experimental studies of syntactic and lexical processes in language comprehension. Unpublished Ph.D. dissertation, M.I.T. Psychology Department, 1975.

Conrad, C.: Context effects in sentence comprehension: A study of the subjective lexicon. Memory and Cognition, **2**, No. 1A, 130–138 (1974).

Cutler, A., Foss, D.J.: Comprehension of ambiguous sentences: The locus of context effects. Paper presented to the 46th annual meeting of the Midwestern Psych. Ass. Chicago, May 2–4, 1974.

Eriksen, B.A., Eriksen, C.W.: The importance of being first: A tachistoscopic study of the contribution of each letter to the recognition of four-letter words. Perception & Psychophysics, **15**, 66–72 (1974).

Fay, D., Cutler, A.: You have a dictionary in your head, not a thesaurus. Paper presented at the 46th annual meeting of the Midwestern Psych. Ass. Chicago, May 2–4, 1974.

Fodor, J., Bever, T., Garrett, M.: The Psychology of Language. McGraw-Hill, 1974.

Forster, K.I.: Visual perception of rapidly presented word sequences of varying complexity. Perception & Psychophysics, **8**, 215–221 (1970).

Forster, K.I.: Separation of effects of meaning on word recognition and sentence processing. Paper presented at the First Melbourne Experimental Psych. Conf. September, 1974.

Forster, K.I., Chambers, S.M.: Lexical access and naming time. JVLVB, **12**, 627–635 (1973).

Forster, K.I., Olbrei, I.F.: Semantic heuristics and syntactic analysis. Cognition **2**, 319–347 (1973).

Forster, K.I., Ryder, L.A.: Perceiving the structure and meaning of sentences. JVLVB, **10**, 285–296 (1971).

Foss, D.J.: Some effects of ambiguity upon sentence comprehension. JVLVB, **9**, 699–706 (1970).

Foss, D.J., Jenkins, C.M.: Some effects of context on the comprehension of ambiguous sentences. JVLVB, **12**, 577–589 (1973).

Fromkin, V.: The non-anamalous nature of anomalous utterances. Language, **47**, 27–52 (1971).

Garrett, M.: Does ambiguity complicate the perception of sentences? In: Advances in Psycholinguistics, G., Flores d'Arcais and W. Levelt (eds.). Amsterdam: North Holland Co., 1970.

Garrett, M.: The analysis of sentence production. In: Advances in Learning and Motivation, Vol. 9, G. Bower (ed.). Academic Press, in press.

Holmes, V., Garrett, M., Arwas, J.: Prior context and the perception of lexically ambiguous words in sentences. Paper presented at the first experimental psychology congress. Melbourne, September, 1974.

Jarvella, R., Snodgrass, J.: Seeing "ring" in "rang" and "retain" in "retention": On recognizing stem morphemes in printed words. JVLVB, **13**, 590–598 (1974).

Lackner, J., Garrett, M.: Resolving ambiguity: Effects of biasing context in the unattended ear. Cognition, **2**, 15–47 (1972).

MacKay, D.G.: Behavioral hybrids: The problem of synonymy in speech perception. Mimeo, Psychol. Dpt. UCLA, 1972.

MacKay, D.G.: Derivational rules: Dead souls or real people in the production of complex nouns. Mimeo, UCLA Psy. Dpt., 1974.

Marslen-Wilson, W.: Sentence perception as an interactive parallel process. Science, 1975, in press.

Meyer, D.E., Schvaneveldt, R.W.: Facilitation in recognizing pairs of words: Evidence of a dependence between retrieval operations. J. of Exp. Psy., **90**, 227–234 (1971).

Miller, G.A.: Some psychologic studies of grammar. Amer. Psych., **17**, 748–762 (1967).

Osgood, C.E., Hoosain, R.: Salience of the two as a unit in the perception of language. Perc. & Psychophys. **15**, 168–192 (1974).

Razran,: Semantic and phonetographic generalization of salivary conditioning to verbal stimuli. J. of Exp. Psy. **39**, 642–652 (1949).

Schank, R.: Conceptual dependency: A theory of natural language understanding. Cognitive Psy. **3**, 552–631 (1972).

Taft, M., Forster, K.I.: Lexical storage and retrieval of prefixed words. Mimeo, Monash Univ. Psych. Dpt., 1975.

2. Spatio-Temporal Patterns

Chapter 20

Visual Masking

ROBERT FOX, Nashville (Tennessee)

With 2 Figures

Contents

Masking is the destructive interaction or interference that occurs among stimuli when their impingements on a receptor are closely coupled in space or time. This interaction is a general perceptual phenomenon operative in all modalities. It has been studied most extensively, however, in audition and vision, with vision receiving the greatest amount of attention. The work reviewed in this chapter is confined to masking in vision.

One striking characteristic of visual masking is that the interaction among stimuli consumes so much space and time relative to the physical characteristics of the stimulus. Consider a brief light flash of moderate intensity, a few milliseconds duration, and a few minutes visual angle—its perception seems immediate and effortless, yet this tiny stimulus may interact for a duration of 50 to 100 ms and over a spatial extent measurable in degrees. Presumably, upon entering the nervous system a physical stimulus is enlarged and enveloped within spatial and temporal boundaries. If these borders are violated, the perception of even the simplest stimulus can be degraded. Thus, masking reveals a fundamental limitation on the rate at which information can be processed by the visual system. This limitation, while of great intrinsic importance, also provides a powerful analytic tool for delimiting the functional stages that process information within the visual system. Moreover, masking is a ubiquitous phenomenon, not confined to the conditions of laboratory stimulation. Whenever there is a sudden change in ambient illumination, as in the glare of passing headlights, or whenever contours sweep the retina, as when the eyes scan a printed page, the essential conditions of masking are met, and they may exert a major influence on the ultimate percept.

The ubiquity of masking and the promise it holds for uncovering fundamental mechanisms of perception have inspired considerable research interest. Over the years a voluminous literature has accumulated. Research on masking has been the subject of a number of excellent reviews (e.g., ALPERN, 1952; BLANC-GARIN, 1967; KAHNEMAN, 1968; LEFTON, 1972; RAAB, 1963; and WEISSTEIN, 1972), which not only provide the reader with a detailed commentary on the field but also impose organization upon it. The availability of these review articles makes it unnecessary for this chapter to be encyclopedic and therefore permits the emphasis to be placed upon subsequent developments.

As a preface to describing these recent developments, it would be helpful to define and illustrate some of the stimulus situations or paradigms most widely used in masking research.

A. Masking Paradigms

Since masking is an omnibus term encompassing all conceivable ways stimuli can be presented to produce interactions, it has proved useful to subdivide and sharpen its definition. The major subdivision is concerned with where the stimuli impinge upon the retina. If nonoverlapping retinal areas are stimulated, the paradigm is referred to as metacontrast. A succinct term for the alternative paradigm, where stimulated retinal areas overlap, has not emerged; hence, authors frequently refer to this situation as masking, using appropriate descriptive terms such as masking by pattern, masking by light flash, and so on. Figure 1 shows two widely used spatial arrangements of stimuli for metacontrast investigations and a stimulus configuration that would conform to the nonmetacontrast paradigm. The designations "mask" and "target" in Figure 1 are somewhat arbitrarily chosen in that the stimuli mutually interact, but it is conventional to designate as target the stimulus upon the fate of which the subject is requested to report. In effect, the target is the dependent variable and the mask the independent variable. A defining characteristic of masking is that both target and mask are transient presentations of brief duration—impulses that perturb the visual system. If the stimuli were not transient, the stimulus configurations would be classified under rubrics other than masking. For example, steady-state presentations of the metacontrast arrangements of Figure 1 would represent the conditions for simultaneous contrast. With respect to measuring the time delay between target and mask, two conventions are used in current research. One measure, called stimulus onset asynchrony (SOA), is the difference in time between the onsets of the two stimuli. The second measure, known as the

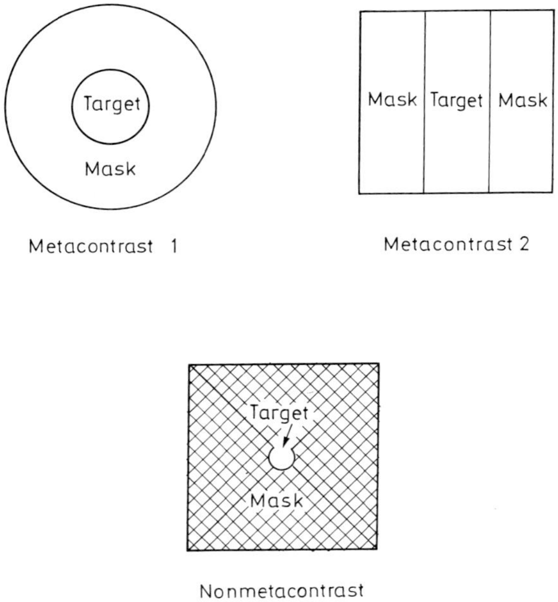

interstimulus interval (ISI), refers to the time between offset of the first stimulus and onset of the second. Attention to which measure is employed is important in comparing the results of various studies because the measures may not be equivalent if stimulus duration is varied to manipulate stimulus energy. With respect to the order of stimulus presentation, mask before target or target before mask, the term "backward masking" is used to designate the case where the target occurs before the mask. The label "backward" results from the fact that the mask appears to operate backward in time upon the target. By that same logic, forward masking occurs when the mask is presented prior to the target. Within the metacontrast paradigm, forward masking is sometimes referred to as paracontrast. Although further refinements of terminology can be made, such distinctions can most readily be introduced as specific topics when the masking literature is considered.

B. Masking of Light by Light

One of the simplest masking situations, yet one with profound implications, is the case where both the mask and the target are light flashes superimposed on the same retinal area. A classic investigation of this kind of nonmetacontrast masking was carried out by CRAWFORD (1947), who used a relatively small (30-min) circular test flash and a large (12-degree) intense circular light flash as the mask, with both stimuli concentrically arranged. It is of interest that the impetus for Crawford's investigations was quite practical, following from pressing military questions concerning the duration and the amplitude of visual impairment a gunner might suffer as a consequence of flashes produced by weapons fire and explosives. Indeed, in Crawford's extensive investigations stimuli included simulated targets such as silhouettes of ships and airplanes. The general effect of the intense masking flash was to raise the threshold for detection of the target, and the temporal course of the threshold elevation yielded considerable information about the operation of rapid light adaptation. An unexpected finding was the evidence for backward masking, whereby the target threshold starts to rise about 100 ms prior to onset of the masking flash. This ostensibly premature rise in threshold, the Crawford effect, stimulated considerable research. These investigations, as well as Crawford's monograph itself, have been conceptualized within the framework of rapid light adaptation produced by neural activity rather than by photochemical changes. In that context, the Crawford effect is interpreted parsimoniously as an interaction between the shorter latency of neural response to the mask and the longer latency to the target. When mask and target are presented to separate eyes (dichoptic stimulation) and contour interaction is minimized, only negligible masking is found, which implies that the sites of masking are at more peripheral neural stages. Research continues, and BOYNTON (1972) has provided a comprehensive review of the area.

There are other active lines of inquiry in vision that employ successive stimulation techniques operationally quite similar to the masking paradigm, even though the work is not always classified as part of the literature on masking. For instance, WESTHEIMER (1965, 1967) has shown that the masking effect of a circular light flash upon a target flash varies nonmonotonically as a function of the diameter of the masking flash, a relationship often referred to as the Westheimer effect. The extent to which the mask is presumed to stimulate excitatory and inhibitory portions of concentric receptive fields provides the theoretical context for the effect. TELLER and her colleagues (e.g., ALEXANDER, 1974; STURR and TELLER, 1973; TELLER, 1971), among others, have pursued related research. Their work provides a good entry point to this literature.

Recent investigations of rod-cone interaction have used a metacontrast stimulation paradigm (e.g., ALPERN, 1965; ALPERN and RUSHTON, 1967; RUSHTON, 1972), although these workers refer to their technique as contrast-flash analysis.

C. Masking of Contours by Adjacent Contours

Of all the stimulus arrangements used in masking research, the one that has received the greatest attention is the metacontrast paradigm, where target and mask stimulate adjacent but nonoverlapping retinal areas. One reason for

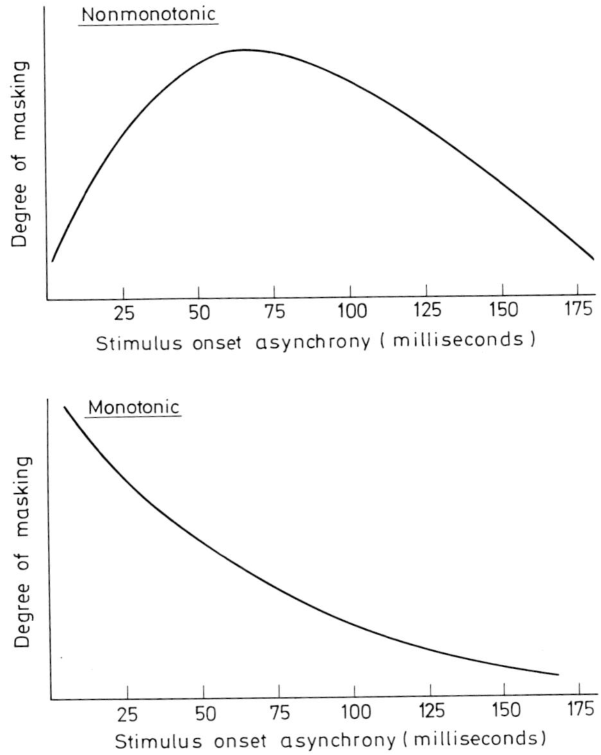

the extraordinary interest in metacontrast is the unusual way that mask and target interact during backward masking as the time interval between target onset and mask onset is systematically varied. The mask reduces the brightness of the target, but maximal reduction of target brightness does not occur with simultaneous onset of target and mask. Rather, maximal reduction occurs when the mask follows the target by about 50 to 75 ms; at greater temporal separations target brightness increases and finally returns to normal. Thus, if target brightness is plotted as a function of time between target and mask onset (either ISI or SOA), the function will be nonmonotonic. A typical nonmonotonic function for backward masking is shown in Figure 2, along with a typical monotonic function. Following KOLERS (1962), monotonic functions are sometimes referred to as "type A" functions; "type B" refers to nonmonotonic functions. The difference between the two kinds of function poses intriguing questions of interpretation, and it is not surprising that a considerable amount of the research on metacontrast has been concerned with temporal relationships between mask and target.

I. Temporal Variables

The nonmonotonic reduction in brightness of the target has been observed many times (e.g., ALPERN, 1953; KOLERS and ROSNER, 1960) under conditions where the target is of sufficient energy to be suprathreshold when presented alone and when the energy of the mask and the target are not too different. If mask energy is high and target energy is low, monotonic masking functions may be obtained (e.g., FEHRER and SMITH, 1962; KOLERS, 1962), monotonic in the sense that masking is greatest when target and mask are presented together and becomes progressively less as the temporal distance between them increases. It is worth noting that earlier theoretic treatments of metacontrast made the quite reasonable assumption that reduction in brightness of the target, even to the point where it appeared to be completely absent, was the defining feature of metacontrast masking. But several developments have required reexamination of that assumption.

One development was the demonstration by FEHRER and RAAB (1962) that reaction time to a target is the same regardless of the brightness reduction produced by the mask. This result has been replicated by FEHRER and BIEDERMAN (1962), HARRISON and FOX (1966), and SCHILLER and SMITH (1966). Recently PROCTOR et al. (1974), using a design with additional controls, have shown a statistically significant effect of the mask on reaction time (RT) to the target, but the absolute size of the effect is slight enough that the main conclusion—that RT is independent of phenomenal brightness—remains valid. The dissociation between reaction time and brightness is similar to the independence between brightness and luminance effects on the increment threshold reported by CORNSWEET and TELLER (1965). The implication for masking is that the attenuation of target brightness cannot be interpreted to mean that all target information is lost or suppressed by the mask.

A second development was the introduction into the metacontrast paradigm of targets requiring a recognition or identification response; for instance, letters of the alphabet, Landolt rings, contour orientation, etc. AVERBACH and CORIELL (1961), using an annulus mask and alphabet letter targets, obtained a nonmonotonic masking function. Yet ERIKSEN and colleagues (e.g., ERIKSEN and COLLINS, 1964, 1965; ERIKSEN and HOFFMAN, 1963) have consistently obtained only monotonic functions for alphabet targets. They attribute the difference between their results and those that have produced U-shaped masking functions to their use of forced-choice response indicators selected to eliminate response bias and to other methodologic refinements designed to enhance the sensitivity of their experiments.

Another explanation for the difference in results has been offered by WEISSTEIN (1968), who described a model of the masking process based on reciprocal inhibition within a network of hypothetic neurons assumed to differ in the rates at which excitation and inhibition develop. Weisstein used the characteristics of the WEISSTEIN and HABER (1965) experiment to fix the parameters of the network and carried out a computer simulation to determine how well the model could accommodate the temporal course of masking found in a large number of published experiments. Excellent qualitative agreement between the model predictions and these data was found. The critical factor that determined whether monotonic or nonmonotonic masking functions would be obtained was the ratio of target energy to mask energy, energy being defined in terms of time-intensity reciprocity. Nonmonotonic masking functions were predicted when target and mask energies were approximately equal, but as the target/mask ratio became smaller monotonic functions were predicted. Unfortunately, this powerful simplifying generalization regarding target/mask energy does not always appear to hold. Efforts to replicate the Weisstein and Haber experiment have not always been successful (e.g., ERIKSEN, BECKER and HOFFMAN, 1970; ERIKSEN et al., 1967; SCHURMAN, 1972). Some methodological issues attendant to this work have been discussed by WEISSTEIN (1972) and LEFTON (1972).

Still another explanation for the differences attendant upon monotonic and nonmonotonic functions that has been suggested in various forms by a number of workers (e.g., ERIKSEN et al., 1970; LEFTON 1972; SCHILLER and SMITH, 1966, 1968) is that brightness detection and target detection are parallel quasi-independent processes that have different time courses. On this view, when an observer attends to target brightness nonmonotonic functions will be obtained, while if the observer attempts to detect the presence of the target monotonic functions will be obtained. Unfortunately, both monotonic and nonmonotonic masking functions continue to be found in detection situations that use indicator methods that presumably control for observer response bias. Lefton, in his continuing series of investigations on configuration and spatial variables influencing masking, has reported monotonic functions (LEFTON, 1970, 1973, 1974; LEFTON and ORR, 1975). Yet COX and DEMBER (1972) found nonmonotonic functions under certain luminance conditions with a forced-choice detection task, as did BURCHARD and LAWSON (1973). Further, the research team of PURCELL and STEWART generally has found nonmonotonic functions for both metacontrast and nonmetacontrast paradigms under a variety of conditions (PURCELL and STEWART, 1970; PURCELL et al. 1974; STEWART and PURCELL, 1970, 1974). So it would appear that providing observers with a detection set and using appropriate detection response methods does not ensure the attainment of monotonic functions.

The differences among studies in terms of the shape of the masking function is puzzling, and one result of the puzzle is to force very careful definition of what kind of masking is involved in a particular experiment, including not only the distinction between metacontrast and nonmetacontrast masking in terms of spatial position of target and mask but also the characteristics of the target and mask and of the response required of the observer. The literature must be read rather carefully with regard to these points to avoid misunderstanding. It should be emphasized, however, that no one has ever questioned the existence of nonmonotonic functions in the case where apparent brightness of the target is assessed. The question arises only in the case where recognition or identification of the target is measured. Needless to say, investigators active in the area are vigorously attempting to identify the critical but presumably subtle variables that yield these differences in the masking function. The configuration of target and mask, luminance levels, and the degree of practice given observers are some of the variables that have been suggested as essentially operative.

Almost all the experiments on masking have presented target and mask only once during any given observation period. The effect of presenting a second mask immediately after the first mask has been explored by ROBINSON (1966) and by DEMBER and PURCELL (1967), who found that the second mask enhanced perception of the target relative to the case where only one mask was presented, a phenomenon they refer to as "disinhibition" or "backward facilitation." SCHILLER and GREENFIELD (1969) have examined stimulus variables responsible for the effect, and SCHURMAN and ERIKSEN (1969) have examined the dependence of the effect upon response methods.

MAYZNER and his colleagues (MAYZNER and TRESSELT, 1970; MAYZNER et al., 1972) have systematically examined a phenomenon they refer to as "sequential blanking," which is quite similar in many ways to metacontrast masking as a number of persons have pointed out (e.g., KAHNEMAN, 1968; LEFTON, 1972). The general approach involves sequentially displaying at rapid rates alphanumeric characters that form words and coherent number series. As a function of such variables as presentation rate and spacing between characters, some of the elements are suppressed or blanked. Presumably the characters adjacent to a blanked character act as a mask. POLLACK (1972) has positively replicated some of the main results obtained by MAYZNER and colleagues, but elaborated upon them by showing that the presence of the blanked elements can be detected through the use of a forced-choice testing procedure.

II. Spatial Variables

Spatial variables encompass a large number of manipulations of mask and target stimuli, including mask and target similarity, distance between mask and target contours, contour sharpness, and retinal locus. The effects of these kinds of manipulations on the magnitude of masking, using both metacontrast and nonmetacontrast masking paradigms, have been investigated in a number of recent experiments. Much of this work has taken as its historical point of departure the hypothesis advanced by WERNER (1935) that masking is primarily a process involving the interaction between adjacent edges of target and mask—in terms of his stimuli, the interaction between the edge of the disk target and the inner perimeter of the surrounding annulus mask.

The effect of similarity between mask and target has been examined a number of times (e.g., FEHRER, 1966; SEKULER, 1965), and the general result is that masking declines as similarity decreases. UTTAL (1970) used dynamic dot patterns to construct target and mask figures that varied in shape and has found strong masking for forms with similar shapes and little masking when shapes differed. For instance, rectangles masked rectangles and triangles masked triangles, but little masking occurred between rectangle-triangle combinations. Again using patterns formed from dots, UTTAL (1971) has investigated the degree to which a dotted triangular target could be masked by random dot patterns as a function of completeness of the triangle; that is, portions of the target triangle were systematically deleted. Masking was found to vary as a function of deletions, with the removal of side portions rather than angles serving to render the target most susceptible to masking. Recently, SHERRICK (1972) has examined the susceptibility to masking of a triangular target form constructed from conventional solid contours and successfully replicated and extended Uttal's observations.

DEMBER and colleagues, using a metacontrast design with a disk target and an annulus mask, have examined the effects of such variables as number of contours within the target and contrast relationships between target and mask (COX and DEMBER, 1970; DEMBER and CHAMBERS, 1975; DEMBER et al., 1973; DEMBER et al., 1974; SHERRICK and DEMBER, 1970a, b; SHERRICK et al., 1974). Although the results are difficult to summarize succinctly, it is clear that these manipulations have strong effects upon masking, some of which are not easily predictable from psychophysical data obtained in nonmasking situations.

Several investigators have examined the effects of spacing between mask and target contours and width of mask, independently or in combination with other variables such as luminance and ISI (COX and DEMBER, 1971; COX et al., 1969; GROWNEY and WEISSTEIN, 1972; KAO and DEMBER, 1973; LEFTON, 1973, 1974; MATTESON, 1969). Although the results are not completely congruent, it does appear that masking declines as distance between target and mask contours increases and that, up to some limit, mask width is a critical variable.

The contribution of target and mask edges to metacontrast masking has been investigated directly by GROWNEY (1976), who manipulated luminance gradients at the stimulus edges while keeping the average or mean luminance constant; the three edge manipulations were (a) blurred edge, where the luminance profile of the stimulus was sinusoidal, (b) sharp edge, where the luminance profile was a square wave, and (c) supersharp edge, where the luminance profile showed a peaked luminance increment at each edge. The major finding of Growney's extensive investigation was that masking occurred only for stimuli with sharp or supersharp edges; essentially no masking was found for targets with gradual or blurred edges. These data support the hypothesis that edge luminance is a critical variable in controlling metacontrast masking defined in terms of reduction of apparent brightness.

As noted earlier, research on spatial variables is concerned with the similarity or lack of it between target and mask, with similarity defined by the physically measurable differences between stimuli. An ingenious alternative approach developed by WEISSTEIN and colleagues is concerned with magnitude of masking as a function of target and mask similarity defined in terms of their Fourier spectrum. The starting point is recent psychophysical and neurophysiologic research that suggests that the recognition of visual patterns involves a kind of Fourier analysis by the visual system, breaking down the pattern into its constituent spatial frequency components (see Chapter 1 of this volume for a summary of this work). Weisstein points out that stimuli that clearly look different and those that occur in different portions of the visual field may be quite similar in terms of a Fourier transform. Further, if the hypothesis of Fourier analysis by the visual system is correct, the masking of a target by a mask might be predicted in terms of their similarity in Fourier space. Pursuing this idea, several investigations (Weisstein, 1973; Weisstein et al., 1974; Weisstein and Bisaha, 1972; Weisstein et al., 1976; Weisstein et al., 1973), using a nonmetacontrast paradigm with reduction in apparent brightness of the target as the indicator of masking, have shown that considerable masking occurs when mask and target are similar in terms of their Fourier spectrum. Some of the rather interesting and counter-intuitive results have included strong masking of a large bull's eye target by a small dot mask, and strong masking despite considerable spatial separation between target and mask. Weisstein is careful to point out that while these data do not confirm the hypothesis of Fourier analysis they are clearly consistent with it.

Dichoptic Masking. Presenting target and mask stimuli to separate eyes is one technique for inferring the stage in the visual system where the interaction occurs. If masking is found under dichoptic conditions, there are reasonable grounds for asserting that at least one mechanism underlying masking is located no earlier than the stage where information from the two eyes is combined. Several investigators have found masking under dichoptic conditions when masking is defined as brightness reduction of the target (e.g., Kolers and Rosner, 1960; Schiller and Smith, 1968; Weisstein, 1972; Weisstein and Growney, 1969). But some differences in both the magnitude of masking and in its temporal course have been observed between monocular and dichoptic presentation conditions (Schiller and Smith, 1968; Weisstein, 1972). Schiller and Smith suggest that binocular rivalry may be operative during dichoptic masking, an hypothesis congruent with the evidence that rivalry suppression is inhibitory (e.g., Blake and Fox, 1974). But it is not certain that the inhibition of rivalry is generated rapidly enough to influence the brief transient stimulus presentations that characterize masking.

Dichoptic masking has also been investigated in nonmetacontrast masking situations, where the target is an alphabet letter form and the mask is either a light flash or an array of contours. When a contoured or patterned mask is used, dichoptic masking can be obtained (Schiller, 1965; Smith and Schiller, 1966; Turvey, 1973). Under monocular presentation conditions light flashes can induce masking, but under dichoptic presentation conditions masking does not occur (Schiller, 1965; Smith and Schiller, 1966).

III. Physiologic Investigations

A small number of investigations have examined physiologic correlates of metacontrast and nonmetacontrast masking. The visually evoked cortical response has been obtained concurrently with behavioral responses in humans (e.g., Schiller and Chorover, 1966; Vaughn and Silverstein, 1968) and in cats (e.g., Lindsley, 1961). Several studies have recorded the responses of single neurons to stimulus arrangements temporally and spatially similar those used to induce masking in humans (e.g., Grüsser et al., 1965; Schiller, 1968).

BRIDGEMAN (1975) summarizes earlier physiologic work on masking and describes an experiment in which he recorded single-unit responses in the cat from the optic tract, the dorsal lateral geniculate nucleus, and the striate cortex during metacontrast stimulation conditions. The response of cortical units could be classified into two groups on the basis of responses latency. Bridgeman suggests that the short latency response might be related to detection of the target and the longer latency response related to brightness reduction of the target.

The interpretation of physiologic data in terms of psychophysical data obtained from humans must of course be done with great caution in all areas of research, as the investigators themselves are well aware. The response from a single neuron obtained from a paralyzed cat with immobile eyes is a datum not easily related to the behavioral response of a conscious human observer. One line of inquiry that has not yet been pursued systematically is the concurrent recording of behavioral and neurophysiologic data from animals trained to make masking discriminations. Techniques for animal testing and for recording from chronic preparations have developed sufficiently to make these kinds of experiments feasible. This kind of combined behavioral-physiologic investigation could shed considerable light on the mechanisms underlying masking, and hopefully such investigations will be mounted in the future.

IV. Extension of Masking to Other Phenomena

The purpose of this section is simply to point out the relevance of masking to topics that previously have been conceptualized within other theoretic frameworks.

Figural aftereffects, the apparent spatial displacement of a contour as a result of prolonged viewing of an adjacent contour, have received considerable experimental attention ever since KOHLER and WALLACH (1944) encompassed these aftereffects and many related phenomena within their satiation theory. An important parameter of the theory, which constituted a physiologic embodiment of Gestalt organizational principles, was the time required for induction of the satiation presumed to be responsible for contour displacement. Many studies suggested that satiation developed over a time course on the order of 5–60 s. So it was of particular interest to find evidence implying that satiation developed rapidly when inspection and test figures were presented briefly, on the order of milliseconds (e.g., IKEDA and OBANAI, 1953, 1955; OYAMA, 1953; SAGARA and OYAMA, 1957; see also Chapter 17 in this volume). Although these data were originally interpreted within the context of the Kohler-Wallach theory, E. MATIN (1974a) has pointed out the compelling operational similarity between these experiments and those expressly concerned with visual masking. Presumably, the mechanisms operative in masking may also be applicable to these figural aftereffects. Matin has also reported data on the temporal course of one particular form of figural aftereffect, the tilt aftereffect, and noted its similarity to the temporal pattern found in certain kinds of masking studies.

Visual sensitivity declines during saccadic eye movements, a phenomenon known as saccadic suppression. A recent review of the extensive research on saccadic suppression has been made by MATIN (1974b). There is considerable agreement that saccadic movements are accompanied by an inhibitory state that attenuates visual input, but there is less agreement about the mechanisms responsible for the inhibition. MATIN et al. (1972) have suggested a relationship between saccadic suppression and metacontrast masking for the case where the eye sweeps across stationary contours, the central idea being that sequential stimulation of the moving eye by stationary contours effectively produces the successive temporal stimulation conditions of metacontrast masking. A novel masking paradigm described by WHITE (1974) also links saccadic suppression and masking. Data that can be interpreted as connecting saccadic suppression to masking have been provided by MACKAY (1970a, 1970b) and by MITRANI and colleagues (e.g., MITRANI et al., 1970). Although suppression can occur when moving eyes are not stimulated by contours (see, for example, RIGGS et al., 1974), the general suggestion (see MATIN, 1974b) is that masking may contribute to the saccadic suppression effect when there is relative movement of contours across the retina.

The perception of motion, both real and apparent, is among the oldest research topics that have received systematic attention. Recent reviews have been provided by KOLERS (1972), SEKULER (1975), and SEKULER and colleagues (Chapter 3 in this volume). The connection between apparent movement and masking, particularly within the metacontrast paradigm, comes about because the successive presentation of spatially adjacent target and mask stimuli is frequently accompanied by a strong impression of apparent motion, an effect that has been mentioned by many investigators. KAHNEMAN (1967, 1968) has suggested that apparent motion may contribute to the masking of the target because motion gives rise to an impossible percept. WEISSTEIN and GROWNEY (1969), however, have shown that apparent movement can occur over a much broader range of space and time parameters than those that induce masking. ERIKSEN and COLGATE (1970) have shown that movement in itself does not impair target detectability. But BREITMEYER et al. (1974) have described ways in which apparent movement could play a contributory role, at least for certain masking situations.

A recent approach to the investigation of motion perception involves rapid successive presentation of random dot patterns similar to the random dot stereograms described by JULESZ (1971). Questions of interest include the kind of apparent motion induced by these patterns and the ability of observers to extract information about pattern differences. Although this work is not directly concerned with masking there are many operational similarities, and the investigators acknowledge the general relevance of their inquiry to masking. Some representative examples of this research provided by ANSTIS (1970), ANSTIS and ROGERS (1975), BELL and LAPPIN (1973), BRADDICK (1973), PHILLIPS and SINGER (1974), and LAPPIN and BELL (1972, 1975).

D. Masking by Overlapping Contours

The rather large number of experiments that can be grouped under this rubric have several defining characteristics. The principal consideration is that mask and target are superimposed on the same retinal area—the nonmetacontrast paradigm. The target usually requires a recognition or detection response—for example, recognition of letter forms. The mask usually consists of an array of contour elements varying in orientation and spatial frequency, selected to obscure recognition of the target. The temporal sequence of the backward masking paradigm is typically employed, with target preceding mask.

In order to appreciate the literature on this kind of masking, it is helpful to have some knowledge of the theoretic context that generated it. Many of the studies have not been directly concerned with understanding the masking process itself; rather, masking was used as a technique for investigating the way in which the visual system processes perceptual information. The general assumption is that the perceptual process can be conceptualized as a series of functional stages that interact to transmit, store, and transform incoming perceptual information. HABER (1969) and HABER and HERSHENSON (1973), among others, have discussed the major tenets of the information-processing approach to visual perception.

Much of the work in this area uses, as a starting point, the classic monograph by SPERLING (1960), which concerns itself with the amount of information an observer can extract from a briefly presented visual display such as a haphazard collection of alphanumeric symbols. The question is closely related to the classic problem of the span of apprehension—how much can one take in at a single glance? Sperling showed through an ingenious partial-report procedure that all the information in a large array persists for several hundred milliseconds after display offset and is potentially available to the observer. Not all items in a display, however, can subsequently be reported by the observer because of limits on memory and fading of the initial representation of the display. The initial representation of the display, likened by SPERLING to the buffer storage of a computer, has been termed an iconic memory or simply icon by NEISSER (1967). The phrase "iconic memory" has gained wide acceptance in the field, and it can serve as a convenient entry point to the literature. Note that iconic memory refers to the aftermath of visual stimulation presented at quite moderate levels of intensity. As such, it differs from the classic afterimage, which is typically produced by high intensity stimulation and which can endure for hours (see, for example, the review of the afterimage research by J.L. BROWN, 1965).

The relationship between masking and iconic memory comes about largely through the use of masking as a technique for controlling the duration and the clarity of iconic memory. A masking stimulus presented immediately after the stimulus array that forms the icon can act to render iconic memory unavailable for further processing. The exact way in which masking does this is the subject of a considerable amount of research. Under some conditions, the mask may fuse with the icon over time, thereby forming a montage that degrades the clarity of the icon. Under other conditions the mask may stop processing of information from the icon by forcing some central processing mechanism to switch its attention to processing the mask. Within the context of research on information processing, iconic memory is the first in a series of processes or stages that ultimately govern the responses of the observer. These subsequent stages involve higher order cognitive variables, such as short term memory and the active maintenance of items in such a memory through rehearsal by the observer; moreover, other cognitive variables may be introduced through the use of stimuli, such as words, that have symbolic attributes that can interact with the observer's prior experience. Research on information processing is a very active area and clearly involves many variables in addition to those specifically related to masking. Representative examples of models developed within this framework are described by SPERLING (1963, 1967). Since research within information processing involves many variables in addition to masking, this active field of research requires a separate review. But several recent articles that can serve to introduce the reader to the field, particularly with respect to the relationship between masking and iconic memory, are those by COLTHEART (1975a, b) and HOLDING (1975a, b, c), and SAKITT's (1976) discussion of the neural basis for iconic memory.

E. Theories of Masking

As befitting the research interest in masking, a considerable number of theoretic formulations of varying degrees of complexity and of breadth has been advanced. Backward masking has attracted particular attention because of the seemingly paradoxical reversal of temporal relationships wherein the mask, presented after the target, apparently moves forward in time to influence the target. Paracontrast, where the mask precedes the target, has attracted less interest, even though it may pose difficult problems for a comprehensive theory.

One influential class of theoretic formulations, known collectively as integration theory, resolves the time paradox in the most direct way. The central assumption is that, while there is a physical difference in time between test and mask, this temporal difference disappears after both stimuli have entered the nervous system. The "integration" of integration theory refers to some kind of fusion or combination of the neural representations of test and mask. Since the latency of neural responses is an inverse function of stimulus energy, it is not unreasonable to assume that a mask of higher energy and faster latency can overtake a target of lower energy and longer latency. These conditions of energy and latency differences were present in CRAWFORD's (1947) experiments as well as in many subsequent investigations and would seem to meet the essential requirements of integration theory. But integration could also occur when the latency differential between target and mask is not likely to be operative. BOYNTON (1961) and ERIKSEN and COLLINS (1965) have pointed out that if physically successive events are processed quantally, in accord with the concept of psychologic moment (see KRISTOFFERSON, 1967a, b, for evidence on this point), then target and mask could fall within the same processing interval and be treated as simultaneous events. A specific version of integration theory, known as the luminance summation-contrast reduction hypothesis, has been described by ERIKSEN (1966), who has pointed out that certain methods for exposing target and mask permit their respective luminance levels to summate over time, thereby reducing the physical contrast. Under these conditions the most parsimonious explanation of masking is that the target is physically attenuated by the exposure conditions, thereby making it unnecessary to posit a more complex masking process operating within the receiver. Integration theory is not confined, however, to situations where target contrast can be reduced by luminance summation. KINSBOURNE and WARRINGTON (1962a, b) were among the first to outline an integration theory, and ERIKSEN and his colleagues (ERIKSEN and ERIKSEN, 1971) have systematically developed several lines of evidence compatible with the theory. In particular they note that the relatively coarse temporal resolution of the visual system, together with evidence that the representation of a physical stimulus can persist for several hundred milliseconds, provides the conditions for integration of target and mask. On the assumption that integration of target and mask is a linear process, monotonic masking functions are predicted. STEWART and PURCELL (1974), however, have outlined a version of integration theory that assumes nonlinear summation between target and mask in such a way that nonmonotonic masking functions are predicted under certain conditions. It should be emphasized that applications of integration theory have been made only to masking situations involving detection or recognition of the target; reductions in target brightness are not encompassed by the theory.

In KAHNEMAN's (1968) review of the masking literature he used the term "interruption theory" to identify a set of theoretic formulations frequently considered to be competing alternatives to integration theories. As Kahneman notes, the particular versions of interruption theory offered by various workers differ in detail yet share the underlying concept that the mask acts to stop or interrupt processing of the target by some means other than degradation of the target posited by integration theory.

Interruption theories have been applied to both metacontrast and nonmetacontrast masking situations, although they have special relevance for theories of information processing because they address the question of the fate of iconic memory. Accordingly, assumptions made about the properties of iconic memory and the extraction of information from it can be important considerations in evaluating the status of any particular interruption theory. For some masking situations, interruption and integration theories appear to be in direct conflict, but there is no intrinsic reason why both processes could not be operative under certain conditions. Indeed, SPENCER and SHUNTICH (1970) have shown that integration and interruption processes may both be operative, depending upon the characteristics of the mask, the information in the target, and time interval between mask and target. TURVEY (1973) has carried out an extended series of experiments on masking by contour, and from these data has developed what he calls a concurrent-contingent model that incorporates concepts from both integration and interruption theories. As in the case of integration theories, interruption theories are concerned with masking of the target when detection or recognition responses are required and do not directly address brightness changes of the target.

Integration and interruption theories do not place strong emphasis upon neurophysiologic phenomena and take into account only very general neurophysiologic considerations. In contrast, there are several theories or models of masking that rely heavily on neural processes. Anatomic and electrophysiologic data are explicitly transformed into theoretic constructs that are used to account for the psychophysical relationships that characterize masking. An appropriate label for this kind of theory is the term "neural model."

PURCELL et al. (1968) have described a neural model for metacontrast masking that is based upon lateral inhibition among neurons assumed to be differentially affected by the luminance and contrast of target and mask stimuli; differences in these stimulus variables alter the rates at which inhibition develops and decays. The model has been used to account for the effect of a second mask upon the masking power of a first mask (i.e., the backward enhancement effect) and for changes in brightness of the target.

Perhaps the most sophisticated neural model is one developed by WEISSTEIN, first described in 1968 and subsequently modified (WEISSTEIN, 1972; WEISSTEIN et al., 1975). The model is composed of a network of five hypothetic neurons with both excitatory and inhibitory outputs that operate in accord with the well-defined mathematical assumptions of the idealized two-factor neurons described by RASHEVSKY (1948) and by LANDAHL (1967). Two neurons are peripheral in the sense that each carries initial information about the target and mask, respectively, to second-order neurons. One second-order neuron (t_2) carries information about the target and terminates upon a decision neuron (d_1). An inhibitory collateral from the other second-order neuron (m_2), which conveys information about the mask, also terminates on the decision neuron d_1. The algebraic summation of excitation from t_2 and inhibition from m_2 controls the response of d_1, which, in turn, determines the fate of the target stimulus. The response of each neuron can be calculated, and the response of the network can be simulated on an analog computer. Because such a model necessarily has a large number of free parameters, Weisstein used the conditions of the WEISSTEIN and HABER (1965) metacontrast detection experiment to fix the parameters and assess how well the network could simulate the masking functions for 26 studies extant in the literature. The qualitative agreement between the predicted shape of the masking function and the published data was quite close, thus providing compelling support for the model.

In a subsequent elaboration of the model (WEISSTEIN, 1972), additional data in support of the model were described, the issues involved in expanding the model to include spatial as well as temporal variables were discussed, and the suggestion was offered that the model was principally concerned with metacontrast masking situations where phenomenal appearance of the target was of major interest. In the most recent statement (WEISSTEIN et al., 1975), the model is characterized as multiple channel, meaning that it operates according to the assumption that the visual system processes information through an array of independent functional channels, each sensitive to a narrow range of spatial and temporal frequencies. The data and theory attendant on the concept of multiple-channel processing is discussed elsewhere; see, for example, Chapters 2 and 3 in this volume. Although the assumptions of multiple-channel processing have not yet been incorporated into the Weisstein model through computer simulation of the neural network, it is clear that the addition of these assumptions provides the model with greater flexibility and the potential for testing many of the spatial and configurational aspects of metacontrast masking.

In their discussion of the model, WEISSTEIN et al. (1975) placed considerable emphasis upon changes in apparent brightness of the target induced by masking, and it is possible to gain the impression that the model has been restricted to brightness changes, a restriction that would leave the data on target recognition, for which the model was initially established, without a theoretic home. But that impression would be incorrect (WEISSTEIN, personal communication). The model still encompasses conditions where masking influences target recognition or discrimination, such as forced-choice recognition of which of several forms (e.g., alphabet letters) was presented. It does not, however, deal with target detection, defined as discerning the presence or absence of a target.

Computer simulation of a neural network is also the approach taken by BRIDGEMAN (1971) in developing a model of metacontrast based upon lateral inhibition. Although inspired by Weisstein's earlier work, Bridgeman based his physiologic assumptions upon the lateral inhibitory interactions found in the eye of the horseshoe crab. The elements of the simulation were the equations developed by RATLIFF (1965) describing these interactions, although some modifications of the equations were required for compatibility with mammalian neurophysiology. The results of the simulation, together with related assumptions about the masking process, led Bridgeman to conclude that such a neural network could account for many of the characteristics of metacontrast masking. He offers the interesting hypothesis that the target might be represented by two kinds of neural signals, one concurrent with it and one representing it after it becomes physically absent. It is suggested that monotonic masking functions will be obtained when the observer attends to the concurrent representation (which occurs earlier in time), while nonmonotonic functions will be obtained when the observer attends to the later-occurring representation. The observer's response criterion is assumed to determine which of the two representations is used.

While not offering an explicit model of masking, MATIN (1975) has thoughtfully discussed the logic of the metacontrast masking paradigm, treating it as a special case of what she calls the two-transient paradigm. The two-transient paradigm refers to the many stimulus situations in several modalities in which two transient stimuli are presented in rapid succession. Matin reviews recent neurophysiologic evidence indicating the existence of neurons that seem maximally responsive to successive stimulation closely coupled in space and time. These neurons, sometimes called motion detectors, may be operative during masking and could provide the basis for a more comprehensive theory of masking. Matin explores the implications of this approach and indicates that the relationships among apparent movement, saccadic suppression and masking might be rationalized through this approach.

A comprehensive neural model of masking has been outlined by Breitmeyer and Ganz (1976), who show how recent neurophysiologic data can be used to account for the major psychophysical relationships that characterize masking. The most relevant data is the evidence that the retinal-lateral geniculate-striate cortex pathway is composed of two parallel and functionally distinct systems. This distinction was first noted by Enroth-Cugell and Robson (1966), who observed that the ganglion cells of the cat retina could be divided into two classes, X cells, which give a sustained response of relatively slow latency, and Y cells, which give a transient response with a faster latency. Subsequent inquiry, carried out primarily in the cat, has revealed other attributes of these two cell classes and established that they are present throughout the visual system. Recent investigations have found X and Y cells in primates (e.g., Sherman et al., 1975, 1976) and it may well be that they are a fundamental feature of mammalian vision. Breitmeyer and Ganz point out that the sustained and the transient responses, together with inhibition between and within cell types, could be the substrate for masking phenomena. It is not possible within this brief space to do justice to their ingenious and detailed reasoning. But to suggest the spirit of their approach, it can be pointed out that the time paradox of backward masking can be resolved if the assumption is made that the target is mediated by the slower latency sustained system and the mask is mediated by the faster latency transient system.

It should be noted that, while neural theories emphasize neurophysiologic phenomena, they are not neurophysiologic theories in the sense that they are vulnerable to disconfirmation by direct neurophysiologic investigations. Rather, they are psychophysical or behavioral theories that can be tested by behavioral experiments.

A class of theoretic suggestions that are complementary to the neural models may aptly be called "response theories." Response means a concern with how an observer translates phenomenal experience into response. Response theories complement neural models in the same way that methods for scaling perceived color contribute to an understanding of neurophysiologic data on color vision. The general idea that the attitude, set, or response criteria of the observer is important in masking has been voiced many times—indeed, anyone who has observed visual masking comes away with the impression that many complex things are occurring quickly. The brightness of the targets may change dramatically and strong apparent movement is seen, and these effects vary considerably as a function of the time between target and mask onsets. Kahneman (1968) was among the first to point out explicitly the importance of the observer's response criterion in determining the results of specific experiments, and Kahneman's suggestion that apparent movement, which can lead to an incomprehensible percept, may contribute to masking can be thought of as an example of a response-theory hypothesis. Moreover, the practice of using a forced-choice response method with extremely well trained observers can be thought of as being guided by the tenets of a response theory, even though the assumptions are implicit. In this approach, the observer combines all the information that can be extracted from the display to assist in deciding whether or not a designated kind of target was present. While this method optimizes correct performance, it does not reveal what features of the display contributed to that performance. A quantitative response model developed by BERNSTEIN and colleagues (e.g., BERNSTEIN et al., 1973, 1974, 1976a, b) attempts to specify the kinds of information components and their strength that are available to an observer. The model has been applied to the case where the brightness of the target changes nonmonotonically during metacontrast. The general approach is that brightness judgments are strongly influenced by the character of the information available to the observer at any given instant, this information varying as a function of such parameters as the time between target and mask onsets. For instance, simultaneous comparisons are possible when mask and target are temporally close, but greater reliance upon absolute judgment is necessary as temporal distance increases. Although the model has been applied only to brightness change, it could be expanded to include other masking situations.

F. Conclusion

This review of research on visual masking has necessarily been brief—no attempt has been made to provide exhaustive coverage of the literature. Nevertheless, the main lines of inquiry and the investigators pursuing them have been identified. Hopefully, sufficient information has been offered to permit the interested reader to gain access to the field.

One impression about research on masking, unavoidable in even a brief review, is that the field is complex and contains numerous unresolved questions. One source of difficulty is simply the many terms and definitions that have arisen to characterize the phenomena associated with specific kinds of masking. The diversity in definition also carries over to the theoretic formulations advanced to accommodate the phenomena of masking. All this means that the reader must approach the literature with particular care to avoid generalizations or extrapolations that are neither warranted by the data nor intended by the authors. A particularly perplexing problem is, of course, the difference in results obtained in ostensibly similar experiments directed toward the same questions, as, for example, the question of the temporal course of masking. It is unlikely that these differences can be attributed to methodologic artifacts, but rather that they represent genuine differences brought about by the action of subtle variables, the effects of which are not yet clearly understood. One source of variation here might reside within the observer, and in particular in the observer's prior exposure to masking situations. As noted in the review, the question of the observer's response criterion has been raised a number of times, and the point has been made that masking is a transient process within which a number of different phenomenal events appear to be occurring simultaneously. It may be that these events can act to mask one another and that, through experience, an observer may undergo a kind of perceptual learning, during which the power of these events to interact would be altered. On this view, differences in the reports of observers would be attributable to authentic differences in their perceptual states rather than to differences in the way they choose to respond. Similar kinds of problems have arisen in other areas of vision, and through such strategies as exchanging observers between laboratories deeper understanding has been achieved.

Finally, the complexity associated with research on masking comes about because a number of important issues in vision are brought together within the masking paradigms. These include the relationship between real motion and apparent motion, the relationship between brightness and luminance, and the distinction between the loss of stimulus information and the transformation of such information. One of the benefits of the continuing inquiry into masking is to focus attention on these issues, thereby contributing to their clarification.

Acknowledgment. I would like to thank a number of people who have helped in the preparation of this work, some by careful reading of the manuscript and some by illuminating discussions of specific issues. These include not only the editors, Hans-Lukas Teuber, Richard Held, and Herschel Leibowitz, but also Bruno Breitmeyer, William Dember, Joseph Lappin, Dean Purcell, and Naomi Weisstein.

Preparation of the work was aided by PHS grant EY00590.

References

Alexander, K.R.: Sensitization by annular surrounds: Sensitization and the contrast-flash effect. Vision Research. **14**, 623–631 (1974).

Alpern, M.: Metacontrast: Historical introduction. American Journal of Optometry. **29**, 631–646 (1952).

Alpern, M.: Metacontrast. Journal of the Optical Society of America. **43**, 648–657 (1953).

Alpern, M.: Rod-cone independence in the after-flash effect. Journal of Physiology **176**, 462–472 (1965).

Alpern, M., and Rushton, W.A.H.: The nature of the rise in threshold produced by contrast flashes. Journal of Physiology. **189**, 519–534 (1967).

Anstis, S.M.: Phi movement as a subtraction process. Vision Research. **10**, 1411–1430 (1970).

Anstis, S.M., and Rogers, B.J.: Illusory reversal of visual depth and movement during changes of contrast. Vision Research. **15**, 957–961 (1975).

Averbach, E., and Coriell, A.S.: Short-term memory in vision. Bell System Technical Journal. **40**, 309–328 (1961).

Bell, H.H., and Lappin, J.S.: Sufficient conditions for the discrimination of motion. Perception and Psychophysics. **14**, 45–50 (1973).

Bernstein, I.H., Fisicaro, S.A., and Fox, J.A.: A multivariate analysis of metacontrast suppression. Paper presented to the Association for Research in Vision and Ophthalmology, Sarasota, April, 1976.

Bernstein, I.H., Proctor, R.W., Belcher, J., and Schurman, D.L.: An analysis of U-shaped metacontrast. Perception and Psychophysics. **16**, 329–336 (1974).

Bernstein, I.H., Proctor, J.D., Proctor, R.W., and Schurman, D.L.: Metacontrast and brightness discrimination. Perception and Psychophysics. **14**, 293–297 (1973).

Bernstein, I.H., Smith, D.B., and Adey, M.: Perceptual and response interdependencies in visual masking. In Attention and Performance. (vol. 6). New York: Academic Press, in press.

Blake, R., and Fox, R.: Binocular rivalry suppression: Insensitive to spatial frequency and orientation change. Vision Research. **14**, 687–692 (1974).

Blanc-Garin, J.: Le Masquage visuel rétroactif. L'Année Psychologique. **67**, 153–193 (1967).

Boynton, R.M.: Some temporal factors in vision. In: Sensory Communication. Rosenblith, W.A. (ed.). New York: Wiley 1961.

Boynton, R.M.: Discrimination of homogeneous double pulses of light. In: Handbook of Sensory Physiology, vol. **7**, part 4, visual psychophysics. Jameson, D., and Hurvich, L. (eds.). Berlin: Springer 1972.

Braddick, O.: The masking of apparent motion in random-dot patterns. Vision Research. **13**, 355–369 (1973).

Breitmeyer, B.G., and Ganz, L.: Implications of sustained and transient channels for theories of visual pattern masking, saccadic suppression, and information processing. Psychological Review. **83**, 1–36 (1976).

Breitmeyer, B.G., Love, R., and Wepman, B.: Contour suppression during stroboscopic motion and metacontrast. Vision Research. **14**, 1451–1456 (1974).

Bridgeman, B.: Metacontrast and lateral inhibition. Psychological Review. **78**, 528–539 (1971).

Bridgeman, B.: Correlates of metacontrast in single cells of the cat visual system. Vision Research. **15**, 91–99 (1975).

Brown, J.L.: The structure of the visual system. In: Vision and Visual Perception. Graham, L.H. (ed.). New York: Wiley 1965.

Burchard, S., and Lawson, R.B.: A U-shaped detection function for backward masking of similar contours. Journal of Experimental Psychology. **99**, 35–41 (1973).

Coltheart, M.: Iconic memory: A reply to Professor Holding. Memory and Cognition. **3**, 42–48 (1975a).

Coltheart, M.: Doubts about iconic memory: A reply to Holding. Quarterly Journal of Experimental Psychology. **27**, 511–512 (1975b).

Cornsweet, T., and Teller, D.Y.: Relation of increment thresholds to brightness and luminance. Journal of the Optical Society of America. **55**, 1303–1308 (1965).

Cox, S.I., and Dember, W.N.: Backward masking of visual targets with internal contours. Psychonomic Science. **19**, 255–256 (1970).

Cox, S.I., and Dember, W.N.: Effects of target-field luminance, interstimulus interval, and target-mask separation on extent of visual backward masking. Psychonomic Science. **22**, 79–80 (1971).

Cox, S.I., and Dember, W.N.: U-shaped metacontrast functions with a detection task. Journal of Experimental Psychology. **95**, 327–333 (1972).

Cox, S.I., Dember, W.N., and Sherrick, M.F.: Effect on backward masking of spatial separation between target and mask contours and of target size. Psychonomic Science, **17**, 205–206 (1969).

Crawford, B.H.: Visual adaptation in relation to brief conditioning stimuli. Proceedings of the Royal Society of London, Series B. **134**, 283–302 (1947).

Dember, W.N., and Chambers, J.: Maskability of visual targets varying in brightness contrast. Bulletin of the Psychonomic Society. **5**, 51–52 (1975).

Dember, W.N., Mathews, W.D., and Stefl, M.: Backward masking and enhancement of multisegmented targets. Bulletin of the Psychonomic Society. **1**, 45–47 (1973).

Dember, W.N., and Purcell, D.G.: Recovery of masked visual targets by inhibition of the masking stimulus. Science. **157**, 1335–1336 (1967).

Dember, W.N., Stefl, M., and Kao, K.C.: Backward masking of gratings varying in spatial frequency. Bulletin of the Psychonomic Society. **3**, 439–441 (1974).

Enroth-Cugell, C., and Robson, J.G.: The contrast sensitivity of retinal ganglion cells of the cat. Journal of Physiology. **187**, 517–552 (1966).

Eriksen, C.W.: Temporal luminance summation effects of backward and forward masking. Perception and Psychophysics. **1**, 87–92 (1966).

Eriksen, C.W., Becker, B.B., and Hoffman, J.E.: Safari to masking land: A hunt for the elusive U. Perception and Psychophysics. **8**, 245–250 (1970).

Eriksen, C.W., and Colgate, R.L.: Identification of forms at brief durations when seen in apparent motion. Journal of Experimental Psychology. **84**, 137–140 (1970).

Eriksen, C.W., and Collins, J.F.: Backward masking in vision. Psychonomic Science. **1**, 101–102 (1964).

Eriksen, C.W., and Collins, J.F.: A reinterpretation of one form of backward and forward masking in visual perception. Journal of Experimental Psychology. **70**, 343–351 (1965).

Eriksen, C.W., Collins, J.F., and Greenspon, T.S.: An analysis of certain factors responsible for nonmonotonic backward masking functions. Journal of Experimental Psychology. **75**, 500–507 (1967).

Eriksen, C.W., and Eriksen, B.A.: Visual perceptual processing rates and backward and forward masking. Journal of Experimental Psychology. **89**, 306–313 (1971).

Eriksen, C.W., and Hoffman, M.: Form recognition at brief durations as a function of adapting field and interval between stimulations. Journal of Experimental Psychology. **66**, 485–499 (1963).

Fehrer, E.: Effect of stimulus similarity on retroactive masking. Journal of Experimental Psychology. **71**, 612–615 (1966).

Fehrer, E., and Biederman, I.: A comparison of reaction and verbal report in the detection of masked stimuli. Journal of Experimental Psychology. **64**, 126–130 (1962).

Fehrer, E., and Raab, D.: Reaction time to stimuli masked by metacontrast. Journal of Experimental Psychology. **63**, 143–147 (1962).

Fehrer, E., and Smith, E.: Effect of luminance ratio on masking. Perceptual and Motor Skills. **14**, 243–253 (1962).

Growney, R.: The function of contour in metacontrast. Vision Research. **16**, 253–261 (1976).

Growney, R.L., and Weisstein, N.: Spatial characteristics of metacontrast. Journal of the Optical Society of America. **62**, 690–696 (1972).

Grüsser, O.-J., Peterson, A., and Sasowski, R.: Neurophysiologische Grundlagen des Metakontrastes. Pflügers Arch. F. Physiol. 1965, **283**, R50.

Haber, R.N.: Information-Processing Approaches to Visual Perception. New York: Holt, Rinehart and Winston 1969.

Haber, R.N., and Hershenson, M.: The Psychology of Visual Perception. New York: Holt, Rinehart and Winston 1973.

Harrison, K., and Fox, R.: Replication of reaction time to stimuli masked by metacontrast. Journal of Experimental Psychology. **71**, 162–163 (1966).

Holding, D.H.: Sensory storage reconsidered. Memory and Cognition. **3**, 31–41 (1975a).

Holding, D.H.: A rejoinder. Memory and Cognition. **3**, 49–50 (1975b).

Holding, D.H.: Doubts about iconic memory: A reply to Coltheart, Lead, and Thompson. Quarterly Journal of Experimental Psychology. **27**, 507–509 (1975c).

Ikeda, H., and Obanai, T.: The quantitative analysis of figural aftereffects (1) The process of growth and decay of figural aftereffects. Japanese Journal of Psychology. **24**, 59–66 (1953).

Ikeda, H., and Obanai, T.: Figural aftereffects, retroactive effect and simultaneous illusion. Japanese Journal of Psychology. **26**, 235–246 (1955).

Julesz, B.: Foundations of Cyclopean Perception. Chicago: University of Chicago Press 1971.

Kahneman, D.: An onset-offset law for one case of apparent motion and metacontrast. Perception and Psychophysics. **2**, 577–584 (1967).

Kahneman, D.: Method, findings, and theory in studies of visual masking. Psychological Bulletin. **70**, 404–425 (1968).

Kao, K.C., and Dember, W.N.: Effects of size of ring on backward masking of a disk by a ring. Bulletin of the Psychonomic Society. **2**, 15–17 (1973).

Kinsbourne, M., and Warrington, E.K.: The effect of an aftercoming random pattern on the perception of brief visual stimuli. Quarterly Journal of Experimental Psychology. **14**, 223–234 (1962a).

Kinsbourne, M., and Warrington, E.K.: Further studies on the masking of brief visual stimuli by a random pattern. Quarterly Journal of Experimental Psychology. **14**, 235–245 (1962b).

Kohler, W., and Wallach, H.: Figural aftereffects: An investigation of visual processes. Proceedings of the American Philosophical Society. **88**, 269–357 (1944).

Kolers, P.A.: Intensity and contour effects in visual masking. Vision Research. **2**, 277–294 (1962).

Kolers, P.A.: Aspects of Motion Perception. New York: Pergamon Press 1972.

Kolers, P.A., and Rosner, B.: On visual masking (metacontrast): Dichoptic observation. American Journal of Psychology. **73**, 2–21 (1960).

Kristofferson, A.B.: Attention and physical time. In: Attention and Performance. Sanders, A. (ed.). Amsterdam: North Holland 1967a.

Kristofferson, A.B.: Successive discrimination as a two-state quantal process. Science. **158**, 1337–1340 (1967b).

Landahl, H.D.: A neural net for masking phenomena. Bulletin of Mathematical Biophysics. **29**, 227–232 (1967).

Lappin, J.S., and Bell, H.H.: Perceptual differentiation of sequential visual patterns. Perception and Psychophysics. **12**, 129–134 (1972).

Lappin, J.S., and Bell, H.H.: The detection of coherence in moving random-dot patterns. Vision Research. **16**, 161–168 (1976).

Lefton, L.A.: Metacontrast: Further evidence for monotonic functions. Psychonomic Science. **21**, 85–87 (1970).

Lefton, L.A.: Metacontrast: A review. Psychonomic Monograph Supplements. **4** (14, whole no. 62 (1972). Republished in Perception and Psychophysics. **13**, 161–171 (1973).

Lefton, L.A.: Spatial factors in metacontrast. Perception and Psychophysics. **14**, 497–500 (1973).

Lefton, L.A.: Internal contours, intercontour distance, and interstimulus intervals: The complex interaction in metacontrast. Journal of Experimental Psychology. **103**, 891–895 (1974).

Lefton, L.A., and Orr, T.B.: Metacontrast can be obtained in the fovea: An examination of retinal location and target size. Bulletin of the Psychonomic Society. **6**, 169–172 (1975).

Lindsley, D.B.: Electrophysiology of the visual system and its relation to perceptual phenomena. In: Brain and Behavior, vol. 1, Brazier, M.A.B. (ed.). Washington, D.C.: American Institute of Biological Sciences 1961.

Mackay, D.: Elevation of visual threshold by displacement of retinal image. Nature. **225**, 90–92 (1970a).

Mackay, D.: Interocular transfer of suppressive effects of retinal image displacements. Nature. **225**, 872–873 (1970b).

Matin, E.: Light adaptation and the dynamics of induced tilt. Vision Research. **14**, 255–265 (1974a).

Matin, E.: Saccadic suppression: A review and an analysis. Psychological Bulletin. **81**, 899–917 (1974).

Matin, E.: The two-transient (masking) paradigm. Psychological Review. **82**, 451–461 (1975).

Matin, E., Clymer, A.B., and Matin, L.: Metacontrast and saccadic suppression. Science. **178**, 179–182 (1972).

Matteson, H.H.: Effects of surround size and luminance on metacontrast. Journal of the Optical Society of America. **59**, 1461–1468 (1969).

Mayzner, M.S., and Tresselt, M.E.: Visual information processing with sequential inputs: A general model for sequential blanking, displacement, and overprinting phenomena. Annals of the New York Academy of Sciences. **169**, 599–619 (1970).

Mayzner, M.S., Tresselt, M.E., and Helfner, M.: A provisional model of visual information processing with sequential inputs. Psychonomic Monograph Supplements. **2** (7, whole no. 23) (1972).

Mitrani, L., Yakimoff, N., and Mateeff, St.: Dependence of visual suppression on the angular size of voluntary saccadic eye movements. Vision Research. **10**, 411–415 (1970).

Neisser, U.: Cognitive Psychology. New York: Appleton Century Crofts 1967.

Oyama, T.: Experimental studies of figural aftereffects. 1. Temporal factors. Japanese Journal of Psychology. **23**, 239–245 (1953).

Phillips, W.A., and Singer, W.: Function and interaction of On and Off transients in vision. 1. Psychophysics. Experimental Brain Research. **19**, 493–506 (1974).

Pollack, I.: Visual discrimination of 'unseen' objects: Forced-choice testing of Mayzner-Tresselt sequential blanking. Perception and Psychophysics. **11**, 121–128 (1972).

Proctor, R.W., Bernstein, I.H., and Schurman, D.L.: Metacontrast and simple reaction time: A reexamination. Journal of Experimental Psychology. **103**, 498–502 (1974).

Purcell, D.G., and Stewart, A.L.: U-shaped backward masking functions with nonmetacontrast paradigms. Psychonomic Science. **21**, 361–363 (1970).

Purcell, D.G., Stewart, A.L., and Brunner, R.L.: Metacontrast target detection under light and dark adaptation. Bulletin of the Psychonomic Society. **3**, 199–201 (1974).

Purcell, D.G., Stewart, A.L., and Dember, W.N.: Spatial effectiveness of the mask: Lateral inhibition in visual backward masking. Perception and Psychophysics. **4**, 344–346 (1968).

Raab, D.: Backward masking. Psychological Bulletin. **60**, 118–129 (1963).

Rashevsky, N.: Mathematical Biophysics. Chicago: University of Chicago Press 1948.

Ratliff, F.: Mach Bands: Quantitative studies on neural networks in the retina, Chapter 3. San Francisco: Holden-Day 1965.

Riggs, L., Merton, P., and Morton, H.: Suppression of visual phosphenes during saccadic eye movements. Vision Research. **14**, 997–1011 (1974).

Robinson, D.N.: Disinhibition of visually masked stimuli. Science. **154**, 157–158 (1966).

Rushton, W.A.H.: Light and dark adaptation. Investigative Ophthalmology. **11**, 503–517 (1972).

Sagara, M., and Oyama, T.: Experimental studies on figural aftereffects in Japan. Psychological Bulletin. **54**, 327–338 (1957).

• Sakitt, B.: Iconic memory. Psychological Review. **83**, 257–276 (1976).

Schiller, P.H.: Monoptic and dichoptic visual masking by patterns and flashes. Journal of Experimental Psychology. **69**, 193–199 (1965).

Schiller, P.H.: Single-unit analysis of backward visual masking and metacontrast in the cat lateral geniculate nucleus. Vision Research. **8**, 855–866 (1968).

Schiller, P.H., and Chorover, S.L.: Metacontrast: Its relation to evoked potentials. Science. **153**, 1398–1401 (1966).

Schiller, P.H., and Greenfield, A.: Visual masking and the recovery phenomenon. Perception and Psychophysics. **6**, 182–184 (1969).

Schiller, P.H., and Smith, M.: Detection in metacontrast. Journal of Experimental Psychology. **71**, 32–46 (1966).

Schiller, P.H., and Smith, M.C.: Monoptic and dichoptic metacontrast. Perception and Psychophysics. **3**, 237–239 (1968).

Schurman, D.L.: Predictive validity of a Rashevsky-Landahl neural net: Test of a model of masking for form. Perception and Psychophysics. **12**, 183–186 (1972).

Schurman, D.L., and Eriksen, C.W.: Summation and interaction of successive masking stimuli in visual perception. American Journal of Psychology. **82**, 320–332 (1969).

Sekuler, R.W.: Spatial and temporal determinants of visual backward masking. Journal of Experimental Psychology. **70**, 401–406 (1965).

• Sekuler, R.W.: Visual motion perception. In: Handbook of Perception, vol. 5. Carterette, E.C., and Friedman, M.P. (eds.). New York: Academic Press 1975.

Sherman, S.M., Norton, T.T., and Casagrande, V.A.: X- and Y-cells in the dorsal lateral geniculate nucleus of the tree shrew (*Tupaia glis*). Brain Research. **93**, 152–157 (1975).

Sherman, S.M., Wilson, J.R., Kaas, J.H., and Webb, S.V.: X- and Y-cells in the dorsal lateral geniculate nucleus of the owl monkey (*Aotus trivirgatus*). Science. **192**, 415–417 (1976).

Sherrick, M.F.: Visual backward masking and the perception of form (doctoral dissertation, University of Cincinnati, 1972). Dissertation Abstracts International, **33**, University Microfilms no. 73–3832 (1973).

Sherrick, M.F., and Dember, W.N.: Completeness and spatial distribution of mask contours as factors in visual backward masking. Journal of Experimental Psychology. **84**, 179–180 (1970a).

Sherrick, M.F., and Dember, W.N.: Visual backward masking and the area-detection relation. Psychonomic Science. **19**, 127–128 (1970a).

Sherrick, M.F., Keating, J.K., and Dember, W.N.: Metacontrast with black and white stimuli. Canadian Journal of Psychology. **28**, 438–445 (1974).

Smith, M.C., and Schiller, P.H.: Forward and backward masking: A comparison. Canadian Journal of Psychology. **20**, 191–197 (1966).

Spencer, T.J., and Shuntich, R.: Evidence for an interruption theory of backward masking. Journal of Experimental Psychology. **85**, 198–203 (1970).

• Sperling, G.: The information available in brief visual presentations. Psychological Monographs. **74**, 1–29 (1960).

• Sperling, G.: A model for visual memory tasks. Human Factors. **5**, 19–31 (1963).

• Sperling, G.: Successive approximations to a model for short-term memory. Acta Psychologica. **27**, 285–292 (1967).

Stewart, A.L., and Purcell, D.G.: U-shaped functions in visual backward masking: Effects of target configuration and retinal position. Perception and Psychophysics. **7**, 253–256 (1970).

Stewart, A.L., and Purcell, D.G.: Visual backward masking by a flash of light: A study of U-shaped detection functions. Journal of Experimental Psychology. **103**, 553–566 (1974).

Sturr, J.F., and Teller, D.Y.: Sensitization by annular surrounds: Dichoptic properties. Vision Research. **13**, 909–918 (1973).

Teller, D.Y.: Sensitization by annular surrounds: Temporal (masking) properties. Vision Research. **11**, 1325–1335 (1971).

Turvey, M.T.: On peripheral and central processes in vision: Inferences from an information-processing analysis of masking with patterned stimuli. Psychological Review. **80**, 1–52 (1973).

Uttal, W.R.: On the physiological basis of masking with dotted visual noise. Perception and Psychophysics. **7**, 321–327 (1970).

Uttal, W.R.: The effect of interval and number on masking with dot bursts. Perception and Psychophysics. **9**, 469–473 (1971).

Vaughn, H.G., and Silverstein, L.: Metacontrast and evoked potentials: A reappraisal. Science. **160**. 207–208 (1968).

Weisstein, N.: A Rashevsky-Landahl neural net: Simulation of metacontrast. Psychological Review. **75**, 494–521 (1968).

Weisstein, N.: Metacontrast. In: Handbook of Sensory Physiology (vol. **7**, part 4, visual psychophysics). Jameson, L., and Hurvich, L. (eds.). Berlin: Springer 1972.

Weisstein, N., Berbaum, K., Ozog, G., Williams, A., and Tangney, J.: What do subjects mean by 'uniformly faded contrast'? Paper presented to the Association for Research in Vision and Ophthalmology, Sarasota, April, 1974.

Weisstein, N., and Bisaha, J.: Gratings mask bars and bars mask gratings: Visual frequency response to aperiodic stimuli. Science. **176**, 1047–1049 (1972).

Weisstein, N., and Growney, R.L.: Apparent movement and metacontrast: A note on Kahneman's formulation. Perception and Psychophysics. **5**, 321–328 (1969).

Weisstein, N., and Haber, R.N.: A U-shaped backward masking function in vision. Psychonomic Science. **2**, 75–76 (1965).

Weisstein, N., Harris, C.S., Berbaum, K., Tangney, J., and Williams, A.: Masking across extensive areas of the visual field by small, localized stimuli. Vision Research. In press.

Weisstein, N., Ozog, G., and Szoc, R.: A comparison and elaboration of two models of metacontrast. Psychological Review, **82**, 325–343 (1975).

Weisstein, N., Szoc, R., Williams, A., and Tangney, J.: Masking of bars and gratings by radially symmetric and aperiodic patterns. Paper presented to the Association for Research in Vision and Ophthalmology, Sarasota, May, 1973.

Werner, H.: Studies on contour: 1. Qualitative analyses. American Journal of Psychology. **47**, 40–64 (1935).

Westheimer, G.: Spatial interaction in the human retina during scotopic vision. Journal of Physiology. **181**, 881–894 (1965).

Westheimer, G.: Spatial interaction in human cone vision. Journal of Physiology. **190**, 139–154 (1967).

White, C.W.: Backward masking: Perceived location or retinal contiguity? Paper presented to the Association for Research in Vision and Ophthalmology, Sarasota, April, 1974.

Chapter 21

Apparent Movement*

STUART M. ANSTIS, Downsview, Ontario, Canada

With 6 Figures and 2 Tables

Contents

* This article reviews some recent experiments and theories on stroboscopic or phi movement. The earlier literature has been revised by NEFF (1936), AARONS (1964), SPIGEL (1965), and GRAHAM (1965). KOLER's book (1972) combines a comprehensive review with many original experiments on apparent movement, and several recent text books (ROBINSON, 1972; KAUFMAN, 1974; ROCK, 1975) contain excellent general chapters on movement perception.

You can say, 'Something, as distinct from nothing, *phies*' (that is, '*Phi*-ers are non-null', '$(\exists x)(\phi x)$') without saying either 'Something, for instance *alpha, phies*' or 'Something, though I have no particular instance in mind, *phies*'. However you cannot think the first of those things without also thinking one of the others. You cannot, you cannot be said to, we will not let you be said to, think only that *phi*-ers are non-null. For it is a fact that either you have at least one particular instance, *alpha,* in mind as *phi*-ing or you don't. And if you do, we will say your whole thought is 'Something, for instance *alpha, phies'*, while if you don't, we will say your whole thought is 'Something, though I have no particular instance in mind, *phies'*. (This does not mean that you can only say, not think, that 'for some x, x is an egg-laying mammal' ...

HINTON, 1974

A. Introduction

The flashing lights on a cinema marquee, which seem to move inward toward the lobby and entice us to follow them, are an example of apparent movement. If we go in and watch the movie, we experience two hours of apparent movement: each movie frame projected on the screen is actually stationary whenever the projector shutter is open. If we stay at home and watch TV instead, we are once again experiencing apparent movement. Films and TV, as they exist today, are possible only because of a quirk in our visual systems. It so happens that these inventions were developed in the early years of this century at a time when WERTHEIMER (1912) and KORTE (1915) first studied apparent movement in their laboratories. Although rule-of-thumb empiricism has developed movies into a brilliant fusion of art and technology, psychophysical methods have still not revealed the mechanisms of apparent movement perception.

If we experience motion when an object is continuously displaced across the visual field, we speak of "real movement" (RM); but if the displacement of the object is discontinuous or intermittent and we still perceive motion, then we speak of "apparent movement" (AM) or stroboscopic movement (KAUFMAN et al., 1971).

An intermittent stimulus gives rise to a sensation of continuous movement, but this is not caused merely by lack of resolution, since the size of the step or jump can be orders greater than the finest resolvable static detail. Two spots that can very easily be resolved give good AM when exposed in alternation. On the other hand, EXNER noticed in 1875 that two successive electric sparks in different positions were seen as a single object in motion, even for time intervals as short as 14 ms. These intervals were too brief to allow perception of sequence or of order, so EXNER concluded that motion is a primary sensation which is not dependent on memory for position nor on the perception of order.

Movement perception is in no way a failure to resolve time and space, but rather an active integration of the two. The integrative processes can be destroyed by damage to certain parts of the brain (BENDER and TEUBER, 1949). Normal subjects perceive real movement as a smooth, continuous transition, but BENDER and TEUBER's brain-damaged subject saw only a sequence of stationary objects, as though lit by a slowly flashing stroboscope. Although he saw the separate, static, resolved positions of an object, as normal people do, he lacked the triggering of some kind of movement-sensing system which would normally integrate or link together these positions into a connected, continuous sequence. For most of us, both real and apparent movements become integrated, but the nature of this integration is quite mysterious.

I. The Relationship Between Real Movement and Apparent Movement

The visual system treats RM and AM as though they are, in some sense, equivalent. This article is mostly about the relationship between apparent movement (AM) and real movement (RM). Doing rough justice to some psychologists, I have classified their widely differing viewpoints either as theories which assert that the mechanisms for perceiving AM and RM are basically the same (Table 1,

Table 1. Theories of apparent movement (AM)

AM same as RM	AM different from RM
Rival one-process theories	
Lock and key (GREGORY, 1966) Shift and subtract (possible embodiment of lock and key)	Figural reconstruction (KOLERS, 1972)
Two-process theory (BRADDICK, 1974)	
Short-range process (15′ arc)	Long-range process
Evidence	
Stimulates motion detectors (GRÜSSER and GRÜSSER-CORNEHLS, 1973)	Does not stimulate motion detectors
Produces motion aftereffects (BANKS and KANE, 1972)	No motion aftereffects
Point-for-point similarity between picture is necessary for AM	Any similarity between pictures can suffice for AM, e.g., cyclopean contours
Motion perception (between pictures) *precedes* form perception (within pictures) (ANSTIS, 1970)	Form segregation (within pictures) *precedes* motion perception (between pictures) (RAMACHANDRAN et al., 1973; PANTLE, 1973)
Motion (between pictures) *predominates* over form (within pictures) (PANTLE and PICCIANO, 1976)	Form (within pictures) *predominates* over motion (between pictures) (PANTLE and PICCIANO, 1976)

left hand column), or else as theories which assert that the mechanisms are basically different (Table 1, right hand column). For example, psychologists such as GREGORY (1966) and FRISBY (1972) believe that the perception of RM and AM are parallel processes with the same underlying mechanisms—perhaps fairly simple, hard-wired neural circuitry. Others, such as KOLERS (1972) and KAUFMAN et al. (1971) are equally convinced that AM is mediated by mechanisms quite different from RM. Authors share a column only because I have put them there. They may well disagree among themselves.

In this article I shall discuss both types of theory and conclude that both types have some truth to them.

B. One-Process Theory: Apparent Movement Has the Same Mechanism as Real Movement

I. AM=RM: the Lock-and-Key Theory

The only current theory asserting the identity of AM and RM is GREGORY'S lock-and-key theory (1966). He has suggested that the visual system will accept stroboscopic movement as a close approximation to real movement, rather as a lock needs to accept a range of slightly varying keys if it is to be of any practical use. Thus an AM stimulus falls within the input tolerances of the RM detecting system. Prima facie evidence for this theory is that AM and RM (1) look alike, (2) can both produce aftereffects of movement, (3) can both produce a response from motion-sensitive neurons in the visual system. In the following, each of these lines of evidence are examined.

AM and RM look alike. From the earliest days (WERTHEIMER, 1912; DE SILVA, 1929) it has been noticed that apparent movement subjectively resembles real movement. With a modern movie, the resemblance is well nigh perfect. The lock-and-key theory is easy to believe where movie frames follow each other very closely in space and time: The staircase of tiny steps or jerks is a close technical approximation to the smooth ramp of a continuous real movement. The key is such an excellent fit that nothing seems to require explanation. An isolated spot which jumps by tens of degrees but is seen as moving, is a more interesting and surprising phenomenon, more worthy of explanation. However, it does not always look exactly like RM, and in fact we shall describe evidence later that AM over long distances is *not* handled by the RM mechanism.

Motion aftereffects. A motion aftereffect is sometimes thought to require continuous real movement of contours across the retina (ANSTIS and GREGORY,

1965), but in fact stroboscopic movement will do almost as well. BANKS and KANE (1972) found that a moving pattern of collapsing circles can give aftereffects of movement in either continuous or stroboscopic illumination, provided that the spatial discontinuity of the stroboscopic stimuli is less than 12.5′ of arc. The apparent movement obtained with wider spatial discontinuities gives only small aftereffects of movement (ANSTIS and MOULDEN, 1970).

Since motion aftereffects are almost certainly caused by adaptation or fatiguing of motion-sensitive neurons (BARLOW and HILL, 1963), this is prima facie evidence that such cases of apparent movement have the same physiologic basis as RM.

Motion-sensitive neurons. Indeed, there is direct evidence that single units which respond to real movement will also respond to stroboscopic movement. Retinal motion-detecting ganglion cells in the frog, rabbit, pigeon, or ground squirrel will all respond to spots flashed in sequence within their receptive fields (see review by GRÜSSER and GRÜSSER-CORNEHLS, 1973). There is no doubt that in many cases stroboscopic movement is an adequate stimulus to movement-detecting systems in many species.

II. AM = RM: a Shift-and-Subtract Model

The lock-and-key theory is simple and plausible, but too general to be easily tested. To make it more specific, we shall embody it in a "shift-and-subtract" model, which can be built as a hardware model. We shall see that although succeeding to explain some examples of human AM perception, it fails instructively on others.

It is thought that retinal motion detectors operate by sampling activity in two nearby retinal areas, A and B, delaying one message and subtracting the other message from it (BARLOW and LEVICK, 1965). Machines have been built which use a similar process of polarized lateral inhibition, or "delay-and-subtract."

It is not difficult to design a device which distinguishes moving from stationary patterns in a visual scene. For instance, photographs can be taken which emphasize stationary objects and reject moving objects, simply by the use of a long exposure time. Figure 1a is a photograph of a traffic island, busy with traffic, taken with a conventional short exposure time. With a long exposure time of several seconds, the moving traffic disappears from the picture (Fig. 1b). The first daguerreotypes used exposures of several minutes, owing to the insensitivity of the earliest photographic emulsions, and critics complained that Daguerre's street scenes never showed any people, since the people moved along the street during the exposure time and blurred out. (The first man to appear in a photograph was a pedestrian who happened to be standing still for a few minutes having his shoes shined while Daguerre's camera shutter was open.)

(a)  (b)

Fig. 1. (a) Photograph of traffic island with moving traffic. (b) Time exposure leaves buildings unaffected, but makes moving traffic disappear (NATKIN, 1939)

Thus a photograph with long exposure time emphasizes stationary objects and rejects moving objects. We would have similar results if we filmed a moving scene, and then *added up* successive frames of the movie by sandwiching together two or more tiny pieces of film. Conversely, we can emphasize moving objects and reject stationary ones by *subtracting* one movie frame from its successor. If a *negative* movie frame is superimposed on a *positive* of the following frame, then for any stationary parts of the scene the black parts of one picture will coincide with the white parts of the other, so that all these stationary parts will cancel out and disappear from the resulting composite picture. But where an object has moved between the taking of the two frames, its positive and negative image will be out of register, and light or dark fringes will appear in the composite picture (MACKAY, 1959).

Movement and change in TV pictures can be detected by electronic subtraction of successive TV frames (MOUNTS, 1969; CANDY et al., 1971). Most of a TV picture is highly redundant, since the stationary parts of a TV picture are the same in each successive frame. MOUNTS and colleagues found that they could transmit TV pictures with eight times the usual efficiency by transmitting only those picture elements which *changed* between successive frames—about 4% of picture elements for a person conversing on a picturephone. They were able to isolate these moving or changing points by subtracting each frame from its successor electronically. Incidentally, they reported that there was usually more correlation between picture elements in the frame-to-frame time dimension than there was between adjacent elements in a single frame In other words, an area is more likely to be stationary than to be spatially uniform: movement is rarer than texture.

Oosterkamp et al. (1966) report a medical application for the same picture-subtraction technique. X-ray photographs of the blood vessels inside the head, called angiograms, are made by injecting a radio-opaque substance into the arteries. Unfortunately, shadows of the skull bones often obscure details of the blood vessels. To avoid this, a television photograph was taken of the head *before* the injection, and then subtracted electronically from the skull-plus-blood vessels, leaving a clear, sharp "subtraction angiogram" of the desired blood vessels. By taking a series of TV angiograms at different times, as the radio-opaque dye moved through the vessels, Oosterkamp found he could display the arteries in red and the veins in blue on a TV color monitor.

This subtraction method detects the presence of a change (a temporal event). To discriminate the direction and velocity of a movement (a spatiotemporal event), the negative picture must be shifted around spatially until it matches the positive. The velocity can then be calculated from the amount of shift. Billingsley (1973) has done this on a computer. Traffic moving along a highway was filmed from directly overhead by a helicopter. When one movie frame was subtracted from its predecessor, using computer methods, the highway and any stationary cars disappeared from the difference picture, whereas cars which had moved between frames showed fringes where the positive was displaced from the negative. If one frame was shifted prior to subtraction by an amount corresponding to a speed of 30 mph, then cars traveling at that speed would disappear from the difference picture. A series of shifts and subtractions would reveal the speed of each car on the road. (In principle, this technique might be extended to provide the police with a color TV picture in which all cars exceeding the speed limit turned red.)

A visual system which shifted and subtracted its successive inputs would really be searching for shifted zones containing point-for-point brightness correlations. Continuously moving real objects (RM) contain such zones, and the shifts between successive instants of time are negligibly small (except in special cases such as occluded movement, where a man walks behind a wall and then reappears on the other side). An isolated jumping spot (AM) also contains such zones, but the shifts are large and discontinuous. A shift-and-subtract model can handle such a case on a lock-and-key basis, but later we shall review evidence that large jumps, say greater than 1/4°, are handled by a different mechanism (Braddick, 1974). In fact, an isolated jumping spot is not the best stimulus to help us decide how the visual system responds to AM.

The really interesting AM stimuli, which the shift-and-subtract model cannot explain, are of three kinds. The first kind involves stimuli which move very fast—too fast for the RM system to handle. The second kind involves figural perceptual processes, which clearly go beyond the simple image processing comprising shift-and-subtract. The responses to these types of stimulation will be discussed next: They lead to theories that AM and RM are detected by quite different mechanisms. After that we shall discuss the third kind of AM stimuli, which are selectively manipulated local (point-by-point) and global correlations between pictures. These special stimuli lead to a two-process theory of two AM mechanisms, one being the same as for RM but the other quite different.

C. One-Process Theory: Apparent Movement Has a Different Mechanism From Real Movement

A. AM≠RM: Theory and Evidence

Reasons for believing that AM and RM have different mechanisms have been set out by KOLERS in his excellent book (1972), which the reader can consult for further details. The main evidence is that AM and RM (1) have different equivalent velocities, (2) have different masking effects on stationary stimuli, and (3) look different from each other after prolonged fixation. (In addition, AM is thought to involve figural perceptual processes: these are discussed in the next section.)

KAUFMAN et al. (1971) compared the velocities at which RM and AM could be seen. They used a rotating wheel with slits in it to produce three conditions which are diagrammed in Figure 2: (a) a spot moving to and fro horizontally between two fixed end points about 2° apart with a delay at each end (RM′ condition); (b) the same as condition (a) but with the end points hidden, so that the spot was visible only while it was moving (RM condition); (c) in this condition the spot was visible only while stationary at the end points (AM condition). The velocity of the display was gradually increased and the subject was asked to report on the clarity of the perceived RM and AM. In conditions (a) and (b) the (real) movement was seen clearly up to a speed of about 8°–10°/s, but above this speed the moving object became blurred or streaked, with a comet's tail. However, in condition (c) the (apparent) movement of a spot from one position to the other was not reported until its equivalent velocity was 8°–10° or faster. (All three conditions degenerated into a diffuse blinking or flickering at around 17°–27°/s.) So the apparent movement began to be visible at a speed where the real movement began to disappear. KAUFMAN et al. suggest that the processes of RM and AM are not parallel, but complementary, with AM taking over when RM becomes inefficient. This indicates that

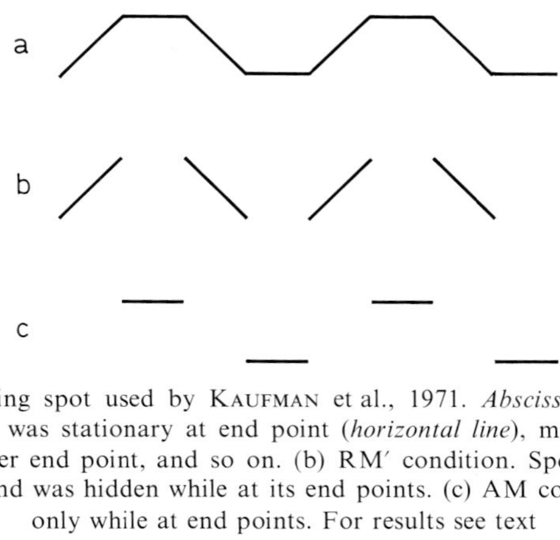

Fig. 2a–c. Path of moving spot used by KAUFMAN et al., 1971. *Abscissa,* time; *ordinate,* space. (a) RM condition. Spot was stationary at end point (*horizontal line*), moved at uniform velocity (*slanting line*) to the other end point, and so on. (b) RM′ condition. Spot was visible only while moving (*slanting lines*) and was hidden while at its end points. (c) AM condition. Spot was visible only while at end points. For results see text

AM may serve biologically for the detection of very rapid movement, thus extending the range of motion perception beyond that allowed by the time constants early in the visual system.

KOLERS (1963, 1964) has questioned the identity of RM and AM. He reported a masking experiment in which a vertical bar moved across a display, either in real movement, or else in apparent movement by being flashed first in one position and then in another. A small test line was flashed briefly somewhere along the path of the movement, and its detection threshold was measured. During real movement of the bar, the threshold for seeing the test line was raised most when it was exposed just as the moving bar passed over it. During apparent movement, the threshold for the test line was not affected. KOLERS concluded that AM differs in some way from RM. However, his results do not compel us to accept his conclusions. First, the timing of AM cannot be mapped on to the timing of RM, as KOLERS tries to do, since the position of a really moving spot changes continuously with time, but the direction and perceived position (if any) of an AM spot are undetermined until the onset of the second (not the first) flash. Second, the experiment shows that AM and RM are physically different stimuli which differ in *some* of their effects—in this case, in their masking effects. But this does not prove that they activate motion-sensitive channels differently.

AM and RM look subjectively different after periods of prolonged fixation (KOLERS, 1964). If an observer looks fixedly at a point marking one end of the path of a sinusoidally oscillating spot, then his perception of sinusoidal RM continues indefinitely. But if the spot is driven to and fro (say on an oscilloscope screen) by a square wave, so that it jumps to and fro in AM, it is found that the perception of continuous pendular movement disappears after 30–60 s and is replaced by the percept of two points flashing on and off in their terminal positions. KOLERS construes this subjective difference as evidence for the nonidentity of the AM and RM mechanisms. But FRISBY (1972) and CLATWORTHY and FRISBY (1973) suggest that RM detectors may underlie both phenomena, but become adapted or fatigued (BARLOW and HILL, 1963), so that the AM stimulation, which is only marginally strong enough to give perceived movement, gradually becomes inadequate to keep the RM detectors responding consistently, whereas RM stimulation remains adequate. Thus the differences may reflect not two mechanisms, but simply the unusual operation of the RM/AM mechanism when fed with AM stimuli close to its limits of tolerance—similar to a lock with a badly fitting key.

II. AM $\neq$ RM: Figural Processes in AM

KOLERS and POMERANTZ (1971) and KOLERS (1972) presented pairs of stimuli flashed sequentially—either identical pairs consisting of squares, circles, triangles, or arrows, or else different pairs, such as a square followed by a circle, or an arrow followed by a triangle, and so on. These dissimilar pairs gave AM just as readily as the identical pairs. It was found that a red square followed

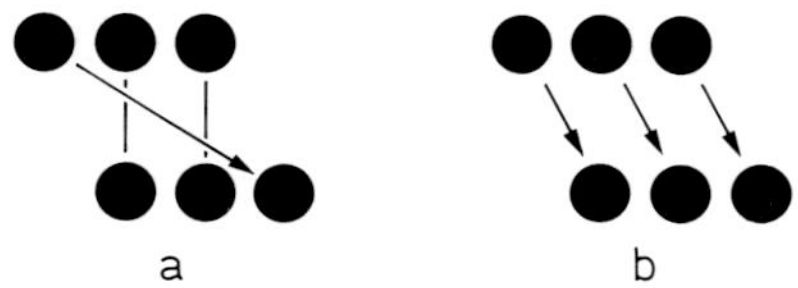

Fig. 3a and b. (PANTLE and PICCIANO, 1976). Three spots at positions a, b, c were exposed in alternation with three spots at positions b′, c′, d.
(a) Short interstimulus intervals and monocular viewing gave "element motion." End spot appeared to jump back and forth.
(b) Longer interstimulus intervals or dichoptic viewing gave "group motion" with all three dots jumping as a triplet

by a displaced green circle showed an apparently continuous plastic deformation as it jumped across the gap, whereas an abrupt change was perceived in midtransit as the color changed from red to green, without passing through grey (or yellow).

Figural perceptual processes must be involved here. However, it is not clear whether these tell us about the way in which motion is signaled, or about the way later stages of visual processing try to make sense of these signals.

SIGMAN and ROCK (1974) were able to demonstrate a direct role for perceptual intelligence in identifying objects and seeing AM between them. If two spots were exposed alternately at a suitable rate, they were perceived as a single jumping spot. But if an opaque object was moved to and fro, alternately covering and uncovering the two (stationary) spots, then subjects did not report movement of the spots, but rather saw the two spots as being continuously present but alternately covered and uncovered by the moving object. The same retinal stimulation from the two spots led to very different perceptual "solutions" to the problems posed by the two displays.

PANTLE and PICCIANO (1976) found that small stimulus changes could alter the whole perceptual organization of an AM display. They presented three spots, a, b, c, in alternation with three displaced spots, b′, c′, d (Fig. 3). When the pictures were presented in rapid alternation to the same eye (making it easy, so to speak, to compare the successive pictures), subjects reported "element motion" of a spot jumping back and forth from a to d, across two stationary spots at b and c. When the interstimulus intervals were increased, or when the two patterns were presented dichoptically (when the first pattern was presented to one eye and the second pattern to the other eye, thus making perceptual comparisons between the pictures more difficult), "group motion" was reported, with all three spots jumping to and fro as a group. Conceivably, rapid alternations in the first case enhance the perceptual links between the pictures, so that in the ensuing "element motion", movement perception predominates over form perception and allows a breakup of the triplet of spots, whereas *dichoptic* presentation in the second case allows cohesion within each picture to hold the triplets together in "group motion", so that form perception predominates over motion perception. These findings demonstrate global and Gestalt factors which cannot be explained by a lock-and-key or shift-and-subtract theory.

D. Two-Process Theory: Apparent Movement Has Same Mechanism as Real Movement for Short-Range Displacements, but Different Mechanism for Long-Range Displacements

HELMHOLTZ and HERING argued for years about color vision. Each considered only part of the evidence, and eventually both of them were proved to be right! Helmholtz was right (regarding the retina) and HERING was also right (regarding the lateral geniculate body). Perhaps the same will prove true for the rivaling AM theorists. BRADDICK (1974) has put forward the hypothesis that AM is mediated by two processes instead of one. He proposes a "short-range" process, which also handles RM and a "long-range" process, which does not.

BRADDICK's theory is that the "short-range" process is a lock-and-key approximation to RM perception. It operates only over a distance of 15′ arc or less, so it would operate, for example, every time we go to the movies. It is probably based upon the stimulation of motion sensitive units and can give rise to motion aftereffects. It is known that motion-detecting neurons do respond to stroboscopic movement (GRÜSSER and GRÜSSER-CORNEHLS, 1973), and prolonged stimulation of these neurons does give rise to motion aftereffects (BARLOW and HILL, 1963). Furthermore, AM stimulation can produce motion aftereffects in human observers, but only if the AM jumps are kept below 12.5′ arc (BANKS and KANE, 1972).

The "long-range" process is thought to respond to stimuli such as a spot which jumps across a large distance—anything from, say, 20′ arc to 20° or more. Such stimuli are not thought to stimulate motion detectors, and there is no evidence that they produce motion aftereffects.

Evidence to disentangle these two processes has come from special AM stimuli—not the isolated spots and lines of classic perceptual psychology, but complex textured patterns. Evidence for the "short-range" process comes from random-dot, Julesz patterns (presented in alternation, not in a stereoscope). These pairs of patterns contain local point-by-point correlation and produce local, short-range AM responses. Evidence for the "long-range" process comes from clusters of points which can evoke subjective contours. These contain global correlations which produce global, long-range AM responses. These are illustrated later in Figure 5 and are described in more detail below.

I. Correlation Within Pictures (=Form) vs. Between Pictures (=Motion)

Visual responses to AM between pairs of pictures can be studied by manipulating the correlation, or similarity, between pictures. In general, how similar must successive pictures be if AM is to be seen between them? Provided that

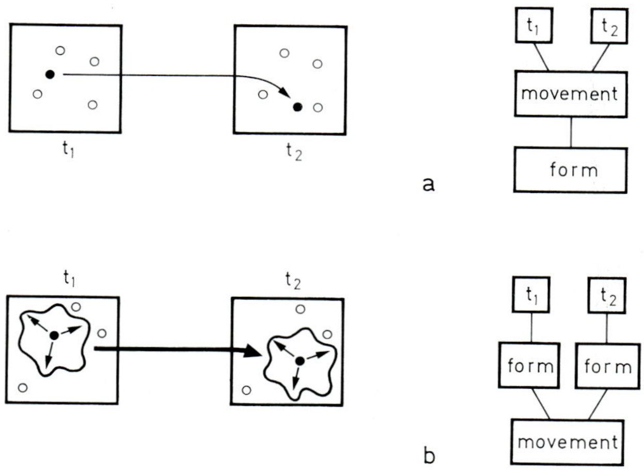

Fig. 4a and b. Two ways of seeing apparent movement. *Left*: two pictures exposed at times t1, t2. Though drawn side by side, pictures are really superimposed. *Right:* hypothetical perceptual processes.
(a) Visual system might compare pictures point by point (*left*), for instance when viewing random-dot stereograms flashed in alternation. AM is seen, showing that motion between pictures is seen prior to any analysis of form (*right*).
(b) Visual system might analyze each picture into forms, patterns or clusters, and then look for motion between these clusters (e.g., cyclopean contours). In this case, form perception must precede motion perception (*right*) (ANSTIS, 1970)

correlated zones of similar brightness exist, the visual system will accept some surprising plastic deformations or mismatches. A ball thrown in a movie retains its circular shape, so AM is easily seen. A running man in a movie changes the relative positions of his limbs, hence his overall shape, but motion is still easy to see. Even when a projected slide of a frowning face fades or dissolves to a superimposed smiling face which is of a different person, the visual system accepts the plastic deformation as being merely a changing expression, although the face itself is also changing: perceptual identity is conferred on faces which do not actually belong to the same person (ANSTIS, 1970).

Can we quantify how much object identity is necessary to carry the percept of movement? In principle, there are two different ways in which the visual system might extract AM from successive, superimposed pictures: 1. The shift-and-subtract method, based on point-by-point comparisons of brightness between the two pictures (Fig. 4a). A point of a given brightness would be compared with nearby points of similar brightness in the next picture, and the best correlation chosen. Thus each dark point in a face would be seen as moving to a nearby dark point in a subsequently presented face on a local point by point basis. No preprocessing or global form recognition *within* each picture is necessary: Only local correlations *between* pictures are used. Once motions are detected, some further perceptual stages might exist to favor coherent moving zones which share a common fate over incoherent motion of points in random directions; but these would occur after the shift-and-subtract stage.

2. Forms or patterns within each picture might be analyzed first, and then motion seen between these patterns. Thus dark points within a face might be perceptually segregated as an eyebrow, and motion then seen between successive eyebrows, not between successive points (Fig. 4b).

The first of these processes detects local movements between points, and the second process detects global movements between preprocessed forms, blobs, or clusters. AM patterns have been devised which selectively forbid one or the other of these processes in turn. Since AM is still seen, we can conclude that either process alone can lead to AM perception. The patterns are described below.

1. Motion Perception Can Precede Form Perception

JULESZ (1971) has devised random-dot stereograms in which both eyes see a random-dot pattern not unlike sandpaper, but in the pattern seen by one eye a square central zone has been uniformly displaced sideways by a few dot diameters. When the patterns are fused binocularly in a stereoscope, a central square is seen floating in depth above the plane of the background. The central square is not present in either pattern taken alone, since it is defined only by the relationship of displacement between the patterns. JULESZ (1971) concludes that stereoscopic depth can be seen without monocular cues, without any prior pattern analysis of the monocular picture seen by each eye.

HOCHBERG (1968), ANSTIS (1970), and JULESZ (1971) all presented Julesz' random-dot patterns in alternation to the same eye. All obtained reports of a central random-dot square in apparent motion. This is a most interesting result, since it shows that the visual system can compare successive patterns to extract the displacement relationship. Perception of motion here must logically precede the perception of the square form, which is created only by the movement. In this case (Fig. 4a), instead of object identity carrying the motion, it is motion which defines the square object that the subject sees (although admittedly not the microtexture of the dot pattern, which must be resolvable in each picture). The square is invisible in each picture on its own—there are no correlations *within* each picture to reveal it: It exists only by virtue of the correlations *between* the pictures, which the visual system picks up as apparent movement.

Any pair of random-dot patterns which give depth when presented to the two eyes in a stereoscope will also give AM when presented to one eye in alternation (ANSTIS, 1970). Perhaps the neural processing of motion resembles that for depth, except that motion perception must include some kind of short-term memory. In fact JULESZ (1971) has presented a shift-and-subtract model for depth perception which is essentially the same as the movement model presented here. One could speculate that stereo vision, which developed much later than motion perception on an evolutionary time scale, took over and adapted many of the technical tricks which the visual system had already devised for seeing movement. It is interesting to note in this connection that retinal ganglion cells that respond to movement of an object in a particular direction are common in the pigeon, the rabbit, and the ground squirrel, animals whose laterally placed eyes look at different parts of the environment, but they seem to be absent in the cat and higher animals with binocular fields (MILNER, 1970). Is it conceivable that stereo vision might have preempted some of the neural circuitry which was originally devoted to motion perception?

The random-dot moving square can be seen only if both patterns are presented to the same eye. AM is lost with dichoptic presentation. Also, the displacement between the two successive pictures must be kept small—below about 15′ arc (BRADDICK, 1974) or perhaps a few dot diameters (LAPPIN and BELL, 1972). So these random-dot displays demonstrate the "short-range" process, in which motion perception—the detection of correlations between pictures—must precede form perception—the detection of correlations within pictures (Fig. 4a). It may also be related to PANTLE and PICCIANO's (1976) mechanism for detecting "element motion" in which motion perception *predominates* over form perception; this also fails to operate under dichoptic viewing conditions.

2. Form Perception Can Precede Motion Perception

RAMACHANDRAN et al. (1973) devised a neat inversion of these random-dot experiments. They presented in alternation two random-dot patterns which were uncorrelated, like two different sheets of sandpaper (Fig. 5a). Each contained 50% black and 50% white dots, distributed at random. The central square in one pattern consisted of random horizontal dashes, and in the other pattern of random vertical dashes. The dashes were 50% black and 50% white, so that there was no overall brightness difference between a central square and its background. The situation was the exact opposite of the random-dot stereograms, in that the central square could now be clearly discerned within each picture, since dashes look different from dots, but there was no point-by-point correlation between the two pictures (Table 2). However, when the two pictures were alternated, a square could be clearly seen jumping back and forth. The straightforward shift-and-subtract model cannot handle this case, because there was no point-for-point correspondence between the two pictures. PANTLE (1973) likewise obtained AM between two uncorrelated patterns, each containing a cluster of red dots against a background of green dots (Fig. 5b). Subjects reported a cluster of red dots moving back and forth in toto. In both these experiments, the perceived movement of a cluster of elements was dependent upon global information within each successively presented pattern rather than a local point-by-point comparison process. It follows that perceptual segregation of the square form within each picture must logically *precede* the perception of motion between the pictures (Fig. 4b). The stimulus constrains the subject first to isolate clusters within each picture on the basis of some visual property ("filled with dashes" or "filled with red dots"), and only then can he see AM between these clusters.

It follows that in this process, perceptual segregation of the square form *within* each picture must precede the perception of motion *between* the pictures (Fig. 4b). We believe that this global process can be identified with BRADDICK's

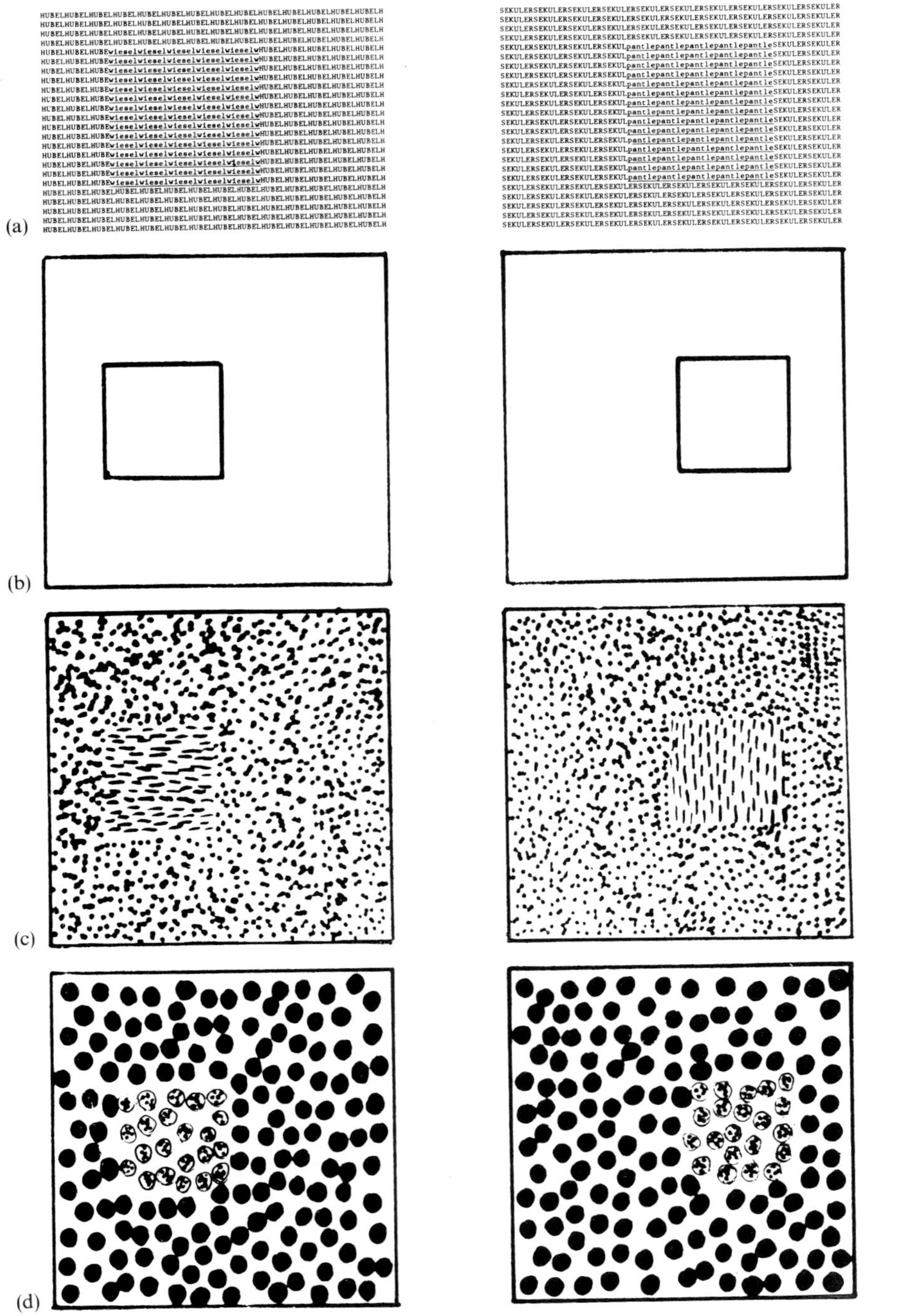

Fig. 5a–d. Patterns containing subjective or cyclopean contours. These contours must be analyzed within each pattern before motion can be seen between patterns, since there is little or no direct correlation between patterns. (c) From RAMACHANDRAN et al. (1973). (d) From PANTLE (1973). Visual system extracts subjective outline of square in each pattern, then sees motion between two squares. In general, any type of visual activity confined to zone x, which can be discriminated from a different visual activity donfined to zone y, might serve as basis for perception of AM

Table 2. Does square area of correlation exist?

Stimulus	Within pictures (form)	Between pictures (motion)	Remarks
Isolated squares/spots/lines (many authors)	Yes	Yes	Site of motion perception cannot be determined
Random-dot stereograms (HOCHBERG, 1968; JULESZ, 1971; ANSTIS, 1970; LAPPIN and BELL, 1972; BRADDICK, 1974)	Yes	No	Motion perception precedes form perception
Dot-dash textures (RAMACHANDRAN et al., 1973)	No	Yes	Form perception precedes motion perception
Red/green spots (PANTLE, 1973)			

"long-range" process. It may also be related to PANTLE and PICCIANO's mechanism for detecting "group motion", in which form perception *predominates* over motion perception.

In these examples, the square zone was defined by dashes or red dots, but in general any visual property will do, provided it makes the zone stand out immediately without prolonged scrutiny. Here is a fanciful example: Suppose you go to Buckingham Palace to see the Queen's coach drive by. If you arrive early, you see the coach moving across your visual field (RM). But if you arrive late, you see only the backs of a crowd of spectators. Even so, you can still observe the progress of the coach indirectly, by observing the wave of excitement (signaled by cheering, gesticulations, etc.) which runs through the crowd opposite the coach. Nobody is moving along—the crowd is too dense—but a wave is moving. In a wave, energy travels although matter does not. Perceptually, you can segregate a zone or traveling wave of "excitement" as it moves (in AM) through the medium of the crowd.

II. A New Phenomenon: Reversed Apparent Movement

Good AM can be produced with the Victorian technique of "dissolving views." Two identical slides are projected on a screen, overlapping but slightly displaced, and one slide is gradually dimmed as the other is brightened. The picture appears to glide rather than jump. ANSTIS (1970) and ANSTIS and ROGERS (1975) reported a curious phenomenon: If a black and white slide dissolved to its own photographic negative, superimposed with a very small displacement (15′ arc or less), then very strong, compelling AM was seen toward the earlier stimulus, i.e., in the *opposite* direction to the physical displacement. It made no difference whether the positive or negative picture came first; in fact with abstract patterns it is arbitrary which picture is called the positive and which

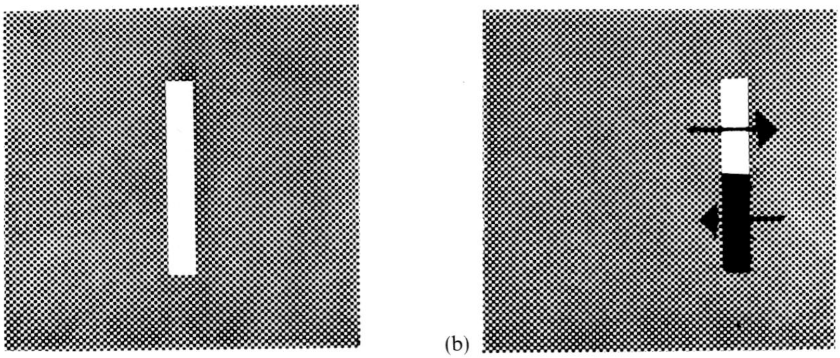

Fig. 6a and b. Reversed apparent movement. The *black/white bar* (b) is superimposed on the *white bar* (a), but with a tiny displacement to the right. Result: when the white bar is replaced via a dissolve by the black/white bar, the upper part of the bar appears to move to the right (normal AM), but the bottom part of the bar appears to move to the left (reversed AM), as indicated by the *arrows*. (ANSTIS, 1970; ANSTIS and ROGERS, 1975)

the negative. Suppose that the two pictures in Figure 6 are superimposed, with the black/white bar displaced by a few min arc to the right. During a dissolve from the first picture to the second the upper part of the white bar is replaced by an identical positive copy displaced to the right and AM is seen to the right. The lower half of the white bar is replaced by a black (negative) bar, also displaced to the right, and strong AM is seen to the *left*. There is no vernier misalignment within either bar on its own, yet the two halves of the bar appear to shear in opposite directions during the dissolve.

Reversed AM is probably a short-range physiologic process occurring early in the visual system. It is probably caused by neural blurring or spatial summation which shifts the effective position of superimposed positive-negative contours (ROGERS and ANSTIS, 1975). Positive-negative dissolves produce the same reversed responses in motion detectors in the cat cortex as they do in human observers (BLAKEMORE and ANSTIS, unpublished results), and in humans they produce motion aftereffects in a direction appropriate to the illusory reversed AM, not to the physical displacement.

E. Conclusion

We have presented evidence that the visual system has two separate mechanisms for seeing AM: a short-range process, in which motion perception precedes form perception and which responds both to AM and RM; and a long-range process, in which form perception precedes motion perception, and which does not respond to RM. It is probably economical for the visual system to change its strategy according to the size of the spatial jump. For an object in real movement, the jumps between successive instants in time are extremely small. A built-in safety factor permits us to tolerate jumps of up to 1/4°, e.g., of a random-dot field. For bigger jumps the visual system loses track of which dot is which and incoherent motion (LAPPIN and BELL, 1972) is seen. Since the computing or search time to keep track of jumps through n dot diameters will increase according to n^2, it becomes more efficient to switch to a strategy of looking for clusters of dots which are labeled, e.g., in red, and then look for motion between clusters. So it makes sense to have a set of hard-wired detectors for real movements which are extremely common visual events. These detectors will accept small displacements on a lock-and-key basis. A secondary, global system deals with large displacements, which are much rarer events since there are no stroboscopes in nature.

References

Aarons, L.: Visual apparent movement research: review, 1935–1955, and bibliography, 1965-63. Percept. Mot. Skills (Monogr. Suppl. 2-V18) **18**, 239–274 (1964).

Anstis, S.M.: Phi movement as a subtraction process. Vision Res. **10**, 1411–1430 (1970).

Anstis, S.M., Gregory, R.L.: The after effect of seen movement: the role of retinal stimulation and of eye movements. Q. J. Exp. Psychol. **17**, 173–174 (1965).

Anstis, S.M., Moulden, B.P.: Aftereffect of seen movement: evidence for peripheral and central components. Q. J. Exp. Psychol. **22**, 222–229 (1970).

Anstis, S.M., Rogers, B.J.: Illusory reversal of visual depth and movement during changes of contrast. Vision Res. **15**, 957–961 (1975).

Banks, W.P., Kane, D.A.: Discontinuity of seen motion reduces the visual motion aftereffect. Percept. Psychophys. **12**, 69–72 (1972).

Barlow, H.B., Hill, R.M.: Evidence for a physiological explanation of the waterfall phenomenon and figural aftereffects. Nature **200**, 1345–1347 (1963).

Barlow, H.B., Levick, W.R.: The mechanism of directionally selective units in rabbit's retina. J. Physiol. (Lond.) **178**, 477–504 (1965).

Bender, M.B., Teuber, H.-L.: Disturbances in visual perception following brain damage. J. Psychol. **28**, 223–233 (1949).

Billingsley, F.C.: Digital image processing for information extraction. J. Man-Machine Studies **5**, 203–214 (1973).

Braddick, O.: A short-range process in apparent motion. Vision Res. **14**, 519–528 (1974).

Candy, J.C., Franke, M.A., Haskell, B.J., Mounts, F.W.: Transmitting television as clusters of frame-to-frame differences. Bell System Techn. J. **50**, 1889–1917 (1971).

Clatworthy, J.L., Frisby, J.P.: Real and apparent movement: evidence for a unitary mechanism. Perception **2**, 161–164 (1973).

Exner, S.: Über das Sehen von Bewegungen und die Theorie des zusammengesetzten Auges. Sitzungsberichte Akademie Wissenschaft Wien, **72**, 156–190 (1875).

Frisby, J.P.: Real and apparent movement—same or different mechanisms? Vision Res. **12**, 1051–1052 (1972).

Graham, C.H.: Perception of movement. In: Vision and Visual Perception. New York: Wiley 1965, pp. 575–588.

Gregory, R.L.: Eye and Brain: The Psychology of Seeing. London: Weidenfeld & Nicolson 1966.

Grüsser, O.-J., Grüsser-Cornehls, U.: Neuronal mechanisms of visual movement perception and some psychophysical and behavioral correlations. In: Handbook of Sensory Physiology, Vol. VII/3A: Central Processing of Information. Jung, R. (ed.). New York: Springer-Verlag 1973.

Hinton, J.M.: This is visual sensation. In: Wisdom: Twelve Essays. Bambrough, R. (ed.). Oxford: Basil Blackwell 1974, pp. 161–162.

Hochberg, J.E.: In the mind's eye. In: Contemporary Theory and Research in Visual Perception. Haber, R.N. (ed.). New York: Holt, Rinehart and Winston 1968, pp. 309–331.

Julesz, B.: Foundations of Cyclopean Perception. Chicago: U. of Chicago Pr. 1971.

Kaufman, L.: Sight and Mind. Fair Lawn, N.J.: Oxford U. Pr. 1974.

Kaufman, L., Cyrulnick, I., Kaplowitz, L., Melnick, G., Stof, D.: The complementarity of apparent and real motion. Psychol. Forsch. **34**, 343–348 (1971).

Kolers, P.A.: Some differences between real and apparent movement. Vision Res. **3**, 191–206 (1963).

Kolers, P.A.: Some illusions of movement. Sci. Am. **211**, (4), 98–106 (1964).

Kolers, P.A.: Aspects of Motion Perception. Oxford: Pergamon 1972.

Kolers, P.A., Pomerantz, J.R.: Figural change in apparent motion. J. Exp. Psychol. **87**, 99–108 (1971).

Korte, A.: Kinematoskopische Untersuchungen. Z. Psychol. **72**, 193–206 (1915).

Lappin, J.S., Bell, H.H.: Perceptual differentiation of sequential visual patterns. Percept. Psychophys. **12**, 129–134 (1972).

Mackay, R.S.: Display of moving parts of a scene. Science **130**, 223–224 (1959).

Milner, P.: Physiological Psychology. New York: Holt, Rinehart & Winston 1970.

Mounts, F.W.: A video encoding system with conditional picture-element replenishment. Bell System Techn. J. **48**, 2545–2554 (1969).

Natkin, M.: Fascinating Fakes in Photography. London: Fountain Pr. 1939.

Neff, W.S.: A critical investigation of the visual apprehension of movement. Am. J. Psychol. **48**, 1–42 (1936).

Oosterkamp, W.J., Van't Hof, A.P.M., Scheren, W.J.L.: X-Ray pictures in colour. Phillips Techn. Rev. **27**, 228–230 (1966).

Pantle, A.J.: Stroboscopic movement based upon global information in successively presented visual patterns. J. Opt. Soc. Am. **63**, 1280A (1973).

Pantle, A.J., Picciano, L.: A multi-stable movement display: evidence for two separate motion systems in humans. Science **193**, 500–502 (1976).

Ramachandran, V.S., Rao, V.M., Vidyasagar, T.R.: Apparent movement with subjective contours. Vision Res. **13**, 1399–1401 (1973).

Robinson, J.O.: The Psychology of Visual Illusions. London: Hutchinson 1972.

Rock, I.: An Introduction to Perception. New York: MacMillan 1975.

Rogers, B.J., Anstis, S.M.: Reversed apparent depth from positive and negative stereograms. Perception **4**, 193–201 (1975).

Sigman, E., Rock, I.: Stroboscopic movement based on perceptual intelligence. Perception **3**, 9–28 (1974).

Silva, H.R. de: An analysis of the visual perception of movement. Br. J. Psychol. **19**, 265–305 (1929).

Spigel, I.M.: Problems in the study of visually perceived movement: an introduction. In: Readings in the Study of Visually Perceived Movement. Spigel, I.M. (ed.). New York: Harper and Row 1965.

Wertheimer, M.: Experimentelle Studien über das Sehen von Bewegung. Z. Psychol. **61**, 161–278 (1912). [Excerpted and transl. in: Classics in Psychology. Shipley, T. (ed.). New York: Philos. Lib. 1961.]

Chapter 22

Visual Event Perception

GUNNAR JOHANSSON, Uppsala (Sweden)

With 15 Figures

Contents

A. Introduction

This chapter deals with an aspect of sensory information which in the past has been rather neglected, namely the perception of continuous changes in the environment and of the perceiver's own displacements in his environment.

The spatial environment of most species of animals is seldom wholly static or "frozen." Animal life generally implies that the animal has the ability to move in its environment, and its ability to react purposively to environmental changes signalled by sensory input is equally fundamental. We regard as something of a biologic axiom that all types of life adapt in this way to the environment, whether it is a question of phylogeny or of ontogeny.

I would like to base our discussion here on these two essential results of phylogenetic and/or ontogenetic adaptation to the environment: ability to move and ability to gain sensory information about the environment. The main sensory channel in this latter respect is usually vision. We can easily establish that these consequences of biologic adaptation are closely interrelated. Purposive motion of an animal most often presupposes simultaneous information about its own motion and about motions of other animals.

Due to general biologic processes, other animals are often to be regarded as potential predators or potential prey, or as mates if they are of the same species. In all these functions, detection of other animals in motion and information about the direction, velocity, etc., of their motions are, together with a control of its own locomotion, of primary importance for survival of the individual and of the species.

Such considerations make it clear that sensory motion detection must be regarded as one of the most important sensory achievements. In addition to motion information received from the visual input, used here as a typical example, we must consider kinetic responses from other sense channels: vestibular, kinesthetic, tactual, and auditory. However, in most species vision is the most important single channel in this respect, which makes it natural to concentrate our treatment on this modality. It is important, however, also to stress the intimate interaction or coaction of different sensory modalities for establishing spatial orientation. For an advanced and highly significant discussion about such sensory coaction and integration of information see GIBSON (1966). Recent experimental evidence combining visual and kinesthetic signals was found by among others, LISHMAN and LEE (1973) and JOHANSSON (1973a).

I. Events as Stimuli and as Percepts

We used motion perception as an example of the most typical and important dimension of perceived change during the time flow. However, as is well known, other dimensions of perceptual change over time also exist. The generic term for all these types of perception of change over time is *event perception*.

As a conceptual complement to event perception we usually use the term *static perception*. Thus, the difference between these two concepts is that, while the time dimension is essential in event perception, this dimension is assumed not to contribute sensory information in static perception.

Before proceeding with our discussion, it may be profitable to be more specific about the terms "event perception" and "stimulus event." The term "event" is defined as a generic concept denoting various kinds of relational change over time in a structure. In perceptual psychology the concepts "distal" and "proximal" are in general use in describing stimuli. We will also use these concepts here and distinguish among (1) *distal events:* the physical events about which the organism needs information, (2) *proximal events:* the pattern of energy flow available at the sense organ, and (3) *perceptual events:* the sensory information obtained from proximal events.

II. The Temporal Aspect

Perceived change implies that the change in the stimulus structure passes a threshold level during a time interval acceptable for immediate perception. This time span is rather short, on the order of a few seconds. The example with the hands of a watch is well known. We perceive the motion of the second hand but not of the hour and minute hand in spite of the fact that from the physical point of view these are also moving. When a cloud passes the sun we perceive the change in illumination but the illumination change at dawn or sunset is not immediately perceived. Evidently, there are numerous physical events which do not evoke event perception but for which we must rely on cognitive processes as mediators of information.

The old concept of "present time" (Präsenzzeit, see, e.g., Fröbes, 1923) as well as the more recent concept, "iconic memory" (Neisser, 1967) has a bearing on this distinction between immediately perceived change and indirect sensory information. It seems to be the span of a perceptual short-term memory which is essential for event perception. This perceptual memory also provides the temporal continuity necessary for event perception.

III. Static Perception and Event Perception

Systematic experimental studies on perception started in the last part of the nineteenth century. The basic types of theories, still dominating, were developed in the laboratories of von Helmholtz, Wundt, Hering, G.E. Müller, and a few others. The laboratory facilities, of course, were rather limited at that time, but in spite of this drawback a number of important problems were successfully investigated. For several reasons however, it was mainly static perception, as already defined, which attracted the main interest: e.g., threshold measurements, static distance perception, principles for structuring static perception, and all the static visual illusions.

At the same time, very few advanced studies on perception of change, e.g., motion, had appeared. Therefore, the more or less explicit theoretic models developed in this research were concerned primarily with static perception. In vision, the retinal image was treated as distinct and unchanging. Retinal localization of image elements and relative retinal size of projections were some main components in the theoretic treatment on space perception. When the problems of motion perception were touched on they were usually treated in terms of some kind of temporal integration of static patterns.

A common way of dealing with visual motion perception in the early perceptual theory was to assume that perceived motion had no direct physiologic correlate in the sensory response but was the result of some kind of "higher" activity of a cognitive nature. Representative of this viewpoint were, e.g., BENUSSI (1917), WITTMAN (1921), and DIMMICK (1920) together with many other psychologists. Essentially VON HELMHOLTZ also belongs to this group. Since he also did not find valid reasons to regard visual motion perception as an immediate sensory response to continuously transforming proximal stimulation (c.f. VON HELMHOLTZ, 1925, pp. 295–296). WUNDT too, was of the opinion that motion perception is the result of some kind of integration of static responses. This position was introduced by TITCHENER in the United States (1910) and there we find it clearly supported (cf. DIMMICK, 1920).

On the other hand, MACH and physiologists such as EXNER and HERING at an early date expressed an opposing opinion. They postulated a direct physiologic correlate for visually perceived motion. ERNST MACH, the famous physicist and advanced psychologist, felt free to introduce the concept "motion sensation" ("*Bewegungsempfindung*"). EXNER also used this term, programmatically.

Recent neurophysiologic research on vision dealing with receptive fields and recording from single units has decisively terminated this old controversy. (For excellent reviews see GRÜSSER and GRÜSSER-CORNEHLS, 1969, 1973). This comprehensive research has clearly demonstrated how certain single brain cells in the visual system of a number of animals (frog, cat, squirrel, monkey, etc.) respond in a differentiated way to motion over extended retinal areas (receptive fields). This indicates that there exists, at least in these animals, an anatomic apparatus which is physiologically adapted for direct visual response to motion stimulation, thus giving decisive empirical support to MACH's old hypothetical construct of *Bewegungsempfindung*. Additional and very strong indications in the same direction are found also in current research in the field of motion perception (cf. JOHANSSON, 1975).

B. Perceptual Kinetics

I. The Eye as a Receiver of Optic Information

Many principles determining biologic functioning of animals can be traced back to the first primitive stages of animal life. A basic functional principle, once established, is in general maintained throughout evolution. This explicitly holds true when it is a question of the optical basis of vision in man. The anatomic structure of the typical vertebrate eye with chambered lens and retina was established very early. In these eyes all rays reflected from the environment cross at the nodal point of the refracting system and reach the retina in distinct points, thus determining the directions of the rays in space. However, exactly the same optical principle is typical in the most primitive open eyes of the chamber type. The opening of the chamber determines the directions of the incoming rays in approximately the same way as the aperture in a pinhole camera and the nodal point of a lens. Throughout the evolution of the eye we also encounter advanced pinhole eyes like the eyes of some mollusks. The geometric principle of projection common to all chambered eyes, both open and equipped with a lens, as well as for the pinhole camera and the lens camera is *the principle of central (polar) projection.*

Central projection determines one-to-one mapping of a figure from one plane to another via rays crossing in a distinct point which is not on either plane. This mapping represents a perspective transformation of a figure. Evidently this geometric principle was "detected" and found useful during the first stages of animal life and was never abandoned. In the following discussion, this principle, as well as the projective geometry based on it, will play an important role in our analyses.

Because of the optical similarity between the vertebrate eye and the ordinary camera, the camera has very often been used as a model for the functioning of the eye. The analogy, however, is far less complete than has usually been observed. It is relevant when it is a question of the optical functioning of the two devices but is inaccurate when applied to the principles for recording optical information. The camera is an instrument for recording static images with sharp contours; this is also true for the motion picture camera. The scenes to be pictured usually include some moving components and, furthermore, the camera as a rule is not stationary while photographing. Therefore, the shutter is a necessary component. The photo with its sharp contours plainly is the result of a nullifying of the temporal aspect in the optical information by means of the shutter.

The eye is also usually in motion relative to the environment and it most often records scenes including objects in motion. However, it lacks the shutter function, which means that, in contrast to the camera, it must deal with the temporal aspect of stimulation; it is constructed for a continuous recording of optical change over time. Far from neutralizing the spatiotemporal flow in the incoming array of light, such changes are a necessary condition for the neural recording of the message in the array. This dependence of changing stimulation is well known from numerous studies of the effects from stabilized retinal images (DITCHBURN and GINSBURG, 1952; RIGGS et al., 1953; YARBUS, 1967).

Eyes with "shutters" do not exist (the eyelid is analogous to a lens cover) and we are free to conclude that the eye from the very beginning was developed for the recording of information abstracted from continuous changes in the distribution of optical energy passing through the pupil. We define this energy flow as the total flow passing the nodal point of the eye and term it the *optical flow*. This flow is the real proximal stimulus and *optical flow* will here be used as term for the optical energy to be analyzed by the visual system.

The eye of man is more or less continuously executing saccadic or pursuit movements and the eye rotates in its socket about a center of rotation very close to the optic nodal point. This means that the retina describes scanning motions relative to the incoming array of light and that the excitation pattern on the retina differs from the optical flow. We will call this excitation pattern the *retinal flow* in order to make a distinction between the two aspects of stimulus description. GIBSON (1968) has very explicitly discussed how the retina scans over the optical flow in order to abstract spatial information.

The optical flows generated when the eye moves relative to a rigid environment or when a rigid object moves relative to the eye, geometrically represent *continuous perspective transformations.* This statement follows from our discussion on page 679 and the fact that we are dealing with continuous processes.

There is an important difference between continuous perspective transformations generated by the motion of the perceiver and that from motion of a perceived object. It is easily seen that a displacement of the eye generates a flow over the total retina but that the motion of objects gives rise to localized flow patterns. In addition, a moving perceiver often has moving objects in his field of vision. In this case we get a total optical flow locally overlaid by, or rather combined with, local flow patterns.

II. Relativity of Reference Frames in Motion Perception

In physics, the term motion denotes displacement of a particle (object) relative to a chosen reference system. A basic proposition is that there is no absolute or ultimate reference system; a physicist is free to choose the reference system for his description of a motion which best fits his purpose. He often works with reference systems which are moving relative to each other and thus also with hierarchies of reference systems.

It is a common misconception that visual perception is at variance with physics in this respect: the static ground then is thought of as representing the absolute frame of reference for motion perception. It is easily found, however, that this conception is erroneous. As passengers in a train or in a car, for instance, we can often simultaneously perceive motion relative to two different reference systems. When we drop a match-box in a moving vehicle we say that it is moving vertically. We invariably see it falling in this way, also in an open car or when it is passing a window in the railway coach. Physically it is of course moving in a parabola-shaped path relative to the earth—like a very slow bullet. Evidently the vehicle perceptually acts as the frame of reference for the falling match-box. The perception of falling relative to this frame of reference, however, is not disturbed by our simultaneous perception through the same window, etc., of our own motion relative to the earth, nor does it disturb our perception of the motion of a flying bird or of a running dog relative to the same static background.

Evidently, the visual system is able to deal simultaneously with more than one reference system, just as the physicist or mathematician does. However, there is also an important difference. In perception the choice of a reference system is not optional and it is not possible to transpose freely from one frame of reference to another. No effort can bring us to *see* the parabolic motion path of the falling match-box or to *see* the dog move backward over the ground. In this respect the visual system follows its own specific rules and any theory of visual motion perception must take these facts into consideration.

In the forthcoming material we will find that the visual system in its treatment of optical impingement in an exclusive way deals with relations among optical structures rather than with absolute measurement of such structures.

III. The Principle of Relativity in Frontoparallel Motion

In the preceeding section we saw from an example that the visual system can simultaneously report motion of the observer relative to the stationary ground and the motion of an object relative to the observer motion. The example given was the simplest possible case of a hierarchical organization of reference frames in visual perception. In daily life we most often encounter far more complex hierarchies. The experimental study of principles underlying this perceptual structuring forms an important branch in the study of visual event perception. I will summarize this research in three steps starting with the simple case of frontoparallel motion.

Traditionally in studies of motion perception the stimulus presentation is classified in two categories: 1) motion in a frontoparallel plane and 2) motion in depth. The reason for this classification is that the former type of projection implies a geometric analysis which from the point of view of Euclidean geometry is far simpler than the latter. Frontoparallel motion brings about displacement of the projected figure but leaves its shape and size invariant, thus dealing with rigid motions of the figure, while projections from motion in depth result in nonrigid motions in the form of changes in shape and/or size of the projected figure.

Accepting the description of proximal stimulus as a product of central projection means that the classification mentioned lacks theoretical relevance. However, because of the advantage of initial exemplifying with the most simple variant, this classification will be provisionally accepted here. Frontoparallel projection affords the simplest possible way of abstracting a basic principle of relativity in the perceptual decoding of the optical flow because we can apply the Euclidean metric in description of projected figures.

One of the first experimental studies of this perceptual principle of abstracting relative motions from a total stimulus flow was carried out by DUNCKER (1929) who introduced the term "*simultane Systemtrennung*" (simultaneous dissociation of systems) for the effect studied. Some years earlier RUBIN (1927) had

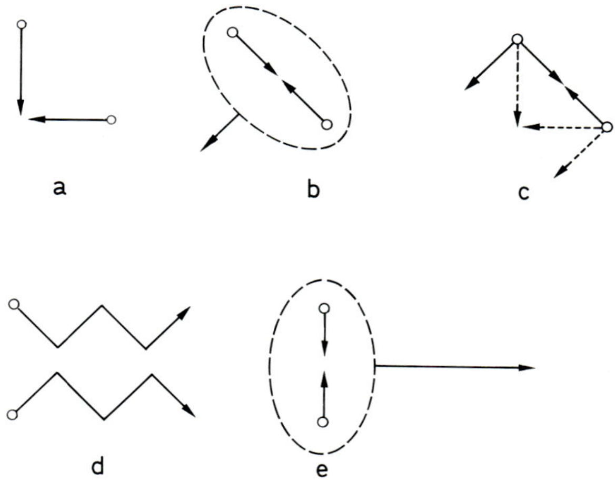

Fig. 1 a–e. Examples of perceptual vector analysis in motion perception. (a) and (d) show the simultaneous motions of two bright dots on a frontal screen, (b) and (e) illustrate the percepts and (c) shows how the percepts represent a correct vector analysis in relative and common components

published a closely related study where he simply but ingeniously demonstrated the perceptual splitting of a motion pattern in independent parts and in fact also the *Systemtrennung*. RUBIN used the term "*Bewegungsanalyse*" (motion analysis) for the effect.

JOHANSSON (1950b) published a monograph reporting a large number of experiments, all dealing with the effects mentioned: motion analysis and its consequences in dissociation of reference frames. As stimuli JOHANSSON used dark dots seen as moving on a bright homogeneous screen. The method of using simple elements such as dots as carriers of motion has been found to be advantageous in many motion studies. This method often helps, in an unproblematic way, to reveal the organizational principles sought for. When using this type of display, perceptual organization due to motion can be studied independent of "pictorial" factors.

From this monograph we choose two simple but informative experiments on frontoparallel motion, one dealing with perception of translatory motion and the other including rotary motion. Figures 1 (a) and (d) show two closely related display patterns evoking simultaneous perception of two different translatory motions in the same couple of elements. The dots move along the indicated tracks in accordance with a sinusoidal or triangular function. They have the same frequency, about 1 p/s. Both displays are easily reproduced on a double beam oscilloscope.

Perceptually, the dots are not seen as moving along the tracks indicated. Figure 1 (a) is seen as two dots moving diagonally toward and away from each other, while this unit of two moving dots is seen as moving to and fro along the other diagonal, as diagrammed in Figure 1 (b). A similar display, 1 (d), is seen as two dots moving vertically toward and from each other and simultaneously together moving along a horizontal track. Thus the "display"

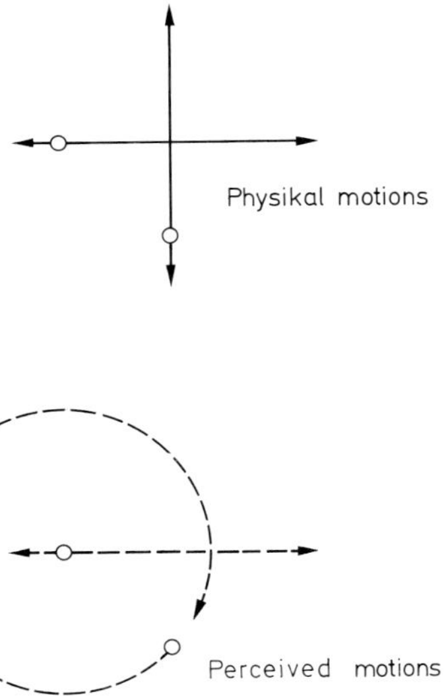

Fig. 2. Example of combinations of sinusoidal motions in two dots yielding perception of rotation of one dot (the not fixated one) about the fixated dot and a translation of this system while the latter is describing a translatory motion. See text

motions are perceptually dissociated in two independent components. One of these components (and the perceptually dominating one) is the motion of the elements *relative to each other* and the residual component is a motion *common for both elements* as shown in the figure. Evidently the common motion component forms the frame of reference for the relative motion. Figure 1 (c) and (e) also show how this perceptual system dissociation represents a mathematically correct vector analysis of the display motions. We will find that this perceptual analysis represents a general principle also found in more complex combinations of motions. A component in the flow pattern common for all elements always is partialled out and acts as a moving frame of reference for the relative motions.

The next example deals with rotary motion in a rather ambiguous type of perception. It is especially interesting because the perceptual choice of alternative was found to depend on eye movement. Figure 2 illustrates the stimulus pattern and presents diagrams of the possible perceptual outcome.

The two dots are moving to and fro in accordance with a sinusoidal function in the vertical and horizontal directions, respectively. They have the same frequency, about 1 cycle/s, but have a phase difference of 90°. From mathematics we know that two such motions given to the same particle result in a circular motion of the particle and in fact we also find something of this effect in the perception of the pattern under study. When one of the points is fixated and followed by the gaze this motion acts as a common component and a frame of reference for the nonfixated motion. Mathematically, this motion, as pointed out, will form a circular orbit round a center located on the fixated point. Also, the percept is mathematically correct here. The nonfixated point is seen as describing an orbital motion about the fixated one while this circular motion is simultaneously anchored to the translatory motion (Fig. 2). Change of fixation from one point to the other immediately results in change of roles of the two dots. The fixated element always determines the perceptual frame of reference. We will return to this effect of eye-movement information.

The perceptual interaction among stimulus elements described above under the term "motion analysis" implies that the distance in visual angle between the elements stays within certain restricted limits. It has been found that distances larger than about 3°–5° only furnish suboptimal results. GOGEL (1974) studied the effect of relative nearness between two moving dots over about 15° and also arranged a conflict between three dots moving at different distances from each other. He found that the degree of interaction among motions faded out with growing angular distance.

The experiments described indicate a fundamental principle in perceptual stimulus decoding. We have found that when two elements are seen in motion against a common frame of reference they are (1) primarily seen as moving relative to each other, i.e., they act as reference frames for each other; furthermore, that (2) the residual component in the display motion remaining after subtraction of this relative motion component in accordance with vector algebra is seen as a motion common to both elements. Let us in the following denote component (1) *the relative motion component* and (2) *the common motion component*. Evidently, the static background acts as a frame of reference for the common motion component and the common motion has the same function for the relative motion component. If one of the two dots represents the moving car in our example above, (p. 680) and the second dot the falling match-box, we are evidently, dealing with one and the same type of perceptual decoding in both cases.

Taking away one of the two interacting elements always results in correct perception of the displayed motion track. This also follows from the above analysis. As observed in the experiments already described, a minimum of two elements is necessary for perceptual interaction of the type studied. This leads to the question of the perceptual effect from displays with a larger number of moving elements. The outcome from some recent experiments (JOHANSSON, 1973b) on motion analysis in the perception of "biological motion" provide an answer to this question. In these experiments, motion patterns representing, e.g., the walking pattern in man, were presented without any concomitant pictorial information by means of the moving-dot technique mentioned above. The theoretic background to the approach was as follows: The human skeleton can be looked upon as a technical device built up from a large number of rigid elements, the bones, connected by joints. In activity, these elements describe more or less pronounced pendulum motions about the joints. All types of bodily activity like walking, running, jumping, etc., bring about a spatiotemporal sequential interaction among the elements in this system which, when described in technical terms, are extremely complex.

If the principle of perceptual vector analysis really is a general principle for motion perception, we must predict that it also determines perception of motions of these skeletal components in motion relative to each other in all types of motion patterns in man and animals. Thus, the study of perception

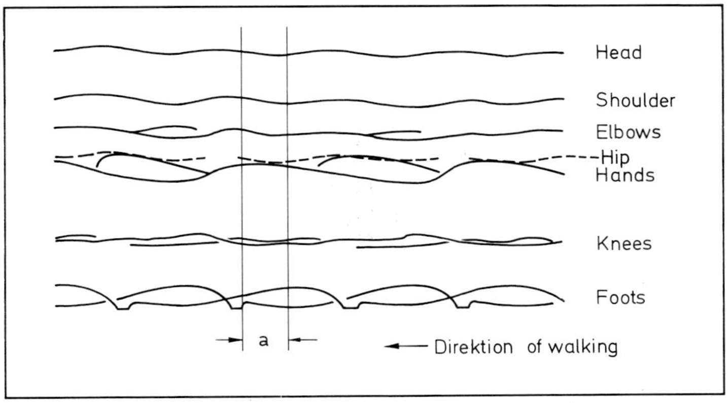

Fig. 3. Open-camera record of the light tracks over about two steps of a walking person. The interval indicated (a) covers the spot motions over 0.2 s which has been found to be sufficient for perceptual integration of the motion pattern to perception of a walking person

of walking patterns can provide a critical test for the general validity of this principle. This was the rationale behind the experiments on biologic motion.

Small luminous points were attached to the main-limb joints of an actor and the actor was filmed in near-darkness while walking, running, dancing, etc. For studies of frontoparallel motion, which is our present concern, ten spots were used, on the shoulder and hip facing the camera and on the camera side of both elbows, wrists, knees, and ankles. Thus, nothing was recorded on the film but a group of ten bright spots, each moving in its own path, but representing the limb joints of a two-dimensional man. The perceptual outcome from watching this movie was extremely positive for the vector analysis model. The swarm of dots on the movie screen was never seen as such. Instead, they were immediately and without option integrated into a structured unit in accordance with the principles for visual vector analysis and seen as a walking person. The perceptual analysis can be briefly described as follows: The stationary background is seen as a reference frame for the hip and shoulder points. This motion acts as a frame of reference for the knee (elbow) motion and finally these latter motions on their part act as reference for the perceived motion of the ankle and wrist elements. A formal vector analysis of the motion of one leg during a short time interval is carried out (see JOHANSSON, 1975).

What is the liminal time for the perceptual organization of such a dot pattern? This question was taken up in a subsequent investigation (JOHANSSON, 1975) where the model for vector analysis was further elaborated. The type of pattern described, representing frontoparallel walking, was used (visual angle distance shoulder-to-ankle was about 3°). In a single blind study, this pattern was shown for short time intervals (0.1–0.5 s) to a group of school children. The result was astonishing: At an exposure time of 0.2 s of the dot pattern all subjects reported seeing a walking man and 40% already saw the man after an exposure of one-tenth of a second. Figure 3 shows an open-camera record of a walking pattern with a time interval of 0.2 s indicated.

One may well ask whether it is really possible perceptually to integrate those short element displacements into a coherent pattern. It is interesting to note that the same type of pattern, presented for 0.25 s, has been included in an educational film [1]. Thousands or viewers spontaneously perceived a walking man from this presentation, so that we may regard the experimental results discussed as well established. These data are also of immediate interest in the study of the neurophysiology of vision, and later some remarks on this aspect will be given.

IV. Stereokinetic Motion Perception From Perspective Transformation

In contrast to central projections from rigid motions in the frontoparallel plane, such projections from rigid motions in all other directions (thus, motions in depth), give rise to size and/or form changes in the projected images. It is easily observed that a central projection from an object in *translatory motion* in depth brings about a shrinking (growing) image on a picture plane and generally also a lateral displacement, and that *rotary motion* of the object results in form changes in the projected image. It is also evident that combinations of translatory and rotary motions of the object result in corresponding combinations of size changes, lateral motion and form changes in the projected image, i.e., rather complex events.

In what respect or to what extent can the eye analyze such a proximal pattern for valid information about the shape and motion of the distal object? This is one of the most important questions for understanding the functioning of the visual system. It is Berkeley's problem applied to kinetic perception.

During the last 40 years, this problem has been attacked in various laboratories. The result is that now at least some basic principles of this aspect of visual functioning have begun to emerge. A good summary of the more important contributions up to 1960 is given by BRAUNSTEIN (1962a).

A frequently used technique in these studies has been the shadow-caster technique. A point source of light throws a shadow of a moving object (the shadow caster) on a translucent screen. This shadow with continuously changing form and/or size is used as stimulus. It represents (or, rather, can be brought to represent) the retinal projection of the object in motion with the traditional depth cues excluded. Two different types of such shadow projection have been applied. In the original one applied among others by METZGER (1934) the light source is set at a considerable distance from the shadow-casting object and the projection screen (see Fig. 5, p. 688), yielding an approximation to a parallel projection. At the Cornell laboratory (GIBSON, 1957), a method for perfect polar projection in the form of shadows was developed. Further theoretic treatments on this method have been brought forward by GOGEL and MERTENS (1966) and by LEE (1969). This method for polar projection is diagrammed in Figure 4.

[1] James B. Maas; Motion Perception I, II, Houghton Mifflin Co. 2 Park Street, Boston, Mass. 02107, USA.

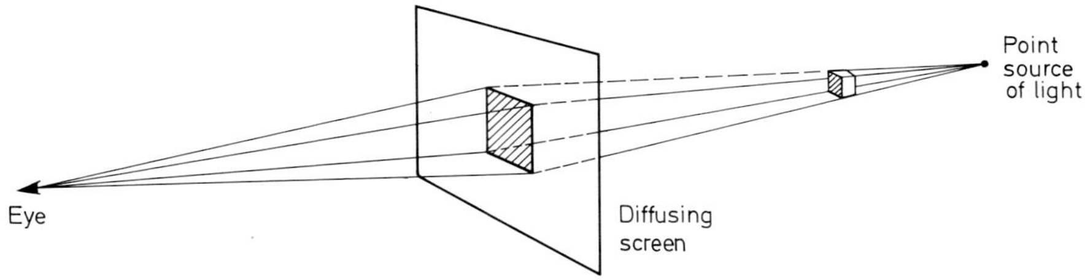

Fig. 4. Simple type example of Gibson's shadow-caster technique with polar projection

Figures drawn on cardboard which are fixed on a rotating turntable and rotating fluorescent objects have also been used as stimuli. In a few cases film technique has been applied. After about 1960, electronic displays controlled by more or less sophisticated devices were found to provide very expedient ways of producing stimulus patterns. The first early example of application of electronic devices is FISICHELLI (1946). GREEN (1961) and BRAUNSTEIN (1962b) first applied digital technique combined with film and JOHANSSON (1964) introduced an analog technique. Since 1970, computer technique has become more and more common as a consequence of the availability of laboratory computers.

After these notes on techniques a look at a number of basic experiments on rotary motion would be useful. Over half a century ago, MUSATTI (1924) studied depth perception from slowly rotating frontal patterns and coined the term "stereokinetic phenomena." His results indicate that proximal transformations representing rigid objects in motion evoked in his subjects perception of rigid objects in motion.

METZGER applied the shadow-caster technique ten years later in some now classic studies. Parallel projection of shadows from groups of vertical rods standing on a rotating horizontal turntable were presented on a translucent screen (see Fig. 5) (METZGER, 1934a, cf. also 1953).

The most general result from METZGER's experiments was that all subjects saw rotary motions in depth, but that the perceived grouping of elements was highly flexible. WHITE and MUESER (1960) have tried to carry the analysis of such patterns a step further. They also found that such stimuli are always perceived as rigid three-dimensional object combinations, but that the percepts in many cases are nonveridical as regards the physical arrangement of rods on the turntable.

An important theoretic discussion this type of stimulus pattern is given by TOSHIMA (1965). As a result of his analysis, TOSHIMA finds that the higher the number of moving elements, the higher are the ratings of rigidity and depth in the percepts. He concludes that factors which strengthen the impression of depth also strengthen the impression of rigidity.

We can regard this latter finding as an indication that the visual system works in accordance with its own geometric rules. It shows that perceived rigidity is filtered out from the proximal event. Geometrically it is of course also possible to describe the pattern under discussion as the projection of elastic structures moving on a frontoparallel plane.

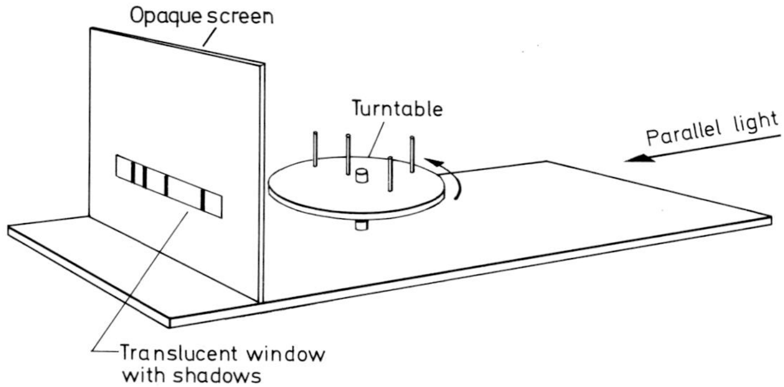

Fig. 5. Sketch of Metzger's experimental setup. See text

WALLACH and his co-workers (WALLACH and O'CONNEL, 1953; WALLACH et al., 1953; WALLACH et al., 1956), have carried out significant studies along the lines drawn by MUSATTI (1924). They coined the term "kinetic depth effect" (KDE) using the shadow-caster technique with approximately parallel projections of rotating objects. WALLACH et al. introduced a great variety of objects and forms as shadow-casters: bent wires, wire outlines, and solid objects.

As a main result they found a strong general trend to perceive the proximal transformations as rigid objects in motion, (objects of the type used as shadow-casters), as soon as the stimulus pattern changed in two dimensions, but to perceive a two-dimensional change when there was a stimulus change in only one dimension. Analogous results were obtained by JOHANSSON (1964), JOHANSSON and Jansson JANSSON (1968) and BÖRJESSON and VON HOFSTEN (1972, 1973) with other techniques.

Two essential conclusions can be drawn from these experiments as compared with the above experiments of the METZGER type. First, we can state that in experiments with displays of the METZGER type there is in fact change mainly in one spatial dimension: the shadows move to and fro but do not change in length (and not effectively in width). However, in the change of velocity, important information is added. WALLACH et al. found, as mentioned above, that changes in only one dimension often result in perceived elasticity instead of rigidity, while simultaneous changes in two dimensions brought about perception of rigid objects. On the other hand we have also found that combinations of a sufficient number of elements in unidimensional change are also effective in this respect. The visual system seems to be able to analyze the relations among the elements in terms of mutually invariant distances, yielding spatial rigidity. Rigidity during rotation implies a common motion of all elements in the perceived structure relative to the center of rotation. Therefore, it is evident that we are in touch with principles for stimulus analysis closely related to the principles established in our analysis of frontoparallel motion.

The second conclusion concerns the degree of specificity (and veridicality) gained from the two-dimensional changes in most of WALLACH's shadow patterns and the patterns of METZGER's type. The first type of stimuli has built in perceptually effective information about the distal stimuli. It results in rather specific and also veridical percepts in spite of the impoverished stimulation, while the latter type is far more nonspecific.

Parallel projection as applied b by METZGER and by WALLACH and his co-workers brings about a certain degree of elasticity and also ambiguity if treated as central projection. (Parallel projection can be looked upon as a central projection with the center of projection at an infinite distance.)

The merit of making a strong point of perspectivity as the principal source of information in visual space perception derives from J.J. GIBSON. In *The Perception of the Visual World* (1950) he already drew heavily on principles of central perspective in his analyses of visual stimulus, and his "gradient theory" is essentially an application of these principles. Prior to any other perceptionist, he also stressed the fundamental importance of characteristics in continuous perspective transformations as a probable basis for stereokinetic perception. Early source papers in this respect are GIBSON (1957) and GIBSON and GIBSON (1957). A broad review of GIBSON's theoretic position is given in GIBSON (1966), and further developed in GIBSON (1968).

In GIBSON and GIBSON (1957) a correct central projection with the shadow caster technique was put into practice for the first time. One of the problems raised in this paper was: "Does the appropriate parameter of continuous perspective transformations with polar projection always give the perception of the changing slant of a constant shape?" Various types of two-dimensional patterns were used (size about 7° visual angle), both squares and "ameboid" forms, and the surfaces were rotated about a central vertical axis over a series of angles from the frontoparallel plane (15°–70°). The result was that all subjects during most part of the exposure saw rigid figures changing their slant. About one-third of the subjects reported seeing two-dimensional form changes for some short time intervals. Thus, if we substitute "nearly always" for "always" in the above question, its experimental answer is affirmative. The perceived slants were in fairly good correspondence with the object slants, but with some underestimation, as shown in Figure 6.

EPSTEIN (1964) conducted a very similar experiment. He found that his 75 subjects perceived rigid objects in motion and that they could identify the shape of the projected objects. EPSTEIN obtained estimates of the angles which, when plotted in the same diagram as the GIBSON and GIBSON one, result in practically the same function. Later GIBSON's theoretic analysis was further elaborated by HAY (1966). Also TOSHIMA (1965), BRAUNSTEIN (1966, 1968, 1972), JOHANSSON and JANSSON (1968), JANSSON (1969), JOHANSSON (1974a, 1974b) and SHAW, MCINTYRE and MACE (1974) treated the problem about perceptual information from perspective transformations from a theoretic point of view.

The next important theoretic progress is found in a paper by VON FIEANDT and GIBSON (1959). These authors studied perceptual sensitivity to differences between perspective and nonperspective transformations, using the shadow-caster technique with one rigid and one elastic two-dimensional shadow-caster. They found that their subjects were capable of seeing differences between these two types of transformation, cf. also VON FIEANDT, 1961. GREEN's (1961) investigation on figural coherence from polar and parallel projection as well as BRAUNSTEIN's (1962) are relevant in this context.

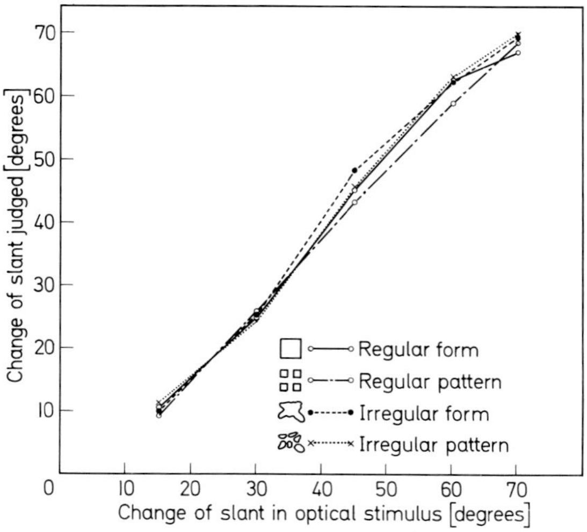

Fig. 6. Relations between projected and perceived slant under kinetic conditions. (From GIBSON and GIBSON, 1957)

Similarly related are a number of investigations on the difference between central and parallel projection of rotary motion regarding the question of perceptual ambiguity of direction of rotation. See BRAUNSTEIN (1966, 1972), HERSCHBERGER (1967), HERSCHBERGER et al. (1974) and JANSSON and BÖRJESSON (1969). A general result from these investigations is that parallel projection of rotary motion brings about total ambiguity of direction of rotation. However, they also indicate that central projection under small angles is equally ineffective for purposes of specifying in this respect. Projections under angles of less than 15° have a very limited effect.

The above review of research on stereokinetic perception is far from complete, but most of the material of essential interest from a theoretic point of view has been included. Thus, we can proceed with the summarizing of some main results.

A general finding is that optical flows representing perspective transformations projected from rigid objects rotating in depth yield perception of objects of constant shape which perform rotary (oscillatory) motions. An important restriction in the generality of this rule, however, is that if the proximal pattern changes only in one dimension there is a reduced probability of seeing rigid relations. It seems as if the visual system has only a limited capacity for abstracting spatial invariance from one-dimensional transformations. Geometrically, such projections can be described as anomalous.

At small angles there is hardly any perceptible difference between central and parallel projection. It has also been found that continuous transformations under parallel projection induce perception of an almost rigid object in about the same way as do continuous transformations under central projection and visual angles of less than 5°.

V. Stereokinesis From Nonperspective Transformations

The investigations reported so far have a serious experimental limitation in common. They are all restricted to stimulus material representing correct (or semicorrect) perspective projections from rigid objects. The problem of stimuli representing form changes of objects was not studied. This limitation was fully acceptable in the exploratory phases of research. The experiments reported brought about some important answers concerning visual information processing of perspective transformations.

However, as soon as we ask for the perceptual principles of this procedure, the experimental restriction mentioned must be removed. Only when projections from both rigid motions and form changes are introduced as experimental variables and when, furthermore, these conditions can be mixed in the same projections, will we get material for a more general conclusion about the principles of perception of motion and form changes.

As far as I know, it was VON FIEANDT and GIBSON (1959; cf. also VON FIEANDT, 1961) who took the first step toward in investigating perceptual effects of nonperspective transformations. They asked for visual sensitivity for perspective transformations as compared with elastic transformations and found that their subjects could differentiate between these two conditions. VON FIEANDT's and GIBSON's results show that the visual system is able to differentiate rigidity during motion from elastic changes. However, in everyday experience perceived objects reveal not only form changes *or* motion but often also form changes *during* motions. Furthermore, most often the motion of an object is a combination of translation and rotation. In everyday perception the eye is certainly able to separate these different types of events from a complex proximal pattern of change. As examples we may think of the perceived movements of most living beings, which combine translations, partial rotations and elastic deformations, or imagine a tree in the wind simultaneously describing both gross pendulum motions and silhouette changes. Waves or whorls on a water surface, flames, the motion and form changes of cigarette smoke or of a cloud in storm, and many other nonmechanical changes like the locomotion of larvas are additional examples. Apparently, man and all kinds of animals are able to pick up specific and valid information from these patterns of change. How is this possible?

This problem was raised explicitly by JOHANSSON (1964). When form changes are accepted as a possible perceptual category, there is no specific geometric information in the proximal pattern of change even if we accept an ability to recognize perspective transformations. This fact was a starting point for an experimental analysis. The following problem was raised: How does the visual apparatus react to nonperspective proximal patterns of change, never met outside the laboratory?

A new type of proximal stimulus patterns was introduced. Bright homogeneous parallelograms (usually rectangles) were generated on a CRT and projected into a perceptually empty space. These parallelograms changed continuously and independently in both the vertical and horizontal dimension (0.5 Hz). In

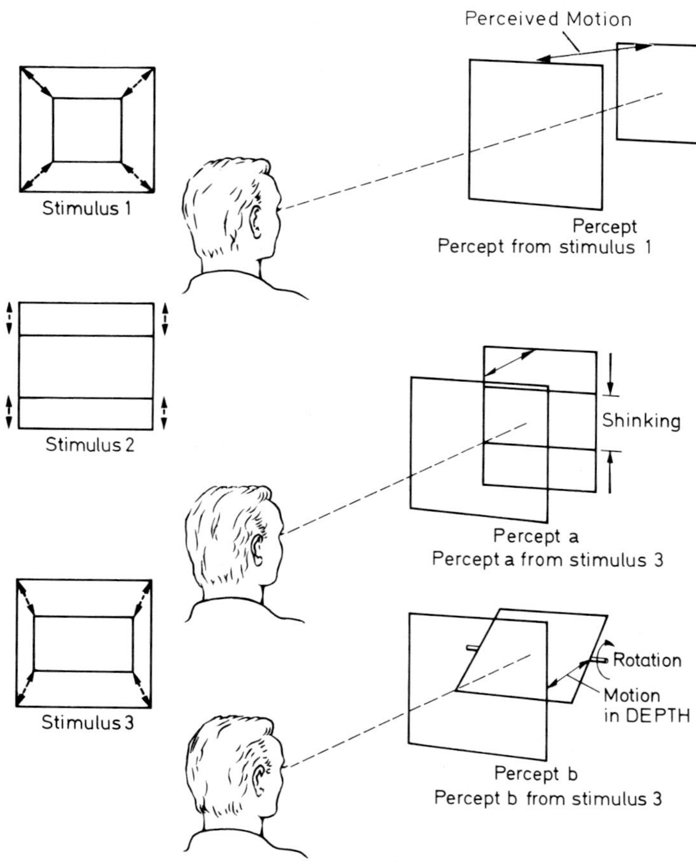

Fig. 7. Diagrams of size or/and shape changes in a frontal stimulus square together with illustrations of corresponding percepts. See text. (From JOHANSSON, 1964 and 1975)

some experiments the two changes had the same frequency, in other cases different frequencies were introduced. Figure 7 gives some examples of such stimulus transformations. The perception of a frontal screen carrying the stimulus patterns was avoided. A kind of telescope projected the pattern as a virtual image directly into the eye. Thus, the pattern was seen as freely hanging in a dark empty space.

The outcome from this set of experiments was instructive. In most cases the visual apparatus responds in a specific way: At maximal rigid motion, translation and/or rotation of approximately form-constant objects was perceived, but often a "rigid" motion together with a simultaneous change of shape of the artificial objects was seen as well.

The perceptually most simple of these displays is diagrammed in Figure 7 (a). The figure undergoes a proportionally equal shrinking-growing in the vertical and the horizontal dimension, thus, only a change in size. This pattern is always seen as a sagittal motion in depth.

Figure 7(b) shows a pattern of change where the y-motion is the same as in Figure 7(a), but where there is no change in the x-dimension. This evokes an ambiguous percept. About 50% of the subjects saw a motion in depth and preferably a rotation of a rigid or semirigid square about a central horizontal axis. The other group perceived a frontal surface changing its shape from a square to a rectangle, etc. Thus, in this experiment as well, change in only one dimension was not an efficient signal for rigid motion.

In Figure 7(c) we find a more complex type of figural change. The x- and y-changes are in phase but they are not proportionally equal and thus, this pattern also represents a change of shape of the surface. The perceptual response to this type of pattern is of decisive importance for an understanding of the geometric principles underlying the perceptual decoding of optical flows. The perceived event is in fact a perfect combination of the percept from Figures 7(a) and (b). The subjects report seeing a surface moving backward and simultaneously 1) rotating or 2) shrinking. The relative length of the perceived backward motion corresponds with the relative size change in the dimension with the least amount of change. Both alternatives are equally interesting. In the first case we find from a mathematical view point that two rigid motions are more or less accurately abstracted from a nonperspective pattern, as if the pattern were a combination of two perspective transformations. In the second case a continuous perspective transformation representing a translatory motion in depth is abstracted from the stimulus pattern and the entire residual change is seen as a form change.

Thus, instead of reacting on a nonperspective transformation with perception of a surface changing its shape, the visual system in a seemingly far more complicated way abstracts as much of continuous perspective transformations as is actually possible. In this respect, we can regard the visual analysis as somewhat more efficient in the perceivers' reporting translation and rotation of a semirigid object as compared with the translation-plus-form-change group.

Another still more drastic example of a sensory analysis of a proximal event in mutually independent components is taken from the same investigation (JOHANSSON, 1964). Figure 8 shows the proximal pattern of change over time of a homogeneous square surface. The frequency of the x-change was 0.9 Hz and of the y-change 0.3 Hz, which bring about a continuous complex change of shape and size. The description of the percept elicited by this pattern was summarized as follows:

"A rectangular surface rotates about one of its vertical edges. The axis of rotation moves continuously toward and away from the observer. During this motion and synchronous with it, the surface shrinks and grows in the horizontal dimension. When it is far away it has the shape of a horizontally oriented rectangle and when it is at the closest turning point it has the form of a square", (p. 199). Thus, in this case, we find a simultaneous translation in depth, a rotation in depth and a form change in the same perceptual object.

JOHANSSON (1964) introduced a vector model for the description of the proximal event in a way corresponding to the perceptual events. This model can be regarded as an elaboration of the model for two-dimensional vector analysis described above (p. 681 ff.). Proportionally equal vectors in x- and y-dimension

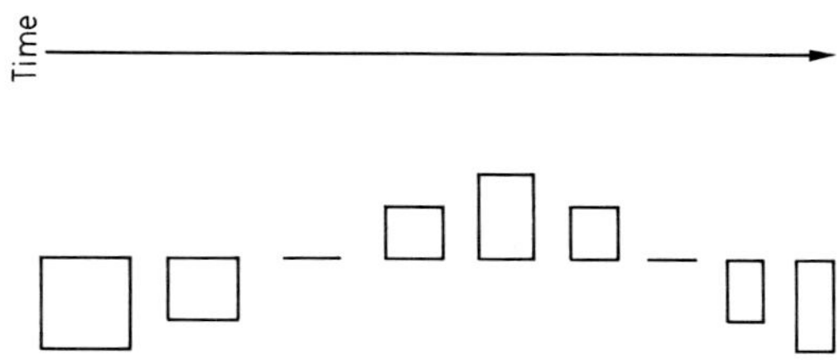

Fig. 8. Diagram of a continuous form change and displacement of a rectangle. It is perceived as a rectangular surface rotating about one of its vertical sides while the axis is moving sagittally in depth and the rectangle changes its shape. See text. (After JOHANSSON, 1964)

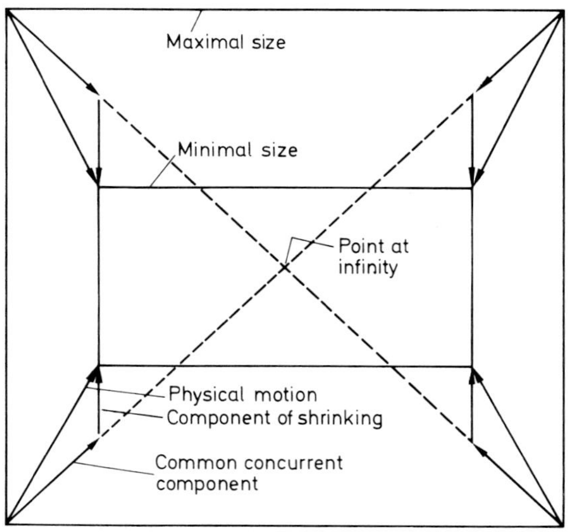

Fig. 9. A vector analysis of non-proportional change in the stimulus (see Fig. 7 c) corresponding to the perceptual analysis of such stimulus changes in common and relative motions. See text

were abstracted and added and their sum interpreted as stimulus for translation in depth. The residuals were treated as stimuli for rotation, if this was projectively possible, and otherwise as form change, (see Fig. 9). Predictions from this model proved to correspond closely with the actual percepts.

While this model was given in strictly quantitative terms, the experimental data were at best semiquantitative. In order to confirm, reject, or modify, this model when it is a question of translatory motion in depth, MARMOLIN and ULFBERG (1972) and MARMOLIN (1973a, b) carried out a series of quantitative experiments. The result was that the basic structure of the model proposed was found to be valid but it also demonstrated that the model was, to a certain extent, a simplification. When the linear change of the pattern was more than about 40%, a certain underestimation of the computed translatory motion in depth was evident. MARMOLIN (1973b) was able to derive a formula including a component of perceived form change which was shown to describe the stimulus-percept relations even when the stimulus pattern contracted down to 5% of its original linear size.

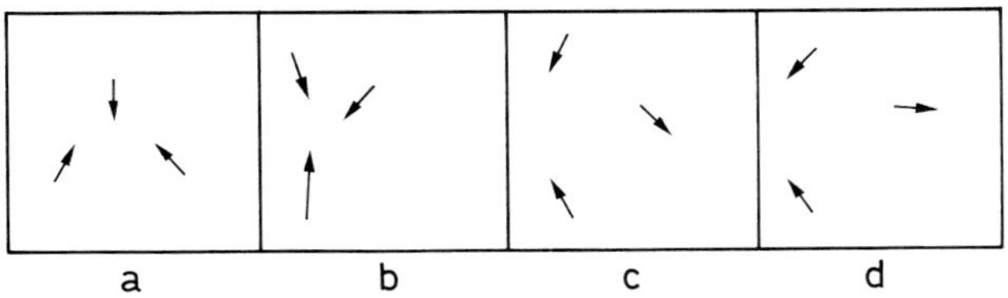

Fig. 10a–d. Combinations of motions of three dots (BÖRJESSON and VON HOFSTEN, 1973b). (a) and (b) generally were perceived as form constant triangles in simultaneous rotation and translation in depth, while (c) and (d) most often were seen as triangles rotating in depth and changing their shape at the same time. (After BÖRJESSON and VON HOFSTEN, 1973b)

BÖRJESSON and VON HOFSTEN (1972, 1973) also dealt with the problem of spontaneous sensory organization in motion perception. They used an reduced type of display with only two or three dots moving in rectilinear paths in a homogeneous frontal plane. Figure 10 shows some of their three-dot patterns.

These papers represent an important contribution to our knowledge about spontaneous perceptual organization of geometrically fully inspecific stimuli. The gross results again were that also under these extremely impoverished stimulus conditions, two-dimensional change in distance and/or direction in such patterns, in most cases evoke perception of rigid or more-or-less rigid objects, rods or triangles. One-dimensional changes again brought about ambiguity between rigid motions and form changes. As in JOHANSSON's investigation, the three-dot patterns are liable to effect perception of simultaneous rotations and translations but may also bring about deformations.

The authors also elaborated a vector model describing the proximal event in correspondence with the percepts. This, like JOHANSSON's model, separates relative and common vectors in the proximal events.

The vector models commented on above have a further characteristic in common. They abstract components of rigid motion under central projection but do so in the framework of Cartesian vector fields. JOHANSSON (1974a, 1974b) discussed the theoretic advantages of a more direct application of projective geometry in the study of visual space perception. The relational invariances under central projection which are fundamental in this geometry are, as we have found above, in far better correspondence with visual stimulus analysis than are the Euclidean conditions for similarity and congruence. Therefore, it was argued that a model founded on the abstracting of these invariances in the optical flow provided a far more adequate and simple starting point than the Euclidean analysis of the proximal stimulus.

In this connection JOHANSSON studied the perceptual relevance for perception of rotation of the projective invariances of central projections of all types of conic sections. One of these experiments (1974b) is of considerable interest for our present analysis of visual data treatment. In this experiment the visual system was enforced to choose between two ways of interpreting a proximal event, one in terms of Euclidean invariance and the other in terms of projective invariance. The display was simple and similar to the BÖRJESSON and VON HOFSTEN dot patterns. Two bright dots, moving with constant speed, traced a frontal rectangle as diagrammed in Figure 11a. The display was seen in parallel light through a collimator which had a homogeneous, empty space as a background.

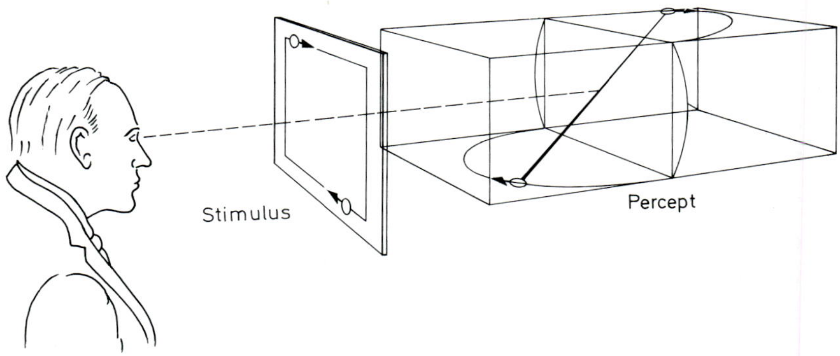

Fig. 11. Stimulus consisting of two bright dots synchronously tracing a rectangle is perceived as end points of an invisible rigid rod rotating in a jerky manner like tracing the inside of a rectangular cube. (From JOHANSSON, 1975)

When only one of the dots was displayed, there was no problem to see the tracing of a frontal, rectangular path and it was the only possible percept. Adding the second dot drastically changed the percept. Now a complex rotary motion was seen. The two dots became end points on an otherwise invisible straight line or rod of constant length. This rod was seen as performing an extremely jerky double rotation, which might be equalled to rotation on an oscillating plane (see Fig. 11).

Our conclusion is bound to be that the primary concern for the visual system in this case was not a Euclidean description of the motion but, instead, projectively invariant relations between the two dots. Indeed, it seems as if the visual network were wired exclusively for this projective type of analysis.

Finally, we will use JOHANSSON'S (1973b) study of biologic motion as a further indication information spontaneous sensory decoding of the optical flow in terms of hierarchical sets of relative projective invariances. Not only stimulus patterns representing frontoparallel walking were analyzed in this paper but also patterns generated from walking in other directions (45°, 90°, etc.) from the frontal plane. The perceptual analysis of these patterns was equally efficient, spontaneous and rapid as in the frontoparallel case. Evidently the frontoparallel case is simply a special case of projective stimulus decoding.

VI. Perception of Bending Motion

So far we have dealt with only two categories of perceptual events: rigid motion and form change. Let us finally pay some attention to stimulus patterns eliciting a third interesting category, namely the bending of a surface like a sheet of paper or metal foil.

JANSSON and JOHANSSON (1973) studied various proximal events that give rise to such percepts. The stimulus patterns were initial outline squares changing their shapes in various ways as exemplified in Figure 12.

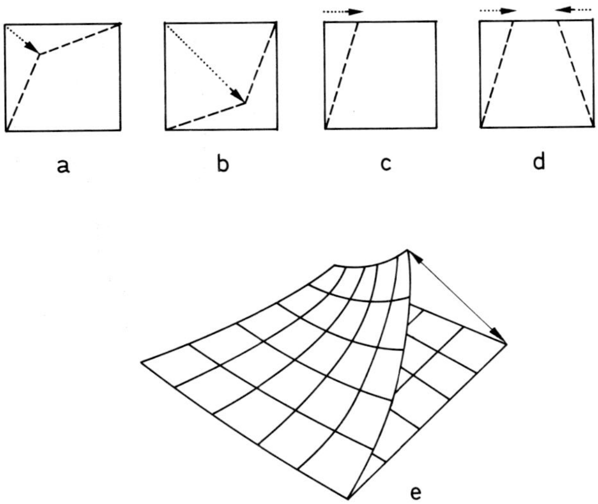

Fig. 12a–e. Examples of form changes of a frontal square (a to d) evoking perception of bending of a flexible surface. (e) illustrates the percept from (a)

Of these stimuli, (a) and (b) were generally perceived as a surface of constant but flexible form, being bent along the diagonal AC. (Three subjects out of 30 reported seeing (b) as a stretching.) The displays (c) and (d) were perceptually ambiguous. About 50% of the subjects reported being of a surface while another group (about 40%) saw stretching of a frontal surface.

Interestingly enough, Figures 12(a) and (b) are easily described as a projection of a static triangle ADC and another triangle ABC rotating about the common line AC. In this way we find that this pattern represents a correct projection of a bending or folding of a surface. We also find that Figures 12(c) and (d) can only be regarded as rough and rather incorrect approximations to such projections. In spite of this, a majority of the subjects perceived bending instead of simple stretching.

The results from these experiments on bending motion are in agreement with the other experiments on nonperspective transformations described above. We are now able to summarize these results: Neither distal object constancy nor proximal perspective transformation are prerequisites for perception of objects moving in a specific way in three-dimensional space. Instead, we must establish that we have a situation as if the sensory apparatus were programmed to abstract motion (translations and/or rotations) by separating out from every kind of optical flow hierarchic sets of components representing perspective transformations. This would explain why we can see, for instance, a ring of cigarette smoke move through the air and simultaneously change its shape in a complex way.

From early research on effects of *perspective* transformations of the type of the "kinetic depth effect" it was reasonable to conclude that such stimuli were a necessary condition for perception of rigid objects moving in depth. In this respect, the studies on *nonperspective* transformations have extended our knowledge significantly. They demonstrate that this conclusion was far too restrictive. Instead, we can now say that *the visual system is constructed for abstracting projective invariances from any type of optical flows.*

Furthermore, the extensive set of data from three-dimensional motion perception presented here allows a second conclusion. The traditional description of proximal stimulus in terms of retinal images paired with the equally traditional Euclidean analysis and comparison of these images in terms of congruence and incongruence is inadequate. For the visual system, as we have established, invariance is of the relative type basic to projective geometry. Applying the absolute measurements of Euclidean geometry as a model for sensory analysis of the stimulus flow has hardly any biologic support and results in the most unwieldy theoretic constructs.

Possibly the most convenient way of dealing with these complex transformation patterns will be to leave the basis in absolute coordinates and apply description in relative, homogeneous coordinates.

VII. Visual Information about Locomotion

In our treatment of the eye as a receiver of optical information, (pp. 678–680) we stated that the optical center of the eye, the nodal point, is seldom at rest relative to the environment. We also underlined that—in accordance with the principles of projective geometry—the optical flow determined by a nodal point moving relative to a stationary environment represents a continuous perspective transformation in the whole array of incoming light. Motion of an organism in the environment is called *locomotion*. In this term we will include both locomotion proper, i.e., displacement of the whole body and partial locomotion in the form of such motion of parts of the body: the head and the limbs.

GIBSON and his co-workers have made an impressive contribution to the study of visual information during motion and have introduced the term *motion perspective* for the systematic retinal flow of differential element motion (GIBSON et al., 1955; GIBSON et al., 1959; GIBSON, 1966). Especially important is the paper with OLUM and ROSENBLATT (GIBSON et al., 1955) in which a mathematical analysis of the stimulus flow in the eyes of an airplane pilot was carried out. Figure 13 is a graphic illustration of such an analysis in terms of motion vectors given in angular coordinates. A closely related analysis of the information contained in the flow pattern generated at the driver's place in a moving car is presented by GORDON and MICHAELS (1963). GORDON (1965) rigorously specified a spheric representation of the optical flow due to locomotion. LEE (1974) has recently presented an elegant and highly instructive analysis of the optical flow from locomotion by applying cylindrical coordinates, which seems to have great didactic advantages.

Another important study of visual locomotion information has been presented by NAKAYAMA and LOOMIS (1974). They applied an analysis of the Gordon type, thus sticking to the spheric model. The most interesting aspect

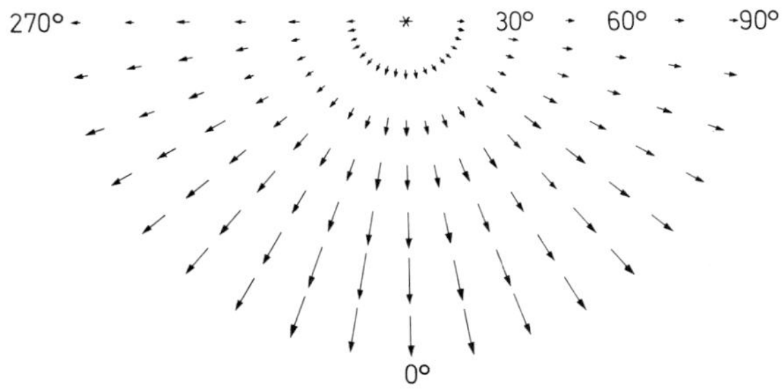

Fig. 13. The flow pattern into the eyes of a pilot during level flight; angular coordinate system. (From GIBSON, OLUM and ROSENBLATT)

of this contribution is the elaboration of a physiologic model for sensory analysis of the flow able to abstract relative projective invariances. They propose a "convexity function," representing a model for center-surround interaction in receptive units. I regard this as a highly promising contribution in this field.

While we find a number of sophisticated treatments on the geometry of locomotion stimulation there exist, to my knowledge, very few experimental contributions. LISHMAN and LEE (1973) have introduced an experimental device for studies of visual locomotion effects which has already produced results important. Experimental studies, however, are mainly found in the applied sector in connection with studies on aircraft landing problems. In a more or less direct way they are based on GIBSON's "center-of-expansion" theory.

VIII. Neurophysiological Aspects Related to the Relativistic Theory of Motion Perception

Nowadays a substantial amount of neurophysiologic knowledge about visual feature detectors sensitive to direction of motion, velocity of motion, orientation of moving contours etc., and even about cells which interact with, and respond to, simultaneous visual and vestibular signals, has been gained. For a comprehensive review and list of references see GRÜSSER and GRÜSSER-CORNEHLS (1969, 1973).

In spite of the extraordinary advancement in this field, the implicit model for sensory stimulus processing underlying its current experimental paradigms is rather unsophisticated. Generally, this model seems to be an absolute-motion model, or more specifically, a motion-over-the retina model. This type of model seems to have been regarded as self-evident in most parts of the research on motion-sensitive cells. In the few cases where two spots in motion over the same area were introduced, the experiment—at least to my knowledge—deal not with responses to relative motion, but rather with inhibition effects, summation effects, etc.

This abolute-motion model, however, is clearly at variance with the relativistic theory for motion perception discussed above. In our analysis, we found good experimental evidence that the perceptual organization of complex systems of relative motions is an automatic and extremely rapid process just as if it were already accomplished in the initial phase of sensory response. Thus, we can reasonably assume that this seemingly automatic perceptual organization is a consequence of a primary neural "wiring" of the type investigated in receptive-field research, and I will give this hypothesis special consideration.

Moreover, if this hypothesis is correct, it has important consequences for neurophysiologic research. It clearly implies that the recording of single-cell responses from a single element in motion represents only a very special and very simple case of neural processing of moving stimuli. It also means that it would be misleading to regard these responses as end products in cases of relative motion as well, and it is equally misleading to assume that adding the second element in the above studies of perceptual vector analysis would not influence the perception of the motion of the first element. Therefore we must hypothesize that adding a second element within a receptive field, moving relative to the first, will drastically change the neural response at some specific point in the receptive system.

C. Perceptual Dynamics in Vision

It is a tradition in physics to break up the study of the motions of material bodies into two subdisciplines: *kinematics* and *dynamics*. Kinematics describes possible motions of material bodies, and dynamics is the study of motions of bodies as a result of forces. Thus, in kinematics there is no reference to force acting on the body, while in dynamics the concept of force is of central importance.

Our above analysis of perceived motion from information in the stimulus can be said to constitute some main features of perceptual kinematics representing a perceptual counterpart to physical kinematics. However, there also exists a perceptual analogy to dynamics, namely, a study of perceived physical forces in moving perceptual objects. I will comment briefly on two types of such studies: perceived causality in moving objects and perception of the gravitational force.

I. Perception of Causality

ALBERT MICHOTTE is a most prominent name in the study of causality perception. His book *La perception de la causalité* (1946, English translation *The Perception of Causality*, 1963) elegantly initiated this area of research.

The basic event studied by MICHOTTE is an application of the old Hume example of causality. A billiard ball is seen moving toward a second ball at rest. The first ball hits the second one and stops, while the second starts moving. The motion of this second ball is perceived as *caused* by energy released from the first ball. MICHOTTE simulated this event by curves on a large disk rotating behind a screen with a horizontal slot.

MICHOTTE's technique was somewhat primitive but it produced acceptable results. Today, electronic techniques have been developed using a CRT as the primary display, which avoids disturbing artifacts in the initial method.

MICHOTTE worked in a highly systematic way and was able to isolate the main factors in causality perception. He investigated mechanical causality, always including some type of motion, but he also tried to establish causality effects from coordinated changes in perceptual qualities. While he was highly successful in establishing a mechanical causality response, the endeavor to demonstrate a causality perception from coordinated quality changes was in vain. For instance, a temporally correct relation between color changes of two objects does not produce any impression of causal relations between the two events.

The mechanical causality perception from different types of stimuli was found to follow given spatiotemporal rules. Rather strict relations were demonstrated between, e.g., speed of the active part and the appearance of perceived causality.

Among the essential conditions for mechanical causality mentioned by MICHOTTE is the existence in the perceptual field of two objects, one active and one passive, and that the active object be in motion before the passive object starts. This is demonstrated by a systematic variation of the experimental conditions.

An important conclusion reached is that the perception of causality seems to follow rigid and rather mechanical rules of a noncognitive character. MICHOTTE regards some such principles as basic functions of the visual system, and not determined by cognitive factors. One argument is the existence of so-called paradoxical causality where the passive element is given higher speed than the elements causing its motion. When the appropriate spatiotemporal conditions are given, a causal process is perceived.

MICHOTTE's primary work has been followed up by himself and a large number of other investigators. A most comprehensive list of investigations of perception of causality including about 40 titles is given in CRABBÉ (1967).

II. Perception of the *g*-Force

The perception of mechanical causality represents perception of conservation of physical force in the form of a transfer of such a force from one object to another. JOHANSSON and JANSSON (1968) have carried out related preliminary investigations with the goal of studying a possible perceptual identification of a motion due to the *g*-force. The subject's task was to adjust the speed of a falling body until it simulates a free fall. Thus, he has to produce the constant 9.8 in the equation: $g = 9.8\ \text{m/s}^2$. The results collected imply a fairly good ability to identify a correct fall. When the constant is higher than 9.8, an extra force acting on the object is perceived and when it is low, the motion seems to be retarded by an invisible medium more dense than air.

D. Perception of Velocity

In a classic study J.F. BROWN (1931) found that the same physical velocity was perceived differently depending on the actual of frame reference. A row of small squares was seen as moving through a window. Doubling all linear dimensions in a comparison field, and thus the size of both the window and the squares, resulted in the physical speed of the targets also having to be roughly doubled before the subjects reported equal velocity when successively comparing the two fields.

This finding implies that perception of velocity is not, as was traditionally assumed, a question of absolute rate of displacement relative to the retinal surface but rather depends on the rate of displacement relative to a frame of reference. Perception of velocity depends on spatial relations rather than absolute speed. Of course, this is what also follows from our accepting perspectivity as determining space perception.

That velocity perception depends on relative rather than absolute change is also clearly demonstrated in an experiment by JOHANSSON (1950a) and in similar experiments by COHEN (1964). In these experiments, subjects were asked to match successively the velocity in two fields, one with only one dot moving to and fro in accordance with a sine function and the other with two such dots moving along the same line in opposite phase or some other phase relations. Under these conditions also it was the relative velocity in the two-dot display which determined the perception of velocity in this field. Thus, when the two dots moved in opposite phase, the velocity of the single dot had to be approximately doubled before a match between the two displays was obtained.

RUNESON (1974) has demonstrated that at the onset of motion of a dot constant physical speed is not perceived as such. After the first moment there is usually a rather sudden reduction of the perceived velocity. RUNESON identified a type of acceleration which he terms "natural motion" which is perceived as constant from the onset. In the equation of this motion a factor representing natural inertia is included (cf. also JOHANSSON, 1950a and GOLDSTEIN and WIENER 1963).

E. Apparent Visual Motion

The distinction between perceived real motion and apparent motion is well established. The main difference between these two categories is found in the proximal event, not in the perceptual event. In the first case we are dealing with a continuous motion or form change in the proximal stimulus while in the second case it is a temporal coordination of brightness changes in static proximal patterns that produces motion perception. I will briefly comment on two types of apparent motion which are of special interest for our discussion.

I. Stroboscopic Motion

If a surface *A* is exposed on a screen for a short time interval, e.g., 0.1 s, and after a short delay of about the same length (0.06–0.2 s) a surface *B* at some distance from A is flashed, an observer sees a surface move from *A* to *B*. This is a typical laboratory example of stroboscopic motion.

The stroboscope was long regarded as something of a curiosity, but when the photographic film technique was introduced its principle was carried over to the film projector. We know that the stroboscopic technique very rapidly became established throughout western culture. Thus, it is easy to understand that psychologists with an interest in visual perception turned their attention to this useful perceptual effect. For a historical review, see BORING (1942).

Some more or less sporadic studies of stroboscopic motion preceded WERTHEIMER's famous study (1912) which is also regarded as the starting point for Gestalt psychology. WERTHEIMER was the first scientist to analyze the effect systematically in terms of the relationship between the stimulus and the percept. In experiments he established how the perceptual outcome was due to strict conditions regarding temporal and spatial relations among stimulus elements.

WERTHEIMER was, for instance, able to demonstrate how time intervals shorter than 0.06 s brought about simultaneous perception of two static surfaces, while intervals longer than 0.2 s resulted in perception of two static surfaces flashing successively. The time intervals between these limits gave rise to perceptual motion. Perception of motion was also dependent on spatial distance between the stimuli.

WERTHEIMER stressed that under special suboptimal conditions (between optimal motion and succession) the subject could see motion without any moving object. This was what he called the pure ϕ. In his hypothetic neurophysiologic construct this pure ϕ was an indication of a neuroelectrical shortcircuiting in the cortex, a wandering of an electrical potential from one stimulus localization in the brain to the other.

WERTHEIMER was also able to demonstrate that, contrary to a previous assumption, motion perception from stroboscopic stimulation was not dependent on eye movements. He proposed that there was no real difference, from the physiologic point of view, between perception of real motion and stroboscopic motion.

WERTHEIMER's study was followed by a very large number of studies on stroboscopic motion. KORTE (1915) tried to establish the relation between the relevant factors and gave the formulations known as "Korte's laws." Nowadays it is accepted that these principles are not laws but approximations lacking strict validity.

Good summaries regarding stroboscopic motion and extensive reference lists are found in NEFF (1937) and LEHMANN (1938–39). Recently, KOLERS (1972) has published a monograph on his studies of motion perception using the stroboscopic method. His monograph affords an extensive review of motion perception but includes perception of real motion as well, while intermodal stroboscopic motion is also reviewed and evaluated. Because of its broad theoretic approach it is one of the most important contributions to the study of motion perception from stroboscopic stimulation.

II. Neurophysiologic Background for Stroboscopic Motion

As mentioned earlier, WERTHEIMER hypothetized that a kind of electrical shortcircuiting of the brain potentials evoked by stimuli is a substratum for motion perception. His lead was elaborated by KÖHLER (1923) and by KOFFKA (1935) and there have been a number of experiments in connection with this theory (see KOFFKA, 1935). It is further elaborated in KÖHLER's and WALLACH's theory of figural aftereffects.

In an investigation on receptive fields in the retina and their central representations, GRÜSSER-CORNEHLS et al. (1963) introduced stroboscopic stimulation in their neurophysiologic research on vision. They found similar responses in the same tectal cells in frogs (*Rana pipiens*) from both real motion and stroboscopic stimulation in the appropriate receptive field. As a stimulus they used a spot (black or white) moving with an angular velocity of about 10°/s in steady light and the same spot moving in flashing stroboscopic illumination (flashes <10 ms). The team was able to state: "All neurons investigated of classes 1 to 3 respond under these conditions to movement of small dark or white spots within the receptive field. Furthermore, the discharges during the activation period after change of position within the receptive field (object stationary) are grouped in the rhythm of the light flashes, if the flash frequency was not higher than 10 to 15 flashes per second. These results indicate that change of position within the receptive field is the true stimulus, which is, of course, under normal conditions, identical with movement within the receptive field. However, there was a maximum time interval for this response to change in position; values depend on other parameters but flashes can be at least 1 s apart. Because large jumps during the interval between two flashes (so long as they are within the receptive field) still elicit a response, the change in position necessary to elicit movement response can be said not to require the successive activation of neighboring or adjacent-but-one receptors."

After so much theoretic speculation about the neurophysiologic basis for stroboscopic motion and about its relation to real motion we now possess some direct empirical material for such discussions.

III. Apparent w-Motion

Other types of apparent motion in vision have also been studied, although most of them are of limited interest in the present context. There is, however, one special type of apparent motion which is of primary interest for our discussion. It is an apparent motion due to slow continuous changes in brightness in one or more stimulus surfaces. This effect was demonstrated by JOHANSSON (1950b); cf. also EKMAN (1952), HALL et al. (1952), HALL and EARLE (1952). It has been discussed under the term "wandering motion," abbreviated to w-motion because of its resemblance with previously known related apparent motion in the tactual field (KATZ, 1927). We will use the term w-motion here for this type of apparent motion.

This apparent motion can be presented both as a motion in a frontoparallel plane and as a radial motion. The frontoparallel motion is produced when the subjects see on a screen two or more bright surfaces in a row changing their brightness. Under reduced illumination, or with an optical arrangement a frequency of 0.3–1 c/s has been found to be optimal. Under these conditions the subject sees a light (or a shadow) moving to and fro in a pendulum motion behind the screen with the bright surfaces seen as transparent windows in an opaque screen. It is not possible to see the pattern as merely surfaces changing their brightness. Under reduced illumination, or with an optical arrangement which excludes the perception of the screen, depth motion is perceived. This also holds true for a single stimulus surface.

The w-motion is being further investigated at the Uppsala laboratory. It is of primary interest to us that the w-motion implies a perceptual decoding yielding constant objects in motion instead of continuously changing luminance on a static surface. This is a good example on the general perceptual principle of decoding as much as possible of stimulus changes to represent motion of constant objects (spatial objects or lights).

F. Motion Thresholds

One of the classical branches of the study of sensory responses to the environment is the investigation of various types of thresholds. In the study of visual motion perception we can mention thresholds for perceived velocity, or for acceleration perception for the shortest perceptible motion in one element, and differential thresholds in comparison of motions, etc.

The subject of motion thresholds is rather complex because of their (spatial and temporal) character. The thresholds always vary with different combinations of these two parameters of sensory recording. GIBSON has emphatically stressed that it is more-or-less meaningless to specify thresholds in motion perception (GIBSON, 1966). Even adopting a less rigorous view than GIBSON's in this respect, it is of great importance to remember that generally the motion thresholds studied are valid only for the stimulus context in which they are recorded.

I. Velocity Thresholds

The first—and still valid—investigations of these types of thresholds stem from the last decades of the nineteenth century. AUBERT (1886) found that for central vision and high contrast an angular stimulus velocity of about 1′/s was the lowest perceptible velocity. For peripheral vision the threshold is reached at around 10′/s–20′/s. AUBERT's results have been supported by later investigators such as BOURDON (1902), GRIM (1911), LEIBOWITZ (1955). LEIBOWITZ has shown how stimulus luminance influences the velocity thresholds to a considerable extent.

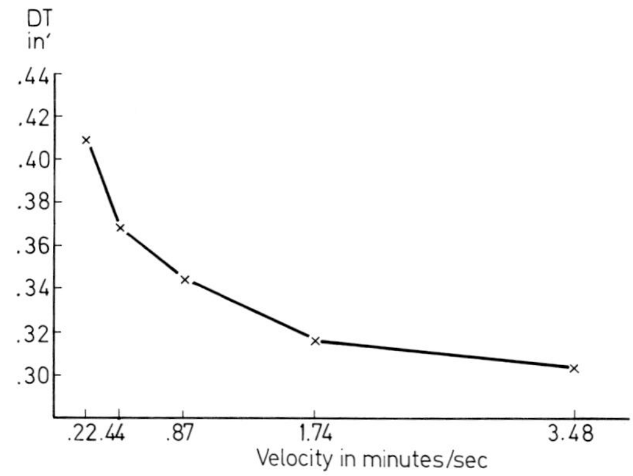

Fig. 14. Displacement thresholds as a function of stimulus velocity. (From JOHANSSON, BÄCKLUND and BERGSTRÖM, 1969)

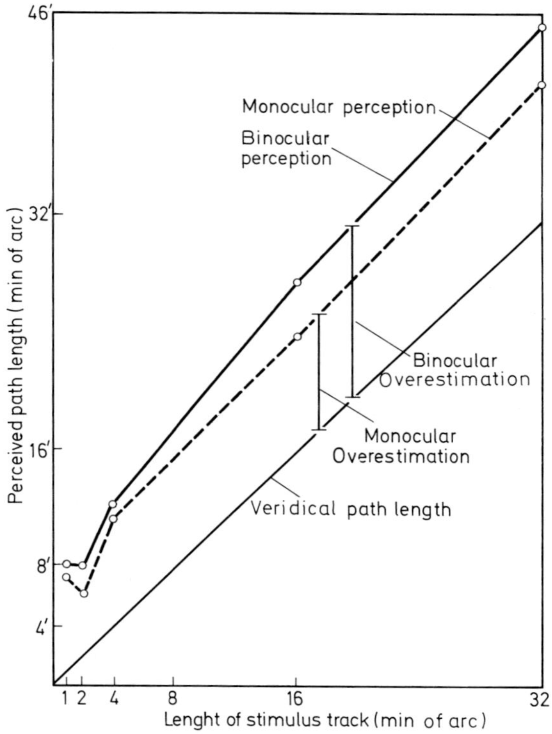

Fig. 15. Perceptual overestimation of short motion tracks in binocular and monocular vision. Stimulus velocity is 16′ visual angle/s. (Replotted from JOHANSSON, 1960)

II. The Displacement Thresholds

Here we find a number of early but reliable results, too. Exner (1875), Stern (1894), and Basler (1906) measured the shortest perceptible motion track. Stern, somewhat surprisingly, found that the displacement threshold is very low, about 15″ of visual angle; Johansson et al. (1970) found that the shortest visible motion track under "hair cross" conditions was of the size order 6–40", verifying Stern's result. They were also able to show that this threshold varies with stimulus angular velocity. This relationship is given in Figure 14. R.H. Brown (1954, 1955, 1958) investigated the effect of luminance, duration, etc., on threshold levels.

Close to the displacement threshold level the length of motion tracks is vastly overestimated, as established by Johansson (1962). This perceptual overestimation plotted as a function of path length (Figure 15) indicates the existence of something like a displacement quantum in the visual processing of motion. Furthermore, this effect is to a certain extent binocularly additive, as shown in the figure, which probably reflects a direct neural amplification of liminal displacement signals.

III. The Differential Thresholds

The least perceptible difference in angular velocity between two elements in motion has been investigated under the notation differential threshold. Because motion is always spatial change relative to a reference frame, velocity thresholds (see above p. 705), and differential thresholds belong to the same category. The difference between these two is that while the reference frame for the classical velocity threshold is the static background, the differential threshold is measured relative to a moving reference frame.

The differential threshold is far more important than the absolute one. The latter must be regarded as rather special, while information about three-dimensional space, as indicated by motion parallax, is due to differential velocities in perceptual elements. Graham et al. (1948) are the best source of knowledge about differential thresholds under various parametric conditions (see also Graham, 1951, 1965).

IV. Acceleration Thresholds

Hick (1950) has studied thresholds for sudden changes and found that the eye is highly sensitive to such changes in velocity. A change of velocity of about 2.5% was enough for perceptual reaction. Thresholds for continuous changes in velocity have been extensively studied by Gottsdanker (1956). He found that the visual sensitivity for such changes is astonishingly high when there are no reference motions available in the visual field. However, also see Runeson (1974) for comparison.

References

Akishige, Y.: Poincare's problem and the law of conservation of perceptual information. In: Contemporary research in psychology and perception. In honorem Kai von Fieandt sexagenarii. Werner Söderström (ed.). Helsinki 1969.

Ames, A.: Visual perception and the rotating trapezoidal window. Psychol. Monogr. **65**, Whole No. 324 (1951).

Aubert, H.: Die Bewegungsempfindung. Pflüger's Arch. ges. Physiol. **39**, 582–601 1886.

Bartley, S.H.: Principles of perception. N.Y.: Harper & Brothers 1958.

Benussi, V.: Versuche zur Analyse taktil erweckter Scheinbewegungen. Archiv f. d. ges. Psychol. **36** (1917).

Boring, E.G.: Sensation and Perception in the History of Experimental Psychology. New York: Appleton-Centuro Co. 1942.

Bourdon, B.: La Perception visuelle de l'espace. Paris: Libraire C. Reinwald, 1902.

Braunstein, M.: The perception of depth through motion. Psychol. Bull. **59**, No. 5, 422–433 (1962).

Braunstein, M.L.: Depth perception in rotating dot patterns. J. Exp. Psychol. **64**, 415–420 (1962).

Braunstein, M.L.: Sensitivity of the observer to transformations of the visual field. J. Exp. Psychol. **73**, 683–687 (1966).

Braunstein, U.L.: Motion and texture as sources of slant information. J. Exp. Psychol. **78**, 247–253 (1968).

Braunstein, M.L.: Perception of rotation in depth. A process model. Psychol. Rev. **79**, 6, 510–524 (1972).

Brown, J.F.: The visual perception of velocity. Psychol. Forsch. **14**, 199–232 (1931).

Brown, R.H.: Velocity discrimination and the intensity-time relation. J. Opt. Soc. Am. **45**, 189–192 (1955).

Börjesson, E. & von Hofsten, C.: Spatial determinants of depth perception in two-dot motion patterns. Perc. & Psychophys. **11**, 4, 263–268 (1972).

Börjesson, E., von Hofsten, C.: Visual perception of motion in depth: Application of a vector model to three-dot motion patterns. Perc. & Psychophys. **13**, 2, 169–179 (1973).

Cohen, R.L.: Problems in motion perception. Uppsala: Lundequistska Bokhandeln 1964.

Crabbé, G.: Les conditions d'une perception de la causalité. Paris: Centre Nat. de la Res. Sc. 1967.

Cross, J., Cross, J.: The misinterpretation of rotary motion. Perc. & Psychophys. **5**, (2), 94–96 (1969).

Day, R.H., Power, R.P.: Frequency of apparent reversal of rotary motion in depth as a function of shape and pattern. Austral. J. Psychol. **15**, 162–174 (1963).

Day, R.H., Power, R.P.: Apparent reversal (Oscillation) of rotary motion in depth: an investigation and a general theory. Psychol. Rev. **72**, 117–127 (1965).

Dimmick, F.L.: An experimental study of visual movement and the phi phenomenon. Amer. J. Psychol. **31**, 317–332 (1920).

Ditchburn, R.W., Ginsburg, B.L.: Vision with a stabilized retinal image. Nature **170**, 36–37 (1952).

Duncker, K.: Über induzierte Bewegung. Psychol. Forsch. **12** (1929).

Ekman, G.: The laws of the wandering phenomenon. Acta Psychol. **8** (1951).

Epstein, W.: Perceptual invariance in the kinetic depth effect. Amer. J. Psychol. **78**, 301–303 (1965).

Epstein, W., Jansson, G., Johansson, G.: Perceived angle of oscillatory motion. Perc. & Psychophys. **3**, 12–16 (1968).

Fieandt, K. von: The perception of a visual shape and of its frame-surface during continuous transformations. Scand. J. Psychol. **2** (1961).

Fieandt, K. von, Gibson, J.J.: The sensitivity of the eye to two kinds of continuous transformations of a shadow-pattern. J. Exp. Psychol. **57**, 344–347 (1959).

Fisichelli, V.R.: Effects of rotational axis and dimensional variations on the reversal of apparent movements in tissajous figures. Amer. J. Psychol. **59**, 669–675 (1946).

Fröbes, S.J.: Lehrbuch der experimentellen Psychologie I, Freiburg: Herder & Co. 1923.

Gibson, J.J.: The perception of the visual world. Houghton Boston: Mifflin Co. 1950.

Gibson, J.J.: Optical motions and transformations as stimuli for visual perception. Psychol. Rev. **64**, 288–295 (1957).

Gibson, J.J.: The senses considered as perceptual systems, New York: Houghton Mifflin Co. 1966.

Gibson, J.J.: What gives rise to perception of motion? Psychol. Rev. **75**, 335–346 (1968).

Gibson, J.J., Gibson, E.J.: Continuous perspective transformations and the perception of rigid motion. J. Exp. Psychol. **54**, 129–138 (1957).

Gibson, E.J., Gibson, J.J., Smith, O.W., Flock, H.: Motion parallax as a determinant of perceived depth. J. Exp. Psychol. **58**, 40–51 (1959).

Gibson, J.J., Olum, P., Rosenblatt, F.: Parallax and perspective during aircraft landings. American Journal of Psychology **68**, 372–385 (1955).

Gogel, W., Mertens, H.: A method of simulating objects moving in depth. Perc. & Mot. Skills **23**, 371–377 (1966).

Gogel, W.: Relative motion and the adjacency principle. Quarterly Journal of Experimental Psychology, **26**, 425–437, 1974.

Goldstein, J., Wiener, C.: On some relations between the perception of depth and of movement. J. Psychol. **55**, 3–23 (1963).

Gordon, D.A.: Static and dynamic visual fields in human space perception. J. Opt. Soc. Am. **55**, 1296–1303 (1965).

Gordon, D.A., Michaels, R.M.: Static and dynamic visual fields in vehicular guidance. Highway Research Record **84**, 1–15 (1963).

Gottsdanker, R.M.: Detection of acceleration of target motion. Psychol. Bull. **53**, 477–487 (1956).

Graham, C.H., Baker, K.E., Hecht, M., Lloyd, V.V.: Factors influencing thresholds for monocular movement parallax. J. Exp. Psychol. **38**, 205–223 (1948).

Graham, C.H.: Visual perception. In Stevens, S.S. (ed.). Handbook of experimental psychology, New York: J. Wiley & Sons 1951.

Graham, C.H.: On some aspects of real and apparent visual movement. J. Opt. Soc. Am. **53**, 1019–1025 (1963).

Graham, C.H.: Vision and visual behavior, New York: John Wiley & Sons 1965.

Green, B.F. Jr.: Figure coherence in the kinetic depth effect. J. Exp. Psychol. **62**, 272–282 (1961).

Grim, K.: Über die Genauigkeit der Wahrnehmung und Ausführung von Augenbewegungen. Z. Sinnesphysiol. **45**, 9–26 (1911).

Grüsser-Cornehls, W., Grüsser, O.-J., Bullock, T.H.: Unit responses in the frogs tectum to moving and non-moving visual stimuli. Science **141**, 3583, 820–822 (1963).

Grüsser, O.-J., Grüsser-Cornehls, W.: Neurophysiologie des Bewegungssehens. Ergebnisse der Physiologie, biologischen Chemie und experimentellen Pharmakologie, **61**, 178–265 (1969).

Grüsser, O.-J., Grüsser-Cornehls, W.: Neuronal mechanisms of visual movement perception and some psychophysical and behavioral correlations. In: Handbook of Sensory Physiology, (Ed. R. Jung), vol. VII/3A, Springer-Verlag, New York, 333–426, 1973.

Hall, K.R.L., Earlie, A.E., Cookes, T.G.: A pendulum phenomenon in the visual perception of apparent movement. Quart. J. Exp. Psychol. **4** (1952).

Hall, K.R.L., Earlie, A.E.: A further study of the pendulum phenomenon. Quart. J. Exp. Psychol. **6** (1954).

Hay, J.C.: Optical motions and space perception. Psychol. Rev. **73**, 6, 550–565 (1966).

Helmholtz, H. von: Physiological Optics. vol. III, Dover-New York: Willy & Sons, 1962.

Herschberger, W.A.: Comment on "apparent reversal (oscillation) of rotary motion in depth". Psychol. Rev. **74**, 3, 235–238 (1967).

Herschberger, W.A., Carpenter, D.C., Starzec, J., Langhlin, N.K.: Simulation of an object rotating in depth: constant and reversal projection ratios. J. Exp. Psychol. **103**, 5, 844–853 (1974).

Hick, W.E.: The thresholds for sudden changes in the velocity of a seen object. Quart. J. Exp. Psychol. **11**, 33–41 (1959).

Hubel, D.H., Wiesel, T.N.: Receptive fields, binocular interaction and functional architecture in the cat's visual cortex. J. Physiol. **160**, 106–123 (1962).

Hubel, D.H., Wiesel, T.N.: Receptive fields and functional architecture of monkey striate cortex. J. Physiol. **195**, 215–243 (1968).

Ittelson, W.H.: The Ames' demonstrations in perception. Princeton: Princeton Univ. Press 1952.

Jansson, G., Runeson, S.: Measurement of perceived oscillation. Dept. of Psychol. Uppsala, 1967, Rep. No. 41.

Jansson, G.: Perceived rotary motion. Acta Univ. Upsaliensis 1969.

Jansson, G., Börjesson, E.: Perceived direction of rotary motion. Perc. & Psychophys. 19–26 (1969).
Jansson, G., Johansson, G.: Visual perception of bending motion. Perception **2**, 321–326 (1973).
Johansson, G.: Configurations in the perception of velocity. Acta Psychologica **7**, 25–79 (1950).
Johansson, G.: Configurations in event perception. Almqvist & Wiksell, Uppsala: Almquist & Wiksell 1950.
Johansson, G.: Rigidity, stability and motion in perceptual space. Acta Psychologica **14**, 359–370 (1958).
Johansson, G.: Binocular interaction in motion perception. Scand. J. Psychool. **1** (1960).
Johansson, G.: Perceptual overestimation of small motion tracks. Psychol. Beiträge: **6**, perception, 3/4, 570–580 (1962).
Johansson, G.: Perception of motion and changing form. Scand. J. Psychol. **5**, 181–208 (1964).
Johansson, G.: Monocular movement parallax and near-space perception. Perception **2**, 135–146 (1973a).
Johansson,G.: Visual perception of biological motion and a model for its analysis. Percept. & Psychophys. **14**, 201–211 (1973b).
Johansson, G.: Projective transformations as determining visual space perception. In: Perception. Essays in honor of J.J. Gibson, eds. R.B. MacLeod and H.L. Pick, Jr., Cornell University Press, Ithaca and London (1974a).
Johansson, G.: Visual perception of rotary motion as transformations of conic sections. Psychologica **17**, 226–237 (1974b).
Johansson, G.: Spatio-temporal differentiation and integration in visual motion perception. Psychol. Res. (in press) 1975.
Johansson, G., Backlund, F., Bergström, S.S.: Shortest perceptible length of motion track as a function of stimulus velocity. Contemporary Research in Psychology of Perception in honorem Kai von Fieandt sexagenarii, 1969.
Johansson, G. & Jansson, G.: Perceived rotary motion from changes in a straight line. Percept. & Psychophys. **4**, 165–170 (1968).
Katz, D.: Über den Vibrationssinn. VIIIth International Congress of Psychology 1926. Proceedings and Papers, Groningen, p. 312, 1927.
Kilpatrick, F.P., Ittelson, W.H.: Three demonstrations involving the visual perception of movement. J. Exp. Psychol. **42**, 394–402 (1951).
Koffka, K.: Principles of Gestalt Psychology, Routledge and Kegan Paul LTD, London (1935) 1950.
Kolers, P.A.: Aspects of motion perception, edition: Pergamon Press. New York: Pergamon Press 1972.
Korte, A.: Kinematoskopische Untersuchungen. Z. Psychol. **72**, 193–296 (1915).
Köhler, W.: Zur Theorie der stroboskopischen Bewegung. Psychol. Forsch. **3**, 397–406 (1923).
Köhler, W.: Die physischen Gestalten in Ruhe und im stationären Zustand. Erlangen: Verlag der philosophischen Akademie 1924.
Langdon, J.: The perception of a changing shape. Quart. J. Exp. Psychol. **3**, 157–165 (1951).
Lee, D.N.: Theory of the stereoscopic shadow-caster. Vision Res. **9**, 145–156 (1969).
Lee, D.N.: Visual information during locomotion. In: Perception. Essays in honor of J.J. Gibson. R.B. MacLeod and H.L. Pick, Jr. (eds.). Ithaca and London: Cornell University Press. Volume pp. 250–267 (1974).
Lehmann, H.: Wesen und Entstehung der Scheinbewegung im Lichte neuer Versuche. Archiv f. d. ges. Psychol. **102**, 1938–39.
Leibowitz, H.W.: The relation between the rate threshold for the perception of movement and luminance of various durations of exposure. J. Exp. Psychol. **49**, 209–214 (1955).
Lettvin, J.Y., Maturana, H.R., McCulloch, W.S., Pitts, W.H.: What the frog's eye tells the frog's brain. Proc. IRE **17**, 1940–1951 (1959).
Lishman, J.R., Lee, D.N.: The autonomy of visual kinaestetics. Perception **2**, 287–294 (1973).
Mach, E.: Analyse der Empfindungen, 1885–1922. English translat. N.Y.: Dover Publ. Inc. 1959.
Marmolin, H., Ulfberg, S.: Motion perception and form change. Quantitative studies of a projection geometric model. 1967 (unpublished report).
Marmolin, H., Ulfberg, S.: Proximal changes and perceived distance of motion in depth. Dept. of Psychol., Uppsala, Rep. No. 125, 1972.

Marmolin, H.: Visually perceived motion in depth resulting from proximal changes. I. Percept. & Psychophys. **14**, 1, 133–142 (1973).
Marmolin, H.: Visually perceived motion in depth resulting from proximal changes. II. Percept. & Psychophys. **14**, 1, 143–148 (1973).
Marshall, W.H., Talbot, S.A.: Recent evidence for neural mechanisms in vision leading to a general theory of sensory acuity. In: H. Klüver (ed.), Visual mechanisms. Lancaster, Pa.: Catell 1942.
Mefford, R.B. Jr., Wieland, B.A.: Perception of depth in rotating objects. Percept. & Motor Skills. **25**, 621–628 (1967).
Mefford, R.B., Jr.: Perception of depth in rotating objects IV. Fluctuating stereokinetic perceptual variants. Percept. & Motor Skills. **27**, 255–276 (1968).
Metzger, W.: Betrachtungen über phänomenale Identität. Psychol. Forsch. **19**, 1–60 (a) (1934).
Metzger, W.: Tiefen-Erscheinungen in optischen Bewegungsfeldern. Psychol. Forsch. **20**, 195–260(b) (1934).
Metzger, W.: Gesetze des Sehens. 2nd edition. Frankfurt: W. Kramer.
Michotte, A.: The Perception of Causality (Transl.) London: Methnen 1963.
Musatti, C.L.: Sui fenomeni stereocinetici. Arch. Ital. Psicol. **3**, 105–120 (1924).
Nakayama, K., Loomis, J.M.: Optical velocity patterns, velocity sensitive neurons and space perception: a hypothesis. Perception **3**, 63–80 (1974).
Neff, W.: A critical investigation of the visual apprehension of movement. Am. J. Psychol. **48**, 1–42, 1936.
Neisser, U.: Cognitive Psychology, edition. New York: John Wiley & Sons 1967.
Reynolds, H.N.: A Study over age groups of the visual perception of motion from changing two-dimensional stimulus patterns. Unpublished thesis, Cornell University, USA, 1963.
Riggs, L.A., Ratliff, F., Cornsweet, J.C., Cornsweet, T.N.: The disappearance of steadily fixated visual test objects. J. Opt. Soc. Am. **43**, 495–501 (1953).
Rubin, E.: Visuell wahrgenommene wirkliche Bewegungen. Z. für Psychol. 1927, **I**, 103 (1927).
Runeson, S.: Constant velocity—not perceived as such. Psychol. Res. **37**, 3–23 (1974).
Shannon, C.E.: A mathematical theory of communication. Bell System Tech. J. 1948, **27** (1948).
Shaw, R., McIntyre, Mace, W.: The role of symmetry in event perception. In: Perception, Essays in honor of J.J. Gibson. MacLeod, R.B. & Pick, H.L. Jr. (eds.). Ithaca and London: Cornell University Press 1974, pp. 277–310.
Sholz, W.: Experimentelle Untersuchungen über die phänomenale Größe von Raumstrecken, die durch Successiv-Darbietung zweier Reize begrenzt werden. Psychol. Forsch. **5**, 219–272 (1925).
Titchener, E.B.: Text book of Psychology, Macmillan, New York (1910).
Toshima, Y.: Perceptual rigid transformation of a moving object in the two-dimensional space. Kynshu Psychol. Studies. III, 259–288 (1965).
Wallach, H., O'Connell, D.N.: The kinetic depth effect. J. Exp. Psychol. **45**, 205–217 (1953).
Wallach, H., O'Connell, D.N., Neisser, U.: The memory effect of visual perception of three-dimensional form. J. Exp. Psychol. **45**, 360–368 (1953).
Wallach, H., Weisz, A., Adams, P.: Circles and derived figures in rotation. Am. J. Psychol. **69**, 48–59 (1956).
Wertheimer, M.: Experimentelle Studien über das Sehen von Bewegung. Z. Psychol. **61**, 161–265 (1912).
White, B.J., Mueser, G.E.: Accuracy in reconstructing the arrangement of elements generating kinetic depth displays. J. Exp. Psychol. **60**, 1–11 (1960).
Wieland, B.A., Mefford, R.B., Jr.: Perception of depth in rotating objects: A symmetry and velocity as the determinant of the stereokinetic effect. Percept. & Motor Skills **26**, 671–681 (1968).
Wittman, J.: Über das Sehen von Scheinbewegungen und Scheinkörpern. Archiv d. ges. Psychol., 1921.
Woodworth, R.S., Schlosberg, H.: Experimental Psychology, edition. New York: H. Holt & Co. 1954.
Yarbus, A.L.: Eye movements and vision. New York: Plenum Press 1967.

Chapter 23

Time Perception

ERNST PÖPPEL, München, Germany

With 1 Figure

Time is not a thing that,
like an apple, may be perceived.
H. WOODROW, 1951

Contents

A. Introduction

The experience of time and how it might be explained has always been a persistent challenge. One of the most compelling analyses of subjective time is the one given by AUGUSTINUS (397/398 A.D.) in the 11th book of his "Confessions." His ideas about the subjective measurement of time are still impressive today; he relates time to the perception of events, an idea that recently has been discussed by GIBSON (1973, "Events are perceivable but time is not"). This chapter has been written in order to argue for such a substitution of time perception by event perception. It shall further be argued that in order to deal with human time perception one has to establish a *taxonomy* of temporal experiences. It appears that different unrelated temporal experiences are often subsumed under the term time perception and that many controversies found in the literature on subjective time stem from an absence of such a taxonomy of temporal experiences.

The exploration of human time perception and temporal organization of behavior in general had a magnificent start in the last century. In 1860, KARL ERNST VON BAER gave an important lecture in St. Petersburg on „Welche Auffassung der lebenden Natur ist die richtige?" where he introduced the concept of time quanta; this concept is in the center of modern theorizing on time perception (cf., STROUD, 1955; SHALLICE, 1964). Even as early as 1865, MACH showed that Weber's law does not hold true for time perception but that there is an interval (in his case 300 to 400 ms) for which there is maximal differential sensitivity, below and above which differential sensitivity is worse; he also pointed out how variable subjective time estimates can be and that the temporal acuity for audition is much better than for the other senses. Within the same decade, DONDERS (1868) tried to measure the "speed of mental processes" using the subtraction method in reaction time experiments, and VIERORDT (1868) published his work on the time sense where he described the "indifference interval" still persecuting the experimentalists today.

Unfortunately, the interest in problems of time perception has declined over the last decades, perhaps because of the many controversies not only over theories but also data. If one reads introductory books, chapters or articles on time perception (e.g., JAMES, 1890; NICHOLS, 1891; WEBER, 1933; WOODROW, 1951; WALLACE and RABIN, 1960; FRAISSE, 1964; COHEN, 1967; MICHON, 1967; GOODDY, 1969; HOLUBÁŘ, 1969; ORME, 1969; ORNSTEIN, 1969; DOOB, 1971; ALLAN and KRISTOFFERSON, 1974), one notices how subjective the selection and presentation of problems often is. One reason why the exploration of time perception might have led to a state of confusion might have been the misconception that time actually is a thing that, like an apple, can be perceived (cf., WOODROW, 1951). On the basis of this misconception, the psychophysical methods developed in the last century were used in the same way as in other psychophysical experiments, such as studies of brightness perception (see for instance WUNDT, 1881); subjective time was looked upon (and still is) as a prothetic continuum (STEVENS, 1957) and a stationary process (PÖPPEL, 1972). The experiments of MACH (1865), however, should have made clear from the beginning that there is something peculiar about subjective time and that discrimination of durations is not analogous to the discrimination of intensities.

What is needed appears to be a *taxonomy* of "elementary time experiences." The only purpose of this chapter is the attempt to provide such a taxonomy. The basic assumption is that time perception has to be related to the occurrence of events as they are perceived and actions taken by the subject. In order to outline the taxonomy, it might be helpful to use a simple scheme (Fig. 1) in which different elementary time experiences are related to such events or actions. The arrow from the left to the right in Figure 1 represents the continuum of time in the sense of classical physics, *past* being represented on the left and *future* on the right. The long vertical line in the middle represents the *now*, conceived of as a point in time without duration. The sequence of events (past) and actions to be taken by the subject (future) is indicated above the time line by a row of small circles. The taxonomy consists basically of five elementary time experiences; these will be briefly characterized now and in more detail in the following sections.

One elementary time experience is *duration estimation;* it refers to our ability to estimate how much time has elapsed between two specified events by using, for instance, conventional time units (like seconds, hours, or weeks). The bulk of research on time perception is actually performed on duration estimation, and for some investigators, duration estimation is the only interesting aspect

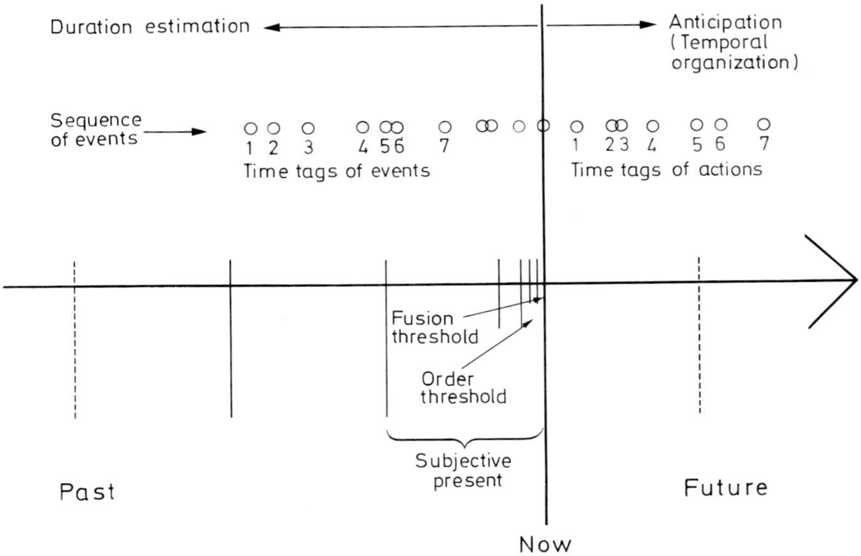

Fig. 1. Graphic representation of elementary time experiences. The arrow from the left to the right represents the continuum of time in the sense of classical physics. Above this line, the sequence of events is shown by small circles. The continuum of time is divided by a vertical line, representing the *now*, into *past* and *future*. The different elementary time experiences (duration estimation, perception of sequences of events, anticipation, or temporal organization of actions to be taken, the experiences of successiveness and of order, and the subjective present) are explained in the text

of human time experience. Duration estimation of longer intervals (minutes or hours) appears to be mainly determined by the amount of information processed (and/or stored) or by the "mental content." This view has been advocated by Guyau (1890) and Sturt (1925) and is presently supported, for instance, by Ornstein (1969) and Michon (1970). The phenomenon of boredom appears to be partly caused by a lack of information during a specific time interval, and a characterization of boredom as given by Hoche (1923) will be reported below.

Events occurring in a rapid succession may not necessarily be experienced successively but may appear subjectively simultaneous. In order to be actually perceived as different events, they must be separated by a minimal temporal interval. This minimal interval is of different duration for the different senses ("fusion threshold"). However, even if events are perceived as different, they must be separated by at least 20 ms or so—this number seems to be the same for different modalities—if their order is to be indicated (Hirsh and Sherrick, 1961). This last observation on the "order threshold" and many other experimental results have suggested the idea of central *temporal processing units* or subjective time quanta with a duration in the range of 20–40 ms. It may be that the experience of "instantaneousness" is related to such subjective time quanta; for very short stimuli neither a beginning nor an end is experienced, and thus no experience of duration is provided (Rubin, 1935).

Another elementary time experience besides duration estimation and the experience of simultaneity and successiveness is characterized by our ability to record the sequence of events. Apparently, not only events as such are recorded in memory, but their time of occurrence as well. Under certain pathologic conditions, as has been suggested for patients with Korsakoff psychosis (e.g., VAN DER HORST, 1932), the *time tags* of events might be lost. Although the events themselves can still be recalled, these patients are said to be no longer able to indicate their sequence.

The experiences of duration, simultaneity/successiveness, and sequence have to be distinguished from one temporal experience which is perhaps the most basic time experience of all and which might be described as the "feeling of nowness." The experience of nowness appears to be embedded in a temporal interval which has been called the "specious" or the *subjective present*. JAMES (1890) called this interval that we experience as present "a sort of saddle-back of time with a certain length of its own, on which we sit perched, and from which we look in two directions into time." It has been suggested (FRAISSE, 1963) that the term time perception should be restricted to those short intervals (a few seconds in duration) when we have this feeling of nowness (this interval of subjective present obviously has nothing to do with the now point (Fig. 1) on the physical time scale).

Thus far, only those aspects of subjective time have been mentioned that refer to whatever lies in the past or in the present on the physical time scale. However, in order to discuss time perception appropriately, the future must also be considered. The elementary time experience that refers to the *temporal organization* of future actions can be called anticipation or planning. The problem of serial organization or preprogramming of behavior has been discussed in a very important article by LASHLEY (1951). He suggested that temporal organization of behavior might be understood by assuming rhythmic mechanisms. If indeed rhythmic mechanisms are basic for the programming of behavioral sequences in the immediate future, they might be expected to influence the experience of temporal intervals in the immediate past as well. The possibility of such a relationship between rhythmic temporal organization of actions and time perception had been suggested a long time ago by MACH (1885), and Pavlov was convinced that rhythmic phenomena might be important in the establishment of temporally conditioned reflexes (see HOLUBÁŘ, 1969).

Each of the five elementary time experiences mentioned (experience of duration, simultaneity/successiveness, sequence, present, and anticipation) is discussed in more detail in the following sections. It will be obvious that the diverse types of time perception preclude any general theory on how time might be perceived. The different elementary time experiences appear to be independent of each other and should be treated as such.

One may miss in such a report (in addition, perhaps, to other matters) a review of methods used in time perception studies. Methodologic questions have been discussed many times, and the interested reader is referred to the following works: WUNDT, 1881; CLAUSEN, 1950; GREGG, 1951; ROSS and KATCHMAR, 1951; BINDRA and WAKSBERG, 1956; FRAISSE et al., 1962; DANZIGER and DU PREEZ, 1963; CARLSON and FEINBERG, 1970; HORNSTEIN and ROTTER, 1969; DOOB, 1971; PÖPPEL, 1972; EISLER, 1976.

B. Duration Estimation

Everybody is aware of the fact that our experience of passing time is influenced by what we are doing. SWIFT and MCGEOCH (1925) pointed out that a speaker may think he is talking only for a few minutes while members of the audience are already checking their watches. These authors asked subjects to read short stories or to listen to them; they observed that doing something actively (such as reading) results in an impression that less time has passed than if one listens passively to what is being read. AXEL (1925) obtained similar results in more standardized experiments and argued that the "level of behavioral activity" determines the experience of time. If one is engaged in a higher level of behavioral activity, time appears to pass rapidly, whereas a low level of behavioral activity, when one is bored for instance, results in the impression that time is dragging.

It is important to note that these experiences of a fast or slow passage of time are present only during the activity (or nonactivity). Retrospectively, the experience of the passage of time is reversed. A period devoid of interesting events that appeared never to end is estimated as having had a very short duration if one looks back on it. On the other hand, time during a day full of new experiences may seem to fly, but the retrospective estimation of time is that of a long duration. The idea that the number of recorded events determines our estimation of time has been analyzed by STURT (1925). She thought that exogenous events as well as thoughts (endogenous events) determine duration estimates. "In estimating time we rely on the amount of mental content experienced during that time ... Time which has been filled by many thoughts appears longer whereas time occupied by few thoughts appears shorter" (STURT, 1925; p. 101).

In more recent discussions of human temporal experience (e.g., FRANKENHAEUSER, 1959; ORNSTEIN, 1969; MICHON, 1970; VROON, 1970), this notion of mental content plays an important role. Duration estimation is treated as an aspect of cognitive organization, and it is stressed that in order to understand duration estimates it may be unnecessary to assume (biologic) time units. With regard to this, the recent book by ORNSTEIN "On the Experience of Time" has greatly influenced modern thought. He shows how powerful the metaphor of *storage size* can be, if one deals with duration estimates.

> We ... relate the experience of duration of a given interval to the size of the storage space for that interval in general information-processing terms. In the storage of a given interval, either increasing the number of stored events or the complexity of those events will increase the size of the storage, and as storage size increases the experience of duration lengthens (ORNSTEIN, 1969; p. 41).

In several experiments, he tested his hypothesis directly, and the results strongly support the hypothesis that the storage size essentially determines the estimates of durations.

Some aspects of estimating duration are revealed by the experience of boredom. HOCHE (1923) pointed out that there is a lack of events (exogenous and endogenous) in relation to what one expects; during boredom, one is prevented from escaping the situation or changing it. As an example, he described how he was sitting in the first row during a lecture listening to an endless talk which he could not follow. Because of the lack of information and because one is trapped in a situation, one's attention is focused on the passage of time. When one concentrates on the passage of time, it appears to move even more slowly—as has been portrayed, for instance, in Morgenstern's poem "Die Zeit." Essentially, boredom is a consequence of a severe mismatch between two time scales, i.e., between "personal" and "government" time as Gooddy (1969) calls it. It takes some time before this mismatch is recognized; Hoche (1923) suggested that at least a few minutes have to pass before boredom can be experienced. Psychotic patients apparently are not bored when they stay in an institution for a long time; Hoche suggested that it is a sign of improvement when psychotic patients become bored.

In order to be able to estimate time on the basis of events that occurred during an interval, a mechanism of *temporal integration* (Hearnshaw, 1956) has to be assumed. Such a mechanism must exist—but there is nothing known about it. The scope of the problem can be appreciated when one reads:

"Temporal integration involves essentially the formation, from temporally disparate units, of configurations, in which the present moment and immediate stimuli lose the dominance they possess at the perceptual level. The capacity to form and to scan such temporal configurations frees the organism from control by the present situation (Hearnshaw, 1956; p. 17).

On a descriptive level, one can distinguish at least two aspects of temporal integration as being relevant for duration estimates, and these two aspects must entail two different mechanisms. If duration estimates are based on the "size of storage" as Ornstein (1969) suggests, there must be some kind of *summative* temporal integration adding up exogenous and endogenous events; the result of such an integration would be the basis of duration estimates. Summative temporal integration has to be distinguished from *averaging* temporal integration, as is implied, for instance, in the adaptation level theory (Helson, 1964). It is assumed in this theory that information processed about past events generates a personal reference system of subjective time (or brightness, weight, etc.). Duration estimates are made by comparing the storage size produced by the events within a particular interval with the subjective frame of reference developed by averaging the durations of different time intervals experienced in the past (Goldstone, 1967). Each act of duration estimates would thus be dependent on both temporal integration mechanisms, the long term *averaging* temporal integration responsible for the "frame of reference," and the short term *summative* temporal integration that determines the storage size. Some specific predictions of the adaptation level theory, such as anchor effects (Postman and Miller, 1945; Adamson, 1967), have been verified in experiments on duration estimates. Some advocates of the theory also claim that it explains the *indifference interval* (Vierordt, 1868). This might be true for longer time intervals in the range of minutes. It will be seen in the section on the subjective present, however, that other explanations not related to averaging temporal integration of events must be invoked in order to understand the indifference interval observed in the range of 2–3 seconds.

C. Temporal Processing Units

A century ago, EXNER (1875) observed that the temporal fusion threshold is different in the different sense modalities; two auditory stimuli must be separated by 1–2 msec in order to be heard as successive, but visual or tactile stimuli separated by such short intervals are still experienced as simultaneous. The auditory system has apparently the best and the visual system the worst "temporal acuity." Temporal fusion thresholds mainly reflect peripheral sensory mechanisms, although central mechanisms can influence them as well. LACKNER and TEUBER (1973), for instance, observed an impaired auditory fusion threshold in patients with left temporal lobe lesions, and it is a well-known fact that critical flicker fusion is affected by lesions in the occipital areas of the brain (e.g., PÖPPEL et al., 1975).

Temporal resolving power must be broken down into two measures as HIRSH and SHERRICK (1961) have pointed out. One of these two aspects of temporal resolving power has just been mentioned, i.e., the minimum time interval that can separate two events so that they are just perceived as nonsimultaneous or successive. The second aspect of temporal acuity refers to the experience of temporal order. Given that two events are perceived as successive, a judgment has to be made as to their temporal order, i.e., which of the two events comes first and which comes second. Experimental observations indicate that measurements of fusion and order thresholds give quite different results. When the temporal order of events is to be recognized, the events must be distinctive so that they can be labeled differently. HIRSH and SHERRICK (1961) observed in their experiments that different events must be separated by 20 ms in order to be reported in their correct temporal order 75% of the time. In contrast to fusion threshold, order threshold has the same numerical value in all modalities tested (vision, hearing, touch); it even has the same value for judgments across modalities. "It is reasonable to hypothesize that a single quantitative process is shared by all three modalities at some point" (HIRSH and SHERRICK, 1961; p. 430). Some kind of time-organizing system is suggested by their results on temporal order threshold that is independent of purely sensory mechanisms, and, presumably, more central.

Time-organizing systems such as these have been suggested under various headings, i.e., biologic clocks, subjective time quanta, processing units, perceptual moments, central oscillations, or excitability cycles. It has been pointed out by WIENER (1958) and SHALLICE (1964) that central clocks allow for a much more economical organization of behavior. WIENER is often quoted as one of the important advocates of biologic clocks:

"The brain has much in common with the computing or control machine, in which various incoming impulses are combined to make outgoing impulses. Such a combination of impulses may take place in at least two ways. One possibility is that the impulses are stored up in the machine or the brain until the proper combination has been recorded, and they go out at whatever time the process is complete. This is a suitable means of computing by means of impulses of a continuing nature. However, there are very considerable advantages in having the impulses of the nature of pulses of brief duration. The proper combination of these involves that they should come in at the proper tick of a clock. Such a mechanism is likely to be more economical in the use of time than control by continuing impulses, and accordingly most forms of control and computation machinery do in fact deal with pulsed impulses and contain a clock as an intrinsic part" (WIENER, 1958).

SHALLICE (1964) showed in his analyses that the detection of change can be done in the fastest and most reliable way if one assumes central oscillations, i.e., that the perceptual input is processed in discrete temporal steps. There is less of a computable load for the brain, and the empirical evidence that SHALLICE discusses suggests that the perceptual moment hypothesis is most satisfactory.

If these central processing units do, in fact, exist, one would expect that different studies show approximately the same numerical value for their duration. This, however, is not the case, although there is a strong bias that favors a duration similar to the order threshold described above (HIRSH and SHERRICK, 1961). Several years ago, attempts were made to relate the duration of these hypothetic processing units (or perceptual moments) to the period of the alpha rhythm of the EEG (e.g., HOLUBÁŘ and MACHEK, 1962; WHITE, 1963) or to the half-period of the alpha rhythm (KRISTOFFERSON, 1967). In most studies, however, a value close to 30 ms, or to be more conservative, between 20 and 40 ms, has been suggested. For instance, when using a reaction time paradigm in memory studies, STERNBERG (1975) observed that the scanning process which is exhaustive has an approximate speed of 30 ms per item. In well-trained tasks such as typing or piano playing, up to 30 bits per second are transferred; within approximately 30 ms one-bit decisions can be made (AUGENSTINE, 1962). LATOUR (1967) observed that visual thresholds oscillate with a period close to 30 ms. If two random patterns that together form a word are shown for 6 ms, each with temporal intervals of 25 ms, 50 ms, etc., the words will be recognized perfectly with a 25 ms interval, but much less often with a 50 ms interval (ERIKSEN and COLLINS, 1968). Two experiences that can be distinguished from each other are reported when the overall duration of two stimuli is 60 ms, i.e., 30 ms for each of the temporally contiguous stimulus events (EFRON, 1967). PODVIGIN (1972) has speculated that oscillations with a frequency of approximately 30 Hz might serve the neuronal identification of specific features of sensory events; his neurophysiologic observations suggest the existence of a visual memory operating in a rhythmic fashion with such a frequency.

Finally, the work on reaction time supports the notion that 30 ms is a basic temporal processing unit (e.g., HARTER and WHITE, 1968; PÖPPEL, 1968, 1970). It has been shown that histograms of choice reaction time are in most instances multimodal with a 30–40 ms temporal interval between adjacent modes. The histograms on choice reaction time can be used to decide between two different alternatives of how the biologic clocks or processing units operate. The question is, in terms of oscillation theory, whether the temporal processing units behave more like relaxation or more like pendulum oscillators (WEVER, 1965), or in psychophysiologic terms, whether they are excitability or scanning cycles (HARTER, 1967). Excitability cycles, but not scanning cycles, can be instantaneously entrained by exogenous stimuli. The multimodal histograms suggest that entrainable temporal processing units have the characteristics of relaxation oscillations or excitability cycles. "If the eye is to respond to external stimuli, it must be assumed that the internal clock is synchronized with the external event . . . If this resetting tendency is not present we shall never find periodicities in the reaction time" (LATOUR, 1967; p. 347). PÖPPEL (1970) demonstrated with the so-called "paternoster" model that scanning cycles (where the periods are not synchronized by the stimulus) cannot explain the multimodal response distributions; scansion is therefore inappropriate as a model for central intermittency. Some authors apparently refer only to scanning cycles when discussing the concept of subjective time quanta. Thus, some of the contradictions in the literature may have resulted from the fact that the important distinction between instantaneously entrainable excitability cycles and continuous scanning cycles has not been made (e.g., ALLPORT, 1968). The point made by VROON (1974) that time quanta might be artificial is hardly convincing, because the evidence is based on numerous, quite different experimental paradigms. In the specific case, however, that he is discussing, he may certainly be right that "time quanta" may be the "result" of statistical manipulations.

Changes in the duration of temporal processing units as a result of physiologic changes in the organism or of lesions in the brain have often been suggested. HOAGLAND's paper (1933) has played an influential role; its subject is a theoretical chemical clock in the organism that is temperature-dependent. His interest had been aroused by his wife who reported a change in the subjective passage of time while she had a fever. Some observations of patients with injuries of the brain indicate that the assumption of central temporal processing units might be helpful in trying to understand certain behavioral aberrations. ALBERT and BEAR (1974), for instance, described a case of word deafness in which the understanding of speech was improved when the examiner spoke very slowly. The authors point out that normal comprehension of speech depends on intact functioning of two components of the "time sense," i.e., sequencing and temporal resolution. One can interpret these observations by assuming that in their patient temporal resolution was decreased, i.e., temporal processing units were prolonged. Different speech sounds produced at regular speed might have fallen into one processing unit and could, therefore, not be decoded properly. The patient was only able to understand when speech was adapted in speed to the prolonged temporal processing units.

D. Time Tags

When we recall a telephone number, we not only remember the numbers themselves, but also their sequence. Reversing two digits would be as big a mistake as replacing one; it would not be possible to place the call. If the digits were given in a random sequence, the particular message would be destroyed. In most messages, units must occur in a specified sequence, like the words of a sentence. A melody changes its character completely if the sequence of tones is changed; the gestalt of a melody is lost if it is played backwards.

Until recently, this specific problem of *time tags* for events has been neglected in studies on time perception. Important contributions, however, have come and can certainly be expected from the psycholinguistic work (e.g., FODOR et al., 1974), since one basic aspect of speech perception and speech production is its sequential order. Trouble with sequencing has been proposed as one aspect of dyslexia (CORKIN, 1974; ZURIF and CARSON, 1970). "It is reasonable to suggest that developmental dyslexia is more parsimoniously related to trouble with the apprehension of temporal sequences within a given sense modality than to the consequent disturbances of crossmodal matching" (ZURIF and CARSON, 1970; p. 359). It has also been observed that patients with left hemispheric lesions do worse than controls in reproducing sequences of three to five visual or auditory stimuli (CARMON and NACHSHON, 1971). These observations may suggest that the time tags defining the position of events in a sequence can be selectively destroyed because of brain injuries. Apparently it is a non-trivial task for the nervous system to keep track of the sequence of events.

The existence of a dissociation of memory for events and the times at which the events happened has also been claimed on the basis of some characteristics of the Korsakoff psychosis. It has been said that in Korsakoff psychosis a selective loss of time tags for events occurs (VAN DER HORST, 1932; WILLIAMS and ZANGWILL, 1950). The basic disturbance, according to VAN DER HORST, would be a loss of time tags; the events themselves can still be remembered. This dissociation between actual events and the times at which they happened would result in confabulation and account for the disorientated impression the patients make. This view, however, has been criticized by TALLAND (1961) who maintains that the Korsakoff psychosis is a result of a more general memory disturbance. Observations on recency discrimination (MILNER, 1974) suggest a selective impairment of time tags that occur after frontal lobe lesions, specifically after left frontal lobectomy.

One problem which might be interesting to investigate is whether sequences are coded in a different way when they are a result of event perception (like in speech perception) or a result of one's own actions. For instance, is one's performance better when repeating the sequence of self-produced actions, or is it better when repeating the sequence of another person's perceived actions? In one case, the time tags are actively selected at the stage of the planning of a sequence, in the other case they have to be perceived.

E. Subjective Present

Temporal intervals up to a few seconds are experienced in a way qualitatively different from longer temporal intervals. This has already been stressed by JAMES (1890) who maintained that there are different mechanisms in time perception. Intervals of up to approximately 5 s can be experienced as a unit, whereas longer intervals are coded symbolically and can only be estimated and not perceived. Completely different mechanisms of temporal integration have to be assumed for short and long temporal intervals. EDGELL and WALLER (1903) tried to answer the question of why short and long temporal intervals are experienced in different ways. They believed that during short intervals of a few seconds, it is possible to focus one's attention on specific events, whereas this is impossible during longer intervals of time.

The short temporal interval of up to a few seconds in duration, experienced as a temporal unit, is usually referred to as the *subjective present* (STERN, 1897; WUNDT, 1911; QUASEBARTH, 1924). There are different means of estimating the duration of this subjective present. BORING (1942) has suggested that the subjective present is associated with the indifference interval (VIERORDT, 1868). If the method of reproduction is used, the indifference interval is that duration which is reproduced correctly. In general, stimuli shorter than the indifference interval are reproduced as longer, and stimuli longer than the indifference interval are reproduced as shorter. In most of the studies, however, there is mixed opinion concerning the duration of the indifference interval (WOODROW, 1934). If the subjective present is not some kind of time constant in our nervous system, then a physiologically oriented explanation like the one based on the theory of a fading trace (KÖHLER, 1923) would appear rather unlikely, and one might perhaps consider the applicability of the adaptation level theory (HELSON, 1964). However, most of the experiments in which the indifference interval was measured cannot be assessed with respect to the subjective present, because the experimental design selectively favored results that would fit the adaptation level theory.

With a different design conceptually similar to the one previously employed by WOODROW (1934), PÖPPEL (1972) tried to test the appropriateness of the adaptation level theory for interpretations of the indifference interval. On the basis of this theory, a specific prediction can be made: an indifference interval should only be established when a subject is required to make a series of reproductions of different intervals. No such indifference interval would be expected when each subject in a group reproduces only one interval, even though collectively the group reproduces intervals over a given range. If in such a situation an indifference interval would be obtained, this observation would be incompatible with the adaptation level theory, since no individual reference system could have been built up in such a test situation. Furthermore, according to the adaptation level theory, indifference intervals should be obtained in any temporal range, whereas if the indifference interval is a temporal constant (related to the subjective present), one would expect it in one temporal range only and not in another. The predictions made by the adaptation level theory were tested using two experimental groups. The range of reproduced intervals for one experimental group was 0.5–5.0 s in steps of 0.5 s; the range for the other experimental group was 10.5–15.0 s. Each subject reproduced once only one temporal interval; there were 38 subjects in the first and 28 subjects in the second experimental group. The results show a clear indifference interval for the experimental group which reproduced intervals between 0.5 and 5.0 s;

no indifference interval was seen for the other experimental group. The indifference interval was observed between 2.0 and 2.5 s. Intervals of up to 2.0 s were reproduced by longer periods, and intervals of 2.5 s and more were reproduced by shorter ones. These results show that the adaptation level theory cannot explain the existence of an indifference interval in the lower range; one has to acknowledge a specific temporal mechanism in the range of a few seconds which might perhaps be related to the subjective present, as BORING (1942) suggested. The results do not, of course, contradict the existence of indifference intervals at other temporal ranges obtained with other experimental paradigms. It is interesting to note that WOODROW (1934) also obtained an interindividual indifference interval with his experimental paradigm, in essence similar to the one used by PÖPPEL (1972), however, at approximately 600 ms. Possibly, a second interindividual indifference interval exists at a much shorter duration. Another explanation for the different outcome of the experiments might be that the number of trials and the stimulus presentation were rather different in both experiments.

There are a number of additional observations that indicate that there is something peculiar about the subjective experience of temporal intervals in the range of 2 s. For instance, GETTY (1975) maintains that Weber's law describes time discriminations much better than CREELMAN'S (1962) model; however, both models cannot deal with a duration of time longer than 2 s. Another mechanism of temporal experience apparently applies for longer intervals. In another experiment, BECHINGER et al. (1969) tested "the hypothesis that the 2 s duration is the most common natural unit time (cycle time) in time judging experiments" (p. 419). They measured information transmission and observed that channel capacity is maximal with the category interval of 2 s (i.e., stimuli had a duration of 2,4,6,... s). A slightly shorter value (1.5 s) has been suggested by RICHARDS (1964) on the basis of time reproduction experiments.

These experiments suggest that time intervals of approximately 2 s are experienced differently, and perhaps the experiments give a good measure of the subjective present. There are some observations that might indicate some specific features of the temporal mechanism underlying the subjective present. In the discussion of temporal processing units, we made a distinction between excitability and scanning cycles. The same question can be asked here. Is the subjective present a "traveling" time interval (ALLPORT, 1968) that always has the same duration, or is it organized as an oscillatory process as suggested by RICHARDS (1964), BECHINGER et al. (1969), and PÖPPEL (1972)? Using the reproduction paradigm, this question was tested (PÖPPEL, 1973), and the observations strongly support an oscillatory model using the excitability or relaxation mode.

Some temporal aspects of behavior that have been found in other areas might be intimately related to the subjective present. Stimuli with a regular pattern, such as the beating of a metronome, are subjectively grouped into units; temporal grouping may override contiguity (MÜLLER and SCHUMANN, 1894). The temporal grouping of successive stimuli, however, has a temporal limit of approximately 2.5 s, as WUNDT (1911) pointed out. Finally, there is a very old observations which appears to be relevant in this context. URBANTSCHITSCH (1875) described that a very weak auditory stimulus would only be heard periodically; he maintained that central effects must be responsible for this oscillatory phenomenon with a period of a few seconds.

F. Temporal Organization

So far our discussion of human time experience has been limited to the apprehension of past or present events, yet time also relates to actions that lie in the future. To what extent is it appropriate to consider the programming of behavioral sequences as it appears, for instance, in speech production (e.g., LASHLEY, 1951) as yet another aspect of time perception?

It has been shown that articulatory sequences must be preprogrammed because there is not enough time for feedback (KENT and MOLL, 1975). Thus, not only the proper phonemes have to be selected but in addition *time tags* have to be distributed in advance in order to produce meaningful words and sentences. It has been suggested by GOLDMAN-EISLER (1967) that the planning of utterances occurs during hesitation pauses and that spontaneous speech is characterized by a rhythmic organization, i.e., alteration between hesitation pauses and fluent speech. The notion that preprogramming of speech occurs in a rhythmic fashion has been strongly suggested by LASHLEY (1951) and recently been discussed by MARTIN (1972) and ALLEN (1975). MARTIN maintains that speaking and listening are dynamically coupled rhythmic activities. Equal-interval accents in speech are a language universal. "Speech utterances are temporally patterned, and many of their elements are temporally predictable" (MARTIN, 1972; p. 489). A listener given initial cues actively enters into the speaker's tempo; such an adaptation of the listener to the speaker with respect to temporal aspects might greatly facilitate the understanding of speech.

In experiments on verbal random number generation, it was observed that subjects are not able to produce sequences of numbers in which the single numbers are independent of the preceding ones (PÖPPEL, 1972). The number sequences that were produced by the subjects, who intended to select randomly, showed marked periodicities. The duration of these periodicities was in the range of a few seconds. It was specifically tested whether the duration of the periodicities is a function of the number of alternatives that are to be brought into a random sequence or whether it is a function of time. When the production rate of the numbers was increased, i.e., the subjects "spoke" faster, the length of the periodicity within the subjective random sequence increased; however, the actual time for the periodicity produced unintentionally under the two conditions remained constant. It is tempting to argue that such periodicities are a reflection of the rhythmic temporal organization suggested, for instance, by LASHLEY (1951) in the programming of speech or all skilled acts. The duration of these periodicities of a few seconds is reminiscent of the duration of the subjective present, and one should, therefore, ask the question of whether the duration of the subjective present might not be a consequence the programming of a behavioral sequence. It could be suggested that the rhythmic organization of speech that entails programming of future events produces a temporal framework that is also the basis of the subjective present.

G. Conclusion

One assumption of this chapter has been that there is no such thing as time perception. If one deals with problems of subjective time, it is suggested that one begin with "event perception." In so doing, one is automatically led to distinguish one *elementary temporal experience* from another. Such experiences, as they relate to the occurrence of events, are graphically illustrated in Figure 1, and it was the intention of this chapter to characterize them. There may be other elementary temporal experiences, and there may be better names for the ones discussed here; however, it is believed that time perception can be explained only if the different aspects of subjective time are first identified, before asking the question of how these relate to each other. It does not appear to be a fruitful strategy (as has often been followed in the past) to seek an understanding of time perception on the basis of only one elementary temporal experience. The mechanisms underlying the different elementary temporal experiences may well be completely different in nature, and this should be acknowledged in the experimental approach. For instance, the basis of the experience of simultaneity, successiveness, or order might be studied on a neuropsychologic or even neurophysiologic level, whereas investigating duration estimation mainly requires the experimental techniques of cognitive psychology. The approach of this chapter has been obviously phenomenologic. However, it is believed that the search for mechanisms and the elaboration of neuronal models entails such a preparatory descriptive attempt.

References

Adamson, R.: Anchor effect limits. Psychon. Sci. **9**, 179–180 (1967).

Albert, M.L., Bear, D.: Time to understand—a case study of word deafness with reference to the role of time in auditory comprehension. Brain **97**, 373–384 (1974).

Allan, L.G., Kristofferson, A.B.: Psychophysical theories of duration discrimination. Perception & Psychophysics **16**, 26–34 (1974).

Allen, G.D.: Speech rhythm: its relation to performance universals and articulatory timing. J. Phonetics **3**, 75–86 (1975).

Allport, D.A.: Phenomenal simultaneity and the perceptual moment hypothesis. Br. J. Psychol. **59**, 395–406 (1968).

Augenstine, L.G.: A model of how humans process information. Biometrics **18**, 420–421 (1962).

Augustinus: Confessiones. Book 11. 397/398

Axel, R.: Estimation of time. In: Archives of psychology. **12**, 5–77 (1925).

Baer, K.E. von: Welche Auffassung der lebenden Natur ist die richtige? Und wie ist diese Auffassung auf die Entomologie anzuwenden? Speech in St. Petersburg 1860. Schmitzdorff, H. (ed.).St. Petersburg Verlag der kaiserl. Hofbuchhandl. 1864, pp. 237–284.

Bechinger, D., Kongehl, G., Kornhuber, H.H.: Natural 2-second cycle in time perception and human information transmission. Die Naturwissenschaften **56**, 419 (1969).

Bindra, D., Waksberg, H.: Methods and terminology in studies of time estimation. Psychol. Bull. **53**, 155–159 (1956).

Boring, E.G.: Sensation and perception in the history of experimental psychology. New York: Appleton-Century-Crofts 1942.

Carlson, V.R., Feinberg, I.: Time judgment as a function of method, practice, and sex. J. exp. Psychol. **85**, 171–180 (1970).

Carmon, A., Nachshon, I.: Effect of unilateral brain damage on perception of temporal order. Cortex **7**, 410–418 (1971).

Clausen, J.: An evaluation of experimental methods of time estimation. J. exp. Psychol. **40**, 756–761 (1950).

Cohen, J.: Psychological time in health and disease. Springfield, Ill.: Charles C. Thomas 1967.

Corkin, S.: Serial-ordering deficits in inferior readers. Neuropsychologia **12**, 347–354 (1974).

Creelman, C.D.: Human discrimination of auditory duration. J. of the Acoustical Soc. of America **34**, 582–593 (1962).

Danziger, K., du Preez, P.D.: Reliability of time estimation by the method of reproduction. Perc. & mot. skills **16**, 879–884 (1963).

Donders, F.C.: On the speed of mental processes. Acta Psychologica **30**, 412–431 (1969). (Orig. 1868).

Doob, L.W.: Patterning of time. New Haven and London: Yale University Press 1971.

Edgell, B., Waller, A.W.: On time judgments. Am. J. Psychol. **14**, 154–174 (1903).

Efron, R.: The duration of the present. Annals of the New York Academy of Sciences **138**, 713–729 (1967).

Eisler, H.: Experiments on subjective duration 1868–1975: a collection of power function exponents. Psychol. Bulletin **83**, 1154–1171 (1976).

Eriksen, C.W., Collins, J.F.: Sensory traces versus the psychological moment in the temporal organization of form. J. exp. Psychol. **77**, 376–382 (1968).

Exner, S.: Experimentelle Untersuchung der einfachsten psychischen Prozesse. Pflügers Archiv ges. Physiol. **11**, 403–432 (1875).

Fodor, J., Bever, T.G., Garrett, M.F.: The psychology of language. An introduction to psycholinguistics and generative grammar. New York: McGraw-Hill 1974.

Fraisse, P.: Perception et estimation du temps. In: Fraisse, P., Piaget, J. Traité de psychologie expérimentale. (eds.). Paris: Presses Universitaires 1963, Vol. VI, pp. 60–95.

Fraisse, P.: The psychology of time. London: Eyre & Spottiswoode 1964.

Fraisse, P., Bonnet, C., Gelly, N., Michon, G.: Vergleich der Zeitschätzungsmethoden. Zeitschrift Psychol. **167**, 268–277 (1962).

Frankenhaeuser, M.: Estimation of time. An experimental study. Stockholm: Almqvist and Wiksel 1959.

Getty, D.J.: Discrimination of short temporal intervals: a comparison of two models. Perception and Psychophysics **18**, 1–8 (1975).

Gibson, J.J.: Events are perceivable but time is not. Paper presented at a meeting of the International Society for the Study of Time, Japan 1973.

Goldman-Eisler, F.: Sequential temporal patterns and cognitive processes in speech. Acta neurologica and psychiatrica. Belgica **67**, 841–851 (1967).

Goldstone, S.: The human clock: a framework for the study of healthy and deviant time perception. Annals New York Acad. Sci. **138**, 767–783 (1967).

Gooddy, W.: Disorders of the time sense. In: Handbook of clinical neurology. P.J. Vinken and G.W. Bruyn (eds.). Amsterdam: North Holland Publishing 1969, Vol. III, pp. 229–250.

Gregg, L.W.: Fractionation of temporal intervals. J. exp. Psychol. **42**, 307–312 (1951).
Guyau, M.: La genése de l'idée de temps. Paris: F. Alcan 1890.
Harter, M.R.: Excitability cycles and cortical scanning: a review of two hypotheses of central intermittency in perception. Psychol. Bull. **68**, 47–58 (1967).
Harter, R., White, C.T.: Periodicity within reaction time distributions and electromyograms. Q. J. exp. Psychol. **20**, 157–166 (1968).
Hearnshaw, L.S.: Temporal integration and behaviour. Bulletin of the British Psychological Society **30**, 1–20 (1956).
Helson, H.: Adaptation-level theory. New York: Harper and Row 1964.
Hirsh, I.J., Sherrick, C.E., Jr.: Perceived order in different sense modalities. J. exp. Psychol. **62**, 423–432 (1961).
Hoagland, H.: The physiological control of judgments of duration: evidence for a chemical clock. J. genet. Psychol. **9**, 267–287 (1933).
Hoche, A.: Langeweile. Psychol. Forschung **3**, 258–271 (1923).
Holubář, J.: The sense of time. Cambridge, Mass.-London: M.I.T. Press 1969.
Holubář, J., Machek, J.: Time sense and epileptic EEG activity. Epilepsia **3**, 323–328 (1962).
Hornstein, A.D., Rotter, G.S.: Research methodology in temporal perception. J. exp. Psychol. **79**, 561–564 (1969).
Horst, L. van der: Über die Psychologie des Korsakowsyndroms. Monatsschrift für Psychiatrie und Neurologie **83**, 65–84 (1932).
James, W.: The principles of psychology. New York: Henry Holt 1890, Vol. I.
Kent, R.D., Moll, K.L.: Articulatory timing in selected consonant sequences. Brain and Language **2**, 304–323 (1975).
Köhler, W.: Zur Theorie des Sukzessivvergleichs und der Zeitfehler. Psychol. Forschung **4**, 115–175 (1923).
Kristofferson, A.B.: Attention and psychophysical time. Acta psychol. **27**, 93–100 (1967)
Lackner, J.R., Teuber, H.-L.: Alterations in auditory fusion thresholds after cerebral injury in man. Neuropsychologia **11**, 409–415 (1973).
Lashley, K.S.: The problem of serial order in behavior. In: Cerebral mechanisms in behavior. Jeffress, L.A. (ed.). New York: Wiley 1951, pp. 112–136.
Latour, P.L.: Evidence of internal clocks in the human operator. Acta psychol. **27**, 341–348 (1967).
Mach, E.: Untersuchungen über den Zeitsinn des Ohres. Sitzungsberichte der mathem.-naturwiss. Classe d. Kaiserl. Akademie d. Wissenschaften **51**, II. Abt. Heft 1–5, 133–150 (1865).
Mach, E.: Die Analyse der Empfindungen und das Verhältnis des Physischen zum Psychischen. Jena: G. Fischer 1885.
Martin, J.G.: Rhythmic (hierarchical) versus serial structure in speech and other behavior. Psychol. Review **79**, 487–509 (1972).
Michon, J.A.: Timing in temporal tracking. Soesterberg: Institute of Perception RVO-TNO 1967.
Michon, J.A.: Processing of temporal information and the cognitive theory of time experience. Studium Generale **23**, 249–265 (1970).
Milner, B.: Hemispheric specialization: scope and limits. In: The neurosciences: third study program. Schmitt, F.O., Worden, F.G. (eds.). Cambridge-London: M.I.T. Press 1974, pp. 75–89.
Müller, G.E., Schumann, F.: Experimentelle Beiträge zur Untersuchung des Gedächtnisses. Zeitschrift für Psychologie **6**, 81–190 (1894).
Nichols, H.: The psychology of time. Amer. J. Psychol. **3**, 453–530 (1891).
Orme, J.E.: Time, experience and behaviour. London: Iliffe Books 1969.
Ornstein, R.E.: On the experience of time. Harmondsworth: Penguin Books 1969.
Podvigin, N.F.: On the mechanism of operative memory in the visual system. Sechenov Physiological Journal of the USSR **58**, 592–594 (1972).
Pöppel, E.: Oszillatorische Komponenten in Reaktionszeiten. Naturwissenschaften **55**, 449–450 (1968).
Pöppel, E.: Excitability cycles in central intermittency. Psychol. Forschung **34**, 1–9 (1970).
Pöppel, E.: Oscillations as possible basis for time perception. In: The study of time. Fraser, J.T., Huber, F.C., Müller, G.H. (eds.). Berlin: Springer 1972, pp. 219–241.
Pöppel, E.: Influence of pause duration on the reproduction of a 2-second interval. Bull. Psychon. Soc. **2**, 291–292 (1973).

Pöppel, E., Cramon, D., von, Backmund, H.: Eccentricity-specific dissociation of visual functions in patients with lesions of the central visual pathways. Nature **256**, 489–490 (1975).

Postman, L., Miller, G.A.: Anchoring of temporal judgments. Amer. J. Psychol. **58**, 43–53 (1945).

Quasebarth, K.: Zeitschätzung und Zeitauffassung optisch und akustisch ausgefüllter Intervalle. Arch. ges. Psychol. **49**, 379–432 (1924).

Richards, W.: Time estimates measured by reproduction. Perceptual and motor skills **18**, 929–943 (1964).

Ross, S., Katchmar, L.: The construction of a magnitude function for short time-intervals. Amer. J. Psychol. **64**, 397–401 (1951).

Rubin, E.: Some elementary time experiences. Acta psychol. **1**, 206–211 (1935).

Shallice, T.: The detection of change and the perceptual moment hypothesis. The British J. of Statistical Psychol. **17**, 113–135 (1964).

Stern, L.W.: Psychische Präsenzzeit. Zeitschrift für Psychologie und Physiologie der Sinnesorgane **13**, 325–349 (1897).

Sternberg, S.: Memory scanning: new findings and current controversies. Quart. J. exp. Psychol. **27**, 1–32 (1975).

Stevens, S.S.: On the psychophysical law. Psychol. Review **64**, 153–181 (1957).

Stroud, J.M.: The fine structure of psychological time. In: Information theory in psychology. Quastler, H. (ed.). Glencoe, Ill.: Free Press 1955, pp. 174–205.

Sturt, M.: The psychology of time. London: Kegan Paul 1925.

Swift, E.J., McGeoch, J.A.: An experimental study of the perception of filled and empty time. J. exp. Psychol. **8**, 240–249 (1925).

Talland, G.A.: Les troubles de l'orientation temporelle dans le syndrome amnésique. L'encéphale **50**, 450–470 (1961).

Urbantschitsch, V.: Über eine Eigenthümlichkeit der Schallempfindungen geringster Intensität. Centralbl. f. d. med. Wissensch. **13**, 625–628 (1875).

Vierordt, K.: Der Zeitsinn nach Versuchen. Tübingen: Laupp 1868.

Vroon, P.A.: Effects of presented and processed information on duration experience. Acta Psychol. **34**, 115–121 (1970).

Vroon, P.A.: Is there a time quantum in duration experience? Am. J. Psychol. **87**, 237–245 (1974).

Wallace, M., Rabin, A.I.: Temporal experience. Psychol. Bull. **57**, 213–236 (1960).

Weber, A.O.: Estimation of time. Psychol. Bull. **30**, 233–252 (1933).

Wever, R.: Pendulum versus relaxation oscillation. In: Circadian Clocks. Aschoff, J. (ed.). Amsterdam: North-Holland Publ. 1965, pp. 74–83.

White, C.T.: Temporal numerosity and the psychological unit of duration. Psychological Monographs: General and Applied **77**, 1–37 (1963).

Wiener, N.: Time and the science of organization. Scientia **93**, 199–205 (1958).

Williams, M., Zangwill, O.L.: Disorders of temporal judgment associated with amnesic states. J. ment. Sci. **96**, 484–493 (1950).

Woodrow, H.: The temporal indifference interval determined by the method of mean error. J. exp. Psychol. **17**, 167–188 (1934).

Woodrow, H.: Time perception. In: Handbook of experimental psychology. Stevens, S.S. (ed.). New York, London: Wiley 1951, pp. 1224–1236.

Wundt, W.: Ueber psychologische Methoden. Philosophische Studien **1**, 1–38 (1881).

Wundt, W.: Einführung in die Psychologie. Leipzig: Voigtländer 1911.

Zurif, E.B., Carson, G.: Dyslexia in relation to cerebral dominance and temporal analysis. Neuropsychologia **8**, 351–361 (1970).

Chapter 24

Perceptual Aspects of the Reading Process and Its Development

E.J. GIBSON, Ithaca, N.Y. (USA)

With 3 Figures

Contents

A. Perception and Reading

An acceptable definition of reading would necessarily be broad enough to include many processes: perceiving, comprehending, remembering, and even making inferences. These cognitive processes would be accompanied by other processes which might be said to serve them such as orienting the head, fixating and moving the eyes, and articulating subvocally. Learning to read, therefore, involves more than perceptual learning. Nevertheless, perception is propaedeutic to any other process involved in reading. The information on the printed page must be extracted; it is embodied in the printed stimulus and can only be picked up by perceptual processes. These processes vary tremendously in efficiency: in skill of discrimination; in the way the page is scanned; in the size of the unit extracted; and in flexibility of attention. Perceptual learning takes place in improving these skills and will thus be stressed. Since reading requires extraction of information from visual displays, visual perception will be considered primarily, but phonologic aspects of words and larger speech units must be related to corresponding visual units and will be considered briefly.

B. Development of Discrimination of Written Symbols

I. Spontaneous Recognition and Production of "Writing" in Young Children

It has often been assumed that learning to differentiate one graphic character from another is a major hurdle in acquisition of literacy. If so, man has evolved a highly adaptive kind of behavior to assist the learning. A child given a writing tool and some paper will scribble spontaneously by 18 months (GIBSON and YONAS, 1968). He is interested in more than guiding the pencil, for he looks at his production and ceases if the tool ceases to leave traces. His scribbling evolves from the "fundamental graphic act" of leaving a trace to controlled guidance. Patterning of scribbles in relation to the paper's edge begins at about 2 years, and diversity of patterns including single lines at various orientations, crossings, and closed forms appear between 2 and 3 years, with increasingly clear-cut form (less and less overlay). KELLOGG (1969) classifies "basic scribbles" into 20 categories, but the number would be fewer if they were arranged as contrastive pattern properties (e.g., dot vs. line, straight vs. curved, open vs. closed). What could afford a better opportunity for learning about the features that alphabets use to differentiate letters? Scribbling resembles actual writing more and more closely, incorporating real letters by 5 years if the child has models at hand (HILDRETH, 1936; LEGRÜN, 1932; WHEELER, 1971).

Does this spontaneous production actually result in learning how to discriminate any features of writing? LAVINE (1977) asked this question in a comparative study of children's recognition of "writing" as distinct from pictures. Children between 3 and $6^1/_2$ years were shown a number of graphic displays to see whether they would classify them as "writing." Features of the displays were varied, such as pictorial representativeness, multiplicity of units, variety of units, linearity, and graphic characteristics of actual writing systems (see GIBSON and LEVIN (1975) for a summary). The 3-year-olds distinguished correctly between pictorial displays and letters (either single letters or a word), although they could not name a letter or read a word. Linear arrangement of subunits, multiple unit displays, and variety of units influenced the child's categorization as writing increasingly until 5 years, when presence of actual letters became important. Knowledge of the unique pattern of features for the Roman alphabet was still incomplete for most children, however. All the 5-year-olds classified a six-letter word in Roman script as writing, but so did they ones in Hebrew script. They could not read the words nor identify the scripts. It seems, then, that children learn spontaneously to recognize global features of writing (e.g., multiple units, linearity) and the set of internal contrastive features used to distinguish units. But this knowledge is based on opportunity to view appropriate specimens. Children in a remote rural village of Yucatan where there was very limited exposure to print and writing were by no means as knowledgeable as children in a middle-class group where exposure was pervasive.

II. Learning to Discriminate Letters

Children thus progress in discrimination of writing when the culture provides opportunity for spontaneous perceptual learning. But the unique shape of each letter, and the features that define a particular set are not necessarily mastered when reading instruction is begun. Sensitivity to differences in letter-like forms increases up to the age of eight or so (GIBSON et al., 1962a). A set of 12 graphic forms comparable to roman capital letters was constructed. These "standards" were then subjected to various transformations, some appropriate to critical features of writing (straight-curve), some not (perspective transformations); some which have been considered to give children trouble (right-left reversals) and some which generally have not (open-closed). The 12 standards were compared in a discrimination test with 12 transformations by children aged 4–8 years. Errors declined with age from a large number at 4 years to only a few at 8. The degree of change (represented by the number of straight-curve transformations, which varied from 1 to 3) was important, and interacted with age. Either sensitivity to degree of similarity or the child's criterion of "same" (or probably, both) changed developmentally. But the rate of improvement with age also depended on the way the standard had been transformed. Figure 1 shows the decline of errors with age grouped into four classes of transformation, pooling specific types within a class.

Perspective transformations were hard to detect at all ages. Although there was a decrease with age, it was not striking. Any kind of foreshortening of a letter is irrelevant for reading, varying with the page's slant, and it is ignored by most readers. Rotations and reversals, on the other hand, were responsible for many errors at 4 and 5 years. That they should be is to be expected, since children have learned about object constancies by this time and know that an object is the same despite rotation. But they have to learn that such identity is not conserved for a frozen, two-dimensional shape on a piece of paper. Most children have learned the difference by 8 years, as the curve shows. Break

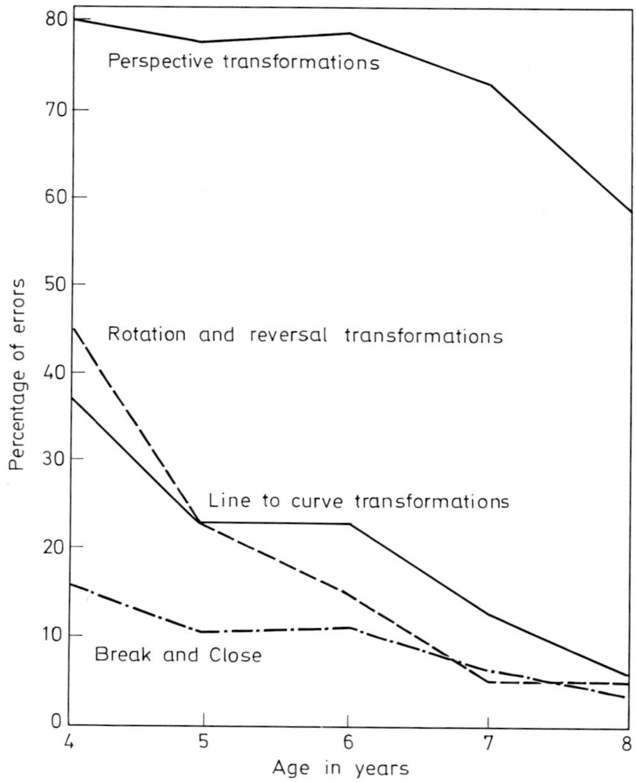

Fig. 1. Types of errors in discrimination of letter-like forms and their decline with age. (From GIBSON et al., 1962a)

and close transformations produced few errors even at 4 years. They are critical features for differentiating solid objects and the knowledge carries over to graphic items.

Other research has examined the ability of kindergarten children to match letters (CALFEE et al., 1972). When single letters were to be matched to one of a series of five, as in the example below,

b – h d b f k

the error rate was quite low (83% and 87% correct matches in two different groups). The major source of error was the right-left mirror image transformation (e.g., b vs. d). Errors on these items were high (about 40%). But by 7 years even this type of error has dropped sharply. With artificial graphemes, GIBSON et al. (1962a) found less than 10% such errors, and with familiar letters the number might be less. SHANKWEILER and LIBERMAN (1972) found only 10% reversal errors for a selected group of very poor readers.

What do children learn when they learn to differentiate and identify individual letters? Do they discover the critical dimensions of difference, or do they learn a figural scheme for each letter? It seems reasonable that they do both,

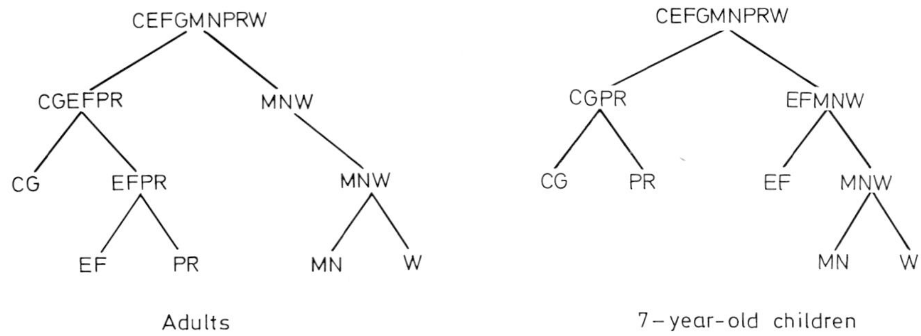

Fig. 2. Tree structures resulting from hierarchical cluster analyses of latencies for letter comparisons by adults and 7-year-old children. (From GIBSON et al., 1968)

with feature differences predominating in early learning, at least. Experiments by PICK (1965) compared the transfer value of discrimination training with letter-like forms and three transformations of them to (1) discrimination of new forms from the old transformations of them versus (2) the old forms from new transformations. There was positive transfer in both cases, but the effect was significantly larger when the familiar transformations were preserved. Detecting dimensions of difference seems thus to be of fundamental importance for discriminating letters, but a figural scheme seems to be formed as well. It would serve a functional role, presumably, in production of a letter.

What exactly are the critical properties that differentiate letters? The research described above was not addressed to this problem, but knowledge of them would be useful. GIBSON (1969) speculated that they are contrastive features analogous to distinctive features of phonemes. They would not be structural elements, in such a case, but rather binary properties that are abstracted by a comparison process. A straight vs. curve opposition might be one; a closed-open opposition another. It is possible to generate, intuitively, a feature chart that will provide a unique pattern of contrastive properties for each letter, but whether such properties are used for differentiation is another question. GIBSON et al. (1968) attacked this problem obtaining confusion matrices for sets of letters presented in pairs. *Ss* made same-different judgments, and latency of responses, as well as errors, were measured. The *Ss* were adults and 1-year-old children. A hierarchical cluster analysis was performed on the error and latency data. Figure 2 shows structures resulting from the latency analysis for children and for adults with a set of nine letters. The nodes in the structure suggest that the straight-curve contrast is highly salient for children and that diagonality is a secondary feature. Diagonality appears to be a salient property for adults, as does intersection, since letters with intersections, vs. "round" ones are clustered at one node.

Similar analyses with other letters, and on data[1] obtained with another judgment (sorting) yielded highly similar contrasts at nodes. There appeared to be some age differences, but probably not after second grade.

---

[1] Data obtained by G. LEHNE. See GIBSON and LEVIN (1975) for a full discussion of results of analyses of confusion matrices.

Contrastive features do appear to be used, then, in processing same-different judgments and sorting of letters. Nodine and his coworkers (Nodine and Stuerle, 1973; Nodine and Simmons, 1974) studied eye-movements of children looking at pairs of letter strings and pairs of single letters during same-different judgments. The quality of the scanning improved from kindergarten to third grade, the older children attending selectively to more informative details, such as areas providing information for feature contrasts, and tending to ignore irrelevant and redundant details. Increased economy of processing was the most noticeable change, however; the older children sometimes made a decision based on only one fixation (often between the letters). The younger children were apt to scan repeatedly between the same target areas, not necessarily very informative ones. How the distinguishing properties are processed in a same-different judgment does not seem to come out clearly from eye-movement photography, suggesting that processing of critical features occurs at a deeper level than peripheral directing of eye movements.

III. Teaching Letter Discrimination

Although most children appear to become competent in letter discrimination without any formal training, there are cases where confusions persist and help is called for. The obvious remedy for such cases appears to be contrastive presentation of confusable pairs with attention directed to the critical contrasts (Samuels, 1970). Some kind of enhancement of the contrastive property, such as a redundant display combining a more salient property (e.g., a color difference) with the areas containing the essential information might facilitate its abstraction. There is a drawback to this method, however. Combining a redundant but salient contrast with a more subtle one may result in nothing but pick-up of the salient one and continued disregard of the critical one (Gibson and Shepela, 1968; Samuels, 1968).

The use of "fading" techniques, as in errorless discrimination learning, is a possibility when enhancing properties are combined with the critical ones. Properly used, it can avoid reinforcement of discriminations based on incorrect "cues." Egeland et al. (1973) compared an errorless discrimination training technique with simple reinforcement or nonreinforcement of discrimination of confusible letters. The judgment was matching to sample, and *Ss* were prekindergarten children. In the errorless discrimination condition, the relevant "cue" was highlighted in bright red, but on subsequent trials it was gradually faded until the entire letter was black. No feedback was given during errorless training. The mean number of errors during training and during a posttest in which neither group received reinforcement was significantly less for the errorless discrimination group.

Fernald (1943) favored the value of motor practice in helping retarded readers to distinguish confusible letters and words. But Williams (1970) found that tracing an outline or copying was not particularly effective for developing recognition of letters in preschool children. Practice in discrimination without reproduction was more effective. Neither does motor pretraining on an artificial grapheme make it easier to associate afterward with an arbitrary response (LEVIN et al., 1963). If the motor responses are directed at calling attention to the perceptually relevant features, however, some benefit may result (HENDRICKSON and MUEHL, 1962). It is not the response as such that matters, but judgmental factors required to make a response that is relevant to the distinguishing property.

IV. Discrimination of Letter Strings

Although discrimination of single letters is seldom a problem for most children, discrimination of letter strings is. When letters are presented in a sequence—even a sequence of two—error rates for matching from a sample increase sharply. CALFEE et al. (1972) found with a matching set, like the one below, that correct choices ranged from 36% to 48% in two groups of kindergarten

CQ... OQ-OC-QC-CQ-CO

children. For sets of three and four letters, the percent dropped lower (30–35%). Performance was no worse when the child had to match from memory, so there must be difficulty in extracting order information, not only in preserving it. SHANKWEILER and LIBERMAN (1972) found that matching words and matching letter strings was still a prime source of difficulty for third graders who read poorly, although matching single letters was not. The errors were not necessarily reversals, but permutations of other types as well.

Experienced readers recognize words by means of orthographic patterns larger than the letter, but beginning readers and poor readers do not. Information about order in the letter string involves knowledge of constraints and structural rules of orthography, even above knowledge of sequential probabilities. More about this later. But first, why is the serial order hard to process, and why is it the locus of developmental lags?

The answer is complex, but at an early perceptual stage it seems that it may be related to masking effects in sequential processing of the letters. Fixations are more frequent in young readers and in poor readers, and duration of the fixation is longer, both handicaps to easy perception of letter order and accurate perception of chunks larger than a letter. Assuming that the individual letters must be processed at some level (or familiar small clumps of them that have become units), there could be both forward and backward masking effects within the word if the scan rate is too fast. Errors in reading are notoriously fewer at the beginning and ends of words, where there is a white space on one side.

What are the facts of masking, considered developmentally? Studies of backward masking comparing different age groups differ in ages of the subjects compared, in the nature of the target (e.g., letter or letters, geometric forms, line orientation, presence or absence of a disc, etc.), in the nature of the mask (e.g., letters, geometric forms, composites of forms, matrices, etc.) in stimulus duration, in ISI duration (time between target and mask presentation), and in the response measure (e.g., detection, judgment of separation, identification, etc.). But every one of these studies (POLLACK, 1965; SPITZ and THOR, 1968; LISS and HAITH, 1970; GUMMERMAN and GRAY, 1972; MILLER, 1972; BLAKE, 1974) found that the masking threshold (interval between the target and the mask that is sufficient to permit a successful judgment with respect to the target) decreased with age, at least up to 15 years (SPITZ and THOR, 1968). The effect of the mask is more harmful with younger *Ss*, shorter ISI intervals, and a more demanding judgment (identification vs. detection). Probably size of the target array (BLAKE, 1974) and other factors (similarity of target to mask) are important as well. Intelligence (IQ) does not seem to be important, but M.A. is (POLLACK, 1965; SPITZ and THOR, 1968).

These facts are of interest because it has been found that dyslexics have a longer masking threshold than normal readers of comparable C.A. and average or better performance in other academic subjects (STANLEY and HALL, 1973). They found that an ISI long enough to judge mere separation for a short word was significantly longer than for normal readers of equivalent C.A.; and the ISI for identification was nearly twice as long (363.6 ms vs 191.5 ms). A difficulty in sequential processing similar to a developmental lag appears to exist for these retarded readers although their performances on other tasks may be unimpaired. Many unanswered questions, such as the relation of this lag to "chunking" and to extraction of spelling patterns exist. Would the lag appear if context were available? The role of forward masking in development has been scarcely touched, but the fact that the end of a word, although followed by a white space, is at a disadvantage with respect to the beginning makes one suspect that forward masking plays a role as well.

C. Perception of Phonologic Features of Words

It is clear that perceptual analysis, as well as perception of superordinate graphic units, is essential for the development of reading skill. Something analogous is demanded for phonologic features of the verbal material. It is less obvious to the layman that a problem exists here, since a child entering school has been comprehending and speaking the language and showing his ability to fit words into new sentence contexts for several years. Surely he perceives the words he hears as integral units? But research has shown that he does not always divide a sentence into words correctly and often has no concept of a "word." Segmenting a word into syllables is a still more abstract task for him; and segmentation of syllables into smaller units approaching a phoneme is for most children an incomprehensible, artificial, and formidable task.

I. Recognition of English Phonology

A child as young as four has been shown to have good appreciation of English phonology. WHORF (1956) developed a useful and quite precise formula for generating all legal sound sequences in the English monosyllable. Using pairs of nonwords, half legal by WHORF's formula and half violating it, MESSER (1967) found that preschool children were able to select the words that conformed to English phonologic rules. MENYUK (1969) found that children from preschool through second grade could imitate nonsense words better when they conformed to the rules of English phonology. Thus 4-year old children do distinguish English from non-English sound sequences, and they assimilate their productions toward legal English. Nevertheless, analysis of both perception and production of these sequences is lacking.

II. Syllable and Phoneme Segmentation

It is generally assumed that in learning to read, children must learn the correspondences between the spoken and the written form of the language. When do children extract from the speech stream the units that are appropriate for learning to read? The question is a hard one to answer, because it is unnatural (and in the case of stop-consonants impossible) to utter a single phoneme in isolation (LIBERMAN et al., 1967). One is perceived, even, only in the process of abstraction from a contrasting pair of monosyllables like *pit-bit*. It is hardly surprising, therefore, that children do not automatically segment speech into individual phonemes. It may be surprising that they do not automatically segment speech into words and syllables (not such a difficult task), until one remembers that the unique purpose of speech for a child is communication—to understand what someone else is saying, or to make his own wants and observations understood. Breaking the speech stream into words, as demonstrated by reversing a pair of words uttered to him, is not easy for many 5-year-old children (HUTTENLOCHER, 1964), especially when the words form a sensible sequence such as "man runs." Segmenting words into syllables is also a task requiring practice at an early age, but at least syllables are unitary constituents and can be uttered in isolation. Japanese children are taught syllable segmentation before learning the two syllabary systems for writing Japanese at the age of 5 (MURAISHI, 1972), apparently without difficulty. Although English syllabification has decidedly more complex rules than Japanese, English-speaking children learn to segment a word into syllables with far greater ease than they learn to segment a word or a syllable into phonemic constituents (LIBERMAN, 1973; SAVIN, 1972; BRUCE, 1964). Difficulty in teaching children to analyze a word into constituent sounds has also been documented for Russian by ZHUROVA (1963). A major feature of Russian prereading training involves practice in segmenting words into phonemes (ELKONIN, 1963).

III. Recognition of Rhyming Similarity

Although children appear to enjoy rhymes at an early age, confuse rhyming substitutions in recognition (CRAMER, 1972), and give spontaneous rhyming free associations (ENTWISTLE, 1966; TENNEY, 1975), they nevertheless as preschoolers do not have the ability to match sounds for similarity when asked to (SAVIN, 1972).

IV. Role of "Awareness"

Why is it that analysis of the acoustic aspect of the speech stream is so much more difficult than the graphic aspect of written language? It seems to have a kind of inscrutability to a child despite his competence in speaking and comprehension. On the other hand, comprehension of the written version is not easy to come by, although analysis (except for serial order) is relatively easy. We can only speculate at present that speech, *prima facie,* carries *meaning* for the child. The physical aspect is not attended to as such and indeed is ephemeral. Writing carries no message when reading instruction is begun; but it is permanent and can be attended to at length.

V. "Cross-modal" Matching

Many experiments have been conducted on the assumption that reading requires some kind of matching of written constituents to acoustic ones. The "elements" chosen for such tests are usually meaningless patterns of dots and dashes. The acoustic patterns are, of course, presented over time, whereas the visual patterns may be a spatial arrangement of dots and dashes, or flashes presented over time. Ability to match patterns across modes is thought by many to be a skill basic to learning to read. The results do not support the hypothesis that intermodal integration is a skill uniquely related to reading (e.g., BRYDEN, 1972; VANDE VOORT et al., 1972). But there is evidence that poor matching ability, even in these rather meaningless tasks, predicts reading ability in *poor* readers. Why? At a guess, it seems likely that extraction of *structure* of patterned information, and perception of the *relations* between subordinate units over time (and space) are requisite for reading. Both the analysis of a pattern and perception of the higher-order structure of a pattern are essentials for skilled reading.

D. Recognition of Words

Despite the need for some analysis of the spoken and written messages in teaching a child the complex nature of the correspondence between the speech code and the written code, it is clearly the coincidence of the *messages* that counts. This semantic relationship exceeds the bounds of perceptual processing, but even in perceiving it is important to remember that a good reader does not process the information letter by letter. The English orthographic system has its own rules which are not adequately described as single letter to single sound matching. The English monosyllable always has a vocalic center, which may or may not be preceded or followed by a consonant or a consonant cluster of as many as five letters when spelled (e.g., "twelfths"). It is a useful characteristic of English that these clusters are nearly all (all but 3 out of 150 common ones [FRIES, 1962/63]) constrained as to initial or final position. Incorporation of this distributive rule decreases alternatives and promotes economical pick-up of syllables as units.

I. The Word-Superiority Effect: How is it to be Explained?

Experiments by CATTELL (1885) nearly a century ago showed that we can perceive words exposed very briefly much more accurately than a string of unconnected letters and that it takes longer to name a letter than to name a word. ERDMANN and DODGE (1898) found that eye movements in reading are fast jumps (saccades) and that the information is extracted almost entirely during the fixations. A good reader makes about seven fixations per line (plus or minus two or more, depending on the length of the line, the text and other factors), usually fewer than the number of words. CATTELL thought that extraction of the higher-order units depended on meaningfulness and familiarity, but later research, especially in the last decade, has not only confirmed CATTELL's results but made it clear that factors other than meaningfulness are involved in what is often referred to as the "word-apprehension effect" or the "word-superiority" effect (see GIBSON and LEVIN, 1975, Chap. 7, for a detailed discussion).

The word-superiority effect has been demonstrated by many methods: identification with a short (tachistoscopic) exposure (CATTELL, 1885, and many others); reaction time (CATTELL, 1886, and others); threshold measures using increasing exposure time or brightness contrast (GIBSON et al., 1964); scanning for a word or nonword target (NEISSER, 1963; CLARE, 1969); latency for same-different judgments (BARRON and PITTENGER, 1974); "word likeness" and "is it a word" judgments (ROSINSKI and WHEELER, 1972; RUBENSTEIN et al., 1970); and detection of a letter embedded in a word versus detection of a letter presented in isolation.

The latter judgment has provided dramatic demonstrations. That a single letter is detected with greater accuracy in a short exposure when it is presented as part of a word, rather than in isolation or in a collection of meaningless symbols has received support from REICHER, 1969; LOTT and SMITH, 1970; WHEELER, 1970; KRUEGER, 1970; JOHNSTON and MCCLELLAND, 1973. JOHNSTON and MCCLELLAND (1974) provided an especially convincing demonstration. Words were presented tachistoscopically, followed by a mask in which letter positions were clearly indicated. In half the trials, *Ss* were told to try to see the whole word. In the other half, *S* was instructed to inspect only one given letter position in the word; the other letters would be irrelevant. After exposure, *S* made a forced choice between two words differing by only one letter (the correct one or an alternative). Performance was better with whole word instructions. Thus, to quote these authors, the "processing of any given stimulus letter must depend critically on the larger stimulus of which it is a part" (p. 1192).

When a string of unrelated letters was presented, in contrast with a word or a single letter, Johnston and McClelland (1974) found the converse result. Letters were detected better when presented alone, despite being part of a longer string. Does it follow that the "word-letter phenomenon" as they term the "word-superiority effect" is explained by the fact that a word is meaningful and familiar, whereas a string of unrelated letters is not? These two features of a word are undoubtedly of importance (Gibson et al., 1964, showed with familiar initials such as *FBI* that meaning of a string of letters, without legal word structure, facilitated threshold of identification), and word frequency (albeit usually confounded with other factors) has been shown again and again to facilitate detection and recognition of words. Nevertheless, two other factors are outstanding candidates for understanding the effect: orthographic legality, and pronounceability.

The effect of orthographic legality (confounded with pronounceability and originally dubbed as such) was studied in 1962 by Gibson et al. A series of orthographically legal nonwords, four to eight letters in length, was constructed by placing appropriately constrained consonants or consonant clusters at the beginnings and similarly constrained consonants at the end, with a vowel or vowel cluster in the center (e.g., *sland, glurk*). An illegal, unpronounceable control list was constructed by inverting the position of the clusters (e.g., *ndasl, rkugl*). The two lists were presented in mixed order at five exposure durations (30–250 ms). The percentage of legal "pronounceable" nonwords read correctly was greater at all exposure durations. A forced choice judgment from a selection of four alternatives yielded the same result. Baron and Thurston (1973) also questioned the sufficiency of meaningfulness and familiarity to explain the "word superiority" effect. They performed experiments comparable to Reicher's (1969) and Wheeler's (1970), embedding target letters in legal and illegal nonwords as well as real words. The legal nonword condition was superior to an illegal nonword condition and to a single-letter condition, and did not differ from a real-word condition.

But orthographic legality implies, *ipso facto*, pronounceability of a word string. Is it effective because *S* pronounces the letter string to himwelf as he reads it and finds it phonetically acceptable (and perhaps, therefore, more memorable as a "chunk")? Gibson et al. (1970) compared tachistoscopic recognition of "pronounceable" vs. "unpronounceable" nonwords in congenitally deaf college students. The deaf *Ss* profited as much from "pronounceability" as did hearing *Ss* of comparable age and education. For the deaf *Ss*, the two types of nonsense words must have been differentiated by orthographic structure alone. Baron (1974a) presented evidence to show that orthographic regularity affected time taken to compare two strings of letters for identity or to search for a letter in a string, but the comparison was not affected by "wordness." On the other hand, comparing the *sound* of two strings (phonetic comparison) was affected by "wordness." BARON (1973) also tested *Ss*' judgments of whether a phrase "sounded" sensible, regardless of how it looked (was spelled correctly or incorrectly via substitution of homophones). *Ss* were faster on phrases that "looked" sensible as well as sounded sensible. "Pronounceability," if one means by it subvocal or auditory representation, seems not to be a necessary factor in explaining the superiority of words and regularly spelled letter strings in experimental manipulations with adults.

II. Units vs. Rules in Word Perception

We have argued on the basis of fairly compelling evidence that neither meaningfulness, familiarity, or pronounceability are sufficient to explain the word-superiority effect although all of them can be shown to have a role in various tasks. Orthography itself contains regularities that affect ease of perceptual pick-up of words, legally constructed letter strings, and letters within such strings. What is the nature of these regularities? When communication theory was being developed it was fashionable to argue that digram frequency and sequential probabilities were the important factors. GIBSON et al. (1970) showed in a step-wise regression analysis that summed digram frequency and even trigram frequency accounted for an insignificant percentage of the variance in tachistoscopic recognition of pseudo-words, whereas rated "pronounceability" (or orthographic regularity in this case) accounted for a highly significant proportion. Positional constraints of consonants, consonant clusters, and certain vowels and vowel clusters provide rules for the English monosyllable and are far better candidates for predicting the effect.

It has been argued that constrained clusters or highly frequent combinations of letters (e.g., *er* or *th*) or the syllables that constitute a word are perceived as units and account for economical perception of orthographically well-structured letter-strings by reducing the number of units to be processed (SMITH and HAVILAND, 1972). This is a rather attractive hypothesis, since syllables of a word (provided one can agree on the definition of a syllable) appear to function as structural units (ZEITLER, 1900; SPOEHR and SMITH, 1973). Furthermore, suffixes and roots appear to function as independent unitary constituents of words (GIBSON and GUINET, 1971). In the latter case, semantic factors undoubtedly play a role. The English monosyllable is often (though not always) a morpheme, and thus has semantic features to confer unity and identity upon it (e.g., a suffix like *ing* or a root word like *walk*). But it also has orthographic constraints which must be observed. The *ng* in the progressive inflection must be at the end of the syllable and the presence of the vowel is imperative. The *lk* in *walk* is constrained to final position in a syllable. Constraints such as these were tested by BARON (1974b) in artificial word lists, with digram frequency and sequential probability controlled. Constrained consonant clusters were shown to possess an advantage for recognition over unconstrained ones following tachistoscopic exposure. BARON concluded that "conformity to rules specifying the order of letters or letter groups" was a spelling regularity that affected perception (see GIBSON and LEVIN, 1975, for a more detailed discussion of this issue).

SMITH and SPOEHR (1974) discussed models of word perception in some detail, contrasting letter perception and word perception. Theories emphasizing higher order units (for either decision or matching) are one class of model. These models (especially decision models) do not rule out guessing, and rather than define higher-order units, they are apt to rely on properties of single letters within the word such as frequency, predictability, and confusability of one letter with another. Tests of the models have generally relied on recognition of three-letter sequences, not the ideal vehicle for finding higher-order units (except regularity across categories of words, which is, in fact, a useful type of spelling redundancy but not truly an intraword unit).

"Spelling patterns" defined as subordinate groups of letters within a word that have invariant correspondence with pronunciation in a given position within a word were at one time proposed by GIBSON et al. (1962) as potential subunits. The fact that congenitally deaf subjects profited equally well from constrained clusters rendered this idea far less attractive. SPOEHR and SMITH (1974) also objected on the grounds that the letters as such must have been perceived first. This objection may not be serious, since letters are probably seen at some level of processing even when identification is facilitated beyond the letter for a legal group.

SMITH and SPOEHR (1973) suggested that syllables are the effective units in word perception and that "parsing rules" can be generated to divide letter-strings into syllables. These rules, however, require that consonants and vowels first be discriminated in the string (a much more difficult task for a child than single letter identification). Also, the superiority of reading a letter in a word is as effective for monosyllables as for multisyllabic words. Knowledge of rules for the structure of monosyllables seems necessary for explaining the easy perception of legal spellings.

SMITH and SPOEHR (1974) reconsidered a grapheme-phoneme translation process, assuming that lexical information is accessed via a phonologic code, but we have already pointed out objections to such a model. A formula for the structure of an English monosyllable (designed for phonology, but nevertheless easily adjusted to orthography) was formulated by WHORF (1940) and it is possible that the rules for this formula become ingrained in the reader and are as unconsciously called into operation as the rules of grammar. But however well founded the facts of the word-superiority effect, its explanation is still moot.

III. Development of Word Recognition

All the previous studies were performed on adult readers. If we knew how reading in larger structures was developed, we might understand the final process. GIBSON et al. (1963) compared first and third grade children at the end of the year on three-letter strings presented tachistoscopically, including real words, pronounceable nonwords, and unpronounceable nonwords. A few longer nonwords of both types were also presented. Even the first graders read the real familiar words and the three-letter pronounceable nonwords (all in CVC format) better than the unpronounceable ones, but did not differentiate the longer nonwords. The third-grade girls did. ROSINSKI and WHEELER (1972) compared first, third, and fifth-grade children on a word-likeness task. Children were shown pairs of nonwords typed on cards, one legally spelled and one illegally, and asked "which is more like a word." The first-grade children performed at a chance level, but the other two groups performed better than chance (70% and 80% correct choices). Length was not a factor. GOLINKOFF (1974) replicated the experiment with first and second-grade children. Pairs of words of varied length contained the same letters, one member orthographically and phonologically legal but the other illegal. Presentation was visual only, auditory only, or visual-auditory-redundant. First-grade children did not perform significantly better than chance with visual or auditory presentation alone but were significantly better (72% correct) with bimodal redundancy. Second graders were significantly better with visual presentation alone (82.5% correct as compared with 65% for auditory and 70% for bimodal presentation). Either bimodal presentation reinforced critical features of "wordness" for first-graders, or they were able to process selectively the preferred mode of presentation; and thus, averaged together, gave the impression of having profited by bimodal redundancy. Visual information for the older children, at any rate, appeared to have surpassed auditory information in defining "wordness." Scores on judgments of word-likeness had a significant relationship ($r=0.50$) with reading achievement scores.

How is knowledge of legal spelling patterns abstracted? GIBSON, with a number of colleagues (see GIBSON and LEVIN, 1975, for a summary), tried varied forms of training in abstracting and generalizing spelling patterns in children learning to read (the majority of experiments were performed on children during the second term of first grade). The experiments typically used a "learning set" procedure with a series of problems: a sorting technique, correction, and opportunities to transfer a principle, if learned, to new problems (a variation of a concept learning paradigm). These experiments so far have been disappointing, yielding primarily negative knowledge. Abstracting a spelling pattern is extremely difficult for most first-grade children. A common, constrained pattern of letters in varied contexts is not salient. Telling the child may be effective for a single problem but has no transfer value. Auditory redundancy (so far, at least) has not been shown to help. Yet, by third grade, children (middle-class children in a good school at least) are able to generalize a lot of information about word likeness. It is only safe to say at this point that reinforcing responses to specific patterns is not the mechanism of the learning, that children appear to learn on their own as a result of extended exposure, and that the knowledge is acquired and used automatically with little awareness of doing so.

E. Meaning

Words, as well as actual events and happenings in the world, convey meaning. But in this writer's view (only one of hundreds, for meaning is an age-old problem for philosophers, linguists, and psychologists), meaning conveyed by words is "mediated" rather than directly perceived, and has its roots in perception of the adaptive significance of relations within events (appearance, disappearance, reappearance; agent→action, action→object, etc.; Brown, 1973). If this be the case, a single word, except in a situational context, is not a good candidate for revealing the apprehension of meaning. Yet words do have meanings; even constituent morphemes within a word do. How words acquire meaning is not within the scope of this chapter, but how we pick up the meaning of a written word would be a highly appropriate topic if we knew the answer. The problem is neatly skirted by many psychologists by assuming that the written word is decoded to a phonetic representation, for which the meaning is already known, so there is, de facto, no problem for reading. This solution is probably vastly oversimplified for the adult reader, at least, for whom access to meaning seems often to proceed directly from the written message.

Moore (1919), a student of Külpe, published a monograph describing experiments in which reaction time was measured as soon as a *S* reported a meaning following presentation of a picture or a word. Reaction time was also measured separately for an image to occur to a word, or a name to occur to a picture. Invariably, the latency for a report of meaning was shorter than that for occurrence of a name or a report of an image. Moore concluded that meaning was abstract, neither an image, nor verbal content. That meaning is abstract is concurred with by many psychologists. But how meaning is extracted from printed words is still a problem. Gibson et al. (1972) thought that printed words and pictures were matched more readily to the same common abstract meaning by adults than by children; evidence suggested that the children processed the bimodal comparison differently than adults, probably naming the picture to match the word (and possibly never really matching on the basis of meaning). That recoding of written words to speech is a mediating stage in comprehension for children seems plausible (perhaps as a result of the way reading is taught) and that it occurs in many adults "when the going gets hard" (Hardyck and Petrinovich, 1970) is also likely. Baron and McKillop (1975) found individual differences in adults in classifying phrases as "making sense" or not. Some *Ss* apparently made the decision on the basis of a "visual strategy" and some on the basis of a "phonemic strategy." The visual strategy (skipping subvocal mediation) appeared to be the more economical one.

Extraction of meaning is clearly one of the important unsolved problems. It should be reiterated that phrase, clause, and sentence context are essential factors in extracting the meaning of a message. Syntactic and semantic analysis of much larger units than the word are still rooted in perception, however, when veridical extraction of knowledge is achieved.

F. Attentional Strategies in Reading

I. Eye Movements

The most easily observed change in attentional strategies as reading skill increases is the achievement of a more systematic and economical eye-movement pattern. Studies by BUSWELL (1922) and others agreed in finding decreases in fixation frequency, number of regressions, and duration of pauses through the fourth grade. The major improvement in oculomotor behavior appears to have occurred by that time, and according to BUSWELL, the pattern has become stable by eighth grade. Figure 3 from TINKER (1965) illustrates differences in scan pattern between good and poor readers. Perception time is less for good readers and regressions are fewer. Apparent improvement of scanning in cross-sectional studies beyond the eighth grade is probably due to selective factors—the improved reading ability of the more able pupils who remain in school (TINKER). TINKER emphasized that good reading is a cause of efficient eye movements, rather than vice versa.

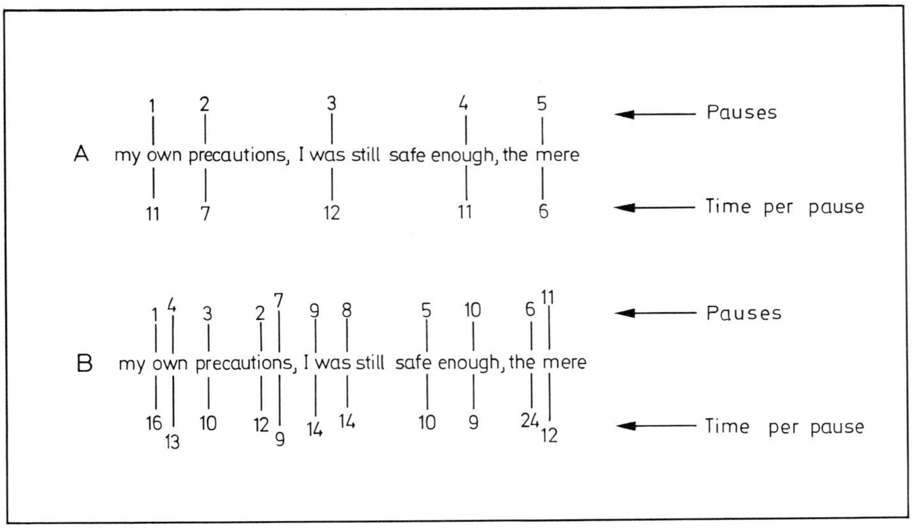

Fig. 3. Scan patterns of good and poor readers (TINKER, 1965)

II. Selective Processing

Written text can be processed selectively in many ways—probably in as many ways as there are different kinds of text, different readers, and different purposes for reading the text. Whether the reader is reading to learn something (facts, principles, lines of a play), to entertain himself, to find a single wanted piece of information, and so on will produce a variety of strategies in a well-trained reader. Focussing attention on what is wanted and ignoring what is not would seem to be an essential process in achieving flexible and economical reading. Improvement with development is characteristic of attentional strategies (GIBSON, 1969; GIBSON and LEVIN, 1975; PICK and FRANKEL, 1973). Such development occurs with improvement of reading skill, but it should be pointed out that the changes are not simple and uni-directional. Attention is at first focussed on meaning (BIEMILLER, 1970) to the neglect of graphic information; graphic and phonologic information after a time are attended to; but eventually, the reader progresses to automatic handling of such information and typically returns to the extraction of a meaningful message (WILLOWS and MACKINNON, 1973; WILLOWS, 1974).

G. Conclusion

Changes in perceptual (as well as other) aspects of reading skill can be characterized as finer differentiation of information in stimulation, both graphic and auditory (e.g., discrimination of distinctive features of letters, segmentation of sounds into subunits, distinguishing of confusible letter-orders); optimization of attention to wanted information (barely touched on here, since it transcends perception); and increasing economy of processing, especially in extracting information from larger, higher-order units. The term higher-order is used advisedly, since language, and especially written language, epitomizes ordered information in sequential presentation. Structure, describable in relations and rules, exists at many levels. In written language, there is structure at the low level of distinctive features of graphemes; there is structure in orthography; there is structure in syntax and punctuation; there is structure in the semantic relations within phrases, sentences, and long passages of discourse. Extracting this order from written language is the mark of economical perception in the skilled reader. The difference between a reader who uses the redundancy given by all these kinds of structure efficiently and automatically, and a beginning scholar who stumbles along decoding letter by letter into speech sounds cannot be exaggerated. The accomplishment of reading and comprehending the text of *War and Peace* is as wonderful as reading the score of a symphony, which does not come through note by note any more than the former comes through letter by letter.

References

Baron, J.: Phonemic stage not necessary for reading. Quart. J. exp. Psychol. **25**, 241–246 (1973).

Baron, J.: Successive stages in word recognition. In: Attention and performance. Dornic, S. and Rabbit, P.M.A. (eds.). New York: Academic Press, 1974a.

Baron, J.: Facilitation of perception by spelling constraints. Canad. J. Psychol. **28**, 37–50 (1974b).

Baron, J., McKillop, B.J.: Individual differences in speed of phonemic analysis, visual analysis and reading. Acta Psychologica **39**, 91–96 (1975)

Baron, J., Thurston, I.: An analysis of the word-superiority effect. Cog. Psychol. **4**, 207–228 (1973).

Barron, R.W., Pittinger, J.B.: The effect of orthographic structure and lexical meaning on *same-different* judgments. Quart. J. Exper. Psychol. **26**, 566–581 (1974).

Biemiller, A.: The development of the use of graphic and contextual information as children learn to read. Reading Res. Quart. **6**, 75–96 (1970).

Blake, J.: Developmental change in visual information processing under backward masking. J. exp. Child Psychol. **17**, 133–146 (1974).

Brown, R.: A first language. Cambridge: Harvard Univ. Press 1973.

Bruce, D.J.: Analysis of word sounds by young children. Brit. J. Educ. Psychol. **34**, 158–169 (1964).

Bryden, M.P.: Auditory-visual and sequential-spatial matching in relation to reading ability. Child Develpm. **43**, 824–832 (1972).

Buswell, G.T.: Fundamental reading habits: A study of their development. Suppl. Educ. Monogr. No. 21 (1922).

Calfee, R.C., Chapman, R.S., Venezky, R.L.: How a child needs to think to learn to read. In: Cognition in learning and memory. Gregg, L.W. (ed.). New York: John Wiley and Sons 1972.

Cattell, J.M.: Über die Zeit der Erkennung und Benennung von Schriftzeichen, Bildern und Farben. Philosophische Studien **2**, 635–650 (1885).

Chase, W.G., Clark, H.H.: Mental operations in the comparison of sentences and pictures. In: Cognition in learning and memory. Gregg, L.W. (ed.). New York: John Wiley and Sons 1972.

Clare, D.A.: A study of principles of integration in the perception of written verbal items. Unpublished Ph.D. Dissertation, Cornell Univ. (1969).

Cramer, P.: A developmental study of errors in memory. Develop. Psychol. **7**, 204–209 (1972).

Egeland, B., Braggins, J., Powalski, J.: Teaching children to discriminate letters of the alphabet through errorless discrimination training. Paper presented at the Biennial Meeting of the Society for Research in Child Development, Philadelphia, Pa. (March 30, 1973).

Entwistle, D.R.: Word associations of young children. Baltimore, MD.: Johns Hopkins Press 1966.

Elkonin, D.B.: The psychology of mastering the elements of reading. In: Education in the U.S.S.R. Simon, B. and Simon, J. (eds.). London: Routledge & Kegan Paul, 1963.

Erdmann, B., Dodge, R.: Psychologische Untersuchungen über das Leben, auf experimenteller Grundlage. Halle (1898).

Fernald, G.: Remedial techniques in basic school subjects. New York: McGraw-Hill 1943.

Fries, C.C.: Linguistics and reading. New York: Holt, Rhinehart & Winston, Inc. 1962/63.

Gibson, E.J.: Principles of perceptual learning and development. New York: Appleton-Century-Crofts, 1969.

Gibson, E.J., Barron, R.W., Garber, E.E.: The developmental convergence of meaning for words and pictures. In: Appendix to Final Report, The relationship between perceptual development and the acquisition of reading skill. Project No. 90046, Grant No. OEG-2-9-420446-1071 (010) between Cornell University and the U.S. Office of Education, 1972.

Gibson, E.J., Bishop, C.H., Schiff, W., Smith, J.: Comparison of meaningfulness and pronunciability as grouping principles in the perception and retention of verbal material. J. exp. Psychol. **67**, 173–182 (1964).

Gibson, E.J., Gibson, J.J., Pick, A.D., Osser, H.: A developmental study of the discrimination of letter-like forms. J. comp. physiol. Psychol. **55**, 897–906 (1962a).

Gibson, E.J., Guinet, L.: Perception of inflections in brief visual presentations of words. J. Verb. Learn. and Verb. Behav. **10**, 182–189 (1971).

Gibson, E.J., Levin, H.: The psychology of reading. Cambridge: MIT Press, 1975.

Gibson, E.J., Osser, H., Pick, A.D.: A study in the development of grapheme-phoneme correspondences. J. Verb. Learn. and Verb. Behav. **2**, 142–146 (1963).

Gibson, E.J., Pick, A.D., Osser, H.T., Hammond, M.: The role of grapheme-phoneme correspondence in the perception of words. Amer. J. Psychol. **75**, 554–570 (1962b).

Gibson, E.J., Schapiro, F., Yonas, A.: Confusion matrices for graphic patterns obtained with a latency measure. In: The analysis of reading skill: A program of basic and applied research. Final Report, Project No. 5-1213, Cornell Univ. and U.S. Office of Education, 1968.

Gibson, E.J., Shepela, S.: Some effects of redundant stimulus information on learning to identify letters. In: The analysis of reading skill: A program of basic and applied research. Final Report, Project No. 5-1213, Cornell Univ. and U.S. Office of Education, 1968.

Gibson, E.J., Shurcliff, A., Yonas, A.: Utilization of spelling patterns by deaf and hearing subjects. In: Basic studies on reading. Levin, H. and Williams, J.P. (eds.). New York: Basic Books, 1970.

Gibson, J.J., Yonas, P.: A new theory of scribbling and drawing in children. In: The analysis of reading skill: A program of basic and applied research. Final Report, Project No. 5-1213, Cornell Univ. and U.S. Office of Education, 1968.

Golinkoff, R.M.: Children's discrimination of English spelling patterns with redundant auditory information. Paper presented at American Educational Research Association, 1974.

Gummerman, K., Gray, C.R.: Age, iconic storage, and visual information processing. J. exp. Child Psychol. **13**, 165–170 (1972).

Hardyck, C.D., Petrinovich, L.F.: Subvocal speech and comprehension level as a function of the difficulty level of reading material. J. Verb. Learn. and Verb. Behav. **9**, 647–652 (1970).

Hendrickson, L.N., Muehl, S.: The effect of attention and motor response pretraining on learning to discriminate B and D in kindergarten children. J. Educ. Psychol. **53**, 236–241 (1962).

Hildreth, G.: Developmental sequences in naive writing. Child Develpm. **7**, 291–303 (1936).

Huttenlocher, J.: Children's language: Word-phrase relationships. Science **143**, 264–265 (1964).

Johnston, J.C., McClelland, J.L.: Visual factors in word perception. Percep. Psychophys. **14**, 365–370 (1973).

Johnston, J.C., McClelland, J.L.: Perception of letters in words: seek not and ye shall find. Science **184**, 1192–1194 (1974).

Kellogg, R.: Analyzing children's art. Palo Alto, Calif.: National Press Books, 1969.

Krueger, L.E.: Search time in a redundant visual display. J. exp. Psychol. **83**, 391–399 (1970).

Lavine, L.O.: Differentiation of letter-like forms in prereading children. Developm. Psychology, **13**, 89–94 (1977).

Legrün, A.: Wie und was „schreiben" Kindergarten-Zöglinge? Z. pädagog. Psychol. **33**, 322–331 (1932).

Levin, H., Watson, J.S., Feldman, M.: Writing as pretraining for association learning. In: A basic research program on reading. Final Report, Project No. 639, Cornell Univ. and U.S. Office of Education, 1963.

Liberman, A.M., Cooper, F.S., Shankweiler, D.P., Studdert-Kennedy, M.: Perception of the speech code. Psychol. Rev. **74**, 431–461 (1967).

Liberman, I.Y.: Segmentation of the spoken word and reading acquisition. Paper presented to the Society for Research in Child Development, Philadelphia, Pa., March 31, 1973.

Liss, P.H., Haith, M.H.: The speed of visual processing in children and adults: Effects of backward and forward masking. Percep. Psychophys. **8**, 396–398 (1970).

Lott, D., Smith, F.: Knowledge of intraword redundancy by beginning readers. Psychon. Sci. **19**, 343–344 (1970).

Menyuk, P.: Sentences children use. Cambridge: MIT Press, 1969.

Messer, S.: Implicit phonology in children. J. Verb. Learn. and Verb. Behav. **6**, 609–613 (1967).

Miller, L.K.: Visual masking and developmental differences in information processing. Child Develpm. **43**, 704–709 (1972).

Moore, T.V.: Image and meaning in memory and perception. Psychol. Monogr. **27**, No. 119 (1919).

Muraishi, S.: Acquisition of reading Japanese syllabic characters in preschool children in Japan. Paper presented at XXth International Congress of Psychology, Toyko, 1972.

Neisser, U.: Decision time without reaction time: Experiments in visual scanning. Amer. J. Psychol. **76**, 376–385 (1963).

Nodine, C.F., Simmons, F.: Processing distinctive features in the differentiation of letter-like symbols. J. exp. Psychol. **103**, 21–28 (1974).

Nodine, C.F., Stuerle, N.L.: Development of perceptual and cognitive strategies for differentiating graphemes. J. exp. Psychol. **97**, 158–166 (1973).

Pick, A.D.: Improvement of visual and tactual form discrimination. J. exp. Psychol. **69**, 331–339 (1965).

Pick, A.D., Frankel, G.: A study of strategies of visual attention in children. Develop. Psychol. **9**, 348–357 (1973).

Pollack, R.H.: Backward figural masking as a function of chronological age and intelligence. Psychon. Science **3**, 65–66 (1965).

Reicher, G.M.: Perceptual recognition as a function of meaningfulness of stimulus material. J. exp. Psychol. **81**, 275–280 (1969).

Rosinski, R.R., Wheeler, K.E.: Children's use of orthographic structure in word discrimination. Psychon. Sci. **26**, 97–98 (1972).

Rubenstein, H., Garfield, L., Millikan, J.A.: Homographic entries in the internal lexicon. J. Verb. Learn. and Verb. Behav. **9**, 487–494 (1970).

Samuels, S.J.: Relationship between formal intralist similarity and the von Restorff effect. J. Educ. Psychol. **59**, 432–437 (1968).

Samuels, S.J.: An experimental program for teaching letter names of the alphabet. Project No. 9-F-009. Washington, D.C.: U.S. Office of Education, 1970.

Savin, H.B.: What the child knows about speech when he starts to learn to read. In: Language by ear and by eye. Kavanagh, J.F. and Mattingly, I.G. (eds.). Cambridge: MIT Press, 1972.

Shankweiler, D., Liberman, I.Y.: Misreading: A search for causes, pp. 293–317. In: Language by ear and by eye. Kavanagh, J.F. and Mattingly, I.G. (eds.). Cambridge: MIT Press, 1972.

Smith, E.E., Haviland, S.E.: Why words are perceived more accurately than non-words: Inference vs. unitization. J. exp. Psychol. **92**, 59–64 (1972).

Smith, E.E., Spoehr, K.T.: The perception of printed English: A theoretical perspective. In: Human information processing: Tutorials in performance and cognition. Kantowitz, B.H. (ed.). Potomac, Md: Erlbaum Press, 1974.

Spoehr, K.T., Smith, E.E.: The role of syllables in perceptual processing. Cog. Psychol. **5**, 71–89 (1973).

Spitz, H.N., Thor, D.H.: Backward masking in retardates and normals. Percep. Psychophys. **4**, 245–246 (1968).

Stanley, G., Hall, R.: Short-term visual information processing in dyslexics. Child Develpm. **44**, 841–844 (1973).

Tenney, Y.J.: The child's conception of organization and recall. J. Exper. Child Psychol., **19**, 100–114 (1975).

Tinker, M.A.: Bases for effective reading. Minneapolis: Univ. Minnesota Press, 1965.

Vande Voort, L., Senf, G.M., Benton, A.L.: Development of audio-visual integration in normal and retarded readers. Child Develpm. **43**, 1260–1272 (1972).

Wheeler, D.D.: Processes in word recognition. Cog. Psychol. **1**, 59–85 (1970).

Wheeler, M.E.: Untutored acquisition of writing skill. Unpublished doctoral dissertation, Cornell University, 1971.

Whorf, B.L.: Linguistics as an exact science. Technol. Rev. **43**, 61–63, 80–83 (1940). Reprinted in: Language, thought and reality. J.B. Carroll Ed. Cambridge: MIT Press, 1956, pp. 220–232.

Williams, J.P.: Training kindergarten children to discriminate letter-like forms. Amer. Educ. Res. J. **6**, 501–514 (1969).

Willows, D.M.: Reading between the lines: selective attention in good and poor readers. Child Develpm. **45**, 408–415 (1974).

Willows, D.M., Mackinnon, G.E.: Selective reading: attention to the "unattended" lines. Canad. J. Psychol. **27**, 292–304 (1973).

Zeitler, J.: Takistokopische Versuche über das Lesen. Wundt's Philosoph. Studien **16**, 380–463 (1900).

Zhurova, L.E.: The development of analysis of words into their sounds by preschool children. Soviet Psychol. Psychiat. **2**, 17–27 (1963/64).

C. Intermodal Effects

Chapter 25

Visual-Vestibular Interaction: Effects on Self-Motion Perception and Postural Control

JOHANNES DICHGANS, Tübingen and THOMAS BRANDT, Essen (Germany)

With 13 Figures

Contents

A. Introduction

The sensation of self-motion is a common visual illusion which allows inferences concerning visual-vestibular interaction. It may be perceived while gazing at moving clouds, streaming water, or when a train moves on the adjacent track in a railway station. This compelling sensation of body movement can even affect postural balance. On first approaching the problem, a psychologic explanation could be suggested in the sense of HELMHOLTZ's (1896) *Urteilstäuschung*. One might assume that these illusions are inferences based upon the conscious or unconscious assumption of a stable environment, so that when the environment does in fact move, the observer infers that he himself is moving. This interpretation would be consistent with the individual's past experience as the entire visual surround seldom moves uniformly under natural conditions unless the body moves relative to the earth.

However, as in the case of other illusions, physiologic explanations may be more rewarding than psychologic ones. As PURKINJE suggested, visual illusions reveal the truth about the visual system *(Gesichtstäuschungen sind Sinneswahrheiten)*. An analysis consistent with his view takes into account that in the visually induced perception of self-motion, the term illusion only applies to the case in which the surround moves exclusively, and recognizes that identical visual stimulation occurs during actual body motion in which instance the same physiologic mechanism may maintain the veridical perception of body motion at constant velocity. The assumption of such a mechanism of visual-vestibular interaction, common to both illusion and veridicality, may lead to a better understanding of sensory control of body movement and spatial orientation than the psychologic explanation.

Under natural conditions with the eyes open, active as well as passive body motion is adequately perceived, be it of constant or varying velocity (Fig. 1 B). While riding in a vehicle with the eyes closed, however, the deficiencies of the vestibular system become apparent. Vestibular information about motion then is evoked only through acceleration or deceleration and dies out as the cupulae within the semicircular canals, or the otoliths, progressively return to their resting position during constant velocity. Consequently, constant velocity in the dark cannot be discriminated from rest for any extended period of time. Due to this lack of sustained labyrinthine information about constant velocity, deceleration from constant velocity is misinterpreted as acceleration in the opposite direction (Fig. 1 A). These two observations support the assumption that visual inputs are directly integrated with vestibular afferents. If so, the visual responses overcome the vestibular organ's deficiency for constant velocity discrimination. Such a concept might also entail inborn neuronal networks for visual-vestibular interaction rather than solely experience and learning. Thus, the aforementioned illusion (see also Fig. 1 C) may in fact indicate a functionally important mechanism of multisensory interaction.

This chapter follows this line of reasoning. First, psychophysic evidence is presented indicating that motion-vision plays a predominant role not only in the perception of self-motion but much more generally, in dynamic spatial orientation and postural control. It will become apparent from this that visual

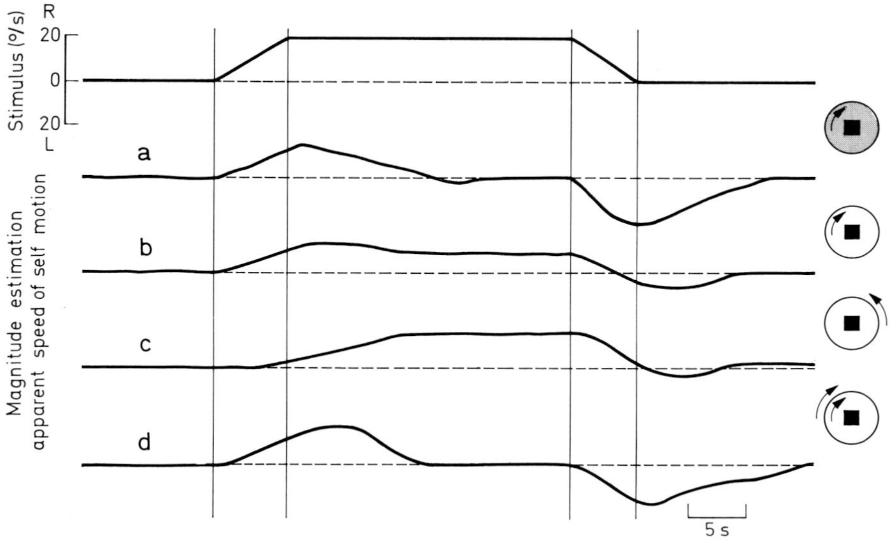

Fig. 1. Original recording of continuous tracking of perceived self-motion velocity and direction during chair and/or surround motion (trapezoid velocity profile, top trace). During chair rotation in dark *A* velocity profile roughly follows mechanical characteristics of cupula-endolymph system, resulting in lack of constant velocity discrimination and consequent misinterpretation of deceleration. With visible surround providing adequate optokinetic information these deficiencies are largely compensated *B*. Net visual effect is demonstrated in *C* where (with considerable latency) apparent self-rotation is elicited in a stationary observer through exclusive surround motion in opposite direction. If visual surround moves with observer as in vehicles *D* motion perception is again erroneous since, as in *A*, it exclusively relies on vestibular inputs

and vestibular information must converge on the same locus somewhere in the brain where they are integrated to provide the basis for a unitary model of dynamic and static orientation in space. Second, neurophysiologic experiments, most of which were designed to test this postulate, are discussed. The results demonstrate the existence of at least one site of interaction within the central nervous system which is common to all vertebrate species tested so far: the vestibular nuclei.

In order to discuss the psychophysical evidence, it is necessary to first describe the various sorts of subjective localization and motion perception with their related reference systems, as well as the terminology.

B. Spatial Localization and Related Types of Motion Perception

The location in space of objects and their observer can be unequivocally specified in terms of physics. Space perception and subjective localization, however, are the conscious result of a transformation of physical characteristics into percepts through sense organs and the subsequent information processing within the pathways to association cortex. Due to the structural and neurophysiologic qualities of the nervous system, the perceived orientation, e.g., of a physically vertical line, may be different from the objective orientation as is shown by the Aubert- (1861) and Müller- (1916) phenomena. This chapter will illustrate that space perception is particularly subject to such perceptual distortion (see also GUEDRY, 1974; GRAYBIEL, 1974; BISCHOF, 1974; LACKNER, Chap. 26, this Vol.). Since perception guides behavior, it consequently seems to be wise to maintain TSCHERMAK's (1921) standpoint of exact subjectivism.

I. Absolute, Relative, and Egocentric Localization

Perceived localization in space and motion perception are relative since they require subjective reference systems just as their physical counterparts can be specified only in relation to a particular coordinate system. Several perceptual reference systems anchored either to the observer or the environment are possible. *Absolute localization*, a term used by TSCHERMAK (1931), refers to subjective orientation with respect to vertical and horizontal (gravity) and the apparent position of objects and the observer on the earth surface. The subjective coordinates of absolute localization do not necessarily coincide with the physical ones. Measurements, e.g. of the perceived vertical, then determine the angle of displacement. *Relative localization* attempts to determine the position not only of objects one to another (HERING, 1879; HOFMANN, 1920) but also parts of the body to the ego (V. KRIES, 1923). The latter implies that the ego is a reference system, which is nicely called to mind by MÜLLER'S (1916) term *egocentric localization*. Egocentric localization, however, also signifies the sensed position of objects with respect to the observer. To complicate matters, the ego still comprises several possible reference systems: MÜLLER's head (k) system, gaze (B) system, and the standpoint (S) system. The latter according to MÜLLER determines subjective directions such as right, left, upward, downward, forward, and backward. But this clearly is still an idealized conceptualization since, when the three coordinate systems are not aligned, there is a complex interaction among them.

It is obvious that egocentric localization does not necessarily presuppose the subject's awareness of absolute localization. Visual grasp and manual reach for example are based on egocentric localization independent of absolute localization as long as the subject is stationary. During locomotion, eye and reaching movements are adjusted according to the concurrent change of absolute localization.

The segmented information gathered during exploration of (visual) space in time must be reevaluated according to the specified reference systems before it is used for the continuous updating of the internal model of space. This model clearly comprises more than any single "segment" registered at a given moment in time.

II. Several Kinds of Motion Perception

According to the aforementioned principles of localization, one may distinguish three kinds of motion perception:

1. The Perception of Self-motion or Vection

Vection, as it is called by TSCHERMAK (1931), this may result from rotation about one or several of the three body axes (x, y, and z, corresponding to roll, pitch, and yaw respectively) in which case it is referred to as *circular vection* (CV) (FISCHER and KORNMÜLLER, 1930a). Linear motion along those axes (to the right/left, forward/backward, upward/downward) is called *linear vection* (LV). A widely accepted and useful nomenclature for the planes and cardinal axes, as well as the polarity conventions for head-referenced movement, has been proposed by HIXSON et al. (1966).

The term *self-motion perception* is equivalent to von KRIES's (1923) *absolute motion perception* and the *exocentric motion perception* of FISCHER and KORNMÜLLER (1930a). The term exocentric also used by the authors of this chapter in earlier publications (BRANDT et al., 1971, 1973) is ambiguous. It should be avoided since it suggests motion with respect to one central locus, whereas it is the entire surround in relation to which motion is perceived. We therefore prefer the descriptive term self-motion perception whether the motion is real or illusory as in the case of visually induced apparent self-motion.

2. The Perception of Relative Motion Between Objects

This perception (DUNCKER's object-relative motion, 1929) again can be veridical or illusory as in the case of induced motion where the actually moving frame (e.g., clouds) may induce apparent motion of the surrounded object (the moon). In this instance then, the relative motion is perceptible but the motion over the ground is not. The relativity of movement perception is well-illustrated if one considers the case in which the eye follows a moving object with a pursuit movement that keeps the image fairly precisely on the fovea. The image of the stationary background then moves across the retina, but the object does not. Nevertheless, the background is perceived as stationary and the object as moving. Perhaps the observer senses the motion of the background and perceives the relative motion of the object (GIBSON, 1954). One could just as well assume that a signal corollary to oculomotor commands (*Efferenzkopie*, VON HOLST und MITTELSTAEDT, 1950; corollary discharge, TEUBER, 1960) supplies the information about object motion while relative background motion is canceled by the same signal.

3. The Perception of Object Motion Relative to the Observer or Egocentric Motion Perception

This perception (VON KRIES, 1923; FISCHER and KORNMÜLLER, 1930a) corresponds to DUNCKER'S (1929) *subject-relative* motion. In this case, motion is phenomenally in reference to the observer regardless of whether he perceives himself as stationary or not.

III. Subjective and Objective Stationarity

"Perceived motion occurs in a perceptually stable space or environment. Another way of saying this is to assert that the perception of stability is part and parcel of the perception of motion" (GIBSON, 1954). The optical conditions for a stable environment seem to be a retinal image containing many elements rather than a few. The disappearance of the autokinetic illusion when the dark room is slightly illuminated is consistent with this hypothesis. So is the moon-in-the-clouds-illusion and also the railroad-train-illusion when we take the clouds or the window-filling train on the next track as motionless (GIBSON, 1954). GIBSON'S assumption has since been substantiated and extended. It has been shown that it is not only the extent and amount of texture that determines the phenomenal environment but also the distribution of contrasts within the visual field and in depth are critical. The retinal periphery as opposed to the center of the visual field dominates the perception of stationarity as well as CV (BRANDT et al., 1973), roll vection (RV) (DICHGANS and BRANDT, 1974; HELD et al., 1975), and LV (LESTIENNE et al., 1977). The dominance of the periphery also applies to what we may term the depth periphery, in that the background, be it moving or not, is much more easily accepted as being stationary than the foreground (BRANDT et al., 1975). Thus, it is neither stationarity (motion) with respect to the earth nor stationarity (motion) on the retina that exclusively determine the phenomenal stability of the environment sensed.

A hypothetic explanation for the sensed stability of the actually moving visual environment during CV might be that the motion information arriving at the visual cortex is neutralized by a collateral signal deriving from the vestibular system. As will be shown later in this chapter, the activity of neurons in the vestibular nuclei is tonically influenced by motion of the seen environment, a fact that could provide a neurophysiologic basis for the illusion of self-motion. The hypothesis presupposes a collateral pathway to carry the neutralizing signal to the visual association cortex whereas the self-motion signal is assumed to reach the vestibular association cortex. Such an intersensory neutralization should not be confused with the model of VON HOLST and MITTELSTAEDT (1950), who discussed cancellation of sensory inflow by an *Efferenzkopie* of motor commands. The hypothesized model depicted in Figure 2 presupposes the reevaluation of retinotopic visual information on the basis of a holistic visually induced self-motion signal. It would also explain the puzzling fact that during visually induced self-motion perception, small contrasts that are stationary on

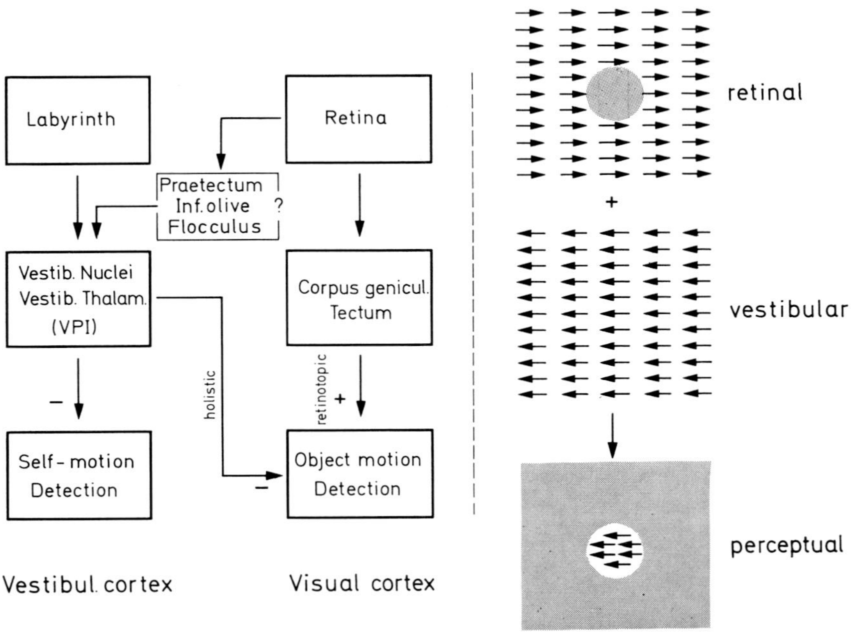

Fig. 2. Schematic diagram of visual-vestibular interaction in object motion detection and dynamic spatial orientation. Combination of holistic self-motion information via vestibular system and retinotopic visual afferents determines visual perception. Depending on stimulus area and its location in the visual field this perception may be veridical or illusory

the retina such as a fixation point, connected to the subject's chair, seem to move with the observer. In this instance the visual perception of stationarity would be reevaluated on the basis of a signal originating from the vestibular system. Such a model could also explain the apparent movement of a stationary visual object during fixation while the labyrinth is stimulated.

Stationarity may also be defined as the zero point within the subjective scale of velocities. Shift of the entire scale including perceived stationarity may be caused by prolonged motion stimulation as demonstrated by the occurrence of velocity adaptation and motion aftereffects (Brandt et al., 1974a).

IV. Effects of Seen Motion and Body Acceleration on Egocentric Localization of Objects

The judgment of *straight ahead (subjektives Geradeaus)* determines the subjective localization of objects in space. It is entirely egocentric, demanding for its definition no reference system outside the human body. Nevertheless, the apparent straight ahead is subject to external influences, in particular those due to motion.

1. Labyrinthine Stimulation

Passive rotary acceleration of the body about its vertical axis has been found to displace the apparent straight ahead in a direction opposite to that of body acceleration, i.e. the light appears to move in the direction of acceleration (FISCHER and KORNMÜLLER, 1931; MORANT, 1959; BRECHER et al., 1972). The lag displacement of apparent straight ahead, tested by pointing, causes an apparent lead dislocation of small visual objects actually positioned in the median plane. Afterimages, in contrast to real visual objects, seem to be displaced in a direction opposite to that of body acceleration (FISCHER, 1928). This might be related to the similar displacement of the straight ahead. GRAYBIEL and HUPP (1946), who first studied this effect in great detail, coined the name *oculogyral illusion*. Earlier descriptions of this apparent displacement had, however, been presented long before (PURKINJE, 1820; MACH, 1875; KLEINT, 1938; CHRISTIAN, 1940), but the statements regarding displacement direction were controversial in the older literature. The illusion is not solely caused by movement of the retinal image due to the slow phase of vestibular nystagmus (VAN DISHOECK et al., 1954; BYFORD, 1963; CAWTHORNE et al., 1956). The evidence for this is that thresholds for the illusion are lower than those for nystagmus and self-motion sensation (ROGGEVEEN and NIJHOFF, 1956; CLARK and STEWART, 1969). Related effects due to otolith rather than semicircular canal stimulation have been observed. They affect absolute instead of egocentric localization. Changes in direction of the gravity vector with respect to the head cause the Aubert- (1861) and Müller- (1916) phenomenon. Changes in direction as well as magnitude of the gravitoinertial vector, e.g., in a human centrifuge result in an apparent tilt of subjective vertical and the horizon corresponding in direction: *oculogravic illusion* (MACH, 1875; CLARK and GRAYBIEL, 1951; GRAYBIEL, 1952). If only the magnitude of gravity force changes as in parabolic flight or in an elevator, an apparent vertical movement of visual objects is sensed: *elevator illusion* (WHITESIDE, 1961). The object will seem to move up if G increases and vice versa. Under the condition of weightlessness during parabolic flight (GRAYBIEL and KELLOGG, 1967) or transiently during space missions (MILLER and GRAYBIEL, 1973), an *illusion of inversion* occurs. A possible correspondence in animal behavior may be the forward looping observed in blindfolded goldfishes under this condition (CAMPBELL, 1962; V. BAUMGARTEN et al., 1972). Pigeons, however, loop backwards (OOSTERVELD and GREVEN, 1975). Finally, linear acceleration may modify the perceived velocity of a moving visual scene (PAVARD and BERTHOZ, 1977).

2. Visual Stimulation

If apparent self-motion is induced by *rotation of the surround* about the vertical axis of a stationary observer, the visual stimulus *causes displacement of the subjective straight* ahead. Displacement is again opposite in direction to the perceived self-motion (lag), in other words, it corresponds in direction to the environment motion causing the sensation of ego motion (FISCHER and KORNMÜLLER, 1931; THURLOW and KERR, 1970; BRECHER et al., 1972).

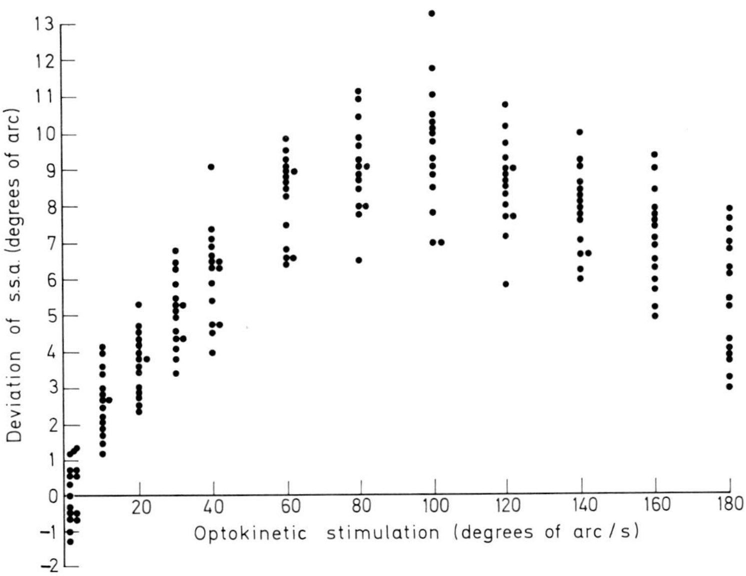

Fig. 3. Graph of individual data points illustrating deviation of "subjective straight ahead" (s.s.a.) from median plane of body when total visual environment (optokinetic drum) is moved around quietly sitting test subject. Each point represents one measurement. For each speed, 15 measurements were made. Different speeds were presented at random. When drum is stationary, points lie close together and are scattered about objective median. With clockwise rotation of drum at various speeds, s.s.a. shows deviation in direction of rotation. Values deviating to right of objective median are shown on ordinate as "plus" points. When drum is set in motion, data points are more scattered than when drum is stationary. (From BRECHER et al., 1972)

BRECHER et al. (1972) asked their subjects to walk backward and forward in a straight line inside an optokinetic drum painted with vertical black and white stripes rotating slowly in a horizontal direction. Deprived of vision of any stationary objects outside the drum, each person consistently deviated from a straight path toward the direction of the drum motion without being aware of it. The deviation of the apparent straight ahead from the objective median plane (for definition, see HOWARD and TEMPLETON, 1966) was then experimentally determined. Subjects were asked to set a luminous line to apparent straight ahead while the drum was stationary or in motion. Figure 3 shows the results of BRECHER et al. (1972), who found an increase in deviation with increasing drum velocity up to a rotation speed of 100°/s followed by a progressive decrease. Their maximal amounts of induced deviation ranging around 9° from the median plane correspond fairly well to the results of an earlier study by THURLOW and KERR (1970). Since perceived velocity of CV exhibits the same dependency on angular stimulus velocity with a maximum at about 100°/s (BRANDT et al., 1973; DICHGANS and BRANDT, 1974), one can assume a close relationship between perceived velocity of CV and the deviation of subjective straight ahead.

Taken together, the results of visual and vestibular stimulation on egocentric localization indicate the close similarity in the perceptual consequences of stimulation of the two sensory organs. The assumption of a unitary central representation of egocentric space based on visual and vestibular (as well as acoustic and somatosensory) afferents is perceptually obvious. Experimentally its existence is further substantiated by the demonstration of analogous effects of visual scenes rotating in a vertical plane as described below in this chapter.

There is, however, one interesting difference between the effect of visual and vestibular stimulation on visual and auditory localizations, respectively. Whereas a stationary light source in an otherwise unstructured visual environment seems to move with the direction of body acceleration (oculogyral illusion, GRAYBIEL and HUPP, 1946) the *audiogyral illusion* (CLARK and GRAYBIEL, 1949) consists in an apparent displacement of a stationary sound source in a direction *opposite* to the direction of body acceleration (MÜNSTERBERG and PIERCE, 1894; CHRISTIAN, 1940). Results consistent with the above have been obtained by THURLOW and KERR (1970) when the visual surround was moved around the stationary subject. They observed that a sound source *and* straight ahead as well seemed to be displaced opposite in direction to the induced perception of self-motion. Similar observations have been made by GEMELLI (1951), whereas ARNOULT's (1952) data indicate the reverse directional relationship. The directional discrepancy between the oculogyral illusion and the audiogyral illusion so far has not been convincingly explained.

C. Visually Induced Perception of Self-Motion (Vection)

I. History of the Self-Motion Illusion

When a stationary observer views a large scene moving uniformly in one direction, he soon feels himself moving in the opposite direction while the scene itself may appear to stop moving. Illusions of this sort were reported long ago since they occur under natural conditions, such as gazing down on a river when standing on a bridge or viewing a train starting on the adjacent track (MACH, 1875; HELMHOLTZ, 1896). MACH was the first to demonstrate this illusion in the laboratory. In his experiments, he used a rotating striped cylinder surrounding the stationary observer (1875) and later a large endless belt horizontally moving across two rollers (1922) to induce the sensation of self-motion opposite in direction to the actual motion of the visual stimulus. FISCHER and KORNMÜLLER (1930a, 1930b) later gave a more complete description of this illusion which, in reference to TSCHERMAK (1931), was named *circular vection* (CV) or *linear vection* (LV), respectively, by these authors. In subsequent years, the illusion of self-motion as induced by a large moving scene seems to have been widely known among experimental psychologists but its detailed psychophysical characteristics and its neurophysiologic basis were not further investigated until very recently.

The sensation of self-motion as induced by displacing the acoustic surround—*audiokinetic* CV (URBANTSCHITSCH, 1897; VON STEIN, 1910; DODGE, 1923)—is less compelling. It is unknown whether its physiologic basis is similar to that of the visually induced vection discussed later (see p. 781). The occurrence of *audiokinetic nystagmus* (VON STEIN, 1910; DODGE, 1923; HENNEBERT, 1960), however, may be considered suggestive of an audio-vestibular convergence. But nystagmus has also been observed during imagination of moving visual scenes (ZIKMUND, 1966) or their hypnotic suggestion (BRADY and LEVITT, 1964). A more compelling illusion of body rotation and nystagmus can be induced when the horizontally extended arm of a stationary subject sitting in the dark is passively rotated about a vertical axis through the shoulder joint: arthrokinetic vection and arthrokinetic nystagmus (BRANDT et al., 1977).

Finally, we have observed that a weak sensation of body motion can also be induced through tactile motion stimulation of a large part of the body surface: *haptokinetic vection*. Systematic investigations of this latter phenomenon, however, have still to be done.

In the past, mainly those investigators interested in the influence of self-rotation perception on auditory localization have used the visually induced sensation of self-motion as a means of dissecting the influences of actual vestibular stimulation from those of self-motion sensation as such (WALLACH, 1940; GEMELLI, 1951; ARNOULT, 1952; THURLOW and KERR, 1970). Now that we know that large moving visual fields also cause a modulation of discharge activity in the vestibular nuclei (see p. 781), this method of separation is no longer justified.

MACH (1875) was the first to observe that the *sensation of self-motion* is *facilitated by fixation of a stationary target*. This facilitation was confirmed later by WARREN (1895), FISCHER and KORNMÜLLER (1930), and WALLACH (1940). In their experiments, the stationary target was perceived as seemingly moving with the observer opposite in direction to the moving pattern. Even the stable contours of the surrounding stationary room appeared to move along with the subject. The result was that the stable spatial relationship between the stationary observer and his surroundings perceptually remained unaltered. Both MACH (1922) and FISCHER and KORNMÜLLER (1930a) attributed the sensation of self-motion to collateral information of oculomotor commands that would come to perceptual awareness. MACH, obviously because of the rather small stimulus area, observed the illusion of self-motion only when the stationary target was fixated and not when the pattern was pursued. He assumed that the illusion was due to the subject's *Innervationsstrom,* the continuous innervation necessary to counteract the reflex-like tendency to pursue the moving belt with the eyes. FISCHER and KORNMÜLLER (1930a) further developed this concept. Working with a slowly rotating and rather dimly lit drum that hung from the ceiling of their laboratory, they discovered that the illusion could still be elicited when the subject pursued the moving pattern by means of optokinetic nystagmus or by fixation of a single stripe while pursuing it with the head. But, since they observed that the sensation of self-motion seemed to occur only intermittently in temporal coincidence with the fast phases of nystagmus,

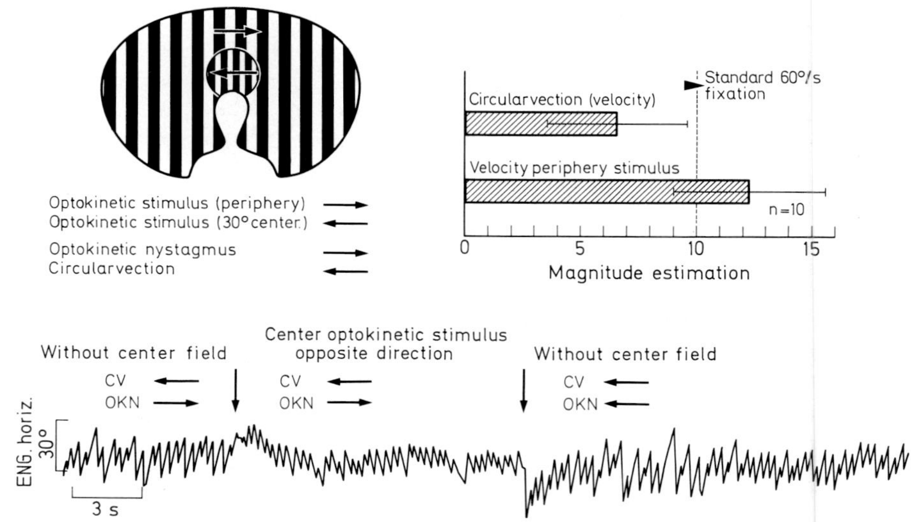

Fig. 4. Optokinetic stimulation of center and periphery in opposite directions by means of centrally located mirror. In this situation CV is determined by peripheral stimulus while optokinetic nystagmus (*OKN*, lower graph), is guided by central stimulus. As soon as central stimulus is introduced, direction of OKN reverses, whereas velocity of CV is only slightly decreased (see magnitude estimation in relation to unindirectional full-field stimulation at upper right). Since eye movements are in direction opposite to movement of peripheral stimulus, its velocity is overestimated. (From BRANDT et al., 1973)

this was taken as evidence for the assumption that the illusion was due to the perception of a central command signal responsible for the eye saccades. The fact that with higher stimulus velocities a continuous self-motion was perceived was explained as the result of fusion of the discontinuous perception occurring at lower stimulus velocities. That this explanation is erroneous was later demonstrated by BRANDT et al. (1973) who were able to dissociate eye movements and CV by presenting a small pattern in the center that moved opposite in direction to a large surrounding pattern subtending the rest of the subject's visual field (Fig. 4). In their experiment, optokinetic nystagmus followed the direction of the central pattern, whereas circular vection depended on the peripheral stimulus which moved in the opposite direction. Consequently, *vection is basically independent of the direction of eye movements.* It is true, however, that image motion across the retina facilitates CV which can be measured in terms of a decreased CV latency from stimulus onset. Facilitation is not dependent on fixation but may also be experienced if one inattentively stares at the pattern (FISCHER and KORNMÜLLER, 1930a; HOOD and LEECH, 1974) in which case the slow phase velocity of optokinetic nystagmus considerably lags behind stimulus speed (KÖRNER and DICHGANS, 1967; DICHGANS and JUNG, 1969). With the entire field of view stimulated by well-structured moving contrasts, CV is mostly "saturated" regardless of whether retinal slippage occurs or not.

II. Circular Vection in a Horizontal Plane

Using a system in which a rotatable chair is surrounded by a concentric drum whose patterned inner surface covers the entire field of vision (Fig. 5), circular motion of the drum invariably leads to an apparent self-rotation opposite in direction to that of the visual stimulus. CV thus induced in a stationary subject is phenomenally equivalent to the sensation induced during slowly accelerated or constant velocity actual chair rotation (BRANDT et al., 1971). With faster changes in body velocity, however, the sensation of acceleration is different from that caused by a velocity step of the visual stimulus.

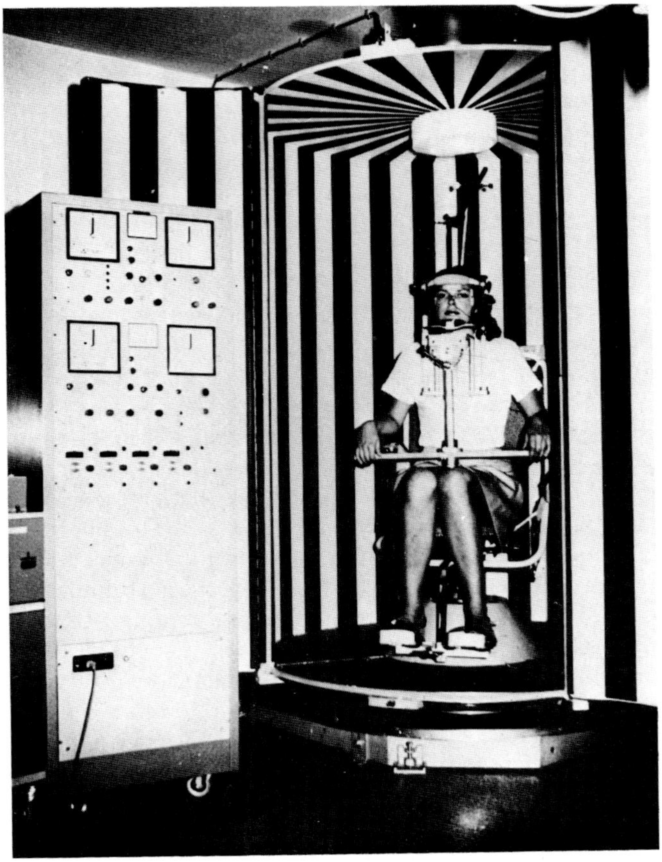

Fig. 5. Chair- and drum-system for exclusive vestibular and/or optokinetic stimulation. Chair and drum can be rotated at servo-controlled angular accelerations and velocities independently or conjointly in various combinations. Drum with its doors closed provides optokinetic stimulation. Luminance is controllable from outside. Eye movements and tracking data may be recorded via slip rings

1. Time Course

A stationary subject *suddenly* exposed to the moving pattern initially experiences movement of the surroundings. This sensation also occurs with a constant angular velocity body rotation in the dark when the lights are switched on, because the two situations are physiologically equivalent with regard to their consequences upon visual and vestibular inputs. Thus, the neurophysiologic processes transforming afferent visual information into what underlies self-motion sensation are slower than those mediating the egocentric perception of surround motion. Using the above-described equipment, *latencies* from onset of the velocity step (lights on) to the start of CV ranged from 1–10 s among subjects. Thereafter, there follows a period of apparent rotary body acceleration during which the surroundings seem to decelerate at the same rate. Exclusive self-rotation is reached within 5–15 s after stimulus onset, then the drum appears to be stationary.

After stimulus termination (lights off) CV continues in the same direction for up to 30 s. CV aftereffects are strongly dependent upon stimulus duration (see p. 779). The typical time course of CV with long latencies for onset and *longtime constants for saturation and fading* is independent of stimulus velocities within a range of 10–120°/s (Dichgans and Brandt, 1972; Brandt et al., 1973). But latencies do depend on other stimulus characteristics like stimulus texture and stimulus area and location within the visual field. In fact, latencies can be taken as a measure of the potency of a visual stimulus in inducing CV. The shortening of CV latencies by moving retinal images as opposed to smooth pursuit has already been mentioned above.

The functional significance of visual-vestibular interaction for spatial orientation during active and passive body movements and for postural stabilization would be enhanced if latencies of visually induced self-motion sensation were shortened by a corresponding vestibular input or vice versa. Such a shortening actually occurs if an impulse acceleration is applied by a sudden stop from a constant velocity body rotation. In this instance, a confirming surround motion (toward the direction of the previous body rotation) is immediately experienced as self-motion by the observer who then interprets the surround as being stationary (Brandt et al., 1974a). Corresponding observations have been made in patients suffering from an acute vestibular lesion, in whom CV latencies are shortened when CV toward the direction of spontaneous nystagmus is elicited (Hökendorf et al., 1977). On the other hand, acceleration patterns producing vestibular stimuli which are contradictory to the visual stimulus (in direction as well as magnitude) frequently destroy the self-rotation sensation precipitously (Young et al., 1973). Conversely, for the visual system's interaction on the vestibular system, the results of Young et al. (1973) do not indicate a facilitation of detection thresholds for body accelerations toward the direction of an already established CV, but rather show an inhibitory influence on acceleration thresholds opposite to the CV direction. This was also measured in terms of an increase in detection latency. The long latencies of CV cannot be ascribed to the net neuronal delay of the visual-vestibular loop, but must result from a temporal summation that may be shortened by a confirming vestibular signal.

One could hypothesize that the lack of a confirming vestibular signal in the case where a moving visual scene is suddenly presented is responsible for the long latencies observed for CV onset. But CV latencies do not increase with the amount of conflict between the presence of a visual stimulus and the absence of a corresponding vestibular stimulus created by increasing speeds of the velocity step presented (BRANDT et al., 1973).

Finally, the lack of true vestibular input is not apt to inform the subject about his actual stationarity (BRANDT et al., 1973), a fact underlining the psychophysical identity of visual and vestibular inputs under these circumstances.

2. Relation to Stimulus Velocities

As in object-motion perception, *the perceived velocity of self-rotation* during constant velocity drum rotation within a certain range is *linearly related to stimulus speed* (BRANDT et al., 1973; DICHGANS and BRANDT, 1974). With the entire surround rotating, CV, in contrast to LV (DENTON, 1971) and postural reactions to LV (LESTIENNE et al., 1976), does not exhibit the strong dependency of apparent velocity upon the spatial frequency of the optokinetic pattern which has been observed in object-motion perception (DIENER et al., 1976) and the adaptation experiments of BREITMEYER (1973) and PANTLE (1974). DIENER et al. (1976), in scaling experiments found, in addition to the linear relationship between stimulus speed and perceived speed (MASHHOUR, 1964; RACHLIN, 1966; DICHGANS et al., 1969; KENNEDY et al., 1972) a *linear relationship between the spatial frequency of the moving pattern and its perceived speed* (Fig. 6). Doubling the frequency of contrasts per unit area of a pattern moving at a given speed caused an average increase in perceived speed of 61%. The relationship between perceived speed (m′), angular speed (ω), and spatial frequency (fs) was expressed by the following equation: $m' = 0.61\ fs \cdot \omega + b \cdot \omega$ (for $0.011 \leqq fs \leqq 0.066$ cycles per degree). In this equation $fs \cdot \omega$ represents the temporal frequency of local retinal stimulation by the successively passing visual contrasts. If a moving pattern contains several spatial frequencies, perceived velocity is dominated by its low frequency components.

For angular velocities below 90°/s, perceived velocity of CV is independent of whether the subject fixates on a stationary target (eyes at rest) or tracks the moving pattern (optokinetic nystagmus). This again is in contrast to object-motion perception in which the perceived velocity of the stimulus is greater by a factor of 1.6–1.9 when the eyes are kept stationary as compared to when optokinetic nystagmus occurs (KÖRNER and DICHGANS, 1967; DICHGANS et al., 1969). This so-called *Aubert-Fleischl paradox* in object-motion perception has recently been shown to also be a function of temporal frequency stimulation on the retina (DICHGANS et al., 1975b). It does not occur if a single edge moves across the retina. The absence of the Aubert-Fleischl paradox in CV can be assumed to be due to the exclusive evaluation of the $b \cdot \omega$ term of the above equation for CV.

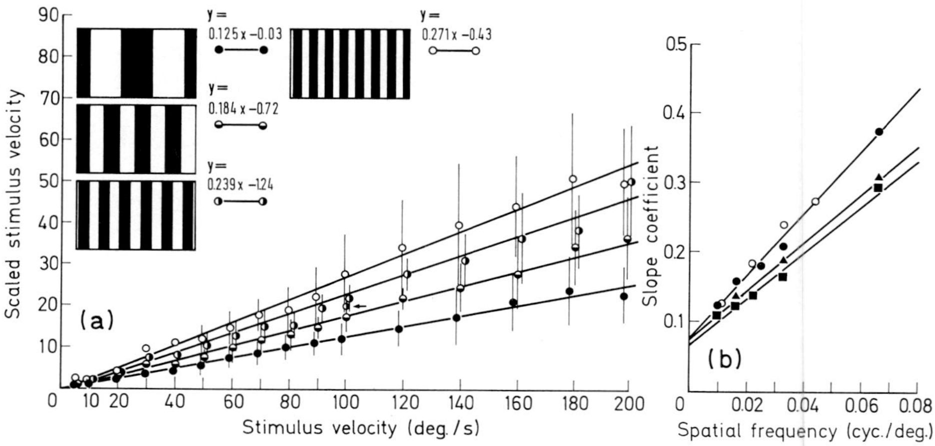

Fig. 6. Effect of spatial frequency of black and white stripes within continuously moving pattern on perceived speed. In A, linear scaling curves relating perceived (ordinate) and physical (abscissa) angular speeds are presented. Data points represent average magnitude estimations with standard deviations of velocity ($N = 10$) in relation to standard stimulus (arrow) which was assigned arbitrary value of 20. Four spatial frequencies (upper left inserts) were used. These were 0.011 cycles/deg, 0.022 c/deg, 0.033 c/deg, and 0.044 c/deg respectively. They were all presented in 50 × 50 deg stimulus field. Figure indicates that slope of scaling functions increases with their spatial frequency. This relationship is more clearly shown in B where slope (ordinate) is related to spatial frequency (abscissa) of stimuli. Open circles represent slopes from A. It is evident that within frequency range tested, slope coefficients linearly relate to spatial frequency of stimulus. Three regression lines apply to scaling curves for 30 × 40 deg and 50 × 50 deg central stimulus (●, ○), 30 × 40 deg peripheral field (▲) centered on 45 deg peripherally and large stimulus field subtending 165 × 100 deg (■). (After DIENER et al., 1976)

The *"saturation" velocity* of CV,[1] however, is slightly higher with pursuit movements than with pure afferent motion information through retinal image motion. As soon as drum speed exceeds 120°/s (with stationary eyes already at 90°/s), subjective speed of CV lags behind stimulus speed and does not increase beyond 180°/s (BRANDT et al., 1973; DICHGANS and BRANDT, 1974). A mixed sensation then occurs whereby the drum appears to rotate in the direction opposite to the perceived CV. The sum of the velocities of these apparent motions seems to correspond roughly to the phenomenal velocity of a stimulus that appears to move in reference to the stationary observer. The laboratory findings of a simultaneous perception of self- and object-motion at higher stimulus velocities can also easily be experienced while riding in a train. Looking out a window one may perceive that nearby objects, e.g., the walls of a tunnel, seem to stream backward in space. The parallelism of the upper limit for CV velocity and the maximal velocity of slow phases of opto-kinetic nystagmus, which also ranges between 90° and 120°/s (GRÜTTNER, 1939; MACKENSEN, 1954; DICHGANS et al., 1973a) is interesting, but does not necessarily imply a causal relationship between the two.

---

[1] CV is saturated if the entire stimulus velocity is apparently taken on by the observer. Saturation does not refer to the peak CV velocity, which is reached below 180°/s stimulus velocity.

3. Motion Constancy

The investigation of CV velocity and the determination of its upper limit becomes more complicated and interesting if one considers the recent finding that *in rotary self-motion, perceived speed derives from the apparent linear speed rather than the angular velocity of the image on the retina* (WIST et al., 1975). When the perceived distance of a visual surround rotating around the observer at a constant angular velocity increases, the perceived velocity of self-motion increases proportional to the shift in apparent distance. This happens even if the angular velocity of the projected image and its spatial pattern characteristics on the retina are unaltered. In the experiments of WIST et al. (1975), this was achieved by use of the Pulfrich effect (PULFRICH, 1922; LIT, 1949). But, accommodative and fusional convergence as well as increasing the inner diameter of the moving drum resulted in a similar change in perceived velocity. Such a mechanism may subserve *motion constancy in case of LV* or the perception of object velocity at different distances from the observer. But it has no overt adaptive function in case of rotary motion where angular velocity does not vary with distance. Apparently, the central nervous system cannot switch off this constancy mechanism in the special case of rotary motion.

The spatial frequency effect described by DIENER et al. (1976) may also subserve motion constancy both in object motion perception (WIST et al., 1976) and LV as well (LESTIENNE et al., 1977). A pattern of constant physical size, if placed at a farther distance, will be imaged with a higher spatial frequency on the retina as compared to the closer pattern. The increase in spatial frequency will tend to compensate for the decrease in angular velocity by keeping the temporal frequency of local contrast changes constant. A distance- and frequency-contingent mechanism supplement each other for velocity constancy in object-motion perception (BROWN, 1931; WIST et al., 1976).

III. Linear Vection

Under natural conditions, LV results from a highly complex pattern of motion stimulation. Motion parallax and motion perspective within the "flow of the ambient visual array from the centrifugal to the centripetal pole" are pattern characteristics that have been extensively discussed by GIBSON (1958, 1966) as the basis of "visual kinesthesis" (visually induced self-motion sensation) in active and passive locomotion. Under laboratory conditions, however, LV in a stationary observer can be evoked by large striped or checkerboard patterns as well as through quasi-natural stimuli like motion pictures taken from a moving vehicle (GIBSON, 1947) or a swinging room surrounding the subject (WOOD, 1895; LISHMAN and LEE, 1973). BERTHOZ et al. (1975) elicited LV through projection of a moving stripe pattern on the lateral and ceiling surfaces of a surrounding box. In this latter instance, it is just the linear movement of the pattern that is sufficient to evoke the illusion. Perspective cues, still present in the early LV experiments of FISCHER and KORNMÜLLER (1930a), are not a necessary requirement for its elicitation. LV in a vertical direction—lift sensation—may equally be elicited through projection of vertically moving stripes onto the windows of an airplane trainer.

The frequency responses for sinusoidal motion of the visual stimulus have been studied for horizontal LV by BERTHOZ et al. (1975) and for motion along a vertical axis by YOUNG and CHU (1976). The fact that LV can be visually elicited proves that not only simulated semicircular canal activity as in CV, but also simulated otolithic activity may result from an appropriate visual stimulation. Latencies for LV may be a little shorter than those for CV. BERTHOZ et al. (1975) found them to range around 1.5 s irrespective of stimulus velocity. Saturation velocities for LV, however, seem to be similar to those of CV as may be calculated from BERTHOZ et al.'s data. BERTHOZ et al. (1975) also determined the velocity and *luminance thresholds* for LV which they found to be close to those for image motion detection. LEIBOWITZ and DICHGANS (1977) found similar results for CV. Latencies for onset and saturation as well as the duration of aftereffects were the same even in low scotopic vision[2].

The powerful role of "visual kinesthesis" in perceived spatial constancy is well-illustrated in an experiment by LISHMAN and LEE (1973). If their subjects walked forward on the ground while the visual environment (a large box) was moving with them instead of moving backward relatively, they believed the floor to be moving backward as on a treadmill while they experienced no self-movement in inertial space. In this instance again, vision determined what was taken as the stationary spatial reference.

HELMHOLTZ (1896) and FISCHER and KORNMÜLLER (1930b) probably were the first to observe an *influence of LV on postural balance,* a phenomenon that was later rediscovered by LEE and ARONSON (1974) and LESTIENNE et al. (1976). When they visually induced the sensation of forward motion through divergent horizontal motion of their pattern of vertical stripes, subjects showed a considerable tendency to fall backward. The postural imbalance is most probably the reaction to a misperception of postural vertical, induced by the moving visual stimulus. In analogy to the tilt phenomena found during circular motion of a visual surround around a horizontal axis, the illusory body tilt might be explained as the consequence of a central recomputation of orientation with respect to gravity based on vision (see p. 773).

At this point it may be useful to remember that during actual linear body motion, say forward, the gravity pull and inertial forces, by way of vector summation, determine not only the sensation of linear motion but also perceived orientation with respect to gravity (JONGKEES and GROEN, 1946; LANSBERG, 1954). In our example, this results in a pitch-up sensation of the body (oculogravic illusion) eventually counteracted by a reflex-like foreward inclination of the trunk. An analogous phenomenon occasionally observed in pilots is a disastrous diving into the sea after takeoff from an aircraft carrier in the case of missing visual or instrumental control (PETERS, 1969). Vision of the

---

[2] LEIBOWITZ and DICHGANS (1977) also tested for any possible influence of refractive error. Blurring the stimulus image by lenses of up to 20 diopters was without appreciable influence on CV latencies.

moving surround, it seems, by means of the induced tilt perception, would tend to counteract the apparent backward tilt, thus stabilizing the pilot's perception of gravitational orientation.

IV. Roll and Pitch Vection

The sensation of continuous roll motion (about the sagittal, or x-axis) may be elicited in a stationary observer while viewing a large disk or a hemispheric dome rotating around his line of sight (DICHGANS et al., 1972; HELD et al., 1975). Pitch vection results from viewing a large pattern that moves around the y-axis (YOUNG et al., 1975). In both instances, as in CV, the induced motion sensation is opposite to the direction of pattern motion. In contrast to CV, however, subjects experience only *limited displacement despite a continuous sensation of self-motion* (Fig. 7a). The constraint on displacement is probably

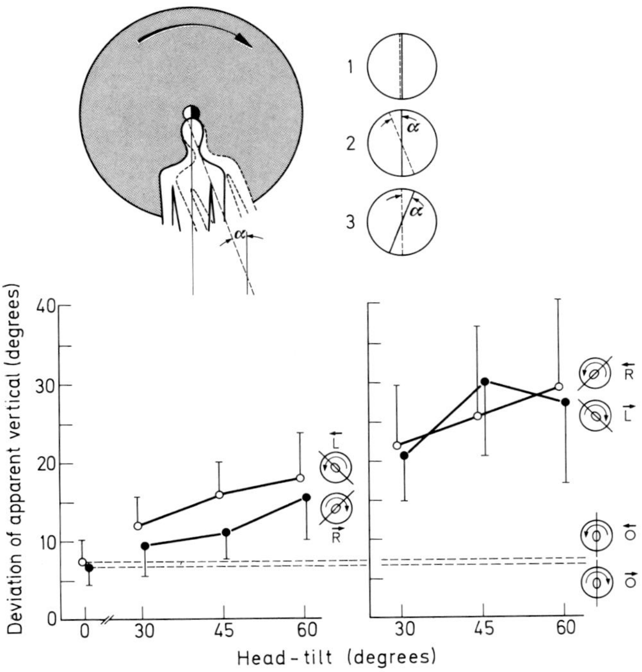

Fig. 7. Displacement of perceived vertical during roll vection induced by large disk rotating around subject's line of sight. Clockwise rotation causes apparent counterclockwise tilt of observer's body (dashed line drawing upper left). Vertical edge (1) separating black and white halves of test target appears similarly tilted (2). Perceived tilt is measured by having subject adjust test edge to apparent vertical (3). Lower half-figure depicts deviation of apparent vertical induced by rotating visual display with different angles of head inclination (abscissa) after subtracting corresponding "A" or "E" effects. Disk rotation and head inclination in same direction (*left panel*) and in opposite directions (*right panel*), for deviations of apparent vertical to right (*black dots*) or to left (*open circles*). Dashed lines depict deviation with head erect and only disk moving (means and standard deviations)

due to the inputs from otoliths and somatosensory gravireceptors, conflicting with the visual effect. The apparent position, consequently, may be conceptualized as the result of a compromise weighing the different and, in part, contradictory sensory inputs for gravitational orientation. Another consequence of the conflict during vections around a horizontal axis is their considerably lower saturation velocity (10°/s, HELD et al., 1975), at which the actually rotating stimulus display looks stationary while the subject experiences roll vection. At higher velocities, the subject experiences both roll vection and stimulus motion.

Induced displacement can be measured in terms of tilt angles of apparent visual and postural vertical from gravitational upright. These are indicated by the adjustments subjects perform in an attempt to compensate for an apparent inclination of both (DICHGANS et al., 1972). Tilts of visual vertical measured during roll vection ranged up to 40° and saturated at an average of 15° at 30–40°/s stimulus velocity. YOUNG et al. (1975), using magnitude estimations, obtained higher values. Tilt angles for pitch were smaller than those for roll and in addition exhibited an unexplained asymmetry between the *smaller pitch-up and larger pitch-down* angles. This asymmetry in pitch sensitivity appeared fixed with respect to the body (egocentric localization), rather than with the direction of down (absolute localization), since in the head inverted position the induced pitch-forward (up) was significantly larger than pitch-backward (down). This asymmetry may be caused by an asymmetry in the visual system that, due to the predominance of forward locomotion, is adapted to downward motion of the "seen" environment (primarily in the lower half of the visual field).

A similar asymmetry is observed for postural reactions to an LV stimulus. With this the tendency to fall backward is considerably stronger then the one to fall forward (LESTIENNE et al., 1977).

Studies with sinusoidal roll-motion stimuli showed that the angle of induced tilt of apparent vertical linearly increases with the logarithm of the stimulus oscillation amplitude (MAURITZ et al., 1977). Such a system integrating stimulus velocity over time could subserve the visual feedback stabilizing posture by visual detection of the displacement angle (see p. 778).

The apparent displacement of both visual and postural vertical has been explained as the result of a central recomputation of the orientation of the gravity vector based on vision (DICHGANS et al., 1972). In this respect, the effect of the moving surround seems to be equivalent to displacing the direction of the gravitational force in the direction of pattern motion. This effect on gravitational orientation may be interpreted as the dynamic counterpart of the much weaker effects caused by the static reorientation of a visual frame or surrounding room (literature reviewed by HOWARD and TEMPLETON, 1966; BISCHOF, 1974). HUGHES et al. (1972), who independently discovered the effect of a rotating background on perception of verticality, used smaller stimuli and therefore obtained minute tilts. They consequently were able to relate their phenomenon to optokinetically induced ocular torsion. This explanation, however, is counterindicated by the large tilt angles observed (DICHGANS et al., 1972).

The fact that displacement is limited has been explained as the result of the conflict between visually induced roll vection (simulated semicircular canal information) on the one hand, and otolithic as well as somatosensory graviceptive information on the other (DICHGANS et al., 1972). This interpretation is supported by the finding that the visually induced tilt markedly increases when the otoliths are placed in a less favorable position by lateral head tilt (DICHGANS et al., 1974; YOUNG et al., 1975). In this situation, the otolith signal possesses a proportionately lower sensory weight and accuracy (COLENBRANDER, 1963/64; GRAYBIEL and CLARK, 1962; GRAYBIEL and PATTERSON, 1955; QUIX and EIJSVOGEL, 1929; SCHÖNE, 1964). The fact that both roll and pitch displacements are reduced if the head is tilted 25° forward—so as to put the dominant plane of the utricular otoliths in an optimal earth horizontal position—may vote for their predominant role in visual-graviceptive interaction (YOUNG et al., 1975).

The potentation of the net visual effect on apparent vertical in an inclined head position is maximal if the visual stimulus is moving opposite to the head tilt (DICHGANS et al., 1974). This asymmetry has been interpreted as the functional hypertrophy of a biologically adaptive mechanism (DICHGANS et al., 1975a). In normal life, body sway causes a relative counterrotation of the visual surround. The visually induced tilt perception then would add to the otolith information and would assist postural righting. Whereas with head inclination and simultaneous visual motion toward the same side—an artificial situation occurring only in the laboratory—postural uprighting caused by graviceptive inputs would be opposed by the effect of motion vision.

D. Retinal and Depth Periphery Dominate Self-Motion Perception and Spatial Orientation

It seems plausible that "tunnel vision" limited to the central parts of the visual field should impair dynamic spatial orientation *(Bewegungsorientierung im Sehraum)* and consequently locomotion. In fact, patients with retinitis pigmentosa, which abolishes peripheral vision, may show this disability; but orientation will be largely preserved if, as it occasionally happens, a small peripheral strip of vision remains intact. That the periphery of the visual field—and also the periphery in depth, corresponding to the background in visual space—play a decisive role in dynamic spatial orientation during active as well as passive locomotion, has been experimentally determined. This was done by way of STEVENS's (1957) magnitude estimations of illusionary CV velocity (BRANDT et al., 1973) and measurements of the tilt angle (DICHGANS and BRANDT, 1974; BRANDT et al., 1975; HELD et al., 1975) induced by the different visual stimuli tested[3]. The results of these experiments demonstrate that mainly area, contrast density,

[3] The occurrence of CV, or optokinetically induced displacement of perceived vertical and posture, or visual stabilization of posture may be used to evaluate residual functions of the peripheral retina that are not detected by traditional perimetry. These tests may be employed in patients while the consciously seeing parts of the visual field are masked. The results may help to explain the sometimes surprisingly good spatial orientation and locomotion among patients with extremely poor foveal vision or perimetrically narrow visual fields.

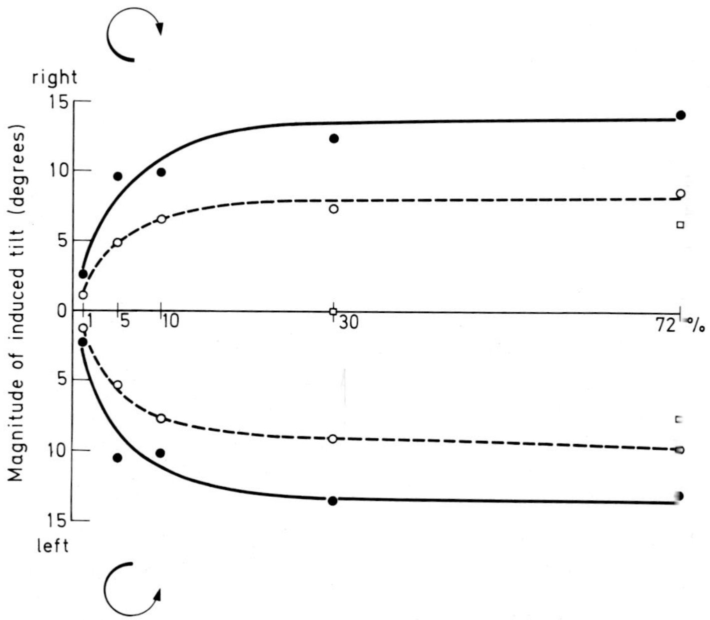

Fig. 8. Mean magnitude of induced tilt of apparent vertical as function of density of colored circles on transparent disk rotating around *S*'s line of sight in front of a stationary background. Abscissa represents the percentage of the total area moved, with area divided into randomly distributed circles, each covering $^1/_4$% of field. Results for three background conditions are shown: solid dots for plain white background, open dots for stationary background carrying 8 circles (2%), open squares for stationary background carrying 288 circles (72%). Early saturation of tilt effect (120 circles corresponding to 30% of total area moving) and inhibitory effect of stationary background are evident

location within the visual field, and the spatial arrangement in depth of a visual stimulus determine whether and how much of the stimulus motion is taken on by the observer or whether the stimulus is exclusively perceived as moving in relation to the stationary subject.

I. The Area Effect

An area effect may be inferred from the older literature in that it was consistently observed that visually induced self-motion preception requires movement of a large portion of the seen environment. Quantitative results, however, were first presented by BRANDT et al. (1973) for CV and were later extended to induced tilt during roll vection by HELD et al. (1975) who found an almost linear increase of the tilt angle with a logarithmic augmentation of the total area moving (as measured in steradians). These results were obtained by use of coherent areas of constant contrast density whose movement was confined to a specific location within the visual field. BRANDT et al. (1975) then determined how induced self-motion relates to the *number and density of moving contrasts* randomly distributed within the visual field. Figures 8 and 9 indicate that the threshold total area for induction of roll vection and apparent tilt is below 1% (of the visual field) if this area is split into four equally sized portions. A single visual object of the same area moving in front of an unstructured background, however, does not induce apparent tilt. With this method, tilt was found to be saturated if 30% of the visual field (scattered into 120 visual objects) were subtended by moving randomly distributed contrasts. It can be inferred from those data that the threshold area and the saturation area are even less if split into a still greater number of smaller contrast objects. In the experiments of HELD et al. (1975), who used coherent areas, the effect of a moving area subtending 30% of the visual field was far from being saturated. Therefore, increasing the number of randomly distributed contrasts in addition to producing an area effect must involve another influence related to the average density of seen elements within the visual field. The *density effect* seems to indicate that a large number of retinal elements has to be simultaneously stimulated as to produce the maximal tilt angle.

II. The Retinal Location Effect

Using moving stimuli equal in area it was shown that the *peripheral retina dominates visually induced vection and spatial orientation* (BRANDT et al., 1973; DICHGANS and BRANDT, 1974; HELD et al., 1975) whereas central vision dominates pattern perception and egocentric (body centered) object motion detection. According to BRANDT et al. (1973), stimulation of the central visual field up to 30° in diameter almost never leads to CV, whereas exposure of the same stimulus to the retinal periphery may be quite effective. Conversely, masking the central field up to 60° in diameter does not impair CV and diminishes the apparent self-motion velocity only slightly with the mask subtending 120° (Fig. 8). The dominance of the retinal periphery for dynamic spatial orientation is further illustrated when one considers that any increase in stimulus area will progressively invade the peripheral visual field.

In the laboratory situation of an *opposite motion stimulation* of the center and periphery (Fig. 4), spatial orientation relies on the peripheral stimulus whereas optokinetic nystagmus, pattern-, and object-motion perception depend on the central stimulus (BRANDT et al., 1973). This experiment illustrates that both mechanisms of motion perception may work in parallel as they frequently do in real life, enabling man to perceive motion of objects while experiencing active locomotion.

III. The Inhibitory Effect of Stationary Contrasts

The inhibitory effect of simultaneously presented stationary contrasts on vections is demonstrated in Figure 8. This effect is to be expected since it simply reflects the two visual mechanisms for static and dynamic spatial orientation which interact in a normal environment. Apparent self-motion and position in space are principally determined by the *proportional distribution of stationary*

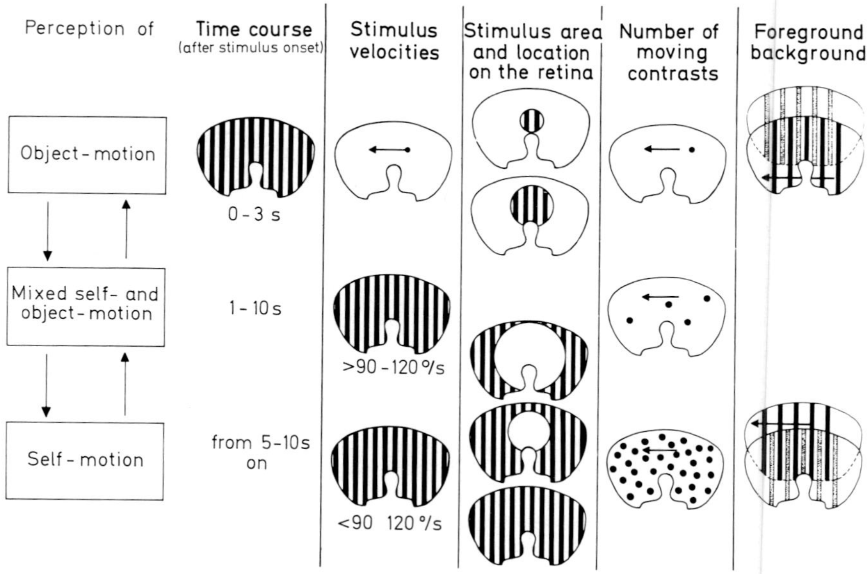

Fig. 9. Schematic drawing summarizing critical optokinetic stimulus properties which determine whether object- or self-motion is perceived

and moving visual contrasts within the seen environment and secondly, by their *spatial arrangement in depth* (BRANDT et al., 1975). *Background* information is of much greater significance than is *foreground* information (Fig. 9). CV may be elicited in spite of a stationary foreground which then appears to move with the observer. But CV is strongly inhibited in the presence of a stationary background. Pattern contrast and average luminosity seem not to be critical within wide limits of photopic vision (LEIBOWITZ and DICHGANS, 1977).

Thus, visually induced self-motion and spatial orientation rely mainly on the information from the seen periphery, both the retinal periphery and the periphery in depth (BRANDT et al., 1975). The existence of such a dominance of the periphery is obviously biologically adaptive. Self-motion is perceived when sizable portions of the depth and/or the retinal periphery are in motion since this is the inevitable consequence of movement of the body in space, even if the foreground is stationary with respect to the observer as in passive movement in a vehicle. On the contrary, stationary contrasts in the retinal and depth periphery, with the movement restricted to contrasts in the foreground, normally exist when an object moves and should thus be associated with object-motion perception. The foreground within the center of the visual field should typically be reserved for the observation and fixation of moving objects localized in body rather than spatial coordinates, thus allowing for reaching and grasping as well as avoidance movements. Interesting in this regard is the observation that stationary contrasts located in the foreground are perceived to move with the observer during CV, thus indicating a localization in terms of body coordinates. This conceptual scheme implies that the two functions of *spatial localization and spatial orientation are preferentially associated with different regions in space*, the former mainly with the central foreground, and the latter mainly with the retinal and depth periphery (background in a broader sense). Periphery-determined spatial orientation thus appears to take advantage of the physical fact that the density per unit visual angle of objects in the background is greater than in the foreground, and consequently provides a larger and, therefore, more reliable sample of the visual environment (BRANDT et al., 1975).

The above-mentioned critical stimulus characteristics illustrate the complexity of man's visual surround, a fact that contrasts to the simplicity of a vestibular stimulus defined entirely by the magnitude and direction of body acceleration. They also give an idea of the difficulties to be expected in an attempt to model visual-vestibular interaction. In spite of this complexity, the central nervous system manages to extract the adequate visual information thus supplementing vestibular and somatosensory senses in their effect on spatial orientation.

E. Aftereffects and Habituation of Self-Motion

Perceptual aftereffects of seen pattern motion are frequently observed after prolonged stimulation. They constitute an apparent motion of reversed direction after the cessation of pattern motion. Since motion aftereffects can be produced both by apparent as well as real movement, they must originate from the net displacement across the retina (see SEKULER and PANTLE, Chap. 3 and ANSTIS, Chap. 21, this Vol.). It seems to be generally accepted that motion aftereffects are caused by selective adaptation or fatigue of movement sensitive neural units within the visual system (BARLOW and HILL, 1963; RICHARDS and SMITH, 1969; WALLS, 1969).

The aftereffects of visually induced self-motion sensation (and optokinetic nystagmus), however, very probably involve the vestibular system (BRANDT and DICHGANS, 1972; COHEN et al., 1973; UEMURA and COHEN, 1973; BRANDT et al., 1974a; WAESPE and HENN, 1977). In contrast to the spiral aftereffect (HOLLAND, 1965), for example, the CV aftereffect is observed in complete darkness, thus not requiring actual information about an external (visual) object and it usually continues in the same direction after stimulus termination. If, however, a stationary visual surround is presented, the self-motion sensation reverses immediately (THALMANN, 1921; BRANDT et al., 1973). Again in contrast to the traditional motion aftereffects, the poststimulus self-motion sensation in the dark usually contains two phases instead of one: an *initial positive phase*, during which aftersensation corresponds in direction to the previous stimulus is followed by a *negative phase*, which is defined by the reversal in motion sensation.

Optokinetic afternystagmus displays a very similar time course with an analogous reversal of direction (in man: ASCHAN and BERGSTEDT, 1955; MACKENSEN and WIEGMANN, 1959; KORNHUBER, 1962; in the rabbit: COLLEWIJN, 1969; in the monkey: KÖRNER and SCHILLER, 1972).

Recently, BRANDT et al. (1974a), studying the perceptual as well as the oculomotor aftereffects induced by rotary motion of the entire visual surround, have shown that duration and intensity of both phases depend on stimulus duration. They observed an increase of the positive phase with increasing stimulus durations up to 1 min whereas the negative component was found to still increase with the longest stimulus duration tested (15 min). The stronger habituative "reverse" tendency shortened the positive aftereffects if stimuli lasted for more than 3 min. Qualitatively similar results have been obtained for the generally more pronounced optokinetic afternystagmus in the monkey (BÜTTNER et al., 1976).

It may be concluded from those studies that the processes that reverse perceptual and oculomotor aftereffects require a longer stimulus duration for saturation and have a longer decay time constant after stimulus termination as compared to the positive aftereffects. These latter processes eventually may be interpreted as a central counterregulation to the visually induced excitation of the vestibular system which becomes also apparent *during* prolonged stimulation (BRANDT et al., 1974a). This interpretation is also supported by the results of YOUNG and HENN (1974), PFALTZ and KATO (1974), and PFALTZ and OHTSUKA (1975), who showed an adaptation transfer from visually induced CV to vestibular nystagmus.

During long lasting exposure to seen motion of the entire visual surround, one may observe a slow tonic decrease in perceived velocity of CV, and, after several minutes, periodic reversals of the direction of perceived self-motion, concurrent with a shift in average eye position, the *Schlagfeld* of JUNG and MITTERMAIER (1939) toward the slow instead of the quick phase of OKN.

The velocity adaptation in CV was demonstrated in scaling experiments or, better, through calculations based on the subjective duration of an apparent 360° revolution (BÜCHELE, 1977). Tonic velocity adaptation in LV has been investigated in field experiments with vehicle drivers (DENTON, 1971; SALVATORE, 1968; SCHMIDT and TIFFIN, 1969) and the short-term adaptation experiments in the laboratory of BERTHOZ et al. (1975).

The intermittent occurrence of *inverted self-motion perception* (BRANDT et al., 1974a) may be interpreted as the result of rivalry between the outlasting activity of actual stimulus excitation and the habituative central counterregulation. The central counterregulation may act as to recreate subjective stationarity and to finally accept physical motion as normal, internally defined as stationarity. The results further illustrate the great amount of plasticity within the central nervous system, which manages not only to adapt its motor outputs to rearrangement of the perceived world (HELD and HEIN, 1963; GONSHOR and MELVILL-JONES, 1971), but also the perception itself (KOHLER, 1956; GRAYBIEL et al., 1960).

F. Neurophysiologic Evidence of Visual-Vestibular Interaction

The psychophysical results discussed so far strongly suggest that visual information about motion of one's surroundings converges onto vestibular structures and is evaluated by cortical areas that "normally" process vestibular input. The psychophysical arguments for this are mainly based on the perceptual similarity of the consequences of an appropriate visual stimulus and vestibular excitation and the way the two interact. Such a concept implies a compartmentalization of motion perception within the cerebral cortex. Self-motion perception is supposed to reside in the parietal "vestibular" cortex, whereas the perception of object motion is assumed to be localized within the visual cortex. Recent neurophysiologic experiments and cytoarchitectonic studies in monkeys by ZEKI (1974) have shown that motion information may be processed beyond the visual areas 17–19 (HUBEL and WIESEL, 1968). ZEKI found that the majority of the neurons in the posterior bank of the superior temporal sulcus responded specifically to the direction of movement. This region may correspond to visual areas of the parietal cortex in man.

I. Neuronal Correlates of Circular Vection

So far only a few neurophysiologic experiments in animals have examined the visual-vestibular interaction in the brainstem. A *direction-specific modulation* of resting discharge has been *evoked by the movement of an ample visual surround* in the vestibular nerve (KLINKE and SCHMIDT, 1970), the vestibular nuclei of the goldfish (DICHGANS et al., 1973b; ALLUM et al., 1976), and the medial and lateral vestibular nuclei of the rabbit (DICHGANS and BRANDT, 1972; LEOPOLD et al., 1973; LEOPOLD, 1974), the cat (LEOPOLD, 1974; BAUER, 1976; DAUNTON and THOMSEN, 1976), and the monkey (HENN et al., 1974; WAESPE and HENN, 1977), and the vestibular part (VPI) of the monkey's thalamus (BÜTTNER and HENN, 1976). The early report by CHANG and WU (1959), who recorded responses to optic stimuli from units in the toad's vestibular nucleus with latencies of about 300 ms and the later recordings from the pretectum and the mesencephalic reticular formation (POTTHOFF et al., 1967), as well as the vestibular cortex (KORNHUBER and DA FONSECA, 1964), are less conclusive since they have been obtained using unstructured and stationary visual (flash) and inadequate vestibular (galvanic) stimulation. These stimuli clearly are not suitable to test multisensory integration of movement information. Thus, it remains open whether there are other sites in the brain at which visual and vestibular inputs converge or to which the already integrated information is transmitted.

All of the recent studies performed in awake animals show a tonic modulation of resting discharge of vestibular units in *response to exclusive constant velocity*

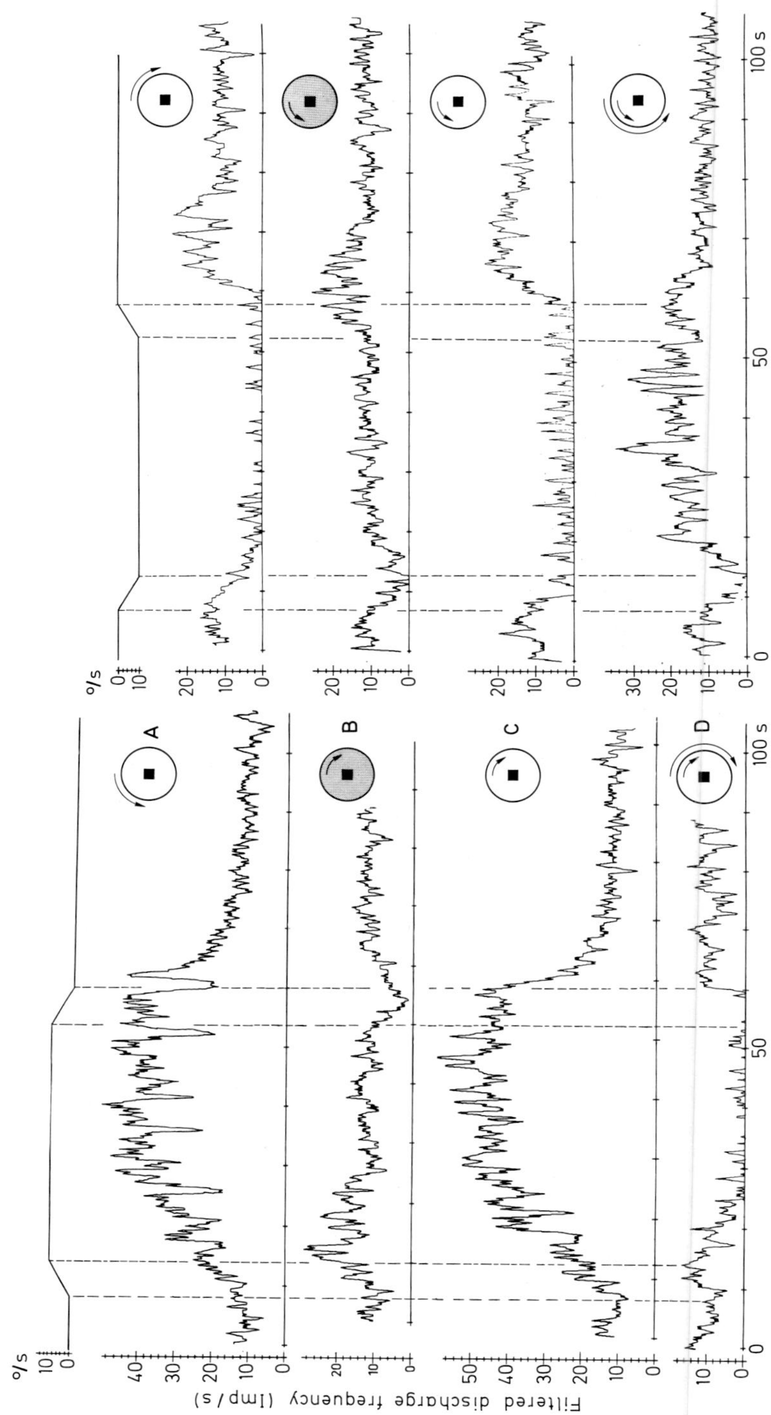
A
B
C
D
°/s
Filtered discharge frequency (Imp/s)
0
50
100 s

motion of the visual surround (Fig. 10A). The modulation, although to a variable degree, seems to occur in the great majority of horizontal semicircular canal-dependent units of all the vertebrate species tested. A unit which is excited by a head acceleration, say, to the left is also excited by motion of the surround to the right, which represents the optokinetic stimulus that in man would cause the sensation of turning to the left. Both type I as well as the inverse type II units (classification following DUENSING and SCHÄFER, 1958) specifically respond to visual motion with an inverse directional response characteristic. Thus, the visually induced effect facilitates the vestibular response to body rotation. Directional asymmetries in the amount of modulation occur in most of the neurons (DICHGANS et al., 1973b; LEOPOLD, 1974; HENN et al., 1974). In the rabbit, about one-quarter of the neurons observed have only an excitatory or an inhibitory response to optokinetic stimuli regardless of their direction. When the stimulus is in one direction, the maximum response for some neurons is greater than the response for the opposite direction (LEOPOLD, 1974; similar results in the goldfish by ALLUM et al., 1976). This difference thus may still provide information about the direction of movement. The visually induced discharge modulation is not only obtained in the animal immobilized by Flaxedil (KLINKE and SCHMIDT, 1970; DICHGANS and BRANDT, 1972; DICHGANS et al., 1973b) where retinal image motion is maximal, but also in the awake and unrelaxed rabbit (LEOPOLD, 1974) and monkey (HENN et al., 1974; WAESPE and HENN, 1977) during optokinetic nystagmus. In the rabbit's vestibular nucleus, a tonic bias modulation has been found in addition to the eye movement correlated activity changes observed earlier by ECKEL (1954) and DUENSING and SCHÄFER (1958). Modulation of vestibular neuron activity follows optokinetic stimulus onset with a latency of up to several seconds (LEOPOLD, 1974; ALLUM et al., 1976; WAESPE and HENN, 1977). Time constants, which can be calculated from the modulation during a constant velocity optokinetic stimulus or after stimulus offset, have been employed to classify neuron responses into three types in the goldfish (ALLUM et al., 1976). The first response type A (25%) is observed to increase its resting discharge rate, approximately exponentially, to a steady state level during constant velocity (Fig. 10A). The time constant

---

◁ Fig. 10. Filtered discharge frequency (ordinate) of type I unit from right vestibular nucleus in unanesthetized, relaxed goldfish in response to trapezoid velocity profiles shown in top lines (acceleration 1.5°/s^2, constant velocity 10°/s for total time of 45 s, deceleration 1.5°/s^2. Corresponding responses to stimuli to right and left are presented adjacently. During exclusive surround motion to left, *A*, unit activity increases beyond termination of acceleration. Subsequently, increased discharge level is maintained throughout constant velocity and deceleration period and is followed by positive aftereffect. During animal rotation to right in dark, *B*, activity approximately follows mechanical properties of cupula-endolymph system. If animal is rotated in light (with respect to his stationary visual horizon), *C*, vestibular responses to acceleration and deceleration combine with visual constant velocity response. If surround rotates twice as fast as animal to right, *D*, visual stimulus dominates unit activity during constant velocity period and attenuates body acceleration responses (evaluation of unit activity through zero phase double lag filter, time constant 200 ms). Comparison with Fig. 1 shows similarities of neuronal discharge profiles in fish and perceived velocities in man during identical stimulus situations associated with this increase is on the average 6.9 s. Type A shows the most intense optokinetic modulation. Type B neurons are rare (16%). They decrease their modulation to a steady state level above resting discharge once constant velocity has been reached (time constant 5.6 s). The most common type C (59%) is characterized by a comparatively smaller amount of optokinetic discharge modulation and short time constants mostly below 1 s.

The principle by which visually induced self-motion velocity is coded at the level of the vestibular nuclei is not completely understood. It seems as if in the relaxed fish (ALLUM et al., 1976) and the rabbit (LEOPOLD, 1974) the optokinetic effect upon vestibular units is saturated at velocites below 10°/s. This may explain why the small velocity lag during smooth pursuit still contains a constant velocity response during body rotation in the light. In the unrelaxed monkey, velocity is coded up to 45–120°/s (WAESPE and HENN, 1977). Also unknown is how stimulus qualities like area and location of motion within visual space affect the modulation. Tuning curves for the rotation-plane specificity of the visual modulation as yet have not been determined.

II. Interaction of Visual and Vestibular Stimulation

Interaction has been tested using either velocity trapezoids as in Figure 10 (DICHGANS et al., 1973b; HENN et al., 1974; ALLUM et al., 1976; WAESPE and HENN, 1977) or sinusoidal body and surround rotation (HENN et al., 1974). It has been shown that in the low frequency range, adequate visual inputs (animal rotation in a lit environment) reinforce the vestibular response and with sinusoidal stimulation abolish the phase lead characteristic for low frequency pure vestibular stimulation (HENN et al., 1974). Assuming that a velocity signal might be the important parameter for the animal, the combination of visual and vestibular inputs reduces the shortcomings of either transfer characteristic alone, i.e., the poor vestibular response at low frequencies and the poor visual one at frequencies exceeding 1 Hz.

Figure 10 illustrates the functional importance of the convergent visual input proposed in the introduction. It shows the great importance of vision for the detection of the steady state (and low frequency) components of body motion compensating for the vestibular system's deficiency in this respect.

Figure 10 B shows how during animal rotation in the dark, the neuronal discharge profile follows the mechanical characteristics of the cupula-endolymph system. This, acting as an overdamped torsion pendulum (STEINHAUSEN, 1933), responds to accelerations only, and within a limited frequency range integrates accelerations to create velocity correspondent frequency profiles in primary vestibular afferents (FERNANDEZ and GOLDBERG, 1971) and second order units in the vestibular nuclei (MELVILL-JONES and MILSUM, 1971; SCHNEIDER and ANDERSON, 1976). As can be seen from Figure 10, the lack of steady state response results in the system's failure not only to detect constant velocity but also to discriminate between deceleration from constant velocity and acceleration in the opposite direction from zero velocity. These deficiencies are compensated for as soon as the animal is rotated in the light relative to the stationary surround (Fig. 10C). Now, the neuronal discharge approximately follows the velocity profile of the stimulus. Even the aftereffect due to the cupula's restoring force is overcompensated. LEOPOLD (1974) demonstrated that in the rabbit vestibular neuron thresholds for horizontal body acceleration are lowered in the presence of a stationary visual environment. The mathematical analysis and modeling of the very probably nonlinear interaction of visual and vestibular afferents in the vestibular nuclei so far has not been completed.

Similar effects of combined stimulation have been shown for the interaction of optokinetic and vestibular stimuli in nystagmus (MOWRER, 1937; JUNG, 1948; RADEMAKER and TER BRAAK, 1948; for a detailed review, see COHEN, 1974).

III. Possible Pathways

The pathways along which visual information reaches the vestibular nuclei are still to be investigated. Direct connections from either the retina, the geniculate body, pretectum, or superior colliculus are unknown. The long latencies for the induction of CV and apparent tilt of the vertical, as well as for the neuronal discharge modulation, would suggest a multisynaptic pathway, possibly through the reticular formation. The hypothesis that the superior colliculus serves as an important relay to the vestibular system for the purpose of dynamic spatial orientation is attractive, for this structure reportedly represents a major center for ambient vision and spatial orientation within a static environment (TREVARTHEN, 1968). This idea, however, still lacks experimental support.

The preference of neurons in the *superior colliculus* for moving, as opposed to stationary, visual stimuli is evident in all mammalian species so far investigated. SPRAGUE et al. (1972) pointed out that "it is only in the superior colliculus that movement is a specific trigger for the great majority of neurons," and they suggested "that behavioral performance involving detection of motion or rates of motion is at least in part integrated by neuronal circuits taking an obligatory route through the superior colliculus." In view of this hypothesis, one may consider anatomic and neurophysiologic evidence for the existence of different retinal cell types (ENROTH-CUGELL and ROBSON, 1966; STONE and HOFFMANN, 1972; BOYCOTT and WÄSSLE, 1974), the axons of which reach different regions within the brain. HOFFMANN (1973) and FUKUDA and STONE (1974), for example, have shown that in the cat an x- or small cell system projects only to the geniculate body, whereas a w-cell system projects only to the midbrain and not to the geniculate. The third, y-cell, system projects to both. It is reasonable to assume that the different spatially overlapping systems subserve separate functions, one of which could be spatial orientation. However, in order to have visual-vestibular interaction for CV, the presence of directional and velocity selective visual neurons seems to be required. But in the monkey, as opposed to the cat, such units are rare in the superior colliculus: SCHILLER and KÖRNER

(1972) found none, and GOLDBERG and WURTZ (1972) observed only 10% direction-specific neurons.

The results of KLINKE and SCHMIDT (1970) in the goldfish and indirect evidence presented by UEMURA and COHEN (1973) and COHEN et al. (1973) in the monkey suggest that the *efferent vestibular system,* which sends its fibers to the labyrinthine receptors, is one of the structures which presumably carry visual information into the vestibular system. More recent studies with single unit recordings from the vestibular nerve of the monkey did not show any visual modulation and therefore suggest that in higher animals the vestibular nuclei are the most peripheral site of visual-vestibular convergence (KELLER, 1976). In man, CV and visually induced tilt may still be induced after bilateral transection of the vestibular nerves (DICHGANS and BRANDT, 1974; ZEE et al., 1976).

The circuit discovered by MAEKAWA and SIMPSON (1972), who showed that visual signals activate Purkinje cells in the *flocculus* via the accessory optic system (MIZUNO et al., 1973; TAKEDA and MAEKAWA, 1976) and the inferior olive (dorsal cap region, ALLEY et al., 1975), at present is to be considered the most likely "visual" pathway to the vestibular nuclei. Recordings by COLLEWIJN (1975) in the rabbit, and by HOFFMANN and SCHOPPMANN (1975) in the cat from the nucleus of the optic tract, which probably represents the pretectal relay station of the MAEKAWA-SIMPSON pathway, indicate a direction-specific reaction to optokinetic stimuli that saturates at low velocities. This saturation is also observed in the visually modulated vestibular nucleus units of the rabbit (LEOPOLD, 1974). It remains open whether this circuit mediates the neurophysiologic correlate for CV (facilitation) and/or whether it subserves fixation suppression (inhibition) of vestibular nystagmus as indicated by ablation studies (TAKEMORI and COHEN, 1974), as well as recordings from floccular cortex (LISBERGER and FUCHS, 1974). Since Purkinje cell axons inhibit the ipsilateral vestibular nuclei (ITO et al., 1970, 1973; BAKER et al., 1972; FUKUDA et al., 1972) and since Purkinje cells of the flocculus are preferentially activated by motion of the visual surround toward the contralateral side (SIMPSON and ALLEY, 1974), this loop could at least in part serve to suppress direct vestibulo-ocular reflexes dependent on vestibular type I units during fixation, or to optimize and control the vestibulo-ocular reflex (GHELARDUCCI et al., 1975).

The descending extrageniculate "visual" pathways to the pontine reticular formation and the nucleus papillioformis described by GRAYBIEL (1972) may indirectly reach the vestibular nuclei, but the possible physiologic significance of these pathways has not been examined. A more interesting possibility are the cortical projections from primary visual areas to the pontine nuclei (BRODAL, 1972a, 1972b) onto regions from which connections to the cerebellar vermis and the cerebellar hemispheres originate (BRODAL and JANSEN, 1976). The rostral pontine nuclei of the cat contain cells that selectively respond to optokinetic stimulation and have large receptive fields frequently crossing the midline (BAKER et al., 1976).

The converse interaction of the vestibular afferences upon visual centers has been demonstrated for the lateral geniculate body (PAPAIOANNOU, 1973;

MAGNIN et al., 1974) and the superior colliculus (BISTI et al., 1974). Whether there is any specific interaction of the two inputs in the visual cortex as suggested by GRÜSSER et al. (1959), and authors investigating changes of visual receptive field characteristics contingent on body tilt (HORN and HILL, 1969; SPINELLI, 1970; DENNEY and ADORJANI, 1972), is still controversial (SCHWARTZKROIN, 1973).

G. Visual Stabilization of Posture

The powerful stabilizing effect of vision on posture is well-known to clinicians. It is particularly apparent in patients with diseases involving proprioceptive joint and muscle afferents as in tabes dorsalis (DUCHENNE, 1858; FRENKEL, 1907; ANDRÉ-THOMAS, 1940). The stabilizing effect of vision on postural imbalance is not quite as strong in patients with vestibular lesions (BARRÉ, 1949; DE HAAN, 1959), but according to our own recordings is still stronger than in normals.

Slight postural instability is provoked also in normals once the eyes are closed or in the dark. In healthy adults, the body sway occurring with eyes open has been quoted as 50–65% less than with eyes closed (TRAVIS, 1945; EDWARDS, 1946). A similar attenuation through vision may be demonstrated in the Fourier spectrum of postural sway (Fig. 11 A), a method of analysis that has been used by others earlier to quantify postural sway (BENSEL and DZENDOLET, 1968; NASHNER, 1970). With this method, one may observe that on the average a subject's attempt to limit his self-generated lateral sway, with eyes open, leads to about a 50% sway amplitude attenuation up to frequencies of about 1.2 Hz when compared with eyes-closed-sway. Comparable results have been obtained from experiments in dogs by TALBOT (1974). NASHNER (1970) concluded on the basis of his data on fore-aft sway, which entailed work on reflex responses to platform displacement in normals and labyrinthine-diseased subjects, that the normal subject regulates postural sway with a combination of high-frequency (semicircular canal and somatosensory receptors) and low-frequency (otoliths and visual receptors) stabilization. NASHNER's (1970) conclusions are supported by the data depicted in Figure 11 A.

Where the semicircular canals are at their optimal velocity performance (above 0.3 Hz, NASHNER's high frequency range), the spectral plots illustrate a moderate amplification of the canal-dependent postural control through vision. Amplification has to be assumed since with eyes open, small sway divergences are corrected more rapidly. The stabilizing effect of vision is much stronger in the low-frequency range which is the domain of the otolith receptors. This becomes evident if one measures the absolute difference in sway amplitude (eyes open vs. eyes closed) and not the ratio (Fig. 11 C). As compared to the efficiency of semicircular canal and somatosensory inputs in sway regulations at the higher frequencies, one may note from the figure that the stabilizing effect of the otoliths in the dark is less. Nonetheless, otolithic receptors must have a role in postural stabilization as patients without normal labyrinthine function have impaired low-frequency stabilization with eyes closed compared to normals.

That it is the visual motion information and not just information about the orientation of contours that stabilizes posture is suggested by experiments with stroboscopic surround illumination. AMBLARD and CREMIEUX (1976) found that visual stabilization was practically absent at strobe frequencies up to 6 Hz, which was the highest frequency they tested. Our own results indicate that postural stabilization by vision starts at about 8–10 Hz, at which frequency motion perception, roll vection, and the visually induced displacement of subjective vertical as well as CV also begin to be observed. It is very likely that the afferent physiologic mechanisms subserving roll vection and apparent vertical displacement are identical with those stabilizing posture by way of visual feedback about the self-generated body sway.

Deceptive visual motion impressions cause a displacement of both perceived visual and postural vertical (DICHGANS et al., 1972) and as a reflex-like reaction, body sway and eventually fall toward the direction of image motion[4] (FISCHER and KORNMÜLLER, 1930b; EDWARDS, 1946; DE WIT, 1972; LEE and ARONSON, 1974; DICHGANS et al., 1975a, 1976; BLES and DE WIT, 1976). A roll-vection stimulus has been presumed to produce a conflict between graviceptive and visual cues (DICHGANS et al., 1972). This conflict can be examined both in the power spectrum (Fig. 11A) of the sway response to a step change in velocity of a visual roll-vection stimulus and in the frequency response (Fig. 11D) to sinusoidal roll-vection perturbations (MAURITZ et al., 1975). Figure 11B shows the original recording of the sway response to such a stimulus. The displacement of perceived vertical elicits the lateral deviation of the center of gravity. The conflict limits its amount and may cause the periodic resetting in Figure 11B (0.03 Hz, MAURITZ et al., 1977) of the displacement of visual vertical and the body's center of gravity. Resonant frequencies of the postural control system may account for the sway amplitude peaks (0.1 and 1 Hz) depicted in Figure 11A. A more general attenuation of postural sway receptor responses during the roll-vection disturbance over a frequency range up to 7 Hz is also illustrated in the Figure.

The frequency response of body sway to the disturbance may be demonstrated using a sinusoidally rotating visual screen. The results for such stimuli are shown by the typical Bode and phase plots in Figure 11D. The Bode plot shows a steep amplitude decrement above 0.1 Hz (MAURITZ et al., 1975; LESTIENNE et al., 1977). The increasing phase lag at higher frequencies reflects the delay of the sway response to the onset of roll vection. The steep decay in induced sway amplitude with frequencies above 0.1 Hz is only seen with the disturbing stimulus. It reflects the counteracting stabilization by parallel loops (probably proprioception in the higher frequency range). The physiologic frequency response, however, deals with confirming and not conflicting visual

[4] In the cat exposed to a roll vection stimulus a direction specific bias of spinal motoneuron reflex excitability may be visually elicited. Its strength is comparable to the vestibular effects of static lateral tilt of the animal (Thoden et al., 1977).

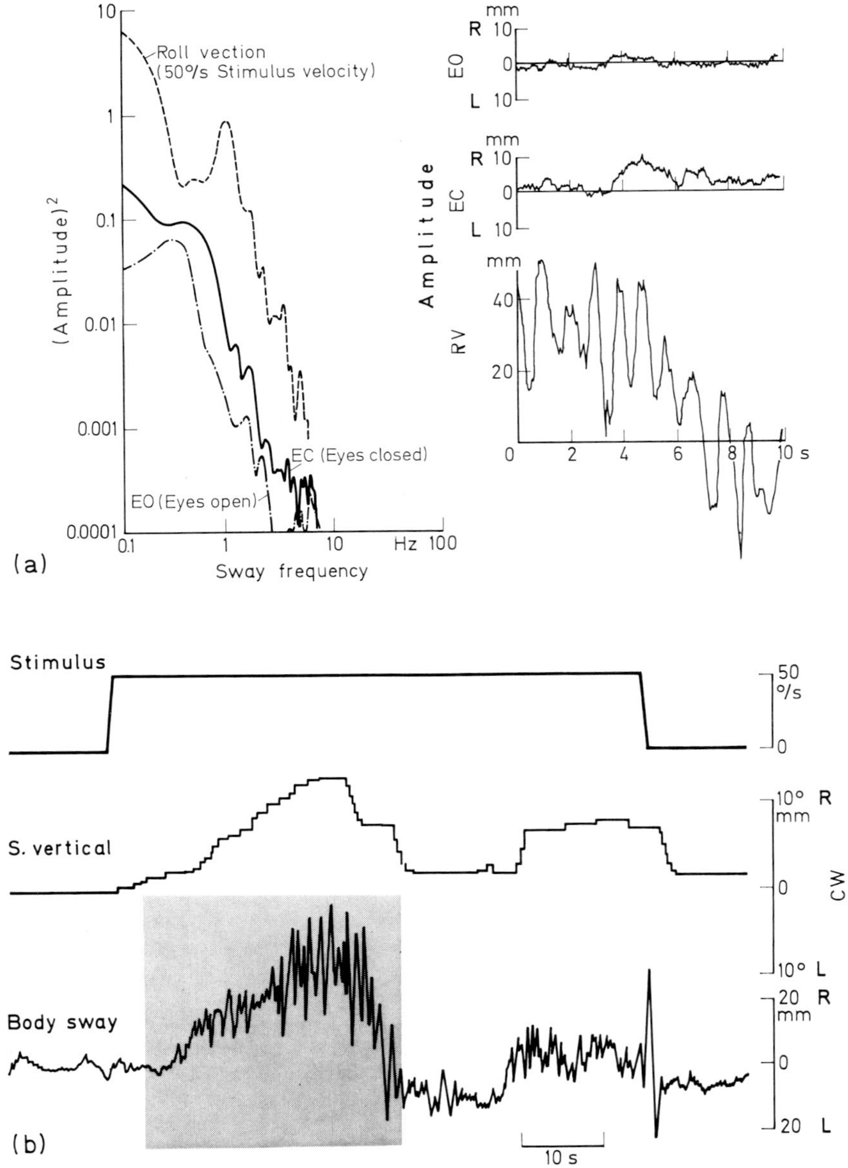

Fig. 11a–e. Posture and perceived vertical in response to visual stimuli. (a) *On left: Fourier power spectrum* of lateral body sway with eyes open, eyes closed, and during visually induced roll vection, 50°/s, of single subject (analyzed period: 30 s). *On right: original traces* representing last 10 s from each of analyzed postural sway responses. (b) Simultaneous recording of apparent vertical and lateral body sway (displacement of center of gravity) in response to constant velocity visual roll stimulus (50°/s to right, same subject as in (a). Deviations of subjective and postural vertical parallel each other and are characterized by their long latencies and periodic breakdown during prolonged stimulation. Period analyzed for body sway power spectrum in a is indicated by shaded area. (c) Amplitude difference between power spectra of lateral sway with eyes closed and with eyes open (average from 10 subjects). Plot clearly indicates corner frequency of about 1 Hz, above which sway stabilization through vision decreases in gain. (d) Bode plot for postural sway and apparent vertical displacement in response to sinusoidal roll-vection stimulus (0.01 Hz–0.25 Hz, constant peak velocity of input 50°/s, 5 subjects). (e) Corresponding records showing large interindividual difference in amplitude of postural sway in response to visual disturbance (upper trace)

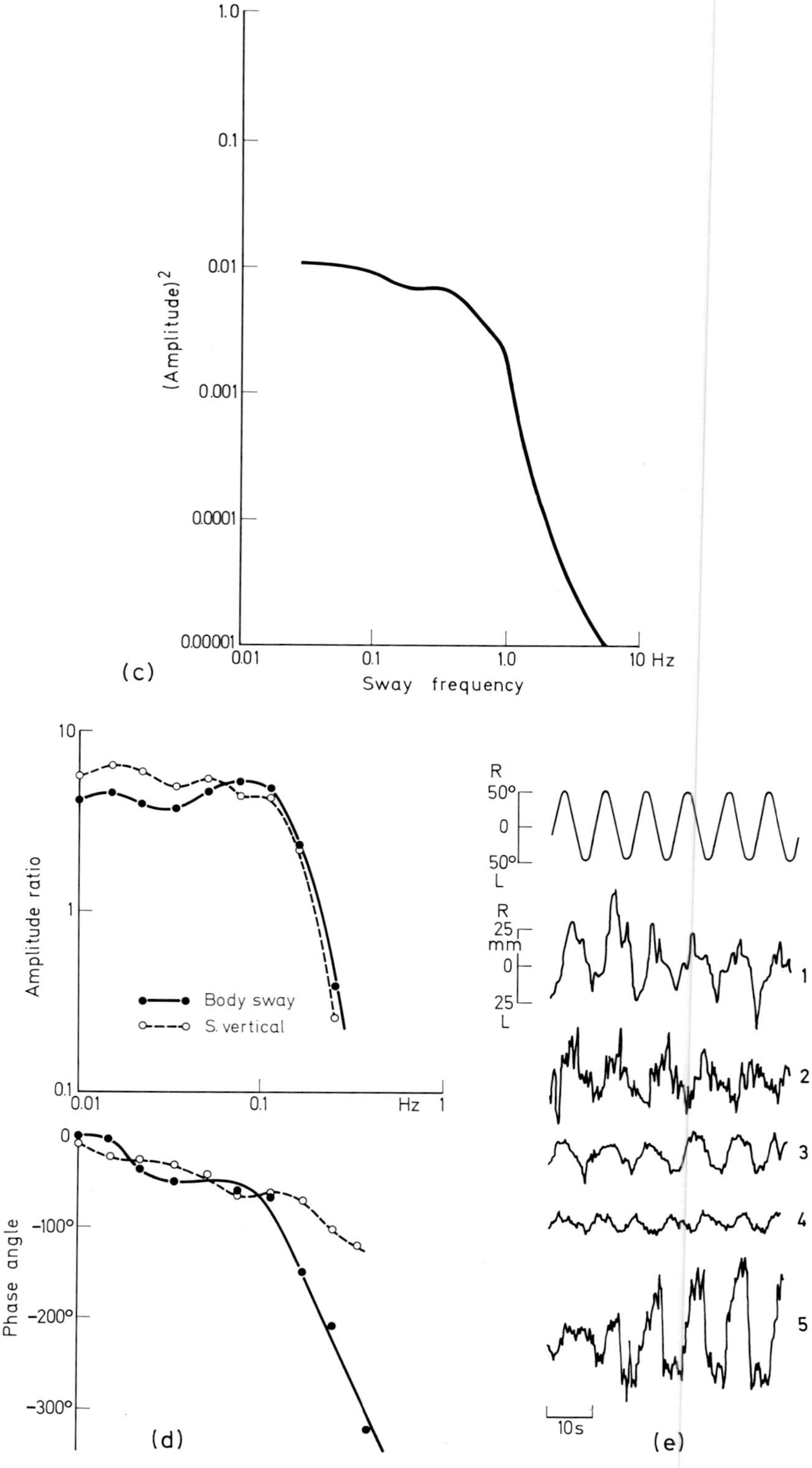

1.0
0.1
0.01
0.001
0.0001
0.00001
(Amplitude)²
0.01
0.1
1.0
10 Hz
Sway frequency
(c)
10
1
0.1
Amplitude ratio
Body sway
S. vertical
0.01
0.1
Hz
0
-100°
-200°
-300°
Phase angle
(d)
R
50°
0
50°
L
R
25
mm
0
25
L
1
2
3
4
5
10s
(e)

Fig. 11c–e

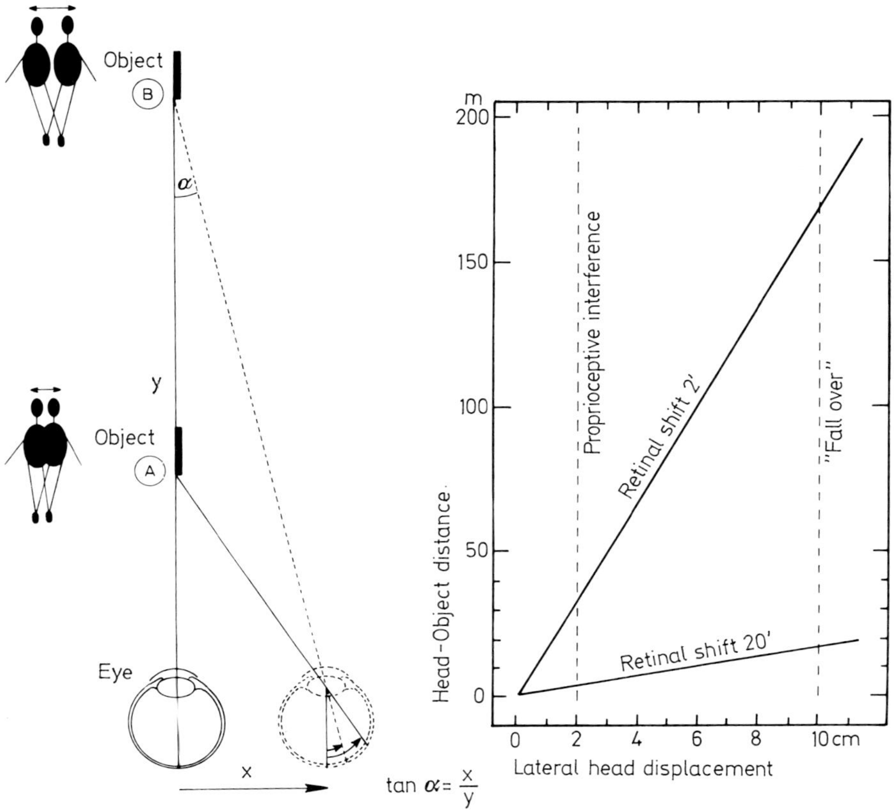

Fig. 12. Distance dependent height vertigo: Geometrical analysis showing that by increasing the distance between eyes and stationary surroundings body sway must also increase in order to be visually detected and to be used for postural stabilization. For a given retinal displacement threshold of between 2 and 20 minutes of arc, normal lateral head sway of 2 cm is visually not detected at a distance of a few meters. Theoretically height-vertigo is maximal well below 20 or 200 meters respectively (after BRANDT et al., 1978)

and proprioceptive signals and therefore exhibits a high gain up to 1 Hz (Fig. 11C). A similar frequency response has been observed for another visuomotor task, the tracking of a sinusoidally moving visual target (SÜNDERHAUF, 1960; FENDER and NYE, 1961). Otolithic responses are ambiguous since their signal is highly dependent on the ankle reaction torque and may be negative, zero, or positive during a sway divergence to one side. Vision relieves this ambiguity. However, if the visual signal itself is in conflict, it may enhance low-frequency instability within the postural control system (DICHGANS et al., 1976). Whether this instability is exclusive to visual-otolithic interactions, or represents cross-coupling effects on neuromuscular and semicircular canal systems, has yet to be investigated.

Visual effects on posture probably are also involved in the pathogenesis of *height vertigo* (LEE and LISHMAN, 1975; BRANDT, 1976). A simple geometrical analysis as presented in Figure 12 shows that if the distance between the eyes and the stationary visual surroundings is increased, body sway must also increase in order to cause a suprathreshold displacement of the retinal image. Thus, in case of large distances, posture stabilizing vestibular and somatosensory information about lateral and foreaft body shift are not assisted by vision, but are in conflict with the visual illusion of no change in position. Geometrically, height vertigo should begin at a few meters distance and should be maximal below a distance of 20 or 200 meters depending on which movement detection threshold is assumed. Using a force measuring platform on a high building BRANDT et al. (1978) demonstrated an increase of body sway with increasing altitude and distance to the stationary visual surround.

Experiments on *the development of visual stabilization of posture* in infants suggest that the usual contribution to this multi-loop control comes in rather late (BRANDT et al., 1976). Scalings of postural reactions to visual roll motion in children revealed three phases: (1) 6–12 month-old-babies show no or very little optokinetic disturbance of their newly acquired ability to sit. (2) Children between the age of 2–5 years show a marked dependence of postural stability on vision with an ipsilateral deviation. (3) From 5 to 15 years of age visual effects slowly decrease to their final strength in adulthood: a moderate head and body tilt. It was concluded that the calibration of the three main loops controlling upright stance occurs sequentially and is mutually interactive. Optimal functioning requires the continuous evaluation of the reafferent consequences of self-generated body movements (BRANDT et al., 1976).

H. Optokinetic Pseudo-Coriolis Effects and Motion Sickness

So far only the role of vision in spatial orientation has been discussed. This chapter should not be concluded, however, without a brief mention of the visual effects on disorientation (dizziness) and motion sickness. *The necessity of vestibular stimulation* for provoking motion sickness is indicated by the observation that motion sickness does not occur in individuals who lack a functional vestibular apparatus (JAMES, 1882; BROWN et al., 1941; GRAYBIEL, 1964; COLEHOUR, 1965; KENNEDY et al., 1968; MONEY, 1970). That *vision is not an essential* but rather a secondary etiologic factor in the genesis of (vestibular) motion sickness was concluded from the fact that blind persons are susceptible to acute motion sickness (DESNOES, 1926; TYLER and BARD, 1949; CHINN and SMITH, 1955) and even in comparison with a control group of normal subjects show no significant difference in incidence rate (GRAYBIEL, 1970).

The role of vision in motion sickness primarily caused by body accelerations so far has been controversial. Under some circumstances, vision has been reported to promote sickness (SJÖBERG, 1931; MANNING and STEWARD, 1949; KOTTENHOFF and LINDAHL, 1958; KENNEDY et al., 1965; OOSTERFELD et al., 1972). In other circumstances, at least when visual motion information is in "physiologic agreement" with vestibular input, there is evidence that sickness is suppressed (ARMSTRONG, 1939; MANNING and STEWARD, 1949; JOHNSON and TAYLOR, 1961; BROWN and CRAMPTON, 1966; MARSHALL and BROWN, 1966; REASON and DIAZ, 1970). Even in the absence of actual body movements, sickness has been reported in persons viewing a tilting or swinging room (WOOD, 1895; WITKIN, 1949; LISHMAN and LEE, 1973), a rotating cylinder from inside (CRAMPTON and YOUNG, 1953), wide screen movie theaters (MONEY, 1970), or the moving scene on the screen of a flight simulator (MILLER and GOODSON, 1960; BARRET and THORNTON, 1968; REASON and DIAZ, 1971). BRANDT et al. (1975) found that *optokinetic motion sickness* could be induced through prolonged angular oscillations of the visual surround around the vertical axis of a stationary subject. A quantitative comparison of optokinetic motion sickness with the motion sickness elicited through body oscillations in the dark at the same frequency and amplitude (0.02 Hz, peak velocity 100°/s) showed a tendency for the optokinetic stimuli to be more effective than the vestibular ones.

Opto-vestibular interaction in motion sickness was quantitatively investigated by DICHGANS and BRANDT (1973), who used their device depicted in Figure 5 which allowed for independent adjustment of chair and surround speed as well as direction. They demonstrated the powerful role of vision in inducing or inhibiting motion sickness depending upon the stimulus conditions. Bending the head during an apparent self-rotation, induced by exclusive rotatory motion of the visual surround, elicits *pseudo-Coriolis effects* in the stationary observer, which perceptually cannot be distinguished from the well-known vestibular Coriolis effects. The latter are known to be a very powerful stimulus for motion sickness. While vestibular Coriolis effects (CE) arise from cross-coupled angular accelerations sensed by the different semicircular canals during real body rotation (GROEN, 1961; MELVILL-JONES, 1970), optokinetic pseudo-Coriolis effects (PCE) are thought to be based on a visually induced central vestibular excitation which is combined with actual information generated through the head movements itself (BRANDT et al., 1971; DICHGANS and BRANDT, 1972, 1973). With regard to their mechanisms, however, PCEs may be more analogous to an effect described by PURKINJE (1820), which is caused by a head movement during a postrotational semicircular canal response. In the Purkinje effect, a persisting angular velocity vector is located by the canals relative to the skull, and the position of this vector relative to the earth is signaled by gravity detectors. The resulting tumbling sensation then conflicts with the no-change-in-position information from the graviceptors (GUEDRY, 1974). In PCE, supposedly the semicircular canal response is centrally simulated by visual inputs, the graviceptive information is identical with that evoked in the corresponding Purkinje effect. The surprising conformity of direction of the illusory tilt in CE and PCE cannot yet be sufficiently explained. The fact that PCE, as well as CE, may not be observed after bilateral labyrinthectomy or eight's nerve transection (DICHGANS and BRANDT, 1973) proves the necessity of primary vestibular input for elicitation of PCE. PCE are of smaller magnitude than CE and saturate at lower angular velocities. Severe *optokinetic motion sickness* can be elicited through repeated provocation and summation of PCE (DICHGANS and BRANDT, 1973). PCEs, depending upon "illusory" CV, share its prolonged time course

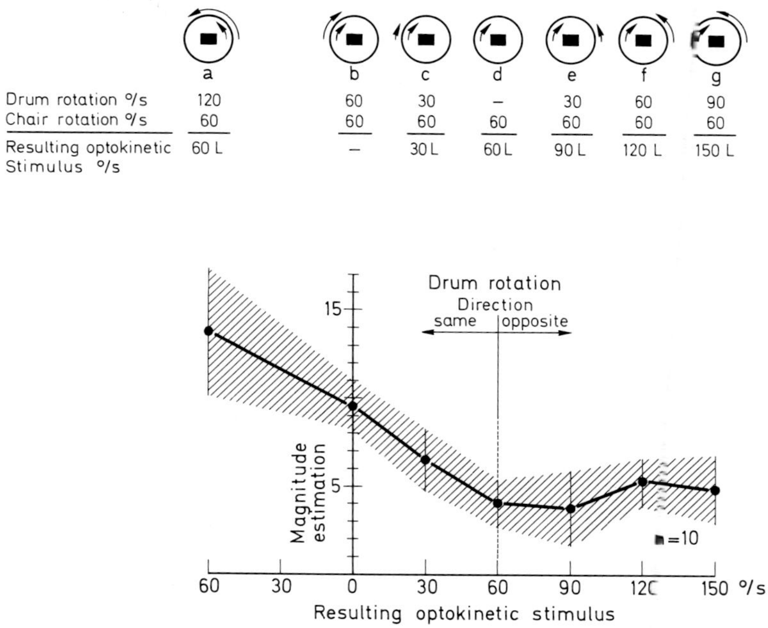

Fig. 13. Magnitude estimation of Coriolis effects, induced by head movements during constant velocity (60°/s) chair rotation while direction and velocity of optokinetic stimulus, provided by additional surround motion, are varied (means and standard deviations). Stimuli are listed in upper part of Figure. Weakest effects occur if relative backward motion of surround is in physiologic agreement with real body rotation (*d*); optokinetic inhibition of "vestibular" Coriolis effects is not enhanced by unproportional increase of velocity beyond 90°/s (*e–g*). Inhibition is reduced if velocity of relative backward motion lags actual chair rotation (*c*). Coriolis effects, however, are markedly enhanced if direction of CV is opposite to actual chair rotation (*a*). Direction-specific interaction of two stimuli is roughly linear within range of ±60 deg of relative velocity (*a–d*)

after stimulus onset and termination, its relation to stimulus velocities and its dependency on stimulus area with predominance of the seen periphery. If a subject is simultaneously exposed to rotation of the visual surround about the line of sight during body angular acceleration about an earth vertical axis then an unpleasant perception of rotation about an off vertical axis and severe nausea occur (ARNOLD et al., 1976). This second type of a FCE has been called *pseudo-Purkinje-effect*.

The visual influence on vestibular CE and motion sickness depends on the direction and speed of the optokinetic stimulus resulting in either inhibition or facilitation (Fig. 13). Apparent tilt and nausea are markedly inhibited if as under natural conditions, surround motion opposite to actual body rotation is presented, but enhanced if the surround moves toward the direction of body rotation, thus resulting in apparent self-rotation opposite to the real rotation. The *direction-specific inhibition of CE and motion sickness* can be practically used in order to avoid sickness in vehicles by providing ample peripheral vision of the relatively moving surround. A hypothetic model for the direction-specific visual-vestibular interaction on CE has been presented by DICHGANS and BRANDT (1973). In this, it is assumed that the visually induced modulation of vestibular unit activity, because of its long decay time, counteracts the momentum excess in the horizontal canals due to the head movement. Consequently, it seems reasonable to distinguish between three basic kinds of so-called Coriolis effects, according to their causal mechanisms, which through summation finally lead to motion sickness: 1) *vestibular CE*, which occur during body rotation in the absence of visual cues, 2) *optokinetico-vestibular CE*, which are inhibited by relative backward motion of a visual scene and enhanced in directionally conflicting situations, and 3) *optokinetic pseudo-Coriolis effects* (PCE), which are elicited in stationary persons during visually induced CV. This classification – referring to stimulus conditions – might help to clarify some of the seemingly contradictory results in the literature. Vestibular and optokinetic motion sickness phenomenologically are identical and are also equally prevented by anti-motion-sickness drugs (BRANDT et al., 1974b).

Acknowledgements: We are grateful to Dr. J. ALLUM, Prof. P. GOURAS, Prof. R. JUNG, Prof. H. LEIBOWITZ, and Prof. E. WIST for criticism of the manuscript and helpful suggestions. The preparation of this chapter was financially supported by the Deutsche Forschungsgemeinschaft (Sonderforschungsbereich 70: Hirnforschung und Sinnesphysiologie).

References

Alley, K., Baker, R., Simpson, J.I.: Afferents to the vestibulo-cerebellum and the origin of the visual climbing fibers in the rabbit. Brain Res. **98**, 582–589 (1975).

Allum, J.H.J., Graf, W., Dichgans, J., Schmidt, C.L.: Visual-vestibular interactions in the vestibular nuclei of the goldfish. Exp. Brain Res. **26**, 463–485 (1976).

André-Thomas: Equilibre et équilibration. Paris: Massion 1940.

Anstis, S.: Apparent motion. In: Handbook of sensory physiology, Held, R., Leibowitz, H.W., Teuber, H.L. (eds.) Berlin-Heidelberg-Göttingen: Springer 1978, Vol. VIII.

Armstrong, H.G.: Principles and practice of aviation medicine. Baltimore: Williams & Wilkins 1939.

Arnold, F., Büchele, W., Brandt, Th.: An optokinetically induced "pseudo Purkinje" effect. Pflügers Arch. Suppl. 368, R 45 (1977)

Arnoult, M.D.: Localization of sound during rotation of the visual environment. Amer. J. Psychol. **65**, 40–58 (1952).

Aschan, G., Bergstedt, M.: The genesis of secondary nystagmus induced by vestibular stimuli. Acta Soc. Med. Upsalien. **60**, 1–13 (1955).

Aubert, H.: Eine scheinbare bedeutende Drehung von Objekten bei Neigung des Kopfes nach rechts oder links. Virchows Arch. **20**, 381–393 (1861).

Baker, J., Gibson, A., Glickstein, M., Stein, J.: Visual cells in the pontine nuclei of the cat. J. Physiol. **255**, 415–433 (1976).

Baker, R.G., Precht, W., Llinás, R.: Cerebellar modulatory action of the vestibulo-trochlear pathway in cat. Exp. Brain Res. **15**, 364–385 (1972).

Barlow, H.B., Hill, R.M.: Evidence for a physiological explanation of the waterfall phenomenon and figural aftereffects. Nature (Lond.) **200**, 1345–1347 (1963).

Barré, J.A.: Épreuve de Romberg vestibulaire. Nouv. Tr. Méd. **15**, 105 (1949).

Barret, G.V., Thornthon, C.L.: Relationship between perceptual style and simulator sickness. J. appl. Psychol. **52**, 304–308 (1968).

Bauer, R.: Optisch-vestibuläre Interaction an Einzelneuronen der Vestibulariskerne und des Vestibulocerebellums bei der Katze. Biol. Diss. Freiburg, 1976.

BENSEL, C.K., DZENDOLET, E.: Power spectral density analysis of the standing sway of males. Percept. Psychophys. **4**, 285–288 (1968).

Berthoz, A., Pavard, B., Young, L.R.: Perception of linear horizontal self-motion induced by peripheral vision (Linearvection). Basic characteristics and visual-vestibular interactions. Exp. Brain Res. **23**, 471–489 (1975).

Bischof, N.: Optic-vestibular orientation to the vertical. In: Handbook of sensory physiology. Kornhuber, H.H. (ed.). Berlin-Heidelberg-New York: Springer 1974, Vol. VI.

Bisti, S., Maffei, L., Piccolino, M.: Visuo-vestibular interactions in the cat's superior colliculus. J. Neurophysiol. **37**, 146–155 (1974).

Bles, W., DeWit, G.: Study of the effects of optic stimuli on standing. Agressologie **17C**; 1–5 (1976).

Boycott, B.B., Wässle, E.: The morphological types of ganglion cells of the domestic cat's retina. J. Physiol. (Lond.) **240**, 397–419 (1974).

Brady, J.P., Levitt, E.E.: Nystagmus as a criterion of hypnotically induced visual hallucinations. Science **146**, 85–86 (1964).

Brandt, Th.: Optisch-vestibuläre Bewegungskrankheit, Höhenschwindel und klinische Schwindelformen, Fortschr. Med. **94**, 1177–1182 (1976).

Brandt, Th., Arnold, F., Bles, W., Kapteyn, T.S.: Height vertigo, a distance-vertigo through visual destabilization of free stance. In: Disorders of ocular motility. Neurophysiological and clinical aspects. Kommerell, G. (ed.) München: Bergmann 1978.

Brandt, Th., Büchele, W., Arnold, F.: Arthrokinetic nystagmus and ego-motion sensation. Exp. Brain Res. **30**, 331–338 (1977)

Brandt, Th., Dichgans, J.: Circularvection, optische Pseudocoriolis-Effekte und optokinetischer Nachnystagmus: Eine vergleichende Untersuchung subjektiver und objektiver optokinetischer Nacheffekte. Albrecht v. Graefes Arch. Klin. exp. Ophthal. **184**, 42–57 (1972).

Brandt, Th., Dichgans, J., Büchele, W.: Motion habituation: inverted self-motion perception and optokinetic after-nystagmus. Exp. Brain Res. **21**, 337–352 (1974a).

Brandt, Th., Dichgans, J., Koenig, E.: Differential effects of central versus peripheral vision on egocentric and exocentric motion perception. Exp. Brain Res. **16**, 476–491 (1973).

Brandt, Th., Dichgans, J., Wagner, W.: Drug effectiveness on experimental optokinetic and vestibular motion sickness. Aerosp. Med. **45**, 1291–1297 (1974b).

Brandt, Th., Diener, H.C., Dichgans, J.: Motion sickness induced through angular oscillations of the body or the visual surround in normals and after labyrinthine lesions. XXIII International Congress of Aviation and Space Medicine Acapulco (1975).

Brandt, Th., Wenzel, D., Dichgans, J.: Die Entwicklung der visuellen Stabilisation des aufrechten Standes beim Kind: Ein Reifezeichen in der Kinderneurologie Arch. Psychiat. Nervenkr. **223**, 1–13 (1976).

Brandt, Th., Wist, E.R., Dichgans, J.: Optisch induzierte Pseudocoriolis-Effekte und Circularvection. Ein Beitrag zur optisch-vestibulären Interaktion. Arch. Psychiat. Nervenkr. **214**, 365–389 (1971).

Brandt, Th., Wist, E.R., Dichgans, J.: Foreground and background in dynamic spatial orientation. Percept. Psychophys. **17**, 497–503 (1975).

Brecher, G.A., Brecher, M.H., Kommerell, G., Sauter, F.A., Sellerbeck, J.: Relation of optical and labyrinthean orientation. Opt. acta **19**, 467–471 (1972).

Breitmeyer, B.G.: A relationship between the detection of size, rate, orientation and direction of motion in the human visual system. Vision Res. **13**, 41–58 (1973).

Brodal, A., Jansen, J.: The pontocerebellar projection in the rabbit and cat. Experimental investigations. J. comp. Neurol. **84**, 31–118 (1946).

Brodal, P.: The corticopontine projection from the visual cortex of the cat. I. The total projection and the projection from area 17. Brain Res. **39**, 297–317 (1972a).

Brodal, P.: The corticopontine projection from the visual cortex of the cat. II. The projection from areas 18 and 19. Brain Res. **39**, 319–335 (1972b).

Brown, G.L., McArdle, B., Magladery, J.W.: Interim report on clinical investigations into airsickness. FPRC Rep. No. 410 (1941).

Brown, J.F.: The visual perception of velocity. Psychol. Forsch. **14**, 199–232 (1931).

Brown, J.H., Crampton, G.H.: Concomitant visual stimulation does not alter habituation of nystagmic oculogyral or psychophysical responses to angular acceleration. Acta oto-laryng. (Stockh.) **61**, 80–91 (1966).

Büchele, W.: Optokinetischer Nachnystagmus und Bewegungshabituation beim Menschen in Abhängigkeit von der Reizdauer. Med. Diss. Freiburg, 1977.

Büttner, U., Henn, V.: Thalamic unit activity in the alert monkey during natural vestibular stimulation. Brain Res. **103**, 127–132 (1976).

Büttner, U., Waespe, W., Henn, V.: Duration and direction of optokinetic afternystagmus as a function of stimulus exposure time in monkeys. Arch. Psychiat. Nervenkr. **222**, 281–291 (1976).

Byford, G.H.: Eye movements and the optogyral illusion. Aerosp. Med. **34**, 119–123 (1963).

Campbell, P.A.: The hunting phenomenon during flight in the weightless state. Presented at AGARD-NATO, Paris, July, 1962.

Cawthorne, T., Dix, M.R., Hallpike, C.S., Hood, J.D.: Vestibular function. Brit. med. Bull. **12**, 131–142 (1956).

Chang, H., Wu, C.: Optic activation of cerebellar and vestibular neurons in the toad. Sci. Rec. **3**, 640–644 (1959).

Chinn, H.J., Smith, P.K.: Motion sickness. Pharmacol. Rev. **7**, 33–83 (1955).

Christian, P.: Experimentelle Beiträge zur intermodalen vestibulo-optischen Wechselbeziehung der Sinnesorgane. Pflügers Arch. ges. Physiol. **243**, 370–387 (1940).

Clark, B., Graybiel, A.: The effect of angular acceleration on sound localization: the audiogyral illusion. J. Psychol. **28**, 235–244 (1949).

Clark, B., Graybiel, A.: Visual perception of the horizontal following exposure to radial acceleration on a centrifuge. J. comp. physiol. Psychol. **44**, 525–534 (1951).

Clark, B., Stewart, J.D.: Effects of angular acceleration on man: thresholds for the perception of rotation and the oculogyral illusion. Aerosp. Med. **40**, 952–956 (1969).

Cohen, B.: The vestibulo-ocular reflex arc. In: Handbook of sensory physiology Kornhuber, H.H. (ed.). Berlin-Heidelberg-New York: Springer 1974, pp. 477–540.

Cohen, B., Uemura, T., Takemori, S.: Effects of labyrinthectomy on optokinetic nystagmus (OKN) and optokinetic afternystagmus (OKAN). Equil. Res. **3**, 80–93 (1973).

Colenbrander, A.: Eye and otoliths. A centrifuge study on the ocular response to otolith stimulation. Aeromed. Acta (Soesterberg) **9**, 45–91 (1963/1964).

Colehour, J.K.: Stress measurements in normal and labyrinthine defective subjects in unusual force environments. In: The role of the vestibular organs in the exploration of space. Washington, NASA SP-**77**, 347–355 (1965).

Colewijn, H.: Optokinetic eye movements in the rabbit: input-output relations. Vision Res. **9**, 117–132 (1969).

Collewijn, H.: Direction-selective units in the rabbit's nucleus of the optic tract. Brain Res. **100**, 489–508 (1975).

Crampton, G.H., Young, F.A.: The differential effects of a rotary visual field on susceptibles and nonsusceptibles to motion sickness. J. comp. physiol. Psychol. **46**, 451–453 (1953).

Daunton, N.G., Thomsen, D.D.: Otolith-visual interactions in single units of cat vestibular nuclei. Neuroscience Abstracts II, **2**, 1526 (1976).

De Haan, P.: The significance of optic stimuli in maintaining the equilibrium. Acta oto-laryng. (Stockh.) **50**, 109–115 (1959).

De Wit, G.: Optic versus vestibular and proprioceptive impulses measured by posturometry. Agressologie **13**, B, 75–79 (1972).

Denney, D., Adorjani, C.: Orientation specificity of visual cortical neurons after head tilt. Exp. Brain Res. **14**, 312–317 (1972).

Denton, G.C.: The influence of visual pattern on perceived speed. Road Research Laboratory Report, Cawthorne G.B.L.R., 409–420 (1971).

Denton, G.C.: Moving road simulator. Ergonomics **9**, 517–520 (1966).

Desnoes, P.H.: Sea sickness. J. Amer. med. Ass. **86**, 319–324 (1926).

Dichgans, J., Brandt, Th.: Visual-vestibular interaction and motion perception. In: Cerebral control of eye movements and motion perception. Dichgans, J. and Bizzi, E. (eds.). Basel-New York: S. Karger 1972, pp. 327–338.

Dichgans, J., Brandt, Th.: Optokinetic motion sickness and pseudo-Coriolis effects induced by moving visual stimuli. Acta oto-laryng. (Stockh.) **76**, 339–348 (1973).

•Dichgans, J., Brandt, Th.: The psychophysics of visually induced perception of self-motion and

tilt. In: The Neurosciences. Schmidt, F.O., Worden, F.G. (eds.). Cambridge, Mass.: MIT Press 1974, Vol. III, pp. 123–129.
Dichgans, J., Brandt, Th., Held, R.: The role of vision in gravitational orientation. In: Mechanisms of spatial perception and orientation as related to gravity. Schöne, H. (ed.). Fortschr. Zool. **23**, 255–263 (1975a).
Dichgans, J., Diener, H.C., Brandt, Th.: Optokinetic graviceptive interaction in different head positions. Acta oto-laryng. (Stockh.) **78**, 391–398 (1974).
Dichgans, J., Held, R., Young, L.R., Brandt, Th.: Moving visual scenes influence the apparent direction of gravity. Science **178**, 1217–1219 (1972).
Dichgans, J., Jung, R.: Attention, eye movements and motion detection: facilitation and selection in optokinetic nystagmus and railway nystagmus. In: Attention in Neurophysiology. Evans, C.R. and Mullholland, T.B. (eds.). London: Butterworth, 1969, pp. 348–375.
Dichgans, J., Körner, F., Voigt, K.: Vergleichende Skalierung des afferenten und efferenten Bewegungssehens beim Menschen: lineare Funktionen mit verschiedener Anstiegssteilheit. Psychol. Forsch. **32**, 277–295 (1969).
Dichgans, J., Mauritz, K.H., Allum, J.H.J., Brandt, Th.: Postural sway in normals and atactic patients: analysis of the stabilizing effects of vision. Agressologie **17**, C, 15–24 (1976).
Dichgans, J., Nauck, B., Wolpert, E.: The influence of attention, vigilance and stimulus area on optokinetic and vestibular nystagmus and voluntary saccades. In: The oculomotor System and brain function. Zikmund, V. (ed.). London: Butterworth 1973a, pp. 281–294.
Dichgans, J., Schmidt, C.L., Graf, W.: Visual input improves the speedometer function of the vestibular nuclei in the goldfish. Exp. Brain Res. **18**, 319–322 (1973b).
Dichgans, J., Wist, E.R., Diener, H.C., Brandt, Th.: The Aubert-Fleischl paradox: a temporal frequency effect on perceived velocity in afferent motion perception. Exp. Brain Res. **23**, 529–533 (1975b).
Dishoek, H.A.E. van, Spoor, A., Nijhoff, P.: The opto-gyral illusion and its relation to the nystagmus of the eyes. Acta oto-laryng. (Stockh.) **44**, 597–607 (1954).
Diener, H.C., Wist, E.R., Dichgans, J., Brandt, Th.: The spatial-frequency effect on perceived velocity. Vision Res. **16**, 169–176 (1976).
Dodge, R.: Thresholds of rotation. J. exp. Psychol. **6**, 107–137 (1923).
Duchenne, G.B.A.: De l'ataxie locomotrice progressive. Recherches sur une maladie caracterisée spécialement par des troubles généraux de la coordination des mouvements. Arch. gén. Méd. 641–652 (1858).
Duensing, F., Schäfer, K.P.: Die Aktivität einzelner Neurone im Bereich der Vestibulariskerne unter besonderer Berücksichtigung des vestibulären Nystagmus. Arch. Psychiat. Nervenkr. **198**, 224–252 (1958).
Duncker, K.: Über induzierte Bewegung. Psychol. Forsch. **12**, 180–259 (1929).
Eckel, W.: Elektrophysiologische und histologische Untersuchungen im Vestibulariskerngebiet bei Drehreizen. Arch. Ohr-, Nas.- u. Kehlk.-Heilk. **164**, 487–513 (1954).
Edwards, A.S.: Body sway and vision. J. exp. Psychol. **36**, 526–535 (1946).
Enroth-Cugell, C., Robson, J.G.: The contrast sensitivity of retinal ganglion cells of the cat. J. Physiol. (Lond.) **187**, 517–552 (1966).
Fender, D.H., Nye, P.W.: An investigation of the mechanisms of eye movement control. Kybernetik **1**, 81–88 (1961).
Fernandez, C., Goldberg, J.M.: Physiology of peripheral neurons innervating semicircular canals of the squirrel monkey. II. Response to sinusoidal stimulation and dynamics of peripheral vestibular system. J. Neurophysiol. **34**, 661–675 (1971).
Fischer, M.H.: Die Regulationsfunktionen des menschlichen Labyrinthes und die Zusammenhänge mit verwandten Funktionen. In: Ergebnisse der Physiologie. Asher, L., Spiro, K. (eds.). München: Bergmann 1928, p. 27.
Fischer, M.H., Kornmüller, A.E.: Optokinetisch ausgelöste Bewegungswahrnehmung und optokinetischer Nystagmus. J. Psychol. Neurol. (Lpz.) **41**, 273–308 (1930a).
Fischer, M.H., Kornmüller, A.E.: Der Schwindel. In: Handbuch der normalen und pathologischen Physiologie. Bethe, A., von Bergmann, G., Embden, G., Ellinger, A. (eds.). Berlin Springer 1930b, Vol. XV/1, pp. 442–494.
Fischer, M.H., Kornmüller, A.E.: Egozentrische Lokalisation. 2. Mitteilung (optische Richtungslokalisation beim vestibulären Nystagmus). J. Psychol. Neurol. (Lpz.) **41**, 383–420 (193).

Fredrickson, J.M., Kornhuber, H.H.: Cortical projections of the vestibular nerve. In: Handbook of sensory physiology, Kornhuber, H.H. (ed.). Berlin-Heidelberg-New York: Springer 1974, Vol. VI/2, pp. 565–582.

Frenkel, H.S.: L'ataxie tabétique. Paris: Alcan 1907.

Fukuda, Y., Highstein, S.M., Ito, M.: Cerebellar inhibitory control of the vestibulo-ocular reflex investigated in rabbit. IIIrd. nucleus. Exp. Brain Res. **14**, 511–526 (1972).

Fukuda, Y., Stone, J.: Retinal distribution and central projections of y-, x-, and w-cells of the cat's retina. J. Neurophysiol. **37**, 749–772 (1974).

Gemelli, A.: The effect of illusory perception of movement on sound localization. In: Essays in psychology. Katz, D. (ed.). Uppsala: Almquist and Wiksell 1951, pp. 104–117.

Ghelarducci, B., Ito, M., Yogi, N.: Impulse discharges from flocculus Purkinje cells of alert rabbits during visual stimulation combined with horizontal head rotation. Brain Res. **87**, 66–72 (1975).

Gibson, J.J. (ed.): Motion picture testing and research. Washington D.C.: Government Printing Office AAF Aviat. Psychol. Program Res. Rep. No. 7, 1947.

Gibson, J.J.: The visual perception of objective motion and subjective movement. Psychol. Rev. **61**, 304–314 (1954).

Gibson, J.J.: Visually controlled locomotion and visual orientation in animals. Brit. J. Psychol. **49**, 182–194 (1958).

•Gibson, J.J.: The senses as perceptual systems. Boston: Houghton Mifflin 1966.

Goldberg, M.E., Wurtz, R.H.: Activity of superior colliculus in behaving monkey. I. Visual receptive fields of single neurons. J. Neurophysiol. **35**, 542–559 (1972).

Gonshor, A., Melvill-Jones, G.: Plasticity in the adult vestibulo-ocular reflex arc. Proc. Canad. Sed. Biol. Soc. **14**, 25 (1971).

Graybiel, A.: Oculogravic illusion. Albrecht v. Graefes Arch. klin. exp. Ophthal. **48**, 605–615 (1952).

Graybiel, A.: Vestibular sickness and some of its implications for space flight. In: Neurological aspects of auditory and vestibular disorders. Fields, W.F., Alford, B.R. (eds.). Springfield: Thomas 1964, Vol. III, Chap. XI.

Graybiel, A.: Susceptibility to acute motion sickness in blind persons. Aerosp. Med. **41**, 650–653 (1970).

Graybiel, A.: Measurement of otolith function in man. In: Handbook of sensory physiology. Kornhuber, H.H. (ed.). Berlin-Heidelberg-New York: Springer 1974, Vol. VI/2, pp. 233–266.

Graybiel, A., Clark, B.: Perception of the horizontal or vertical with head upright, on the side, and inverted under static conditions, and during exposure to centripetal force. Aerosp. Med. **33**, 147–155 (1962).

Graybiel, A., Clark, B., Zariello, J.J.: Observations on human subjects living in a "slow rotation room" for periods of two days. Arch. Neurol. (Chicago) **3**, 55–73 (1960).

Graybiel, A., Hupp, D.I.: The oculo-gyral illusion; a form of apparent motion which may be observed following stimulation of the semicircular canals. J. Aviat. Med. **17**, 3–27 (1946).

Graybiel, A., Kellog, R.S.: The inversion illusion in parabolic flight: its probable dependence on otolith function. Aerosp. Med. **38**, 1099–1103 (1967).

Graybiel, A., Patterson, J.L.: Thresholds of stimulation of the otolith organs as indicated by the oculogravic illusion. J. appl. Physiol. **7**, 666–670 (1955).

Graybiel, A.M.: Some extrageniculate visual pathways in the cat. Invest. Ophthal. **11**, 322–332 (1972).

Groen, J.J.: The problems of the spinning top applied to the semicircular canals. Confin. neurol. (Basel) **21**, 454–455 (1961).

Grüsser, O.J., Grüsser-Cornehls, U., Saur, G.: Reaktionen einzelner Neurone im optischen Cortex der Katze nach elektrischer Polarisation des Labyrinths. Pflügers Arch. ges. Physiol. **269**, 593–612 (1959).

Grüttner, R.: Experimentelle Untersuchungen über den optokinetischen Nystagmus. Z. Sinnesphysiol. **68**, 1–48 (1939).

Guedry, F.: Psychophysics of vestibular sensation. In: Handbook of sensory physiology. Kornhuber, H.H. (ed). Berlin-Heidelberg-New York: Springer 1974, Vol. VI/2, pp. 3–154.

•Held, R., Hein, A.: Movement produced stimulation in the development of visually guided behaviour. J. comp. physiol. Psychol. **56**, 872–876 (1963).

Held, R. Dichgans, J., Bauer, J.: Characteristics of moving visual scenes influencing spatial orientation. Vision Res. **15**, 357–365 (1975).
Helmholtz, H. von: Handbuch der physiologischen Optik. Hamburg-Leipzig: L. Voss 1896.
Henn, V., Young, L.R., Finley, C.: Vestibular nucleus units in alert monkeys are also influenced by moving visual fields. Brain Res. **71**, 144–149 (1974).
Hennebert, P.E.: Nystagmus audiocinétique. Acta oto-laryng. (Stockh.), **51**, 412–415 (1960).
Hering, E.: Der Raumsinn und die Bewegungen des Auges. In: Hermanns Handbuch der Physiologie Leipzig: F.C.W. Vogel 1879, Vol. III/1, pp. 343–601.
Hixson, W.C., Niven, J.I., Correia, M.J.: Kinematics nomenclature for psychological accelerations. Monograph 14. Pensacola, Fla.: Naval Aerospace Medical Institute 1966.
Hökendorf, H., Bles, W., Brandt, Th.: Direction specific reduction of circularvection latencies as a measure of latent labyrinthine vertigo. Pflügers Arch. Ges. Physiol. **368**, Suppl. R 45 (1977).
Hoffmann, K.P.: Conduction velocity in pathways from retina to superior colliculus in the cat; a correlation with receptive-field properties. J. Neurophysiol. **36**, 409–424 (1973).
Hoffmann, K.P., Schoppmann, A.: Retinal input to direction selective cells in the nucleus tractus opticus of the cat. Brain Res. **99**, 359–366 (1975).
Hofmann, F.B.: Die Lehre vom Raumsinn des Auges. Springer 1920/25. Berlin-Heidelberg-New York: Springer (Reprint) 1970.
Holland, H.C.: The spiral after-effect. Oxford: Pergamon Press 1965.
Holst, E. von, Mittelstaedt, H.: Das Reafferenzprinzip (Wechselwirkungen zwischen Zentralnervensystem und Peripherie). Naturwissenschaften **37**, 464–476 (1950).
Hood, J.D., Leech, J.: The significance of peripheral vision in the perception of movement. Acta oto-laryng. (Stockh.) **77**, 72–79 (1974).
Horn, G., Hill, R.M.: Modification of receptive fields of cells in the visual cortex occurring spontaneously and associated with body tilt. Nature (Lond.) **221**, 186–188 (1969).
Howard, I.P., Templeton, W.B.: Human spatial orientation. London-New York-Sidney: John Wiley & Sons 1966.
Hubel, D.H., Wiesel, T.N.: Receptive fields and functional architecture of monkey striate cortex. J. Physiol. (Lond.) **195**, 215–243 (1968).
Hughes, P.C., Brecher, G.A., Fischkin, S.M.: Effects of rotating backgrounds upon the perception of verticality. Percept. Psychophys. **11**, 135–138 (1972).
Ito, M., Highstein, S.M., Fukuda, J.: Cerebellar inhibition of the vestibulo-ocular reflex in rabbit and cat and its blockage by picrotoxin. Brain Res. **17**, 524–526 (1970).
Ito, M., Nisimaru, N., Yamamoto, M.: Specific neural connections for the cerebellar control of vestibulo-ocular reflexes. Brain Res. **60**, 238–243 (1973).
James, W.: The sense of dizziness in deaf-mutes. Amer. J. Otol. **4**, 239–254 (1882).
Johnson, W.H., Taylor, N.B.G.: Some experiments on the relative effectiveness of various types of accelerations on motion sickness. Aerosp. Med. **32**, 205–208 (1961).
Jongkees, L.B.W., Groen, J.J.: The nature of the vestibular stimulus. J. Laryng. **61**, 529–541 (1946).
Jung, R.: Die Registrierung des postrotatorischen und optokinetischen Nystagmus und die optisch-vestibuläre Integration beim Menschen. Acta oto-laryng. (Stockh.) **36**, 199–202 (1948).
Jung, R., Mittermaier, R.: Zur objektiven Registrierung und Analyse verschiedener Nystagmusformen: vestibulärer, optokinetischer und spontaner Nystagmus in ihren Wechselbeziehungen. Arch. Ohr.-, Nas.-, u. Kehlk.-Heilk. **146**, 410–439 (1939).
Keller, E.L.: Behavior of horizontal semicircular canal afferents in alert monkey during vestibular and optokinetic stimulation. Exp. Brain Res. **24**, 459–471 (1976).
Kennedy, R.S., Graybiel, A., McDonough, R.C., Beckwith, Fr. D.: Symptomatology under storm conditions in the North Atlantic in control subjects and persons with bilateral labyrinth defects. Acta oto-laryng. (Stockh.) **66**, 533–540 (1968).
Kennedy, R.S., Tolhurst, G.C., Graybiel, A.: The effects of visual deprivation on adaptation to a rotating environment. Pensacola, Fla.: NSAM-918-R-93 (1965).
Kennedy, R.S., Yessenow, M.D., Wendt, G.R.: Magnitude estimation of visual velocity. J. Psychol. **82**, 133–144 (1972).
Kleint, H.: Versuche über die Wahrnehmung. Z. Psychol. **143**, 299–316 (1938).

Klinke, R., Schmidt, C.L.: Efferent influence on the vestibular organ during active movement of the body. Pflügers Arch. ges. Physiol. **318**, 325–332 (1970).

Körner, F., Dichgans, J.: Bewegungswahrnehmung, optokinetischer Nystagmus und retinale Bildwanderung: der Einfluß visueller Aufmerksamkeit auf zwei Mechanismen des Bewegungssehens. Albrecht v. Graefes Arch. klin. exp. Ophthal. **174**, 34–38 (1967).

Körner, F., Schiller, P.H.: The optokinetic response under open and closed loop conditions in the monkey. Exp. Brain Res. **14**, 318–330 (1972).

Kohler, I.: Der Brillenversuch in der Wahrnehmungspsychologie mit Bemerkungen zur Lehre von der Adaptation. Z. exp. angew. Psychol. **3**, 381–417 (1956).

Kornhuber, H.H.: Optokinetischer Nachnystagmus, vestibuläre Übererregbarkeit und periodischer Nystagmus alternans. Klin. Wschr. **40**, 549 (1962).

Kornhuber, H.H., Da Fonseca, J.S.: Optovestibular integration in the cat's cortex: a study of sensory convergence on cortical neurons. In: The Oculomotor System. Bender, M.B. (ed.). New York-Evanston-London: Hoeber, Harper and Row 1964.

Kottenhoff, H., Lindahl, L.E.H.: Visual and emotional factors in motion sickness. Percept. Motor Skills **8**, 173–174 (1958).

Kries, J. von: Allgemeine Sinnesphysiologie. Leipzig: F.C.W. Vogel 1923.

•Lackner, J.R.: Some mechanism underlying sensory and postural stability in man. In: Handbook of sensory physiology, Held, R., Leibowitz, H.W., Teuber, H.L. (eds.). Berlin-Heidelberg-Göttingen: Springer 1977, Vol. VIII.

Lansberg, M.P.: Some considerations and investigations in the field of labyrinthine functioning. Aeromed. Acta (Soesterberg) **3**, 209–267 (1954).

•Lee, D.N., Aronson, E.: Visual proprioceptive control of standing in human infants. Percept. Psychphys. **15**, 529–532 (1974).

Lee, D.N., Lishman, J.R.: Visualproprioceptive control of stance. J. Human Movem. Stud. **1**, 87–95 (1975).

Leibowitz, H., Dichgans, J.: The influence of luminance level and refractive error on circularvection (in preparation).

Leopold, H.C., Schmidt, C.L., Sterc, J., Dichgans, J.: Der Einfluß optokinetischer Reize auf das Entladungsverhalten vestibulärer Kernneurone. Pflügers Arch. ges. Physiol. **339** Suppl. R 77 (1973).

Leopold, H.C.: Visuelle Konvergenz auf die Vestibulariskerne des Kaninchens. Med. Diss. Freiburg, 1974.

Lestienne, F., Soechting, J., Berthoz, A.: Postural readjustments induced by linear motion of visual scenes. Exp. Brain Res. **28**, 363–384 (1977).

Lisberger, S.G., Fuchs, A.F.: Response of flocculus Purkinje cells to adequate vestibular stimulation in the alert monkey: fixation vs. compensatory eye movements. Brain Res. **69**, 347–353 (1974).

•Lishman, J.R., Lee, D.N.: The autonomy of visual kinaesthesis. Perception **2**, 287–294 (1973).

Lit, A.: The magnitude of the Pulfrich stereo phenomenon as a function of binocular differences of retinal illuminance at scotopic and photopic levels. Amer. J. Psychol. **62**, 159–181 (1949).

Mach, E.: Grundlinien der Lehre von den Bewegungsempfindungen. Leipzig: Engelmann 1875.

Mach, E.: Die Analyse der Empfindungen, 9th ed. Jena: G. Fischer 1922.

Mackensen, G.: Untersuchungen zur Physiologie des optokinetischen Nystagmus. Individuell bedingte quantitative Unterschiede im Ablauf des optokinetischen Nystagmus. Albrecht v. Graefes Arch. Ophthal. **155**, 284–313 (1954).

Mackensen, G., Wiegmann, O.: Untersuchungen zur Physiologie des optokinetischen Nachnystagmus. I. Mitteilung. Die Abhängigkeit des optokinetischen Nachnystagmus von der Winkelgeschwindigkeit des Reizmusters. Albrecht v. Graefes Arch. klin. exp. Ophthal. **160**, 497–509 (1959).

Maekawa, K., Simpson, J.I.: Climbing fiber responses evoked in the vestibulocerebellum of rabbit from visual system. J. Neurophysiol. **36**, 649–666 (1973).

Magnin, M., Jeannerod, M., Putkonen, P.T.S.: Vestibular and saccadic influences on dorsal and ventral nuclei of the lateral geniculate body. Exp. Brain Res. **21**, 1–18 (1974).

Manning, G.W., Stewardt, W.G.: Effect of body position on incidence of motion sickness. J. appl. Physiol. **1**, 619–628 (1949).

Marshall, J.E., Brown, J.H.: Visual arousal interaction and specifity of nystagmic habituation. Fort Knox, Ky.: U.S. Army Med. Res. Lab., Rept. No. 688 1966.

Mashhour, M.: Psychophysical relations in the perception of velocity. In: Stockholm studies in psychology. Stockholm: Almquist and Wiksell 1964, Vol. III.

Mauritz, K.H., Dichgans, J., Allum, J., Brandt, Th.: Frequency characteristics of postural sway in response to selfinduced and conflicting visual stimulation. Pflügers Arch. ges. Physiol. **335**, Suppl. R 95 (1975).

Mauritz, K.H., Dichgans, J., Hufschmidt, A.: The angle of visual roll motion determines displacement of subjective vertical. Perception and Psychophysics **22**, 557–562 (1977).

Melvill-Jones, G.: Origin significance and amelioration of Coriolis illusions from semicircular canals: a non-mathematical appraisal. Aerosp. Med. **41**, 482–490 (1970).

Melvill-Jones, G., Milsum, J.H.: Frequency response analysis of central vestibular unit activity resulting from rotational stimulation of the semicircular canals. J. Physiol. (Lond.) **219**, 191–215 (1971).

Miller, J.W., Goodson, J.E.: Motion sickness in a helicopter simulator. Aerosp. Med. **31**, 204 (1960).

Miller, E.F., Graybiel, A.: Experiment M-131—human vestibular function. Aerosp. Med. **44**, 593–608 (1973).

Mizuno, N., Mochizuki, K., Akimoto, C., Matzushima, R.: Pretectal projection to the inferior olive in the rabbit. Exp. Neurol. **39**, 498–506 (1973).

Money, K.E.: Motion sickness. Physiol. Rev. **50**, 1–39 (1970).

Morant, R.B.: The visual perception of median plane as influenced by labyrinthine stimulation. J. Psychol. **47**, 25–35 (1959).

Mowrer, O.H.: The influence of vision during bodily rotation upon the duration of post-rotational vestibular nystagmus. Acta oto-laryng. (Stockh.) **25**, 351–364 (1937).

Müller, G.E.: Über das Aubert'sche Phänomen. Z. Sinnesphysiol. **49**, 109–246 (1916).

Münsterberg, H., Pierce, A.H.: The localization of sound. Psychol. Rev. **1**, 461–476 (1894).

Nashner, L.M.: Sensory feedback in human posture control. MVT 70–3, Cambridge, Mass.: Man Vehicle Lab. M.I.T. 1970.

Oosterveld, W.J., Graybiel, A., Cramer, D.B.: Influence of vision on susceptibility to acute motion sickness studied under quantifiable stimulus-response conditions. Aerosp. Med. **43**, 1005–1007 (1972).

Oosterveld, W.J., Greven, A.J.: Flight behaviour of pigeons during weightlessness. Acta oto-laryng. (Stockh.) **79**, 233–241 (1975).

Pantle, A.: Motion aftereffect magnitude as a measure of the spatiotemporal response properties of direction-sensitive analyzers. Vision Res. **14**, 1229–1236 (1974).

Papaioannou, J.: Effects of caloric labyrinthine stimulation on the spontaneous activity of lateral geniculate nucleus neurons in the cat. Exp. Brain Res. **17**, 1–9 (1973).

Pavard, B., Berthoz, A.: Linear acceleration modifies the perceived velocity of moving visual scenes. Perception

Peters, R.A.: Dynamics of the vestibular system and their relation to motion perception, spatial disorientation, and illusions. NASA, CR-1309 1969.

Pfaltz, C.R., Kato, J.: Interaction of visual and vestibular stimuli in vestibular habituation. Amer. Arch. Otolaryng. (St. Louis) **100**, 444–451 (1974).

Pfaltz, C.R., Ohtsuka, Y.: The influence of optokinetic training upon vestibular habituation. Acta oto-laryng. (Stockh.) **79**, 253–258 (1975).

Potthoff, P.C., Richter, M.P., Burandt, H.R.: Multisensorische Konvergenzen an Hirnstammneuronen der Katze. Arch. Psychiat. u. Z. ges. Neurol. **210**, 36–60 (1967).

Pulfrich, C.: Die Stereoskopie im Dienste der isochromen und heterochromen Photometrie. Naturwissenschaften **10**, 553–564 (1922).

Purkinje, J.E.: Beiträge zur näheren Kenntnis des Schwindels aus heautognostischen Daten. Med. Jb. (Österreich) **6**, 79–125 (1820).

Quix, F.H., Eijsvogel, M.H.P.M.: Experimente über die Funktion des Otolithenapparates beim Menschen. Z. Hals-, Nas.- u. Ohrenheilk. **23**, 68–96 (1929).

Rachlin, H.C.: Scaling subjective velocity, distance and duration. Percept. Psychophys. **1**, 77–82 (1966).

Rademaker, G.G.J., Ter Braak, J.W.G.: On the central mechanism of some optic reactions. Brain **71**, 48–76 (1948).

Reason, J.T., Diaz, E.: The effects of visual reference on adaptation to coriolis accelerations. London: Ministry of Defence, FPRC Rept. No. 1303 1970.
Reason, J.T., Diaz, E.: Simulator sickness in passive observers. London: Ministery of Defence; FPRC, Rept. No. 1310 1971.
Richards, W., Smith, R.A.: Midbrain as a site for the motion after-effect. Nature (Lond.) **223**, 533–534 (1969).
Roggeveen, L.J., Nijhoff, P.: The normal and pathological thresholds of the perception of angular accelerations for the optogyral illusion and the turning sensation. Acta oto-laryng. (Stockh.) **46**, 533–541 (1956).
Salvatore, S.: Velocity sensing. Highway Res. Rec. **282**, 79–90 (1968).
Schiller, P.H., Koerner, F.: Discharge characteristics of single units in superior colliculus of the alert Rhesus monkey. J. Neurophysiol. **34**, 920–936 (1972).
Schmidt, F., Tiffin, J.: Distorsion of drivers' estimates of automobile speed as a function of speed adaptation. J. appl. Psychol. **53**, 536–539 (1969).
Schneider, L.W., Anderson, D.J.: Transfer characteristics of first and second order lateral canal vestibular neurons in gerbils. Brain Res. **112**, 61–76 (1976).
Schöne, H.: On the role of gravity in human spatial orientation. Aerosp. Med. **35**, 764–772 (1964).
Schwartzkroin, P.A.: Effects of round window stimulation on unit discharges in the visual cortex and superior colliculi. Exp. Brain Res. **17**, 527–538 (1973).
Sekuler, R., Pantle, A., Levinson, E.: Physiological basis of motion perception. In: Handbook of sensory physiology. Held, R., Leibowitz, H., Teuber, H.L. (eds.). Berlin-Heidelberg-New York: Springer 1978, Vol. VIII/1.
Simpson, J.I., Alley, K.E.: Visual climbing fiber input to rabbit vestibulo-cerebellum: a source of direction specific information. Brain Res. **82**, 302–308 (1974).
Sjöberg, A.A.: Experimentelle Studien über den Auslösungsmechanismus der Seekrankheit. Acta oto-laryng. (Stockh.) Suppl. **14**, 1–136 (1931).
Spinelli, D.N.: Recognition of visual patterns. In: Perception and its disorders. Hamburg, D.A. (ed.). Baltimore: Williams and Wilkins 1970, pp. 139–149.
Sprague, J.M., Berlucchi, G., Rizzolatti, G.: The role of the superior colliculus and pretectum in vision and visually guided behavior. In: Handbook of sensory physiology. R. Jung (ed). Berlin-Heidelberg-New York: Springer 1973, Vol. VII/3B, pp. 27–102.
Stein, St. von: Schwindel (Autokinesis externa et interna). Leipzig: O. Lessier 1910.
Steinhausen, W.: Über die Beobachtung der Cupula in den Bogengangsampullen des lebenden Hechts. Pflügers Arch. ges. Physiol. **232**, 500–512 (1933).
Stevens, S.S.: On the psychophysical law. Psychol. Rev. **64**, 153–181 (1957).
Stone, J., Hoffmann, K.P.: Very slow conducting ganglion cells in the cat's retina: a major new functional type? Brain Res. **43**, 610–616 (1972).
Sünderhauf, A.: Untersuchungen über die Regelung der Augenbewegungen. Klin. Mbl. Augenheilk. **136**, 837–856 (1960).
Takeda, T., Maekawa, K.: The origin of the pretecto-olivary tract. A study using the horseradish peroxidase method. Brain Res. **117**, 319–325 (1976).
Takemori, S., Cohen, B.: Loss of visual suppression of vestibular nystagmus after flocculus lesions. Brain Res. **72**, 213–224 (1974).
Talbot, R.E.: Modification of postural response of the normal dog by blindfolding. J. Physiol. (Lond.) **243**, 309–320 (1974).
Teuber, H.L.: Perception. In: Handbook of Physiology. Field, J. (ed). Washington: Amer. physiol. Soc. 1960, Vol. III, pp. 1595–1688.
Thalmann, W.A.: The after-effects of seen movement when the whole field is filled by a moving stimulus. Amer. J. Psychol. **32**, 429–441 (1921).
Thoden, U., Dichgans, J., Savidis, Th.: Direction specific optokinetic modulation of monosynpatic hind limb reflexes in cats. Exp. Brain Res. **30**, 155–160 (1977).
Thurlow, W.R., Kerr, Th.P.: Effect of a moving visual environment on localization of sound. Amer. J. Psychol. **83**, 112–118 (1970).
Travis, R.C.: An experimental analysis of dynamic and static equilibrium. J. exp. Psychol. **35**, 216–234 (1945).
Trevarthen, C.B.: Two mechanisms of vision in primate. Psychol. Forsch. **31**, 229–337 (1968).
Tschermak, A.: Der exakte Subjectivismus in der neueren Sinnesphysiologie. Pflügers Arch. ges. Physiol. **188**, 1–20 (1921).

Tschermak, A.: Optischer Raumsinn. In: Handbuch der normalen und pathologischen Physiologie. Bethe, A., Bergmann, G., Embden, G., Ellinger, A. (eds.). Berlin: Springer 1931, Vol. XII/2, pp. 834–1000.

Tyler, D.B., Bard, P.: Motion sickness. Physiol. Rev. **29**, 311–369 (1949).

Uemura, T., Cohen, B.: Effects of vestibular nuclei lesons on vestibulo-ocular reflexes and posture in monkeys. Acta oto-laryng. (Stockh.) Suppl. **315**, 1–71 (1973).

Urbantschitsch, V.: Über Störungen des Gleichgewichtes und Scheinbewegungen. Z. Ohrenheilk. **31**, 234–294 (1897).

Waespe, W., Henn, V.: Behaviour of secondary vestibular units during optokinetic nystagmus and after-nystagmus in alert monkeys. Pflügers Arch. 362, Suppl. R 197 (1976).

Waespe, W., Henn, V.: Neuronal activity in the vestibular nuclei of the alert monkey during vestibular and optokinetic stimulation. Exp. Brain. Res. **27**, 523–538 (1977).

Wallach, H.: The role of head movements and vestibular and visual cues in sound localization. J. exp. Psychol. **27**, 339–368 (1940).

Walls, G.L.: Interocular transfer of the after image. Amer. J. Opt. **30**, 57–64 (1969).

Warren, H.C.: Sensations of rotation. Psychol. Rev. **2**, 273–276 (1895).

Wist, E.R., Diener, H.C., Dichgans, J., Brandt, Th.: Perceived distance and the perceived speed of self-motion: linear versus angular velocity. Percept. Psychophys. **17**, 549–554 (1975).

Wist, E.R., Diener, H.C., Dichgans, J.: Motion constancy dependent upon perceived distance and the spatial frequency of the stimulus pattern. Percept. Psychophys. **19**, 485–491 (1976).

Whiteside, T.C.D.: Hand-eye co-ordination in weightlessness. Aerosp. Med. **32**, 719–725 (1961).

Witkin, H.A.: Perception of body position and of the position of the visual field. Psychol Monogr. **63**, 1–46 (1949).

Wood, R.W.: The "haunted swing" illusion. Psychol. Rev. **2**, 277–278 (1895).

Young, L.R., Chu, W.: Visually induced self-motion sensation in a vertical plane: frequency responses for sinusoidal and random field motion (1976) (in preparation).

Young, L.R., Dichgans, J., Murphy, R., Brandt, Th.: Interaction of optokinetic and vestibular stimuli in motion perception. Acta oto-laryng. (Stockh.) **76**, 24–31 (1973).

Young, L.R., Henn, V.B.: Selective habituation of vestibular nystagmus by visual stimulation. Acta oto-laryng. (Stockh.) **77**, 159–166 (1974).

Young, L.R., Oman, C.M., Dichgans, J.: Influence of head orientation on visually induced pitch and roll sensation. Aviat. Space Environ. Med. **46**, 264–268 (1975).

Zee, D.S., Yee, R.D., Robinson, D.A.: Optokinetic responses in labyrinthine-defective human beings. Brain Res. **113**, 423–428 (1976).

Zeki, S.M.: Functional organization of a visual area in the posterior bank of the superior temporal sulcus of the rhesus monkey. J. Physiol. (Lond.) **236**, 549–573 (1974).

Zikmund, V.: Oculomotor activity during visual imagery of a moving stimulus pattern. Stud. Psychol. **8**, 254–272 (1966).

Chapter 26

Some Mechanisms Underlying Sensory and Postural Stability in Man

JAMES R. LACKNER, Waltham, Massachusetts (USA)

With 14 Figures

Contents

A. Introduction

In order to preserve the spatial stability of our perceptual world, we must continuously relate information about our posture to ongoing patterns of auditory, visual, and somatosensory stimulation. During self-movement, the central nervous system must determine which part of the change in exteroceptive stimulation is the direct consequence of active or passive body movement; were this monitoring to fail, stationary objects in the environment would seem to move every time we moved. The kinds of information available to us concerning our moment-to-moment posture are complex; they include not only proprioceptive and vestibular inputs but also corollary discharges (TEUBER, 1960) signalling intended or ongoing movement patterns. These internal sources of information can, under special circumstances, be overridden by powerful exteroceptive inputs which in turn, therefore, can influence our appreciation of ongoing body posture.

One consequence of this interaction between exteroceptive and internally derived information is that the perceived location of a light or sound is not determined solely by the pattern of physical stimulation at the eyes or ears but also by the registered posture of the head in relation to the trunk and the gravitational vertical. As a consequence, whenever there is an error in the interpretation of head or trunk posture relative to each other or relative to the external force environment, auditory and visual mislocalizations of comparable magnitude and time-course can result.

The mislocalizations and illusions that can result from these interactions show a remarkable degree of plasticity. For example, when a person moves about while wearing prism-spectacles that displace his visual field, he at first is inaccurate when reaching for objects. Gradually, however, these errors decrease or disappear (HELD, 1961; HARRIS, 1965; ROCK, 1966). Similarly, during exposure to rotation on a centrifuge, the complex postural and visual illusion that is initially experienced during movements of the head, the Coriolis oculogyral illusion (GRAYBIEL et al., 1961) attenuates with time until complete adaptation is achieved. The physiological mechanisms underlying such adaptative changes are unknown. As will be discussed in the following account, however, there is reason to think that in situations involving abnormal sensory stimulation, the compensatory changes that occur often involve central reinterpretations of the relationship between patterns of proprioceptive and exteroceptive stimulation generated by movements of the body. Accordingly, errors in the localization of external auditory or visual targets can be eliminated by changes in the registration of head posture relative to the trunk and, correspondingly, errors in the subjective apprehension of ongoing posture can be eliminated by changes in the perceived body orientations signaled by particular proprioceptive patterns of stimulation.

Much of the interest centered on these adaptative modifications stems from the assumption that such compensations reflect the functioning of mechanisms normally responsible for preserving a stable perceptual distinction between changes in sensory stimulation elicited by self-movement and those resulting from movement of the environment with respect to the observer. The operation of these stabilizing mechanisms can perhaps best be appreciated by a systematic consideration of the postural-sensory and sensory-postural interactions that reveal aspects of their functioning.

B. Displacements in Visual and Auditory Localization During Rotation About the Body Axis

The three semicircular canals on either side of the head contain specialized receptors for the detection of angular acceleration. During rotary accelerations of the head, the cupulo-endolymph mechanisms of those canals lying within or near the plane of rotation are activated. Angular acceleration is maintained only briefly during a voluntary head movement; consequently, the rest states of the cupulae are quickly restored by the deceleration terminating the head movement. The magnitudes of such brief head movements are usually correctly perceived and neither auditory nor visual localization is significantly affected.

I. The Oculogyral Illusion

When a subject is gradually accelerated to a constant angular velocity in a dark room, his subjective sensations of rotation do not correspond to the actual pattern of physical stimulation because, as will be described later, the cupulo-endolymph mechanism fails to reflect adequately the stimulus situation. If he is fixating a small target light that is stationary with respect to him, then soon after the initial acceleratory phase has begun he will report that the target is moving with respect to him in the direction of rotation, i.e., the target starts to lead the subject (MACH, 1886). GRAYBIEL and HUPP (1946) rediscovered and systematically investigated this phenomenon, which they named the *Oculogyral illusion*. They found that it has several additional components. During the period of rotation at constant angular velocity immediately following the acceleratory phase, the target appears to move in the direction opposite its original displacement for approximately 30 s; the target then appears stationary until the subject is decelerated to rest. At that time, the subject will see the target undergo two additional movements: initially it appears to move in the direction opposite that of his prior rotation, and then, for about another 30 s, it appears to move in the direction of his prior rotation.

II. The Audiogyral Illusion

Changes in sensory localization during and after rotary stimulation are not confined to the visual modality alone. CLARK and GRAYBIEL (1949) found that a sound source, stationary with respect to a rotating subject, will also be reported to undergo several changes in apparent position. The time courses of these auditory changes are similar to those of the oculogyral illusion, and the phenomenon is known as the *Audiogyral illusion*.

III. Mechanisms Underlying the Oculogyral and Audiogyral Illusions

A characteristic common to both the oculogyral and audiogyral illusions is a subjective misinterpretation of true body-rotation. During the period of constant angular acceleration, the subject comes to feel himself as being accelerated less rapidly than he actually is, and then for about the first 30 s of rotation at constant velocity, he experiences deceleration in the opposite direction. The reverse pattern is experienced during and after return to rest. These false postural sensations are commonly attributed to changes in the registration of cupula position resulting from either 1) a decreased end-organ output for a particular cupular deflection, 2) a change in the central interpretation of (normal) end-organ outputs (EK et al., 1960; HALLPIKE and HOOD, 1953), or 3) an efferent inhibition of the hair cells of the end organ, thereby reducing the neural transfer function (GROEN, 1970).

According to any of these theories, the subject experiences himself as being stationary when the cupulae are still deflected, because this deviated position now indicates "zero angular acceleration"; accordingly, upon return of the cupulae to their physical rest positions, acceleration in the opposite direction is signaled because the cupulae have moved past a floating "physiological zero" position. These interpretations are in accord with the observation that labyrinthine-defective (L-D) subjects experience neither the oculogyral nor the audiogyral illusions (GRAYBIEL, 1967).

C. Shifts in Visual and Auditory Localization During Tilt of the Body Axis

I. The A- and E-Effects

Vertical lines in a fully illuminated environment still appear vertical when the head is tilted, even though the images of these lines no longer fall on the same regions of the retinae that are stimulated when the head is erect. Thus, precise compensation is made for the change in retinal image orientation caused by tilting the head in a lighted environment. However, compensation is less accurate when the contours of the experimental chamber are not visible. For lateral head and body tilts of 50° or less, an observer trying to set a luminous line to the gravitational vertical will set it too far to the side opposite his body tilt (the *E-effect* of MÜLLER); for larger angles of tilt, he will set the line too far in the direction of his tilt (the *Aubert phenomenon* or *A-effect*).

Generally, the *E-effect* persists until the tilt angle exceeds 60° (BAUERMEISTER, 1964; BOURDON, 1906; MÜLLER, 1916); beyond 60° observers exhibit the *A-effect*. Tilted observers making judgments of the visual horizontal show similar patterns of errors (MILLER and GRAYBIEL, 1966; MILLER et al., 1966). The *A-effect* may reach a magnitude of 40 or 50° when the body is nearly inverted; by contrast, the *E-effect* rarely exceeds 7 or 8°. Systematic studies of the time courses of the *A-* and *E-effects* have not been carried out; however, AUBERT (1861) found that when he rapidly tilted his head the phenomenal rotation of a luminous line was not immediate. A more extensive review of these phenomena is available in HOWARD and TEMPLETON (1966) and LACKNER (1976a).

An observer who has been returned to the upright after prolonged body tilt in the dark will make transient errors in setting a luminous line to the visual vertical or horizontal (DAY and WADE, 1966; MCFARLAND and CLARKSON, 1966; WADE, 1968; WADE and DAY, 1968a, 1968b). Only tilt angles of 30° or less have been studied, but the aftereffects indicated by visual settings of the vertical are always opposite in direction to the prior tilt, rarely exceeding 2 or 3°; WADE and DAY (1968b) have attributed these aftereffects to changes in apparent head position. Similar aftereffects have been found following passive lateral tilts of the head or trunk with the observer upright or supine, indicating that both the otolith organs and neck proprioceptors can jointly and independently contribute to these aftereffects (WADE, 1968).

II. Displacements in Auditory Localization During Body Tilt

Changes in tactile and auditory localization also occur during lateral tilts of the body axis in the dark. During moderate body tilts, attempts to set a rod to the apparent gravitational vertical while using only tactile and kinesthetic cues result in settings too far to the opposite side (BAUERMEISTER et al., 1964). Similarly, subjects tilted in a dark room will hear an ambient sound as being in the midline of their head only if the sound source is deviated to the side of their "up ear" (TEUBER and LIEBERT, 1956). The reverse pattern of mislocalization occurs for dichotically presented (stereophonic) sounds; to maintain a subjectively centered sound image, the stimulus to the "down ear" must be given a time lead relative to the values that produce a centered sound image on testing at the upright (TEUBER and DIAMOND, 1956).

The changes in auditory localization that occur during prolonged tilt of the body axis are not immediate but develop over time, reaching a maximum in approximately 2 min (LACKNER, 1970, 1974a). In addition, on return to the true upright, subjects continue to make errors in auditory localization for nearly 30 s (see Fig. 1). It is notable that the magnitudes and time courses of the changes in auditory localization, both during tilt and upon return to the upright, are associated with corresponding changes in subjective posture. After being tilted, the subject quickly comes to underestimate the extent of his tilt; and, when returned to the true upright, initially experiences himself as being tilted to the opposite side (see Fig. 2). When the subject is tilted, turning on the room lights to provide a fully patterned visual surrounding eliminates the errors both in auditory localization and in subjective posture. After the room lights are re-extinguished, it takes almost 2 min before the auditory mislocalizations and misapprehensions of posture again reach a maximum.

It has been found recently that analogous displacements in the apparent locations of visual targets occur during tilt of the body axis (LACKNER, 1976b). A tilted subject fixating a small target light located in the projection of the median plane of his head will soon report the light to be off-center to the "down side." This change in visual localization, which is not dependent on ocular counterrolling, is accompanied by an error in the subject's apprehension of his posture of like time-course and magnitude. As in the auditory case, the visual and postural mislocalizations are abolished if the room lights are turned on and then gradually redevelop when the room lights are again extinguished.

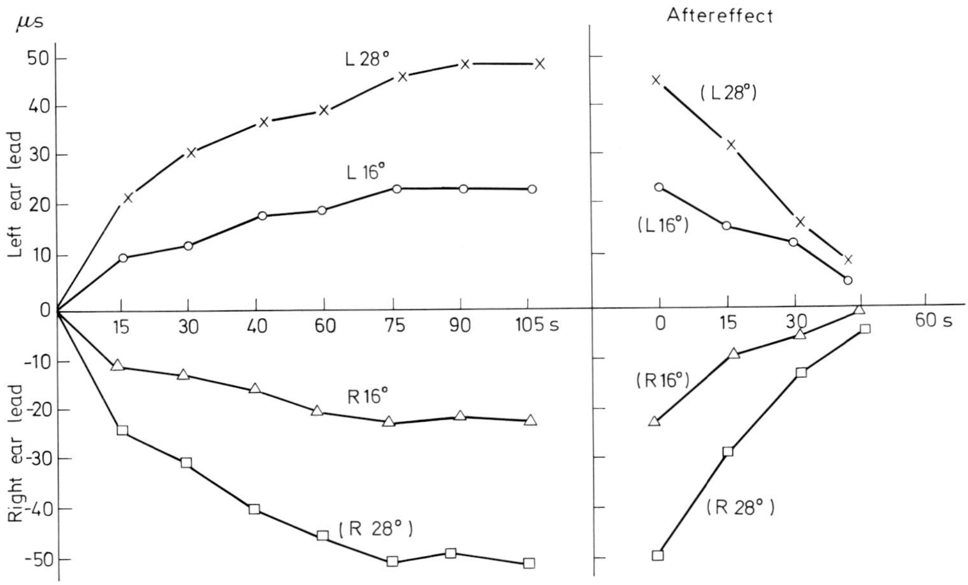

Fig. 1. Changes in arrival times of dichotically presented sounds necessary to maintain a centered sound image as a function of elapsed time during and after tilt of the body axis. (from LACKNER, 1974a)

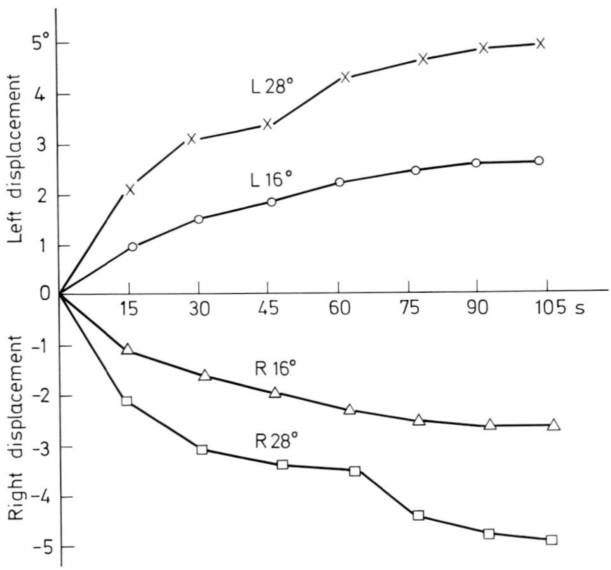

Fig. 2. Changes in the perception of the postural vertical as a function of body tilt and elapsed time. The ordinate specifies the position of the subject's body when he perceives himself as upright. (From LACKNER, 1974a)

III. Relation of Errors in Apparent Posture to Errors in Auditory and Visual Localization

Several observations indicate that abnormal registration or interpretation of proprioceptive information from the neck can lead to errors in visual and auditory localization similar to those resulting from body-axis tilt. As already mentioned, WADE (1968) found that subjects whose heads are kept upright while their trunks are maintained laterally tilted will exhibit systematic errors similar to the *A*- and *E-effects* when indicating the apparent visual vertical with a luminous line. Likewise, electrical stimulation of the sternocleidomastoid muscle in an erect subject (WAPNER et al., 1951), or application of a counterweight to his head so that he has to exert a force to maintain his head vertical (KLEINT, 1937; SCHNEIDER and BARTLEY, 1962), will produce shifts in the apparent visual vertical. Analogous errors in auditory localization result if a blindfolded subject's head is kept horizontally deviated for several minutes; concomitant with these auditory mislocalizations are covarying errors in the apparent position of the head with respect to the trunk (LACKNER, 1973a).

The sensory mechanisms that contribute to these phenomena are extremely complicated. CLARK and GRAYBIEL (1966, 1967, 1968) found that an observer required to tilt his head and body actively while standing (and to maintain one of various combinations of head and trunk angles with respect to the gravitoinertial vertical) will fail to exhibit the *A*- or *E-effects*. Their experimental group, which included L-D as well as normal observers, did exhibit the *E-effect* when passively maintained in a tilted position. To interpret these observations, CLARK and GRAYBIEL (1966) proposed that during "active tilt" the contact cues from the feet, and the kinesthetic cues specifying the relative positions of the head, trunk, and legs are sufficiently rich to permit accurate assessment of body posture; and that, during passive tilt, the contact and kinesthetic cues are too restricted to permit completely veridical judgment of body orientation. Accordingly, many sensory channels influence perception of the postural vertical; and, which ones will have the most influence varies according to the experimental conditions. For example, when immersed in water a blindfolded person has to rely on otolithic information to determine the upright; accordingly, a normal subject can perform with reasonable accuracy (NELSON, 1968), whereas a L-D subject can not (GRAYBIEL et al., 1968; JAMES, 1882), even though he will be almost as accurate under nonimmersed conditions as the normal subject

IV. Sensory Factors Influencing Apparent Posture

Taken together, the foregoing observations indicate that proprioceptive information from joint and muscle receptors as well as somatosensory and vestibular information can influence both apparent posture and visual and auditory localization. In this context, it should be noted that abnormal muscle spindle activity generated by vibrating skeletal muscles can elicit a variety of proprioceptive illusions of limb movement and position, thereby influencing apparent posture

(GOODWIN et al., 1972a, b; LACKNER and LEVINE, 1978). These observations are treated in detail below. In summary, a common theme relates the changes in sensory localization that occur during and after tilt of the body axis, rotation about the body axis, and lateral deviation of the head with respect to the trunk: sensory mislocalizations are associated with errors in apparent posture of similar magnitude and time-course.

D. Changes in Visual and Auditory Localization During Exposure to Centrifugal Rotation

I. The Oculogravic Illusion

Changes in visual orientation during exposure to centripetal acceleration were first reported by MACH (1897). He noticed that whenever a train in which he was riding rounded a sharp turn at high speed, objects outside the train seemed to tilt and he felt tilted as well. This phenomenon was first systematically investigated by CLARK and GRAYBIEL (1949) and later named the *oculogravic illusion* by GRAYBIEL (1952). The direction of the illusion depends on the observer's orientation with respect to the centripetal force vector. For example, during counterclockwise rotation on a centrifuge, an observer seated upright and facing the direction of rotation will feel himself to be tilted rightward and will see a luminous horizontal line as tilted clockwise (see Fig. 3); when facing the direction of clockwise rotation, the opposite pattern is experienced (CLARK and GRAYBIEL, 1951).

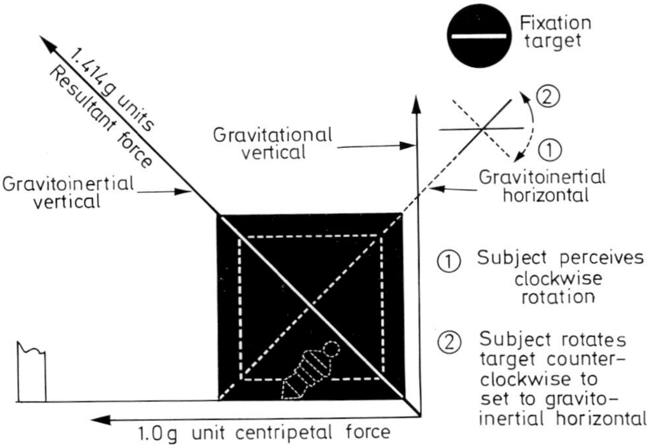

Fig. 3. Illustration of the oculogravic illusion; the vertical subject perceives himself as tilted clockwise and sees a horizontal line as tilted clockwise. (From GRAYBIEL, 1973)

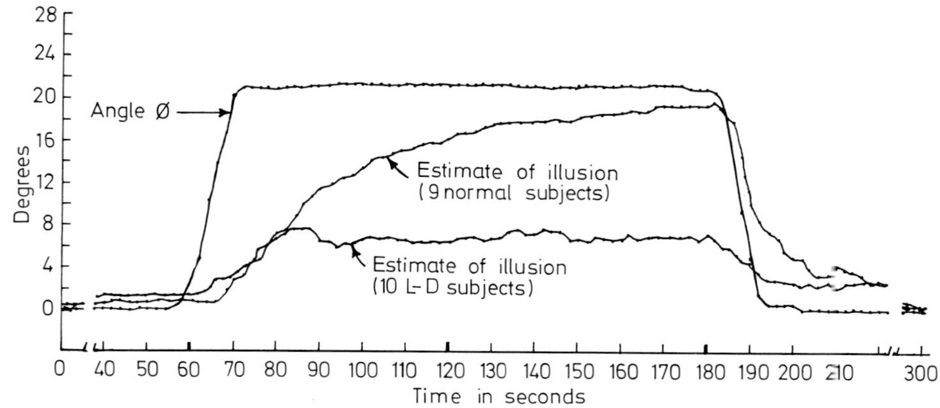

Fig. 4. Gradual development of the oculogravic illusion when subjects are exposed to displacement of the gravitoinertial vertical. (From GRAYBIEL and CLARK, 1965)

The perception of the oculogravic illusion is not immediate: after the force vectors acting on the subject have reached a constant value, there is a lag of approximately 120 s before the illusion is experienced at full strength. Moreover, the illusion is usually smaller in magnitude than the change in the gravitoinertial force vector, i.e., subjects feel less tilted than would be expected on the basis of the change in the force environment (see Fig. 4). CLARK and GRAYBIEL (1963a, 1966a), studying the factors that govern the oculogravic illusion, found that its character is influenced not only by the magnitude of the centripetal force to which the subject is exposed but also by the level of illumination in the centrifuge chamber. For example, if a person is experiencing a stable level of the oculogravic illusion (as indicated by his errors in attempts to set a luminous line to the gravitational horizontal), then the illusion can be abolished — or at least considerably attenuated — by turning on the cabin lights. When the room lights are again extinguished, it takes nearly 2 min before the illusion again reaches a maximum. CLARK and GRAYBIEL (1966a) have indicated that this pattern makes it unlikely that the time lag associated with the oculogravic illusion originates in end-organ response times or in delays attributable to intersensory integration times as once suggested by GRAYBIEL and BROWN (1951). CLARK and GRAYBIEL (1966a) further point out that DEVRIES (1950) has shown that the otoliths takes much less than a second to stabilize in a new position following a change in resultant force.

II. Sensory Mechanisms Involved in the Oculogravic Illusion

Although doubtlessly attributable in part to the labyrinths, the oculogravic illusion is experienced in attenuated form by L-D subjects; it is of interest that for these subjects, the illusion may take 60 min to develop fully.

The ability of L-D subjects to experience the oculogravic illusion has been shown to be related to the touch, pressure, and kinesthetic receptor systems (CLARK and GRAYBIEL, 1966b); in the normal subject, otolithic as well as touch, pressure and kinesthetic information is involved (GRAYBIEL et al., 1968).

The relative contributions of otolithic and nonotolithic cues to the oculogravic illusion have been evaluated by CLARK and GRAYBIEL (1968) in an experiment involving measurements of the subjective visual horizontal in subjects standing on a rotating platform. The ingenious feature of this experiment—in which both L-D and normal subjects participated—was that a subject could be positioned in various voluntarily maintained head-and-trunk orientions in relation to the gravitoinertial force vector. This permitted the specification of postures in which the otolithic and nonotolithic cues were either antagonistic or synergistic. The experimental results are of especial interest: normal and L-D subjects performed identically; both groups were able to set a luminous line accurately to the horizontal. Utilizing tactile and kinesthetic formation, the L-D subjects were able to perform as accurately as the normal subjects who, in certain conditions, actually had to discount misleading otolithic information when judging their orientation.

CLARK and GRAYBIEL (1968) specify six characteristics that distinguish this experiment from others on the oculogravic illusion: 1) the subject actively maintained his head and trunk in the desired postures; 2) the subject was not supported artificially; 3) the subject stood on an inclined plane so that his feet were aligned with the gravitoinertial vertical; 4) the subject supported a luminous rod in his own hands and set it to the apparent horizontal; 5) the subject "... perceived his body as being tilted away from the horizontal floor of the room by his own effort, whereas in the typical experiment on the oculogravic illusion, he perceived the chair, floor, and his body to be tilted outboard ..."; 6) the subject was not subjected to asymmetric pressure cues. From these considerations it can be seen that the organism is not responding passively to changes in vestibular stimulation but is integrating these signals with tactile and kinesthetic accounts of body orientation to determine apparent posture.

III. The Audiogravic Illusion

An auditory counterpart to the oculogravic illusion exists: when a subject is exposed to a change in the resultant linear force acting on his body, he also mislocalizes sounds. This *audiogravic illusion*, first described and named by GRAYBIEL and NIVEN (1951), is similar to the oculogravic illusion; subjects experience tilt of their stationary body and simultaneously hear a stationary sound source move in the direction opposite their subjective change in body posture. To maintain the apparent locus of the sound constant, the source has to be physically displaced in the direction of the change in apparent body position.

IV. Common Factors Underlying the Oculogravic and Audiogravic Illusions and the Shifts in Visual and Auditory Localization During Tilt of the Body Axis

The oculogravic and audiogravic illusions both involve concomitant changes in apparent posture and sensory localization. It should be noted that the changes in visual and auditory localization described above, which occur during prolonged tilt of the body in the dark, have time courses virtually identical with those of the oculogravic and audiogravic illusions, are also abolished if the lights in the experimental chamber are turned on, and likewise redevelop gradually when the lights are again extinguished. These common factors imply similar or identical underlying mechanisms.

E. Adaptation to the Coriolis Oculogyral Illusion

I. The Coriolis Oculogyral Illusion

If a subject some distance from the center of a rotating centrifuge turns his head about an axis other than one parallel to the centrifuge's axis of rotation, he will be subjected to cross-coupling and Coriolis accelerations (GROEN, 1961; MEDA, 1952). These accelerations produce a situation in which the semicircular canals are not signaling the true direction of head displacement (GRAYBIEL et al., 1961). In fact, when a subject turns his head about an axis orthogonal to the axis of rotation of the centrifuge, he will experience turning about a third axis that is orthogonal both to the axis of rotation of the centrifuge and to the axis about which he has turned his head. This incorrectly experienced motion of the head is accompanied by illusory motion of the visual environment. For example, if a subject facing the center of rotation of a clockwise-turning centrifuge fixates a small target light while tilting his head to his left shoulder, he will simultaneously feel his head move diagonally backwards to the left and see the target light rise diagonally forward to the right. GRAYBIEL (1962) has designated this visual and postural illusion the *Coriolis oculogyral illusion*. Although the possibility has not been investigated, presumably there is a *Coriolis audiogyral illusion*.

II. Vestibular Adaptation to Coriolis and Cross-Coupling Accelerations

Subjects who continue to make head movements during rotation gradually experience less aberrant motion of their head and the visual environment until, at length, their head motions are correctly perceived and the visual environment

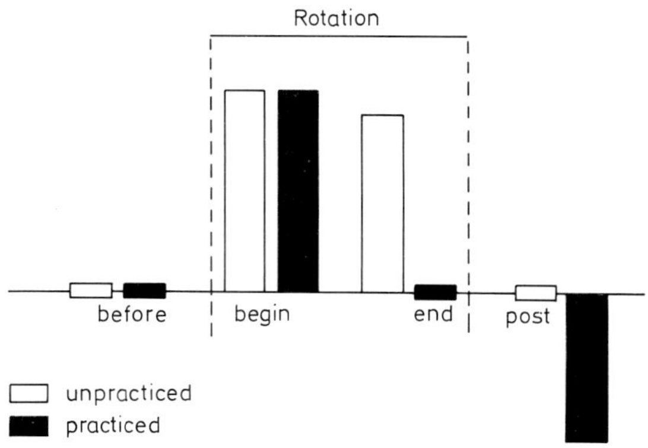

Fig. 5. Adaptation of the Coriolis oculogyral illusion occurs for that quadrant in which many head movements have been made. (From GRAYBIEL, 1964)

remains stable (GRAYBIEL et al., 1961). Adaptation occurs for those directions in which the subjects make a large number of head movements, although there is generalization to nearby directions. If head movements are made in four quadrants—fore-aft, left-right—then adaptation generalizes for all other directions of head displacement. Such "adapted" subjects experience strong negative aftereffects when the centrifuge is stopped: head movements elicit a pattern of illusory head-and-visual motion opposite in sign to that initially experienced before adaptation was achieved (see Fig. 5). The Coriolis oculogyral illusion is much stronger and adaptation takes much longer for higher rotary velocities of the centrifuge.

The nystagmus that accompanies the Coriolis oculogyral illusion also abates after the subject has made many head movements (GUEDRY and GRAYBIEL, 1962; GUEDRY et al., 1962). Initially, such nystagmus occurs in the plane specified by the effective stimulation of the semicircular canals rather than by the actual trajectory of the head. GUEDRY and GRAYBIEL (1962) found that during the course of a 64 h experiment, this nystagmus decreased slowly in intensity; after cessation of rotation, a nystagmus of opposite sign was present during head movements and was still apparent an hour later. GROEN (1970) has suggested that such adaptive changes in vestibular response which leave negative aftereffects on return to normal stimulus situations result from centrally generated "patterns of opposite sign" which effectively cancel aberrant sensory signals of a predictable nature.

III. Influence of Continuous Changes in Centripetal Acceleration on Apparent Posture and Visual Localization

GRAYBIEL and JOHNSON (1963) created an unique experimental situation to study the effect of continuous changes in centripetal acceleration on a subject's perception of his own posture and the apparent direction of visual targets.

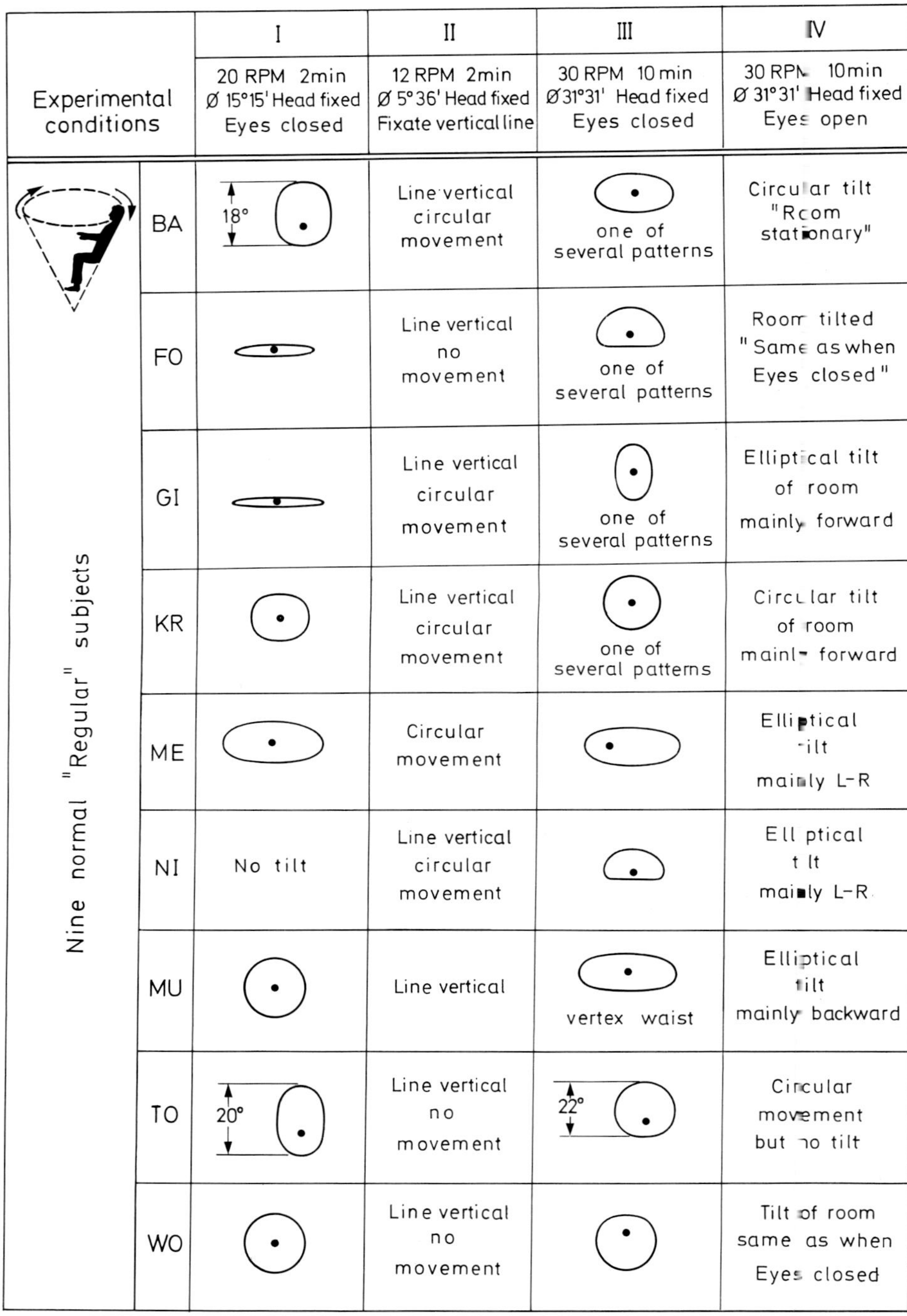

Experimental conditions		I	II	III	IV
		20 RPM 2min Ø 15°15' Head fixed Eyes closed	12 RPM 2min Ø 5°36' Head fixed Fixate vertical line	30 RPM 10 min Ø 31°31' Head fixed Eyes closed	30 RPM 10min Ø 31°31' Head fixed Eyes open
Nine normal "Regular" subjects	BA	18°	Line vertical circular movement	one of several patterns	Circular tilt "Room stationary"
	FO		Line vertical no movement	one of several patterns	Room tilted "Same as when Eyes closed"
	GI		Line vertical circular movement	one of several patterns	Elliptical tilt of room mainly forward
	KR		Line vertical circular movement	one of several patterns	Circular tilt of room mainly forward
	ME		Circular movement		Elliptical tilt mainly L-R
	NI	No tilt	Line vertical circular movement		Elliptical tilt mainly L-R
	MU		Line vertical	vertex waist	Elliptical tilt mainly backward
	TO	20°	Line vertical no movement	22°	Circular movement but no tilt
	WO		Line vertical no movement		Tilt of room same as when Eyes closed

Fig. 6. Visual and postural illusions experienced by normal and labyrinthine-defective subjects exposed to a "rotating" linear acceleration vector. (From GRAYBIEL and JOHNSON, 1963)

Periodic changes in centripetal acceleration were achieved by seating subjects in a counter-rotating room that was mounted on the arm of a centrifuge. The room and the centrifuge were rotated at the same rate but in opposite directions; consequently, the centripetal acceleration vector changed systematically, but the net angular acceleration was zero. All subjects, including the L-D subjects that participated, experienced sensations of "simultaneously tilting and rotating" in an elliptical or circular pattern, with the head describing a path considerably larger than the waist and feet. This pattern is illustrated in Figure 6. The L-D subjects experienced the postural illusions as clearly as the subjects with functioning labyrinths; accordingly, the otoliths can not be solely responsible for the illusion. Coupled with the postural illusion was illusory motion of a vertical luminous line—the normal subjects saw the stimulus line describe a circular or elliptical pattern; the L-D subjects also experienced the illusory visual motion.

IV. Adaptation to a Rotating Environment

The existence of the Coriolis oculogyral illusion seemed at one time to preclude adjustment to living in a rotating environment, e.g., a spacecraft that was being rotated to generate "artificial gravity" (GRAYBIEL, 1965). Early studies

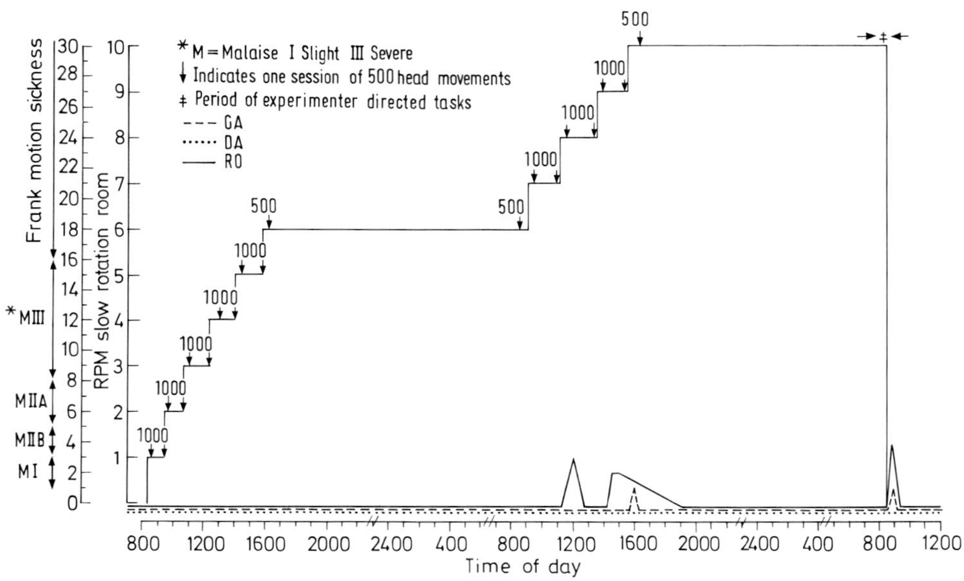

Fig. 7. Stress profile of three subjects who received stepwise increases in rotational speed to a terminal velocity of 10 rpm. The rapid adaptation is attributable to the large number of head movements executed at each dwell velocity. (From GRAYBIEL, 1969)

of man's tolerance to a rotating environment indicated that above 5 rpm performance was severely disrupted and that subjects not only experienced the Coriolis oculogyral illusion but also progressively cold sweating, increased salivation, drowsiness, stomach awareness, stomach discomfort, nausea, and finally severe nausea with vomiting (GRAYBIEL et al., 1960)—this pattern of symptoms constitutes the syndrome of motion sickness (GRAYBIEL, 1969). Subjects tend to be somewhat less susceptible to motion sickness if they keep their eyes closed while moving their heads (OOSTERVELD et al., 1972), possibly because they are then not experiencing the visual component of the Coriolis oculogyral illusion. Most subjects, even those very susceptible to motion sickness, can adapt to rotation at 5 rpm if they are permitted to make a large number of head movements: few, however, can adapt to 10 rpm stimulation if they are exposed in a single-step change from 0 to 10 rpm.

GRAYBIEL and his colleagues have recently shown, however, that nearly all subjects, including those highly susceptible to motion sickness, can be adapted to rotation at 10 rpm if they are brought up to terminal velocity in small increments (e.g., 1 rpm) and are required to make many head movements (several hundred) at each new dwell velocity (GRAYBIEL, 1971; GRAYBIEL and WOOD, 1969; GRAYBIEL et al., 1969). Subjects exposed in this incremental fashion can actually be taken beyond 10 rpm without ever exhibiting signs of reflex vestibular disturbances (i.e., nystagmus, Coriolis oculogyral illusion, and postural disequilibrium) or motion sickness (see Fig. 7). That adaptation to the gradually altered force environment actually has taken place is shown by the fact that, upon return to 0-rpm in one step, all subjects experience reflex vestibular disturbances when they move their heads.

V. Incremental Exposure Facilitates Vestibular Adaptation

Exposure to one complete incremental adaptation series leads to more rapid adaptation during exposure to another incremental exposure series regardless of whether it involves rotation in the same or opposite direction. That is, subjects can be brought up to terminal velocity more rapidly in the second incremental exposure series, because they can make fewer head movements at each dwell velocity than in their first exposure series and still remain immune from reflex vestibular disturbances and symptoms of motion sickness. It appears, therefore, that incremental exposure hastens adaptation to direction-specific, reflex-vestibular disturbances as well as to nondirection-specific, vestibular side-effects, such as motion sickness. The possibility that incremental exposure may hasten adaptation to other conditions of unusual postural and sensory stimulation deserves investigation.

F. Adaptation to Visual Rearrangement

I. Adaptation to Altered Retinal-Image Motion

The adaptive changes leading to attenuation of the Coriolis oculogyral illusion would appear to be related to a form of adaptation seen by WALLACH and KRAVITZ (1965a) when they altered the relationship between a subject's head movements and retinal-image motion. In these experiments, whenever the subject turned his head, the image of an external target that he was viewing was displaced by a fractional amount of his head motion in the same or opposite direction. Under these conditions, the subject on moving his head will at first correctly see the target move in the same or opposite direction; however, with longer exposure, the target will appear stationary. When adaptation is complete, if the physical motion of the target is eliminated, the subject on moving his head will see the target displace in the direction opposite that in which it appeared to move before adaptation was achieved (WALLACH and KRAVITZ, 1975a, b; HAY, 1968). Similar results occur within this exposure paradigm if auditory rather than visual targets are used (WALLACH and KRAVITZ, 1968). Such compensatory changes, like those leading to attenuation of the Coriolis oculogyral illusion, are clearly dependent on the dynamic mechanisms by which an organism discriminates between 1) changes in sensory stimulation, normal or abnormal, contingent on its own movements and 2) changes in sensory stimulation resulting from independent physical movements of external objects.

II. Adaptation to Retinal-Image Reversal and Inversion

STRATTON's early observations on adaptation to visual rearrangement are important in this context. In a pioneering set of experiments, STRATTON (1897a, b) fitted himself with a monocular lens system that both reversed and inverted the visual field, and wore the device for a number of days while keeping his other eye occluded. Because the device was attached to his head it reversed the relationship between head movement and retinal image motion; consequently, every time STRATTON turned his head and eye to fixate a target, the visual world seemed to move in the same direction but at twice the rate [see CARR (1935) for an explanation of the optical situation]. After prolonged exposure, the visual world again appeared stationary during head movements; however, the visual motion had been replaced by a postural illusion: STRATTON found that when he turned his head in one direction he felt it to be moving in the opposite direction (STRATTON, 1907). The illusion of visual movement during head movements returned, with opposite sign, as soon as the lens system was removed, and only gradually disappeared.

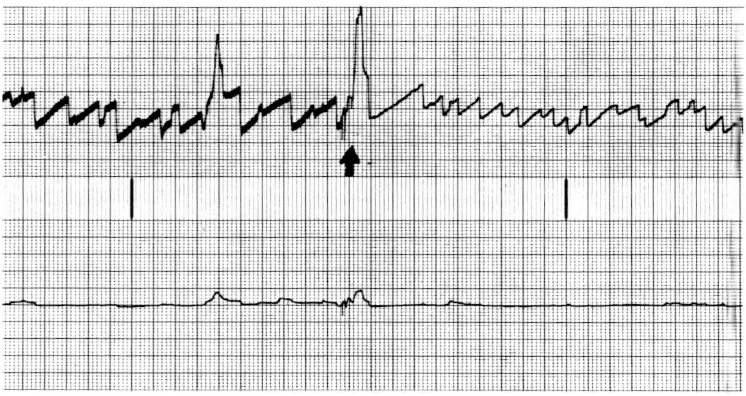

Fig. 8. Record of horizontal nystagmus produced by applying a physiotherapy vibrator to a subject's right cheek bone; arrow indicates cessation of stimulation. During vibration, the subject was experiencing self-movement to the left; when the vibration was stopped he experienced self-movement to the right. His nystagmus had its slow phase to the right at all times. Calibration: 10 mm = 10 degrees; paper speed 10 mm/s. (From LACKNER and GRAYBIEL, 1974)

Recently, DOLEZAL (1971) and MELVILL-JONES and GONSHOR (1972) have shown that sensory-postural compensation, at the reflex level, underlie part of the adaptative changes described by STRATTON. MELVILL-JONES and GONSHOR found that prolonged wearing of right-left reversing spectacles will change the direction of the slow-phase of vestibular nystagmus so that it is in the direction of body rotation rather than in the opposite direction. DOLEZAL has shown similar reversals in sign for compensatory eye movements during active head movements. It seems apparent, therefore, that modification of the vestibulo-ocular reflex arc underlies at least in part the adaptation to reversal of the visual field originally described by STRATTON. In this context, it is notable that LACKNER and GRAYBIEL (1974), who demonstrated that it is possible to stimulate the semicircular canals with regional vibration of the head, found that the direction of sensed self-rotation and the direction of vestibular nystagmus can easily be dissociated (see Fig. 8).

III. Compensatory Postural Changes During Adaptation to Visual Rearrangement

Compensatory postural changes occur as well in freely moving subjects who are wearing prism spectacles that laterally displace the visual field. Typically, as they walk about, such subjects begin to deviate their heads in the direction of the visual displacement (HARRIS, 1965; KOHLER, 1964; LACKNER, 1970, 1973b, 1976a). After adaptation is complete, the subject will accept a laterally deviated position of his head as being "straight ahead" with respect to his trunk. EBENHOLTZ (1966) and MORANT and BELLER (1965) have noted similar compensatory changes in subjects wearing lens systems that rotate the optic array; subjects soon tilt their heads in the direction of the optic rotation. Such changes in

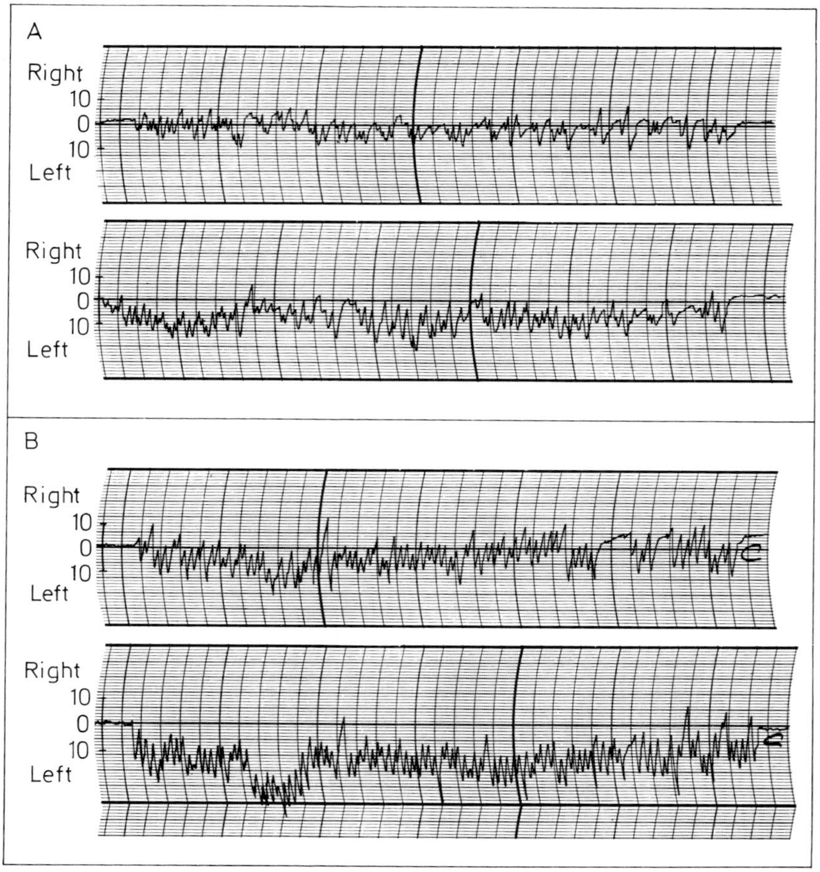

Fig. 9a and b. Typical nystagmus patterns recorded during pre- and post-trials for the two experimental conditions. Calibration legends indicate eye positions 10° leftward and 10° rightward with respect to the head median plane. (a) Representative 30-s trials from one subject in physical head deviation condition. Upper trace was recorded with the subject's head fixed straight ahead with respect to the trunk. Lower trace was recorded with the head deviated 45° to the right of the trunk median plane. (b) Representative 30-s trials from one subject in apparent head deviation condition. Upper trace and lower trace were both recorded with the subject's head oriented straight ahead in relation to his trunk. The upper trace was recorded prior to the subject's being exposed to a 13° leftward displacement of his visual world for 3 h. The lower trace was recorded after the subject had adapted to the visual rearrangement and the prisms had been removed; under this circumstance, the subject experiences his head to be deviated rightward although it is physically aligned with the median plane of his trunk. (From Teixeira and Lackner, 1976)

registered head posture always serve to eliminate the consequences of the optical displacement and to restore accurate sensory-motor coordination to external visual stimuli. Teixeira and Lackner (1976) have recently found that after periods of exposure to visual displacement in which subjects are free to move about, there is associated with the change in apparent head position a displacement of the return position of the fast phase of optokinetic nystagmus (see Fig. 9). Their observation indicates that reflex oculomotor adjustments related to tonic neck reflexes are involved in adaptation to visual displacement.

IV. Compensatory Postural Changes in Patients with Sensory and Motor Deficits

It should be noted that postural adjustments also compensate for sensory rearrangements arising from neurologic damage. For example, patients with homonymous hemianopsias or extra-ocular muscle defects show compensatory changes in head posture; these changes are such as to center the remaining visual field with respect to the trunk, or in the case of a paralyzed muscle to restore ocular motility in the affected direction by deviating the head in the direction of the paralyzed muscle's action and then achieving control by modulating the activity level of the antagonist muscle (COGAN, 1956; URIST, 1970).

V. Influence of Visual Rearrangement on Auditory Localization

Although the effect is less familiar, the localization of auditory stimuli is also influenced by visual rearrangement. Initially, ambient sounds are misheard in the direction and by the amount of the visual displacement (LACKNER, 1973c); but, as adaptation proceeds and there is a change in the interpretation of head posture, auditory localization improves in accuracy, *pari passu*, until, when adaptation is complete, auditory localization is again veridical (LACKNER, 1973b, 1976a). After removal of the prism spectacles, transient negative aftereffects in the localization of auditory stimuli continue until registered head posture again corresponds to true head posture (see Fig. 10). The directions of displacement are opposite for dichotically presented and for ambient sounds.

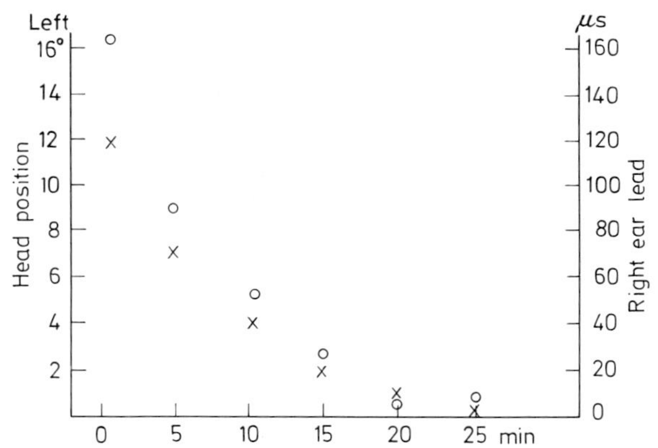

Fig. 10. Restitution of normal head posture and auditory localization after exposure to visual rearrangement. X's represent the true position of the head in relation to the trunk when it is perceived to be straight ahead; O's represent arrival time lead (right ordinate) to one ear necessary to produce a centered sound image for dichotically presented clicks. Abscissa indicates time elapsed since removal of prism spectacles. (From LACKNER, 1973b)

G. Influence of Optokinetic Stimulation on Sensory Localization and Posture

I. Illusory Self-Rotation Induced by Optokinetic Stimulation

Movement of the entire visual field, or a portion of it, can induce apparent self-movement in a stationary observer (MACH, 1897; HELMHOLTZ, 1866). Anyone who has been looking out the window of a stationary train as an adjacent train began to move past in the opposite direction can testify to the strength and compellingness of this illusory self-motion — it feels as if the cushion of the seat is pushing into one's back. The haunted-swing illusion of WOOD (1895), in which observers seated in a stationary swing feel themselves moving back and forth when the walls of the enclosing experimental chamber are rocked, indicates that oscillatory as well as unidirectional visual stimulation can induce apparent self-motion. The direction of apparent self-motion is always opposite to that of the visual stimulation.

II. Illusory Self-Rotation Induced by Auditory and by Tactile Stimulation

DODGE (1923) found that illusory self-rotation could be induced by a rotating sound field. Although apparatus limitations prevented DODGE from eliciting strong illusions of rotation, he obtained recordings of eye movements which indicated that nystagmoid movements of the eyes were occurring during apparent

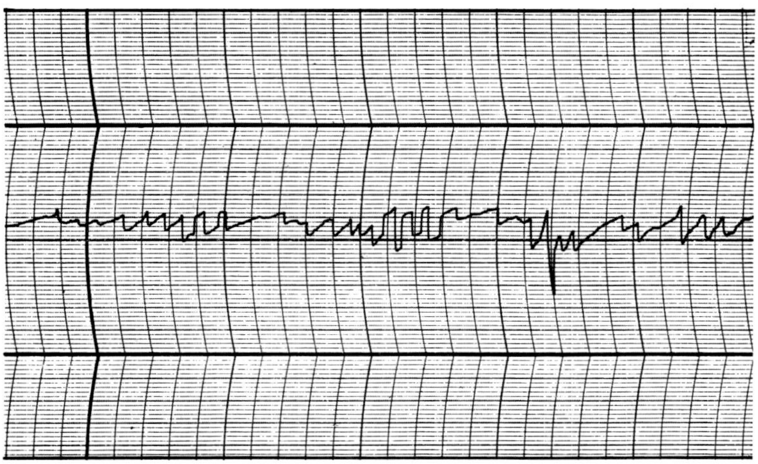

Fig. 11. Nystagmoid eye movements of subject experiencing illusory selfrotation to the left induced by a sound field rotating clockwise, 60°/s. Calibration: Each small division = 1°; up = rightward deviation of eyes; chart speed = 6 mm/s = 1 horizontal division. (From LACKNER, 1977)

self-rotation. His observations have recently been confirmed and extended (LACKNER, 1977). A nystagmus pattern recorded from a subject experiencing illusory self-rotation during auditory stimulation is shown in Fig. 11. Apparent self-rotation can also be induced by revolving tactile stimulation, and an illusion of self-rotation that has been induced by optokinetic stimulation can be maintained without lapse by tactile stimulation. Nystagmoid movements of the eyes also occur during illusory self-rotation that is elicited by tactile stimulation (LACKNER, 1977).

These observations indicate that illusory body motion can be induced in situations involving a uniformly changing input from the visual, auditory, or somatosensory realms in the absence of changes in canalicular or otolith input. Such situations are ambiguous with regard to the specification of orientation, because non-changing vestibular inputs can be associated with being stationary, being rotated, or being displaced at constant velocity, whereas movement of the entire visual, auditory, or tactile field generally takes place only during movement of the body in relation to a stationary environment; consequently, "figure-ground" type reversals of apparent movement of self and surroundings can result.

III. Influence of Optokinetic Stimulation on Auditory Localization and Appreciation of Body Position

Exposure to optokinetic stimulation, in addition to inducing illusory self motion, affects the localization of sounds and the judgment of "straight-ahead." THURLOW and KERR (1970) found that sounds were heard too far in the direction of apparent self-motion, and that the apparent straight-ahead was similarly displaced. ARNOULT (1952) and GEMELLI (1951) and WALLACH (1940) earlier made extensive observations on these same phenomena. Powerful influences of moving visual scenes on the judgment of locomotion within inertial space have been demonstrated by LISHMAN and LEE (1973). In their experiment, as subjects walked forward the walls of the experimental chamber were displaced forward as well; the subjects experienced themselves to be standing in the same place and walking on a treadmill. In a related experiment, LEE and ARONSON (1974) found that the ability of infants to stand was disrupted by the presentation of visual patterns that normally signal movement of the observer. Together these experiments emphasize the compelling influence of vision on posture (cf. LACKNER, 1973a, b, c, 1976a; NIELSEN, 1963; TASTEVIN, 1937).

IV. Differential Effectiveness of Optokinetic Stimulation of Central and Peripheral Retinal Areas in Eliciting Illusory Self-Motion

The central and peripheral areas of the retina are not equally effective in eliciting illusory self-rotation (BRANDT et al., 1975). In fact, when the central and peripheral regions of the retina are stimulated with patterns moving in opposite directions, the peripheral stimulation determines the direction of apparent self-rotation, and the central stimulation determines the direction of optokinetic nystagmus (BRANDT et al., 1973). These facts—taken with another, namely that illusory self-rotation can be induced by moving visual patterns when the eyes are fixating a stationary target—indicate that illusory self-rotation is not contingent on eye movements. It has been reported that when subjects are exposed suddenly to optokinetic stimulation, the latencies before their first reports of illusory self-rotation range between 1–10 s and are independent of stimulus velocity over the range 10°–120°/s (DICHGANS and BRANDT, 1972; BRANDT et al., 1973).

V. Properties of Illusory Self-Motion Depend on the Direction and Velocity of Visual Stimulation

MACH (1897) found that the direction of illusory self-movement is dependent on the direction and character of visual stimulation. He described illusory linear self-displacement in the horizontal as well as vertical direction. His observations have been confirmed and extended by FISCHER and KORNMÜLLER (1930), LISHMAN and LEE (1973), and BERTHOZ et al. (1975). In related experiments, DICHGANS et al. (1972) and HELD et al. (1975) have found that illusory tilt motion can be induced by viewing a large striped disc rotating in the frontal plane; continuous motion is experienced but only a limited amount of tilt. Sinusoidal displacement of visual patterns can elicit illusory self-displacement of a similar nature (WOOD, 1895; GURNEE, 1931; BERTHOZ et al., 1975).

When rotation of the visual environment is coupled with actual rotation of the observer, augmentation or diminution of apparent self-rotation will result, depending on whether the observer and surroundings are being displaced in the same or in the opposite direction (BRANDT et al., 1974a; YOUNG et al., 1973). GURNEE's (1931) classic observation that illusory self-motion induced by visual stimulation raises the threshold for detection of angular acceleration in the direction opposite the illusory self-rotation has recently been confirmed by YOUNG et al. (1973). Although detection thresholds for angular acceleration can be elevated, a lowering of thresholds has not been found during concordant visual and vestibular stimulation.

VI. The Pseudo-Coriolis Illusion

If an observer experiencing optokinetically induced, apparent self-rotation tilts his head to the side, he may see the visual-array tilt and experience simultaneously a direction of head tilt that does not correspond to the true trajectory. This pattern has been named the pseudo-Coriolis illusion by DICHGANS and BRANDT (1973) who first described it. They consider it and the Coriolis oculogyral illusion to be virtually identical qualitatively, although the pseudo-Coriolis illusion tends to be less strong.

VII. Pseudo-Coriolis Illusion and Motion Sickness

DICHGANS and BRANDT (1973) found that, like the Coriolis illusion, periodic elicitation of the pseudo-Coriolis effect leads to acute motion sickness. They believe that the motion sickness symptoms elicited by these two forms of stimulation are qualitatively identical and differ only quantitatively, the effects induced by pseudo-Coriolis stimulation being weaker; nevertheless, the aftereffects of optokinetically induced motion sickness, including headache, nausea, drowsiness, and dizziness were often found to persist for many hours after stimulation. The similarities between the Coriolis and pseudo-Coriolis effects are of interest because of reports that visual and vestibular information converge in the vestibular nuclei (cf. DICHGANS and BRANDT, 1972; DICHGANS et al., 1973, HENN et al., 1974; KLINKE and SCHMIDT, 1970). The Coriolis and pseudo-Coriolis illusions are thought to arise because the same neuronal mechanisms within the vestibular system have been accessed by different routes.

It is probably inappropriate, however, to equate the mechanisms of the Coriolis and pseudo-Coriolis illusions in this fashion. LACKNER and TEIXEIRA (1977) have found that the appearance of motion sickness symptoms is different for optokinetically and vestibularly induced motion sickness. During vestibular

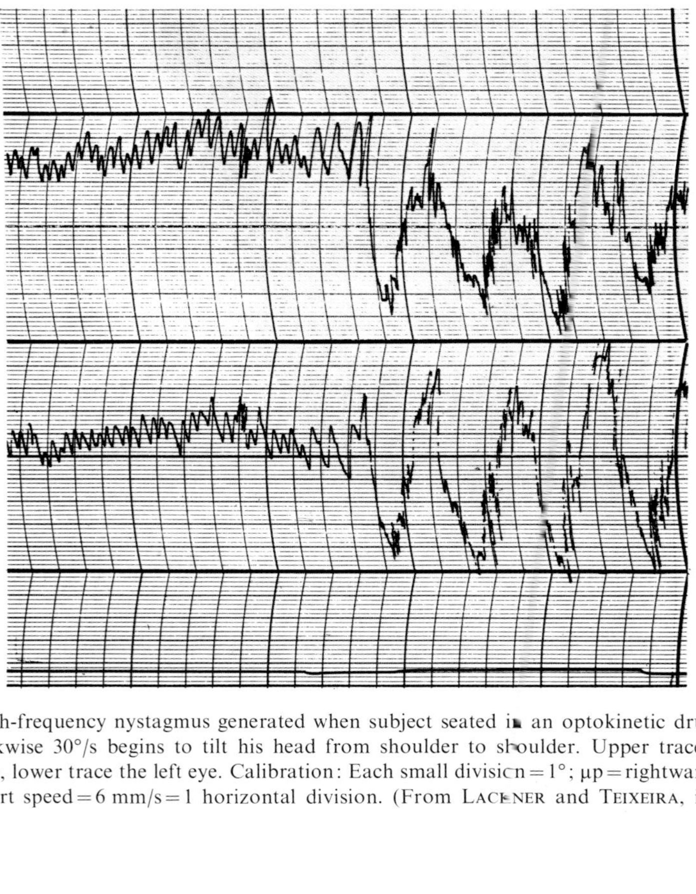

Fig. 12. High-frequency nystagmus generated when subject seated in an optokinetic drum rotating counterclockwise 30°/s begins to tilt his head from shoulder to shoulder. Upper trace represents the right eye, lower trace the left eye. Calibration: Each small division = 1°; µp = rightward deviation of eyes; chart speed = 6 mm/s = 1 horizontal division. (From LACKNER and TEIXEIRA, in progress)

stimulation, there is a rather orderly appearance of signs of motion sickness: cold sweating, pallor, increased salivation, drowsiness, stomach awareness, stomach distress, nausea, severe nausea, and vomiting; occasionally dizziness and headache accompany the severe nausea (GRAYBIEL, 1969). By contrast, during optokinetic stimulation, dizziness and headache, or dizziness, headache, and stomach awareness often develop without any of the intermediate signs. Moreover, these symptoms may develop or get progressively worse over time after removal from the optokinetic drum. After cessation of vestibular stimulation, symptoms of motion sickness generally abate rapidly or stay the same. The symptoms of motion-sickness elicited during pseudo-Coriolis stimulation may be related to the high-frequency nystagmus generated when head movements are made in an optokinetic drum—such a nystagmus record is presented in Fig. 12; when optokinetic stimulation is terminated an afternystagmus can be measured that often persists for several days (LACKNER and TEIXEIRA, 1977). Accordingly, the severe dizziness and headache experienced by subjects tilting their heads during exposure to optokinetic stimulation may very well depend in part on the resulting oculomotor disturbance.

VIII. Suppression of Illusory Self-Motion by Head Movements

LACKNER and TEIXEIRA (1977) found that subjects making continuous head movements can suppress the induction of illusory self-rotation; some subjects can be exposed to 10°/s increments in optokinetic stimulation every few minutes, up to velocities of 80°/s, the highest velocity tested, without experiencing self-rotation or the pseudo-Coriolis illusion. As the speed of optokinetic stimulation is increased, the subjects have to increase the frequency of their head movements to prevent apparent self-rotation. Subjects who make head movements in this fashion, from shoulder to shoulder, experience fewer symptoms of motion sickness than subjects who receive the same optokinetic stimulation but who do not move their heads. The suppression of illusory self-rotation is not contingent on voluntary movements of the head but occurs during passive head movements as well. LACKNER and TEIXEIRA (in progress) found that subjects exposed to high velocity optokinetic stimulation (e.g., 60°/s) would initially experience the pseudo-Coriolis illusion when they tilted their heads from side to side every few seconds. However, with continued exposure the pseudo-Coriolis illusion will rapidly diminish in intensity and in a few minutes not be noticeable. A subject who has "adapted" to the pseudo-Coriolis illusion will not, when tilting his head in a stationary visual environment, experience a profound aftereffect of opposite sign such as is experienced by subjects who have adapted to the Coriolis oculogyral illusion (see section on adaptation to the Coriolis oculogyral illusion, above). These observations emphasize the very considerable differences between the Coriolis and Pseudo-Coriolis illusions and imply distinct, although perhaps related, underlying mechanisms.

IX. Mechanisms Underlying Induction of Illusory Self-Motion

The induction of apparent self-motion by visual, auditory, or haptic stimulation represents one aspect of the way in which sensory information is related to apparent body orientation. A continuous change in visual, auditory, or haptic stimulation ordinarily occurs only when an observer is moving at constant velocity in relation to a stable environment; in such a situation, the observer does not have other sources of sensory information to indicate that he is truly stationary. However, as soon as the observer's head is moved actively or passively, there is a pattern of input from joint receptors of the neck and from the semicircular canals and otolith organs specifying that the observer's body is stationary and that he has moved his head through a particular trajectory; this pattern would be different if the observer were in fact rotating. Such a dynamic change in proprioceptive and vestibular input is sufficient to override an ambiguous pattern of visual, auditory, or haptic stimulation. In this context, it should be recalled that CLARK and GRAYBIEL (1966, 1967, 1968) demonstrated that normal as well as L-D subjects who are actively maintaining their postures do not experience the *A* and *E-effects* or the oculogravic illusion. Their observations and those of LACKNER and TEIXEIRA (1977) hence emphasize the dynamic characteristics of the mechanisms underlying spatial orientation—no single sensory input determines apparent body orientation, but rather a complex assessment of the pattern of all inputs takes place. Determining the specific nature of this assessment constitutes a problem of formidable complexity.

H. Postural and Sensory Illusions Evoked by Skeletal Muscle Vibration

I. The Tonic Vibration Reflex

Vibration of a skeletal muscle elicits a reflex contraction of that muscle, the tonic vibration reflex (HAGBARTH and EKLUND, 1966). A high-frequency vibration of 100 Hz activates the primary endings of the spindle receptors within the muscle, leading thereby to a direct monosynaptic activation of the alpha motoneurons of the vibrated muscle and indirectly to an inhibition of the alpha motoneurons of the antagonist muscle; lower frequency vibration activates both spindle secondary and primary endings (MATTHEWS, 1972). The strength of tonic vibration reflexes is influenced by a variety of factors, including the length of the vibrated muscle, the state of innervation of that muscle and its antagonist, the temperature of the muscle, and the tonic level of gamma-efferent activity (HAGBARTH and EKLUND, 1966, 1968; MARSDEN et al., 1969).

II. Contribution of Muscle-Afferent Information to Position Sense

GOODWIN et al. (1972a, b) recently discovered that if the action of a muscle contracting under a tonic vibration reflex is resisted by restraining the controlled limb, then that limb will be experienced as moving. The direction of the apparent motion corresponds to the direction of movement that would occur if the vibrated muscle were actually lengthening. Their observation indicates that muscle-afferent information can influence conscious position sense; for example, muscle-spindle information can be used to control pursuit eye movements in total darkness (LACKNER, 1975) or to stabilize eye position (LACKNER and ZABKAR, 1977). Until GOODWIN and his colleagues' experiments, informed opinion held that muscle-afferent information played no role in position sense but was part of a reflex-control system not accessible to consciousness (cf. MERTON, 1953, 1954, 1970; MOUNTCASTLE, 1974). The effects of vibration are not confined to eliciting local segmental reflexes, i.e., tonic vibration reflexes, but implicate other muscle groups as well because of modified activity in supraspinal structures (EKLUND, 1972, 1973).

III. Postural Illusions Related to Abnormal Muscle-Spindle Feedback

The importance of muscle-spindle information in human spatial orientation has been underscored by some recent developments. If a standing subject's achilles tendons are vibrated, the tonic vibration reflexes generated will cause him to sway backwards and, if vibration is maintained, he will have to make postural adjustments to prevent himself from falling over backwards (EKLUND, 1969, 1972, 1973). GOODWIN (1973) found that if he prevented backwards motion of a blindfolded subject whose achilles tendons were being vibrated, then the stationary subject would experience himself as falling forward.

LACKNER and LEVINE (1978) have confirmed and extended GOODWIN's observation. By vibrating different muscle groups they could elicit predictable patterns of apparent motion of the body in almost any direction; such apparent motion often continues during prolonged periods of stimulation, e.g., five or more minutes. Although continuous movement is experienced, the change in apparent position is much less than would be expected on the basis of the apparent velocity of movement; in fact, the experienced positional change is usually small. When the contours of the experimental chamber are visible, illusory self-motion cannot be elicited by muscle vibration.

IV. Visual Illusions and Nystagmus Related to Abnormal Muscle-Spindle Feedback

If a subject experiencing strong self-motion is presented a dim target light, he will see the target light as moving in pace with his own apparent body motion, but like himself, the target will not appear to be undergoing much displacement. By contrast, if a subject is experiencing only slight apparent motion, then turning on a bright target light will abolish his illusory motion. Presumably, similar effects would occur if auditory targets were substituted for the visual ones. Dissociations of apparent movement and apparent displacement are also characteristics of the oculogyral illusion (GRAYBIEL et al., 1946) and of the illusory motion of the forearm evoked by muscle vibration (McCLOSKEY, 1975).

LACKNER and LEVINE (1978) have found that illusory movement induced by muscle vibration is sometimes accompanied by nystagmoid movements of the subject's eyes. The slow phase of the nystagmus is often compensatory, i.e., in the direction opposite the experienced body motion. Vertical nystagmus is occasionally elicited when the subject's apparent motion is fore-aft or up-down, and horizontal nystagmus can appear during experienced rotary motion. A representative nystagmus record is presented in Fig. 13. After vibration is stopped, an after-nystagmus will persist many seconds if the subject is kept in darkness; the after-nystagmus has the same sign as the primary nystagmus, although the subject will experience a postural motion aftereffect of opposite sign. Vibration of neck muscles controlling the roll position of the head can evoke illusory head tilt and rotary nystagmoid movements of the eyes.

The threshold for evoking apparent body motion by vibration is lower than that for eliciting nystagmus; subjects generally have to experience decided self-

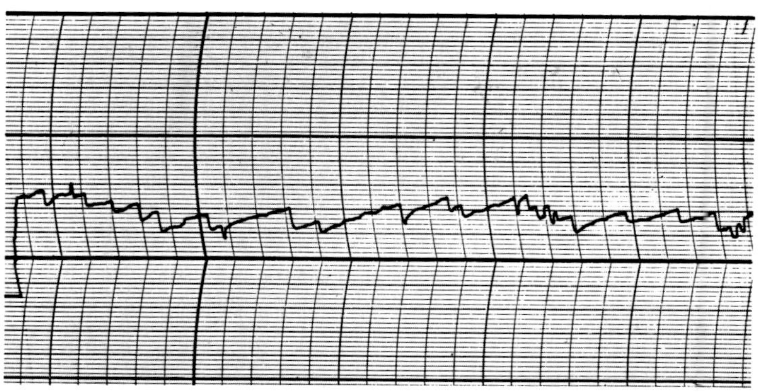

Fig. 13. Nystagmoid eye movements of subject experiencing illusory leftward rotation induced by vibration (120 pulses/s) of the right gluteus minimus. Subject's eyes are moving in compensatory fashion, slow phase rightward, fast phase leftward. Calibration: Each small division = 1°; up = rightward deviation of eyes; chart speed = 6 mm/s = 1 horizontal division. (From LACKNER and LEVINE, 1978)

motion before nystagmus appears (LACKNER and LEVINE, 1978); such a difference in thresholds is also found when the body is actually exposed to angular or linear acceleration (GRAYBIEL and BARTLEY, 1948; GRAYBIEL and PATTERSON, 1954; VAN DISHOECK et al., 1954). Not all subjects exhibit strong tonic vibration reflexes nor is it possible in all subjects who do exhibit such reflexes to induce illusory self-movement.

V. Basis for Muscle-Spindle Feedback Illusions

The existence of muscle-spindle feedback illusions of movement emphasizes the complexity of the sensory factors that can influence spatial orientation. When the sensory input from other modalities is constant and consistent with the body being either stationary or moving at constant velocity, a level of muscle afferent activity that is normally associated with actual movement of the body can be interpreted as movement of the stationary body. Associated with this apparent body motion is apparent movement of a stationary visual target and, if no target is present, nystagmoid movements of the eyes. Such a pattern of changes in apparent posture and sensory localization, although evoked by different sensory mechanisms, is virtually identical to that of the oculogyral illusion described by GRAYBIEL and HUPP (1946).

I. Sensory-Motor Performance During Parabolic and Space Flight

Ordinarily, there is a concordance or synergy among the visual, vestibular, proprioceptive, kinesthetic, and somatosensory cues specifying body orientation. However, in the unusual gravitational conditions encountered during space flight, this normal relationship is altered; and, as a consequence, changes in eye-hand coordination, apparent body orientation, and visual localization result.

I. Eye-Hand Coordination During Aerospace Flight

Most studies of visuomotor coordination in weightlessness have been conducted during the short periods, 10–30 s, of zero-g that alternate with periods of supra-g when an aircraft flies a Keplerian trajectory (HABER and HABER,

1950). In the earliest of these studies (BALLINGER, 1952), little disruption of performance was found during the 20-s periods of weightlessness that were achieved. Later, VON BECKH (1954) measured the accuracy of visuomotor coordination in both humans and snapping turtles (*Hydromedusa tectifera*) during parabolic flight. This particular species of turtle normally shows great accuracy in snapping at bait; however, during zero-g the animals had difficulty in orienting and controlling their strike, although they slowly retained their accuracy over the course of about 30 zero-g flights. A L-D turtle that had been included with the other turtles was not affected by variations in g-load. VON BECKH's human subjects were required to point in various predetermined patterns; they were reasonably accurate when their eyes were open and visual feedback about response accuracy was permitted, but with eyes closed they tended to deviate upwards when pointing. Performance improved after the subjects repeated the task over the course of several flights.

GERATHEWOHL et al. (1957), extending some earlier experiments of GERATHEWOHL (1954), studied the accuracy with which subjects could point to a bull's-eye pattern during different levels of g-loading. At zero-g subjects consistently pointed too high, at 3 g they pointed too low, striking the pattern below the bull's eye. After six or seven exposures to the task, the subjects returned to normal accuracy under zero-g; however, they failed to show any improvement under the 3-g condition, even with continued practice, despite the fact that, as in the zero-g condition, they had visual feedback about their response accuracy.

In two related experiments, WHITESIDE (1960, 1961) investigated tonus changes in postural muscles and changes in eye-hand coordination during parabolic flight maneuvers. During zero-g, the balance of activity in antigravity muscles was disturbed yielding inaccuracies on pointing tasks. The ankle jerk was absent for the first 100 ms of weightlessness; WHITESIDE attributes its later restoration to a reestablishment of muscle tone by suprasegmental, rather than spinal, reflexes. WHITESIDE's pointing experiments, unlike those of earlier investigators, had the advantage that the subjects marked the virtual image of a visual target while being denied sight of the hand. During zero-g, his subjects pointed too low; when exposed to 2 g they pointed too high. The directions of these shifts are opposite to those observed in the experiments of VON BECKH (1954), GERATHEWOHL (1954), and GERATHEWOHL et al. (1957); raising the possibility that the subjects of the latter studies were consciously attempting to correct their pointing responses to the targets.

WHITESIDE, like GERATHEWOHL and STALLINGS (1958), found that during the transition from 1 g to zero-g, the apparent position of a stationary visual target appears to move upward. WHITESIDE felt that his subjects were actually pointing accurately at the *apparent* position of the visual target during the periods of zero- and 2 g. No improvement in pointing accuracy occurred over successive trials in WHITESIDE's experiment — this lack of improvement is related undoubtedly to the absence of available visual feedback about pointing accuracy.

The relatively minor errors in sensory-motor coordination found in these early studies suggested that subjects permitted visual feedback should be able to perform visuomotor tasks adequately during prolonged exposure to weightlessness. This assumption was borne out by the performance of astronauts in Gemini Flights V and VII (GRAYBIEL et al., 1967), and in the four Skylab missions (GRAYBIEL et al., 1975; MILLER and GRAYBIEL, 1973).

II. Perception of Body Orientation During Aerospace Flight

GRAYBIEL (1966) has described an unusual postural illusion experienced by Russian cosmonauts during an orbital flight. When their eyes were closed, the cosmonauts felt upside down within their space capsule. They could attenuate or abolish this illusion by pushing themselves firmly against their chairs or by opening their eyes. Several cosmonauts in a later flight experienced the same illusion, but for them the illusion developed slowly during the course of the mission and persisted whether their eyes were open or closed. In both flights the illusion ceased during re-entry.

GRAYBIEL and KELLOGG (1967) utilized the zero-g phase of parabolic flight to study the factors which give rise to this illusion—named by them the *inversion illusion*. A comparison of the performances of normal and L-D subjects who were 1) free floating, 2) encased in a fiberglass mold oriented at various angles in relation to the aircraft cabin, and 3) "standing" on the cabin ceiling, showed that the L-D subjects never experienced the inversion illusion, whereas several normal subjects experienced the illusion under every experimental condition. GRAYBIEL and KELLOGG concluded that the inversion illusion likely depends on decreases in otolith activity, a conclusion supported as well by the observations of MILLER et al. (1965) on ocular counterrolling during zero- and 0.5 g.

It seems likely that other animals also experience the inversion illusion. OOSTERVELD and GREVEN (1975), studying the flight behavior of pigeons during the zero-g phase of parabolic flight, found that normal pigeons permitted free vision would take to flight as the g-load approached 0.06 g and would then fly upside down during zero-g. They attribute this flight pattern to the animals experiencing postural illusions like those experienced by man under comparable conditions. Alterations in the swimming patterns of fish have also been observed during exposure to reduced or absent g-loads (VON BAUMGARTEN et al., 1971; VON BAUMGARTEN et al., 1975) and have similarly been related to changes in apparent orientation.

III. Changes in Visual Localization During Parabolic Flight

The apparent positions of afterimages and external visual targets change during the magnitude variations in force produced by parabolic flight. During the increased-g phase, an afterimage projected against a contourless background

Vertical displacement of real target, visual after-image, or VAI, superimposed on RT during change in magnitude but not in direction of gravitational-inertial force

Investigator	Experimental vehicle	>1.0 G			<1.0 G			Zero-G		
		RT	VAI	RT and VAI	RT	VAI	RT and VAI	RT	VAI	RT and VAI
CLARK et al.	Aircraft	↑								
GERATHEWOHL AND STALLINGS	AIRCRAFT		↓						↑	
SCHOCK	Aircraft	↓			↓			Osc.[1]		
WHITESIDE	Elevator									
	Centrifuge	↑								
	Aircraft	↑	↓	↑	↓			↓		
NIVEN et al.	Elevator		↓	↑		↑	↓			
Present experiment	Aircraft	↑	↓	↑	↓	↑	↓	↓	↑	↓

[1] Small up-down oscillations.

Fig. 14. Illusory visual motion experienced during magnitude changes in gravitoinertial force. (From ROMAN et al., 1963)

will appear to move downward; during zero-g the afterimage will appear to move upward (GERATHEWOHL and STALLINGS, 1959). Under comparable observation conditions, WHITESIDE (1961) found that afterimages changed position in the fashion just described and that external visual targets underwent the opposite pattern of apparent displacement.

ROMAN et al. (1963) extended these observations by studying the apparent movement of a real target and an afterimage both separately and simultaneously during variations in g-loading. An external visual target appeared to move downward during zero-g, whereas an afterimage seemed to move upward regardless of whether the observer's eyes were open or closed (see Fig. 14). The displacement of the afterimage under these conditions is likely related to the upward deviation of the eyes that occurs on transition to zero-g (cf. SHILLINGER et al., 1973; VON BAUMGARTEN et al., 1975). However, when a real target and an afterimage were overlapped, the two moved together and remained overlapped during variations in g-load – the conjoint movement was always that characteristic of the real target in isolation. ROMAN et al. (1963) found that the external target and the afterimage appeared to move in opposite directions if the real target was not being fixated; the reason for these differences remains unknown. WARREN et al. (1963) proved that angular accelerations are not involved in the genesis of these illusions.

These experiments indicate that illusory visual movement can be evoked by magnitude changes in the gravitoinertial force vector. WHITESIDE (1961), who noticed comparable changes in visual direction during rapid force changes in an elevator, has suggested the term *elevator illusion* for these phenomena. The elevator illusion, the autokinetic effect, and the oculogyral and oculogravic illusions have been subsumed within a common explanatory framework based on interacting patterns of reflex and voluntary activation of the extraocular muscles and their central consequences by WHITESIDE et al. (1965). Strong support for their theory has recently been provided by VON BAUMGARTEN et al. (1975) and SHILLINGER et al. (1973), who found that in the absence of a visual fixation target a subject's eyes will deviate during variations in g-load. During exposure to increased-g levels, the eyes move downward, whereas during transition into weightlessness, they move upward. It should be noted that these changes are compensatory in terms of the subject's apparent posture in these situations, i.e., they are field-holding reflexes (WALLS, 1962).

IV. Otolith Activity in Zero-g

Exposure to subgravity conditions evokes a variety of correlated postural and visual changes that are associated with errors in visuomotor coordination; these changes are related in part to reductions in otolith activity that occur on transition into sub-gravity states. Subjects permitted visual feedback can adapt rapidly to the unusual force environment and their eye-hand coordination will rapidly return to normal. This form of adaptation is probably similar or identical to that which occurs when the visual array is displaced by means of prism spectacles (LACKNER, 1976a). It should be noted that in zero-g the otoliths are not "functionally de-afferented" because they will still respond to the forces generated when head movements are made with respect to the aircraft or space vehicle.

J. Discussion

The theme of a bidirectional relationship between postural and sensory mechanisms unites the varied experimental paradigms and observations that have been described. Many of the experiments highlighted the influence of postural information on sensory localization. For example, during tilt of the body axis in the dark, it was found that subjects soon come to underestimate their tilt and to mislocalize auditory and visual targets by a comparable amount; similarly, during rotation about the vertical body axis in the dark, subjects experience postural illusions that are accompanied by changes in visual and auditory localization, the oculogyral and audiogyral illusions. Subjects on a centrifuge exposed to a change in the gravitoinertial force vector experience body tilt and show related changes in visual and auditory localization, the oculogravic and audiogravic illusions; moreover, when such subjects turn their heads about an axis that is not parallel to the axis of rotation, they will feel their heads move through a different path and see the visual world move in a direction determined by their experienced head motion, the Coriolis oculogyral illusion.

In all of these situations, abnormal registration or interpretation of head and trunk posture is paralleled by errors in visual and auditory localization of comparable magnitude and time course. It is notable that, except in the case of the Coriolis oculogyral illusion—in which a massive conflicting stimulation of the semicircular canals and otolith organs is involved—the presence of a fully illuminated and patterned environment will prevent or attenuate errors in the interpretation of posture and accordingly in visual and auditory localization as well. In this context, it should be recalled that visual information can override vestibular, somatosensory, and proprioceptive information in other situations as well. For example, during exposure to whole-field optokinetic stimulation, stationary subjects will experience themselves as moving (MACH, 1897); and similarly, during exposure to a stepwise deviation (or reversal of the visual field, subjects often experience changes in apparent head posture (LACKNER, 1974b).

These postural-sensory and sensory-postural interactions reflect aspects of the mechanisms responsible for the maintenance of auditory and visual direction constancy. As has been emphasized, ordinarily when a subject moves voluntarily in relation to stationary visual or auditory stimuli, he experiences himself as moving and the stimulus objects as stationary. Consequently, his nervous system must be taking into account the amount of change in activity from his peripheral sense organs that would be expected on the basis of his intended movement (HELMHOLTZ, 1866; MACH, 1897; VON HOLST and MITTELSTAEDT, 1950; SPERRY, 1950; TEUBER, 1960). If such an analysis were not occurring, the subject would be unable to distinguish between changes in sensory stimulation resulting from his own movement and from movement of the stimulus field.

Accordingly, one aspect of maintaining constancy of visual and auditory direction involves the concurrent monitoring both of afferent messages about ongoing body orientation from the vestibular, visual, and proprioceptive systems and efferent messages about intended and ongoing movements, and relating them to incoming sensory stimulation from auditory, visual, and somatosensory sources. Within this framework it can be seen that when an error occurs in the registration of body posture, the error is interpreted as a physical movement of the organism. Accordingly, compensation is made with respect to incoming auditory and visual signals for the amount of change in sensory stimulation that would have resulted if the body were in fact moving; as a consequence, the apparent loci of stationary visual and auditory stimulus objects change.

When the entire visual or auditory environment moves in relation to the stationary observer, this displacement is often interpreted as movement of the organism in relation to a stationary world, because normally—unless being transported in a vehicle of some kind, a situation in which additional sensory and cognitive cues are generally available to reveal the true state of affairs—the only circumstance in which the entire environment moves relative to the observer is when he himself is moving. It is for this reason that sensations of self-rotation and nystagmus can be elicited in a stationary blindfolded subject when an auditory or tactile stimulus is revolved about him.

The adaptive changes that attenuate or eliminate the Coriolis oculogyral illusion and those that compensate for visual rearrangement are also dependent on the functioning of these same spatial constancy mechanisms. Compensatory modifications occur when there is a discordance between the messages provided by different sensory sources (e.g., vision and proprioception, vestibular sensation and proprioception) about moment-to-moment body orientation (see also Harris, 1965; Rock, 1966; Wallach, 1968; Lackner, 1973d, 1974c, 1975b; Mather and Lackner, 1975, 1977). The discordant-sensory inputs trigger a central compensation that involves modifications in the representation of ongoing posture; these reinterpretations of apparent posture lead to changes in visual and auditory localization that eliminate the sensory conflict which initiated the process. The entire sequence is facilitated if exposure is introduced incrementally (Graybiel, 1969, 1971; Lackner and Lobovits, 1978).

Sensory influences on apparent posture and postural influences on sensory localization hence reflect a complex interaction of efferent, vestibular, and proprioceptive information about body orientation with exteroceptive information from the eyes and ears and skin, an interaction that is essential to preserve the long term stability and spatial integrity of the organism's perceptual world.

References

Arnoult, M.D.: Localization of sound during rotation of the visual environment. Amer. J. Psychol. **65**, 48–58 (1952).

Aubert, H.: Eine scheinbare bedeutende Drehung von Objekten bei Neigung des Kopfes nach rechts oder links. Virchows Arch. path. Anat. **20**, 381–393 (1861).

Ballinger, E.R.: Human experiments in subgravity and prolonged acceleration. J. Aviat. Med. **23**, 319–321 (1952).

Bauermeister, M.: Effect of body tilt on apparent verticality, apparent body position, and their relation. J. exp. Psychol. **67**No. 2, 142–147 (1964).

Bauermeister, M., Werner, H., Wapner, S.: The effect of body tilt on tactual-kinesthetic perception of verticality. Amer. J. Psychol. **77**, 451–456 (1964).

Baumgarten, R.J. von, Baldrighi, G., Shillinger, G.L. Jr.: Vestibular function of fish during diminished G-force and weightlessness. Aerosp. Med. **43**, 626–632 (1972).

Baumgarten, R.J. von, Baldrighi, G., Shillinger, G.L.Jr., Harth, O., Thuemler, R.: Vestibular function in the space environment. Acta Astronaut. **2**, 49–58 (1975).

Beckh, H.J.A. von: Experiments with animals and human subjects under sub- and zero-gravity conditions during the dive and parabolic flight. Aviat. Med. **25**, 235–241 (1954).

Berthoz, A., Pavard, B., Young, L.R.: Perception of linear horizontal self-motion induced by peripheral vision (linear vection). Basic characteristics and visual-vestibular interactions. Exp. Brain Res. **23**, 471–489 (1975).

Bourdon, B.: Sur le rôle de la tête dans la perception de l'espace. Rev. Philos. **61**, 526–529 (1906).

Brandt, T., Dichgans, J., Büchele, W.: Motion habituation: Inverted selfmotion perception and optokinetic afternystagmus. Exp. Brain Res. **21**, 337–352 (1974).

Brandt, T., Dichgans, J., Koenig, E.: Differential effects of central versus peripheral vision on egocentric and exocentric motion perception. Exp. Brain Res. **16**, 476–491 (1973).

Carr, H.A.: An introduction to space perception. New York: Longmans, Green, 1935.

Clark, B., Graybiel, A.: The effect of angular acceleration on sound localization: The audiogyral illusion. J. Psychol. **28**, 235–244 (1949a).
Clark, B., Graybiel, A.: Apparent rotation of a fixed target associated with linear acceleration in flight. Amer. J. Ophthal. **32**, 549–557 (1949b).
Clark, B., Graybiel, A.: Visual perception of the horizontal following exposure to radial acceleration on a centrifuge. J. comp. physiol. Psychol. **44**, 525–534 (1951).
Clark, B., Graybiel, A.: Contributing factors in the perception of the oculogravic illusion. Amer. J. Psychol. **76**, 18–27 (1963).
Clark, B., Graybiel, A.: Factors contributing to the delay in the perception of the oculogravic illusion. Amer. J. Psychol. **79**, 377–388 (1966a).
Clark, B., Graybiel, A.: Perception of the visual horizontal in normal and labyrinthine-defective subjects during prolonged rotation. Amer. J. Psychol. **79**, 608–612 (1966b).
Clark, B., Graybiel, A.: Egocentric localization of the visual horizontal in normal and labyrinthine-defective observers as a function of head and body tilt. Percept. and Psychophys. **2**, 609–611 (1967).
Clark, B., Graybiel, A.: Influence of contact cues on the perception of the oculogravic illusion. Acta oto-laryng. (Stockh.) **65**, 373–380 (1968).
Cogan, D.G.: Neurology of the ocular muscles. 2nd Edition. Springfield, Ill.: Chas. C. Thomas, 1956.
Day, R.J., Wade, N.J.: Visual spatial after-effect from prolonged head-tilt. Science, **154**, 1201–1202 (1966).
deVries, H.: The mechanics of labyrinth otoliths. Acta oto-laryng. (Stockh.) **38**, 262–273 (1950).
Dichgans, J., Brandt, T.: Visual-vestibular interaction and motion perception. In: Cerebral control of eye movements and motion perception. Basel: S. Karger, 1972.
Dichgans, J., Brandt, T.: Optokinetic motion sickness and pseudo-coriolis effects induced by moving visual stimuli. Acta oto-laryng. (Stockh.) **76**, 339–348 (1973).
Dichgans, J., Held, R., Young, L.R., Brandt, T.: Moving visual scenes influence the apparent direction of gravity. Science **178**, 1217–1219 (1972).
Dichgans, J., Schmidt, C.L., Graf, W.: Visual input improves the speedometer function of the vestibular nuclei in the goldfish. Exp. Brain Res. **18**, 319–322 (1973).
Dodge, R.: Thresholds of rotation. J. exp. Psychol. **6**, 107–137 (1923).
Dolezal, H.: Long term perceptual and performatory adaptation to wearing up-down reversing prisms in the real world. Unpublished monograph, Cornell University, 1971.
Ebenholtz, S.M.: Adaptation to a rotated visual field as a function of degree of optical tilt and exposure time. J. exp. Psychol. **72**, 629–634 (1966).
Ek, J., Jongkees, L.B.W., Klijn, J.: On the effect of continuous acceleration. Acta oto-laryng. (Stockh). **51**, 416–419 (1960).
Eklund, G.: Influence of muscle vibration on balance in man. Acta Soc. Med. Upsalien **74**, 113–117 (1969).
Eklund, G.: General features of vibration-induced effects on balance. Uppsala J. med. Sci. **77**, 112–124 (1972).
Eklund, G.: Further studies of vibration-induced effects on balance. Uppsala J. med. Sci. **78**, 65–72 (1973).
Fischer, M.H., Kornmüller, A.E.: Optokinetisch ausgelöste Bewegungswahrnehmung und optokinetischer Nystagmus. J. Psychol. Neurol. (Lpz) **41**, 273–308 (1930).
Gemelli, A.: The effect of illusory perception of movement on sound localization. In: Essays in Psychology dedicated to David Katz. Uppsala: Almqvist and Wiksell, 1951.
Gerathewohl, S.: Comparative studies on animals and human subjects in the gravity-free state. J. Aviat. Med. **25**, 412–417 (1954).
Gerathewohl, S., Stallings, H.D.: A study of the oculogravic illusion. J. Aviat. Med. **29**, 504–516 (1958).
Gerathewohl, S.J., Strughold, H., Stallings, H.D.: Sensori-motor performance during weightlessness: Eye-hand coordination. J. Aviat. Med. **28**, 7–12 (1957).
Goodwin, G.M.: Personal Communication. February 6, 1973.
Goodwin, G.M., McCloskey, D.I., Matthews, P.B.C.: Proprioceptive illusions induced by muscle vibration: Contribution to perception by muscle spindles? Science, N.Y. **175**, 1382–1384 (1972a).

Goodwin, G.M., McCloskey, D.I., Matthews, P.B.C.: The contribution of muscle afferents to kinesthesia shown by vibration-induced illusions of movement and by the effects of paralyzing joint afferents. Brain **95**, 705–748 (1972b).

Granit, R.: Constant errors in the execution and appreciation of movement. Brain **95**, 649–660 (1972).

Graybiel, A.: The oculogravic illusion. Arch. Ophthal. **48**, 605–615 (1952).

Graybiel, A.: Vestibular sickness and some of its implications for space flight. In: Neurological aspects of auditory and vestibular disorders. Springfield, Ill.: Charles C. Thomas, 1964.

Graybiel, A.: Functional disturbances of vestibular origin of significance in space flight. In: Second International Symposium on Man in Space, Paris 1965, Proceedings. Vienna and New York: Springer Verlag, 1967, pp. 8–32.

Graybiel, A.: Vestibular problems in relation to space travel. In: The vestibular system and its disorders. Philadelphia: University of Pennsylvania Press, 1966 (443–458).

Graybiel, A.: Structural elements in the concept of motion sickness. Aerosp. Med. **40**, 351–367 (1969).

Graybiel, A.: Prevention of reflex vestibular disturbances and motion sickness by natural means and by drugs. Proc. of the 21st International Astronautical Congress. Amsterdam: North Holland, 1971, pp. 328–348.

Graybiel, A.: Otolith function and human performance. Adv. Otorhinolaryngol. **20**, 485–519 (1973).

Graybiel, A., Brown, R.H.: The delay in visual reorientation following exposure to a change in direction of resultant force on a human centrifuge. J. genet. Psychol. **45**, 143–150 (1951).

Graybiel, A., Clark, B.: The validity of the oculogravic illusion as a specific indicator of otolith function. Aerosp. Med. **36**, 1173–1181 (1965).

Graybiel, A., Clark, B., MacCorquodale, K., Hupp, D.I.: Role of vestibular nystagmus in the visual perception of a moving target in the dark. Am. J. Psychol. **59**, 259–266 (1946).

Graybiel, A., Clark, B., Zarriello, J.J.: Observations on human subjects living in a "slow rotation room" for periods of two days. AMA Arch. Neurol. **3**, 55–73 (1960).

Graybiel, A., Deane, F.R., Colehour, J.K.: Prevention of overt motion sickness by incremental exposure to otherwise highly stressful coriolis accelerations. Aerosp. Med. **40**, 142–148 (1969).

Graybiel, A., Guedry, F., Johnson, W., Kennedy, R.S.: Adaptation to bizarre stimulation of the semicircular canals as indicated by the oculogyral illusion. Aerosp. Med. **32**, 321–327 (1961).

Graybiel, A., Hupp, D.I.: The oculo-gyral illusion: a form of apparent motion which may be observed following stimulation of the semicircular canals. J. Aviat. Med. **17**, 3–27 (1946).

Graybiel, A., Johnson, W.: A comparison of the symptomatology experienced by healthy persons and subjects with loss of labyrinthine function when exposed to unusual patterns of centripetal force in a counter-rotating room. Ann. Otol. Rhinol. Laryngol. **72**, 357–374 (1963).

Graybiel, A., Kellogg, R.S.: Inversion illusion in parabolic flight: Its probable dependence on otolith function. Aerosp. Med. **38**, 1099–1103 (1967).

Graybiel, A., Kerr, W.A., Bartley, S.H.: Stimulus thresholds of the semicircular canals as a function of angular acceleration. Am. J. Psychol. **61**, 21–36 (1948).

Graybiel, A., Miller, E.F. II, Billingham, J., Waite, R., Berry, C.A., Deitlein, L.F.: Vestibular experiments in Gemini flights V and VII. Aerosp. Med. **38**, 360–370 (1967).

Graybiel, A., Miller, E.F. II, Homick, J.L.: Individual differences in susceptibility to motion sickness among six Skylab astronauts. Acta Astronaut. **2**, 155–174 (1975).

Graybiel, A., Miller, E.F. II, Newson, B.D., Kennedy, R.S.: The effect of water immersion on perception of the oculogravic illusion in normal and labyrinthine-defective subjects. Acta oto-laryng. (Stockh.) **65**, 599–610 (1968).

Graybiel, A., Niven, J.I.: The effect of a change in direction of resultant force on sound localization: the audiogravic illusion. J. exp. Psychol. **42**, 227–230 (1951).

Graybiel, A., Patterson, J.L.: Thresholds of stimulation of the otolith organs as indicated by the oculogravic illusion. J. appl. Physiol. **7**, 666–670 (1955).

Graybiel, A., Wood, C.D.: Rapid vestibular adaptation in a rotating environment by means of controlled head movements. Aerosp. Med. **40**, 638–643 (1969).

Groen, J.J.: The problems of the spinning top applied to the semi-circular canals. Confin. neurol. (Basel) **21**, 454–455 (1961).

Groen, J.J.: Central regulation of vestibular function. In: Recent advances in aerospace medicine. Dordrecht-Holland: D. Reidel, 1970.

Guedry, F.E., Graybiel, A.: Compensatory nystagmus conditioned during adaptation to living in a rotating room. J. appl. Physiol. **17**, 398–404 (1962).

Guedry, F.E., Graybiel, A., Collins, W.E.: Reduction of nystagmus and disorientation in human subjects. Aerosp. Med. **33**, 1356–1360 (1962).

Gurnee, H.: The effect of a visual stimulus upon the perception of bodily motion. Amer. J. Psychol. **43**, 26–48 (1931).

Gurnee, H.: Thresholds of vertical movement of the body. J. exp. Psychol. **17**, 270–285 (1934).

Haber, F., Haber, H.: Possible methods of producing the gravity-free state for medical research. J. Aviat. Med. **21**, 395–400 (1950).

Hagbarth, K.E., Eklund, G.: Motor effects of vibratory muscle stimuli in man. In: Muscular afferents and motor control. Stockholm: Almqvist and Wiksell, 1966.

Hagbarth, K.E., Eklund, G.: The effects of muscle vibration in spasticity, rigidity, and cerebellar disorders. J. Neurol. Neurosurg. Psychiat. **31**, 207–213 (1968).

Hallpike, C.S., Hood, J.D.: The speed of the slow component of ocular nystagmus induced by angular acceleration of the head; its experimental determination and application to the physical theory of the cupular mechanism. Proc. roy. Soc., B **141**, 216–230 (1953).

Harris, C.S.: Perceptual adaptation to inverted, reversed, and displaced vision. Psychol. Rev. **72**, 419–444 (1965).

Hay, J.: Visual adaptation to an altered correlation between eye movement and head movement. Science **160**, 429–430 (1968).

Held, R.: Exposure history as a factor in maintaining stability of perception and coordination. J. nerv. ment. Dis. **132**, 26–32 (1961).

Held, R., Dichgans, J., Bauer, J.: Characteristics of moving visual scenes influencing spatial orientation. Vision Res. **15**, 357–365 (1975).

Helmholtz, H. von: Handbuch der Physiologischen Optik. Leipzig: Voss, 1866.

Henn, V., Young, L.R., Finley, C.: Vestibular nucleus units in alert monkeys are also influenced by moving visual scenes. Brain Res. **71**, 144–149 (1974).

Holst, E. von, Mittelstaedt, H.: Das Reafferenzprinzip. Naturwissenschaften **37**, 464–476 (1950).

Howard, I.P., Templeton, W.B.: Human spatial orientation. New York: Wiley, 1966.

James, W.: The sense of dizziness in deaf-mutes. Amer. J. Otol. **4**, 239–254 (1882).

Kleint, H.: Versuche über die Wahrnehmung. Z. Psychol. **140**, 109–138 (1937).

Klinke, R., Schmidt, C.L.: Efferent influence on the vestibular organ during active movements of the body. Pflüger's Arch. **318**, 325–332 (1970).

Kohler, I.: The formation and transformation of the visual world. Psychology Iss. **3**. [First published as Über Aufbau und Wandlungen der Wahrnehmungswelt, S.B. Öst. Akad. Wiss. Wien, math.-nat. Kl. **227**, 1–118 (1951).]

Lackner, J.R.: Influence of posture on the spatial localization of sounds. Ph.D. Thesis, Mass. Inst. Tech. (1970).

Lackner, J.R.: The role of posture in sound localization. Quart J. exp. Psychol. **26**, 235–251 (1973a).

Lackner, J.R.: The role of posture in adaptation to visual rearrangement. Neuropsychologia **11**, 33–44 (1973b).

Lackner, J.R.: Visual rearrangement affects auditory localization. Neuropsychologia **11**, 29–32 (1973c).

Lackner, J.R.: A device for investigating adaptation to visual rearrangement. J. Psychol. **85**, 137–141 (1973d).

Lackner, J.R.: Changes in auditory localization during body tilt. Acta oto-laryng. (Stockh.) **77**, 19–29 (1974a).

Lackner, J.R.: Influence of visual rearrangement and visual motion on sound localization. Neuropsychologia **12**, 291–293 (1974b).

Lackner, J.R.: Adaptation to displaced vision: role of proprioception. Percept. and mot. Skills **38**, 1251–1256 (1974c).

Lackner, J.R.: Pursuit eye movements elicited by muscle afferent information. Neurosci. Letters **1**, 25–28 (1975).

Lackner, J.R.: Influence of abnormal postural and sensory conditions on human sensory motor performance. Environ. Biol. and Med. **2**, 139–177 (1976).

Lackner, J.R.: Changes in visual localization during body tilt. Forthcoming (1976b).

Lackner, J.R.: Induction of nystagmus in stationary subjects with a rotating sound field. Avia. Space and environ. Med. **48**, 129–131 (1977).

Lackner, J.R., Graybiel, A.: Elicitation of vestibular side effects by regional vibration of the head. Aerosp. Med. **45–(11)**, 1267–1272 (1974).

Lackner, J.R., Levine, M.: Changes in apparent body orientation and sensory localization induced by vibration of postural muscles: The propriogyral illusion. Aviat. Space and Environ. Med. In press (1978).

Lackner, J.R., Lobovits, D.: Incremental exposure facilitates adaptation to visual rearrangement. Aviat. Space and Environ. Med. **49** (2), 362–364 (1978).

Lackner, J.R., Teixeira, R.: Visual-vestibular interaction: vestibular stimulation suppresses the visual induction of illusory self-rotation. Avia. Space and Environ. Med. **48**, 248–253 (1977)

Lackner, J.R., Zabkar, J.: A proprioceptive contribution to oculomotor stability. Vision Res. **17**, 1225–1229 (1977).

•Lee, D., Aronson, E.: Visual proprioceptive control of standing in human infants. Percept. and Psychophys. **15**, 529–532 (1974).

•Lishman, J.R., Lee, D.N.: The autonomy of visual kinesthesis. Perception **2**, 287–294 (1973).

Mach, E.: Beiträge zur Analyse der Empfindungen, 1. Jena: Fischer, 1886. [English translation, The analysis of sensations. New York: Dover, 1958].

Mach, E.: Contributions to the analysis of the sensations. Trans. C.M. Williams, Chicago: Open Court Publishing, 1897.

Marsden, C.D., Meadows, J.C., Hodgson, H.J.F.: Observations on the reflex response to muscle vibration in man and its voluntary control. Brain **92**, 829–846 (1969).

Mather, J., Lackner, J.R.: Adaptation to visual rearrangement elicited by tonic vibration reflexes. Exp. Brain Res. **24**, 103–105 (1975).

Mather, J., Lackner, J.R.: Adaptation to visual rearrangement: role of sensory discordance. Quart. J. exp. Psychol. **29**, 237–244 (1977)

Matthews, P.B.C.: Mammalian muscle receptors and their central actions. London: Arnold, 1972.

McCloskey, D.I.: Differences between the senses of movement and position shown by the effects of loading and vibration of muscles in man. Brain Res. **61**, 119–131 (1973).

McFarland, J.H., Clarkson, F.: Perception of orientation: adaptation to lateral body tilt. Am. J. Psychol. **79**, 265–271 (1966).

Meda, E.: A research on the threshold for the coriolis and Purkinje phenomena of excitation of the semicircular canals. Arch. Fisiol. **52**, 116–134 (1952).

Melvill Jones, G., Gonshor, A.: Extreme vestibular habituation to long-term reversal of vision during natural head movements. Proc. Aerosp. Med. Assoc. Ann. Sci. Mtg. Bal Harbour, p. 22 (1972).

Merton, P.A.: Speculations on the servo-control of movement. In: The spinal cord. London: Churchill, 1953.

Merton, P.A.: Human position sense and sense of effort. Symp. Soc. exp. Biol. **18**, 387–400 (1964).

Merton, P.A.: The sense of effort. In: Breathing: Hering-Brewer centenary symposium. London: Churchill, 1970.

Miller, E.F. Jr., Fregly, A.R., Graybiel, A.: Visual horizontal perception in relation to otolith function. Naval Aerosp. Med. Inst., Pensacola NAMI-989 (1966).

Miller, E.F. II, Graybiel, A.: Role of the otolith organs in the perception of horizontality. Am. J. Psychol. **79**, 24–37 (1966).

Miller, E.F. II, Graybiel, A.: Experiment M-131: human vestibular function. Aerosp. Med. **44**, 593–608 (1973).

Miller, E.F. II, Graybiel, A., Kellog, R.S.: Otolith organ activity within earth standard, one-half standard and zero gravity environment. Aerosp. Med. **37**, 399–403 (1965).

Morant, R.B., Beller, H.K.: Adaptation to prismatically rotated visual fields. Science **148**, 530–531 (1965).

Mountcastle, V.B.: Neural mechanisms in somesthesia. In: Medical physiology, 13th Ed. I. St. Louis: C.V. Mosby, 1974.

Müller, G.E.: Über das Aubertsche Phänomen. Z. Sinnensphysiol. **49**, 109–244 (1916).

Nelson, J.G.: Effect of water immersion and body position upon perception of the gravitational vertical. Aerosp. Med. **39**, 806–811 (1968).

Nielsen, T.I.: Volition: a new experimental approach. Scand. J. Psychol. **4**, 225–230 (1963).
Oosterveld, W.J., Graybiel, A., Cramer, D.B.: Influence of vision on susceptibility to acute motion sickness studied under quantifiable stimulus-response conditions. Aerosp. Med. **43**, 1005–1007 (1972).
Oosterveld, W.J., Greven, A.J.: Flight behavior of pigeons during weightlessness. Acta oto-laryng. (Stockh.) **79**, 233–241 (1975).
Rock, I.: The nature of perceptual adaptation. New York: Basic Books, 1966.
Roman, J.A., Warren, B.H., Niven, J.I., Graybiel, A.: Some observations on the behavior of a visual target and a visual afterimage during parabolic flight maneuvers. Aerosp. Med. **34**, 841–846 (1963).
Schneider, C.W., Bartley, S.H.: A study of the effects of mechanically induced tension of the neck muscles on the perception of verticality. J. Psychol. **54**, 245–248 (1962).
Shillinger, G.L. Jr., von Baumgarten, R.J., Baldrighi, G.: The gravity response, the rotation sensation, and other illusory sensations experienced in aircraft and space flight. Space Life Sci. **4**, 368–374 (1973).
Sperry, R.W.: Neural basis of the spontaneous optokinetic response induced by visual inversion. J. comp. physiol. Psychol. **43**, 482–489 (1950).
Stratton, G.M.: Upright vision and the retinal image. Psychol. Rev. **4**, 182–187 (1897a).
Stratton, G.M.: Vision without inversion of the retinal image. Psychol. Rev. **4**, 341–360, 363–481 (1897b).
Stratton, G.M.: Eye movements and visual direction. Psychol. Bull. **4**, 155–158 (1907).
Tastevin, J.: En partant de l'expérience d'Aristote. l'encephale **1**, 57–84, 140–158 (1937).
Teuber, H.-L.: Perception. In: Handbook of physiology, 3, Sec. 1, 1595–1668. Washington: Amer. Physiol. Soc., 1960.
Teuber, H.-L., Diamond, S.: Effects of brain injury in man on binaural localization of sounds. Paper read at EPA Mtg., Atlantic City, 1956.
Teuber, H.-L., Liebert, R.S.: Effects of body tilts on auditory localization (abstract). Amer. Psychol. **11**, 430 (1956).
Teixeira, R., Lackner, J.R.: Influence of apparent head position on optokinetic nystagmus and eye posture. Exp. Brain Res. **24**, 435–439 (1976).
Thurlow, W.R., Kerr, T.P.: Effect of a moving visual environment on localization of sound. Amer. J. Psychol. **83**, 112–118 (1970).
Urist, M.J.: Head tilt in vertical muscle paresis. Am. J. Ophthalmol. **69**, 3, 440–442 (1970).
Van Dishoeck, H.A.E., Spoor, A., Nijhoff, P.: The opto-gyral illusion and its relation to the nystagmus of the eyes. Acta oto-laryng. (Stockh.) **44**, 597–607 (1954).
Wade, N.J.: Visual orientation during and after lateral head, body, and trunk tilt. Percept. and Psychophys. **3**, 215–219 (1968).
Wade, N.J., Day, R.H.: Apparent head position as a basis for a visual after-effect of prolonged head tilt. Percept. and Psychophys. **3**, 324–326 (1968a).
Wade, N.J., Day, R.H.: Development and dissipation of a visual spatial after-effect from prolonged head tilt. J. exp. Psychol. **76**, 439–443 (1968b).
Wallach, H.: The role of head movements and vestibular and visual cues in sound localization. J. exp. Psychol. **27**, 339–368 (1940).
Wallach, H.: Informational discrepancy as a basis of perceptual adaptation. In: The neuropsychology of spatially oriented behavior, 209–229. Homewood, Ill.: Dorsey Press, 1968.
Wallach, H., Kravitz, J.: The measurement of the constancy of visual direction and of its adaptation. Psychon. Sci. **2**, 217–218 (1965a).
Wallach, H., Kravitz, J.: Rapid adaptation in the constancy of visual direction with active and passive rotation. Psychon. Sci. **3**, 165–166 (1965b).
Wallach, H., Kravitz, J.: Adaptation in the constancy of visual direction tested by measuring the constancy of auditory direction. Percept. and Psychophys. **4(5)**, 299–303 (1968).
Walls, G.L.: The evolutionary history of eye movements. Vision Res. **2**, 69–80 (1962).
Wapner, S., Werner, H., Chandler, K.A.: Experiments on sensory-tonic field theory of perception: I. Effect of extraneous stimulation on the visual perception of verticality. J. exp. Psychol. **42**, 341–343 (1951).

Warren, B.H., Roman, J.A., Graybiel, A.: Exclusion of angular accelerations as the principal cause of visual illusions during parabolic flight maneuvers. Joint Report No. SAM-TDR-63-78, USAF School of Aerospace Med. Brooks AF Base, Texas and USN school of Aviation Med, Pensacola, Fla. (1963).

Warren, H.C.: Sensations of rotation. Psychol. Rev. **2**, 273–276 (1895).

Whiteside, T.C.D.: Effect of weightlessness on some postural mechanisms. Aerosp. Med. **31**, 324–325 (1960).

Whiteside, T.C.D.: Hand-eye coordination in weightlessness. Aerosp. Med. **32**, 719–725 (1961).

Whiteside, T.C.D., Graybiel, A., Niven, J.I.: Visual illusions of movement. Brain **88**, 193–210 (1965).

Wood, R.W.: The "haunted swing" illusion. Psychol. Rev. **2**, 277–278 (1895).

Young, C.R., Dichgans, J., Murphy, R. Brandt, T.: Interaction of optokinetic and vestibular stimuli in motion perception. Acta oto-laryng. (Stockh.) **76**, 24–31 (1973).

D. The Problem of Pain

CHAPTER 27

Pain Perception in Man

E.R. HILGARD*, Stanford, Californien (USA)

With 10 Figures

Contents

* Preparation of this chapter has been aided by Grant MH-03859 from the National Institute of Mental Health.

Aversive states in man run the gamut from brief sensory pains produced by pricks, scratches, shocks, or blows associated with specific types of stimulation, to suffering caused by more severe or prolonged stimulation, or long-experienced pain from any source (identified or not). Finally, there is the very different suffering of mental anguish in which the sensory component of pain may be absent, but the person is distressed because of loss of self-esteem owing to disfigurement, social alienation, or other causes. Although these three kinds of aversive states are all in some respects perceptual, the usual conventions for defining a sensory modality relate it to specific sources of stimulation. Pain fits this set of conventions only in part, and its motivational-emotional connotations when it is described as anguish, distress, or suffering go beyond specific modality classification, and lead to some puzzling problems in the interpretation of the totality of aversive states.

Even when pain is correlated with specific sources of stimulation, its status as a separate modality is brought into question because of the association of pain with high intensity of stimulation in other modalities such as vision, audition, or thermal sensitivity. Because of its aversive properties, pain is always incompletely described as an information-processing system, even though it can be shown to be quantitatively correlated with measurable sources of stimulation. However, it is appropriate to begin the discussion of pain perception by treating it as a sensory modality subject to threshold determination and magnitude estimation like any other sense, leaving until later the complicating considerations.

A. Stimuli for Laboratory Pain

Any psychophysical study begins with specifying a stimulus that can be controlled and measured. Much ingenuity has been exercised in attempting to find the appropriate stimulus for the laboratory study of pain, one that will produce graduated pains without cutting, bruising, burning, or in other ways injuring the experimental subject. The following six sources of stimulation have been selected as representative.

I. Radiant Thermal Stimulation

To dissociate the pain response from touch, Hardy et al. (1952) developed a 'dolorimeter' for the study of pain thresholds. The investigator marks an area of the forehead with black India ink to assure constant heat absorption and radiation, and then directs radiant heat from a controlled source to this area. The subject reports when warmth is felt and then when pain is felt, providing in this way a threshold measure that can be expressed in physical units.

II. Electrical Shock

TURSKY and his collaborators (e.g., TURSKY, 1974) have improved on earlier methods in their investigation of pain responses evoked by electric shock applied through standardized electrodes, usually placed on the subject's forearm. The improvements over earlier methods lay in the following two steps: (1) developing a concentric shock electrode, with contact to the skin made through saline-soaked pads of cellulose sponge; (2) reducing the impedance of the electrode-skin circuit to a stable value of about 5000 ohms prior to stimulation by rubbing a small amount of conductive paste into the area about to be stimulated. Unless impedance is controlled, neither constant current nor constant voltage stimulation results in consistent sensory intensities.

III. Pressure Against Bone Surface

Some investigators wish to produce severe pains with a minimum of damage, and a number of devices have been used for placing pressure against bony surfaces, such as a football cleat against the shin bone (RYAN and KOVACIC, 1966), or a band tightened about the head to produce a headache (WOLFF, 1963; DUDLEY et al., 1965), or a wedge bearing upon the phalanx of a finger (FORGIONE and BARBER, 1971).

IV. Cold Water Stimulation ("Cold Pressor Test")

Placing a hand or foot in circulating ice water produces quite severe pain in less than a minute; the maximum is, in fact, reached in about a minute, and the effects after that are more complex because of numbing and other phasic changes in subjective response (WOLF and HARDY, 1941; KUNKLE, 1949). Because of these effects with longer times, the method is not very satisfactory for tolerance (pain endurance) measures; within the first minute, however, the rise in pain is very orderly and the method experimentally convenient.

V. Exercise and Ischemia: the Tourniquet Method

The tourniquet-exercise method has been used in the study of pain in two chief variants.

In the first of these variants, the arm is made ischemic by application of a tourniquet, and then exercise is carried out until no further contractions of the hand are possible. In addition to the time to termination, a record may be kept of the work accomplished through pumping of a liquid by squeezing a bulb as the exercise (instead of lifting a weight). The volume of liquid pumped can then be measured. The subject may report the time at which pain is first felt ("threshold time") and then continue until termination ("tolerance time") (LIBERMAN, 1964; MCGLASHAN et al., 1969).

Because of a preference for magnitude estimates rather than tolerance times, BEECHER and his associates have introduced a different variant of the tourniquet-exercise method (BEECHER, 1966; SMITH et al., 1966). The method is known as the "submaximum effort tourniquet technique," and proceeds as follows. After the blood is removed from the arm by wrapping the arm with an elastic bandage, the tourniquet (an ordinary sphygmomanometer cuff) is inflated above the elbow, the bandage is removed, and the subject squeezes a dynamometer at a standard rate for a set number of trials. He then merely sits quietly, waiting for the pain to mount; there is usually little pain while the preliminary exercise takes place, and the pain thereafter mounts slowly, not becoming extreme for some subjects until 20 to 30 min have passed, by contrast with the continuous exercise method in which the termination comes at a mean of 3 or 4 min. The pain is usually reported on a verbal scale in the submaximum effort tourniquet technique.

VI. Chemical Stimulation

The pain of ischemia probably owes to the release of some sort of chemical agent by the contracting muscle, the role of circulating blood being to eliminate this metabolite; if no exercise is involved, ischemic muscle does not become painful, at least over a period of 10 min or so (RODBARD, 1970).

The direct injection of a number of chemicals into the blood stream, or intraperitoneally, will produce pain in man. These include hypertonic salt solutions, and various amines and peptides, particularly bradykinin. Bradykinin is found in the blisters that form following burns; if the substance produced in the burn blister is injected into the blood stream, it produces a painful reaction. These substances are not very convenient for experiments of the psychophysical type, but they are important in studying the qualities of perceived pain, and in studying the action of analgesics, such as aspirin, which appear to neutralize their effects (LIM and GUZMAN, 1968).

B. Pain Measurement and Psychophysical Functions

Two components of pain are commonly recognized. One of these components is the *sensory-information* one, highly correlated with the nature of the stimulus, its location, and its intensity and duration. The second component, when referred to as the *reaction component*, is said to be a response to the painful information: crying out, wishing to terminate the pain, pleading for sympathy, and so on. Another way of describing the second component, to distinguish it from sensory information, is to label it the affective-motivational component, thus not giving any implication that one component is prior to the other (MELZACK and CASEY, 1968). These issues will come up later; first pain will be treated as though it were a sensory modality.

I. Thresholds of Sensory Pain

The lower threshold of pain is defined, like other absolute thresholds, as that level of stimulus intensity at which pain responses are first given, according to some appropriate psychophysical method. One problem is that there is usually some other response at lower intensities (e.g., cold or warm, if thermal pain is being produced), and the pain response has to be distinguished from the nonpain one. It is because of this problem that verbal responses are commonly used in threshold measurements of this kind, for man by the use of language is able to make these distinctions better than most nonverbal indicators. Absolute thresholds have been best worked out for thermal and electric shock stimulation, and illustrations will be confined to these two.

HARDY et al. (1952), using their dolorimeter, found the threshold for pain in 150 subjects to have a mean of 0.206 g calories per second per cm^2, with a standard deviation of 0.21 g $cal/s/cm^2$.

Because of the uncertainties of the distinctions that the subject is required to make between the threshold for warmth and that for pain, the problem of the subjective criterion becomes important, and the more modern methods of signal detection become relevant. CLARK (1969) investigated the change in thermal pain reports when the pain was modified by a placebo. He found that the placebo changed the criterion for pain, hence the usual verbal report, but did not change the sensitivity to pain as measured by d'. Ordinary psychophysical methods do not make this distinction, and some of the experimenter-bias effects attributed by BEECHER (1968) to the HARDY et al. method may very well be a consequence of the failure to make this distinction [1]. Another signal detection experiment will be considered later (page 865).

TURSKY and O'CONNELL (1972) used their concentric electrode-controlled impedance method to determine thresholds to electric shocks, in which threshold was defined by the instruction: "Tell us when you feel any sensation under the electrode on your right (or left) arm." This is a sensory threshold, not necessarily a pain threshold, and hence may not be comparable to the radiant heat pain threshold of HARDY et al. The values found, with 10 subjects, had a mean of 0.33 milliamperes on the first day, with a range of 0.20 to 0.56, and a mean of 0.44 on the second day, with a range of 0.24 to 0.64.

An electric shock can be presented very briefly and terminated quickly, so that it can be given at fairly high levels of discomfort. TURSKY and O'CONNELL

[1] Despite BEECHER's (1968) citation of 14 investigations refuting the HARDY et al. (1952) claims for their radiant heat method, the situation may not be as confused as he believed it to be. BEECHER and his associates have now been able to use electric shock in a laboratory setting to provide dose specific curves for morphine (SMITH et al., 1970), so that laboratory methods upon which he once frowned are now becoming more acceptable.

(1972) reported the tolerance level according to the instruction: "Now we will gradually increase the intensity of the stimulation until you tell us that you don't want to go any higher." They found this level at a mean of 9.0 ma. on the first day, with a range of 5.7 to 14.1 for their 10 subjects, and a mean of 9.4 on the second day, with a range of 5.1 to 14.1. Reliabilities were much more satisfactory than those for the absolute threshold, with correlations of 0.95 to 1.00 within days (all significant at $p=0.001$) and correlations of 0.73 to 0.87 between days (all significant at $p=0.01$ or better).

Tolerance levels in the exercise-ischemia situation, with exercise carried to termination, were found in one investigation to vary from 1.7 to 4.2 min, with pumping of water from 182 to 402 ml (McGlashan et al., 1969). Retest reliability on separate days was reported to be satisfactory (Caldwell and Smith, 1966).

II. Correlation Between Threshold and Tolerance Measures

In general, correlations between threshold measures and tolerance measures are low or nonsignificant (Gelfand, 1964), although some small positive relationships may be found. Tursky and O'Connell (1972) found within-day correlations ranging from 0.3 to 0.66 between their measures of threshold and tolerance for shock, with 8 of 10 correlations significant at the 0.05 level, while between days the small positive correlations were mostly not significant.

III. Magnitude Estimation

The course of suprathreshold pain with changes in stimulus intensity is more informative than either threshold or tolerance levels, because it yields information about lawful relationships between experienced pain and several levels of stimulation, and has practical applicability to pain management for pains that in surgical and medical conditions are often at intermediate suprathreshold levels. Data are available for radiant heat pain, electric shock, cold pressor response, and exercise-ischemia.

Data from the radiant heat method, as reported by Hardy et al. (1952), have been replotted as a power function in Figure 1. The fit is satisfactory in the lower part of the curve, where the exponent is 1.00, as found later by Adair et al. (1968).

Using the method of electrical stimulation, Sternbach and Tursky (1964) demonstrated a power function for magnitude estimates of pain when shocks were delivered at various levels. The high exponents (mostly 1.8–1.9), mean that the rise in pain is an increasing function of shock intensity, by contrast with the exponent of about one for the radiant heat data. Just because power functions end up as straight lines does not mean that the functions are alike when not plotted in log-log form.

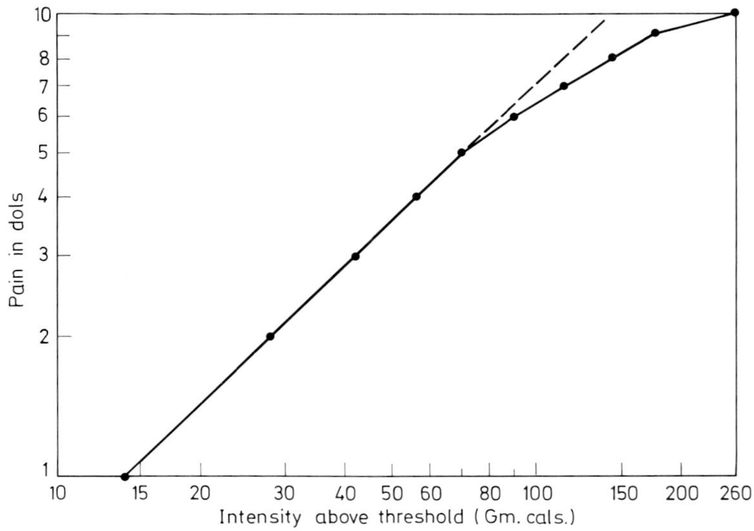

Fig. 1. Increase in pain on dol scale as a function of radiant heat: data from HARDY et al. (1952) replotted as a power function

The cold pressor test requires that the hand be cooled continuously, so that the tendency for a monotonic report, as in the case of radiant heat, is very strong. The same kind of orderliness is found, with the increases in magnitude estimates showing a power function with a slope less than 1.00 (HILGARD, 1969). Results at three water temperatures are shown in Figure 2. These curves use time in the water as though it were equivalent to an increase in stimulus intensity, which indeed it is. This is, however, an unconventional use of stimulus intensity. Another possibility is to take some specific time and plot intensity as a function of temperature. This has been done in Figure 3 for 25 s in the water. If water temperature is measured as a departure from the pain threshold value of 18° C, the points project to a minimum report of pain near this value.

A methodologic point in connection with magnitude estimation is worth noting. If an upper limit to the scale is used (such as the limit of 10 on the dol scale), changes in the function arise as the limit is approached (as in Fig. 1). Even a "reference value," to keep subjects using similar ranges of magnitude estimates, produces some distortion, as shown in Figure 4. In the experiments from which the pain reports of Figure 4 were obtained, the subject was asked to report on a scale in which 0 meant no pain and 10 was a reference or anchoring value of a pain so severe that he would very much like to remove his hand and forearm from the ice water, but he should keep it in a little longer if he reached that point and continue to count as the pain mounted. The three panels of Figure 4 show three types of response for 47 subjects whose pain exceeded the anchoring value. For some, the value made little difference, but for others it exerted a depressing effect and for still others became the occasion for a sharp upturn in magnitude estimates. Because of

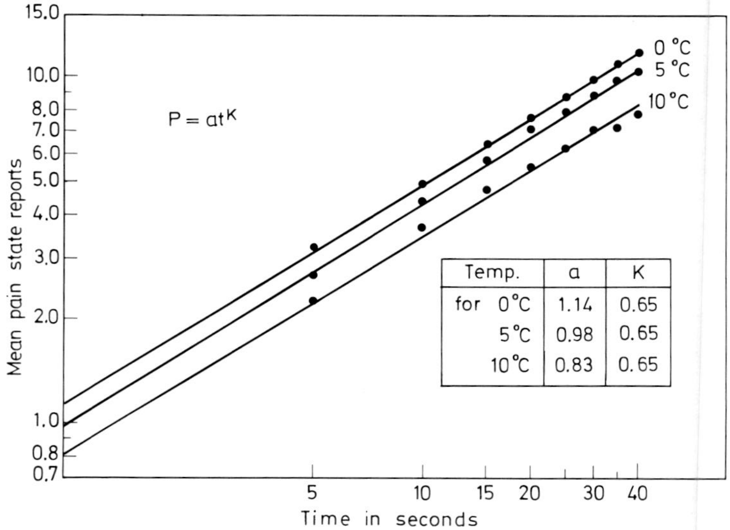

Fig. 2. Increase in pain with time in circulating cold water as a function of water temperature, plotted as power functions. (23 subjects, serving in all conditions.) LANGE and HILGARD (1968)

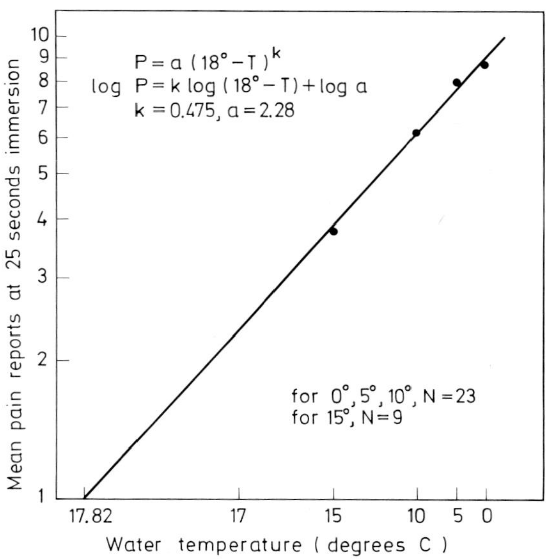

Fig. 3. Pain reports as a function of temperature difference from threshold at 18° C. Same subjects as in Figure 2 for 0°, 5°, and 10° C; means for 9 additional subjects at 15° C. (HILGARD et al. (1974) b)

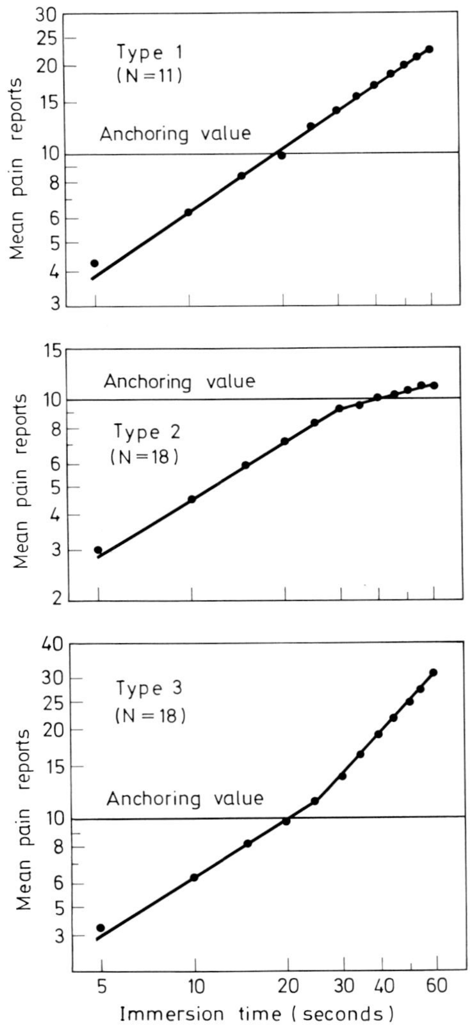

Fig. 4. Differential effect of anchoring value on inflection of power function as anchoring value is approached and exceeded. After HILGARD et al. (1974b)

the general orderliness within the first 25 or 30 seconds, for many purposes it has seemed wise to limit quantitative comparisons to this initial period of immersion.

If magnitude estimates are used in ischemic pain, in the submaximum effort tourniquet method, the course of the pain rise also fits a power function with time (Fig. 5). The pain increase is orderly, and retest reliabilities are satisfactory (LENOX, 1970).

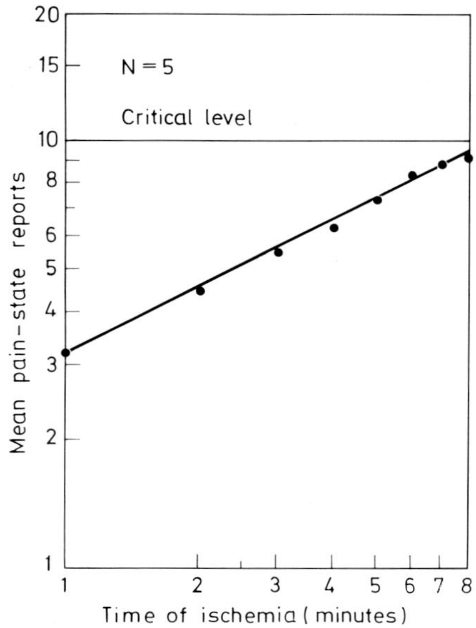

Fig. 5. Pain as a function of time in ischemia. HILGARD (1969), Figure 4, page 107

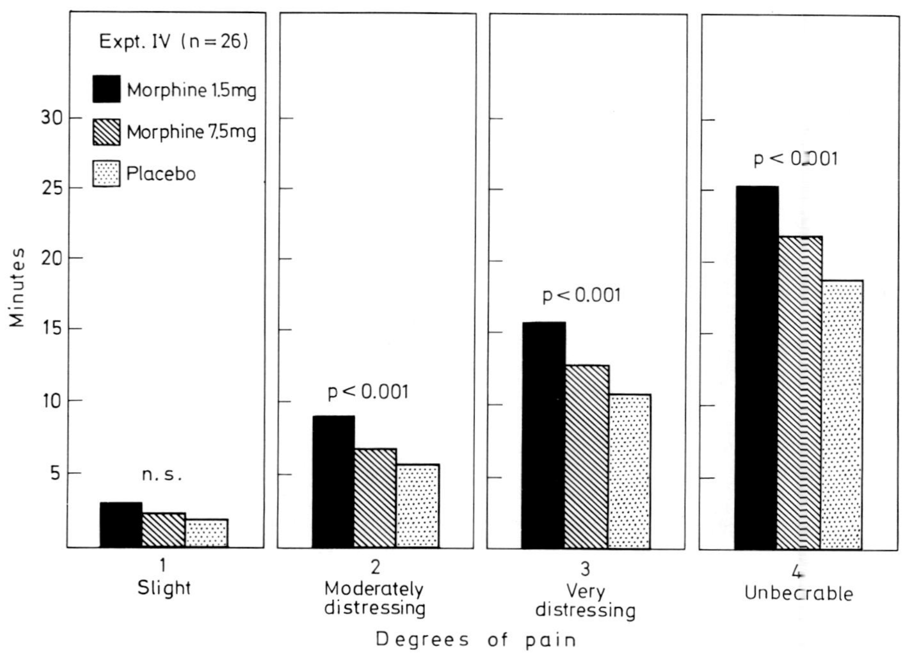

Fig. 6. Dose-effect curves; minutes of submaximum exercise tourniquet ischemia to various pain levels for 26 subjects. Morphine at two dosages and placebo. From BEECHER (1968), page 209

IV. Dose-Specific Analgesic Effects as Validation of Pain Measures

One method of testing the validity of laboratory pain measures is to find whether or not the laboratory pains as measured are modified by the analgesics known to be effective in the clinic.

Representative findings in which magnitude estimation has been used are available from a number of studies, of which one example may serve to show the practical use of such an indicator.

In their presentation of the submaximum effort tourniquet method, SMITH et al., (1966) showed that the method was sensitive to morphine in doses of 10 mg/70 kg b.wt. (Fig. 6). It was not, however, sensitive to a 5 mg dose, sufficient to produce relief for patients. They believed that the lesser anxiety on the part of experimental subjects may have been responsible for this lesser sensitivity.

The same laboratory later tested electrical shock, using TURSKY's procedures, and again reported dose-specific effects from morphine upon magnitude estimation (SMITH et al., 1970).

C. Modifiers of Laboratory Pain

There are many influences upon pain that go beyond those commonly controlled in laboratory experiments dealing with other sensory phenomena. A few of these will serve to call attention to the wide range of possibilities.

I. Concurrent Sources of Stimulation

Pain relief through the use of counterirritants is a practice widely used in folk medicine; witness mustard plasters, liniments, hot and cold compresses, all of which provide superficial stimulation to relieve deeper pains. Only in recent years have these effects been studied under controlled conditions, and a rationale provided through neurophysiologic knowledge.

Although electrical stimulation to relieve symptoms also has a long history, (e.g., GAMMON and STARR, 1941), many investigators in recent years have tested the use of superficial self-stimulation over sites of pain to relieve the underlying pain (CAMPBELL and TAUB, 1973; KRASNEGOR et al., 1972; MEYER and FIELDS, 1972; SHEALY, 1974; SHELDON et al., 1967; SWEET and WEPSIC, 1968; WALL and SWEET, 1967). In general, a low intensity of electrical stimulation, pulsing at around 100 Hz, which feels to the subject something like a mild massage (attracting attention, but not painful), is delivered near the site of pain and adjusted by the subject to the appropriate level. For some fraction of pain-sufferers, such stimulation may also reduce the underlying deep pain not only while the stimulation is on, but also for some time thereafter.

A flurry of interest was generated a few years ago when it was announced that audio stimulation by white noise or music, with intensity controlled by the patient, could be used for analgesia in dental operations (GARDNER and LICKLIDER, 1959). Soon, equipment was made available to the dental profession and, for a time, was widely used. It gradually fell into disuse because it was effective for some patients only, and there was some danger of damage to the ears produced by continuous stimulation at high levels.

When the method was effective, results were indeed dramatic, and MELZACK et al. (1963) set out to discover the basis for its occasional effectiveness. Using a careful design, the results were quite clearcut. Audio-stimulation and pain alone, without suggestions, and placebo audio with suggestions had no effect on pain tolerance time. Only the combination of audio-analgesia with suggestions of effectiveness worked, and, of course, not for all subjects. The authors interpreted the effect as owing to a turning of attention away from the pain to the tracking of the auditory inputs, especially with the music, which gave an opportunity for singing, keeping time, and so on.

II. Suggestion and Hypnosis

The specific effects of suggestion and hypnosis for the control of pain have long been known, but in recent years there have been a number of investigators subjecting these effects to quantitative study. Scales have been devised to measure hypnotic susceptibility. They consist of a series of suggestions that represent a sample of the kinds of behavior shown by hypnotically responsive subjects, such as arm movements to suggestion, inhibited voluntary control, hallucinatory behavior, age regression, posthypnotic amnesia, and the carrying out of posthypnotic suggestions. The subject receives a score based on the number of items "passed," that is, responded to in the manner of a hypnotically responsive person. Such scores show wide individual differences and satisfactory retest reliabilities (e.g., HILGARD, 1965). When subjects of known hypnotic responsiveness, as measured by these scales, are subjected to laboratory pain with and without suggestions for pain reduction, the amount that the pain is reduced by suggestion is found to correlate with their hypnotizability, whether or not there has been a prior induction of hypnosis. In the cold pressor test, the amount of reduction in pain correlates about 0.50 with measured hypnotic responsiveness (HILGARD, 1967; EVANS and PAUL, 1970; HILGARD et al., 1974b) (Fig. 7). Although when measured over random groups the amount of pain reduction is not significantly affected by a hypnotic induction before the analgesia suggestions are given, for highly responsive subjects pain is reduced more, when the subject is hypnotized than when he is not hypnotized (HILGARD et al., 1975).

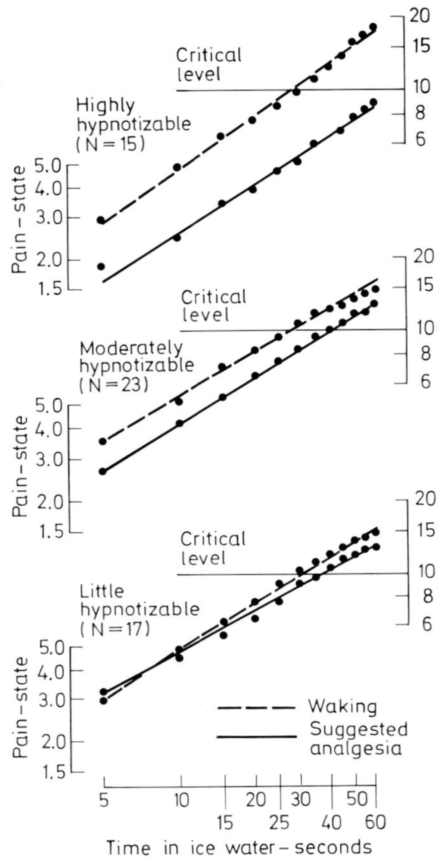

Fig. 7. Pain reduction as related to hypnotic susceptibility. (HILGARD, 1967)

Within the usual level of pain reduction, an interesting finding is that the reduced pain, when plotted as a power function of time in the ice water, as in Figure 7, shows a change in the value of the intercept with the y-axis, but yields the same exponent (slope) as when the full pain is experienced. This means that reduction through the course is as though a filter had been placed between the stimulus and response, reducing the response by a constant fraction at each level of experienced pain. A similar result is found with hallucinated pain, in which the hallucinated pain of ice water yields a function also parallel to that of physically produced pain, but typically at a somewhat lower level of pain (Fig. 8).

A practical implication of the orderliness of these results is that satisfactory pain studies can be conducted without exposing the subject to severe pains, because the trends are already evident when very modest suprathreshold pains are being felt. The point has also been noted by TURSKY (1974) in reference to electrodermal pain.

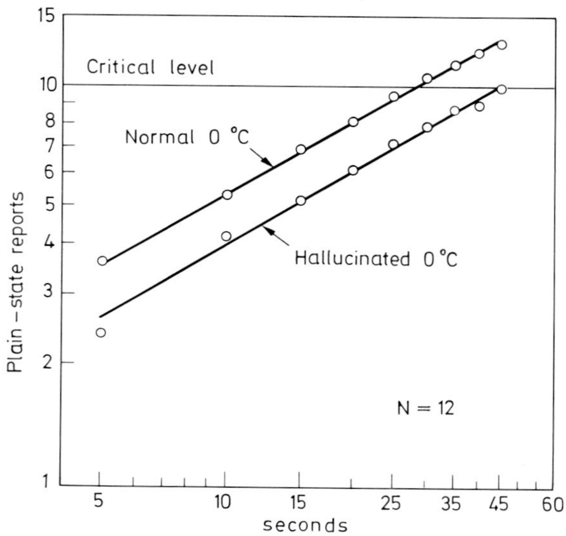

Fig. 8. Course of pain reports, normal pain in ice water, and hallucinated pain. (HILGARD, 1971, Figure 3, page 472)

III. Placebo Effects

The nature of a placebo response is not well understood, despite the consider-able attention placebos have received through the years (e.g., SHAPIRO, 1964). A peculiar quantitative relationship was noted by EVANS (1974) in reviewing the literature on the size of the placebo effect. Regardless of the strength of the analgesic agent being tested, the placebo appears to reduce the pain by a nearly constant fraction as inferred from the ratio of pain reduction by placebo to pain reduction by an active drug. This ratio in double-blind studies turns out to be 0.56 for a strong analgesic (morphine), and the same for milder analgesics (aspirin, 0.54, Darvon, 0.56). EVANS interprets this as a consequence of some subtle communication from the physician to the patient about the expected potency of the drug being used.

A careful experiment by MCGLASHAN et al. (1969) shows that response to placebo differs from hypnotic response to suggested analgesia by having the subject squeeze a bulb, pumping water, while his arm was occluded by a tourni-quet, and took measures of threshold time (and volume of liquid displaced) and tolerance time (to termination), with volume of liquid. To simplify the discussion, we may consider only the tolerance time [2]. The essential findings are illustrated in Figure 9. For subjects highly susceptible to hypnosis, the mean pain reduction, as shown by increased tolerance time, is substantially greater than pain reduction by placebo; for less susceptible subjects the response to both hypnosis and placebo is slight, but equal.

[2] I wish to thank Dr. Frederick J. EVANS for making the original data available to me so that I could prepare this revised presentation.

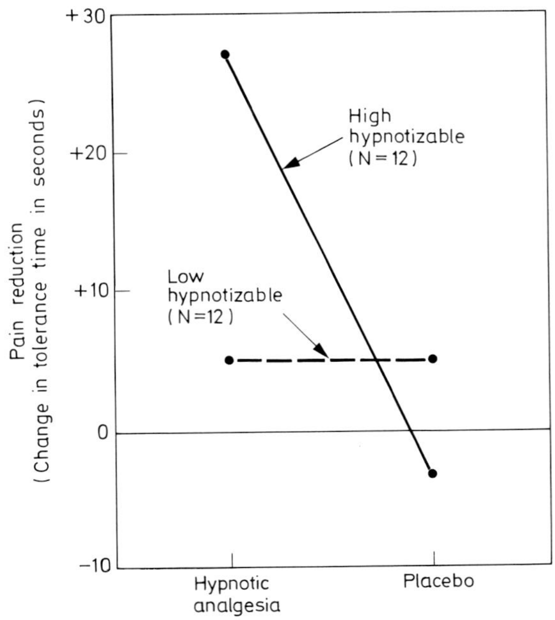

Fig. 9. Pain tolerance time in tourniquet-exercise ischemia: Differential effects of hypnotic analgesia and placebo on subjects selected as high and low in hypnotic responsiveness. Plotted from data of McGlashan et al. (1969), as supplied by Frederick J. Evans

IV. Motivational, Affective, and Cognitive Aspects

A large literature centers on the relationship between anxiety and pain, with some indication that the higher the anxiety, the higher the pain (Shor, 1962; Sternbach, 1965). Evans (1974) has pointed out that the relationship is not a simple one, for in the placebo study previously referred to, subjects high in chronic anxiety increased their pain tolerance following the placebo significantly more than subjects low in anxiety. Hilgard et al. (1974a) have noted that substantial increases in physiologic responses, such as heart rate or blood pressure, often arise in anticipation of the control of pain by subjects well able to reduce their pain through hypnotic analgesia suggestions; it is hard to believe that these are anxiety-free subjects when they show these signs of stress in anticipation of reduced pain.

Preparedness for what is to follow has been shown in a number of studies to affect the response to painful stimulation. Hill et al. (1952a, b) gave subjects control over the painful stimulus, after which a given level of electrical shock or thermal radiation was perceived as less painful than without that assurance. Staub et al. (1971) found no difference in tolerance to electric shock by giving subjects simple control of onset, intensity, and time between shocks, but found a significant reduction in tolerance levels when the subjects, originally having had control, were made to relinquish control.

Pain responses are subject to the kinds of motivational influences that are encompassed by theories of cognitive consistency. For example, the pain reported appears to correspond to the amount of pay received for participating in an experiment on pain—the greater the pay the greater the pain—as though some suffering is consistent with the higher pay for participating (LEWIN, 1965; ZIMBARDO et al., 1966; ZIMBARDO, 1969).

Life experiences that are related to growing up in different subcultures have been shown to affect responsiveness to pain (ZBOROWSKI, 1969). In laboratory investigations, STERNBACH and TURSKY (1965) and TURSKY and STERNBACH (1967) showed no consistent differences at threshold level for reactions to shock by housewives from Yankee, Irish, Jewish, and Italian subcultures, but showed marked differences in pain tolerance, especially engendered by the low tolerance of the Italian women in this comparison [3].

It is evident that in studying responsiveness to pain we are not dealing with a simple function dependent solely on the sensitivity of receptor mechanisms and intactness of conduction pathways.

D. Central Factors in Pain and Suffering

Much of the prior discussion has related pain perception to the conditions of stimulation, appropriate to a discussion of a sense-perception modality. There are, however, many pains experienced by human subjects that are very loosely correlated, if at all, with peripheral stimulation. These pains of ill-defined origin are commonly called central pains, but this designation does little but relabel them, for where they "center" is often itself obscure.

The first point to be noted is that pains may be delayed and appear many seconds after the termination of stimulation (LIVINGSTON, 1943), and pains originally dependent on some focal source of stimulation may recur when that stimulation is no longer present. Much of the evidence comes from pathologic pain, particularly phantom limb pain, causalgia, and neuralgia (MELZACK, 1973).

In a recent discussion, MELZACK (1974) lists four properties of phantom limb-pain:

1. The pain persists long after the healing of the injured tissues, continuing for more than a year after onset in about 70% of the patients.

2. Trigger zones may spread to healthy areas of the body, so that a gentle pressure or pin prick on another limb or head may cause pain in the phantom.

[3] Subjective scales in this study (motivated and unmotivated tolerance levels) showed group differences, while the slopes of the power functions based on magnitude estimation did not differ. TURSKY (1974) interprets this as evidence for a separation between the sensory and reactive components of the pain experience. This interpretation is not entirely convincing, in view of the possibility of a filtering process that could reduce the total experience without modifying the slope of the power function. (See p. 861).

3. Phantom limb pain is more likely to develop in those patients who experienced pain in the amputated limb prior to its surgical removal.

4. Treatment success is quite variable, although success is sometimes dramatic. For example, a procaine block locally into the stump may have no effect or it may stop the pain, sometimes for long periods of time or even permanently, although the drug wears off within hours.

Surgical intervention is seldom successful; hypnotic treatment may be (CEDERCREUTZ and UUSITALO, 1967).

That there are a whole range of psychogenic pains is clear to anyone in clinical practice with an estimate that pain affects more than 60% of the patients in psychiatric clinics (MERSKEY, 1974). It does little good to dismiss them as hysterical or imaginary; it is probably better to use a classification such as learned pains, which suggests that they can also be unlearned (FORDYCE, 1974a).

The complexity of subjective aspects of the pain experience has emerged through the reexamination of something reported occasionally by clinicians over the years. As far back as JAMES (1889) it was shown that a hypnotized person, feeling no pain as a consequence of analgesic suggestions, may actually report the experience of pain if given the opportunity to do so through a dissociated activity such as automatic writing. By subjecting this possibility to quantitative laboratory study, it has been shown, at least for some very highly hypnotizable subjects, that pain that is consciously denied, and not at all overtly reacted to, may be reported at nearly its full strength through automatic writing, or a related method of automatic talking in which a "hidden observer" reports (HILGARD, 1973, 1974; HILGARD et al., 1975; KNOX et al., 1974). Some ambiguity arises over the distinction between the sensory-information aspect of pain and the reactive or suffering aspect in this setting. Even though reported as intense in its sensory aspects, the pain is often not troublesome under these circumstances. In this respect, the reports correspond with those who received frontal lobe operations to reduce pain and reported that the "pain" persisted but the "anguish" disappeared (FREEMAN and WATTS, 1950). This distinction is not universally made in our laboratory studies, however, and many uncertainties of interpretation persist.

The dual nature of pain—its sensory aspects and its other aspects—may appear in conventional experiments studying human pain, without the complications of hypnotic analgesia. For example, the sensory-decision or signal detection methods derive a measure of d', inferred to be a measure of sensory discrimination. The ordinary verbal report, as used in classical psychophysics experiments, may disagree with d'; when pain is involved this difference is subject to interpretation and may reflect the duality of pain. CHAPMAN et al. (1973) used signal detection methods in a study of the effects of 33% nitrous oxide on thermal pain from a radiant source. When d' was used as the measure, reports of both "hot" and "pain" were discriminated as in the control (non nitrous oxide) condition, with the absolute sensitivity reduced for both by the gas. However, when a bias measure was studied, it was found that reports of "hot" were not changed but reports of "pain" were significantly changed. By this measure, subjects reported *less* pain or discomfort with nitrous oxide than would be inferred from d' and the reports of "hot." In decision-theory terms this represents a "response bias" as an operator characteristic in reporting pain, but such a bias may be psychologically significant as indicating that the subject is genuinely less troubled by the stressful stimulus under nitrous oxide, in disagreement with the preservation of his discrimination of its sensory aspects.

E. Theories of Pain

The gate control theory of pain, proposed by MELZACK and WALL (1965) is, at the time of writing, the most discussed of pain theories, and the one that appears to be guiding much of experimental work and some of the clinical approaches to pain alleviation. It must not be assumed, however, that insofar as it is true it is a completed theory, nor that it is without its points of difficulty. Before turning to this prevalent theory, mention may be made of its predecessors. In this, I follow the historical discussion in MELZACK (1973).

I. The Specificity Theory

The specificity theory, going back to Descartes, makes the plausible assumption that something happens at the site of injury that sends a message to a brain center evolved to apprehend pain; after central processing of the pain information, which includes both the quality of the pain and its local signs, appropriate motor action is produced to deal with the injury through withdrawal (when possible), or crying out, or diffuse discharge if escape is blocked. This is all so plausible that it must in some sense be correct, but the problem becomes one of identifying the specific receptors and pathways involved, and the center that is specialized for pain. The next important step in the theory was taken by VON FREY (1895), who identified the free nerve endings as the receptors for cutaneous pain. His arguments, following in part from MÜLLER's doctrine of specific nerve energies, were reviewed carefully by BORING (1942).

The notion of a straight-through, relatively rigid pain system, implied by the specificity theory, has been seriously criticized by MELZACK and WALL (1962, 1965).

II. Pattern Theory

Contemporary with VON FREY's theory, GOLDSCHEIDER's (1894) pattern theory has survived as a rival of the specificity theory. His pattern (or summation) theory proposed that pain depended upon a summation of inputs that had to reach a critical level for pain to be felt, and central systems were important in this summation. Modern pattern theories also recognize peripheral summation, interpreted centrally as pain (WEDELL, 1955; SINCLAIR, 1955). Central summation (returning closer to GOLDSCHEIDER) was proposed in somewhat different ways by LIVINGSTON (1943), HEBB (1949), and GERARD (1951), all recognizing the enduring nature of some pains beyond focal stimulation.

It may be noted that both types of theory are concerned with pain as a sensory process. Those who have recognized the affective-motivational components have also commonly returned to the linear assumption that the order of events is first some pain response in a pain center, followed by evaluation and motivational responses as reactions to the pain, rather than as inherent components of the pain experience. The distinction may be enhanced even by those, such as BEECHER (1959), who have deplored the emphasis upon the sensory components to the neglect of the "reactive" components. A different approach is taken in the gate-control theory, in which the distinction between the sensory-information and the motivational-affective components is preserved, but where they are thought of as simultaneous and not successive, so that the implications of a sensation followed by a reaction are not retained.

III. The Gate-Control Theory

The gate-control theory, proposed by MELZACK and WALL (1965), and discussed frequently since then, is the last in a long series of two-component theories, but with a great deal of new data to give it greater clarity and plausibility. Two systems had earlier been identified as epicritic and protopathic (HEAD, 1920), fast and slow (BISHOP, 1946), or based on myelinated and unmyelinated fibers with small fibers carrying pain in a network, while large fibers are inhibitory (NOORDENBOOS, 1959).

The theory begins with a now widely accepted distinction between two conducting systems from the spinal cord to the higher centers that are involved in pain, a sensory-discriminative system, and a motivational-affective system (CASEY, 1973).

The sensory-discriminative system begins with large fibers (A-alpha) entering the dorsal columns, most of them traveling without synapse, up the ipsilateral dorsal and dorsolateral spinal cord, making a synapse in the dorsal column nucleus in the lower brain stem. Here the second-order neurons cross over to the ventral posterior lateral nucleus of the opposite side; fibers from the nucleus project to the parietal lobe somatosensory area of the cortex. This, then, is the kind of direct system that we commonly associate with sensory afferent processes; it conducts rapidly, and yields information about peripheral stimulation, information that may in itself be innocuous. Although most of the fibers travel up the cord as indicated, some of the A-fibers send collaterals that make synapse in the dorsal horn; these are the fibers involved in the interactions of the gate mechanism.

The motivational-affective system is more complex. It receives its input from the smaller fibers (C and A-delta). The A-delta fibers are somewhat larger than the C-fibers, representing about 15% of the fibers in cats and monkeys, but these are also responsive to pain. These C and A-delta make synapse with the short fibers of the dorsal horn cells, lamina 5 cells, which form a gray-matter column running the length of the cord. Some short transmission cells, called

T-cells by MELZACK and WALL, are located in the substantia gelatinosa of the dorsal horn. Fibers from cells synapsing with them cross the midline to the ventrolateral part of the spinal cord to make up the ascending ventrolateral spinothalamic tract, commonly identified as the pain tract. This ascending system has projections to the posterior lateral thalamus, and has rich connections to the paramedial system in the core of the brain stem subserving motivational and affective functions: the reticular formation, hypothalamus, medial and intralaminar thalamic structures, and (via thalamic structures) the limbic forebrain structures. Because of the small fibers and many synapses this is a relatively slowly acting system.

One feature of the gate-control mechanism rests on the hypothesis that some of the modulation of pain occurs through an interaction between the two systems at the intrasegmental level, that is, in the dorsal horn where the two kinds of fibers have entered through the same dorsal root (Fig. 10).

The total amount and balance of activity from the large fiber system (L) and the small fiber system (S) is said to affect some sort of gating mechanism in the substantia gelatinosa, influencing discharges in the first transmission cells (T cells) that then send the pain impulses on their way. The central control mechanism will be discussed presently. The practical consequence of this portion of the theory has been to accelerate the use of various superficial counterirritants, either to large fiber nerves or to the skin (which is served by large fibers), in an effort to counteract deep and persistent pains, as indicated earlier (p. 859). The successes are great enough to give some support to the theory.

The central control mechanisms represent another set of pain modifiers. There are many possible pathways by which impulses from higher centers can descend to modify activity at the level of the cord, from the ventral posterior lateral nucleus, for example, where the innocuous information arrives speedily, perhaps before the motivation and affective processing have been integrated. REYNOLDS (1969), for example, electrically stimulated the midbrain central gray of rats by way of implanted electrodes and was able to carry out a laparotomy without the use of chemical anesthetics, with no evidence of responsiveness as long as the electrical stimulation was continued; once it was discontinued, responses to aversive stimuli reappeared. More recently, LIEBESKIND et al. (1973) have shown the same thing for the cat; stimulation through electrodes surrounding the cerebral aqueduct in the core of the brainstem abolish reactions to pain for the duration of the stimulation. These cells are also thought to be the biochemical receptors for morphine, whose analgesic properties are well known.

These, then, are the neurophysiologic roots of the gate-control theory. Three types of difficulty and unsolved problems have been listed by CASEY (1973) as follows: (1) the complexity of interconnections in the dorsal spinal gray matter makes critical anatomical specification of the gate-control mechanism extremely difficult; (2) interneurons with all the necessary properties have not yet been located; (3) some of the presynaptic and intraspinal interactions have not supported some of the details of the theory. To this may be added the largely undeveloped theory of central control. What seems to be quite well established can be stated in three propositions:

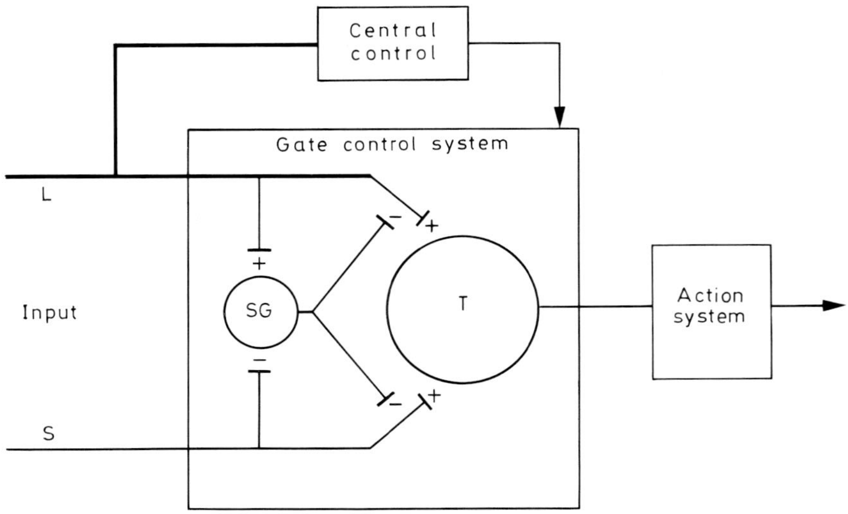

Fig. 10. Gate theory of pain. Large fibers (L) ascend the cord without synapse, carrying innocuous sensory information, but some collaterals enter the dorsal horn, where they are said to be inhibitory, closing the pain gate (G). Small fibers (S) tend to keep gate open. Transmitting fibers (T) are affected by the consequences of this interaction. The transmitted impulses activate both the sensory-discriminative pain system and the motivational affective system. There are also some central controls from above. MELZACK and WALL (1965)

1. Two distinctive mechanisms, one informative, one motivational-emotional, appear to be involved in the total pattern of pain perception.
2. Deep and persistent pain can be modified by concurrent stimulation of large fibers, and the pain reduction outlasts the counterirritant, so that some process enduring in time must be present to moderate responses to a continuing pain source.
3. Central control processes, whether of a psychologically recognized kind, or of brain stimulation, can clearly affect the perception of noxious stimulation.

These three features have to be included in any satisfactory pain theory; the popularity of the gate-control theory rests in part on the fact that it is the only theory that recognizes this total obligation.

F. Clinical Treatment of Pain: Its Lessons for a Basic Science of Pain Perception

The bridge between the laboratory and the clinic is a two-way street, and basic knowledge about pain can contribute to practical treatment, and practical experience in controlling pain can validate basic science findings, or propose limits to them and raise new questions.

I. Pharmacology of Pain

Because pain can be controlled by chemical agents, the use of various drugs with patients has given an important impetus to pain study. Some aspects of the pharmacology of pain have been largely neglected by psychologists, such as the intravenous or intraperitoneal injections of various substances, although the findings have a considerable bearing on the nature of the stimulus to pain (e.g., LIM, 1966). The neglect has not, of course, been complete (e.g., WOLFF and JARVIK, 1961; 1964; KANTOR et al., 1967).

II. Lessons From Pain Surgery

It is a reasonable conjecture that half the surgical operations for pain, particularly for undiagnosed intractable pain, have not resulted in permanent relief, and unfortunately, a reasonable number of these have left the patient worse off than he was before (SHEALY, 1974; WHITE, 1968). This should not be interpreted as an indictment of the surgical profession, but as an indication that when the surgeon has operated according to somebody's theory about pain tracts or pain centers, his operation, even though successful, has often not relieved the pain. Such a result calls for a modification of the anatomical-physiologic theory.

III. Acupuncture

The faddist nature of the current interest in acupuncture is a problem for the social psychology of science. Although acupuncture has been widely known and widely practiced all along, not only in mainland China, but in Japan, in France, and elsewhere, the American interest was not aroused until a popular columnist, James Reston, had his appendix removed with the aid of acupuncture in China, as reported by him in the *New York Times* on July 26 and August 22, 1971. WALL (1972), reporting on some of his own observations made in Bangkok, as well as conjecturing freely about the motivation circumstances in China, assigned a large share of the success of acupuncture to a hypnotic (or placebo) effect.

The admixture of credulity with science is illustrated by a development in France known as auriculotherapy (NOGIER, 1972). NOGIER contends that the ear lobe is shaped like the human fetus placed upside down, the head represented by the ear lobe, the body bending around the ear canal. Hence points for insertion of needles can be determined by the homologous points on the ear. Placing needles only in the ear, his success with auriculotherapy is said to match that of classical acupuncture, and one book on classical acupuncture indicates that the Chinese have in part adopted NOGIER's method, having performed 3,379 surgical interventions in Nanking with needles in the ear only between 1965 and 1972 (NIBOYET, 1973).

WALL's prediction that some relation to hypnosis might be found has been borne out by a study in which success in acupuncture was compared with success in hypnosis. Of 13 subjects rated as little susceptible to hypnosis, only one had partial relief of pain through acupuncture; of the 36 most highly susceptible to hypnosis, 19 experienced nearly complete relief through acupuncture, 12 partial relief, and for 5 acupuncture failed entirely. Because reduction of pain was not attempted under hypnosis we have no way of knowing how comparable the two procedures might have been (KATZ et al., 1974).

MELZACK, the other member of the MELZACK-WALL team, appears to favor a hyperstimulation-analgesia theory of the action of acupuncture over the hypnosis theory (MELZACK, 1973, 185–190). This would accord with the gate-theory of a central biasing mechanism.

IV. Hypnosis

Hypnosis is widely successful in the treatment of clinical pain, including the pain of obstetrics (AUGUST, 1961), burns (CRASILNECK et al., 1955), migraine (HARDING, 1967), phantom limb pains (CEDERCREUTZ and UUSILATO, 1967), terminal cancer (SACERDOTE, 1966), and various types of major surgery (SCOTT, 1973). Here again the issue is not whether or not it "works," but the conditions under which it works, and what patient selection has to be involved. For reviews of hypnosis in the control of pain, see HILGARD and HILGARD (1975) and BARBER (1963).

V. Behavior Therapy

The many successes in pain clinics using behavior therapy for persons with long histories of intractable pain play up very strongly the importance of learned responsiveness to pain, and, therefore, bear upon central controls in pain (FORDYCE, 1974b). The methods of reinforcement and extinction are often quite ingenious, with dramatic results. Patients not only learn to live with their pains, but they often learn to rid themselves of the pain experience.

VI. Psychiatry

The association of depression with pain (whether cause or effect) has been noted particularly by STERNBACH (1970), who sees this as one problem for the psychiatrist. According to KOLB (1954), a psychiatrist can often be helpful in cases of phantom limb pain where physical methods have proved ineffective.

Perhaps the main teaching of the clinic today is that the central and subjective aspects of pain are of enormous importance. They should be dealt with before surgery is attempted, rather than the other way around.

References

Adair, E.R., Stevens, J.C., Marks, L.E.: Thermally induced pain, the Dol Scale, and the psychophysical power law. Amer. J. Psychol. **81**, 147–164 (1968).

August, R.V.: Hypnosis in obstetrics. New York: McGraw-Hill, 1961.

Barber, T.X.: The effects of "hypnosis" on pain: A critical review of experimental and clinical findings. Psychosom. Med. **25**, 303–333 (1963).

Beecher, H.K.: Measurement of subjective responses: Quantitative effects of drugs. New York: Oxford Press, 1959.

Beecher, H.K.: Pain: One mystery solved. Science, **151**, 840–841 (1966).

Beecher, H.K.: The measurement of pain in man: A re-inspection of the work of the Harvard group. In Soulairac, A., Cahn, J., and Charpentier, J. (eds.) Pain, 201–213. New York: Academic Press, 1968.

Bishop, G.H.: Neural mechanisms of cutaneous sense. Physiol. Rev. **26**, 77–102 (1946).

Bonica, J.J. (ed.) International symposium on pain. (Advances in Neurology, Vol. 4). New York: Raven Press 1974.

Boring, E.G.: Sensation and perception in the history of experimental psychology. New York: Appleton-Century-Crofts 1942.

Caldwell, L.S., Smith, R.P.: Pain and endurance of isometric muscle contractions. J. Eng. Psychol. **5**, 25–32 (1966).

Campbell, J.N., Taub, A.: Local analgesia from percutaneous electrical stimulation: A peripheral mechanism. Arch. Neurol. **28**, 347–350 (1973).

Casey, K.L.: Pain: A current view of neural mechanisms. Amer. Sci. **61**, 194–200 (1973).

Cedercreutz, C., Uusitalo, E.: Hypnotic treatment of phantom sensations in 37 amputees. In Lassner, J. (ed.) Hypnosis and psychosomatic medicine, 65–66, New York: Springer-Verlag 1967.

Chapman, C.R., Murphy, T.M., Butler, S.H.: Analgesic strength of 33 percent nitrous-oxide: A signal detection evaluation. Science, **179**, 1246–1248 (1973).

Clark, W.C.: Sensory-decision theory analysis of the placebo effect on the criterion pain and thermal sensitivity (d′). J. abnorm. Psychol. **74**, 363–371 (1969).

Crasilneck, H.B., Stirman, J.A., Wilson, B.J., McCranie, E.J., Fogelman, M.J.: Use of hypnosis in the management of patients with burns. J. Amer. med. Ass. **158**, 103–106 (1955).

Dudley, D.L., Masuda, M., Martin, C.J., Holmes, T.H.: Psychophysiological studies of experimentally induced action oriented behavior. J. psychosom. Res. **9**, 209–221 (1965).

Evans, F.J.: The placebo response in pain reduction. In Bonica 289–296 (1974).

Evans, M.B., Paul, G.L.: Effects of hypnotically suggested analgesia on physiological and subjective responses to cold stress. J. cons. clin. Psychol. **35**, 362–371 (1970).

Fordyce, W.E.: Pain viewed as learned behavior. In Bonica 415–422 (a) (1974).

Fordyce, W.E.: Treating chronic pain by contingency management. In Bonica 583–589 (b) 1974.

Forgione, A.G., Barber, T.X.: A strain gauge pain stimulator. Psychophysiology, **8**, 102–106 (1971).

Freeman, W., Watts, J.W.: Psychosurgery in the treatment of mental disorders and intractable pain. Springfield, Ill.: Thomas 1950.

Gammon, G.D., Starr, I.: Studies in the relief of pain by counterirritation. J. clin. Invest. **20**, 13–20 (1941).

Gardner, W.J., Licklider, J.C.R.: Auditory analgesia in dental operations. J. Amer. dent. Ass. **59**, 1144–1149 (1959).

Gelfand, S.: The relationship of experimental pain tolerance to pain threshold. Canad. J. Psychol. **18**, 36–42 (1964).

Gerard, R.W.: The physiology of pain: Abnormal neuron states in causalgia and related phenomena. Anesthesiology, **12**, 1–13 (1951).

Goldscheider, A.: Ueber den Schmerz in physiologischer und klinischer Hinsicht. Berlin: Hirschwald (1894).

Harding, H.C.: Hypnosis in the treatment of migraine. In: Lassner, J. (ed.) Hypnosis and psychosomatic medicine, 131–134. New York: Springer-Verlag 1967.

Hardy, J.D., Wolff, H.G., Goodell, H.: Pain sensations and reactions. Baltimore, Md. Williams and Wilkins 1952.

Head, H.: Studies in neurology. London: Kegan Paul 1920.

Hebb, D.O.: The organization of behavior. New York: Wiley 1949.

Hilgard, E.R.: Hypnotic susceptibility. New York: Harcourt Brace Jovanovich 1965.

Hilgard, E.R.: A quantitative study of pain and its reduction through hypnotic suggestion. Proc. nat. Acad. Sci. (Wash.) **57**, 1581–1586 (1967).

Hilgard, E.R.: Pain as a puzzle for psychology and physiology. Amer. Psychol. **24**, 103–113 (1969).

Hilgard, E.R.: Pain: Its reduction and production under hypnosis. Proc. Amer. phil. Soc. **115**, 470–476 (1971).

Hilgard, E.R.: A neodissociation interpretation of pain reduction in hypnosis. Psychol. Rev. **80**, 396–411 (1973).

Hilgard, E.R.: Toward a neodissociation theory: Multiple cognitive controls in human functioning. Perspect. Biol. Med. **17**, 301–316 (1974).

Hilgard, E.R., Hilgard, J.R.: Hypnosis in the relief of pain. Los Altos, Calif.: Wm. Kaufmann, Inc. (1975).

Hilgard, E.R., Macdonald, H., Marshall, G., Morgan, A.H.: The anticipation of pain and pain control under hypnosis: Heart rate and blood pressure responses in the cold pressor test. J. abnorm. Psychol. **83**, 561–568 (1974a).

Hilgard, E.R., Morgan, A.H., Macdonald, H.: Pain and dissociation in the cold pressor test: A study of hypnotic analgesia with "hidden reports" through automatic key-pressing and automatic talking. J. abnorm. Psychol. **84**, 280–289 (1975).

Hilgard, E.R., Ruch, J.C., Lange, A.F., Lenox, J.R., Morgan, A.H., Sachs, L.B.: The psychophysics of cold pressor pain and its modification through hypnotic suggestion. Amer. J. Psychol. **87**, 17–32 (1974b).

Hill, H.E., Kornetsky, G., Flanary, H.G., Wikler, A.: Studies on anxiety associated with anticipation of pain. Arch. Neurol. Psychiat. (Chicago) 67, 612–619 (1952b).

Hill, H.E., Kornetsky, C.H., Flanary, H.G., Wikler, A.: Effects of anxiety and morphine on discrimination of intensites of painful stimuli. J. clin. Invest. **31**, 473–480 (1952a).

James, W.: Automatic writing. Proc. Amer. Soc. psych. Res. **1**, 548–564 (1889).

Kantor, T.G., Jarvik, M.E., Wolff, B.E.: Bradykinin as a mediator of human pain. Proc. Soc. exp. Biol. (N.Y.) **126**, 505–507 (1967).

Katz, R.L., Kao, C.Y., Spiegel, H., Katz, G.J.: Pain, acupuncture, hypnosis. In Bonica 819–825 (1974).

Knox, V.J., Morgan, A.H., Hilgard, E.R.: Pain and suffering in ischemia: The paradox of hypnotically suggested anesthesia as contradicted by reports from "the hidden observer" Arch. gen. Psychiat. **30**, 840–847 (1974).

Kolb, L.C.: The painful phantom: Psychology, physiology, and treatment. Springfield, Ill.: Thomas 1954.

Krasnegor, N.A., Jennings, J.R., Orr, W.C., Fields, H.L.: The after-effects of peripheral nerve stimulation: Changes in psychophysical judgments and autonomic reactions during the scaling of cutaneous pain. Psychon. Sci. **26**, 74–76 (1972).

Kunkle, E.C.: Phasic pains induced by cold. J. appl. Physiol. **1**, 811–824 (1949).

Lange, A.F., Hilgard, E.R.: Pain response to the immersion of a hand and forearm in cold water at 0°, 5°, and 10° Centigrade: I. Pain state reports. Unpublished. Hawthorne House Research Memorandum # 74 (1968).

Lenox, J.R.: Effect of hypnotic analgesia on verbal report and cardiovascular responses to ischemic pain. J. abnorm. Psychol. **75**, 199–206 (1970).

Lewin, I.: The effect of reward on the experience of pain. In Dissertations in cognitive processes. Detroit, Mich.: Center for Cognitive Processes, Wayne State University 1965.

Liberman, R.: An experimental study of the placebo response under three different situations of pain. J. psychiat. Res. **2**, 233–246 (1964).

Liebeskind, J.C., Guilbaud, G., Besson, J.M., Oliveras, J.L.: Analgesia from electrical stimulation of the periaqueductal gray matter in the cat: Behavioral observations and inhibitory effects on spinal cord interneurons. Brain. Res. **50**, 441–446 (1973).

Lim, R.S.: A revised concept of the mechanism of analgesia and pain. In Knighton, R.S., and Dumke, P.R. (eds.). Pain. Boston: Little Brown 1966.

Lim, R.S., Guzman, F.: Manifestations of pain in analgesic evaluation in animals and man. In Soulairac, A., Cahn, J., and Charpentier, J. (eds.) Pain, 119–152. New York: Academic Press 1968.

Livingston, W.K.: Pain mechanisms. New York: Macmillan 1943.

McGlashan, T.H., Evans, F.J., Orne, M.T.: The nature of hypnotic analgesia and placebo response to experimental pain. Psychosom. Med. **31**, 227–246 (1969).

Melzack, R.: The puzzle of pain. New York: Basic Books 1973.
Melzack, R.: Central neural mechanisms in phantom limb pain. In Bonica 319–326 (1974).
Melzack, R., Casey, K.L.: Sensory, motivational, and central control determinants of pain: A new conceptual model. In Kenshalo, D. (ed.). The skin senses. Springfield, Ill.: Thomas 1968.
Melzack, R., Wall, P.D.: On the nature of cutaneous sensory mechanisms. Brain, **85**, 331–356 (1962).
Melzack, R., Wall, P.D.: Pain mechanisms: A new theory. Science, **150**, 971–979 (1965).
Melzack, R., Weisz, A.Z., Sprague, L.T.: Stratagems for controlling pain: Contributions of auditory stimulation and suggestion. Exp. Neurol. **8**, 239–247 (1963).
Merskey, H.: The contribution of the psychiatrist to the treatment of pain. In Bonica (1974), 605–609.
Meyer, G.A., Fields, H.L.: Causalgia treated by selective large fiber stimulation of peripheral nerve. Brain, **95**, 163–168 (1972).
Niboyet, J.E.H.: L'anesthésie par l'acupuncture. Sainte-Ruffine, France: Maisonneuve 1973.
Nogier, P.F.M.: Treatise of auriculotherapy. Moulins-lés-Metz, France: Maisonneuve 1972.
Noordenboos, W.: Pain: Problems pertaining to the transmission of nerve impulses which give rise to pain. Amsterdam: Elsevier Press 1959.
Reynolds, D.V.: Surgery in the rat during electrical analgesia induced by focal brain stimulation. Science, **164**, 444–445 (1969).
Rodbard, S.: Muscle pain. In Crue, B.J., Jr. (ed.) Pain and suffering: Selected aspects, 154–167. Springfield, Ill.: Thomas 1970.
Ryan, E.D., Kovacic, C.R.: Pain tolerance and athletic participation. Percept. Mot. Skills, **22**, 383–390 (1966).
Sacerdote, P.: Hypnosis in cancer patients. Amer. J. clin. Hypnos. **9**, 100–108 (1966).
Scott, D.L.: Hypnoanalgesia for major surgery: A psychodynamic process. Amer. J. clin. Hypnos. **16**, 84–91 (1973).
Shapiro, A.K.: Factors contributing to the placebo effect: Their implications for psychotherapy. Amer. J. Psychother. **18**, (Suppl. 1), 73–88 (1964).
Shealy, C.N.: Six years' experience with electrical stimulation for control of pain. In Bonica (1974), 775–782.
Sheldon, C.H., Pudenz, R.H., Doyle, J.: Electrical control of facial pain. Amer. J. Surg. **114**, 209–212 (1967).
Shor, R.E.: Physiological effects of painful stimulation during hypnotic analgesia under conditions designed to minimize anxiety. Int. J. clin. exp. Hypnos. **10**, 183–202 (1967).
Sinclair, D.C.: Cutaneous sensation and the doctrine of specific nerve energies. Brain, **78**, 584–614 (1955).
Smith, G.M., Lawrence, D.E., Markowitz, R.Z., Mosteller, F., Beecher, H.K.: An experimental pain method sensitive to morphine in man: The submaximum effort tourniquet technique. J. Pharmacol. **154**, 324–332 (1966).
Smith, G.M., Parry, W.L., Denton, J.E., Beecher, H.K.: Effect of morphine on pain produced in man by electric shock delivered through an annular-disc electrode. Proc. 78th Annual Convention, Amer. psychol. Ass. 819–820 (1970).
Staub, E., Tursky, B., Schwartz, G.E.: Self-control and predictability: Their effects on reactions to aversive stimulation. J. Pers. soc. Psychol. **18**, 157–162 (1971).
Sternbach, R.A.: Autonomic responsivity and the concept of sets. In Greenfield, N.S., and Lewis, W.C. (eds.) Psychoanalysis and current biological thought. Madison, Wis.: Univ. of Wisconsin Press 1965.
Sternbach, R.A.: Strategies and tactics in the treatment of patients with pain. In Crue, B.L. (ed.) Pain and suffering: Selected aspects. Springfield, Ill.: Thomas 1970.
Sternbach, R.A., Tursky, B.: On the psychophysical power function in electric shock. Psychon. Sci. **1**, 217–218 (1969).
Sternbach, R.A., Tursky, B.: Ethnic differences among housewives in psychophysical and skin potential responses to electric shock. Psychophysiology, **1**, 241–246 (1965).
Sweet, W.H., Wepsic, J.G.: Treatment of chronic pain by stimulation of fibers of primary afferent neuron. Trans. Amer. neurol. Ass. **93**, 103–107 (1968).
Tursky, B.: Physical, physiological, and psychological factors that affect pain reaction to electric shock. Psychophysiology, **2**, 95–112 (1974).

Tursky, B., O'Connell, D.: Reliability and interjudgment predictability of subjective judgments of electrocutaneous stimulation. Psychophysiology, **9**, 290–295 (1972).

Tursky, B., Sternbach, R.A.: Further physiological correlates of ethnic differences in responses to shock. Psychophysiology, **4**, 67–74 (1967).

Wall, P.: An eye on the needle. New Scientist, July 20, 129–131 (1972).

Wall, P.D., Sweet, W.H.: Temporary abolition of pain in man. Science, **155**, 108–109 (1967).

Wedell, G.: Somesthesis and the chemical senses. Ann. Rev. Psychol. **6**, 119–136 (1955).

White, J.C.: Operations for the relief of pain in the torso and extremities: Evaluation of their effectiveness over long periods. In Soulairac, A., Cahn, J., and Charpentier, J. (eds.) Pain, 503–519. New York: Academic Press 1968.

Wolf, S., Hardy, J.D.: Studies on pain. Observations on pain due to local cooling and on factors involved in the "cold pressor" effect. J. clin. Invest. **20**, 521–533 (1941).

Wolff, B.B., Jarvik, M.E.: A quantitative measure of deep somatic pain. Arthr. Rheum. **4**, 126–127 (1961).

Wolff, B.B., Jarvik, M.E.: Relationship between superficial and deep somatic thresholds of pain with a note on handedness. Amer. J. Psychol. **77**, 589–599 (1964).

Wolff, H.G.: Headache and other head pains (2nd ed.). New York: Oxford Univ. Press 1963.

Zborowski, M.: People in pain. San Francisco: Jossey-Bass 1969.

Zimbardo, P.G.: Cognitive control of motivation. Chicago: Scott, Foresman 1969.

Zimbardo, P.G., Cohen, A.R., Weisenberg, M., Dworkin, L., Fireston, I.: Control of pain motivation by cognitive dissonance. Science, **151**, 217–219 (1966).

E. Perceptuan Effects of Cerebral Lesions

Chapter 28

The Brain and Human Behavior

Invited evening address at the 21st International Psychological Congress, Paris, July 20, 1976

HANS-LUKAS TEUBER† Cambridge, Mass. USA

With 14 Figures and 2 Tables

Contents

Introduction

The topic of "brain and human behavior" leads us into problems as vast as our entire field, as difficult, and as unfinished. Concern with human behavior may be as old as humankind, but the attempt to understand ourselves by means of experimental science is young: My father still listened to WUNDT, my grandfather could have listened to HELMHOLTZ. For only a few generations have we seen truly systematic efforts at relating aspects of behavior to aspects of brain function. The ultimate coalescence of psychology and neurology that my own teacher, LASHLEY, demanded (1941a) is still a long way off. Why then try to survey where we are, if we are so very much at the start?

The reasons for such an attempt are simple: We are dealing with a part of behavioral science where discoveries are being made at a rate that seems to double every few years and where the problems are fundamental. They are of the sort GEORGE WALD characterized (1958) when he wrote that "the great questions (in any field) are those an intelligent child asks, and getting no answers, learns to stop asking." Our field is young enough not to have stopped. What we want to know is nothing less than what goes on within ourselves (and by that we mean within our central nervous system), when we perceive, when we move, when we feel (or express) emotions, and when we learn or remember.

It needs little reflection to realize how far we are from having real answers to any of these questions, but there are glimpses, perhaps more for perception and movement, and less for memory and mood. To ask such broad questions may seem hopelessly premature, but it remains unfortunately true that the answers one gets depend on the way our questions are being asked. Nor is it wise to tackle our questions separately, since the answers will turn out to be interrelated. As I have often argued, we cannot look at perception without considering coordinated movement, with its own perceptual consequences, and both perception and movement involve memory and often mood. By keeping in mind this kinship among our questions, we are more likely to turn up unitary explanatory principles, particularly if we are vigilant in trying to match thorough analyses of brain structure with equally thorough analyses of behavior.

To illustrate such attempts I invite you to consider some crucial problems in perception: how we see dots as dots, and lines as lines, and a face as a face, and as *that* face among a thousand faces; how we move in deliberate ("voluntary") movements, and how we experience or display emotion, and, lastly, and necessarily still more briefly, how we learn or remember. We shall look at each of these interrelated aspects of our behavior from several vantage points. First of all, we ask what happens to the behavior in question after particular *brain injuries*, or differently put, we try to see how function proceeds in the presence of a gap in the living tissue (cf. HECAEN, 1962, 1972). Second, we try to marshal some of the relevant information about the *structure* involved in the lesion, the connections of that region with other areas and its intricate microanatomy, the normal physiological action of single cells within the region, and, occasionally, considerations of neurochemistry. In addition, both of these accounts, those focusing on the changes of the individual's behavior, and those focusing on neuronal structures and physiology, will be amplified by brief reviews of comparative and developmental issues. Thus, we shall bring in observations on how the behavior in question might appear in lower forms, *across species*, or how it might be acquired by young children in their *early development*.

We thus select the lessons to be drawn from lesions, the lessons of an emerging anatomy and physiology, and the lessons that can be derived from comparative and developmental studies. Yet in all this the cases of altered behavior after brain lesions mark our starting point. For that I stand in debt to the more than 500 people with penetrating brain wounds who have permitted me to study their conditions, often for decades after they had sustained their injury in the various terrible wars, from the Second World War to the Korean campaign, and to the endless war in Vietnam.

With exemplary unselfishness, these men have allowed me to examine the effects of their injuries, fully knowing they were being asked to *help me* to understand, not so much how function breaks down in the presence of brain injury, but rather how the human brain works when it does. The continuing study of these groups of adult patients was supplemented by that of similar groups of patients with civilian accidents or with brain disease, and of children with very early brain damage. Throughout, we can say what HENRY HEAD was fond of saying, that it is not primarily the disease that engages our attention, but the way in which by injury or disease "normal physiology is laid bare" (1920).

In this way, we have studied how sight is affected by wounds of the human visual pathways, or memory and mood by lesions of what we have been calling the limbic parts of the brain. I shall try to convince you that certain kinds of *blindness can illuminate sight*, and certain forms of paralysis can tell us something about the normal bases of voluntary movement. And I shall argue that abnormal forgetfulness, the acquired amnesias of the brain injured, can point us in the direction in which answers to the riddle of memory can be sought.

A. Perception: Elementary Aspects

How, then, do I see a dot, or a line as a line, and in *that* place, and as vertical even if I move my eyes or head or entire body, or incline my head?

I. Effects of Lesions

Let me begin with an observation now 30 years old (Fig. 1). Here we have a classical situation: a gap in the living substrate of vision, owing to the passage of a small shell fragment through the most posterior part of the occipital lobe; the fragment, in a young man, destroyed the lips of the calcarine fissure to which the visual pathways from both eyes project. As a result, the patient has a permanent gap in his visual fields, in their very center. Yet what is important here is not the acquired island of blindness (the scotoma) as such, but the fact that *it is not seen*: the patient insists that his visual field is whole (TEUBER, 1966; TEUBER et al., 1960). When shown a vertical line, crossing the area of blindness, he insists he sees the line unbroken. When given two lines

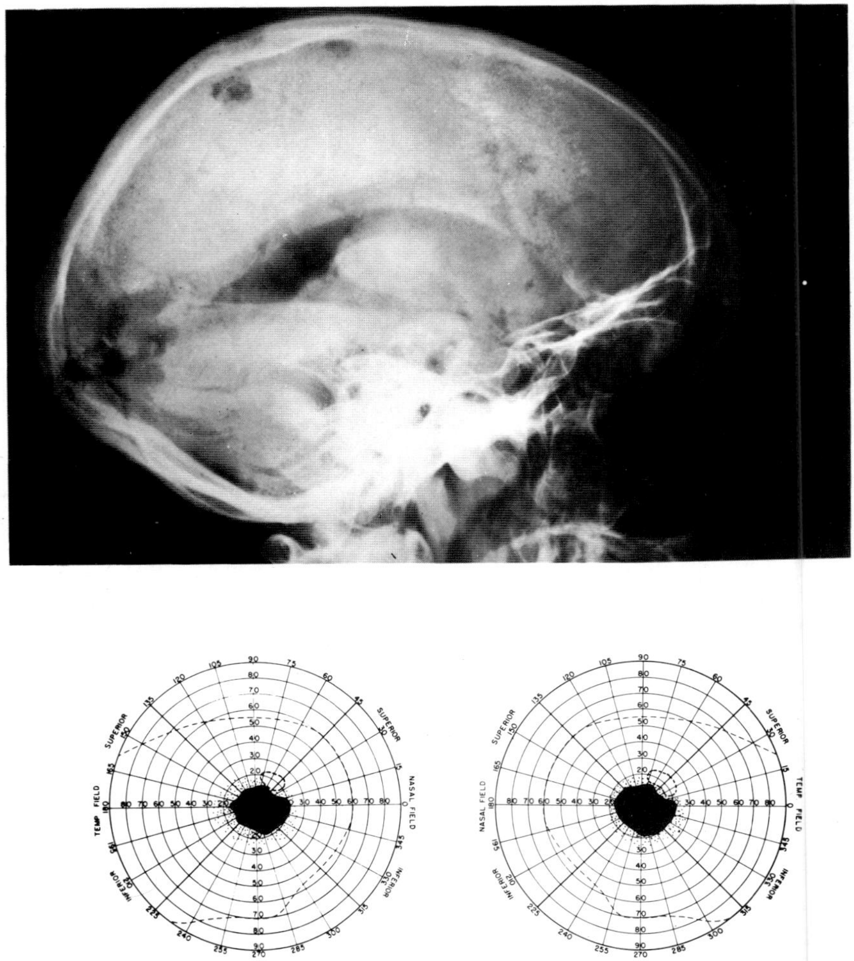

Fig. 1. Acquired island of blindness (central scotoma) in the visual field (*below*), after penetrating shell fragment wound of occipital lobes as seen in X-ray of skull (above). (From: TEUBER, 1960)

to fixate, one horizontal and one vertical, but intersecting, he claims he sees a cross, and he still does so even if the intersection at the center is replaced by an objective gap. When asked to gaze upon the familiar redundant line pattern introduced by MACKAY (1957), he reports multiple intersecting lines but fails to perceive the bull's-eye in the center. In fact, he also "completes" a random noise field, noting no irregularity in the center (Fig. 2).

Yet if you invite him to look at your face against some uniformly patterned background, and your face is kept at a distance such that it fits inside the scotoma, he exclaims that he fails to see the face—only your headless shoulders against a complete background. What is vision here, and what is blindness?

Fig. 2. Redundant line pattern introduced by MacKay (1957), suitable for testing "completion" of contours across acquired blind spots. (See text for details; also Gerrits and Vendrik, 1970)

Lastly, if you superimpose, as MacKay did first, the visual noise and the redundant line pattern, an extraordinary thing happens. The patient manages to perceive, for the first time, his own scotoma, "entoptically." Like you and I, he obtains the normal illusion of streaming, circling dots (at right angles to the lines) over his visual field outside the scotoma, but within the scotoma, so to speak, he still completes the lines and the randomly bobbing dots, without, however, the induced streaming of the dots. Clearly, such phenomena suggest a differential fragility of visual function, with some aspects dependent on the integrity of primary visual cortex, and others bypassing that part of the visual nervous system. But how can we account for these observations in terms of normal function?

II. Convergent Evidence from Single-Unit Studies and Other Recent Visual Physiology and Anatomy

The phenomenon of "completion" is nearly ubiquitous in central scotomata and must be related to the intrinsic organization of the visual pathways. In fact, the primary visual cortex, with its characteristic stripe in the fourth cortical layer (the stripe of Gennari) has been subjected to more detailed anatomic and neurophysiologic scrutiny than nearly any other part of the cerebral mantle. Consider only that the discovery of this characteristic stripe in that part of the cortex antedated the invention of the compound microscope, having been seen by GENNARI (1782) with a hand lens, exactly 200 years ago, in 1776! Yet both the horizontal layering of this cortex, and its vertical organization in palisade-like structures, have defied interpretation until two independent and equally important events occurred—the introduction of the microelectrode, enabling us to tap the electric activity of single nerve cells in the brain (including those in the striate cortex), and the discovery by HUBEL of the *question* to put to the individual neurons from which one records: namely, that the adequate stimulus is *not* flux of light, or sudden darkness, but a specific visual pattern.

The audience knows how this story unfolded: how KUFFLER (1953) showed the importance of dots and contrast for the mammalian retina, and how this finding was subsequently extended to other lower way-stations along the visual pathways; how our Boston colleagues HUBEL and WIESEL (1960, 1962, 1969) have demonstrated the clustering of orientation-specific cells, responding maximally to vertical edges, or to various obliques, or to horizontals, in "*columns*" of cortex, so that cells in a given column may prefer, say, vertical bars, and in another, obliques at a particular angle, and in still another column, horizontals.

Perhaps we should interpolate here a recent discovery by PATRICIA GOLDMAN (from the National Institute of Health) and Professor WALLE NAUTA, at our laboratories at M.I.T. (1977) according to their findings, not only the visual cortex and the sensorimotor strip are organized in columns (as has now been known for nearly 20 years) but also, and quite unexpectedly, the frontal cortex and even the limbic cortex, in the primate. Thus, the principle of *columnar organization* (first found by MOUNTCASTLE for the sensory cortex, 1957) extends much more widely, and possibly to the cortex in its entirety. The cortex now appears as an enormous array of microorgans, each a fifth to half a millimeter wide and cylindrical in shape, whose modes of information processing, undoubtedly radically different in different cortical areas, remain to be uncovered.

But to return to the visual proper: I put it to you that the *beginnings* of a more fundamental understanding of certain phenomena encountered after partial visual field destruction may be close at hand: these include (a) the tendency to continue or complete simple contours into areas of the visual field corresponding to the scotoma, (b) the survival of capacity to locate and perhaps even perceive dots,[1] and (c) the remarkable filling-in of visual noise. What

[1] The capacity to locate visual targets shone into areas of scotoma may be distinct from the completion of patterns, since orienting to light sources is known to survive total loss of visual cortex in monkeys (see KLÜVER, 1942; PASIK and PASIK, 1968; WEISKRANTZ, 1963; HUMPHREY and WEISKRANTZ, 1967; WEISKRANTZ and COWEY, 1970). Ability to move one's eyes toward "unseen" targets flashed into the blind regions of the field has been shown in some of our patients (see KÖRNER and TEUBER, 1973; PÖPPEL et al., 1973), a phenomenon confirmed by WEISKRANTZ and his colleagues (SANDERS et al., 1974) and dubbed "blindsight" (see also PERENIN and JEANNEROD, 1975). A particularly strong interpretation of such residual "vision," after striate-cortex destruction can be found in the hypothesis of (at least) "two visual systems," one for locating, the other for discriminating patterns (HELD et al., 1967–1968). SCHNEIDER (1969; see also DIAMOND and

one would have to assume is that those columns that are left intact around the gap in the tissue, with their various specifications, are still capable of processing information about orientation of lines, or about direction of movement, and this despite the lack of those units that signal the length of contours.

At the same time, we must realize how far we still are from having exhausted the marvelous intricacy and orderliness of the visual cortex. The eminently teachable hierarchy postulated for classes of cells, from "simple" to "complex" and "hypercomplex." undoubtedly needs revision. So-called complex cells (often with wider receptive fields than simple ones) are sensitive to visual noise, whereas simple cells are not (HAMMOND and MACKAY, 1975), and the simple cells, in turn, have now been further subdivided, for the adult monkey's visual cortex, into at least seven subclasses (called "S" cells, from S_1 to S_7, by SCHILLER et al., 1976), with increasing internal structure in their receptive fields (e.g., with multiple, parallel excitatory ridges, and the ridges sensitive to stimulus movement in the same and in opposite directions, etc.)

Certainly, among themselves, these "S" cells may still stand in a hierarchical relation (each higher class receiving combined output from the ones below), in line with what I have often called the principle of "cascade specification of inputs." What is most arresting, however, is the very recent observation by SCHILLER that a given "S" cell in the monkey's striate cortex may be responsive to one kind of orientation (for a stationary edge) and to another kind of directed movement (SCHILLER et al., 1976). This observation has prompted him to develop the elegant, if tentative, model shown in Figure 3.

None of these recent disclosures detract from the fundamental importance of HUBEL and WIESEL's original discoveries. What the new disclosures are doing, however, is rather obvious: we are beginning to understand why certain unexpected "dissociations" in perception after brain injury can be observed (e.g., the differential reactions to stationary edges and to visual noise, or the perversion of movement perception in the absence of similarly severe disorders in the perception of stationary patterns). Furthermore, the new and steadily increasing information about single-cell activity forces us to be cautious in identifying the edge-sensitive cells in the visual cortex, without further proof, with "edge-*detectors*" (CREUTZFELDT and ITO, 1968). Before we can do so, we must prove that one cannot see contours without these cells, and that contour perception would be altered with changes in the distribution of these orientation-sensitive elements in the visual cortex.

HALL, 1969) argued with especial force for such a separation of systems in the hamster, one for telling the animal "where" things are (a pathway involving the superior colliculi in the midbrain, and extra-striate cortex), and another for "what" they are (involving the lateral geniculate in the thalamus, and the striate cortex). Undercutting the colliculus produced trouble with visually guided orientational movements, whereas visual-cortex destruction produced no trouble with orientation but considerable deficits in the discrimination of visual patterns. Though still under active controversy, at least in its applicability across species, the "multiple systems" hypothesis has had considerable heuristic value (e.g., GRAYBIEL, 1974; SCHNEIDER, 1970, 1975); in its original form it provides one of the clearest instances of what I called (in 1955) the principle of "double dissociation of symptoms" (contrasting sets of behavioral symptoms with contrasting cerebral lesions).

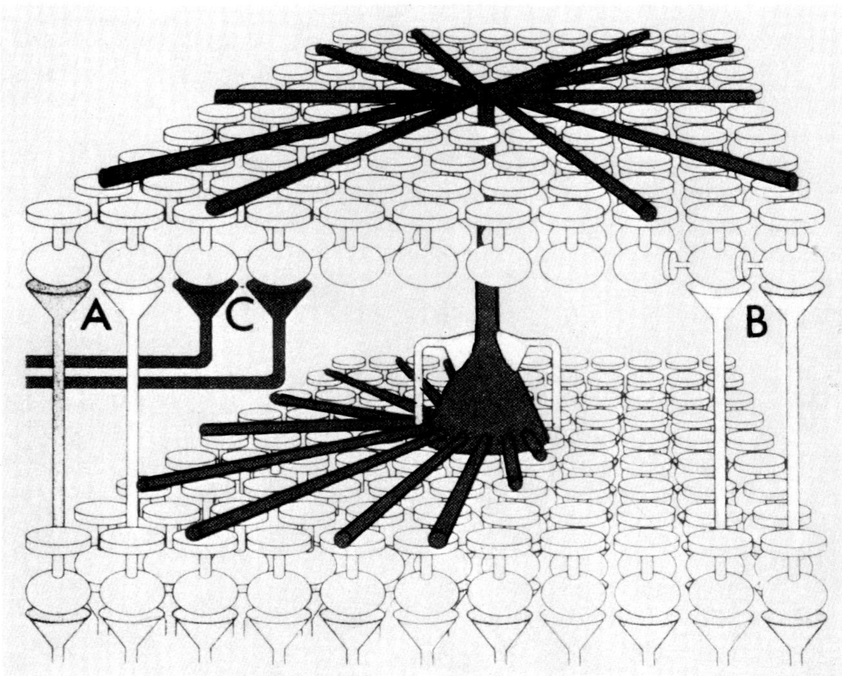

Fig. 3. Schematic model of a neuron of the S_1 type in the monkey's visual cortex (according to SCHILLER, 1976). The S_1 cell is shown in the center in black, with its basal dendrites (*in black, below*), and its apical dendrites (*in black, above*). Interneurons are shown as continuous layers above and below. Selective connections made by the dendrites of the S_1 cell account for its selective response, to direction (of moving stimuli) in the lower layers, and to orientation (of stationary edges) in the upper layer of neurons. The axis of orientation is also the perspective line where inhibition is ineffective on the cell. Diverse inputs from the subcortex are shown at *A* and *B*, whereas transcortical input from other pyramidal cells is shown at *C*.

III. Developmental and Comparative Aspects

The experiments most suitable in this respect are either comparative in nature, that is, assessing the perceptual capacities, particularly of invertebrates, against the presence or absence of the appropriate neuronal arrangements—or developmental, such as noting changes in perceptual capacities with changes in the neuronal equipment during normal ontogeny, or interfering experimentally with this equipment by selective deprivation or appropriately biased input.

Very tight couplings between the feature sensitivity of single neurons and those of whole organisms do exist, undoubtedly, in the invertebrates with image-forming eyes, as in the remarkably specialized reactions of jumping spiders, or in the now-classic demonstrations by SUTHERLAND (1957) of selective pattern blindness for obliques in the octopus—a difficulty curiously reminiscent of the trouble normal children have with mirror-image obliques (RUDEL and TEUBER, 1963).

In lower vertebrates, the work of LETTVIN and colleagues (1959) at M.I.T. (done independently of the HUBEL-WIESEL experiments) seemed to suggest an equally exciting parallelism between the pattern-specific responses of different neurons in the frog's visual nervous system, and the visually guided behavior of the entire frog. As LETTVIN likes to point out, he approached the individual neurons in the spirit of an ethologist, intent upon discovering "releasing stimuli," and he tried to detect the candidate stimuli by thinking about the "ethogram" of the entire frog.[2]

The most critical points, however, for our present purpose, are those that one can raise concerning carnivore and primate visual systems subjected to special visual environments. Close coupling between unit activity and behavior was suggested by the ingenious if sometimes controversial experiments of BLAKEMORE and his colleagues (1970, 1973). They raised kittens in cylinders bearing only, for example, vertical stripes, and were able to induce a parallel change in cortical unit-physiology and in total-kitten behavior. For the visual cortex, they reported a marked increase in verticality-sensitive neurons (after rearing in the presence of vertical stripes), and a loss of responses to obliques and horizontals. In the kitten's behavior, they saw a tendency to play with vertically held sticks and to bump into horizontals. Unexpectedly, STRYKER and SHERK (1975) in our laboratories at M.I.T. found their kittens' brains quite resistant to this treatment: rearing in striped cylinders was ineffective in "warping" their kittens' cortices. Still more recently though (and in collaboration with HIRSCH), SHERK and STRYKER (unpublished data) were able to alter the cellular responses in the kitten cortex by rearing the animal with goggles over its eyes; the goggles exposed vertical stripes to one eye and horizontal ones to the other eye, or even just vertical stripes to both. These results do confirm and extend the early demonstrations by HIRSCH and SPINELLI (1970), who found cortical (but only very slight behavioral) changes in kittens raised with goggles bearing stripes.

---

[2] On the other hand, though the examination of these early discoveries helps one to understand the hyperbolic descriptions (e.g., of individual cells as "bug detectors"), real bugs always activate more than one class of neurons in the frog's visual nervous system. The "bug-detecting" cells do prefer dark dots that move against a light background, but the frequency of the neuronal discharges also depends on contrast and angular size of the dots, and on the velocity of their movement (cf. GRÜSSER and GRÜSSER-CORNEHLS, 1973). In fact, which classes of neurons are activated usually depends on more than one stimulus dimension. We thus must avoid a premature one-to-one equation of classes of neurons, on one side, with singular stimulus dimensions on the other, just as we have no real right to speak of "bug detectors"—LETTVIN prefers to speak jokingly of grandmother(-detecting) cells!—at the level of an individual neuron or of a singular neuronal class. The problem of universals (how we extract such higher-order percepts) is still unsolved, even though it can now be much more sharply posed.

Similarly, rearing kittens in stroboscopic light or in front of a uniformly moving visual field has drastic effects on movement-sensitive cells cf. CYNADER, 1975; CYNADER et al., 1973, 1976; also JEANNEROD's group, e.g., VITAL-DURAND and JEANNEROD, 1974), although, here too, the behavioral correlations still need to be worked out.

Some crucial experimental issues, thus, remain unsettled; we have not fully ascertained for higher forms whether, and (if so) which of the various classes of feature-sensitive elements are truly necessary for the detection of corresponding environmental features by the organism as a whole. We also need to know how strictly innate these various cell types are, and to what extent and under what conditions they can be shown to be "plastic."

Under certain extreme conditions, oriented lines can certainly gain powerful control over human behavior: two decades ago, two patients presented themselves to us in rapid succession with complaints of brief episodes of unconsciousness elicited by looking at vertically oriented grid patterns. These patients were promptly relieved when such patterns were rotated out of the vertical. Here, the entire patient acted transiently like a Hubel-Wiesel cell, with the EEG showing markedly abnormal discharges during the patient's exposure to vertical lines. But the Hubel-Wiesel cells had not yet been discovered, and so the matter was left to rest (however, others had the courage to publish similar cases, see BICKFORD et al., 1969; CHATRIAN et al., 1970; and more recently in a systematic study, WILKINS et al., 1975).

Most to the point, however, are two very recent series of experiments, one done in Cambridge, England, and Halifax, Nova Scotia, the other in my colleague Richard Held's laboratories at M.I.T. in Cambridge, Massachusetts. To begin with the latter experiments, HELD and his co-workers were able to show strong predilections for gazing upon vertical or horizontal gratings, rather than obliques, on the part of young infants (down to 2 weeks of age, see LEEHEY et al., 1975, Fig. 4). Such surprisingly "nativistic" findings are in line with current work in the M.I.T. laboratories by SHERK and STRYKER (1976) who demonstrate for the kitten cortex that even in the newborn, and in kittens raised for the first 5 weeks in the dark, the various classes of feature-sensitive neurons are present, though not as well tuned as they will be later on (see also BUISSERET and IMBERT, 1976). Taken together, these experiments rather detract from the earlier criticisms by BARLOW and PETTIGREW (1971) who had questioned the original observations of HUBEL and WIESEL of an essentially innate complement of such specific cells in the newborn.

At the same time, however, an importantly different light is cast on all of this by the experiment of MITCHELL, BLAKEMORE, and their colleagues (1976), in England and Nova Scotia, showing that rotating one eye in the kitten ("torting" the eye in its orbit, about 90°), so that vertical lines on the retina become horizontal, does *not* prevent these animals from treating objectively vertical lines as still vertical through the torted eye. This adaptation occurred, even though BLAKEMORE himself (with ALAN HEIN and others, 1975) had previously shown that such visual torting of the eye leaves the receptive-field characteristics of the visual cortex quite unchanged: verticality-sensitive neurons react to retinal (and therefore not to environmental) verticals and continue to do so. Clearly

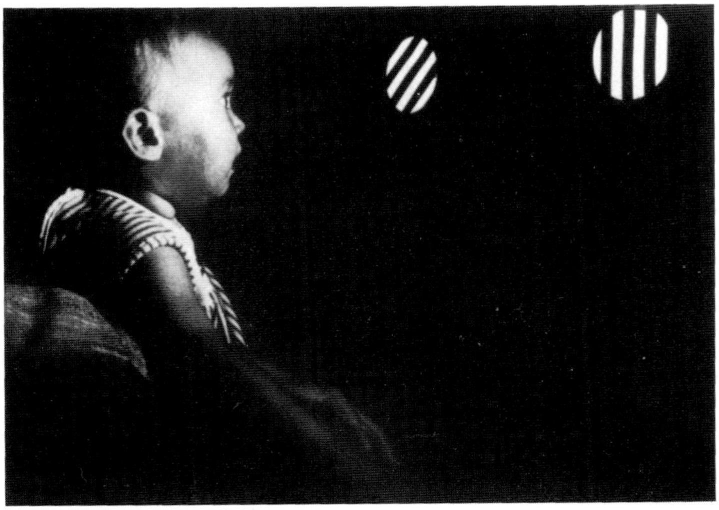

Fig. 4. Test situation used by HELD (see LEEHEY et al., 1975) in order to determine preferential fixations by infants seated in front of vertical and oblique gratings. A preference for verticals (or horizontals) is demonstrable with this technique for the appropriate spatial frequencies of the gratings, from 2 weeks of age onward, and probably earlier. The method of "preferential looking" becomes unsuitable for children above the age of 1 year.

a different system and a different level is involved in the reevaluation of verticality that must underlie the animal's adaptation to the altered visual input (see also YINON, 1975).

B. Complex Perceptual Achievements: Faces

Our account of perception of patterns has so far been limited to edges and moving dots—but we have said nothing of how we manage to comprehend what these patterns might signify. How do we recognize faces or understand words?

I. Effects of Lesions

Remember that our patient with his magnificent completion for dots and lines failed to complete a face—much like my teacher LASHLEY who enjoyed "beheading" people during his migraine attacks when he would insist that he could see the wallpaper patterns behind our headless shoulders (1941b).

But what do we make of a case like that of a young man, with a radical right temporal-lobe amputation following a civilian car accident, who had only relatively small visual-field defects (even on the special perimeter constructed for us by Professor HARMS, 1965), yet insisted that he could not recognize his own parents by simply looking at their faces, and could not tell who they were until he heard their voices?

In fact, when shown the schematic face constructed by BRUNSWIK and REITER (1937) (Fig. 5), he complained that he saw lines that might form an apple, or possibly a pear, but not a very good pear, because there was a break in the skin below (pointing at the mouth), the stem was folded over (pointing at the nose), and there were two wormholes (the eyes). I hasten to add that he had other perceptual difficulties with complex pictures and with real scenes *not* containing faces, but it was hard to resist the impression that his trouble with faces was somewhat out of proportion not only to his elementary visual capacities, which were so largely intact, but also to his other perceptual impairments (KÖRNER and TEUBER, 1973; TEUBER, 1975a).

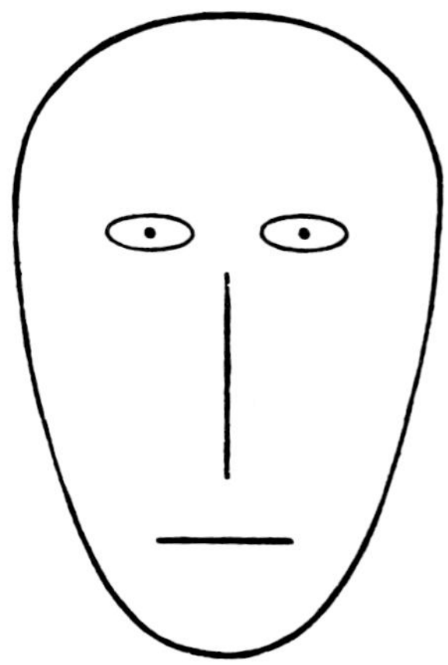

Fig. 5. Schematic face (after BRUNSWIK and REITER, 1937), called by a patient "an apple, or perhaps a pear"

How do we, in fact, see the transition from face to pear in the familiar set of Charivari cartoons of LOUIS PHILIPPE (Fig. 6)? Are faces, with their relatively greater dependence on the right hemisphere, "special," in a similar way to that in which speech, with its dependence (in most of us) on the left hemisphere, is said to be "special"? Seven years ago, my student ROBERT YIN began to tackle that question. He first noted (as had others before him) that certain transformations such as spatial inversions—turning a snapshot of a face upside down—were surprisingly destructive of one's ability to recognize a face. He then proceeded to show that otherwise normal adults who were

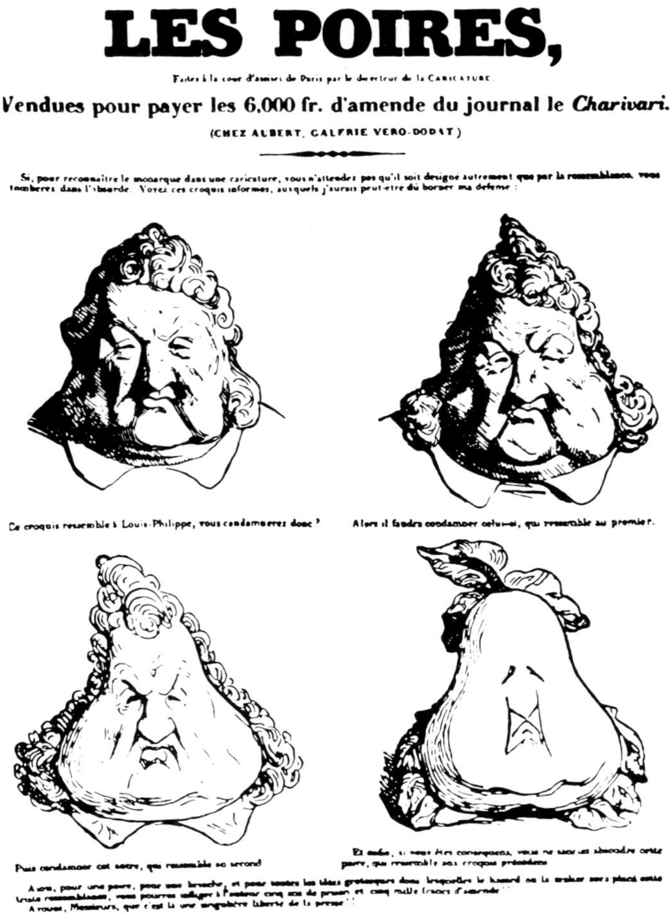

Fig. 6. Charivari cartoons of Louis Philippe by Charles Philipon, 1834. (See text for comments; also GOMBRICH, 1972)

poor at distinguishing faces were actually *less* bothered by inversion, as though they processed faces in a manner somewhat different from that adopted by those who were more efficient (YIN, 1969). Then he went on to prove that brain-injured men with long-standing injuries of the *right* posterior sector of their brain were worse at memorizing and recognizing previously unfamiliar faces (snapshots) shown in normal orientation, but were abnormally tolerant (less bothered) when those faces were shown upside down (YIN, 1970). Such differential effects of inversion were not found by YIN for similarly mono-oriented control materials such as pictures of houses or airplanes or costumes, or stick figures of people.[3]

It looked then, and again later when my colleague, Dr. Suzanne CORKIN, and I repeated and extended these studies in larger numbers of brain-injured men (TEUBER, 1975b), as though the right-hemisphere lesions entailed a change in processing, from the configurational approach critically dependent on upright position, to an approach that relies, often less efficiently, on this or that detail.

II. Clues from Physiology, Including Single-Unit Studies

No one has ever tried to record from single units in a primate in the presence of faces, but we know that the inferior temporal (IT) cortex in the monkey is important for higher-order visual processing (GROSS, 1973), with the integrity of the posterior portions of that cortex in the monkey perhaps more important for the solving of perceptual tasks, and the more anterior portions, for adequate performance on relatively simple, concurrent visual tasks, suggesting trouble with visual memory (IWAI, and MISHKIN, 1969). The striking results of GROSS et al. (1972), working with IT cortex in adult monkeys and recording from single neurons there, will have to be brought into contact with these results of lesion experiments: GROSS found exceedingly complex trigger features for individual IT neurons, almost reminiscent of the differential releasers for predatory versus courtship behavior in jumping spiders (Figs. 7 and 8). More recently, MISHKIN and his co-workers (personal communication) have launched a systematic study of such single-unit responses in the inferior portion of the temporal lobes of alert monkeys seated in restraining chairs in front of complex visual

[3] It must be pointed out that these relatively subtle changes in perception of faces are quite different from the (rare) instances of near-complete breakdown in face recognition. The latter condition is typically associated with damage to both sides of the brain, a situation that obtained in the case of severe imperception we have just described. Moreover, the more common, if subtle changes in face perception described by YIN and others, after right-hemisphere involvement (see, e.g., BENTON and VAN ALLEN, 1968; DE RENZI and SPINNLER, 1966; MILNER, 1960, 1968; TZAVARAS et al., 1970; WARRINGTON and JAMES, 1967), are probably best interpreted as a change in the "strategy" of face perception, and may not be readily dissociated from the equally subtle changes in the perception of other objects, e.g., those depicted in atypical views ("noncanonical" pictures, as introduced in an ingenious study by WARRINGTON and TAYLOR, 1973). It thus means using a shorthand expression (and a potentially misleading one), if one calls face perception an exclusive right-hemisphere function, even though it is clearly more vulnerable to right-sided than to left-sided lesions. Face recognition is not abolished by complete removal of a right hemisphere. Moreover, patients with surgical division of the large commissural fiber systems between their two hemispheres, studied by SPERRY (1974) and his colleagues (e.g., LEVY et al., 1972), can be shown to react quite predictably to composite ("chimeric") faces: when asked to match a composite snapshot against other snapshots, they rely on the left half of the composite face; when asked to name the face, they rely on the right half. The same, however, is true for other chimeric patterns, such as different flowers (e.g., the left half of a rose placed against the right half of another flower). Again, instructions to match elicit reliance on the right hemisphere (left half of visual field), and instructions to name, reliance on the left hemisphere (right half of visual field).

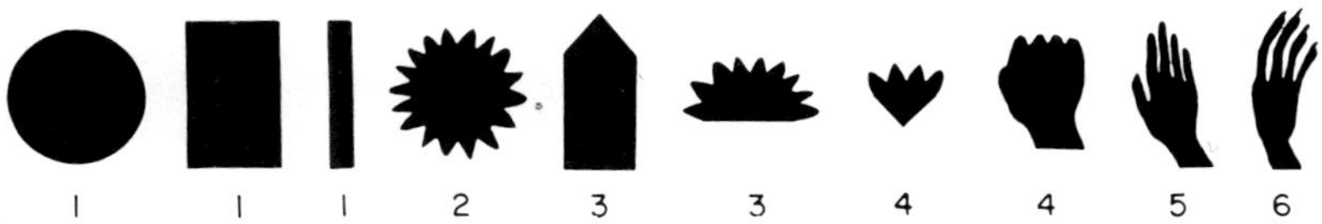

Fig. 7. Stimulus patterns (cardboard cutouts) used by GROSS and co-workers (1972) to elicit discharges in a single neuron in the rhesus monkey's inferotemporal (*IT*) cortex. Relative effectiveness increases from left to right, as noted below the patterns

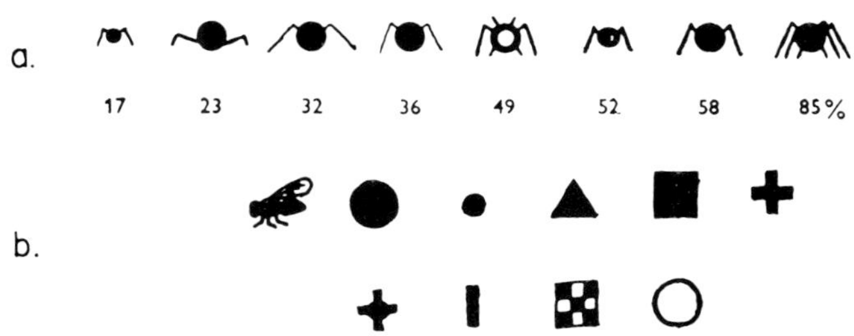

Fig. 8. Dummy stimuli (cardboard cutouts) used to demonstrate relative effectiveness of various patterns in releasing mating display (*above*, row *a*) and predatory stalking behavior (*below*, row *b*) in spiders. (After DREES, 1952)

patterns. The experiments are done in the hope of finding neural correlates of "complex representations." Obviously, the crucial issue remains that of identifying what it is that releases the cellular discharge. The neurons in GROSS' monkeys are not necessarily what they seem to be, i.e., not canonical detectors for hands, or even monkey hands; they could still be sensitive to, say, repetitive line patterns. But the findings nevertheless suggest neuronal arrangements capable of much higher-order classifications (see MISHKIN, 1966) than those provided by occipital feature-detecting elements with their sensitivities for orientation and direction, or velocity of movement, or color. What if these IT units were studied in the very young animal, or in those reared with selective visual deprivation? We can only guess.

III. Developmental Aspects

Yet we do know a bit more about the later stages in the development of face recognition by young children, thanks to the very recent work of my younger colleagues at M.I.T., Susan Carey-Block, Rhea Gendzier, and Bryan Woods, who are studying the reaction of normal and brain-injured children to snapshots of faces. They have found that young children, up to the age of 9 or 10, are rather poor at learning to recognize snapshots of unfamiliar faces in normal orientation, and, much like Yin's adults with right posterior brain injuries, normal children below 8 years of age are much less bothered by spatial inversion than are normal adults.

This prompted them to take a lead from the important work, here in Paris, by Ariane Lévy-Schoen (1964) and to ask children of different ages to identify snapshots of people's faces in spite of varying paraphernalia, such as hats, or changing hairstyles or eye glasses, or mustaches, or varying facial expressions. Carey and Diamond (1977) were then able to show that at the earlier ages whenever children were tolerant of inversion of snapshots, they were also most *intolerant* of (most readily folled by) changes in paraphernalia, whereas they were curiously uninfluenced by (or able to abstract from) changes in facial expression.

Obviously, this evidence fits together, if we assume that the early development of face perception goes from a rather piecemeal to an increasingly schematic and configurational mode of processing. Thus, paraphernalia that do not fool the adult are significant sources of confusion for the child, because the younger they are, the more likely they are to look for distinctive details rather than forming an overall complex impression (see also Vurpillot, 1972).

Clearly, this cannot be true in absolute terms, but only for *un*familiar faces, and perhaps only for the markedly reduced form of stimuli represented by snapshots. Accordingly, John Samuelson obtained Polaroid pictures of children with varying disguises, in playgroups, developing the pictures in front of the children so that no question of the origin of the picture could arise. When the snapshots depicted such thoroughly familiar faces as those of playmates or siblings, even 6-year-old children behaved more like normal adults: they could "see through" the varying paraphernalia, and they were disturbed by inversion. This was not true for Polaroid pictures taken in one playgroup and then shown to members of another group on the other side of town.

The early development of face perception is thus not adequately described if we were to say that young children could never adopt a schematic (rather than piecemeal) way of looking at snapshots of faces. What seems to grow, as the child grows in the first decade, is the capacity to *extend* the schematic manner of looking at faces from familiar to increasingly unfamiliar portraits. This would be compatible with the assumption of a rather slow postnatal maturation of certain systems in the nonspeech, right cerebral hemisphere.

C. Language and the Left Hemisphere

Ever since the pivotal discovery by Broca 115 years ago in Paris (1861), we have associated language capacities in the majority of adults with the integrity of important regions of the left cerebral hemisphere. But it is only fair to point out that after more than a century of investigation and debate, we are still unsure about nearly every important issue here. We are still ignorant of the precise structures that underlie different aspects of normal language performance, the mechanisms of first-language learning, and even the very *nature* of what it is we are losing when, after certain left-hemisphere lesions, we suffer impairments of production or reception of speech.

I. Effects of Lesions

Let me again begin the discussion with a singular case: a young soldier comes around in a battalion aid-station in Southeast Asia and concludes that he has been taken prisoner, because everyone seems to speak with abnormal rapidity and in what is obviously a foreign, incomprehensible tongue, even though all of the people about him are wearing American uniforms. He had sustained a penetrating shell-fragment wound of the left temporal lobe and did recover, as did most of these men (persistent aphasia, receptive or productive, being fortunately rather rare, in most of these cases). Yet to this day, he retains the impression that people talk abnormally fast.

This case prompted us to revive an exceedingly simple test, that of telling two clicks apart, one presented to one ear, in earphones, the other to the other, with varying brief time intervals between the clicks (LACKNER and TEUBER, 1973). Our patient in fact showed an extreme difficulty in separating the two clicks, much like the failure of certain patients with parietal-lobe injury to resolve the two points of a touch compass (Fig. 9). But is the breakdown in temporal resolution after certain left-hemisphere lesions (cf also TALLAL and PIERCY, 1975) all that is needed to understand the main features of receptive aphasias? Probably not; there are good reasons not to abandon Professor LU-

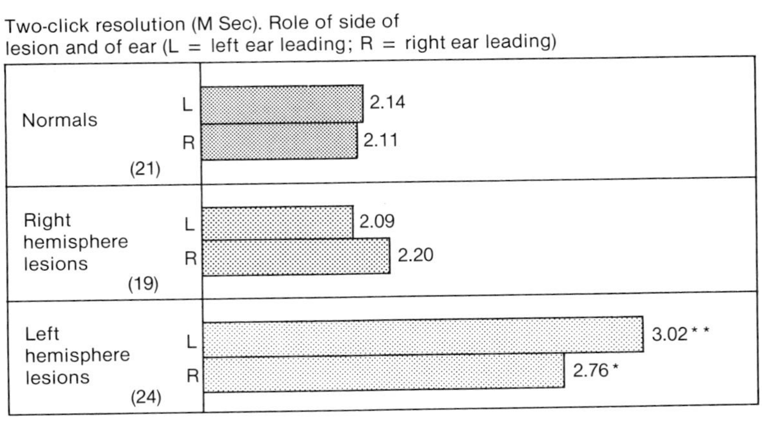

Fig. 9. Time intervals (in ms) needed to separate two clicks delivered (for 1 ms each) in brief succession, one to each ear (based on LACKNER and TEUBER, 1973). *L* left ear leading; *R* right ear leading

RIA's (1966) suggestion of a loss, at least in some of these cases, of "templates" for detecting the distinctive features out of which the phonemes of a language are built.[4]

II. Anatomical and Physiologic Aspects, Including Single-Unit Studies

It is obvious that we have little to say about possible neuronal mechanisms for speech perception or production. Vocal language in the human sense of that term is not known to exist in any other species, so that direct approaches to single-unit recording in the relevant cerebral regions can only be made in our own species where there are very few clinical situations that would justify such procedures. Nevertheless, we can derive some (admittedly distant) analogies for a microphysiology of reception of complex sounds from studies of neuronal reactions to species-specific sound patterns in animals (cf. review by WORDEN and GALAMBOS, 1972): the ingenious observations on specific auditory reactions in the bullfrog to the frog's croak, in CAPRANICA's (1965) and in FRISHKOPF's and GOLDSTEIN's work at M.I.T. (1963); the studies of squirrel monkey calls in Ploog's laboratory in Munich (WINTER et al., 1966; see also WOLLBERG and NEWMAN, 1972) and the still more recent work on the learned songs of canaries, where NOTTEBOHM et al. (1976) can now show so clearly a greater dependence of the song on the intactness of regions in the *left* rather than right cerebral hemisphere.

While some of these animal studies may eventually help us in understanding central neuronal arrangements for filtering complex sounds, they bear of course only very indirectly on the essential features of human language: the code-value of "phonemes," the universal and creative use of grammar, and the unsolved problem of semantics. It is probably far from being an evolutionary accident that the rich, vocal repertoires of squirrel monkeys depend on the integrity of so-called limbic regions of their brain (that is, on areas and pathways one associates ordinarily with the life of the emotions), and much less on anatomic structures which, in man, become essential for language. Such observations are in line with the deliberately provocative notion of Norbert Bischoff (personal communication), who believes that human language evolved quite apart from primarily emotional expression and social signals, and thus not as an elaboration of primate communication but as a tool for thought. Yet there is one respect in which the recent discoveries about birdsong do provide leads towards a possible physiology and anatomy of human language, and that is the extraordinary role played in both species, the songbird and the human, by the left rather than right cerebral hemisphere.

---

[4] It should nevertheless be noted that BLUMSTEIN and her colleagues (1977a, b) devoted two important studies to this very issue: they found that patients with posterior brain damage in the left hemisphere and marked difficulties in understanding speech were still able to discriminate between various pairs of phonemes, but were then not able to label the phonemes, indicating that the trouble in their cases seemed to lie on a higher level. In fact, even categorical perception of phonemes may be preserved in the absence of appropriate use of these phonemes in speech-comprehension.

III. Developmental and Comparative Aspects

The parallel here with early human development goes even further (NOTTEBOHM, 1971; NOTTEBOHM et al., 1976): it appears more and more likely that if unilateral lesions are placed in the avian brain *before* song has crystallized, the lesions cannot prevent full song from developing; presumably, song then develops on the other side of the bird's nervous system. Such plasticity is largely lost once the song has become established. In our own species, the relative sparing of language after early, but not after late left-hemisphere lesions is of course well known, but as MILNER has so strikingly demonstrated (1974a, b), early impingement on these left-sided language areas appears to be required before one can observe an atypical (right-hemisphere) representation of speech. It is as if the presence of an intact language zone on the left normally inhibits a latent potential for language on the right.

Very recently, BRYAN WOODS and I have noted (1973), much in line with some of MILNER's observations, that such "escape" of language is often achieved only at a price, and that this price then tends to be borne by functions that would normally depend on the integrity of the right (nonspeech) hemisphere (a point also made by SPERRY, 1974). Thus, we were able to determine, in yet unpublished work, that very early lesions of *either* hemisphere in children can permanently impair their performance on the "paraphernalia" test for unfamiliar faces. In fact, our observations on very early lesions seem to suggest a primacy of language that will develop even under the handicap of massive left-sided cerebral destruction but with consequent impairment on various non-language tasks. There appears to be less of a corresponding plasticity for certain right-hemisphere functions, in cases where there is early damage to the right side, and the intact left hemisphere is already largely committed to speech.

But, whatever one thinks of these claims for developmental asymmetries, it is clear to me that we may have to take some of my colleague CHOMSKY's warnings (1968) very seriously: the tremendous achievements of the normal child in the acquisition of language *must* require an intricate, and essentially innate, apparatus shared by all of humankind, for the extraction of linguistic features, and for the production of grammatically ordered speech. It is for this reasons that we have set up a little cradle in which FODOR et al. (1969) in our department, years ago, used to place very young infants to test their reaction to speech sounds, and we have dubbed this little cradle a "hotbed of nativism," and the particular laboratory in our building where this work takes place the "cave of Plato."

In FODOR's and GARRETT's work at M.I.T. (e.g., FODOR et al., 1975) and in the more extensive work of PETER EIMAS and his colleagues at Brown University (1971), a strong case has been made for categorical perception of phonemes by infants, even before their babbling stage: these babies readily distinguish "p" from "k" across different vowel environments, though the physical waveforms of *p* in front of *ee* and *oo* vary greatly as LIBERMAN and COOPER and their colleagues at the Haskins Laboratory (1967) have so convincingly established.

If the categorical perception of phonemes in the preverbal child can be accepted (and there is still some controversy), how should it be explained? For those who believe in a motor theory of speech perception, the distinctive features that determine what phonemes we hear simply reflect the principal ways in which we articulate speech sounds (cf. LIBERMAN et al., 1967). Thus, the "distinctive features" would be more than a universal schema for classifying phonemes, in all their diversity, across languages; the features would be "real," in the sense of being universal neuronal mechanisms for producing *and* for perceiving sounds of speech. This seminal idea was at the center of ROMAN JAKOBSON's argument made over 30 years ago (1942), when he drew attention to the universality, all over the world, of baby talk. Clearly, however, as JAKOBSON already pointed out then, a strong form of such a motor theory of speech perception must be impossible; we obviously hear some phonemic distinctions we cannot make.

The case of the preverbal child, with his amazing ways of classifying speech sounds that he cannot yet articulate, certainly detracts from any idea that we pattern our perceptions of speech sounds only *after* we have managed to adopt correctly the corresponding gestures of our vocal apparatus. But this is not to say that there could not be a genetically anchored preadaptation (of what we can learn to hear in the rapid and complex flow of speech) to whatever we can *potentially* articulate. Just as earlier evolution has fashioned the feature-sensitive neuronal elements, in all species that can see patterns, even so our hearing of "speech as speech" may well have required an evolution that built internal templates for the distinctive features of phonemes, in a manner that fits the *making* of these features, by the speaker, like key and lock.

A recent example bears on this issue: In a series of studies in our department, WILLIAM COOPER (1974) demonstrated (as had EIMAS' group) that we can "adapt" to speech sounds; that is, the normal adult listener, after hearing a "tee" sound eight or more times over, will require a different acoustic wave pattern at the end of the exposure, if the syllable is to sound to him the same as before the exposure. What COOPER adds is the proof that this change is not limited to what the listener hears after having been saturated with "tee," but that the change also infects (i.e., distorts transiently) how he pronounces that very sound.

D. From Perception to Motion

Even if only a weak form of the motor theory of speech perception can be admitted, there is further accumulating evidence that central motor programs for producing speech sounds must play a role in the ways the sounds of speech can be perceived. And this evidence fits with the more general idea that the problems of patterning of movements and patterning in perception are intimately related one to another.

I. Effects of Lesions

Close linkage between the patterning of perception and of movement can be seen in a truly amazing disclosure by LAUGHLIN TAYLOR, BRENDA MILNER, and CHRISTOPHER DARWIN (personal communication, but see also ETTLINGER et al., 1975): Small cortical removals (performed in patients for the control of focal epilepsy) from the "face area" on the left side of the brain (within the sensorimotor strip) are followed by severe and characteristic discorders of *spelling*. These patients make many errors on both oral and written spelling tests, and they have remarkable difficulties in deciding which embedded stop-consonant has been heard, when you expose them to bisyllabic utterances, such as "a*g*ma," "a*t*ma," "a*p*ma."

Yet the close connection between perception and movement does not need to be explored exclusively in the realm of speech. As I said earlier, even the most elementary acts of seeing a line in a particular place, in spite of eye movements or head tilts on our part, already point to a fundamental aspect of sensorimotor interaction that must enter into all perception and play its role in all perceptually guided movement. In order to know where things are, in relation to ourselves, we must know where *we* are, at any given moment; our own positions and postures, and any changes in posture, are thus part and parcel of both perception *and* action. Usually, these considerations are subsumed under the rubric of proprioception and particularly vestibular *in*flow during changes in posture; but beyond these sorts of simple considerations, a central *out*flow of signals, *re*setting and even *pre*setting the sensory mechanisms in our central nervous system, may have to be assumed. Thus, in addition to the elementary processing of inputs, and to the elaboration of complex perceptual patterns (which we have considered so far in this lecture), we must ask by what neuronal arrangements our brain manages to take "into account" (MACKAY, 1972) those continual transformations of the scene that are the result of our own motor output. For a long time, I have assigned a special role in this outflow regulation to the more anterior portions of the forebrain (TEUBER, 1960, 1964, 1971a, b).

Let me start, here too, close to the beginning of my own work, and rapidly trace the evolution of my thoughts on the frontal and parietal lobes up to the present. In 1954, MISHKIN and I observed how deep frontal lesions, in previously healthy men, especially in the acute phase after their injury, interfered with the setting of the subjective visual vertical when the head and body were tilted. This was a most unexpected finding, since the perception of the vertical was already known to be very resistant to posterior brain lesions, even in the presence of large scotomata or more complex perceptual difficulties. Note that these patients with acute frontal injury had no difficulty in setting the visual vertical as long as they themselves were upright, nor in setting themselves upright in the dark. The trouble seemed to be specific to the visuopostural version of the task, in which they had to take their own (tilted) posture into account while producing a visual judgement. This strange symptom might still have been interpreted as a difficulty in dealing with two kinds of concurrent sensory inflow: visual and postural information, but other tasks were soon discovered for which an interpretation in terms of altered outflow signals seemed more compelling (TEUBER, 1964, 1972).

Similar perceptual-motor difficulties have been demonstrated in patients after damage to the basal ganglia beneath the frontal cortex (TEUBER and PROCTOR, 1964), as would have been predicted by Richard JUNG (cf. JUNG and HASSLER, 1960), except that, in the case of the basal ganglia lesion, purely postural tasks (such as righting oneself in the dark) may also be impaired. We have since then (1976) attempted to relate many of our observations in men with frontal or basal ganglia disorders to the impressively systematic observations on the effects of experimental removals from these structures in monkeys (see MISHKIN and PRIBRAM, 1956; ROSVOLD, 1972).

Obviously, this enormously large and complex apparatus in the primate forebrain cannot be analyzed in terms of any single contribution to behavior. Still, we cling to our belief that many symptoms of frontal-lobe disorders, both in man and in monkey, could be covered by a proposal that goes back to views expressed by HELMHOLTZ in the last century (1867), and by VON HOLST and MITTELSTAEDT (1950), as well as, independently, Roger SPERRY (1950), in the middle of the present century. Specifically, we postulate that when we make deliberate voluntary movements (e.g., shift our eyes across the room), *two* streams of signals are initiated within our nervous system, and not only one. One of these two is of course the classical motor outflow to the effector organs. The other set of signals is sent, directly and centrally, to the sensory systems, so that the consequences of the intended action can be taken into account.

We call these discharges "corollary" when they are essentially derivations of momentary motor commands, and "anticipatory" when more remote consequences of the impending action are being computed. In either case, these signals (which we believe originate at least in part from the more anterior portions of the forebrain) involve an information flow that is the reverse of the classical, Sherringtonian one: not from sensory to motor, from back to front, so to speak, but in the opposite direction, from motor and premotor to sensory, and therefore from front to back.

Several points need to be made about these conjectures. I no longer believe, as I did for many years, that such corollary and anticipatory mechanisms should be vested entirely into the anterior portions of the cerebral mantle; not only frontal, but also parietal mechanisms may be important (MOUNTCASTLE, 1976). But I still believe that these mechanisms, even though unproven, will be found, since only they can provide the requisite stability for our perceptions, and the spatial and temporal framework for action.

The notions certainly helped us to understand the curious, though often transitory difficulties in *visual searching* which can be seen in monkey and man after certain frontal lesions (but more severely and persistently after mid- and posterior parietal damage), in which the failure of search seems best interpreted as a more fundamental failure in properly adjusting self-produced output to recurrent input (TEUBER, 1964, 1972). The concepts have helped us to accept, as a symptom of certain frontal lesions, the curious abnormalities in the reversal of certain reversible figures, and these concepts might even be extended to the more complex breakdown in performance on tests of sorting and categorizing, such as the familiar Wisconsin version of Weigl's famous test (GRANT and BERG, 1948).

As MILNER (1963, 1964) has demonstrated, superior convexity lesions of the frontal lobes (even if unilateral) can disrupt performance on this task. The failure is not in categorical thinking as such, but in the execution of the task. I often cite those of my patients with frontal lesions who indicate that they "know" what to do. The patient might say, "You can do this according to color, form, or number," yet he fails again and again, saying, "It must be color, so if I do this (sorting, e.g., to form), I'll be wrong. See – I'm right – I'm wrong" (TEUBER, 1964). This extremely baffling and tragic perversion of action is of course exactly what our friend LURIA has described again and again for cases of massive (often neoplastic) involvement of the frontal lobes in man, perhaps most explicitly in *his* evening address to the International Congress of Psychology, held in London in 1969 (LURIA, 1971).

II. Single-Unit and Microanatomical Studies

Yet we are certainly far from having any notion of how we should picture these corollary and anticipatory discharges, or more broadly put, programs for action, in any specific detail within the nervous system. We know, however, thanks to the work of BIZZI and SCHILLER in the M.I.T. laboratories (1970), that the frontal eye fields contain numerous cells that discharge not *before*, like motor neurons, but *during* particular eye and head movements, as if accompanying the action and announcing it to the animal while the action proceeds (Fig. 10). Further forward, in the banks of the principal sulcus, Peter Schiller (unpublished data) found cells that discharge, if and only if the monkey looks at an object *and* reaches for it, but the units become silent when the monkey looks without reaching or reaches without looking. It may be important to note that these regions of the frontal cortex project (as GOLDMAN and NAUTA have just shown again with careful radioisotope studies, 1976) into the depths of the superior colliculus in the midbrain and into the pons in the brain stem, where they can influence ongoing eye-movement-related activity. Also, there is little question that individual superior-colliculus cells can be identified that *turn off* when the eye moves relative to a fixed visible target, and discharge vigorously to the same movement, when it is produced by a real motion of the target across the stationary eye (ROBINSON and WURTZ, 1976).

At least as exciting, though still open to alternative interpretations, is the emerging story of the mode of action of cells in the so-called parietal association cortex (areas 5 and 7 on the standard cortical maps), where MOUNTCASTLE and his group at JOHNS HOPKINS (1975, 1976) are finding numerous cells akin to the few seen by SCHILLER in the midfrontal region: cells that discharge when the animal looks at an object within reach, or moves his hand to grasp it.

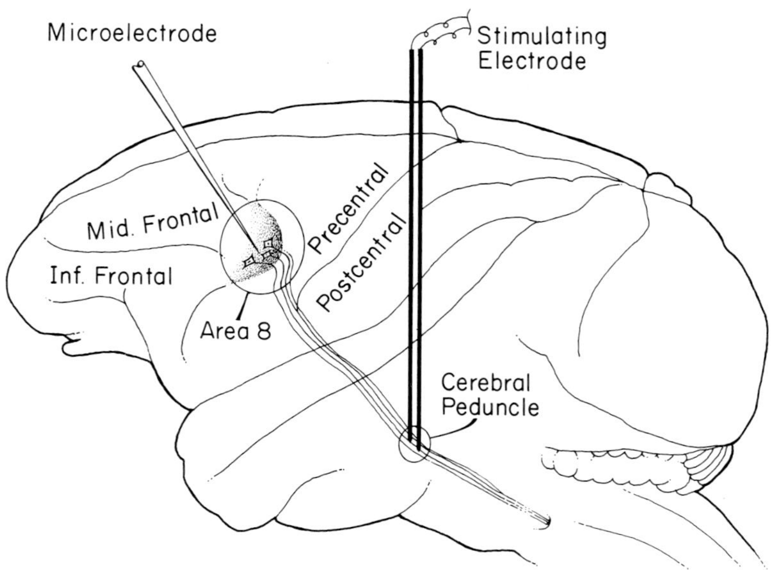

Fig. 10. Experimental arrangement for recording single-unit responses from the monkey's frontal eye fields (see, e.g., BIZZI and SCHILLER, 1970). A stimulating electrode is used to trigger impulses that are conducted upward (against their normal direction) into the cells of origin of the descending fibers stimulated. In this way, one can prove that the cells in the frontal lobe ("area 8"), from which the microelectrode records, are in fact sending their efferents to the brain stem. The microelectrode records before, during, and after various eye and head movements initiated by the monkey. Occasionally, neurons are found in the principal horizontal sulcus which discharge conjointly to eye and hand movements. (See text for details)

Obviously, we have known for a long time that these mid- and posterior parietal regions are crucially important for orienting ourselves to our own bodies and to external space. The behavioral tests developed years ago by my colleagues JOSEPHINE SEMMES, LILA GHENT, SIDNEY WEINSTEIN, and myself (1955), have made it clear that even decades after parietal gunshot wounds, subtle but significant difficulties can exist in the finding of routes by means of maps. The deficit is not due to any trouble with memory, since the defect exists even though the maps are carried by the patient and continuously inspected (as in the case of visually presented maps), or palpated by one or the other hand (in the case of maps made in raised relief). Nor are these cerebral systems so organized that the orientation in external space is inexorably bound up with orientation to one's own body (SEMMES et al., 1963). A slow-growing tumor in the posterior sector of the brain may gradually produce total blindness in a patient (once it involves more than the visual cortex proper) and also simultaneously destroy all capacity for spatial orientation, even in the most familiar of surroundings; yet it can leave orientation to one's own body quite intact. Orientation to the body (personal orientation) is thus evidently dissociable from orientation to extrapersonal space, and depends on the integrity of more anterior parts of the cerebral convexity.

III. Developmental and Comparative Aspects

Much remains to be done to explore the early developmental status of human frontal and parietal-lobe functions. RITA RUDEL and I have applied the Tilting Chair Rest (TEUBER and RUDEL, 1962) as well as the Route-Finding and Body Scheme Task (RUDEL and TEUBER, 1971) to normal children and young adults and to those with early lesions of their brains, and found a surprisingly slow development of adult-like performance in the normal child and devastating effects on these capacities after early cerebral lesions. What is most intriguing, however, is the question of how—quite generally in the young and in the old—motor and perceptual systems interact. It is clear that the complex evolution of a normal infant's reach takes him through stages reminiscent of a patient with deep frontal-lobe lesions. Infants quite normally exhibit grasping automatisms, and even visually-elicited groping: a magnetlike reaction, as if they were still incapable of disenthralling themselves from the overpowering presence of the desired stimulus object. Such behavior (described years ago in our laboratories by THOMAS TWITCHELL, 1965) resembles the breakdown in reaching seen in adult patients with deep frontal lesions who grasp your hand and cannot release their grasp, or follow the reflex hammer as if drawn by a magnet—a performance that would make sense if there were in those cases no corollary or anticipatory discharges whereby the person could take the impending consequences of his own action into account.

In fact, my colleague NAUTA has recently extended our corollary-discharge notion (as a maker of voluntariness of voluntary action) to the baffling effects or *orbital*-frontal lesions in man where we sometimes, unfortunately, see long-lasting disturbances in the capacity to conform to the values of society. A similar lack of compliance to the norms of behavior is brought out even in the laboratory in the curious "rule-breaking behavior" on simple tests, as has been noted by MILNER (1965), peculiar to patients with massive frontal-lobe excisions. NAUTA now proposes (1971) that many neurons in the *orbital*-frontal cortex with their intimate relations to the visceral organs within the body, might discharge in a manner that would permit the organism to compute in advance what it would feel like, in one's viscera, if one were about to adopt this or that course of action.

Much of this is admittedly conjecture, but you can see, perhaps, how without such conjectures or "anticipatory" glimpses of what might be the case we would not be able to formulate appropriate experimental questions, whether addressed to the behavior of the whole organism or to the individual neurons. It may be a fair guess that the next series of discoveries will uncover the adequate stimuli for diverse neuronal units in the vast associative and limbic regions of the forebrain.

E. Mood, Memory, and the Limbic System

All of the so-called association areas—temporal, parietal, frontal—discharge massively (as has been shown with the Nauta technique by PANDYA et al., 1971, and by JONES and POWELL, 1970, and others besides them) into what we call since BROCA the *limbic* regions of our brain (Fig. 11). And these limbic regions in turn, as well as the neocortex, are in receipt of profuse input from below, from those chemically specific pathways so recently described that take their origin in the brain stem and carry the so-called biogenic amines, noradrenalin, dopamine, serotonin and perhaps others, over most of the forebrain (see, e.g., FUXE, 1965; UNGERSTEDT, 1971). Few would deny the affinity of these systems to processes involved in the regulation of mood and motives, their importance for memory, their role in self-stimulation (OLDS and MILNER, 1954), and particularly for aminergic brain stem structures, a role in wakefulness and sleep (JOUVET, 1973).

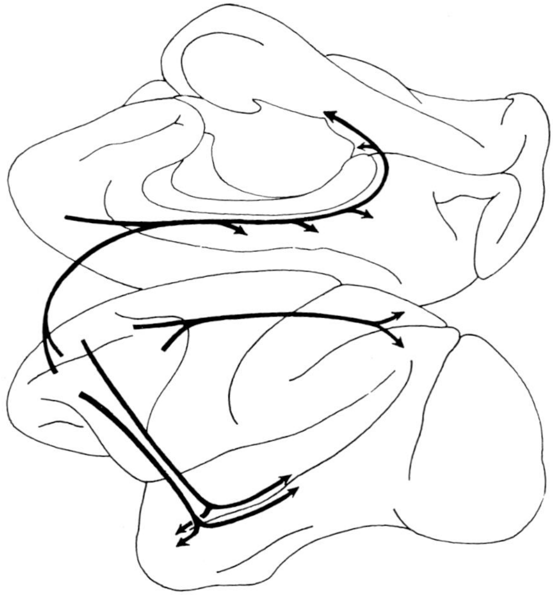

Fig. 11. Diagram of direct fiber connections (as established by modified NAUTA techniques) originating from the frontal cortex of the monkey, and projecting to other neocortical and limbic areas (from: NAUTA, 1971). Note how the frontal cortex sends fibers back to the temporal and parietal lobes, and down into the "limbic belt," i.e., into the presubiculum and thence into the hippocampus. A similar outflow of fibers towards the hippocampal region can also be shown for the temporal and the parietal "association cortex." Other projections, from cortex to subcortex, and from subcortex upwards, or from nonfrontal regions towards the frontal lobe, are omitted from this diagram

I. Effects of Lesions

The interpretation of lesion effects in limbic areas is still beset with controversy, perhaps even more than for the neocortical systems we have treated primarily so far in this lecture. But let me give a few possible instances here, again starting with some of my earliest observations. Toward the end of the Second World War, I encountered a patient with a shell fragment balloting freely in the third ventricle of his brain, as illustrated in Figure 12. As my former colleague BENDER and I have described on many occasions (TEUBER et al., 1960), this patient presented the kind of global disorder one is not likely to see after a focal lesion of the cerebral convexity: abrupt mood swings, forced crying and laughter, and inappropriate sadness or elation, together with all sorts of fluctuations in vital regulatory activities, such as blood pressure and body temperature. What is remarkable here is that the patient was at first

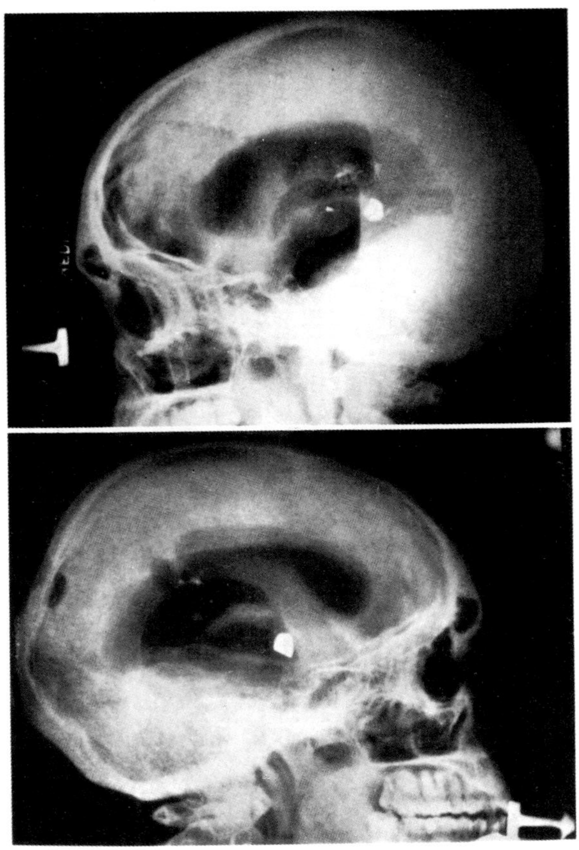

Fig. 12. Metallic foreign body balloting in a markedly enlarged third ventricle of the brain (compare skull X-rays taken with patient in the brow-up and in the brow-down positions), following head injury incurred by shell fragments in World War II. (After TEUBER et al., 1960). (For Behavioral symptoms; i.e., mood swings, memory disturbances, failure of vital regulations, see text)

(and for several weeks), quite capable of maintaining a critical outlook, saying when he cried, "It cries in me," only to begin to invent reasons for his unmotivated sadness later on, just as patients with freely arising, so-called endogenous, depressions tend to do, inventing, after a while, reasons for being sad.

Yet at the same time, this man exhibited a severe anterograde amnesia. He was forgetful to the point where people had to be reintroduced to him after brief absences from the testing room. To me, as a student of Lashley and of Goldstein, this amnesia seemed to be merely an essential part of the patient's general disturbance in mood and of his post-traumatic confusion, but events have since shown me that these different components of such a global disorder are strongly dissociable.

For one thing, at least temporary modifications in abnormal mood can apparently be produced by relatively minor assaults on parts of the limbic system (Fig. 13). In an attempt to relieve long-lasting depression, obsessive-

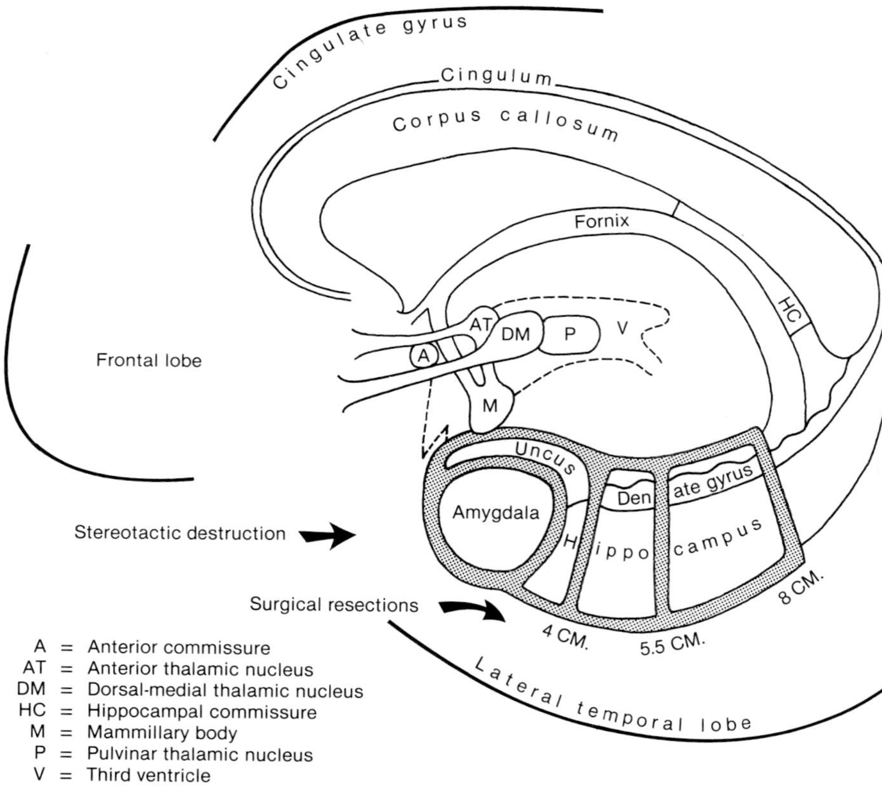

Fig. 13. Diagram of major-way stations in limbic cortex and in various subcortical cell groups that have been implicated at various times in lesions (surgical or accidental) followed by alterations in memory or mood. (After OJEMAN, 1966) Note the cingulate cortex and cingulum bundle (*top*), where lesions are being placed in cases of cingulotomy (see also Figure 14, and text). Note also areas labeled amygdala, uncus, hippocampus (*lower part of diagram, largest resection*), which were removed, as indicated, in SCOVILLE's patient H.M. (See SCOVILLE and MILNER, 1957), together with parahippocampal gyrus (not shown)

compulsive disorders, or persistent pain, our colleague Thomas Ballantine has made small bilateral lesions in the cingulum, within the limbic belt (Fig. 14). These lesions are followed by surprisingly little (and essentially transient) effects on complex intellectual achievements or memory processes, but there are often quite noticeable modifications of mood (TEUBER et al., 1977). Thus, in 11 recently studied cases of persistent and totally disabling pain, refractory to all sorts of other treatments over the years, "cingulotomy" was said by nine of the patients to have abolished or markedly altered their pain, by removing the intolerable quality of the experience, even though "new" pains from other sources could readily be felt. In those cases where there had been severe addiction to pain-relieving drugs before the surgery, the addiction vanished afterwards, since the patients could be taken abruptly off their drugs without any withdrawal symptoms.

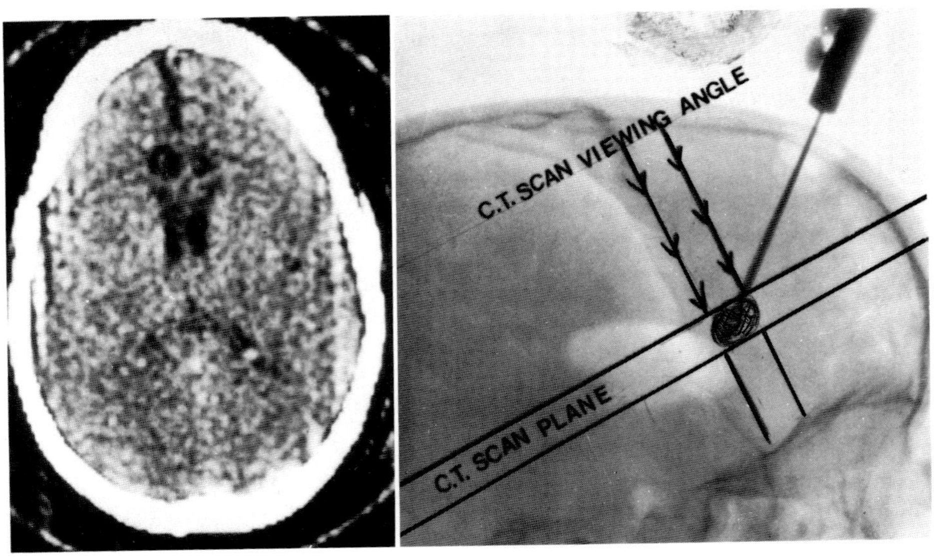

Fig. 14. Computerized X-ray (by computer-assisted tomography) (*left*), showing anterior horns of ventricular system in brain, and two circular areas in front (*top*), corresponding to surgically produced lesions in cingulate region and cingulum bundle. For comparison, conventional X-rays (air studies) are shown on right taken during the operation. (Courtesy of Dr. T. BALLANTINE, Massachusetts General Hospital, Boston, Mass., USA.)

This is not to say that such destructive procedures on the human brain are the answer to addiction, or the ultimate answer to intractable pain or other persistent disorders of mood; I cite these cases only to underscore the subtlety and apparent selectivity in the effects of certain circumscribed limbic lesions. Perhaps we should not have been surprised in view of the far-reaching resiliency we had observed after many of the small lesions in our series of young patients with cerebral trauma.

On the other hand, devastating and virtually irreversible effects on memory can result from bilateral limbic lesions that are differently placed in the medial temporal regions (see again Fig. 13), or from damage to midline structures in the thalamus (ADAMS et al., 1962) or in the tegmental regions of the midbrain (TEUBER et al., 1969). Perhaps the best known instance of such memory disorder is the much-cited case of H.M., a patient of SCOVILLE and MILNER (1957), in whom uncus, amygdala, hippocampus, and parahippocampal gyrus were resected bilaterally in 1953. This surgery was performed by SCOVILLE as a last resort in attempting to control epilepsy (see again Fig. 13).

As Professor MILNER has shown, in numerous systematic examinations in the follow-up of this case (MILNER, 1962; MILNER et al., 1968), H.M. presents more than a mere sum of the contrasting material-specific memory disorders she has described for cases of unilateral (left or right) anterior temporal lobectomy where the removal encroached upon the hippocampus (MILNER, 1971). H.M.'s extreme forgetfulness after this bilateral medial temporal removal is clearly different from the changes in the perceptual or linguistic processing one sees after various neocortical lesions, because these specific perceptual or linguistic troubles can be absent in a global amnesia such as H.M's, yet little of ongoing events can be recalled.

In a case such as H.M.'s, it does not matter whether the events he seems to forget were seen, heard, or felt, or whether they could be put into words or not. Still more baffling is a further aspect of such a global amnesia: H.M. has similar trouble with recall for events that *antedate* his operation by a year and a half. He thus shows a retrograde amnesia in addition to his continuing anterograde amnesia, as did other cases of amnesia resulting from bilateral medial temporal lesions (PENFIELD and MILNER, 1958; PENFIELD and MATHIESON, 1974).

These retrograde amnesias within the amnesic state represent a special feature that any theory of memory will have to explain. The phenomenon was already known to RIBOT (1881), though he cannot have had any inkling of a relationship between amnesic states and the integrity of various limbic structures. Unfortunately, some of the basic facts are still in dispute. SANDERS and WARRINGTON (1971) reported that their amnesic patients actually did equally badly on tests of recognition for photographs of famous public figures across all premorbid epochs for which the patients were tested. Others (SELTZER and BENSON, 1974; MARSLEN-WILSON and TEUBER, 1975; SQUIRE et al., 1975), using somewhat different techniques and different kinds of amnesic patients, have come instead to the conclusion (much in line with RIBOT's original view) that there is a "gradient" of retrograde effects on memory: events closest to the onset of the illness are least likely to be recalled.

The same claim of a greater vulnerability of recent over older pretraumatic material in memory has been made for the reversible effects upon memory of bilateral hippocampal stimulation through indwelling electrodes in epileptic patients (see BICKFORD et al., 1960; CHAPMAN et al., 1967). In these studies (which are probably experimental duplications of what one witnesses in spontaneously occurring episodes of ictal amnesia in temporal-lobe epilepsy or in transient bilateral troubles with cerebral circulation), the patients develop both anterograde and retrograde memory gaps; the longer the period of electric stimulation, the greater the retroactive gap in their memory. Thus seconds of current flow are sometimes reported to "erase" hours of events preceding the maneuver, and minutes of current flow, entire days.

A rather concordant picture emerged from repeated quantitative studies of these phenomena of anterograde and retrograde amnesias in our brain-injured patient population. In several earlier surveys of the amnesia-inducing effects of head injuries, we found (TEUBER, 1968, 1969) that although post-traumatic amnesia can readily appear without retrograde amnesia, the converse situation of retrograde amnesia without post-traumatic amnesia does not seem to hold (see Tables 1 and 2). But to what question is this an answer? This asymmetry clearly must contain a clue to the physiology of memory—but what is that clue?

Table 1. Memory disorders[a] in 100 consecutive cases of penetrating brain injury in young adults (World War II series)

None	38
RA alone	0
PTA alone	15
RA and PTA	21
AA (and RA and PTA)	19
Undefined	7
	100

[a] Definitions:
Retrograde amnesia (RA)—Inability to recall events that occurred *before* the brain trauma.
Post-traumatic amnesia (PTA)—Inability to recall events that occurred *after* the trauma.
Anterograde amnesia (AA)—Persistent post-traumatic amnesia

Table 2. Relationship between duration of retrograde amnesia and duration of post-traumatic amnesia of immediate onset in 88 consecutive cases of head injury sustained in Korean War

Retrograde amnesia	Post-traumatic amnesia			
	None	Seconds to 1 day	>1 Day to 1 week	>1 week
None	25 (28%)	3 (3%)	9 (10%)	5 (6%)
Seconds		6 (7%)	10 (12%)	10 (12%)
Minutes		3 (3%)	5 (6%)	2 (2%)
Hours, days, weeks, months			3 (3%)	7 (8%)

The crucial issue, here as elsewhere, is the question of how to analyze the altered behavior. Can we identify a root symptom in amnesia (or, at least, in some forms of amnesia) from which everything else about the condition would follow? At this stage, these questions of interpretation are still a matter of strenuous debate, even though most of us will admit that there is simply no single interpretation that fits all aspects of this tragic condition.[5] Among the interpretations proposed are those that put trouble with consolidation of memory traces into the center: the hippocampus and related structures would then be thought to "boost" traces during the early stages of their becoming established so that loss of such "boosting" activity would lead to insufficient consolidation (see MILNER et al., 1968). Others prefer more semantic interpretations and invoke insufficient depths of initial encoding as the root failure in many amnesic states (BUTTERS and CERMAK, 1974). In some ways, the most radical and the most ingenious interpretation is that advanced by WARRINGTON and WEISKRANTZ (1970), who consider trouble with retrieval rather than with initial encoding or storage as the outstanding feature of the amnesic state. Each of these interpretations (and there are others, e.g., GAFFAN's 1974 proposal of selective failure of recognition memory) can account for some aspects of abnormal forgetfulness but not for others.

A further complication is the obvious possibility that the amnesic state itself might not be unitary but appears in qualitatively different forms associated with different lesions (LHERMITTE and SIGNORET, 1972; MILNER 1966; MILNER and TEUBER 1968; ZANGWILL, 1966).

The amnesia of the Korsakoff syndrome (brain damage in severe alcoholism) certainly differs from that of patients such as H.M. by virtue of H.M.'s profound self-consciousness and anguish about the possible social consequences of his morbid forgetfulness and by his continual but insuccessful efforts to remember; both the awareness of illness and the efforts to remember are typically absent in the postalcoholic Korsakoff syndrome.

II. Limbic Unit Activity and Related Physiologic Issues

A major obstacle in the search for physiologic correlates of human amnesia after bilateral medial temporal destruction is the absence of similarly severe or obvious memory losses in animals after bilateral hippocampectomies. This may be due to a genuine species difference in cerebral organization, or to

[5] Thus, H.M. did generally well on our test of famous faces (i.e., was good at retrieval) for the faces known up to, but not beyond, the beginning of the 1950s, showing a precipitous decline in unprompted recognition for faces that had become publicly known in the 1950s and 1960s (MARSLEN-WILSON and TEUBER, 1975). On the other hand, he profited better with letter prompts than with circumstantial (semantic) prompts for faces he did not recognize. On tests that required him to learn strings of words beyond his span (cf. HEBB, 1961) he failed to show ultra-span learning (DRACHMAN and ARBIT, 1966) but he did produce quite remarkable responses that show preservation of nearly all of the constituent phonemes, though recombined into new words, e.g., when the examiners gave him "store tree camp earth rain eye," H.M. responded with "storm key train birth plain eye" (MARSLEN-WILSON and TEUBER, in preparation).

an incomparability of behavioral tasks when applied across different species. In this respect, the proposal of WARRINGTON and WEISKRANTZ (1970)—that the essence of human amnesia is a failure in retrieval—is particularly attractive, since it would bring the effects of bimesial temporal-lobe lesions in man much more in line with what is so far known to happen after similar lesions in subhuman forms, where no global amnesias have yet been demonstrated. In animals with hippocampal removals, the picture seems to be instead one of trouble with response selection, or with inhibition of irrelevant responses.

Analogously, WARRINGTON and WEISKRANTZ (1970) can show for amnesic patients that seemingly forgotten material is brought out by methods of prompting that exclude potentially interfering or intrusive material. Yet greater success in the retrieval of traces when sources of interference are eliminated could also be taken to mean that the traces are weak or fragmentary to begin with (a view preferred by ZANGWILL, 1943, 1966; MILNER, 1962; HUPPERT and PIERCY, 1976, and by WILLIAMS, 1950, in their earlier descriptions of the amnesic state). None of these continuing perplexities detract from the fundamental importance of the discovery that the hippocampus and related structures are so crucial for normal memory in man; what the perplexities do is to hamper our inquiry into the specific physiology of these vital limbic structures.

If there is, as yet, even less certainty about the activity of single units in limbic structures as compared with other brain regions, then it is not for want of observations and often bold hypotheses. For the rodent's hippocampal formation, for instance, single-unit activity has been brought into correlation with various stages in conditioning (e.g., SEGAL et al., 1972), or with more elementary appetitive activities such as eating and drinking (RANCK, 1975). Others have invoked a more generalized response to "familiarity," or to "place" (GAGE and OLTON, 1975; O'KEEFE and DOSTROVSKY, 1971), yet the vehemence of the controversy (e.g., NADEL et al., 1975) suggests that we have not yet converged on the most appropriate ways of putting our question to the hippocampal units. Perhaps it will help to renew the long-discredited notion of a close relation between the hippocampus and the olfactory system, in line with Kipling's verses that "smells are surer than sights or sounds to make our heart strings crack." For some time now, colleagues of ours in the M.I.T. laboratories, under the direction of S.L. CHOROVER, have been looking at the mode of action of individual units of the rodent's and rabbit's olfactory bulb and olfactory brain during reception of biologically important odors (odors of the mate or the litter), and they have looked for longer-lasting changes in these activities during simple forms of olfactory discrimination learning.

It is after all well established that exposure to the odor of an individual male pocket mouse during mating will enable the female mouse to recognize the odor of her partner afterwards, for at least 24–36 hours, because the odor of any other male mouse will make this female terminate her pregnancy. This pregnancy block (PARKES and BRUCE, 1962) is surely a remarkable case of acquired distinctiveness of cues but still refractory to detailed analysis because we know as yet so little about the primary input transduction in the olfactory system. Yet somehow one thinks that a major revelation about memory is to be found in that system, if we only focus on the sufficiently basic questions.

III. Developmental and Comparative Issues

Least of all is known about the ontogeny of various aspects of learning, yet it is here that important clues might be obtained. The relatively slow postnatal differentiation of hippocampal granule cells in rodents has been brought into relation with the delayed emergence of certain learning capacities (e.g., BAYER et al., 1973; DOUGLAS et al., 1973; EGGER et al., 1973), and the affinities of the structure to particular monoamine systems (e.g., MOORE and HALARIS, 1975) would suggest that even in our own species the early postnatal development of these limbic structures might be closely correlated with changing behavioral repertoires and changing susceptibilities to various behavior-modifying drugs. We know how different early learning, in the very young child, can be from that in the older child and adult, but the tracing out of the corresponding brain-behavior relationships has barely begun.

Conclusion

In looking back over the road we have traveled, I am aware of how small a part of the total territory has been traversed. The experiments we have reviewed are mostly those of one laboratory and are in any case seen from one vantage point. Yet such a personal view of a growing field is inevitable and perhaps not entirely undesirable. Our work produces us, even more than we can be said to produce our work, and the work becomes a filter through which we look at our field.

The key questions about perception and movement, memory and mood remain unanswered, but I have tried to indicate why I believe we must keep them before us as we proceed. We have emphasized the role of feature detectors in vision and possibly in language but admitted to the uncertainties that still cling to their role in global behavior. We discussed their relative innateness and the apparent limits of their modifiability. All these unresolved issues are powerful sources of experiment. So are the residual problems concerning the patterning of voluntary movement and the ways in which incipient motor acts might transform our perception. Normal and abnormal moods, in relation to the developing neurotransmitter story, take us even further beyond what we know, although new and fundamental disclosures are imminent, and cannot help but reflect as well on the refractory problems of memory and learning. Though all of our questions remain, there have been spectacular advances since the days of HELMHOLTZ and WUNDT, or of PIÉRON when he wrote about *Le cerveau et la pensée* (1923). The converging evolutions of experimental psychology, physiology and microanatomy, together with comparative and developmental studies, are bound to take us ever closer toward our common goal: that of gaining a rational understanding of ourselves.

For millennia, we have tried to comprehend the universe around us; the time has come, during this last century, and is now here, to attempt to comprehend ourselves. To this end, all of the sciences have to be put into the service of man's understanding of man. Psychology finds its identity, I propose, by its subject matter not by its methods.

It is clear that our particular science is as central as physics, and ultimately more so. But it is also capable of as much abuse as physics. As Lord Adrian once said, "He who can first explain and control paranoia will have found the means of producing it." Yet just for that reason, all of us here who are concerned with furthering man's understanding of man will have to abide by a new kind of hippocratic oath: never to do harm, always to heal rather than hinder, to make human life richer, and to make it free.

Acknowledgments

Some of the work reviewed in this lecture has been aided by grants from the U.S. National Institute of Mental Health (MH 2433), the Institute of Neurological and Communicative Disorders and Stroke (1 PO1 NS12336), and the N.I.H. Division of Research Resources (General Clinical Research Center Program, RR-88). The work has also been supported in various years by the Grant and Sloan Foundations of New York, and, most recently, the Spencer Foundation of Chicago.

The author is indebted for discussions of points raised in this paper and for helpful criticism to many of his colleagues, and particularly to SUZANNE CORKIN, OTTO-JOACHIM GRÜSSER, RICHARD HELD, BRENDA MILNER, WALLE NAUTA, and MARIANNE L. TEUBER.

References

Adams, R.D., Collins, G.H., Victor, M.: Troubles de la mémoire et de l'apprentissage chez l'homme: leurs relations avec lésions des lobes temporaux et du diencéphale. In: Physiologie de l'Hippocampe. Paris: Centre National de la Recherche Scientifique 1962, pp. 273–295.

•Barlow, H.B., Pettigrew, J.D.: Lack of specificity of neurons in the visual cortex of young kittens. J. Physiol. **218**, 98–100 (1971).

Bayer, S.A., Brunner, R.L., Hine, R., Altman, J.: Behavioral effects of interference with the postnatal acquisition of hippocampal granule cells. Nature [New Biol.] **242**, 222–224 (1973).

Benton, A.L., Van Allen, M.W.: Impairment in facial recognition in patients with cerebral disease. Cortex **4**, 344–358 (1968).

Bickford, R.G., Daly, D., Keith, M.M.: Sensory precipitation and reflex mechanisms. In: Jasper, H.H., Ward, A.A., Pope, A., (eds.), Basic Mechanisms of the Epilepsies. London: Churchill 1969.

Bickford, R.G., Dodge, H.W., Uhlein, A.: Electrographic and behavioral effects related to depth stimulation in human patients. In: Ramsey, E.R., O'Doherty, D.S., (eds.), Electrical Studies of the Unanesthetized Brain. New York: Hoeber 1960.

Bizzi, E., Schiller, P.H.: Single unit activity in the frontal eye fields of unanaesthetized monkeys during eye and head movement. Exp. Brain Res. **10**, 151–158 (1970).

•Blakemore, C., Cooper, G.F.: Development of the brain depends on the visual environment. Nature **228**, 477–478 (1970).

- Blakemore, C., Mitchell, D.: Environmental modification of the visual cortex and the neural basis of learning and memory. Nature **241**, 467–468 (1973).
- Blakemore, C., Van Sluyters, R.C., Peck, C.K., Hein, A.: Development of cat visual cortex following rotation of one eye. Nature **257**, 584–586 (1975).
- Blumstein, S.E., Baker, E., Goodglass, H.: Phonological factors in auditory comprehension in aphasia. Neuropsychologia **15**, 19–30 (1977a).
- Blumstein, S.E., Cooper, W.E., Zurif, E., Caramazza, A.: The perception and production of voice-onset time on aphasia. Neuropsychologia **15**, 371–383 (1977b).
- Broca, P.: Perte de la parole. Bull. Soc. Anthropol. **2**, 235–237 (1861) More complete account: Remarques sur le siège de la faculté du langage articulé suivies d'une observation d'aphémie (perte de la parole). Bull. Soc. Anthropol. **4**, 330–357 (1861).
- Brunswik, E., Reiter, L.: Eindruckscharaktere schematisierter Gesichter. Z. Psychol. **142**, 67–134 (1937)
- Buisseret, P., Imbert, M.: Visual cortical cells: the developmental properties in normal and dark-reared kitten. J. Physiol. **225**, 511–525 (1976).
- Butters, N., Cermak, L.S.: The role of cognitive factors in the memory disorders of alcoholic patients with the Korsakoff syndrome. Ann. N.Y. Acad. Sci. **233**, 61–75 (1974).
- Capranica, R.R.: The Evoked Vocal Response of the Bullfrog. Cambridge: M.I.T. Press 1965.
- Carey, S., Diamond, R.: From piecemeal to configurational representation of faces. Science **195**, 312–314 (1977).
- Chapman, L.F., Walter, R.D., Rand, R.W., Markham, C.H., Crandall, P.H.: Memory changes induced by stimulation of hippocampus or amygdala in epilepsy patients with implanted electrodes. Trans. Am. Neurol. Assoc. **92**, 50–56 (1967).
- Chatrian, G.E., Lettich, E., Miller, L.H., Green, J.F.: Pattern-sensitive epilepsy. Epilepsia **11**, 125–262 (1970).
- Chomsky, N.: Language and Mind. New York: Harcourt, Brace World 1968.
- Cooper, W.E.: Perceptuomotor adaptation to a speech feature. Percept. Psychophys. **16**, 229–234 (1974).
- Creutzfeldt, O.D., Ito, M.: Functional synaptic organization of primary visual cortex neurons in the cat. Exp. Brain Res. **6**, 324–352 (1968).
- Cynader, M.: Selective abolition of direction specificity in cat visual cortex. Neuroscience Abstracts. **1**, 84 (1975).
- Cynader, M., Berman, N., Hein, A.: Cats reared in stroboscopic illumination: effects on receptive fields in visual cortex. Proc. Natl. Acad. Sci. U.S.A. **70**, 1353–1354 (1973).
- Cynader, M., Berman, N., Hein, A.: Recovery of function in cat visual cortex following prolonged deprivation. Exp. Brain Res. **25**, 139–156 (1976).
- DeRenzi, E., Spinnler, H.: Facial recognition in brain-damaged patients. Neurology **16**, 145–152 (1966).
- Diamond, I.T., Hall, W.C.: Evolution of neocortex. Science **164**, 251–262 (1969).
- Douglas, R.J., Peterson, J., Douglas, D.: The ontogeny of a hippocampus-dependent response in two rodent species. Behav. Biol. **8**, 27–37 (1973).
- Drachman, D.A., Arbit, J.: Memory and the hippocampal complex. Arch. Neurol. **15**, 52–61 (1966).
- Drees, O.: Untersuchungen über die angeborenen Verhaltensweisen bei Springspinnen (Salticidae). Z. Tierpsychol. **9**, 169–207 (1952).
- Egger, G.J., Livesey, P.J., Dawson, R.G.: Ontogenetic aspects of central cholinergic involvement in spontaneous alternation. Dev. Psychobiol. **6**, 289–299 (1973).
- Eimas, P.D., Siqueland, E.R., Jusczyk, P., Vigorito, J.: Speech perception in infants. Science **171**, 303–306 (1971).
- Ettlinger, G., Teuber, H.-L. Milner, B.: The 17th international symposium of neuropsychology. Neuropsychologia **13**, 125–133 (1975).
- Fodor, J.A., Garrett, M., Shapero, D.B.: Discrimination among phonemes by infants. Q. Prog. Rep. **96**, Research Laboratory of Electronics. M.I.T. (1969).
- Fodor, J.A., Garrett, M., Brill, S.: Pi ka pu: the perception of speech sounds by prelinguistic infants. Perception and Psychophysics **18**, 74–78 (1975).
- Frishkopf, L.S., Goldstein, Jr., M.H.: Responses to acoustic stimuli from single units in the eighth nerve of the bullfrog. J. Acoust. Soc. Am. **35**, 1219–1228 (1963).

Fuxe, K.: Evidence for the existence of monoamine neurons in the central nervous system. IV. Distribution of monoamine nerve terminals in the central nervous system. Acta Physiol. Scand. [Suppl.] **247**, 37–84 (1965).

Gaffan, D.: Recognition impaired and association intact in the memory of monkey after transection of the fornix. J. Comp. Physiol. Psychol. **86**, 1100–1109 (1974).

Gage, F.H., III, Olton, D.S.: Hippocampal influence on hyperactivity induced by septal lesions. Brain Res. **98**, 311–325 (1975).

Gennari, F.: De Peculiari Structura Cerebri Nonnullisque Ejus Morbis. Paucae Aliae Anatom. Observat. Accedunt. Parma, Regio Typographeo (Bodoni) 1782, Vol. XVI, 87.

Gerrits, H.J.M., Vendrik, A.J.H.: Simultaneous contrast, filling-in process and information processing in man's visual system. Exp. Brain Res. **11**, 411–430 (1970).

Goldman, P.S., Nauta, W.J.H.: Autoradiographic demonstration of a projection from prefrontal association cortex to the superior colliculus in the rhesus monkey. Brain Res. **116**, 145–149 (1976).

Goldman, P.S., Nauta, W.J.H.: Columnar distribution of cortico-cortical fibers in the frontal association, limbic, and motor cortex of the developing rhesus monkey. Brain Res. **122**, 393–413 (1977).

Gombrich, E.H.: The mask and the face: the perception of physiognomic likeness in life and art. In: Gombrich, E.H., Hochberg, J., Black, M., Perception and Reality. Baltimore: Johns Hopkins Press 1972, pp. 1–46.

Grant, D.A., Berg, E.A.: A behavioral analysis of degree of reinforcement and ease of shifting to new responses in a Weigl-type card-sorting problem. J. Exp. Psychol. **38**, 404–411 (1948).

Graybiel, A.M.: Studies of the anatomical organization of posterior association cortex. In: Schmitt, F.O., Worden, F.G., (eds.), The Neurosciences. Third Study Program. Cambridge: M.I.T. Press 1974, pp. 205–214.

Gross, C.G.: Visual functions of inferotemporal cortex. In: Jung, R., (ed.), Handbook of Sensory Physiology. New York: Springer-Verlag 1973, Vol. VII, 3B, pp. 451–482.

Gross, C.H., Rocha-Miranda, C.E., Bender, D.B.: Visual properties of neurons in inferotemporal cortex of the macaque. J. Neurophysiol. **35**, 96–111 (1972).

Grüsser, O.-J., Grüsser-Cornehls, U.: Neural mechanisms of visual movement perception and some psychophysical and behavioral correlations. In: Autrum, H., Jung, R., Loewenstein, W.R., MacKay, D.M., Teuber, H.-L., (eds.), Handbook of Sensory Physiology. New York: Springer-Verlag 1973, Vol. VII, 3A. pp. 333–429.

Hammond, P., MacKay, D.M.: Differential responses of cat visual cortical cells to textured stimuli. Exp. Brain Res. **22**, 427–430 (1975).

Harms, H.: Visuelle und pupillomotorische Störungen bei Veränderungen des Okzipitallappens. Proc. 8th Internat. Congr. Neurol. **5**, 57–78 (1965).

Head, H.: Studies in Neurology. London: Oxford Medical Publications 1920.

Hebb, D.O.: Distinctive features of learning in the higher animal. In: Delafresnaye, J.F., (ed.), Brain Mechanisms and Learning. London-New York: Oxford Univ. Press 1961, pp. 37–51.

Hécaen, H.: Clinical symptomatology in right and left hemispheric lesions. In: Mountcastle, V.B., (ed.), Interhemispheric Relations and Cerebral Dominance. Baltimore: Johns Hopkins Press 1962.

Hécaen, H.: Introduction à la Neuropsychologie. Paris: Librairie Larousse 1972.

Held, R., Ingle, D., Schneider, G.E., Trevarthen, C.B.: Locating and identifying: Two modes of visual processing. Psychol. Forsch. **31**, 44–62; 299–348 (1967–1968).

Hirsch, H.V.B., Spinelli, D.N.: Visual experience modifies distribution of horizontally and vertically oriented receptive fields in cats. Science **168**, 869–871 (1970).

Hubel, D.H., Wiesel, T.N.: Receptive fields of single neurons in the cat's striate cortex. J. Physiol. **150**, 91–104 (1960).

Hubel, D.H., Wiesel, T.N.: Receptive fields, binocular interaction and functional architecture in the cat's visual cortex. J. Physiol. **160**, 106–154 (1962).

Hubel, D.H., Wiesel, T.N.: An anatomical demonstration of columns in the monkey striate cortex. Nature **221**, 747–750 (1969).

Humphrey, N.K., Weiskrantz, L.: Vision in monkeys after removal of the striate cortex. Nature **215**, 595–597 (1967).

Huppert, F.A., Piercy, M.: Recognition memory in amnesic patients: effect of the temporal context and familiarity of material. Cortex **12**, 3–20 (1976).

Iwai, E., Mishkin, M.: Further evidence on the locus of the visual area in the temporal lobe of the monkey. Exp. Neurol. **25**, 585–594 (1969).

Jakobson, R.: Kindersprache, Aphasie und allgemeine Lautgesetze. Sprakvetenskapliga Sällskapets i Uppsala Förhandlingar, Universitets Åvsskrift **9**, 1–83 (1942). English translation (revised): Child Language, Aphasia and Phonological Universals. The Hague: Mouton 1968, 99. pp. French translation: Le Langage Enfantin et l'Aphasie. Paris: Éditions de Minuit 1969.

Jones, E.G., Powell, T.P.S.: An anatomical study of converging sensory pathways within the cerebral cortex of the monkey. Brain **93**, 793–820 (1970).

Jouvet, M.: Essai sur le rève. Arch. Ital. Biol. **111**, 564–576 (1973).

Jung, R., Hassler, R.: The extra-pyramidal motor system. In: Magoun, H.W., Hall, V.E., (eds.), Handbook of Neurophysiology. Washington, D.C.: Am. Physiol. Soc. 1960, Vol. II, pp. 893–928.

Klüver, H.: Functional significance of the geniculo-striate system. Biol. Symposia **7**, 253–299 (1942).

Körner, F., Teuber, H.-L.: Visual field defects after missile injuries to the geniculo-striate pathway in man. Exp. Brain Res. **18**, 88–113 (1973).

• Kuffler, S.W.: Discharge patterns and functional organization of mammalian retina. J. Neurophysiol. **16**, 37–68 (1953).

Lackner, J.R., Teuber, H.-L.: Alterations in auditory fusion thresholds after cerebral injury in man. Neuropsychologia **11**, 409–415 (1973).

Lashley, K.S.: Coalescence of neurology and psychology. Proc. Am. Phil. Soc. **84**, 461–470 (1941a).

Lashley, K.S.: Patterns of cerebral integration indicated by the scotomas of migraine. Arch. Neurol. Psychiat. **46**, 331–339 (1941b).

Leehey, S.C., Moskowitz-Cook, A., Brill, S., Held, R.: Orientational anisotropy in infant vision. Science **190**, 900–902 (1975).

• Lettvin, J.Y., Maturana, H.R., McCulloch, W.S., Pitts, W.H.: What the frog's eye tells the frog's brain. Proc. Inst. Radio Engin. **4**, 1940–1951 (1959).

Lévy-Schoen, A.: L-Image d'Autrui Chez l'Enfant. Paris: Presses Universitaires de France 1964.

Levy, J., Trevarthen, C., Sperry, R.W.: Perception of bilateral chimeric figures following hemisphere deconnection. Brain **95**, 61–78 (1972).

Lhermitte, F., Signoret, J.-L.: Analyse neuropsychologique et différenciation des syndromes amnésiques. Rev. Neurol. (Paris) **126**, 161–178 (1972).

Liberman, A., Cooper, F.S., Shankweiler, D., Studdert-Kennedy, M.: Perception of the speech code. Psychol. Rev. **74**, 431–461 (1967).

• Luria, A.R.: Higher Cortical Function in Man. New York: Basic Books 1966.

Luria, A.R.: The Origin and Cerebral Organization of Man's Conscious Action. Dorchester: Dorset Press 1971, pp. 37–52.

MacKay, D.M.: Moving visual images produced by regular stationary patterns. Nature **180**, 849–850 (1957).

MacKay, D.M.: Visual stability and voluntary eye movements. In: Autrum, H., Jung, R., Loewenstein, W.R., MacKay, D.M., Teuber, H.-L., (eds.), Handbook of Sensory Physiology. New York: Springer-Verlag 1973, Vol. VII, 3A, pp. 307–331.

Marslen-Wilson, W.D., Teuber, H.-L.: Memory for remote events in anterograde amnesia: recognition of public figures from news photographs. Neuropsychologia **13**, 353–365 (1975).

Milner, B.: Impairment of visual recognition and recall after right temporal lobectomy in man. Paper read at Psychonomic Soc. 1st Ann. Mtg., Chicago, Sept. 1960.

Milner, B.: Les troubles de la mémoire accompagnant des lésions hippocampiques bilatérales. In: Physiologie de l'Hippocampe. Paris: Centre National de la Recherche Scientifique 1962, pp. 257–272.

Milner, B.: Effects of different brain lesions on card sorting. Arch. Neurol. **9**, 90–100 (1963).

Milner, B.: Some effects of frontal lobectomy in man. In: Warren, J.M., Akert, K., (eds.), The Frontal Granular Cortex and Behavior. New York: McGraw-Hill 1964, pp. 313–334.

Milner, B.: Visually-guided maze learning in man: effects of bilateral hippocampal, bilateral frontal and unilateral cerebral lesions. Neuropsychologia **3**, 317–338 (1965).

Milner, B.: Amnesia following operations on the temporal lobes. In: Whitty, C.W.M., Zangwill, O.L., (eds.), Amnesia. London: Butterworth 1966, pp. 109–133.

Milner, B.: Visual recognition and recall after right temporal-lobe excision in man. Neuropsychologia **6**, 191–209 (1968).

Milner, B.: Interhemispheric differences and psychological processes in man. Br. Med. Bull. **27**, 272–277 (1971).

•Milner, B.: Hemispheric specialization: scope and limits. In: Schmitt, F.O., Worden, F.G., (eds.), The Neurosciences. Third study program. Cambridge: M.I.T. Press 1974a, pp. 75–89.

Milner, B.: Sparing of language functions after early unilateral brain damage. Neurosci. Res. Program Bull. **2**, 213–217 (1974b).

Milner, B., Corkin, S., Teuber, H.-L.: Further analysis of the hippocampal amnesic syndrome: 14-year follow-up study of H.M. Neuropsychologia **6**, 215–234 (1968).

•Milner, B., Teuber, H.-L.: Alterations of perception and memory in man. In: Weiskrantz, L., (ed.), Analysis of Behavioral Change. New York: Harper and Row 1968, pp. 268–375.

•Mishkin, M.: Visual mechanisms beyond the striate cortex. In: Russell, R.W., (ed.), Frontiers of Physiological Psychology. New York: Academic Press 1966, pp. 93–116.

Mishkin, M., Pribram, K.H.: Analysis of effects of frontal lesions in the monkey: II. Variations of delayed response. J. Comp. Physiol. Psychol. **49**, 36–40 (1956).

Mitchell, D.E., Griffin, F., Muir, D., Blakemore, C., Van Sluyters, R.C.: Behavioral compensation of cats after early rotation of one eye Exp. Brain Res. **25**, 109–113 (1976).

Moore, R.Y., Halaris, A.E.: Hippocampal innervation by serotonin neurons of the midbrain raphe in the rat. J. Comp. Neurol. **164**, 171–184 (1975).

Mountcastle, V.B.: Modality and topographic properties of single neurons of cat's somatic sensory cortex. J. Neurophysiol. **20**, 408–434 (1957).

Mountcastle, V.B.: The world around us; neural command functions for selective attention. Neurosci. Res. Program Bull. **14** (April Suppl.), 1–47 (1976).

Mountcastle, V.B., Lynch, J.C., Georgopoulos, A., Sakata, H., Acuna, C.: Posterior parietal association cortex of the monkey: command functions for operations within extrapersonal space. J. Neurophysiol. **38**, 871–908 (1975).

Nadel, L., O'Keefe, J., Black, A.: Slam on the brakes: a critique of Altman, Brunner and Bayer's response inhibition model of hippocampal function. Behav. Biol. **14**, 151–162 (1975).

Nauta, W.J.H.: The problem of the frontal lobe: a reinterpretation. J. Psychiat. Res. **8**, 167–187 (1971).

•Nottebohm, F.: Ontogeny of bird song: different strategies in vocal development are reflected in learning stages, critical periods, and neural lateralization. Science **167**, 950–956 (1970).

Nottebohm, F., Stokes, T.M., Leonard, C.M.: Central control of song in the canary, Serinus canarius. J. Comp. Neurol. **165**, 457–486 (1976).

Ojeman, R.G.: Correlation between specific human brain lesions and memory changes. Neurosci. Res. Program Bull. **4**, (July Suppl.), 1–70 (1966).

O'Keefe, J., Dostrovsky, J.: The hippocampus as a spatial map. Preliminary evidence from unit activity in the freely-moving rat. Brain Res. **34**, 171–175 (1971).

•Olds, J., Milner, P.: Positive reinforcement produced by electrical stimulation of septal area and other regions of rat brain. J. Comp. Physiol. Psychol. **47**, 419–427 (1954).

Pandya, D.N., Dye, P., Butters, N.: Efferent cortico-cortical projections of the prefrontal cortex in the rhesus monkey. Brain Res. **31**, 21–34 (1971).

Parkes, A.S., Bruce, H.M.: Pregnancy block in female mice placed in boxes soiled by males. J. Reprod. Fertil. **4**, 303–308 (1962).

Pasik, P., Pasik, T.: Further studies of extrageniculate vision in the monkey. Trans. Am. Neurol. Assoc. **93**, 262–264 (1968).

Penfield, W., Mathieson, G.: Memory: autopsy findings and comments on the role of hippocampus in experimental recall. Arch. Neurol. **31**, 145–154 (1974).

Penfield, W., Milner, B.: Memory deficit produced by bilateral lesions in the hippocampal zone. Arch. Neurol. Psychiat. **79**, 475–497 (1958).

Perenin, M.T., Jeannerod, M.: Residual vision in blind hemifields. Neuropsychologia **13**, 1–8 (1975).

Piéron, H.: Le Cerveau et la Pensée. Paris: Alcan 1923.

•Pöppel, E., Held, R., Frost, D.: Residual visual functions after brain wound involving the central visual pathways in man. Nature **243**, 295–296 (1973).

Ranck, Jr., J.B.: Behavioral correlates and firing repertoires of neurons in the dorsal hippocampal formation and septum of unrestrained rats. In: Isaacson, R.L. Pribram, K.H., (eds.), The Hippocampus. New York: Plenum Press 1975, Vol. II, pp. 207–244.

Ribot, T.: Les Maladies de la Mémoire. Paris: G. Baillière 1881.

Robinson, D.L., Wurtz, R.H.: Use of an extraretinal signal by monkey superior colliculus neurons toinguish real from self-induced movements. J. Neurophysiol. **39**, 852–870 (1976).

Rosvold, H.E.: The frontal lobe system: cortical-subcortical interrelationships. Acta Neurobiol. Exp. **32**, 439–460 (1972).

Rudel, R.G., Teuber, H.-L.: Discrimination of direction of line in children. J. Comp. Physiol. Psychol. **56**, 892–898 (1963).

Rudel, R.G., Teuber, H.-L.: Spatial orientation in normal children and in children with early brain injury. Neuropsychologia. **9**, 401–407 (1971).

Sanders, H.I., Warrington, E.K.: Memory for remote events in amnesic patients. Brain **94**, 661–668 (1971).

Sanders, M.D., Warrington, E.K., Marshall, J., Weiskrantz, L.: *Blindsight*: vision in a field defect. Lancet *1974/Apr. 20*, 707–708.

Schiller, P.H., Finlay, B.L., Volman, S.F.: Quantitative studies of single cell properties in monkey striate cortex. V. Multivariate statistical analyses and models. J. Neurophysiol **39**, 1288–1373 (1976).

Schneider, G.E.: Two visual systems: brain mechanisms for localization and discrimination are dissociated by tectal and cortical lesions. Science **163**, 895–902 (1969).

Schneider, G.E.: Mechanisms of functional recovery following lesions of visual cortex or superior colliculus in neonate and adult hamsters. Brain Behav. Evol. **3**, 295–323 (1970).

Schneider, G.E.: Anomalous axonal connections implicated in sparing and alteration of function after early lesions. Neurosci. Res. Program Bull. **12**, 222–227 (1975).

Scoville, W.B., Milner, B.: Loss of recent memory after bilateral hippocampal lesions. J. Neurol. Neurosurg. Psychiatry **20**, 11–21 (1957).

Segal, M., Disterhoft, J.F., Olds, J.: Hippocampal unit activity during classical aversive and appetitive conditioning. Science **175**, 792–794 (1972).

Seltzer, B., Benson, D.F.: The temporal pattern of retrograde amnesia in Korsakoff's disease. Neurology **24**, 527–530 (1974).

Semmes, J., Weinstein, S., Ghent, L., Teuber, H.-L.: Spatial orientation in man after cerebral injury: I. Analyses by locus of lesion. J. Psychol. **39**, 227–244 (1955).

Semmes, J., Weinstein, S., Ghent, L., Teuber, H.-L.: Correlates of impaired orientation in personal and extrapersonal space. Brain **86**, 742–772 (1963).

Sherk, H., Stryker, M.P.: Quantitative study of cortical orientation selectivity in visually inexperienced kitten. J. Neurophysiol. **39**, 63–70 (1976).

Sperry, R.W.: Neural basis of the spontaneous optokinetic response produced by visual inversion. J. Comp. Physiol. Psychol. **43**, 482–489 (1950).

Sperry, R.W.: Lateral specialization in the surgically separated hemispheres. In: Schmitt, F.O., Worden, F.G., (eds.), The Neurosciences. Third Study Program. Cambridge: M.I.T. Press 1974, pp. 5–19.

Squire, L.R., Slater, P.C., Chace, P.M.: Retrograde amnesia: temporal gradient in very long-term memory following electroconvulsive therapy. Science **187**, 77–79 (1975).

Stryker, M.P., Sherk, H.: Modification of cortical orientation selectivity in the cat by restricted visual experience: a re-examination. Science **190**, 904–905 (1975).

Sutherland, N.S.: Visual discrimination of orientation and shape by the octopus. Nature **179**, 11–13 (1957).

Tallal, P., Piercy, M.: Developmental aphasia: the perception of brief vowels and extended consonants. Neuropsychologia **13**, 69–74 (1975).

Teuber, H.-L.: Physiological psychology. Ann. Rev. Psychol. **6**, 267–296 (1955).

Teuber, H.-L.: Perception. In: Field, J., Magoun, H.W., Hall, V.E., (eds.), Handbook of Physiology. Section of Neurophysiology. Washington, D.C.: Am. Physiol. Soc. 1960, Vol. III, pp. 1595–1688.

Teuber, H.-L.: The riddle of frontal lobe function in man. In: Warren, J.M., Akert, K., (eds.), The Frontal Granular Cortex and Behavior. New York: McGraw-Hill 1964, pp. 410–444.

Teuber, H.-L.: Alterations in perception after brain injury. In: Eccles, J.C., (ed.), Brain and Conscious Experience. New York: Springer-Verlag 1966, pp. 182–216.

Teuber, H.-L.: Disorders of memory following penetrating missile wounds of the brain. Neurology **18** (Abstract), 267–268 (1968).

Teuber, H.L.: Neglected aspects of the posttraumatic syndrome. In Walker, A.E., Caveness, W.F., Critchley, M., (eds.), The Late Effects of Head Injury. Springfield, Ill.: C.C. Thomas 1969, 13–34.
Teuber, H.-L.: L'hypothèse des décharges corollaires. In: Dubois-Poulsen, A., Lairy, G.-C., Rémond, A., (eds.), La Fonction du Regard. Paris: I.N.S.E.R.M. 1971a, pp. 187–198.
Teuber, H.-L.: Perception et mouvement. Aspets neurophysiologiques et psychophysiologiques. In: Hécaen, H., (ed.), Neuropsychologie de la Perception Visuelle. Paris: Masson 1971b, pp. 187–221.
Teuber, H.-L.: Unity and diversity of frontal lobe functions. Acta Neurobiol. Exp. **32**, 615–656 (1972).
Teuber, H.-L.: Effects of focal brain injury on human behavior. In: Tower, D.B., (ed.), The Nervous System. The Clinical Neurosciences. New York: Raven Press 1975a, Vol. II, pp. 457–480.
Teuber, H.-L.: Recovery of function after brain injury in man. In: Plum, F., (ed.), Outcome of Severe Damage to the Central Nervous System. Ciba Found. Symp. **34** (New Series). Amsterdam: Elsevier 1975b, pp. 159–190.
Teuber, H.-L.: Complex functions of basal ganglia. In: Yahr, M.D., (ed.), The Basal Ganglia. New York: Raven Press 1976, pp. 151–168.
Teuber, H.-L., Proctor (Bowen), F.: Some effects of basal ganglia lesions in subhuman primates and man. Neuropsychologia. **2**, 85–93 (1964).
Teuber, H.-L., Rudel, R.G.: Behavior after cerebral lesions in children and adults. Dev. Med. Child Neurol. **4**, 3–20 (1962).
Teuber, H.-L., Battersby, W.S., Bender, M.B.: Visual Field Defects After Penetrating Missile Wounds of the Brain. Cambridge: Harvard Univ. Press 1960, 143 p.
Teuber, H.-L., Milner, B., Vaughan, Jr., H.G.: Persistent anterograde amnesia after stab wound of the basal brain. Neuropsychologia **6**, 267–282 (1968).
Teuber, H.-L., Corkin, S., Twitchell..E.: A study of vklotomy in man. In: Sweet, W.H., (ed.), Neurosurgicalreatment in Psychiatry, Pain and Epilepsy. Baltimore: Univ. Park Press 1977, pp. 355–362 (in press).
Twitchell, T.E.: The automatic grasping responses of infants. Neuropsychologia, 247–259 (1965).
Tzavaras, A., Hécaen, H., LeBras, H.: Le problème de la spécifité du déficit dereconnaissance du visage humain lors des lésions hémisphériques unilatérales. Neuropsychologia **8**, 403–416 (1970).
Ungerstedt, U.: Stereotaxic mapping of the monoamine pathways in the rat brain. Acta Physiol. Scand. **367**, [Suppl.] 1–48 (1971).
Vital-Durand, F., Jeannerod, M.: Role of visual experience in the development of optokinetic response in kittens. Exp. Brain Res. **20**, 297–302 (1974).
Von Helmholtz, H.: Handbuch der Physiologischen Optik. Leipzig: Leopold Voss 1867, Vol. III.
Von Holst, E., Mittelstaedt, H.: Das Reafferenzprinzip (Wechselwirkungen zwischen Zentralnervensystem und Peripherie). Naturwissenschaften **37**, 464–476 (1950).
Vurpillot, E.: Le Monde Visuel du Jeune Enfant. Paris: Presses Universitaires de France 1972. (Translated as: The Visual World of the Child, by W.E.C. Gilham, with forewords by J. Bruner and P. Fraisse. New York: International Universities Press 1976).
Wald, G.: Introduction to: Henderson, L.J. The Fitness of the Environment. Boston: Beacon Press 1958.
Warrington, E.K., James, M.: An experimental investigation of facial recognition in patients with unilateral cerebral lesions. Cortex **3**, 317–326 (1967).
Warrington, E.K., Sanders, H.I.: The fate of old memories. Q. J. Exp. Psychol. **23**, 432–442 (1971).
Warrington, E.K., Taylor, A.M.: The contribution of the right parietal lobe to object recognition. Cortex **9**, 152–164 (1973).
Warrington, E.K., Weiskrantz, L.: Amnesic syndrome: consolidation or retrieval? Nature **228**, 628–630 (1970).
Weiskrantz, L.: Contour discrimination in a young monkey with striate cortex ablation. Neuropsychologia **1**, 145–165 (1963).
Weiskrantz, L., Cowey, A.: Filling in the scotoma: a study of residual vision after striate cortex lesions in monkeys. In: Stellar, E., Sprague, J., (eds.), Progress in Physiological Psychology 1970, Vol. III, pp. 237–260.

Wilkins, A.J., Andermann, F., Ives, J.: Stripes, complex cells and seizures—an attempt to determine the locus and nature of the trigger mechanism in pattern-sensitive epilepsy. Brain **98**, 365–380 (1975).

Williams, M.: Memory studies in ECT. J. Neurol., Neurosurg., Psychiatry **13**, 314–319 (1950).

Winter, P., Ploog, D., Latta, J.: Vocal repertoire of the squirrel monkey (Saimiri sciureus), its analysis and significance. Exp. Brain Res. **1**, 359–384 (1966).

Wollberg, Z., Newman, J.D.: Auditory cortex of squirrel monkey: Response patterns of single cells to species-specific vocalization. Science **175**, 212–214 (1972).

Woods, B.T., Teuber, H.-L.: Early onset of complementary specialization of cerebral hemispheres in man. Trans. Am. Neurol. Assoc. **98**, 113–117 (1973).

Worden, F.G., Galambos, R. (eds.): Auditory processing of biologically significant sounds. Neurosci. Res. Program Bull. **10**, 1–110 (1972).

Yin, R.K.: Looking at upside-down faces. J. Exp. Psychol. **81**, 141–145 (1969).

Yin, R.K.: Face recognition by brain-injured patients: a dissociable disability? Neuropsychologia **8**, 395–402 (1970).

Yinon, U.: Eye rotation in developing kittens: The effect on ocular dominance and receptive field organization of cortical cells. Exp. Brain Res. **24**, 215–218 (1975).

Zangwill, O.L.: Clinical tests of memory impairment. Proc. Roy. Soc. Med. **36**, 576–580 (1943).

Zangwill, O.L.: The amnesic syndrome. In: Whitty C.W.M., Zangwill, O.L., (eds.), Amnesia. London: Butterworth 1966.

Author Index

Subject Index

Handbook of Sensory Physiology

A General Survey

Volume I
Principles of Receptor Physiology
Editor: W.R. Loewenstein
ISBN 3-540-05144-9

Volume II
Somatosensory System
Editor: A. Iggo
ISBN 3-540-05941-5

Volume III

Part 1: **Enteroceptors**
Editor: E. Neil
ISBN 3-540-05523-1

Part 2: **Muscle Receptors**
Editor: C.C. Hunt
ISBN 3-540-06891-0

Part 3: **Electroreceptors and Other Specialized Receptors in Lower Vertebrates**
Editor: A. Fessard
ISBN 3-540-06872-4

Volume IV
Chemical Senses

Part 1: **Olfaction**
Editor: L.M. Beidler
ISBN 3-540-05291-7

Part 2: **Taste**
Editor: L.M. Beidler
ISBN 3-540-05501-0

Volume V
Auditory System
Editors: W.D. Keidel, W.D. Neff

Part 1: **Anatomy, Physiology (Ear)**
ISBN 3-540-06676-4

Part 2: **Physiology (CNS), Behavioral Studies, Psychoacoustics**
ISBN 3-540-07000-1

Part 3: **Clinical and Special Topics**
ISBN 3-540-07129-6

Volume VI
Vestibular System
Editor: H.H. Kornhuber

Part 1: **Basic Mechanisms**
ISBN 3-540-06889-9

Part 2: **Psychophysics, Applied Aspects and General Interpretations**
ISBN 3-540-06864-3

Volume VII

Part 1: **Photochemistry of Vision**
Editor: H.J.A. Dartnall
ISBN 3-540-05145-7

Part 2: **Physiology of Photoreceptor Organs**
Editor: M.G.F. Fuortes
ISBN 3-540-05743-9

Part 3: **Central Processing of Visual Information**
Editor: R. Jung

Part 3/A: **Integrative Functions and Comparative Data**
ISBN 3-540-05769-2

Part 3/B: **Visual Centers in the Brain**
ISBN 3-540-06056-1

Part 4: **Visual Psychophysics**
Editors: D. Jameson, L.M. Hurvich
ISBN 3-540-05146-5

Part 5: **The Visual System in Vertebrates**
Editor: F. Crescitelli
ISBN 3-540-07908-4

Part 6: **Comparative Physiology and Evolution of Vision in Invertebrates**

Part 6/A: **Invertebrate Photoreceptors**
ISBN 3-540-08837-7

Part 6/B: **Invertebrate Visual Centers and Behavior**
ISBN 3-540-08703-6

Volume VIII
Perception
Editors: R. Held, H.W. Leibowitz, H.-L. Teuber
ISBN 3-540-08300-6

Volume IX
Development of Sensory Systems
Editor: M. Jacobson
ISBN 3-540-08632-3

Springer-Verlag
Berlin
Heidelberg
New York